The Moral Life

The Moral Life

An Introductory Reader in Ethics and Literature

THIRD EDITION

LOUIS P. POJMAN
LEWIS VAUGHN

New York   Oxford
OXFORD UNIVERSITY PRESS
2007

Oxford University Press, Inc., publishes works that further Oxford University's objective of excellence in research, scholarship, and education.

Oxford New York
Auckland Cape Town Dar es Salaam Hong Kong Karachi
Kuala Lumpur Madrid Melbourne Mexico City Nairobi
New Delhi Shanghai Taipei Toronto

With offices in
Argentina Austria Brazil Chile Czech Republic France Greece
Guatemala Hungary Italy Japan Poland Portugal Singapore
South Korea Switzerland Thailand Turkey Ukraine Vietnam

Copyright © 2007 by Oxford University Press, Inc.

Published by Oxford University Press, Inc.
198 Madison Avenue, New York, New York, 10016
http://www.oup.com

Oxford is a registered trademark of Oxford University Press

Library of Congress Cataloging-in-Publication Data

The moral life : an introductory reader in ethics and literature / [compiled] by Louis P. Pojman, Lewis Vaughn.—3rd ed.
      p. cm.
   Includes bibliographical references.
   ISBN-13: 978-0-19-530851-8
      1. Ethics. I. Pojman, Louis P. II. Vaughn, Lewis.

BJ1025.M665 2007
170—dc22   2006048281

Printing number: 9 8 7 6 5 4 3

Printed in the United States of America
on acid-free paper

Dedicated to
my colleagues in the English Department
United States Military Academy
West Point

•

Where Philosophy and English
cross-fertilize each other
in a magnificent manner

CONTENTS

PREFACE TO THE THIRD EDITION

This new edition of *The Moral Life* is a continuation and expansion of Louis Pojman's unique project of harnessing both literature and philosophy to deepen students' understanding of moral concepts and issues. He recognized that literature can often show life in vivid relief and unnerving detail—and reveal how the moral life is, or could be, or should be lived. And he knew well, as all good moral philosophers do, that philosophy can help us make sense of the complexities and conflicts of this moral experience, guiding us to moral principles, theories, or insights beneath the everyday confusion of feelings, prejudice, and custom.

Most textbooks never live past the first edition, and many that do survive beyond this benchmark cease to be as useful as they once were. But some books make such a valuable contribution to teaching that they deserve to continue indefinitely, even if their authors do not. I believe that *The Moral Life* is such a text, and Professor Pojman thought so too. Before his death in late 2005, we agreed that I would continue his work on the book and manage future editions. This third edition has been the immediate result, a work fully in keeping with his original vision and, I hope, at least a modest improvement on an already excellent volume.

For this edition, eleven new selections have been added, including several classic articles, along with a new chapter on euthanasia. The new readings are: Mary Midgley, "Trying Out One's New Sword"; John Stuart Mill, "Utilitarianism Refined"; William K. Frankena, "Kant's Theory"; J. O. Urmson, "Saints and Heroes"; Jane English, "What Do Grown Children Owe Their Parents?"; Don Marquis, "Why Abortion Is Immoral"; Judith Jarvis Thomson, "A Defense of Abortion"; Dan W. Brock, "Voluntary Active Euthanasia"; J. Gay-Williams, "The Wrongfullness of Euthanasia"; James Rachels, "Active and Passive Euthanasia"; and Thomas Nagel, "What Is Wrong with Terrorism?"

Lewis Vaughn
March 2006

PREFACE

This is a book integrating literature with philosophy, while also covering both classical and contemporary ethical theory and applied topics. Literature often highlights moral ideas, focusing on particular people in their dilemmas, awakening our imagination to new possibilities, and enabling us to understand the moral life in fresh and creative ways. Good literature compels us to rethink and revise our everyday assumptions. It sets before us powerful particularities that serve both as reinforcers and counterexamples to our sweeping principles. Harriet Beecher Stowe's *Uncle Tom's Cabin* challenged the assumptions of antebellum America and created great sympathy for the abolitionist cause. Arthur Koestler's *Darkness at Noon* and George Orwell's *Animal Farm* and *1984* brought clearly home to millions the dangers of totalitarianism. Dostoevsky's *Crime and Punishment* made us aware of the haunting voice of conscience that could overturn our best rationalization. William Golding's *Lord of the Flies* is like a picture worth a thousand arguments about why we need morality. William Styron's *Sophie's Choice* confronts us with the tragedy of moral choice when all options are unacceptable. Aldous Huxley's *Brave New World* highlights the paradox of freedom and welfare better than any political philosophy book I've ever read. Victor Hugo's Bishop of Digne encountering Jean Valjean is a more eloquent statement on the virtuous person than anything ever published in professional journals on virtue ethics. Tolstoy's short stories on greed and love leave their indelible marks on our souls. And so it goes. Good literature is the contemporary equivalent of the parables of the New Testament. They make the abstract concrete, bring it home to the heart, and force us to think with innovative imagination.

Yet, acknowledging the element of truth in Kant's rejection of the empirical and the need for examples in ethics, particularity often is one-sided and passion ridden. If it leaves us merely with gut reactions to particular tragedy, it tends toward bias and irrationality. One needs cool-headed philosophical analysis to play a sturdy role in sorting out the ambiguities and ambivalences in literature, to abstract from particulars and universalize principles, to generate wide-ranging intellectual theories. To paraphrase Kant, the passionate imagination of literature is blind without the cool head of philosophy, but the cool head of philosophy is sterile and as frigid as an iceberg without the passions of life, conveyed in literature.

I have endeavored to join forces, to unite literature and philosophy in the service of ethical understanding. Most sections of this work open with literary pieces.

This work is divided into four parts:

I *The Nature of Morality.* This part emphasizes the central problems: What is morality? What is it for? What is its scope and force? I use Golding's *Lord of the Flies,* Melville's *Billy Budd,* and Styron's *Sophie's Choice* to highlight central themes. These are followed by philosophical essays that delve more systematically into the nature of morality, the nature of good and evil, and, relating to the scope and force of morality, moral relativism and objectivism. One might wonder why the latter issue comes in so soon, but there may be no issue more in dispute among young people today than this topic. Hence its prominence.

II *Moral Theories and Moral Character.* This part emphasizes the three classic ethical theories: utilitarianism, deontological ethics, and virtue ethics. I have used philosophical classics, supplemented by poignant selections from literature, such as Ursula Le Guin's "The Ones Who Walk Away from Omelas" and an excerpt from Aldous Huxley's *Brave New World.* Following the chapter on virtue ethics, I have included essays on particular virtues and vices, such as Tolstoy's "How Much Land Does a Man Need?" and Kant's "Jealousy, Malice, and Ingratitude," Helen Keller's "Three Days to See," Plutarch's "In Consolation to His Wife," and Vice Admiral Stockdale's "The World of Epictetus."

III *Moral Issues.* This part treats the questions: Why be moral? What is the meaning of life? and What is important about freedom, autonomy, and self-respect? I have included Plato's classic discussion of "The Ring of Gyges," a selection from Ayn Rand's *Atlas Shrugged,* followed by critiques by Louis P. Pojman and James Rachels. Under the heading "Does Life Have Meaning?" I have included selections from the writings of Epicurus, Albert Camus, Viktor Frankl, the Buddha, and Robert Nozick. Under "Freedom, Autonomy, and Self-Respect," I have included selections from Martin Luther King, Jr., Maya Angelou, Jean-Paul Sartre, Thomas Hill, and Kurt Vonnegut.

IV *Applied Ethics.* This part treats contemporary issues such as sex, love and marriage, abortion, euthanasia, animal rights, the environment, and terrorism. I have chosen issues that relate primarily to personal, rather than social, morality, including selections from John Barth, Kant, C. S. Lewis, and George Orwell.

Many people have helped with this project. Robert Miller, executive editor at Oxford University Press, first proposed the idea of this anthology and gave enormous support to it. I also thank my colleagues in the English Department (an umbrella department for philosophy at West Point—we have seventeen philosophers in the English Department—this must be a record—plus a lot of English faculty who are addicted to philosophy). This book is dedicated to all the members of my department, who are as collegial, honorable, and unpretentious as any colleagues I have had the pleasure of working with. Capt. Jowell Parks, Ltc. Janice Hudley, Ltc. Mike Owens, Ltc. Al Bishop, and Ltc. Mike Burke all made excellent suggestions along the way. Col. Peter Stromberg and Col. Anthony Hartle, our chairmen, have supported my work with wonderful generosity. Robert Audi, Margarita Levin, Robert van Wyk, Bonnie Steinbock, several anonymous reviewers, and, especially, Mary Gilbertson offered good advice. My wife, Trudy, who has been my deepest friend and inspiration for forty years worked closely with me through every step of this project.

> Louis P. Pojman
> U.S. Military Academy
> West Point, NY

Introduction
On the Nature of Morality

Morality is about good and evil, and right and wrong action. What exactly are these? It is not always easy to say. Various religions and philosophies differ. What is the good? Religious people identify it with God, the source of all being and value. Plato thought the good was a transcendent, indefinable mystery, the source of all being and value. It is the absolute truth, higher even than God and discoverable by reason and intuition. Plato's follower, the Cambridge philosopher G. E. Moore, modified Plato's formula, omitting the transcendent dimension. The good, he thought, was a nonnatural, indefinable property like the color yellow. It was not the source of all reality, only of morality and aesthetic reality. On the other hand, Jeremy Bentham (chapter 4) and Richard Taylor (chapter 2) deny there is anything mysterious or transcendent about goodness. They hold that the good is a definable, natural property. It refers to pleasure or the object of desire—*good* is a functional term that refers to the satisfaction of our desires, the pleasure we feel when satisfied. Variations on this basic hedonism appear in the literature; the human good for Mill consists not just in any kind of pleasure but in certain qualities of pleasure—a deep sense of well-being or happiness spread over a lifetime, not necessarily a life of ecstatic rapture, "but moments of such, in an existence made up of few and transitory pains, many and various pleasures, with a decided predominance of the active over the passive, and having as the foundation of the whole, not to expect more from life than it is capable of bestowing."* For Nietzsche (chap-

*John Stuart Mill, *Utilitarianism* (1863, chapter 2). Mill elaborates on his functional hedonism: "Happiness is a life in which exist free action (includter 2) goodness has nothing to do with pleasure or happiness ("Only the Englishman wants that") but power, the sense of dominating, of being in control, of being the alpha male in the pack. Goodness derives from the will to power that we all deeply crave. As such it is hierarchical and inegalitarian. But the envious mediocre masses detest this natural good, and so are determined to crush it. Morality, according to Nietzsche, is the herd's attempt to institutionalize mediocrity and protect the sheep from the more excellent wolves. The priests, both religious and secular moralizers, invent the soft moral virtues (pity, patience, peace, kindness, forgiveness, and tolerance) in order to protect themselves from their betters. Helping the worst off, redeeming the worthless, forgiving the criminal, maintaining the lives of sick bodies and diseased souls—the criminals, the stupid, and the mediocre. The ideas of good and evil must be understood in the clash between the superior overmen, and the priests who represent the masses. Right and wrong action, then, become a kind of politically correct ideology which, ironically, proves the Nietzschean point of the will to power. For the moralists invent good and evil in order to empower themselves and their clientele against their superior enemy.

Where does the truth lie in these matters? One thing everyone engaged in the debate recognizes: morality is both personal and social. It is personal in that it has to do with how we should live our lives, what we should strive to become. It is social in that it recognizes that we are not hermits or gods, independent beings with no need for each other. We are centers of conscious striving, desire, who have wills of our own but have to adjust the pursuit of our goals in the light of other people's desires and interests. How to reconcile and adjust these twin forces, the personal and the social, is the central domain of ethics. It is the central concern of this anthology. Many works of ethics emphasize the broader areas of social policy or social ethics: just-war theory, economic relations, punishment, political arrangements, and institutional justice. There is a place for that. But what I want us to focus on in this work is the more personal dimension of ethics: its raison d'être, its fundamental purposes. We want to build from the ground up, for unless we get our foundations firmly laid, our structure will be in danger

---

ing meaningful work), loving relations, and moral character, and in which the individual is not plagued by guilt and anxiety but is blessed with peace and satisfaction."

of capsizing. We will first study the nature of morality, beginning with a sizable selection from William Golding's moral allegory, *Lord of the Flies*. After a commentary, we will examine the philosophical analogue to Golding's work, Thomas Hobbes's *Leviathan,* written three hundred years earlier. In chapter 2 we examine the nature of Good and Evil. After this we raise one of the most crucial questions about morality: is it universally valid or only relative to individual choice or one's culture?

In Part II we progress to the three classic moral theories: *utilitarianism,* which aims at maximizing good consequences, usually defined in terms of pleasure or happiness; *deontological ethics,* which focuses on the individual act (its inherent rightness or wrongness) and the individual (his or her inherent dignity or value); and *virtue ethics,* which focuses on character, the kind of qualities we should inculcate, the kind of people we should become. But all of these theories recognize the role of virtue and vice—morally significant character traits. So in chapter 7 we examine several classic virtues and vices.

In Part III we consider theoretical issues that are implicit in our study of the nature of morality and moral theories, enlarging on what was said earlier. If the first two parts constituted the foundations and formal structure of moral theory, Part III deals with the materials in our building. First we examine the idea of the self in relation to others. Sometimes we can flout moral rules when it is in our perceived interest to do so. Should we do so? Why should we be moral whenever we can enhance personal gain by disregarding morality's requirements? This problem is related to the second—what really is important about life, what, if anything, gives it meaning? Or is it merely "a tale told by an idiot, full of sound and fury, signifying nothing"? Here we look at various worldviews about the nature and destiny of humanity: Epicureanism, Stoicism, Theism, Buddhism, Existentialism, and others. In chapter 10 we examine the importance of freedom and autonomy.

Finally, in Part IV we examine six practical moral issues—perhaps, continuing our metaphor of the house, these constitute the inner dynamics, the plumbing, electricity, and furniture. In chapter 11 we examine the meaning of human sexuality in relation to love and marriage. What does morality permit and forbid? In chapter 12 we analyze the difficult problem of abortion. What rights, if any, do fetuses have? In chapter 13 we look at euthanasia. Chapter 14 deals with our duties to animals, including whether we should be vegetarians. Chapter 15 considers our duties to the environment. How should we relate to nature and the general environment? Do we have obligations to future generations to leave this world a safe place in which to live? Finally, chapter 16 deals with the pressing issue of global terrorism in relation to the quest for justice.

I have generally included readings that take opposing stands on the issues at hand, though sometimes I have simply included a reading to stimulate thinking. The main purpose of this work is to help you think through some of the most difficult and exciting issues of our time. Hence the use of literature to supplement philosophical analysis.

Literature particularizes the general problem and brings it home to us, enlivening the imagination so that we see and feel nuances that are vital to resolving difficult moral issues, possibilities that we might not have considered in our abstract thinking about moral dilemmas. But it is no substitute for philosophical analysis, so while many chapters begin with a literary work, the philosophical essays are where most of the necessary argument and theory take place.

Part I

The Nature of Morality
Good and Evil

In this part of our work we consider three fundamental questions relating to morality: What is the purpose of morality? What are good and evil? Is morality essentially relative or are there objective moral truths? We begin each chapter with a literary selection and then go on to provide a philosophical analysis.

CHAPTER 1

What Is the Purpose of Morality?

What is the purpose of morality? What is morality for? It seems to have many purposes. These include enabling us to reach our goals in socially acceptable ways, enabling us to resolve conflicts of interests fairly, developing certain kinds of positive character, promoting human happiness, enabling society to survive. You can probably think of others. But just as a picture is worth a thousand words, a good story may do more to illuminate the purpose of morality than a thousand disquisitions on the subject. So we begin our book with a sizable selection from William Golding's *Lord of the Flies*, a modern allegory on the nature and purpose of morality. A group of British private school boys are marooned on an island; detached from the constraints of civilization, they turn into savages. Whether or not human nature is as depraved as Golding makes it out to be, the significance of the book lies in the fact that it illuminates the need for and purpose of ethical codes. After Golding's novel, Louis Pojman gives an analysis on its meaning for our understanding of morality. This is followed by a selection from Thomas Hobbes's classic work *Leviathan* (1651), which, in seventeenth-century prose, poignantly sets forth a similar message to Golding's.

These three readings center on the foundational problems of moral philosophy. It is imperative that we think clearly about them before we tackle normative theories and applied ethics. Let us turn now to one of the great moral allegories of our time, William Golding's *Lord of the Flies*.

Lord of the Flies
A Moral Allegory

WILLIAM GOLDING

William Golding is considered one of the most profoundly insightful writers of our age. His works explore the human condition and the need for moral consciousness. In this work, published in 1954, Golding describes a situation in which the veneer of civilization is stripped away from children and a primordial evil emerges out of the depths of the human heart.

An indeterminate number of schoolboys, ranging in age from six to twelve, are cast adrift on an uninhabited island in the Pacific, after being evacuated from England during the next world war. They are forced to create their own social system. All begins well, as Ralph is democratically chosen leader of the group and appropriate rules are agreed upon: keep the fire going, use proper sanitation, obey proper authority and orderly procedures in the assembly. Bereft of modern technology, they must reinvent simple tools or use tools for innovative purposes: eyeglasses to focus the sun's light to start a fire, sticks for spears. They construct shelters and build a fire on the top of the mountain in order to signal their presence to passing ships. They miss simple conveniences: scissors to cut their long, knotty hair, toothbrushes, sanitary facilities, and clothes.

For a while the constraints of civilized society prevent total chaos. While the youngest children, "littluns," are frightened and homesick, the older boys entertain them. They seem ready to make the best out of their fate, and recognize the necessity of substantive and procedural rules. Only he who has the white conch, the symbol of authority, may speak at an assembly, and the democratically chosen leader is invested with limited powers. Even the sadistic Roger, while taunting little Henry by throwing stones near him, manages to keep the stones from harming the child.

Here, invisible yet strong, was the taboo of the old life. Round the squatting child was the protection of parents and school and policemen and the law. Roger's arm was conditioned by a civilization that knew nothing of him and was in ruins. (p. 78)

After some initial euphoria at being liberated from the adult world of constraints into an exciting world of fun in the sun, the children come up against the usual banes of social existence: filth, competition for power and status, neglect of social responsibility, failure of public policy, and escalating violence. Two boys, Ralph, the son of a naval officer, and Jack, the head choirboy, vie for leadership and a bitter rivalry emerges between them. As a compromise, a division of labor ensues in which Jack's choirboy hunters refuse to help Ralph and a few others in constructing shelters. Piggy, the bespectacled asthmatic, acts as the wise and rational counselor, and Simon, an epileptic, is portrayed as possessing special spiritual insight, but these qualities, rationality and spirituality, are tested by the Lord of the Flies. Freeloading soon becomes a common phenomenon as the majority of children leave their tasks to play on the beach. Sanitation becomes a problem, as the diarrheal children defecate all over the beach. Neglect of the fire causes it to burn out, which, in turn, results in failure to be rescued by a passing ship. We enter the novel as Jack returns with his choirboy hunters, having slain their first pig, only to be reprimanded by Ralph for not tending the fire.

The hunters were more silent now, but at this they buzzed again. Ralph flung back his hair. One arm pointed at the empty horizon. His voice was loud and savage, and struck them into silence.

"There was a ship."

Jack, faced at once with too many awful implications, ducked away from them. He laid a hand on the pig and drew his knife. Ralph brought his arm down, fist clenched, and his voice shook.

"There was a ship. Out there. You said you'd keep the fire going and you let it out!" He took a step towards Jack who turned and faced him.

"They might have seen us. We might have gone home—"

This was too bitter for Piggy, who forgot his timidity in the agony of his loss. He began to cry out, shrilly:

"You and your blood, Jack Merridew! You and your hunting! We might have gone home——"

Ralph pushed Piggy on one side.

"I was chief; and you were going to do what I said. You talk. But you can't even build huts—then you go off hunting and let out the fire——"

He turned away, silent for a moment. Then his voice came again on a peak of feeling.

"There was a ship——"

One of the smaller hunters began to wail. The dismal truth was filtering through to everybody. Jack went very red as he hacked and pulled at the pig.

"The job was too much. We needed everyone."

Ralph turned.

"You could have had everyone when the shelters were finished. But you had to hunt—"

"We needed meat."

Jack stood up as he said this, the bloodied knife in his hand. The two boys faced each other. There was the brilliant world of hunting, tactics, fierce exhilaration, skill; and there was the world of longing and baffled common-sense. Jack transferred the knife to his left hand and smudged blood over his forehead as he pushed down the plastered hair.

Piggy began again.

"You didn't ought to have let that fire out. You said you'd keep the smoke going——"

This from Piggy, and the wails of agreement from some of the hunters drove Jack to violence. The bolting look came into his blue eyes. He took a step, and able at last to hit someone, stuck his fist into Piggy's stomach. Piggy sat down with a grunt. Jack stood over him. His voice was vicious with humiliation.

"You would, would you? Fatty!"

Ralph made a step forward and Jack smacked Piggy's head. Piggy's glasses flew off and tinkled on the rocks. Piggy cried out in terror:

"My specs!"

He went crouching and feeling over the rocks but Simon, who got there first, found them for him. Passions beat about Simon on the mountain-top with awful wings.

"One side's broken."

Piggy grabbed and put on the glasses. He looked malevolently at Jack.

"I got to have them specs. Now I only got one eye. Jus' you wait——"

Jack made a move towards Piggy who scrambled away till a great rock lay between them. He thrust his head over the top and glared at Jack through his one flashing glass.

"Now I only got one eye. Just you wait——"

Jack mimicked the whine and scramble.

"Jus' you wait—yah!"

Piggy and the parody were so funny that the hunters began to laugh. Jack felt encouraged. He went on scrambling and the laughter rose to a gale of hysteria. Unwillingly Ralph felt his lips twitch; he was angry with himself for giving way.

He muttered.

"That was a dirty trick."

Jack broke out of his gyration and stood facing Ralph. His words came in a shout.

"All right, all right!"

He looked at Piggy, at the hunters, at Ralph.

"I'm sorry. About the fire, I mean. There. I——"

He drew himself up.

"—I apologize."

The buzz from the hunters was one of admiration at this handsome behaviour. Clearly they were of the opinion that Jack had done the decent thing, had put himself in the right by his generous apology and Ralph, obscurely, in the wrong. They waited for an appropriately decent answer.

Yet Ralph's throat refused to pass one. He resented, as an addition to Jack's misbehaviour, this verbal trick. The fire was dead, the ship was gone. Could they not see? Anger instead of decency passed his throat.

"That was a dirty trick."

They were silent on the mountain-top while the opaque look appeared in Jack's eyes and passed away.

Ralph's final word was an ungracious mutter.

"All right. Light the fire."

With some positive action before them, a little of the tension died. Ralph said no more, did nothing, stood looking down at the ashes round his feet. Jack was loud and active. He gave orders, sang, whistled, threw remarks at the silent Ralph—remarks that did not need an answer, and therefore could not invite a snub; and still Ralph was silent. No one, not even Jack, would ask him to move and in the end they had to build the fire three yards away and in a place not really as convenient. So Ralph asserted his chieftainship and could not have chosen a better way if he had thought for days. Against this weapon, so indefinable and so effective, Jack was powerless and raged without knowing why. By the time the pile was built, they were on different sides of a high barrier.

When they had dealt with the fire another crisis arose. Jack had no means of lighting it. Then to his surprise, Ralph went to Piggy and took the glasses from him. Not even Ralph knew how a link between him and Jack had been snapped and fastened elsewhere.

"I'll bring 'em back."

"I'll come too."

Piggy stood behind him, islanded in a sea of meaningless colour, while Ralph knelt and focused the glossy spot. Instantly the fire was alight Piggy held out his hands and grabbed the glasses back.

Before these fantastically attractive flowers of violet and red and yellow, unkindness melted away. They became a circle of boys round a camp fire and even Piggy and Ralph were half-drawn in. Soon some of the boys were rushing down the slope for more wood while Jack hacked the pig. They tried holding the whole carcass on a stake over the fire, but the stake burnt more quickly than the pig roasted. In the end they skewered bits of meat on branches and held them in the flames: and even then almost as much boy was roasted as meat.

Ralph dribbled. He meant to refuse meat but his past diet of fruit and nuts, with an odd crab or fish, gave him too little resistance. He accepted a piece of half-raw meat and gnawed it like a wolf.

Piggy spoke, also dribbling.

"Aren't I having none?"

Jack had meant to leave him in doubt, as an assertion of power; but Piggy by advertising his omission made more cruelty necessary.

"You didn't hunt."

"No more did Ralph," said Piggy wetly, "nor Simon." He amplified. "There isn't more than a ha'porth of meat in a crab."

Ralph stirred uneasily. Simon, sitting between the twins and Piggy, wiped his mouth and shoved his piece of meat over the rocks to Piggy, who grabbed it. The twins giggled and Simon lowered his face in shame.

Then Jack leapt to his feet, slashed off a great hunk of meat, and flung it down at Simon's feet.

"Eat! Damn you!"

He glared at Simon.

"Take it!"

He spun on his heel, centre of a bewildered circle of boys.

"I got you meat!"

Numberless and inexpressible frustrations combined to make his rage elemental and awe-inspiring.

"I painted my face—I stole up. Now you eat—all of you—and I——"

Slowly the silence on the mountain-top deepened till the click of the fire and the soft hiss of roasting meat could be heard clearly. Jack looked round for understanding but found only respect. Ralph stood among the ashes of the signal fire, his hands full of meat, saying nothing.

Then at last Maurice broke the silence. He changed the subject to the only one that could bring the majority of them together.

"Where did you find the pig?"

Roger pointed down the unfriendly side.

"They were there—by the sea."

Jack, recovering, could not bear to have his story told. He broke in quickly.

"We spread round. I crept, on hands and knees. The spears fell out because they hadn't barbs on. The pig ran away and made an awful noise——"

"It turned back and ran into the circle, bleeding——"

All the boys were talking at once, relieved and excited.

"We closed in——"

The first blow had paralysed its hind quarters, so then the circle could close in and beat and beat—

"I cut the pig's throat——"

The twins, still sharing their identical grin, jumped up and ran round each other. Then the rest joined in, making pig-dying noises and shouting.

"One for his nob!"

"Give him a fourpenny one!"

Then Maurice pretended to be the pig and ran squealing into the centre, and the hunters, circling still, pretended to beat him. As they danced, they sang.

"*Kill the pig. Cut her throat. Bash her in.*"

Ralph watched them, envious and resentful. Not till they flagged and the chant died away, did he speak.

"I'm calling an assembly."

One by one, they halted, and stood watching him.

"With the conch. I'm calling a meeting even if we have to go on into the dark. Down on the platform. When I blow it. Now." He turned away and walked off, down the mountain.

[Things degenerate. The fire, the symbol of hope, is left unattended, and the conch, the symbol of orderly governance, is disdained by Jack's group. With the diminished symbols, Ralph's authority, and the rational procedures he stands for, become undermined. Frightened little Percival reports that he has seen the beast, a preternatural creature who bodes no good. Piggy dismisses such talk as superstitious and assures the group that life follows scientific laws that exclude the preternatural. Ghosts and beasts can't exist. Why not?

> *"'Cos things wouldn't make sense. Houses an' streets, an' TV—they wouldn't work."*
> *But Simon thinks differently. "Maybe there is a beast."*
> *The assembly cried out savagely and Ralph stood up in amazement. "You, Simon? You believe in this?"*
> *... "What I mean is ... maybe it's only us."*
> *"Nuts" [responded] Piggy shocked out of decorum ...*
> *Simon became inarticulate in his effort to express mankind's essential illness.*

Eventually Jack succeeds in winning all but five of the boys to his cause. Only Simon, Piggy, and the twins, Sam and Eric ("Samneric"), remain with Ralph in his project of keeping the fire burning and living by the rule of law, though Simon has gone off on a venture. The crowd has joined Jack and his hunters. Jack rules by charismatic might, livening their spirits with pig hunts and orgies, but treating the littluns cruelly. Needing a magnifying glass to start their fire for the pig roast, three hunters, Jack, Roger, and Maurice, steal into Ralph and Piggy's shelter, attack Ralph and Piggy, and steal Piggy's glasses. We enter (chapter 11) where Ralph and his friends are grieving the loss of the glasses and the fire. Piggy, complains that without his glasses he can't see, and demands that they confront Jack with his crime. He speaks:]

"I got the conch. I'm going to that Jack Merridew an' tell him, I am."
"You'll get hurt."

"What can he do more than he has? I'll tell him what's what. You let me carry the conch, Ralph. I'll show him the one thing he hasn't got."

Piggy paused for a moment and peered round at the dim figures. The shape of the old assembly, trodden in the grass, listened to him.

"I'm going to him with this conch in my hands. I'm going to hold it out. Look, I'm goin' to say, you're stronger than I am and you haven't got asthma. You can see, I'm goin' to say, and with both eyes. But I don't ask for my glasses back, not as a favour. I don't ask you to be a sport, I'll say, not because you're strong, but because what's right's right. Give me my glasses, I'm going to say— you got to!"

Piggy ended, flushed and trembling. He pushed the conch quickly into Ralph's hands as though in a hurry to be rid of it and wiped the tears from his eyes. The green light was gentle about them and the conch lay at Ralph's feet, fragile and white. A single drop of water that had escaped Piggy's fingers now flashed on the delicate curve like a star.

At last Ralph sat up straight and drew back his hair.

"All right. I mean—you can try if you like. We'll go with you."

"He'll be painted," said Sam, timidly. "You know how he'll be——"

"—he won't think much of us——"

"—if he gets waxy we've had it——"

Ralph scowled at Sam. Dimly he remembered something that Simon had said to him once, by the rocks.

"Don't be silly," he said. And then he added quickly, "Let's go."

He held out the conch to Piggy who flushed, this time with pride.

"You must carry it."

"When we're ready I'll carry it——"

Piggy sought in his mind for words to convey his passionate willingness to carry the conch against all odds.

"—I don't mind. I'll be glad, Ralph, only I'll have to be led."

Ralph put the conch back on the shining log.

"We better eat and then get ready."

They made their way to the devastated fruit trees. Piggy was helped to his food and found some by touch. While they ate, Ralph thought of the afternoon.

"We'll be like we were. We'll wash——"

Sam gulped down a mouthful and protested.

"But we bathe every day!"

Ralph looked at the filthy objects before him and sighed.

"We ought to comb our hair. Only it's too long."

"I've got both socks left in the shelter," said Eric, "so we could pull them over our heads like caps, sort of."

"We could find some stuff," said Piggy, "and tie your hair back."

"Like a girl!"

"No. 'Course not."

"Then we must go as we are," said Ralph, "and they won't be any better."

Eric made a detaining gesture.

"But they'll be painted! You know how it is——"

The others nodded. They understood only too well the liberation into savagery that the concealing paint brought.

"Well, we won't be painted," said Ralph, "because we aren't savages."

Samneric looked at each other.

"All the same——"

Ralph shouted.

"No paint!" . . .

They set off along the beach in formation. Ralph went first, limping a little, his spear carried over one shoulder. He saw things partially through the tremble of the heat haze over the flashing sands, and his own long hair and injuries. Behind him came the twins, worried now for a while but full of unquenchable vitality. They said little but trailed the butts of their wooden spears; for Piggy had found, that looking down, shielding his tired sight from the sun, he could just see these moving along the sand. He walked between the trailing butts, therefore, the conch held carefully between his two hands. The boys made a compact little group that moved over the beach, four plate-like shadows dancing and mingling beneath them. There was no sign left of the storm, and the beach was swept clean like a blade that has been scoured. The sky and the mountain were at an immense distance, shimmering in the heat; and the reef was lifted by mirage, floating in a kind of silver pool half-way up the sky.

They passed the place where the tribe had danced. The charred sticks still lay on the rocks where the rain had quenched them but the sand by the water was smooth again. They passed this in silence. No one doubted that the tribe would be found at the Castle Rock and when they came in sight of it they stopped with one accord. The densest tangle on the island, a mass of twisted stems, black and green and impenetrable, lay on their left and tall grass swayed before them. Now Ralph went forward.

Here was the crushed grass where they had all lain when he had gone to prospect. There was the neck of land, the ledge skirting the rock, up there were the red pinnacles.

Sam touched his arm.

"Smoke."

There was a tiny smudge of smoke wavering into the air on the other side of the rock.

"Some fire—I don't think."

Ralph turned.

"What are we hiding for?"

He stepped through the screen of grass on to the little open space that led to the narrow neck.

"You two follow behind. I'll go first, then Piggy a pace behind me. Keep your spears ready."

Piggy peered anxiously into the luminous veil that hung between him and the world.

"Is it safe? Ain't there a cliff? I can hear the sea."

"You keep right close to me."

Ralph moved forward on to the neck. He kicked a stone and it bounded into the water. Then the sea sucked down, revealing a red, weedy square forty feet beneath Ralph's left arm.

"Am I safe?" quavered Piggy. "I feel awful——"

High above them from the pinnacles came a sudden shout and then an imitation war-cry that was answered by a dozen voices from behind the rock.

"Give me the conch and stay still."

"Halt! Who goes there?"

Ralph bent back his head and glimpsed Roger's dark face at the top.

"You can see who I am!" he shouted. "Stop being silly!"

He put the conch to his lips and began to blow. Savages appeared, painted out of recognition, edging round the ledge towards the neck. They carried spears and disposed themselves to defend the entrance. Ralph went on blowing and ignored Piggy's terrors.

Roger was shouting.

"You mind out—see?"

At length Ralph took his lips away and paused to get his breath back. His first words were a gasp, but audible.

"—calling an assembly."

The savages guarding the neck muttered among themselves but made no motion. Ralph walked forwards a couple of steps. A voice whispered urgently behind him.

"Don't leave me, Ralph."

"You kneel down," said Ralph sideways, "and wait till I come back."

He stood half-way along the neck and gazed at the savages intently. Freed by the paint, they had tied their hair back and were more comfortable than he was. Ralph made a resolution to tie his own back afterwards. Indeed he felt like telling them to wait and doing it there and then; but that was impossible. The savages sniggered a bit and one gestured at Ralph with his spear. High above, Roger took his hands off the lever and leaned out to see what was going on. The boys on the neck stood in a pool of their own shadow, diminished to shaggy heads. Piggy crouched, his back shapeless as a sack.

"I'm calling an assembly."

Silence.

Roger took up a small stone and flung it between the twins, aiming to miss. They started and Sam only just kept his footing. Some source of power began to pulse in Roger's body.

Ralph spoke again, loudly.

"I'm calling an assembly."

He ran his eye over them.

"Where's Jack?"

The group of boys stirred and consulted. A painted face spoke with the voice of Robert.

"He's hunting. And he said we weren't to let you in."

"I've come to see about the fire," said Ralph, "and about Piggy's specs."

The group in front of him shifted and laughter shivered outwards from among them, light, excited laughter that went echoing among the tall rocks.

A voice spoke from behind Ralph.

"What do you want?"

The twins made a bolt past Ralph and got between him and the entry. He turned quickly. Jack, identifiable by personality and red hair, was advancing from the forest. A hunter crouched on either side. All three were masked in black and green. Behind them on the grass the headless and paunched body of a sow lay where they had dropped it.

Piggy wailed.

"Ralph! Don't leave me!"

With ludicrous care he embraced the rock, pressing himself to it above the sucking sea. The sniggering of the savages became a loud derisive jeer.

Jack shouted above the noise.

"You go away, Ralph. You keep to your end. This is my end and my tribe. You leave me alone."

The jeering died away.

"You pinched Piggy's specs," said Ralph, breathlessly. "You've got to give them back."

"Got to? Who says?"

Ralph's temper blazed out.

"I say! You voted for me for Chief. Didn't you hear the conch? You played a dirty trick—we'd have given you fire if you'd asked for it——"

The blood was flowing in his cheeks and the bunged-up eye throbbed.

"You could have had fire whenever you wanted. But you didn't. You came sneaking up like a thief and stole Piggy's glasses!"

"Say that again!"

"Thief! Thief!"

Piggy screamed.

"Ralph! Mind me!"

Jack made a rush and stabbed at Ralph's chest with his spear. Ralph sensed the position of the weapon from the glimpse he caught of Jack's arm and put the thrust aside with his own butt. Then he brought the end round and caught Jack a stinger across the ear. They were chest to chest, breathing fiercely, pushing and glaring.

"Who's a thief?"

"You are!"

Jack wrenched free and swung at Ralph with his spear. By common consent they were using the spears as sabres now, no longer daring the lethal points. The blow struck Ralph's spear and slid down, to fall agonizingly on his fingers. Then they were apart once more, their positions reversed, Jack towards the Castle Rock and Ralph on the outside towards the island.

Both boys were breathing very heavily.

"Come on then——"

"Come on——"

Truculently they squared up to each other but kept just out of fighting distance.

"You come on and see what you get!"

"You come on——"

Piggy clutching the ground was trying to attract Ralph's attention. Ralph moved, bent down, kept a wary eye on Jack.

"Ralph—remember what we came for. The fire. My specs."

Ralph nodded. He relaxed his fighting muscles, stood easily and grounded the butt of his spear. Jack watched him inscrutably through his paint. Ralph glanced up at the pinnacles, then towards the group of savages.

"Listen. We've come to say this. First you've got to give back Piggy's specs. If he hasn't got them he can't see. You aren't playing the game——"

The tribe of painted savages giggled and Ralph's mind faltered. He pushed his hair up and gazed at the green and black mask before him, trying to remember what Jack looked like.

Piggy whispered.

"And the fire."

"Oh yes. Then about the fire. I say this again. I've been saying it ever since we dropped in."

He held out his spear and pointed at the savages.

"Your only hope is keeping a signal fire going as long as there's light to see. Then maybe a ship'll notice the smoke and come and rescue us and take us home. But without that smoke we've got to wait till some ship comes by accident. We might wait years; till we were old——"

The shivering, silvery, unreal laughter of the savages sprayed out and echoed away. A gust of rage shook Ralph. His voice cracked.

"Don't you understand, you painted fools? Sam, Eric, Piggy and me—we aren't enough. We tried to keep the fire going, but we couldn't. And then you, playing at hunting. . . ."

He pointed past them to where the trickle of smoke dispersed in the pearly air.

"Look at that! Call that a signal fire? That's a cooking fire. Now you'll eat and there'll be no smoke. Don't you understand? There may be a ship out there——"

He paused, defeated by the silence and the painted anonymity of the group guarding the entry. The chief opened a pink mouth and addressed Samneric who were between him and his tribe.

"You two. Get back."

No one answered him. The twins, puzzled, looked at each other; while Piggy, reassured by the cessation of violence, stood up carefully. Jack glanced back at Ralph and then at the twins.

"Grab them!"

No one moved. Jack shouted angrily.

"I said 'grab them'!"

The painted group moved round Samneric nervously a. unhandily. Once more the silvery laughter scattered.

Samneric protested out of the heart of civilization.

"Oh, I say!"

"—honestly!"

Their spears were taken from them.

"Tie them up!"

Ralph cried out hopelessly against the black and green mask.

"Jack!"

"Go on. Tie them."

Now the painted group felt the otherness of Samneric, felt the power in their own hands. They felled the twins clumsily and excitedly. Jack was inspired. He knew that Ralph would attempt a rescue. He struck in a humming circle behind him and Ralph only just parried the blow. Beyond them the tribe and the twins were a loud and writhing heap. Piggy crouched again. Then the twins lay, astonished, and the tribe stood round them. Jack turned to Ralph and spoke between his teeth.

"See? They do what I want."

There was silence again. The twins lay, inexpertly tied up, and the tribe watched Ralph to see what he would do. He numbered them through his fringe, glimpsed the ineffectual smoke.

His temper broke. He screamed at Jack.

"You're a beast and a swine and a bloody, bloody thief!"

He charged.

Jack, knowing this was the crisis, charged too. They met with a jolt and bounced apart. Jack swung with his fist at Ralph and caught him on the ear. Ralph hit Jack in the stomach and made him grunt. Then they were facing each other again, panting and furious, but unnerved by each other's ferocity. They became aware of the noise that was the background to this fight, the steady shrill cheering of the tribe behind them.

Piggy's voice penetrated to Ralph.

"Let me speak."

He was standing in the dust of the fight, and as the tribe saw his intention the shrill cheer changed to a steady booing.

Piggy held up the conch and the booing sagged a little, then came up again to strength.

"I got the conch!"

e shouted.

I tell you, I got the conch!"

Surprisingly, there was silence now; the tribe were curious to hear what amusing thing he might have to say.

Silence and pause; but in the silence a curious air-noise, close by Ralph's head. He gave it half his attention—and there it was again; a faint "Zup!" Someone was throwing stones: Roger was dropping them, his one hand still on the lever. Below him, Ralph was a shock of hair and Piggy a bag of fat.

"I got this to say. You're acting like a crowd of kids."

The booing rose and died again as Piggy lifted the white, magic shell.

"Which is better—to be a pack of painted niggers like you are, or to be sensible like Ralph is?"

A great clamour rose among the savages. Piggy shouted again.

"Which is better—to have rules and agree, or to hunt and kill?"

Again the clamour and again—"Zup!"

Ralph shouted against the noise.

"Which is better, law and rescue, or hunting and breaking things up?"

Now Jack was yelling too and Ralph could no longer make himself heard. Jack had backed right against the tribe and they were a solid mass of menace that bristled with spears. The intention of a charge was forming among them; they were working up to it and the neck would be swept clear. Ralph stood facing them, a little to one side, his spear ready. By him stood Piggy still holding out the talisman, the fragile, shining beauty of the shell. The storm of sound beat at them, an incantation of hatred. High overhead, Roger, with a sense of delirious abandonment, leaned all his weight on the lever.

Ralph heard the great rock long before he saw it. He was aware of a jolt in the earth that came to him through the soles of his feet, and the breaking sound of stones at the top of the cliff. Then the monstrous red thing bounded across the neck and he flung himself flat while the tribe shrieked.

The rock struck Piggy a glancing blow from chin to knee: the conch exploded into a thousand white fragments and ceased to exist. Piggy, saying nothing, with no time for even a grunt, travelled through the air sideways from the rock, turning over as he went. The rock bounded twice and was lost in the forest. Piggy fell forty feet and landed on his back across that square, red rock in the sea. His head opened and stuff came out and turned red. Piggy's arms and legs twitched a bit, like a pig's after it has been killed. Then the sea breathed again in a long, slow sigh, the water boiled white and pink over the rock; and when it went, sucking back again, the body of Piggy was gone.

This time the silence was complete. Ralph's lips formed a word but no sound came.

Suddenly Jack bounded out from the tribe and began screaming wildly.

"See? See? That's what you'll get! I meant that! There isn't a tribe for you any more! The conch is gone—"

He ran forward, stooping.

"I'm Chief!"

Viciously, with full intention, he hurled his spear at Ralph. The point tore the skin and flesh over Ralph's ribs, then sheared off and fell in the water. Ralph stumbled, feeling not pain but panic, and the tribe, screaming now like the Chief, began to advance. Another spear, a bent one that would not fly straight, went past his face and one fell from on high where Roger was. The twins lay hidden behind the tribe and the anonymous devils' faces swarmed across the neck. Ralph turned and ran. A great noise as of sea-gulls rose behind him. He obeyed an instinct that he did not know he possessed and swerved over the open space so that the spears went wide. He saw the headless body of the sow and jumped in time. Then he was crashing through foliage and small boughs and was hidden by the forest.

The Chief stopped by the pig, turned and held up his hands.

"Back! Back to the fort!"

Presently the tribe returned noisily to the neck where Roger joined them.

The Chief spoke to him angrily.

"Why aren't you on watch?"

Roger looked at him gravely.

"I just came down——"

The hangman's horror clung round him. The Chief said no more to him but looked down at Samneric.

"You got to join the tribe."

"You lemme go——"

"—and me."

The Chief snatched one of the few spears that were left and poked Sam in the ribs.

"What d'you mean by it, eh?" said the Chief fiercely. "What d'you mean by coming with spears? What d'you mean by not joining my tribe?"

The prodding became rhythmic. Sam yelled.

"That's not the way."

Roger edged past the Chief, only just avoiding pushing him with his shoulder. The yelling ceased, and Samneric lay looking up in quiet terror. Roger advanced upon them as one wielding a nameless authority.

CRY OF THE HUNTERS

Ralph lay in a covert, wondering about his wounds. The bruised flesh was inches in diameter over his right ribs, with a swollen and bloody scar where the spear had hit him. His hair was full of dirt and tapped like the tendrils of a creeper. All over he was scratched and bruised from his flight through the forest. By the time his breathing was normal again, he had worked out that bathing these injuries would have to wait. How could you listen for naked feet if you were splashing in water? How could you be safe by the little stream or on the open beach?

Ralph listened. He was not really far from the Castle Rock, and during the first panic he had thought he heard sounds of pursuit. But the hunters had only sneaked into the fringes of the greenery, retrieving spears perhaps, and then had rushed back to the sunny rock as if terrified of the darkness under the leaves. He had even glimpsed one of them, striped brown, black, and red, and had judged that it was Bill. But really, thought Ralph, this was not Bill. This was a savage whose image refused to blend with that ancient picture of a boy in shorts and shirt.

The afternoon died away; the circular spots of sunlight moved steadily over green fronds and brown fibre but no sound came from behind the Rock. At last Ralph wormed out of the ferns and sneaked forward to the edge of that impenetrable thicket that fronted the neck of land. He peered with elaborate caution between branches at the edge and could see Robert sitting on guard at the top of the cliff. He held a spear in his left hand and was tossing up a pebble and catching it again with the right. Behind him a column of smoke rose thickly, so that Ralph's nostrils flared and his mouth dribbled. He wiped his nose and mouth with the back of his hand and for the first time since the morning felt hungry. The tribe must be sitting round the gutted pig, watching the fat ooze and burn among the ashes. They would be intent.

Another figure, an unrecognizable one, appeared by Robert and gave him something, then turned and went back behind the rock. Robert laid his spear on the rock beside him and began to gnaw between his raised hands. So the feast was beginning and the watchman had been given his portion.

Ralph saw that for the time being he was safe. He limped away through the fruit trees, drawn by the thought of the poor food yet bitter when he remembered the feast. Feast to-day, and then to-morrow. . . .

He argued unconvincingly that they would let him alone; perhaps even make an outlaw of him. But then the fatal unreasoning knowledge came to him again. The breaking of the conch and the deaths of Piggy and Simon lay over the island like a vapour. These painted savages would go further and further. Then there was that indefinable connection between himself and Jack; who therefore would never let him alone; never.

He paused, sun-flecked, holding up a bough, prepared to duck under it. A spasm of terror set him shaking and he cried aloud.

"No. They're not as bad as that. It was an accident."

He ducked under the bough, ran clumsily, then stopped and listened.

He came to the smashed acres of fruit and ate greedily. He saw two littluns and, not having any idea of his own appearance, wondered why they screamed and ran.

When he had eaten he went towards the beach. The sunlight was slanting now into the palms by the wrecked shelter. There was the platform and the pool. The best thing to do was to ignore this leaden feeling about the heart and rely on their common sense, their daylight sanity. Now that the tribe had eaten, the thing to do was to try again. And anyway, he couldn't stay here all night in an empty shelter by the deserted platform. His flesh crept and he shivered in the evening sun. No fire; no smoke; no rescue.

[Jack launches a murderous manhunt for Ralph, who hides in the forest. After a time, he hears "a curious trickling sound and then a louder crepitation as if someone were unwrapping great sheets of cellophane." Smoke was flowing through the branches "in white and yellow wisps." Jack had started

a forest fire in order to smoke Ralph out into the open. What could he do? He was beginning to panic. He might find a place away from the fire and climb a tree or he could try to burst their line. A third idea was to find a hiding place somewhere and hope his pursuers would pass by him.]

A nearer cry stood him on his feet and immediately he was away again, running fast among thorns and brambles. Suddenly he blundered into the open, found himself again in that open space—and there was the fathom-wide grin of the skull, no longer ridiculing a deep blue patch of sky but jeering up into a blanket of smoke. Then Ralph was running beneath trees, with the grumble of the forest explained. They had smoked him out and set the island on fire.

Hide was better than a tree because you had a chance of breaking the line if you were discovered.

Hide, then.

He wondered if a pig would agree, and grimaced at nothing. Find the deepest thicket, the darkest hole on the island, and creep in. Now, as he ran, he peered about him. Bars and splashes of sunlight flitted over him and sweat made glistening streaks on his dirty body. The cries were far now, and faint.

At last he found what seemed to him the right place, though the decision was desperate. Here, bushes and a wild tangle of creeper made a mat that kept out all the light of the sun. Beneath it was a space, perhaps a foot high, though it was pierced everywhere by parallel and rising stems. If you wormed into the middle of that you would be five yards from the edge, and hidden, unless the savage chose to lie down and look for you; and even then, you would be in darkness—and if the worst happened and he saw you, then you had a chance to burst out at him, fling the whole line out of step and double back.

Cautiously, his stick trailing behind him, Ralph wormed between the rising stems. When he reached the middle of the mat he lay and listened.

The fire was a big one and the drum-roll that he had thought was left so far behind was nearer. Couldn't a fire out-run a galloping horse? He could see the sun-splashed ground over an area of perhaps fifty yards from where he lay: and as he watched, the sunlight in every patch blinked at him. This was so like the curtain that flapped in his brain that for a moment he thought the blinking was inside him. But then the patches blinked more rapidly, dulled and went out, so that he saw that a great heaviness of smoke lay between the island and the sun.

If anyone peered under the bushes and chanced to glimpse human flesh it might be Samneric who would pretend not to see and say nothing. He laid his cheek against the chocolate-coloured earth, licked his dry lips and closed his eyes. Under the thicket, the earth was vibrating very slightly; or perhaps there was a sound beneath the obvious thunder of the fire and scribbled ululations that was too low to hear.

Someone cried out. Ralph jerked his cheek off the earth and looked into the dulled light. They must be near now, he thought, and his chest began to thump. Hide, break the line, climb a tree—which was the best after all? The trouble was you only had one chance.

Now the fire was nearer; those volleying shots were great limbs, trunks even, bursting. The fools! The fools! The fire must be almost at the fruit trees—what would they eat to-morrow?

Ralph stirred restlessly in his narrow bed. One chanced nothing! What could they do? Beat him? So what? Kill him? A stick sharpened at both ends.

The cries, suddenly nearer, jerked him up. He could see a striped savage moving hastily out of a green tangle, and coming towards the mat where he hid, a savage who carried a spear. Ralph gripped his fingers into the earth. Be ready now, in case.

Ralph fumbled to hold his spear so that it was point foremost; and now he saw that the stick was sharpened at both ends.

The savage stopped fifteen yards away and uttered his cry.

Perhaps he can hear my heart over the noises of the fire. Don't scream. Get ready.

The savage moved forward so that you could only see him from the waist down. That was the butt of his spear. Now you could see him from the knee down. Don't scream.

A herd of pigs came squealing out of the greenery behind the savage and rushed away into the forest. Birds were screaming, mice shrieking, and a little hopping thing came under the mat and cowered.

Five yards away the savage stopped, standing right by the thicket, and cried out. Ralph drew his feet up and crouched. The stake was in his hands, the stake sharpened at both ends, the stake that vibrated so wildly, that grew long, short, light, heavy, light again.

The ululation spread from shore to shore. The savage knelt down by the edge of the thicket, and there were lights flickering in the forest behind him. You could see a knee disturb the mould. Now the other. Two hands. A spear.

A face.

The savage peered into the obscurity beneath the thicket. You could tell that he saw light on this side and on that, but not in the middle—there. In the middle was a blob of dark and the savage wrinkled up his face, trying to decipher the darkness.

The seconds lengthened. Ralph was looking straight into the savage's eyes.

Don't scream.

You'll get back.

Now he's seen you. He's making sure. A stick sharpened.

Ralph screamed, a scream of fright and anger and desperation. His legs straightened, the screams became continuous and foaming. He shot forward, burst the thicket, was in the open, screaming, snarling, bloody. He swung the stake and the savage tumbled over; but there were others coming towards him, crying out. He swerved as a spear flew past and then was silent, running. All at once the lights flickering ahead of him merged together, the roar of the forest rose to thunder and a tall bush directly in his path burst into a great fan-shaped flame. He swung to the right, running desperately fast, with the heat beating on his left side and the fire racing forward like a tide. The ululation rose behind him and spread along, a series of short sharp cries, the sighting call. A brown figure showed up at his right and fell away. They were all running, all crying out madly. He could hear them crashing in the undergrowth and on the left was the hot, bright thunder of the fire. He forgot his wounds, his hunger and thirst, and became fear; hopeless fear on flying feet, rushing through the forest towards the open beach. Spots jumped before his eyes and turned into red circles that expanded quickly till they passed out of sight. Below him, someone's legs were getting tired and the desperate ululation advanced like a jagged fringe of menace and was almost overhead.

He stumbled over a root and the cry that pursued him rose even higher. He saw a shelter burst into flames and the fire flapped at his right shoulder and there was the glitter of water. Then he was down, rolling over and over in the warm sand, crouching with arm up to ward off, trying to cry for mercy.

He staggered to his feet, tensed for more terrors, and looked up at a huge peaked cap. It was a white-topped cap, and above the green shade of the peak was a crown, an anchor, gold foliage. He saw white drill, epaulettes, a revolver, a row of gilt buttons down the front of a uniform.

A naval officer stood on the sand, looking down at Ralph in wary astonishment. On the beach behind him was a cutter, her bows hauled up and held by two ratings. In the stern-sheets another rating held a sub-machine gun.

The ululation faltered and died away.

The officer looked at Ralph doubtfully for a moment, then took his hand away from the butt of the revolver.

"Hullo."

Squirming a little, conscious of his filthy appearance, Ralph answered shyly.

"Hullo."

The officer nodded, as if a question had been answered.

"Are there any adults—any grown-ups with you?"

Dumbly, Ralph shook his head. He turned a half-pace on the sand. A semicircle of little boys, their bodies streaked with coloured clay, sharp sticks in their hands, were standing on the beach making no noise at all.

"Fun and games," said the officer.

The fire reached the coco-nut palms by the beach and swallowed them noisily. A flame, seemingly detached, swung like an acrobat and licked up the palm heads on the platform. The sky was black.

The officer grinned cheerfully at Ralph.

"We saw your smoke. What have you been doing? Having a war or something?"

Ralph nodded.

The officer inspected the little scarecrow in front of him. The kid needed a bath, a hair-cut, a nose-wipe and a good deal of ointment.

"Nobody killed, I hope? Any dead bodies?"

"Only two. And they've gone."

The officer leaned down and looked closely at Ralph.

"Two? Killed?"

Ralph nodded again. Behind him, the whole island was shuddering with flame. The officer knew, as a rule, when people were telling the truth. He whistled softly.

Other boys were appearing now, tiny tots some of them, brown, with the distended bellies of small savages. One of them came close to the officer and looked up.

"I'm, I'm——"

But there was no more to come. Percival Wemys Madison sought in his head for an incantation that had faded clean away.

The officer turned back to Ralph.

"We'll take you off. How many of you are there?"

Ralph shook his head. The officer looked past him to the group of painted boys.

"Who's boss here?"

"I am," said Ralph loudly.

A little boy who wore the remains of an extraordinary black cap on his red hair and who carried the remains of a pair of spectacles at his waist, started forward, then changed his mind and stood still.

"We saw your smoke. And you don't know how many of you there are?"

"No, sir."

"I should have thought," said the officer as he visualized the search before him, "I should have thought that a pack of British boys—you're all British aren't you?—would have been able to put up a better show than that—I mean——"

"It was like that at first," said Ralph, "before things——"

He stopped.

"We were together then——"

The officer nodded helpfully.

"I know. Jolly good show. Like the Coral Island."

Ralph looked at him dumbly. For a moment he had a fleeting picture of the strange glamour that had once invested the beaches. But the island was scorched up like dead wood—Simon was dead—and Jack had. . . . The tears began to flow and sobs shook him. He gave himself up to them now for the first time on the island; great, shuddering spasms of grief that seemed to wrench his whole body. His voice rose under the black smoke before the burning wreckage of the island; and infected by that emotion, the other little boys began to shake and sob too. And in the middle of them, with filthy body, matted hair, and unwiped nose, Ralph wept for the end of innocence, the darkness of man's heart, and the fall through the air of the true, wise friend called Piggy.

The officer, surrounded by these noises, was moved and a little embarrassed. He turned away to give them time to pull themselves together; and waited, allowing his eyes to rest on the trim cruiser in the distance.

For Further Reflection

1. What is the main idea about morality that you get out of this selection from *Lord of the Flies?*

2. Piggy tells Ralph that he is going to Jack to order him to return his glasses. "I don't ask for my glasses back as a favor . . . but because what's right's right. Give me my glasses. . . . You got to." What is Piggy presupposing about the situation and about the significance of morality? What is Jack's response? How does he further respond upon being called a thief? Why is he infuriated by that charge?

3. Compare Ralph's understanding of morality with Piggy's and Jack's. How do they exhibit different moral positions?

4. What, if anything, is the significance of the conch and how do you interpret its destruction?

On the Nature and Purpose of Morality
Reflections on William Golding's
Lord of the Flies

LOUIS P. POJMAN

Louis P. Pojman was professor of philosophy at the United States Military Academy and the editor of this volume. In this essay he analyzes Golding's novel in terms of the nature and purpose of morality. He relates it to Hobbes's account in the *Leviathan* (see the next reading) and identifies the larger purposes of morality.

This essay was written specifically for this volume. Copyright © 2000 Louis P. Pojman.

> Which is better—to have rules and agree, or to hunt
> and kill?
>
> —Piggy

> Morality is more honored in the breach than in the
> observance.
>
> —Thomas Hobbes

Why exactly do we need moral codes? What function do they play
in our lives and in society in general? William Golding's classic
novel *Lord of the Flies* (1954), a modern moral allegory, abridged
in the previous reading, may provide us with a clue to the answer
to these questions.

Golding's allegory is a response to a Victorian British children's
classic, *The Coral Island* (1858), by Robert Ballantyne, in which
three teenage boys are shipwrecked on an unidentified Pacific
island. Ralph Rover, the fifteen-year-old narrator, Jack Martin, and
the creative and wise Peterkin Gay. These boys prove to be ideal
Englishmen and live in uninterrupted harmony, a utopia, until they
encounter cannibals who capture them. But just when the cannibals are about to boil them for dinner, missionaries arrive who convert the cannibals and liberate them from heathen darkness and the
boys from the dark cauldron. The book was written as a refutation
of the prevailing Calvinist and Puritan doctrine of original sin, which
holds that human nature is ineluctably perverse. In *The Coral Island,*
human nature is essentially good.

Since then, two traumatic, cataclysmic world wars have disabused
us of such Pollyanna-like humanism and the age of innocence.
Golding transforms Ralph Rover into Ralph, the commonsensical,
decent, and likable leader; Jack Martin into the rapacious and
Dionysian Jack Merridew, redheaded rival of Ralph, who demands
the position of leadership because he is head choirboy and can
sing C-sharp; and creative and wise Peterkin into two persons,
Simon, the clairvoyant, mystical epileptic, and Piggy, the asthmatic,
myopic philosopher, the conscience of Ralph.

Lord of the Flies is the antithesis of *The Coral Island.* It portrays the
very opposite of the Victorian utopia, a dystopia, a virtual hell. Jack
overthrows Ralph as the leader, and with him, humane rules. The
unbridled lust for excitement leads to the great orgiastic pig-kills,
the sodomizing of a female pig, and finally, at its nadir, to the thirst

for human blood. They turn into savages, sadistically hunting, "Kill the beast! Cut its throat! Spill its blood!" In their Dionysian frenzy, they mistake Simon for a beast and kill him. Piggy has his glasses stolen with impunity and is sadistically murdered. Ralph, who resists the depravity to the end, is hunted like a pig and is about to be destroyed when the British navy, seeing the smoke of the burning jungle, comes to the rescue.

What is Golding trying to tell us? E. L. Epstein comments on his work:

> The theme is an attempt to trace the defects of society back to the defects of human nature. The moral is that the shape of a society must depend on the ethical nature of the individual and not only any political system however apparently logical or respectable. The whole book is symbolic in nature except the rescue in the end where adult life appears, dignified and capable, but in reality enmeshed in the same evil as the symbolic life of the children on the island. The officer, having interrupted a manhunt [of Ralph], prepares to take the children off the island in a cruiser which will presently be hunting its enemy in the same implacable way. And who will rescue the adult and his cruiser?[1]

Civilization's power is weak and vulnerable to atavistic, volcanic passions. The sensitive Simon, the symbol of religious consciousness (as in "Simon Peter," the first disciple of Jesus), who prophesies that Ralph will be saved and is the first to discover and fight against the "ancient, inescapable recognition" of the beast in us, is slaughtered by the group in a wild frenzy. Only Piggy and Ralph, mere observers of the orgiastic homicide, feel vicarious pangs of guilt at this atrocity.

The incarnation of philosophy and culture—poor, fat, nearsighted Piggy, with his broken spectacles and asthma—becomes ever more pathetic as the chaos increases. The nadir of his ridiculous position is reached after the rebels, led by Jack, steal his spectacles in order to harness the sun's rays for starting fires. After Ralph, the emblem of not too bright but morally good civilized leadership, fails to persuade Jack to return the glasses, Piggy asserts his moral right to them:

> You're stronger than I am and you haven't got asthma. You can see. . . . But I don't ask for my glasses back, not as a favour. I don't ask you to be a sport . . . not because you're strong, but because what's right's right. Give me my glasses. . . . You got to. (p. 211)

---

[1]E. L. Epstein, "Notes on *Lord of the Flies,*" in William Golding, *Lord of the Flies* (New York: G. P. Putnam, 1959), p. 250–51.

Piggy might as well have addressed the fire itself, for in this state of anarchy moral discourse is a foreign tongue that only incites the worst elements to greater immorality. Roger, Jack's sadistic lieutenant, perched on a cliff above, finally liberated from the constraints which held back his arm from harming little Henry, responds to moral reasoning by dislodging a huge rock from a cliff that hits Piggy and flings him to his death forty feet below.

The title *Lord of the Flies* comes from a translation of the Greek *Beelzebub,* which is a name for the devil. The boys are frightened by shadowy figures which they imagine to be a supernatural beast, but, as the prophetic Simon points out, "Maybe [the beast] is only us." We need no external devil to bring about evil. We have found the devil and, in the words of Pogo, "he is us." Ubiquitous, ever waiting for a moment to strike out, he emerges from the depths of the subconscious whenever there is a conflict of interest or a moment of moral lassitude. As E. L. Epstein says, "The tenets of civilization, the moral and social codes, the Ego, the intelligence itself, form only a veneer over this white-hot power, this uncontrollable force, 'the fury and the mire of human veins.'"[2]

Beelzebub's ascendancy proceeds through fear, hysteria, violence, and death. A delegation starts out hunting pigs for meat. The hunters quickly find themselves enjoying the excitement, the violence, the bloody destruction of the pig, the symbol of the beast. In order to drown the incipient shame over bloodthirstiness, and take on a persona more compatible with their deed, the children paint themselves with colored mud. Their lusting for the kill takes on all the powerful overtones of an orgiastic sexual ritual, including ritual, sadistic sodomy, as they lunge the wooden spear up the rectum of the female pig. Liberated from their social selves, they kill without remorse whoever gets in their way. The death of Simon and Piggy (the symbols of the religious and the philosophical, the two great fences blocking the descent to hell) and the final orgiastic hunt with the "spear sharpened at both ends" signal for Ralph the depths of evil in the human heart.

Ironically, it is the British navy that finally comes to the rescue and saves Ralph (civilization) just when all seems lost. But the symbol of the navy is a Janus-faced omen. On the one hand it may symbolize the fact that a military defense is, unfortunately, sometimes needed to save civilization from the barbarians (Hilter's Nazis or Jack and Roger's allies), but on the other hand it symbolizes the quest for blood and vengeance latent in contemporary civilization. The children's world is really only a stage lower than the adult world whence they come, and that shallow civilization could very well regress to tooth and claw if it were scratched too sharply. The children were saved by the adults, but who will save the adults, who put so much emphasis in military enterprises and weapons systems—in the euphemistic name of "defense"? To quote Epstein:

> The officer, having interrupted a man-hunt, prepares to take the children off the island in a cruiser which will presently be hunting its enemy in the same implacable way. And who will rescue the adult and his cruiser?[3]

The fundamental ambiguity of human existence is seen in every section of the book, poignantly mirroring the human condition. Even Piggy's spectacles, the sole example of modern technology on the island, become a bane for the island as Jack uses them to ignite a forest fire that will smoke out their prey, Ralph, and that ends up burning down the entire forest and destroying the island's animal life. The spectacles are a symbol both of our penchant for misusing technology to vitiate the environment and of our ability to create weapons that will lead to global suicide.

Golding is trying to place his finger on a defect of human nature. What exactly is that defect? An older theological term for it is *original sin,* a certain tendency to assert one's ego against God and the social good. One need not be a theist with a concept of sin to accept this message: human nature has a tendency to selfishness, to a desperate egotism, which, in appropriate circumstances, is all too willing to harm others unjustly. Cut off from the sanctions of adult civilization, these preteens lack the resources to sustain the institutions that would mitigate the damage of unbridled egoism.

Ask yourself, What could make the difference between the dystopia of *Lord of the Flies* and the utopia of *Coral Island.* Could you rewrite Golding's book in order to achieve an opposite ending? I had a conversation with a Bucknell University philosophy student, Coleen Zoller, who said that she thinks *Lord of the Flies* is a very male book, illustrating the worst kind of male behavior. "Women would typically act differently. They would stress cooperation and caring

[3]Op. cit., p. 251.

for one another. The process would be quite different." Do you think this is true? Can you imagine different young people acting better?

WHY DO WE NEED MORALITY?
HOBBES'S ACCOUNT

Why do we need morality? What is its nature and purpose? What does it do for us that no other social arrangement does? There are many philosophical replies to these questions, but a classic reply, one relevant to the situation of *Lord of the Flies,* is that given by the English philosopher Thomas Hobbes (1588–1679) in his book *Leviathan* (1651). Hobbes believed that human beings always act out of perceived self-interest, that is, they invariably seek gratification and avoid harm. His argument goes like this:

Nature has made us basically equal in physical and mental abilities, so that while one person may be somewhat stronger or have a higher IQ than another, each has the ability to harm, even kill, the other, if not alone, then in confederacy with others. Furthermore, we all want to attain our goals, including sufficient food, shelter, security, power, wealth, and other scarce resources. These two facts, equality of ability to harm and desire to attain our goals, lead to an unstable state.

From this equality of ability arises equality of hope in the attaining of our ends. And therefore if any two people desire the same thing, which nevertheless they cannot both enjoy, they become enemies; and in the way to their end, which is principally their own preservation and sometimes their enjoyment only, endeavor to destroy, or subdue one another. And from hence it comes to pass, that where an invader hath no more to fear, than another man's single power; if one plant, sow, build, or possess a convenient seat, others may probably be expected to come prepared with forces united, to dispossess, and deprive him, not only of the fruit of his labor, but also of his life or liberty. And the invader again is in the like danger of another.[4]

Given this state of insecurity, people have reason to fear one another. Hobbes calls this a "state of nature," one in which there

[4]Thomas Hobbes, *Leviathan* (1651), chapter 13.

are no common ways of life, no laws or moral rules which are enforced, no justice or injustice, for these concepts lack application. There are no reliable expectations about other people's behavior—except that they will follow their own inclinations and perceived interests, tending to be arbitrary, violent, and capricious.

> Hereby it is manifest, that during the time men live without a common power to keep them all in awe, they are in that condition which is called war; and such a war, as is for *every man, against every man*. For war consists not in battle only or in the act of fighting; but in a tract of time, wherein the will to contend in battle is sufficiently known: and therefore the notion of *time,* is to be considered in the nature of war; as it is in the nature of weather. For as the nature of foul weather lies not in the shower or two of rain, but in an inclination thereto of many days together; so the nature of war consists not in actual fighting, but in the known disposition thereto, during all the time there is no disposition to the contrary.

The consequence of the state of nature, this war of all against all, is described thusly:

> In such a condition, there is no place for industry; because the fruit thereof is uncertain: and consequently no cultivating of the earth; no navigation, nor use of the comfortable buildings; no instruments of moving, and removing, such things as require much force; no knowledge of the face of the earth; no account of time; no arts; no literature; no society; and which is worst of all, continual fear, and danger of violent death; and the life of man solitary, poor, nasty, brutish and short.

But this state of nature, or more exactly, state of anarchy and chaos, is in no one's interest. We can all do better if we compromise, give up some of our natural liberty—to do as we please—so that we will all be more likely to get what we want: security, happiness, power, prosperity, and peace. So rational egoists that we are, according to Hobbes, we exchange some of our liberty for a *social contract* or *covenant,* wherein a ruler and rules are set over us, which we are to obey, since they are enforced by a mighty ruler, the State, the *Leviathan.* Only within this contract does morality arise and do justice, and injustice come into being. Where there is no enforceable law, there is neither right nor wrong, justice nor injustice.

So morality is a form of social control. We all opt for an enforceable set of rules which *if almost all of us obey almost all of the time almost all will be better off almost all of the time.* A select few, conceivably, might be better off in the state of nature, but the vast majority will be better off in a situation of security and mutual cooperation. It may turn out that some people cheat, renege on their contract, but so long as the adherence is widespread by most of us most of the time, we will all flourish.

Hobbes didn't claim that a pure state of nature ever existed or that humanity ever really formally entered into such a contract, though he notes that among nations such a state actually exists, so that a "cold war" keeps us all in fear. Rather, Hobbes is offering an explanation of the function of morality. He is answering the question, Why do we need morality. Why? Because without it existence would be an unbearable hell in which life was "solitary, poor, nasty, brutish and short."

THE PURPOSES OF MORALITY

What is the role of morality in human existence? What are little boys and girls and big men and women made of that requires ethical consciousness? Ralph answers these questions at the end of *Lord of the Flies.*

> And in the middle of [the children], with filthy body, matted hair, and unwiped nose, Ralph wept for the end of innocence, the darkness of man's heart, and the fall through the air of the true, wise friend called Piggy. (p. 248)

In this wise modern moral allegory, we catch a glimpse of some of the purposes of morality. Rules formed over the ages and internalized within us hold us back and hopefully defeat the "Lord of the Flies" in society, whether he be inherent in us individually or an emergent property of corporate existence. The moral code restrains even the sadistic Rogers of society from evil until untoward social conditions open up the sluice gates of sadism and random violence. Morality is the force that enables Piggy and Ralph to maintain a modicum of order within their dwindling society, first motivating them to compromise with Jack and then keeping things in a wider perspective.

In Golding's allegory, morality is "honored more in the breach than in the observance," for we see the consequences of not having rules and principles and virtuous character. As Piggy says, "Which is better—to have rules and agree, or to hunt and kill [each other]?" Morality consists of a set of rules which if followed by nearly everyone will promote the flourishing of nearly everyone. These rules restrict our freedom but only in order to promote greater freedom and well-being. More specifically morality seems to have these five purposes:

1. To keep society from falling apart.
2. To ameliorate human suffering.
3. To promote human flourishing.
4. To resolve conflicts of interest in just and orderly ways.
5. To assign praise and blame, reward the good and punish the guilty.

Let us elaborate these purposes. Imagine what society would be if everyone or nearly everyone did whatever he or she pleased, disregarding basic moral rules. I would make a promise to you to help you with your philosophy homework tomorrow if you fix my car today. You believe me. So you fix my car, but you are deeply angry when I laugh at you on the morrow when I drive away to the beach instead of helping you with your homework. Or you loan me money but I run off with it. Or I lie to you or harm you when it is in my interest or even kill you when I feel the urge.

In such a society parents would abandon or abuse their children and spouses betray each other whenever it was convenient. The very notion of a *spouse* would be meaningless, since it connotes commitment, loyalty, fidelity, all of which are *moral* notions. No one would have an incentive to cooperate or help anyone else because reciprocity (a moral principle) would not be recognized. Great suffering would go largely unameliorated and, certainly, people would not be very happy. We would not flourish or reach our highest potential. Under such circumstances society would break down. Even thieves must adhere to moral rules with each other, if they have any hope of robbing others.

In 1995 I visited the former USSR countries Kazakhstan and Russia, which are undergoing a difficult transition from communism to democracy (which hopefully will be resolved favorably). In this transition, with the state's power considerably withdrawn, crime is on the increase and distrust is prevalent. At night I had to navigate my way up the staircases in our apartment building in complete darkness. I inquired as to why there were no light bulbs in the stairwells, only to be told that the residents stole them, believing that if they did not take them, their neighbors would. Without a dominant authority, the former Communist authorities, the social contract has eroded and everyone must struggle alone in the darkness.

We need moral rules to guide our actions in ways that light up our paths and prevent and reduce suffering, that enhance human (and animal, for that matter) well-being, that allow us to resolve our conflicts of interests according to recognizably fair rules, and to assign responsibility for actions, so that we can praise and blame, reward and punish people according to how their actions reflect moral principles.

Even though these five purposes are related, they are not identical, and different moral theories emphasize different purposes and in different ways. Utilitarianism stresses human flourishing and the amelioration of suffering, whereas contractual systems rooted in rational self-interest accent the role of resolving conflicts of interest. A complete moral theory would include a place for each of these purposes. Such a system has the goal of internalizing the rules that promote these principles in each moral person's life, producing the virtuous person, someone who is "a jewel that shines in [morality's] own light," to paraphrase Kant. It is fair to say that morality is a necessary condition for happiness. Whether it is also a sufficient condition for happiness is more controversial, a question we shall consider in Part III. The goal of morality is to create happy and virtuous people, the kind that create flourishing communities. That's why it is the most important subject on earth.

For Further Reflection

1. What, according to Pojman, is the main message of *Lord of the Flies?* Do you agree? Explain.

2. How does Pojman relate Golding's novel to Hobbes's account of morality?

3. Discuss Pojman's five purposes of morality. Do you agree morality has all of these purposes? If not, explain. Can you think of other purposes it has?

On the State of Nature

THOMAS HOBBES

Thomas Hobbes (1588–1679), the greatest English political philosopher, set forth the classic version of the idea that morality and politics arise out of a social contract. He was born on Good Friday, April 5, 1588, in Westbury, England, the son of an eccentric vicar. On the day of his birth the Spanish Armada, the greatest naval fleet the world had then seen, was spotted off the coast of southern England. The chronicler John Aubrey reports that Hobbes's mother, only seven months pregnant, startled by the news, fell into labor and delivered him. Hobbes wrote of this experience, "Unbeknownst to my mother at that time she gave birth to twins, myself and fear. And fear has been my constant companion throughout life." Hobbes's lifetime was filled with the dangers of war, the invading Spanish Armada, the religious wars of Europe, the Civil War in England. His political philosophy may be read as a cure against the fear and insecurity of people desperately in need of peace and tranquility. Hobbes was educated at Oxford University, and lived through an era of political revolutions as a scholar and tutor (to the future Charles II).

Hobbes is known today primarily for his masterpiece in political theory, *Leviathan* (1651), a book written during the English civil wars (1642–1652), sometimes referred to as "the Great Rebellion," which pitted the forces of monarchy (the Royalists) under Charles I against those of Parliament under Oliver Cromwell. Hobbes's work was intended to support the Royalists, as he believed that the monarchy was the best guarantee for orderly and stable government. Yet the Royalists misconstrued his interpretation as supporting the rebels, no doubt because Hobbes rejected the usual grounds for the monarchy, the divine right of kings. For this reason, and because the book conveyed a materialist view of human nature, thought to be dangerous to religion, it was suppressed or violently attacked throughout Hobbes's lifetime.

From Thomas Hobbes, *Leviathan,* 1651.

What are the doctrines his contemporaries found so controversial? First of all, Hobbes breaks from the medieval notion that the state is a natural organism, based on natural devotion and interdependence. He develops a moral and political theory based not on natural affection, but on psychological egoism. Hobbes argues that people are all egoists who always act in their own self-interest, to obtain gratification and avoid harm. However, we cannot obtain any of the basic goods because of the inherent fear of harm and death, the insecurity in an unregulated "state of nature," in which life is "solitary, poor, nasty, brutish and short." We cannot relax our guard, for everyone is constantly in fear of everyone else. In this state of anarchy the prudent person concludes that it really is in all our self-interest to make a contract to keep to a minimal morality of respecting human life, keeping covenants made, and obeying the laws of the society. This minimal morality, which Hobbes refers to as "the laws of nature" is nothing more than a set of maxims of prudence. In order to ensure that we all obey this covenant Hobbes proposes a strong sovereign or "Leviathan" to impose severe penalties on those who disobey the laws, for "covenants without the sword are but words."*

---

*The term *Leviathan* refers to the sea monster (or whale) referred to in the Book of Job:

Let those curse the day who are skilled to rouse up Leviathan (3:8) . . .
Can you draw out Leviathan with a fishhook or press down his tongue with a cord?
Can you put a rope in his nose or pierce his jaw with a hook? . . .
Will he make a covenant with you to take him for your servant for ever? . . .
His sneezings flash forth light, and his eyes are like the eyelids of the dawn.
Out of his mouth go flaming torches; sparks of fire leap forth.
Out of his nostrils comes forth smoke, as from a boiling pot and burning rushes.
His breath kindles coals, and flame comes forth from his mouth . . .
When he raises himself up the mighty are afraid; at the crashing they are beside themselves . . .
Upon earth there is not his like, a creature without fear.
He beholds everything that is high; he is king over all the sons of pride. (Job 41)

OF THE NATURAL CONDITION
OF MANKIND AS CONCERNING
THEIR FELICITY, AND MISERY

Nature hath made men so equal, in the faculties of the body, and mind; as that though there be found one man sometimes manifestly stronger in body, or of quicker mind than another; yet when all is reckoned together, the difference between man, and man, is not so considerable, as that one man can thereupon claim to himself any benefit, to which another may not pretend, as well as he. For as to the strength of body, the weakest has strength enough to kill the strongest, either by secret machination, or by confederacy with others, that are in the same danger with himself.

And as to the faculties of the mind, setting aside the arts grounded upon words, and especially that skill of proceeding upon general, and infallible rules, called science; which very few have, and but in few things; as being not a native faculty, born with us; nor attained, as prudence, while we look after somewhat else, I find yet a greater equality amongst men, than that of strength. For prudence, is but experience; which equal time, equally bestows on all men, in those things they equally apply themselves unto. That which may perhaps make such equality incredible, is but a vain conceit of one's own wisdom, which almost all men think they have in a greater degree, than the vulgar; that is, than all men but themselves, and a few others, whom by fame, or for concurring with themselves, they approve. For such is the nature of men, that howsoever they may acknowledge many others to be more witty, or more eloquent, or more learned; yet they will hardly believe there be many so wise as themselves; for they see their own wit at hand, and other men's at a distance. But this proveth rather that men are in that point equal, than unequal. For there is not ordinarily a greater sign of the equal distribution of any thing, than that every man is contented with his share.

From this equality of ability, ariseth equality of hope in the attaining of our ends. And therefore if any two men desire the same thing, which nevertheless they cannot both enjoy, they become enemies; and in the way to their end, which is principally their own conservation, and sometimes their delectation only, endeavour to destroy, or subdue one another. And from hence it comes to pass, that where an invader hath no more to fear, than another man's single power; if one plant, sow, build, or possess a convenient seat, others may probably be expected to come prepared with forces united, to dispossess, and deprive him, not only of the fruit of his labour, but also of his life, or liberty. And the invader again is in the like danger of another.

And from this diffidence of one another, there is no way for any man to secure himself, so reasonable, as anticipation; that is, by force, or wiles, to master the persons of all men he can, so long, till he see no other power great enough to endanger him: and this is no more than his own conservation requireth, and is generally allowed. Also because there be some, that taking pleasure in contemplating their own power in the acts of conquest, which they pursue farther than their security requires; if others, that otherwise would be glad to be at ease within modest bounds, should not by invasion increase their power, they would not be able, long time, by standing only on their defence, to subsist. And by consequence, such augmentation of dominion over men being necessary to a man's conservation, it ought to be allowed him.

Again, men have no pleasure, but on the contrary a great deal of grief, in keeping company, where there is no power able to over-awe them all. For every man looketh that his companion should value him, at the same rate he sets upon himself: and upon all signs of contempt, or undervaluing, naturally endeavours, as far as he dares, (which amongst them that have no common power to keep them in quiet, is far enough to make them destroy each other), to extort a greater value from his contemners, by damage; and from others, by the example.

So that in the nature of man, we find three principal causes of quarrel. First, competition; secondly, diffidence; thirdly, glory.

The first, maketh men invade for gain; the second, for safety; and the third, for reputation. The first use violence, to make themselves masters of other men's persons, wives, children, and cattle; the second, defend them; the third, for trifles, as a word, a smile, a different opinion, and any other sign of undervalue, either direct in their persons, or by reflection in their kindred, their friends, their nation, their profession, or their name.

Hereby it is manifest, that during the time men live without a common power to keep them all in awe, they are in that condition which is called war; and such a war, as is of every man, against every man. For war, consisteth not in battle only, or the act of fighting; but in a tract of time, wherein the will to contend by battle is sufficiently known: and therefore the notion of *time,* is to be considered in the nature of war; as it is in the nature of weather. For as the nature of foul weather, lieth not in the shower or two of rain; but in an inclination thereto of many days together: so the nature of war, consisteth not in actual fighting; but in the known disposition thereto, during all the time there is no assurance to the contrary. All other time is PEACE.

Whatsoever therefore is consequent to a time of war, where every man is enemy to every man; the same is consequent to the time, wherein men live without other security, than what their own strength, and their own invention shall furnish them withal. In such condition, there is no place for industry; because the fruit thereof is uncertain: and consequently no culture of the earth; no navigation, nor use of the commodities that may be imported by sea; no commodious building; no instruments of moving, and removing, such things as require much force; no knowledge of the face of the earth; no account of time; no arts; no letters; no society; and which is worst of all, continual fear, and danger of violent death; and the life of man, solitary, poor, nasty, brutish, and short.

It may seem strange to some man, that has not well weighed these things; that nature should thus dissociate, and render men apt to invade, and destroy one another: and he may therefore, not trusting to this inference, made from the passions, desire perhaps to have the same confirmed by experience. Let him therefore consider with himself, when taking a journey, he arms himself, and seeks to go well accompanied; when going to sleep, he locks his doors; when even in his house he locks his chests; and this when he knows there be laws, and public officers, armed, to revenge all injuries shall be done him; what opinion he has of his fellow-subjects, when he rides armed; of his fellow citizens, when he locks his doors; and of his children, and servants, when he locks his chests. Does he not there as much accuse mankind by his actions, as I do by my words? But neither of us accuse man's nature in it. The desires, and other passions of man, are in themselves no sin. No more are the actions, that proceed from those passions, till they know a law that forbids them: which till laws be made they cannot know: nor can any law be made, till they have agreed upon the person that shall make it.

It may peradventure be thought, there was never such a time, nor condition of war as this; and I believe it was never generally so, over all the world: but there are many places, where they live so now. For the savage people in many places of America, except the government of small families, the concord whereof dependeth on natural lust, have no government at all; and live at this day in that brutish manner, as I said before. Howsoever, it may be perceived what manner of life there would be, where there were no common power to fear, by the manner of life, which men that have formerly lived under a peaceful government, use to degenerate into, in a civil war.

But though there had never been any time, wherein particular men were in a condition of war one against another; yet in all times, kings, and persons of sovereign authority, because of their independency, are in continual jealousies, and in the state and posture of gladiators; having their weapons pointing, and their eyes fixed on one another; that is, their forts, garrisons, and guns upon the frontiers of their kingdoms; and continual spies upon their neighbours; which is a posture of war. But because they uphold thereby, the industry of their subjects; there does not follow from it, that misery, which accompanies the liberty of particular men.

To this war of every man, against every man, this also is consequent; that nothing can be unjust. The notions of right and wrong, justice and injustice have there no place. Where there is no common power, there is no law: where no law, no injustice. Force, and fraud, are in war the two cardinal virtues. Justice, and injustice are none of the faculties neither of the body, nor mind. If they were, they might be in a man that were alone in the world, as well as his senses, and passions. They are qualities, that relate to men in society, not in solitude. It is consequent also to the same condition, that there be no propriety, no dominion, no *mine* and *thine* distinct; but only that to be every man's, that he can get; and for so long, as he can keep it. And thus much for the ill condition, which man by mere nature is actually placed in; though with a possibility to come out of it, consisting partly in the passions, partly in his reason.

The passions that incline men to peace, are fear of death; desire of such things as are necessary to commodious living; and a hope by their industry to obtain them. And reason suggesteth convenient articles of peace, upon which men may be drawn to agreement. These articles, are they, which otherwise are called the Laws of Nature: whereof I shall speak more particularly, in the two following chapters.

OF THE FIRST AND SECOND NATURAL LAWS, AND OF CONTRACTS

The right of nature, which writers commonly call *jus naturale,* is the liberty each man hath, to use his own power, as he will himself, for the preservation of his own nature; that is to say, of his own life; and consequently, of doing any thing, which in his own judgment, and reason, he shall conceive to be the aptest means thereunto.

By LIBERTY, is understood, according to the proper signification of the word, the absence of external impediments: which impediments, may oft take away part of a man's power to do what he would; but cannot hinder him from using the power left him, according as his judgment, and reason shall dictate to him.

A LAW OF NATURE, *lex naturalis,* is a precept or general rule, found out by reason, by which a man is forbidden to do that, which is destructive of his life, or taketh away the means of preserving the same; and to omit that, by which he thinketh it may be best preserved. For though they that speak of this subject, use to confound *jus,* and *lex, right* and *law:* yet they ought to be distinguished; because RIGHT, consisteth in liberty to do, or to forbear; whereas LAW, determineth, and bindeth to one of them: so that law, and right, differ as much, as obligation, and liberty; which in one and the same matter are inconsistent.

And because the condition of man, as hath been declared in the precedent chapter, is a condition of war of every one against every one; in which case every one is governed by his own reason; and there is nothing he can make use of, that may not be a help unto him, in preserving his life against his enemies; it followeth, that in such a condition, every man has a right to every thing; even to one another's body. And therefore, as long as this natural right of every man to every thing endureth, there can be no security to any man, how strong or wise soever he be, of living out the time, which nature ordinarily alloweth men to live. And consequently it is a precept, or general rule of reason, *that every man, ought to endeavour peace, as far as he has hope of obtaining it; and when he cannot obtain it, that he may seek, and use, all helps, and advantages of war.* The first branch of which rule, containeth the first, and fundamental law of nature; which is, *to seek peace, and follow it.* The second, the sum of the right of nature; which is, *by all means we can, to defend ourselves.*

From this fundamental law of nature, by which men are commanded to endeavour peace, is derived this second law; *that a man be willing, when others are so too, as far-forth, as for peace, and defence of himself he shall think it necessary, to lay down this right to all things; and be contented with so much liberty against other men, as he would allow other men against himself.* For as long as every man holdeth this right, of doing any thing he liketh; so long are all men in the condition of war. But if other men will not lay down their right, as well as he; then there is no reason for any one, to divest himself of his: for that were to expose himself to prey, which no man is bound to, rather than to dispose himself to peace. This is that law of the Gospel; *whatsoever you require that others should do to you, that do ye to them. And that law of all men, quod tibi fieri non vis, alteri ne feceris.*[1]

To *lay down* a man's *right* to any thing, is to *divest* himself of the *liberty,* of hindering another of the benefit of his own right to the same. For he that renounceth, or passeth away his right, giveth not to any other man a right which he had not before; because there is nothing to which every man had not right by nature: but only standeth out of his way, that he may enjoy his own original right, without hindrance from him; not without hindrance from another. So that the effect which redoundeth to one man, by another man's defect of right, is but so much diminution of impediments to the use of his own right original.

Right is laid aside, either by simply renouncing it; or by transferring it to another. By *simply* RENOUNCING; when he cares not to whom the benefit thereof redoundeth. By TRANSFERRING; when he intendeth the benefit thereof to some certain person, or persons. And when a man hath in either manner abandoned, or granted away his right; then is he said to be OBLIGED, or BOUND, not to hinder those, to whom such right is granted, or abandoned, from the benefit of it: and that he *ought,* and it is his DUTY, not to make void that voluntary act of his own: and that such hindrance is INJUSTICE, and INJURY, as being *sine jure,*[2] the right being before renounced, or transferred. So that *injury,* or *injustice,* in the controversies of the world, is somewhat like to that, which in the disputations of scholars is called *absurdity.* For as it is there called an absurdity,

---

[1]["What you do not want done to you, do not do to others."—ed. note]
[2][That is, without right.—ed. note]

to contradict what one maintained in the beginning: so in the world, it is called injustice, and injury, voluntarily to undo that, which from the beginning he had voluntarily done. The way by which a man either simply renounceth, or transferreth his right, is a declaration, or signification, by some voluntary and sufficient sign, or signs, that he doth so renounce, or transfer; or hath so renounced, or transferred the same, to him that accepteth it. And these signs are either words only, or actions only; or, as it happeneth most often, both words, and actions. And the same are the BONDS, by which men are bound, and obliged: bonds, that have their strength, not from their own nature, for nothing is more easily broken than a man's word, but from fear of some evil consequence upon the rupture.

Whensoever a man transferreth his right, or renounceth it; it is either in consideration of some right reciprocally transferred to himself; or for some other good he hopeth for thereby. For it is a voluntary act: and of the voluntary acts of every man, the object is some *good to himself.* And therefore there be some rights, which no man can be understood by any words, or other signs, to have abandoned, or transferred. At first a man cannot lay down the right of resisting them, that assault him by force, to take away his life; because he cannot be understood to aim thereby, at any good to himself. The same may be said of wounds, and chains, and imprisonment; both because there is no benefit consequent to such patience; as there is to the patience of suffering another to be wounded, or imprisoned: as also because a man cannot tell, when he seeth men proceed against him by violence, whether they intend his death or not. And lastly the motive, and end for which this renouncing, and transferring of right is introduced, is nothing else but the security of a man's person, in his life, and in the means of so preserving life, as not to be weary of it. And therefore if a man by words, or other signs, seem to despoil himself of the end, for which those signs were intended; he is not to be understood as if he meant it, or that it was his will; but that he was ignorant of how such words and actions were to be interpreted.

The mutual transferring of right, is that which men call CONTRACT.

There is a difference between transferring of right to the thing; and transferring, or tradition, that is delivery of the thing itself. For the thing may be delivered together with the translation of the right; as in buying and selling with ready-money; or exchange of goods, or lands: and it may be delivered some time after.

Again, one of the contractors, may deliver the thing contracted for on his part, and leave the other to perform his part at some determinate time after, and in the mean time be trusted; and then the contract on his part, is called PACT, or COVENANT: or both parts may contract now, to perform hereafter: in which cases, he that is to perform in time to come, being trusted, his performance is called *keeping of promise*, or faith; and the failing of performance, if it be voluntary, *violation of faith*.

When the transferring of right, is not mutual: but one of the parties transferreth, in hope to gain thereby friendship, or service from another, or from his friends; or in hope to gain the reputation of charity, or magnanimity; or to deliver his mind from the pain of compassion; or in hope of reward in heaven, this is not contract, but GIFT, FREE-GIFT, GRACE: which words signify one and the same thing.

Signs of contract, are either *express,* or *by inference.* Express, are words spoken with understanding of what they signify: and such words are either of the time *present,* or *past;* as, *I give, I grant, I have given, I have granted, I will that this be yours:* or of the future; as, *I will give, I will grant:* which words of the future are called PROMISE.

If a covenant be made, wherein neither of the parties perform presently, but trust one another; in the condition of mere nature, which is a condition of war of every man against every man, upon any reasonable suspicion, it is void: but if there be a common power set over them both, with right and force sufficient to compel performance, it is not void. For he that performeth first, has no assurance the other will perform after; because the bonds of words are too weak to bridle men's ambition, avarice, anger, and other passions, without the fear of some coercive power; which in the condition of mere nature, where all men are equal, and judges of the justness of their own fears, cannot possibly be supposed. And therefore he which performeth first, does but betray himself to his enemy; contrary to the right, he can never abandon, of defending his life, and means of living.

But in a civil estate, where there is a power set up to constrain those that would otherwise violate their faith, that fear is no more reasonable: and for that cause, he which by the covenant is to perform first, is obliged so to do.

The cause of fear, which maketh such a covenant invalid, must be always something arising after the covenant made; as some new fact, or other sign of the will not to perform: else it cannot make the covenant void. For that which could not hinder a man from promising, ought not to be admitted as a hindrance of performing.

OF OTHER LAWS OF NATURE

From that law of nature, by which we are obliged to transfer to another, such rights, as being retained, hinder the peace of mankind, there followeth a third; which is this, *that men perform their covenants made:* without which, covenants are in vain, and but empty words; and the right of all men to all things remaining, we are still in the condition of war.

And in this law of nature, consisteth the fountain and original of JUSTICE. For where no covenant hath preceded, there hath no right been transferred, and every man has right to every thing; and consequently, no action can be unjust. But when a covenant is made, then to break it is *unjust:* and the definition of INJUSTICE, is no other than *the not performance of covenant.* And whatsoever is not unjust, is *just.*

But because covenants of mutual trust, where there is a fear of not performance on either part, as hath been said in the former chapter, are invalid; though the original of justice be the making of covenants; yet injustice actually there can be none, till the cause of such fear be taken away; which while men are in the natural condition of war, cannot be done. Therefore before the names of just, and unjust can have place, there must be some coercive power, to compel men equally to the performance of their covenants, by the terror of some punishment, greater than the benefit they expect by the breach of their covenant; and to make good that propriety, which by mutual contract men acquire, in recompense of the universal right they abandon: and such power there is none before the erection of a commonwealth. And this is also to be gathered out of the ordinary definition of justice in the Schools: for they say, that *justice is the constant will of giving to every man his own,* and therefore where there is no *own,* that is, no propriety, there is no injustice; and where there is no coercive power erected, that is, where there is no commonwealth, there is no propriety; all men having right to all things: therefore where there is no commonwealth, there nothing is unjust. So that the nature of justice, consisteth in keeping of valid covenants: but the validity of covenants begins not but with the constitution of a civil power, sufficient to compel men to keep them: and then it is also that propriety begins. . . .

For Further Reflection

1. Hobbes wrote, "The utility of morality and civil philosophy is to be estimated, not so much by the commodities we have by knowing these sciences, as by the calamities we receive from not knowing them." What does he mean by this, and does the selection above illustrate it?

2. Is Hobbes's view of human nature accurate? Do we always act out of the motivations of fear and distrust? Are people entirely self-interested egoists? Is psychological egoism, the view that we always do what we perceive to be in our best interest, too bleak and one-sided?

3. Hobbes thought that only an absolute sovereign could establish or ensure peace and civil society. Is he correct? What would his estimation of democracy be? Could democratic society make use of his analysis? How would democrats modify Hobbes's theory?

4. David Hume criticized the idea that contract theories provide a justification of political authority. First of all, there is no evidence of an original contract ever being made and, secondly, even if our ancestors did sign an original contract, why should that give us any reason for obeying the laws of the state? Even as we are not bound by the marriage or business contracts of our ancestors, why should we be obligated by their political contracts?

Further Readings for Chapter 1

Baier, Kurt. *The Moral Point of View.* Ithaca, N.Y.: Cornell University Press, 1958. This influential work sees morality primarily in terms of social control.

Frankena, William K. *Ethics.* 2nd ed. Englewood Cliffs, N.J.: Prentice-Hall, 1973. A succinct, reliable guide.

Gert, Bernard. *Morality: A New Justification of the Moral Rules.* 2nd ed. Oxford: Oxford University Press, 1988. A clear and comprehensive discussion of the nature of morality.

MacIntyre, Alasdair. *A Short History of Ethics*. New York: Macmillan, 1966. A lucid, if uneven, survey of the history of Western ethics.

Mackie, J. L. *Ethics: Inventing Right and Wrong*. New York: Penguin, 1976. This book takes a very different view of ethics from mine, viewing ethics from a skeptical perspective.

Pojman, Louis. *Ethics: Discovering Right and Wrong*. 4th ed. Belmont, Calif.: Wadsworth Publishing Company, 2002. An objectivist perspective.

Singer, Peter. *The Expanding Circle: Ethics and Sociobiology*. Oxford: Oxford University Press, 1983. A fascinating attempt to relate ethics to sociobiology.

Taylor, Paul. *Principles of Ethics*. Evanston, Ill.: Dickerson, 1975. This work covers many of the same topics as my book, usually from a different perspective. His discussion of the principle of universalizability (pp. 95–105) is especially useful.

Taylor, Richard, *Good and Evil*. Buffalo, N.Y.: Prometheus, 1970. A lively, easy-to-read work that sees the main role of morality to be the resolution of conflicts of interest.

Turnbull, Colin. *The Mountain People*. New York: Simon & Schuster, 1972. An excellent anthropological study of a people living on the edge of morality.

Van Wyk, Robert. *Introduction to Ethics*. New York: St. Martin's Press, 1990. A clearly written recent introduction to the subject.

Warnock, G. J. *The Object of Morality*. London: Methuen, 1971. A clearly written, well-argued analysis of the nature of morality.

CHAPTER 2

Good and Evil

What are good and evil? In the general introduction we contrasted two classical notions of the good: Plato's transcendent notion that the good was the source of all being and morality, and the hedonic notion that the good is defined as pleasure (and, by extension, happiness). Plato and religious theories have a common thesis, that good is transcendent. It has a source beyond the empirical, in God or in a world of ideas. Similarly, for transcendentalists, the opposite of goodness, evil, is preternatural, inexplicable by ordinary understanding, mysterious. The third-century Manicheans and Zoroastrians believed that good and evil were two independent, equally powerful forces, always in conflict. St. Augustine (354–430), partly in response to the Manicheans, a group to which he had formerly belonged, developed the idea that evil was not a real being at all, but merely an absence of the good. It is parasitic on the good, a state of deprivation. Others attribute evil to the devil. On the other hand, the hedonist tradition rejects this transcendental approach and identifies the good with pleasure and happiness and evil with pain and suffering, purely empirical experiences. There is nothing mysterious about evil. It is, in the hedonist account, merely a problem of socializing human beings to take others into due consideration.

For many people, the hedonist account lacks sufficient explanatory power. Evil is a profound mystery, more perplexing than the nature of good, for it seems gratuitous. How could a good God permit evil? This is the question raised in our second reading from Dostoevsky's *Brothers Karamazov,* where the cynical philosopher Ivan asks his religious brother Alyosha how he can explain the problem of evil in the world.

Something bewildering and fascinating does surround evil. We are shocked, even horrified, at the brutalities of the Nazis or Pol Pot's atrocities. Shakespeare's Iago is one of the most frightening

characters in literature, for he seems to carry sadism to an unprecedented height, or, at least, approaching Milton's Satan, who cries
out in *Paradise Lost* "Evil be thou my good." Is this ugly feature,
malignity, in all of us to some extent? Is it a primordial force that
civilization constantly represses? Or is it simply an outcome of frustrated endeavors, a result of a failed upbringing? Yet we sometimes
discover families in which love and consideration are strong, though
one child develops into a moral monster. This was apparently the
case of the youth in Washington state who killed his two parents,
both teachers, who, it is reported, gave him enormous love and
care. Yet, he was an ornery child from early childhood. Sometimes
good children grow up in neglected environments and bad people
grow up in good environments. What accounts for this?

We begin chapter 2 with a selection from Herman Melville's *Billy
Budd,* the story of a seemingly innocent, beautiful youth, Billy Budd,
who becomes entrapped in evil, in the guise of master-at-arms John
Claggart. It is Billy's inner nobility that brings out Claggart's venom
and leads to the tragedy of the story. The third reading is from
William Styron's *Sophie's Choice,* in which a young Polish mother,
Sophie, is forced by a Nazi doctor at Auschwitz to make a terrible
choice in sacrificing the life of one of her children. Our fourth reading by Kevin Bales reports on the tragic reappearance of slavery in
the world.

The very opposite of the evil of John Claggart and the Nazi doctor are the Protestant Pastor Trocme and the people of La Chambon, France, who, at enormous personal risk, save the lives of six
thousand Jews from the Nazis. Philip Hallie analyzes the situation
in our fifth reading. In our sixth reading, the Australian philosopher Stanley Benn analyzes wickedness and classifies it into four
distinct types: selfishness, conscientious wickedness, heteronomous
wickedness, and pathological wickedness. Benn gives a purely naturalistic account of evil, defining it as "any object, property or happening about which it is both intelligible and correct to say that it
would be a better state of affairs if that object, et cetera, did not
exist or occur." Benn's article includes an insightful account of malignity, including Claggart and Iago.

In our seventh reading, the German philosopher Friedrich Nietzsche offers a radically different analysis of good and evil, as con-
structions of a weak, herd morality, fearful of the superior ability
of the natural aristocrat, whose master morality transcends what we
now call good and evil. It is no accident that Nietzsche names his

hero "Zarathustra," the name of the ancient Zoroastrian leader who believed that good and evil were independent, eternally co-present forces in the universe. Finally, in our last reading, Richard Taylor gives a thoroughly naturalistic account of the origin of good and evil, as based on our interests and preferences.

Billy Budd

HERMAN MELVILLE

Herman Melville (1819–1891), the American novelist, wrote *Billy Budd* late in life. It was not published until Melville had been dead more than thirty years. The story takes place in 1797, a time when the British navy was threatened by mutinies, in which its very authority was at stake. It was the custom of naval ships to stop merchant vessels at sea and impress sailors into its service. Such occurred when men from the British man-of-war the HMS *Indomitable* went on board a merchant ship and impressed one sailor into His Majesty's service. The sailor was Billy Budd, a handsome and guileless twenty-one-year-old orphan, known for his affable nature and inability to speak clearly. He was illiterate and stammered, but nevertheless communicated such genuine good will that he was the darling of his mates. When informed by his new masters that he would not be returning home but out to sea, Billy changed his plans cheerfully and devoted himself to his duties as a good citizen and sailor. He soon became immensely popular on board the *Indomitable*.

One man, however, despised Billy. He was John Claggart, master-at-arms. Perhaps Claggart was jealous of Billy's good looks and popularity. We are not told the exact reasons, but Claggart loathed Billy to the point of concocting a fantastic story of mutiny, supposedly instigated by Billy. Claggart went to the captain of the *Indomitable,* Captain Vere, and reported an alleged meeting between Billy and another sailor discussing mutiny. There was such a meeting, only it was instigated by Claggart, and Billy renounced the suggestion of rebellion without hesitation.

Captain Vere was an honorable, fair-minded man of good will, who liked Billy and suspected that Claggart was lying. He warned his master-at-arms that bearing false witness

From Herman Melville, *Billy Budd*. The manuscript of *Billy Budd* was found among Melville's possessions after he died. It was not published until 1924.

against a fellow sailor at sea merited the death penalty. Then he invited Billy into his office and instructed Claggart to face him with the charges. We enter as Billy is being accused of plotting to mutiny.

With the measured step and calm collected air of an asylum physician approaching in the public hall some patient beginning to show indications of a coming paroxysm, Claggart deliberately advanced within short range of Billy, and mesmerically looking him in the eye, briefly recapitulated the accusation.

Not at first did Billy take it in. When he did the rose-tan of his cheek looked struck as by white leprosy. He stood like one impaled and gagged. Meanwhile the accuser's eyes, removing not as yet from the blue, dilated ones, underwent a phenomenal change, their wonted rich violet color blurring into a muddy purple. Those lights of human intelligence losing human expression, icily protruding like alien eyes of certain uncatalogued creatures of the deep.

The first mesmeric glance was one of surprised fascination; the last was as the hungry lurch of the torpedo-fish.

"Speak, man!" said Captain Vere to the transfixed one, struck by his aspect even more than by Claggart's. "Speak! defend yourself." Which appeal caused but a strange, dumb gesturing and gurgling in Billy; amazement at such an accusation so suddenly sprung on inexperienced nonage; this, and it may be horror at the accuser, serving to bring out his lurking defect, and in this instance for the time intensifying it into a convulsed tongue-tie; while the intent head and entire form, straining forward in an agony of ineffectual eagerness to obey the injunction to speak and defend himself, gave an expression to the face like that of a condemned vestal priestess in the moment of being buried alive, and in the first struggle against suffocation.

Though at the time Captain Vere was quite ignorant of Billy's liability to vocal impediment, he now immediately divined it, since vividly Billy's aspect recalled to him that of a bright young schoolmate of his whom he had seen struck by much the same startling impotence in the act of eagerly rising in the class to be foremost in response to a testing question put to it by the master. Going close up to the young sailor, and laying a soothing hand on his shoulder, he said, "There is no hurry, my boy. Take your time, take your time." Contrary to the effect intended, these words, so fatherly in tone, doubtless touching Billy's heart to the quick, prompted yet more violent efforts at utterance—efforts soon ending for the time in confirming the paralysis, and bringing to the face an expression which was as a crucifixation to behold. The next instant, quick as the flame from a discharged cannon at night, his right arm shot out, and Claggart dropped to the deck. Whether intentionally, or but owing to the young athlete's superior height, the blow had taken effect full upon the forehead, so shapely and intellectual-looking a feature in the master-at-arms; so that the body fell over lengthwise, like a heavy plank tilted from erectness. A gasp or two, and he lay motionless.

"Fated boy," breathed Captain Vere, in tone so low as to be almost a whisper. . . .

Who in the rainbow can draw the line where the violet tint ends and the orange tint begins? Distinctly we see the difference of the colors, but where exactly does the one first blendingly enter into the other? So with sanity and insanity. In pronounced cases there is no question about them. But in some supposed cases, in various degrees supposedly less pronounced, to draw the exact line of demarcation few will undertake, though for a fee becoming considerate some professional experts will. There is nothing namable but that some men will, or undertake to, do it for pay.

Whether Captain Vere, as the surgeon professionally and privately surmised, was really the sudden victim of any degree of aberration, every one must determine for himself by such light as this narrative may afford.

That the unhappy event which has been narrated could not have happened at a worse juncture was but too true. For it was close on the heel of the suppressed insurrections, an aftertime very critical to naval authority, demanding from every English sea commander two qualities not readily interfusable—prudence and rigor. Moreover, there was something crucial in the case.

In the jugglery of circumstances preceding and attending the event on board the *Indomitable,* and in the light of that martial code whereby it was formally to be judged, innocence and guilt personified in Claggart and Budd in effect changed places. In a legal view the apparent victim of the tragedy was he who had sought to victimize a man blameless; and the indisputable deed of the latter, navally regarded, constituted the most heinous of military crimes. Yet more. The essential right and wrong involved in the matter, the clearer that might be, so much the worse for the responsibility of a loyal sea commander, inasmuch as he was not authorized to determine the matter on that primitive basis.

Small wonder then that the *Indomitable*'s captain, though in general a man of rapid decision, felt that circumspectness not less than
promptitude was necessary. Until he could decide upon his course,
and in each detail; and not only so, but until the concluding measure was upon the point of being enacted, he deemed it advisable,
in view of all the circumstances, to guard as much as possible
against publicity. Here he may or may not have erred. Certain it is,
however, that subsequently in the confidential talk of more than
one or two gun rooms and cabins he was not a little criticized by
some officers, a fact imputed by his friends and vehemently by his
cousin Jack Denton to professional jealousy of Starry Vere. Some
imaginative ground for invidious comment there was. The maintenance of secrecy in the matter, the confining all knowledge of it
for a time to the place where the homicide occurred, the quarter-
deck cabin; in these particulars lurked some resemblance to the
policy adopted in those tragedies of the palace which have occurred
more than once in the capital founded by Peter the Barbarian.

The case indeed was such that fain would the *Indomitable*'s captain have deferred taking any action whatever respecting it further
than to keep the foretopman a close prisoner till the ship rejoined
the squadron and then submitting the matter to the judgment of
his admiral.

But a true military officer is in one particular like a true monk.
Not with more of self-abnegation will the latter keep his vows of
monastic obedience than the former his vows of allegiance to martial duty.

Feeling that unless quick action was taken on it, the deed of the
foretopman, so soon as it should be known on the gun decks, would
tend to awaken any slumbering embers of the Nore[1] among the crew,
a sense of the urgency of the case overruled in Captain Vere every
other consideration. But though a conscientious disciplinarian, he
was no lover of authority for mere authority's sake. Very far was he
from embracing opportunities for monopolizing to himself the perils of moral responsibility, none at least that could properly be
referred to an official superior or shared with him by his official
equals or even subordinates. So thinking, he was glad it would not
be at variance with usage to turn the matter over to a summary court

---

[1] The mutiny on the ship *Nore* shook the British navy's authority and created a spirit of insurrection among its seamen.

of his own officers, reserving to himself, as the one on whom the ultimate accountability would rest, the right of maintaining a supervision of it, or formally or informally interposing at need. Accordingly a drumhead court was summarily convened, he electing the individuals composing it: the first lieutenant, the captain of marines, and the sailing master.

In associating an officer of marines with the sea lieutenant and the sailing master in a case having to do with a sailor, the commander perhaps deviated from general custom. He was prompted thereto by the circumstance that he took that soldier to be a judicious person, thoughtful, and not altogether incapable of grappling with a difficult case unprecedented in his prior experience. Yet even as to him he was not without some latent misgiving, for withal he was an extremely good-natured man, an enjoyer of his dinner, a sound sleeper, and inclined to obesity—a man who though he would always maintain his manhood in battle might not prove altogether reliable in a moral dilemma involving aught of the tragic. As to the first lieutenant and the sailing master, Captain Vere could not but be aware that though honest natures, of approved gallantry upon occasion, their intelligence was mostly confined to the matter of active seamanship and the fighting demands of their profession.

The court was held in the same cabin where the unfortunate affair had taken place. This cabin, the commander's, embraced the entire area under the poop deck. Aft, and on either side, was a small stateroom, the one now temporarily a jail and the other a dead-house, and a yet smaller compartment, leaving a space between expanding forward into a goodly oblong of length coinciding with the ship's beam. A skylight of moderate dimension was overhead, and at each end of the oblong space were two sashed porthole windows easily convertible back into embrasures for short carronades.

All being quickly in readiness, Billy Budd was arraigned, Captain Vere necessarily appearing as the sole witness in the case, and as such temporarily sinking his rank, though singularly maintaining it in a matter apparently trivial, namely, that he testified from the ship's weather side, with that object having caused the court to sit on the lee side. Concisely he narrated all that had led up to the catastrophe, omitting nothing in Claggart's accusation and deposing as to the manner in which the prisoner had received it. At this testimony the three officers glanced with no little surprise at Billy Budd, the last man they would have suspected either of the mutinous design alleged by Claggart or the undeniable deed he himself had done. The first lieutenant, taking judicial primacy and turning toward the prisoner, said, "Captain Vere has spoken. Is it or is it not as Captain Vere says?"

In response came syllables not so much impeded in the utterance as might have been anticipated. They were these: "Captain Vere tells the truth. It is just as Captain Vere says, but it is not as the master-at-arms said. I have eaten the King's bread and I am true to the King."

"I believe you, my man," said the witness, his voice indicating a suppressed emotion not otherwise betrayed.

"God will bless you for that, your honor!" not without stammering said Billy, and all but broke down. But immediately he was recalled to self-control by another question, to which with the same emotional difficulty of utterance he said, "No, there was no malice between us. I never bore malice against the master-at-arms. I am sorry that he is dead. I did not mean to kill him. Could I have used my tongue I would not have struck him. But he foully lied to my face and in presence of my captain, and I had to say something, and I could only say it with a blow, God help me!"

In the impulsive aboveboard manner of the frank one the court saw confirmed all that was implied in words that just previously had perplexed them, coming as they did from the testifier to the tragedy and promptly following Billy's impassioned disclaimer of mutinous intent—Captain Vere's words, "I believe you, my man."

Next it was asked of him whether he knew of or suspected aught savoring of incipient trouble (meaning mutiny, though the explicit term was avoided) going on in any section of the ship's company.

The reply lingered. This was naturally imputed by the court to the same vocal embarrassment which had retarded or obstructed previous answers. But in main it was otherwise here, the question immediately recalling to Billy's mind the interview with the after-guardsman in the forechains. But an innate repugnance to playing a part at all approaching that of an informer against one's own shipmates—the same erring sense of uninstructed honor which had stood in the way of his reporting the matter at the time, though as a loyal man-of-war's man it was incumbent on him, and failure so to do, if charged against him and proven, would have subjected him to the heaviest of penalties; this, with the blind feeling now his that nothing really was being hatched, prevailed with him. When the answer came it was a negative.

"One question more," said the officer of marines, now first speaking and with a troubled earnestness. "You tell us that what the master-at-arms said against you was a lie. Now why should he have so lied, so maliciously lied, since you declare there was no malice between you?"

At that question, unintentionally touching on a spiritual sphere wholly obscure to Billy's thoughts, he was nonplussed, evincing a confusion indeed that some observers, such as can readily be imagined, would have construed into involuntary evidence of hidden guilt. Nevertheless, he strove some way to answer, but all at once relinquished the vain endeavor, at the same time turning an appealing glance toward Captain Vere as deeming him his best helper and friend. Captain Vere, who had been seated for a time, rose to his feet, addressing the interrogator. "The question you put to him comes naturally enough. But how can he rightly answer it?—or anybody else, unless indeed it be he who lies within there," designating the compartment where lay the corpse. "But the prone one there will not rise to our summons. In effect, though, as it seems to me, the point you make is hardly material. Quite aside from any conceivable motive actuating the master-at-arms, and irrespective of the provocation to the blow, a martial court must needs in the present case confine its attention to the blow's consequence, which consequence justly is to be deemed not otherwise than as the striker's deed."

This utterance, the full significance of which it was not at all likely that Billy took in, nevertheless caused him to turn a wistful interrogative look toward the speaker, a look in its dumb expressiveness not unlike that which a dog of generous breed might turn upon his master, seeking in his face some elucidation of a previous gesture ambiguous to the canine intelligence. Nor was the same utterance without marked effect upon the three officers, more especially the soldier. Couched in it seemed to them a meaning unanticipated, involving a prejudgment on the speaker's part. It served to augment a mental disturbance previously evident enough.

The soldier once more spoke, in a tone of suggestive dubiety addressing at once his associates and Captain Vere: "Nobody is present—none of the ship's company, I mean—who might shed lateral light, if any is to be had, upon what remains mysterious in this matter."

"That is thoughtfully put," said Captain Vere; "I see your drift. Ay, there is a mystery; but, to use a scriptural phrase, it is a 'mystery of iniquity,' a matter for psychologic theologians to discuss. But what has a military court to do with it? Not to add that for us any possible investigation of it is cut off by the lasting tongue-tie of—him—in yonder," again designating the mortuary stateroom. "The prisoner's deed—with that alone we have to do."

To this, and particularly the closing reiteration, the marine soldier, knowing not how aptly to reply, sadly abstained from saying aught. The first lieutenant, who at the outset had not unnaturally assumed primacy in the court, now overrulingly instructed by a glance from Captain Vere, a glance more effective than words, resumed that primacy. Turning to the prisoner, "Budd," he said, and scarce in equable tones, "Budd, if you have aught further to say for yourself, say it now."

Upon this the young sailor turned another quick glance toward Captain Vere; then, as taking a hint from that aspect, a hint confirming his own instinct that silence was now best, replied to the lieutenant, "I have said all, sir."

The marine—the same who had been the sentinel without the cabin door at the time that the foretopman, followed by the master-at-arms, entered it—he, standing by the sailor throughout these judicial proceedings, was now directed to take him back to the after compartment originally assigned to the prisoner and his custodian. As the twain disappeared from view, the three officers, as partially liberated from some inward constraint associated with Billy's mere presence, simultaneously stirred in their seats. They exchanged looks of troubled indecision, yet feeling that decide they must and without long delay. For Captain Vere, he for the time stood—unconsciously with his back toward them, apparently in one of his absent fits—gazing out from a sashed porthole to windward upon the monotonous blank of the twilight sea. But the court's silence continuing, broken only at moments by brief consultations, in low earnest tones, this served to arouse him and energize him. Turning, he to-and-fro paced the cabin athwart; in the returning ascent to windward climbing the slant deck in the ship's lee roll, without knowing it symbolizing thus in his action a mind resolute to surmount difficulties even if against primitive instincts strong as the wind and the sea. Presently he came to a stand before the three. After scanning their faces he stood less as mustering his thoughts for expression than as one only deliberating how best to put them to well-meaning men not intellectually mature, men with whom it was necessary to demonstrate certain principles that were axioms to himself. Similar impatience as to talking is perhaps one reason that deters some minds from addressing any popular assemblies.

When speak he did, something, both in the substance of what he said and his manner of saying it, showed the influence of un-shared studies modifying and tempering the practical training of an active career. This, along with his phraseology, now and then was suggestive of the grounds whereon rested that imputation of a certain pedantry socially alleged against him by certain naval men of wholly practical cast, captains who nevertheless would frankly concede that His Majesty's navy mustered no more efficient officer of their grade than Starry Vere.

What he said was to this effect: "Hitherto I have been but the witness, little more; and I should hardly think now to take another tone, that of your coadjutor for the time, did I not perceive in you—at the crisis too—a troubled hesitancy, proceeding, I doubt not, from the clash of military duty with moral scruple—scruple vitalized by compassion. For the compassion, how can I otherwise than share it? But, mindful of paramount obligations, I strive against scruples that may tend to enervate decision. Not, gentlemen, that I hide from myself that the case is an exceptional one. Speculatively regarded, it well might be referred to a jury of casuists. But for us here, acting not as casuists or moralists, it is a case practical, and under martial law practically to be dealt with.

"But your scruples: do they move as in a dusk? Challenge them. Make them advance and declare themselves. Come now; do they import something like this: If, mindless of palliating circumstances, we are bound to regard the death of the master-at-arms as the prisoner's deed, then does that deed constitute a capital crime whereof the penalty is a mortal one. But in natural justice is nothing but the prisoner's overt act to be considered? How can we adjudge to summary and shameful death a fellow creature innocent before God, and whom we feel to be so?—Does that state it aright? You sign sad assent. Well, I too feel that, the full force of that. It is Nature. But do these buttons that we wear attest that our allegiance is to Nature? No, to the King. Though the ocean, which is inviolate Nature primeval, though this be the element where we move and have our being as sailors, yet as the King's officers lies our duty in a sphere correspondingly natural? So little is that true, that in receiving our commissions we in the most important regards ceased to be natural free agents. When war is declared are we the commissioned fighters previously consulted? We fight at command. If our judgments approve the war, that is but coincidence. So in other particulars. So now. For suppose condemnation to follow these present proceedings. Would it be so much we ourselves that would condemn as it would be martial law operating through us? For that law and the rigor of it, we are not responsible. Our vowed responsibility is in this: That however pitilessly that law may operate in any instances, we nevertheless adhere to it and administer it.

"But the exceptional in the matter moves the hearts within you. Even so too is mine moved. But let not warm hearts betray heads that should be cool. Ashore in a criminal case, will an upright judge allow himself off the bench to be waylaid by some tender kinswoman of the accused seeking to touch him with her tearful plea? Well, the heart here, sometimes the feminine in man, is as that piteous woman, and hard though it be, she must here be ruled out."

He paused, earnestly studying them for a moment; then resumed.

"But something in your aspect seems to urge that it is not solely the heart that moves in you, but also the conscience, the private conscience. But tell me whether or not, occupying the position we do, private conscience should not yield to that imperial one formulated in the mode under which alone we officially proceed?"

Here the three men moved in their seats, less convinced than agitated by the course of an argument troubling but the more the spontaneous conflict within.

Perceiving which, the speaker paused for a moment; then abruptly changing his tone, went on.

"To steady us a bit, let us recur to the facts.—In wartime at sea a man-of-war's man strikes his superior in grade, and the blow kills. Apart from its effect the blow itself is, according to the Articles of War, a capital crime. Furthermore—"

"Ay, sir," emotionally broke in the officer of marines, "in one sense it was. But surely Budd purposed neither mutiny nor homicide."

"Surely not, my good man. And before a court less arbitrary and more merciful than a martial one, that plea would largely extenuate. At the Last Assizes it shall acquit. But how here? We proceed under the law of the Mutiny Act. In feature no child can resemble his father more than that Act resembles in spirit the thing from which it derives—War. In His Majesty's service—in this ship, indeed—there are Englishmen forced to fight for the King against their will. Against their conscience, for aught we know. Though as their fellow creatures some of us may appreciate their position, yet as navy officers what reck we of it? Still less recks the enemy. Our impressed men he would fain cut down in the same swath with our volunteers. As regards the enemy's naval conscripts, some of whom may even share our own abhorrence of the regicidal French Directory, it is the same on our side. War looks but to the frontage, the appearance. And the Mutiny Act, War's child, takes after the father. Budd's intent or non-intent is nothing to the purpose.

"But while, put to it by those anxieties in you which I cannot but respect, I only repeat myself—while thus strangely we prolong proceedings that should be summary—the enemy may be sighted and an engagement result. We must do; and one of two things must we do—condemn or let go."

"Can we not convict and yet mitigate the penalty?" asked the sailing master, here speaking, and falteringly, for the first.

"Gentlemen, were that clearly lawful for us under the circumstances, consider the consequences of such clemency. The people" (meaning the ship's company) "have native sense; most of them are familiar with our naval usage and tradition; and how would they take it? Even could you explain to them—which our official position forbids—they, long molded by arbitrary discipline, have not that kind of intelligent responsiveness that might qualify them to comprehend and discriminate. No, to the people the foretopman's deed, however it be worded in the announcement, will be plain homicide committed in a flagrant act of mutiny. What penalty for that should follow, they know. But it does not follow. *Why?* they will ruminate. You know what sailors are. Will they not revert to the recent outbreak at the Nore? Ay. They know the well-founded alarm—the panic it struck throughout England. Your clement sentence they would account pusillanimous. They would think that we flinch, that we are afraid of them—afraid of practicing a lawful rigor singularly demanded at this juncture, lest it should provoke new troubles. What shame to us such a conjecture on their part, and how deadly to discipline. You see then, whither, prompted by duty and the law, I steadfastly drive. But I beseech you, my friends, do not take me amiss. I feel as you do for this unfortunate boy. But did he know our hearts, I take him to be of that generous nature that he would feel even for us on whom this military necessity so heavy a compulsion is laid."

With that, crossing the deck he resumed his place by the sashed porthole, tacitly leaving the three to come to a decision. On the cabin's opposite side the troubled court sat silent. Loyal lieges, plain and practical, though at bottom they dissented from some points Captain Vere had put to them, they were without the faculty, hardly had the inclination, to gainsay one whom they felt to be an earnest man, one too not less their superior in mind than in naval rank. But it is not improbable that even such of his words as were not without influence over them, less came home to them than his closing appeal to their instinct as sea officers: in the forethought he threw out as to the practical consequences to discipline, considering the unconfirmed tone of the fleet at the time, should a man-of-war's man's violent killing at sea of a superior in grade be allowed to pass for aught else than a capital crime demanding prompt infliction of the penalty. . . .

In brief, Billy Budd was formally convicted and sentenced to be hung at the yardarm in the early morning watch, it being now night. Otherwise, as is customary in such cases, the sentence would forthwith have been carried out. In wartime on the field or in the fleet, a mortal punishment decreed by a drumhead court—on the field sometimes decreed by but a nod from the general—follows without delay on the heel of conviction, without appeal. . . .

The next morning Billy Budd was hanged. His last words were "God bless Captain Vere!"

For Further Reflection

1. Normally we think that one must intend to kill a victim before one can be guilty of murder, as opposed to involuntary manslaughter. But Budd never intended to kill Claggart. Should he have been charged with murder?

2. Why did Captain Vere take the stance he did against Billy? Was he concerned with the deterrent effect an execution would have at a time when mutiny was a serious problem or did he think he was bound to carry out the letter of the law? What should he have done? Why?

3. Perhaps the most interesting thing about this story is the stark contrast between Claggart and Billy Budd. What are some of the moral lessons we may learn from this contrast and how they encounter one another?

Why Is There Evil?

FYODOR DOSTOEVSKY

Fyodor Dostoevsky (1822–1881), the great Russian novelist, was born in Moscow. His revolutionary sympathies and a penchant for gambling managed to keep him in constant danger. Among his famous novels are *Crime and Punishment* (1866) and *The Brothers Karamazov* (1880), from which our reading is taken.

In this scene, the philosophical cynic Ivan Karamazov explains to his devoutly religious brother, Alyosha, a Christian monk, why the problem of evil prevents him from accepting God.

"Well, tell me where to begin, give your orders. The existence of God, eh?"

"Begin where you like. You declared yesterday at father's that there was no God." Alyosha looked searchingly at his brother.

"I said that yesterday at dinner on purpose to tease you and I saw your eyes glow. But now I've no objection to discussing with you, and I say so very seriously. I want to be friends with you, Alyosha, for I have no friends and want to try it. Well, only fancy, perhaps I too accept God," laughed Ivan, "that's a surprise for you, isn't it?"

"Yes of course, if you are not joking now."

"Joking? I was told at the elder's yesterday that I was joking. You know, dear boy, there was an old sinner in the eighteenth century who declared that, if there were no God, he would have to be invented. . . . And man has actually invented God. And what's strange, what would be marvelous, is not that God should really exist; the marvel is that such an idea, the idea of the necessity of God, could enter the head of such a savage, vicious beast as man. So holy it is, so touching, so wise and so great a credit it does to man. As for me, I've long resolved not to think whether man created God or God man. . . . For what are we aiming at now? I am trying to explain as quickly as possible my essential nature, that is what manner of man I am, what I believe in, and for what I hope, that's it, isn't it? And

From Fyodor Dostoevsky, *The Brothers Karamazov,* translated by Constance Garnett (London: Heinemann, 1912).

therefore I tell you that I accept God simply. But you must note this: if God exists and if He really did create the world, then, as we all know, He created it according to the geometry of Euclid and the human mind with the conception of only three dimensions in space. Yet there have been and still are geometricians and philosophers, and even some of the most distinguished, who doubt whether the whole universe, or to speak more widely the whole of being, was only created in Euclid's geometry; they even dare to dream that two parallel lines, which according to Euclid can never meet on earth, may meet somewhere in infinity. I have come to the conclusion that, since I can't understand even that, I can't expect to understand about God. I acknowledge humbly that I have no faculty for settling such questions. I have a Euclidian earthly mind, and how could I solve problems that are not of this world? And I advise you never to think about it either, my dear Alyosha, especially about God, whether He exists or not. All such questions are utterly inappropriate for a mind created with an idea of only three dimensions. And so I accept God and am glad to, and what's more I accept His wisdom, His purpose— which are utterly beyond our ken; I believe in the underlying order and the meaning of life; I believe in the eternal harmony in which they say we shall one day be blended. I believe in the Word to Which the universe is striving, and Which Itself was 'with God,' and Which Itself is God and so on, and so on, to infinity. There are all sorts of phrases for it. I seem to be on the right path, don't I? Yet would you believe it, in the final result I don't accept this world of God's, and, although I know it exists, I don't accept it at all. It's not that I don't accept God, you must understand, it's the world created by Him I don't and cannot accept. Let me make it plain. I believe like a child that suffering will be healed and made up for, that all the humiliating absurdity of human contradictions will vanish like a piti- ful mirage, like the despicable fabrication of the impotent and infi- nitely small Euclidian mind of man, that in the world's finale, at the moment of eternal harmony, something so precious will come to pass that it will suffice for all hearts, for the comforting of all resentments, for the atonement of all the crimes of humanity, of all the blood they've shed; that it will make it not only possible to forgive but to justify all that has happened with men—but though all that may come to pass, I don't accept it. I won't accept it. Even if parallel lines do meet and I see it myself, I shall see it and say that they've met, but still I won't accept it. That's what's at the root of me, Alyosha; that's my creed.

" . . . Do you understand why this infamy must be and is permitted? Without it, I am told, man could not have known good and evil. Why should he know that diabolical good and evil when it costs so much? Why, the whole world of knowledge is not worth that child's prayer to 'dear, Kind God'! I say nothing of the sufferings of grown-up people, they have eaten the apple, damn them, and the devil take them all! But these little ones! I am making you suffer, Alyosha, you are not yourself. I'll leave off if you like."

"Never mind. I want to suffer too," muttered Alyosha.

"One picture, only one more, because it's so curious, so characteristic, and I have only just read it in some collection of Russian antiquities. I've forgotten the name. I must look it up. It was in the darkest days of serfdom at the beginning of the century, and long live the Liberator of the People! There was in those days a general of aristocratic connections, the owner of great estates, one of these men—somewhat exceptional, I believe, even then—who, retiring from the service into a life of leisure, are convinced that they've earned absolute power over the lives of their subjects. There were such men then. So our general, settled on his property of two thousand souls, lives in pomp and domineers over his poor neighbors as though they were dependents and buffoons. He has kennels of hundreds of hounds and nearly a hundred dog-boys—all mounted, and in uniform. One day a serf boy, a little child of eight, threw a stone in play and hurt the paw of the general's favorite hound. 'Why is my favorite dog lame?' He is told that the boy threw a stone that hurt the dog's paw. 'So you did it.' The general looked the child up and down. 'Take him.' He was taken—taken from his mother and kept shut up all night. Early that morning the general comes out on horseback, with the hounds, his dependents, dog-boys, and huntsmen, all mounted around him in full hunting parade. The servants are summoned for their edification, and in front of them all stands the mother of the child. The child is brought from the lockup. It's a gloomy, cold, foggy autumn day, a capital day for hunting. The general orders the child to be undressed; the child is stripped naked. He shivers, numb with terror not daring to cry. . . . 'Make him run,' commands the general. 'Run! run!' shout the dog-boys. The boy runs. . . . 'At him!' yells the general, and he sets the whole pack of hounds on the child. The hounds catch him, and tear him to pieces before his mother's eyes! . . . I believe the general was afterwards declared incapable of administering his estates. Well—what did he deserve? To be shot? to be shot for the satisfaction of our moral feelings? Speak, Alyosha!"

"To be shot," murmured Alyosha, lifting his eyes to Ivan with a pale twisted smile.

"Bravo!" cried Ivan delighted. "If even you say so . . . You're a pretty monk! So there is a little devil sitting in your heart, Alyosha Karamazov!"

"What I said was absurd, but—"

"That's just the point that 'but'!" cried Ivan. "Let me tell you, novice, that the absurd is only too necessary on earth. The world stands on absurdities, and perhaps nothing would have come to pass in it without them. We know what we know!"

"What do you know?"

"I understand nothing," Ivan went on, as though in delirium. "I don't want to understand anything now. I want to stick to the fact. I made up my mind long ago not to understand. If I try to understand anything, I shall be false to the fact and I have determined to stick to the fact."

"Why are you trying me?" Alyosha cried, with sudden distress. "Will you say what you mean at last?"

"Of course, I will; that's what I've been leading up to. You are dear to me, I don't want to let you go, and I won't give you up to your Zossima."

Ivan for a minute was silent, his face became all at once very sad.

"Listen! I took the case of the children only to make my case clearer. Of the other tears of humanity with which the earth is soaked from its crust to its center, I will say nothing. I have narrowed my subject on purpose. I am a bug, and I recognize in all humility that I cannot understand why the world is arranged as it is. Men are themselves to blame, I suppose; they were given paradise, they wanted freedom, and stole fire from heaven, though they knew they would become unhappy, so there is no need to pity them. With my pitiful, earthly, Euclidian understanding, all I know is that there is suffering and that there are none guilty; that cause follows effect, simply and directly; that everything flows and finds its level—but that's only Euclidian nonsense, I know that, and I can't consent to live by it! What comfort is it to me that there are none guilty and that cause follows effect simply and directly, and that I know it—I must have justice, or I will destroy myself. And not justice in some remote infinite time and space, but here on earth, and that I could see myself. I have believed in it. I want to see it, and if I am dead by then, let me rise again, for if it all happens without me, it will be too unfair. Surely I haven't suffered, simply that I, my crimes and my sufferings, may manure the soil of the future harmony for somebody else. I want to see with my own eyes the hind lie down with the lion and the victim rise up and embrace his murderer. I want to be there when everyone suddenly understands what it has all been for. All the religions of the world are built on this longing, and I am a believer. But then there are the children, and what am I to do about them? That's a question I can't answer. For the hundredth time I repeat, there are numbers of questions, but I've only taken the children, because in their case what I mean is so unanswerably clear. Listen! If all must suffer to pay for the eternal harmony, what have children to do with it, tell me, please? It's beyond all comprehension why they should suffer, and why they should pay for the harmony. Why should they, too, furnish material to enrich the soil for the harmony of the future? I understand solidarity in sin among men. I understand solidarity in retribution, too; but there can be no such solidarity with children. And if it is really true that they must share responsibility for all their fathers' crimes, such a truth is not of this world and is beyond my comprehension. Some jester will say, perhaps, that the child would have grown up and have sinned, but you see he didn't grow up, he was torn to pieces by the dogs, at eight years old. Oh, Alyosha, I am not blaspheming! I understand, of course, what an upheaval of the universe it will be, when everything in heaven and earth blends in one hymn of praise and everything that lives and has lived cries aloud: 'Thou art just, O Lord, for Thy ways are revealed,' when the mother embraces the fiend who threw her child to the dogs, and all three cry aloud with tears, 'Thou are just, O Lord!' then, of course, the crown of knowledge will be reached and all will be made clear. But what pulls me up here is that I can't accept that harmony. And while I am on earth, I make haste to take my own measures. You see, Alyosha, perhaps it really may happen that if I live to that moment, or rise again to see it, I, too, perhaps, may cry aloud with the rest, looking at the mother embracing the child's torturer, 'Thou art just, O Lord!' but I don't want to cry aloud then. While there is still time, I hasten to protect myself and so I renounce the higher harmony altogether. It's not worth the tears of that one tortured child who beat itself on the breast with its little fist and prayed in its stinking outhouse, with its unexpiated tears to 'dear, kind God'! It's not worth it, because those tears are unatoned for. They must be atoned for, or there can be no harmony. But how? How are you going to atone for them? Is it possible? By their being avenged? But what do

I care for avenging them? What do I care for a hell for oppressors? What good can hell do, since those children have already been tortured? And what becomes of harmony, if there is hell? I want to forgive. I want to embrace. I don't want more suffering. And if the sufferings of children go to swell the sum of sufferings which was necessary to pay for truth, then I protest that the truth is not worth such a price. I don't want the mother to embrace the oppressor who threw her son to the dogs! She dare not forgive him! Let her forgive him for herself, if she will, let her forgive the torturer for the immeasurable suffering of her mother's heart. But the sufferings of her tortured child she has no right to forgive; she dare not forgive the torturer, even if the child were to forgive him! And if that is so, if they dare not forgive, what becomes of harmony? Is there in the whole world a being who would have the right to forgive and could forgive? I don't want harmony. From love for humanity I don't want it. I would rather be left with the unavenged suffering. I would rather remain with my unavenged suffering and unsatisfied indignation, *even if I were wrong*. Besides, too high a price is asked for harmony; it's beyond our means to pay so much to enter on it. And so I hasten to give back my entrance ticket, and if I am an honest man I am bound to give it back as soon as possible. And that I am doing. It's not God that I don't accept, Alyosha, only I most respectfully return Him the ticket."

"That's rebellion," murmured Alyosha, looking down.

"Rebellion? I am sorry you call it that," said Ivan earnestly. "One can hardly live in rebellion, and I want to live. Tell me yourself, I challenge you—answer. Imagine that you are creating a fabric of human destiny with the object of making men happy in the end, giving them peace and rest at last, but that it was essential and inevitable to torture to death only one tiny creature—that baby beating its breast with its fist, for instance—and to found that edifice on its unavenged tears, would you consent to be the architect on those conditions? Tell me, and tell the truth."

"No, I wouldn't consent," said Alyosha softly.

For Further Reflection

1. There are three propositions involved in the traditional formulation of the problem of evil:

    God is all-powerful (including being all-knowing).

God is perfectly good.
Evil exists.
These premises seem to be mutually incompatible, for if God
is all-good, he will not allow evil if he can help it. And if he
is all-powerful, he is able to prevent evil. But evil exists. Hence,
the problem of evil. How does Ivan deal with these premises?
Is there any way to resolve this problem that makes sense of
all the premises?

2. Do you think that the existence of enormous evil, such as Ivan
    portrays, counts against the existence of God? Explain why or
    why not.

Sophie's Choice

WILLIAM STYRON

William Styron, the well-known American novelist, received
the Pulitzer Prize in 1967 for *The Confessions of Nat Turner*.
In this *Sophie's Choice* excerpt he describes a young Polish mother, Sophie, with her two small children, being transported in a crowded train by German soldiers during World
War II to Auschwitz, the Nazi concentration camp. There
she is examined by a doctor, whom she calls *Jemand von
Niemand* (literally, every man of no man), who first tries
to seduce her but shortly after offers her a fateful choice.
We enter the story with Sophie and her two children, Jan
and Eva, on the train.

The name Oświęcim—Auschwitz—which had at first murmured its
way through the compartment made [Sophie] weak with fear, but she
had no doubt whatever that that was where the train was going. A
minuscule sliver of light, catching her eye, drew her attention to a

tiny crack in the plywood board across the window, and during the
first hour of the journey she was able to see enough by the dawn's
glow to tell their direction: south. Due south past the country villages
that crowd around Warsaw in place of the usual suburban outskirts,
due south past greening fields and copses crowded with birch trees,
south in the direction of Cracow. Only Auschwitz, of all their plausible destinations, lay south, and she recalled the despair she felt
when with her own eyes she verified where they were going. The
reputation of Auschwitz was ominous, vile, terrifying. Although in
the Gestapo prison rumors had tended to support Auschwitz as the
place where they would eventually be shipped, she had hoped inces-
santly and prayed for a labor camp in Germany, where so many Poles
had been transported and where, according to other rumor, conditions were less brutal, less harsh. But as Auschwitz loomed more and
more inevitably and now, on the train, made itself inescapable,
Sophie was smothered by the realization that she was victim of punishment by association, retribution through chance concurrence. She
kept saying to herself: I don't belong here. If she had not had the
misfortune of being taken prisoner at the same time as so many of
the Home Army members (a stroke of bad luck further complicated
by her connection with Wanda, and their common dwelling place,
even though she had not lifted a finger to help the Resistance), she
might have been adjudged guilty of the serious crime of meat smug-
gling but not of the infinitely more grave crime of subversion, and
hence might not be headed for a destination so forbiddingly malign.
But among other ironies, she realized, was this one: she had not been
judged guilty of anything, merely interrogated and forgotten. She had
then been thrown in haphazardly among these partisans, where she
was victim less of any specific retributive justice than of a general
rage—a kind of berserk lust for complete domination and oppression which seized the Nazis whenever they scored a win over the
Resistance, and which this time had even extended to the several
hundred bedraggled Poles ensnared in that last savage roundup.

Certain things about the trip she remembered with utter clarity.
The stench, the airlessness, the endless shifting of positions—stand
up, sit down, stand up again. At the moment of a sudden stop a
box toppling down on her head, not stunning her, not hurting too
much, but raising an egg-size bulge at the top of her skull. The
view outside the crack, where spring sunlight darkened into driz-
zling rain: through the film of rain, birch trees still tormented by
the past winter's crushing snowfall, bent into shapes of white par-
abolic arches, strongbows, catapults, beautiful broken skeletons,

whips. Lemon dots of forsythia everywhere. Delicate green fields blending into distant forests of spruce and larch and pine. Sunshine again. Jan's books, which he tried to read in the feeble light as he sat on her lap: *The Swiss Family Robinson* in German; Polish editions of *White Fang* and *Penrod and Sam*. Eva's two possessions, which she refused to park in the luggage rack but clutched fiercely as if any moment they might be wrested from her hands: the flute in its leather case and her *mis*—the one-eared, one-eyed teddy bear she had kept since the cradle.

More rain outside, a torrent. Now the odor of vomit, pervasive, unextinguishable, cheesy. Fellow passengers: two frightened convent girls of sixteen or so, sobbing, sleeping, waking to murmur prayers to the Holy Virgin; Wiktor, a black-haired, intense, infuriated young Home Army member already plotting revolt or escape, ceaselessly scribbling messages on slips of paper to be passed to Wanda in another compartment; a fear-maddened shriveled old lady claiming to be the niece of Wieniawski, claiming the bundle of parchment she kept pressed close to her to be the original manuscript of his famous *Polonaise,* claiming some kind of immunity, dissolving into tears like the schoolgirls at Wiktor's snarled remark that the Nazis would wipe their asses on the worthless *Polonaise.* Hunger pangs beginning. Nothing at all to eat. Another old woman—quite dead— laid out in the exterior aisle on the spot where her heart attack had felled her, her hands frozen around a crucifix and her chalk-white face already smudged by the boots and shoes of people treading over and around her. Through her crevice once more: Cracow at night, the familiar station, moonlit railroad yards where they lay stranded hour after hour. In the greenish moonglow an extraordinary sight: a German soldier standing in *feldgrau* uniform and with slung rifle, masturbating with steady beat in the half-light of the deserted yard, grinningly exhibiting himself to such curious or indifferent or bemused prisoners as might be looking through the peepholes. An hour's sleep, then the morning's brightness. Crossing the Vistula, murky and steaming. Two small towns she recognized as the train moved westward through the dusty pollen-gold morning: Skawina, Zator. Eva beginning to cry for the first time, torn by spasms of hunger. Hush, baby. A few more moments' drowse riven by a sun-flooded, splendid, heart-wrenching, manic dream: herself begowned and bediademed, seated at the keyboard before ten thousand onlookers, yet somehow—astoundingly—flying, *flying,* soaring to deliverance on the celestial measures of the Emperor Concerto. Eyelids fluttering apart. A slamming, braking stop. Auschwitz.

They waited in the car during most of the rest of the day. At an early moment the generators ceased working; the bulbs went out in the compartment and what remaining light there was cast a milky pallor, filtering through the cracks in the plywood shutters. The distant sound of band music made its way into the compartment. There was a vibration of panic in the car; it was almost palpable, like the prickling of hair all over one's body, and in the near-darkness there came a surge of anxious whispering—hoarse, rising, but as incomprehensible as the rustle of an army of leaves. The convent girls began to wail in unison, beseeching the Holy Mother. Wiktor loudly told them to shut up, while at the same instant Sophie took courage from Wanda's voice, faint from the other end of the car, begging Resistance members and deportees alike to stay calm, stay quiet.

It must have been early in the afternoon when word came regarding the hundreds upon hundreds of Jews from Malkinia in the forward cars. *All Jews in vans* came a note to Wiktor, a note which he read aloud in the gloom and which Sophie, too numb with fright to even clutch Jan and Eva close against her breast for consolation, immediately translated into: All the Jews have gone to the gas. Sophie joined with the convent girls in prayer. It was while she was praying that Eva began to wail loudly. The children had been brave during the trip, but now the little girl's hunger blossomed into real pain. She squealed in anguish while Sophie tried to rock and soothe her, but nothing seemed to work; the child's screams were for a moment more terrifying to Sophie than the word about the doomed Jews. But soon they stopped. Oddly, it was Jan who came to the rescue. He had a way with his sister and now he took over—at first shushing her in the words of some private language they shared, then pressing next to her with his book. In the pale light he began reading to her from the story of Penrod, about little boys' pranks in the leafy Elysian small-town marrow of America; he was able to laugh and giggle, and his thin soprano singsong cast a gentle spell, combining with Eva's exhaustion to lull her to sleep.

Several hours passed. It was late afternoon. Finally another slip of paper was passed to Wiktor: *AK first car in vans.* This plainly meant one thing—that, like the Jews, the several hundred Home Army members in the car just forward had been transported to Birkenau and the crematoriums. Sophie stared straight ahead, composed her hands in her lap and prepared for death, feeling inexpressible terror but for the first time, too, tasting faintly the blessed bitter relief of acceptance. The old niece of Wieniawski had fallen into a comalike stupor, the *Polonaise* in crumpled disarray, rivulets of drool flowing from the corners of her lips. In trying to reconstruct that moment a long time later, Sophie wondered whether she might not then have become unconscious herself, for the next thing she remembered was her own daylight-dazzled presence outside on the ramp with Jan and Eva, and coming face to face with Hauptsturmführer Fritz Jemand von Niemand, doctor of medicine.

Sophie did not know his name then, nor did she ever see him again. I have christened him Fritz Jemand von Niemand because it seems as good a name as any for an SS doctor—for one who appeared to Sophie as if from nowhere and vanished likewise forever from her sight, yet who left a few interesting traces of himself behind. One trace: the recollected impression of relative youth—thirty-five, forty—and the unwelcome good looks of a delicate and disturbing sort. Indeed, traces of Dr. Jemand von Niemand and his appearance and his voice and his manner and other attributes would remain with Sophie forever. The first words he said to her, for example: "*Ich möchte mit dir schlafen.*" Which means, as bluntly and as unseductively as possible: "I'd like to get you into bed with me." Dreary loutish words, spoken from an intimidating vantage point, no finesse, no class, callow and cruel, an utterance one might expect from a B-grade movie Nazi *Schweinhund*. But these, according to Sophie, were the words he first said. Ugly talk for a doctor and a gentleman (perhaps even an aristocrat), although he was visibly, indisputably drunk, which might help explain such coarseness. Why Sophie, at first glance, thought he might be an aristocrat—Prussian perhaps, or of Prussian origin—was because of his extremely close resemblance to a Junker officer, a friend of her father's, whom she had seen once as a girl of sixteen or so on a summer visit to Berlin. Very "Nordic"-looking, attractive in a thin-lipped, austere, unbending way, the young officer had treated her frostily during their brief meeting, almost to the point of contempt and boorishness; nonetheless, she could not help but be taken by his arresting handsomeness, by—surprisingly—something not really effeminate but rather silkily feminine about his face in repose. He looked a bit like a militarized Leslie Howard, whom she had had a mild crush on ever since *The Petrified Forest*. Despite the dislike he had inspired in her, and her satisfaction in not having to see this German officer again, she remembered thinking about him later rather disturbingly: If he had been a woman, he would have been a person I think I might have felt drawn to. But now here was his counterpart, almost his replica,

standing in his slightly askew SS uniform on the dusty concrete platform at five in the afternoon, flushed with wine or brandy or
schnapps and mouthing his unpatrician words in an indolently patri-
cian, Berlin-accented voice: "I'd like to get you into bed with me."

Sophie ignored what he was saying, but as he spoke she glimpsed
one of those insignificant but ineffaceable details—another spectral
trace of the doctor—that would always spring out in vivid trompe
l'oeil from the confused surface of the day: a sprinkling of boiled-
rice grains on the lapel of the SS tunic. There were only four or
five of these; shiny with moisture still, they looked like maggots.
She gave them her dazed scrutiny, and while doing so she realized
for the first time that the piece of music being played just then by
the welcoming prisoners' band—hopelessly off-key and disorgan-
ized, yet flaying her nerves with its erotic sorrow and turgid beat
as it had even in the darkened car—was the Argentine tango "La
Cumparsita." Why had she not been able to name it before? Ba-
dum-*ba*-dum!

"*Du bist eine Polack,*" said the doctor. "*Bist du auch eine Kom-
munistin?*" Sophie placed one arm around Eva's shoulders, the
other arm around Jan's waist, saying nothing. The doctor belched,
then more sharply elaborated: "I know you're a Polack, but are you
also another one of these filthy Communists?" And then in his fog
he turned toward the next prisoners, seeming almost to forget
Sophie.

Why hadn't she played dumb? "*Nicht sprecht Deutsch.*" It could
have saved the moment. There was such a press of people. Had she
not answered in German he might have let the three of them pass
through. But there was the cold fact of her terror, and the terror
caused her to behave unwisely. She knew now what blind and merciful ignorance had prevented very few Jews who arrived here from
knowing, but which her association with Wanda and the others had
caused her to know and to dread with fear beyond utterance: a selection. She and the children were undergoing at this very moment the
ordeal she had heard about—rumored in Warsaw a score of times in
whispers—but which had seemed at once so unbearable and
unlikely to happen to her that she had thrust it out of her mind. But
here she was, and here was the doctor. While over there—just
beyond the roofs of the boxcars recently vacated by the death-bound
Malkinia Jews—was Birkenau, and the doctor could select for its
abyssal doors anyone whom he desired. This thought caused her
such terror that instead of keeping her mouth shut she said, "*Ich bin*

polnisch! In Krakow geboren!" Then she blurted helplessly, "I'm not Jewish! Or my children—they're not Jewish either." And added, "They are racially pure. They speak German." Finally she announced, "I'm a Christian. I'm a devout Catholic."

The doctor turned again. His eyebrows arched and he looked at Sophie with inebriate, wet, fugitive eyes, unsmiling. He was now so close to her that she smelled plainly the alcoholic vapor—a rancid fragrance of barley or rye—and she was not strong enough to return his gaze. It was then that she knew she had said something wrong, perhaps fatally wrong. She averted her face for an instant, glancing at an adjoining line of prisoners shambling through the golgotha of their selection, and saw Eva's flute teacher Zaorski at the precise congealed instant of his doom—dispatched to the left and to Birkenau by an almost imperceptible nod of a doctor's head. Now, turning back, she heard Dr. Jemand von Niemand say, "So you're not a Communist. You're a believer."

"Ja, mein Hauptmann. I believe in Christ." What folly! She sensed from his manner, his gaze—the new look in his eye of luminous intensity—that everything she was saying, far from helping her, from protecting her, was leading somehow to her swift undoing. She thought: Let me be struck dumb.

The doctor was a little unsteady on his feet. He leaned over for a moment to an enlisted underling with a clipboard and murmured something, meanwhile absorbedly picking his nose. Eva, pressing heavily against Sophie's leg, began to cry. "So you believe in Christ the Redeemer?" the doctor said in a thick-tongued but oddly abstract voice, like that of a lecturer examining the delicately shaded facet of a proposition in logic. Then he said something which for an instant was totally mystifying: "Did He not say, 'Suffer the little children to come unto Me'?" He turned back to her, moving with the twitchy methodicalness of a drunk.

Sophie, with an inanity poised on her tongue and choked with fear, was about to attempt a reply when the doctor said, "You may keep one of your children."

"Bitte?" said Sophie.

"You may keep one of your children," he repeated. "The other one will have to go. Which one will you keep?"

"You mean, I have to choose?"

"You're a Polack, not a Yid. That gives you a privilege—a choice."

Her thought processes dwindled, ceased. Then she felt her legs crumple. "I can't choose! I can't choose!" She began to scream. Oh,

how she recalled her own screams! Tormented angels never
screeched so loudly above hell's pandemonium. "*Ich kann nicht
wählen!*" she screamed.

The doctor was aware of unwanted attention. "Shut up!" he
ordered. "Hurry now and choose. Choose, goddamnit, or I'll send
them both over there. Quick!"

She could not believe any of this. She could not believe that she
was now kneeling on the hurtful, abrading concrete, drawing her
children toward her so smotheringly tight that she felt that their flesh
might be engrafted to hers even through layers of clothes. Her disbelief was total, deranged. It was disbelief reflected in the eyes of
the gaunt, waxy-skinned young Rottenführer, the doctor's aide, to
whom she inexplicably found herself looking upward in supplica-
tion. He appeared stunned, and he returned her gaze with a wide-
eyed baffled expression, as if to say: I can't understand this either.

"Don't make me choose," she heard herself plead in a whisper,
"I can't choose."

"Send them both over there, then," the doctor said to the aide,
"*nach links.*"

"Mama!" She heard Eva's thin but soaring cry at the instant that
she thrust the child away from her and rose from the concrete with
a clumsy stumbling motion. "Take the baby!" she called out. "Take
my little girl!"

At this point the aide—with a careful gentleness that Sophie would
try without success to forget—tugged at Eva's hand and led her away
into the waiting legion of the damned. She would forever retain a
dim impression that the child had continued to look back, beseeching. But because she was now almost completely blinded by salty,
thick, copious tears she was spared whatever expression Eva wore,
and she was always grateful for that. For in the bleakest honesty of
her heart she knew that she would never have been able to tolerate
it, driven nearly mad as she was by her last glimpse of that vanishing small form.

For Further Reflection

1. This is a classic moral dilemma in which both options are bad:
   either *actively* condemn one of your children to death, or by
   refusing to choose have both killed. What should Sophie have
   done? What would you do? Why?

The New Slavery

KEVIN BALES

Kevin Bales is principal lecturer at the Roehampton Institute of Surrey, England, and one of the world's leading authorities on contemporary slavery. In this essay, he explains the manner in which slavery still exists in the world, especially in Southeast Asia and Sub-Saharan Africa, but also in South America, East Asia, Europe, and America.

The French Countryside in summer lives up to its reputation. As we sit outdoors in little village about one hundred miles from Paris, the breeze brings us the scent of apples from the orchard next door. I have come here to meet Seba, a newly freed slave. She is a handsome and animated young woman of twenty-two, but as she tells me her story she draws into herself, smoking furiously, trembling, and then the tears come.

> I was raised by my grandmother in Mali, and when I was still a little girl a woman my family knew came and asked her if she could take me to Paris to care for her children. She told my grandmother that she would put me in school and that I would learn French. But when I came to Paris I was not sent to school, I had to work every day. In their house I did all the work; I cleaned the house, cooked the meals, cared for the children, and washed and fed the baby. Every day I started work before 7 A.M. and finished about 11 P.M.; I never had a day off. My mistress did nothing; she slept late and then watched television or went out.
>
> One day I told her that I wanted to go to school. She replied that she had not brought me to France to go to school but to take care of her children. I was so tired and run-down. I had problems with my teeth; sometimes my cheek would swell and the pain would be terrible. Sometimes I had stomachaches, but when I was ill I still had to work. Sometimes when I was in pain I would cry, but my mistress would shout at me.

Reprinted from Kevin Bales, *Disposable People* (Berkeley: University of California Press, 1999), by permission.

I slept on the floor in one of the children's bedrooms; my food was their leftovers. I was not allowed to take food from the refrigerator like the children. If I took food she would beat me. She often beat me. She would slap me all the time. She beat me with the broom, with kitchen tools, or whipped me with electric cable. Sometimes I would bleed; I still have marks on my body.

Once in 1992 I was late going to get the children from school; my mistress and her husband were furious with me and beat and then threw me out on the street. I had nowhere to go; I didn't understand anything, and I wandered on the streets. After some time her husband found me and took me back to their house. There they stripped me naked, tied my hands behind my back, and began to whip me with a wire attached to a broomstick. Both of them were beating me at the same time. I was bleeding a lot and screaming, but they continued to beat me. Then she rubbed chili pepper into my wounds and stuck it in my vagina. I lost consciousness.

Sometime later one of the children came and untied me. I lay on the floor where they had left me for several days. The pain was terrible but no one treated my wounds. When I was able to stand I had to start work again, but after this I was always locked in the apartment. They continued to beat me.

Seba was finally freed when a neighbor, after hearing the sounds of abuse and beating, managed to talk to her. Seeing her scars and wounds, the neighbor called the police and the French Committee against Modern Slavery (CCEM), who brought a case and took Seba into their care. Medical examinations confirmed that she had been tortured.

Today Seba is well cared for, living with a volunteer family. She is receiving counseling and is learning to read and write. Recovery will take years, but she is a remarkably strong young woman. What amazed me was how far Seba still needs to go. As we talked I realized that though she was twenty-two and intelligent, her understanding of the world was less developed than the average five-year-old's. For example, until she was freed she had little understanding of time—no knowledge of weeks, months, or years. For Seba there was only the endless round of work and sleep. She knew that there were hot days and cold days, but never learned that the seasons follow a pattern. If she ever knew her birthday she had forgotten it, and she did not know her age. She is baffled by the idea of "choice." Her volunteer family tries to help her make choices, but she still can't grasp it. I asked Seba to draw the best picture of a person that she could. She told me it was the first time she had ever tried to draw a person. This was the result:

If Seba's case were unique it would be shocking enough, but Seba is one of perhaps 3,000 household slaves in Paris. Nor is such slavery unique to that city. In London, New York, Zurich, Los Angeles, and across the world, children are brutalized as household slaves. And they are just one small group of the world's slaves.

Slavery is not a horror safely consigned to the past; it continues to exist throughout the world, even in developed countries like France and the United States. Across the world slaves work and sweat and build and suffer. Slaves in Pakistan may have made the shoes you are wearing and the carpet you stand on. Slaves in the Caribbean may have put sugar in your kitchen and toys in the hands of your children. In India they may have sewn the shirt on your back and polished the ring on your finger. They are paid nothing.

Slaves touch your life indirectly as well. They made the bricks for the factory that made the TV you watch. In Brazil slaves made the charcoal that tempered the steel that made the springs in your car and the blade on your lawnmower. Slaves grew the rice that fed the woman that wove the lovely cloth you've put up as curtains. Your investment portfolio and your mutual fund pension own stock in companies using slave labor in the developing world. Slaves keep your costs low and returns on your investments high.

Slavery is a booming business and the number of slaves is increasing. People get rich by using slaves. And when they've finished with their slaves, they just throw these people away. This is the new slavery, which focuses on big profits and cheap lives. It is not about owning people in the traditional sense of the old slavery, but about controlling them completely. People become completely disposable tools for making money.

> On more than ten occasions I woke early in the morning to find the corpse of a young girl floating in the water by the barge. Nobody bothered to bury the girls. They just threw their bodies in the river to be eaten by the fish.

This was the fate of young girls enslaved as prostitutes in the gold mining towns of the Amazon, explained Antonia Pinto, who worked there as a cook and a procurer. While the developed world bemoans the destruction of the rain forests, few people realize that slave labor is used to destroy them. Men are lured to the region by promises of riches in gold dust, and girls as young as eleven are offered jobs in the offices and restaurants that serve the mines. When they arrive in the remote mining areas, the men are locked up and forced to work in the mines; the girls are beaten, raped, and put to work as prostitutes. Their "recruitment agents" are paid a small amount for each body, perhaps $150. The "recruits" have become slaves—not through legal ownership, but through the final authority of violence. The local police act as enforcers to control the slaves. As one young woman explained, "Here the brothel owners send the police to beat us . . . if we flee they go after us, if they find us they kill us, or if they don't kill us they beat us all the way back to the brothel.

The brothels are incredibly lucrative. The girl who "cost" $150 can be sold for sex up to ten times a night and bring in $10,000 per month. The only expenses are payments to the police and a pittance for food. If a girl is a troublemaker, runs away, or gets sick, she is easy to get rid of and replace. Antonia Pinto described what happened to an eleven-year-old girl when she refused to have sex with a miner: "After decapitating her with his machete, the miner drove around in his speedboat, showing off her head to the other miners, who clapped and shouted their approval.

As the story of these girls shows, slavery has not, as most of us have been led to believe, ended. To be sure, the word *slavery* continues to be used to mean all sorts of things and all too often it has been applied as an easy metaphor. Having just enough money to get by, receiving wages that barely keep you alive, may be called wage slavery, but it is not slavery. Sharecroppers have a hard life, but they are not slaves. Child labor is terrible, but it is not necessarily slavery.

We might think slavery is a matter of ownership, but that depends on what we mean by *ownership*. In the past, slavery entailed one person legally owning another person, but modern slavery is different. Today slavery is illegal everywhere, and there is no more *legal* ownership of human beings. When people buy slaves today they don't ask for a receipt or ownership papers, but they do gain *control*—and they use violence to maintain this control. Slaveholders have all of the benefits of ownership without the legalities. Indeed, for the slaveholders, not having legal ownership is an improvement because they get total control without any responsibility for what they own. For that reason I tend to use the term slave*holder* instead of slave*owner*.

In spite of this difference between the new and the old slavery, I think everyone would agree that what I am talking about is slavery: the total control of one person by another for the purpose of economic exploitation. Modern slavery hides behind different masks, using clever lawyers and legal smoke screens, but when we strip away the lies, we find someone controlled by violence and denied all of their personal freedom to make money for someone else. As I traveled around the world to study the new slavery, I looked behind the legal masks and I saw people in chains. Of course, many people think there is no such thing as slavery anymore, and I was one of those people just a few years ago.

FIRST COME, FIRST SERVED

I first encountered the vestiges of the old slavery when I was four years old. What happened is one of my strongest memories. It was the 1950s in the American South and my family was having dinner in a cafeteria. As we started down the serving line I saw another family standing behind a chain, waiting as others moved through with their trays. With the certainty of a four-year-old, I knew that they had arrived first and should be ahead of us. The *fairness* of first come, first served had been drummed into me. So I unhooked the chain and said, "You were here first, you should go ahead." The father of this African American family looked down at me with eyes full of feeling, just as my own father came up and put his hand on my shoulder. Suddenly the atmosphere was thick with unspoken emotion. Tension mixed with bittersweet approval as both fathers grappled with the innocent ignorance of a child who had never heard of segregation. No one spoke, until finally the black father said, "That's OK, we're waiting on someone; go ahead."

My parents were not radicals, but they had taught me the value of fairness and equal treatment. They believed that the idea of our equality was one of the best things about America, and they never approved of the racism of segregation. But sometimes it takes a child's simplicity to cut through the weight of custom. The intensity of that moment stayed with me, though it was years before I began to understand what those two sets of parents were feeling. As I grew up I was glad to see such blatant segregation coming to an end. The idea that there might still be actual slavery—quite apart from segregation—never crossed my mind. Everyone knew that in the United States slavery had ended in 1865.

Of course, the gross inequalities in American society brought the slavery of the past to mind. I realized that the United States, once a large-scale slave society, was still suffering from a botched emancipation program. Soon after Abraham Lincoln's celebrated proclamation, Jim Crow laws and oppression took over to keep ex-slaves from economic and political power. I came to understand that emancipation was a *process,* not an event—a process that still had a way to go. As a young social researcher, I generally held jobs concerned with the residue of this unfinished process: I studied bad housing, health differences between the races, problems in integrated schools, and racism in the legal system. But I still saw all this as the vestiges of slavery, as problems that were tough but not intractable.

It was only after I moved to England in the early 1980s that I became aware of real slavery. At a large public event I came across a small table set up by Anti-Slavery International. I picked up some leaflets in passing, and I was amazed by what I read. There was no flash-of-light experience, but I developed a gnawing desire to find out more. I was perplexed that this most fundamental human right was still not assured—and that no one seemed to know or care about it. Millions of people were actively working against the nuclear threat, against apartheid in South Africa, against famine in Ethiopia, yet *slavery* wasn't even on the map. The more this realization dug into me, the more I knew I had to do something. Slavery is an obscenity. It is not just stealing someone's labor; it is the theft of an entire life. It is more closely related to the concentration camp than to questions of bad working conditions. There seems nothing to debate about slavery: it must stop. My question became: What can I do to bring an end to slavery? I decided to use my skills as a social researcher, and I embarked on the project that led to this book.

HOW MANY SLAVES?

For several years I collected every scrap of information I could find about modern slavery. I went to the United Nations and the British Library; I trawled through the International Labour Office and visited human rights organizations and charities. I talked to anthropologists and economists. Getting useful, reliable information on slavery is very difficult. Even when shown photographs and affidavits, nations' officials deny its existence. Human rights organizations, in contrast, want to expose the existence of slavery. They report what they are told by the victims of slavery, and it is their business to counter government denials with evidence of widespread slavery. Who and what can we believe?

My approach was to pull together all the evidence I could find, country by country. When someone gave reasons why a number of people were in slavery, I took note. When two people independently stated they had good reasons to think that there was a certain amount of slavery, I began to feel more convinced. Sometimes I found that researchers were working on slavery in two different parts of the same country without knowing about each other. I looked at every report I could find and asked, "What can I feel sure about? Which numbers do I trust?" Then I added up what I had found, taking care to be conservative. If I had any doubts about a report, I left it out of my calculations. It's important to remember that slavery is a shadowy, illegal enterprise, so statistics are hard to come by. I can only make a good guess at the numbers.

My best estimate of the number of slaves in the world today is 27 million.

This number is much smaller than the estimates put forward by some activists, who give a range as high as 200 million, but it is the number I feel I can trust; it is also the number that fits my strict definition of slavery. The biggest part of that 27 million, perhaps 15 to 20 million, is represented by *bonded labor* in India, Pakistan, Bangladesh, and Nepal. Bonded labor or debt bondage happens when people give themselves into slavery as security against a loan or when they inherit a debt from a relative (we'll look at this more closely later). Otherwise slavery tends to be concentrated in Southeast Asia, northern and western Africa, and parts of South America (but there are some slaves in almost every country in the world, including the United States, Japan, and many European countries). There are more slaves alive today than all the people stolen from Africa in the time of the transatlantic slave trade. Put another way, today's slave population is greater than the population of Canada, and six times greater than the population of Israel.

These slaves tend to be used in simple, nontechnological, and traditional work. The largest group work in agriculture. But slaves are used in many other kinds of labor: brickmaking, mining or quarrying, prostitution, gem working and jewelry making, cloth and carpet making, and domestic service; they clear forests, make charcoal, and work in shops. Much of this work is aimed at local sale and consumption, but slave-made goods reach into homes around the world. Carpets, fireworks, jewelry, and metal goods made by slave labor, as well as grains, sugar, and other foods harvested by slaves, are imported directly to North America and Europe. In addition, large international corporations, acting through subsidiaries in the developing world, take advantage of slave labor to improve their bottom line and increase the dividends to their shareholders.

But the value of slaves lies not so much in the particular products they make as in their sweat, in the volume of work squeezed out of them. Slaves are often forced to sleep next to their looms or brick kilns; some are even chained to their work tables. All their waking hours may be turned into working hours. In our global economy one of the standard explanations that multinational corporations give for closing factories in the "first world" and opening them in the "third world" is the lower labor cost. Slavery can constitute a significant part of these savings. No paid workers, no matter how efficient, can compete economically with unpaid workers—slaves.

WHAT DOES RACE HAVE TO DO WITH IT?

In the new slavery race means little. In the past, ethnic and racial differences were used to explain and excuse slavery. These differences allowed slaveholders to make up reasons why slavery was acceptable, or even a good thing for the slaves. The *otherness* of the slaves made it easier to employ the violence and cruelty necessary for total control. This otherness could be defined in almost any way—a different religion, tribe, skin color, language, custom, or economic class. Any of these differences could be and were used to separate the slaves from the slaveholders. Maintaining these differences required tremendous investment in some very irrational ideas—and the crazier the justifying idea, the more vehemently it was insisted upon. The American Founding Fathers had to go through moral, linguistic, and political contortions to explain why their "land of the free" was only for white people. Many of them knew that by allowing slavery they were betraying their most cherished ideals. They were driven to it because slavery was worth a lot of money to a lot of people in North America at the time. But they went to the trouble of devising legal and political excuses because they felt they had to justify their economic decisions morally.

Today the morality of money overrides other concerns. Most slaveholders feel no need to explain or defend their chosen method of labor recruitment and management. Slavery is a very profitable business, and a good bottom line is justification enough. Freed of ideas that restrict the status of slave to *others,* modern slaveholders use other criteria to choose slaves. Indeed, they enjoy a great advantage: being able to enslave people from one's own country helps keep costs down. Slaves in the American South in the nineteenth century were very expensive, in part because they originally had to be shipped thousands of miles from Africa. When slaves can be gotten from the next town or region, transportation costs fall. The question isn't "Are they the right color to be slaves?" but "Are they vulnerable enough to be enslaved?" The criteria of enslavement today do not concern color, tribe, or religion; they focus on weakness, gullibility, and deprivation.

It is true that in some countries there are ethnic or religious differences between slaves and slaveholders. In Pakistan, for example, many enslaved brickmakers are Christians while the slaveholders are Muslim. In India slave and slaveholder may be from different castes. In Thailand they may come from different regions of the country and are much more likely to be women. But in Pakistan there are Christians who are not slaves, in India members of the same caste who are free. Their caste or religion simply reflects their vulnerability to enslavement; it doesn't cause it. Only in one country, Mauritania, does the racism of the old slavery persist—there black slaves are held by Arab slaveholders, and race is a key division. To be sure, some cultures are more divided along racial lines than others. Japanese culture strongly distinguishes the Japanese as different from everyone else, and so enslaved prostitutes in Japan are more likely to be Thai, Philippine, or European women—although they may be Japanese. Even here, the key difference is not racial but economic: Japanese women are not nearly so vulnerable and desperate as Thais or Filipinas. And the Thai women are available for shipment to Japan because Thais are enslaving Thais. The same pattern occurs in the oil-rich states of Saudi Arabia and Kuwait, where Muslim Arabs promiscuously enslave Sri Lankan Hindus, Filipino Christians, and Nigerian Muslims. The common denominator is poverty, not color. Behind every assertion of ethnic difference is the reality of economic disparity. If all left-handed people in the world became destitute tomorrow, there would soon be slaveholders taking advantage of them. Modern slaveholders are predators keenly aware of weakness; they are rapidly adapting an ancient practice to the new global economy.

For Further Reflection

1. Read over Seba's story. What light does it shed on the human condition? Does this story shed any light on what morality is for?

2. According to Bales, how many slaves are in the world today? How does their existence affect our lives?

3. Discuss the causes of modern slavery. How can this institution exist in today's world? What, if anything, can be done about it?

From Cruelty to Goodness

PHILIP HALLIE

Philip Hallie grew up in Chicago and earned his degrees
at Grinnell, Oxford, and Harvard. For many years he was
professor of philosophy at Wesleyan University. Among his
many works are *The Paradox of Cruelty* (1969) and *Lest
Innocent Blood Be Shed* (1979).

In this essay Hallie examines the reality of cruelty, especially institutional cruelty, such as that of slavery and the
Nazi treatment of Jews during World War II. Institutionalized cruelty involves the undermining of dignity by perpetrating a false inequality of worth and power. By degrading the victim, the victimizer exalts his own perception of
self-worth, but in reality becomes evil. As an example of
the kind of goodness necessary to defeat cruelty, Hallie describes the Protestant citizens, especially Pastor Trocme, of
the village of Le Chambon, who risked their lives to save
six thousand Jews from the Nazis.

I am a student of ethics, of good and evil; but my approach to these
two rather melodramatic terms is skeptical. I am in the tradition of
the ancient Greek *skeptikoi,* whose name means "inquirers" or "inves-
tigators." And what we investigate is relationships among particular
facts. What we put into doubt are the intricate webs of high-level
abstractions that passed for philosophizing in the ancient world, and
that still pass for philosophizing. My approach to good and evil
emphasizes not abstract common nouns like "justice," but proper
names and verbs. Names and verbs keep us close to the facts better
than do our highfalutin common nouns. Names refer to particular
people, and verbs connect subjects with predicates *in time,* while
common nouns are above all this.

One of the words that is important to me is my own name. For
me, philosophy is personal; it is closer to literature and history than
it is to the exact sciences, closer to the passions, actions, and common sense of individual persons than to a dispassionate technical

Reprinted from "From Cruelty to Goodness" © 1981 The Hastings Center by permission of The Hastings Center.

science. It has to do with the personal matter of wisdom. And so ethics for me is personal—my story, and not necessarily (though possibly) yours. It concerns particular people at particular times.

But ethics is more than such particulars. It involves abstractions, that is, rules, laws, ideals. When you look at the ethical magnates of history you see in their words and deeds two sorts of ethical rules: negative and positive. The negative rules are scattered throughout the Bible, but Moses brought down from Mount Sinai the main negative ethical rules of the West: Thou shalt not murder; thou shalt not betray. . . . The positive injunctions are similarly spread throughout the Bible. In the first chapter of the book of Isaiah we are told to ". . . defend the fatherless, plead for the widow." The negative ethic forbids certain actions; the positive ethic demands certain actions. To follow the negative ethic is to be decent, to have clean hands. But to follow the positive ethic, to be one's brother's keeper, is to be more than decent—it is to be active, even aggressive. If the negative ethic is one of decency, the positive one is the ethic of riskful, strenuous nobility.

In my early studies of particularized ethical terms, I found myself dwelling upon negative ethics, upon prohibitions. And among the most conspicuous prohibitions I found embodied in history was the prohibition against deliberate harmdoing, against cruelty. "Thou shalt not be cruel" had as much to do with the nightmare of history as did the prohibitions against murder and betrayal. In fact, many of the Ten Commandments—especially those against murder, adultery, stealing, and betrayal—were ways of prohibiting cruelty.

Early in my research it became clear that there are various approaches to cruelty, as the different commandments suggest. For instance, there is the way reflected in the origins of the word "cruel." The Latin *crudus* is related to still older words standing for bloodshed, or raw flesh. According to the etymology of the word, cruelty involves the spilling of blood.

But modern dictionaries give the word a different meaning. They define it as "disposed to giving pain." They emphasize awareness, not simply bloodshed. After all, they seem to say, you cannot be cruel to a dead body. There is no cruelty without consciousness.

And so I found myself studying the kinds of awareness associated with the hurting of human beings. It is certainly true that for millennia in history and literature people have been torturing each other not only with hard weapons but also with hard words.

Still, the word "pain" seemed to be a simplistic and superficial way of describing the many different sorts of cruelty. In Reska Weiss's *Journey Through Hell* (London, 1961) there is a brief passage of one of the deepest cruelties that Nazis perpetrated upon extermination camp inmates. On a march

> Urine and excreta poured down the prisoners' legs, and by nightfall the excrement, which had frozen to our limbs, gave off its stench.

And Weiss goes on to talk not in terms of "pain" or bloodshed, but in other terms:

> . . . We were really no longer human beings in the accepted sense. Not even animals, but putrefying corpses moving on two legs.

There is one factor that the idea of "pain" and the simpler idea of bloodshed do not touch: cruelty, not playful, quotidian teasing or raging, but cruelty (what the anti-cruelty societies usually call "substantial cruelty") involves the maiming of a person's dignity, the crushing of a person's self-respect. Bloodshed, the idea of pain (which is usually something involving a localizable occurrence, localizable in a tooth, in a head, in short, in the body), these are superficial ideas of cruelty. A whip, bleeding flesh, these are what the journalists of cruelty emphasize, following the etymology and dictionary meaning of the word. But the depths of an understanding of cruelty lie in the depths of an understanding of human dignity and of how you can maim it without bloodshed, and often without localizable bodily pain.

In excremental assault, in the process of keeping camp inmates from wiping themselves or from going to the latrine, and in making them drink water from a toilet bowl full of excreta (and the excreta of the guards at that) localizable pain is nothing. Deep humiliation is everything. We human beings believe in hierarchies, whether we are skeptics or not about human value. There is a hierarchical gap between shit and me. We are even above using the word. We are "above" walking around besmirched with feces. Our dignity, whatever the origins of that dignity may be, does not permit it. In order to be able to want to live, in order to be able to walk erect, we must respect ourselves as beings "higher" than our feces. When we feel that we are not "higher" than dirt or filth, then our lives are maimed at the very center, in the very depths, not merely in some localizable portion of our bodies. And when our lives are so maimed we become things, slaves, instruments. From ancient times until this moment, and as long as there will be human beings on this planet, there are those who know this and will use it, just as the Roman slave owners and the Southern American slave owners knew it when—one time a year—they encouraged the slaves to drink all the alcohol they could drink so that they could get bestially drunk and then even more bestially sick afterwards, under the eyes of their generous owners. The self-hatred, the loss of self-respect that the Saturnalia created in ancient Rome, say, made it possible to continue using the slaves as things, since they themselves came to think of themselves as things, as sub-human tools of the owners and the overseers.

Institutionalized cruelty, I learned, is the subtlest kind of cruelty. In episodic cruelty the victim knows he is being hurt, and his victimizer knows it too. But in a persistent pattern of humiliation that endures for years in a community, both the victim and the victimizer find ways of obscuring the harm that is being done. Blacks come to think of themselves as inferior, even esthetically inferior (black is "dirty"); and Jews come to think of themselves as inferior, even esthetically (dark hair and aquiline noses are "ugly"), so that the way they are being treated is justified by their "actual" inferiority, by the inferiority they themselves feel.

A similar process happens in the minds of the victimizers in institutionalized cruelty. They feel that since they are superior, even esthetically ("to be blonde is to be beautiful"), they deserve to do what they wish, deserve to have these lower creatures under their control. The words of Heinrich Himmler, head of the Nazi SS, in Posen in the year 1943 in a speech to his SS subordinates in a closed session, show how institutionalized cruelty can obscure harmdoing:

> . . . the words come so easily. "The Jewish people will be exterminated," says every party member, "of course. It's in our program . . . extermination. We'll take care of it." And then they come, these nice 80 million Germans, and every one of them has his decent Jew. Sure the others are swine, but his one is a fine Jew . . . Most of you will know what it means to have seen 100 corpses together, or 500 to 1000. To have made one's way through that, and . . . to have remained a decent person throughout, that is what has made us hard. That is a page of glory in our history. . . .

In this speech he was making a sharp distinction between the program of crushing the Jews and the personal sentiments of individual Germans. The program stretched over years; personal senti-

ments were momentary. He was pleading for the program, for institutionalized destruction.

But one of the most interesting parts of the speech occurs toward
the end of it:

> . . . in sum, we can say that we fulfilled the heaviest of tasks [destroy-
> ing the Jews] in love to our people. And we suffered no harm in
> our essence, in our soul, in our character. . . .

Commitment that overrides all sentimentality transforms cruelty and
destruction into moral nobility, and commitment is the lifeblood of
an institution.

CRUELTY AND THE POWER RELATIONSHIPS

But when I studied all these ways that we have used the word
"cruelty," I was nagged by the feeling that I had not penetrated
into its inner structure. I was classifying, sorting out symptoms; but
symptoms are signals, and what were the symptoms signals *of?* I
felt like a person who had been studying cancer by sorting out
brief pains from persistent pains, pains in the belly from pains in
the head. I was being superficial, and I was not asking the question, "What are the forces behind these kinds of cruelty?" I felt that
there were such forces, but as yet I had not touched them.

Then one day I was reading in one of the great autobiographies
of western civilization, Frederick Douglass's *Life and Times.* The
passage I was reading was about Douglass's thoughts on the origins of slavery. He was asking himself: "How could these whites
keep us enslaved?" And he suddenly realized:

> My faculties and powers of body and soul are not my own, but are
> the property of a fellow-mortal in no sense superior to me, except
> that he has the physical power to compel me to be owned and con-
> trolled by him. By the combined physical force of the community I
> am his slave—a slave for life.

And then I saw that a disparity in power lay at the center of the
dynamism of cruelty. If it was institutional cruelty it was in all likelihood a difference involving both verbal and physical power that kept
the cruelty going. The power of the majority and the weakness of a
minority were at the center of the institutional cruelty of slavery and
of Nazi anti-Semitism. The whites not only outnumbered the blacks

in America, but had economic and political ascendancy over them.
But just as important as these "physical" powers was the power that
words like "nigger" and "slave" gave the white majority. Their language sanctified if it did not create their power ascendancy over the
blacks, and one of the most important projects of the slave-holders
and their allies was that of seeing to it that the blacks themselves
thought of themselves in just these powerless terms. They utilized
the language to convince not only the whites but the blacks themselves that blacks were weak in mind, in will power, and in worth.
These words were like the excremental assault in the killing camps
of the Nazis: they diminished both the respect the victimizers
might have for their victims and the respect the victims might have
for themselves.

It occurred to me that if a power differential is crucial to the
idea of cruelty, then when that power differential is maintained,
cruelty will tend to be maintained, and when that power differential is eliminated, cruelty will tend to be eliminated. And this seemed
to work. In all kinds of cruelty, violent and polite, episodic and
institutional, when the victim arms himself with the appropriate
strength, the cruelty diminishes or disappears. When Jews joined
the Bush Warriors of France, the Maquis, and became powerful
enough to strike at Vichy or the Nazis, they stopped being victims
of French and Nazi cruelty. When Frederick Douglass learned to
use the language with great skill and expressiveness, and when he
learned to use his physical strength against his masters, the power
differential between him and his masters diminished, and so did
their cruelty to him. In his autobiography he wrote:

> A man without force is without the essential dignity of humanity.
> Human nature is so constituted that it cannot honor a helpless man,
> though it can pity him, and even this it cannot do long if signs of
> power do not arise.

When I looked back at my own childhood in Chicago, I remembered that the physical and mental cruelties that I suffered in the
slums of the southwest side when I was about ten years old sharply
diminished and finally disappeared when I learned how to defend
myself physically and verbally. It is exactly this lesson that Douglass learned while growing up in the cruel institution of slavery.

Cruelty then, whatever else it is, is a kind of power relationship,
an imbalance of power wherein the stronger party becomes the

victimizer and the weaker becomes the victim. And since many general terms are most swiftly understood in relationship with their opposites (just as "heavy" can be understood most handily in relationship with what we mean by "light") the opposite of cruelty lay in a situation where there is no imbalance of power. The opposite of cruelty, I learned, was freedom from that unbalanced power relationship. Either the victim should get stronger and stand up to the victimizer, and thereby bring about a balance of their powers, or the victim should free himself from the whole relationship by flight.

In pursuing this line of thought, I came to believe that, again, dictionaries are misleading: many of them give "kindness" as the antonym for "cruelty." In studying slavery in America and the concentration camps of central Europe I found that kindness could be the ultimate cruelty, especially when it was given within that unbalanced power relationship. A kind overseer or a kind camp guard can exacerbate cruelty, can remind his victim that there are other relationships than the relationship of cruelty, and can make the victim deeply bitter, especially when he sees the self-satisfied smile of his victimizer. He is being cruelly treated when he is given a penny or a bun after having endured the crushing and grinding of his mental and bodily well-being. As Frederick Douglass put it:

> The kindness of the slave-master only gilded the chain. It detracted nothing from its weight or strength. The thought that men are for other and better uses than slavery throve best under the gentle treatment of a kind master.

No, I learned, the opposite of cruelty is not kindness. The opposite of the cruelty of the overseer in American slavery was not the kindness of that overseer for a moment or for a day. An episodic kindness is not the opposite of an institutionalized cruelty. The opposite of institutionalized cruelty is freedom from the cruel relationship.

It is important to see how perspectival the whole meaning of cruelty is. From the perspective of the SS guard or the southern overseer, a bit of bread, a smile is indeed a diminution of cruelty. But in the relationship of cruelty, the point of view of the victimizer is of only minor importance; it is the point of view of the victim that is authoritative. The victim feels the suffering in his own mind and body, whereas the victimizer, like Himmler's "hard" and "decent" Nazi, can be quite unaware of that suffering. The sword does not feel the pain that it inflicts. Do not ask it about suffering.

GOODNESS PERSONIFIED IN LE CHAMBON

All these considerations drove me to write my book *The Paradox of Cruelty*. But with the book behind me, I felt a deep discontent. I saw cruelty as an embodiment, a particular case of evil. But if cruelty is one of the main evils of human history, why is the opposite of cruelty not one of the key goods of human history? Freedom from the cruel relationship, either by escaping it or by redressing the imbalance of power, was not essential to what western philosophers and theologians have thought of as goodness. Escape is a negative affair. Goodness has something positive in it, something triumphantly affirmative.

Hoping for a hint of goodness in the very center of evil, I started looking closely at the so-called "medical experiments" of the Nazis upon children, usually Jewish and Gypsy children, in the death camps. Here were the weakest of the weak. Not only were they despised minorities, but they were, as individuals, still in their nonage. They were dependents. Here the power imbalance between the cruel experimenters and their victims was at its greatest. But instead of seeing light or finding insight by going down into this hell, into the deepest depth of cruelty, I found myself unwillingly becoming part of the world I was studying. I found myself either yearning to be viciously cruel to the victimizers of the children, or I found myself feeling compassion for the children, feeling their despair and pain as they looked up at the men and women in white coats cutting off their fingertips one at a time, or breaking their slender bones, or wounding their internal organs. Either I became a would-be victimizer or one more Jewish victim, and in either case I was not achieving insight, only misery, like so many other students of the Holocaust. And when I was trying to be "objective" about my studies, when I was succeeding at being indifferent to both the victimizers and the victims of these cruel relationships, I became cold; I became another monster who could look upon the maiming of a child with an indifferent eye.

To relieve this unending suffering, from time to time I would turn to the literature of the French resistance to the Nazis. I had been trained by the U.S. Army to understand it. The resistance was a way of trying to redress the power imbalance between Hitler's Fortress Europe and Hitler's victims, and so I saw it as an enemy of cruelty. Still, its methods were often cruel like the methods of most power struggles, and I had little hope of finding goodness here. We soldiers violated the negative ethic forbidding killing in order, we thought, to follow the positive ethic of being our brothers' keepers.

And then one gray April afternoon I found a brief article on the French village of Le Chambon-sur-Lignon. I shall not analyze here the tears of amazement and gladness and release from despair—in short, of joy—that I shed when I first read that story. Tears themselves interest me greatly—but not the tears of melancholy hindsight and existential despair; rather the tears of awe you experience when the realization of an ideal suddenly appears before your very eyes or thunders inside your mind; these tears interest me.

And one of the reasons I wept at first reading about Le Chambon in those brief, inaccurate pages was that at last I had discovered an embodiment of goodness in opposition to cruelty. I had discovered in the flesh and blood of history, in people with definite names in a definite place at a definite time in the nightmare of history, what no classical or religious ethicist could deny was goodness.

The French Protestant village of Le Chambon, located in the Cévennes Mountains of southeastern France, and with a population of about 3,500, saved the lives of about 6,000 people, most of them Jewish children whose parents had been murdered in the killing camps of central Europe. Under a national government which was not only collaborating with the Nazi conquerors of France but frequently trying to outdo the Germans in anti-Semitism in order to please their conquerors, and later under the day-to-day threat of destruction by the German Armed SS, they started to save children in the winter of 1940, the winter after the fall of France, and they continued to do so until the war in France was over. They sheltered the refugees in their own homes and in various houses they established especially for them; and they took many of them across the terrible mountains to neutral Geneva, Switzerland, in the teeth of French and German police and military power. The people of Le Chambon are poor, and the Huguenot faith to which they belong is a diminishing faith in Catholic and atheist France; but their spiritual power, their capacity to act in unison against the victimizers who surrounded them, was immense, and more than a match for the military power of those victimizers.

But for me as an ethicist the heart of the matter was not only their special power. What interested me was that they obeyed *both* the negative and the positive injunctions of ethics; they were good

not only in the sense of trying to be their brothers' keepers, protecting the victim, "defending the fatherless," to use the language
of Isaiah; they were also good in the sense that they obeyed the
negative injunctions against killing and betraying. While those
around them—including myself—were murdering in order presumably, to help mankind in some way or other, they murdered
nobody, and betrayed not a single child in those long and dangerous four years. For me as an ethicist they were the embodiment
of unambiguous goodness.

But for me as a student of cruelty they were something more:
they were an embodiment of the opposite of cruelty. And so, somehow, at last, I had found goodness in opposition to cruelty. In
studying their story, and in telling it in *Lest Innocent Blood Be Shed,*
I learned that the opposite of cruelty is not simply freedom from
the cruel relationship; it is *hospitality.* It lies not only in something
negative, an absence of cruelty or of imbalance; it lies in unsenti-
mental, efficacious love. The opposite of the cruelties of the camps
was not the liberation of the camps, the cleaning out of the barracks and the cessation of the horrors. All of this was the *end* of
the cruelty relationship, not the opposite of that relationship. And
it was not even the end of it, because the victims would never forget and would remain in agony as long as they remembered their
humiliation and suffering. No, the opposite of cruelty was not the
liberation of the camps, not freedom; it was the hospitality of the
people of Chambon, and of very few others during the Holocaust.
The opposite of cruelty was the kind of goodness that happened
in Chambon.

Let me explain the difference between liberation and hospitality
by telling you about a letter I received a year ago from a woman
who had been saved by the people of Le Chambon when she was
a young girl. She wrote:

> Never was there a question that the Chambonnais would not share
> all they had with us, meager as it was. One Chambonnais once told
> me that even if there was less, they still would want more for us.

And she goes on:

> It was indeed a very different attitude from the one in Switzerland,
> which while saving us also resented us so much.
>   If today we are not bitter people like most survivors it can only
> be due to the fact that we met people like the people of Le Cham-

bon, who showed to us simply that life can be different, that there are people who care, that people can live together and even risk their own lives for their fellow man.

The Swiss liberated refugees and removed them from the cruel relationship; the people of Le Chambon did more. They taught them that goodness could conquer cruelty, that loving hospitality could remove them from the cruel relationship. And they taught me this, too.

It is important to emphasize that cruelty is not simply an episodic, momentary matter, especially institutional cruelty like that of Nazism or slavery. As we have seen throughout this essay, not only does it persist while it is being exerted upon the weak; *it can persist in the survivors* after they have escaped the power relationship. The survivors torture themselves, continue to suffer, continue to maim their own lives long after the actual torture is finished. The self-hatred and rage of the blacks and the despair of the native Americans and the Jews who have suffered under institutional crushing and maiming are continuations of original cruelties. And these continuations exist because only a superficial liberation from torture has occurred. The sword has stopped falling on their flesh in the old obvious ways, but the wounds still bleed. I am not saying that the village of Chambon healed these wounds—they go too deep. What I am saying is that the people I have talked to who were once children in Le Chambon have more hope for their species and more respect for themselves as human beings than most other survivors I have met. The enduring hospitality they met in Le Chambon helped them find realistic hope in a world of persisting cruelty.

What was the nature of this hospitality that saved and deeply changed so many lives? It is hard to summarize briefly what the Chambonnais did, and above all how they did it. The morning after a new refugee family came to town they would find on their front door a wreath with *"Bienvenue!"* "Welcome!" painted on a piece of cardboard attached to the wreath. Nobody knew who had brought the wreath; in effect, the whole town had brought it.

It was mainly the women of Chambon who gave so much more than shelter to these, the most hated enemies of the Nazis. There was Madame Barraud, a tiny Alsatian, who cared for the refugee boys in her house with all the love such a tiny body could hold, and who cared for the way they felt day and night. And there were others.

But there was one person without whom Le Chambon could not have become the safest place in Europe for Jews: the Huguenot minister of the village, André Trocmé. Trocmé was a passionately religious man. He was massive, more than six feet tall, blonde, with a quick temper. Once long after the war, while he was lecturing on the main project of his life, the promotion of the idea of nonviolence in international relations, one of the members of his audience started to whisper a few words to his neighbor. Trocmé let this go on for a few moments, then interrupted his speech, walked up to the astonished whisperer, raised his massive arm, pointed toward the door, and yelled, "Out! Out! Get out!" And the lecture was on nonviolence.

The center of his thought was the belief that God showed how important man was by becoming Himself a human being, and by becoming a particular sort of human being who was the embodiment of sacrificially generous love. For Trocmé, every human being was like Jesus, had God in him or her, and was just as precious as God Himself. And when Trocmé with the help of the Quakers and others organized his village into the most efficient rescue machine in Europe, he did so not only to save the Jews, but also to save the Nazis and their collaborators. He wanted to keep them from blackening their souls with more evil—he wanted to save them, the victimizers, from evil.

One of the reasons he was successful was that the Huguenots had been themselves persecuted for hundreds of years by the kings of France, and they knew what persecution was. In fact, when the people of Chambon took Jewish children and whole families across the mountains of southeastern France into neutral Switzerland, they often followed pathways that had been taken by Huguenots in their flight from the Dragoons of the French kings.

A particular incident from the story of Le Chambon during the Nazi occupation of France will explain succinctly why he was successful in making the village a village of refuge. But before I relate the story, I must point out that the people of the village did not think of themselves as "successful," let alone as "good." From their point of view, they did not do anything that required elaborate explanation. When I asked them why they helped these dangerous guests, they invariably answered, "What do you mean, 'Why'? Where else could they go? How could you turn them away? What is so special about being ready to help (*prête à servir*)? There was nothing else to do." And some of them laughed in amazement when I told them that I thought they were "good people." They saw no alternative to their actions and to the way they acted, and therefore they saw what they did as necessary, not something to be picked out for praise. Helping these guests was for them as natural as breathing or eating—one does not think of alternatives to these functions; they did not think of alternatives to sheltering people who were endangering not only the lives of their hosts but the lives of all the people of the village.

And now the story. One afternoon a refugee woman knocked on the door of a farmhouse outside the village. The farmers around the village proper were Protestants like most of the others in Chambon, but with one difference: they were mostly "Darbystes," followers of a strange Scot named Darby, who taught their ancestors in the nineteenth century to believe every word of the Bible, and indeed, who had them memorize the Bible. They were literal fundamentalists. The farm-woman opened the door to the refugee and invited her into the kitchen where it was warm. Standing in the middle of the floor the refugee, in heavily accented French, asked for eggs for her children. In those days of very short supplies, people with children often went to the farmers in the "gray market" (neither black nor exactly legal) to get necessary food. This was early in 1941, and the farmers were not yet accustomed to the refugees. The farm-woman looked into the eyes of the shawled refugee and asked, "Are you Jewish?" The woman started to tremble, but she could not lie, even though that question was usually the beginning of the end of life for Jews in Hitler's Fortress Europe. She answered, "Yes."

The woman ran from the kitchen to the staircase nearby, and while the refugee trembled with terror in the kitchen, she called up the stairs, "Husband, children, come down, come down! We have in our house at this very moment a representative of the Chosen People!"

Not all the Protestants in Chambon were Darbyste fundamentalists; but almost all were convinced that people are the children of God, and are as precious as God Himself. Their leaders were Huguenot preachers and their following of the negative and positive commandments of the Bible came in part from their personal generosity and courage, but also in part from the depths of their religious conviction that we are all children of God, and we must take care of each other lovingly. This combined with the ancient and deep historical ties between the Huguenots and the Jews of France and their own centuries of persecution by the Dragoons and Kings of France helped make them what they were, "always ready to help," as the Chambonnais saying goes.

A CHOICE OF PERSPECTIVES

We have come a long way from cruelty to the people of Chambon, just as I have come a long way in my research from concrete evil to concrete goodness. Let me conclude with a point that has been alternately hinted at and stressed in the course of this essay.

A few months after *Lest Innocent Blood Be Shed* was published I received a letter from Massachusetts that opened as follows:

> I have read your book, and I believe that you mushy-minded moralists should be awakened to the facts. Nothing happened in Le Chambon, nothing of any importance whatsoever.
>
> The Holocaust, dear Professor, was like a geological event, like an earthquake. No person could start it; no person could change it; and no person could end it. And no small group of persons could do so either. It was the armies and the nations that performed actions that counted. Individuals did nothing. You sentimentalists have got to learn that the great masses and big political ideas make the difference. Your people and the people they saved simply do not exist.

Now between this position and mine there is an abyss that no amount of shouted arguments or facts can cross. And so I shall not answer this letter with a tightly organized reply. I shall answer it only by telling you that one of the reasons institutional cruelty exists and persists is that people believe that individuals can do nothing, that only vast ideologies and armies can act meaningfully. Every act of institutional cruelty—Nazism, slavery, and all the others—lives not with people in the concrete, but with abstractions that blind people to individuals. Himmler's speech to the SS leadership in 1943 is full of phrases like "exterminating a bacillus," and "The Jewish people will be exterminated." And in that speech he attacks any German who believes in "his decent Jew." Institutional cruelty, like other misleading approaches to ethics, blinds us to the victim's point of view; and when we are blind to that point of view we can countenance and perpetrate cruelty with impunity.

I have told you that I cannot and will not try to refute the letter from Massachusetts. I shall only summarize the point of view of this essay with another story.

I was lecturing a few months ago in Minneapolis, and when I finished talking about the Holocaust and the village of Le Chambon, a woman stood up and asked me if the village of Le Chambon was in the Department of Haute-Loire, the high sources of the Loire River. Obviously she was French, with her accent; and all French people know that there are many villages called "Le Chambon" in France, just as any American knows that there are many "Main Streets" in the United States. I said that Le Chambon was indeed in the Haute-Loire.

She said, "Then you have been speaking about the village that saved all three of my children. I want to thank you for writing this book, not only because the story will now be permanent, but also because I shall be able to talk about those terrible days with Americans now, for they will understand those days better than they have. You see, you Americans, though you sometimes cross the oceans, live on an island here as far as war is concerned . . ."

Then she asked to come up and say one sentence. There was not a sound, not even breathing, to be heard in the room. She came to the front of the room and said, "The Holocaust was storm, lightning, thunder, wind, rain, yes. And Le Chambon was the rainbow."

Only from her perspective can you understand the cruelty and the goodness I have been talking about, not from the point of view of the gentleman from Massachusetts. You must choose which perspective is best, and your choice will have much to do with your feelings about the preciousness of life, and not only the preciousness of other people's lives. If the lives of others are precious to you, your life will become more precious to you.

For Further Reflection

1. What does Hallie mean when he says that "philosophy is personal; it is closer to literature and history than it is to the exact sciences"?

2. How does Hallie characterize cruelty? Why does he think that institutionalized cruelty is the worst kind of cruelty?

3. Explain Hallie's notion of power relations and how they bear on the reality of cruelty.

4. Reflect on the story of the people of Le Chambon, who saved thousands of Jews. What were their motives? What lessons can we learn from them?

5. How does Hallie use this story to illustrate the antidote to cruelty? Compare the letter from Massachusetts with the statement of the woman in Minneapolis: "The Holocaust was storm, lightning, thunder, wind, rain, yes. And Le Chambon was the rainbow."

Wickedness

STANLEY BENN

Stanley Benn (1921–1986) was a research fellow in philosophy at the Australian National University, Canberra. He was the author of several important works in social and political philosophy. In this essay Benn analyzes the concept of wickedness, describing four types: (1) selfishness: the person pursues his or her own good, disregarding the rights and good of others; (2) conscientious wickedness: the person is unconditionally loyal to a person or group, even when it does evil; (3) heteronomous wickedness: the person abdicates personal responsibility for his or her actions. Adolph Eichmann is an example—a Nazi who freely gave up his personal moral moorings in complete obedience to authority. See Stanley Milgram's essay (chapter 10) for an interesting study of this kind of vice. (4) pathological wickedness: the person makes evil his or her highest value, as Satan does in Milton's *Paradise Lost* when he cries, "Evil be thou my good!" This is the worst kind of wickedness because it inverts evil into a value to be sought for its own sake.

EVILS IN NATURE AND EVILS IN PERSONS

When philosophers talk of the problem of evil, they generally mean a problem in theodicy. Anyone who believes in a morally perfect, omniscient, and omnipotent God needs to explain and justify the existence of evils in the world. Unbelievers have no such problem. Nevertheless there are still uses to which the concept of evil can be put. Diseases, deformities, earthquakes and floods that destroy crops and wreck cities—these are, for anyone, too intelligibly evils, instances of what I shall term "evils in nature." I do not confine that term, however, to what we commonly call "natural disasters" but use it to denote any object, property, or happening about which it is both intelligible and correct to say that it would be a better state of affairs if that object et cetera did not exist or occur.

Reprinted from Stanley Benn, *Ethics* (Chicago: University of Chicago Press, 1985): 795–809. Reprinted by permission of The University of Chicago Press.

I take evil in nature to be a simple fact. It is a feature of the world that animals and human beings alike suffer pain, that there is ugliness as well as beauty, that there are bereavements and grievous disappointments. These things simply happen and are no less natural evils for their happening to conscious and rational beings. I do not mean, of course, that consciousness of the evil is never a necessary constituent: clearly this must be so in the case of a bereavement or a disappointment, though it is more problematic in cases of evils of ugliness. But bereavements and disappointments, while evils for human beings, are not evils in human beings. I shall make no attempt to say why such things are accounted evil; on the contrary, evil in nature I take for present purposes to be unproblematic, so that I shall not consider that I am begging any questions if I use that concept in explicating evil in human beings.

One kind of evil in human beings is "wickedness"—a word that has fallen undeservedly on bad times with the secularization of moral discourse. Wickedness in human beings is still a new kind of evil in nature, but one which raises special problems because, having in general a capacity for rational action and judgment, wicked people not merely are evil but also do evil, with evil intent. My purpose in this article is to inquire into forms of human wickedness, their relation with other evils in human beings, and their relation to freedom of choice and motivation to evil.

By "wickedness" I mean whatever it is about someone that warrants our calling him a wicked person. It is therefore a different notion from what makes an action an evil deed, for an evil deed may be done by someone who is not wicked but only weak or misguided. Neither is every wrongdoer evil, for one may do wrong with good intentions or even (some would say) because in some situations whatever one did would be wrong. And conversely, someone who was fully conscious and rational but also completely paralyzed and aphasic, who spent his life hating everyone about him, rejoicing in their misfortune, wishing them ill, and reveling in malignant fantasies, would be a wicked person who did no wrong at all. Indispensable, however, to the notion of a wicked person is a cognitive capacity, or at least a capacity to envisage states of affairs in the imagination, conjoined with a set of attitudes toward such states of affairs. G. E. Moore, whose account of evil is in terms not of persons but of "states of things," nevertheless describes the "great positive evils" as "organic unities" constituted by "cognitions of some

object, accompanied by some emotion," where "emotion" is roughly
equivalent to what I mean by "attitude."[1]

Common, however, to both wickedness in action and wickedness
in attitude is an evil maxim, in something like Kant's sense. A person
perceives situations, real or imagined, under certain descriptions and
has attitudes in respect of them in accordance with general maxims.
If I recognize someone as virtuous and hate him just for being virtuous, I have the maxim, Virtuous people are to be hated. Vandals act
on the maxim, Beautiful objects are to be destroyed, racists on the
maxim, Blacks are to be despised or hurt, egoists on the maxim, No
one's interests but my own are to count. In each case the gerundival
form of the maxim specifies a kind of action or attitudinal response,
in accordance with what that person takes as a rule of life.

A person may be wicked because the maxims that order his life
are, by and large, evil maxims, that is, maxims that no one ought
to act on at all. Sometimes this may be seen as a kind of mistake
on his part; he may believe to be good what is really evil, and vice
versa. And then we may need some way of distinguishing culpable and nonculpable mistakes. But in other instances there is no
mistake: a person may act on an evil maxim, knowing it to be so.
That is the nature of malignant or Satanic wickedness. These are
both problematic issues to which I return.

It is possible, however, for a person to be wicked not because
the first-order maxims of his actions are inherently wicked but
because they are regulated by some higher-order maxim which systematically excludes consideration of any good which might circumscribe his first-order maxims. An example of such a restrictive
higher-order maxim might be, No maxim is to be entertained as a
rule of conduct that would circumscribe the duty to obey the orders
of superior officers. Selfish wickedness and conscientious wickedness, which I shall consider a little later, are restrictive in much the
same way, for whether or not, in either case, the maxims of action
are inherently evil, the regulating principle will be found to be
excluding in the required sense. These forms of wickedness I shall
term "wickednesses of exclusion."

By contrast with those who act on evil first-order maxims, or who
so order their first-order maxims as to exclude what ought nevertheless to be taken account of, the merely weak willed and the

---

[1]G. E. Moore, *Principia Ethica* (Cambridge: Cambridge University Press,
1903), p. 208.

morally indolent and the people who cannot control their passions are not wicked people, for the maxims they really do acknowledge and on which they would wish to act are good ones. Such people are morally defective, and therefore bad, precisely because their actions fall short of their good intentions. That very incoherence is a mitigating condition, though not, of course, an excusing one.

I shall outline, in most of the remainder of this article, a typology of wickedness, which will shed some light on the difficult moral and philosophical questions of responsibility and culpability and on the possibility of evil actions knowingly performed. The primary distinctions are between self-centered, conscientious, and malignant forms of wickedness. In each case I shall ask how far ignorance, error, or incapacity is necessarily or possibly a feature of the actions and maxims of action under discussion and what difference it could make to the judgment of wickedness.

SELF-CENTERED FORMS OF WICKEDNESS

The least problematic kind of self-centered wicked person is the selfish one, but the category includes as well any person whose maxims are regulated by a higher-order maxim restricting consideration to goods and evils respecting only subjects and groups defined by reference to the agent himself. So a person who devoted himself exclusively to promoting the interests of his family or of his firm or to the aggrandizement of his nation might be wicked in this way if he did so with a ruthless unconcern for whether other people might be entitled or required to act on corresponding maxims of their own. The cruder kind of chauvinist or jingoist—My country, right or wrong—acts on just such a self-centered principle, providing he does not universalize it for citizens of others countries too.

The merely selfish person recognizes his own well-being as a good and acts for the sake of it. That is to say, in being selfish he does not embrace evil as such, under that description. Self-interest is not merely an intelligible motive but also one that many philosophers have thought to be a paradigm of a motive, the motive of self-love. Selfishness is wicked not on account of its end but for what it excludes, for it consists in closing one's eyes and one's heart to any good but a self-centered good. In Kant's view, this is the most characteristic form of human wickedness.

According to Kant, the moral law, as the law of reason, is not merely accessible to any rational being but also, for human beings at least, always one spring of action, necessarily motivating in some degree. So it is not that the selfishly wicked person is motivated by a perverse antagonism to the moral law. Rather, self-love, which is for any rational person a genuine spring, assumes an irrational precedence over the moral law. Accordingly, a wicked person is not one whom the law cannot motivate but rather someone who "reverses the moral order of the springs in adopting them into his maxims: he adopts, indeed, the moral law along with that of self-love; but. . . . he makes the spring of self-love and its inclinations the condition of obedience to the moral law; whereas, on the contrary, the latter ought to be adopted. . . . as the sole spring, being the *supreme condition* of the satisfaction of the former."[2]

The selfish person may, however, be mistaken in his belief that what he intends is really good, even from his own narrow perspective; it may in reality be damaging, even to himself. Someone altogether committed to increasing his own wealth or power—a miser or a megalomaniac—may be wrong to value such things, at any rate as ends instead of as means to other goods. That error is not, however, an excuse for his wickedness since his specific wickedness as a selfish person derives from what is excluded rather than from the end he actually seeks. That, of course, can add to his wickedness. Sadistic wickedness is more shocking, perhaps, than miserliness because the suffering of others, to which the miser or the vain person may be merely indifferent and inattentive, is for the sadist itself the source of the pleasure which makes it seem a good. In taking it to be so, however, the sadist may still be mistaken, even in his own terms, if, for instance, the pleasure is part of a self-destructive rake's progress of personal degradation. There would be no inconsistency, however, in deeming the sadist wicked on account both of the intrinsic evil and of the exclusiveness of his maxim while yet feeling compassion for someone who is destroying himself so worthlessly.

PSYCHOPATHY

In contrast to selfish wickedness, the form of self-centered evil in persons manifested in a psychopathic personality may not count as wickedness at all. This takes the form of a kind of moral imbecil-

[2]I. Kant, "Of the Indwelling of the Bad Principle along with the Good, or On the Radical Evil in Human Nature," in *Kant's Theory of Ethics*, trans. T. K. Abbot (London: Longman, Green & Co., 1927), p. 343.

ity. The psychopath, like the selfishly wicked person, acts from self-love. His is capable, at least within limits, of instrumental deliberation, though he may be prone to discount future satisfactions heavily in favor of immediate gratification. So he may be liable to do evil impulsively to satisfy a whim. But the more significant point is that he does not see it as evil, except, perhaps, in a conventional sense: This is something that I know most people do not like being done, so I had better conceal the body. But the kind of considerations that might justify and rationalize conventional disapproval can get no purchase on his understanding. To the extent that the psychopath has, and perceives in himself, the capacity to make decisions which can make a difference to the way things turn out—to the extent that he is capable of forming beliefs taking account of evidence and argument and of acting on those beliefs—he satisfies the minimal conditions for being a rational chooser or, one may say, a natural person.[3] Full rationality does not, however, consist only in the capacity to take account of relevant considerations advanced by others. It includes also the capacity to decenter: to conceive of ways of looking at the world, and at oneself, from someone else's standpoint or from no particular standpoint at all—from the standpoint of anyone. It is this capacity that the psychopath lacks. Whereas the selfish person understands well enough how the well-being of other persons can be a reason for someone's action or forbearance but disregards such reasons, the psychopath is simply unable to see how that could be a reason for him at all. To be asked to take account of such a reason would be, to him, like being asked to have regard to sensibilities of a stone or, perhaps, to the relevance of the color of someone's hair when deciding whether to make off with his wallet. While it would be wrong to say that the psychopath has no view of good and evil (for he knows what he would enjoy and what he would prefer not to suffer), he is incapable of understanding that distinction in any but a self-centered way. So though his maxims never take account of others' interests, it is not because a higher-order maxim excludes them; it is that first-order maxims embodying them are simply unintelligible to him. Such a person does not act on an evil maxim, know-

---

[3]For a fuller statement of the theory of natural and moral personality on which this article relies, see S. I. Benn, "Freedom, Autonomy, and the Concept of a Person," *Aristotelian Society Proceedings* (1975–76) 76 (1976): 109–30.

ing it to be evil, nor does he act on a self-centered second-order maxim that excludes relevant first-order maxims since he can hardly be said to have any second-order maxims at all. Such a person cannot be wicked. Nevertheless, he may be both an evil in nature and an instance of evil in a person.

Moral imbecility may well fill us with horror; certainly it is frightening. As much might be said, however, of other evils in nature, such as cancers or leprosy. But there may be something besides to account for our special hostility toward the moral imbecile. It is hard to see him simply as an evil but amoral force, like a man-eating tiger in a Bengal village, for he is defective in a capacity without which people in society could not live together. He seems at once to claim consideration as a fellow person and to disqualify himself from that consideration. Because he satisfies the minimal conditions for a rational chooser, he qualifies for the respect due to a person and is a bearer of rights, but as a moral defective, he is incompetent to bear the corresponding obligations and responsibilities. In assessing his moral status, it is hard not to judge him by the standards appropriate to a person of normal capacities, of which he is a monstrously deformed travesty. Nevertheless, though qualified as a person, he is disqualified from counting as a wicked one. And precisely because he is a person, we are subject to moral constraints in dealing with this evil that do not apply to our dealings with man-eating tigers.

CONSCIENTIOUS WICKEDNESS

The conscientiously wicked person is distinguished from the self-centered one in that the maxims of his actions are seen by him as universally valid and applicable. Unlike the crude chauvinist's complete indifference to other nations' claims, the conscientiously wicked nationalist might hold that his nation's supremacy would be universally valid and overriding good, perhaps because it would be good for all humanity, perhaps because it had some excellence which any rational being would have to recognize as generating an overriding claim. The higher-order maxim by which the conscientiously wicked person lives is not self-centered; rather, it rules that all considerations not directly validated by his primary ideal goal or principle are necessarily subordinate when they conflict with it. So a conscientious Nazi need not always be indifferent to the claims of humanity instantiated in the plight of Jews. Were they anywhere but in Germany, or perhaps anywhere but in Europe, and were they not (as the Nazis claimed) an international conspiracy against the German nation, there would be a case for not exterminating them, perhaps even for manifesting concern for their well-being; but any such considerations were necessarily and totally overridden by the Herrenvolk ideal, which thus, in a Nazi's view, legitimated the Final Solution. Of course, the conscientious Nazi was himself one of the Herrenvolk, but it was not for that self-centered reason that he maintained its exclusive moral priority.

As with self-centered wickedness, conscientious wickedness can arise when the putative ideal is genuinely a good but is pursued with a ruthlessness that excludes other goods which ought to be taken account of. But it is also possible that the putative ideal is itself a monstrous error. In both cases it is alike necessary to build into the analysis criteria of culpability for the misjudgment of values. Suppose, for instance, that Aztec priests truly believed that human sacrifice gave pleasure to the god and that to please the god was good not because that way the harvests would be good (an acceptably valuable if not always an acceptably overriding end) but just as a good in itself and, further, that individual human beings as such were of subordinate concern. But suppose, also, that there was nothing in their moral consciousness with which such beliefs would not cohere. It is hard to see how they could then be called wicked. It is that reservation, however, that their moral consciousness be coherent, that makes their case problematic, where the case of Adolf Hitler is not. We must deplore murderous behavior as evil since slaying human beings is evil in nature, and if it is the result of intentional action, it must count as an evil in persons that they could act like that. But for it to count as a wickedness in persons, they must have within their repertoire some humane principles that the Aztecs (at least the Aztecs of my hypothesis) did not have. That exoneration cannot be extended, however, to tyrants and fanatics nearer home—Adolf Hitler, for instance. The resources of the European moral tradition afforded him ample reasons for treating the sufferings of Jews as of some account even set against the objective of racial purity, itself an end which that tradition provided ample grounds for questioning.

Conscientious wickedness is rarely a case of pursuing an end unaware of attendant consequences as evils; it is more often a case of a single-minded pursuit of an objective which (unlike racial purity) can reasonably be seen as good, but at the cost of a callous insensitivity to evil done by the way. It is not that the person believes the incidental evil to be itself good but rather that, having reason to think it evil, he nevertheless systematically disregards it. It is not that one cannot honestly believe with Robespierre and Saint-Just, that out of a Terror can emerge a Republic of virtue or, with the IRA, that only through indiscriminate violence can a united Ireland arise but that to go through with it one must almost certainly stifle sensibility to the horrors through which one must wade to bring it about. That sensibility, too, is a part of one's moral consciousness, no less than the perceived ideal. For a person whose conception of the moral law has developed within a moral tradition that recognizes indiscriminate murder as evil, such single-mindedness may be possible only if he has a sense of mission so great or an arrogance so overwhelming that he can desensitize himself, school himself to a callous disregard for considerations to which he nevertheless can and ought to attend.

Doing evil that good may come of it, or a greater evil be avoided, is not, however, a sufficient condition for wickedness in a person. Everyone responsible for major political decisions is likely to have been confronted with such difficult and painful choices. The history of atomic warfare is a record of one such dilemma after another. The mark of the wicked person is that such choices are for him neither difficult nor painful since the considerations that would make them so are systematically neutralized. It may, indeed, be a causally necessary condition for making such choices that one make of oneself a wicked person in this sense; in an evil world, perhaps only the wicked are callous enough to do the evil that needs to be done. "Whoever wants to engage in politics at all," wrote Max Weber, ". . . . must know that he is responsible for what may become of himself under the impact of these paradoxes. . . . He lets himself in for the diabolical forces lurking in all violence. . . . Everything that is striven for through political action operating with violent means and following an ethic of responsibility endangers the 'salvation of the soul.' "[4]

Conscientious wickedness is not so radically different, then, from selfish wickedness. In both cases it is the refusal to acknowledge the moral significance of evils which one nevertheless knows or could reasonably be expected to know as evils that constitutes the person's wickedness.

[4]Max Weber, "Politics as a Vocation," in *From Max Weber*, ed. H. H. Gerth and C. Wright Mills (London: Kegan Paul, Trench, Trubner & Co., 1948), pp. 125–26.

HETERONOMOUS WICKEDNESS

The kinds of wickedness identified so far are manifested in peopl
whose responses to situations, whether active or merely contempl:
tive, are their own; theirs is the judgment, theirs the act, theirs the
wickedness. But if the Nuremberg defendants were arguably like
that, Eichmann in Jerusalem pleaded that he simply obeyed orders
and could not therefore be responsible for the evils in which he had
participated. He had not, he said, felt any hatred of the Jews or any
pleasure from their sufferings and destruction. He had committed
himself conscientiously to a line of duty, but unlike Hitler and his
leading henchmen, he could plausibly disclaim responsibility for having adopted the aims to which his official duties directed him. His
defense amounted to the claim that what he did must be seen under
the global description of doing his duty, not of pursuing evil, and the
former is not itself a description of wickedness, not in any of the
terms that I have set out so far. If, then, wickedness in a person
requires that he adopt an evil maxim, how was Eichmann wicked?
In a perceptive discussion of Hannah Arendt's report of the Eichmann Trial, Barry Clarke has created the category of "heteronomous
evil" to cover such a case, and I shall follow him in this, though I
shall call it "heteronomous wickedness."[5]

Clarke's argument depends on a distinction between acting spontaneously and acting autonomously. Eichmann not only relied utterly on his superiors for directions for acting in all relevant regards
but in joining the Nazi Party and the bureaucracy also opted out
of critical judgment in all matters affecting his official duties. He
had chosen heteronomy, and the evil that he did followed from
that decision.[6] Could he be said, then, to have possessed the capacity for free choice that is the mark of a person, the condition for

[5]Barry Clarke, "Beyond 'The Banality of Evil,'" *British Journal of Political
Science* 10 (1980): 417–39 (on Hannah Arendt, *Eichmann in Jerusalem: A
Report on the Banality of Evil* [London: Faber & Faber, 1963]).
[6]"Eichmann made two exceptions in his merciless anti-Semitic programme,
once when he helped a half-Jewish cousin, and another time when at his
uncle's request he helped a Viennese Jewish couple: but his conscience
bothered him so much afterwards that he 'confessed his sins' (Eichmann's
phrase) to his superiors" (John Kleinig, "Always Let Your Conscience Be
Your Guide?" *Interchange* 1 [1967]: 107, referring to the account in Arendt,
p. 131).

esponsibility for oneself, and therefore a necessary condition for one's being a wicked person?

A correct perspective on such an argument must distinguish between the ordinary practical capacity of a normal minimally rational chooser to make decisions (which I have elsewhere called "autarchy"—a self-directing condition) and the capacity to make autonomous judgments.[7] The salient conditions for autarchy were outlined above, in discussing the moral status of the psychopath, who in my view satisfies them while yet lacking moral responsibility. In some people, however, autarchy is impaired, in various degrees ranging from catatonia through autism to compulsions of various kinds. Under hypnosis, a person loses autarchy to a considerable degree; a person acting under posthypnotic suggestion less so. Such people are programmed—and by other people—and are therefore heterarchic. To the extent that one is autistic, compulsive, or heterarchic, one lacks the capacity to decide for oneself, which is the condition for free, responsible action, and to just that extent one lacks the capacity for wickedness. But Eichmann was heteronomous, not heterarchic, and heteronomy is not merely consistent with autarchy—it requires it.

By autonomy I understand a character trait amounting to a capacity to act on principles (i.e., in accordance with a *nomos*) that are one's own because one has made them so by a process of rational reflection on the complex of principles and values that one has assimilated from one's social environment. It is a process in which one confronts the incoherences and conflicts within that complex and works to resolve them into something like a coherent set of moral attitudes. We do not invent our morality ex nihilo; we make it our own by creatively testing it for consistency. Now Eichmann certainly did nothing like that. On the contrary, he handed over his conscience to the care of the party, the state, and the Fuehrer, thereby imposing on his power of autarchic decision (which remained all the same quite unimpaired) constraints which he thereafter would not look at critically. But, of course, nothing made it impossible for him to do so. He had, as Clarke puts it, elected for heteronomy, and though as time went on it no doubt became increasingly difficult, psychologically speaking, to challenge the system to which he had put himself in thrall, still he had made it so

---

[7]See my analysis of autarchy and autonomy, heterarchy and heteronomy, set out at greater length in Benn.

himself; he had willfully made himself the compliant and flecting tool of wickedness, which is a perversion of the n nature of persons as choosers.

I do not mean that one may never accept moral leadership fr others or commit oneself to a role in a movement or an organiz tion, nor do I mean that in the performance of the duties of a office one must always do precisely what one would have chosen to do irrespective of the requirements of the office. Social practices and institutions would lose their point if that were the case; they are, after all, ways of coordinating the acts of many people toward common goals and will work as such only if people can rely on one another to do what is expected of them. But this does not entail a duty to suspend all judgment. In accepting the guidance of an authority, we are responsible for satisfying ourselves that the principles for which it stands are ones which in general we can endorse; though its particular injunctions may sometimes puzzle us, we must be prepared to monitor its performance over all.

We have to distinguish, therefore, between a conditional and an absolute heteronomy. A person who chooses a conditional heteronomy may reasonably submit to the guidance of the party or the church, providing he does not surrender the power to judge whether it remains true to the principles that led him to choose just that one as the good one. We resign ourselves absolutely to heteronomy at the risk of becoming, like Eichmann, people of evil will, with a capacity in no way impaired to grasp the evil that we do in obeying wicked orders but willfully disregarding it as evil. As with the conscientiously and the selfishly wicked persons, the heteronomously wicked has become insensitive to certain morally significant states of affairs just because the maxim of his actions and attitudes leaves no place for them in his moral constitution.

WICKEDNESS AND MORAL LUCK

Of course, not every absolutely heteronomous person is necessarily wicked. Someone who submits in this total fashion to the guidance of a saint may be less than admirable as a person; but it would be both perverse and wildly censorious to call him wicked. For that one must be disposed to act, or respond, in accordance with evil maxims or in disregard of good ones. The saint's disciple will do neither. But a person who does evil by reason of having elected o put his moral judgment into the keeping of evil persons or institutions has taken a gamble that, as a morally responsible person, he is not entitled to take—and has lost.

This qualification suggests a more general and far-reaching one, affecting all the categories of wickedness discussed so far. Selfish people, people dedicated solely to their families or to the interests of their firms or their countries, and fanatics conscientiously pursuing a blinkered ideal all have it in them to be wicked people. But if the actions picked out for them by their restrictive second-order maxims happened never to be evil actions, it would be harsh to call such people wicked, even if their first-order maxims were always self-centered or narrowly principled. For, as I suggested earlier, such maxims are not always intrinsically bad. Imagine someone who acted single-mindedly on a maxim of self-interest but whose actions were, by social circumstances, under such close scrutiny that any action that damaged someone else, or any denial of help to someone in need, would invite the penalties of public censure. He would have reasons for taking account of appropriate other-regarding maxims, though they would be reasons encapsulated in a self-interested strategy. Such a person would be morally unworthy, but his social institutions would save him from actualizing the wickedness which was latent in him. The Puritan communities of the seventeenth century maintained strict moral surveillance over their members because they were more concerned with saving people from doing wickedness of which they were capable than with moral worth, which, they believed, few, if any, people possessed, and then only by divine election. But we do not have to accept the doctrine of predestination to believe that what preserves many quite ordinary people from wickedness is the good fortune of their circumstances and that in a Belsen or an Auschwitz they might be capable not merely of the desperate meanness of so many of the inmates but also of the wickedness of very nearly all the guards.

MALIGNITY

In all the forms of wickedness treated so far, the regulative maxim has been directed to something understood by the agent, however perversely, as a good. For some philosophers, as we shall see, this has been held to be a necessary condition for any rational action at all. The kind of wickedness, however, which Coleridge saw instantiated in Iago as "motiveless malignity," and which Milton's Satan epitomize in "Evil be thou my good," throws doubt on this supposition.

Iago and Satan are, of course, the paradigm instances in literature of the unalloyed wickedness of malignity, of pursuing evil under the aspect of evil. According to Kant, "In order to call a man bad, it should be possible to argue a priori from some actions, or from a single consciously bad action to a bad maxim as its foundation, and from this to a general source in the actor of all particular morally bad maxims, this source again being itself a maxim."[8] But Kant denies that human beings can adopt as a fundamental maxim, informing all rational choices as a kind of perverse moral law, the maxim, Do evil for evil's sake. A "malignant reason," a "bad Rational Will," would require that "antagonism to the law would itself be made a spring of action . . . so that the subject would be made a *devilish* being."[9] Kant believes that human beings cannot be like this yet it is not easy to see why since he believes that devils who are presumably also rational, can be. Perhaps to be a devil is to be irrational in the special way that, while apprehending the moral law, one responds to it, like Satan, antagonistically, finding in it not a spring of action but a spring of counteraction. I shall consider in a moment whether it is logically possible to make evil one's end, but if it is not, then it must be impossible for devils too. And if the impossibility is not of this kind, I cannot see why human beings may not also be Satanic.

I suggested earlier that the attitudes and actions of a selfishly wicked person are governed by a conception of the good, albeit the good of the agent himself; his wickedness consists in his indifference to other values. A malignant person, by contrast, should take account of the suffering of someone else as a reason for action, irrespective of self-love, just as much as would a benevolent person. But unlike the latter, he would promote it. It is as evil that he rejoices in the suffering and not because he sees it, in some partial or distorted way, as a good, even for himself. He does not think himself better off for it; he is no less disinterested in rejoicing in it than is a benevolent person who rejoices in someone else's good fortune. Just as the prospect of satisfying one's own sexual desire is pleasurable to contemplate, as a good, so, for the malignant person, someone else's suffering is a pleasure to contemplate, but as an evil, apprehended

[8]Kant, p. 327.
[9]Ibid., p. 342.

as such. Correspondingly, it is unalloyed wickedness to hate the good, apprehended as good, and because it is good, and to seek its destruction on that account.

The unalloyed wickedness of malignity presents a logical or a psychological problem, not a moral one. The difficulty is not to decide what attitude to adopt toward it; if it exists at all, it is to be totally abhorred. The problem is rather to understand its motivation or, indeed, to decide whether the very description of it is coherent. Is it perhaps that we perceive something as unalloyed wickedness only because we haven't fully understood it?

According to Socrates, a man who knows the good cannot choose to do evil; no one intentionally chooses evil knowing it to be so.[10] Since my account of unalloyed wickedness implicitly denies this claim, it is necessary to consider why Socrates may have made it. But more than that, what account can we give of motivation to evil if the one given by Socrates turns out not to be true?

Socrates' paradox can be made plausible given a certain view of the motives of action. If we suppose that all intentional or voluntary action is undertaken with some aim, it must be supposed that what is aimed at must be desired; and if someone desires it, he must see it as a good thing to bring it about.[11] Accordingly, for Socrates, whoever aims at evil does so in ignorance of its true nature, under the misapprehension of it as good.

The trouble with Socrates' story is that it distorts the nature of true malignity. I said earlier that a malignant person recognizes the suffering of someone else as an evil and rejoices in it just because it is evil and that he would not rejoice in it were it not that he saw it as such. Even more perplexing, on Socrates' account, is the case of self-destructive action prompted by self-hatred. One must go a long and devious way round to find a good that such a person might believe that he was promoting in spiting himself. Clearly if

---

[10]See Plato, *Protagoras* 352a–358d. In the *Laws,* Plato asserts: "No wrongdoer is so of deliberation. For no man will ever deliberately admit supreme evil, and least of all in his most precious possessions. But every man's most precious possession, as we said, is his soul; no man, then, we may be sure, will of set purpose receive the supreme evil into this most precious thing and live with it there all his life through" (731c).

[11]Michael Stocker has examined the claim that it is not possible to desire the bad in "Desiring the Bad: An Essay in Moral Psychology," *Journal of Philosophy* 76 (1979): 738–53.

one aims at an outcome then, in a rather weak sense, one must desire it; but it is not, even for the person desiring it, necessarily desirable on that account. For what is desirable is what it is appropriate to desire, and the malignant person desires things very often precisely because they are not appropriate. Consider the case of Claggart, the master-at-arms, in Herman Melville's story *Billy Budd*. Claggart conceives a hatred of "the Handsome Sailor," "who in Claggart's own phrase was 'the sweet and pleasant young fellow,'" and falsely charges him with sedition in order to destroy him.[12] Claggart has no reason to hate Billy if by "reason" we mean reason of interest. There is no apparent good that can come to him, or to anyone else, from the evil that will come about. So far from moving him to act for the sake of something he sees as a good, his hatred moves him to spite and to destroy it.[13]

Claggart's reason for hating Billy is precisely his goodness. He can appreciate it only as a reproach, as something that diminishes him, that he must therefore hate and destroy.[14] There is a passage in Schopenhauer that expresses this state of mind most eloquently: "Very bad men bear the stamp of inward suffering in the very expression of the countenance. . . . From this inward torment, which is absolutely and directly essential to them, there finally proceeds that delight in the suffering of others which does not spring from mere egoism, but is disinterested, and which constitutes wickedness proper, rising to the pitch of cruelty. For this the suffering of others is not a means for the attainment of the ends of its own will, but an end in itself."[15] Schopenhauer's explanation is that such wicked persons suffer "an intensity of will" that nothing could assuage. "Every privation" (every frustration of desire) "is infinitely increased by the enjoyment of others, and relieved by the knowledge that others suffer the same privation." Moreover, an "attained

[12]Herman Melville, *Billy Budd and Other Tales* (New York: New American Library of World Literature, Inc., 1961), chap. 11, p. 35.

[13]See Peter Kivy, "Melville's *Billy* and the Secular Problem of Evil: The Worm in the Bud," *Monist* 63 (1980): 480–93, for a stimulating discussion of the problem of malignity in general and Claggart in particular.

[14]Compare Iago, of Cassio: "He hath a daily beauty in his life that makes me ugly" (Othello, 5.1.19–20).

[15]A. Schopenhauer, *The World as Will and Idea,* in *The Philosophy of Schopenhauer,* ed. Irwin Edman (New York: Modern Library, 1928), p. 293.

end never fulfills the promise of the desired object." From "a manifestation of will reaching the point of extraordinary wickedness, there necessarily springs an excessive inward misery, an eternal unrest, an incurable pain; he seeks indirectly the alleviation which directly is denied him,—seeks to mitigate his own suffering by the sight of the suffering of others, which at the same time he recognises as an expression of his power. The suffering of others now becomes for him an end in itself, and is a spectacle in which he delights; and thus arises the phenomenon of pure cruelty, blood thirstiness, which history exhibits so often in the Neros and Domitians, in the African Deis, in Robespierre, and the like."[16]

Of course, one might say that Coleridge was mistaken and that the malignity of Iago and Claggart, with which Schopenhauer's story accords so well, was not "motiveless" but was motivated by envy or resentment. But these motives are not motives of interest, prompted by a good to be brought about by action. They explain the action only by filling out further the description of what is done by giving us a better grasp of the organic relation between the state of affairs, the beliefs of the agent, and the attitude that binds us together. Envious and resentful people are not aiming to bring about a good; nor does the good that they recognize appeal to them. On the contrary, it inflames and enrages them.

I have interpreted the Socratic position up to this point as a psychological theory about how an end must be perceived for it to be a motivating cause, and I have tried to rebut this theory by showing that one can grasp the motives of Iago and Claggart without having to convert them into perceived goods, whether goods for the agents themselves or goods that the agents themselves perceived as appropriately desired.[17] Suppose, however, that we take

---

[16]Ibid., p. 294.

[17]Iago makes some pretense that his animosity toward Othello is prompted by a report that the latter had seduced his wife. Supposing him really to have believed that, it is interesting to see how that could change our judgment of Iago. It would still be the case that he knowingly wished an evil on Othello, but not now simply for evil's sake. Revenge, responding to an injury, represents a primitive kind of justice; the maxim of his action would then have been not to do evil for evil's sake but to exact just recompense. And this, presumably, is where a retributivist's defense of punishment must begin since he defends the inflicting of evil not, like the malignant, for evil's sake but in the name of justice. To satisfy one's

the Socratic claim to be logical rather that psychological. On this interpretation, seeing something as good is to acknowledge that there is the strongest possible practical reason for seeking it, however one may fail in practice through weakness of will. Conversely, to see something as evil would be to recognize that there is a reason not to seek it. So it would be incoherent to adopt Satan's policy of pursuing evil for its own sake since this would be to have as one's reason for action what was logically a reason against action.

Schopenhauer's account of malignity is too plausible, however, for the logical objection to clinch the matter. That objection depends on an assumed nexus between recognizing that there is a reason for action, having that reason as one's own, and being motivated to act on it. There seem to be two ways, though, in which one could recognize the good (or the desirable) and the evil (the undesirable). Paradigmatically, it is true, to see a state of affairs as desirable is to acknowledge that, by criteria of value and appropriateness that one can acknowledge as one's own, there is a reason for desiring things so. But we can envisage a person imagining very well what it would be like to have such a moral experience, to make the appraisals that most people make, and to see why, indeed, they found desirable the things that they did, given the kind of people that they were. And he could envy them for being as they are while being filled, like Claggart, with resentment and hate for them and the things they love and value just because he knows that there is no possibility that he could be like them, think like them, feel like them, or care like them. Precisely because the good that he sees cannot motivate him, he hates it for its very inaccessibility. He grasps the attraction of the good and knows its opposite as evil, but in an encapsulated way that prevents its being also—for him—a reason for action in the way that it is for them. His acknowledging it as good amounts to seeing that it is a reason, but it is not a reason that he can have or that could be his motive.

---

claim to vengeance is thus not merely an intelligible motive but also one that in some measure redeems malignity, as envy does not. Resentment straddles these two possibilities. Like Claggart and Iago, one can resent being diminished by goodness, which is no injury, but one can also resent a real injury, and someone who wished another ill on that account, though falling short of charity, would be a wicked person only to the extent that his justified grievance made him insensitive to counterconsiderations.

The way in which the malignant subject experiences such a rancorous motivation to evil may be set out schematically as follows:

1. Properties $C_1 \ldots C_n$ in a person are virtues (V).
2. Anyone is a good person (G) if and only if he has properties V.
3. For any G, X is a reason for action (e.g., the principle that one should turn the other cheek).
4. I value someone's being a G if and only if I believe I could myself succeed in being a G.
5. I value V if and only if I can be a G.
6. I do not believe I can have X as my reason for action.
7. Therefore I do not believe I could succeed in being a G.
8'. Any properties that I would value if I had them (P), but which I believe I cannot succeed in having, are to be despised (maxim 1).
8''. Any person (S) who succeeds in having P is to be made to suffer for having them (maxim 2).
8'''. Any action that only an S would have a reason for doing is to be avoided, and the contrary action is to be done (maxim 3).
9. To despise virtue, to cause good people to suffer, and to do wrong, that is, to act on maxims 1, 2, and 3, is evil.
10. So evil is to be done (maxim 4).

It might be objected that anyone adopting maxims 1–4 would do so only in order to assuage a sense of his own inadequacy and that this amounts to embracing evil only for the sake of a perceived good. But of course, if one knew that this was what one was doing—crying "sour grapes"—the strategy would be ineffective. The malignant could assuage a sense of inadequacy only if he was really unaware of this aspect of his motivation; otherwise he would know when he said that he detested virtue that he really admired it. The explanatory methods of depth psychology consist precisely in constructing scenarios such that the end of every action is an intelligible good or the relief of an intelligible unease. But the putative unconscious strategies are by no means always successful—the malignant's rancor is not assuaged, nor does he feel any the less inadequate when his rival is laid low; for if it is indeed his own moral failing in comparison with his rival's virtue that dismays him, acting viciously as a reprisal can only aggravate the sense of inferiority. The method of depth psychology must explain, therefore, why the good that is the imputed objective is so ineffectually pursued. Meanwhile, whatever the psychiatric explanation, there can be little doubt that the malignant subject really is hating good and delighting in evil under precisely these descriptions, without feeling that there is anything logically incoherent in doing so. And while the phenomenology of rancor may not apply in precisely the same way to every instance of malignancy, it is enough to suggest that the nexus between recognition of a reason, having it as one's own, and being motivated to act on it can be broken.

For Further Reflection

1. What is Benn's definition of evil? How is it related to wickedness? Do you agree with his analysis?

2. Analyze Benn's four types of wickedness. Do they overlap? Do they help us understand the nature of evil?

3. Examine Benn's concept of malignity. Some philosophers argue that it is not possible knowingly to choose evil as one's goal. What does Benn think about this thesis and how does he treat it? Do you agree with him?

Beyond Good and Evil

FRIEDRICH NIETZSCHE

Friedrich Nietzsche (1844–1900) was a German philosopher and a forerunner of existentialism. Descended through both of his parents from Lutheran ministers, Nietzsche was raised in a devout Christian home and was known as "the little Jesus" by his schoolmates. He studied theology at the University of Bonn and philology at Leipzig, becoming an athe-

Reprinted from *The Complete Works of Nietzsche,* ed. Oscar Levy, vols. 10 and 11 (New York: T. Foulis, 1910).

ist in the process. At the age of twenty-four he was appointed professor of classical philology at the University of Basel in Switzerland, where he taught for ten years until forced by ill health to retire. Eventually he became mentally ill.

Nietzsche believes that the fundamental creative force that motivates all creation is the will to power. We all seek not happiness but to affirm ourselves, to flourish and dominate. Since we are essentially unequal in ability, intelligence, and imagination, it follows that the fittest will survive and be victorious in the contest with the weaker and the baser. Great beauty inheres in the struggle of noble spirits ascending to a pinnacle on the trunks of lesser beings, including lesser human beings. But this process is hampered by Judeo-Christian morality, which Nietzsche labels "slave morality." Slave morality, which is the invention of jealous priests, envious and resentful of the excellent and the powerful, advocates that we become meek and mild, that we believe the lie of all humans having equal worth. He sometimes, as in our reading, refers to this as the ethics of "resentment." The herd resents their superior competitors.

Nietzsche's idea of an inegalitarian, aesthetic ethic assumes the thesis that God is dead. God plays no vital role in our culture—except as a protector of the slave morality, including the idea of equal worth of all persons. If we recognize that there is no rational basis for believing in God, we will see that the whole edifice of slave morality must crumble and with it the notion of equal worth. In its place will arise the morality of the noble person based on the virtues of high courage, disciplined passion, pride, and intelligence, in the pursuit of affirmation and excellence.

We begin this section with Nietzsche's famous description of the madman who announces the death of God; we then turn to selections from *Beyond Good and Evil*.

THE MADMAN AND THE DEATH OF GOD

Have you ever heard of the madman who on a bright morning lighted a lantern and ran to the market-place calling out unceasingly: "I seek God! I seek God!"—As there were many people standing about who did not believe in God, he caused a great deal of amusement. Why! is he lost? said one. Has he strayed away like a child? said another. Or does he keep himself hidden? Is he afraid of us? Has he taken a seavoyage? Has he emigrated?—the people cried out laughingly, all in a hubbub. The insane man jumped into their midst and transfixed them with his glances. "Where is God gone?" he called out. "I mean to tell you! *We have killed him,*—you and I! We are all his murderers! But how have we done it? How were we able to drink up the sea? Who gave us the sponge to wipe away the whole horizon? What did we do when we loosened this earth from its sun? Whither does it now move? Whither do we move? Away from all suns? Do we not dash on unceasingly? Backwards, side-ways, forwards, in all directions? Is there still an above and below? Do we not stray, as through infinite nothingness? Does not empty space breathe upon us? Has it not become colder? Does not night come on continually, darker and darker? Shall we not have to light lanterns in the morning? Do we not hear the noise of the grave-diggers who are burying God? Do we not smell the divine putrefaction?—for even Gods putrefy! God is dead! God remains dead! And we have killed him! How shall we console ourselves, the most murderous of all murderers? The holiest and the mightiest that the world has hitherto possessed, has bled to death under our knife—who will wipe the blood from us? With what water could we cleanse ourselves? What lustrums, what sacred games shall we have to devise? Is not the magnitude of this deed too great for us? Shall we not ourselves have to become Gods, merely to seem worthy of it? There never was a greater event—and on account of it, all who are born after us belong to a higher history than any history hitherto!"—Here the madman was silent and looked again at his hearers; they also were silent and looked at him in surprise. At last he threw his lantern on the ground, so that it broke in pieces and was extinguished. "I come too early," he then said, "I am not yet at the right time. This prodigious event is still on its way, and is travelling—it has not yet reached men's ears. Lightning and thunder need time, the light of the stars needs time, deeds need time, even after they are done, to be seen and heard. This deed is as yet further from them than the furthest star—*and yet they have done it!*"—It is further stated that the madman made his way into different churches on the same day, and there intoned his *Requiem aeternam deo*. When led out and called to account, he always gave the reply: "What are these churches now, if they are not the tombs and monuments of God?"— . . .

WHAT IS NOBLE?

Every elevation of the type "man," has hitherto been the work of an aristocratic society and so it will always be—a society believing in a long scale of gradations of rank and differences of worth among human beings, and requiring slavery in some form or other. Without the *pathos of distance,* such as grows out of the incarnated difference of classes, out of the constant outlooking and downlooking of the ruling caste on subordinates and instruments, and out of their equally constant practice of obeying and commanding, of keeping down and keeping at a distance—that other more mysterious pathos could never have arisen, the longing for an ever new widening of distance within the soul itself, the formation of ever higher, rarer, further, more extended, more comprehensive states, in short, just the elevation of the type "man," the continued "self-surmounting of man," to use a moral formula in a super-moral sense. To be sure, one must not resign oneself to any humanitarian illusions about the history of the origin of an aristocratic society (that is to say, of the preliminary condition for the elevation of the type "man"): the truth is hard. Let us acknowledge unprejudicedly how ever higher civilisation hitherto has *originated!* Men with a still natural nature, barbarians in every terrible sense of the word, men of prey, still in possession of unbroken strength of will and desire for power, threw themselves upon weaker, more moral, more peaceful races (perhaps trading or cattle-rearing communities), or upon old mellow civilisations in which the final vital force was flickering out in brilliant fireworks of wit and depravity. At the commencement, the noble caste was always the barbarian caste: their superiority did not consist first of all in their physical, but in their psychical power—they were more *complete* men (which at every point also implies the same as "more complete beasts").

Corruption—as the indication that anarchy threatens to break out among the instincts, and that the foundation of the emotions, called "life," is convulsed—is something radically different according to the organisation in which it manifests itself. When, for instance, an aristocracy like that of France at the beginning of the Revolution, flung away its privileges with sublime disgust and sacrificed itself to an excess of its moral sentiments, it was corruption:—it was really only the closing act of the corruption which had existed for centuries, by virtue of which that aristocracy had abdicated step by step its lordly prerogatives and lowered itself to a *function* of royalty (in the end even to its decoration and parade-dress). The essential thing, however, in a good and healthy aristocracy is that it should *not* regard itself as a function either of the kingship or the commonwealth, but as the *significance* and highest justification thereof—that it should therefore accept with a good conscience the sacrifice of a legion of individuals, who, *for its sake,* must be suppressed and reduced to imperfect men, to slaves and instruments. Its fundamental belief must be precisely that society is *not* allowed to exist for its own sake, but only as a foundation and scaffolding, by means of which a select class of beings may be able to elevate themselves to their higher duties, and in general to a higher *existence:* like those sun-seeking climbing plants in Java—they are called *Sipo Matador*—which encircle an oak so long and so often with their arms, until at last, high above it, but supported by it, they can unfold their tops in the open light, and exhibit their happiness.

To refrain mutually from injury, from violence, from exploitation, and put one's will on a par with that of others: this may result in a certain rough sense in good conduct among individuals when the necessary conditions are given (namely, the actual similarity of the individuals in amount of force and degree of worth, and their co-relation within one organisation). As soon, however, as one wished to take this principle more generally, and if possible even as *the fundamental principle of society,* it would immediately disclose what it really is—namely, a Will to the *denial* of life, a principle of dissolution and decay. Here one must think profoundly to the very basis and resist all sentimental weakness: life itself is *essentially* appropriation, injury, conquest of the strange and weak, suppression, severity, obtrusion of peculiar forms, incorporation, and at the least, putting it mildest, exploitation;—but why should one for ever use precisely these words on which for ages a disparaging purpose has been stamped? Even the organisation within which, as was previously supposed, the individuals treat each other as equal—it takes place in every healthy aristocracy—must itself, if it be a living and not a dying organisation, do all that towards other bodies, which the individuals within it refrain from doing to each other: it will have to be the incarnated Will to Power, it will endeavour to grow, to gain ground, attract to itself and acquire ascendency—not owing to any morality or immorality, but because it *lives,* and because life *is* precisely Will to Power. On no point, however, is the ordinary consciousness of Europeans more unwilling to be corrected than on this matter; people now rave everywhere, even under the guise of science, about coming conditions of society in which "the exploiting character" is to be absent:—that sounds to my ears as if they promised to invent a mode of life which should refrain from all organic functions. "Exploitation" does not belong to a depraved, or imperfect and primitive society: it belongs to the *nature* of the living being as a primary organic function; it is a consequence of the intrinsic Will to Power, which is precisely the Will to Life.—Granting that as a theory this is a novelty—as a reality it is the *fundamental fact* of all history: let us be so far honest towards ourselves!

MASTER AND SLAVE MORALITY

In a tour through the many finer and coarser moralities which have hitherto prevailed or still prevail on the earth, I found certain traits recurring regularly together, and connected with one another, until finally two primary types revealed themselves to me, and a radical distinction was brought to light. There is *master-morality* and *slave-morality;*—I would at once add, however, that in all higher and mixed civilisations, there are also attempts at the reconciliation of the two moralities; but one finds still oftener the confusion and mutual misunderstanding of them, indeed, sometimes their close juxtaposition—even in the same man, within one soul. The distinctions of moral values have either originated in a ruling caste, pleasantly conscious of being different from the ruled—or among the ruled class, the slaves and dependents of all sorts. In the first case, when it is the rulers who determine the conception "good," it is the exalted, proud disposition which is regarded as the distinguishing feature, and that which determines the order of rank. The noble type of man separates from himself the beings in whom the opposite of this exalted, proud disposition displays itself: he despises them. Let it at once be noted that in this first kind of morality the antithesis "good" and "bad" means practically the same as "noble" and "despicable";—the antithesis *"good"* and *"evil"* is of a different origin. The cowardly, the timid, the insignificant, and those thinking merely of narrow utility are despised; moreover, also, the distrustful, with their constrained glances, the self-abasing, the dog-like kind of men who let themselves be abused, the mendicant flatterers, and above all the liars:— it is a fundamental belief of all aristocrats that the common people are untruthful. "We truthful ones"—the nobility in ancient Greece called themselves. It is obvious that everywhere the designations of

moral value were at first applied to *men,* and were only derivatively
and at a later period applied to *actions;* it is a gross mistake, therefore, when historians of morals start with questions like, "Why have
sympathetic actions been praised?" The noble type of man regards
himself as a determiner of values; he does not require to be approved
of; he passes the judgment: "What is injurious to me is injurious in
itself"; he knows that it is he himself only who confers honour on
things; he is a *creator of values.* He honours whatever he recognises
in himself: such morality is self-glorification. In the foreground there
is the feeling of plenitude, of power, which seeks to overflow, the
happiness of high tension, the consciousness of a wealth which
would fain give and bestow:—the noble man also helps the unfortunate, but not—or scarcely—out of pity, but rather from an impulse
generated by the superabundance of power. The noble man honours in himself the powerful one, him also who has power over himself, who knows how to speak and how to keep silence, who takes
pleasure in subjecting himself to severity and hardness, and has reverence for all that is severe and hard. "Wotan placed a hard heart in
my breast," says an old Scandinavian Saga: it is thus rightly expressed
from the soul of a proud Viking. Such a type of man is even proud
of *not* being made for sympathy; the hero of the Saga therefore adds
warningly: "He who has not a hard heart when young, will never
have one." The noble and brave who think thus are the furthest
removed from the morality which sees precisely in sympathy, or
in acting for the good of others, or in *désintéressement,* the characteristic of the moral; faith in oneself, pride in oneself, a radical enmity and irony towards "selflessness," belong as definitely to noble
morality, as do a careless scorn and precaution in presence of
sympathy and the "warm heart."—It is the powerful who *know* how
to honour, it is their art, their domain for invention. The profound
reverence for age and for tradition—all law rests on this double reverence—the belief and prejudice in favour of ancestors and unfavourable to newcomers, is typical in the morality of the powerful;
and if, reversely, men of "modern ideas" believe almost instinctively
in "progress" and the "future," and are more and more lacking in
respect for old age, the ignoble origin of these "ideas" has compla-
cently betrayed itself thereby. A morality of the ruling class, however,
is more especially foreign and irritating to present-day taste in the
sternness of its principle that one has duties only to one's equals; that
one may act towards beings of a lower rank, towards all that is foreign, just as seems good to one, or "as the heart desires," and in any

case "beyond good and evil": it is here that sympathy and similar sentiments can have a place. The ability and obligation to exercise prolonged gratitude and prolonged revenge—both only within the circle of equals—artfulness in retaliation, *raffinement* of the idea in friendship, a certain necessity to have enemies (as outlets for the emotions of envy, quarrelsomeness, arrogance—in fact, in order to be a good *friend*): all these are typical characteristics of the noble morality, which, as has been pointed out, is not the morality of "modern ideas," and is therefore at present difficult to realise and also to unearth and disclose.—It is otherwise with the second type of morality, *slave-morality*. Supposing that the abused, the oppressed, the suffering, the unemancipated, the weary, and those uncertain of themselves, should moralise, what will be the common element in their moral estimates? Probably a pessimistic suspicion with regard to the entire situation of man will find expression, perhaps a condemnation of man, together with his situation. The slave has an unfavourable eye for the virtues of the powerful; he has a scepticism and distrust, a *refinement* of distrust of everything "good" that is there honoured— he would fain persuade himself that the very happiness there is not genuine. On the other hand, *those* qualities which serve to alleviate the existence of sufferers are brought into prominence and flooded with light; it is here that sympathy, the kind, helping hand, the warm heart, patience, diligence, humility, and friendliness attain to honour; for here these are the most useful qualities, and almost the only means of supporting the burden of existence. Slave-morality is essentially the morality of utility. Here is the seat of the origin of the famous antithesis "good" and "evil":—power and dangerousness are assumed to reside in the evil, a certain dreadfulness, subtlety, and strength, which do not admit of being despised. According to slave-morality, therefore, the "evil" man arouses fear; according to master-morality, it is precisely the "good" man who arouses fear and seeks to arouse it, while the bad man is regarded as the despicable being. The contrast attains its maximum when, in accordance with the logical consequences of slave-morality, a shade of depreciation—it may be slight and well-intentioned—at last attaches itself to the "good" man of this morality; because, according to the servile mode of thought, the good man must in any case be the *safe* man: he is good-natured, easily deceived, perhaps a little stupid, *un bonhomme*. Everywhere that slave-morality gains the ascendency, language shows a tendency to approximate the significations of the words "good" and "stupid."—A last fundamental difference: the desire for *freedom,* the instinct for happiness and the refinements of the feeling of liberty belong as necessarily to slave-morals and morality, as artifice and enthusiasm in reverence and devotion are the regular symptoms of an aristocratic mode of thinking and estimating.— Hence we can understand without further detail why love *as a passion*—it is our European specialty—must absolutely be of noble origin; as is well known, its invention is due to the Provençal poet-cavaliers, those brilliant, ingenious men of the *"gai saber,"* to whom Europe owes so much, and almost owes itself. . . .

There is an *instinct for rank,* which more than anything else is already the sign of a *high* rank; there is a *delight* in the *nuances* of reverence which leads one to infer noble origin and habits. The refinement, goodness, and loftiness of a soul are put to a perilous test when something passes by that is of the highest rank, but is not yet protected by the awe of authority from obtrusive touches and incivilities: something that goes its way like a living touchstone, undistinguished, undiscovered, and tentative, perhaps voluntarily veiled and disguised. He whose task and practice it is to investigate souls, will avail himself of many varieties of this very art to determine the ultimate value of a soul, the unalterable, innate order of rank to which it belongs: he will test it by its *instinct for reverence. Différence engendre haine* [Difference engenders hate.—ED.]: the vulgarity of many a nature spurts up suddenly like dirty water, when any holy vessel, any jewel from closed shrines, any book bearing the marks of great destiny, is brought before it; while on the other hand, there is an involuntary silence, a hesitation of the eye, a cessation of all gestures, by which it is indicated that a soul *feels* the nearness of what is worthiest of respect. . . .

The revolt of the slaves in morals begins in the very principle of *resentment* becoming creative and giving birth to values—a resentment experienced by creatures who, deprived as they are of the proper outlet of action, are forced to find their compensation in an imaginary revenge. While every aristocratic morality springs from a triumphant affirmation of its own demands, the slave-morality says "no" from the very outset to what is "outside itself," "different from itself," and "not itself": and this "no" is its creative deed. This reversal of the valuing standpoint—this *inevitable* gravitation to the objective instead of back to the subjective—is typical of "resentment": the slave-morality requires as the condition of its existence an external and objective world, to employ physiological terminology, it requires objective stimuli to be capable of action at all—its action is fundamentally a reaction. The contrary is the case when we come to the aristocrat's system of values: it acts and grows spontaneously, it merely seeks its antithesis in order to pronounce a more grateful and exultant "yes" to its own self;—its negative conception, "low," "vulgar," "bad," is merely a pale late-born foil in comparison with its positive and fundamental conception (saturated as it is with life and passion), of "we aristocrats, we good ones, we beautiful ones, we happy ones."

When the aristocratic morality goes astray and commits sacrilege on reality, this is limited to that particular sphere with which it is *not* sufficiently acquainted—a sphere, in fact, from the real knowledge of which it disdainfully defends itself. It misjudges, in some cases, the sphere which it despises, the sphere of the common vulgar man and the low people: on the other hand, due weight should be given to the consideration that in any case the mood of contempt, of disdain, of superciliousness, even on the supposition that it *falsely* portrays the object of its contempt, will always be far removed from that degree of falsity which will always characterise the attacks—in effigy, of course—of the vindictive hatred and revengefulness of the weak in onslaughts on their enemies. In point of fact, there is in contempt too strong an admixture of nonchalance, of casualness, of boredom, of impatience, even of personal exultation, for it to be capable of distorting its victim into a real caricature or a real monstrosity. Attention again should be paid to the almost benevolent *nuances* which, for instance, the Greek nobility imports into all the words by which it distinguishes the common people from itself; note how continuously a kind of pity, care, and consideration imparts its honeyed *flavour,* until at last almost all the words which are applied to the vulgar man survive finally as expressions for "unhappy," "worthy of pity" . . . —and how, conversely, "bad," "low," "unhappy" have never ceased to ring in the Greek ear with a tone in which "unhappy" is the predominant note: this is a heritage of the old noble aristocratic morality, which remains true to itself even in contempt. . . . The "well-born" simply *felt* themselves the "happy"; they did not have to manufacture their happiness artificially through looking at their enemies, or in cases to talk and lie themselves into happiness (as is the custom with all resentful men); and similarly, complete men as they were, exuberant with strength, and consequently *necessarily* energetic, they were too wise to dissociate happiness from action—activity becomes in their minds necessarily counted as happiness (that is the etymology of εὖ πράττειν—all in sharp contrast to the "happiness" of the weak and the oppressed, with their festering venom and malignity, among whom happiness appears essentially as a narcotic, a deadening, a quietude, a peace, a "Sabbath," an enervation of the mind and relaxation of the limbs—in short, a purely *passive* phenomenon. While the aristocratic man lived in confidence and openness with himself γεν-ναῖος, "noble-born," emphasises the nuance "sincere," and perhaps also "naïf"), the resentful man, on the other hand, is neither sincere nor naïf, nor honest and candid with himself. His soul *squints;* his mind loves hidden crannies, tortuous paths and backdoors, everything secret appeals to him as *his* world, *his* safety, *his* balm; he is past master in silence, in not forgetting, in waiting, in provisional self-depreciation and self-abasement. A race of such *resentful* men will of necessity eventually prove more *prudent* than any aristocratic race, it will honour prudence on quite a distinct scale, as, in fact, a paramount condition of existence, while prudence among aristocratic men is apt to be tinged with a delicate flavour of luxury and refinement; so among them it plays nothing like so integral a part as that complete certainty of function of the governing *unconscious* instincts, or as indeed a certain lack of prudence, such as a vehement and valiant charge, whether against danger or the enemy, or as those ecstatic bursts of rage, love, reverence, gratitude, by which at all times noble souls have recognised each other. When the resentment of the aristocratic man manifests itself, it fulfils and exhausts itself in an immediate reaction, and consequently instills no *venom:* on the other hand, it never manifests itself at all in countless instances, when in the case of the feeble and weak it would be inevitable. An inability to take seriously for any length of time their enemies, their disasters, their *misdeeds*—that is the sign of the full strong natures who possess a superfluity of moulding plastic force, that heals completely and produces forgetfulness: a good example of this in the modern world is Mirabeau, who had no memory for any insults and meannesses which were practised on him, and who was only incapable of forgiving because he forgot. Such a man indeed shakes off with a shrug many a worm which would have buried itself in another; it is only in characters like these that we see the possibility (supposing, of course, that there is such a possibility in the world) of the real *"love* of one's enemies." What respect for his enemies is found, forsooth, in an aristocratic man—and such a reverence is already a bridge to love! He insists on having his enemy to himself as his distinction. He tol-

erates no other enemy but a man in whose character there is nothing to despise and *much* to honour! On the other hand, imagine
the "enemy" as the resentful man conceives him—and it is here
exactly that we see his work, his creativeness; he has conceived
"the evil enemy," the "evil one," and indeed that is the root idea
from which he now evolves as a contrasting and corresponding figure a "good one," himself—his very self!

The method of this man is quite contrary to that of the aristocratic man, who conceives the root idea "good" spontaneously and
straight away, that is to say, out of himself, and from that material
then creates for himself a concept of "bad"! This "bad" of aristocratic origin and that "evil" out of the cauldron of unsatisfied
hatred—the former an imitation, an "extra," an additional nuance;
the latter, on the other hand, the original, the beginning, the essential act in the conception of a slave-morality—these two words "bad"
and "evil," how great a difference do they mark, in spite of the fact
that they have an identical contrary in the idea "good." But the idea
"good" is *not* the same: much rather let the question be asked,
"Who is really evil according to the meaning of the morality of
resentment?" In all sternness let it be answered thus:—*just* the good
man of the other morality, just the aristocrat, the powerful one, the
one who rules, but who is distorted by the venomous eye of resent-
fulness, into a new colour, a new signification, a new appearance.
This particular point we would be the last to deny: the man who
learnt to know those "good" ones only as enemies, learnt at the
same time not to know them only as *"evil enemies,"* and the same
men who . . . were kept so rigorously in bounds through convention, respect, custom, and gratitude, though much more through
mutual vigilance and jealousy, . . . these men who in their relations
with each other find so many new ways of manifesting consideration, self-control, delicacy, loyalty, pride, and friendship, these men
are in reference to what is outside their circle (where the foreign
element, a *foreign* country, begins), not much better than beasts of
prey, which have been let loose. They enjoy there freedom from
all social control, they feel that in the wilderness they can give vent
with impunity to that tension which is produced by enclosure and
imprisonment in the peace of society, they *revert* to the innocence
of the beast-of-prey conscience, like jubilant monsters, who perhaps come from a ghostly bout of murder, arson, rape, and torture,
with bravado and a moral equanimity, as though merely some wild
student's prank had been played, perfectly convinced that the poets

have now an ample theme to sing and celebrate. It is impossible not to recognise at the core of all these aristocratic races the beast of prey; the magnificent *blonde brute,* avidly rampant for spoil and victory; this hidden core needed an outlet from time to time, the beast must get loose again, must return into the wilderness—the Roman, Arabic, German, and Japanese nobility, the Homeric heroes, the Scandinavian Vikings, are all alike in this need. It is the aristocratic races who have left the idea "Barbarian" on all the tracks in which they have marched; nay, a consciousness of this very barbarianism, and even a pride in it, manifests itself even in their highest civilisation (for example, when Pericles says to his Athenians in that celebrated funeral oration, "Our audacity has forced a way over every land and sea, rearing everywhere imperishable memorials of itself for *good* and for *evil"*). This audacity of aristocratic races, mad, absurd, and spasmodic as may be its expression; the incalculable and fantastic nature of their enterprises, . . . their nonchalance and contempt for safety, body, life, and comfort, their awful joy and intense delight in all destruction, in all the ecstasies of victory and cruelty,—all these features become crystallised, for those who suffered thereby in the picture of the "barbarian," of the "evil enemy," perhaps of the "Goth" and of the "Vandal." The profound, icy mistrust which the German provokes, as soon as he arrives at power— even at the present time—is always still an aftermath of that inextinguishable horror with which for whole centuries Europe has regarded the wrath of the blonde Teuton beast. . . .

. . . One may be perfectly justified in being always afraid of the blonde beast that lies at the core of all aristocratic races, and in being on one's guard: but who would not a hundred times prefer to be afraid, when one at the same time admires, than to be immune from fear, at the cost of being perpetually obsessed with the loathsome spectacle of the distorted, the dwarfed, the stunted, the envenomed? And is that not our fate? What produces to-day our repulsion towards "man"?—for we *suffer* from "man," there is no doubt about it. It is not fear; it is rather that we have nothing more to fear from men; it is that the worm "man" is in the foreground and pullulates; it is that the "tame man," the wretched mediocre and unedifying creature, has learnt to consider himself a goal and a pinnacle, an inner meaning, an historic principle, a "higher man"; yes, it is that he has a certain right so to consider himself, in so far as he feels that in contrast to that excess of deformity, disease, exhaustion, and effeteness whose odour is beginning to pollute present-day Europe, he at any rate has achieved a relative success, he at any rate still says "yes" to life.

GOODNESS AND THE WILL TO POWER

What is good?—All that enhances the feeling of power, the Will to Power, and the power itself in man. What is bad?—All that proceeds from weakness. What is happiness?—The feeling that power is increasing—that resistance has been overcome.

Not contentment, but more power; not peace at any price but war; not virtue, but competence (virtue in the Renaissance sense, *virtu,* free from all moralistic acid). The first principle of our humanism: The weak and the failures shall perish. They ought even to be helped to perish.

What is more harmful than any vice?—Practical sympathy and pity for all the failures and all the weak: Christianity.

Christianity is the religion of pity. Pity opposes the noble passions which heighten our vitality. It has a depressing effect, depriving us of strength. As we multiply the instances of pity we gradually lose our strength of nobility. Pity makes suffering contagious and under certain conditions it may cause a total loss of life and vitality out of all proportion to the magnitude of the cause. . . . Pity is the practice of nihilism.

For Further Reflection

1. What do you make of the parable of God's death? What is its significance for ethics?

2. A good exercise for getting a grip on the radicality of Nietzsche's ethics is to read Jesus's Sermon on the Mount (chapter 7) after reading Nietzsche. Discuss the contrast.

3. Compare Nietzsche's ethics with Aristotle's ethics of virtue (chapter 6). What are the similarities and differences? How might Aristotle respond to the charge that his ethics are really a "gentleman's" version of Nietzsche's more shocking ideas?

On the Origin of Good and Evil

RICHARD TAYLOR

Richard Taylor taught philosophy at Brown University, Rochester University, and Union College. In this essay he argues that morality, especially good and evil, is not a transcendental but a naturalistic reality, something that originates in the fact that we are *conative* beings (having desires and felt needs). If we had no desires, no values would exist—no good and evil, which are functional terms, referring to our goals and interests. Right and wrong emerge in social situations, as rules for behavior. They are based on common goals and interests. The rules and practices that either promote cooperation toward meeting our desires or resolve interpersonal conflict are *right* rules and practices, and those rules and practices that hinder cooperation and conflict resolution are *wrong* ones.

It has, as we have seen, been fairly characteristic of moral philosophers to begin with an assumed dichotomy between what *is* and what *ought* to be. Having turned their backs on the former as having little relevance to philosophical ethics, they have proclaimed the content of the latter as the unique realm of ethics. Some, in fact, have declared it a fallacy even to attempt to derive any philosophy of what ought to be from what in fact is, which pretty much amounts to declaring that facts can have little bearing upon ethics. One result of this is that moral philosophy has all too often resembled declamation. The advocates for the various and conflicting programs have had little to appeal to other than their own intuitions of things, these being sometimes baptized as the deliverances of "practical reason" and the like.

I am now going to remove this distinction between *is* and *ought*. More precisely, I shall show that all moral distinctions, beginning with the basic distinction between good and evil, are based entirely on certain facts and, in particular, on facts concerning human nature. It is because men are the kind of beings they are—namely, what

I have called conative beings—that the distinction between good and evil arises in the first place. Once this has been seen, we can see what good and evil in fact are. This basic distinction then having been made clear—and having been based not on intuitions and sentiments or abstract reasoning but on a certain conception of human nature—we can derive the further distinctions between moral right and wrong and give a fairly clear content to the idea of the common good.

MEN AS CONATIVE BEINGS

Men are rational or cognitive beings, but to say this is very far from stating the whole truth about them. So far as ethics is concerned, it leaves entirely out of account the most important fact about men, that they are desiderative or conative beings as well. I have already explained what this means, but it needs to be briefly reiterated here, as it is crucial to establishing the distinction between good and evil.

To describe men as conative is not to say anything at all abstruse or metaphysical, as this bit of terminology might suggest. It is only to call attention to a fact of human nature with which everyone is perfectly familiar: men have needs, desires, and goals; they pursue ends; they have certain wants and generally go about trying to satisfy them in various ways. Psychologists, metaphysicians, and others might have conflicting theories concerning how this fact is to be understood and explained, but the fact itself is hardly open to any question. It is more obvious that men are, in the sense just explained, conative beings, than that they are rational ones. There are men whom one might genuinely doubt to be rational, but it is doubtful whether anyone has ever seen a living man whom he suspected had no needs, desires, or wants. Such a man would be totally inactive and resemble a statue more than a man.

Thus, when a man is seen doing anything, it can generally be asked why he is doing it, what he is doing it for, or what he is trying to accomplish. This need not suggest that his behavior is not caused in the usual ways, although some might want to maintain this. What it does mean is that there is some point to what he is doing, some outcome that he intends. It implies nothing more.

For example, a man is seen operating a typewriter. Why is he doing that? Perhaps he is writing a letter, or an editorial, or something of that sort. In short, he has some purpose, and his typewriting activity is his means to fulfilling it. Or a man is seen running. What for? Perhaps to get to a store before it closes, or to catch a bus. Again, he has some purpose and is trying to fulfill it by running. Or once more, a man is seen walking toward a pump with an empty bucket. What for? Presumably, to fill the bucket (a goal) to enable himself to drink, wash, and so on (further purposes or goals).

I have used these exceedingly commonplace examples of human activity to illustrate three points. The first is that voluntary or deliberate human activity is generally interpreted as goal-directed. When we ask why a man is doing whatever it is that he is doing, we are usually seeking some explanation in terms of what he is trying to accomplish by that activity. This presupposes something about men that is universally taken for granted: men have goals and purposes and wants and desires, and they generally act in ways they consider appropriate to fulfilling them. It presupposes, in fact, that they are conative beings or, as I shall sometimes express it, that they are beings having desires and wants.

The second point is that, in speaking of a man's goals or purposes, one need not be referring to some *ultimate* goal, or even to any that is very important. The goal of one's activity might be exceedingly trivial and of only momentary significance, as in the foregoing examples. It could hardly be one's ultimate goal, or the goal of one's lifetime, to fill a bucket with water or to catch a bus. Yet, that might be precisely what his goal is then and there. Of course most men do have larger, more long-range goals. A man will spend years struggling, for example, in pursuit of some objective important to him, such as a degree in medicine, or perhaps fame as an author. Some men do devote the better part of their lives to ends having that kind of personal importance. In speaking of human behavior as goal-directed, however, I do not have this sort of thing primarily in mind, even though I include it. What I am calling attention to is much simpler and more commonplace. The conative aspect of human nature is as well exhibited by a man munching an apple or swatting a fly as it is by someone devoting his lifetime to a great ambition.

And the third point is that reason appears to enter into men's purposeful activity primarily to devise the means to attain the ends and has little to do with ends themselves. Thus, if a man wants to fill a bucket with water, it is in the clearest sense rational that he should carry it to the pump, as the most elementary reason or intelligence indicates that this is the appropriate means to that end. Merely wishing that pail might become filled, or trying to find some way to bring the pump to the pail, would be unreasonable, precisely in the sense that these are not means that give much promise of working. There is not, however, any reason for filling the pail in the first place. There is, to be sure, some further purpose that can thus be fulfilled—the purpose of drinking, for example, or of washing—but this only indicates that filling the pail, which is his immediate purpose, is in turn a means to still some further purpose. It is, for example, neither rational nor irrational that one should want to drink; it is merely an expression of fact that he is thirsty. In the same sense, it is neither rational nor irrational that a man should want to swat a fly, or catch a bus, or become a physician, or attain fame as an author. These are simply statements of this or that man's aims or goals, both trivial and great, and they have nothing to do with reason. How they are to be reached, on the other hand, has a great deal to do with reason, for in general, one can set about trying to accomplish whatever it is he wants to accomplish in either an intelligent and rational way or otherwise. To say he is pursuing his goals in an intelligent way is only to say, as an inference from experience, that the means he adopts has some promise of succeeding.

CONATION AS THE PRECONDITION OF GOOD AND EVIL

With these rather commonplace observations in mind, let us now ask what conditions are necessary in order that any distinction between good and evil and between right and wrong can be made. That is, what must be presupposed in saying of something that it is good, or that it is bad, or in saying of an action that it is morally right or morally wrong?

Unthinking men have a tendency to assume that some things are just naturally good and others bad, and some actions right and some wrong, and that we need only to discover which are which. Even some of the most thoughtful philosophers, as we have seen, have started out with the same assumption. Thus, it is supposed that men are born into a world in which these distinctions already hold. Many have insisted that these distinctions cannot either have been contrived by men, or have awaited man's invention of laws, conventions, and customs. Ever so many things are man-made, including laws and moral customs; however, it is often thought that we cannot suppose the ultimate distinctions between good and evil or right and wrong to be such, for this would render all ethics, all justice, and all morality entirely relative. Indeed, most philosophers have thought that the problem of the moralist is simply to discover the true nature of goodness and rightness; they have disagreed not on whether such things exist independently of men, but on what *is* truly good, and what is truly right.

But now let us note that the basic distinction between good and evil could not even theoretically be drawn in a world that we imagined to be devoid of all life. That is, if we suppose the world to be exactly as it is, except that it contains not one living thing, it seems clear that nothing in it would be good and nothing bad. It would just be a dead world, turning through space with a lifeless atmosphere. Having deprived our imagined world of all life, we can modify it in numberless ways, but by no such modification can we ever produce the slightest hint of good or evil in it until we introduce at least one living being capable of reacting in one way or another to the world as that being finds it. Thus, we can imagine on the one hand that it is filled with things satisfying, lovely, and beautiful—with sunrises and sunsets, pleasing sights and sounds and fragrant odors, and with all things that beings like ourselves would find necessary and agreeable to life. Or we can imagine the opposite—a world that is dark and cold, filled with nauseous smells and barren of anything that would redeem such bleak aspects. But so long as we suppose that neither of these worlds does contain any being like ourselves, or any sentient being whatever, then neither world is *better* or *worse* than the other. Each is simply a world of facts, neutral with respect to good or evil, and destined to remain so until we suppose at least one onlooker capable of some sort of reaction to such facts.

Next we note that, if we begin to add inhabitants to this world who are, like ourselves, more or less rational, intelligent, and capable of perception but who, unlike ourselves, have no needs, purposes, or desires, the distinction between good and evil still does not arise. Imagine, for example, a whole colony of machinelike beings, living together and interacting in various ways. These beings, we can suppose, can perceive what is going on around them, distinguish between true and false, and make various inferences; but they are machinelike in that nothing matters to them, nothing makes any difference so far as their needs and purposes are concerned, because they have no needs or purposes, they do not care about anything. If it is raining, they observe that it is raining, but they seek no shelter, for they have no interest in being dry. If it is bitterly cold, then again they note this fact, but make no attempt to warm themselves because they care not whether they are warm or cold. If one of these beings observes another moving with great speed and force toward itself, it infers that a collision is impending, but makes no attempt to step aside, because it has no purpose that would be frustrated by such a collision. It has not even the desire to perpetuate its own existence, because it has no desires whatever. Having then been run down and broken by the onrushing being, losing a few limbs perhaps, it simply notes that this has happened, but it does not retaliate, because it had no interest in preserving any of its limbs or other parts anyway; and so on.

Such beings are, to be sure, difficult to imagine, for if we suppose them to be capable of perceiving, then we seem to imagine them to be living things, and it is difficult to imagine *any* living thing having no interests or purposes whatever, not even an interest in self-preservation. But of course we need not imagine that they are living things; we can instead suppose that they are enormously complicated machines, if that makes it easier. And then we need only suppose that they share with certain living things, such as ourselves, the capacity to perceive what is going on and to draw certain conclusions from what they perceive, but that they do *not* share with other living things, such as ourselves, any interest in what is going on. They are, in short, possessed of some degree of intelligence, but of no will whatever.

Now I think it is clear that a world inhabited by such beings would still be a world devoid of any good or evil. Like the first world we imagined, which did not even contain any beings of the most elementary intelligence, this one might contain anything we care to put into it without there arising the least semblance of good or of evil—until we imagine it to contain at least one being having some need, interest, or purpose. It would not matter to the beings just described whether their world was one filled with sunlight, warmth, and beauty, or dark and cold and filled with nauseous smells, because nothing would matter to them. They could tell the difference between sunlight and darkness, between warmth and cold, but they could in no way tell the difference between good and bad. Such a distinction would in fact have no meaning to them, and if they found their world dark, smelly, and cold they would have no basis for pronouncing it bad, simply because they would have no preference for any other kind of world.

THE EMERGENCE OF GOOD AND EVIL

Thus far, then, there is no good and no evil; there is nothing but bare facts of this kind or that.

But now let us suppose a world, much like our own, except that it contains throughout its vastness just one sentient being, a being who, like ourselves, cannot only perceive what is contained in the world around him and make certain inferences, but one to whom what he finds makes a difference. Suddenly, with the introduction of just one such being, certain things in the world do acquire the aspect of good and evil. Those things are good that this one being finds satisfying to his needs and desires, and those bad to which he reacts in the opposite way. Things in the world are not merely perceived by this being, but perceived as holding promise or threat to whatever interests him. Thus, the things that nourish and give warmth and enhance life are deemed good, and those that frustrate and threaten are deemed bad. The distinction between good and evil in a world containing only one living being possessed of needs and wants arises, then, only in relation to those needs and wants, and in no way existed in their absence. In the most general terms, those things are good that satisfy this being's actual wants, those that frustrate them are bad.

Now, with this picture still before us, let us note two things that are highly significant for the problems before us. The first is that the judgments of this solitary being concerning good and evil are as *absolute* as any judgment can be. Such a being is, indeed, the measure of all things: of good things as good and of bad things as bad. Whatever this being finds and declares to be good *is* good, and what he similarly finds to be evil, *is* evil. No distinction can be made, in terms of this being, between what is merely good *for him* and what is good *absolutely*. Whatever is good for him is good absolutely; there is no higher standard of goodness. For what could it be? If good and evil in this world arise only in relation to this being's wants and needs, then what could it possibly mean to say that something satisfies these but is nevertheless bad, or that something frustrates them but is nevertheless good? There simply is nothing else, apart from these wants and needs, in terms of which good and evil can possibly be measured, or even exist.

The second thing to note is that, even though good and evil have emerged with the appearance in this world of a single living being having wants and needs, no moral obligation has similarly arisen. The distinction between moral *right* and *wrong* has not yet come into the picture at all. That such a being should find something useful and agreeable and subsequently seize it, or find something threatening and shun it, is neither right nor wrong. Whatever he finds and wants is his for the taking, by a kind of natural right that is nothing but the absence of any natural wrong, and he cannot possibly have an obligation to undertake what would injure him, or even so much as make him the least uncomfortable. Although he can in this moral solitude create good and evil for himself, merely by his own declaration of what he finds things to be, he can in no way inflict them. For who could be his beneficiary or victim, besides himself? To whom could he owe any obligation to do anything? And by what standard, other than good and evil themselves, over which he is the sole judge, could any action of his be deemed right or wrong? He could, to be sure, fail to act in his own best interest, or even injure himself through neglect or stupidity, for which he would be accountable to no one. It would be as inappropriate to ascribe any moral responsibility to this solitary being as to the merest insect crawling through the grass.

Our next step, then, is to add another being like ourselves, another conative being with his own feelings, wants, and interests, and to suppose that the two who now inhabit our world have some interaction with each other. No new distinction between good and evil is introduced with the introduction of this new inhabitant, for that distinction emerged, complete and perfect, as soon as we assumed the existence of but one such inhabitant. With this small plurality of beings, it remains just what it was before. The first inhabitant deemed those things good that he found agreeable to his needs and purposes, and those things bad that threatened the opposite, and in this judgment he was absolutely correct. For him, the good and evil of things consisted of precisely such promise and threat to his interests. Such, accordingly, will it also be for our second sentient and goal-directed inhabitant. Those things will be good for him that promise fulfillment of his aims, whether grand or trifling, and those that threaten the opposite will be bad. In this judgment he, too, cannot err. For this will be precisely what the distinction between good and evil will mean to him, as it is what it means to the first; it will be the condition, and the only condition, of such a distinction being drawn by either of them. And we are not, it should be noted, here supposing any power of reasoning in either of our two beings. We do not suppose them to be appraising the various features of their common environment in terms of what they promise or threaten, and then *inferring* from such features that they have the moral qualities of good or evil. We do not even assume these two beings to be rational, though the picture is not altered in case they are. We only assume them to be sentient beings with needs, or in other words, beings who desire and shun, and can feel it when their needs are fulfilled, and when they are not.

THE EMERGENCE OF RIGHT AND WRONG

There was, we noted, no place for such ethical notions as right and wrong or for moral obligation, so long as we imagined a world containing only one purposeful and sentient being, although the presence of such a being was enough to produce good and evil. With the introduction of a multiplicity of such beings, however, we have supplied the foundation for these additional notions, for they are based on the fact that the aims or purposes of such beings can conflict. Thus, two or more such beings can covet the same thing. In that case each will deem it a good, but it can easily arise that not both can possess it, that its possession by one will mean deprivation for the other. The result is a conflict of wills, which can lead to a mutual aggression in which each stands to lose more than the thing for which they are contending is worth to either of them. Such a situation can produce a threat to life itself, for example, and without life all good and evil are reduced to zero.

There is, moreover, another side to the coin. For just as the wills of two purposeful beings can conflict, in the manner just suggested, so also can they coincide in a very significant way. That is, situations can arise in which each of two such beings needs the help of the other in order to attain what it wants, or to ward off some evil. They may, for example, be threatened by some force, animate or inanimate, that the strength of neither is sufficient to overcome, but from which their combined strength offers some hope of safety. Or again, each may find that he possesses in excess of his own needs something that the other requires. One, for example, may possess an excess of food, of which the other has none, while the latter one possesses an excess of the requirements for shelter, entirely lacking to the former. The possibility of mutual giving and taking thus presents itself, wherein each can benefit greatly at small cost to himself. Or again, two such beings may have some common end, such as the begetting of children, for which some sort of cooperation is needed by the very nature of things, and so on.

The supposition of a multiplicity of beings, each with its own needs and purposes, presents, in short, numberless possibilities for (1) conflict, and (2) cooperation. Possibilities of the first kind are loaded with the threat of evil, and those of the second kind with the promise of good, still thinking of good and evil in the sense already adduced—namely, as that which satisfies or fulfills, and that which frustrates felt needs and goals.

RIGHT AND WRONG AS RELATIVE TO RULES

If needs are to be satisfied and goals fulfilled, however, then situations of conflict and, particularly, situations of cooperation must be resolved in the context of *rules,* using the notion of rules in an extremely broad sense that encompasses any regular and predictable behavior. Thus, it becomes a "rule" that two or more such beings, faced with a common threat, shall abstain from attacking each other until that threat is overcome. It becomes another rule that they shall meet the threat together by combining their resources, inasmuch as acting in accordance with such rules will enable each to avoid what appears as an evil. When two such beings each covet the same thing, and not both can possess it, it may become a rule that it remains with him who first possessed it. The underlying basis for such a rule is that, if it is disregarded, the coveted thing may end up in the hands of neither, and that evils even greater than this, such as mutual injury or even death, may follow instead. When each of two such beings possesses an excess of what is sought by the other, a rule of trading becomes obviously advantageous to both. Through such behavior, the good of each is enhanced at no significant cost. The alternative is combat, in which each would be faced with the possibility of total loss.

Now it should be clear from this that by rules I do not mean rational principles of conduct, in the sense that it would require any powers of reason to discover them, much less do I mean principles that are set forth in any coherent writing or speech. They need not be things that are formulated at all. Rules, in the sense that I am now considering them, are nothing but practices or ways of behaving that are more or less regular and that can, therefore, be expected. They are, on the other hand, rational in this sense: such behavior offers promise, to those who behave in the manner in question, of avoiding evil and attaining good. Mutual aggression, for example, always presents the threat of great and unpredictable evil to each aggressor, and the possibility of such evil is almost certain to outweigh any possibility of good. To the extent, therefore, that some good can be ensured by a certain mode of behavior or, as I am using the term, by action in accordance with a rule, and that such behavior will remove the threat of evil contained in any situation of combat, then action in accordance with the rule is better than combat. In that sense, but only in that sense, it is more rational.

Suppose, for example, that among a certain people the practice arises that men, on approaching one another, extend a forearm with the palm of the hand open and exposed to view, each thus indicating that he is unarmed. The gesture is recognized and acknowledged by each then grasping the other's open hand, that is, by shaking hands. Now here, clearly, is a rule, as I am using the term, even though it does not need to be formulated or embodied in any code. It is simply a regular mode of behavior. It has as its obvious purpose the avoidance of evil and the advancement of good and is in that sense, but that sense only, rational. It would be most treacherously violated by one who, extending his open hand of friendship, assaulted his greeter with a weapon concealed in his other hand. The treachery of this would consist in using the rule to promote the very evil the rule was meant to avoid.

THE WORLD AS IT IS

We have been imagining, then, a world, at first lifeless and barren, that gradually becomes occupied with beings having needs, feelings, and purposes. Until the appearance of the first such being, that world contains no hint of good or evil, but both arise the moment he comes into the picture. With the multiplication of such beings, the possibilities of further goods and evils arise with the appearance of situations of cooperation and conflict. Good is increased and enhanced by the former and evil by the latter. Cooperation, however, and the safe resolution of conflict obviously require certain regular modes of behavior, or what I have called rules. These notions having been made tolerably clear, we can now refine and elaborate on the imaginary picture with which we began until it begins to resemble the world of men in which we actually live.

Thus, we can suppose that the multiplicity of sentient and purposeful beings by which our imaginary world is inhabited are men like ourselves, for we, too, are sentient and purposeful beings. We can suppose that those modes of behavior required for cooperation and the resolution of conflict situations become actual precepts, conveyed by one generation to the next, and that the most important of them come to be rules embodied in traditional literature for which men have a certain awe. They are, thus, passed from generation to generation, like the Ten Commandments of scripture. Others come to assume the form of written laws, and various practical means are hit on for securing, as nearly as possible, the adherence to them on the part of all. Groupings of men are formed for the attainment of the maximum of good for some or all and the minimization of evil. Thus do societies arise, by their common adherence to rules that become more elaborate as the societies themselves become larger and more complex. The behavior required by such rules rises, by some degree or other, to that level we call civilized conduct; but the basic principle of those rules remains exactly what it was from the outset: the minimization of conflict and its consequent evil, and the maximization of cooperation and its consequent good.

All this is, of course, but a sketch, and a very superficial one, but no more is really needed for our present purpose, which is to explain good and evil and moral right and wrong.

How, then, do moral right and wrong arise? The answer is fairly obvious in the light of what has been said. Right is simply the adherence to rule, and wrong is violation of it. The notions of right and wrong absolutely presuppose the existence of rules, at least in the broad sense of rule with which we began. That two beings should fight and injure each other in their contest for something that each covets, and thereby, perhaps, each lose the good he wanted to seize, is clearly an evil to both. But in the absence of a rule of behavior—that is, some anticipated behavior to the contrary—no wrong has been done; only an evil has been produced. Given such a rule, however—for example, given the simple and rudimentary expectation that the thing in question shall be his who first took it—then a wrong is committed by the one who attempts to divest the holder of that good. The wrong comes into being with the violation of the rule, and in no way existed ahead of the rule. The same is, of course, true of right. If, for example, we presuppose no expectation that a good may be enjoyed in peace by whoever first seizes it, then, if another nevertheless, in the absence of any such rule, abstains from seizing that good from its first possessor, this potential aggressor has clearly fostered a good, simply by eschewing an evil. But he has in no way done "the right thing," for the notion of *right* conduct can have no meaning in the absence of some sort of rule. If one is tempted to say that this would-be aggressor has done something morally right, then one will find that all he means is that he has produced an effect that was good. That is something entirely different. One also may be reading into a situation, in which, by hypothesis, there is no rule to which to adhere, certain rules of right and wrong that one has learned to respect.

For Further Reflection

1. Examine Taylor's theory of good and evil and right and wrong. First, note that he claims that humans are basically conative beings—moved by will and desire—rather than rational beings. Do you agree with this? What role does he think reason plays in life?

2. Outline the four stages in the thought process, from a universe with no conscious beings to his final stage. Where do good and evil enter in? Where do right and wrong enter in? How are the two categories related to each other? Do you agree with Taylor's analysis? Explain your answer.

3. What, according to Taylor, is the purpose of rules? Give an example of a rule to illustrate his point. Do you find his analysis convincing? Explain your answer.

4. Are some rules better than others?

Further Readings for Chapter 2

Hallie, Philip P. *Cruelty.* Middletown, Conn.: Wesleyan University Press, 1982.
Kekes, John. "The Reflexivity of Evil." *Social Philosophy and Policy* 15, no. 1 (1998).
Midgley, Mary. *Wickedness: A Philosophical Essay.* Boston: Routledge and Kegan Paul, 1984.
Milo, Ronald. *Immorality.* Princeton, N.J.: Princeton University Press, 1984.

Milo, Ronald. "Virtue, Knowledge and Wickedness." *Social Philosophy and Policy* 15, no. 1 (1998).

Nietzsche, Frederich. *Beyond Good and Evil.* Translated by R. J. Hollingdale. Penguin, 1990.

Taylor, Richard. *Good and Evil.* Buffalo, N.Y.: Prometheus, 1970.

CHAPTER 3

Is Everything Relative?

Is morality essentially relative or are there objective moral truths? This question haunts contemporary society. On the one hand, anthropologists have uncovered a multitudinous array of variegated cultural codes and moral practices. Who are we to judge another culture? Tolerance would seem to require that we allow for a plethora of practices and ways of expressing morality. We've been taught that multicultural diversity is a good in its own right, so we should be accepting of difference. On the other hand, some actions seem wrong in principle (torturing or killing the innocent, breaking promises, lying, and destroying other people's property) and some actions seem morally good (helping people who are in need, keeping contracts, cooperating for mutual benefit, and promoting justice). How do we reconcile these opposing insights?

The readings in this chapter inquire into the strengths and weaknesses of moral relativism, the theory that the validity of moral principles is dependent on cultural or subjective acceptance. Our first reading is an ancient observation of the Greek historian Herodotus on how different cultures project their customs onto the heavens, identifying them with eternal verities. Our second reading is a defense of relativism by the cultural anthropologist Ruth Benedict, who develops the theme set forth by Herodotus. Cultural norms are the colored glasses through which we view all our world. In our third reading, Louis Pojman critiques moral relativism and defends its opposite, moral objectivism. He argues, that while some things are relative, there are universal moral truths, valid for all people at all times. In our fourth reading, "Judge Not?," Jean Bethke Elshtain questions the dictum which is at the heart of relativism. In our fifth reading, "Trying Out One's New Sword," Mary Midgley uses a compelling example from Japanese history to argue that understanding and judging other cultures are not only possible but inescapable. And, finally, Henrik Ibsen illustrates the philosophy of moral objectivism in the person of Dr. Stockmann, who defies his culture in the name of truth.

Custom Is King

HERODOTUS

Herodotus (485–430 B.C.), a Greek and the first Western historian, in this brief passage from his *Histories* illustrates cultural relativism and may suggest that ethical relativism is the correct view ("culture is king").

Thus it appears certain to me, by a great variety of proofs, that Cambyses was raving mad; he would not else have set himself to make a mock of holy rites and long-established usages. For if one were to offer men to choose out of all the customs in the world such as seemed to them the best, they would examine the whole number, and end by preferring their own; so convinced are they that their own usages far surpass those of all others. Unless, therefore, a man was mad, it is not likely that he would make sport of such matters. That people have this feeling about their laws may be seen by very many proofs: among others, by the following. Darius, after he had got the kingdom, called into his presence certain Greeks who were at hand, and asked—"What he should pay them to eat the bodies of their fathers when they died?" To which they answered, that there was no sum that would tempt them to do such a thing. He then sent for certain Indians, of the race called Callatians, men who eat their fathers, and asked them, while the Greeks stood by, and knew by the help of an interpreter all that was said— "What he should give them to burn the bodies of their fathers at their decease?" The Indians exclaimed aloud, and bade him forbear such language. Such is men's wont herein; and Pindar was right, in my judgment, when he said, "Custom is the king o'er all."

From Herodotus, *The Histories of Herodotus,* translated by George Rawlinson (New York: Appleton, 1859).

The Case for Moral Relativism

RUTH BENEDICT

Ruth Benedict (1887–1948), an American anthropologist, taught at Columbia University and is best known for her book *Patterns of Culture* (1934). Benedict sets forth a theory of moral relativism in which moral principles are based on the common beliefs and practices of social systems. Since these systems or cultures can vary, so can morality. Like a work of art, the social system chooses which theme of its repertoire of basic tendencies to emphasize and then goes about to create a more or less comprehensive system of mores to support those tendencies. What is considered normal or abnormal behavior will depend on the choices of these social systems, or what Benedict calls the "idea-practice pattern of the culture."

In this selection Benedict assembles a varied array of cultural data from her research of tribal behavior on an island in northwest Melanesia from which she draws her conclusions that moral relativism is the correct view of morality.

Modern social anthropology has become more and more a study of the varieties and common elements of cultural environment and the consequences of these in human behavior. For such a study of diverse social orders primitive peoples fortunately provide a laboratory not yet entirely vitiated by the spread of a standardized worldwide civilization. Dyaks and Hopis, Fijians and Yakuts are significant for psychological and sociological study because only among these simpler peoples has there been sufficient isolation to give opportunity for the development of localized social forms. In the higher cultures the standardization of custom and belief over a couple of continents has given a false sense of the inevitability of the particular forms that have gained currency, and we need to turn to a wider survey in order to check the conclusions we hastily base upon this near-universality of familiar customs. Most of the simpler

From "Anthropology and the Abnormal," by Ruth Benedict, in *The Journal of General Psychology* 10 (1934): 59–82, a publication of the Helen Dwight Reid Educational Foundation.

cultures did not gain the wide currency of the one which, out of our experience, we identify with human nature, but this was for various historical reasons, and certainly not for any that gives us as its carriers a monopoly of social good or of social sanity. Modern civilization, from this point of view, becomes not a necessary pinnacle of human achievement but one entry in a long series of possible adjustments.

These adjustments, whether they are in mannerisms like the ways of showing anger, or joy, or grief in any society, or in major human drives like those of sex, prove to be far more variable than experience in any one culture would suggest. In certain fields, such as that of religion or of formal marriage arrangements, these wide limits of variability are well known and can be fairly described. In others it is not yet possible to give a generalized account, but that does not absolve us of the task of indicating the significance of the work that has been done and of the problems that have arisen.

One of these problems relates to the customary modern normal-abnormal categories and our conclusions regarding them. In how far are such categories culturally determined, or in how far can we with assurance regard them as absolute? In how far can we regard inability to function socially as diagnostic of abnormality, or in how far is it necessary to regard this as a function of the culture?

As a matter of fact, one of the most striking facts that emerge from a study of widely varying cultures is the ease with which our abnormals function in other cultures. It does not matter what kind of "abnormality" we choose for illustration, those which indicate extreme instability, or those which are more in the nature of character traits like sadism or delusions of grandeur or of persecution, there are well-described cultures in which these abnormals function at ease and with honor, and apparently without danger or difficulty to the society. . . .

The most notorious of these is trance and catalepsy. Even a very mild mystic is aberrant in our culture. But most peoples have regarded even extreme psychic manifestations not only as normal and desirable, but even as characteristic of highly valued and gifted individuals. This was true even in our own cultural background in that period when Catholicism made the ecstatic experience the mark of sainthood. It is hard for us, born and brought up in a culture that makes no use of the experience, to realize how important a role it may play and how many individuals are capable of it, once it has been given an honorable place in any society. . . .

Cataleptic and trance phenomena are, of course, only one illustration of the fact that those whom we regard as abnormals may function adequately in other cultures. Many of our culturally discarded traits are selected for elaboration in different societies. Homosexuality is an excellent example, for in this case our attention is not constantly diverted, as in the consideration of trance, to the interruption of routine activity which it implies. Homosexuality poses the problem very simply. A tendency toward this trait in our culture exposes an individual to all the conflicts to which all aberrants are always exposed, and we tend to identify the consequences of this conflict with homosexuality. But these consequences are obviously local and cultural. Homosexuals in many societies are not incompetent, but they may be such if the culture asks adjustments of them that would strain any man's vitality. Wherever homosexuality has been given an honorable place in any society, those to whom it is congenial have filled adequately the honorable roles society assigns to them. Plato's *Republic* is, of course, the most convincing statement of such a reading of homosexuality. It is presented as one of the major means to the good life, and it was generally so regarded in Greece at that time.

The cultural attitude toward homosexuals has not always been on such a high ethical plane, but it has been very varied. Among many American Indian tribes there exists the institution of the berdache, as the French called them. These men-women were men who at puberty or thereafter took the dress and the occupations of women. Sometimes they married other men and lived with them. Sometimes they were men with no inversion, persons of weak sexual endowment who chose this role to avoid the jeers of the women. The berdaches were never regarded as of first-rate supernatural power, as similar men-women were in Siberia, but rather as leaders in women's occupations, good healers in certain diseases, or, among certain tribes, as the genial organizers of social affairs. In any case, they were socially placed. They were not left exposed to the conflicts that visit the deviant who is excluded from participation in the recognized patterns of his society.

The most spectacular illustrations of the extent to which normality may be culturally defined are those cultures where an abnormality of our culture is the cornerstone of their social structure. It is not possible to do justice to these possibilities in a short discussion. A recent study of an island of northwest Melanesia by Fortune describes a society built upon traits which we regard as beyond the border of paranoia. In this tribe the exogamic groups look upon each other as prime manipulators of black magic, so that one marries always into an enemy group which remains for life one's deadly and unappeasable foes. They look upon a good garden crop as a confession of theft, for everyone is engaged in making magic to induce into his garden the productiveness of his neighbors'; therefore no secrecy in the island is so rigidly insisted upon as the secrecy of a man's harvesting of his yams. Their polite phrase at the acceptance of a gift is, "And if you now poison me, how shall I repay you this present?" Their preoccupation with poisoning is constant; no woman ever leaves her cooking pot for a moment untended. Even the great affinal economic exchanges that are characteristic of this Melanesian culture area are quite altered in Dobu since they are incompatible with this fear and distrust that pervades the culture. They go farther and people the whole world outside their own quarters with such malignant spirits that all-night feasts and ceremonials simply do not occur here. They have even rigorous religiously enforced customs that forbid the sharing of seed even in one family group. Anyone else's food is deadly poison to you, so that communality of stores is out of the question. For some months before harvest the whole society is on the verge of starvation, but if one falls to the temptation and eats up one's seed yams, one is an outcast and a beachcomber for life. There is no coming back. It involves, as a matter of course, divorce and the breaking of all social ties.

Now in this society where no one may work with another and no one may share with another, Fortune describes the individual who was regarded by all his fellows as crazy. He was not one of those who periodically ran amok and, beside himself and frothing at the mouth, fell with a knife upon anyone he could reach. Such behavior they did not regard as putting anyone outside the pale. They did not even put the individuals who were known to be liable to these attacks under any kind of control. They merely fled when they saw the attack coming on and kept out of the way. "He would be all right tomorrow." But there was one man of sunny, kindly disposition who liked work and liked to be helpful. The compulsion was too strong for him to repress it in favor of the opposite tendencies of his culture. Men and women never spoke of him without laughing; he was silly and simple and definitely crazy. Nevertheless, to the ethnologist used to a culture that has, in Christianity, made his type the model of all virtue, he seemed a pleasant fellow. . . .

. . . Among the Kwakiutl it did not matter whether a relative had died in bed of disease, or by the hand of an enemy, in either case death was an affront to be wiped out by the death of another person. The fact that one had been caused to mourn was proof that one had been put upon. A chief's sister and her daughter had gone up to Victoria, and either because they drank bad whiskey or because their boat capsized they never came back. The chief called together his warriors, "Now I ask you, tribes, who shall wail? Shall I do it or shall another?" The spokesman answered, of course, "Not you, Chief. Let some other of the tribes." Immediately they set up the war pole to announce their intention of wiping out the injury, and gathered a war party. They set out, and found seven men and two children asleep and killed them. "Then they felt good when they arrived at Sebaa in the evening."

The point which is of interest to us is that in our society those who on that occasion would feel good when they arrived at Sebaa that evening would be the definitely abnormal. There would be some, even in our society, but it is not a recognized and approved mood under the circumstances. On the Northwest Coast those are favored and fortunate to whom that mood under those circumstances is congenial, and those to whom it is repugnant are unlucky. This latter minority can register in their own culture only by doing violence to their congenial responses and acquiring others that are difficult for them. The person, for instance, who, like a Plains Indian whose wife has been taken from him, is too proud to fight, can deal with the Northwest Coast civilization only by ignoring its strongest bents. If he cannot achieve it, he is the deviant in that culture, their instance of abnormality.

This head-hunting that takes place on the Northwest Coast after a death is no matter of blood revenge or of organized vengeance. There is no effort to tie up the subsequent killing with any responsibility on the part of the victim for the death of the person who is being mourned. A chief whose son has died goes visiting wherever his fancy dictates, and he says to his host, "My prince has died today, and you go with him." Then he kills him. In this, according to their interpretation, he acts nobly because he has not been downed. He has thrust back in return. The whole procedure is meaningless without the fundamental paranoid reading of bereavement. Death, like all the other untoward accidents of existence, confounds man's pride and can only be handled in the category of insults.

Behavior honored upon the Northwest Coast is one which is recognized as abnormal in our civilization, and yet it is sufficiently close to the attitudes of our own culture to be intelligible to us and to have a definite vocabulary with which we may discuss it. The megalomaniac paranoid trend is a definite danger in our society. It is encouraged by some of our major preoccupations, and it confronts us with a choice of two possible attitudes. One is to brand it as abnormal and reprehensible, and is the attitude we have chosen in our civilization. The other is to make it an essential attribute of ideal man, and this is the solution in the culture of the Northwest Coast.

These illustrations, which it has been possible to indicate only in the briefest manner, force upon us the fact that normality is culturally defined. An adult shaped to the drives and standards of either of these cultures, if he were transported into our civilization, would fall into our categories of abnormality. He would be faced with the psychic dilemmas of the socially unavailable. In his own culture, however, he is the pillar of society, the end result of socially inculcated mores, and the problem of personal instability in his case simply does not arise.

No one civilization can possibly utilize in its mores the whole potential range of human behavior. Just as there are great numbers of possible phonetic articulations, and the possibility of language depends on a selection and standardization of a few of these in order that speech communication may be possible at all, so the possibility of organized behavior of every sort, from the fashions of local dress and houses to the dicta of a people's ethics and religion, depends upon a similar selection among the possible behavior traits. In the field of recognized economic obligations or sex taboos this selection is as nonrational and subconscious a process as it is in the field of phonetics. It is a process which goes on in the group for long periods of time and is historically conditioned by innumerable accidents of isolation or of contact of peoples. In any comprehensive study of psychology, the selection that different cultures have made in the course of history within the great circumference of potential behavior is of great significance.

Every society, beginning with some slight inclination in one direction or another, carries its preference farther and farther, integrating itself more and more completely upon its chosen basis, and discarding those types of behavior that are uncongenial. Most of those organizations of personality that seem to us most uncontrovertibly abnormal have been used by different civilizations in the very foundations of their institutional life. Conversely the most valued traits of our normal individuals have been looked on in differently organized cultures as aberrant. Normality, in short, within a very wide range, is culturally defined. It is primarily a term for the socially elaborated segment of human behavior in any culture; and abnormality, a term for the segment that that particular civilization does not use. The very eyes with which we see the problem are conditioned by the long traditional habits of our own society.

It is a point that has been made more often in relation to ethics than in relation to psychiatry. We do not any longer make the mistake of deriving the morality of our locality and decade directly from the inevitable constitution of human nature. We do not elevate it to the dignity of a first principle. We recognize that morality differs in every society, and is a convenient term for socially approved habits. Mankind has always preferred to say, "It is morally good," rather than "It is habitual," and the fact of this preference is matter enough for a critical science of ethics. But historically the two phrases are synonymous.

The concept of the normal is properly a variant of the concept of the good. It is that which society has approved. A normal action is one which falls well within the limits of expected behavior for a particular society. Its variability among different peoples is essentially a function of the variability of the behavior patterns that different societies have created for themselves, and can never be wholly divorced from a consideration of culturally institutionalized types of behavior.

Each culture is a more or less elaborate working-out of the potentialities of the segment it has chosen. In so far as a civilization is well integrated and consistent within itself, it will tend to carry farther and farther, according to its nature, its initial impulse toward a particular type of action, and from the point of view of any other culture those elaborations will include more and more extreme and aberrant traits.

Each of these traits, in proportion as it reinforces the chosen behavior patterns of that culture, is for that culture normal. Those individuals to whom it is congenial either congenitally, or as the result of childhood sets, are accorded prestige in that culture, and are not visited with the social contempt or disapproval which their traits would call down upon them in a society that was differently organized. On the other hand, those individuals whose characteristics are not congenial to the selected type of human behavior in that community are the deviants, no matter how valued their personality traits may be in a contrasted civilization.

The Dobuan who is not easily susceptible to fear of treachery, who enjoys work and likes to be helpful, is their neurotic and regarded as silly. On the Northwest Coast the person who finds it difficult to read life in terms of an insult contest will be the person upon whom fall all the difficulties of the culturally unprovided for. The person who does not find it easy to humiliate a neighbor, nor to see humiliation in his own experience, who is genial and loving, may, of course, find some unstandardized way of achieving satisfactions in his society, but not in the major patterned responses that his culture requires of him. If he is born to play an important role in a family with many hereditary privileges, he can succeed only by doing violence to his whole personality. If he does not succeed, he has betrayed his culture; that is, he is abnormal.

I have spoken of individuals as having sets toward certain types of behavior, and of these sets as running sometimes counter to the types of behavior which are institutionalized in the culture to which they belong. From all that we know of contrasting cultures it seems clear that differences of temperament occur in every society. The matter has never been made the subject of investigation, but from the available material it would appear that these temperament types are very likely of universal recurrence. That is, there is an ascertainable range of human behavior that is found wherever a sufficiently large series of individuals is observed. But the proportion in which behavior types stand to one another in different societies is not universal. The vast majority of individuals in any group are shaped to the fashion of that culture. In other words, most individuals are plastic to the moulding force of the society into which they are born. In a society that values trance, as in India, they will have supernormal experience. In a society that institutionalizes homosexuality, they will be homosexual. In a society that sets the gathering of possessions as the chief human objective, they will amass property. The deviants, whatever the type of behavior the culture has institutionalized, will remain few in number, and there seems no more difficulty in moulding the vast malleable majority to the "normality" of what we consider an aberrant trait, such as delusions of reference, than to the normality of such accepted behavior patterns as acquisitiveness. The small proportion of the number of the deviants in any culture is not a function of the sure instinct with which that society has built itself upon the fundamental sanities, but of the universal fact that, happily, the majority of mankind quite readily take any shape that is presented to them. . . .

For Further Reflection

1. Is Benedict correct in saying that our culture is "but one entry in a long series of possible adjustments"? What are the implications of this statement?

2. Can we separate the descriptive (or fact-stating) aspect of anthropological study from the prescriptive (evaluative) aspect of evaluating cultures? Are there some independent criteria by which we can say that some cultures are better than others? Can you think how this project might begin?

3. What are the implications of Benedict's claim that morality is simply whatever a culture deems normal behavior? Is this a satisfactory equation? Can you apply it to the institution of slavery or the Nazi policy of anti-Semitism?

4. What is the significance of Benedict's statement, "The very eyes with which we see the problem are conditioned by the long traditional habits of our own society"? Can we apply the conceptual relativism embodied in this statement to her own position?

The Case Against Moral Relativism

LOUIS P. POJMAN

In this article Pojman analyzes the structure of ethical relativism as constituted by two theses: the diversity thesis and
the dependency thesis. Then he examines two types of ethical relativism: subjectivism and conventionalism, arguing
that both types have serious problems. Next he indicates a
way of taking into account the insights of relativism while
maintaining an objectivist position. Pojman outlines two
objectivist arguments and concludes by suggesting some reasons why people have been misled by relativist arguments.

"WHO'S TO JUDGE WHAT'S RIGHT OR WRONG?"

Like many people, I have always been instinctively a moral
relativist. As far back as I can remember . . . it has always
seemed to be obvious that the dictates of morality arise from
some sort of convention or understanding among people,
that different people arrive at different understandings, and
that there are no basic moral demands that apply to everyone. This seemed so obvious to me I assumed it was everyone's instinctive view, or at least everyone who gave the
matter any thought in this day and age.

—Gilbert Harman[1]

Ethical relativism is the doctrine that the moral rightness
and wrongness of actions vary from society to society and
that there are not absolute universal moral standards on all
men at all times. Accordingly, it holds that whether or not
it is right for an individual to act in a certain way depends
on or is relative to the society to which he belongs.

—John Ladd[2]

---

[1]Gilbert Harman, "Is There a Single True Morality?" in *Morality, Reason and
Truth*, eds. David Copp and David Zimmerman (Rowman & Allenheld,
1984).
[2]John Ladd, *Ethical Relativism* (Wadsworth, 1973).

Gilbert Harman's intuitions about the self-evidence of ethical relativism contrast strikingly with Plato's or Kant's equal certainty about the truth of objectivism, the doctrine that universally valid or true ethical principles exist.[3] "Two things fill the soul with ever new and increasing wonder and reverence the oftener and more fervently reflection ponders on it: the starry heavens above and the moral law within," wrote Kant. On the basis of polls taken in my ethics and introduction to philosophy classes in recent years, Harman's views may signal a shift in contemporary society's moral understanding. The polls show a two-to-one ratio in favor of moral relativism over moral absolutism, with fewer than five percent of the respondents recognizing that a third position between these two polar opposites might exist. Of course, I'm not suggesting that all of these students had a clear understanding of what relativism entails, for many who said they were relativists also contended in the same polls that abortion except to save the mother's life is always wrong, that capital punishment is always wrong, or that suicide is never morally permissible.

Among my university colleagues, a growing number also seem to embrace moral relativism. Recently one of my nonphilosopher colleagues voted to turn down a doctoral dissertation proposal because the student assumed an objectivist position in ethics. (Ironically, I found in this same colleague's work rhetorical treatment of individual liberty that raised it to the level of a non-negotiable absolute). But irony and inconsistency aside, many relativists are aware of the tension between their own subjective positions and their metatheory

---

[3]Lest I be misunderstood, in this essay I will generally be speaking about the validity rather than the truth of moral principles. Validity holds that they are proper guides to action, whereas truth presupposes something more. It presupposes Moral Realism, the theory that moral principles have special ontological status. Although this may be true, not all objectivists agree. R. M. Hare, for instance, argues that moral principles, while valid, do not have truth value. They are like imperatives which have practical application but cannot be said to be true. Also, I am mainly concerned with the status of *principles,* not theories themselves. There may be a plurality of valid moral theories, all containing the same objective principles. I am grateful to Edward Sherline for drawing this distinction to my attention.

that entails relativism. I confess that I too am tempted by the allurements of this view and find some forms of it plausible and worthy of serious examination. However, I also find it deeply troubling.

In this essay I will examine the central notions of ethical relativism and look at the implications that seem to follow from it. Then I will present the outline of a very modest objectivism, one that takes into account many of the insights of relativism and yet stands as a viable option to it.

1. An Analysis of Relativism

Let us examine the theses contained in John Ladd's succinct statement on ethical (conventional) relativism that appears at the beginning of this essay. If we analyze it, we derive the following argument:

1. Moral rightness and wrongness of actions vary from society to society, so there are no universal moral standards held by all societies.
2. Whether or not it is right for individuals to act in a certain way depends on (or is relative to) the society to which they belong.
3. Therefore, there are no absolute or objective moral standards that apply to all people everywhere.

1. The first thesis, which may be called the *diversity thesis,* is simply a description that acknowledges the fact that moral rules differ from society to society. The Spartans of ancient Greece and the Dobu of New Guinea believe that stealing is morally right, but we believe it is wrong. The Roman father had the power of life and death (*just vitae necisque*) over his children, whereas we condemn parents for abusing their children. A tribe in East Africa once threw deformed infants to the hippopotamuses, and in ancient Greece and Rome infants were regularly exposed, while we abhor infanticide. Ruth Benedict describes a tribe in Melanesia that views cooperation and kindness as vices, whereas we see them as virtues. While in ancient Greece, Rome, China and Korea parricide was condemned as "the most execrable of crimes," among Northern Indians aged persons, persons who were no longer capable of walking, were left alone to starve. Among the California Gallinomero, when fathers became feeble, a burden to their sons, "the poor old wretch is not infrequently thrown down on his back and securely held while a stick is placed across his throat, and two of them seat themselves on the ends of it until he ceases to breathe."[4] Sexual practices vary over time and place. Some cultures permit homosexual behavior, while others condemn it. Some cultures practice polygamy, while others view it as immoral. Some cultures condone while others condemn premarital sex. Some cultures accept cannibalism, while the very idea revolts us. Some West African tribes perform clitoridectomies on girls, whereas we deplore such practices. Cultural relativism is well documented, and "custom is the king o'er all." There may or may not be moral principles that are held in common by every society, but if there are any, they seem to be few at best. Certainly it would be very difficult to derive any single "true" morality by observing various societies' moral standards.

2. The second thesis, *the dependency thesis,* asserts that individual acts are right or wrong depending on the nature of the society from which they emanate. Morality does not occur in a vacuum, and what is considered morally right or wrong must be seen in a context that depends on the goals, wants, beliefs, history, and environment of the society in question. As William G. Sumner says,

> We learn the morals as unconsciously as we learn to walk and hear and breathe, and [we] never know any reason why the [morals] are what they are. The justification of them is that when we wake to consciousness of life we find them facts which already hold us in the bonds of tradition, custom, and habit.[5]

Trying to see things from an independent, noncultural point of view would be like taking out our eyes in order to examine their contours and qualities. There is no "innocent eye." We are simply culturally determined beings.

We could, of course, distinguish between a weak and a strong thesis of dependency, for the nonrelativist can accept a certain degree of relativity in the way moral principles are *applied* in various cultures, depending on beliefs, history, and environment. For example, Jewish men express reverence for God by covering their

---

[4]Reported by the anthropologist Powers, *Tribes of California,* p. 178. Quoted in E. Westermarck, *Origin and Development of Moral Ideals* (London, 1906), p. 386. This work is a mine of examples of cultural diversity.
[5]W. G. Sumner, *Folkways* (Ginn & Co., 1906), p. 76.

heads when entering places of worship, whereas Christian men uncover their heads when entering places of worship. Westerners shake hands upon greeting each other, whereas Hindus place their hands together and point them toward the person to be greeted. Both sides adhere to principles of reverence and respect but apply them differently. But the ethical relativist must maintain a stronger thesis, one that insists that the moral principles themselves are products of the cultures and may vary from society to society. The ethical relativist contends that even beyond environmental factors and differences in beliefs, a fundamental disagreement exists among societies. One way for the relativist to support this thesis is by appealing to an indeterminacy of translation thesis, which maintains that there is a conceptual relativity among language groups so that we cannot even translate into our language the worldviews of a culture with a radically different language.

In a sense we all live in radically different worlds. But the relativist wants to go further and maintain that there is something conventional about *any* morality, so that every morality really depends on a level of social acceptance. Not only do various societies adhere to different moral systems, but the very same society could (and often does) change its moral views over place and time. For example, the majority of people in the southern United States now view slavery as immoral, whereas one hundred and forty years ago they did not. Our society's views on divorce, sexuality, abortion, and assisted suicide have changed somewhat as well—and they are still changing.

3. The conclusion that there are no absolute or objective moral standards binding on all people follows from the first two propositions. Combining cultural relativism (*the diversity thesis*) with *the dependency thesis* yields ethical relativism in its classic form. If there are different moral principles from culture to culture and if all morality is rooted in culture, then it follows that there are no universal moral principles that are valid (or true) for all cultures and peoples at all times.

2. Subjectivism

Some people think that this conclusion is still too tame, and they maintain that morality is dependent not on the society but rather on the individual. As my students sometimes maintain, "Morality is in the eye of the beholder." They treat morality like taste or aesthetic judgments—person relative. This form of moral subjectivism has the sorry consequence that it makes morality a very useless concept, for, on its premises, little or no interpersonal criticism or judgment is logically possible. Suppose that you are repulsed by observing John torturing a child. You cannot condemn him if one of his principles is "torture little children for the fun of it." The only basis for judging him wrong might be that he was a hypocrite who condemned others for torturing. But suppose that another of his principles is that hypocrisy is morally permissible (for him); thus we cannot condemn him for condemning others for doing what he does.

On the basis of subjectivism Adolf Hitler and the serial murderer Ted Bundy could be considered as moral as Gandhi, so long as each lived by his own standards, whatever those might be. Witness the following paraphrase of a tape-recorded conversation between Ted Bundy and one of his victims in which Bundy justifies his murder:

> Then I learned that all moral judgments are "value judgments," that all value judgments are subjective, and that none can be proved to be either 'right' or 'wrong.' I even read somewhere that the Chief Justice of the United States had written that the American Constitution expressed nothing more than collective value judgments. Believe it or not, I figured out for myself—what apparently the Chief Justice couldn't figure out for himself—that if the rationality of one value judgment was zero, multiplying it by millions would not make it one whit more rational. Nor is there any 'reason' to obey the law for anyone, like myself, who has the boldness and daring—the strength of character—to throw off its shackles. . . . I discovered that to become truly free, truly unfettered, I had to become truly uninhibited. And I quickly discovered that the greatest obstacle to my freedom, the greatest block and limitation to it, consists in the insupportable 'value judgment' that I was bound to respect the rights of others. I asked myself, who were these 'others'? Other human beings, with human rights? Why is it more wrong to kill a human animal than any other animal, a pig or a sheep or a steer? Is your life more to you than a hog's life to a hog? Why should I be willing to sacrifice my pleasure more for the one than for the other? Surely you would not, in this age of scientific enlightenment, declare that God or nature has marked some pleasures as 'moral' or 'good' and others as 'immoral' or 'bad'? In any case, let me assure you, my dear young lady, that there is absolutely no comparison between the pleasure I might take in eating ham and the pleasure I anticipate in raping and murdering you. That is the honest conclusion to which my education has led me—

after the most conscientious examination of my spontaneous and uninhibited self.[6]

Notions of good and bad, or right and wrong, cease to have interpersonal evaluative meaning. We might be revulsed by the views of Ted Bundy, but that is just a matter of taste. A student might not like it when her teacher gives her an F on a test paper, while he gives another student an A for a similar paper, but there is no way to criticize him for injustice, because justice is not one of his chosen principles.

Absurd consequences follow from subjectivism. If it is correct, then morality reduces to aesthetic tastes about which there can be neither argument nor interpersonal judgment. Although many students say they espouse subjectivism, there is evidence that it conflicts with other of their moral views. They typically condemn Hitler as an evil man for his genocidal policies. A contradiction seems to exist between subjectivism and the very concept of morality, which it is supposed to characterize, for morality has to do with *proper* resolution of interpersonal conflict and the amelioration of the human predicament (both deontological and teleological systems do this, but in different ways—see chapters 4 and 5 of Part II). Whatever else it does, morality has a minimal aim of preventing a Hobbesian state of nature (see chapter 1), wherein life is "solitary, poor, nasty, brutish, and short." But if so, subjectivism is no help at all, for it rests neither on social agreement of principle (as the conventionalist maintains) nor on an objectively independent set of norms that bind all people for the common good. If there were only one person on earth, there would be no occasion for morality, because there wouldn't be any interpersonal conflicts to resolve or others whose suffering he or she would have a duty to ameliorate. Subjectivism implicitly assumes something of this solipsism, an atomism in which isolated individuals make up separate universes.

Subjectivism treats individuals like billiard balls on a societal pool table where they meet only in radical collisions, each aimed at his or her own goal and striving to do in the others before they themselves are done in. This atomistic view of personality is belied by the facts that we develop in families and mutually dependent communities in which we share a common language, common institutions, and similar rituals and habits, and that we often feel one another's joys and

[6]This is a paraphrased and rewritten statement of Ted Bundy by Harry V. Jaffa, *Homosexuality and the Natural Law* (Claremont, CA: The Claremont Institute of the Study of Statesmanship and Political Philosophy, 1990), 3–4.

sorrows. As the poet John Donne wrote, "No man is an island, entire of itself; every man is a piece of the continent."

Radical individualistic ethical relativism is incoherent. If so, it follows that the only plausible view of ethical relativism must be one that grounds morality in the group or culture. This form is called *conventionalism*.

3. Conventionalism

Conventional ethical relativism, the view that there are no objective moral principles but that all valid moral principles are justified (or are made true) by virtue of their cultural acceptance, recognizes the social nature of morality. That is precisely its power and virtue. It does not seem subject to the same absurd consequences which plague subjectivism. Recognizing the importance of our social environment in generating customs and beliefs, many people suppose that ethical relativism is the correct metaethical theory. Furthermore, they are drawn to it for its liberal philosophical stance. It seems to be an enlightened response to the sin of ethnocentricity, and it seems to entail or strongly imply an attitude of tolerance toward other cultures. Anthropologist Ruth Benedict says, that in recognizing ethical relativity, "We shall arrive at a more realistic social faith, accepting as grounds of hope and as new bases for tolerance the coexisting and equally valid patterns of life which mankind has created for itself from the raw materials of existence."[7] The most famous of those holding this position is the anthropologist Melville Herskovits, who argues even more explicitly than Benedict that ethical relativism entails intercultural tolerance.

1. If morality is relative to its culture, then there is no independent basis for criticizing the morality of any other culture but one's own.
2. If there is no independent way of criticizing any other culture, we ought to be *tolerant* of the moralities of other cultures.
3. Morality is relative to its culture. Therefore,
4. We ought to be *tolerant* of the moralities of other cultures.[8]

Tolerance is certainly a virtue, but is this a good argument for it? I think not. If morality simply is relative to each culture, then if the

[7]Ruth Benedict, *Patterns of Culture* (New American Library, 1934), p. 257.
[8]Melville Herskovits, *Cultural Relativism* (Random House, 1972).

culture in question does not have a principle of tolerance, its members have no obligation to be tolerant. Herskovits seems to be treating the *principle of tolerance* as the one exception to his relativism. He seems to be treating it as an absolute moral principle. But from a relativistic point of view there is no more reason to be tolerant than to be intolerant and neither stance is objectively morally better than the other.

Not only do relativists fail to offer a basis for criticizing those who are intolerant, but they cannot rationally criticize anyone who espouses what they might regard as a heinous principle. If, as seems to be the case, valid criticism supposes an objective or impartial standard, relativists cannot morally criticize anyone outside their own culture. Adolf Hitler's genocidal actions, so long as they are culturally accepted, are as morally legitimate as Mother Teresa's works of mercy. If Conventional Relativism is accepted, racism, genocide of unpopular minorities, oppression of the poor, slavery, and even the advocacy of war for its own sake are as equally moral as their opposites. And if a subculture decided that starting a nuclear war was somehow morally acceptable, we could not morally criticize these people. Any actual morality, whatever its content, is as valid as every other, and more valid than ideal moralities—since the latter aren't adhered to by any culture.

There are other disturbing consequences of ethical relativism. It seems to entail that reformers are always (morally) wrong since they go against the tide of cultural standards. William Wilberforce was wrong in the eighteenth century to oppose slavery; the British were immoral in opposing *suttee* in India (the burning of widows, which is now illegal in India). The early Christians were wrong in refusing to serve in the Roman army or to bow down to Caesar, since the majority in the Roman Empire believed that these two acts were moral duties. In fact, Jesus himself was immoral in breaking the law of His day by healing on the Sabbath day and by advocating the principles of the Sermon on the Mount, since it is clear that few in His time (or in ours) accepted them.

Yet we normally feel just the opposite, that the reformer is a courageous innovator who is right, who has the truth, against the mindless majority. Sometimes the individual must stand alone with the truth, risking social censure and persecution. As Dr. Stockman says in Ibsen's *Enemy of the People,* after he loses the battle to declare his town's profitable but polluted tourist spa unsanitary, "The most dangerous enemy of the truth and freedom among us—is the compact majority. Yes, the damned, compact and liberal majority. The majority has *might*—unfortunately—but *right* it is not. Right—are I and a few others." Yet if relativism is correct, the opposite is necessarily the case. Truth is with the crowd and error with the individual.

Similarly, conventional ethical relativism entails disturbing judgments about the law. Our normal view is that we have a prima facie duty to obey the law, because law, in general, promotes the human good. According to most objective systems, this obligation is not absolute but relative to the particular law's relation to a wider moral order. Civil disobedience is warranted in some cases where the law seems to be in serious conflict with morality. However, if moral relativism is true, then neither law nor civil disobedience has a firm foundation. On the one hand, from the side of the society at large, civil disobedience will be morally wrong, so long as the majority culture agrees with the law in question. On the other hand, if you belong to the relevant subculture which doesn't recognize the particular law in question (because it is unjust from your point of view), disobedience will be morally mandated. The Ku Klux Klan, which believes that Jews, Catholics and Blacks are evil or undeserving of high regard, are, given conventionalism, morally permitted or required to break the laws which protect these endangered groups. Why should I obey a law that my group doesn't recognize as valid?

To sum up, unless we have an independent moral basis for law, it is hard to see why we have any general duty to obey it; and unless we recognize the priority of a universal moral law, we have no firm basis to justify our acts of civil disobedience against "unjust laws." Both the validity of law and morally motivated disobedience of unjust laws are annulled in favor of a power struggle.

There is an even more basic problem with the notion that morality is dependent on cultural acceptance for its validity. The problem is that the notion of a *culture* or *society* is notoriously difficult to define. This is especially so in a pluralistic society like our own where the notion seems to be vague with unclear boundary lines. One person may belong to several societies (subcultures) with different value emphases and arrangements of principles. A person may belong to the nation as a single society with certain values of patriotism, honor, courage, laws (including some which are controversial but have majority acceptance, such as the current law on abortion). But he or she may also belong to a church which opposes some of the laws of the State. He may also be an integral member of a socially mixed community where different principles hold sway, and he may belong to clubs and a family where still other rules are adhered to. Relativism would seem to tell us that where he is a member of societies with conflicting moralities he must be judged both wrong and not-wrong whatever he does. For example, if Mary is a U.S. citizen and a member of the Roman Catholic Church, she is wrong (qua Catholic) if she chooses to have an abortion and not-wrong (qua citizen of the U.S.A.) if she acts against the teaching of the Church on abortion. As a member of a racist university fraternity, KKK, John has no obligation to treat his fellow Black student as an equal, but as a member of the university community itself (where the principle of equal rights is accepted) he does have the obligation; but as a member of the surrounding community (which may reject the principle of equal rights) he again has no such obligation; but then again as a member of the nation at large (which accepts the principle) he is obligated to treat his fellow with respect. What is the morally right thing for John to do? The question no longer makes much sense in this moral Babel. It has lost its action-guiding function.

Perhaps the relativist would adhere to a principle which says that in such cases the individual may choose which group to belong to as primary. If Mary chooses to have an abortion, she is choosing to belong to the general society relative to that principle. And John must likewise choose among groups. The trouble with this option is that it seems to lead back to counter-intuitive results. If Murder Mike of Murder, Incorporated, feels like killing Bank President Ortcutt and wants to feel good about it, he identifies with the Murder, Incorporated society rather than the general public morality. Does this justify the killing? In fact, couldn't one justify anything simply by forming a small subculture that approved of it? Ted Bundy would be morally pure in raping and killing innocents simply by virtue of forming a little coterie. How large must the group be in order to be a legitimate subculture or society? Does it need ten or fifteen people? How about just three? Come to think about it, why can't my burglary partner and I found our own society with a morality of its own? Of course, if my partner dies, I could still claim that I was acting from an originally social set of norms. But why can't I dispense with the interpersonal agreements altogether and invent my own morality—since morality, on this view, is only an invention anyway? Conventionalist relativism seems to reduce to subjectivism. And subjectivism leads, as we have seen, to moral solipsism, to the demise of morality altogether.

Should one object that this is an instance of the *Slippery Slope Fal-*

lacy,[9] let that person give an alternative analysis of what constitutes a viable social basis for generating valid (or true) moral principles. Perhaps we might agree (for the sake of argument, at least) that the very nature of morality entails two people making an agreement. This move saves the conventionalist from moral solipsism, but it still permits almost any principle at all to count as moral. And what's more, those principles can be thrown out and their contraries substituted for them as the need arises. If two or three people decide that they will make cheating on exams morally acceptable for themselves, via forming a fraternity "Cheaters Anonymous" at their university, then cheating becomes moral. Why not? Why not rape, as well?

However, I don't think you can stop the move from conventionalism to subjectivism. The essential force of the validity of the chosen moral principle is that it is dependent on *choice*. The conventionalist holds that it is the choice of the group, but why should I accept the group's silly choice, when my own is better (for me)? Why should anyone give such august authority to a culture of society? If this is all morality comes to, why not reject it altogether—even though one might want to adhere to its directives when others are looking in order to escape sanctions?

4. A Critique of Ethical Relativism

However, while we may fear the demise of morality, as we have known it, this in itself may not be a good reason for rejecting relativism. That is, for judging it false. Alas, truth may not always be edifying. But the consequences of this position are sufficiently alarming to prompt us to look carefully for some weakness in the relativist's argument. So let us examine the premises and conclusion listed at the beginning of this essay as the three theses of relativism.

1. *The Diversity Thesis.* What is considered morally right and wrong varies from society to society, so that there are no moral principles accepted by all societies.
2. *The Dependency Thesis.* All moral principles derive their validity from cultural acceptance.

---

[9]The fallacy of objecting to a proposition on the erroneous grounds that, if accepted, it will lead to a chain of states of affairs which are absurd or unacceptable.

3. *Ethical Relativism.* Therefore, there are no universally valid moral principles, objective standards which apply to all people everywhere and at all times.

Does any one of these seem problematic? Let us consider the first thesis, the diversity thesis, which we have also called cultural relativism. Perhaps there is not as much diversity as anthropologists like Sumner and Benedict suppose. One can also see great similarities between the moral codes of various cultures. E. O. Wilson has identified over a score of common features,[10] and before him Clyde Kluckhohn has noted much significant common ground between cultures.

> Every culture has a concept of murder, distinguishing this from execution, killing in war, and other "justifiable homicides." The notions of incest and other regulations upon sexual behavior, the prohibitions upon untruth under defined circumstances, of restitution and reciprocity, of mutual obligations between parents and children— these and many other moral concepts are altogether universal.[11]

Colin Turnbull's description of the sadistic, semidisplaced, disintegrating Ik in Northern Uganda supports the view that a people without principles of kindness, loyalty, and cooperation will degenerate into a Hobbesian state of nature.[12] But he has also produced evidence that underneath the surface of this dying society, there is a deeper moral code from a time when the tribe flourished, which occasionally surfaces and shows its nobler face.

On the other hand, there is enormous cultural diversity and many societies have radically different moral codes. Cultural relativism seems to be a fact, but, even if it is, it does not by itself establish the truth of ethical relativism. Cultural diversity in itself is neutral between theories. For the objectivist could concede complete cultural relativism, but still defend a form of universalism; for he or she could argue that some cultures simply lack correct moral principles.

On the other hand, a denial of complete cultural relativism (i.e., an admission of some universal principles) does not disprove ethical relativism. For even if we did find one or more universal principles, this would not prove that they had any objective status. We

---

[10]E. O. Wilson, *On Human Nature* (Bantam Books, 1979), pp. 22–23.
[11]Clyde Kluckhohn, "Ethical Relativity: Sic et Non," *Journal of Philosophy,* LII (1955).
[12]Colin Turnbull, *The Mountain People* (New York: Simon & Schuster, 1972).

could still *imagine* a culture that was an exception to the rule and be unable to criticize it. So the first premise doesn't by itself imply ethical relativism and its denial doesn't disprove ethical relativism.

We turn to the crucial second thesis, the dependency thesis. Morality does not occur in a vacuum, but rather what is considered morally right or wrong must be seen in a context, depending on the goals, wants, beliefs, history, and environment of the society in question. We distinguished a *weak* and a *strong* thesis of dependency. The weak thesis says that the application of principles depends on the particular cultural predicament, whereas the strong thesis affirms that the principles themselves depend on that predicament. The nonrelativist can accept a certain relativity in the way moral principles are *applied* in various cultures, depending on beliefs, history, and environment. For example, a raw environment with scarce natural resources may justify the Eskimos' brand of euthanasia to the objectivist, who in another environment would consistently reject that practice. The members of a tribe in the Sudan throw their deformed children into the river because of their belief that such infants *belong* to the hippopotamus, the god of the river. We believe that they have a false belief about this, but the point is that the same principles of respect for property and respect for human life are operative in these contrary practices. They differ with us only in belief, not in substantive moral principle. This is an illustration of how nonmoral beliefs (e.g., deformed children belong to the hippopotamus) when applied to common moral principles (e.g., give to each his due) generate different actions in different cultures. In our own culture the difference in the nonmoral belief about the status of a fetus generates opposite moral prescriptions. The major difference between pro-choicers and pro-lifers is not whether we should kill persons but whether fetuses are really persons. It is a debate about the facts of the matter, not the principle of killing innocent persons.

So the fact that moral principles are weakly dependent doesn't show that ethical relativism is valid. In spite of this weak dependency on nonmoral factors, there could still be a set of general moral norms applicable to all cultures and even recognized in most, which are disregarded at a culture's own expense.

What the relativist needs is a strong thesis of dependency, that somehow all principles are essentially cultural inventions. But why should we choose to view morality this way? Is there anything to recommend the strong thesis over the weak thesis of dependency? The relativist may argue that in fact we don't have an obvious impartial standard from which to judge. "Who's to say which culture is right and which is wrong?" But this seems to be dubious. We can reason and perform thought experiments in order to make a case for one system over another. We may not be able to *know* with certainty that our moral beliefs are closer to the truth than those of another culture or those of others within our own culture, but we may be *justified* in believing that they are. If we can be closer to the truth regarding factual or scientific matters, why can't we be closer to the truth on moral matters? Why can't a culture be simply confused or wrong about its moral perceptions? Why can't we say that the society like the Ik which sees nothing wrong with enjoying watching its own children fall into fires is less moral in that regard than the culture that cherishes children and grants them protection and equal rights? To take such a stand is not to commit the fallacy of ethnocentricism, for we are seeking to derive principles through critical reason, not simply uncritical acceptance of one's own mores.

Many relativists embrace relativism as a default position. Objectivism makes no sense to them. I think this is Ladd and Harman's position, as the latter's quotation at the beginning of this article seems to indicate. Objectivism has insuperable problems, so the answer must be relativism. The only positive argument I know for the strong dependency thesis upon which ethical relativism rests is that of the indeterminacy of translation thesis. This theory, set forth by B. L. Whorf and W. V. Quine,[13] holds that languages are often so fundamentally different from one another that we cannot accurately translate concepts from one to another. But this thesis, while relatively true even within a language (each of us has an idiolect), seems falsified by experience. We do learn foreign languages and learn to translate across linguistic frameworks. For example, people from a myriad of language groups come to the United States and learn English and communicate perfectly well. Rather than a complete hiatus, the interplay between these other cultures eventually enriches the English language with new concepts (for example, *forte/foible, taboo,* and *coup de grâce*), even as English has enriched (or "corrupted" as the French might argue) other languages. Even if it turns out that there is some indeterminacy of translation between language users,

[13]See Benjamin Whorf, *Language, Thought and Reality* (MIT Press, 1956); and W. V. Quine, *Word and Object* (MIT Press, 1960), and *Ontological Relativity* (Columbia University Press, 1969).

we should not infer from this that no translation or communication is possible. It seems reasonable to believe that general moral principles are precisely those things that can be communicated transculturally. The kind of common features that Kluckhohn and Wilson advance—duties of restitution and reciprocity, regulations on sexual behavior, obligations of parents to children, a no-unnecessary-harm principle, and a sense that the good should flourish and the guilty be punished—these and others constitute a common human experience, a common set of values within a common human predicament of struggling to survive and flourish in a world of scarce resources.[14] So it is possible to communicate cross-culturally and find that we agree on many of the important things in life. If this is so, then the indeterminacy of translation thesis, upon which relativism rests, must itself be relativized to the point where it is no objection to objective morality.

5. *The Case for Moral Objectivism*

If nonrelativists are to make their case, they will have to offer a better explanation of cultural diversity and why we should nevertheless adhere to moral objectivism. One way of doing this is to appeal to a divine law, and human sin, which causes deviation from that law. Although I think that human greed, selfishness, pride, self-deception and other maladies have a great deal to do with moral differences and that religion may lend great support to morality, I don't think that a religious justification is necessary for the

---

[14]David Hume gave the classic expression to this idea of a common human nature when he wrote:

> It is universally acknowledged that there is a great uniformity among the actions of men, in all nations and ages, and that human nature remains still the same, in its principles and operations. The same events follow from the same causes. Ambition, avarice, self-love, vanity, friendship, generosity, public spirit; these passions, mixed in various degrees, and distributed through society, have been, from the beginning of the world, and still are, the source of all the actions and enterprises which have ever been observed among mankind. Would you know the sentiments, inclinations, and course of life of the Greeks and Romans? Study well the temper and actions of the French and English: you cannot be much mistaken in transferring to the former most of the observations which you have made with regard to the latter. Mankind are so much the same, in all times and places, that history informs us of nothing new or strange in that particular. Its chief use is only to discover the constant and uni-

validity of moral principles. In any case, in this section I shall outline a modest nonreligious objectivism, first by appealing to our
intuitions and secondly by giving a naturalist account of morality
that transcends individual cultures.

First, I must make it clear that I am distinguishing moral *absolutism* from moral *objectivism*. The absolutist believes that there are
nonoverrideable moral principles which ought never to be violated.
Kant's system, or one version of it, is a good example. One ought
never to break a promise, no matter what. Act utilitarianism also
seems absolutist, for the principle, Do that act that has the most
promise of yielding the most utility, is nonoverrideable. An objectivist need not posit any nonoverrideable principles, at least not in
unqualified general form, and so need not be an absolutist. As Ren-
ford Bambrough put it,

> To suggest that there is a *right* answer to a moral problem is at once
> to be accused of or credited with a belief in moral absolutes. But it
> is no more necessary to believe in moral absolutes in order to believe
> in moral objectivity than it is to believe in the existence of absolute
> space or absolute time in order to believe in the objectivity of tem-
> poral and spatial relations and of judgments about them.[15]

On the objectivist's account moral principles are what William
Ross refers to as *prima facie* principles, valid rules of action which
should generally be adhered to, but which may be overridden by
another moral principle in cases of moral conflict. For example,

---

versal principles of human nature, by showing men in all varieties of
circumstances and situations, and furnishing us with materials, from
which we may form our observations, and become acquainted with the
regular springs of human action and behavior. These records of wars,
intrigues, factions, and revolutions, are so many collections of experiments by which the politician or moral philosopher fixes the principles
of his science; in the same manner as the physician or natural philosopher becomes acquainted with the nature of plants, minerals, and other
external objects, by the experiments which he forms concerning them.
Nor are the earth, water, and other elements examined by Aristotle and
Hippocrates more like to those which at present lie under our observation than the men described by Polybius and Tacitus are to those who
now govern the world. *Essays, Moral, Political and Literary* (Longman,
Green, 1875).

[15]Renford Bambrough, *Moral Skepticism and Moral Knowledge* (London: Routledge & Kegan Paul, 1979), p. 33.

while a principle of justice may generally outweigh a principle of benevolence, there are times when enormous good could be done by sacrificing a small amount of justice, so that an objectivist would be inclined to act according to the principle of benevolence. There may be some absolute or nonoverrideable principles, but there need not be many or any for objectivism to be true.[16]

If we can establish or show that it is reasonable to believe that there is at least one objective moral principle which is binding on all people everywhere in some ideal sense, we shall have shown that relativism is probably false and that a limited objectivism is true. Actually, I believe that there are many qualified general ethical principles which are binding on all rational beings, but one will suffice to refute relativism. The principle I've chosen is the following:

A. It is morally wrong to torture people for the fun of it.

I claim that this principle is binding on all rational agents, so that if some agent, S, rejects A, we should not let that affect our intuition that A is a true principle but rather try to explain S's behavior as perverse, ignorant, or irrational instead. For example, suppose Adolf Hitler doesn't accept A. Should that affect our confidence in the truth of A? Is it not more reasonable to infer that Adolf is morally deficient, morally blind, ignorant, or irrational than to suppose that his noncompliance is evidence against the truth of A?

Suppose further that there is a tribe of Hitlerites somewhere who enjoy torturing people. The whole culture accepts torturing others for the fun of it. Suppose that Mother Teresa or Gandhi tries unsuccessfully to convince them that they should stop torturing people altogether, and they respond by torturing the reformers. Should this affect our confidence in A? Would it not be more reasonable to look for some explanation of Hitlerite behavior? For example, we might hypothesize that this tribe lacked a developed sense of sympathetic imagination which is necessary for the moral life. Or we might theorize that this tribe was on a lower evolutionary level than most *Homo sapiens*. Or we might simply conclude that the tribe was closer to a Hobbesian state of nature than most societies, and as such probably would not survive. But we need not know the correct answer as to why the tribe was in such bad shape in order to maintain our confidence in A as a moral principle. If A is a basic or core belief for

---

[16]William Ross, *The Right and the Good* (Oxford University Press, 1930), p. 18f.

us, we will be more likely to doubt the Hitlerites' sanity or ability to think morally than to doubt the validity of A.

We can perhaps produce other candidates for membership in our minimally basic objective moral set. For example:

1. Do not kill innocent people.
2. Do not cause unnecessary pain or suffering.
3. Do not cheat or steal.
4. Keep your promises and honor your contracts.
5. Do not deprive another person of his or her freedom.
6. Do justice, treating equals equally and unequals unequally.
7. Tell the truth.
8. Help other people, at least when the cost to oneself is minimal.
9. Reciprocate (show gratitude for services rendered).
10. Obey just laws.

These ten principles are examples of the *core morality,* principles necessary for the good life. They are not arbitrary, for we can give reasons why they are necessary to social cohesion and human flourishing. Principles like the Golden Rule, not killing innocent people, treating equals equally, truth telling, promise keeping, and the like are central to the fluid progression of social interaction and the resolution of conflicts of which ethics are about (at least minimal morality is, even though there may be more to morality than simply these kinds of concerns). For example, language itself depends on a general and implicit commitment to the principle of truth telling. Accuracy of expression is a primitive form of truthfulness. Hence, every time we use words correctly we are telling the truth. Without this behavior, language wouldn't be possible. Likewise, without the recognition of a rule of promise keeping, contracts are of no avail and cooperation is less likely to occur. And without the protection of life and liberty, we could not secure our other goals.

A moral code or theory would be adequate if it contained a requisite set of these objective principles or the core morality, but there could be more than one adequate moral code or theory which contained different rankings of these principles and other principles consistent with *core morality*. That is, there may be a certain relativity to secondary principles (whether to opt for monogamy rather than polygamy, whether to include a principle of high altruism in the set of moral duties, whether to allocate more resources to medical care than to environmental concerns, whether to institute a law to drive on the left side of the road or the right side of the road, and so forth), but in every morality a certain core will remain, though applied somewhat differently because of differences in environment, belief, tradition, and the like.

The core moral rules are analogous to the set of vitamins necessary for a healthy diet. We need an adequate amount of each vitamin—some humans more of one than another—but in prescribing a nutritional diet we don't have to set forth recipes, specific foods, place settings, or culinary habits. Gourmets will meet the requirements differently than ascetics and vegetarians, but the basic nutrients may be had by all without rigid regimentation or an absolute set of recipes.

Stated more positively, an objectivist who bases his or her moral system on a common human nature with common needs and desires might argue for objectivism somewhat in this manner:

1. Human nature is relatively similar in essential respects, having a common set of needs and interests.
2. Moral principles are functions of human needs and interests, instituted by reason in order to promote the most significant interests and needs of rational beings (and perhaps others).
3. Some moral principles will promote human interests and meet human needs better than others.
4. Those principles which will meet essential needs and promote the most significant interests of humans in optimal ways can be said to be objectively valid moral principles.
5. Therefore, since there is a common human nature, there is an objectively valid set of moral principles, applicable to all humanity.

This argument assumes that there is a common human nature. In a sense, I accept a *strong dependency thesis*—morality *depends* on human nature and the needs and interests of humans in general, but not on any specific cultural choice. There is only one large human framework to which moral principles are relative.[17] I have

[17]In his essay "Moral Relativism" in *Moral Relativism and Moral Objectivity* (Blackwell, 1996) by Gilbert Harman and Judith Jarvis Thomson, Harman defines moral relativism as the claim that "There is no single true

considered the evidence for this claim toward the end of Section 4, but the relativist may object. I cannot defend it any further in this paper, but suppose we content ourselves with a less controversial first premise, stating that some principles will tend to promote the most significant interests of persons. The revised argument would go like this:

1. Objectively valid moral principles are those adherence to which meets the needs and promotes the most significant interests of persons.
2. Some principles are such that adherence to them meets the needs and promotes the most significant interests of persons.
3. Therefore, there are some objectively valid moral principles.

Either argument would satisfy objectivism, but the former makes it clearer that it is our common human nature that generates the common principles.[18] However, as I mentioned, some philosophers might not like to be tied down to the concept of a common human nature, in which case the second version of the argument may be used. It has the advantage that even if it turned out that we did have somewhat different natures or that other creatures in the universe had somewhat different natures, some of the basic moral principles would still survive.

If this argument succeeds, there are ideal moralities (and not simply adequate ones). Of course, there could still be more than one ideal morality, from which presumably an ideal observer would choose under optimal conditions. The ideal observer may conclude that out of an infinite set of moralities two, three, or more combinations would tie for first place. One would expect that these would

---

morality. There are many different moral frameworks, none of which is more correct than the others." (p. 5) I hold that morality has a function of serving the needs and interests of human beings, so that some frameworks do this better than others. Essentially, all adequate theories will contain the principles I have identified in this essay.

[18]I owe the reformulation of the argument to Bruce Russell. Edward Sherline has objected (in correspondence) that assuming a common human nature in the first argument begs the question against the relativist. You may be the judge.

be similar, but there is every reason to believe that all of these would contain the set of core principles.

Of course, we don't know what an ideal observer would choose, but we can imagine that the conditions under which such an observer would choose would be conditions of maximal knowledge about the consequences of action-types and impartiality, second-order qualities which ensure that agents have the best chance of making the best decisions. If this is so, then the more we learn to judge impartially and the more we know about possible forms of life, the better chance we have to approximate an ideal moral system. And if there is the possibility of approximating ideal moral systems with an objective core and other objective components, then ethical relativism is certainly false. We can confidently dismiss it as an aberration and get on with the job of working out better moral systems.

Let me make the same point by appealing to your intuitions in another way. Imagine that you have been miraculously transported to the dark kingdom of hell, and there you get a glimpse of the sufferings of the damned. What is their punishment? Well, they have eternal back itches which ebb and flow constantly. But they cannot scratch their backs, for their arms are paralyzed in a frontal position, so they writhe with itchiness throughout eternity. But just as you are beginning to feel the itch in your own back, you are suddenly transported to heaven. What do you see in the kingdom of the blessed? Well, you see people with eternal back itches, who cannot scratch their own backs. But they are all smiling instead of writhing. Why? Because everyone has his or her arms stretched out to scratch someone else's back, and, so arranged in one big circle, a hell is turned into a heaven of ecstasy.

If we can imagine some states of affairs or cultures that are better than others in a way that depends on human action, we can ask what are those character traits that make them so. In our story people in heaven, but not in hell, cooperate for the amelioration of suffering and the production of pleasure. These are very primitive goods, not sufficient for a full-blown morality, but they give us a hint as to the objectivity of morality. Moral goodness has something to do with the ameliorating of suffering, the resolution of conflict, and the promotion of human flourishing. If our heaven is really better than the eternal itchiness of hell, then whatever makes it so is constitutively related to moral rightness.

6. An Explanation of the Attraction
of Ethical Relativism

Why, then, is there such a strong inclination toward ethical relativism? I think that there are four reasons, which haven't been adequately emphasized. One is the fact that the options are usually
presented as though absolutism and relativism were the only alternatives, so conventionalism wins out against an implausible com-
petitor. At the beginning of this paper I referred to a student questionnaire that I have been giving for twenty years. It reads as follows:
"Are there any ethical absolutes, moral duties binding on all persons at all times, or are moral duties relative to culture? Is there
any alternative to these two positions?" Fewer than five percent suggest a third position and very few of them identify objectivism.
Granted, it takes a little philosophical sophistication to make the
crucial distinctions, and it is precisely for lack of this sophistication
or reflection that relativism has procured its enormous prestige. But,
as Ross and others have shown and as I have argued in this paper,
one can have an objective morality without being absolutist.

The second reason for an inclination toward ethical relativism is
the confusion of moral objectivism with moral realism. A realist is
a person who holds that moral values have independent existence,
if only as emergent properties. The anti-realist claims that they do
not have independent existence. But objectivism is compatible with
either of these views. All it calls for is deep intersubjective agreement among humans because of a common nature and common
goals and needs.

An example of a philosopher who confuses objectivity with realism is the late J. L. Mackie, who rejects objectivism because there
are no good arguments for the independent existence of moral values. He admits, however, that there is a great deal of intersubjectivity in ethics. "There could be agreement in valuing even if valuing is just something people do, even if this activity is not further
validated. Subjective agreement would give intersubjective values,
but intersubjectivity is not objectivity."[19] But Mackie fails to note
that there are two kinds of intersubjectivity, and that one of them
gives all that the objectivist wants for a moral theory. Consider the
following situations of intersubjective agreement:

---

[19]J. L. Mackie, *Ethics: Inventing Right and Wrong* (Penguin, 1977), p. 22.

Set A

A1. All the children in first grade at School S would agree that playing in the mud is preferable to learning arithmetic.

A2. All the youth in the district would rather take drugs than go to school.

A3. All the people in Jonestown, British Guiana, agree that the Rev. Jones is a prophet from God, and they love him dearly.

A4. Almost all the people in community C voted for George Bush.

Set B

B1. All the thirsty desire water to quench their thirst.

B2. All humans (and animals) prefer pleasure to pain.

B3. Almost all people agree that living in society is more satisfying than living as hermits alone.

The naturalist contrasts these two sets of intersubjective agreements and says that the first set is accidental, not part of what it means to be a person, whereas the agreements in the second set are basic to being a person, basic to our nature. Agreement on the essence of morality, the core set, is the kind of intersubjective agreement more like the second kind, not the first. It is part of the essence of a human in community, part of what it means to flourish as a person, to agree and adhere to the moral code.

The third reason is that our recent sensitivity to cultural relativism and the evils of ethnocentricism, which have plagued the relations of Europeans and Americans with those of other cultures, has made us conscious of the frailty of many aspects of our moral repertoire, so that there is a tendency to wonder "Who's to judge what's really right or wrong?" However, the move from a reasonable cultural relativism, which rightly causes us to rethink our moral systems, to an ethical relativism, which causes us to give up the heart of morality altogether, is an instance of the fallacy of confusing factual or descriptive statements with normative ones. Cultural relativism doesn't entail ethical relativism. The very reason that we are against ethnocentricism constitutes the same basis for our being for an objective moral system: that impartial reason draws us to it.

We may well agree that cultures differ and that we ought to be cautious in condemning what we don't understand, but this in no way need imply that there are not better and worse ways of living.

We can understand and excuse, to some degree at least, those who differ from our best notions of morality, without abdicating the notion that cultures without principles of justice or promise keeping or protection of the innocent are morally poorer for these omissions.

A fourth reason, which has driven some to moral nihilism and others to relativism, is the decline of religion in Western society. As one of Dostoevsky's characters has said, "If God is dead, all things are permitted." The person who has lost religious faith feels a deep vacuum and understandably confuses it with a moral vacuum, or he or she finally resigns to a form of secular conventionalism. Such people reason that if there is no God to guarantee the validity of the moral order, there must not be a universal moral order. There is just radical cultural diversity and death at the end. But even if there turns out to be no God and no immortality, we still will want to live happy, meaningful lives during our fourscore years on earth. If this is true, then it matters by which principles we live, and those which win out in the test of time will be objectively valid principles.

In conclusion I have argued (1) that cultural relativism (the fact that there are cultural differences regarding moral principles) does not entail ethical relativism (the thesis that there are no objectively valid universal moral principles); (2) that the dependency thesis (that morality derives its legitimacy from individual cultural acceptance) is mistaken; and (3) that there are universal moral principles based on a common human nature and a need to solve conflicts of interest and flourish.

So "Who's to judge what's right or wrong?" We are. We are to do so on the basis of the best reasoning we can bring forth, and with sympathy and understanding.[20]

For Further Reflection

1. Is Pojman correct in thinking most American students tend to be moral relativists? If he is, why is this? What is the attraction of relativism? If he's not correct, explain your answer.

2. Explain the difference between subjective ethical relativism and conventionalism.

[20]Bruce Russell, Morton Winston, Edward Sherline, and an anonymous reviewer made important criticisms on earlier versions of this article, issuing in this revision.

3. Sometimes people argue that since there are no universal moral truths, each culture's morality is as good as every other, so we ought not to interfere in its practices. Assess this argument.

4. Does moral relativism have a bad effect on society? Reread the tape-recorded conversation between serial murderer Ted Bundy and one of his victims (pages 171–172) in which Bundy attempts to justify the murder of his victim on the basis of the idea that all moral values are subjective. Analyze Bundy's discussion. How would the relativist respond to Bundy's claim that relativism justifies rape and murder? What do you think? Why?

Judge Not?

JEAN BETHKE ELSHTAIN

Jean Bethke Elshtain, who was born in Germany, is Laura Spelman Rockefeller professor of social and political ethics at the University of Chicago. She is the author of several works in social ethics, including *Democracy on Trial*. In this essay she examines the platitude that we should not judge other people and gives reasons for thinking that we are not only permitted to make moral judgments but have an obligation to do so.

We are a society awash in exculpatory strategies. We've devised lots of fascinating ways to let ourselves or others off the hook: all one need do is think of recent, well-publicized trials to appreciate the truth of this. We Americans are at present being bombarded with sensationalistic tales of victimization and equally sensationalistic proclamations of immunity from responsibility. Alternately

Reprinted from Jean Bethke Elshtain, "Judge Not?" *First Things* (October 1994) with permission of the Institute on Religion & Public Life, New York, N.Y.

bemused and troubled by the Oprah Winfreyization of American life, I sometimes think of my grandmother.

Dear Grandma (may she rest in peace) knew how to judge. She was tough as nails on people she found despicable or merely wanting. She chewed them out in her low German dialect (being a Volga German, *hochdeutsch* was not her tongue), and we grandchildren could figure out a thing or two. We knew when she was describing someone as "swinish" or "dirty," these being ways to characterize those who stole from others, beat their wives or their livestock, or abused their children. (Women, of course, could be abusers, too.) We missed a good bit of her assessments, though, as it was the policy of my grandmother, my mother, and Aunts Mary and Martha not to teach us *plattdeutsch*. When Grandma was really on a roll and wanted nothing less than to condemn someone to perdition, her favorite judging word was "Russki." Hearing it sent a frisson through our tender flesh and bones. The last time I heard her say this I was forty-three or forty-four years old and it still frightened me, not quite out of my wits, but I remained convinced, as I had been since the age of five or six when I had acquired some inkling of what was at stake, that that person was doomed, no two ways about it.

"Russki" was her shorthand judgment on the garden-variety cheat, the ordinary bum, the farmer who shortchanged his hired hands, or the mother who kept her kids in dirty clothes, let their noses run, and never washed their hair. Why "Russki" as a term of judgment? That was historic overdetermination. It was the Russians who had begun to undermine the historic immunities of the Volga German communities. Under Tsar Nicholas, on the throne when my grandparents' families emigrated to the New Country from what my grandmother always called the Old Country, their sons were being drafted into the Russian Army; and they were so fearful that they hid their Bibles (Luther's German translation) in secret places.

I suppose my grandmother would be a good candidate for sensitivity training. She is beyond the reach of the enthusiasts of pop psychology with its quivering "non-judgmentalism," having died at the age of ninety-four two years ago, but it gives me a shiver of another sort (one of delight) to imagine a confrontation between Grandma and a "facilitator," eyes agleam with programmed goodness, saying things like, "Now, Mrs. Lind, *why* do you feel that way?" Or: "Don't you think that's a little harsh? Have you considered how hurtful such words can be?" Probably the facilitator would want to take a good look at my mother, and, in addition to Aunts Mary and Martha, Uncle

Bill and Uncle Ted, too, no doubt damaged beyond repair, having been reared by such a no-nonsense judger. Good luck! I doubt they would have the slightest inkling of what she was going on about. There was no room in the family idiom for evasions of responsibility and you would find yourself the subject of an assessment of a rather decisive sort if you tried one.

No doubt from time to time my grandmother and her children rushed to judgment. I know my sisters and brothers and I sometimes wished Mom wouldn't embarrass us in public by being so, well, *decisive* in her assessment of things—more than once delivered up in front of those being assessed, too. I recall wanting to seek the nearest exit on more than one occasion. But then I thought, even at the time, better this than someone agreeable and eternally smiling, like my nemesis, the mother of Judy Belcher (not her real name), who was a "pal" to her daughter. They "talked about everything," especially "boyfriends" and "fashion," and they liked to "have fun together." I found this pretty disgusting. I still do. Judging seems to run in the family.

But to say this is not to say much. For what is at stake is the capacity to make judgments as an ethical issue of the gravest sort, and along with it, the discernment of what it means to judge well. In other words, we need a clear sense of why judging is important and what is involved in the activity of judging, and we need a way to distinguish between rash judging—not judging well—and the kind of judging that lies at the heart of what it means to be a self-respecting human subject in a community of other equally self-respecting subjects.

Judging has been in bad odor for quite some time in American culture. It is equated with being punitive, or with insensitivity, or with various "phobias" and "isms." It is the mark of antiquated ways of thinking, feeling, and willing. Better, no doubt, to be something called "open-minded," a trait thought to be characteristic of sensitive and supportive persons. A young woman well known to me reports that she and her fellow teachers at one of the elite New York public high schools were enjoined not to make students "feel bad" by being too decisive in their assessments of student work and effort. I breathed a sigh of recognition when she told me this; it is the sort of thing one hears in the higher reaches of the academy, too. In fact, this attitude is everywhere, even on bumper stickers. At least some of the readers of this essay will have sighted a bumper sticker that reads: "A Mind Is Like a Parachute. It Works Best When It Is Open."

Yes, indeed, one wants to counter, the more open—meaning the more porous and thin—the better. A rather more convenient way of being in the world than being called upon to discriminate in the old—best—sense of the word. An open mind of the sort celebrated by the bumper sticker may signify an empty head, a person incapable of those acts of discernment we call "judging," one who is, in fact, driven to see in such acts mere prejudice.

But prejudice and judgment are two very different human possibilities; indeed, the more we proliferate prejudices, free from the scrutiny of that discernment we aim to evade, the less capable we are, over time, of making judgments. An example or two, in line with Kant's insistence that "Examples are the go-cart of judgments," may suffice. When I first began university teaching, in 1973, I taught a course called "Feminist Politics and Theory." I taught it for several years until I decided the tumult was too much to put up with semester after semester. One problem I encountered went like this. I had designed the course as a sustained exercise in assessing, and critically contrasting, competing feminist accounts of culture and politics. I asked my students to engage certain questions that presupposed their capacity for judgment: What sort of picture of the human condition is presented by this theorist? Could her prescription for change be implemented? How? What would the world look like if it were? And so on. But I ran into trouble straight-off for, in the eyes of many of my students, what I was supposed to be doing was condemning that big booming abstraction, Patriarchy, for fifty minutes three times a week. I was supposed to embrace, not criticize, feminist doctrines—all of them—even though the ideas of the radical separatist feminists scarcely comported with those of liberal feminists on many issues. Needless to say, the Marxist feminists and the eco-feminists didn't see eye-to-eye on lots of things either.

Students sometimes showed up in my office bereft and troubled. One told me she had been a feminist since she was fourteen and didn't need to hear feminism criticized. Another told me she was so "upset" by my criticism of the text of a feminist who proposed test-tube reproduction and a world run by beneficent cyber-engineers, and so "shocked" at my insistence that she respond to a series of questions asking her to sift, discriminate, and assess this text and others, that she had complained to, and sought refuge in, a support group at the women's center. Yet another refused to write a paper contrasting Freud's essays on female development with what the psychoanalytic feminists were doing with Freud because

"Freud was a cancer-ridden, cigar-smoking misogynist." This expression of prejudice was not an authentic moment of judging, of course, not least because the student had refused to read the assigned texts. She was repeating a prejudice, not forming a judgment.

A teacher quickly wearies of this sort of thing because it undermines the presuppositions that guide and help to constitute the pedagogical enterprise, one of the most important of these suppositions being that students are capable of weighing alternatives with a generosity of spirit and quality of discernment that makes their subsequent judgments at least plausible if not unassailable. I have always been fond of a pithy sentence in a letter Freud wrote to his fiancee, Martha: "A human being must be able to pull himself together to form a judgment, otherwise he turns into what we Viennese call a *guten Potschen* [doormat]." Apart from being stepped on, what is the problem with persons as doormats? Precisely this: they have sloughed off that which is theirs to do—to enter a community of judging, meaning that one can see error and try to put it right, one can distinguish the more from the less important, one can appropriately name phenomena and act accordingly. As an example of the latter, think of the distinction to be marked between "misfortune" and an "injustice" and what we are enjoined to do whether we confront one or the other. Now Freud was not urging Martha to be cruel or incapable of compassion or forgiveness; rather, he was urging her to stiffen her spine a bit, to stand up for herself, and not to shrink from acts of assessment and discernment.

Judging involves calling things by their real names, embracing the difficult recognition that what Hannah Arendt called "an enormously enlarged empathy" does not in itself suffice to sustain the capacity for that critical thinking we call judging. Arendt had little use for those who treated adults as if they were children by spoon-feeding them palatable "truths" rather than the harder truths of life and politics. If we over-assimilate our situation to that of others, and pretend that we are "at one" with them, we may lose the point at which we leave off and they begin. We are then in danger of losing the faculty of judgment that, for Arendt, consists in "thinking the particular" and through this concrete act reaching for more general conclusions and truths.

Why is judging—what Arendt called the preeminent political faculty—at a nadir among us? Surely much of the explanation lies in the triumph of the ideology of victimization coupled with self-esteem mania. The two are, of course, closely linked. Examples are so numerous it is hard to pick and choose. Take one from the public schools. By now most discerning citizens are familiar with the study showing that American schoolchildren scored much lower on math accomplishment tests than did their counterparts from several other societies—even while these same Americans were the ones who "felt best" about their math ability. Here the emphasis on "feeling good" by contrast to concrete accomplishment results in students being incapable of an accurate discernment of where they really stand on their math ability. Here is a second story, this from the literary front. My son is an aspiring poet and he finds increasingly depressing the many moments, whether in class or out, when a poem that is weak in execution and flat in evocative power is embraced as something "real" and important because it speaks about the poet's own undigested experiences, which by definition can never be assessed and criticized. In other words, the self-referential prejudices of our time swamp a cooler set of criticisms and judgments, and wind up making a triumph of something rather petty. In the process, the work of those young men and women who really struggle with form and language and getting it right is trivialized, their accomplishments discounted. In some circles, if you carefully and precisely criticize a weak poem, you may face censure because the poem and its author's psyche or identity are at one; thus, you find yourself in the position of criticizing her (or his) life, given the utter collapse of one into the other, when what you really want to do is to explain why you think this isn't a very good poem.

The culture of victimization, then, and the triumph of pop-psych notions of "self-esteem," in contrast to a self capable of discernment and judging well, seems a pretty clear source of our discontents in this matter. Of course, any decent person is concerned about victims, and there are *real* victims in our less than perfect world. But that is not the issue. An ideology of victimization (of the feminist sort) casts women as victims of male oppression from the very beginning of time; indeed, female victimization has taken on foundational status. But this victim ideology diverts attention from concrete and specific instances of female victimization in favor of pushing a relentless worldview structured around such dichotomies as victim/victimizer, guilty/innocent, tainted/pure. The female victim, construed as innocent, remains somehow free from sin. Remember Arendt's insistence, following Kant, that judging "is the faculty of thinking the particular." An ideology of victimization—with its harsh and exaggerated polemicism—actually hurts the cause of women's rights, for it provides grounds for callous or sexist individuals to deprecate the claims of actual victims.

Victimization ideology is little more than a politics of resentment, given the growing body of evidence demonstrating that women, though they often have been victims of injustice, have played a variety of active roles throughout history and in every culture. Of course, who didn't know that? It is quite incredible that one must make this point against those who, in the name of feminism, promote the generic prejudice that women are victims *simpliciter*. Our world is filled with noisy forces urging us to refrain from judging precisely in the name of justice. This dangerous nonsense is in evidence in every issue of any daily newspaper anywhere. The jurors in the Reginald Denny beating case decided not to convict because the thugs who smashed a man's face to an unrecognizable pulp and exulted for the cameras as if they had just made the winning touchdown at a Superbowl Game were in the grip of a "mob psychology" and could not, therefore, be judged for their specific acts of wanton, and repeated, violence. The Menendez brothers were "victims" who, although they blasted their parents numerous times with a shotgun, were not to be held accountable. We cannot judge them given what they "went through," as one juror put it.

Take another case, one worth looking at in some detail. A woman in Nashville, Tennessee, starved her infant son to death. Turned into a robot, so it was claimed, she was unable to feed the infant even though the husband was away at work all day. Her defense was based on her having been abused by this husband even though when he got home from work, the two of them would dress up and go out on the town, frequenting sleazy bars, looking for men and women for three-way sex. Meanwhile, a baby is starving to death. Of this terrible story, victimization doctrine holds that as a victim of abuse herself, the woman, by definition, could not in turn be victimizing another. We cannot judge her actions because she is oppressed. According to her lawyers, who are now mounting an appeal, the jury that found her guilty has victimized her twice. But one who looks at victimization as a concrete and specific act would argue that, although it is terrible to be abused, for a twenty-three-year old woman with a range of options open to her (she might have given the infant to her mother to care for, as she had done with an older child) to starve an infant to death is more terrible yet. Surely, to make that assessment is not an act prompted by a harsh desire for revenge. It flows, rather, from a recognition that we are able to distinguish real victims from rhetorical ones, evil acts and crimes from less serious misdeeds.

As the lawyers for this woman said, the woman cannot be "held accountable," and to do so is a "male deal . . . or a society deal, but some people just don't get it." Now, we are told, the perpetrator is a victim twice or even thrice—of that amorphous entity, society, of her husband, and of the jury that found her guilty. The woman's mother has stepped in, proclaiming that she, too, is a "victim" for she "lost a grandson." Notice the language: she "lost" the grandson, as if he had been misplaced, not knowingly, over a six-week period, starved to death as he lay, immobile, listless, no longer able to cry, in his own waste in a filthy crib in a locked room as his parents played out their fantasies with male and female prostitutes. This is nigh unbelievable, but there it is. Even if this awful case gets turned back on appeal, we—all of us—are in danger of being worn down by arguments of this sort; hence, the more likely it is that, at some future point, we will have forgotten what it means to hold *this* person accountable in *this* situation for *this* particular horrible deed.

Let's pursue this just a bit further, depressing as it is, because the elimination of the possibility of judgment, the evacuation of the very capacity of judging would spell the end of the human subject as a self-respecting accountable being. Judging is a sign, a mark, of our respect for the dignity of others and ourselves. We are surrounded by various strategies of exculpation—ways to evade responsibility for a situation or an outcome should one happen to be a member of an "oppressed" or "victimized" group. In a recent book, *The Alchemy of Race and Rights,* the author, Patricia Williams, plays the victim card to achieve both ends simultaneously. Acknowledging that the Tawana Brawley accusations in the now-notorious 1988 scandal were part of a hoax, Williams suggests that that doesn't really matter. For Brawley was a victim of "some unspeakable crime." "No matter how she got there. No matter who did it to her—and even if she did it to herself." That is, even if Brawley injured herself, "her condition was clearly the expression of some crime against her, some tremendous violence, some great violation that challenges comprehension." Brawley was the victim of a "meta-rape," and this secures both her victim status and legitimates the power plays of those who cynically manipulated the situation. These latter escape judgment; and Brawley cannot be judged either. But the "society" that somehow "did" this to her on a "meta" level becomes responsible given the prejudice that in a "racist" society all African Americans are victims of the dominant "metanarrative." Consider the alternative view of black possibility and responsibility noted by Stephen Carter:

> We must never lose the capacity for judgment, especially the capacity to judge ourselves and our people. . . . Standards of morality matter no less than standards of excellence. There are black people who commit heinous crimes, and not all of them are driven by hunger and neglect. . . . We are not automatons. To understand all may indeed be to forgive all, but no civilization can survive when the capacity for understanding is allowed to supersede the capacity for judgment. Otherwise, at the end of the line lies a pile of garbage: Hitler wasn't evil, just insane.

"When the capacity for understanding is allowed to supersede the capacity for judgment"—let the words linger for a moment. Then conjure with the teaching of Jesus: "Judge not that ye be not judged," this, of course, from the Sermon on the Mount. These, too, are words I grew up with. And I pondered them, wondering if my mother's "judgmental" attitude was compatible with Jesus' injunction. We were also told: "There but for the grace of God go I." We were told to "walk around in the other guy's shoes" before we judged severely or before we judged at all. Squaring this with Grandma's dismissive "Russki" was no easy matter. I sometimes repaired to Lincoln, one of my childhood heroes. I especially loved the magnificent Second Inaugural, "With malice toward none, with charity for all . . ." Those words I could square with judgment. Malice and judgment: the punitive and the fair are not the same. Lincoln had, after all, insisted that the nations were under God's judgment, and our terrible Civil War, the war he was prosecuting in terms of "unconditional surrender," was our punishment for chattel slavery. Lincoln was no value-free, laid-back kind of guy: compassion with judgment, this framed his life and work. "Judge not" is, then, not an injunction to spineless acceptance but a caution against peremptory legalisms that leave no space for acts of compassion and witness.

I have also found helpful the discussion of the lively British philosopher, Mary Midgley. In her book *Can't We Make Moral Judgments?* Midgley notes our contemporary search for a nonjudgmental politics and quotes all those people who cry, in effect, "But surely it's always wrong to make moral judgments." We are not permitted to make anyone uncomfortable, to be "insensitive." Yet moral judgment of "some kind," says Midgley, "is a necessary element to our thinking." Judging involves our whole nature—it isn't just icing on the cake of self-identity. Judging makes it possible for us to "find our way through a whole forest of possibilities."

Midgley argues that Jesus was taking aim at sweeping condemnations and vindictiveness: he was not trashing the "whole faculty of judgment." Indeed, Jesus is making the "subtle point that while we cannot possibly avoid judging, we can see to it that we judge fairly, as we would expect others to do to us." This is part and parcel, then, of justice as fairness, as a discernment about a particular case and person and deed. Subjectivism in such matters—of the "I'm okay, you're okay," variety—is a cop-out, a way to stop forming and expressing moral judgments altogether. This strange suspension of specific moments of judgment goes hand-in-glove, of course, with an often violent rhetoric of condemnation of whole categories of persons, past and present—that all-purpose villain, the Dead White European Male, comes to mind.

Perhaps this is the point at which we might recall Tocqueville's warnings about "What Sort of Despotism Democratic Nations Have to Fear," for Tocqueville's worst-case scenario has quite a bit to do with judging or, better put, no longer being able to distinguish the better from the worse, the excellent from the mediocre, slavishness from self-responsibility. Democratic despotism, according to Tocqueville, would have a "different character" from the tyranny of the Old World. "It would be more widespread and milder; it would degrade men rather than torment them." Thus, Tocqueville sees citizens withdrawing into themselves, circling around one another in pursuit of "the petty and banal pleasures with which they glut their souls." The exercise of genuine free choice becomes rarer, the activity of free will occurs "within a narrower compass, and little by little robs each citizen of the proper use of his own faculties." The words Tocqueville uses to describe this state of things are "hinder . . . restrain . . . enervate . . . stultify." Losing over time the "faculty of thinking, feeling, and acting for themselves," these citizens "slowly fall below the level of humanity." Tocqueville nowhere talks about collapse of the faculty of judgment in a specific sense but that, surely, is much of what is at stake. Judging is central to, indeed constitutive of, both our self-identity *and* our sociality: it helps us to disentangle, analyze, separate, discern and, in so doing, puts us smack dab in a world of others—not apart, not above, not below, but *among.*

Told that, if we are "powerful" we cannot judge others but can only be judged, and on the other hand that if we are "powerless" we can judge totally but cannot be judged—since the "powerful" by definition "don't get it"—we fall into an intellectual laziness that is itself ethically corrupt and corrupting. As Midgley notes, Jesus' message was: do not stone people, do not cast them out, do not write them off. His target was punitive self-righteousness. With such self-righteousness now a major cottage industry, are we in the danger zone imagined by Tocqueville? That is the question to which sober reflection on judging leads us—or at least where it should.

For Further Reflection

1. Why does judging have a bad odor in American culture?

2. Examine Elshtain's reasons for being judgmental, and for thinking nonjudgmentalism is "dangerous nonsense." Are they convincing? Explain your answer.

Trying Out One's New Sword

MARY MIDGLEY

> Mary Midgley is a British moral philosopher known for her provocative writings on religion and science. Her books include *Heart and Mind: The Varieties of Moral Experience* (1981), *Evolution as a Religion* (1985), and *Myths We Live By* (2003). In this selection, Midgley criticizes what she calls "moral isolationism," the notion that cultures are isolated entities that can neither understand nor legitimately make moral judgments about each other.

All of us are, more or less, in trouble today about trying to understand cultures strange to us. We hear constantly of alien customs. We see changes in our lifetime which would have astonished our

---

From *Heart and Mind: The Varieties of Moral Experience* (Brighton, Sussex: Harvester Press, 1981).

parents. I want to discuss here one very short way of dealing with this difficulty, a drastic way which many people now theoretically favour. It consists in simply denying that we can ever understand any culture except our own well enough to make judgements about it. Those who recommend this hold that the world is sharply divided into separate societies, scaled units, each with its own system of thought. They feel that the respect and tolerance due from one system to another forbid us ever to take up a critical position to any other culture. Moral judgement, they suggest, is a kind of coinage valid only in its country of origin.

I shall call this position "moral isolationism." I shall suggest that it is certainly not forced upon us, and indeed that it makes no sense at all. People usually take it up because they think it is a respectful attitude to other cultures. In fact, however, it is not respectful. Nobody can respect what is entirely unintelligible to them. To respect someone, we have to know enough about him to make a *favourable* judgement, however general and tentative. And we do understand people in other cultures to this extent. Otherwise a great mass of our most valuable thinking would be paralysed.

To show this, I shall take a remote example, because we shall probably find it easier to think calmly about it than we should with a contemporary one, such as female circumcision in Africa or the Chinese Cultural Revolution. The principles involved will still be the same. My example is this. There is, it seems, a verb in classical Japanese which means "to try out one's new sword on a chance wayfarer." (The word is *tsujigiri,* literally "crossroads-cut"). A samurai sword had to be tried out because, if it was to work properly, it had to slice through someone at a single blow, from the shoulder to the opposite flank. Otherwise, the warrior bungled his stroke. This could injure his honour, offend his ancestors, and even let down his emperor. So tests were needed, and wayfarers had to be expended. Any wayfarer would do—provided, of course, that he was not another Samurai. Scientists will recognize a familiar problem about the rights of experimental subjects.

Now when we hear of a custom like this, we may well reflect that we simply do not understand it; and therefore are not qualified to criticize it at all, because we are not members of that culture. But we are not members of any other culture either, except our own. So we extend the principle to cover all extraneous cultures, and we seem therefore to be moral isolationists. But this is, as we shall see, an impossible position. Let us ask what it would involve.

We must ask first: Does the isolating barrier work both ways? Are people in other cultures equally unable to criticize *us?* This question struck me sharply when I read a remark in *The Guardian* by an anthropologist about a South American Indian who had been taken into a Brazilian town for an operation, which saved his life. When he came back to his village, he made several highly critical remarks about the white Brazilians' way of life. They may very well have been justified. But the interesting point was that the anthropologist called these remarks "a damning indictment of Western civilization." Now the Indian had been in that town about two weeks. Was he in a position to deliver a damning indictment? Would we ourselves be qualified to deliver such an indictment on the Samurai, provided we could spend two weeks in ancient Japan? What do we really think about this?

My own impression is that we believe that outsiders can, in principle, deliver perfectly good indictments—only, it usually takes more than two weeks to make them damning. Understanding has degrees. It is not a slapdash yes-or-no matter. Intelligent outsiders can progress in it, and in some ways will be at an advantage over the locals. But if this is so, it must clearly apply to ourselves as much as anybody else.

Our next question is this: Does the isolating barrier between cultures block praise as well as blame? If I want to say that the Samurai culture has many virtues, or to praise the South American Indians, am I prevented from doing *that* by my outside status? Now, we certainly do need to praise other societies in this way. But it is hardly possible that we could praise them effectively if we could not, in principle, criticize them. Our praise would be worthless if it rested on no definite grounds, if it did not flow from some understanding. Certainly we may need to praise things which we do not *fully* understand. We say "there's something very good here, but I can't quite make out what it is yet." This happens when we want to learn from strangers. And we can learn from strangers. But to do this we have to distinguish between those strangers who are worth learning from and those who are not. Can we then judge which is which?

This brings us to our third question: What is involved in judging? Now plainly there is no question here of sitting on a bench in a red robe and sentencing people. Judging simply means forming an opinion, and expressing it if it is called for. Is there anything wrong about this? Naturally, we ought to avoid forming—and expressing—*crude* opinions, like that of a simple-minded missionary, who might dismiss the whole Samurai culture as entirely bad, because non-Christian. But this is a different objection. The trouble with crude opinions is that they are crude, whoever forms them, not that they are formed by the wrong people. Anthropologists, after all, are outsiders quite as much as missionaries. Moral isolationism forbids us to form *any* opinions on these matters. Its ground for doing so is that we don't understand them. But there is much that we don't understand in our own culture too. This brings us to our last question: If we can't judge other cultures, can we really judge our own? Our efforts to do so will be much damaged if we are really deprived of our opinions about other societies, because these provide the range of comparison, the spectrum of alternatives against which we set what we want to understand. We would have to stop using the mirror which anthropology so helpfully holds up to us.

In short, moral isolationism would lay down a general ban on moral reasoning. Essentially, this is the programme of immoralism, and it carries a distressing logical difficulty. Immoralists like Nietzsche are actually just a rather specialized sect of moralists. They can no more afford to put moralizing out of business than smugglers can afford to abolish customs regulations. The power of moral judgement is, in fact, not a luxury, not a perverse indulgence of the self-righteous. It is a necessity. When we judge something to be bad or good, better or worse than something else, we are taking it as an example to aim at or avoid. Without opinions of this sort, we would have no framework of comparison for our own policy, no chance of profiting by other people's insights or mistakes. In this vacuum, we could form no judgements on our own actions.

Now it would be odd if Homo sapiens had really got himself into a position as bad as this—a position where his main evolutionary asset, his brain, was so little use to him. None of us is going to accept this sceptical diagnosis. We cannot do so, because our involvement in moral isolationism does not flow from apathy, but from a rather acute concern about human hypocrisy and other forms of wickedness. But we polarize that concern around a few selected moral truths. We are rightly angry with those who despise, oppress or steamroll other cultures. We think that doing these things is actually *wrong*. But this is itself a moral judgement. We could not condemn oppression and insolence if we thought that all our condemnations were just a trivial local quirk of our own culture. We could still less do it if we tried to stop judging altogether.

Real moral scepticism, in fact, could lead only to inaction, to our losing all interest in moral questions, most of all in those which concern other societies. When we discuss these things, it becomes instantly clear how far we are from doing this. Suppose, for instance, that I criticize the bisecting Samurai, that I say his behaviour is brutal. What will usually happen next is that someone will protest, will say that I have no right to make criticisms like that of another culture. But it is most unlikely that he will use this move to end the discussion of the subject. Instead, he will justify the Samurai. He will try to fill in the background, to make me understand the custom, by explaining the exalted ideals of discipline and devotion which produced it. He will probably talk of the lower value which the ancient Japanese placed on individual life generally. He may well suggest that this is a healthier attitude than our own obsession with security. He may add, too, that the wayfarers did not seriously mind being bisected, that in principle they accepted the whole arrangement.

Now an objector who talks like this is implying that it *is* possible to understand alien customs. That is just what he is trying to make me do. And he implies, too, that if I do succeed in understanding them, I shall do something better than giving up judging them. He expects me to change my present judgement to a truer one—namely, one that is favourable. And the standards I must use to do this cannot just be Samurai standards. They have to be ones current in my own culture. Ideals like discipline and devotion will not move anybody unless he himself accepts them. As it happens, neither discipline nor devotion is very popular in the West at present. Anyone who appeals to them may well have to do some more arguing to make *them* acceptable, before he can use them to explain the Samurai. But if he does succeed here, he will have persuaded us, not just that there was something to be said for them in ancient Japan, but that there would be here as well.

Isolating barriers simply cannot arise here. If we accept something as a serious moral truth about one culture, we can't refuse to apply it—in however different an outward form—to other cultures as well, wherever circumstance admit it. If we refuse to do this, we just are not taking the other culture seriously. This becomes clear if we look at the last argument used by my objector—that of justification by consent of the victim. It is suggested that sudden bisection is quite in order, *provided* that it takes place between consenting adults. I cannot now discuss how conclusive this justification is. What I am pointing out is simply that it can only work if we believe that *consent* can make such a transaction respectable—and this is a thoroughly modern and Western idea. It would probably never occur to a Samurai; if it did, it would surprise him very much. It is *our* standard. In applying it, too, we are likely to make another typically Western demand. We shall ask for good factual evidence that the wayfarers actually do have this rather surprising taste—that they are really willing to be bisected. In applying Western standards in this way, we are not being confused or irrelevant. We are asking the questions which arise *from where we stand,* questions which we can see the sense of. We do this because asking questions which you can't see the sense of is humbug. Certainly we can extend our questioning by imaginative effort. We can come to understand other societies better. By doing so, we may make their questions our own, or we may see that they are really forms of the questions which we are asking already. This is not impossible. It is just very hard work. The obstacles which often prevent it are simply those of ordinary ignorance, laziness and prejudice.

If there were really an isolating barrier, of course, our own culture could never have been formed. It is no sealed box, but a fertile jungle of different influences—Greek, Jewish, Roman, Norse, Celtic and so forth, into which further influences are still pouring—American, Indian, Japanese, Jamaican, you name it. The moral isolationist's picture of separate, unmixable cultures is quite unreal. People who talk about British history usually stress the value of this fertilizing mix, no doubt rightly. But this is not just an odd fact about Britain. Except for the very smallest and most remote, all cultures are formed out of many streams. All have the problem of digesting and assimilating things which, at the start, they do not understand. All have the choice of learning something from this challenge, or, alternatively, of refusing to learn, and fighting it mindlessly instead.

This universal predicament has been obscured by the fact that anthropologists used to concentrate largely on very small and remote cultures, which did not seem to have this problem. These tiny societies, which had often forgotten their own history, made neat, self-contained subjects for study. No doubt it was valuable to emphasize their remoteness, their extreme strangeness, their independence of our cultural tradition. This emphasis was, I think, the root of moral isolationism. But, as the tribal studies themselves showed, even there the anthropologists were able to interpret what they saw and make judgements—often favorable—about the tribesmen. And the tribesmen, too, were quite equal to making judgements about the anthropologists—and about the tourists and Coca-Cola salesmen who followed them. Both sets of judgements, no doubt, were somewhat hasty, both have been refined in the light of further experience. A similar transaction between us and the Samurai might take even longer. But that is no reason at all for deeming it impossible. Morally as well as physically, there is only one world, and we all have to live in it.

For Further Reflection

1. What are Midgley's arguments against moral isolationism?

2. Why does Midgley say that moral isolationism is an impossible position?

3. If we can praise other cultures, can't we also blame them? Why or why not?

4. Do you believe that the behavior of the "bisecting Samurai" is brutal? If so, do you believe that you understand enough about the behavior to make such a judgment? Are you a moral isolationist?

5. Suppose someone accuses you of misunderstanding the true nature of the Samurai's actions. What would this response imply about your accuser's views toward other cultures?

The Enemy of the People

HENRIK IBSEN

Henrik Ibsen (1828–1906), a Norwegian, is considered one of the greatest dramatists of all time. He was influenced by the Danish existentialist Søren Kierkegaard, who held that truth is unpopular and lonely. Kierkegaard wanted inscribed on his tombstone the epitaph THE INDIVIDUAL, signifying the idea of individual integrity in the face of the corrupt masses. Several of Ibsen's plays convey this idea, including the one excerpted here.

Our story takes place in a small Norwegian town that has become prosperous thanks to its baths, which bring people from miles around to seek their healing powers. Dr. Thomas Stockmann, the medical officer in charge of overseeing the baths, is also credited with founding them. His brother Peter is the mayor of the town. Noticing that during the previous summer visitors to the baths contracted typhus, Stockmann sends water samples to the university. He has just received the university report stating that the water is dangerously polluted. Dr. Stockmann prepares an article on the problem, which the liberal editor Hovstad is delighted to print in the progressive newspaper the *People's Messenger*. Aslaksen, the printer, and leader of the skilled workers' guild, is also strongly behind Stockmann in his endeavor to reveal the truth, seeing it as a means to undermine the power of the old guard and capitalists. However, when these established powers get wind of Stockmann's news, they exert their influence by informing the town that in order to redesign the piping system, the town will have to tax the people for some twenty thousand pounds and the baths will have to be closed for two years. The message is clear: cleaning up the polluted baths will have a severe economic cost.

Suddenly, the liberals switch sides. Peter, the mayor, warns his brother against publishing the article. Hovstad squirms and reneges on his promise to publish the exposé.

From *The Best Known Works of Henrik Ibsen* (New York: Blue Ribbon Books, 1928).

Aslaksen pleads for moderation. Even Stockmann's wife, Katherine, pleads with him to drop the matter. Only his daughter, Petra, stands squarely behind him. We enter with Peter discussing the report with Stockmann.

PETER. Was it necessary to make all these investigations behind my back?

DR. STO. Yes, because until I was absolutely certain about it—

PETER. Then you mean that you are absolutely certain now?

DR. STO. Surely you are convinced of that.

PETER. Is it your intention to bring this document before the Baths Committee as a sort of official communication?

DR. STO. Certainly. Something must be done in the matter—and that quickly.

PETER. As usual, you employ violent expressions in your report. You say, amongst other things, that what we offer visitors in our Baths is a permanent supply of poison.

DR. STO. Well, can you describe it any other way, Peter? Just think—water that is poisonous, whether you drink it or bathe in it! And this we offer to the poor sick folk who come to us trustfully and pay us at an exorbitant rate to be made well again!

PETER. And your reasoning leads you to this conclusion, that we must build a sewer to draw off the alleged impurities from Mölledal and must relay the water-conduits.

DR. STO. Yes. Do you see any other way out of it? I don't.

PETER. I made a pretext this morning to go and see the town engineer, and, as if only half seriously, broached the subject of these proposals as a thing we might perhaps have to take under consideration some time later on.

DR. STO. Some time later on!

PETER. He smiled at what he considered to be my extravagance, naturally. Have you taken the trouble to consider what your proposed alterations would cost? According to the information I obtained, the expenses would probably mount up to fifteen or twenty thousand pounds.

DR. STO. Would it cost so much?

PETER. Yes; and the worst part of it would be that the work would take at least two years.

DR. STO. Two years? Two whole years?

PETER. At least. And what are we to with the Baths in the meantime? Close them? Indeed we should be obliged to. And do you suppose any one would come near the place after it had got about that the water was dangerous?

DR. STO.   Yes, but, Peter, that is what it is.

PETER.   And all this at this juncture—just as the Baths are beginning to be known. There are other towns in the neighborhood with qualifications to attract visitors for bathing purposes. Don't you suppose they would immediately strain every nerve to divert the entire stream of strangers to themselves? Unquestionably they would; and then where should we be? We should probably have to abandon the whole thing, which has cost us so much money—and then you would have ruined your native town.

DR. STO.   I—should have ruined—!

PETER.   It is simply and solely through the Baths that the town has before it any future worth mentioning. You know that just as well as I.

DR. STO.   But what do you think ought to be done, then?

PETER.   Your report has not convinced me that the condition of the water at the Baths is as bad as you represent it to be.

DR. STO.   I tell you it is even worse!—or at all events it will be in summer, when the warm weather comes.

PETER.   As I said, I believe you exaggerate the matter considerably. A capable physician ought to know what measures to take—he ought to be capable of preventing injurious influences or of remedying them if they become obviously persistent.

DR. STO.   Well? What more?

PETER.   The water supply for the Baths is now an established fact, and in consequence must be treated as such. But probably the Committee, at its discretion, will not be disinclined to consider the question of how far it might be possible to introduce certain improvements consistently with a reasonable expenditure.

DR. STO.   And do you suppose that I will have anything to do with such a piece of trickery as that?

PETER.   Trickery!!

DR. STO.   Yes, it would be a trick—a fraud, a lie, a downright crime towards the public, towards the whole community!

PETER.   I have not, as I remarked before, been able to convince myself that there is actually any imminent danger.

DR. STO.   You have! It is impossible that you should not be convinced. I know I have represented the facts absolutely truthfully and fairly. And you know it very well, Peter, only you won't acknowledge it. It was owing to your action that both the Baths and the water-conduits were built where they are; and that is what you won't acknowledge—that damnable blunder of yours. Pooh!—do you suppose I don't see through you?

PETER.   And even if that were true? If I perhaps guard my reputation somewhat anxiously, it is in the interests of the town. Without moral authority I am powerless to direct public affairs as seems, to my judgment, to be best for the common good. And on that account—and for various other reasons too—it appears to me to be a matter of importance that your report should not be delivered to the Committee. In the interests of the public, you must withhold it. Then, later on, I will raise the question and we will do our best, privately; but nothing of this unfortunate affair—not a single word of it—must come to the ears of the public.

DR. STO.   I am afraid you will not be able to prevent that now, my dear Peter.

PETER.   It must and shall be prevented.

DR. STO.   It is no use, I tell you. There are too many people that know about it.

PETER.   That know about it? Who? Surely you don't mean those fellows on the "People's Messenger"?

DR. STO.   Yes, they know. The liberal-minded independent press is going to see that you do your duty.

PETER   [*after a short pause*].   You are an extraordinarily independent man, Thomas. Have you given no thought to the consequences this may have for yourself?

DR. STO.   Consequences?—for me?

PETER.   For you and yours, yes.

DR. STO.   What the deuce do you mean?

PETER.   I believe I have always behaved in a brotherly way to you— have always been ready to oblige or to help you?

DR. STO.   Yes, you have, and I am grateful to you for it.

PETER.   There is no need. Indeed, to some extent I was forced to do so—for my own sake. I always hoped that, if I helped to improve your financial position, I should be able to keep some check on you.

DR. STO.   What!! Then it was only for your own sake—!

PETER.   Up to a certain point, yes. It is painful for a man in an official position to have his nearest relative compromising himself time after time.

DR. STO.   And do you consider that I do that?

PETER.   Yes, unfortunately, you do, without even being aware of it. You have a restless, pugnacious, rebellious disposition. And then there is that disastrous propensity of yours to want to write about every sort of possible and impossible thing. The moment an idea comes into your head, you must needs go and write a newspaper article or a whole pamphlet about it.

DR. STO. Well, but is it not the duty of a citizen to let the public share in any new ideas he may have?

PETER. Oh, the public doesn't require any new ideas. The public is best served by the good, old-established ideas it already has.

DR. STO. And that is your honest opinion?

PETER. Yes, and for once I must talk frankly to you. Hitherto I have tried to avoid doing so, because I know how irritable you are; but now I must tell you the truth, Thomas. You have no conception what an amount of harm you do yourself by your impetuosity. You complain of the authorities, you even complain of the government—you are always pulling them to pieces; you insist that you have been neglected and persecuted. But what else can such a cantankerous man as you expect?

DR. STO. What next? Cantankerous, am I?

PETER. Yes, Thomas, you are an extremely cantankerous man to work with—I know that to my cost. You disregard everything that you ought to have consideration for. You seem completely to forget that it is me you have to thank for your appointment here as medical officer to the Baths.—

DR. STO. I was entitled to it as a matter of course!—I and nobody else! I was the first person to see that the town could be made into a flourishing wateringplace, and I was the only one who saw it at that time. I had to fight single-handed in support of the idea for many years; and I wrote and wrote—

PETER. Undoubtedly. But things were not ripe for the scheme then—though, of course, you could not judge of that in your out-of-the-way corner up north. But as soon as the opportune moment came I—and the others—took the matter into our hands—

DR. STO. Yes, and made this mess of all my beautiful plan. It is pretty obvious now what clever fellows you were!

PETER. To my mind the whole thing only seems to mean that you are seeking another outlet for your combativeness. You want to pick a quarrel with your superiors—an old habit of yours. You cannot put up with any authority over you. You look askance at anyone who occupies a superior official position; you regard him as a personal enemy, and then any stick is good enough to beat him with. But now I have called your attention to the fact that the town's interests are at stake—and, incidentally, my own too. And therefore I must tell you, Thomas, that you will find me inexorable with regard to what I am about to require you to do.

DR. STO.   And what is that?

PETER.   As you have been so indiscreet as to speak of this delicate matter to outsiders, despite the fact that you ought to have treated it as entirely official and confidential, it is obviously impossible to hush it up now. All sorts of rumours will get about directly, and everybody who has a grudge against us will take care to embellish these rumours. So it will be necessary for you to refute them publicly.

DR. STO.   I! How? I don't understand.

PETER.   What we shall expect is that, after making further investigations, you will come to the conclusion that the matter is not by any means as dangerous or as critical as you imagined in the first instance.

DR. STO.   Oho!—so that is what you expect!

PETER.   And, what is more, we shall expect you to make public profession of your confidence in the Committee and in their readiness to consider fully and conscientiously what steps may be necessary to remedy any possible defects.

DR. STO.   But you will never be able to do that by patching and tinkering at it—never! Take my word for it, Peter; I mean what I say, as deliberately and emphatically as possible.

PETER.   As an officer under the Committee, you have no right to any individual opinion.

DR. STO. [*amazed*].   No right?

PETER.   In your official capacity, no. As a private person, it is quite another matter. But as a subordinate member of the staff of the Baths, you have no right to express any opinion which runs contrary to that of your superiors.

DR. STO.   This is too much! I, a doctor, a man of science, have no right to—!

PETER.   The matter in hand is not simply a scientific one. It is a complicated matter, and has its economic as well as its technical side.

DR. STO.   I don't care what it is! I intend to be free to express my opinion on any subject under the sun.

PETER.   As you please—but not on any subject concerning the Baths. That we forbid.

DR. STO. [*shouting*].   You forbid—! You! A pack of—

PETER.   *I* forbid it—I, your chief; and if I forbid it, you have to obey.

DR. STO. [*controlling himself*]. Peter—if you were not my brother—

PETRA [*throwing open the door*]. Father, you shan't stand this!

MRS. STO. [*coming in after her*]. Petra, Petra!

PETER. Oh, so you have been eavesdropping.

MRS. STO. You were talking so loud, we couldn't help—

PETRA. Yes, I was listening.

PETER. Well, after all, I am very glad—

DR. STO. [*going up to him*]. You were saying something about forbidding and obeying?

PETER. You obliged me to take that tone with you.

DR. STO. And so I am to give myself the lie, publicly?

PETER. We consider it absolutely necessary that you should make some public statement as I have asked for.

DR. STO. And if I do not—obey?

PETER. Then we shall publish a statement ourselves to reassure the public.

DR. STO. Very well; but in that case I shall use my pen against you. I stick to what I have said; I will show that I am right and that you are wrong. And what will you do then?

PETER. Then I shall not be able to prevent your being dismissed.

DR. STO. What—?

PETRA. Father—dismissed!

MRS. STO. Dismissed!

PETER. Dismissed from the staff of the Baths. I shall be obliged to propose that you shall immediately be given notice, and shall not be allowed any further participation in the Baths' affairs.

DR. STO. You would dare to do that!

PETER. It is you that are playing the daring game.

PETRA. Uncle, that is a shameful way to treat a man like father!

MRS. STO. Do hold your tongue, Petra!

PETER [*looking at* PETRA]. Oh, so we volunteer our opinions already, do we? Of course. [*To* MRS. STOCKMANN.] Katherine, I imagine you are the most sensible person in this house. Use any influence you may have over your husband, and make him see what this will entail for his family as well as—

DR. STO. My family is my own concern and nobody else's!

PETER. —for his own family, as I was saying, as well as for the town he lives in.

DR. STO. It is I who have the real good of the town at heart! I want to lay bare the defects that sooner or later must come to the light of day. I will show whether I love my native town.

PETER.   You, who in your blind obstinacy want to cut off the most important source of the town's welfare?

DR. STO.   The source is poisoned, man! Are you mad? We are making our living by retailing filth and corruption! The whole of our flourishing municipal life derives its sustenance from a lie!

PETER.   All imagination—or something even worse. The man who can throw out such offensive insinuations about his native town must be an enemy to our community.

DR. STO. [*going up to him*].   Do you dare to—!

MRS. STO. [*throwing herself between them*].   Thomas!

PETRA [*catching her father by the arm*].   Don't lose your temper, father!

PETER.   I will not expose myself to violence. Now you have had a warning; so reflect on what you owe to yourself and your family. Good-bye. [*Goes out.*]

DR. STO. [*walking up and down*].   Am I to put up with such treatment as this? In my own house, Katherine! What do you think of that!

MRS. STO.   Indeed it is both shameful and absurd Thomas—

PETRA.   If only I could give uncle a piece of my mind—

DR. STO.   It is my own fault. I ought to have flown out at him long ago!—shown my teeth!—bitten! To hear him call me an enemy to our community! Me! I shall not take that lying down, upon my soul!

MRS. STO.   But, dear Thomas, your brother has power on his side—

DR. STO.   Yes, but I have right on mine, I tell you.

MRS. STO.   Oh! yes, right—right. What is the use of having right on your side if you have not got might?

PETRA.   Oh, mother!—how can you say such a thing!

DR. STO.   Do you imagine that in a free country it is no use having right on your side? You are absurd, Katherine. Besides, haven't I got the liberal-minded, independent press to lead the way, and the compact majority behind me? That is might enough, I should think!

MRS. STO.   But, good heavens, Thomas, you don't mean to—?

DR. STO.   Don't mean to what?

MRS. STO.   To set yourself up in opposition to your brother.

DR. STO.   In God's name, what else do you suppose I should do but take my stand on right and truth?

PETRA.   Yes, I was just going to say that.

MRS. STO.   But it won't do you any earthly good. If they won't do it, they won't.

Dr. Sto.   Oho, Katherine! Just give me time, and you will see how I will carry the war into their camp.

Mrs. Sto.   Yes, you carry the war into their camp, and you get your dismissal—that is what you will do.

Dr. Sto.   In any case I shall have done my duty towards the public—towards the community. I, who am called its enemy!

Mrs. Sto.   But towards your family, Thomas? Towards your own home! Do you think that is doing your duty towards those you have to provide for?

Petra.   Ah, don't think always first of us, mother.

Mrs. Sto.   Oh, it is easy for you to talk; you are able to shift for yourself, if need be. But remember the boys, Thomas; and think a little too of yourself, and of me—

Dr. Sto.   I think you are out of your senses, Katherine! If I were to be such a miserable coward as to go on my knees to Peter and his damned crew, do you suppose I should ever know an hour's peace of mind all my life afterwards?

Mrs. Sto.   I don't know anything about that; but God preserve us from the peace of mind we shall have, all the same, if you go on defying him! You will find yourself again without the means of subsistence, with no income to count upon. I should think we had had enough of that in the old days. Remember that, Thomas; think what that means.

Dr. Sto. [*collecting himself with a struggle and clenching his fists*]. And this is what this slavery can bring upon a free, honourable man! Isn't it horrible, Katherine?

Mrs. Sto.   Yes, it is sinful to treat you so, it is perfectly true. But, good heavens, one has to put up with so much injustice in this world.—There are the boys, Thomas! Look at them! What is to become of them? Oh, no, no, you can never have the heart—. [Ejlif and Morten *have come in while she was speaking, with their school books in their hands*].

Dr. Sto.   The boys—! [*Recovers himself suddenly.*] No, even if the whole world goes to pieces, I will never bow my neck to this yoke! [*Goes towards his room.*]

Mrs. Sto. [*following him*].   Thomas—what are you going to do!

Dr. Sto. [*at his door*].   I mean to have the right to look my sons in the face when they are grown men. [*Goes into his room.*]

Mrs. Sto. [*bursting into tears*].   God help us all!

Petra.   Father is splendid! He will not give in.

[*The boys look on in amazement;* Petra *signs to them not to speak!* . . .

[Stockmann is outraged at the moral cowardice of the "progressives." Leaving the Baths polluted in this way will put the unwitting visitors, seeking health, in grave danger. He tries to rent a hall, but the town leaders are united against him. Finally, an old sea captain, Horster, opens his hall to him to reveal his findings. A crowd gathers, including Hovstad and his brother Peter. After an attempt to muzzle him fails, Dr. Stockmann speaks.]

Asl. [*ringing his bell*]. Dr. Stockmann will address the meeting.

Dr. Sto. I should like to have seen anyone, a few days ago, dare to attempt to silence me as has been done to-night! I would have defended my sacred rights as a man, like a lion! But now it is all one to me; I have something of even weightier importance to say to you.

[*The crowd presses nearer to him,* Morten Kiil *conspicuous among them.*]

Dr. Sto. [*continuing*]. I have thought and pondered a great deal, these last few days—pondered over such a variety of things that in the end my head seemed too full to hold them—

Peter [*with a cough*]. Ahem!

Dr. Sto. —but I got them clear in my mind at last, and then I saw the whole situation lucidly. And that is why I am standing here to-night. I have a great revelation to make to you, my fellow-citizens! I will impart to you a discovery of a far wider scope than the trifling matter that our water-supply is poisoned and our medicinal Baths are standing on pestiferous soil.

A number of voices [*shouting*]. Don't talk about the Baths! We won't hear you! None of that!

Dr. Sto. I have already told you that what I want to speak about is the great discovery I have made lately—the discovery that all the sources of our moral life are poisoned and that the whole fabric of our civic community is founded on the pestiferous soil of falsehood.

Voices of disconcerted Citizens. What is that he says?

Peter. Such an insinuation—!

Asl. [*with his hand on his bell*]. I call upon the speaker to moderate his language.

Dr. Sto. I have always loved my native town as a man only can love the home of his youthful days. I was not old when I went away from here; and exile, longing and memories cast as it were an additional halo over both the town and its inhabitants. [*Some clapping and applause.*] And there I stayed, for many years, in a horrible hole far away up north. When I came into contact with some of the people that lived scattered about among the rocks, I often thought it would of been more service to the poor half-starved creatures if a veterinary doctor had been sent up there, instead of a man like me. [*Murmurs among the crowd.*]

BILL. [*laying down his pen*].   I'm damned if I have ever heard—!

HOV.   It is an insult to a respectable population!

DR. STO.   Wait a bit! I do not think anyone will charge me with having forgotten my native town up there. I was like one of the eider-ducks brooding on its nest, and what I hatched was—the plans for these Baths. [*Applause and protests.*] And then when fate at last decreed for me the great happiness of coming home again—I assure you, gentlemen, I thought I had nothing more in the world to wish for. Or rather, there was one thing I wished for—eagerly, untiringly, ardently—and that was to be able to be of service to my native town and the good of the community.

PETER [*looking at the ceiling*].   You chose a strange way of doing it—ahem!

DR. STO.   And so, with my eyes blinded to the real facts, I revelled in happiness. But yesterday morning—no, to be precise, it was yesterday afternoon—the eyes of my mind were opened wide, and the first thing I realised was the colossal stupidity of the authorities—. [*Uproar, shouts and laughter.* MRS. STOCKMANN *coughs persistently.*]

PETER.   Mr. Chairman!

ASL. [*ringing his bell*].   By virtue of my authority—!

DR. STO.   It is a petty thing to catch me up on a word, Mr. Aslaksen. What I mean is only that I got scent of the unbelievable piggishness our leading men had been responsible for down at the Baths. I can't stand leading men at any price!—I have had enough of such people in my time. They are like billy-goats in a young plantation; they do mischief everywhere. They stand in a free man's way, whichever way he turns, and what I should like best would be to see them exterminated like any other vermin—. [*Uproar.*]

PETER.   Mr. Chairman, can we allow such expressions to pass?

ASL. [*with his hand on his bell*].   Doctor—!

DR. STO.   I cannot understand how it is that I have only now acquired a clear conception of what these gentry are, when I had almost daily before my eyes in this town such an excellent specimen of them—my brother Peter—slow-witted and hide-bound in prejudice—. [*Laughter, uproar and hisses.* Mrs. Stockmann *sits coughing assiduously.* Aslaksen *rings his bell violently.*]

The Drunken Man [*who has got in again*].   Is it me he is talking about? My name's Petersen, all right—but devil take me if I—

Angry Voices.   Turn out that drunken man! Turn him out. [*He is turned out again.*]

Peter.   Who was that person?

1st Citizen.   I don't know who he is, Mr. Mayor.

2nd Citizen.   He doesn't belong here.

3rd Citizen.   I expect he is a navvy from over at [*the rest is inaudible*].

Asl.   He had obviously had too much beer.—Proceed, Doctor, but please strive to be moderate in your language.

Dr. Sto.   Very well, gentlemen, I will say no more about our leading men. And if anyone imagines, from what I have just said, that my object is to attack these people this evening, he is wrong—absolutely wide of the mark. For I cherish the comforting conviction that these parasites—all these venerable relics of a dying school of thought—are most admirably paving the way for their own extinction; they need no doctor's help to hasten their end. Nor is it folk of that kind who constitute the most pressing danger to the community. It is not they who are most instrumental in poisoning the sources of our moral life and directing the ground on which we stand. It is not they who are the most dangerous enemies of truth and freedom amongst us.

Shouts from all sides.   Who then? Who is it? Name! Name!

Dr. Sto.   You may depend upon it I shall name them! That is precisely the great discovery I made yesterday. [*Raises his voice.*] The most dangerous enemy to truth and freedom amongst us is the compact majority—yes, the damned compact Liberal majority—that is it! Now you know; [*Tremendous uproar. Most of the crowd are shouting, stamping and hissing. Some of the older men among them exchange stolen glances and seem to be enjoying themselves.* Mrs. Stockmann *gets up, looking anxious.* Ejlif *and* Morten *advance threateningly upon some schoolboys who are playing pranks.* Aslaksen *rings his bell and begs for silence.* Hovstad *and* Billing *both talk at once, but are inaudible. At last quiet is restored.*]

Asl.   As chairman, I call upon the speaker to withdraw the ill-considered expressions he has just used.

Dr. Sto.   Never, Mr. Aslaksen! It is the majority in our community that denies me my freedom and seeks to prevent my speaking the truth.

Hov.   The majority always has right on its side.

Bill.   And truth too, by God!

Dr. Sto.   The majority *never* has right on its side. Never, I say! That is one of these social lies against which an independent, intelligent man must wage war. Who is it that constitute the majority of the population in a country? Is it the clever folk or the stupid? I don't imagine you will dispute the fact that at present the stupid people are in an absolutely overwhelming majority all the world over. But, good Lord!—you can never pretend that it is right that the stupid folk should govern the clever ones! [*Up-roar and cries.*] Oh. yes—you can shout me down, I know! but you cannot answer me. The majority has *might* on its side—unfortunately; but *right* it has *not*. I am in the right—I and a few other scattered individuals. The minority is always in the right. [*Renewed uproar.*]

Hov.   Aha!—so Dr. Stockmann has become an aristocrat since the day before yesterday!

Dr. Sto.   I have already said that I don't intend to waste a word on the puny, narrow-chested, short-winded crew whom we are leaving astern. Pulsating life no longer concerns itself with them. I am thinking of the few, the scattered few amongst us, who have absorbed new and vigorous truths. Such men stand, as it were, at the outposts, so far ahead that the compact majority has not yet been able to come up with them; and there they are fighting for truths that are too newly-born into the world of consciousness to have any considerable number of people on their side as yet.

Hov.   So the Doctor is a revolutionary now!

Dr. Sto.   Good heavens—of course I am, Mr. Hovstad! I propose to raise a revolution against the lie that the majority has the monopoly of the truth. What sort of truths are they that the majority usually supports? They are truths that are of such advanced age that they are beginning to break up. And if a truth is as old as that, it is also in a fair way to become a lie, gentlemen. [*Laughter and mocking cries.*] Yes, believe me or not, as you like; but truths are by no means as long-lived as Methuselah—as some folk imagine. A normally constituted truth lives, let us say, as a rule seventeen or eighteen, or at most twenty years; seldom longer. But truths as aged as that are always worn frightfully thin, and nevertheless it is only then that the majority recognises them and recommends them to the community as wholesome moral nourishment. There is no great nutritive value in that sort of fare, I can assure you; and, as a doctor, I ought to know. These "majority truths" are like last year's cured meat—like rancid, tainted ham; and they are the origin of the moral scurvy that is rampant in our communities.

ASL.   It appears to me that the speaker is wandering a long way from his subject.

PETER.   I quite agree with the Chairman.

DR. STO.   Have you gone clean out of your senses, Peter? I am sticking as closely to my subject as I can; for my subject is precisely this, that it is the masses, the majority—this infernal compact majority—that poisons the sources of our moral life and infects the ground we stand on.

HOV.   And all this because the great, broad-minded majority of the people is prudent enough to show deference only to well-ascertained and well-approved truths?

DR. STO.   Ah, my good Mr. Hovstad, don't talk nonsense about well-ascertained truths! The truths of which the masses now approve are the very truths that the fighters at the outposts held to in the days of our grandfathers. We fighters at the outposts nowadays no longer approve of them; and I do not believe there is any other well-ascertained truth except this, that no community can live a healthy life if it is nourished only on such old marrowless truths.

HOV.   But instead of standing there using vague generalities, it would be interesting if you would tell us what these old marrowless truths are, that we are nourished on.

[*Applause from many quarters.*]

DR. STO.   Oh, I could give you a whole string of such abominations; but to begin with I will confine myself to one well-approved truth, which at bottom is a foul lie, but upon which nevertheless Mr. Hovstad and the "People's Messenger" and all the "Messenger's" supporters are nourished.

HOV.   And that is—?

DR. STO.   That is, the doctrine you have inherited from your forefathers and proclaim thoughtlessly far and wide—the doctrine that the public, the crowd, the masses, are the essential part of the population—that they constitute the People—that the common folk, the ignorant and incomplete element in the community, have the same right to pronounce judgment and to approve, to direct and to govern, as the isolated, intellectually superior personalities in it.

BILL.   Well, damn me if ever I—

Hov. [*at the same time, shouting out.*]   Fellow-citizens, take good note of that!

A NUMBER OF VOICES [*angrily*].   Oho!—we are not the People! Only the superior folk are to govern, are they!

A WORKMAN.   Turn the fellow out, for talking such rubbish!

ANOTHER.   Out with him!

ANOTHER [*calling out*].   Blow your horn, Evensen!

[*A horn is blown loudly, amidst hisses and an angry uproar.*]

DR. STO. [*when the noise has somewhat abated*].   Be reasonable! Can't you stand hearing the voice of truth for once? I don't in the least expect you to agree with me all at once; but I must say I did expect Mr. Hovstad to admit I was right, when he had recovered his composure a little. He claims to be a freethinker—

VOICES [*in murmurs of astonishment*].   Freethinker, did he say? Is Hovstad a freethinker?

Hov. [*shouting*].   Prove it, Dr. Stockmann! When have I said so in print?

DR. STO. [*reflecting*].   No, confound it, you are right!—you have never had the courage to. Well, I won't put you in a hole, Mr. Hovstad. Let us say it is I that am the freethinker, then. I am going to prove to you, scientifically, that the "People's Messenger" leads you by the nose in a shameful manner when it tells you that you— that the common people, the crowd, the masses, are the real essence of the People. That is only a newspaper lie, I tell you! The common people are nothing more than the raw material of which a People is made. [*Groans, laughter and uproar.*] Well, isn't that the case? Isn't there an enormous difference between a well-bred and an ill-bred strain of animals? Take, for instance, a common barn-door hen. What sort of eating do you get from a shrivelled up old scrag of a fowl like that? Not much, do you! And what sort of eggs does it lay? A fairly good crow or a raven can lay pretty nearly as good an egg. But take a well-bred Spanish or Japanese hen, or a good pheasant or a turkey—then you will see the difference. Or take the case of dogs, with whom we humans are on such intimate terms. Think first of an ordinary common cur—I mean one of the horrible, coarse-haired, low-bred curs that do nothing but run about the streets and befoul the walls of the houses. Compare one of these curs with a poodle whose sires for many generations have been bred in a gentleman's house, where they have had the best of food and had the opportunity of hearing soft voices and music. Do you not think that the poodle's brain is developed to quite a different degree from that of the cur? Of course it is. It is puppies of well-bred poodles like that, that showmen train to do incredibly clever tricks—things that a common cur could never learn to do even if it stood on its head. [*Uproar and mocking cries.*]

A CITIZEN [*calls out*]. Are you going to make out we are dogs, now?

ANOTHER CITIZEN. We are not animals, Doctor!

DR. STO. Yes, but, bless my soul, we *are,* my friend! It is true we are the finest animals anyone could wish for; but, even amongst us, exceptionally fine animals are rare. There is a tremendous difference between poodle-men and cur-men. And the amusing part of it is, that Mr. Hovstad quite agrees with me as long as it is a question of four-footed animals—

HOV. Yes, it is true enough as far as they are concerned.

DR. STO. Very well. But as soon as I extend the principle and apply it to two-legged animals, Mr. Hovstad stops short. He no longer dares to think independently, or to pursue his ideas to their logical conclusion; so he turns the whole theory upside down and proclaims in the "People's Messenger" that it is the barn-door hens and street curs that are the finest specimens in the menagerie. But that is always the way, as long as a man retains the traces of common origin and has not worked his way up to intellectual distinction.

HOV. I lay no claim to any sort of distinction. I am the son of humble countryfolk, and I am proud that the stock I come from is rooted deep among the common people he insults.

VOICES. Bravo, Hovstad! Bravo! Bravo!

DR. STO. The kind of common people I mean are not only to be found low down in the social scale; they crawl and swarm all around us—even in the highest social positions. You have only to look at your own fine, distinguished Mayor! My brother Peter is every bit as plebeian as anyone that walks in two shoes—[*laughter and hisses*].

PETER. I protest against personal allusions of this kind.

DR. STO. [*imperturbably*]. —and that, not because he is, like myself, descended from some old rascal of a pirate from Pomerania or thereabouts—because that is who we are descended from—

PETER.   An absurd legend. I deny it!

DR. STO.   —but because he thinks what his superiors think and holds the same opinions as they. People who do that are, intellectually speaking, common people; and that is why my magnificent brother Peter is in reality so very far from any distinction—and consequently also so far from being liberal-minded.

PETER.   Mr. Chairman—!

HOV.   So it is only the distinguished men that are liberal-minded in this country? We are learning something quite new! [*Laughter.*]

DR. STO.   Yes, that is part of my new discovery too. And another part of it is that broad-mindedness is almost precisely the same thing as morality. That is why I maintain that it is absolutely inexcusable in the "People's Messenger" to proclaim, day in and day out, the false doctrine that it is the masses, the crowd, the compact majority, that have the monopoly of broad-mindedness and morality—and that vice and corruption and every kind of intellectual depravity are the result of culture, just as the filth that is draining into our Baths is the result of the tanneries up at Mölledal! [*Uproar and interruptions.* DR. STOCKMANN *is undisturbed, and goes on, carried away by his ardour, with a smile.*] And yet this same "People's Messenger" can go on preaching that the masses ought to be elevated to higher conditions of life! But, bless my soul, if the "Messenger's" teaching is to be depended upon, this very raising up the masses would mean nothing more or less than setting them straightway upon the paths of depravity! Happily the theory that culture demoralises is only an old falsehood that our forefathers believed in and we have inherited. No, it is ignorance, poverty, ugly conditions of life, that do the devil's work! In a house which does not get aired and swept every day—my wife Katherine maintains that the floor ought to be scrubbed as well, but that is a debatable question—in such a house, let me tell you, people will lose within two or three years the power of thinking or acting in a moral manner. Lack of oxygen weakens the conscience. And there must be a plentiful lack of oxygen in very many houses in this town, I should think, judging from the fact that the whole compact majority can be unconscientious enough to wish to build the town's prosperity on a quagmire of falsehood and deceit.

ASL.   We cannot allow such a grave accusation to be flung at a citizen community.

A Citizen.   I move that the Chairman direct the speaker to sit down.

Voices [*angrily*].   Hear, hear! Quite right! Make him sit down!

Dr. Sto. [*losing his self-control*].   Then I will go and shout the truth at every street corner! I will write it in other towns' newspapers! The whole country shall know what is going on here.

Hov.   It almost seems as if Dr. Stockmann's intentions were to ruin the town.

Dr. Sto.   Yes, my native town is so dear to me that I would rather ruin it than see it flourishing upon a lie.

Asl.   This is really serious. [*Uproar and cat-calls.* Mrs. Stockmann *coughs, but to no purpose; her husband does not listen to her any longer.*]

Hov. [*shouting above the din.*]   A man must be a public enemy to wish to ruin a whole community!

Dr. Sto. [*with growing fervour*].   What does the destruction of a community matter, I tell you! All who live by lies ought to be exterminated like vermin! You will end by infecting the whole country; you will bring about such a state of things that the whole country will deserve to be ruined. And if things come to that pass, I shall say from the bottom of my heart: Let the whole country perish, let all these people be exterminated!

Voices from the crowd.   That is talking like an out-and-out enemy of the people!

Bill.   There sounded the voice of the people, by all that's holy!

The whole crowd [*shouting*].   Yes, yes! He is an enemy of the people! He hates his country! He hates his own people!

Asl.   Both as a citizen and as an individual, I am profoundly disturbed by what we have had to listen to. Dr. Stockmann has shown himself in a light I should never have dreamed of. I am unhappily obliged to subscribe to the opinion which I have just heard my estimable fellow-citizens utter; and I propose that we should give expression to that opinion in a resolution. I propose a resolution as follows: "This meeting declares that it considers Dr. Thomas Stockmann, Medical Officer of the Baths, to be an enemy of the people." [*A storm of cheers and applause. A number of men surround the* Doctor *and hiss him.* Mrs. Stockmann *and* Petra *have got up from their seats.* Morten *and* Ejlif *are fighting the other schoolboys for hissing; some of their elders separate them.*]

Dr. Sto. [*to the men who are hissing him*].   Oh, you fools! I tell you that—

ASL. [*ringing his bell*]. We cannot hear you now, Doctor. A formal vote is about to be taken; but, out of regard for personal feelings, it shall be by ballot and not verbal. Have you any clean paper, Mr. Billing?

BILL. I have both blue and white here.

ASL. [*going to him*]. That will do nicely; we shall get on more quickly that way. Cut it up into small strips—yes, that's it. [*To the meeting.*] Blue means no; white means yes. I will come round myself and collect votes. [PETER STOCKMANN *leaves the hall.* ASLAKSEN *and one or two others go around the room with the slips of paper in their hats.*]

1ST CITIZEN [*to* HOVSTAD]. I say, what has come to the Doctor? What are we to think of it?

HOV. Oh, you know how headstrong he is.

2ND CITIZEN [*to* BILLING]. Billing, you go to their house—have you ever noticed if the fellow drinks?

BILL. Well I'm hanged if I know what to say. There are always spirits on the table when you go.

3RD CITIZEN. I rather think he goes quite off his head sometimes.

1ST CITIZEN. I wonder if there is any madness in his family?

BILL. I shouldn't wonder if there were.

4TH CITIZEN. No, it is nothing more than sheer malice; he wants to get even with somebody for something or other.

BILL. Well certainly he suggested a rise in his salary on one occasion lately, and did not get it.

THE CITIZENS [*together*]. Ah!—then it is easy to understand how it is!

THE DRUNKEN MAN [*who has got amongst the audience again*]. I want a blue one, I do! And I want a white one too!

VOICES. It's that drunken chap again! Turn him out!

MORTEN KIIL [*going up to* DR. STOCKMANN.] Well, Stockmann, do you see what these monkey tricks of yours lead to?

DR. STO. I have done my duty.

MORTEN KIIL. What was that you said about the tanneries at Mölledal?

DR. STO. You heard well enough. I said they were the source of all the filth.

MORTEN KIIL. My tannery too?

DR. STO. Unfortunately your tannery is by far the worst.

MORTEN KIIL. Are you going to put that in the papers?

DR. STO. I shall conceal nothing.

MORTEN KIIL. That may cost you dear, Stockmann. [*Goes out.*]

A STOUT MAN [*going up to* CAPTAIN HORSTER, *without taking any notice of the ladies.*] Well, Captain, so you lend your house to enemies of the people?

HORS. I imagine I can do what I like with my own possessions, Mr. Vik.

THE STOUT MAN. Then you can have no objection to my doing the same with mine.

HORS. What do you mean, sir?

THE STOUT MAN. You shall hear from me in the morning. [*Turns his back on him and moves off.*]

PETRA. Was that not your owner, Captain Horster?

HORS. Yes, that was Mr. Vik the ship-owner.

ASL. [*with the voting-papers in his hands, gets up on to the platform and rings his bell.*] Gentlemen, allow me to announce the result. By the votes of every one here except one person—

A YOUNG MAN. That is the drunk chap!

ASL. By the votes of every one here except a tipsy man, this meeting of citizens declares Dr. Thomas Stockmann to be an enemy of the people. [*Shouts and applause.*] Three cheers for our ancient and honourable citizen community! [*Renewed applause.*] Three cheers for our able and energetic Mayor, who has so loyally suppressed the promptings of family feeling! [*Cheers.*] The meeting is dissolved. [*Gets down.*]

BILL. Three cheers for the Chairman!

THE WHOLE CROWD. Three cheers for Aslaksen! Hurrah!

DR. STO. My hat and coat, Petra! Captain, have you room on your ship for passengers to the New World?

HORS. For you and yours we will make room, Doctor. . . .

[*Horn-blowing, hisses, and wild cries.* DR. STOCKMANN *goes out through the hall with his family,* HORSTER *elbowing a way for them.*]

THE WHOLE CROWD [*howling after as they go.*] Enemy of the People! Enemy of the People!

BILL. [*as he puts his papers together*]. Well, I'm damned if I go and drink toddy with the Stockmanns tonight!

[*The crowd press towards the exit. The uproar continues outside; shouts of* "Enemy of the People!" *are heard from without.*] . . .

[Dr. Stockmann is declared an enemy of the people and is ostracized by the community. He tells Katherine, "You should never wear your best trousers when you go out to fight for freedom and truth. It is not that I care so much about the trousers, you know; you can always sew them up again for me. But that the common herd should dare to make this attack on me, as if they were my equals—that is what I cannot, for the life of me, swallow!"

He is fired from his post and informed that his patients have been instructed to boycott him. His two sons are attacked at school and Petra is fired from her teaching position. His wife wants the family to move away from this town, and his brother, Peter, agrees. But Dr. Stockmann refuses to leave. He will open up a school and serve the poor. He will fight the battle to its finish.]

For Further Reflection

1. What is the key conflict in this play? How well does Dr. Stockmann deal with it?

2. What virtues and vices are exemplified in this play? Assess the various characters, especially Dr. Stockmann. Do you agree with Aslaksen that he should be more moderate? Or is Stockmann a man of rare courage and integrity?

3. What would you do in this situation? Should he leave town as his wife and brother advise?

4. What are the implications of Dr. Stockmann's actions for the issue of moral relativism?

5. Is the problem portrayed in this play relevant today? If so, what are we doing about it? Explain your answer.

6. How important is it to proclaim the truth even when it may have social repercussions?

Further Readings for Chapter 3

Brink, David. *Moral Realism and the Foundation of Ethics.* Cambridge: Cambridge University Press, 1989.

Fishkin, James. *Beyond Subjective Morality.* New Haven: Yale University Press, 1984.

Harman, Gilbert. "Moral Relativism Defended." *Philosophical Review* 84 (1975).

Ladd, John, ed. *Ethical Relativism.* Belmont, Calif.: Wadsworth Publishing Company, 1973. A good collection of basic readings.

Westermarck, Edward. *Ethical Relativity.* Atlantic Highlands, N.J.: Humanities Press, 1960.

Williams, Bernard. *Morality.* New York: Harper Torchbooks, 1972.

Wong, David. *Moral Relativity.* Berkeley and Los Angeles: University of California Press, 1985.

Part II

Moral Theories
and Moral Character

Suppose you are on an island with a dying millionaire. As he lies dying, he entreats you for one final favor: "I've dedicated my whole life to baseball and have gotten endless pleasure, and some pain, rooting for the New York Yankees for fifty years. Now that I am dying, I want to give all my assets, $6 million, to the Yankees. Would you take this money [he indicates a box containing the money in large bills] back to New York and give it to the New York Yankees' owner, George Steinbrenner, so that he can buy better players?" You agree to carry out his wish, at which point a huge smile of relief and gratitude breaks out on his face as he expires in your arms. After returning to New York, you see a newspaper advertisement placed by the World Hunger Relief Organization (whose integrity you do not doubt) pleading for $6 million to be used to save 100,000 people dying of starvation in East Africa. Not only will the $6 million save their lives, but it will be used to purchase small technology and the kinds of fertilizers necessary to build a sustainable economy. You reconsider your promise to the dying Yankees fan in the light of this consideration. What should you do with the money?

What is the right thing to do in this kind of situation? Consider some traditional moral principles and see if they help you come to a decision. One principle often given to guide action is "Let your conscience be your guide." But does it help here? No. Since conscience is primarily a function of our upbringing, people's consciences will speak to them in different ways according to how they were brought up. Depending on their upbringing, some people feel no qualms about terrorist acts, whereas others feel the torments of conscience over stepping on a gnat. Suppose your conscience tells you to give the money to the Yankees and my conscience tells me to give the money to the World Hunger Relief Organization. How can we ever discuss the matter? If conscience is the end of the matter, we're left mute.

Another principle urged on us is "Do whatever is most loving." St. Augustine (354–430) said, "Love God and do whatever you want." Love is surely a wonderful value, but is it enough to guide our actions where there is a conflict of interest? "Love is blind," it has been said, "but reason, like marriage, is an eye opener." Whom should I love in the case of the disbursement of the millionaire's money? The millionaire or the starving people? It's not clear how love alone will settle anything. In fact, it is not obvious that we must always do what is most loving. Should we always treat our enemies in loving ways? Or is it morally acceptable to hate those who have purposefully and unjustly harmed us, our loved ones, and other innocent people? Should the survivors of Auschwitz love Adolf Hitler? We will deal with these questions later. Here we must be content to notice that love alone does not solve difficult moral issues.

A third principle often given to guide us in moral actions is the Golden Rule: "Do unto others as you would have them do unto you." We will look more closely at this principle in chapter 5, but for the moment we should note that it has problems. First of all, it cannot be taken literally. Suppose John loves to hear loud rock music. John would love you to play it loud for him, so he reasons that he should play it loud for you—even though he knows that you hate it. So the rule must be modified: "Do unto others as you would have them do unto you if you were in their shoes." But this still has problems. If John were in the shoes of Sirhan Sirhan (the assassin of Robert Kennedy), he'd want to be released from the penitentiary, but it's not clear that Sirhan should be. If John puts himself in a sex-starved person's shoes, he'd want the next available person to have sex with him, but it's not obvious that he needs to comply with that want.

Similarly, the Golden Rule doesn't tell us to whom to give the millionaire's money.

Conscience, love, the Golden Rule are all worthy rules of thumb to help us through life. They work for most of us most of the time over ordinary moral situations. But in more complicated cases, especially where there are legitimate conflicts of interests, they are limited.

A more promising strategy for solving dilemmas is that of following definite moral rules. Suppose you decide to give the millionaire's money to the Yankees in order to keep your promise or because to do otherwise would be stealing. The principle you followed would be "Always keep your promise" and/or "Thou shalt not steal" (the Eighth Commandment). Principles are important in life. All learning involves understanding a set of rules. As Oxford University philosopher R. M. Hare says,

> To learn to do anything is never to learn to do an individual act; it is always to learn to do acts of a certain kind in a certain kind of situation; and this is to learn a principle. . . . Without principles we could not learn anything whatever from our elders. . . . Every generation would have to start from scratch and teach itself. But . . . self-teaching, like all other teaching, is the teaching of principles.[1]

If you decide to act on the principle of promise-keeping or not stealing in the case of the millionaire's money, then you adhere to a type of moral theory called *deontology.*

If, on the other hand, you decide to give the money to the World Hunger Relief Organization in order to save an enormous number of lives and restore economic solvency to the region, you side with a type of theory called *teleology* or *teleological ethics.*

Traditionally, two major types of ethical systems have dominated the field. In one, the locus of value is the act or kind of act, and in the other, the locus of value is the outcome or consequences of the act. The former type of theory is called deontological (from the Greek *deon,* meaning "duty," and *logos* meaning "logic"), and the latter is called teleological (from the Greek *teleos,* meaning "having reached one's end" or "finished"). Whereas teleological systems see the ultimate criterion of morality in some nonmoral value that results from acts, deontological systems see certain features in the act itself as having intrinsic value. For example, a teleologist would judge whether lying was morally right or wrong by the consequences it produced, but a deontologist would see something intrinsically wrong in the very act of lying. In the next chapter we will consider the dominant version of teleological ethics, utilitarianism. In chapter 5, we'll examine Immanuel Kant's ethics as the major form of deontological ethics. Then in chapter 6 we shall examine a third

[1]R. M. Hare, *The Language of Morals* (Oxford University Press, 1952), p. 60.

theory, virtue ethics, that holds that what is important is moral character—virtue, not (primarily) rules. It rejects the emphasis on rules set forth in these first two theories. But before we turn to this alternative, let us say a few words about teleological ethics, especially utilitarianism.

As we mentioned earlier, a teleologist is a person whose ethical decision-making aims solely at maximizing nonmoral goods such as pleasure, happiness, welfare, and the amelioration of suffering. That is, the standard of right or wrong action for the teleologist is the comparative consequences of the available actions. The act that produces the best consequences is right. Whereas the deontologist is concerned only with the rightness of the act itself, the teleologist asserts that there is no such thing as an act having intrinsic worth. Whereas for the deontologist there is something intrinsically bad about lying, for the teleologist the only thing wrong with lying is the bad consequences it produces. If you can reasonably calculate that a lie will do even slightly more good than telling the truth, you have an obligation to lie. We will examine a deontological account of lying in Charles Fried's article in chapter 5.

Chapter 6 deals with virtue ethics, the theory that character, not rules, is the basis of morality.

CHAPTER 4

Utilitarianism

Utilitarianism is a consequentialist theory which aims at maximizing happiness or "utility." The founders, Jeremy Bentham (1748–1832) and John Stuart Mill (1806–1873), were humanist reformers, who believed that the letter of the law was often a serious impediment to social progress. "The greatest happiness for the greatest number" was their motto. Morality should serve humanity, not vice versa. They were active in promoting penal reform, animal welfare, and women's rights. According to their theory, we should punish criminals not for retributive (or backward-looking) reasons, but simply to prevent their further crimes and to deter others (forward-looking reasons). The classic version of utilitarianism, called *act utilitarianism,* states that an act is right to the extent that it promotes the most overall happiness. So before you do anything, you ought to consider if other acts might better promote utility. If there are, you have a duty to do them. For example, you should give the money you promised to give to the New York Yankees (in our opening thought-experiment) to the starving people if you think more good will come of it. The atomic bombing of Hiroshima and Nagasaki during World War II was justified on utilitarian grounds. A more moderate version of utilitarianism is called *rule utilitarianism,* which holds that we must choose a set of rules that promise to result in the greatest overall happiness, and follow them even when a given instance is unlikely to result in the greatest happiness for the most people.

A common criticism of utilitarianism is that it fails to take human rights seriously. Bentham thought all rights were legal rather than moral. He said that human rights were nonsense and inalienable rights "nonsense on stilts." What is important is responsibility, not rights. We are to take responsibility both for what we do and for

235

what we allow to happen. A discussion of utilitarianism and justice will occur in some of our selections.

We turn first to a famous incident that occurred on the open seas in which Seaman Holmes was confronted with a dilemma of having his longboat sink or throwing passengers overboard. After this, we consider Bentham's classical exposition of utilitarianism, Mill's further development of the doctrine, and then Kai Nielsen's modern defense. Then we examine Bernard Williams's critique of utilitarianism and Ursula Le Guin's short story about a town whose utilitarian happiness was predicated on the suffering of a child. Finally, we examine Aldous Huxley's dialogue between the utilitarian social engineer of the brave new world, Mustapha Mond, and the savage, who chooses freedom over happiness.

We turn first to a moral dilemma which brings out utilitarian calculations: the case of Seaman Holmes and the longboat of the *William Brown.*

Seaman Holmes and the Longboat of William Brown, Reported by John William Wallace

The American ship *William Brown* left Liverpool on March 13, 1841, bound for Philadelphia. She had on board (besides a heavy cargo) a crew of seventeen and sixty-five passengers. About ten o'clock on the night of April 19, when distant 250 miles southwest of Cape Race, Newfoundland, the vessel struck an iceberg and began to sink rapidly. The longboat and the jolly-boat were cleared away and lowered. The captain, the second mate, seven of the crew, and one passenger got into the jolly-boat. The first-mate, eight seamen, including Holmes, and thirty-two passengers (forty-one in all) got into the long-boat. This was about twice as many passengers as the boat was made to hold. The remaining thirty-one passengers were forced to stay with the sinking ship and soon perished. On the following morning (Tuesday) the captain, being about to part company with the long-boat, gave its crew several directions, and, among other counsel, advised them to obey all the orders of the first-mate, as they would obey his, the captain's. The crew promised that they would do so.

The long-boat was believed to be in generally good condition, but it turned out that she had a leak. The passengers had buckets and bailed so that the vessel remained afloat. However, the captain and mate reported that "a very little irregularity in the stowage would have capsized the long-boat" and "if she had struck any piece of ice she would inevitably have gone down. There was great peril of ice for any boat."

Having survived for 24 hours, on Tuesday night heavy rain fell, and the boat began to sink lower into the sea. The first-mate concluded that the men must be thrown overboard to save the boat.

United States v. Holmes (case no. 15,383), Circuit Court E. d. Pennsylvania, April 22, 1842. Reported by John William Wallace.

He ordered the crew to throw the male passengers overboard. They hesitated. The first-mate repeated the order. "Men, you must go to work, or we shall all perish." They then went to work; and threw out 14 male passengers. Two sisters of one of the men voluntarily dove into the sea. Two married men and a boy were spared, as well as the women. The long-boat stayed afloat. The next morning Holmes discovered a ship in the distance and drew its attention to the long-boat, so that everyone on board was saved.

After the ship reached Philadelphia, the first-mate and most of the seamen, aware of the impending trial, disappeared. Holmes alone was present to be tried for manslaughter. The judge instructed the jury that the law of the sea required that passengers must always be saved in preference to seamen except those indispensable for operating the boat. If, after sacrificing the lives of the expendable sailors, passengers still must be sacrificed, lots must be drawn, assuming there is time to do so.

The survivors testified that Holmes acquitted himself heroically and compassionately during this ordeal. As the boat was about to pull away from the wreck, Holmes, hearing the desperate cry of a mother for her little daughter, who had been left behind, dashed back at the risk of his life, found the girl, and carried her in his arms to the long-boat.

The jury found Holmes guilty of manslaughter but recommended mercy. He was sentenced to six months' imprisonment at hard labor, in addition to the nine months he had already served in prison while waiting for the trial.

For Further Reflection

1. Discuss the various aspects of this case. What are the salient features? What should the first mate have done? What should Holmes have done? What would you have done in Holmes's place? Do you agree with the law that passengers' lives should be preferred to seamen's? Why or why not?

Classical Utilitarianism

JEREMY BENTHAM

Jeremy Bentham (1748–1832) was a British utilitarian and legal reformer. In this essay from *An Introduction to the Principles of Morals and Legislation,* he argues that pleasure is the only intrinsic value and pain the only intrinsic evil. All other goods and evils are derived from these two qualities. Moral rightness and wrongness are defined in his hedonistic utilitarian approach according to their consequences in producing pleasure and pain.

OF THE PRINCIPLE OF UTILITY

I. Nature has placed mankind under the governance of two sovereign masters, *pain* and *pleasure*. It is for them alone to point out what we ought to do, as well as to determine what we shall do. On the one hand the standard of right and wrong, on the other the chain of causes and effects, are fastened to their throne. They govern us in all we do, in all we say, in all we think: every effort we can make to throw off our subjection, will serve but to demonstrate and confirm it. In words a man may pretend to abjure their empire: but in reality he will remain subject to it all the while. The *principle of utility* recognizes this subjection, and assumes it for the foundation of that system, the object of which is to rear the fabric of felicity by the hands of reason and of law. Systems which attempt to question it, deal in sounds instead of sense, in caprice instead of reason, in darkness instead of light.

But enough of metaphor and declamation: it is not by such means that moral science is to be improved.

II. The principle of utility is the foundation of the present work: it will be proper therefore at the outset to give an explicit and determinate account of what is meant by it. By the principle of utility is meant that principle which approves or disapproves of every action whatsoever, according to the tendency which it appears to have to augment or diminish the happiness of the party whose

Excerpted from *An Introduction to the Principles of Morals and Legislation* (1789).

interest is in question: or, what is the same thing in other words, to promote or to oppose that happiness. I say of every action whatsoever; and therefore not only of every action of a private individual, but of every measure of government.

III. By utility is meant that property in any object, whereby it tends to produce benefit, advantage, pleasure, good, or happiness, (all this in the present case comes to the same thing) or (what comes again to the same thing) to prevent the happening of mischief, pain, evil, or unhappiness to the party whose interest is considered: if that party be the community in general, then the happiness of the community: if a particular individual, then the happiness of that individual.

VALUE OF A LOT OF PLEASURE OR PAIN, HOW TO BE MEASURED

I. Pleasures then, and the avoidance of pains, are the ends which the legislator has in view: it behoves him therefore to understand their *value*. Pleasures and pains are the *instruments* he has to work with; it behoves him therefore to understand their force, which is again, in other words, their value.

II. To a person considered *by himself,* the value of a pleasure or pain considered *by itself,* will be greater or less, according to the four following circumstances:

1. Its *intensity.*
2. Its *duration.*
3. Its *certainty* or *uncertainty.*
4. Its *propinquity* or *remoteness.*

III. These are the circumstances which are to be considered in estimating a pleasure or a pain considered each of them by itself. But when the value of any pleasure or pain is considered for the purpose of estimating the tendency of any *act* by which it is produced, there are two other circumstances to be taken into the account; these are,

5. Its *fecundity,* or the chance it has of being followed by sensations of the *same* kind: that is, pleasures, if it be a pleasure: pains, if it be a pain.
6. Its *purity,* or the chance it has of *not* being followed by sensations of the *opposite* kind: that is, pains, if it be a pleasure: pleasures, if it be a pain.

These two last, however, are in strictness scarcely to be deemed properties of the pleasure or the pain itself; they are not, therefore, in strictness to be taken into the account of the value of that pleasure or that pain. They are in strictness to be deemed properties only of the act, or other event, by which such pleasure or pain has been produced; and accordingly are only to be taken into the account of the tendency of such act or such event.

IV. To a *number* of persons, with reference of each of whom the value of a pleasure or a pain is considered, it will be greater or less, according to seven circumstances: to wit, the six preceding ones; *viz.*

1. Its *intensity.*
2. Its *duration.*
3. Its *certainty* or *uncertainty.*
4. Its *propinquity* or *remoteness.*
5. Its *fecundity.*
6. Its *purity.*

And one other; to wit:

7. Its *extent;* that is, the number of persons to whom it *extends;* or (in other words) who are affected by it.

V. To take an exact account then of the general tendency of any act, by which the interests of a community are affected, proceed as follows. Begin with any one person of those whose interests seem most immediately to be affected by it: and take an account,

1. Of the value of each distinguishable pleasure which appears to be produced by it in the first instance.

2. Of the value of each *pain* which appears to be produced by it in the *first* instance.

3. Of the value of each pleasure which appears to be produced by it *after* the first. This constitutes the *fecundity* of the first *pleasure* and the *impurity* of the first *pain.*

4. Of the value of each *pain* which appears to be produced by it after the first. This constitutes the *fecundity* of the first *pain,* and the *impurity* of the first pleasure.

5. Sum up all the values of all the *pleasures* on the one side, and those of all the pains on the other. The balance, if it be on the side of pleasure, will give the *good* tendency of the act upon the whole, with respect to the interests of that *individual* person; if on the side of pain, the *bad* tendency of it upon the whole.

6. Take an account of the *number* of persons whose interests appear to be concerned; and repeat the above process with respect to each. *Sum up* the numbers expressive of the degrees of *good* tendency, which the act has, with respect to each individual, in regard to whom the tendency of it is *good* upon the whole: do this again with respect to each individual, in regard to whom the tendency of it is *bad* upon the whole. Take the *balance;* which, if on the side of *pleasure,* will give the general *good tendency* of the act, with respect to the total number or community of individuals concerned; if on the side of pain, the general *evil tendency,* with respect to the same community.

VI. It is not to be expected that this process should be strictly pursued previously to every moral judgment, or to every legislative or judicial operation. It may, however, be always kept in view: and as near as the process actually pursued on these occasions approaches to it, so near will such process approach to the character of an exact one.

VII. The same process is alike applicable to pleasure and pain, in whatever shape they appear: and by whatever denomination they are distinguished: to pleasure, whether it be called *good* (which is properly the cause or instrument of pleasure) or *profit* (which is distant pleasure, or the cause or instrument of distant pleasure), or *convenience,* or *advantage, benefit, emolument, happiness,* and so forth: to pain, whether it be called *evil,* (which corresponds to *good*) or *mischief,* or *inconvenience,* or *disadvantage,* or *loss,* or *unhappiness,* and so forth.

VIII. Nor is this a novel and unwarranted, any more than it is a useless, theory. In all this there is nothing but what the practice of mankind, wheresoever they have a clear view of their own interest, is perfectly conformable to. An article of property, an estate in land, for instance, is valuable, on what account? On account of the pleasures of all kinds which it enables a man to produce, and what comes to the same thing the pains of all kinds which it enables him to avert. But the value of such an article of property is universally understood to rise or fall according to the length or shortness of the time which a man had in it: the certainty or uncertainty of its coming into possession: and the nearness or remoteness of the time at which, if at all, it is to come into possession. As to the *intensity* of the pleasures which a man may derive from it, this is never thought of, because it depends upon the use which each particular person may come to make of it; which cannot be estimated till the particular pleasures he may come to derive from it, or the particular pains he may come to exclude by means of it, are brought to view. For the same reason, neither does he think of the *fecundity* or *purity* of those pleasures.

Thus much for pleasure and pain, happiness and unhappiness, in *general*. . . .

XVII. Under the Gentoo and Mahometan religions, the interests of the rest of the animal creation seem to have met with some attention. Why have they not, universally, with as much as those of human creatures, allowance made for the difference in point of sensibility? Because the laws that are have been the work of mutual fear; a sentiment which the less rational animals have not had the same means as man has of turning to account. Why **ought** they not? No reason can be given. If the being eaten were all, there is very good reason why we should be suffered to eat such of them as we like to eat: we are the better for it, and they are never the worse. They have none of those long-protracted anticipations of future misery which we have. The death they suffer in our hands commonly is, and always may be, a speedier, and by that means a less painful one, than that which would await them in the inevitable course of nature. If the being killed were all, there is very good reason why we should be suffered to kill such as molest us: we should be the worse for their living, and they are never the worse for being dead. But is there any reason why we should be suffered to torment them? Not any that I can see. Are there any why we should **not** be suffered to torment them? Yes, several. The day has been, I grieve to say in many places it is not yet past, in which the greater part of the species, under the denomination of slaves, have been treated by the law exactly upon the same footing, as, in England for example, the inferior races of animals are still. The day may come, when the rest of the animal creation may acquire those rights which never could have been withholden from them but by the hand of tyranny. The French have already discovered that the blackness of the skin is no reason why a human being should be abandoned without redress to the caprice of a tormentor. It may come one day to be recognized, that the number of the legs, the villosity of the skin, or the termination of the **os**

sacrum, are reasons equally insufficient for abandoning a sensitive being to the same fate. What else is it that should trace the insuperable line? Is it the faculty of reason, or, perhaps, the faculty of discourse? But a full-grown horse or dog is beyond comparison a more rational, as well as a more conversable animal, than an infant of a day, or a week, or even a month, old. But suppose the case were otherwise, what would it avail? The question is not, Can they **reason**? nor, Can they *talk*? but, Can they **suffer**?

For Further Reflection

1. Analyze Bentham's utilitarianism. Do you agree with him that "pain and pleasure" are our "two sovereign masters"? What does he mean by *pain* and *pleasure?* Note that *pleasure* is an ambiguous word. It can mean "sensuous titillation" or "satisfaction." Which does Bentham mean? Which concept does he need for his theory?

2. In his own time Bentham was criticized for setting forth a "pig philosophy," since his "simplistic" notions of motivation by pain and pleasure are more suited to pigs than humans. Do you agree with this judgment?

3. Bentham's utilitarianism requires that we perform a hedonic calculus, summing up all the prospective pleasures likely to result from an act and subtracting the pains. Go over his process and note the difficulties of doing this.

4. Reread the last paragraph regarding the criterion of suffering as the basis for moral consideration. What are the implications of this principle for ethics? For our relations with animals?

Utilitarianism Refined

JOHN STUART MILL

English philosopher John Stuart Mill (1806–1873) has earned a prestigious place in the pantheon of respected philosophers for his work in epistemology (the study of knowledge), deductive and inductive logic, political thought, and ethics. The centerpiece of the latter is, of course, his *Utilitarianism* (1861), in which he articulates a more sophisticated version of Jeremy Bentham's views. In this excerpt from the book, Mill tries to improve on Bentham's one-dimensional concept of happiness.

. . . The creed which accepts as the foundation of morals, Utility, or the Greatest Happiness Principle, holds that actions are right in proportion as they tend to promote happiness, wrong as they tend to produce the reverse of happiness. By happiness is intended pleasure, and the absence of pain; by unhappiness, pain, and the privation of pleasure. To give a clear view of the moral standard set up by the theory, much more requires to be said; in particular, what things it includes in the ideas of pain and pleasure; and to what extent this is left an open question. But these supplementary explanations do not affect the theory of life on which this theory of morality is grounded—namely, that pleasure, and freedom from pain, are the only things desirable as ends; and that all desirable things (which are as numerous in the utilitarian as in any other scheme) are desirable either for the pleasure inherent in themselves, or as means to the promotion of pleasure and the prevention of pain.

Now, such a theory of life excites in many minds, and among them in some of the most estimable in feeling and purpose, inveterate dislike. To suppose that life has (as they express it) no higher end than pleasure—no better and nobler object of desire and pursuit—they designate as utterly mean and grovelling; as a doctrine worthy only of swine, to whom the followers of Epicurus were, at a very early period, contemptuously likened; and modern holders of the doctrine are occasionally made the subject of equally polite comparisons by its German, French, and English assailants.

From *Utilitarianism,* 7th ed. (London: Longmans, Green, and Co., 1879).

When thus attacked, the Epicureans have always answered, that it is not they, but their accusers, who represent human nature in a degrading light; since the accusation supposes human beings to be capable of no pleasures except those of which swine are capable. If this supposition were true, the charge could not be gainsaid, but would then be no longer an imputation; for if the sources of pleasure were precisely the same to human beings and to swine, the rule of life which is good enough for the one would be good enough for the other. The comparison of the Epicurean life to that of beasts is felt as degrading, precisely because a beast's pleasures do not satisfy a human being's conceptions of happiness. Human beings have faculties more elevated than the animal appetites, and when once made conscious of them, do not regard anything as happiness which does not include their gratification. I do not, indeed, consider the Epicureans to have been by any means fault-less in drawing out their scheme of consequences from the utili-tarian principle. To do this in any sufficient manner, many Stoic, as well as Christian elements require to be included. But there is no known Epicurean theory of life which does not assign to the pleasures of the intellect; of the feelings and imagination, and of the moral sentiments, a much higher value as pleasures than to those of mere sensation. It must be admitted, however, that utili-tarian writers in general have placed the superiority of mental over bodily pleasures chiefly in the greater permanency, safety, uncost-liness, &c., of the former—that is, in their circumstantial advantages rather than in their intrinsic nature. And on all these points utili-tarians have fully proved their case; but they might have taken the other, and, as it may be called, higher ground, with entire consis-tency. It is quite compatible with the principle of utility to recog-nise the fact, that some *kinds* of pleasure are more desirable and more valuable than others. It would be absurd that while, in esti-mating all other things, quality is considered as well as quantity, the estimation of pleasures should be supposed to depend on quan-tity alone.

If I am asked, what I mean by difference of quality in pleasures, or what makes one pleasure more valuable than another, merely as a pleasure, except its being greater in amount, there is but one possible answer. Of two pleasures, if there be one to which all or almost all who have experience of both give a decided preference, irrespective of any feeling of moral obligation to prefer it, that is the more desirable pleasure. If one of the two is, by those who are competently acquainted with both, placed so far above the other that they prefer it, even though knowing it to be attended with a greater amount of discontent, and would not resign it for any quantity of the other pleasure which their nature is capable of, we are justified in ascribing to the preferred enjoyment a superiority in quality, so far outweighing quantity as to render it, in comparison, of small account.

Now it is an unquestionable fact that those who are equally acquainted with, and equally capable of appreciating and enjoying, both, do give a most marked preference to the manner of existence which employs their higher faculties. Few human creatures would consent to be changed into any of the lower animals, for a promise of the fullest allowance of a beast's pleasures; no intelligent human being would consent to be a fool, no instructed person would be an ignoramus, no person of feeling and conscience would be selfish and base, even though they should be persuaded that the fool, the dunce, or the rascal is better satisfied with his lot than they are with theirs. They would not resign what they possess more than he, for the most complete satisfaction of all the desires which they have in common with him. If they ever fancy they would, it is only in cases of unhappiness so extreme, that to escape from it they would exchange their lot for almost any other, however undesirable in their own eyes. A being of higher faculties requires more to make him happy, is capable probably of more acute suffering, and is certainly accessible to it at more points, than one of an inferior type; but in spite of these liabilities, he can never really wish to sink into what he feels to be a lower grade of existence. We may give what explanation we please of this unwillingness; we may attribute it to pride, a name which is given indiscriminately to some of the most and to some of the least estimable feelings of which mankind are capable; we may refer it to the love of liberty and personal independence, an appeal to which was with the Stoics one of the most effective means for the inculcation of it; to the love of power, or to the love of excitement, both of which do really enter into and contribute to it: but its most appropriate appellation is a sense of dignity, which all human beings possess in one form or other, and in some, though by no means in exact, proportion to their higher faculties, and which is so essential a part of the happiness of those in whom it is strong, that nothing which conflicts with it could be, otherwise than momentarily, an object of desire to them. Whoever supposes that this preference takes place at a sacrifice of happiness—that the superior being, in anything like equal circumstances, is not happier than the inferior—confounds the two very different ideas, of happiness, and content. It is indisputable that the being whose capacities of enjoyment are low, has the greatest chance of having them fully satisfied; and a highly-endowed being will always feel that any happiness which he can look for, as the world is constituted, is imperfect. But he can learn to bear its imperfections, if they are at all bearable; and they will not make him envy the being who is indeed unconscious of the imperfections, but only because he feels not at all the good which those imperfections qualify. It is better to be a human being dissatisfied than a pig satisfied; better to be Socrates dissatisfied than a fool satisfied. And if the fool, or the pig, is of a different opinion, it is because they only know their own side of the question. The other party to the comparison knows both sides.

It may be objected, that many who are capable of the higher pleasures, occasionally, under the influence of temptation, postpone them to the lower. But this is quite compatible with a full appreciation of the intrinsic superiority of the higher. Men often, from infirmity of character, make their election for the nearer good, though they know it to be the less valuable; and this no less when the choice is between two bodily pleasures, than when it is between bodily and mental. They pursue sensual indulgences to the injury of health, though perfectly aware that health is the greater good. It may be further objected, that many who begin with youthful enthusiasm for everything noble, as they advance in years sink into indolence and selfishness. But I do not believe that those who undergo this very common change, voluntarily choose the lower description of pleasures in preference to the higher. I believe that before they devote themselves exclusively to the one, they have already become incapable of the other. Capacity for the nobler feelings is in most natures a very tender plant, easily killed, not only by hostile influences, but by mere want of sustenance; and in the majority of young persons it speedily dies away if the occupations to which their position in life has devoted them, and the society into which it has thrown them, are not favourable to keeping that higher capacity in exercise. Men lose their high aspirations as they lose their intellectual tastes, because they have not time or opportunity for indulging them; and they addict themselves to inferior pleasures, not because they deliberately prefer them, but because they are either the only ones to which they have access, or the only ones which they are any longer capable of enjoying. It may be questioned whether any one who has remained equally susceptible to both classes of pleasures, ever knowingly and calmly preferred the lower; though many, in all ages, have broken down in an ineffectual attempt to combine both.

From this verdict of the only competent judges, I apprehend there can be no appeal. On a question which is the best worth having of two pleasures, or which of two modes of existence is the most grateful to the feelings, apart from its moral attributes and from its consequences, the judgment of those who are qualified by knowledge of both, or, if they differ, that of the majority among them, must be admitted as final. And there needs be the less hesitation to accept this judgment respecting the quality of pleasures, since there is no other tribunal to be referred to even on the question of quantity. What means are there of determining which is the acutest of two pains, or the intensest of two pleasurable sensations, except the general suffrage of those who are familiar with both? Neither pains nor pleasures are homogeneous, and pain is always heterogeneous with pleasure. What is there to decide whether a particular pleasure is worth purchasing at the cost of a particular pain, except the feelings and judgment of the experienced? When, therefore, those feelings and judgment declare the pleasures derived from the higher faculties to be preferable *in kind,* apart from the question of intensity, to those of which the animal nature, disjoined from the higher faculties, is susceptible, they are entitled on this subject to the same regard. . . .

For Further Reflection

1. According to Mill, in what ways can the experience of happiness vary? Do you agree?

2. What does Mill mean by "It is better to be a human being dissatisfied than a pig satisfied; better to be Socrates dissatisfied than a fool satisfied"?

3. In Mill's view, who is to be the judge of the desirability of different forms of pleasure?

4. Do you believe that the quantity of happiness is more important than its quality? Why or why not?

A Defense of Utilitarianism

KAI NIELSEN

Kai Nielsen, until his retirement, was professor of philosophy at Calgary University. He has written important works in the philosophy of religion and in political theory, as well as in ethics. This essay is a clear example of act utilitarianism, the doctrine that we ought to evaluate each act on its own merits, those merits consisting in whether the act maximizes utility. Nielsen sets forth his theory as a credible alternative to moral conservativism or deontological ethics, which maintains that there are "moral principles, prescribing determinate actions, with which it would always be wrong not to act in accordance no matter what the consequences." He argues, to the contrary, that it is the consequences that determine the moral worth of an action.

Nielsen's arguments in favor of utilitarianism partly depend on the notion of negative responsibility. That is, we are responsible not only for the consequences of our actions, but also for the consequences of our *nonactions*.

I

It is sometimes claimed that any consequentialist view of ethics has monstrous implications which make such a conception of morality untenable. What we must do—so the claim goes—is reject all forms of consequentialism and accept what has been labeled 'conservatism' or 'moral absolutism.' By 'conservatism' is meant, here, a normative ethical theory which maintains that there is a privileged moral principle or cluster of moral principles, prescribing determinate actions, with which it would always be wrong not to act in accordance no matter what the consequences. A key example of such a principle is the claim that it is always wrong to kill an innocent human, whatever the consequences of not doing so.

I will argue that such moral conservatism is itself unjustified and, indeed, has morally unacceptable consequences, while consequen-

From *Ethics* 82 (1972): 113–124. Reprinted by permission of The University of Chicago Press.

tialism does not have implications which are morally monstrous and does not contain evident moral mistakes.

A consequentialist maintains that actions, rules, policies, practices, and moral principles are ultimately to be judged by certain consequences: to wit (for a very influential kind of consequentialism), by whether doing them more than, or at least as much as doing anything else, or acting in accordance with them more than or at least as much as acting in accordance with alternative policies, practices, rules or principles, tends, on the whole, and for *everyone* involved, to maximize satisfaction and minimize dissatisfaction. The states of affairs to be sought are those which maximize these things to the greatest extent possible for all mankind. But while this all sounds very humane and humanitarian, when its implications are thought through, it has been forcefully argued, it will be seen actually to have inhumane and morally intolerable implications. Circumstances could arise in which one holding such a view would have to assert that one was justified in punishing, killing, torturing, or deliberately harming the innocent, and such a consequence is, morally speaking, unacceptable.[1] As Anscombe has put it, anyone who "really thinks, *in advance,* that it is open to question whether such an action as procuring the judicial execution of the innocent should be quite excluded from consideration—I do not want to argue with him; he shows a corrupt mind."[2]

At the risk of being thought to exhibit a corrupt mind and a shallow consequentialist morality, I should like to argue that things are not as simple and straightforward as Anscombe seems to believe.

Surely, every moral man must be appalled at the judicial execution of the innocent or at the punishment, torture, and killing of the innocent. Indeed, being appalled by such behavior partially defines what it is to be a moral agent. And a consequentialist has very good utilitarian grounds for being so appalled, namely, that it is always wrong to inflict pain for its own sake. But this does not get to the core considerations which divide a conservative position such as Anscombe's from a consequentialist view. There are a series

---

[1]Alan Donagan, "Is There a Credible Form of Utilitarianism?," and H. J. McCloskey, "A Non-Utilitarian Approach to Punishment," both in Michael D. Bayles, ed. *Contemporary Utilitarianism* (Garden City, N.Y.: Doubleday, 1968).

[2]Elizabeth Anscombe, "Modern Moral Philosophy," *Philosophy 23* (January 1957): 16–17.

of tough cases that need to be taken to heart and their implications thought through by any reflective person, be he a conservative or a consequentialist. By doing this, we can get to the heart of the issue between conservatism and consequentialism. Consider this clash between conservatism and consequentialism arising over the problem of a 'just war.'

> If we deliberately bomb civilian targets, we do not pretend that civilians are combatants in any simple fashion, but argue that this bombing will terminate hostilities more quickly, and will minimize all around suffering. It is hard to see how any brand of utilitarian will escape Miss Anscombe's objections. We are certainly killing the innocent . . . we are not killing them for the sake of killing them, but to save the lives of other innocent persons. Utilitarians, I think, grit their teeth and put up with this as part of the logic of total war; Miss Anscombe and anyone who thinks like her surely has to either redescribe the situation to ascribe guilt to the civilians or else she has to refuse to accept this sort of military tactics as simply wrong.[3]

It is indeed true that we cannot but feel the force of Anscombe's objections here. But is it the case that anyone shows a corrupt mind if he defends such bombing when, horrible as it is, it will quite definitely lessen appreciably the total amount of suffering and death in the long run, and if he is sufficiently nonevasive not to rationalize such a bombing of civilians into a situation in which all the putatively innocent people—children and all—are somehow in some measure judged guilty? Must such a man exhibit a corrupt moral sense if he refuses to hold that such military tactics are never morally justified? Must this be the monstrous view of a fanatical man devoid of any proper moral awareness? It is difficult for me to believe that this must be so.

Consider the quite parallel actions of guerrilla fighters and terrorists in wars of national liberation. In certain almost unavoidable circumstances, they must deliberately kill the innocent. We need to see some cases in detail here to get the necessary contextual background, and for this reason the motion picture *The Battle of Algiers* can be taken as a convenient point of reference. There we saw Algerian women—gentle, kindly women with children of their own and plainly people of moral sensitivity—with evident heaviness of

[3]Alan Ryan, "Review of Jan Narveson's *Morality and Utility,*" *Philosophical Books 9,* no. 3 (October 1958): 14.

heart, plant bombs which they had every good reason to believe would kill innocent people, including children; and we also saw a French general, also a human being of moral fiber and integrity, order the torture of Arab terrorists and threaten the bombing of houses in which terrorists were concealed but which also contained innocent people, including children. There are indeed many people involved in such activities who are cruel, sadistic beasts, or simply morally indifferent or, in important ways, morally uncomprehending. But the characters I have referred to from *The Battle of Algiers* were not of that stamp. They were plainly moral agents of a high degree of sensitivity, and yet they deliberately killed or were prepared to kill the innocent. And, with inessential variations, this is a recurrent phenomenon of human living in extreme situations. Such cases are by no means desert-island or esoteric cases.

It is indeed arguable whether such actions are always morally wrong—whether anyone should ever act as the Arab women or French general acted. But what could not be reasonably maintained, *pace* Anscombe, by any stretch of the imagination, is that the characters I described from *The Battle of Algiers* exhibited corrupt minds. Possibly morally mistaken, yes; guilty of moral corruption, no.

Dropping the charge of moral corruption but sticking with the moral issue about what actions are right, is it not the case that my consequentialist position logically forces me to conclude that under some circumstances—where the good to be achieved is great enough—I must not only countenance but actually advocate such violence toward the innocent? But is it not always, no matter what the circumstances or consequences, wrong to countenance, advocate, or engage in such violence? To answer such a question affirmatively is to commit oneself to the kind of moral absolutism or conservatism which Anscombe advocates. But, given the alternatives, should not one be such a conservative or at least hold that certain deontological principles must never be overridden?

I will take, so to speak, the papal bull by the horns and answer that there are circumstances when such violence must be reluctantly assented to or even taken to be something that one, morally speaking, must do. But, *pace* Anscombe, this very much needs arguing, and I shall argue it; but first I would like to set out some further but simpler cases which have a similar bearing. They are, by contrast, artificial cases. I use them because, in their greater simplicity, by contrast with my above examples, there are fewer variables to control and I can more conveniently make the essential conceptual and moral points. But, if my argument is correct for these simpler cases, the line of reasoning employed is intended to be applicable to those more complex cases as well.

II

Consider the following cases embedded in their exemplary tales:

1. *The Case of the Innocent Fat Man*

Consider the story (well known to philosophers) of the fat man stuck in the mouth of a cave on a coast. He was leading a group of people out of the cave when he got stuck in the mouth of the cave and in a very short time high tide will be upon them, and unless he is promptly unstuck, they all will be drowned except the fat man, whose head is out of the cave. But, fortunately or unfortunately, someone has with him a stick of dynamite. The short of the matter is, either they use the dynamite and blast the poor innocent fat man out of the mouth of the cave or everyone else drowns. Either one life or many lives. Our conservative presumably would take the attitude that it is all in God's hands and say that he ought never to blast the fat man out, for it is always wrong to kill the innocent. Must or should a moral man come to that conclusion? I shall argue that he should not.

My first exemplary tale was designed to show that our normal, immediate, rather absolutistic, moral reactions need to be questioned along with such principles as 'The direct intention of the death of an innocent person is never justifiable.' I have hinted (and later shall argue) that we should *beware* of our moral outrage here—our naturally conservative and unreflective moral reactions—for here the consequentialist has a strong case for what I shall call 'moral radicalism.' But, before turning to a defense of that, I want to tell another story taken from Philippa Foot but used for my own purposes.[4] This tale, I shall argue, has a different import than our previous tale. Here our unrehearsed, commonsense moral reactions will stand up under

---

[4] Philippa Foot, "The Problem of Abortion and the Doctrine of the Double Effect," *Oxford Review,* no. 5 (1967): 5–15.

moral scrutiny. But, I shall also argue when I consider them in Section III, that our commonsense moral reactions here, initial expectations to the contrary notwithstanding, can be shown to be justified on consequentialist grounds. The thrust of my argument for this case is that we are not justified in opting for a theistic and/or deontological absolutism or in rejecting consequentialism.

2. *The Magistrate and the Threatening Mob*

A magistrate or judge is faced with a very real threat from a large and uncontrollable mob of rioters demanding a culprit for a crime. Unless the criminal is produced, promptly tried, and executed, they will take their own bloody revenge on a much smaller and quite vulnerable section of the community (a kind of frenzied pogrom). The judge knows that the real culprit is unknown and that the authorities do not even have a good clue as to who he may be. But he also knows that there is within easy reach a disreputable, thoroughly disliked, and useless man, who, though innocent, could easily be blamed so that the mob would be quite convinced that he was guilty and would be pacified if he were promptly executed. Recognizing that he can prevent the occurrence of extensive carnage only by framing some innocent person, the magistrate has him framed, goes through the mockery of a trial, and has him executed. Most of us regard such a framing and execution of such a man in such circumstances as totally unacceptable.[5] There are some who would say that it is categorically wrong—morally inexcusable—*whatever the circumstances.* Indeed, such a case remains a problem for the consequentialist, but here again, I shall argue, one can consistently remain a consequentialist and continue to accept commonsense moral convictions about such matters.

My storytelling is at an end. The job is to see what the stories imply. We must try to determine whether thinking through their implications should lead a clear-headed and morally sensitive man to abandon consequentialism and to adopt some form of theistic absolutism and/or deontological absolutism. I shall argue that it does not.

[5]Later, I shall show that there are desert-island circumstances—i.e., highly improbable situations—in which such judicial railroading might be a moral necessity. But I also show what little force desert-island cases have in the articulation and defense of a normative ethical theory.

III

I shall consider the last case first because there are good reasons why the consequentialist should stick with commonsense moral convictions for such cases. I shall start by giving my rationale for that claim. If the magistrate were a tough-minded but morally conscientious consequentialist, he could still, on straightforward consequentialist grounds, refuse to frame and execute the innocent man, even knowing that this would unleash the mob and cause much suffering and many deaths. The rationale for his particular moral stand would be that, by so framing and then executing such an innocent man, he would, in the long run, cause still more suffering through the resultant corrupting effect on the institution of justice. That is, in a case involving such extensive general interest in the issue—without that, there would be no problem about preventing the carnage or call for such extreme measures—knowledge that the man was framed, that the law had prostituted itself, would, surely, eventually leak out. This would encourage mob action in other circumstances, would lead to an increased skepticism about the incorruptibility or even the reliability of the judicial process, and would set a dangerous precedent for less clearheaded or less scrupulously humane magistrates. Given such a potential for the corruption of justice, a utilitarian or consequentialist judge or magistrate could, on good utilitarian or consequentialist grounds, argue that it was morally wrong to frame an innocent man. If the mob must rampage if such a sacrificial lamb is not provided, then the mob must rampage.

Must a utilitarian or consequentialist come to such a conclusion? The answer is no. It is the conclusion which is, as things stand, the most reasonable conclusion, but that he *must* come to it is far too strong a claim. A consequentialist could *consistently*—I did not say successfully—argue that, in taking the above tough-minded utilitarian position, we have overestimated the corrupting effects of such judicial railroading. His circumstance was an extreme one: a situation not often to be repeated even if, instead of acting as he did, he had set a precedent by such an act of judicial murder. A utilitarian rather more skeptical than most utilitarians about the claims of commonsense morality might reason that the lesser evil here is the judicial murder of an innocent man, vile as it is. He would persist in his moral iconoclasm by standing on the consequentialist rock that the lesser evil is always to be preferred to the greater evil.

The short of it is that utilitarians could disagree, as other consequentialists could disagree, about what is morally required of us in that case. The disagreement here between utilitarians or consequentialists of the same type is not one concerning fundamental moral principles but a disagreement about the empirical facts, about what course of action would in the long run produce the least suffering and the most happiness for *everyone* involved.[6]

However, considering the effect advocating the deliberate judicial killing of an innocent man would have on the reliance people put on commonsense moral beliefs of such a ubiquitous sort as the belief that the innocent must not be harmed, a utilitarian who defended the centrality of commonsense moral beliefs would indeed have a strong utilitarian case here. But the most crucial thing to recognize is that, to regard such judicial bowing to such a threatening mob as unqualifiedly wrong, as morally intolerable, one need not reject utilitarianism and accept some form of theistic or deontological absolutism.

It has been argued, however, that, in taking such a stance, I still have not squarely faced the moral conservative's central objection to the judicial railroading of the innocent. I allow, as a consequentialist, that there could be circumstances, at least as far as logical possibilities are concerned, in which such a railroading would be justified but that, as things actually go, it is not and probably never in fact will be justified. But the conservative's point is that in *no circumstances, either actual or conceivable, would it be justified*. No matter what the consequences, it is unqualifiedly unjustified. To say, as I do, that the situations in which it might be justified are desert-island, esoteric cases which do not occur in life, is not to the point, for, as Alan Donagan argues, "Moral theory is *a priori,* as clear-headed utilitarians like Henry Sidgwick recognized. It is, as Leibniz would say, 'true of all possible worlds.' "[7] Thus, to argue as I have and as others have that the counterexamples directed against the consequentialists appeal to conditions which are never in fact fulfilled or are unlikely to be fulfilled is beside the point.[8]

[6]'Everyone' here is used distributively, i.e., I am talking about the interests of each and every one. In that sense, everyone's interests need to be considered.

[7]Donagan, op. cit., p. 189.

[8]T. L. S. Sprigge argues in such a manner in his "A Utilitarian Reply to Dr. McCloskey" in Michael D. Bayles, ed. *Contemporary Utilitarianism* (Garden City, N.Y.: Doubleday, 1968).

Whether "a moral theory is true or false depends on whether its implications for all possible worlds are true. Hence, whether utilitarianism (or consequentialism) is true or false cannot depend on how the actual world is."[9] It is possible to specify logically conceivable situations in which consequentialism would have implications which are monstrous—for example, certain beneficial judicial murders of the innocent (whether they are even remotely likely to obtain is irrelevant)—hence consequentialism must be false.

We should not take such a short way with consequentialists, for what is true in Donagan's claim about moral theory's being a priori will not refute or even render implausible consequentialism, and what would undermine it in such a claim about the a priori nature of moral theory and presumably moral claims is not true.

To say that moral theory is a priori is probably correct if that means that categorical moral claims—fundamental moral statements—cannot be deduced from empirical statements or nonmoral theological statements, such that it is a contradiction to assert the empirical and/or nonmoral theological statements and deny the categorical moral claims or vice versa.[10] In that fundamental sense, it is reasonable and, I believe, justifiable to maintain that moral theory is autonomous and a priori. It is also a priori in the sense that moral statements are not themselves a kind of empirical statement. That is, if I assert 'One ought never to torture any sentient creature' or 'One ought never to kill an innocent man,' I am not trying to predict or describe what people do or are likely to do but am asserting what they are *to do*. It is also true that, if a moral statement is true, it holds for all possible worlds *in which situations are exactly the sort characterized in the statement.* If it is true for one, it is true for all. You cannot consistently say that *A* ought to do *B* in situation **Y** and deny that someone exactly like *A* in a situation exactly like **Y** ought to do *B*.

In these ways, moral claims and indeed moral theory are a priori. But it is also evident that none of these ways will touch the consequentialist or utilitarian arguments. After all, the consequentialist need not be, and typically has not been, an ethical naturalist—he need not think moral claims are derivable from factual claims

[9]Donagan, op. cit., p. 194.
[10]There is considerable recent literature about whether it is possible to derive moral claims from nonmoral claims. See W. D. Hudson, ed., *The Is-Ought Question: A Collection of Papers on the Central Problem in Moral Philosophy* (New York: St. Martin's Press, 1969).

or that moral claims are a subspecies of empirical statement and he could accept—indeed, he must accept—what is an important truism anyway, that you cannot consistently say that A ought to do B in situation Y and deny that someone exactly like A in a situation exactly like Y ought to do B. But he could and should deny that moral claims are a priori in the sense that rational men must or even will make them without regard for the context, the situation, in which they are made. We say people ought not to drive way over the speed limit, or speed on icy roads, or throw knives at each other. But, if human beings had a kind of metallic exoskeleton and would not be hurt, disfigured, or seriously inconvenienced by knives sticking in them or by automobile crashes, we would not—so evidently at least—have good grounds for saying such speeding or knife throwing is wrong. It would not be so obvious that it was unreasonable and immoral to do these things if these conditions obtained.

In the very way we choose to describe the situation when we make ethical remarks, it is important in making this choice that we know what the world is like and what human beings are like. Our understanding of the situation, our understanding of human nature and motivation cannot but affect our structuring of the moral case. The consequentialist is saying that, as the world goes, there are good grounds for holding that judicial killings are morally intolerable, though he would have to admit that if the world (including human beings) were very different, such killings could be something that ought to be done. But, in holding this, he is not committed to denying the universalizability of moral judgments, for, where he would reverse or qualify the moral judgment, the situation must be different. He is only committed to claiming that, where the situation is the same or relevantly similar and the persons are relevantly similar, they must, if they are to act morally, do the same thing. However, he is claiming both (1) that, as things stand, judicial killing of the innocent is always wrong and (2) that it is an irrational moral judgment to assert of reasonably determinate actions (e.g., killing an innocent man) that they are unjustifiable and morally unacceptable on all *possible* worlds, whatever the situation and whatever the consequences.

Donagan's claims about the a priori nature of moral theories do not show such a consequentialist claim to be mistaken or even give us the slightest reason for thinking that it is mistaken. What is brutal and vile, for example, throwing a knife at a human being just for the fun of it, would not be so, if human beings were invulnerable to harm from such a direction because they had a metallic exoskeleton. Similarly, what is, as things are, morally intolerable, for example, the judicial killing of the innocent, need not be morally intolerable in all conceivable circumstances.

Such considerations support the utilitarian or consequentialist skeptical of simply taking the claims of our commonsense morality as a rock-bottom ground of appeal for moral theorizing. Yet it may also well be the case—given our extensive cruelty any way—that, if we ever start sanctioning such behavior, an even greater callousness toward life than the very extensive callousness extant now will, as a matter of fact, develop. Given a normative ethical theory which sanctions, *under certain circumstances,* such judicial murders, there may occur an undermining of our moral disapproval of killing and our absolutely essential moral principle that all human beings, great and small, are deserving of respect. This is surely enough, together with the not unimportant weight of even our unrehearsed moral feelings, to give strong utilitarian weight *here* to the dictates of our commonsense morality. Yet, I think I have also said enough to show that someone who questions their 'unquestionableness' in such a context does not thereby exhibit a 'corrupt mind' and that it is an open question whether he must be conceptually confused or morally mistaken over this matter.

IV

So far, I have tried to show with reference to the case of the magistrate and the threatening mob how consequentialists can reasonably square their normative ethical theories with an important range of commonsense moral convictions. Now, I wish by reference to the case of the innocent fat man to establish that there is at least a serious question concerning whether such fundamental commonsense moral convictions should always function as 'moral facts' or a kind of moral ground to test the adequacy of normative ethical theories or positions. I want to establish that careful attention to such cases shows that we are not justified in taking the principles embodied in our commonsense moral reasoning about such cases as normative for all moral decisions. That a normative ethical theory is incompatible with some of our 'moral intuitions' (moral feelings or convictions) does not refute the normative ethical theory. What I will try to do here is to establish that this case, no more than the case examined in Section III, gives us adequate grounds for abandoning consequentialism and for adopting moral conservativism.

Forget the levity of the example and consider the case of the innocent fat man. If there really is no other way of unsticking our fat man and if plainly, without blasting him out, everyone in the cave will drown, then, innocent or not, he should be blasted out. This indeed overrides the principle that the innocent should never be deliberately killed, but it does not reveal a callousness toward life, for the people involved are caught in a desperate situation in which, if such extreme action is not taken, many lives will be lost and far greater misery will obtain. Moreover, the people who do such a horrible thing or acquiesce in the doing of it are not likely to be rendered more callous about human life and human suffering as a result. Its occurrence will haunt them for the rest of their lives and is as likely as not to make them more rather than less morally sensitive. It is not even correct to say that such a desperate act shows a lack of respect for persons. We are not treating the fat man merely as a means. The fat man's person—his interests and rights—are not ignored. Killing him is something which is undertaken with the greatest reluctance. It is only when it is quite certain that there is no other way to save the lives of the others that such a violent course of action is justifiably undertaken.

Alan Donagan, arguing rather as Anscombe argues, maintains that "to use any innocent man ill for the sake of some public good is directly to degrade him to being a mere means" and to do this is of course to violate a principle essential to morality, that is, that human beings should never merely be treated as means but should be treated as ends in themselves (as persons worthy of respect.)[11] But, as my above remarks show, it need not be the case, and in the above situation it is not the case, that in killing such an innocent man we are treating him *merely* as a means. The action is universalizable, all alternative actions which would save his life are duly considered, the blasting out is done only as a last and desperate resort with the minimum of harshness and indifference to his suffering and the like. It indeed sounds ironical to talk this way, given what is done to him. But if such a terrible situation were to arise, there would always be more or less humane ways of going about one's grim task. And in acting in the more humane ways

[11]Donagan, op. cit., pp. 199–200.

toward the fat man, as we do what we must do and would have done to ourselves were the roles reversed, we show a respect for his person.[12]

In so treating the fat man—not just to further the public good but to prevent the certain death of a whole group of people (that is, to prevent an even greater evil than his being killed in this way)—the claims of justice are not overridden either, for each individual involved, if he is reasoning correctly, should realize that if he were so stuck rather than the fat man, he should in such situations be blasted out. Thus, there is no question of being unfair. Surely we must choose between evils here, but is there anything more reasonable, more morally appropriate, than choosing the lesser evil when doing or allowing some evil cannot be avoided? That is, where there is no avoiding both and where our actions can determine whether a greater or lesser evil obtains, should we not plainly always opt for the lesser evil? And is it not obviously a greater evil that all those other innocent people should suffer and die than that the fat man should suffer and die? Blowing up the fat man is indeed monstrous. But letting him remain stuck while the whole group drowns is still more monstrous.

The consequentialist is on strong moral ground here, and, if his reflective moral convictions do not square either with certain unrehearsed or with certain reflective particular moral convictions of human beings, so much the worse for such commonsense moral convictions. One could even usefully and relevantly adapt here—though for a quite different purpose—an argument of Donagan's. Consequentialism of the kind I have been arguing for provides so persuasive "a theoretical basis for common morality that when it contradicts some moral intuition, it is natural to suspect that intuition, not theory, is corrupt."[13] Given the comprehensiveness, plausibility, and overall rationality of consequentialism, it is not unreasonable to override even a deeply felt moral conviction if it does not square with such a theory, though, if it made no sense or overrode the bulk of or even a great many of our considered moral convictions, that would be another matter indeed.

Anticonsequentialists often point to the inhumanity of people

---

[12]Again, I am not asserting that we would have enough fortitude to assent to it were the roles actually reversed. I am making a conceptual remark about what as moral beings we must try to do and not a psychological observation about what we can do.

[13]Donagan, op. cit., p. 198.

who will sanction such killing of the innocent, but cannot the compliment be returned by speaking of the even greater inhumanity, conjoined with evasiveness, of those who will allow even more death and far greater misery and then excuse themselves on the ground that they did not intend the death and misery but merely forbore to prevent it? In such a context, such reasoning and such forbearing to prevent seems to me to constitute a moral evasion. I say it is evasive because rather than steeling himself to do what in normal circumstances would be a horrible and vile act but in this circumstance is a harsh moral necessity, he allows, when he has the power to prevent it, a situation which is still many times worse. He tries to keep his 'moral purity' and avoid 'dirty hands' at the price of utter moral failure and what Kierkegaard called 'double-mindedness.' It is understandable that people should act in this morally evasive way but this does not make it right.

My consequentialist reasoning about such cases as the case of the innocent fat man is very often resisted on the grounds that it starts a very dangerous precedent. People rationalize wildly and irrationally in their own favor in such situations. To avoid such rationalization, we must stubbornly stick to our deontological principles and recognize as well that very frequently, if people will put their wits to work or just endure, such admittedly monstrous actions done to prevent still greater evils will turn out to be unnecessary.

The general moral principles surrounding bans on killing the innocent are strong and play such a crucial role in the ever-floundering effort to humanize the savage mind—savage as a primitive and savage again as a contemporary in industrial society—that it is of the utmost social utility, it can be argued, that such bans against killing the innocent not be called into question in any practical manner by consequentialist reasoning.

However, in arguing in this way, the moral conservative has plainly shifted his ground, and he is himself arguing on consequentialist grounds that we must treat certain nonconsequentialist moral principles as absolute (as principles which can never *in fact,* from a reasonable moral point of view, be overridden, for it would be just too disastrous to do so).[14] But now he is on my home court, and my reply is that there is no good evidence at all that in the

[14]Jonathan Bennett, "Whatever the Consequences" *Analysis* 26 (1966), has shown that this is a very common equivocation for the conservative and makes, when unnoticed, his position seem more plausible than it actually is.

circumstances I characterized, overriding these deontological principles would have this disastrous effect. I am aware that a bad
precedent could be set. Such judgments must not be made for more
doubtful cases. But my telling my two stories in some detail, and
my contrasting them, was done in order to make evident the type
of situation, with its attendant rationale, in which the overriding of
those deontological principles can be seen clearly to be justified
and the situations in which this does obtain and why. My point
was to specify the situations in which we ought to override our
commonsense moral convictions about those matters, and the contexts in which we are not so justified or at least in which it is not
clear which course of action is justified.[15]

If people are able to be sufficiently clear-headed about these
matters, they can see that there are relevant differences between
the two sorts of cases. But I was also carefully guarding against
extending such 'moral radicalism'—if such it should be called—to
other and more doubtful cases. Unless solid empirical evidence can
be given that such a 'moral radicalism' would—if it were to gain a
toehold in the community—overflow destructively and inhumanely
into the other doubtful and positively unjustifiable situations, nothing has been said to undermine the correctness of my consequentialist defense of 'moral radicalism' in the contexts in which I defended it.

For Further Reflection

1. Analyze Nielsen's arguments for utilitarianism. What are their
   strengths and weaknesses?

2. Does it make sense to use utilitarian reasoning in deciding how
   to fight a war? How would a deontologist and a utilitarian differ in deciding on the morality of dropping the A-bomb on
   Hiroshima during World War II?

---

[15]I have spoken, conceding this to the Christian absolutist for the sake of the
discussion, as if (1) it is fairly evident what our commonsense moral convictions are here and (2) that they are deontological principles taken to
hold no matter what the consequences. But that either (1) or (2) is clearly
so seems to me very much open to question.

3. Consider the two examples given in this article: the fat man in the cave and the judge and the threatening mob. What is the morally right thing to do in these cases? Does utilitarianism have a better answer than deontological ethics to this question?

4. What is negative responsibility? What are its implications? What are some problems with it?

Against Utilitarianism

BERNARD WILLIAMS

Bernard Williams holds a joint appointment as professor of philosophy at both Oxford University and the University of California at Berkeley. In this selection he argues that utilitarianism is a bad moral theory because it violates moral integrity, itself a deep moral ideal. That is, utilitarians frequently require us to reject conscience and our personal ideals in favor of the "lesser of evils." It is the concept of *negative responsibility* (discussed in Nielsen's article) that is the prime culprit in this degenerate process. Because, according to utilitarianism, we are responsible for evil if we knowingly let it happen when we could do something about it, the utilitarian requires us to do lesser evils—even when they require us to violate moral principles and do great harm. Williams offers two examples of how utilitarianism infringes on our integrity.

It is because consequentialism attaches value ultimately to states of affairs, and its concern is with what states of affairs the world contains, that it essentially involves the notion of *negative responsibil-*

Reprinted with permission from *Utilitarianism: For and Against,* edited by J. J. C. Smart and Bernard Williams (Cambridge University Press, 1973).

ity: that if I am ever responsible for anything, then I must be just as much responsible for things that I allow or fail to prevent, as I am for things that I myself, in the more everyday restricted sense, bring about. Those things also must enter my deliberations, as a responsible moral agent, on the same footing. What matters is what states of affairs the world contains, and so what matters with respect to a given action is what comes about if it is done, and what comes about if it is not done, and those are questions not intrinsically affected by the nature of the causal linkage, in particular by whether the outcome is partly produced by other agents.

The strong doctrine of negative responsibility flows directly from consequentialism's assignment of ultimate value to states of affairs. Looked at from another point of view, it can be seen also as a special application of something that is favoured in many moral outlooks not themselves consequentialist—something which, indeed, some thinkers have been disposed to regard as the essence of morality itself: a principle of impartiality. Such a principle will claim that there can be no relevant difference from a moral point of view which consists just in the fact, not further explicable in general terms, that benefits or harms accrue to one person rather than to another—'it's me' can never in itself be a morally comprehensible reason. [By] this principle, familiar with regard to the reception of harms and benefits, we can see consequentialism as extending to their production: from the moral point of view, there is no comprehensible difference which consists just in my bringing about a certain outcome rather than someone else's producing it. That the doctrine of negative responsibility represents in this way the extreme of impartiality, and abstracts from the identity of the agent, leaving just a locus of causal intervention in the world—that fact is not merely a surface paradox. It helps to explain why consequentialism can seem to some to express a more serious attitude than non-consequentialist views, why part of its appeal is to a certain kind of high-mindedness. Indeed, that is part of what is wrong with it.

Let us look more concretely at two examples, to see what utilitarianism might say about them, what we might say about utilitarianism and, most importantly of all, what would be implied by certain ways of thinking about the situations. . . .

(1) George, who has just taken his Ph.D. in chemistry, finds it extremely difficult to get a job. He is not very robust in health, which cuts down the number of jobs he might be able to do satisfactorily. His wife has to go out to work to keep them, which itself causes a

great deal of strain, since they have small children and there are severe problems about looking after them. The results of all this, especially on the children, are damaging. An older chemist, who knows about this situation, says that he can get George a decently paid job in a certain laboratory, which pursues research into chemical and biological warfare. George says that he cannot accept this, since he is opposed to chemical and biological warfare. The older man replies that he is not too keen on it himself, come to that, but after all George's refusal is not going to make the job or the laboratory go away; what is more, he happens to know that if George refuses the job, it will certainly go to a contemporary of George's who is not inhibited by any such scruples and is likely if appointed to push along the research with greater zeal than George would. Indeed, it is not merely concern for George and his family, but (to speak frankly and in confidence) some alarm about this other man's excess of zeal, which has led the older man to offer to use his influence to get George the job. . . . George's wife, to whom he is deeply attached, has views (the details of which need not concern us) from which it follows that at least there is nothing particularly wrong with research into CBW. What should he do?

(2) Jim finds himself in the central square of a small South American town. Tied up against the wall are a row of twenty Indians, most terrified, a few defiant, in front of them several armed men in uniform. A heavy man in a sweat-stained khaki shirt turns out to be the captain in charge and, after a good deal of questioning of Jim which establishes that he got there by accident while on a botanical expedition, explains that the Indians are a random group of the inhabitants who, after recent acts of protest against the government, are just about to be killed to remind other possible protestors of the advantages of not protesting. However, since Jim is an honoured visitor from another land, the captain is happy to offer him a guest's privilege of killing one of the Indians himself. If Jim accepts, then as a special mark of the occasion, the other Indians will be let off. Of course, if Jim refuses, then there is no special occasion, and Pedro here will do what he was about to do when Jim arrived, and kill them all. Jim, with some desperate recollection of schoolboy fiction, wonders whether if he got hold of a gun, he could hold the captain, Pedro and the rest of the soldiers to threat, but it is quite clear from the set-up that nothing of that kind is going to work: any attempt at that sort of thing will mean that all the Indians will be killed, and himself. The men against the wall,

and the other villagers, understand the situation, and are obviously begging him to accept. What should he do?

To these dilemmas, it seems to me that utilitarianism replies, in the first case, that George should accept the job, and in the second, that Jim should kill the Indian. Not only does utilitarianism give these answers but, if the situations are essentially as described and there are no further special factors, it regards them, it seems to me, as *obviously* the right answers. But many of us would certainly wonder whether, in (1), that could possibly be the right answer at all; and in the case of (2), even one who came to think that perhaps that was the answer, might well wonder whether it was obviously the answer. Nor is it just a question of the rightness or obviousness of these answers. It is also a question of what sort of considerations come into finding the answer. A feature of utilitarianism is that it cuts out a kind of consideration which for some others makes a difference to what they feel about such cases: a consideration involving the idea, as we might first and very simply put it, that each of us is specially responsible for what *he* does, rather than for what other people do. This is an idea closely connected with the value of integrity. It is often suspected that utilitarianism, at least in its direct forms, makes integrity as a value more or less unintelligible. I shall try to show that this suspicion is correct. Of course, even if that is correct, it would not necessarily follow that we should reject utilitarianism; perhaps, as utilitarians sometimes suggest, we should just forget about integrity, in favour of such things as a concern for the general good. However, if I am right, we cannot merely do that, since the reason why utilitarianism cannot understand integrity is that it cannot coherently describe the relations between a man's projects and his actions.

TWO KINDS OF REMOTER EFFECT

A lot of what we have to say about this question will be about the relations between my projects and other people's projects. But before we get on to that, we should first ask whether we are assuming too hastily what the utilitarian answers to the dilemmas will be. In terms of more dire effects of the possible decisions, there does not indeed seem much doubt about the answer in either case; but it might be said that in terms of more remote or less evident effects counterweights might be found to enter the utilitarian scales. Thus the effect on George of a decision to take the job might be invoked, or its effect on others who might know of his decision. The possibility of there being more beneficent labours in the future from which he might be barred or disqualified, might be mentioned; and so forth. Such effects—in particular, possible effects on the agent's character, and effects on the public at large—are often invoked by utilitarian writers dealing with problems about lying or promise-breaking, and some similar considerations might be invoked here.

There is one very general remark that is worth making about arguments of this sort. The certainty that attaches to these hypotheses about possible effects is usually pretty low; in some cases, indeed, the hypothesis invoked is so implausible that it would scarcely pass if it were not being used to deliver the respectable moral answer, as in the standard fantasy that one of the effects of one's telling a particular lie is to weaken the disposition of the world at large to tell the truth. The demands on the certainty or probability of these beliefs as beliefs about particular actions are much milder than they would be on beliefs favouring the unconventional course. It may be said that this is as it should be, since the presumption must be in favour of the conventional course: but that scarcely seems a *utilitarian* answer, unless utilitarianism has already taken off in the direction of not applying the consequences to the particular act at all.

Leaving aside that very general point, I want to consider now two types of effect that are often invoked by utilitarians, and which might be invoked in connection with these imaginary cases. The attitude or tone involved in invoking these effects may sometimes seem peculiar; but that sort of peculiarity soon becomes familiar in utilitarian discussions, and indeed it can be something of an achievement to retain a sense of it.

First, there is the psychological effect on the agent. Our descriptions of these situations have not so far taken account of how George or Jim will be after they have taken the one course or the other; and it might be said that if they take the course which seemed at first the utilitarian one, the effects on them will be in fact bad enough and extensive enough to cancel out the initial utilitarian advantages of that course. Now there is one version of this effect in which, for a utilitarian, some confusion must be involved, namely that in which the agent feels bad, his subsequent conduct and relations are crippled and so on, *because he thinks that he has done the wrong thing*—for if the balance of outcomes was as it appeared to be *before* invoking this effect, then he has not (from the utilitarian point of view) done the wrong thing. So that version of the effect, for a rational and utilitarian agent, could not possibly make any difference to the assessment of right and wrong. However, perhaps he is not a thoroughly rational agent, and is disposed to have bad feelings, whichever he decided to do. Now such feelings, which are from a strictly utilitarian point of view irrational—nothing, a utilitarian can point out, is advanced by having them—cannot, consistently, have any great weight in a utilitarian calculation. I shall consider in a moment an argument to suggest that they should have no weight at all in it. But short of that, the utilitarian could reasonably say that such feelings should not be encouraged, even if we accept their existence, and that to give them a lot of weight is to encourage them. Or, at the very best, even if they are straightforwardly and without any discount to be put into the calculation, their weight must be small: they are after all (and at best) one man's feelings.

That consideration might seem to have particular force in Jim's case. In George's case, his feelings represent a larger proportion of what is to be weighed, and are more commensurate in character with other items in the calculation. In Jim's case, however, his feelings might seem to be of very little weight compared with other things that are at stake. There is a powerful and recognizable appeal that can be made on this point: as that a refusal by Jim to do what he has been invited to do would be a kind of self-indulgent squeamishness. That is an appeal which can be made by other than utilitarians—indeed, there are some uses of it which cannot be consistently made by utilitarians, as when it essentially involves the idea that there is something dishonourable about such self-indulgence. But in some versions it is a familiar, and it must be said a powerful, weapon of utilitarianism. One must be clear, though, about what it can and cannot accomplish. The most it can do, so far as I can see, is to invite one to consider how seriously, and for what reasons, one feels that what one is invited to do is (in these circumstances) wrong, and in particular, to consider that question from the utilitarian point of view. When the agent is not seeing the situation from a utilitarian point of view, the appeal cannot force him to do so; and if he does come round to seeing it from a utilitarian point of view, there is virtually nothing left for the appeal to do. If he does not see it from a utilitarian point of view, he will not see his resistance to the invitation, and the unpleasant feelings he associates with accepting it, *just* as disagreeable experiences of his; they figure rather as emotional expressions of a thought that to accept would be wrong. He may be asked, as by the appeal, to consider whether he is right, and indeed whether he is fully serious, in thinking that. But the assertion of the appeal, that he is being self-indulgently squeamish, will not itself answer that question, or even help to answer it, since it essentially tells him to regard his feelings just as unpleasant experiences of his, and he cannot, by doing that, answer the question they pose when they are precisely not so regarded, but are regarded as indications of what he thinks is right and wrong. If he does come round fully to the utilitarian point of view then of course he will regard these feelings just as unpleasant experiences of his. And once Jim—at least—has come to see them in that light, there is nothing left for the appeal to do, since *of course* his feelings, so regarded, are of virtually no weight at all in relation to the other things at stake. The 'squeamishness' appeal is not an argument which adds in a hitherto neglected consideration. Rather, it is an invitation to consider the situation, and one's own feelings, from a utilitarian point of view.

The reason why the squeamishness appeal can be very unsettling, and one can be unnerved by the suggestion of self-indulgence in going against utilitarian considerations, is not that we are utilitarians who are uncertain what utilitarian value to attach to our moral feelings, but that we are partially at least not utilitarians, and cannot regard our moral feelings merely as objects of utilitarian value. Because our moral relation to the world is partly given by such feelings, and by a sense of what we can or cannot 'live with,' to come to regard those feelings from a purely utilitarian point of view, that is to say, as happenings outside one's moral self, is to lose a sense of one's moral identity; to lose, in the most literal way, one's integrity. At this point utilitarianism alienates one from one's moral feelings; we shall see a little later how, more basically, it alienates one from one's actions as well. . . .

INTEGRITY

The [two] situations have in common that if the agent does not do a certain disagreeable thing, someone else will, and in Jim's situation at least the result, the state of affairs after the other man has acted, if he does, will be worse than after Jim has acted, if Jim does. The same, on a smaller scale, is true of George's case. I have already suggested that it is inherent in consequentialism that it offers a strong doctrine of negative responsibility. If I know that if I do X, O_1 will eventuate, and if I refrain from doing X, O_2 will, and that O_2 is worse than O_1, then I am responsible for O_2 if I refrain voluntarily from doing X. 'You could have prevented it,' as will be said, and truly, to Jim, if he refuses, by the relatives of the other Indians.

In the present cases, the situation of O_2 includes another agent bringing about results worse than O_1. So far as O_2 has been identified up to this point—merely as the worse outcome which will eventuate if I refrain from doing X—we might equally have said that what that other brings about is O_2; but that would be to under-describe the situation. For what occurs if Jim refrains from action is not solely twenty Indians dead, but *Pedro's killing twenty Indians,* and that is not a result which Pedro brings about, though the death of the Indians is. We can say: what one does is not included in the outcome of what one does, while what another does can be included in the outcome of what one does. For that to be so, as the terms are now being used, only a very weak condition has to be satisfied: for Pedro's killing the Indians to be the outcome of Jim's refusal, it only has to be causally true that if Jim had not refused, Pedro would not have done it.

That may be enough for us to speak, in some sense, of Jim's responsibility for that outcome, if it occurs; but it is certainly not enough, it is worth noticing, for us to speak of Jim's *making* those things happen. For granted this way of their coming about, he could have made them happen only by making Pedro shoot, and there is no acceptable sense in which his refusal makes Pedro shoot. If the captain had said on Jim's refusal, 'you leave me with no alternative,' he would have been lying, like most who use that phrase. While the deaths, and the killing, may be the outcome of Jim's refusal, it is misleading to think, in such a case, of Jim having an *effect* on the world through the medium (as it happens) of Pedro's acts; for this is to leave Pedro out of the picture in his essential role of one who has intentions and projects, projects for realizing which Jim's refusal would leave an opportunity. Instead of thinking in terms of supposed effects of Jim's projects on Pedro, it is more revealing to think in terms of the effects of Pedro's projects on Jim's decision.

Utilitarianism would do well then to acknowledge the evident fact that among the things that make people happy is not only making other people happy, but being taken up or involved in any of a vast range of projects, or—if we waive the evangelical and moralizing associations of the word—commitments. One can be committed to such things as a person, a cause, an institution, a career, one's own genius, or the pursuit of danger.

Now none of these is itself the *pursuit of happiness:* by an exceedingly ancient platitude, it is not at all clear that there could be anything which was just that, or at least anything that had the slightest chance of being successful. Happiness, rather, requires being involved in, or at least content with, something else. It is not impossible for utilitarianism to accept that point: it does not have to be saddled with a naive and absurd philosophy of mind about the relation between desire and happiness. What it does have to say is that if such commitments are worthwhile, then pursuing the projects that flow from them, and realizing some of those projects, will make the person for whom they are worthwhile, happy. It may be that to claim that is still wrong: it may well be that a commitment can make sense to a man (can make sense of his life) without his supposing that it will make him *happy.* But that is not the present point; let us grant to utilitarianism that all worthwhile human projects must conduce, one way or another, to happiness. The point is that even if that is true, it does not follow, nor could it possibly be true, that those projects are themselves projects of pursuing happiness. One has to believe in, or at least want, or quite minimally, be content with, other things, for there to be anywhere that happiness can come from.

Utilitarianism, then, should be willing to agree that its general aim of maximizing happiness does not imply that what everyone is doing is just pursuing happiness. On the contrary, people have to be pursuing other things. What those other things may be, utilitarianism, sticking to its professed empirical stance, should be prepared just to find out. No doubt some possible projects it will want to discourage, on the grounds that their being pursued involves a negative balance of happiness to others: though even there, the unblinking accountant's eye of the strict utilitarian will have something to put in the positive column, the satisfactions of the destructive agent. Beyond that, there will be a vast variety of generally beneficent or at least harmless projects; and some no doubt, will take the form not just of tastes or fancies, but of what I have called 'commitments.' It may even be that the utilitarian researcher will find that many of those with commitments, who have really identified themselves with objects outside themselves, who are thoroughly involved with other persons, or institutions, or activities or causes, are actually happier than those whose projects and wants are not like that. If so, that is an important piece of utilitarian empirical lore.

When I say 'happier' here, I have in mind the sort of consideration which any utilitarian would be committed to accepting: as for instance that such people are less likely to have a breakdown or commit suicide. Of course that is not all that is actually involved, but the point in this argument is to use to the maximum degree utilitarian notions, in order to locate a breaking point in utilitarian thought. In appealing to this strictly utilitarian notion, I am being more consistent with utilitarianism than [J.J.C.] Smart is. In his struggles with the problem of the brain-electrode man, Smart commends the idea that 'happy' is a partly evaluative term, in the sense that we call 'happiness' those kinds of satisfaction which, as things are, we approve of. But *by what standard* is this surplus element of approval supposed, from a utilitarian point of view, to be allocated? There is no source for it, on a strictly utilitarian view, except further degrees of satisfaction, but there are none of those available, or the problem would not arise. Nor does it help to appeal to the fact that we dislike in prospect things which we like when we get there, for from a utilitarian point of view it would seem that the original dislike was merely irrational or based on an error. Smart's argument at this point seems to be embarrassed by a well-known utilitarian uneasiness, which comes from a feeling that it is not respectable to ignore the 'deep,' while not having anywhere left in human life to locate it.

Let us now go back to the agent as utilitarian, and his higher-order project of maximizing desirable outcomes. At this level, he is committed only to that: what the outcome will actually consist of will depend entirely on the facts, on what persons with what projects and what potential satisfactions there are within calculable reach of the causal levers near which he finds himself. His own substantial projects and commitments come into it, but only as one lot among others—they potentially provide one set of satisfactions among those which he may be able to assist from where he happens to be. He is the agent of the satisfaction system who happens to be at a particular point at a particular time: in Jim's case, our man in South America. His own decisions as a utilitarian agent are a function of all the satisfactions which he can effect from where he is: and this means that the projects of others, to an indeterminately great extent, determine his decision.

This may be so either positively or negatively. It will be so positively if agents within the causal field of his decision have projects which are at any rate harmless and so should be assisted. It will equally be so, but negatively, if there is an agent within the causal field whose projects are harmful, and have to be frustrated to maximize desirable outcomes. So it is with Jim and the soldier Pedro. On the utilitarian view, the undesirable projects of other people as much determine, in this negative way, one's decisions as the desirable ones do positively: if those people were not there, or had different projects, the causal nexus would be different, and it is the actual state of the causal nexus which determines the decision. The determination to an indefinite degree of my decisions by other people's projects is just another aspect of my unlimited responsibility to act for the best in a causal framework formed to a considerable extent by their projects.

The decision so determined is, for utilitarianism, the right decision. But what if it conflicts with some project of mine? This, the utilitarian will say, has already been dealt with: the satisfaction to you of fulfilling your project, and any satisfactions to others of your so doing, have already been through the calculating device and have been found inadequate. Now in the case of many sorts of projects, that is a perfectly reasonable sort of answer. But in the case of projects of the sort I have called 'commitments,' those with which one is more deeply and extensively involved and identified, this cannot just by itself be an adequate answer, and there may be no adequate answer at all. For, to take the extreme sort of case, how can a man, as a utilitarian agent, come to regard as one satisfaction among others, and a dispensable one, a project or attitude round which he has built his life, just because someone else's projects have so structured the causal scene that that is how the utilitarian sum comes out?

The point here is not, as utilitarians may hasten to say, that if the project or attitude is that central to his life, then to abandon it will be very disagreeable to him and great loss of utility will be involved. I have already argued in section 4 that it is not like that; on the contrary, once he is prepared to look at it like that, the argument in any serious case is over anyway. The point is that he is identified with his actions as flowing from projects and attitudes which in some cases he takes seriously at the deepest level, as what his life is about (or, in some cases, this section of his life—seriousness is not necessarily the same as persistence). It is absurd to demand of such a man, when the sums come in from the utility network which the projects of others have in part determined, that he should just step aside from his own project and decision and acknowledge the decision which utilitarian calculation requires. It is to alienate him in a real sense from his actions and the source of his action in his own convictions. It is to make him into a channel between the input of everyone's projects, including his own, and an output of optimistic decision; but this is to neglect the extent to which *his* actions and *his* decisions have to be seen as the actions and decisions which flow from the projects and attitudes with which he is most closely identified. It is thus, in the most literal sense, an attack on his integrity.

These sorts of considerations do not in themselves give solutions to practical dilemmas such as those provided by our examples; but I hope they help to provide other ways of thinking about them. In fact, it is not hard to see that in George's case, viewed from this perspective, the utilitarian solution would be wrong. Jim's case is different, and harder. But if (as I suppose) the utilitarian is probably right in this case, that is not to be found out just by asking the utilitarian's questions. Discussions of it—and I am not going to try to carry it further here—will have to take seriously the distinction between my killing someone, and its coming about because of what I do that someone else kills them: a distinction based, not so much on the distinction between action and inaction, as on the distinction between my projects and someone else's projects. At least it will have to start by taking that seriously, as utilitarianism does not; but then it will have to build out from there by asking why that distinction seems to have less, or a different, force in this case than it has in George's. One question here would be how far one's powerful objection to killing people just is, in fact, an application of a powerful objection to their being killed. Another dimension of that is the issue of how much it matters that the people at risk are actual, and there, as opposed to hypothetical, or future, or merely elsewhere.

There are many other considerations that could come into such a question, but the immediate point of all this is to draw one particular contrast with utilitarianism: that to reach a grounded decision in such a case should not be regarded as a matter of just discounting one's reactions, impulses and deeply held projects in the face of the pattern of utilities, nor yet merely adding them in—but in the first instance of trying to understand them.

Of course, time and circumstances are unlikely to make a grounded decision, in Jim's case at least, possible. It might not even be decent. Instead of thinking in a rational and systematic way either about utilities or about the value of human life, the relevance of the people at risk being present, and so forth, the presence of the people at risk may just have its effect. The significance of the immediate should not be underestimated. Philosophers, not only utilitarian ones, repeatedly urge one to view the world *sub specie aeternitatis,* but for most human purposes that is not a good *species* to view it under. If we are not agents of the universal satisfaction system, we are not primarily janitors of any system of values, even our own: very often, we just act, as a possibly confused result of the situation in which we are engaged. That, I suspect, is very often an exceedingly good thing.

For Further Reflection

1. Why does Williams reject the utilitarian notion of negative responsibility?

2. What is Williams's main objection to *consequentialism* (his term for utilitarianism)? Examine the cases of George and Jim. What do you think is the right thing to do in these cases? What are Williams's answers? Do you agree with his reasoning?

3. What does Williams mean by *integrity?* What role does this notion play in his argument? Some have criticized Williams for unjustifiably exalting integrity too highly. They say, if my feelings of integrity conflict with making hard but rationally supported choices, I ought to overcome those feelings and do what is right. Here is an illustration. I have given my whole life to support political party X, which had admirable goals and did much good. But the party has been irremediably morally corrupted and now is harming people. Still my sense of integrity is tied up in all the good the party once stood for. I reason that it would be a good thing to destroy the party, for the good of humanity, and I have the opportunity to do so. But my sense of integrity prevents me from easily doing this. I deeply identify with party X. Although this may be a hard decision, many ethicists would argue that I must overcome my squeamishness and do the right thing: destroy party X, so that its present evil will be ineffectual. How would Williams deal with this case? How would you?

The Ones Who Walk Away from Omelas

URSULA LE GUIN

Ursula Le Guin is the author of many novels and short story collections, including *The Wind's Twelve Quarters,* from which this short story is taken. The story is about an ideal utilitarian, utopian society that is dependent on one significant suffering. Le Guin credits a passage from the philosopher William James as the point of departure for this story. James wrote:

> Or if the hypothesis were offered us of a world in which Messr. Fourier's and Bellamy's and Morris's utopias should all be outdone, and millions kept permanently happy on the one simple condition that a certain lost soul on the far-off edge of things should lead a life of lonely torment, what except a special and independent sort of emotion can it be which would make us immediately feel, even though an impulse arose within us to clutch at the happiness so offered, how hideous a thing would be its enjoyment when deliberately accepted as the fruit of such a bargain?

With a clamor of bells that set the swallows soaring, the Festival of Summer came to the city Omelas, bright-towered by the sea. The rigging of the boats in harbor sparkled with flags. In the streets between houses with red roofs and painted walls, between old moss-grown gardens and under avenues of trees, past great parks and public buildings, processions moved. Some were decorous: old people in long stiff robes of mauve and grey, grave master workmen, quiet, merry women carrying their babies and chatting as they walked. In other streets the music beat faster, a shimmering of gong and tambourine, and the people went dancing, the procession was a dance. Children dodged in and out, their high calls rising like the swallows' crossing flights over the music and the singing. All the processions wound towards the north side of the city, where on the great water-meadow called the Green Fields boys and girls, naked in the bright air, with mud-stained feet and ankles and long, lithe arms, exercised their restive horses before the race. The horses wore no gear at all but a halter without bit. Their manes were braided with streamers of silver, gold, and green. They flared their nostrils and pranced and boasted to one another; they were vastly excited, the horse being the only animal who has adopted our ceremonies as his own. Far off to the north and west the mountains stood up half encircling Omelas on her bay. The air of morning was so clear that the snow still crowning the Eighteen Peaks burned with white-gold fire across the miles of sunlit air, under the dark blue of the sky. There was just enough wind to make the banners that marked the racecourse snap and flutter now and then. In the silence of the broad green meadows one could hear the music winding through the city streets, farther and nearer and ever approaching, a cheerful faint sweetness of the air that from time to time trembled and gathered together and broke out into the great joyous clanging of the bells.

Joyous! How is one to tell about joy? How describe the citizens of Omelas?

They were not simple folk, you see, though they were happy. But we do not say the words of cheer much any more. All smiles have become archaic. Given a description such as this one tends to make certain assumptions. Given a description such as this one tends to look next for the King, mounted on a splendid stallion and surrounded by his noble knights, or perhaps in a golden litter borne by great-muscled slaves. But there was no king. They did not use swords, or keep slaves. They were not barbarians. I do not know the rules and laws of their society, but I suspect that they were singularly few. As they did without monarchy and slavery, so they also got on without the stock exchange, the advertisement, the secret police, and the bomb. Yet I repeat that these were not simple folk, not dulcet shepherds, noble savages, bland utopians. They were not less complex than us. The trouble is that we have a bad habit, encouraged by pedants and sophisticates, of considering happiness as something rather stupid. Only pain is intellectual, only evil interesting. This is the treason of the artist: a refusal to admit the banality of evil and the terrible boredom of pain. If you can't lick 'em, join 'em. If it hurts, repeat it. But to praise despair is to condemn delight, to embrace violence is to lose hold of everything else. We have almost lost hold; we can no longer describe a happy man, nor make any celebration of joy. How can I tell you about the people of Omelas? They were not naïve and happy children—though their children were, in fact, happy. They were mature, intelligent, passionate adults whose lives were not wretched. O miracle! but I wish I could describe it better. I wish I could convince you. Omelas sounds in my words like a city in a fairy tale, long ago and far away, once upon a time. Perhaps it would be best if you imagined it as your own fancy bids, assuming it will rise to the occasion, for certainly I cannot suit you all. For instance, how about technology? I think that there would be no cars or helicopters in and above the streets; this follows from the fact that the people of Omelas are happy people. Happiness is based on a just discrimination of what is necessary, what is neither necessary nor destructive, and what is destructive. In the middle category, however—that of the unnecessary but undestructive, that of comfort, luxury, exuberance, etc.—they could perfectly well have central heating, subway trains, washing machines, and all kinds of marvelous devices not yet invented here, floating light-sources, fuelless power, a cure for the common cold. Or they could have none of that: it doesn't matter. As you like it. I incline to think that people from towns up and down the coast have been coming in to Omelas during the last days before the Festival on very fast little trains and double-decked trams, and that the train station of Omelas is actually the handsomest building in town, though plainer than the magnificent Farmers' Market. But even granted trains, I fear that Omelas so far strikes some of you as goody-goody. Smiles, bells, parades, horses, blah. If so, please add an orgy. If an orgy would help, don't hesitate. Let us not, however, have temples from which issue beautiful nude priests and priestesses already half in ecstasy and ready to copulate with any man or woman, lover or stranger, who desires union with the deep godhead of the blood, although that was my first idea. But really it would be better not to have any temples in Omelas—at least, not manned temples. Religion yes, clergy no. Surely the beautiful nudes can just wander about, offering themselves like divine soufflés to the hunger of the needy and the rapture of the flesh. Let them join the processions. Let tambourines be struck above the copulations, and the glory of desire be proclaimed upon the gongs, and (a not unimportant point) let the offspring of these delightful rituals be beloved and looked after by all. One thing I know there is none of in Omelas is guilt. But what else should there be? I thought at first there were no drugs, but that is puritanical. For those who like it, the faint insistent sweetness of *drooz* may perfume the ways of the city, *drooz* which first brings a great lightness and brilliance to the mind and limbs, and then after some hours a dreamy languor, and wonderful visions at last of the very arcana and inmost secrets of the Universe, as well as exciting the pleasure of sex beyond all belief; and it is not habit-forming. For more modest tastes I think there ought to be beer. What else, what else belongs in the joyous city? The sense of victory, surely, the celebration of courage. But as we did without clergy, let us do without soldiers. The joy built upon successful slaughter is not the right kind of joy; it will not do; it is fearful and it is trivial. A boundless and generous contentment, a magnanimous triumph felt not against some outer enemy but in communion with the finest and fairest in the souls of all men everywhere and the splendor of the world's summer: this is what swells the hearts of the people of Omelas, and the victory they celebrate is that of life. I really don't think many of them need to take *drooz*.

Most of the processions have reached the Green Fields by now. A marvelous smell of cooking goes forth from the red and blue tents of the provisioners. The faces of small children are amiably sticky; in the benign grey beard of a man a couple of crumbs of rich pastry are entangled. The youths and girls have mounted their horses and are beginning to group around the starting line of the course. An old woman, small, fat, and laughing, is passing out flowers from a basket, and tall young men wear her flowers in their shining hair. A child of nine or ten sits at the edge of the crowd, alone, playing on a wooden flute. People pause to listen, and they smile, but they do not speak to him, for he never ceases playing and never sees them, his dark eyes wholly rapt in the sweet, thin magic of the tune.

He finishes, and slowly lowers his hands holding the wooden flute.

As if that little private silence were the signal, all at once a trumpet sounds from the pavilion near the starting line: imperious, melancholy, piercing. The horses rear on their slender legs, and some of them neigh in answer. Sober-faced, the young riders stroke the horses' necks and soothe them, whispering, "Quiet, quiet, there my beauty, my hope. . . ." They begin to form in rank along the starting line. The crowds along the racecourse are like a field of grass and flowers in the wind. The Festival of Summer has begun.

Do you believe? Do you accept the festival, the city, the joy? No? Then let me describe one more thing.

In a basement under one of the beautiful public buildings of Omelas, or perhaps in the cellar of one of its spacious private homes, there is a room. It has one locked door, and no window. A little light seeps in dustily between cracks in the boards, secondhand from a cobwebbed window somewhere across the cellar. In one corner of the little room a couple of mops, with stiff, clotted, foul-smelling heads, stand near a rusty bucket. The floor is dirt, a little damp to the touch, as cellar dirt usually is. The room is about three paces long and two wide: a mere broom closet or disused tool room. In the room a child is sitting. It could be a boy or a girl. It looks about six, but actually is nearly ten. It is feeble-minded. Perhaps it was born defective, or perhaps it has become imbecile through fear, malnutrition, and neglect. It picks its nose and occasionally fumbles vaguely with its toes or genitals, as it sits hunched in the corner farthest from the bucket and the two mops. It is afraid of the mops. It finds them horrible. It shuts its eyes, but it knows the mops are still standing there; and the door is locked; and nobody will come. The door is always locked; and nobody ever comes, except that sometimes—the child has no understanding of time or interval—sometimes the door rattles terribly and opens, and a person, or several people, are there. One of them may come in and kick the child to make it stand up. The others never come close, but peer in at it with frightened, disgusted eyes. The food bowl and the water jug are hastily filled, the door is locked, the eyes disappear. The people at the door never say anything, but the child, who has not always lived in the tool room, and can remember sunlight and its mother's voice, sometimes speaks. "I will be good," it says. "Please let me out. I will be good!" They never answer. The child used to scream for help at night, and cry a good deal, but now it only makes a kind of whining, "eh-haa, eh-haa," and it speaks less and less often. It is so thin there are no calves to its legs; its belly protrudes; it lives on a half-bowl of corn meal and grease a day. It is naked. Its buttocks and thighs are a mass of festered sores, as it sits in its own excrement continually.

They all know it is there, all the people of Omelas. Some of them have come to see it, others are content merely to know it is there. They all know that it has to be there. Some of them understand why, and some do not, but they all understand that their happiness, the beauty of their city, the tenderness of their friendships, the health of their children, the wisdom of their scholars, the skill of their makers, even the abundance of their harvest and the kindly weathers of their skies, depend wholly on this child's abominable misery.

This is usually explained to children when they are between

eight and twelve, whenever they seem capable of understanding; and most of those who come to see the child are young people, though often enough an adult comes, or comes back, to see the child. No matter how well the matter has been explained to them, these young spectators are always shocked and sickened at the sight. They feel disgust, which they had thought themselves superior to. They feel anger, outrage, impotence, despite all the explanations. They would like to do something for the child. But there is nothing they can do. If the child were brought up into the sunlight out of that vile place, if it were cleaned and fed and comforted, that would be a good thing, indeed; but if it were done, in that day and hour all the prosperity and beauty and delight of Omelas would wither and be destroyed. Those are the terms. To exchange all the goodness and grace of every life in Omelas for that single, small improvement: to throw away the happiness of thousands for the chance of the happiness of one: that would be to let guilt within the walls indeed.

The terms are strict and absolute; there may not even be a kind word spoken to the child.

Often the young people go home in tears, or in a tearless rage, when they have seen the child and faced this terrible paradox. They may brood over it for weeks or years. But as time goes on they begin to realize that even if the child could be released, it would not get much good of its freedom: a little vague pleasure of warmth and food, no doubt, but little more. It is too degraded and imbecile to know any real joy. It has been afraid too long ever to be free of fear. Its habits are too uncouth for it to respond to humane treatment. Indeed, after so long it would probably be wretched without walls about it to protect it, and darkness for its eyes, and its own excrement to sit in. Their tears at the bitter injustice dry when they begin to perceive the terrible justice of reality, and to accept it. Yet it is their tears and anger, the trying of their generosity and the acceptance of their helplessness, which are perhaps the true source of the splendor of their lives. Theirs is no vapid, irresponsible happiness. They know that they, like the child, are not free. They know compassion. It is the existence of the child, and their knowledge of its existence, that makes possible the nobility of their architecture, the poignancy of their music, the profundity of their science. It is because of the child that they are so gentle with children. They know that if the wretched one were not there snivelling in the dark, the other one, the flute-player, could make no joyful music as the young riders line up in their beauty for the race in the sunlight of the first morning of summer.

Now do you believe in them? Are they not more credible? But there is one more thing to tell, and this is quite incredible.

At times one of the adolescent girls or boys who go to see the child does not go home to weep or rage, does not, in fact, go home at all. Sometimes also a man or woman much older falls silent for a day or two, and then leaves home. These people go out into the street, and walk down the street alone. They keep walking, and walk straight out of the city of Omelas, through the beautiful gates. They keep walking across the farmlands of Omelas. Each one goes alone, youth or girl, man or woman. Night falls; the traveler must pass down village streets, between the houses with yellow-lit windows, and on out into the darkness of the fields. Each alone, they go west or north, towards the mountains. They go on. They leave Omelas, they walk ahead into the darkness, and they do not come back. The place they go towards is a place even less imaginable to most of us than the city of happiness. I cannot describe it at all. It is possible that it does not exist. But they seem to know where they are going, the ones who walk away from Omelas.

For Further Reflection

1. Discuss how this short story applies to the debate over utilitarianism. Would you walk away from Omelas (Salem spelled backward plus O for Oregon)? Explain your answer.

2. Do we already live in a world like Omelas, only not a utopia? Is our happiness predicated on the suffering of poorer nations from whom we get cheap goods?

The Utilitarian Social Engineer and the Savage

ALDOUS HUXLEY

Aldous Huxley (1894–1963) was one of the great prophetic English writers of the twentieth century. In his classic futuristic novel, *Brave New World* (which takes place several hundred years after Ford invented the automobile—the beginning of the technological era), the "year of our Ford" (A.F.) replaces "the year of our Lord" (A.D.) as the prime chronological designator. Sexuality is divorced from procreation. Sexual intercourse is recreational, occurs promiscuously and daily. Children are genetically manufactured by the "Bokanovsky Process" in state hatcheries according to eugenic principles (Alpha Plus intellectuals, Beta and Delta workers . . . Epsilon Minus morons) to fill various state functions. Individualism, especially personal commitments like those of family loyalty, are viewed as repugnant, giving way to the social motto "Community, Identity, Stability." This separation of sex from procreation typically struck people as the most implausible feature of Huxley's 1932 fantasy. But today it is close to a possibility. We have the technological knowledge to be able to produce or manufacture babies with specific genomes. Science fiction may become science.

In the following excerpt we meet the controller of the Brave New World utopia, Mustapha Mond, the utilitarian social engineer, who explains to his troublesome guests, John "the Savage," so named because he was brought up in "uncivilized primitive" American Indian culture, and the two Alpha dissidents, Helmholtz Watson and Bernard Marx, why individual freedom and happiness are incompatible. Mond himself fully understands that social and personal happiness means sacrificing some valuable things, such as personal freedom, Shakespeare, the search for truth, science, and religion; but the quest for truth and beauty lead to social unrest, sickness, old age, and sadness. These constitute the tragedy of freedom. Hence personal freedom has to be reduced to a vanishing point. The motto of *Brave New World* could well be "The Greatest Happiness for the Greatest Number."

John "the Savage" has been brought to the utopia of the Brave New World. While he is in the Hospital for the Dying, where his mother, Linda, has just died, he sees the Delta workers deadening their minds on drugs (*soma*) and impersonal sex. He desperately tries to liberate low-caste Deltas from their bondage to mindless hedonism. We enter the story as the 162 menial workers at the hospital are about to receive their *soma* ration.

The menial staff of the Park Lane Hospital for the Dying consisted of one hundred and sixty-two Deltas divided into two Bokanovsky Groups of eighty-four red-headed female and seventy-eight dark dolychocephalic male twins, respectively. At six, when their working day was over, the two Groups assembled in the vestibule of the Hospital and were served by the Deputy Sub-Bursar with their *soma* ration.

From the lift the Savage stepped out into the midst of them. But his mind was elsewhere—with death, with his grief, and his remorse; mechanically, without consciousness of what he was doing, he began to shoulder his way through the crowd.

"Who are you pushing? Where do you think you're going?"

High, low, from a multitude of separate throats, only two voices squeaked or growled. Repeated indefinitely, as though by a train of mirrors, two faces, one a hairless and freckled moon haloed in orange, the other a thin, beaked bird-mask, stubbly with two days' beard, turned angrily towards him. Their words and, in his ribs, the sharp nudging of elbows, broke through his unawareness. He woke once more to external reality, looked round him, knew what he saw—knew it, with a sinking sense of horror and disgust, for the recurrent delirium of his days and nights, the nightmare of swarming indistinguishable sameness. Twins, twins. . . . Like maggots they had swarmed defilingly over the mystery of Linda's death. Maggots again, but larger, full grown, they now crawled across his grief and his repentance. He halted and, with bewildered and horrified eyes, stared round him at the khaki mob, in the midst of which, overtopping it by a full head, he stood. "How many goodly creatures are there here!" The singing words mocked him derisively. "How beauteous mankind is! O brave new world . . ."

"*Soma* distribution!" shouted a loud voice. "In good order, please. Hurry up there."

A door had been opened, a table and chair carried into the vestibule. The voice was that of a jaunty young Alpha, who had entered carrying a black iron cash-box. A murmur of satisfaction went up from the expectant twins. They forgot all about the Savage. Their attention was now focused on the black cash-box, which the young man had placed on the table, and was now in process of unlocking. The lid was lifted.

"Oo-oh!" said all the hundred and sixty-two simultaneously, as though they were looking at fireworks.

The young man took out a handful of tiny pill-boxes. "Now," he said peremptorily, "step forward, please. One at a time, and no shoving."

One at a time, with no shoving, the twins stepped forward. First two males, then a female, then another male, then three females, then . . .

The Savage stood looking on. "O brave new world, O brave new world . . ." In his mind the singing words seemed to change their tone. They had mocked him through his misery and remorse, mocked him with how hideous a note of cynical derision! Fiendishly laughing, they had insisted on the low squalor, the nauseous ugliness of the nightmare. Now, suddenly, they trumpeted a call to arms. "O brave new world!" Miranda was proclaiming the possibility of loveliness, the possibility of transforming even the nightmare into something fine and noble. "O brave new world!" It was a challenge, a command.

"No shoving there now!" shouted the Deputy Sub-Bursar in a fury. He slammed down the lid of his cash-box. "I shall stop the distribution unless I have good behaviour."

The Deltas muttered, jostled one another a little, and then were still. The threat had been effective. Deprivation of *soma*—appalling thought!

"That's better," said the young man, and reopened his cash-box.

Linda had been a slave, Linda had died; others should live in freedom, and the world be made beautiful. A reparation, a duty. And suddenly it was luminously clear to the Savage what he must do; it was as though a shutter had been opened, a curtain drawn back.

"Now," said the Deputy Sub-Bursar.

Another khaki female stepped forward.

"Stop!" called the Savage in a loud and ringing voice. "Stop!"

He pushed his way to the table; the Deltas stared at him with astonishment.

"Ford!" said the Deputy Sub-Bursar, below his breath. "It's the Savage." He felt scared.

"Listen, I beg of you," cried the Savage earnestly. "Lend me your ears . . ." He had never spoken in public before, and found it very difficult to express what he wanted to say. "Don't take that horrible stuff. It's poison, it's poison."

"I say, Mr. Savage," said the Deputy Sub-Bursar, smiling propitiatingly. "Would you mind letting me . . . "

"Poison to soul as well as body."

"Yes, but let me get on with my distribution, won't you? There's a good fellow." With the cautious tenderness of one who strokes a notoriously vicious animal, he patted the Savage's arm. "Just let me . . ."

"Never!" cried the Savage.

"But look here, old man . . ."

"Throw it all away, that horrible poison."

The words "Throw it all away" pierced through the enfolding layers of incomprehension to the quick of the Delta's consciousness. An angry murmur went up from the crowd.

"I come to bring you freedom," said the Savage, turning back towards the twins. "I come . . ."

The Deputy Sub-Bursar heard no more; he had slipped out of the vestibule and was looking up a number in the telephone book.

"Not in his own rooms," Bernard summed up. "Not in mine, not in yours. Not at the Aphroditæum; not at the Centre or the College. Where can he have got to?"

Helmholtz shrugged his shoulders. They had come back from their work expecting to find the Savage waiting for them at one or other of the usual meeting-places, and there was no sign of the fellow. Which was annoying, as they had meant to nip across to Biarritz in Helmholtz's four-seater sporticopter. They'd be late for dinner if he didn't come soon.

"We'll give him five more minutes, said Helmholtz. "If he doesn't turn up by then we'll . . ."

The ringing of the telephone bell interrupted him. He picked up the receiver. "Hullo. Speaking." Then, after a long interval of listening, "Ford in Flivver!" he swore. "I'll come at once."

"What is it?" Bernard asked

"A fellow I know at the Park Lane Hospital," said Helmholtz. "The Savage is there. Seems to have gone mad. Anyhow, it's urgent. Will you come with me?"

Together they hurried along the corridor to the lifts.

"But do you like being slaves?" the Savage was saying as they entered the Hospital. His face was flushed, his eyes bright with ardour and indignation. "Do you like being babies? Yes, babies. Mewling and puking, he added, exasperated by their bestial stupidity into throwing insults at those he had come to save. The insults bounced off their carapace of thick stupidity; they stared at him with a blank expression of dull and sullen resentment in their eyes. "Yes, puking!" he fairly shouted. Grief and remorse, compassion and duty—all were forgotten now and, as it were, absorbed into an intense overpowering hatred of these less than human monsters. "Don't you want to be free and men? Don't you even understand what manhood and freedom are?" Rage was making him fluent; the words came easily, in a rush. "Don't you?" he repeated, but got no answer to his question. "Very well then," he went on grimly. "I'll teach you; I'll *make* you be free whether you want to or not." And pushing open a window that looked on to the inner court of the Hospital, he began to throw the little pill-boxes of *soma* tablets in handfuls out into the area.

For a moment the khaki mob was silent, petrified, at the spectacle of this wanton sacrilege, with amazement and horror.

"He's mad," whispered Bernard, staring with wide open eyes. "They'll kill him. They'll . . ." A great shout suddenly went up from the mob; a wave of movement drove it menacingly towards the Savage. "Ford help him!" said Bernard, and averted his eyes.

"Ford helps those who help themselves." And with a laugh, actually a laugh of exultation, Helmholtz Watson pushed his way through the crowd.

"Free, free!" the Savage shouted, and with one hand continued to throw the *soma* into the area while, with the other, he punched the indistinguishable faces of his assailants. "Free!" And suddenly there was Helmholtz at his side—"Good old Helmholtz!"—also punching—"Men at last!"—and in the interval also throwing the poison out by handfuls through the open window. "Yes, men! men!"

and there was no more poison left. He picked up the cash-box and showed them its black emptiness. "You're free!"

Howling, the Deltas charged with a redoubled fury.

Hesitant on the fringes of the battle. "They're done for," said Bernard and, urged by a sudden impulse, ran forward to help them; then thought better of it and halted; then, ashamed, stepped forward again; then again thought better of it, and was standing in an agony of humiliated indecision—thinking that *they* might be killed if he didn't help them, and that *he* might be killed if he did—when (Ford be praised!), goggle-eyed and swine-snouted in their gas-masks, in ran the police.

Bernard dashed to meet them. He waved his arms; and it was action, he was doing something. He shouted "Help!" several times, more and more loudly so as to give himself the illusion of helping. "Help! *Help!* Help!"

The policemen pushed him out of the way and got on with their work. Three men with spraying machines buckled to their shoulders pumped thick clouds of *soma* vapour into the air. Two more were busy round the portable Synthetic Music Box. Carrying water pistols charged with a powerful anæsthetic, four others had pushed their way into the crowd and were methodically laying out, squirt by squirt, the more ferocious of the fighters.

"Quick, quick!" yelled Bernard. "They'll be killed if you don't hurry. They'll . . . Oh!" Annoyed by his chatter, one of the policemen had given him a shot from his water pistol. Bernard stood for a second or two wambling unsteadily on legs that seemed to have lost their bones, their tendons, their muscles, to have become mere sticks of jelly, and at last not even jelly—water: he tumbled in a heap on the floor.

Suddenly, from out of the Synthetic Music Box a Voice began to speak. The Voice of Reason, the Voice of Good Feeling. The sound-track roll was unwinding itself in Synthetic Anti-Riot Speech Number Two (Medium Strength). Straight from the depths of a non-existent heart, "My friends, my friends!" said the Voice so pathetically, with a note of such infinitely tender reproach that, behind their gas masks, even the policemen's eyes were momentarily dimmed with tears, "what is the meaning of this? Why aren't you all being happy and good together? Happy and good," the Voice repeated. "At peace, at peace." It trembled, sank into a whisper and momentarily expired. "Oh, I do want you to be happy," it began, with a yearning earnestness. "I do so want you to be good! Please, please be good and . . ."

Two minutes later the Voice and the *soma* vapour had produced their effect. In tears, the Deltas were kissing and hugging one another—half a dozen twins at a time in a comprehensive embrace. Even Helmholtz and the Savage were almost crying. A fresh supply of pill-boxes was brought in from the Bursary; a new distribution was hastily made and, to the sound of the Voice's richly affectionate, baritone valedictions, the twins dispersed, blubbering as though their hearts would break. "Good-bye, my dearest, dearest friends, Ford keep you! Good-bye, my dearest, dearest friends, Ford keep you. Good-bye my dearest, dearest . . ."

When the last of the Deltas had gone the policeman switched off the current. The angelic Voice fell silent.

"Will you come quietly?" asked the Sergeant, "or must we anæsthetize?" He pointed his water pistol menacingly.

"Oh, we'll come quietly," the Savage answered, dabbing alternately a cut lip, a scratched neck, and a bitten left hand. . . .

The room into which the three were ushered was the Controller's study.

"His fordship will be down in a moment." The Gamma butler left them to themselves.

Helmholtz laughed aloud.

"It's more like a caffeine-solution party than a trial," he said, and let himself fall into the most luxurious of the pneumatic arm-chairs. "Cheer up, Bernard," he added, catching sight of his friend's green unhappy face. But Bernard would not be cheered; without answering, without even looking at Helmholtz, he went and sat down on the most uncomfortable chair in the room, carefully chosen in the obscure hope of somehow deprecating the wrath of the higher powers.

The Savage meanwhile wandered restlessly round the room, peering with a vague superficial inquisitiveness at the books in the shelves, at the sound-track rolls and reading machine bobbins in their numbered pigeon-holes. On the table under the window lay a massive volume bound in limp black leather-surrogate, and stamped with large golden T's. He picked it up and opened it. MY LIFE AND WORK, BY OUR FORD. The book had been published at Detroit by the Society for the Propagation of Fordian Knowledge. Idly he turned the pages, read a sentence here, a paragraph there, and had just come to the conclusion that the book didn't interest him, when the door opened, and the Resident World Controller for Western Europe walked briskly into the room.

Mustapha Mond shook hands with all three of them; but it was to the Savage that he addressed himself. "So you don't much like civilization, Mr. Savage," he said.

The Savage looked at him. He had been prepared to lie, to bluster, to remain sullenly unresponsive; but, reassured by the good-humoured intelligence of the Controller's face, he decided to tell the truth, straightforwardly. "No." He shook his head.

Bernard started and looked horrified. What would the Controller think? To be labelled as the friend of a man who said that he didn't like civilization—said it openly and, of all people, to the Controller—it was terrible. "But, John," he began. A look from Mustapha Mond reduced him to an abject silence.

"Of course," the Savage went on to admit, "there are some very nice things. All that music in the air, for instance . . ."

"Sometimes a thousand twangling instruments will hum about my ears and sometimes voices."

The Savage's face lit up with a sudden pleasure. "Have you read it too?" he asked. "I thought nobody knew about that book here, in England."

"Almost nobody. I'm one of the very few. It's prohibited, you see. But as I make the laws here, I can also break them. With impunity, Mr. Marx," he added, turning to Bernard. "Which I'm afraid you *can't* do."

Bernard sank into a yet more hopeless misery.

"But why is it prohibited?" asked the Savage. In the excitement of meeting a man who had read Shakespeare he had momentarily forgotten everything else.

The Controller shrugged his shoulders. "Because it's old; that's the chief reason. We haven't any use for old things here."

"Even when they're beautiful?"

"Particularly when they're beautiful. Beauty's attractive, and we don't want people to be attracted by old things. We want them to like the new ones."

"But the new ones are so stupid and horrible. Those plays, where there's nothing but helicopters flying about and you *feel* the people kissing." He made a grimace. "Goats and monkeys!" Only in Othello's words could he find an adequate vehicle for his contempt and hatred.

"Nice tame animals, anyhow," the Controller murmured parenthetically.

"Why don't you let them see *Othello* instead?"

"I've told you; it's old. Besides, they couldn't understand it."

Yes, that was true. He remembered how Helmholtz had laughed at *Romeo and Juliet.* "Well then," he said, after a pause, "something new that's like *Othello,* and that they could understand."

"That's what we've all been wanting to write," said Helmholtz, breaking a long silence.

"And it's what you never will write," said the Controller. "Because, if it were really like *Othello* nobody could understand it, however new it might be. And if were new, it couldn't possibly be like *Othello.*"

"Why not?"

"Yes, why not?" Helmholtz repeated. He too was forgetting the unpleasant realities of the situation. Green with anxiety and apprehension, only Bernard remembered them; the others ignored him. "Why not?"

"Because our world is not the same as Othello's world. You can't make flivvers without steel—and you can't make tragedies without social instability. The world's stable now. People are happy; they get what they want, and they never want what they can't get. They're well off; they're safe; they're never ill; they're not afraid of death; they're blissfully ignorant of passion and old age; they're plagued with no mothers or fathers; they've got no wives, or children, or lovers to feel strongly about; they're so conditioned that they practically can't help behaving as they ought to behave. And if anything should go wrong, there's *soma.* Which you go and chuck out of the window in the name of liberty, Mr. Savage. *Liberty!*" He laughed. "Expecting Deltas to know what liberty is! And now expecting them to understand *Othello!* My good boy!"

The Savage was silent for a little. "All the same," he insisted obstinately, "*Othello's* good, *Othello's* better than those feelies."

"Of course it is," the Controller agreed. "But that's the price we have to pay for stability. You've got to choose between happiness and what people used to call high art. We've sacrificed the high art. We have the feelies and the scent organ instead."

"But they don't mean anything."

"They mean themselves; they mean a lot of agreeable sensations to the audience."

"But they're . . . they're told by an idiot."

The Controller laughed. "You're not being very polite to your friend, Mr. Watson. One of our most distinguished Emotional Engineers . . ."

"But he's right," said Helmholtz gloomily. "Because it *is* idiotic. Writing when there's nothing to say . . ."

"Precisely. But that requires the most enormous ingenuity. You're making flivvers out of the absolute minimum of steel—works of art out of practically nothing but pure sensation."

The Savage shook his head. "It all seems to me quite horrible."

"Of course it does. Actual happiness always looks pretty squalid in comparison with the over-compensations for misery. And, of course, stability isn't nearly so spectacular as instability. And being contented has none of the glamour of a good fight against misfortune, none of the picturesqueness of a struggle with temptation, or a fatal overthrow by passion or doubt. Happiness is never grand."

"I suppose not," said the Savage after a silence. "But need it be quite so bad as those twins?" He passed his hand over his eyes as though he were trying to wipe away the remembered image of those long rows of identical midgets at the assembling tables, those queued-up twin-herds at the entrance to the Brentford monorail station, those human maggots swarming round Linda's bed of death, the endlessly repeated face of his assailants. He looked at his bandaged left hand and shuddered. "Horrible!"

"But how useful! I see you don't like our Bokanovsky Groups; but, I assure you, they're the foundation on which everything else is built. They're the gyroscope that stabilizes the rocket plane of state on its unswerving course." The deep voice thrillingly vibrated; the gesticulating hand implied all space and the onrush of the irresistible machine. Mustapha Mond's oratory was almost up to synthetic standards.

"I was wondering," said the Savage, "why you had them at all—seeing that you can get whatever you want out of those bottles. Why don't you make everybody an Alpha Double Plus while you're about it?"

Mustapha Mond laughed. "Because we have no wish to have our throats cut," he answered. "We believe in happiness and stability. A society of Alphas couldn't fail to be unstable and miserable. Imagine a factory staffed by Alphas—that is to say by separate and unrelated individuals of good heredity and conditioned so as to be capable (within limits) of making a free choice and assuming responsibilities. Imagine it!" he repeated.

The Savage tried to imagine it, not very successfully.

"It's an absurdity. An Alpha-decanted, Alpha-conditioned man would go mad if he had to do Epsilon Semi-Moron work—go mad, or start smashing things up. Alphas can be completely socialized—but only on condition that you make them do Alpha work. Only an Epsilon can be expected to make Epsilon sacrifices, for the good reason that for him they aren't sacrifices; they're the line of least resistance. His conditioning has laid down rails along which he's got to run. He can't help himself; he's foredoomed. Even after decanting, he's still inside a bottle—an invisible bottle of infantile and embryonic fixations. Each one of us, of course," the Controller meditatively continued, "goes through life inside a bottle. But if we happen to be Alphas, our bottles are, relatively speaking, enormous. We should suffer acutely if we were confined in a narrower space. You cannot pour upper-caste champagne-surrogate into lower-caste bottles. It's obvious theoretically. But it has also been proved in actual practice. The result of the Cyprus experiment was convincing."

"What was that?" asked the Savage.

Mustapha Mond smiled. "Well, you can call it an experiment in rebottling if you like. It began in A.F. 473. The Controllers had the island of Cyprus cleared of all its existing inhabitants and re-colonized with a specially prepared batch of twenty-two thousand Alphas. All agricultural and industrial equipment was handed over to them and they were left to manage their own affairs. The result exactly fulfilled all the theoretical predictions. The land wasn't properly worked; there were strikes in all the factories; the laws were set at naught, orders disobeyed; all the people detailed for a spell of low-grade work were perpetually intriguing for high-grade jobs, and all the people with high-grade jobs were counter-intriguing at all costs to stay where they were. Within six years they were having a first-class civil war. When nineteen out of the twenty-two thousand had been killed, the survivors unanimously petitioned the World Controllers to resume the government of the island. Which they did. And that was the end of the only society of Alphas that the world has ever seen."

The Savage sighed, profoundly.

"The optimum population," said Mustapha Mond, "is modelled on the iceberg—eight-ninths below the water line, one-ninth above."

"And they're happy below the water line?"

"Happier than above it. Happier than your friend here, for example." He pointed.

"In spite of that awful work?"

"Awful? *They* don't find it so. On the contrary, they like it. It's light, it's childishly simple. No strain on the mind or the muscles. Seven and a half hours of mild, unexhausting labour, and then the *soma* ration and games and unrestricted copulation and the feelies. What more can they ask for? True," he added, "they might ask for shorter hours. And of course we could give them shorter hours. Technically, it would be perfectly simple to reduce all lower-caste working hours to three or four a day. But would they be any the happier for that? No, they wouldn't. The experiment was tried, more than a century and a half ago. The whole of Ireland was put on to the four-hour day. What was the result? Unrest and a large increase in the consumption of *soma;* that was all. Those three and a half hours of extra leisure were so far from being a source of happiness, that people felt constrained to take a holiday from them. The Inventions Office is stuffed with plans for labour-saving processes. Thousands of them." Mustapha Mond made a lavish gesture. "And why don't we put them into execution? For the sake of the labourers; it would be sheer cruelty to afflict them with excessive leisure. It's the same with agriculture. We could synthesize every morsel of food, if we wanted to. But we don't. We prefer to keep a third of the population on the land. For their own sakes—because it takes *longer* to get food out of the land than out of a factory. Besides, we have our stability to think of. We don't want to change. Every change is a menace to stability. That's another reason why we're so chary of applying new inventions. Every discovery in pure science is potentially subversive; even science must sometimes be treated as a possible enemy. Yes, even science."

Science? The Savage frowned. He knew the word. But what it exactly signified he could not say. Shakespeare and the old men of the pueblo had never mentioned science, and from Linda he had only gathered the vaguest hints: science was something you made helicopters with, something that caused you to laugh at the Corn Dances, something that prevented you from being wrinkled and losing your teeth. He made a desperate effort to take the Controller's meaning.

"Yes," Mustapha Mond was saying, "that's another item in the cost of stability. It isn't only art that's incompatible with happiness; it's also science. Science is dangerous; we have to keep it most carefully chained and muzzled."

"What?" said Helmholtz, in astonishment. "But we're always saying that science is everything. It's a hypnopædic platitude."

"Three times a week between thirteen and seventeen," put in Bernard.

"And all the science propaganda we do at the College . . ."

"Yes; but what sort of science?" asked Mustapha Mond sarcastically. "You've had no scientific training, so you can't judge. I was a pretty good physicist in my time. Too good—good enough to realize that all our science is just a cookery book, with an orthodox theory of cooking that nobody's allowed to question, and a list of recipes that mustn't be added to except by special permission from the head cook. I'm the head cook now. But I was an inquisitive young scullion once. I started doing a bit of cooking on my own. Unorthodox cooking, illicit cooking. A bit of real science, in fact." He was silent.

"What happened?" asked Helmholtz Watson.

The Controller sighed. "Very nearly what's going to happen to you young men. I was on the point of being sent to an island."

The words galvanized Bernard into violent and unseemly activity. "Send *me* to an island?" He jumped up, ran across the room, and stood gesticulating in front of the Controller. "You can't send *me*. I haven't done anything. It was the others. I swear it was the others." He pointed accusingly to Helmholtz and the Savage. "Oh, please don't send me to Iceland. I promise I'll do what I ought to do. Give me another chance. Please give me another chance." The tears began to flow. "I tell you, it's their fault," he sobbed. "And not to Iceland. Oh please, your fordship, please . . ." And in a paroxysm of abjection he threw himself on his knees before the Controller. Mustapha Mond tried to make him get up; but Bernard persisted in his grovelling; the stream of words poured out inexhaustibly. In the end the Controller had to ring for his fourth secretary.

"Bring three men," he ordered, "and take Mr. Marx into a bedroom. Give him a good *soma* vaporization and then put him to bed and leave him."

The fourth secretary went out and returned with three green-uniformed twin footmen. Still shouting and sobbing, Bernard was carried out.

"One would think he was going to have his throat cut," said the Controller, as the door closed. "Whereas, if he had the smallest sense, he'd understand that his punishment is really a reward. He's being sent to an island. That's to say, he's being sent to a place where he'll meet the most interesting set of men and women to be found anywhere in the world. All the people who, for one reason or another, have got too self-consciously individual to fit into community-life. All the people who aren't satisfied with orthodoxy, who've got independent ideas of their own. Every one, in a word, who's any one. I almost envy you, Mr. Watson."

Helmholtz laughed. "Then why aren't you on an island yourself?"

"Because, finally, I preferred this," the Controller answered. "I was given the choice: to be sent to an island, where I could have got on with my pure science, or to be taken on to the Controllers' Council with the prospect of succeeding in due course to an actual Controllership. I chose this and let the science go." After a little silence, "Sometimes," he added, "I rather regret the science. Happiness is a hard master—particularly other people's happiness. A much harder master, if one isn't conditioned to accept it unquestioningly, than truth." He sighed, fell silent again, then continued in a brisker tone, "Well, duty's duty. One can't consult one's own preference. I'm interested in truth, I like science. But truth's a menace, science is a public danger. As dangerous as it's been beneficent. It has given us the stablest equilibrium in history. China's was hopelessly insecure by comparison; even the primitive matriarchies weren't steadier than we are. Thanks, I repeat, to science. But we can't allow science to undo its own good work. That's why we so carefully limit the scope of its researches—that's why I almost got sent to an island. We don't allow it to deal with any but the most immediate problems of the moment. All other enquiries are most sedulously discouraged. It's curious," he went on after a little pause, "to read what people in the time of Our Ford used to write about scientific progress. They seemed to have imagined that it could be allowed to go on indefinitely, regardless of everything else. Knowledge was the highest good, truth the supreme value; all the rest was secondary and subordinate. True, ideas were beginning to change even then. Our Ford himself did a great deal to shift the emphasis from truth and beauty to comfort and happiness. Mass production demanded the shift. Universal happiness keeps the wheels steadily turning; truth and beauty can't. And, of course, whenever the masses seized political power, then it was happiness rather than truth and beauty that mattered. Still, in spite of everything, unrestricted scientific research was still permitted. People still went on talking about truth and beauty as though they were the sovereign goods. Right up to the time of the Nine Years' War. *That* made them change their tune all right. What's the point of truth or beauty or knowledge when the anthrax bombs are popping all around you? That was when science first began to be controlled—after the Nine Years' War. People were ready to have even their appetites controlled then. Anything for a quiet life. We've gone on controlling ever since. It hasn't been very good for truth, of course. But it's been very good for happiness. One can't have something for nothing. Happiness has got to be paid for. You're paying for it, Mr. Watson—paying because you happen to be too much interested in beauty. I was too much interested in truth; I paid too."

"But *you* didn't go to an island," said the Savage, breaking a long silence.

The Controller smiled. "That's how I paid. By choosing to serve happiness. Other people's—not mine. It's lucky," he added, after a pause, "that there are such a lot of islands in the world. I don't know what we should do without them. Put you all in the lethal chamber, I suppose. By the way, Mr. Watson, would you like a tropical climate? The Marquesas, for example; or Samoa? Or something rather more bracing?"

Helmholtz rose from his pneumatic chair. "I should like a thoroughly bad climate," he answered. "I believe one would write better if the climate were bad. If there were a lot of wind and storms, for example . . ."

The Controller nodded his approbation. "I like your spirit, Mr. Watson. I like it very much indeed. As much as I officially disapprove of it." He smiled. "What about the Falkland Islands?"

"Yes, I think that will do," Helmholtz answered. "And now, if you don't mind, I'll go and see how poor Bernard's getting on."

"Art, science—you seem to have paid a fairly high price for your happiness," said the Savage, when they were alone. "Anything else?"

"Well, religion, of course," replied the Controller. "There used to be something called God—before the Nine Years' War. But I was forgetting; you know all about God, I suppose."

"Well . . ." The Savage hesitated. He would have liked to say something about solitude, about night, about the mesa lying pale under the moon, about the precipice, the plunge into shadowy darkness, about death. He would have liked to speak; but there were no words. Not even in Shakespeare.

The Controller, meanwhile, had crossed to the other side of the room and was unlocking a large safe set into the wall between the bookshelves. The heavy door swung open. Rummaging in the darkness within, "It's a subject," he said, "that has always had a great interest for me." He pulled out a thick black volume. "You've never read this, for example."

The Savage took it. "*The Holy Bible, containing the Old and New Testaments,*" he read aloud from the title-page.

"Nor this." It was a small book and had lost its cover.

"*The Imitation of Christ.*"

"Nor this." He handed out another volume.

"*The Varieties of Religious Experience.* By William James."

"And I've got plenty more," Mustapha Mond continued, resuming his seat. "A whole collection of pornographic old books. God in the safe and Ford on the shelves." He pointed with a laugh to his avowed library—to the shelves of books, the rack full of reading-machine bobbins and sound-track rolls.

"But if you know about God, why don't you tell them?" asked the Savage indignantly. "Why don't you give them these books about God?"

"For the same reason as we don't give them *Othello:* they're old; they're about God hundreds of years ago. Not about God now."

"But God doesn't change."

"Men do, though."

"What difference does that make?"

"All the difference in the world," said Mustapha Mond. He got up again and walked to the safe. "There was a man called Cardinal Newman," he said. "A cardinal," he exclaimed parenthetically, "was a kind of Arch-Community-Songster."

"'I Pandulph, of fair Milan, cardinal.' I've read about them in Shakespeare."

"Of course you have. Well, as I was saying, there was a man called Cardinal Newman. Ah, here's the book." He pulled it out. "And while I'm about it I'll take this one too. It's by a man called Maine de Biran. He was a philosopher, if you know what that was."

"A man who dreams of fewer things than there are in heaven and earth," said the Savage promptly.

"Quite so. I'll read you one of the things he *did* dream of in a moment. Meanwhile, listen to what this old Arch-Community-Songster said." He opened the book at the place marked by a slip of paper and began to read. "'We are not our own any more than what we possess is our own. We did not make ourselves, we cannot be supreme over ourselves. We are not our own masters. We are God's property. Is it not our happiness thus to view the matter? Is it any happiness or any comfort, to consider that we *are* our own? It may be thought so by the young and prosperous. These may think it a great thing to have everything, as they suppose, their own way—to depend on no one—to have to think of nothing out of sight, to be without the irksomeness of continual acknowledgment, continual prayer, continual reference of what they do to the will of another. But as time goes on, they, as all men, will find that independence was not made for man—that it is an unnatural state—will do for a while, but will not carry us on safely to the end . . .'" Mustapha Mond paused, put down the first book and, picking up the other, turned over the pages. "Take this, for example," he said, and in his deep voice once more began to read: "'A man grows old; he feels in himself that radical sense of weakness, of listlessness, of discomfort, which accompanies the advance of age; and, feeling thus, imagines himself merely sick, lulling his fears with the notion that this distressing condition is due to some particular cause, from which, as from an illness, he hopes to recover. Vain imaginings! That sickness is old age; and a horrible disease it is. They say that it is the fear of death and of what comes after death that makes men turn to religion as they advance in years. But my own experience has given me the conviction that, quite apart from any such terrors or imaginings, the religious sentiment tends to develop as we grow older; to develop because, as the passions grow calm, as the fancy and sensibilities are less excited and less excitable, our reason becomes less troubled in its working, less obscured by the images, desires and distractions, in which it used to be absorbed; whereupon God emerges as from behind a cloud; our soul feels, sees, turns towards the source of all light; turns naturally and inevitably; for now that all that gave to the world of sensations its life and charms has begun to leak away from us, now that phenomenal existence is no more bolstered up by impressions from within or from without, we feel the need to lean on something that abides, something that will never play us false—a reality, an absolute and everlasting truth. Yes; we inevitably turn to God; for this religious sentiment is of its nature so pure, so delightful to the soul that experiences it, that it makes up to us for all our other losses.'" Mustapha Mond shut the book and leaned back in his chair. "One of the numerous things in heaven and earth that these philosophers didn't dream about was this" (he waved his hand), "us, the modern world. 'You can only be independent of God while you've got youth and prosperity; independence won't take you safely to the end.' Well, we've now got youth and prosperity right up to the end. What follows? Evidently, that we can be independent of God. 'The religious sentiment will compensate us for all our losses.' But there aren't any losses for us to compensate; religious sentiment is superfluous. And why should we go hunting for a substitute for youthful desires, when youthful desires never fail? A substitute for distractions, when we go on enjoying all the old fooleries to the very last? What need have we of repose when our minds and bodies continue to delight in activity? of consolation, when we have *soma?* of something immovable, when there is the social order?"

"Then you think there is no God?"

"No, I think there quite probably is one."

"Then why? . . ."

Mustapha Mond checked him. "But he manifests himself in different ways to different men. In premodern times he manifested himself as the being that's described in these books. Now . . ."

"How does he manifest himself now?" asked the Savage.

"Well, he manifests himself as an absence; as though he weren't there at all."

"That's your fault."

"Call it the fault of civilization. God isn't compatible with machinery and scientific medicine and universal happiness. You must make your choice. Our civilization has chosen machinery and medicine and happiness. That's why I have to keep these books locked up in the safe. They're smut. People would be shocked it . . ."

The Savage interrupted him. "But isn't it *natural* to feel there's a God?"

"You might as well ask if it's natural to do up one's trousers with zippers," said the Controller sarcastically. "You remind me of another of those old fellows called Bradley. He defined philosophy as the finding of bad reason for what one believes by instinct. As if one believed anything by instinct! One believes things because one has been conditioned to believe them. Finding bad reasons for what one believes for other bad reasons—that's philosophy. People believe in God because they've been conditioned to believe in God."

"But all the same," insisted the Savage, "it is natural to believe in God when you're alone—quite alone, in the night, thinking about death . . ."

"But people never are alone now," said Mustapha Mond. "We make them hate solitude; and we arrange their lives so that it's almost impossible for them ever to have it."

The Savage nodded gloomily. At Malpais he had suffered because they had shut him out from the communal activities of the pueblo, in civilized London he was suffering because he could never escape from those communal activities, never be quietly alone.

"Do you remember that bit in *King Lear?*" said the Savage at last. "'The gods are just and of our pleasant vices make instruments to plague us; the dark and vicious place where thee he got cost him his eyes,' and Edmund answers—you remember, he's wounded, he's dying—'Thou hast spoken right; 'tis true. The wheel has come full circle; I am here.' What about that now? Doesn't there seem to be a God managing things, punishing, rewarding?"

"Well, does there?" questioned the Controller in his turn. "You can indulge in any number of pleasant vices with a freemartin and run no risks of having your eyes put out by your son's mistress. 'The wheel has come full circle; I am here.' But where would Edmund be nowadays? Sitting in a pneumatic chair, with his arm round a girl's waist, sucking away at his sex-hormone chewing-gum and looking at the feelies. The gods are just. No doubt. But their code of law is dictated, in the last resort, by the people who organize society; Providence takes its cue from men."

"Are you sure?" asked the Savage. "Are you quite sure that the Edmund in that pneumatic chair hasn't been just as heavily punished as the Edmund who's wounded and bleeding to death? The gods are just. Haven't they used his pleasant vices as an instrument to degrade him?"

"Degrade him from what position? As a happy, hard-working, goods-consuming citizen he's perfect. Of course, if you choose some other standard than ours, then perhaps you might say he was degraded. But you've got to stick to one set of postulates. You can't play Electro-magnetic Golf according to the rules of Centrifugal Bumble-puppy."

"But value dwells not in particular will," said the Savage. "It holds his estimate and dignity as well wherein 'tis precious of itself as in the prizer."

"Come, come," protested Mustapha Mond, "that's going rather far, isn't it?"

"If you allowed yourselves to think of God, you wouldn't allow yourselves to be degraded by pleasant vices. You'd have a reason for bearing things patiently, for doing things with courage. I've seen it with the Indians."

"I'm sure you have," said Mustapha Mond. "But then we aren't Indians. There isn't any need for a civilized man to bear anything that's seriously unpleasant. And as for doing things—Ford forbid that he should get the idea into his head. It would upset the whole social order if men started doing things on their own."

"What about self-denial, then? If you had a God, you'd have a reason for self-denial."

"But industrial civilization is only possible when there's no self-denial. Self-indulgence up to the very limits imposed by hygiene and economics. Otherwise the wheels stop turning."

"You'd have a reason for chastity!" said the Savage, blushing a little as he spoke the words.

"But chastity means passion, chastity means neurasthenia. And passion and neurasthenia mean instability. And instability means the end of civilization. You can't have a lasting civilization without plenty of pleasant vices."

"But God's the reason for everything noble and fine and heroic. If you had a God . . ."

"My dear young friend," said Mustapha Mond, "civilization has absolutely no need of nobility or heroism. These things are symptoms of political inefficiency. In a properly organized society like ours, nobody has any opportunities for being noble or heroic. Conditions have got to be thoroughly unstable before the occasion can arise. Where there are wars, where there are divided allegiances, where there are temptations to be resisted, objects of love to be fought for or defended—there, obviously, nobility and heroism have some sense. But there aren't any wars nowadays. The greatest care is taken to prevent you from loving any one too much. There's no such thing as a divided allegiance; you're so conditioned that you can't help doing what you ought to do. And what you ought to do is on the whole so pleasant, so many of the natural impulses are allowed free play, that there really aren't any temptations to resist. And if ever, by some unlucky chance, anything unpleasant should somehow happen, why, there's always *soma* to give you a holiday from the facts. And there's always *soma* to calm your anger, to reconcile you to your enemies, to make you patient and long-suffering. In the past you could only accomplish these things by making a great effort and after years of hard moral training. Now, you swallow two or three half-gramme tablets, and there you are. Anybody can be virtuous now. You can carry at least half your morality about in a bottle. Christianity without tears—that's what *soma* is."

"But the tears are necessary. Don't you remember what Othello said? 'If after every tempest came such calms, may the winds blow till they have wakened death.' There's a story one of the old Indians used to tell us, about the Girl of Mátaski. The young men who wanted to marry her had to do a morning's hoeing in her garden. It seemed easy; but there were flies and mosquitoes, magic ones. Most of the young men simply couldn't stand the biting and stinging. But the one that could—he got the girl."

"Charming! But in civilized countries," said the Controller, "you can have girls without hoeing for them; and there aren't any flies or mosquitoes to sting you. We got rid of them all centuries ago."

The Savage nodded, frowning. "You got rid of them. Yes, that's just like you. Getting rid of everything unpleasant instead of learning to put up with it. Whether 'tis better in the mind to suffer the slings and arrows of outrageous fortune, or to take arms against a sea of troubles and by opposing end them . . . But you don't do either. Neither suffer nor oppose. You just abolish the slings and arrows. It's too easy." . . .

"What you need," the Savage went on, "is something *with* tears for a change. Nothing costs enough here."

("Twelve and a half million dollars," Henry Foster had protested when the Savage told him that. "Twelve and a half million—that's what the new Conditioning Centre cost. Not a cent less.")

"Exposing what is mortal and unsure to all that fortune, death and danger dare, even for an eggshell. Isn't there something in that?" he asked, looking up at Mustapha Mond. "Quite apart from God—though of course God would be a reason for it. Isn't there something in living dangerously?"

"There's a great deal in it," the Controller replied. "Men and women must have their adrenals stimulated from time to time."

"What?" questioned the Savage, uncomprehending.

"It's one of the conditions of perfect health. That's why we've made the V.P.S. treatments compulsory."

"V.P.S.?"

"Violent Passion Surrogate. Regularly once a month. We flood the whole system with adrenin. It's the complete physiological equivalent of fear and rage. All the tonic effects of murdering Desdemona and being murdered by Othello, without any of the inconveniences."

"But I like the inconveniences."

"We don't," said the Controller. "We prefer to do things comfortably."

"But I don't want comfort. I want God, I want poetry, I want real danger, I want freedom, I want goodness. I want sin."

"In fact," said Mustapha Mond, "you're claiming the right to be unhappy."

"All right then," said the Savage defiantly, "I'm claiming the right to be unhappy."

"Not to mention the right to grow old and ugly and impotent; the right to have syphilis and cancer; the right to have too little to eat; the right to be lousy; the right to live in constant apprehension of what may happen tomorrow; the right to catch typhoid; the right to be tortured by unspeakable pains of every kind." There was a long silence.

"I claim them all," said the Savage at last.

Mustapha Mond shrugged his shoulders. "You're welcome," he said.

For Further Reflection

1. In *Brave New World* Huxley starkly contrasts freedom and high culture with happiness. Is his description of the tension between these two values accurate, or is it a caricature? Explain your answer.

2. Following up on the first question, is Huxley's satire on utilitarianism insightful, or is it really aimed at a straw man? Note Huxley himself criticized his work as offering the Savage "only two alternatives, an insane life in Utopia, or the life of a primitive in an Indian village, a life more human in some respects, but in other hardly less queer and abnormal. At the time the book was written this idea, that human beings are given free will in order to choose between insanity, on the one hand, and lunacy on the other, was one that I found amusing and regarded as quite possibly true. . . . Today I feel no wish to demonstrate that sanity is impossible. On the contrary, though I remain no less sadly certain than in the past that sanity is a rather rare phenomenon, I am convinced that it can be achieved and would like to see more of it." (Preface to *Brave New World,* 1946 edition) Do you agree with this reflection of Huxley's, that the truth is in the middle—between complete, unregulated freedom of will and social stability wherein we can find happiness?

3. What, if any, are the lessons of Huxley's novel for our age?

Further Readings for Chapter 4

Bentham, Jeremy. *Introduction to the Principles of Morals and Legislation.* Edited by W. Harrison. Oxford: Oxford University Press, 1948.

Hardin, Russell. *Morality Within the Limits of Reason.* Chicago: University of Chicago Press, 1988. A cogent contemporary defense of utilitarianism.

Hare, R. M. *Moral Thinking.* Oxford: Oxford University Press, 1981.

Mill, John Stuart. *Utilitarianism.* Indianapolis: Bobbs-Merrill, 1957.

Quinton, Anthony. *Utilitarian Ethics.* New York: Macmillan, 1973. A clear exposition of classical utilitarianism.

Smart, J. J. C., and Bernard Williams. *Utilitarianism For and Against.* Cambridge: Cambridge University Press, 1973. A classic debate on the subject.

CHAPTER 5

Deontological Ethics

We have already outlined the basic ideas of deontological ethics in the introduction to this part. Deontologists distinguish themselves from consequentialists, like utilitarians, by holding that rightness and wrongness of acts are determined by the intrinsic quality of the act itself or the kind of act it is, not by its consequences. So, recurring to the example in the last chapter, a deontologist would tend to give the millionaire's money to the owner of the New York Yankees, according to the millionaire's request, not to the world hunger organization. There are two classic versions of deontological ethics: Kant's categorical imperative and Ross's intuitionism. Both are featured in this chapter. As you will see from the first reading, Immanuel Kant, the great eighteenth-century German philosopher, held that we may test the moral status of our acts by asking whether we could will the maxim (or principle) of that act to be a universal law of nature. If we can so universalize the principle, the act passes the test of what is morally permissible. If we cannot, then the act is immoral. Kant argued that we cannot will that lying or promise-breaking be universal laws, so that they must be seen as immoral. For Kant, such moral principles are absolute. They have no exceptions. Kant's notion of the categorical imperative is critiqued in the second reading by William Frankena.

The second kind of deontological ethics is that of W. D. Ross, the Oxford philosopher, who in our third reading sets forth an intuitionist morality. If we consult our conscience, we will hit upon obvious moral principles. W. D. Ross, unlike Kant, is not an absolutist. Moral principles have *prima facie* or conditional bindingness. They are valid principles, having universal application, but they may not always win out in the end. Another, more stringent, duty may override the normal duty. So, while we should generally tell the truth, we may be obligated to lie, if by so doing we may save an innocent person's life.

Our fourth reading is R. M. MacIver's "The Deep Beauty of the Golden Rule," an acute defense of that procedure, followed by Richard Whately's classic critique of it. We then examine Ambrose Bierce's Civil War short story "A Horseman in the Sky," which is followed by Charles Fried's discourse on the evil of lying. After this, we encounter Plato's classic Euthyphro Problem, which asks whether religion is the basis of morality or vice versa. We end with Thomas Nagel's provocative essay on moral luck.

The Moral Law

IMMANUEL KANT

Immanuel Kant (1724–1804) was born into a deeply pietis-
tic Lutheran family in Königsberg, Germany, and lived in
that town his entire life. At sixteen he entered the University of Königsberg, where he later taught philosophy. He
is considered the greatest philosopher of the Enlightenment.
Among his works are *Critique of Pure Reason* (1781), *Pro-
legomena to Any Future Metaphysic* (1785), and *Foundations of the Metaphysic of Morals* (1785), from which the
present selection is taken.

In this classic work Kant rejects such ethical theories as
the theory of moral sentiments, set forth by the eighteenth-
century Scottish moralists Francis Hutcheson and David
Hume, in which morality is naturalistic, contingent, and
hypothetical. The moral sentiment view is contingent in that
it is based on human nature and, in particular, on our feelings or sentiments. Had we been created differently, we
would have a different nature and, hence, different moral
duties. Morality in this view consists of hypothetical imperatives in that they depend on our desires for their realization. For example, we should obey the law because we want
a peaceful, orderly society. We should seek peace because
it is necessary for personal happiness. The naturalistic ethicists were typically utilitarians who sought to maximize
human happiness.

Kant rejects this naturalistic, utilitarian account of ethics.
Ethics is not *contingent* but *absolute,* and its duties or
imperatives are not *hypothetical* but *categorical* (noncon-
ditional). Ethics is based not on feeling but on reason. It
is because we are rational beings that we are valuable and
capable of discovering moral laws binding on all persons
at all times. As such, our moral duties are not dependent
on feelings but on reason. They are unconditional, universally valid, and necessary, regardless of the possible consequences or opposition to our inclinations.

Reprinted from *The Foundations of the Metaphysic of Morals,* Translated by T. K. Abbott (this translation first published in 1873).

This is Kant's first formulation of his *categorical imperative:* "Act only on that maxim whereby you can at the same time will that it would become a universal law." This imperative is given as the criterion (or second-order principle) by which to judge all other principles. If we can consistently will that everyone do some type of action, then the categorical imperative enjoins that type of action. If we cannot consistently will that everyone do some type of action, then that type of action is morally wrong. Kant argues, for example, that we cannot consistently will that everyone make false promises, for the very institution of promising entails or depends on general adherence to keeping the promise or intending to do so.

Kant offers a second formulation of the categorical imperative: "So act as to treat humanity, whether in your own person or in that of any other, in every case as an end and never as merely a means only." Each person by virtue of his or her reason has dignity and profound worth, which entail that he or she must never be exploited, manipulated, or merely used as a means to our idea of what is for the general good.

PREFACE

As my concern here is with moral philosophy, I limit the question suggested to this: Whether it is not of the utmost necessity to construct a pure moral philosophy, perfectly cleared of everything which is only empirical, and which belongs to anthropology? for that such a philosophy must be possible is evident from the common idea of duty and of the moral laws. Everyone must admit that if a law is to have moral force, *i.e.* to be the basis of an obligation, it must carry with it absolute necessity; that, for example, the precept, "Thou shall not lie," is not valid for men alone, as if other rational beings had no need to observe it; and so with all the other moral laws properly so called; that, therefore, the basis of obligation must not be sought in the nature of man, or in the circumstances in the world in which he is placed, but *a priori* simply in the conception of pure reason; and although any other precept which is founded on principles of mere experience may be in certain respects universal, yet in as far as it rests even in the least degree on an empirical basis, perhaps only as to a motive, such a precept, while it may be a practical rule, can never be called a moral law. . . .

THE GOOD WILL

Nothing can possibly be conceived in the world, or even out of it, which can be called good, without qualification, except a Good Will. Intelligence, wit, judgment, and the other *talents* of the mind, however they may be named, or courage, resolution, perseverance, as qualities of temperament, are undoubtedly good and desirable in many respects; but these gifts of nature may also become extremely bad and mischievous if the will which is to make use of them, and which, therefore, constitutes what is called *character,* is not good. It is the same with the *gifts of fortune.* Power, riches, honour, even health, and the general well-being and contentment with one's conditions which is called *happiness,* inspire pride, and often presumption, if there is not a good will to correct the influence of these on the mind, and with this also to rectify the whole principle of acting, and adapt it to its end. The sight of a being who is not adorned with a single feature of a pure and good will, enjoying unbroken prosperity, can never give pleasure to an impartial rational spectator. Thus a good will appears to constitute the indispensable condition even of being worthy of happiness.

There are even some qualities which are of service to this good will itself, and may facilitate its action, yet which have no intrinsic unconditional value, but always presuppose a good will, and this qualifies the esteem that we justly have for them, and does not permit us to regard them as absolutely good. Moderation in the affections and passions, self-control, and calm deliberation are not only good in many respects, but even seem to constitute part of the intrinsic worth of the person; but they are far from deserving to be called good without qualification, although they have been so unconditionally praised by the ancients. For without the principles of a good will, they may become extremely bad; and the coolness of a villain not only makes him far more dangerous, but also directly makes him more abominable in our eyes than he would have been without it.

A good will is good not because of what it performs or effects, not by its aptness for the attainment of some proposed end, but simply by virtue of the volition, that is, it is good in itself, and considered by itself to be esteemed much higher than all that can be brought about by it in favour of any inclination, nay, even of the sum-total of all inclinations. Even if it should happen that, owing to special disfavour of fortune, or the niggardly provision of a stepmotherly nature, this will should wholly lack power to accomplish its purpose, if with its greatest efforts it should yet achieve nothing, and there should remain only the good will (not, to be sure, a mere wish, but the summoning of all means in our power), then, like a jewel, it would still shine by its own light, as a thing which has its whole value in itself. Its usefulness or fruitlessness can neither add to nor take away anything from this value. It would be, as it were, only the setting to enable us to handle it the more conveniently in common commerce, or to attract to it the attention of those who are not yet connoisseurs, but not to recommend it to true connoisseurs, or to determine its value.

WHY REASON WAS MADE TO GUIDE THE WILL

There is, however, something so strange in this idea of the absolute value of the mere will, in which no account is taken of its utility, that notwithstanding the thorough assent of even common reason to the idea, yet a suspicion must arise that it may perhaps really be the product of mere high-blown fancy, and that we may have misunderstood the purpose of nature in assigning reason as the governor of our will. Therefore we will examine this idea from this point of view.

    In the physical constitution of an organized being, that is, a being adapted suitably to the purposes of life, we assume it as a fundamental principle that no organ for any purpose will be found but what is also the fittest and best adapted for that purpose. Now in a being which has reason and a will, if the proper object of nature were its *conservatism,* its *welfare,* in a word, its *happiness,* then nature would have hit upon a very bad arrangement in selecting the reason of the creature to carry out this purpose. For all the actions which the creature has to perform with a view to this purpose, and the whole rule of its conduct, would be far more surely prescribed to it by instinct, and that end would have been attained thereby much more certainly than it ever can be by reason. Should reason have been communicated to this favoured creature over and above, it must only have served it to contemplate the happy constitution of its nature, to admire it, to congratulate itself thereon, and to feel thankful for it to the beneficent cause, but not that it should subject its desires to that weak and delusive guidance, and meddle bunglingly with the purpose of nature. In a word, nature would have taken care that reason should not break forth into *practical exercise,* nor have the presumption, with its weak insight, to think out for itself the plan of happiness, and of the means of attaining it. Nature would not only have taken on herself the choice of the ends, but also of the means, and with wise foresight would have entrusted both to instinct.

And, in fact, we find that the more a cultivated reason applies itself with deliberate purpose to the enjoyment of life and happiness, so much the more does the man fail of true satisfaction. And from this circumstance there arises in many, if they are candid enough to confess it, a certain degree of *misology,* that is, hatred of reason, especially in the case of those who are most experienced in the use of it, because after calculating all the advantages they derive, I do not say from the invention of all the arts of common luxury, but even from the sciences (which seem to them to be after all only a luxury of the understanding), they find that they have, in fact, only brought more trouble on their shoulders, rather than gained in happiness; and they end by envying, rather than despising, the more common stamp of men who keep closer to the guidance of mere instinct, and do not allow their reason much influence on their conduct. And this we must admit, that the judgment of those who would very much lower the lofty eulogies of the advantages which reason gives us in regard to the happiness and satisfaction of life, or who would even reduce them below zero, is by no means morose or ungrateful to the goodness with which the world is governed, but that there lies at the root of these judgments the idea that our existence has a different and far nobler end, for which, and not for happiness, reason is properly intended, and which must, therefore, be regarded as the supreme condition to which the private ends of man must, for the most part, be postponed.

For as reason is not competent to guide the will with certainty in regard to its objects and the satisfaction of all our wants (which it to some extent even multiplies), this being an end to which an implanted instinct would have led with much greater certainty; and since, nevertheless, reason is imparted to us as a practical faculty, *i.e.* as one which is to have influence on the *will,* therefore, admitting that nature generally in the distribution of her capacities has adapted the means to the end, its true destination must be to produce a *will,* not merely good as a *means* to something else, but *good in itself,* for which reason was absolutely necessary. This will then, though not indeed the sole and complete good, must be the supreme good and the condition of every other, even of the desire of happiness. Under these circumstances, there is nothing inconsistent with the wisdom of nature in the fact that the cultivation of the reason, which is requisite for the first and unconditional purpose, does in many ways interfere, at least in this life, with the attainment of the second, which is always conditional, namely, happiness. Nay, it may even reduce it to nothing, without nature thereby failing in her purpose. For reason recognizes the establishment of a good will as its highest practical destination, and in attaining this purpose is capable only of a satisfaction of its own proper kind, namely, that from the attainment of an end, which end again is determined by reason only, notwithstanding that this may involve many a disappointment to the ends of inclination.

THE FIRST PROPOSITION OF MORALITY

[An action must be done from a sense of duty, if it is to have moral worth]

We have then to develop the notion of a will which deserves to be highly esteemed for itself, and is good without a view to anything further, a notion which exists already in the sound natural understanding, requiring rather to be cleared up than to be taught, and which in estimating the value of our actions always takes the first place, and constitutes the condition of all the rest. In order to do this, we will take the notion of duty, which includes that of a good will, although implying certain subjective restrictions and hindrances. These, however, far from concealing it, or rendering it unrecognizable, rather bring it out by contrast, and make it shine forth so much the brighter.

I omit here all actions which are already recognized as inconsistent with duty although they may be useful for this or that purpose, for with these the question whether they are done *from duty* cannot arise at all, since they even conflict with it. I also set aside those actions which really conform to duty, but to which men have *no* direct *inclination,* performing them because they are impelled thereto by some other inclination. For in this case we can readily distinguish whether the action which agrees with duty is done *from duty,* or from a selfish view. It is much harder to make this distinction when the action accords with duty, and the subject has besides a *direct* inclination to it. For example, it is always a matter of duty that a dealer should not overcharge an inexperienced purchaser; and wherever there is much commerce the prudent tradesman does not overcharge, but keeps a fixed price for everyone, so that a child buys of him as well as any other. Men are thus *honestly* served; but this is not enough to make us believe that the tradesman has so acted from duty and from principles of honesty: his own advantage required it; it is out of the question in this case to suppose that he might besides have a direct inclination in favour of the buyers, so that, as it were, from love he should give no advantage to one over another. Accordingly the action was done neither from duty nor from direct inclination, but merely with a selfish view.

On the other hand, it is a duty to maintain one's life; and, in addition, everyone has also a direct inclination to do so. But on this account the often anxious care which most men take for it has no intrinsic worth, and their maxim has no moral import. They preserve their life *as duty requires,* no doubt, but not *because duty requires.* On the other hand, if adversity and hopeless sorrow have completely taken away the relish for life; if the unfortunate one, strong in mind, indignant at his fate rather than desponding or dejected, wishes for death, and yet preserves his life without loving it—not from inclination or fear, but from duty—then his maxim has a moral worth.

To be beneficent when we can is a duty; and besides this, there are many minds so sympathetically constituted that, without any other motive of vanity or self-interest, they find a pleasure in spreading joy around them, and can take delight in the satisfaction of others so far as it is their own work. But I maintain that in such a case an action of this kind, however proper, however amiable it may be, has nevertheless no true moral worth, but is on a level with other inclinations, *e.g.* the inclination to honour, which, if it is happily directed to that which is in fact of public utility and accordant with duty, and consequently honourable, deserves praise and encouragement, but not esteem. For the maxim lacks the moral import, namely, that such actions be done *from duty,* not from inclination. Put the case that the mind of that philanthropist was clouded by sorrow of his own, extinguishing all sympathy with the lot of others, and that while he still has the power to benefit others in distress, he is not touched by their trouble because he is absorbed with his own; and now suppose that he tears himself out of this dead insensibility, and performs the action without any inclination to it, but simply from duty, then first has his action its genuine moral worth. Further still; if nature has put little sympathy in the heart of this or that man; if he, supposed to be an upright man, is by temperament cold and indifferent to the sufferings of others, perhaps because in respect of his own he is provided with the special gift of patience and fortitude, and supposes, or even requires, that others should have the same—and such a man would certainly not be the meanest product of nature—but if nature had not specially framed him for a philanthropist, would he not still find in himself a source from whence to give himself a far higher worth than that of a good-natured temperament could be? Unquestionably. It is just in this that the moral worth of the character is brought out which is incomparably the highest of all, namely, that he is beneficent, not from inclination, but from duty.

To secure one's own happiness is a duty, at least indirectly; for discontent with one's condition, under a pressure of many anxieties and amidst unsatisfied wants, might easily become a great *temptation to transgression of duty.* But here again, without looking to duty, all men have already the strongest and most intimate inclination to happiness, because it is just in this idea that all inclinations are combined in one total. But the precept of happiness is often of such a sort that it greatly interferes with some inclinations, and yet a man cannot form any definite and certain conception of the sum of satisfaction of all of them which is called happiness. It is not then to be wondered at that a single inclination, definite both as to what it promises and as to the time within which it can be gratified, is often able to overcome such a fluctuating idea, and that a gouty patient, for instance, can choose to enjoy what he likes, and to suffer what he may, since, according to his calculation, on this occasion at least, he has [only] not sacrificed the enjoyment of the present moment to a possibly mistaken expectation of a happiness which is supposed to be found in health. But even in this case, if the general desire for happiness did not influence his will, and supposing that in his particular case health was not a necessary element in this calculation, there yet remains in this, as in all other cases, this law, namely, that he should promote his happiness not from inclination but from duty, and by this would his conduct first acquire true moral worth.

It is in this manner, undoubtedly, that we are to understand those passages of Scripture also in which we are commanded to love our neighbour, even our enemy. For love, as an affection, cannot be commanded, but beneficence for duty's sake may; even though we are not impelled to it by any inclination—nay, are even repelled by a natural and unconquerable aversion. This is *practical* love, and not *pathological*[1]—a love which is seated in the will, and not in the propensions of sense—in principles of action and not of tender sympathy; and it is this love alone which can be commanded.

THE SECOND PROPOSITION OF MORALITY

The second proposition is: That an action done from duty derives its moral worth, *not from the purpose* which is to be attained by it, but from the maxim by which it is determined, and therefore does not depend on the realization of the object of the action, but merely on the *principle of volition* by which the action has taken place, without regard to any object of desire. It is clear from what precedes that the purposes which we may have in view in our actions, or their effects regarded as ends and springs of the will, cannot give to actions any unconditional or moral worth. In what, then, can their worth lie, if it is not to consist in the will and in reference to its expected effect? It cannot lie anywhere but in the *principle of the will* without regard to the ends which can be attained by the action. For the will stands between its *a priori principle,* which is formal, and its *a posteriori* spring, which is material, as between two roads, and as it must be determined by something, it follows that it must be determined by the formal principle of volition when an action is done from duty, in which case every material principle has been withdrawn from it.

THE THIRD PROPOSITION OF MORALITY

The third proposition, which is a consequence of the two preceding, I would express thus: *Duty is the necessity of acting from respect for the law.* I may have *inclination* for an object as the effect of my proposed action, but I cannot have *respect* for it, just for this reason, that it is an effect and not an energy of will. Similarly, I cannot have respect for inclination, whether my own or another's; I can at most, if my own, approve it; if another's, sometimes even

[1]Passional or emotional

love it; *i.e.* look on it as favourable to my own interest. It is only what is connected with my will as a principle, by no means as an effect—what does not subserve my inclination, but overpowers it, or at least in case of choice excludes it from its calculation—in other words, simply the law of itself, which can be an object of respect, and hence a command. Now an action done from duty must wholly exclude the influence of inclination, and with it every object of the will, so that nothing remains which can determine the will except objectively the *law,* and subjectively *pure respect* for this practical law, and consequently the maxim that I should follow this law even to the thwarting of all my inclinations.

Thus the moral worth of an action does not lie in the effect expected from it, nor in any principle of action which requires to borrow its motive from this expected effect. For all these effects—agreeableness of one's condition, and even the promotion of the happiness of others—could have been also brought about by other causes, so that for this there would have been no need of the will of a rational being; whereas it is in this alone that the supreme and unconditional good can be found. The pre-eminent good which we call moral can therefore consist in nothing else than *the conception of law* in itself, *which certainly is only possible in a rational being,* in so far as this conception, and not the expected effect, determines the will. This is a good which is already present in the person who acts accordingly, and we have not to wait for it to appear first in the result.

THE SUPREME PRINCIPLE OF MORALITY: THE CATEGORICAL IMPERATIVE

But what sort of law can that be, the conception of which must determine the will, even without paying any regard to the effect expected from it, in order that this will may be called good absolutely and without qualification? As I have deprived the will of every impulse which could arise to it from obedience to any law, there remains nothing but the universal conformity of its actions to law in general, which alone is to serve the will as a principle, *i.e.* I am never to act otherwise than so *that I could also will that my maxim should become a universal law.* Here, now, it is the simple conformity to law in general, without assuming any particular law applicable to certain actions, that serves the will as its principle, and must so serve it, if duty is not to be a vain delusion and a chimerical notion. The common reason of men in its practical judgments perfectly coincides with this, and always has in view the principle here suggested. Let the question be, for example: May I when in distress make a promise with the intention not to keep it? I readily distinguish here between the two significations which the question may have: Whether it is prudent, or whether it is right, to make a false promise? The former may undoubtedly often be the case. I see clearly indeed that it is not enough to extricate myself from a present difficulty by means of this subterfuge, but it must be well considered whether there may not hereafter spring from this lie much greater inconvenience than that from which I now free myself, and as, with all my supposed *cunning,* the consequences cannot be so easily foreseen but that credit once lost may be much more injurious to me than any mischief which I seek to avoid at present, it should be considered whether it would not be more *prudent* to act herein according to a universal maxim, and to make it a habit to promise nothing except with the intention of keeping it. But it is soon clear to me that such a maxim will still only be based on the fear of consequences. Now it is a wholly different thing to be truthful from duty, and to be so from apprehension of injurious consequences. In the first case, the very notion of the action already implies a law for me; in the second case, I must first look about elsewhere to see what results may be combined with it which would affect myself. For to deviate from the principle of duty is beyond all doubt wicked; but to be unfaithful to my maxim of prudence may often be very advantageous to me, although to abide by it is certainly safer. The shortest way, however, and an unerring one, to discover the answer to this question whether a lying promise is consistent with duty, is to ask myself, Should I be content that my maxim (to extricate myself from difficulty by a false promise) should hold good as a universal law, for myself as well as for others? and should I be able to say to myself, "Every one may make a deceitful promise when he finds himself in a difficulty from which he cannot otherwise extricate himself"? Then I presently become aware that while I can will the lie, I can by no means will that lying should be a universal law. For with such a law there would be no promises at all, since it would be in vain to allege my intention in regard to my future actions to those who would not believe this allegation, or if they over-hastily did so, would pay me back in my own coin. Hence my maxim, as soon as it should be made a universal law, would necessarily destroy itself.

I do not, therefore, need any far-reaching penetration to discern what I have to do in order that my will may be morally good. Inexperienced in the course of the world, incapable of being prepared for all its contingencies, I only ask myself: Canst thou also will that thy maxim should be a universal law? If not, then it must be rejected, and that not because of a disadvantage accruing from myself or even to others, but because it cannot enter as a principle into a possible universal legislation, and reason extorts from me immediate respect for such legislation. I do not indeed as yet *discern* on what this respect is based (this the philosopher may inquire), but at least I understand this, that it is an estimation of the worth which far outweighs all worth of what is recommended by inclination, and that the necessity of acting from *pure* respect for the practical law is what constitutes duty, to which every other motive must give place, because it is the condition of a will being good *in itself,* and the worth of such a will is above everything.

Thus, then, without quitting the moral knowledge of common human reason, we have arrived at its principle. And although, no doubt, common men do not conceive it in such an abstract and universal form, yet they always have it really before their eyes, and use it as the standard of their decision. . . .

Nor could anything be more fatal to morality than that we should wish to derive it from examples. For every example of it that is set before me must be first itself tested by principles of morality, whether it is worthy to serve as an original example, *i.e.* as a pattern, but by no means can it authoritatively furnish the conception of morality. Even the Holy One of the Gospels must first be compared with our ideal of moral perfection before we can recognize Him as such; and so He says of Himself, "Why call ye Me [whom you see] good; none is good [the model of good] but God only [whom ye do not see]." But whence have we the conception of God as the supreme good? Simply from the *idea* of moral perfection, which reason frames *a priori,* and connects inseparably with the notion of a free will. Imitation finds no place at all in morality, and examples serve only for encouragement, *i.e.* they put beyond doubt the feasibility of what the law commands, they make visible that which the practical rule expresses more generally, but they can never authorize us to set aside the true original which lies in reason, and to guide ourselves by examples.

From what has been said, it is clear that all moral conceptions have their seat and origin completely *a priori* in the reason, and that, moreover, in the commonest reason just as truly as in that which is in the highest degree speculative; that they cannot be obtained by abstraction from any empirical, and therefore merely contingent knowledge; that it is just this purity of their origin that makes them worthy to serve as our supreme practical principle, and that just in proportion as we add anything empirical, we detract from their genuine influence, and from the absolute value of actions; that it is not only of the greatest necessity, in a purely speculative point of view, but is also of the greatest practical importance, to derive these notions and laws from pure reason, to present them pure and unmixed, and even to determine the compass of this practical or pure rational knowledge, *i.e.* to determine the whole faculty of pure practical reason; and, in doing so, we must not make its principles dependent on the particular nature of human reason, though in speculative philosophy this may be permitted, or may even at times be necessary; but since moral laws ought to hold good for every rational creature, we must derive them from the general concept of a rational being. In this way, although for its *application* to man morality has need of anthropology, yet, in the first instance, we must treat it independently as pure philosophy, *i.e.* as metaphysic, complete in itself (a thing which in such distinct branches of science is easily done); knowing well that unless we are in possession of this, it would not only be vain to determine the moral element of duty in right actions for purposes of speculative criticism, but it would be impossible to base morals on their genuine principles, even for common practical purposes, especially of moral instruction, so as to produce pure moral dispositions, and to engraft them on men's minds to the promotion of the greatest possible good in the world. . . .

THE RATIONAL GROUND
OF THE CATEGORICAL IMPERATIVE

. . . [T]he question, how the imperative of *morality* is possible, is undoubtedly one, the only one, demanding a solution, as this is not at all hypothetical, and the objective necessity which it presents cannot rest on any hypothesis, as is the case with the hypothetical imperatives. Only here we must never leave out of consideration that we *cannot* make out *by any example,* in other words empirically, whether there is such an imperative at all; but it is rather to be feared that all those which seem to be categorical may yet be at bottom hypothetical. For instance, when the precept is: Thou shalt not promise deceitfully; and it is assumed that the necessity of this is not a mere counsel to avoid some other evil, so that it should mean: Thou shalt not make a lying promise, lest if it become known thou shouldst destroy thy credit, but that an action of this kind must be regarded as evil in itself, so that the imperative of the prohibition is categorical; then we cannot show with certainty in any example that the will was determined merely by the law, without any other spring of action, although it may appear to be so. For it is always possible that fear of disgrace, perhaps also obscure dread of other dangers, may have a secret influence on the will. Who can prove by experience the nonexistence of a cause when all that experience tells us is that we do not perceive it? But in such a case the so-called moral imperative, which as such appears to be categorical and unconditional, would in reality be only a pragmatic precept, drawing our attention to our own interests, and merely teaching us to take these into consideration.

We shall therefore have to investigate *a priori* the possibility of a categorical imperative, as we have not in this case the advantage of its reality being given in experience, so that [the elucidation of] its possibility should be requisite only for its explanation, not for its establishment. In the meantime it may be discerned beforehand that the categorical imperative alone has the purport of a practical law: all the rest may indeed be called *principles* of the will but not laws, since whatever is only necessary for the attainment of some arbitrary purpose may be considered as in itself contingent, and we can at any time be free from the precept if we give up the purpose: on the contrary, the unconditional command leaves the will no liberty to choose the opposite; consequently it alone carries with it that necessity which we require in a law.

Secondly, in the case of this categorical imperative or law of morality, the difficulty (of discerning its possibility) is a very profound one. It is an *a priori* synthetical practical proposition; and as there is so much difficulty in discerning the possibility of speculative propositions of this kind, it may readily be supposed that the difficulty will be no less with the practical.

FIRST FORMULATION OF THE CATEGORICAL IMPERATIVE: UNIVERSAL LAW

In this problem we will first inquire whether the mere conception of a categorical imperative may not perhaps supply us also with the formula of it, containing the proposition which alone can be a categorical imperative; for even if we know the tenor of such an absolute command, yet how it is possible will require further special and laborious study, which we postpone to the last section.

When I conceive a hypothetical imperative, in general I do not know beforehand what it will contain until I am given the condition. But when I conceive a categorical imperative, I know at once what it contains. For as the imperative contains besides the law only the necessity that the maxims shall conform to this law, while the law contains no conditions restricting it, there remains nothing but the general statement that the maxim of the action should conform to a universal law, and it is this conformity alone that the imperative properly represents as necessary.

There is therefore but one categorical imperative, namely, this: *Act only on that maxim whereby thou canst at the same time will that it should become a universal law.*

Now if all imperatives of duty can be deduced from this one imperative as from their principle, then, although it should remain undecided whether what is called duty is not merely a vain notion, yet at least we shall be able to show what we understand by it and what this notion means.

Since the universality of the law according to which effects are produced constitutes what is properly called *nature* in the most general sense (as to form), that is the existence of things so far as it is determined by general laws, the imperative of duty may be expressed thus: *Act as if the maxim of thy action were to become by thy will a universal law of nature.*

FOUR ILLUSTRATIONS

We will now enumerate a few duties, adopting the usual division of them into duties to ourselves and to others, and into perfect and imperfect duties.

1. A man reduced to despair by a series of misfortunes feels wearied of life, but is still so far in possession of his reason that he can ask himself whether it would not be contrary to his duty to himself to take his own life. Now he inquires whether the maxim of his action could become a universal law of nature. His maxim is: From self-love I adopt it as a principle to shorten my life when its longer duration is likely to bring more evil than satisfaction. It

is asked then simply whether this principle founded on self-love can become a universal law of nature. Now we see at once that a system of nature of which it should be a law to destroy life by means of the very feeling whose special nature it is to impel to the improvement of life would contradict itself, and therefore could not exist as a system of nature; hence that maxim cannot possibly exist as a universal law of nature, and consequently would be wholly inconsistent with the supreme principle of all duty.

2. Another finds himself forced by necessity to borrow money. He knows that he will not be able to repay it, but sees also that nothing will be lent to him, unless he promises stoutly to repay it in a definite time. He desires to make this promise, but he has still so much conscience as to ask himself: Is it not unlawful and inconsistent with duty to get out of a difficulty in this way? Suppose, however, that he resolves to do so, then the maxim of his action would be expressed thus: When I think myself in want of money, I will borrow money and promise to repay it, although I know that I never can do so. Now this principle of self-love or of one's own advantage may perhaps be consistent with my whole future welfare; but the question is, Is it right? I change then the suggestion of self-love into a universal law, and state the question thus: How would it be if my maxim were a universal law? Then I see at once that it could never hold as a universal law of nature, but would necessarily contradict itself. For supposing it to be a universal law that everyone when he thinks himself in a difficulty should be able to promise whatever he pleases, with the purpose of not keeping his promise, the promise itself would become impossible, as well as the end that one might have in view in it, since no one would consider that anything was promised to him, but would ridicule all such statements as vain pretenses.

3. A third finds in himself a talent which with the help of some culture might make him a useful man in many respects. But he finds himself in comfortable circumstances, and prefers to indulge in pleasure rather than to take pains in enlarging and improving his happy natural capacities. He asks, however, whether his maxim of neglect of his natural gifts, besides agreeing with his inclination to indulgence, agrees also with what is called duty. He sees then that a system of nature could indeed subsist with such a universal law although men (like the South Sea islanders) should let their talents rest, and resolve to devote their lives merely to idleness, amuse-

ment, and propagation of their species—in a word, to enjoyment; but he cannot possibly *will* that this should be a universal law of nature, or be implanted in us as such by a natural instinct. For, as a rational being, he necessarily wills that his faculties be developed, since they serve him, and have been given him, for all sorts of possible purposes.

4. A fourth, who is in prosperity, while he sees that others have to contend with great wretchedness and that he could help them, thinks: What concern is it of mine? Let everyone be as happy as Heaven pleases, or as he can make himself; I will take nothing from him nor even envy him, only I do not wish to contribute anything to his welfare or to his assistance in distress! Now no doubt if such a mode of thinking were a universal law, the human race might very well subsist, and doubtless even better than in a state in which everyone talks of sympathy and good-will, or even takes care occasionally to put it into practice, but, on the other side, also cheats when he can, betrays the rights of men, or otherwise violates them. But although it is possible that a universal law of nature might exist in accordance with that maxim, it is impossible to *will* that such a principle should have the universal validity of a law of nature. For a will which resolved this would contradict itself, inasmuch as many cases might occur in which one would have need of the love and sympathy of others, and in which, by such a law of nature, sprung from his own will, he would deprive himself of all hope of the aid he desires.

These are a few of the many actual duties, or at least what we regard as such, which obviously fall into two classes on the one principle that we have laid down. We must be *able to will* that a maxim of our action should be a universal law. This is the canon of the moral appreciation of the action generally. Some actions are of such a character that their maxim cannot without contradiction be even *conceived* as a universal law of nature, far from it being possible that we should *will* that it *should* be so. In others this intrinsic impossibility is not found, but still it is impossible to *will* that their maxim should be raised to the universality of a law of nature, since such a will would contradict itself. It is easily seen that the former violate strict or rigorous (inflexible) duty; the latter only laxer (meritorious) duty. Thus it has been completely shown by these examples how all duties depend as regards the nature of the obligation (not the object of the action) on the same principle.

SECOND FORMULATION
OF THE CATEGORICAL IMPERATIVE:
HUMANITY AS AN END IN ITSELF

. . . Now I say: man and generally any rational being *exists* as an end in himself, *not merely as a means* to be arbitrarily used by this or that will, but in all his actions, whether they concern himself or other rational beings, must be always regarded at the same time as an end. All objects of the inclinations have only a conditional worth; for if the inclinations and the wants founded on them did not exist, then their object would be without value. But the inclinations themselves being sources of want are so far from having an absolute worth for which they should be desired, that, on the contrary, it must be the universal wish of every rational being to be wholly free from them. Thus the worth of any object which is *to be acquired* by our action is always conditional. Beings whose existence depends not on our will but on nature's, have nevertheless, if they are nonrational beings, only a relative value as means, and are therefore called *things;* rational beings, on the contrary, are called *persons,* because their very nature points them out as ends in themselves, that is as something which must not be used merely as means, and so far therefore restricts freedom of action (and is an object of respect). These, therefore, are not merely subjective ends whose existence has a worth *for us* as an effect of our action, but *objective ends,* that is things whose existence is an end in itself: an end moreover for which no other can be substituted, which they should subserve *merely* as means, for otherwise nothing whatever would possess *absolute worth;* but if all worth were conditioned and therefore contingent, then there would be no supreme practical principle of reason whatever.

If then there is a supreme practical principle or, in respect of the human will, a categorical imperative, it must be one which, being drawn from the conception of that which is necessarily an end for everyone because it is *an end in itself,* constitutes an *objective* principle of will, and can therefore serve as a universal practical law. The foundation of this principle is: *rational nature exists as an end in itself.* Man necessarily conceives his own existence as being so: so far then this is a *subjective* principle of human actions. But every other rational being regards its existence similarly, just on the same rational principle that holds for me: so that it is at the same time an objective principle, from which as a supreme practical law all laws of the will must be capable of being deduced. Accordingly the practical imperative will be as follows: *So act as to treat humanity, whether in thine own person or in that of any other, in every case as an end withal, never as means only. . . .*

. . . Looking back now on all previous attempts to discover the principle of morality, we need not wonder why they all failed. It was seen that man was bound to laws by duty, but it was not observed that the laws to which he is subject are *only those of his own giving,* though at the same time they are *universal,* and that he is only bound to act in conformity with his own will; a will, however, which is designed by nature to give universal laws. For when one has conceived man only as subject to a law (no matter what), then this law required some interest, either by way of attraction or constraint, since it did not originate as a law from *his own* will, but his will was according to a law obliged by *something else* to act in a certain manner. Now by this necessary consequence all the labour spent in finding a supreme principle of *duty* was irrevocably lost. For men never elicited duty, but only a necessity of acting from a certain interest. Whether this interest was private or otherwise, in any case the imperative must be conditional, and could not by any means be capable of being a moral command. I will therefore call this the principle of *Autonomy* of the will, in contrast with every other which I accordingly reckon as *Heteronomy.*

THE KINGDOM OF ENDS

The conception of every rational being as one which must consider itself as giving in all the maxims of its will universal laws, so as to judge itself and its actions from this point of view—this conception leads to another which depends on it and is very fruitful, that of a *kingdom of ends.*

By a *kingdom* I understand the union of different rational beings in a system by common laws. Now since it is by laws that ends are determined as regards their universal validity, hence, if we abstract from the personal differences of rational beings, and likewise from all the content of their private ends, we shall be able to conceive all ends combined in a systematic whole (including both rational beings as ends in themselves, and also the special ends which each may propose to himself), that is to say, we can conceive a kingdom of ends, which on the preceding principles is possible.

For all rational beings come under the *law* that each of them must treat itself and all others *never merely as means,* but in every case *at the same time as ends in themselves.* Hence results a systematic union of rational beings by common objective laws, *i.e.,* a kingdom which may be called a kingdom of ends, since what these laws have in view is just the relation of these beings to one another as ends and means. . . .

For Further Reflection

1. Is Kant's philosophy merely a development of the Golden Rule: "Do unto others what you would have them do unto you"? If it is equivalent, does it make Kant's system more intuitively plausible? But does it also lead to problems with what Kant thought to be the implications of his system? For example, on the basis of the Golden Rule one might endorse certain instances of euthanasia, but Kant's discussion of suicide seems to rule this out.

2. Kant's ethics is called deontological (from the Greek word for "duty") because he believes that the value of an act is in the act itself rather than in its consequences (as teleologists hold). Deontological ethics has been criticized as being too rigid. Do you think that this is true? Should the notion of consequences be taken into consideration?

3. How would Kant deal with moral conflicts? When two universal principles conflict, how would Kant resolve the dilemma?

4. Kant's categorical imperative has also been criticized for being more wide open than he realized, for it doesn't limit what could be universalized. How would Kant respond to these counterexamples? (1) Everyone should tie his right shoe before his left shoe; (2) All retarded or senile people should be executed by the government (adding, if I should become retarded or senile, I should also undergo this fate).

Kant's Theory

WILLIAM K. FRANKENA

William Frankena (1908–1994) earned an international reputation for his writings on moral theory and the history of
ethics, including numerous papers and his much-lauded
textbook *Ethics*. For more than four decades he was a highly
regarded teacher of philosophy at the University of Michigan. In this selection taken from his famous text, Frankena
argues that Kant's categorical imperative has several defects
that Kant and his followers have failed to appreciate.

. . . Another example of a monistic kind of rule deontology is presented by Immanuel Kant. We must confine our discussion to what
he calls the first form of the categorical imperative, "Act only on
that maxim which you can at the same time will to be a universal
law." In this dictum, Kant is taking a principle, very similar to those
quoted from Sidgwick and Rashdall, and offering it as the necessary and sufficient criterion for determining what more concrete
maxims or rules we should live by. We have, in effect, already
accepted the principle as *necessary*, the question is whether it is
sufficient. If so, our search for a normative ethics is ended.

There are problems about the interpretation of Kant, but we may
take him as saying, first, that when one acts voluntarily one always
acts on a formulizable maxim or rule; second, that one is choosing and judging from the moral point of view if and only if one is
or would be willing to universalize one's maxim, that is, if he is or
would be willing to see his rule acted on by everyone who is in
a situation of a similar kind, even if he himself turns out to be on
the receiving end on occasion; and, third, that an action is morally
right and/or obligatory if and only if one can consistently will that
the maxim or rule involved be acted on by everyone in similar circumstances, and an action is morally wrong if and only if one cannot consistently will this. Here we are concerned primarily with the
last contention, though we will also have a word to say about the
second. Is Kant's criterion sufficient as well as necessary for determining what is morally right or obligatory?

From *Ethics*, 2nd Edition by William K. Frankena, © 1989. Adapted by
permission of Pearson Education, Inc., Upper Saddle River, NJ.

Let us first take an example of how he applies it. In one of his illustrations he supposes that A makes a promise but is ready to break it if this suits his purposes. A's maxim then may be expressed thus, "When it suits my purposes I will make promises, intending also to break them if this suits my purposes." But A cannot consistently will this maxim to be universally acted on, says Kant.

> . . . could I say to myself that everyone make a false promise when he is in difficulty from which he otherwise cannot escape? I immediately see that I could will the lie but not a universal law to lie. For with such a law [i.e., with such a maxim universally acted on] there would be no promises at all. . . . Thus my maxim would necessarily destroy itself as soon as it was made a universal law.[1]

Kant concludes, therefore, that it is wrong to make deceitful promises. By somewhat similar arguments, he believes he can also show, for example, that it is wrong to commit suicide, that we ought to cultivate our natural gifts or talents, and that we ought to help others who are in trouble.

It is often alleged that Kant is being a utilitarian in these arguments, not a deontologist as he purports to be. This is a mistake. He is not arguing that one must keep one's promises because the results of everyone's breaking them when convenient or advantageous to themselves would be so bad as to be intolerable. This is how a rule-utilitarian would run the argument. Kant, however, is contending that one cannot even will such a maxim to be universally acted on, because in so doing, one would be involved in a contradiction of will; one would be willing both that it be possible to make promises and have them credited (else why make them?) and that everyone be free to break promises to suit his own purposes. In other words, he is arguing, not that the results of everyone's always acting on the deceitful promise maxim are bad, but that the results are self-defeating, since if that maxim were universally acted on, we could not even have the institution of promise making which that maxim presupposes.

It must be admitted that Kant's arguments are not always as convincing as the one against deceitful promising. It must also be

[1]Immanuel Kant, *Foundations of the Metaphysic of Morals,* tr. L. W. Beck (New York: The Liberal Arts Press, 1959), p. 19. See selections in Frankena and Granrose, eds., *Introductory Readings in Ethics* (Englewood Cliffs, N.J.: Prentice-Hall, Inc., 1974), Chap. II.

pointed out that he is not free from the difficulties due to conflicts between duties; it seems possible, at any rate, that keeping a promise might on occasion prevent one from helping someone in trouble. Possibly Kant could argue in this case that it would be right to break the promise and help the person in trouble, since one can will the maxim, "When breaking a promise is required in order to help someone I will break it," to be universally acted on in the situations specified, especially if it is also specified in the maxim that the promise is not crucially important and that the help is. Kant, however, does not take this line, and talks as if he can show that promises ought never to be broken. But this his argument does not suffice to show. As was just indicated, one may be able to will a specific rule that permits promises to be broken in a certain kind of situation to be universally acted on, even though one cannot will a more blanket one to become a universal law.

Thus Kant's arguments, even if good, do not prove as much as he thinks; and in the case just presented, this is just as well, since he thought he could prove too much. Even if we admit that his criterion rules out certain sorts of action as immoral (for example, deceitful promising which does not enable one to help another), must we agree that all of our duties can be established by his test? Take the duty to help others. It is true that if one adopts the maxim of not helping others in need and wills this to be a universal law, he is likely to find himself willing inconsistently to abrogate this rule, since he is likely himself to be in need sometime. Still, it is not hard to imagine a man whose fortune is fairly sure or one who is willing to be consistent and to take the consequences of his maxim's being universally acted on; if there are such people, Kant's test will not suffice to establish benevolence as a duty. Of course, one might conclude that it is not a duty just because it does not pass this test; but this seems a drastic conclusion, and, deontological as he was, even Kant could not draw it.

Is every maxim that does pass Kant's test a duty, as he sometimes seems to think? "When alone in the dark, whistle"—this seems to be a maxim one can will to be a universal law. If not, "Tie your left shoestring first" clearly is. Yet, surely, neither of these rules can be regarded as a duty. One might reply here that such questions about whistling and tying shoestrings are not moral ones, and this is correct, but Kant does not tell us how to determine whether they are moral or not. It might also be argued that Kant was not regarding all maxims one *can* will to be universal laws as *duties,* but only holding that maxims one *cannot* will to be universal laws are *immoral* or *wrong* to act on. That is, Kant meant to say (a) that it is *permissible* to act on a maxim if and only if one can will it to be a universal law, (b) that it is *wrong* to act on a maxim if and only if one cannot will it to be a universal law, and (c) that it is a *duty* to act on a maxim if and only if one cannot will its *opposite* to be a universal law. I am, in fact, inclined to think this is what Kant meant and should have said. But even then his criterion of right and wrong is not sufficient, for it does not actually rule out all immoral maxims, e.g., the maxim of never helping anyone.

In any event, it seems to me that in order for one's maxims to be considered moral duties, it is not enough that one be able consistently to will one's maxims to be universally acted on. Much depends on the point of view from which one wills one's rules to be universally followed. One might do this from the aesthetic point of view or, more probably, from a prudential one. One might, for example, will honesty to be universally practiced because one regards everyone's being honest, including oneself (else one is not universalizing, but making an exception of oneself, which Kant is right in putting out of moral bounds), as being advantageous to oneself. "Everyone's being honest is the best policy from my point of view." If one uses such reasoning, one can hardly claim to be taking the moral point of view. There is more to the moral point of view than being willing to universalize one's rules; Kant and his followers fail to see this fact, although they are right in thinking such a willingness is part of it.

For Further Reflection

1. According to Frankena, what difficulty exists in Kant's theory "due to conflicts between duties"?

2. Why does Frankena suggest that Kant's universalization test may not be enough to establish benevolence as a duty?

3. What does Frankena mean by "There is more to the moral point of view than being willing to universalize one's rules"?

4. Do you agree with Frankena's criticisms of Kant's theory? Explain.

Intuitionism

W. D. ROSS

Sir William D. Ross (1877–1971) was provost of Oriel College, Oxford University. His book *The Right and the Good* (1930), from which the present selection is taken, is a classic treatise in ethical intuitionism. Ross argues against utilitarianism (both hedonistic utilitarianism and Moore's ideal utilitarianism), asserting that optimal consequences have nothing to do with moral rightness or wrongness. We have intuitive knowledge of rightness and wrongness in terms of action-guiding principles, such as to keep promises made, to promote justice, to show gratitude for benefits rendered, and to refrain from harming others. Unlike Kant's principles, however, these principles are not absolutes, that is, duties that must never be overridden by more binding moral duties. Moral principles are *prima facie* duties. That is, while their intrinsic value is not dependent on circumstances, their application is. They can be overridden by other *prima facie* duties. Essentially, these principles are the outcomes of generations of reflection on our duty, and their holistic schema has been internalized within us, so that ultimately, as Aristotle said, the "decision lies in the perception."

. . . A . . . theory has been put forward by Professor Moore that what makes actions right is that they are productive of more *good* than could have been produced by any other action open to the agent.

This theory is in fact the culmination of all the attempts to base rightness on productivity of some sort of result. The first form this attempt takes is the attempt to base rightness on conduciveness to the advantage or pleasure of the agent. This theory comes to grief over the fact, which stares us in the face, that a great part of duty consists in an observance of the rights and a furtherance of the interests of others, whatever the cost to ourselves may be. Plato and others may be right in holding that a regard for the rights of others never in the long run involves a loss of happiness for the agent, that 'the just life profits a man.' But this, even if true, is irrelevant to the rightness of the act. As soon as a man does an action *because* he thinks he will promote his own interests thereby, he is acting not from a sense of its rightness but from self-interest.

To the egoistic theory hedonistic utilitarianism supplies a much-needed amendment. It points out correctly that the fact that a certain pleasure will be enjoyed by the agent is no reason why he *ought* to bring it into being, rather than an equal or greater pleasure to be enjoyed by another, though, human nature being what it is, it makes it not unlikely that he *will* try to bring it into being. But hedonistic utilitarianism in its turn needs a correction. On reflection it seems clear that pleasure is not the only thing in life that we think good in itself, that for instance we think the possession of a good character, or an intelligent understanding of the world, as good or better. A great advance is made by the substitution of 'productive of the greatest good' for 'productive of the greatest pleasure.'

Not only is this theory more attractive than hedonistic utilitarianism, but its logical relation to that theory is such that the latter could not be true unless *it* were true, while it might be true though hedonistic utilitarianism were not. It is in fact one of the logical bases of hedonistic utilitarianism. For the view that what produces the maximum pleasure is right has for its bases the views (1) that what produces the maximum good is right, and (2) that pleasure is the only thing good in itself. If they were not assuming that what produces the maximum *good* is right, the utilitarians' attempt to show that pleasure is the only thing good in itself, which is in fact the point they take most pains to establish, would have been quite irrelevant to their attempt to prove that only what produces the maximum *pleasure* is right. If, therefore, it can be shown that productivity of the maximum good is not what makes all right actions right, we shall *a fortiori* have refuted hedonistic utilitarianism.

When a plain man fulfills a promise because he thinks he ought to do so, it seems clear that he does so with no thought of its total consequences, still less with any opinion that these are likely to be the best possible. He thinks in fact much more of the past than of the future. What makes him think it right to act in a certain way is the fact that he has promised to do so—that and, usually, nothing more. That his act will produce the best possible consequences is not his reason for calling it right. What lends colour to the theory we are examining, then, is not the actions (which form probably a great majority of our actions) in which some such reflection as 'I have promised' is the only reason we give ourselves for thinking a certain action right, but the exceptional cases in which the consequences of fulfilling a promise (for instance) would be so disastrous to others that we judge it right not to do so. It must of course be admitted that such cases exist. If I have promised to meet a friend at a particular time for some trivial purpose, I should certainly think myself justified in breaking my engagement if by doing so I could prevent a serious accident or bring relief to the victims of one. And the supporters of the view we are examining hold that my thinking so is due to my thinking that I shall bring more good into existence by the one action than by the other. A different account may, however, be given of the matter, an account which will, I believe, show itself to be the true one. It may be said that besides the duty of fulfilling promises, I have and recognize a duty of relieving distress, and that when I think it right to do the latter at the cost of not doing the former, it is not because I think I shall produce more good thereby but because I think it the duty which is in the circumstances more of a duty. This account surely corresponds much more closely with what we really think in such a situation. If, so far as I can see, I could bring equal amounts of good into being by fulfilling my promise and by helping someone to whom I had made no promise, I should not hesitate to regard the former as my duty. Yet on the view that what is right is right because it is productive of the most good I should not so regard it.

There are two theories, each in its way simple, that offer a solution of such cases of conscience. One is the view of Kant, that there are certain duties of perfect obligation, such as those of fulfilling promises, of paying debts, of telling the truth, which admit of no exception whatever in favour of duties of imperfect obligation, such as that of relieving distress. The other is the view of, for instance, Professor Moore and Dr. Rashdall, that there is only the duty of producing good, and that all 'conflicts of duties' should be resolved by asking 'By which action will most good be produced?' But it is more important that our theory fit the facts than that it be simple, and the account we have given above corresponds (it seems to me) better than either of the simpler theories with what we really think, viz. that normally promise-keeping, for example, should come before benevolence, but that when and only when the good to be produced by the benevolent act is very great and the promise comparatively trivial, the act of benevolence becomes our duty.

In fact the theory of 'ideal utilitarianism' if I may for brevity refer so to the theory of Professor Moore, seems to simplify unduly our relations to our fellows It says, in effect, that the only morally significant relation in which my neighbours stand to me is that of being possible beneficiaries by my action. They do stand in this relation to me, and this relation is morally significant. But they may also stand to me in the relation of promisee to promiser, of creditor to debtor, of wife to husband, of child to parent, of friend to friend, of fellow countryman to fellow countryman, and the like; and each of these relations is the foundation of a *prima facie* duty which is more or less incumbent on me according to the circumstances of the case. When I am in a situation, as perhaps I always am, in which more than one of these *prima facie* duties is incumbent on me, what I have to do is to study the situation as fully as I can until I form the considered opinion (it is never more) that in the circumstances one of them is more incumbent than any other; then I am bound to think that to do this *prima facie* duty is my duty *sans phrase* in the situation.

I suggest '*prima facie* duty' or 'conditional duty' as a brief way of referring to the characteristic (quite distinct from that of being a duty proper) which an act has, in virtue of being of a certain kind (e.g., the keeping of a promise), of being an act which would be a duty proper if it were not at the same time of another kind which is morally significant. Whether an act is a duty proper or actual duty depends on *all* the morally significant kinds it is an instance of. The phrase '*prima facie* duty' must be apologized for, since (1) it suggests that what we are speaking of is a certain kind of duty, whereas it is in fact not a duty but something related in a special way to duty. Strictly speaking, we want not a phrase in which duty is qualified by an adjective, but a separate noun. (2) '*Prima' facie* suggests that one is speaking only of an appearance which a moral situation presents at first sight, and which may turn out to be illusory; whereas what I am speaking of is an objective fact involved in the nature of the situation, or more strictly in an element of its nature, though not, as duty proper does, arising from its *whole* nature. I can, however, think of no term which fully meets the case. 'Claim' has been suggested by Professor Prichard. The word 'claim' has the advantage of being quite a familiar one in this connexion, and it seems to cover much of the ground. It would be quite natural to say, 'a person to whom I have made a promise has a claim on me,' and also, 'a person whose distress I could relieve (at the cost of breaking the promise) has a claim on me.' But (1) while 'claim' is appropriate from *their* point of view, we want a word to express the corresponding fact from the agent's point of view—the fact of his being subject to claims that can be made against him; and ordinary language provides us with no such correlative to 'claim.' And (2) (what is more important) 'claim' seems inevitably to suggest two persons, one of whom might make a claim on the other; and while this covers the ground of social duty, it is inappropriate in the case of that important part of duty which is the duty of cultivating a certain kind of character in oneself. It would be artificial, I think, and at any rate metaphorical, to say that one's character has a claim on oneself.

There is nothing arbitrary about these *prima facie* duties. Each rests on a definite circumstance which cannot seriously be held to be without moral significance. Of *prima facie* duties I suggest, without claiming completeness or finality for it, the following division.

(1) Some duties rest on previous acts of my own. These duties seem to include two kinds, (*a*) those resting on a promise or what may fairly be called an implicit promise, such as the implicit undertaking not to tell lies which seems to be implied in the act of entering into conversation (at any rate by civilized men), or of writing books that purport to be history and not fiction. These may be called the duties of fidelity. (*b*) Those resting on a previous wrongful act. These may be called the duties of reparation. (2) Some rest on previous acts of other men, i.e. services done by them to me. These may be loosely described as the duties of gratitude. (3) Some rest on the fact or possibility of a distribution of pleasure or happiness (or of the means thereto) which is not in accordance with the merit of the persons concerned; in such cases there arises a duty to upset or prevent such a distribution. These are the duties of justice. (4) Some rest on the mere fact that there are other beings in the world whose condition we can make better in respect of virtue, or of intelligence, or of pleasure. These are the duties of beneficence. (5) Some rest on the fact that we can improve our own condition in respect of virtue or of intelligence. These are the duties of self-improvement. (6) I think that we should distinguish from (4) the duties that may be summed up under the title of 'not injuring others.' No doubt to injure others is incidentally to fail to do them good; but it seems to me clear that non-maleficence is apprehended as a duty distinct from that of beneficence, and as a duty of a more stringent character. It will be noticed that this alone among the types of duty has been stated in a nega-

tive way. An attempt might no doubt be made to state this duty, like the others, in a positive way. It might be said that it is really the duty to prevent ourselves from acting either from an inclination to harm others or from an inclination to seek our own pleasure, in doing which we should incidentally harm them. But on reflection it seems clear that the primary duty here is the duty not to harm others, this being a duty whether or not we have an inclination that if followed would lead to our harming them; and that when we have such an inclination the primary duty not to harm others gives rise to a consequential duty to resist the inclination. The recognition of this duty of non-maleficence is the first step on the way to the recognition of the duty of beneficence; and that accounts for the prominence of the commands 'thou shalt not kill,' 'thou shalt not commit adultery,' 'thou shalt not steal,' 'thou shalt not bear false witness,' in so early a code as the Decalogue. But even when we have come to recognize the duty of beneficence, it appears to me that the duty of non-maleficence is recognized as a distinct one, and as *prima facie* more binding. We should not in general consider it justifiable to kill one person in order to keep another alive, or to steal from one in order to give alms to another.

The essential defect of the 'ideal utilitarian' theory is that it ignores, or at least does not do full justice to, the highly personal character of duty. If the only duty is to produce the maximum of good, the question who is to have the good—whether it is myself, or my benefactor, or a person to whom I have made a promise to confer that good on him, or a mere fellow man to whom I stand in no such special relation—should make no difference to my having a duty to produce that good. But we are all in fact sure that it makes a vast difference.

One or two other comments must be made on this provisional list of the divisions of duty. (1) The nomenclature is not strictly correct. For by 'fidelity' or 'gratitude' we mean, strictly, certain states of motivation; and, as I have urged, it is not our duty to have certain motives, but to do certain acts. By 'fidelity,' for instance, is meant, strictly, the disposition to fulfil promises and implicit promises *because we have made them*. We have no general word to cover the actual fulfilment of promises and implicit promises *irrespective of motive;* and I use 'fidelity,' loosely but perhaps conveniently, to fill this gap. So too I use 'gratitude' for the returning of services, irrespective of motive. The term 'justice' is not so much confined, in ordinary usage, to a certain state of motivation, for we should often talk of a man as acting justly even when we did not think his motive was the wish to do what was just simply for the sake of doing so. Less apology is therefore needed for our use of 'justice' in this sense. And I have used the word 'beneficence' rather than 'benevolence,' in order to emphasize the fact that it is our duty to do certain things, and not to do them from certain motives.

(2) If the objection be made that this catalogue of the main types of duty is an unsystematic one resting on no logical principle, it may be replied, first, that it makes no claim to being ultimate. It is a *prima facie* classification of the duties which reflection on our moral convictions seems actually to reveal. And if these convictions are, as I would claim that they are, of the nature of knowledge, and if I have not misstated them, the list will be a list of authentic conditional duties, correct as far as it goes though not necessarily complete. The list of *goods* put forward by the rival theory is reached by exactly the same method—the only sound one in the circumstances—viz. that of direct reflection on what we really think. Loyalty to the facts is worth more than a symmetrical architectonic or a hastily reached simplicity. If further reflection discovers a perfect logical basis for this or for a better classification, so much the better.

(3) It may, again, be objected that our theory that there are these various and often conflicting types of *prima facie* duty leaves us with no principle upon which to discern what is our actual duty in particular circumstances. But this objection is not one which the rival theory is in a position to bring forward. For when we have to choose between the production of two heterogeneous goods, say knowledge and pleasure, the 'ideal utilitarian' theory can only fall back on an opinion, for which no logical basis can be offered, that one of the goods is the greater; and this is no better than a similar opinion that one of two duties is the more urgent. And again, when we consider the infinite variety of the effects of our actions in a way of pleasure, it must surely be admitted that the claim which *hedonism* sometimes makes, that it offers a readily applicable criterion of right conduct, is quite illusory.

I am unwilling, however, to content myself with an *argumentum ad hominem,* and I would contend that in principle there is no reason to anticipate that every act that is our duty is so for one and the same reason. Why should two sets of circumstances, or one set of circumstances, *not* possess different characteristics, any one of which makes a certain act our *prima facie* duty? When I ask what it is that makes me in certain cases sure that I have a *prima facie* duty to do so and so, I find that it lies in the fact that I have made a promise; when I ask the same question in another case, I find the answer lies in the fact that I have done a wrong. And if on reflection I find (as I think I do) that neither of these reasons is reducible to the other, I must not on any *a priori* ground assume that such a reduction is possible.

It is necessary to say something by way of clearing up the relation between *prima facie* duties and the actual or absolute duty to do one particular act in particular circumstances. If, as almost all moralists except Kant are agreed and as most plain men think, it is sometimes right to tell a lie or to break a promise, it must be maintained that there is a difference between *prima facie* duty and actual or absolute duty. When we think ourselves justified in breaking, and indeed morally obliged to break, a promise in order to relieve someone's distress, we do not for a moment cease to recognize a *prima facie* duty to keep our promise, and this leads us to feel, not indeed shame or repentance, but certainly compunction, for behaving as we do; we recognize, further, that it is our duty to make up somehow to the promise for the breaking of the promise. We have to distinguish from the characteristic of being our duty that of tending to be our duty. Any act that we do contains various elements in virtue of which it falls under various categories. In virtue of being the breaking of a promise, for instance, it tends to be wrong; in virtue of being an instance of relieving distress it tends to be right. Tendency to be one's duty may be called a parti-resultant attribute, i.e. one which belongs to an act in virtue of some one component in its nature. *Being* one's duty is a toti-resultant attribute, one which belongs to an act in virtue of its whole nature and of nothing less than this.

Something should be said of the relation between our apprehension of the *prima facie* rightness of certain types of acts and our mental attitude toward particular acts. It is proper to use the word 'apprehension' in the former case and not in the latter. That an act, *qua* fulfilling a promise, or *qua* effecting a just distribution of good, or *qua* returning services rendered, or *qua* promoting the good of others, or *qua* promoting the virtue or insight of the agent, is *prima facie* right, is self-evident; not in the sense that it is evident from the beginning of our lives, or as soon as we attend to the proposition for the first time, but in the sense that when we have reached sufficient mental maturity and have given sufficient attention to the proposition it is evident without any need of proof, or of evidence beyond itself. It is self-evident, just as a mathematical axiom, or the validity of a form of inference, is evident. The moral order expressed in these propositions is just as much part of the fundamental nature of the universe (and, we may add, of any possible universe in which there were moral agents at all) as is the spatial or numerical structure expressed in the axioms of geometry or arithmetic. In our confidence that these propositions are true there is involved the same trust in our reason that is involved in our confidence in mathematics; and we should have no justification for trusting it in the latter sphere and distrusting it in the former. In both cases we are dealing with propositions that cannot be proved, but that just as certainly need no proof.

Supposing it to be agreed, as I think on reflection it must, that no one *means* by 'right' just 'productive of the best possible consequences,' or 'optimific,' the attributes 'right' and 'optimific' might stand in either of two kinds of relation to each other. (1) They might be so related that we could apprehend *a priori,* either immediately or deductively, that any act that is optimific is right and any act that is right is optimific, as we can apprehend that any triangle that is equilateral is equiangular and *vice versa.* Professor Moore's view is, I think, that the coextensiveness of 'right' and 'optimific' is apprehended immediately. He rejects the possibility of any proof of it. Or (2) the two attributes might be such that the question whether they are invariably connected had to be answered by means of an inductive inquiry. Now at first sight it might seem as if the constant connexion of the two attributes could be immediately apprehended. It might seem absurd to suggest that it could be right for anyone to do an act which would produce consequences less good than those which would be produced by some other act in his power. Yet a little thought will convince us that this is not absurd. The type of case in which it is easiest to see that this is so is, perhaps, that in which one has made a promise. In such a case we all think that *prima facie* it is our duty to fulfil the promise irrespective of the precise goodness of the total consequences. And though we do not think it is necessarily our actual or absolute duty to do so, we are far from thinking that any, even the slightest, gain in the value of the total consequences will necessarily justify us in doing something else instead. Suppose, to simplify the case by abstraction, that the fulfilment of a promise to A would produce 1,000 units of good for him, but that by doing some other act I could produce 1,001 units of good for B, to whom I have made no promise, the other consequences of the two acts being of equal value; should we really think it self-evident that it was our duty to do the second act and not the first? I think not. We should, I fancy, hold that only a much greater disparity of value between the total consequences would justify us in failing to discharge our *prima facie* duty to A. After all, a promise is a promise, and is not to be treated so lightly as the theory we are examining would imply. What, exactly, a promise is, is not so easy to determine, but we are surely agreed that it constitutes a serious moral limitation to our freedom of action. To produce the 1,001 units of good for B rather than fulfil our promise to A would be to take, not perhaps our duty as philanthropists too seriously, but certainly our duty as makers of promises too lightly.

Or consider another phase of the same problem. If I have promised to confer on A a particular benefit containing 1,000 units of good, is it self-evident that if by doing some different act I could produce 1,001 units of good for A himself (the other consequences of the two acts being supposed equal in value), it would be right for me to do so? Again, I think not. Apart from my general *prima facie* duty to do A what goal I can, I have another *prima facie* duty to do him the particular service I have promised to do him, and this is not to be set aside in consequence of a disparity of good of the order of 1,001 to 1,000, though a much greater disparity might justify me in so doing.

Or again, suppose that A is a very good and B a very bad man, should I then, even when I have made no promise, think it self-evidently right to produce 1,001 units of good for B rather than 1,000 for A? Surely not. I should be sensible of a *prima facie* duty of justice, i.e. of producing a distribution of goods in proportion to merit, which is not outweighed by such a slight disparity in the total goods to be produced.

Such instances—and they might easily be added to—make it clear that there is no self-evident connexion between the attributes 'right' and 'optimific.' The theory we are examining has a certain attractiveness when applied to our decision that a particular act is our duty (though I have tried to show that it does not agree with our actual moral judgements even here). But it is not even plausible when applied to our recognition of *prima facie* duty. For if it were self-evident that the right coincides with the optimific, it should be self-evident that what is *prima facie* right is *prima facie* optimific. But whereas we are certain that keeping a promise is *prima facie* right, we are not certain that it is *prima facie* optimific (though we are perhaps certain that it is *prima facie* bonific). Our certainty that it is *prima facie* right depends not on its consequences but on its being the fulfilment of a promise. The theory we are examining involves too much difference between the evident ground of our conviction about *prima facie* duty and the alleged ground of our conviction about actual duty.

The coextensiveness of the right and the optimific is, then, not self-evident. And I can see no way of proving it deductively; nor, so far as I know, has anyone tried to do so. There remains the question whether it can be established inductively. Such an inquiry, to be conclusive, would have to be very thorough and extensive. We should have to take a large variety of the acts which we, to the best of our ability, judge to be right. We should have to trace as far as possible their consequences, not only for the persons directly affected but also for those indirectly affected, and to these no limit can be set. To make our inquiry thoroughly conclusive, we should have to do what we cannot do, viz. trace these consequences into an unending future. And even to make it reasonably conclusive, we should have to trace them far into the future. It is clear that the most we could possibly say is that a large variety of typical acts that are judged right appear, so far as we can trace their consequences, to produce more good than any other acts possible to the agents in the circumstances. And such a result falls far short of proving the constant connexion of the two attributes. But it is surely clear that no inductive inquiry justifying even this result has ever been carried through. The advocates of utilitarian systems have been so much persuaded either of the identity or of the self-evident connexion of the attributes 'right' and 'optimific' (or 'felicific') that they have not attempted even such an inductive inquiry as is possible. And in view of the enormous complexity of the task and the inevitable inconclusiveness of the result, it is worth no one's while to make the attempt. What, after all, would be gained by it? If, as I have tried to show, for an act to be right and to be optimific are not the same thing, and an act's being optimific is not even the ground of its being right, then if we could ask ourselves (though the question is really unmeaning) which we ought to do, right acts because they are right or optimific acts because they are optimific, our answer must be 'the former.' If they are optimific as well as right, that is interesting but not morally important; if not, we still ought to do them (which is only another way of saying that they *are* the right acts), and the question whether they are optimific has no importance for moral theory.

There is one direction in which a fairly serious attempt has been made to show the connexion of the attributes 'right' and 'optimific.' One of the most evident facts of our moral consciousness is the sense which we have of the sanctity of promises, a sense which does not, on the face of it, involve the thought that one will be bringing more good into existence by fulfilling the promise than by breaking it. It is plain, I think, that in our normal thought we consider that the fact that we have made a promise is in itself sufficient to create a duty of keeping it, the sense of duty resting on remembrance of the past promise and not on thoughts of the future consequences of its fulfilment. Utilitarianism tries to show that this is not so, that the sanctity of promises rests on the good consequences of the fulfilment of them and the bad consequences of their nonfulfilment. It does so in this way: it points out that when you break a promise you not only fail to confer a certain advantage on your promisee but you diminish his confidence, and indirectly the confidence of others, in the fulfilment of promises. You thus strike a blow at one of the devices that have been found most useful in the relations between man and man—the device on which, for example, the whole system of commercial credit rests—and you tend to bring about a state of things wherein each man, being entirely unable to rely on the keeping of promises by others, will have to do everything for himself, to the enormous impoverishment of human well-being.

To put the matter otherwise, utilitarians say that when a promise ought to be kept it is because the total good to be produced by keeping it is greater than the total good to be produced by breaking it, the former including as its main element the maintenance and strengthening of general mutual confidence, and the latter being greatly diminished by a weakening of this confidence. They say, in fact, that the case I put some pages back never arises—the case in which by fulfilling a promise I shall bring into being 1,000 units of good for my promisee, and by breaking it 1,001 units of good for someone else, the other effects of the two acts being of equal value. The other effects, they say, never are of equal value. By keeping my promise I am helping to strengthen the system of mutual confidence; by breaking it I am helping to weaken this; so that really the first act produces $1,000 + x$ units of good, and the second $1,001 - y$ units, and the difference between $+x$ and $-y$ is enough to outweigh the slight superiority in the immediate effects of the second act. In answer to this it may be pointed out that there must be *some* amount of good that exceeds the difference between +x and −y (i.e. exceeds $x + y$); say, $x + y + z$. Let us suppose the *immediate* good effects of the second act to be assessed not at 1,001 but at 1,000 + $x + y + z$. Then its *net* good effects are 1,000 + $x + z$, i.e. greater than those of the fulfilment of the promise; and the utilitarian is bound to say forthwith that the promise should be broken. Now, we may ask whether that is really the way we think about promises. Do we really think that the production of the slightest balance of good, no matter who will enjoy it, by the breach of a promise frees us from the obligation to keep our promise? We need not doubt that a system by which promises are made and kept is one that has great advantages for the general well-being. But that is not the whole truth. To make a promise is not merely to adapt an ingenious device for promoting the general well-being; it is to put oneself in a new relation to one person in particular, a relation which creates a specifically new *prima facie* duty to him, not reducible to the duty of promoting the general well-being of society. By all means let us try to foresee the net good effects of keeping one's promise and the net good effects of breaking it, but even if we assess the first at 1,000 + x and the second at 1,000 + x + z, the question still remains whether it is not our duty to fulfil the promise. It may be suspected, too, that the effect of a single keeping or breaking of a promise in strengthening or weakening the fabric of mutual confidence is greatly exaggerated by the theory we are examining. And if we suppose two men dying together alone, do we think that the duty of one to fulfil before he dies a promise he has made to the other would be extinguished by the fact that neither act would have any effect on the general confidence? Anyone who holds this may be suspected of not having reflected on what a promise is.

I conclude that the attributes 'right' and 'optimific' are not identical, and that we do not know either by intuition, by deduction, or by induction that they coincide in their application, still less that the latter is the foundation of the former. It must be added, however, that if we are ever under no special obligation such as that of fidelity to a promisee or of gratitude to a benefactor, we ought to do what will produce most good; and that even when we are under a special obligation the tendency of acts to promote general good is one of the main factors in determining whether they are right.

In what has preceded, a good deal of use has been made of 'what we really think' about moral questions; a certain theory has been rejected because it does not agree with what we really think. It might be said that this is in principle wrong; that we should not be content to expound what our present moral consciousness tells us but should aim at a criticism of our existing moral consciousness in the light of theory. Now I do not doubt that the moral consciousness of men has in detail undergone a good deal of modification as regards the things we think right, at the hands of moral theory. But if we are told, for instance, that we should give up our view that there is a special oblig-atoriness attaching to the keeping of promises because it is self-evident that the only duty is to produce as much good as possible, we have to ask ourselves whether we really, when we reflect, *are* convinced that this is self-evident, and whether we really *can* get rid of our view that promise-keeping has a bindingness independent of productiveness of maximum good. In my own experience I find that I cannot, in spite of a very genuine attempt to do so; and I venture to think that most people will find the same, and that just because they cannot lose the sense of special obligation, they cannot accept as self-evident, or even as true, the theory which would require them to do so. In fact it seems, on reflection, self-evident that a promise, simply as such, is something that *prima facie* ought to be kept, and it does *not,* on reflection, seem self-evident that production of max-imum good is the only thing that makes an act obligatory. And to ask us to give up at the bidding of a theory our actual apprehension of what is right and what is wrong seems like asking people to repu-diate their actual experience of beauty, at the bidding of a theory which says 'only that which satisfies such and such conditions can be beautiful.' If what I have called our actual apprehension is (as I would maintain that it is) truly an apprehension, i.e. an instance of knowledge, the request is nothing less than absurd.

I would maintain, in fact, that what we are apt to describe as 'what we think' about moral questions contains a considerable amount that we do not think but know, and that this forms the standard by reference to which the truth of any moral theory has to be tested, instead of having itself to be tested by reference to any theory. I hope that I have in what precedes indicated what in my view these elements of knowledge are that are involved in our ordinary moral consciousness.

It would be a mistake to found a natural science on 'what we really think,' i.e. on what reasonably thoughtful and well-educated people think about the subjects of the science before they have studied them scientifically. For such opinions are interpretations, and often misinterpretations, of sense-experience; and the man of science must appeal from these to sense-experience itself, which furnishes his real data. In ethics no such appeal is possible. We have no more direct way of access to the facts about rightness and goodness and about what things are right or good, than by thinking about them; the moral convictions of thoughtful and well-educated people are the data of ethics just as sense-perceptions are the data of a natural science. Just as some of the latter have to be rejected as illusory, so have some of the former; but as the latter are rejected only when they are in conflict with other more accurate sense-perceptions, the former are rejected only when they are in conflict with other convictions which stand better the test of reflection. The existing body of moral convictions of the best people is the cumulative product of the moral reflection of many generations, which has developed an extremely delicate power of appreciation of moral distinctions; and this the theorist cannot afford to treat with anything other than the greatest respect. The verdicts of the moral consciousness of the best people are the foundation on which he must build; though he must first compare them with one another and eliminate any contradictions they may contain.

For Further Reflection

1. What is Ross's argument against all types of utilitarianism?

2. Ross is both an intuitionist and a pluralist. He thinks we can acquire knowledge of the correct moral principles by consulting our deepest intuitions and he thinks that by so doing we will discover a plurality of principles, not reducible to a single principle, as utilitarians claim. First of all, do you agree with Ross that we can discover the true principles by consulting our intuitions? And second, do you agree that the principles are, in the last analysis, irreducible to one overarching principle? What are the objections to these positions? Suppose you and I consult our intuitions and come to different conclusions. How can we adjudicate the conflict?

3. What does Ross mean by *prima facie* duty? How does this notion separate his theory from Kant's?

The Deep Beauty of the Golden Rule

R. M. MacIver

R. M. MacIver (1882–1970) was professor of sociology at
Columbia University. MacIver argues that the Golden Rule
is the best method for discovering one's moral duty. By
putting yourself in another person's place you can find
guidance for action.

The subject that learned men call ethics is a wasteland on the philosophical map. Thousands of books have been written on this matter, learned books and popular books, books that argue and books
that exhort. Most of them are empty and nearly all are vain. Some
claim that pleasure is *the* good; some prefer the elusive and more
enticing name of happiness; others reject such principles and speak
of equally elusive goals such as self-fulfillment. Others claim that
the good is to be found in looking away from the self in devotion
to the whole—which whole? in the service of God—whose God?—
even in the service of the State—who prescribes the service? Here
indeed, if anywhere, after listening to the many words of many
apostles, one goes out by the same door as one went in.

The reason is simple. You say: "This is the way you should
behave." But I say: "No, that is not the way." You say: "This is right."
But I say: "No, that is wrong, and this is right." You appeal to experience. I appeal to experience against you. You appeal to authority:
it is not mine. What is left? If you are strong, you can punish me for
behaving my way. But does that prove anything except that you are
stronger than I? Does it prove the absurd dogma that might makes
right? Is the slavemaster right because he owns the whip, or Torque-
mada because he can send his heretics to the flames?

From this impasse no system of ethical rules has been able to
deliver itself. How can ethics lay down final principles of behavior
that are not your values against mine, your group's values against
my group's? . . .

Does all this mean that a universal ethical principle, applicable alike to me and you, even where our values diverge, is impossible? That there is no rule to go by, based on reason itself, in this world of irreconcilable valuations?

There is no rule that can prescribe both my values and yours or decide between them. There is one universal rule, and one only, that can be laid down, on ethical grounds—that is, apart from the creeds of particular religions and apart from the ways of the tribe that falsely and arrogantly universalize themselves.

Do to others as you would have others do to you. This is the only rule that stands by itself in the light of its own reason, the only rule that can stand by itself in the naked, warring universe, in the face of the contending values of men and groups.

What makes it so? Let us first observe that the universal herein laid down is one of procedure. It prescribes a mode of behaving, not a goal of action. On the level of goals, of *final* values, there is irreconcilable conflict. One rule prescribes humility, another pride; one prescribes abstinence, another commends the flesh-pots; and so forth through endless variations. All of us wish that *our* principle could be universal; most of us believe that it *should* be, that our *ought* ought to be all men's *ought,* but since we differ there can be on this level, no possible agreement.

When we want to make our ethical principle prevail we try to persuade others, to "convert" them. Some may freely respond, if their deeper values are near enough to ours. Others will certainly resist and some will seek to persuade us in turn—why shouldn't they? Then we can go no further except by resort to force and fraud. We can, if we are strong, dominate some and we can bribe others. We compromise our own values in doing so and we do not in the end succeed; even if we were masters of the whole world we could never succeed in making our principle universal. We could only make it falsely tyrannous.

So if we look for a principle in the name of which we can appeal to all men, one to which their reason can respond in spite of their differences, we must follow another road. When we try to make our values prevail over those cherished by others, we attack their values, their dynamic of behavior, their living will. If we go far enough we assault their very being. For the will is simply valuation in action. Now the deep beauty of the golden rule is that instead of attacking the will that is in other men, it offers their will a new dimension. "Do as you *would* have others . . ." As *you* would will others to do. It bids you expand your vision, see yourself in new relationships. It bids you transcend your insulation, see yourself in the place of others, see others in your place. It bids you test your values or at least your way of pursuing them. If you would disapprove that another should treat you as you treat him, the situations being reversed is not that a sign that, by the standard of your own values, you are mistreating him?

This principle obviously makes for a vastly greater harmony in the social scheme. At the same time it is the only universal of ethics that does not take sides with or contend with contending values. It contains no dogma. It bids everyone follow his own rule, as it would apply *apart* from the accident of his particular fortunes. It bids him enlarge his own rule, as it would apply whether he is up or whether he is down. It is an accident that you are up and I am down. In another situation you would be down and I would be up. That accident has nothing to do with my *final* values or with yours. . . .

It follows that while this first principle attacks no intrinsic values, no primary attachments of men to goods that reach beyond themselves, it nevertheless purifies every attachment, every creed, of its accidents, its irrelevancies, its excesses, its false reliance on power. It saves every human value from the corruption that comes from the arrogance of detachment and exclusiveness, from the shell of the kind of absolutism that imprisons its vitality.

At this point a word of caution is in order. The golden rule does not solve for us our ethical problems but offers only a way of approach. It does not prescribe our treatment of others but only the spirit in which we should treat them. It has no simple mechanical application and often enough is hard to apply—what general principle is not? It certainly does not bid us treat others as others *want* us to treat them—that would be an absurdity. The convicted criminal wants the judge to set him free. If the judge acts in the spirit of the golden rule, within the limits of the discretion permitted him as judge, he might instead reason somewhat as follows: "How would I feel the judge ought to treat *me* were I in this man's place? What could I—the man I am and yet somehow standing where this criminal stands—properly ask the judge to do for me, to me? In this spirit I shall assess his guilt and his punishment. In this spirit I shall give full consideration to the conditions under which he acted. I shall try to understand *him,* to do what I properly can for him, while at the same time I fulfill my judicial duty in protecting society against the dangers that arise if criminals such as he go free."

"Do to others as you would have others do to you." The disease to which all values are subject is the growth of a hard insulation. "I am right: I have the truth. If you differ from me, you are a heretic, you are in error. *Therefore* while you must allow me every liberty when you are in power I need not, in truth I ought not to, show any similar consideration for you." The barb of falsehood has already begun to vitiate the cherished value. While *you* are in power I advocate the equal rights of all creeds: when *I* am in power, I reject any such claim as ridiculous. This is the position taken by various brands of totalitarianism, and the communists in particular have made it a favorite technique in the process of gaining power, clamoring for rights they will use to destroy the rights of those who grant them. Religious groups have followed the same line. Roman Catholics, Calvinists, Lutherans, Presbyterians, and others have on occasion vociferously advocated religious liberty where they were in the minority, often to curb it where in turn they became dominant.

This gross inconsistency on the part of religious groups was flagrantly displayed in earlier centuries, but examples are still not infrequent. Here is one. *La Civilita Catholicá,* a Jesuit organ published in Rome, has come out as follows:

> The Roman Catholic Church, convinced, through its divine prerogatives, of being the only true church, must demand the right to freedom for herself alone, because such a right can only be possessed by truth, never by error. As to other religions, the church will certainly never draw the sword, but she will require that by legitimate means they shall not be allowed to propagate false doctrine. Consequently, in a state where the majority of the people are Catholic, the Church will require that legal existence be denied to error. . . . In some countries, Catholics will be obliged to ask full religious freedom for all, resigned at being forced to cohabitate where they alone should rightly be allowed to live. . . . The Church cannot blush for her own want of tolerance, as she asserts it in principle and applies it in practice.[1]

Since this statement has the merit of honesty it well illustrates the fundamental lack of rationality that lies behind all such violations of the golden rule. The argument runs: "Roman Catholics know they possess the truth; *therefore* they should not permit others to propagate error." By parity of reasoning why should not Protestants

---

[1]Quoted in the *Christian Century* (June 1948).

say—and indeed they have often said it—"We know we possess the truth; therefore we should not tolerate the errors of Roman Catholics." Why then should not atheists say: "We know we possess the truth; therefore we should not tolerate the errors of dogmatic religion."

No matter what we believe, we are equally convinced that *we* are right. We have to be. That is what belief means, and we must all believe something. The Roman Catholic Church is entitled to declare that all other religious groups are sunk in error. But what follows? That other groups have not the right to believe they are right? That you have the right to repress them while they have no right to repress you? That they should concede to you what you should not concede to them? Such reasoning is mere childishness. Beyond it lies the greater foolishness that truth is advanced by the forceful suppression of those who believe differently from you. Beyond that lies the pernicious distortion of meanings which claims that liberty is only "the liberty to do right"—the "liberty" for me to do what *you* think is right. This perversion of the meaning of liberty has been the delight of all totalitarians. And it might be well to reflect that it was the radical Rousseau who first introduced the doctrine that men could be "forced to be free."

How much do they have truth who think they must guard it within the fortress of their own might? How little that guarding has availed in the past! How often it has kept truth outside while superstition grew moldy within! How often has the false alliance of belief and force led to civil dissension and the futile ruin of war! But if history means nothing to those who call themselves "Christian" and still claim exclusive civil rights for their particular faith, at least they might blush before this word of one they call their Master: "All things therefore whatsoever ye would that men should do unto you, even so do ye also unto them; for this is the law and the prophets."

For Further Reflection

1. According to MacIver, how does the Golden Rule solve the problem of disputes about right and wrong?

2. What is "the deep beauty of the Golden Rule"?

3. How does the Golden Rule apply to religion and totalitarian ideologies?

A Critique of the Golden Rule

RICHARD WHATELY

Richard Whately (1787–1863), English philosopher and logician, and Archbishop of Dublin, was educated and taught at Oxford University. He is best known for his *Elements of Logic.*

Whately argues that the Golden Rule is not a self-sufficient moral principle but presupposes a background of moral principles.

I. THE GOLDEN RULE

That invaluable rule of our Lord's, "To do to others as we would have them do to us," will serve to explain, when rightly understood, the true character of moral instruction. If you were to understand that precept as designed to convey to us the first notions of right and wrong, and to be your sole guide as to what you ought to do and to avoid in your dealings with your neighbor, you would be greatly perplexed. For you would find that a literal compliance with the precept would be sometimes *absurd,* sometimes *wrong,* and sometimes *impossible.* And probably it is through making this mistake that men in general apply the rule so much seldomer than they ought. For the real occasions for its use occur to all of us every day.

Supposing any one should regard this golden rule as designed to answer the purpose of a complete system of morality, and to teach us the difference of right and wrong; then, if he had let his land to a farmer, he might consider that the farmer would be glad to be excused paying any rent for it, since he would himself, if he were the farmer, prefer having the land rent-free; and that, therefore, the rule of doing as he would be done by requires him to give up all his property. So also a shopkeeper might, on the same principle, think that the rule required him to part with his goods under prime cost, or to give them away, and thus to ruin himself. Now such a procedure would be *absurd.*

Again, supposing a jailer who was intrusted with the safe custody of a prisoner should think himself bound to let the man escape, because he himself, if he were a prisoner, would be glad to obtain freedom, he would be guilty of a breach of trust. Such an application of the rule, therefore, would be morally *wrong.*

And again, if you had to decide between two parties who were pleading their cause before you, you might consider that *each* of them wished for a decision in his *own* favor. And how, then, you might ask, would it be possible to apply the rule? since in deciding *for* the one party you could not but decide *against* the other. A literal compliance with the rule, therefore, would be, in such a case, *impossible.*

II.   APPLICATION OF THE GOLDEN RULE

Now, if you were to put such cases as these before any sensible man, he would at once say that you are to consider, not what you might *wish* in each case, but what you would regard as *fair, right, just, reasonable,* if you were in another person's place. If you were a farmer, although you might feel that you would be very glad to have the land rent-free—that is, to become the owner of it—you would not consider that you had any just claim to it, and that you could *fairly expect* the landlord to make you a present of his property. But you would think it reasonable that, if you suffered some great and unexpected loss, from an inundation or any such calamity, he should make an abatement of the rent. And this is what a good landlord generally thinks it right to do, in compliance with the golden rule.

So, also, if you had a cause to be tried, though of course you would *wish* the decision to be in your favor, you would be sensible that all you could *reasonably expect* of the judge would be that he should lay aside all prejudice, and attend impartially and carefully to the evidence, and decide according to the best of his ability. And this— which is what *each* part may fairly claim—is what an upright judge will do. And the like holds good in all the other cases.

III.   DESIGN OF THE GOLDEN RULE

You have seen, then, that the golden rule was far from being designed to impart to men the first notions of justice. On the contrary, it *presupposes* that knowledge; and if we had *no* such notions, we could not properly apply the rule. But the real design of it is to put us on our guard against the danger of being blinded by self-interest. A person who has a good general notion of what is just may often be tempted to act unfairly or unkindly towards his neighbors, when his own interest or gratification is concerned and to overlook the rightful claims of others. When David was guilty of an enormous sin in taking his neighbor's wife, and procuring the death of the husband, he was thinking only of his own gratification, quite forgetful of duty, till his slumbering conscience was roused by the prophet Nathan. On hearing the tale of "the poor man's lamb," his general abhorrence of injustice and cruelty caused him to feel vehement indignation against the supposed offender; but he did not apply his principles to his own case, till the prophet startled him by saying, "Thou art the man!"

And we, if we will make a practice of applying the golden rule, may have a kind of prophet always at hand, to remind us how, and when, to act on our principles of right. We have only to consider, "What should I think were I in the other's place, and he were to do so and so to me? How should I require him to treat me? What could I in fairness claim from him? . . .

For Further Reflection

1. How strong are Whately's arguments? Are they convincing? Can the Golden Rule be suitably set forth, so as to accommodate Whately's criticisms?

2. Consider this counterexample to the Golden Rule: Mrs. Jones feels neglected and wants her husband to talk to her, but Mr. Jones, after a hard day at the office, desperately wants peace and quiet. The criticism states that applying the Golden Rule would yield the following unsatisfactory results: Mrs. Jones would start talking to Mr. Jones, thus making him miserable, while Mr. Jones would remain silent, because that's how he would want Mrs. Jones to treat him. Both are miserable. Is this a fair criticism of the Golden Rule?

A Horseman in the Sky

AMBROSE BIERCE

Ambrose Bierce (1842–?1914) was a journalist who fought in the Civil War. He was famous for his sardonically humorous essays, including *The Devil's Dictionary* (1906). He disappeared into Mexico in 1913 and was presumed dead shortly thereafter.

In this Civil War story Carter Druse, a young Virginian, decides to join the Union Army. He announces this decision to his father, who, though disappointed, instructs him, whatever happens, to do what he conceives to be his duty. The story begins with Carter asleep at his post.

I

One sunny afternoon in the autumn of the year 1861 a soldier lay in a clump of laurel by the side of a road in western Virginia. He lay at full length upon his stomach, his feet resting upon the toes, his head upon the left forearm. His extended right hand loosely grasped his rifle. But for the somewhat methodical disposition of his limbs and a slight rhythmic movement of the cartridge-box at the back of his belt he might have been thought to be dead. He was asleep at his post of duty. But if detected he would be dead shortly afterward, death being the just and legal penalty of his crime.

The clump of laurel in which the criminal lay was in the angle of a road which after ascending southward a steep acclivity to that point turned sharply to the west, running along the summit for perhaps one hundred yards. There it turned southward again and went zigzagging downward through the forest. At the salient of that second angle was a large flat rock, jutting out northward, overlooking the deep valley from which the road ascended. The rock capped a high cliff; a stone dropped from its outer edge would have fallen sheer downward one thousand feet to the tops of the pines. The angle where the soldier lay was on another spur of the same cliff. Had he been awake he would have commanded a view, not only of

---

Reprinted from Ambrose Bierce, *Civil War Stories*.

the short arm of the road and the jutting rock, but of the entire profile of the cliff below it. It might well have made him giddy to look.

The country was wooded everywhere except at the bottom of the valley to the northward, where there was a small natural meadow, through which flowed a stream scarcely visible from the valley's rim. This open ground looked hardly larger than an ordinary door-yard, but was really several acres in extent. Its green was more vivid than that of the inclosing forest. Away beyond it rose a line of giant cliffs similar to those upon which we are supposed to stand in our survey of the savage scene, and through which the road had somehow made its climb to the summit. The configuration of the valley, indeed, was such that from this point of observation it seemed entirely shut in, and one could but have wondered how the road which found a way out of it had found a way into it, and whence came and whither went the waters of the stream that parted the meadow more than a thousand feet below.

No country is so wild and difficult but men will make it a theatre of war; concealed in the forest at the bottom of that military rat-trap, in which half a hundred men in possession of the exits might have starved an army to submission, lay five regiments of Federal infantry. They had marched all the previous day and night and were resting. At nightfall they would take to the road again, climb to the place where their unfaithful sentinel now slept, and descending the other slope of the ridge fall upon a camp of the enemy at about midnight. Their hope was to surprise it, for the road led to the rear of it. In case of failure, their position would be perilous in the extreme; and fail they surely would should accident or vigilance apprise the enemy of the movement.

II

The sleeping sentinel in the clump of laurel was a young Virginian named Carter Druse. He was the son of wealthy parents, an only child, and had known such ease and cultivation and high living as wealth and taste were able to command in the mountain country of western Virginia. His home was but a few miles from where he now lay. One morning he had risen from the breakfast-table and said, quietly but gravely: "Father, a Union regiment has arrived at Grafton. I am going to join it."

The father lifted his leonine head, looked at the son a moment in silence, and replied: "Well, go, sir, and whatever may occur do what you conceive to be your duty. Virginia, to which you are a traitor, must get on without you. Should we both live to the end of the war, we will speak further of the matter. Your mother, as the physician has informed you, is in a most critical condition; at the best she cannot be with us longer than a few weeks, but that time is precious. It would be better not to disturb her."

So Carter Druse, bowing reverently to his father, who returned the salute with a stately courtesy that masked a breaking heart, left the home of his childhood to go soldiering. By conscience and courage, by deeds of devotion and daring, he soon commended himself to his fellows and his officers; and it was to these qualities and to some knowledge of the country that he owed his selection for his present perilous duty at the extreme outpost. Nevertheless, fatigue had been stronger than resolution and he had fallen asleep. What good or bad angel came in a dream to rouse him from his state of crime, who shall say? Without a movement, without a sound, in the profound silence and the languor of the late afternoon, some invisible messenger of fate touched with unsealing finger the eyes of his consciousness—whispered into the ear of his spirit the mysterious awakening word which no human lips ever have spoken, no human memory ever has recalled. He quietly raised his forehead from his arm and looked between the masking stems of the laurels, instinctively closing his right hand about the stock of his rifle.

His first feeling was a keen artistic delight. On a colossal pedestal, the cliff—motionless at the extreme edge of the capping rock and sharply outlined against the sky—was an equestrian statue of impressive dignity. The figure of the man sat on the figure of the horse, straight and soldierly, but with the repose of a Grecian god carved in the marble which limits the suggestion of activity. The gray costume harmonized with its aërial background; the metal of accoutrement and caparison was softened and subdued by the shadow; the animal's skin had no points of high light. A carbine strikingly foreshortened lay across the pommel of the saddle, kept in place by the right hand grasping it at the "grip"; the left hand, holding the bridle rein, was invisible. In silhouette against the sky the profile of the horse was cut with the sharpness of a cameo; it looked across the heights of air to the confronting cliffs beyond. The face of the rider, turned slightly away, showed only an outline of temple and beard; he was looking downward to the bottom of the valley. Magnified by its lift against the sky and by the soldier's testifying sense of the formidableness of a near enemy the group appeared of heroic, almost colossal, size.

For an instant Druse had a strange, half-defined feeling that he had slept to the end of the war and was looking upon a noble work of art reared upon that eminence to commemorate the deeds of an heroic past of which he had been an inglorious part. The feeling was dispelled by a slight movement of the group: the horse, without moving its feet, had drawn its body slightly backward from the verge; the man remained immobile as before. Broad awake and keenly alive to the significance of the situation, Druse now brought the butt of his rifle against his cheek by cautiously pushing the barrel forward through the bushes, cocked the piece, and glancing through the sights covered a vital spot of the horseman's breast. A touch upon the trigger and all would have been well with Carter Druse. At that instant the horseman turned his head and looked in the direction of his concealed foeman—seemed to look into his very face, into his eyes, into his brave, compassionate heart.

Is it then so terrible to kill an enemy in war—an enemy who has surprised a secret vital to the safety of one's self and comrades—an enemy more formidable for his knowledge than all his army for its numbers? Carter Druse grew pale; he shook in every limb, turned faint, and saw the statuesque group before him as black figures, rising, falling, moving unsteadily in arcs of circles in a fiery sky. His hand fell away from his weapon, his head slowly dropped until his face rested on the leaves in which he lay. This courageous gentleman and hardy soldier was near swooning from intensity of emotion.

It was not for long; in another moment his face was raised from earth, his hands resumed their places on the rifle, his forefinger sought the trigger; mind, heart, and eyes were clear, conscience and reason sound. He could not hope to capture that enemy; to alarm him would but send him dashing to his camp with his fatal news. The duty of the soldier was plain: the man must be shot dead from ambush—without warning, without a moment's spiritual preparation, with never so much as an unspoken prayer, he must be sent to his account. But no—there is a hope; he may have discovered nothing—perhaps he is but admiring the sublimity of the landscape. If permitted, he may turn and ride carelessly away in the direction whence he came. Surely it will be possible to judge at the instant of his withdrawing whether he knows. It may well be that his fixity of attention—Druse turned his head and looked through the deeps of air downward, as from the surface to the bottom of a translucent sea. He saw creeping across the green meadow a sinuous line of figures of men and horses—some foolish commander was permitting the soldiers of his escort to water their beasts in the open, in plain view from a dozen summits!

Druse withdrew his eyes from the valley and fixed them again upon the group of man and horse in the sky, and again it was through the sights of his rifle. But this time his aim was at the horse. In his memory, as if they were a divine mandate, rang the words of his father at their parting: "Whatever may occur, do what you conceive to be your duty." He was calm now. His teeth were firmly but not rigidly closed; his nerves were as tranquil as a sleeping babe's—not a tremor affected any muscle of his body; his breathing, until suspended in the act of taking aim, was regular and slow. Duty had conquered; the spirit had said to the body: "Peace, be still." He fired.

III

An officer of the Federal force, who in a spirit of adventure or in quest of knowledge had left the hidden *bivouac* in the valley, and with aimless feet had made his way to the lower edge of a small open space near the foot of the cliff, was considering what he had to gain by pushing his exploration further. At a distance of a quarter-mile before him, but apparently at a stone's throw, rose from its fringe of pines the gigantic face of rock, towering to so great a height above him that it made him giddy to look up to where its edge cut a sharp, rugged line against the sky. It presented a clean, vertical profile against a background of blue sky to a point half the way down, and of distant hills, hardly less blue, thence to the tops of the trees at its base. Lifting his eyes to the dizzy altitude of its summit the officer saw an astonishing sight—a man on horseback riding down into the valley through the air!

Straight upright sat the rider, in military fashion, with a firm seat in the saddle, a strong clutch upon the rein to hold his charger from too impetuous a plunge. From his bare head his long hair streamed upward, waving like a plume. His hands were concealed in the cloud of the horse's lifted mane. The animal's body was as level as if every hoofstroke encountered the resistant earth. Its motions were those of a wild gallop, but even as the officer looked they ceased, with all the legs thrown sharply forward as in the act of alighting from a leap. But this was a flight!

Filled with amazement and terror by this apparition of a horseman in the sky—half believing himself the chosen scribe of some new Apocalypse, the officer was overcome by the intensity of his emotions; his legs failed him and he fell. Almost the same instant he heard a crashing sound in the trees—a sound that died without an echo—and all was still.

The officer rose to his feet, trembling. The familiar sensation of an abraded shin recalled his dazed faculties. Pulling himself together he ran rapidly obliquely away from the cliff to a point distant from its foot; thereabout he expected to find his man; and thereabout he naturally failed. In the fleeting instant of his vision his imagination had been so wrought upon by the apparent grace and ease and intention of the marvelous performance that it did not occur to him that the line of march of aërial cavalry is directly downward, and that he could find the objects of his search at the very foot of the cliff. A half-hour later he returned to camp.

This officer was a wise man; he knew better than to tell an incredible truth. He said nothing of what he had seen. But when the commander asked him if in his scout he had learned anything of advantage to the expedition he answered:

"Yes, sir; there is no road leading down into this valley from the southward."

The commander, knowing better, smiled.

IV

After firing his shot, Private Carter Druse reloaded his rifle and resumed his watch. Ten minutes had hardly passed when a Federal sergeant crept cautiously to him on hands and knees. Druse neither turned his head nor looked at him, but lay without motion or sign of recognition.

"Did you fire?" the sergeant whispered.

"Yes."

"At what?"

"A horse. It was standing on yonder rock—pretty far out. You see it is no longer there. It went over the cliff."

The man's face was white, but he showed no other sign of emotion. Having answered, he turned away his eyes and said no more. The sergeant did not understand.

"See here, Druse," he said, after a moment's silence, "it's no use making a mystery. I order you to report. Was there anybody on the horse?"

"Yes."

"Well?"

"My father."

The sergeant rose to his feet and walked away. "Good God!" he said.

For Further Reflection

1. What was Carter Druse's duty in this situation? Was it different from what he thought it to be? What should he have done? What would you have done?

2. How does this story bear upon deontological ethics? How would a Kantian evaluate Carter Druse's action?

3. What would a utilitarian have done in these circumstances?

The Evil of Lying

CHARLES FRIED

Charles Fried is a professor of law at Harvard University. In this selection from his book *Right and Wrong* he argues that lying is wrong even if it sometimes has good results. However, all things considered, sometimes special other duties override our duty not to lie. Fried defines lying earlier in the book this way: "A person lies when he asserts a proposition

Reprinted by permission of the publishers from *Right and Wrong* by Charles Fried, Cambridge, Mass.: Harvard University Press, copyright © 1978 by the President and Fellows of Harvard College.

he believes to be false." It could turn out that the lie is in fact true, such as when Mary wants to deceive you and tells you that your friend has betrayed you—and it turns out, unbeknownst to Mary, that he really has. Lying is intentional and bad because it fails to respect truth. But it is not only bad, it is morally wrong, since it violates respect for persons.

The evil of lying is as hard to pin down as it is strongly felt. Is lying wrong or is it merely something bad? If it is bad, why is it bad—is it bad in itself or because of some tendency associated with it? Compare lying to physical harm. Harm is a state of the world and so it can only be classified as bad; the wrong I argued for was the *intentional doing* of harm. Lying, on the other hand, can be wrong, since it is an action. But the fact that lying is an action does not mean that it *must* be wrong rather than bad. It might be that the action of lying should be judged as just another state of the world—a time-extended state, to be sure, but there is no problem about that—and as such it would count as a negative element in any set of circumstances in which it occurred. Furthermore, if lying is judged to be bad it can be bad in itself, like something ugly or painful, or it can be bad only because of its tendency to produce results that are bad in themselves.

If lying were bad, not wrong, this would mean only that, other things being equal, we should avoid lies. And if lying were bad not in itself but merely because of its tendencies, we would have to avoid lies only when those tendencies were in fact likely to be realized. In either case lying would be permissible to produce a net benefit, including the prevention of more or worse lies. By contrast the categorical norm "Do not lie" does not evaluate states of affairs but is addressed to moral agents, forbidding lies. Now if lying is wrong it is also bad in itself, for the category of the intrinsically bad is weaker and more inclusive than the category of the wrong. And accordingly, many states of the world are intrinsically bad (such as destruction of valuable property) but intentional acts bringing them about are not necessarily wrong.

Bentham plainly believed that lying is neither wrong nor even intrinsically bad: "Falsehood, take it by itself, consider it as not being accompanied by any other material circumstances, nor therefore productive of any material effects, can never, upon the principle of utility, constitute any offense at all." By contrast, Kant and Augustine argued at length that lying is wrong. Indeed, they held that lying is not only wrong *unless* excused or justified in defined ways (which is my view) but that lying is always wrong. Augustine sees lying as a kind of defilement, the liar being tainted by the lie, quite apart from any consequences of the lie. Kant's views are more complex. He argues at one point that lying undermines confidence and trust among men generally: "Although by making a false statement I do no wrong to him who unjustly compels me to speak, yet I do wrong to men in general . . . I cause that declarations in general find no credit, and hence all rights founded on contract should lose their force; and this is a wrong to mankind." This would seem to be a consequentialist argument, according to which lying is bad only insofar as it produces these bad results. But elsewhere he makes plain that he believes these bad consequences to be necessarily, perhaps even conceptually linked to lying. In this more rigoristic vein, he asserts that lying is a perversion of one's uniquely human capacities irrespective of any consequences of the lie, and thus lying is not only intrinsically bad but wrong.

Finally, a number of writers have taken what looks like an intermediate position: the evil of lying is indeed identified with its consequences, but the connection between lying and those consequences, while not a necessary connection, is close and persistent, and the consequences themselves are pervasive and profound. Consider this passage from a recent work by G. F. Warnock:

> I do not necessarily do you any harm at all by deed or word if I induce you to believe what is not in fact the case; I may even do you good, possibly by way, for example, of consolation or flattery. Nevertheless, though deception is not thus necessarily directly damaging it is easy to see how crucially important it is that the natural inclination to have recourse to it should be counteracted. It is, one might say, not the implanting of false beliefs that is damaging, but rather the generation of the suspicion that they may be being implanted. For this undermines trust; and, to the extent that trust is undermined, all cooperative undertakings, in which what one person can do or has reason to do is dependent on what others have done, are doing, or are going to do, must tend to break down. . . . There is no sense in my asking you for your opinion on some point, if I do not suppose that your answer will actually express your opinion (verbal communication is doubtless the most important of all our co-operative undertakings). (*The Object of Morality* [London: Methuen, 1971], p. 84.)

Warnock does not quite say that truth-telling is good in itself or that lying is wrong, yet the moral quality of truth-telling and lying is not so simply instrumental as it is, for instance, for Bentham. Rather, truth-telling seems to bear a fundamental, pervasive relation to the human enterprise, just as lying appears to be fundamentally subversive of that enterprise. What exactly is the nature of this relation? How does truth-telling bear to human goods a relation which is more than instrumental but less than necessary?

The very definition of lying makes plain that consequences are crucial, for lying is intentional and the intent is an intent to produce a consequence: false belief. But how can I then resist the consequentialist analysis of lying? Lying is an attempt to produce a certain effect on another, and if that effect (consequence) is not bad, how can lying be wrong? I shall have to argue, therefore, that to lie is to intend to produce an effect which always has something bad about it, an effect moreover of the special sort that it is wrong to produce it intentionally. To lay that groundwork for my argument about lying, I must consider first the moral value of truth.

TRUTH AND RATIONALITY

A statement is true when the world is the way the statement says it is. Utilitarians insist (as in the quotation from Bentham above) that truth, like everything else, has value just exactly as it produces value—pleasure, pain, the satisfaction or frustration of desire. And of course it is easy to show that truth (like keeping faith, not harming the innocent, respecting rights) does not always lead to the net satisfactions of desire, to the production of utility. It may *tend* to do so, but that tendency explains only why we should discriminate between occasions when truth does and when it does not have value—an old story. It is an old story, for truth—like justice, respect, and self-respect—has a value which consequentialist analyses (utilitarian or any other) do not capture. Truth, like respect, is a foundational value.

The morality of right and wrong does not count the satisfaction of desire as the overriding value. Rather, the integrity of persons, as agents and as the objects of the intentional agency of others, has priority over the attainment of the goals which agents choose to attain. I have sought to show how respect for physical integrity is related to respect for the person. The person, I argued, is not just a locus of potential pleasure and pain but an entity with determinate characteristics. The person is, among other things, necessarily an incorporated, a physical, not an abstract entity. In relation to truth we touch another necessary aspect of moral personality:

the capacity for judgment, and thus for choice. It is that aspect which Kant used to ground his moral theory, arguing that freedom and rationality are the basis for moral personality. John Rawls makes the same point, arguing that "moral personality and not the capacity for pleasure and pain . . . [is] the fundamental aspect of the self . . . The essential unity of the self is . . . provided by the concept of right." The concept of the self is prior to the goods which the self chooses, and these goods gather their moral significance from the fact that they have been chosen by moral beings—beings capable of understanding and acting on moral principles.

In this view freedom and rationality are complementary capacities, or aspects of the same capacity, which is moral capacity. A man is free insofar as he is able to act on a judgment because he perceives it to be correct; he is free insofar as he may be moved to action by the judgments his reason offers to him. This is the very opposite of the Humean conception of reason as the slave of the passions. There is no slavery here. The man who follows the steps of a mathematical argument to its conclusion because he judges them to be correct is free indeed. To the extent that we choose our ends we are free; and as to objectively valuable ends which we choose because we see their value, we are still free.

Now, rational judgment is true judgment, and so the moral capacity for rational choice implies the capacity to recognize the matter on which choice is to act and to recognize the kind of result our choices will produce. This applies to judgments about other selves and to judgments in which one locates himself as a person among persons, a self among selves. These judgments are not just arbitrary suppositions: *they are judged to be true of the world.* For consider what the self would be like if these judgments were not supposed to be true. Maybe one might be content to be happy in the manner of the fool of Athens who believed all the ships in the harbor to be his. But what of our perceptions of other people? Would we be content to have those whom we love and trust the mere figments of our imaginations? The foundational values of freedom and rationality imply the foundational value of truth, for the rational man is the one who judges aright, that is, truly. Truth is not the same as judgment, as rationality; it is rather the proper subject of judgment. If we did not seek to judge truly, and if we did not believe we could judge truly, the act of judgment would not be what we know it to be at all.

Judgment and thus truth are *part* of a structure which as a whole makes up the concept of self. A person's relation to his body and the fact of being an incorporated self are another part of that structure. These two parts are related. The bodily senses provide matter for judgments of truth, and the body includes the physical organs of judgment.

THE WRONG OF LYING

So our capacity for judgment is foundational and truth is the proper object of that capacity, but how do we get to the badness of lying, much less its categorical wrongness? The crucial step to be supplied has to do not with the value of truth but with the evil of lying. We must show that to lie to someone is to injure him in a way that particularly touches his moral personality. From that, the passage is indeed easy to the conclusion that to inflict such injury intentionally (remember that all lying is by hypothesis intentional) is not only bad but wrong. It is this first, crucial step which is difficult. After all, a person's capacity for true judgment is not necessarily impaired by inducing in him a particular false belief. Nor would it seem that a person suffers a greater injury in respect to that capacity when he is induced to believe a falsity than when we intentionally prevent him from discovering the truth, yet only in the first case do we lie. Do we really do injury to a person's moral personality when we persuade him falsely that it rained yesterday in Bangkok—a fact in which he has no interest? And do we do him more injury than when we fail to answer his request for yesterday's football scores, in which he is mildly interested? Must we not calculate the injury by the *other* harm it does: disappointed expectations, lost property, missed opportunities, physical harm? In this view, lying would be a way of injuring a person in his various substantive interests—a way of stealing from him, hurting his feelings, perhaps poisoning him—but then the evil of lying would be purely instrumental, not wrong at all.

All truth, however irrelevant or trivial, has value, even though we may cheerfully ignore most truths, forget them, erase them as encumbrances from our memories. The value of every truth is shown just in the judgment that the only thing we must not do is falsify truth. Truths are like other people's property, which we can care nothing about but may not use for our own purposes. It is as if the truth were not ours (even truth we have discovered and which is known only to us), and so we may not exercise an unlimited

dominion over it. Our relations to other people have a similar structure: we may perhaps have no duty to them, we may be free to
put them out of our minds to make room for others whom we care
about more, but we may not harm them. And so we may not falsify truth. But enough of metaphors—what does it mean to say that
the truth is not ours?

The capacity for true judgment is the capacity to arrive at judgments which are in fact true of the world as it exists apart from
our desires, our choices, our values. It is the world presented to
us by true judgments—including true judgments about ourselves—
which we then make the subject of our choices, our valuation. Now,
if we treat the truth as our own, it must be according to desire or
valuation. But for rational beings these activities are supposed to
depend on truth; we are supposed to desire and choose according
to the world as it is. To choose that something not be the case
when it is in fact the case is very nearly self-contradictory—for
choice is not *of* truth but *on the basis of* truth. To deliberate about
whether to believe a truth (not whether it is indeed true—another
story altogether) is like deciding whether to cheat at solitaire. All
this is obvious. In fact I suppose one cannot even coherently talk
about choosing to believe something one believes to be false. And
this holds equally for all truths—big and little, useful, and downright inconvenient. But we do and must calculate *about* (and not
just *with*) truths all the time as we decide what truths to acquire,
what to forget. We decide all the time not to pursue some inquiry
because it is not worth it. Such calculations surely must go forward
on the basis of what truths are useful, given one's plans and desires.
Even when we pursue truth for its own sake, we distinguish between
interesting and boring truths.

Considering what truth to acquire or retain differs, however, from
deliberately acquiring false beliefs. All truths are acquired as propositions correctly (truly) corresponding to the world, and in this respect, all truths are equal. A lie, however, has the form and occupies
the role of truth in that it too purports to be a proposition about the
world; only the world does not correspond to it. So the choice of a
lie is not like a choice among truths, for the choice of a lie is a choice
to affirm as the basis for judgment a proposition which does not correspond to the world. So, when I say that truth is foundational, that
truth precedes choice, what I mean is *not* that this or that truth is
foundational but that judging according to the facts is foundational
to judging at all. A scientist may deliberate about which subject to

study and, having chosen his subject, about the data worth acquiring, but he cannot even deliberate as a scientist about whether to acquire false data. Clearly, then, there is something funny (wrong?) about lying to oneself, but how do we go from there to the proposition that it is wrong to lie to someone else? After all, much of the peculiarity about lying to oneself consists in the fact that it seems not so much bad as downright self-contradictory, logically impossible, but that does not support the judgment that it is wrong to lie to another. I cannot marry myself, but that hardly makes it wrong to marry someone else.

Let us imagine a case in which you come as close as you can to lying to yourself: You arrange some operation, some fiddling with your brain that has no effect other than to cause you to believe a proposition you know to be false and also to forget entirely the prior history of how you came to believe that proposition. It seems to me that you do indeed harm yourself in such an operation. This is because a free and rational person wishes to have a certain relation to reality: as nearly perfect as possible. He wishes to build his conception of himself and the world and his conception of the good on the basis of truth. Now if he affirms that the truth is available for fiddling in order to accommodate either his picture of the world or his conception of the good, then this affirms that reality is dependent on what one wants, rather than what one wants being fundamentally constrained by what there is. Rationality is the respect for this fundamental constraint of truth. This is just another way of saying that the truth is prior to our plans and prospects and must be respected whatever our plans might be. What if the truth we "destroy" by this operation is a very trivial and irrelevant truth—the state of the weather in Bangkok on some particular day? There is still an injury to self, because the fiddler must have some purpose in his fiddling. If it is a substantive purpose, then the truth is in fact relevant to that purpose, and my argument holds. If it is just to show it can be done, then he is only trying to show he can do violence to his rationality—a kind of moral blasphemy. Well, what if it is a very *little* truth? Why, then, it is a very little injury he does himself—but that does not undermine my point.

Now, when I lie to you, I do to you what you cannot actually do to yourself—brain-fiddling being only an approximation. The nature of the injury I would do to myself, if I could, explains why lying to you is to do you harm, indeed why it is wrong. The lie is an injury because it produces an effect (or seeks to) which a person as a moral agent should not wish to have produced in him, and thus it is as much an injury as any other effect which a moral agent would not wish to have produced upon his person. To be sure, some people may want to be lied to. That is a special problem; they are like people who want to suffer (not just are willing to risk) physical injury. In general, then, I do not want you to lie to me in the same way that as a rational man I would not lie to myself if I could. But why does this make lying wrong and not merely bad?

Lying is wrong because when I lie I set up a relation which is essentially exploitative. It violates the principle of respect, for I must affirm that the mind of another person is available to me in a way in which I cannot agree my mind would be available to him—for if I do so agree, then I would not expect my lie to be believed. When I lie, I am like a counterfeiter: I do not want the market flooded with counterfeit currency; I do not want to get back my own counterfeit bill. Moreover, in lying to you, I affirm such an unfairly unilateral principle in respect to an interest and capacity which is crucial, as crucial as physical integrity: your freedom and your rationality. When I do intentional physical harm, I say that your body, your person, is available for my purposes. When I lie, I lay claim to your mind.

Lying violates respect and is wrong, as is any breach of trust. Every lie is a broken promise, and the only reason this seems strained is that in lying the promise is made and broken at the same moment. Every lie necessarily implies—as does every assertion—an assurance, a warranty of its truth. The fact that the breach accompanies the making should, however, only strengthen the conclusion that this is wrong. If promise-breaking is wrong, then a lie must be wrong, since there cannot be the supervening factor of changed circumstances which may excuse breaches of promises to perform in the future.

The final one of the convergent strands that make up the wrong of lying is the shared, communal nature of language. This is what I think Kant had in mind when he argued that a lie does wrong "to men in general." If whether people stood behind their statements depended wholly on the particular circumstances of the utterance, then the whole point of communication would be undermined. For every utterance would simply be the occasion for an analysis of the total circumstances (speaker's and hearer's) in order to determine what, if anything, to make of the utterance. And though we do often wonder and calculate whether a person is telling the truth, we do so from a baseline, a presumption that people do stand behind their statements. After all, the speaker surely depends on such a baseline. He wants us to think that he is telling the truth. Speech is a paradigm of communication, and all human relations are based on some form of communication. Our very ability to think, to conceptualize, is related to speech. Speech allows the social to penetrate the intimately personal. Perhaps that is why Kant's dicta seem to vacillate between two positions: lying as a social offense, and lying as an offense against oneself; the requirement of an intent to deceive another, and the insistence that the essence of the wrong is not injury to another but to humanity. Every lie violates the basic commitment to truth which stands behind the social fact of language.

I have already argued that bodily integrity bears a necessary relation to moral integrity, so that an attack upon bodily integrity is wrong, not just bad. The intimate *and* social nature of truth make the argument about lying stronger. For not only is the target aspect of the victim crucial to him as a moral agent but, by lying, we attack that target by a means which itself offends his moral nature; the means of attack are social means which can be said to belong as much to the victim as to his assailant. There is not only the attack at his moral vitals, but an attack with a weapon which belongs to him. Lying is, thus, a kind of treachery. (*Kind of* treachery? Why not treachery pure and simple?) It is as if we not only robbed a man of his treasure but in doing so used his own servants or family as our agents. That speech is our *common* property, that it belongs to the liar, his victim and all of us makes the matter if anything far worse.

So this is why lying is not only bad (a hurt), but wrong, why lying is wrong apart from or in addition to any other injury it does, and why lying seems at once an offense against the victim and against mankind in general, an offense against the liar himself, and against the abstract entity, truth. Whom do you injure when you pass a counterfeit bill?

What about little pointless lies? Do I really mean they are wrong? Well, yes, even a little lie is wrong, *if* it is a true piece of communication, an assertion of its own truth and not just a conventional way of asserting nothing at all or something else (as in the case of polite or diplomatic formulas). A little lie is a little wrong, but it is still something you must not do.

For Further Reflection

1. Evaluate Fried's argument against lying. Why is it always wrong—even if only a little wrong? Is his argument sound? Explain.

2. Fried makes several comparisons of lying with other acts: stealing, injuring, counterfeiting, promise-breaking, and violating the social fact of language. Are these good analogies?

3. Fried says lying is exploitative. Is this always the case? Can you think of cases where one lies not to exploit but to help another?

Does Morality Depend on Religion?

PLATO

Plato (427–347 B.C.) is one of the greatest philosophers who ever lived and the first philosopher to write systematically about metaphysics and ethics. Here we see his mentor, Socrates, engaged in a dialogue with the self-righteously religious Euthyphro, who is going to court to report his father for having killed a slave. In the course of the discussion Socrates raises the question that is known as the question of the divine command theory of ethics: Is the good good because God loves it, or does God love the good because it is good? The doctrine that morality depends on religion is called the Divine Command Theory, since God's commands determine what is right and wrong.

SOCRATES.   But shall we . . . say that whatever all the gods hate is unholy, and whatever they all love is holy: while whatever some

---

Reprinted from the *Euthyphro,* translated by William Jowett (New York: Charles Scribner's Sons, 1889).

of them love, and others hate, is either both or neither? Do you wish us now to define holiness and unholiness in this manner?

EUTHYPHRO. Why not, Socrates?

SOCR. There is no reason why I should not, Euthyphro. It is for you to consider whether that definition will help you to instruct me as you promised.

EUTH. Well, I should say that holiness is what all the gods love, and that unholiness is what they all hate.

SOCR. Are we to examine this definition, Euthyphro, and see if it is a good one? Or are we to be content to accept the bare assertions of other men, or of ourselves, without asking any questions? Or must we examine the assertions?

EUTH. We must examine them. But for my part I think that the definition is right this time.

SOCR. We shall know that better in a little while, my good friend. Now consider this question. Do the gods love holiness because it is holy, or is it holy because they love it?

EUTH. I do not understand you, Socrates.

SOCR. I will try to explain myself: we speak of a thing being carried and carrying, and being led and leading, and being seen and seeing; and you understand that all such expressions mean different things, and what the difference is.

EUTH. Yes, I think I understand.

SOCR. And we talk of a thing being loved, and, which is different, of a thing loving?

EUTH. Of course.

SOCR. Now tell me: is a thing which is being carried in a state of being carried, because it is carried, or for some other reason?

EUTH. No, because it is carried.

SOCR. And a thing is in a state of being led, because it is led, and of being seen, because it is seen?

EUTH. Certainly.

SOCR. Then a thing is not seen because it is in a state of being seen; it is in a state of being seen because it is seen; and a thing is not led because it is in a state of being led; it is in a state of being led because it is led: and a thing is not carried because it is in a state of being carried; it is in a state of being carried because it is carried. Is my meaning clear now, Euthyphro? I mean this: if anything becomes, or is affected, it does not become because it is in a state of becoming; it is in a state of becoming because it becomes; and it is not affected because it is in a state of being affected; it is in a state of being affected because it is affected. Do you not agree?

EUTH. I do.

SOCR. Is not that which is being loved in a state, either of becoming, or of being affected in some way by something?

EUTH. Certainly.

SOCR. Then the same is true here as in the former cases. A thing is not loved by those who love it because it is in a state of being loved. It is in a state of being loved because they love it.

EUTH. Necessarily.

SOCR. Well, then, Euthyphro, what do we say about holiness? Is it not loved by all the gods, according to your definition?

EUTH. Yes.

SOCR. Because it is holy, or for some other reason?

EUTH. No, because it is holy.

SOCR. Then it is loved by the gods because it is holy; it is not holy because it is loved by them?

EUTH. It seems so.

SOCR. But then what is pleasing to the gods is pleasing to them, and is in a state of being loved by them, because they love it?

EUTH. Of course.

SOCR. Then holiness is not what is pleasing to the gods, and what is pleasing to the gods is not holy, as you say, Euthyphro. They are different things.

EUTH. And why, Socrates?

SOCR. Because we are agreed that the gods love holiness because it is holy; and that it is not holy because they love it. Is not this so?

EUTH. Yes.

SOCR. And that what is pleasing to the gods because they love it, is pleasing to them by reason of this same love; and that they do not love it because it is pleasing to them.

EUTH. True.

SOCR. Then, my dear Euthyphro, holiness, and what is pleasing to the gods, are different things. If the gods had loved holiness because it is holy, they would also have loved what is pleasing to them because it is pleasing to them; but if what is pleasing to them had been pleasing to them because they loved it, then holiness too would have been holiness, because they loved it. But now you see that they are opposite things, and wholly different from each other. For the one is of a sort to be loved because it is loved: while the other is loved, because it is of a sort to be loved. My question, Euthyphro, was, What is holiness? But it turns out that you have not explained to me the essence of holiness; you have been content to mention an attribute which belongs to it, namely, that all the gods love it. You have not yet told me what is its essence. Do not, if you please, keep from me what holiness is; begin again and tell me that. Never mind whether the gods love it, or whether it has other attributes: we shall not differ on that point. Do your best to make it clear to me what is holiness and what is unholiness.

For Further Reflection

1. Does morality depend on religion for its validity, or does it have independent validity? In other words, Is the divine command theory true? What does Socrates seem to believe? What do you believe? Why?

2. What are the implications of holding that ethics depends on religion? Could God make rape and murder morally right actions today? How do you know that He hasn't (and kept it a secret)? If it turns out that no God exists, does that mean that morality is an illusion?

3. If Goodness means simply "what God commands," what do we mean when we say that "God is good"?

4. If the divine command theory is true, how is God different from the devil? Is He simply more powerful?

Moral Luck

THOMAS NAGEL

Thomas Nagel is professor of philosophy at New York University and the author of several works in moral and political philosophy. In this selection Nagel challenges the Kantian way of viewing morality, which assumes that we are all equal rational participants in the moral enterprise, each having the same opportunity to be moral. Nagel suggests that this view is simplistic and fails to take into account the manner in which external factors impinge upon us. They introduce the idea of moral luck, which he defines thus: "Where a significant aspect of what someone does depends on factors beyond his control, yet we continue to treat him in that respect as an object of moral judgment, it can be called moral luck."

Four types of moral luck are considered: constitutive luck, circumstantial luck, consequential luck in which consequences retrospectively justify an otherwise immoral act (or fail to justify an otherwise moral act), and consequential luck in which the consequences affect the type of blame or remorse (or moral praise).

Kant believed that good or bad luck should influence neither our moral judgment of a person and his actions, nor his moral assessment of himself.

> The good will is not good because of what it effects or accomplishes or because of its adequacy to achieve some proposed end; it is good only because of its willing, i.e., it is good of itself. And, regarded for itself, it is to be esteemed incomparably higher than anything which could be brought about by it in favor of any inclination or even of the sum total of all inclinations. Even if it should happen that, by a particular unfortunate fate or by the niggardly provision of a stepmotherly nature, this will should be wholly lacking in power to accomplish its purpose, and if even the greatest effort should not

From *Mortal Questions* (Cambridge University Press, 1979). Reprinted by permission of Cambridge University Press. Notes omitted.

avail it to achieve anything of its end, and if there remained only the good will (not as a mere wish but as the summoning of all the means in our power), it would sparkle like a jewel in its own light, as something that had its full worth in itself. Usefulness or fruitlessness can neither diminish nor augment this worth.

He would presumably have said the same thing about a bad will: whether it accomplishes its evil purposes is morally irrelevant. And a course of action that would be condemned if it had a bad outcome cannot be vindicated if by luck it turns out well. There cannot be moral risk. This view seems to be wrong, but it arises in response to a fundamental problem about moral responsibility to which we possess no satisfactory solution.

The problem develops out of the ordinary conditions of moral judgment. Prior to reflection it is intuitively plausible that people cannot be morally assessed for what is not their fault, or for what is due to factors beyond their control. Such judgment is different from the evaluation of something as a good or bad thing, or state of affairs. The latter may be present in addition to moral judgment, but when we blame someone for his actions we are not merely saying it is bad that they happened, or bad that he exists: we are judging *him,* saying he is bad, which is different from his being a bad thing. This kind of judgment takes only a certain kind of object. Without being able to explain exactly why, we feel that the appropriateness of moral assessment is easily undermined by the discovery that the act or attribute, no matter how good or bad, is not under the person's control. While other evaluations remain, this one seems to lose its footing. So a clear absence of control, produced by involuntary movement, physical force, or ignorance of the circumstances, excuses what is done from moral judgment. But what we do depends in many more ways than these on what is not under our control—what is not produced by a good or a bad will in Kant's phrase. And external influences in this broader range are not usually thought to excuse what is done from moral judgment, positive or negative.

Let me give a few examples, beginning with the type of case Kant has in mind. Whether we succeed or fail in what we try to do nearly always depends to some extent on factors beyond our control. This is true of murder, altruism, revolution, the sacrifice of certain interests for the sake of others—almost any morally important act. What has been done, and what is morally judged, is partly determined by external factors. However jewel-like the good will may be in its own right, there is a morally significant difference between rescuing someone from a burning building and dropping him from a twelfth-story window while trying to rescue him. Similarly, there is a morally significant difference between reckless driving and manslaughter. But whether a reckless driver hits a pedestrian depends on the presence of the pedestrian at the point where he recklessly passes a red light. What we do is also limited by the opportunities and choices with which we are faced, and these are largely determined by factors beyond our control. Someone who was an officer in a concentration camp might have led a quiet and harmless life if the Nazis had never come to power in Germany. And someone who led a quiet and harmless life in Argentina might have become an officer in a concentration camp if he had not left Germany for business reasons in 1930.

I shall say more later about these and other examples. I introduce them here to illustrate a general point. Where a significant aspect of what someone does depends on factors beyond his control, yet we continue to treat him in that respect as an object of moral judgment, it can be called moral luck. Such luck can be good or bad. And the problem posed by this phenomenon, which led Kant to deny its possibility, is that the broad range of external influences here identified seems on close examination to undermine moral assessment as surely as does the narrower range of familiar excusing conditions. If the condition of control is consistently applied, it threatens to erode most of the moral assessments we find it natural to make. The things for which people are morally judged are determined in more ways than we at first realize by what is beyond their control. And when the seemingly natural requirement of fault or responsibility is applied in light of these facts, it leaves few pre-reflective moral judgments intact. Ultimately, nothing or almost nothing about what a person does seems to be under his control.

Why not conclude, then, that the condition of control is false—that it is an initially plausible hypothesis refuted by clear counter-examples? One could in that case look instead for a more refined condition which picked out the *kinds* of lack of control that really undermine certain moral judgments, without yielding the unacceptable conclusion derived from the broader condition, that most or all ordinary moral judgments are illegitimate.

What rules out this escape is that we are dealing not with a theoretical conjecture but with a philosophical problem. The condition of control does not suggest itself merely as a generalization from certain clear cases. It seems *correct* in the further cases to which it is extended beyond the original set. When we undermine moral assessment by considering new ways in which control is absent, we are not just discovering what *would* follow given the general hypothesis, but are actually being persuaded that in itself the absence of control is relevant in these cases too. The erosion of moral judgment emerges not as the absurd consequence of an over-simple theory, but as a natural consequence of the ordinary idea of moral assessment, when it is applied in view of a more complete and precise account of the facts. It would therefore be a mistake to argue from the unacceptability of the conclusions to the need for a different account of the conditions of moral responsibility. The view that moral luck is paradoxical is not a *mistake,* ethical or logical, but a perception of one of the ways in which the intuitively acceptable conditions of moral judgment threaten to undermine it all. . . .

[Here Nagel begins his discussion of the four types of moral luck:

1. Luck in the way one's action and projects turn out.
2. Luck in how one is determined by antecedent circumstances.
3. Constitutive luck—"the kind of person you are, where this is not just a question of what you deliberately do, but of your inclinations, capacities, and temperament."
4. Circumstantial luck—if circumstances had been different, the judgment of your act would have been assessed differently.]

Let us first consider luck, good and bad, in the way things turn out. Kant, in the above-quoted passage, has one example of this in mind, but the category covers a wide range. It includes the truck driver who accidentally runs over a child, the artist who abandons his wife and five children to devote himself to painting, and other cases in which the possibilities of success and failure are even greater. The driver, if he is entirely without fault, will feel terrible about his role in the event, but will not have to reproach himself. Therefore this example of agent-regent is not yet a case of *moral* bad luck. However, if the driver was guilty of even a minor degree of negligence—failing to have his brakes checked recently, for example—then if that negligence contributes to the death of the child, he will not merely feel terrible. He will blame himself for the death. And what makes this an example of moral luck is that he would have to blame himself only slightly for the negligence itself if no situation arose which required him to brake suddenly and violently to avoid hitting a child. Yet the *negligence* is the same in both cases, and the driver has no control over whether a child will run into his path.

The same is true at higher levels of negligence. If someone has had too much to drink and his car swerves onto the sidewalk, he can count himself morally lucky if there are no pedestrians in his path. If there were, he would be to blame for their deaths, and would probably be prosecuted for manslaughter. But if he hurts no one, although his recklessness is exactly the same, he is guilty of a far less serious legal offense and will certainly reproach himself and be reproached by others much less severely. To take another legal example, the penalty for attempted murder is less than that for successful murder—however similar the intentions and motives of the assailant may be in the two cases. His degree of culpability can depend, it would seem, on whether the victim happened to be wearing a bullet-proof vest, or whether a bird flew into the path of the bullet—matters beyond his control.

Finally, there are cases of decision under uncertainty—common in public and in private life. Anna Karenina goes off with Vronsky, Gauguin leaves his family, Chamberlain signs the Munich Agreement, the Decembrists persuade the troops under their command to revolt against the czar, the American colonies declare their independence from Britain, you introduce two people in an attempt at matchmaking. It is tempting in all such cases to feel that some decision must be possible, in the light of what is known at the time, which will make reproach unsuitable no matter how things turn out. But this is not true; when someone acts in such ways he takes his life, or his moral position, into his hands, because how things turn out determines what he has done. It is possible *also* to assess the decision from the point of view of what could be known at the time, but this is not the end of the story. If the Decembrists had succeeded in overthrowing Nicholas I in 1825 and establishing a constitutional regime, they would be heroes. As it is, not only did they fail and pay for it, but they bore some responsibility for the terrible punishments meted out to the troops who had been persuaded to follow them. If the American Revolution had been a bloody failure resulting in greater repression, then Jefferson, Franklin, and Washington would still have made a noble attempt, and might not even have regretted it on their way to the scaffold, but they would also have had to blame themselves for what they had helped to bring on their compatriots. (Perhaps peaceful efforts at reform would eventually have succeeded.) If Hitler had not overrun Europe and exterminated millions, but instead had died of a heart attack after occupying the Sudetenland, Chamberlain's action at Munich would still have utterly betrayed the Czechs, but it would not be the great moral disaster that has made his name a household word.

In many cases of difficult choice the outcome cannot be foreseen with certainty. One kind of assessment of the choice is possible in advance, but another kind must await the outcome, because the outcome determines what has been done. The same degree of culpability or estimability in intention, motive, or concern is compatible with a wide range of judgments, positive or negative, depending on what happened beyond the point of decision. The *mens rea* which could have existed in the absence of any consequences does not exhaust the grounds of moral judgment. Actual results influence culpability or esteem in a large class of unquestionably ethical cases ranging from negligence through political choice.

That these are genuine moral judgments rather than expressions of temporary attitude is evident from the fact that one can say *in advance* how the moral verdict will depend on the results. If one negligently leaves the bath running with the baby in it, one will realize, as one bounds up the stairs toward the bathroom, that if the baby has drowned one has done something awful, whereas if it has not one has merely been careless. Someone who launches a violent revolution against an authoritarian regime knows that if he fails he will be responsible for much suffering that is in vain, but if he succeeds he will be justified by the outcome. I do not mean that *any* action can be retroactively justified by history. Certain things are so bad in themselves, or so risky, that no results can make them all right. Nevertheless, when moral judgment does depend on the outcome, it is objective and timeless and not dependent on a change of standpoint produced by success or failure. The judgment after the fact follows from an hypothetical judgment that can be made beforehand, and it can be made as easily by someone else as by the agent.

From the point of view which makes responsibility dependent on control, all this seems absurd. How is it possible to be more or less culpable depending on whether a child gets into the path of one's car, or a bird into the path of one's bullet? Perhaps it is true that what is done depends on more than the agent's state of mind or intention.

The problem then is, why is it not irrational to base moral assessment on what people do, in this broad sense? It amounts to holding them responsible for the contributions of fate as well as for their own—provided they have made some contribution to begin with. If we look at cases of negligence or attempt, the pattern seems to be that overall culpability corresponds to the product of mental or intentional fault and the seriousness of the outcome. Cases of decision under uncertainty are less easily explained in this way, for it seems that the overall judgment can even shift from positive to negative depending on the outcome. But here too it seems rational to subtract the effects of occurrences subsequent to the choice, that were merely possible at the time, and concentrate moral assessment on the actual decision in light of the probabilities. If the object of moral judgment is the *person,* then to hold him accountable for what he has done in the broader sense is akin to strict liability, which may have its legal uses but seems irrational as a moral position.

The result of such a line of thought is to pare down each act to its morally essential core, an inner act of pure will assessed by motive and intention. Adam Smith advocates such a position in *The Theory of Moral Sentiments,* but notes that it runs contrary to our actual judgments.

> But how well soever we may seem to be persuaded of the truth of this equitable maxim, when we consider it after this manner, in abstract, yet when we come to particular cases, the actual consequences which happen to proceed from any action, have a very great effect upon our sentiments concerning its merit or demerit, and almost always either enhance or diminish our sense of both. Scarce, in any one instance, perhaps, will our sentiments be found, after examination, to be entirely regulated by this rule, which we all acknowledge ought entirely to regulate them.

Joel Feinberg points out further that restricting the domain of moral responsibility to the inner world will not immunize it to luck. Factors beyond the agent's control, like a coughing fit, can interfere with his decisions as surely as they can with the path of a bullet from his gun. Nevertheless the tendency to cut down the scope of moral assessment is pervasive, and does not limit itself to the influence of effects. It attempts to isolate the will from the other direction, so to speak, by separating out constitutive luck. Let us consider that next.

Kant was particularly insistent on the moral irrelevance of qualities of temperament and personality that are not under the control of the will. Such qualities as sympathy or coldness might provide the background against which obedience to moral requirements is more or less difficult, but they could not be objects of moral assessment themselves, and might well interfere with confident assessment of its proper object—the determination of the will by the motive of duty. This rules out moral judgment of many of the virtues and vices, which are states of character that influence choice but are certainly not exhausted by dispositions to act deliberately in certain ways. A person may be greedy, envious, cowardly, cold, ungenerous, unkind, vain, or conceited, but *behave* perfectly by a monumental effort of will. To possess these vices is to be unable to help having certain feelings under certain circumstances, and to have strong spontaneous impulses to act badly. Even if one controls the impulses, one still has the vice. An envious person hates the greater success of others. He can be morally condemned as envious even if he congratulates them cordially and does nothing to denigrate or spoil their success. Conceit, likewise, need not be displayed. It is fully present in someone who cannot help dwelling with secret satisfaction on the superiority of his own achievements, talents, beauty, intelligence, or virtue. To some extent such a quality may be the product of earlier choices; to some extent it may be amenable to change by current actions. But it is largely a matter of constitutive bad fortune. Yet people are morally condemned for such qualities, and esteemed for others equally beyond control of the will: they are assessed for what they are *like*.

To Kant this seems incoherent because virtue is enjoined on everyone and therefore must in principle be possible for everyone. It may be easier for some than for others, but it must be possible to achieve it by making the right choices, against whatever temperamental background. One may want to have a generous spirit, or regret not having one, but it makes no sense to condemn oneself or anyone else for a quality which is not within the control of the will. Condemnation implies that you should not be like that, not that it is unfortunate that you are.

Nevertheless, Kant's conclusion remains intuitively unacceptable. We may be persuaded that these moral judgments are irrational, but they reappear involuntarily as soon as the argument is over. This is the pattern throughout the subject.

The third category to consider is luck in one's circumstances, and I shall mention it briefly. The things we are called upon to do, the moral tests we face, are importantly determined by factors beyond our control. It may be true of someone that in a dangerous situation he would behave in a cowardly or heroic fashion, but if the situation never arises, he will never have the chance to distinguish or disgrace himself in this way, and his moral record will be different.

A conspicuous example of this is political. Ordinary citizens of Nazi Germany had an opportunity to behave heroically by opposing the regime. They also had an opportunity to behave badly, and most of them are culpable for having failed this test. But it is a test to which the citizens of other countries were not subjected, with the result that even if they, or some of them, would have behaved as badly as the Germans in like circumstances, they simply did not and therefore are not similarly culpable. Here again one is morally at the mercy of fate, and it may seem irrational upon reflection, but our ordinary moral attitudes would be unrecognizable without it. We judge people for what they actually do or fail to do, not just for what they would have done if circumstances had been different.

This form of moral determination by the actual is also paradoxical, but we can begin to see how deep in the concept of responsibility the paradox is embedded. A person can be morally responsible only for what he does; but what he does results from a great deal that he does not do; therefore he is not morally responsible for what he is and is not responsible for. (This is not a contradiction, but it is a paradox.)

It should be obvious that there is a connection between these problems about responsibility and control and an even more familiar problem, that of freedom of the will. That is the last type of moral luck I want to take up, though I can do no more within the scope of this essay than indicate its connection with the other types.

If one cannot be responsible for consequences of one's acts due to factors beyond one's control, or for antecedents of one's acts that are properties of temperament not subject to one's will, or for the circumstances that pose one's moral choices, then how can one be responsible even for the stripped-down acts of the will itself, if *they* are the product of antecedent circumstances outside of the will's control?

The area of genuine agency, and therefore of legitimate moral judgment, seems to shrink under this scrutiny to an extensionless point. Everything seems to result from the combined influence of factors, antecedent and posterior to action, that are not within the agent's control. Since he cannot be responsible for them, he cannot be responsible for their results—though it may remain possible to take up the aesthetic or other evaluative analogues of the moral attitudes that are thus displaced.

It is also possible, of course, to brazen it out and refuse to accept the results, which indeed seem unacceptable as soon as we stop thinking about the arguments. Admittedly, if certain surrounding circumstances had been different, then no unfortunate consequences would have followed from a wicked intention, and no seriously culpable act would have been performed; but since the circumstances were *not* different, and the agent *in fact* succeeded in perpetrating a particularly cruel murder, *that* is what he did, and that is what he is responsible for. Similarly, we may admit that if certain antecedent circumstances had been different, the agent would never have developed into the sort of person who would do such a thing; but since he *did* develop (as the inevitable result of those antecedent circumstances) into the sort of swine he is, and into the person who committed such a murder, *that* is what he is blamable for. In both cases one is responsible for what one actually does—even if what one actually does depends in important ways on what is not within one's control. This [compatibilist] account of our moral judgments would leave room for the ordinary conditions of responsibility—the absence of coercion, ignorance, or involuntary movement—as part of the determination of what someone has done—but it is understood not to exclude the influence of a great deal that he has not done.

The only thing wrong with this solution is its failure to explain how skeptical problems arise. For they arise not from the imposition of an arbitrary external requirement, but from the nature of moral judgment itself. Something in the ordinary idea of what someone does must explain how it can seem necessary to subtract from it anything that merely happens—even though the ultimate consequence of such subtraction is that nothing remains. And something in the ordinary idea of knowledge must explain why it seems to be undermined by any influences on belief not within the control of the subject—so that knowledge seems impossible without an impossible foundation in autonomous reason. But let us leave epistemology aside and concentrate on action, character, and moral assessment.

The problem arises, I believe, because the self which acts and is the object of moral judgment is threatened with dissolution by the absorption of its acts and impulses into the class of events. Moral judgment of a person is judgment not of what happens to him, but of him. It does not say merely that a certain event or state of affairs is fortunate or unfortunate or even terrible. It is not an evaluation of a state of the world, or of an individual as part of the world. We are not thinking just that it would be better if he were different, or did not exist, or had not done some of the things he has done. We are judging *him,* rather than his existence or characteristics. The effect of concentrating on the influence of what is not under his control is to make this responsible self seem to disappear, swallowed up by the order of mere events.

What, however, do we have in mind that a person must *be* to be the object of these moral attitudes? While the concept of agency is easily undermined, it is very difficult to give it a positive characterization. That is familiar from the literature on Free Will.

I believe that in a sense the problem has no solution, because something in the idea of agency is incompatible with actions being events, or people being things. But as the external determinants of what someone has done are gradually exposed, in their effect on consequences, character, and choice itself, it becomes gradually clear that actions are events and people things. Eventually nothing remains which can be ascribed to the responsible self, and we are left with nothing but a portion of the larger sequences of events, which can be deplored or celebrated, but not blamed or praised.

Though I cannot define the idea of the active self that is thus undermined, it is possible to say something about its sources. There is a close connection between our feelings about ourselves and our feelings about others. Guilt and indignation, shame and contempt, pride and admiration are internal and external sides of the same moral attitudes. We are unable to view ourselves simply as portions of the world, and from inside we have a rough idea of the boundary between what is us and what is not, what we do and what happens to us, what is our personality and what is an accidental handicap. We apply the same essentially internal conception of the self to others. About ourselves we feel pride, shame, guilt, remorse—and agent-regret. We do not regard our actions and our characters merely as fortunate or unfortunate episodes—though they may also be that. We cannot *simply* take an external evaluative view of ourselves—of what we most essentially are and what we do. And this remains true even when we have seen that we are not responsible for our own existence, or our nature, or the choices we have to make, or the circumstances that give our acts the consequences they have. Those acts remain ours and we remain ourselves, despite the persuasiveness of the reasons that seem to argue us out of existence.

It is this internal view that we extend to others in moral judgment—when we judge *them* rather than their desirability or utility. We extend to others the refusal to limit ourselves to external evaluation, and we accord to them selves like our own. But in both cases this comes up against the brutal inclusion of humans and everything about them in a world from which they cannot be separated and of which they are nothing but contents. The external view forces itself on us at the same time that we resist it. One way this occurs is through the gradual erosion of what we do by the subtraction of what happens.

The inclusion of consequences in the conception of what we have done is an acknowledgment that we are parts of the world, but the paradoxical character of moral luck which emerges from this acknowledgment shows that we are unable to operate with such a view, for it leaves us with no one to be. The same thing is revealed in the appearance that determinism obliterates responsibility. Once we see an aspect of what we or someone else does as something that happens, we lose our grip on the idea that it has been done and that we can judge the doer and not just the happening. This explains why the absence of determinism is no more hospitable to the concept of agency than is its presence—a point that has been noticed often. Either way the act is viewed externally, as part of the course of events.

The problem of moral luck cannot be understood without an account of the internal conception of agency and its special connection with the moral attitudes as opposed to other types of value. I do not have such an account. The degree to which the problem has a solution can be determined only by seeing whether in some degree the incompatibility between this conception and the various ways in which we do not control what we do is only apparent. I have nothing to offer on that topic either. But it is not enough to say merely that our basic moral attitudes toward ourselves and others are determined by what is actual; for they are also threatened by the sources of that actuality, and by the external view of action which forces itself on us when we see how everything we do belongs to a world that we have not created.

For Further Reflection

1. What is Nagel's criticism of Kant? Why does he think that Kant's notion of the good will as the sole determinant of moral goodness is simplistic?

2. Go over the types of moral luck that Nagel discusses. Are his arguments cogent and persuasive? It might help to examine the main examples. Take the German who becomes a Nazi officer who does great evil, but who in different, more peaceful circumstances would have been an average citizen with no great moral culpability. Is Nagel correct to say that the officer just had bad moral luck? Or can more be said about this assessment that would make sense of the Kantian idea of moral goodness?

3. Why does Nagel think that our notion of moral responsibility is deeply problematic, even incoherent?

4. Nagel believes that the free-will determinist debate is paradoxical. If we are determined by antecedent circumstances, then we are not responsible for what we do; but if we are not determined by these conditions, then everything seems arbitrary—free will seems to presuppose the very causal structure that it attacks. Does this make sense? Do you believe that you have free will? Explain your answer.

5. Do you believe there is moral luck or can we, in principle, make genuine moral judgments about people and their actions?

Further Readings for Chapter 5

Acton, Harry. *Kant's Moral Philosophy*. New York: Macmillan, 1970.

Broad, C. D. *Five Types of Ethical Theory*. London: Routledge and Kegan Paul, 1930.

Donagan, Alan. *The Theory of Morality*. Chicago: University of Chicago Press, 1977.

Feldman, Fred. *Introductory Ethics*. Englewood Cliffs, N.J.: Prentice-Hall, 1978. Chapters 7 and 8. A clear and critical exposition.

Harris, C. E. *Applying Moral Theories*. Belmont, Calif.: Wadsworth, 1986. Chapter 7. An excellent exposition of contemporary deontological theories, especially of Gewirth's work.

Kant, Immanuel. *Critique of Practical Reason*. Translated by Lewis White Beck. Indianapolis: Bobbs-Merrill, 1956.

——. *Grounding for the Metaphysics of Morals*. Translated by James Ellington. Indianapolis: Hackett Publishing Company, 1981.

——. *Lectures on Ethics*. Translated by Louis Infield. Indianapolis: Hackett Publishing Company, 1963.

Raphael, D. D. *Moral Philosophy*. Oxford: Oxford University Press, 1981. Chapter 6.

Ross, W. D. *Kant's Ethical Theory*. Oxford: Clarendon Press, 1954.

——. *The Right and the Good*. Oxford: Oxford University Press, 1930.

Ward, Keith. *The Development of Kant's Views of Ethics*. Oxford: Blackwell's, 1972.

Wolff, Robert P. *The Autonomy of Reason: A Commentary on Kant's* Groundwork of the Metaphysics of Morals. New York: Harper & Row, 1973.

CHAPTER 6

Virtue Ethics

John hears that 100,000 people are starving in Ethiopia. He feels deep sorrow about this and sends $100 of his hard-earned money to a famine relief project in that country. Joan hears the same news but doesn't feel anything. However, out of a sense of duty she also sends $100 of her hard-earned money to the relief project.

Jack and Jill each have the opportunity to embezzle a million dollars from the bank at which they work. Jill never even considers embezzling; the possibility is not even an option for her. Jack wrestles valiantly with the temptation, almost succumbs to it, but through a grand effort of the will finally succeeds in resisting the temptation.

Who in each case is more moral?

Whereas most ethical theories have been either duty-oriented or action-oriented, that is, either deontological or teleological (utilitarian), there is a third tradition which goes back to Plato and, especially, Aristotle, and which receives support in the writings of the Epicureans, the Stoics, Jesus, and the early Christian church. We refer to *virtue ethics* (sometimes called *aretaic ethics* after the Greek word *arete*, "excellence" or "virtue"). Rather than seeing the heart of ethics in action or duties, virtue ethics centers in the heart and personality of the agent—in his or her character. Whereas the action-based ethics emphasizes *doing*, virtue ethics emphasizes *being*—being a certain kind of person who will no doubt manifest his or her being in actions or nonactions. For traditional duty-based ethics, the question is "What should I do?" For the virtue ethicist, the question is "What sort of person should I become?"

Virtue ethics seeks to produce excellent persons, who act well out of spontaneous goodness and serve as examples to inspire others. It seeks to create people like Moses, Confucius, Socrates, Jesus, Buddha, Albert Schweitzer, Mohandas Gandhi, and Mother Teresa—

people who light up our moral landscape as jewels who shine in their own light.

We begin our study with one of the most poignant examples of virtue, Victor Hugo's good bishop of Digne in *Les Misérables*. Then we examine a classic passage on the virtues by Aristotle and, after that, a modern interpretation by Bernard Mayo. Then we contemplate J. O. Urmson's discussion of moral actions that go beyond the requirements of duty—to saintly or heroic behavior. This is followed by Nathaniel Hawthorne's short story "The Great Stone Face." Our final reading is William Frankena's critique of virtue ethics, in which Frankena argues that while the virtues are important, whatever is valid about virtue ethics should be subordinate to a deontological system.

The Bishop and the Candlesticks

VICTOR HUGO

The French writer Victor Hugo (1802–1885) was one of the greatest novelists of the nineteenth century. His most famous works are *The Hunchback of Notre Dame* and *Les Misérables,* from which this selection is taken.

In this selection we meet Jean Valjean, a forty-six-year-old ex-convict, who, in the year our story opens, 1815, has just been released from the galleys where he was imprisoned for nineteen years.* His original sentence was five years for stealing a loaf of bread to feed his family, but his repeated attempts to escape his cruel prison added fourteen more years to his sentence. Originally a poor but morally uncorrupted laborer, Jean becomes a hardened criminal in the galleys. Now he is released and after four days of weary walking has just entered the French town of Digne. Here is Hugo's description of him:

> A slouched leather cap half hid his face, bronzed by the sun and wind, and dripping with sweat. His shaggy breast was seen through the coarse yellow shirt which at the neck was fastened by a small silver anchor; he wore a cravat twisted like a rope; coarse blue trousers, worn and shabby, white on one knee and with holes in the other; and an old, ragged, gray blouse patched on one side with a piece of green cloth sewed with twine; upon his back was a well-filled knapsack, strongly buckled and quite new. In his hand he carried an enormous knotted stick; his stockingless feet were in hobnailed shoes; his hair was cropped and his beard long. The sweat and heat, his long walk, and the dust added an indescribable meanness to his tattered appearance.

Jean has very little money (109 francs) and knows no one. Famished and exhausted, he seeks food and shelter in the town inns, but is recognized as an unkempt ex-convict and everyone turns him away. Dogs are loosed on him and, barely escaping their jaws, he is heard to comment, "I am not even a dog." He shivers in the Alpine

---

Translated from Victor Hugo, *Les Misérables,* 1863.
*"The galleys" refers to a large, low medieval ship propelled by sails and oars. Prisoners were chained to their seats and required to row the ship.

evening cold. Eventually, an old woman takes pity on him and points him to a house. He knocks on the door.

Unbeknownst to Jean, he has knocked on the door of the bishop of Digne, Monseigneur Charles François-Bienvenu Myriel, also known as M. Bienvenu. The good bishop is dedicated to simple living and helping the poor. His allowance from the state is 3,000 francs a year, but he gives away 2,800 of these francs to the poor. He is known for his humility, kindness, and good works.

His servant, Mme. Magliore, has just entered the house and relates to the bishop and his sister, who lives in the same house, that a terrible-looking ex-convict is in town and has been turned out of all the inns. "Indeed," says the bishop. "Yes," replies the frightened Mme. Magliore. "Something will happen in this town tonight." Just then there is a violent knock on the door. The bishop says, "Come in."

THE HEROISM OF PASSIVE OBEDIENCE

The door opened.

It opened quickly, quite wide, as if pushed by someone boldly and with energy.

A man entered.

That man we know already; it was the traveler we have seen wandering about in search of a lodging.

He came in, took one step, and paused, leaving the door open behind him. He had his knapsack on his back, his stick in his hand, and a rough, hard, tired, and fierce look in his eyes, as seen by the firelight. He was hideous. It was an apparition of ill-omen.

Mme. Magliore had not even the strength to scream. She stood trembling with her mouth open.

Mdlle. Baptistine turned, saw the man enter, and started out half alarmed; then, slowly turning back again toward the fire, she looked at her brother, and her face resumed its usual calmness and serenity.

The bishop looked upon the man with a tranquil eye.

As he was opening his mouth to speak, doubtless to ask the stranger what he wanted, the man, leaning with both hands on his club, glanced from one to another in turn, and, without waiting for the bishop to speak, said, in a loud voice:

"See here! My name is Jean Valjean. I am a convict; I have been nineteen years in the galleys. Four days ago I was set free, and started for Pontarlier, which is my destination; during these four days I have walked from Toulon. To-day I have walked twelve leagues. When I reached this place this evening I went to an inn, and they sent me away on account of my yellow passport, which I had shown at the mayor's office, as was necessary. I went to another inn; they said: 'Get out!' It was the same with one as with another; nobody would have me. I went to the prison and the turnkey would not let me in. I crept into a dog-kennel, the dog bit me, and drove me away as if he had been a man; you would have said that he knew who I was. I went into the fields to sleep beneath the stars; there were no stars. I thought it would rain, and there was no good God to stop the drops, so I came back to the town to get the shelter of some doorway. There in the square I laid down upon a stone; a good woman showed me your house, and said: 'Knock there!' I have knocked. What is this place? Are you an inn? I have money; my savings, 109 francs and 15 sous, which I have earned in the galleys by my work for nineteen years. I will pay. What do I care? I have money. I am very tired—twelve leagues on foot—and I am so hungry. Can I stay?"

"Mme. Magloire," said the bishop, "put on another plate."

The man took three steps and came near the lamp which stood on the table. "Stop," he exclaimed; as if he had not been understood; "not that, did you understand me? I am a galley slave—a convict—I am just from the galleys." He drew from his pocket a large sheet of yellow paper, which he unfolded. "There is my passport, yellow, as you see. That is enough to have me kicked out wherever I go. Will you read it? I know how to read, I do. I learned in the galleys. There is a school there for those who care for it. See, here is what they have put in my passport: 'Jean Valjean, a liberated convict, native of——,' you don't care for that, 'has been nineteen years in the galleys; five years for burglary; fourteen years for having attempted four times to escape. This man is very dangerous.' There you have it! Everybody has thrust me out; will you receive me? Is this an inn? Can you give me something to eat and a place to sleep? Have you a stable?"

"Mme. Magloire," said the bishop, "put some sheets on the bed in the alcove."

We have already described the kind of obedience yielded by these two women.

Mme. Magloire went out to fulfill her orders.

The bishop turned to the man:

"Monsieur, sit down and warm yourself; we are going to take supper presently, and your bed will be made ready while you sup."

At last the man quite understood; his face, the expression of which till then had been gloomy and hard, now expressed stupefaction, doubt and joy, and became absolutely wonderful. He began to stutter like a madman.

"True? What? You will keep me? you won't drive me away—a convict? You call me monsieur and don't say, 'Get out, dog!' as everybody else does. I thought that you would send me away, so I told first off who I am. Oh! the fine woman who sent me here; I shall have a supper! a bed like other people, with mattress and sheets—a bed! It is nineteen years that I have not slept on a bed. You are really willing that I should stay? You are good people! Besides, I have money; I will pay well. I beg your pardon, M. Innkeeper, what is your name? I will pay all you say. You are a fine man. You are an innkeeper, ain't you?"

"I am a priest who lives here," said the bishop.

"A priest," said the man. "Oh, noble priest! Then you do not ask any money? You are the curé, ain't you—the curé of this big church? Yes, that's it. How stupid I am, I didn't notice your cap."

While speaking he had deposited his knapsack and stick in the corner, replaced his passport in his pocket and sat down. Mdlle. Baptistine looked at him pleasantly. He continued:

"You are humane, M. l'Curé; you don't despise me. A good priest is a good thing. Then you don't want me to pay you?"

"No," said the bishop, "keep your money. How much have you? You said 109 francs, I think."

"And 15 sous," added the man.

"One hundred and nine francs and fifteen sous. And how long did it take you to earn that?"

"Nineteen years."

"Nineteen years!"

The bishop sighed deeply.

The man continued: "I have all my money yet. In four days I have spent only 25 sous which I earned by unloading wagons at Grasse. As you are an abbé I must tell you we have an almoner in the galleys. And then one day I saw a bishop; monseigneur, they called him. It was the Bishop of Majore from Marseilles. He is the curé who is over the curés. You see—beg pardon, how I bungle saying it, but for me it is so far off; you know what we are. He said mass in the center of the place on an altar; he had a pointed gold thing on his head that shone in the sun; it was noon. We were drawn up in line on three sides with cannons, and matches lighted before us. We could not see him well. He spoke to us, but he was not near enough, we did not understand him. That is what a bishop is."

While he was talking the bishop shut the door, which he had left wide open.

Mme. Magloire brought in a plate and set it on the table.

"Mme. Magloire," said the bishop, "put this plate as near the fire as you can." Then turning toward his guest, he added: "The night wind is raw in the Alps; you must be cold, monsieur."

Every time he said the word monsieur with his gently solemn and heartily hospitable voice the man's countenance lighted up. Monsieur to a convict is a glass of water to a man dying of thirst at sea. Ignominy thirsts for respect.

"The lamp," said the bishop, "gives a very poor light."

Mme. Magloire understood him, and, going to his bedchamber, took from the mantel the two silver candlesticks, lighted the candles and placed them on the table.

"M. l'Curé," said the man, "you are good; you don't despise me. You take me into your house; you light your candles for me, and I haven't hid from you where I come from, and how miserable I am."

The bishop, who was sitting near him, touched his hand gently and said: "You need not tell me who you are. This is not my house; it is the house of Christ. It does not ask any comer whether he has a name, but whether he has an affliction. You are suffering; you are hungry and thirsty; be welcome. And do not thank me; do not tell me that I take you into my house. This is the home of no man except him who needs an asylum. I tell you, who are a traveler, that you are more at home here than I; whatever is here is yours. What need have I to know your name? Besides, before you told me, I knew it."

The man opened his eyes in astonishment.

"Really? You knew my name?"

"Yes," answered the bishop, "your name is my brother."

"Stop, stop, M. l'Curé," exclaimed the man, "I was famished when I came in, but you are so kind that now I don't know what I am; that is all gone."

The bishop looked at him again and said:

"You have seen much suffering?"

"Oh, the red blouse, the ball and chain, the plank to sleep on, the heat, the cold, the galley's screw, the lash, the double chain for nothing, the dungeon for a word—even when sick in bed, the chain. The dogs, the dogs are happier! nineteen years! and I am 46, and now a yellow passport. That is all."

"Yes," answered the bishop, "you have left a place of suffering. But listen, there will be more joy in heaven over the tears of a repentant sinner than over the white robes of 100 good men. If you are leaving that sorrowful place with hate and anger against men, you are worthy of compassion; if you leave it with good-will, gentleness and peace, you are better than any of us."

Meantime Mme. Magloire had served up supper; it consisted of soup made of water, oil, bread, and salt, a little pork, a scrap of mutton, a few figs, a green cheese, and a large loaf of rye bread. She had, without asking, added to the usual dinner of the bishop a bottle of fine old Mauves wine.

The bishop's countenance was lighted up with this expression of pleasure, peculiar to hospitable natures. "To supper!" he said, briskly, as was his habit when he had a guest. He seated the man at his right. Mdlle. Baptistine, perfectly quiet and natural, took her place at his left.

The bishop said the blessing and then served the soup himself according to his usual custom. The man fell to eating greedily.

Suddenly the bishop said: "It seems to me something is lacking on the table."

The fact was that Mme. Magloire had set out only the three plates which were necessary. Now it was the custom of the house when the bishop had any one to supper to set all six of the silver plates on the table, an innocent display. This graceful appearance of luxury was a sort of child-likeness which was full of charm in this gentle but austere household, which elevated poverty to dignity.

Mme. Magloire understood the remark; without a word she went out, and a moment afterward the three plates for which the bishop had asked were shining on the cloth symmetrically arranged before each of the three diners.

SOME ACCOUNT OF THE DAIRIES
OF PONTARLIER

Now, in order to give an idea of what passed at this table, we cannot do better than to transcribe here a passage in a letter from Mdlle. Baptistine to Mme. de Boischevron, in which the conversation between the convict and the bishop is related with charming minuteness:

"This man paid no attention to any one. He ate with the voracity of a starving man. After supper, however, he said:

"'M. l'Curé, all this is too good for me, but I must say that the wagoners, who wouldn't have me eat with them, live better than you.'

"Between us, the remark shocked me a little. My brother answered:

"'They are more fatigued than I am.'

"'No,' responded this man; 'they have more money. You are poor, I can see. Perhaps you are not a curé even? Are you only a curé? Ah! if God is just, you will deserve to be a curé.'

"'God is more than just,' said my brother.

"A moment after he added:

"'M. Jean Valjean, you are going to Pontarlier?'

"'A compulsory journey.'

"I am pretty sure that is the expression the man used. Then he continued:

"'I must be on the road to-morrow morning by day-break. It is a hard journey. If the nights are cold the days are warm.'

"'You are going,' said my brother, 'to a fine country. During the revolution, when my family was ruined, I took refuge at first in Franche-Comté, and supported myself there for some time by the labor of my hands. There I found plenty of work, and had only to make my choice. There are paper-mills, tanneries, distilleries, oil factories, large clock-making establishments, steel manufactories, copper foundries, at least twenty iron foundries, four of which, at Lods, Châtillion, Audincourt, and Beure, are very large.'

"I think I am not mistaken, and that these are the names that my brother mentioned. Then he broke off and addressed me:

"'Dear sister, have we not relatives in that part of the country?'

"I answered:

"'We had; among others, M. Lucenet, who was captain of the gates at Pontarlier under the old régime.'

"'Yes,' replied my brother, 'but in '93 no one had relatives; every one depended upon his hands. I labored. They have in the region of Pontarlier where you are going, M. Valjean, a business which is quite patriarchal and very charming, sister.'

[The bishop engages Jean in a friendly conversation about dairies.]

". . . One thing struck me. This man was what I have told you. Well, my brother during the supper and during the entire evening, with the exception of a few words about Jesus when he entered, did not say a word which could recall to this man who he himself was, nor indicate to him who my brother was. It was apparently a fine occasion to get in a little sermon and set up the bishop above the convict in order to make an impression upon his mind. It would, perhaps, have appeared to some to be a duty, having this unhappy man in hand, to feed the mind at the same time with the body, and to administer reproof, seasoned with morality and advice, or at least a little pity, accompanied by an exhortation to conduct himself better in future. My brother asked him neither his country nor his history; for his crime lay in his history, and my brother seemed to avoid everything which could recall it to him. At one time as my brother was speaking of the mountaineers of Pontarlier who have a pleasant labor near heaven and who, he added, are happy because they are innocent, he stopped short, fearing there might have been in this word which had escaped him something which could wound the feelings of this man. Upon reflection, I think I understand what was passing in my brother's mind. He thought doubtless, that this man, who called himself Jean Valjean, had his wretchedness too constantly before his mind; that it was best not to distress him by referring to it, and to make him think, if it were only for a moment, that he was a common person like any one else by treating him thus in the ordinary way. Is not this really understanding charity? Is there not, dear madame, something truly evangelical in this delicacy which abstains from sermonizing, moralizing and making allusions, and is not the wisest sympathy when a man has a suffering point not to touch upon it at all? It seems to me that this was my brother's inmost thought. At any rate, all I can say is, if he had all these ideas he did not show them even to me; he was, from beginning to end, the same as on other evenings, and he took supper with this Jean Valjean with the same air and manner that he would have supped with M. Gédéon, the provost, or with the curé of the parish." . . .

TRANQUILLITY

After having said good-night to his sister, Mgr. Bienvenu took one of the silver candlesticks from the table, handed the other to his guest, and said to him:

"Monsieur, I will show you to your room."

The man followed him.

As may have been understood from what has been said before, the house was so arranged that one could reach the alcove in the oratory only by passing through the bishop's sleeping-chamber. Just as they were passing through this room Mme. Magloire was putting up the silver in the cupboard at the head of the bed. It was the last thing she did every night before going to bed.

The bishop left his guest in the alcove before a clean, white bed. The man set down the candlestick upon a small table.

"Come," said the bishop, "a good night's rest to you; to-morrow morning, before you go, you shall have a cup of warm milk from our cows."

"Thank you, M. l'Abbé," said the man.

Scarcely had he pronounced these words of peace when suddenly he made a singular motion which would have chilled the two good women of the house with horror had they witnessed it. Even now it is hard for us to understand what impulse he obeyed at that moment. Did he intend to give a warning or to throw out a menace? Or was he simply obeying a sort of instinctive impulse, obscure even to himself? He turned abruptly toward the old man, crossed his arms, and, casting a wild look upon his host, exclaimed in a harsh voice:

"Ah, now, indeed! You lodge me in your house as near to you as that!"

He checked himself and added with a laugh, in which there was something horrible:

"Have you reflected upon it? Who tells you that I am not a murderer?"

The bishop responded:

"God will take care of that."

Then, with gravity, moving his lips like one praying or talking to himself, he raised two fingers of his right hand and blessed the man, who, however, did not bow; and, without turning his head or looking behind him, went into his chamber.

When the alcove was occupied a heavy serge curtain was drawn in the oratory, concealing the altar. Before this curtain the bishop knelt as he passed out and offered a short prayer.

A moment afterward he was walking in the garden, surrendering mind and soul to a dreamy contemplation of these grand and mysterious works of God which night makes visible to the eye.

As to the man, he was so completely exhausted that he did not even avail himself of the clean white sheets; he blew out the candle with his nostril, after the manner of convicts, and fell on the bed, dressed as he was, into a sound sleep.

Midnight struck as the bishop came back to his chamber.

A few moments afterward all in the little house slept. . . .

THE MAN AWAKES

As the cathedral clock struck two, Jean Valjean awoke.

What awakened him was, too good a bed. For nearly twenty years he had not slept in a bed, and, although he had not undressed, the sensation was too novel not to disturb his sleep.

He had slept something more than four hours. His fatigue had passed away. He was not accustomed to give many hours to repose.

He opened his eyes and looked for a moment into the obscurity about him, then he closed them to go to sleep again.

When many diverse sensations have disturbed the day, when the mind is preoccupied, we can fall asleep once, but not a second time. Sleep comes at first much more readily than it comes again. Such was the case with Jean Valjean. He could not get to sleep again, and so he began to think.

He was in one of those moods in which the ideas we have in our minds are perturbed. There was a kind of vague ebb and flow in his brain. His oldest and his latest memories floated about pell mell, and crossed each other confusedly, losing their own shapes, swelling beyond measure, then disappearing all at once, as if in a muddy and troubled stream. Many thoughts came to him, but there was one which continually presented itself, and which drove away all others. What that thought was we shall tell directly. He had noticed the six silver plates and the large ladle that Mme. Magloire had put on the table.

Those six silver plates took possession of him. There they were within a few steps. At the very moment that he passed through the middle room to reach the one he was now in, the old servant was placing them in a little cupboard at the head of the bed. He had marked that cupboard well; on the right, coming from the dining-room. They were solid, and old silver. With the big ladle they would bring, at least, 200 francs; double what he had got for nineteen years' labor. True; he would have got more if the *government* had not *robbed* him.

His mind wavered a whole hour and a long one, in fluctuation and in struggle. The clock struck three. He opened his eyes, rose up hastily in bed, reached out his arm and felt his knapsack, which he had put into the corner of the alcove, then he thrust out his legs and placed his feet on the floor and found himself, he knew not how, seated on his bed.

He remained for some time lost in thought in that attitude, which would have had a rather ominous look had any one seen him there in the dusk—he only awake in the slumbering house. All at once he stooped down, took off his shoes and put them softly upon the mat in front of the bed, then he resumed his thinking posture and was still again.

In that hideous meditation the ideas which we have pointed out troubled his brain without ceasing, entered, departed, returned and became a sort of weight upon him; and then he thought, too, he knew not why, and with that mechanical obstinacy that belongs to reverie, of a convict named Brevet, whom he had known in the galleys, and whose trousers were only held up by a single knit cotton suspender. The checked pattern of that suspender came continually before his mind.

He continued in this situation and would, perhaps, have remained there until daybreak, if the clock had not struck the quarter or the half-hour. The clock seemed to say to him, "Come along!"

He rose to his feet, hesitated for a moment longer and listened; all was still in the house; he walked straight and cautiously toward the window which he could discern. The night was not very dark; there was a full moon, across which large clouds were driving before the wind. This produced alternations of light and shade, out-of-doors eclipses and illuminations, and indoors a kind of glimmer. This glimmer, enough to enable him to find his way, changing with the passing clouds, resembled that sort of livid light which falls through the window of a dungeon before which men are passing and repassing. On reaching the window Jean Valjean examined it. It had no bars, opened into the garden, and was fastened, according to the fashion of the country, with a little wedge only. He opened it; but as the cold, keen air rushed into the room he closed it again immediately. He looked into the garden with that absorbed look which studies rather than sees. The garden was inclosed with a white wall, quite low and readily scaled. Beyond, against the sky, he distinguished the tops of trees at equal distances apart, which showed that this wall separated the garden from an avenue or a lane planted with trees.

When he had taken this observation he turned like a man whose mind is made up, went to his alcove, took his knapsack, opened it, fumbled in it, took out something which he laid upon the bed, put his shoes into one of his pockets, tied up his bundle, swung it upon his shoulders, put on his cap, and pulled the vizor down over his eyes, felt for his stick, and went and put it in the corner of the window, then returned to the bed, and resolutely took up the object which he had laid on it. It looked like a short iron bar, pointed at one end like a spear.

It would have been hard to distinguish in the darkness for what use this piece of iron had been made. Could it be a lever? Could it be a club?

In the daytime it would have been seen to be nothing but a miner's drill. At that time the convicts were sometimes employed in quarrying stone on the high hills that surround Toulon, and they often had miners' tools in their possession. Miners' drills are of solid iron, terminating at the lower end in a point, by means of which they are sunk into the rock.

He took the drill in his right hand, and, holding his breath, with stealthy steps he moved toward the door of the next room, which was the bishop's, as we know. On reaching the door he found it unlatched. The bishop had not closed it.

WHAT HE DOES

Jean Valjean listened. Not a sound.

He pushed the door.

He pushed it lightly with the end of his finger, with the stealthy and timorous carefulness of a cat. The door yielded to the pressure with a silent, imperceptible movement, which made the opening a little wider.

He waited a moment and then pushed the door again more boldly.

It yielded gradually and silently. The opening was now wide enough for him to pass through; but there was a small table near the door, which with it formed a troublesome angle and which barred the entrance.

Jean Valjean saw the obstacle. At all hazards the opening must be made still wider.

He so determined, and pushed the door a third time, harder than before. This time a rusty hinge suddenly sent out into the darkness a harsh and prolonged creak.

Jean Valjean shivered. The noise of this hinge sounded in his ears as clear and terrible as the trumpet of the judgment day.

In the fantastic exaggeration of the first moment he almost imagined that this hinge had become animate and suddenly endowed with a terrible life; and that it was barking like a dog to warn everybody and rouse the sleepers.

He stopped, shuddering and distracted, and dropped from his tiptoes to his feet. He felt the pulses of his temples beat like triphammers, and it appeared to him that his breath came from his chest with the roar of wind from a cavern. It seemed impossible that the horrible sound of this incensed hinge had not shaken the whole house with the shock of an earthquake; the door pushed by him had taken the alarm, and had called out; the old man would arise; the two old women would scream; help would come; in a quarter of an hour the town would be alive with it and the gendarmes in pursuit. For a moment he thought he was lost.

He stood still, petrified like the pillar of salt, not daring to stir. Some minutes passed. The door was wide open; he ventured to look into the room. Nothing had moved. He listened. Nothing was stirring in the house. The noise of the rusty hinge had awakened nobody.

The first danger was over, but still he felt within him a frightful tumult. Nevertheless he did not flinch. Not even when he thought he was lost had he flinched. His only thought was to make an end of it quickly. He took one step and was in the room.

A deep calm filled the chamber. Here and there indistinct, confused forms could be distinguished; which by day were papers scattered over a table, open folios, books piled on a stool, an armchair with clothes on it, a *prie-Dieu,* but now were only dark corners and whitish spots. Jean Valjean advanced, carefully avoiding the furniture. At the further end of the room he could hear the equal and quiet breathing of the sleeping bishop.

Suddenly he stopped; he was near the bed, he had reached it sooner than he thought.

Nature sometimes joins her effects and her appearances to our acts with a sort of serious and intelligent appropriateness, as if she would compel us to reflect. For nearly a half-hour a great cloud had darkened the sky. At the moment when Jean Valjean paused before the bed the cloud broke as if purposely, and a ray of moonlight crossing the high window, suddenly lighted up the bishop's pale face. He slept tranquilly. He was almost entirely dressed, though in bed, on account of the cold nights of the lower Alps, with a dark woolen garment which covered his arms to the wrists. His head had fallen on the pillow in the unstudied attitude of slumber; over the side of the bed hung his hand, ornamented with the pastoral ring, and which had done so many good deeds, so many pious acts. His entire countenance was lit up with a vague expression of content, hope and happiness. It was more than a smile and almost a radiance. On his forehead rested the indescribable reflection of an unseen light. The souls of the upright in sleep have visions of a mysterious heaven.

A reflection from this heaven shone upon the bishop.

But it was also a luminous transparency, for this heaven was within him; this heaven was his conscience. . . .

There was something of divinity almost in this man, thus unconsciously august.

Jean Valjean was in the shadow with the iron drill in his hand, erect, motionless, terrified at this radiant figure. He had never seen anything comparable to it. This confidence filled him with fear. The moral world has no greater spectacle than this; a troubled and restless conscience on the verge of committing an evil deed, contemplating the sleep of a good man.

This sleep in this solitude, with a neighbor such as he, contained a touch of the sublime, which he felt vaguely but powerfully.

None could have told what was within him, not even himself. To attempt to realize it the utmost violence must be imagined in the presence of the most extreme mildness. In his face nothing could be distinguished with certainty. It was a sort of haggard astonishment. He saw it; that was all. But what were his thoughts? It would have been impossible to guess. It was clear that he was moved and agitated. But of what nature was this emotion?

He did not remove his eyes from the old man. The only thing which was plain from his attitude and his countenance was a strange indecision. You would have said he was hesitating between two realms—that of the doomed and that of the saved. He appeared ready either to cleave this skull or to kiss this hand.

In a few moments he raised his left hand slowly to his forehead and took off his hat; then, letting his hand fall with the same slowness, Jean Valjean resumed his contemplations, his cap in his left hand, his club in his right, and his hair bristling on his fierce-looking head.

Under this frightful gaze the bishop still slept in profoundest peace. The crucifix above the mantel-piece was dimly visible in the

moonlight, apparently extending its arms toward both, with a benediction for one and a pardon for the other.

Suddenly Jean Valjean put on his cap, then passed quickly, without looking at the bishop, along the bed, straight to the cupboard
which he perceived near its head; he raised the drill to force the lock;
the key was in it; he opened it; the first thing he saw was the basket
of silver, he took it, crossed the room with hasty stride, careless of
noise, reached the door, entered the oratory, took his stick, stepped
out, put the silver into his knapsack, threw away the basket, ran
across the garden, leaped over the wall like a tiger and fled.

THE BISHOP AT WORK

The next day at sunrise Mgr. Bienvenu was walking in the garden.
Mme. Magloire ran toward him quite beside herself.

"Monseigneur, monseigneur," cried she, "does your greatness
know where the silver basket is?"

"Yes," said the bishop.

"God be praised!" said she; "I did not know what had become
of it?"

The bishop had just found the basket on a flower-bed. He gave
it to Mme. Magloire and said: "There it is."

"Yes," said she, "but there is nothing in it. The silver?"

"Ah!" said the bishop, "it is the silver, then, that troubles you. I
do not know where that is."

"Good heavens! it is stolen. The man who came last night stole it."

And in the twinkling of an eye, with all the agility of which her
age was capable, Mme. Magloire ran to the oratory, went into the
alcove, and came back to the bishop. The bishop was bending with
some sadness over a cochlearia des Guillons, which the basket had
broken in falling. He looked up at Mme. Magloire's cry:

"Monseigneur, the man has gone! the silver is stolen!"

While she was uttering this exclamation her eyes fell on an angle
of the garden where she saw traces of an escalade. A capstone of
the wall had been thrown down.

"See, there is where he got out; he jumped into Cochefilet lane.
The abominable fellow! he has stolen our silver!"

The bishop was silent for a moment, then, raising his serious
eyes, he said mildly to Mme. Magloire:

"Now, first, did this silver belong to us?"

Mme. Magloire did not answer; after a moment the bishop continued:

"Mme. Magloire: I have for a long time wrongfully withheld this silver; it belonged to the poor. Who was this man? A poor man evidently."

"Alas! alas!" returned Mme. Magloire. "It is not on my account or mademoiselle's; it is all the same to us. But it is on yours, monseigneur. What is monsieur going to eat from now?"

The bishop looked at her with amazement.

"How so! have we no tin plates?"

Mme. Magloire shrugged her shoulders.

"Tin smells."

"Well, then, iron plates."

Mme. Magloire made an expressive gesture.

"Iron tastes."

"Well," said the bishop, "then, wooden plates."

In a few minutes he was breakfasting at the same table at which Jean Valjean sat the night before. While he was breakfasting M. Bienvenu pleasantly remarked to his sister, who said nothing, and Mme. Magloire, who was grumbling to herself, that there was really no need even of a wooden spoon or fork to dip a piece of bread into a cup of milk.

"Was there ever such an idea?" said Mme. Magloire to herself, as she went backward and forward; "to take in a man like that, and to give him a bed beside him; and yet what a blessing it was he did nothing but steal! Oh, my stars! it makes the chills run over me when I think of it!"

Just as the brother and sister were rising from the table there was a knock at the door.

"Come in," said the bishop.

The door opened. A strange, fierce group appeared on the threshold. Three men were holding a fourth by the collar. The three men were gendarmes;[1] the fourth, Jean Valjean.

A brigadier of gendarmes, who appeared to head the group, was near the door. He advanced toward the bishop, giving a military salute:

"Monseigneur," said he.

At this word Jean Valjean, who was sullen, and seemed entirely cast down, raised his head with a stupefied air.

[1]Police.—ed. note

"Monseigneur!" he murmured, "then it is not the curé!"

"Silence!" said a gendarme, "it is monseigneur, the bishop."

In the meantime Mgr. Bienvenu had approached as quickly as his great age permitted;

"Ah, there you are!" said he, looking toward Jean Valjean, "I am glad to see you. But I gave you the candlesticks also, which are silver like the rest, and would bring 200 francs. Why did you not take them along with your plates?"

Jean Valjean opened his eyes and looked at the bishop with an expression which no human tongue could describe.

"Monseigneur," said the brigadier, "then what this man said was true? We met him. He was going like a man who was running away and we arrested him in order to see. He had this silver."

"And he told you," interrupted the bishop, with a smile, "that it had been given him by a good old priest with whom he had passed the night. I see it all. And you brought him back here? It is all a mistake."

"If that is so," said the brigadier, "we can let him go."

"Certainly," replied the bishop.

The gendarmes released Jean Valjean, who shrank back.

"Is it true that they let me go?" he said in voice almost inarticulate, as if he were speaking in his sleep.

"Yes! you can go. Do you not understand?" said a gendarme.

"My friend," said the bishop, "before you go away here are your candlesticks; take them."

He went to the mantel-piece, took the two candlesticks and brought them to Jean Valjean. The two women beheld the action without a word, or gesture, or look that might disturb the bishop.

Jean Valjean was trembling in every limb. He took the two candlesticks mechanically and with a wild appearance.

"Now," said the bishop, "go in peace. By the way, my friend, when you come again you need not come through the garden. You can always come in and go out by the front door. It is closed only with a latch, day or night."

Then turning to the gendarmes, he said:

"Messieurs, you can retire." The gendarmes withdrew.

Jean Valjean felt like a man who is just about to faint.

The bishop approached him and said, in a low voice:

"Forget not, never forget that you have promised me to use this silver to become an honest man."

Jean Valjean, who had no recollection of this promise, stood confounded. The bishop had laid much stress upon these words as he uttered them. He continued, solemnly:

"Jean Valjean, my brother, you belong no longer to evil, but to good. It is your soul that I am buying for you. I withdraw it from dark thoughts and from the spirit of perdition and I give it to God!"

For Further Reflection

1. Jean Valjean is plucked from the kingdom of evil by the good bishop. As the story develops he gradually is transformed into a moral hero, who serves the poor. What message is Victor Hugo trying to convey in this story? What is he suggesting about human nature and our relation to good and evil?

2. Identify the virtues in the bishop of Digne. Note that there is no discussion of moral duties; the bishop acts out of spontaneous goodness, out of saintly character, risking even his own life in the process. Do you think that Hugo has painted an ideal person, or is the bishop an imprudent idealist who is just lucky he hasn't met a worse fate?

3. Ironically, it so happens that the bishop has been working on a book about duty for years. But it never gets finished. Do you see any symbolism in this fact?

Virtue Ethics

ARISTOTLE

Aristotle (384–322 B.C.) was born in Stagira in Macedon, the son of a physician. He was a student of Plato at the Academy in Athens and tutor of Alexander the Great. Aristotle saw ethics as the branch of political philosophy concerned with a good life. It is thus a practical rather than a purely theoretical science. In this selection from *Nicomachean Ethics,* Aristotle considers the nature of ethics in relation to

Reprinted from *Aristotle's Nicomachean Ethics,* translated by James E. C. Weldon (Macmillan, 1897).

human nature. From this same perspective he discusses the nature of virtue, which he defines as traits that enable us to live well in communities. To achieve a state of well-being or happiness, proper social institutions are necessary. Thus, the moral person cannot exist in isolation from a flourishing political community that enables the person to develop the necessary virtues for the good life.

Aristotle goes on to show the difference between moral and intellectual virtues. While the intellectual virtues may be taught directly, the moral ones must be lived in order to be learned. By living well, we acquire the best guarantee to the happy life. But again, happiness requires that one be lucky enough to live in a flourishing state. By considering luck as part of morality, Aristotle distinguishes his position from deontological ones like those of the Bible and Kant, and so defends a point noted in Nagel's article— the importance of luck to morality. In the last analysis, the moral life consists in moderation, living in accordance with the "golden mean," a middle ground between extremes.

BOOK I

All Human Activities Aim at Some Good

Chapter 1. Every art and every scientific inquiry, and similarly every action and purpose, may be said to aim at some good. Hence the good has been well defined as that at which all things aim. But it is clear that there is a difference in ends; for the ends are sometimes activities, and sometimes results beyond the mere activities. Where there are ends beyond the action, the results are naturally superior to the action.

As there are various actions, arts, and sciences, it follows that the ends are also various. Thus health is the end of the medical art, a ship of shipbuilding, victory of strategy, and wealth of economics. It often happens that a number of such arts or sciences combine for a single enterprise, as the art of making bridles and all such other arts as furnish the implements of horsemanship combine for horsemanship, and horsemanship and every military action for strategy; and in the same way, other arts or sciences combine for others. In all these cases, the ends of the master arts or sciences, whatever they may be, are more desirable than those of the subordinate arts or sciences, as it is for the sake of the former that the latter are pursued. It makes no difference to the argument whether the activities themselves are the ends of the action, or something beyond the activities, as in the above-mentioned sciences.

If it is true that in the sphere of action there is some end which we wish for its own sake, and for the sake of which we wish everything else, and if we do not desire everything for the sake of something else (for, if that is so, the process will go on *ad infinitum,* and our desire will be idle and futile), clearly this end will be good and the supreme good. Does it not follow then that the knowledge of this good is of great importance for the conduct of life? Like archers who have a mark at which to aim, shall we not have a better chance of attaining what we want? If this is so, we must endeavor to comprehend, at least in outline, what this good is, and what science or faculty makes it its object.

It would seem that this is the most authoritative science. Such a kind is evidently the political, for it is that which determines what sciences are necessary in states, and what kinds should be studied, and how far they should be studied by each class of inhabitant. We see too that even the faculties held in highest esteem, such as strategy, economics, and rhetoric, are subordinate to it. Then since politics makes use of the other sciences and also rules what people may do and what they may not do, it follows that its end will comprehend the ends of the other sciences, and will therefore be the good of mankind. For even if the good of an individual is identical with the good of a state, yet the good of the state is evidently greater and more perfect to attain or to preserve. For though the good of an individual by himself is something worth working for, to ensure the good of a nation or a state is nobler and more divine.

These then are the objects at which the present inquiry aims, and it is in a sense a political inquiry. . . .

The Science of the Good for Man Is Politics

Chapter 2. As every science and undertaking aims at some good, what is in our view the good at which political science aims, and what is the highest of all practical goods? As to its name there is, I may say, a general agreement. The masses and the cultured classes agree in calling it happiness, and conceive that "to live well" or "to do well" is the same thing as "to be happy." But as to what happiness is they do not agree, nor do the masses give the same account of it as the philosophers. The former take it to be something visible and palpable, such as pleasure, wealth, or honor; different people, however, give different definitions of it, and often even the same man gives different definitions at different times. When he is ill, it is health, when he is poor, it is wealth; if he is conscious of his own ignorance, he envies people who use grand language above his own comprehension. Some philosophers, on the other hand, have held that, besides these various goods, there is an absolute good which is the cause of goodness in them all.[1] It would perhaps be a waste of time to examine all these opinions; it will be enough to examine such as are most popular or as seem to be more or less reasonable.

Chapter 3. Men's conception of the good or of happiness may be read in the lives they lead. Ordinary or vulgar people conceive it to be a pleasure, and accordingly choose a life of enjoyment. For there are, we may say, three conspicuous types of life, the sensual, the political, and, thirdly, the life of thought. Now the mass of men present an absolutely slavish appearance, choosing the life of brute beasts, but they have ground for so doing because so many persons in authority share the tastes of Sardanapalus.[2] Cultivated and energetic people, on the other hand, identify happiness with honor, as honor is the general end of political life. But this seems too superficial an idea for our present purpose; for honor depends more upon the people who pay it than upon the person to whom it is paid, and the good we feel is something which is proper to a man himself and cannot be easily taken away from him. Men too appear to seek honor in order to be assured of their own goodness. Accordingly, they seek it at the hands of the sage and of those who know them well, and they seek it on the ground of their virtue; clearly then, in their judgment at any rate, virtue is better than honor. Perhaps then we might look on virtue rather than honor as the end of political life. Yet even this idea appears not quite complete; for a man may possess virtue and yet be asleep or inactive throughout life, and not only so, but he may experience the greatest calamities and misfortunes. Yet no one would call such a life a life of happiness, unless he were maintaining a paradox. But we need not

[1]Plato

[2]A half-legendary ruler whose name to the Greeks stood for extreme mental luxury and extravagance.

dwell further on this subject, since it is sufficiently discussed in popular philosophical treatises. The third life is the life of thought, which we will discuss later.

The life of money making is a life of constraint; and wealth is obviously not the good of which we are in quest; for it is useful merely as a means to something else. It would be more reasonable to take the things mentioned before—sensual pleasure, honor, and virtue—as ends than wealth, since they are things desired on their own account. Yet these too are evidently not ends, although much argument has been employed to show that they are. . . .

Characteristics of the Good

Chapter 5.   But leaving this subject for the present, let us revert to the good of which we are in quest and consider what it may be. For it seems different in different activities or arts; it is one thing in medicine, another in strategy, and so on. What is the good in each of these instances? It is presumably that for the sake of which all else is done. In medicine this is health, in strategy victory, in architecture a house, and so on. In every activity and undertaking it is the end, since it is for the sake of the end that all people do whatever else they do. If then there is an end for all our activity, this will be the good to be accomplished; and if there are several such ends, it will be these.

Our argument has arrived by a different path at the same point as before; but we must endeavor to make it still plainer. Since there are more ends than one, and some of these ends—for example, wealth, flutes, and instruments generally—we desire as means to something else, it is evident that not all are final ends. But the highest good is clearly something final. Hence if there is only one final end, this will be the object of which we are in search; and if there are more than one, it will be the most final. We call that which is sought after for its own sake more final than that which is sought after as a means to something else; we call that which is never desired as a means to something else more final than things that are desired both for themselves and as means to something else. Therefore, we call absolutely final that which is always desired for itself and never as a means to something else. Now happiness more than anything else answers to this description. For happiness we always desire for its own sake and never as a means to something else, whereas honor, pleasure, intelligence, and every virtue we

desire partly for their own sakes (for we should desire them independently of what might result from them), but partly also as means
to happiness, because we suppose they will prove instruments of
happiness. Happiness, on the other hand, nobody desires for the
sake of these things, nor indeed as a means to anything else at all.

If we start from the point of view of self-sufficiency, we reach
the same conclusion; for we assume that the final good is self-
sufficient. By self-sufficiency we do not mean that a person leads
a solitary life all by himself, but that he has parents, children, wife
and friends and fellow citizens in general, as man is naturally a
social being. Yet here it is necessary to set some limit; for if the
circle must be extended to include ancestors, descendants, and
friends' friends, it will go on indefinitely. Leaving this point, however, for future investigation, we call the self-sufficient that which,
taken even by itself, makes life desirable and wanting nothing at
all; and this is what we mean by happiness.

Again, we think happiness the most desirable of all things, and
that not merely as one good thing among others. If it were only
that, the addition of the smallest more good would increase its de-
sirableness; for the addition would make an increase of goods, and
the greater of two goods is always the more desirable. Happiness
is something final and self-sufficient and the end of all action.

Chapter 6.   Perhaps, however, it seems a commonplace to say that
happiness is the supreme good; what is wanted is to define its
nature a little more clearly. The best way of arriving at such a definition will probably be to ascertain the function of man. For, as
with a flute player, a sculptor, or any artist, or in fact anybody who
has a special function or activity, his goodness and excellence seem
to lie in his function, so it would seem to be with man, if indeed
he has a special function. Can it be said that, while a carpenter and
a cobbler have special functions and activities, man, unlike them,
is naturally functionless? Or, as the eye, the hand, the foot, and
similarly each part of the body has a special function, so may man
be regarded as having a special function apart from all these? What,
then, can this function be? It is not life; for life is apparently something that man shares with plants; and we are looking for something peculiar to him. We must exclude therefore the life of nutrition and growth. There is next what may be called the life of
sensation. But this too, apparently, is shared by man with horses,
cattle, and all other animals. There remains what I may call the

active life of the rational part of man's being. Now this rational part is twofold; one part is rational in the sense of being obedient to reason, and the other in the sense of possessing and exercising reason and intelligence. The active life too may be conceived of in two ways, either as a state of character, or as an activity; but we mean by it the life of activity, as this seems to be the truer form of the conception.

The function of man then is activity of soul in accordance with reason, or not apart from reason. Now, the function of a man of a certain kind, and of a man who is good of that kind—for example, of a harpist and a good harpist—are in our view the same in kind. This is true of all people of all kinds without exception, the superior excellence being only an addition to the function; for it is the function of a harpist to play the harp, and of a good harpist to play the harp well. This being so, if we define the function of man as a kind of life, and this life as an activity of the soul or a course of action in accordance with reason, and if the function of a good man is such activity of a good and noble kind, and if everything is well done when it is done in accordance with its proper excellence, it follows that the good of man is activity of soul in accordance with virtue, or, if there are more virtues than one, in accordance with the best and most complete virtue. But we must add the words "in a complete life." For as one swallow or one day does not make a spring, so one day or a short time does not make a man blessed or happy. . . .

Inasmuch as happiness is an activity of soul in accordance with perfect virtue, we must now consider virtue, as this will perhaps be the best way of studying happiness. . . . Clearly it is human virtue we have to consider; for the good of which we are in search is, as we said, human good, and the happiness, human happiness. By human virtue or excellence we mean not that of the body, but that of the soul, and by happiness we mean an activity of the soul. . . .

BOOK II

Moral virtues can best be acquired by practice and habit. They imply a right attitude toward pleasures and pains. A good man deliberately chooses to do what is noble and right for its own sake. What is right in matters of moral conduct is usually a mean between two extremes.

Chapter 1. Virtue then is twofold, partly intellectual and partly moral, and intellectual virtue is originated and fostered mainly by teaching; it demands therefore experience and time. Moral virtue on the other hand is the outcome of habit, and accordingly its name, *ethike,* is derived by a slight variation from *ethos,* habit. From this fact it is clear that moral virtue is not implanted in us by nature; for nothing that exists by nature can be transformed by habit. Thus a stone, that naturally tends to fall downwards, cannot be habituated or trained to rise upwards, even if we tried to train it by throwing it up ten thousand times. Nor again can fire be trained to sink downwards, nor anything else that follows one natural law be habituated or trained to follow another. It is neither by nature then nor in defiance of nature that virtues grow in us. Nature gives us the capacity to receive them, and that capacity is perfected by habit.

Again, if we take the various natural powers which belong to us, we first possess the proper faculties and afterwards display the activities. It is obviously so with the senses. Not by seeing frequently or hearing frequently do we acquire the sense of seeing or hearing; on the contrary, because we have the senses we make use of them; we do not get them by making use of them. But the virtues we get by first practicing them, as we do in the arts. For it is by doing what we ought to do when we study the arts that we learn the arts themselves; we become builders by building and harpists by playing the harp. Similarly, it is by doing just acts that we become just, by doing temperate acts that we become temperate, by doing brave acts that we become brave. The experience of states confirms this statement, for it is by training in good habits that lawmakers make the citizens good. This is the object all lawmakers have at heart; if they do not succeed in it, they fail of their purpose; and it makes the distinction between a good constitution and a bad one.

Again, the causes and means by which any virtue is produced and destroyed are the same; and equally so in any part. For it is by playing the harp that both good and bad harpists are produced; and the case of builders and others is similar, for it is by building well that they become good builders and by building badly that they become bad builders. If it were not so, there would be no need of anybody to teach them; they would all be born good or bad in their several crafts. The case of the virtues is the same. It is by our actions in dealings between man and man that we become either just or unjust. It is by our actions in the face of danger and by our training ourselves to fear or to courage that we become either cowardly or courageous. It is much the same with our appetites and angry passions. People become temperate and gentle, others licentious and passionate, by behaving in one or the other way in particular circumstances. In a word, moral states are the results of activities like the states themselves. It is our duty therefore to keep a certain character in our activities, since our moral states depend on the differences in our activities. So the difference between one and another training in habits in our childhood is not a light matter, but important, or rather, all-important.

Chapter 2.   Our present study is not, like other studies, purely theoretical in intention; for the object of our inquiry is not to know what virtue is but how to become good, and that is the sole benefit of it. We must, therefore, consider the right way of performing actions, for it is acts, as we have said, that determine the character of the resulting moral states.

That we should act in accordance with right reason is a common general principle, which may here be taken for granted. The nature of right reason, and its relation to the virtues generally, will be discussed later. But first of all it must be admitted that all reasoning on matters of conduct must be like a sketch in outline; it cannot be scientifically exact. We began by laying down the principle that the kind of reasoning demanded in any subject must be such as the subject matter itself allows; and questions of conduct and expediency no more admit of hard and fast rules than questions of health.

If this is true of general reasoning on ethics, still more true is it that scientific exactitude is impossible in treating of particular ethical cases. They do not fall under any art or law, but the actors themselves have always to take account of circumstances, as much as in medicine or navigation. Still, although such is the nature of our present argument, we must try to make the best of it.

The first point to be observed is that in the matters we are now considering deficiency and excess are both fatal. It is so, we see, in questions of health and strength. (We must judge of what we cannot see by the evidence of what we do see.) Too much or too little gymnastic exercise is fatal to strength. Similarly, too much or too little meat and drink is fatal to health, whereas a suitable amount produces, increases, and sustains it. It is the same with temperance, courage, and other moral virtues. A person who avoids and is afraid

of everything and faces nothing becomes a coward; a person who
is not afraid of anything but is ready to face everything becomes
foolhardy. Similarly, he who enjoys every pleasure and abstains
from none is licentious; he who refuses all pleasures, like a boor,
is an insensible sort of person. For temperance and courage are
destroyed by excess and deficiency but preserved by the mean.

Again, not only are the causes and agencies of production,
increase, and destruction in moral states the same, but the field of
their activity is the same also. It is so in other more obvious
instances, as, for example, strength; for strength is produced by taking a great deal of food and undergoing a great deal of exertion,
and it is the strong man who is able to take most food and undergo
most exertion. So too with the virtues. By abstaining from pleasures
we become temperate, and, when we have become temperate, we
are best able to abstain from them. So again with courage; it is by
training ourselves to despise and face terrifying things that we become brave, and when we have become brave, we shall be best
able to face them.

The pleasure or pain which accompanies actions may be
regarded as a test of a person's moral state. He who abstains from
physical pleasures and feels pleasure in so doing is temperate; but
he who feels pain at so doing is licentious. He who faces dangers
with pleasure, or at least without pain, is brave; but he who feels
pain at facing them is a coward. For moral virtue is concerned with
pleasures and pains. It is pleasure which makes us do what is base,
and pain which makes us abstain from doing what is noble. Hence
the importance of having a certain training from very early days,
as Plato says, so that we may feel pleasure and pain at the right
objects; for this is true education. . . .

Chapter 3.   But we may be asked what we mean by saying that
people must become just by doing what is just and temperate by
doing what is temperate. For, it will be said, if they do what is just
and temperate they are already just and temperate themselves, in
the same way as, if they practice grammar and music, they are
grammarians and musicians.

But is this true even in the case of the arts? For a person may
speak grammatically either by chance or at the suggestion of somebody else; hence he will not be a grammarian unless he not only
speaks grammatically but does so in a grammatical manner, that is,
because of the grammatical knowledge which he possesses.

There is a point of difference too between the arts and the virtues. The productions of art have their excellence in themselves. It is enough then that, when they are produced, they themselves should possess a certain character. But acts in accordance with virtue are not justly or temperately performed simply because they are in themselves just or temperate. The doer at the time of performing them must satisfy certain conditions; in the first place, he must know what he is doing; secondly, he must deliberately choose to do it and do it for its own sake; and thirdly, he must do it as part of his own firm and immutable character. If it be a question of art, these conditions, except only the condition of knowledge, are not raised; but if it be a question of virtue, mere knowledge is of little or no avail; it is the other conditions, which are the results of frequently performing just and temperate acts, that are not slightly but all-important. Accordingly, deeds are called just and temperate when they are such as a just and temperate person would do; and a just and temperate person is not merely one who does these deeds but one who does them in the spirit of the just and the temperate.

It may fairly be said that a just man becomes just by doing what is just, and a temperate man becomes temperate by doing what is temperate, and if a man did not so act, he would not have much chance of becoming good. But most people, instead of acting, take refuge in theorizing; they imagine that they are philosophers and that philosophy will make them virtuous; in fact, they behave like people who listen attentively to their doctors but never do anything that their doctors tell them. But a healthy state of the soul will no more be produced by this kind of philosophizing than a healthy state of the body by this kind of medical treatment.

Chapter 4. We have next to consider the nature of virtue. Now, as the properties of the soul are three, namely, emotions, faculties, and moral states, it follows that virtue must be one of the three. By emotions I mean desire, anger, fear, pride, envy, joy, love, hatred, regret, ambition, pity—in a word, whatever feeling is attended by pleasure or pain. I call those faculties through which we are said to be capable of experiencing these emotions, for instance, capable of getting angry or being pained or feeling pity. And I call those moral states through which we are well or ill disposed in our emotions, ill disposed, for instance, in anger, if our anger be too violent or too feeble, and well disposed, if it be rightly moderate; and similarly in our other emotions.

Now neither the virtues nor the vices are emotions; for we are not called good or bad for our emotions but for our virtues or vices. We are not praised or blamed simply for being angry, but only for being angry in a certain way; but we are praised or blamed for our virtues or vices. Again, whereas we are angry or afraid without deliberate purpose, the virtues are matters of deliberate purpose, or require deliberate purpose. Moreover, we are said to be moved by our emotions, but by our virtues or vices we are not said to be moved but to have a certain disposition.

For these reasons the virtues are not faculties. For we are not called either good or bad, nor are we praised or blamed for having simple capacity for emotion. Also while Nature gives us our faculties, it is not Nature that makes us good or bad; but this point we have already discussed. If then the virtues are neither emotions nor faculties, all that remains is that they must be moral states.

Chapter 5.   The nature of virtue has been now described in kind. But it is not enough to say merely that virtue is a moral state; we must also describe the character of that moral state.

We may assert then that every virtue or excellence puts into good condition that of which it is a virtue or excellence, and enables it to perform its work well. Thus excellence in the eye makes the eye good and its function good, for by excellence in the eye we see well. Similarly, excellence of the horse makes a horse excellent himself and good at racing, at carrying its rider and at facing the enemy. If then this rule is universally true, the virtue or excellence of a man will be such a moral state as makes a man good and able to perform his proper function well. How this will be the case we have already explained, but another way of making it clear will be to study the nature or character of virtue.

Now of everything, whether it be continuous or divisible, it is possible to take a greater, a smaller, or an equal amount, and this either in terms of the thing itself or in relation to ourselves, the equal being a mean between too much and too little. By the mean in terms of the thing itself, I understand that which is equally distinct from both its extremes, which is one and the same for every man. By the mean relatively to ourselves, I understand that which is neither too much nor too little for us; but this is not one nor the same for everybody. Thus if 10 be too much and 2 too little, we take 6 as a mean in terms of the thing itself; for 6 is as much greater than 2 as it is less than 10, and this is a mean in arithmetical proportion. But the mean considered relatively to ourselves may not be ascertained in that way. It does not follow that if 10 pounds of meat is too much and 2 too little for a man to eat, the trainer will order him 6 pounds, since this also may be too much or too little for him who is to take it; it will be too little, for example, for Milo but too much for a beginner in gymnastics. The same with running and wrestling; the right amount will vary with the individual. This being so, the skillful in any art avoids alike excess and deficiency; he seeks and chooses the mean, not the absolute mean, but the mean considered relatively to himself.

Every art then does its work well, if it regards the mean and judges the works it produces by the mean. For this reason we often say of successful works of art that it is impossible to take anything from them or to add anything to them, which implies that excess or deficiency is fatal to excellence but that the mean state ensures it. Good artists too, as we say, have an eye to the mean in their works. Now virtue, like Nature herself, is more accurate and better than any art; virtue, therefore, will aim at the mean. I speak of moral virtue, since it is moral virtue which is concerned with emotions and actions, and it is in these we have excess and deficiency and the mean. Thus it is possible to go too far, or not far enough in fear, pride, desire, anger, pity, and pleasure and pain generally, and the excess and the deficiency are alike wrong; but to feel these emotions at the right times, for the right objects, towards the right persons, for the right motives, and in the right manner, is the mean or the best good, which signifies virtue. Similarly, there may be excess, deficiency, or the mean, in acts. Virtue is concerned with both emotions and actions, wherein excess is an error and deficiency a fault, while the mean is successful and praised, and success and praise are both characteristics of virtue.

It appears then that virtue is a kind of mean because it aims at the mean.

On the other hand, there are many different ways of going wrong; for evil is in its nature infinite, to use the Pythagorean phrase, but good is finite and there is only one possible way of going right. So the former is easy and the latter is difficult; it is easy to miss the mark but difficult to hit it. And so by our reasoning excess and deficiency are characteristics of vice and the mean is a characteristic of virtue.

"For good is simple, evil manifold."

Chapter 6. Virtue then is a state of deliberate moral purpose, consisting in a mean relative to ourselves, the mean being determined by reason, or as a prudent man would determine it. It is a mean, firstly, as lying between two vices, the vice of excess on the one hand, the vice of deficiency on the other, and, secondly, because, whereas the vices either fall short of or go beyond what is right in emotion and action, virtue discovers and chooses the mean. Accordingly, virtue, if regarded in its essence or theoretical definition, is a mean, though, if regarded from the point of view of what is best and most excellent, it is an extreme.

But not every action or every emotion admits of a mean. There are some whose very name implies wickedness, as, for example, malice, shamelessness, and envy among the emotions, and adultery, theft, and murder among the actions. All these and others like them are marked as intrinsically wicked, not merely the excesses or deficiencies of them. It is never possible then to be right in them; they are always sinful. Right or wrong in such acts as adultery does not depend on our committing it with the right woman, at the right time, or in the right manner; on the contrary, it is wrong to do it at all. It would be equally false to suppose that there can be a mean or an excess or deficiency in unjust, cowardly or licentious conduct; for, if that were so, it would be a mean of excess and deficiency, an excess of excess and a deficiency of deficiency. But as in temperance and courage there can be no excess or deficiency, because the mean there is in a sense an extreme, so too in these other cases there cannot be a mean or an excess or a deficiency, but however the acts are done, they are wrong. For in general an excess or deficiency does not have a mean, nor a mean an excess or deficiency. . . .

Chapter 8. There are then three dispositions, two being vices, namely, excess and deficiency, and one virtue, which is the mean between them; and they are all in a sense mutually opposed. The extremes are opposed both to the mean and to each other, and the mean is opposed to the extremes. For as the equal if compared with the less is greater, but if compared with the greater is less, so the mean state, whether in emotion or action, if compared with deficiency is excessive, but if compared with excess is deficient. Thus the brave man appears foolhardy compared with the coward, but cowardly compared with the foolhardy. Similarly, the temperate man appears licentious compared with the insensible man but insensible compared with the licentious; and the liberal man appears extravagant compared with the stingy man but stingy compared with the spendthrift. The result is that the extremes each denounce the mean as belonging to the other extreme; the coward calls the brave man foolhardy, and the foolhardy man calls him cowardly; and so on in other cases.

But while there is mutual opposition between the extremes and the mean, there is greater opposition between the two extremes than between extreme and the mean; for they are further removed from each other than from the mean, as the great is further from the small and the small from the great than either from the equal. Again, while some extremes show some likeness to the mean, as foolhardiness to courage and extravagance to liberality, there is the greatest possible dissimilarity between extremes. But things furthest removed from each other are called opposites; hence the further things are removed, the greater is the opposition between them.

In some cases it is deficiency and in others excess which is more opposed to the mean. Thus it is not foolhardiness, an excess, but cowardice, a deficiency, which is more opposed to courage, nor is it insensibility, a deficiency, but licentiousness, an excess, which is more opposed to temperance. There are two reasons why this should be so. One lies in the nature of the matter itself; for when one of two extremes is nearer and more like the mean, it is not this extreme but its opposite that we chiefly contrast with the mean. For instance, as foolhardiness seems more like and nearer to courage than cowardice, it is cowardice that we chiefly contrast with courage; for things further removed from the mean seem to be more opposite to it. This reason lies in the nature of the matter itself; there is a second which lies in our own nature. The things to which we ourselves are naturally more inclined we think more opposed to the mean. Thus we are ourselves naturally more inclined to pleasures than to their opposites, and are more prone therefore to self-indulgence than to moderation. Accordingly we speak of those things in which we are more likely to run to great lengths as more opposed to the mean. Hence licentiousness, which is an excess, seems more opposed to temperance than insensibility.

Chapter 9. We have now sufficiently shown that moral virtue is a mean, and in what sense it is so; that it is a mean as lying between two vices, a vice of excess on the one side and a vice of deficiency on the other, and as aiming at the mean in emotion and action.

That is why it is so hard to be good; for it is always hard to find
the mean in anything; it is not everyone but only a man of science
who can find the mean or center of a circle. So too anybody can
get angry—that is easy—and anybody can give or spend money,
but to give it to the right person, to give the right amount of it, at
the right time, for the right cause and in the right way, this is not
what anybody can do, nor is it easy. That is why goodness is rare
and praise worthy and noble. One then who aims at a mean must
begin by departing from the extreme that is more contrary to the
mean; he must act in the spirit of Calypso's advice,

"Far from this spray and swell hold thou thy ship,"

for of the two extremes one is more wrong than the other. As it is
difficult to hit the mean exactly, we should take the second best
course, as the saying is, and choose the lesser of two evils. This
we shall best do in the way described, that is, steering clear of the
evil which is further from the mean. We must also note the weaknesses to which we are ourselves particularly prone, since different natures tend in different ways; and we may ascertain what our
tendency is by observing our feelings of pleasure and pain. Then
we must drag ourselves away towards the opposite extreme; for by
pulling ourselves as far as possible from what is wrong we shall
arrive at the mean, as we do when we pull a crooked stick straight.

In all cases we must especially be on our guard against the pleasant, or pleasure, for we are not impartial judges of pleasure. Hence
our attitude towards pleasure must be like that of the elders of the
people in the *Iliad* towards Helen, and we must constantly apply
the words they use; for if we dismiss pleasure as they dismissed
Helen, we shall be less likely to go wrong. By action of this kind,
to put it summarily, we shall best succeed in hitting the mean.

Undoubtedly this is a difficult task, especially in individual cases.
It is not easy to determine the right manner, objects, occasion and
duration of anger. Sometimes we praise people who are deficient in
anger, and call them gentle, and at other times we praise people who
exhibit a fierce temper as high spirited. It is not however a man who
deviates a little from goodness, but one who deviates a great deal,
whether on the side of excess or of deficiency, that is blamed; for he
is sure to call attention to himself. It is not easy to decide in theory
how far and to what extent a man may go before he becomes blameworthy, but neither is it easy to define in theory anything else in the

region of the senses; such things depend on circumstances, and our judgment of them depends on our perception.

So much then is plain, that the mean is everywhere praiseworthy, but that we ought to aim at one time towards an excess and at another towards a deficiency; for thus we shall most easily hit the mean, or in other words reach excellence.

For Further Reflection

1. Is Aristotle's concept of happiness clear? Is it a subjective or objective notion? That is, is it subjective, in the mind of the beholder, so one is just as happy as one feels oneself to be; or is it objective, defined by a state of being, and having certain characteristics regardless of how one feels? According to Aristotle, could a criminal be happy?

2. Is Aristotle's ethics sufficiently action guiding? Does it help us make decisions? If I ask what should I do in situation *X*, Aristotle would seem to say, "Do what the virtuous person would do." But if I ask how I am to recognize the virtuous person, he would seem to say, "He is one who acts justly." Is there something circular about this reasoning? Does virtue ethics need supplementation from other ethical systems, or can it solve this problem?

Virtue and the Moral Life

BERNARD MAYO

Bernard Mayo is a British philosopher and the author of *Ethics and the Moral Life,* from which this selection is taken. Mayo contrasts the deontologists' and teleologists' ethics of "doing" with the ethics of "being" or character demonstrated by the saints and heroes. He contends that the saints and

From *Ethics and the Moral Life.* Copyright © 1958 by Macmillan. Reprinted by permission of Palgrave Macmillan.

heroes show us that a living example, not rigid rules, is important in ethics. We learn more about ethics by looking at the lives of such people than by learning a set of principles.

The philosophy of moral principles, which is characteristic of Kant and the post-Kantian era, is something of which hardly a trace exists in Plato. . . . Plato says nothing about rules or principles or laws, except when he is talking politics. Instead he talks about virtues and vices, and about certain types of human character. The key word in Platonic ethics is Virtue; the key word in Kantian ethics is Duty. And modern ethics is a set of footnotes, not to Plato, but to Kant. . . .

Attention to the novelists can be a welcome correction to a tendency of philosophical ethics of the last generation or two to lose contact with the ordinary life of man which is just what the novelists, in their own way, are concerned with. Of course there are writers who can be called in to illustrate problems about Duty (Graham Greene is a good example). But there are more who perhaps never mention the words duty, obligation, or principle. Yet they are all concerned—Jane Austen, for instance, entirely and absolutely—with the moral qualities or defects of their heroes and heroines and other characters. This points to a radical one-sidedness in the philosophers' account of morality in terms of principles: it takes little or no account of qualities, of what people *are*. It is just here that the old-fashioned word Virtue used to have a place; and it is just here that the work of Plato and Aristotle can be instructive. Justice, for Plato, though it is closely connected with acting according to law, does not *mean* acting according to law: it is a quality of character, and a just action is one such as a just man would do. Telling the truth, for Aristotle, is not, as it was for Kant, fulfilling an obligation; again it is a quality of character, or, rather, a whole range of qualities of character, some of which may actually be defects, such as tactlessness, boastfulness, and so on—a point which can be brought out, in terms of principles, only with the greatest complexity and artificiality, but quite simply and naturally in terms of character.

If we wish to enquire about Aristotle's moral views, it is no use looking for a set of principles. Of course we can find *some* principles to which he must have subscribed—for instance, that one ought not to commit adultery. But what we find much more prominently is a set of character-traits, a list of certain types of person—the courageous man, the niggardly man, the boaster, the lavish spender, and so on. The basic moral question, for Aristotle, is not, What shall I do? but, What shall I be?

These contrasts between doing and being, negative and positive, and modern as against Greek morality were noted by John Stuart Mill; I quote from the *Essay on Liberty:*

> Christian morality (so-called) has all the characters of a reaction; it is, in great part, a protest against Paganism. Its ideal is negative rather than positive, passive rather than active; Innocence rather than Noble-ness; Abstinence from Evil, rather than energetic Pursuit of the Good; in its precepts (as has been well said) "Thou shalt not" predominates unduly over "Thou shalt . . ." Whatever exists of magnanimity, high-mindedness, personal dignity, even the sense of honour, is derived from the purely human, not the religious part of our education, and never could have grown out of a standard of ethics in which the only worth, professedly recognized, is that of obedience.

Of course, there are connections between being and doing. It is obvious that a man cannot just *be;* he can only be what he is by doing what he does; his moral qualities are ascribed to him because of his actions, which are said to manifest those qualities. But the point is that an ethics of Being must include this obvious fact, that Being involves Doing; whereas an ethics of Doing, such as I have been examining, may easily overlook it. As I have suggested, a morality of principles is concerned only with what people do or fail to do, since that is what rules are for. And as far as this sort of ethics goes, people might well have no moral qualities at all except the possession of principles and the will (and capacity) to act accordingly.

When we speak of a moral quality such as courage, and say that a certain action was courageous, we are not merely saying something about the action. We are referring, not so much to what is done, as to the kind of person by whom we take it to have been done. We connect, by means of imputed motives and intentions, with the char-acter of the agent as courageous. This explains, incidentally, why both Kantians and Utilitarians encounter, in their different ways, such difficulties in dealing with motives, which their principles, on the face of it, have no room for. A Utilitarian, for example, can only praise a courageous action in some such way as this: the action is of a sort such as a person of courage is likely to perform, and courage is a quality of character the cultivation of which is likely to increase rather than diminish the sum total of human happiness. But Aristotelians have no need of such circumlocution. For them a courageous action just is one which proceeds from and manifests a certain type of character, and is praised because such a character trait is good, or better than others, or is a virtue. An evaluative criterion is sufficient: there is no need to look for an imperative criterion as well, or rather instead, according to which it is not the character which is good, but the cultivation of the character which is right. . . .

No doubt the fundamental moral question is just "What ought I to do?" And according to the philosophy of moral principles, the answer (which must be an imperative "Do this") must be derived from a conjunction of premises consisting (in the simplest case) firstly of a rule, or universal imperative, enjoining (or forbidding) all actions of a certain type in situations of a certain type, and, secondly, a statement to the effect that this is a situation of that type, falling under that rule. In practice the emphasis may be on supplying only one of these premises, the other being assumed or taken for granted: one may answer the question "What ought I to do?" either by quoting a rule which I am to adopt, or by showing that my case is legislated for by a rule which I do adopt. . . . [I]f I am in doubt whether to tell the truth about his condition to a dying man, my doubt may be resolved by showing that the case comes under a rule about the avoidance of unnecessary suffering, which I am assumed to accept. But if the case is without precedent in my moral career, my problem may be soluble only by adopting a new principle about what I am to do now and in the future about cases of this kind.

This second possibility offers a connection with moral ideas. Suppose my perplexity is not merely an unprecedented situation which I could cope with by adopting a new rule. Suppose the new rule is thoroughly inconsistent with my existing moral code. This may happen, for instance, if the moral code is one to which I only pay lip-service, if . . . its authority is not yet internalised, or if it has ceased to be so; it is ready for rejection, but its final rejection awaits a moral crisis such as we are assuming to occur. What I now need is not a rule for deciding how to act in this situation and others of its kind. I need a whole set of rules, a complete morality, new principles to live by.

Now, according to the philosophy of moral character, there is another way of answering the fundamental question "What ought I to do?" Instead of quoting a rule, we quote a quality of character, a virtue: we say "Be brave," or "Be patient" or "Be lenient." We may even say "Be a man": if I am in doubt, say, whether to take a risk, and someone says "Be a man," meaning a morally sound man, in this case a man of sufficient courage. (Compare the very different ideal invoked in "Be a gentleman." I shall not discuss whether this is a *moral* ideal.) Here, too, we have the extreme cases, where a man's moral perplexity extends not merely to a particular situation but to his whole way of living. And now the question "What ought I to do?" turns into the question "What ought I to be?"—as, indeed, it was treated in the first place. ("Be brave.") It is answered, not by quoting a rule or a set of rules, but by describing a quality of character or a type of person. And here the ethics of character gains a practical simplicity which offsets the greater logical simplicity of the ethics of principles. We do not have to give a list of characteristics or virtues, as we might list a set of principles. We can give a unity to our answer.

Of course we can in theory give a unity to our principles: this is implied by speaking of a *set* of principles. But if such a set is to be a system and not merely aggregate, the unity we are looking for is a logical one, namely the possibility that some principles are deductible from others, and ultimately from one. But the attempt to construct a deductive moral system is notoriously difficult, and in any case ill-founded. Why should we expect that all rules of conduct should be ultimately reducible to a few?

SAINTS AND HEROES

But when we are asked "What shall I be?" we can readily give a unity to our answer, though not a logical unity. It is the unity of character. A person's character is not merely a list of dispositions; it has the organic unity of something that is more than the sum of its parts. And we can say, in answer to our morally perplexed questioner, not only "Be this" and "Be that," but also "Be like So-and-So"—where So-and-So is either an ideal type of character, or else an actual person taken as representative of the ideal, as exemplar. Examples of the first are Plato's "just man" in the Republic; Aristotle's man of practical wisdom, in the *Nicomachean Ethics;* Augustine's citizen of the City of God; the good Communist; the American way of life (which is a collective expression for a type of character). Examples of the second kind, the exemplar, are Socrates, Christ, Buddha, St. Francis, the heroes of epic writers and of novelists. Indeed the idea of the Hero, as well as the idea of the Saint, are very much the expression of this attitude to morality. Heroes and saints are not merely people who did things. They are people whom we are expected, and expect ourselves, to imitate. And imitating them means not merely doing what they did; it means being like them. Their status is not in the least like that of legislators whose laws we admire; for the character of a legislator is irrelevant to our judgment about his legislation. The heroes and saints did not merely give us principles to live by (though some of them did that as well): they gave us examples to follow.

Kant, as we should expect, emphatically rejects this attitude as "fatal to morality." According to him, examples serve only to render *visible* an instance of the moral principle, and thereby to demonstrate its practical feasibility. But every exemplar, such as Christ himself, must be judged by the independent criterion of the moral law, before we are entitled to recognize him as worthy of imitation. I am not suggesting that the subordination of exemplars to principles is incorrect, but that it is one-sided and fails to do justice to a large area of moral experience.

Imitation can be more or less successful. And this suggests another defect of the ethics of principles. It has no room for ideals, except the ideal of a perfect set of principles (which, as a matter of fact, is intelligible only in terms of an ideal character or way of life), and the ideal of perfect conscientiousness (which is itself a character-trait). This results, of course, from the "black-or-white" nature of moral verdicts based on rules. There are degrees by which we approach or recede from the attainment of a certain quality or virtue; if there were not, the word "ideal" would have no meaning. Heroes and saints are not people whom we try to be *just* like, since we know that is impossible. It is precisely because it is impossible for ordinary human beings to achieve the same qualities as the saints, and in the same degree, that we do set them apart from the rest of humanity. It is enough if we try to be a little like them. . . .

For Further Reflection

1. How does Mayo contrast rule-governed ethics with virtue ethics? Is this a real difference or an exaggeration? That is, deontologists and utilitarians also promote the virtues, though perhaps

for different reasons than the virtue ethicist. Exactly what are those differences?

2. What are the advantages and what are the weaknesses of virtue ethics?

3. Mayo argues that Kant would reject the insights of virtue ethics, since for him morality has nothing to do with emotions or examples, but with reason. But could Kant still have a significant role for the virtues?

4. What, according to Mayo, is the value of having saints and heroes?

5. Some critics contend that virtue ethics is relativistic—since what is considered virtuous differs from culture to culture. Do you agree? How would a virtue ethicist respond to this charge?

Saints and Heroes

J. O. URMSON

Aristotelian scholar J. O. Urmson was a professor of philosophy at Stanford University and a fellow and tutor in philosophy at Corpus Christi College, Oxford. In this selection, he contends that philosophers have too often ignored an important class of moral actions—*supererogatory* actions, those that are "above and beyond" our duty, such as the conduct of saintly and heroic persons.

Moral philosophers tend to discriminate, explicitly or implicitly, three types of action from the point of view of moral worth. First, they recognize actions that are a duty, or obligatory, or that we ought to perform, treating these terms as approximately synonymous; second, they recognize actions that are right in so far as they

From "Saints and Heroes" by J. O. Urmson in *Essays in Moral Philosophy*, © 1958, University of Washington Press. Reprinted by permission of the publisher.

are permissible from a moral standpoint and not ruled out by moral considerations, but that are not morally required of us, like the lead of this or that card at bridge; third, they recognize actions that are wrong, that we ought not to do. Some moral philosophers, indeed, could hardly discriminate even these three types of action consistently with the rest of their philosophy; Moore, for example, could hardly recognize a class of morally indifferent actions, permissible but not enjoined, since it is to be presumed that good or ill of some sort will result from the most trivial of our actions. But most moral philosophers recognize these three types of action and attempt to provide a moral theory that will make intelligible such a threefold classification.

To my mind this threefold classification, or any classification that is merely a variation on or elaboration of it, is totally inadequate to the facts of morality; any moral theory that leaves room only for such a classification will in consequence also be inadequate. My main task in this paper will be to show the inadequacy of such a classification by drawing attention to two of the types of action that most conspicuously lie outside such a classification; I shall go on to hazard some views on what sort of theory will most easily cope with the facts to which I draw attention, but the facts are here the primary interest.

We sometimes call a person a saint, or an action saintly, using the word "saintly" in a purely moral sense with no religious implications; also we sometimes call a person a hero or an action heroic. It is too clear to need argument that the words "saint" and "hero" are at least normally used in such a way as to be favorably evaluative; it would be impossible to claim that this evaluation is always moral, for clearly we sometimes call a person a saint when evaluating him religiously rather than morally and may call a person the hero of a game or athletic contest in which no moral qualities were displayed, but I shall take it that no formal argument is necessary to show that at least sometimes we use both words for moral evaluation.

If "hero" and "saint" can be words of moral evaluation, we may proceed to the attempt to make explicit the criteria that we implicitly employ for their use in moral contexts. It appears that we so use them in more than one type of situation, and that there is a close parallel between the ways in which the two terms "hero" and "saint" are used; we shall here notice three types of situation in which they are used which seem to be sufficiently different to merit distinction. As the first two types of situation to be noticed are ones that can be readily subsumed under the threefold classification mentioned above, it will be sufficient here to note them and pass on to the third type of situation, which, since it cannot be subsumed under that classification, is for the purposes of this paper the most interesting.

A person may be called a saint (1) if he does his duty regularly in contexts in which inclination, desire, or self-interest would lead most people not to do it, and does so as a result of exercising abnormal self-control; parallel to this a person may be called a hero (1) if he does his duty in contexts in which terror, fear, or a drive to self-preservation would lead most men not to do it, and does so by exercising abnormal self-control. Similarly for actions: an action may be called saintly (1) if it is a case of duty done by virtue of self-control in a context in which most men would be led astray by inclination or self-interest, and an action may be called heroic (1) if it is a case of duty done by virtue of self-control in a context in which most men would be led astray by fear or a drive for self-preservation. The only difference between the saintly and the heroic in this sort of situation is that the one involves resistance to desire and self-interest; the other, resistance to fear and self-preservation. This is quite a clear difference, though there may be marginal cases, or cases in which motives were mixed, in which it would be equally appropriate to call an action indifferently saintly or heroic. It is easy to give examples of both the heroic and the saintly as distinguished above: the unmarried daughter does the saintly deed of staying at home to tend her ailing and widowed father; the terrified doctor heroically stays by his patients in a plague-ridden city.

A person may be called a saint (2) if he does his duty in contexts in which inclination or self-interest would lead most men not to do it, not, as in the previous paragraph, by abnormal self-control, but without effort; parallel to this a person may be called a hero (2) if he does his duty in contexts in which fear would lead most men not to do so, and does so without effort. The corresponding accounts of a saintly (2) or heroic (2) action can easily be derived. Here we have the conspicuously virtuous deed, in the Aristotelian sense, as opposed to the conspicuously self-controlled, encratic deed of the previous paragraph. People thus purged of temptation or disciplined against fear may be rare, but Aristotle thought there could be such; there is a tendency today to think of such people as merely lucky or unimaginative, but Aristotle thought more highly of them than of people who need to exercise self-control.

It is clear that, in the two types of situation so far considered, we are dealing with actions that fall under the concept of duty. Roughly, we are calling a person saintly or heroic because he does his duty in such difficult contexts that most men would fail in them. Since for the purposes of this paper I am merely conceding that we do use the term "saintly" and "heroic" in these ways, it is unnecessary here to spend time arguing that we do so use them or in illustrating such uses. So used, the threefold classification of actions whose adequacy I wish to deny can clearly embrace them. I shall therefore pass immediately to a third use of the terms "heroic" and "saintly" which I am not merely willing to concede but obliged to establish.

I contend, then, that we may also call a person a saint (3) if he does actions that are far beyond the limits of his duty, whether by control of contrary inclination and interest or without effort; parallel to this we may call a person a hero (3) if he does actions that are far beyond the bounds of his duty, whether by control of natural fear or without effort. Such actions are saintly (3) or heroic (3). Here, as it seems to me, we have the hero or saint, heroic or saintly deed, par excellence; until now we have been considering but minor saints and heroes. We have considered the, certainly, heroic action of the doctor who does his duty by sticking to his patients in a plague-stricken city; we have now to consider the case of the doctor who, no differently situated from countless other doctors in other places, volunteers to join the depleted medical forces in that city. Previously we were considering the soldier who heroically does his duty in the face of such dangers as would cause most to shirk—the sort of man who is rightly awarded the Military Medal in the British Army; we have now to consider the case of the soldier who does more than his superior officers would ever ask him to do—the man to whom, often posthumously, the Victoria Cross is awarded. Similarly, we have to turn from saintly self-discipline in the way of duty to the dedicated, self-effacing life in the service of others which is not even contemplated by the majority of upright, kind, and honest men, let alone expected of them.

Let us be clear that we are not now considering cases of natural affection, such as the sacrifice made by a mother for her child; such cases may be said with some justice not to fall under the concept of morality but to be admirable in some different way. Such cases as are here under consideration may be taken to be as little bound up with such emotions as affection as any moral action may be. We may consider an example of what is meant by "heroism" (3) in more detail to bring this out.

We may imagine a squad of soldiers to be practicing the throwing of live hand grenades; a grenade slips from the hand of one of them and rolls on the ground near the squad; one of them sacrifices his life by throwing himself on the grenade and protecting his comrades with his own body. It is quite unreasonable to suppose that such a man must be impelled by the sort of emotion that he might be impelled by if his best friend were in the squad; he might only just have joined the squad; it is clearly an action having moral status. But if the soldier had not thrown himself on the grenade would he have failed in his duty? Though clearly he is superior in some way to his comrades, can we possibly say that they failed in their duty by not trying to be the one who sacrificed himself? If he had not done so, could anyone have said to him, "You ought to have thrown yourself on that grenade"? Could a superior have decently ordered him to do it? The answer to all these questions is plainly negative. We clearly have here a case of a moral action, a heroic action, which cannot be subsumed under the classification whose inadequacy we are exposing.

But someone may not be happy with this conclusion, and for more respectable reasons than a desire to save the traditional doctrine. He may reason as follows: in so far as that soldier had time to feel or think at all, he presumably felt that he ought to do that deed; he considered it the proper thing to do; he, if no one else, might have reproached himself for failing to do his duty if he had shirked the deed. So, it may be argued, if an act presents itself to us in the way this act may be supposed to have presented itself to this soldier, then it is our duty to do it; we have no option. This objection to my thesis clearly has some substance, but it involves a misconception of what is at issue. I have no desire to present the act of heroism as one that is naturally regarded as optional by the hero, as something he might or might not do; I concede that he might regard himself as being obliged to act as he does. But if he were to survive the action only a modesty so excessive as to appear false could make him say, "I only did my duty," for we know, and he knows, that he has done more than duty requires. Further, though he might say to himself that so to act was a duty, he could not say so even beforehand to anyone else, and no one else could ever say it. Subjectively, we may say, at the time of action, the deed presented itself as a duty, but it was not a duty.

Another illustration, this time of saintliness, may help. It is recorded by Bonaventura that after Francis of Assisi had finished preaching to the birds on a celebrated occasion his companions gathered around him to praise and admire. But Francis himself was not a bit pleased; he was full of self-reproach that he had hitherto failed in what he now considered to be his duty to preach to the feathered world. There is indeed no degree of saintliness that a suitable person may not come to consider it to be his duty to achieve. Yet there is a world of difference between this failure to have preached hitherto to the birds and a case of straightforward breach of duty, however venial. First, Francis could without absurdity reproach himself for his failure to do his duty, but it would be quite ridiculous for anyone else to do so, as one could have done if he had failed to keep his vows, for example. Second, it is not recorded that Francis ever reproached anyone else for failure to preach to the birds as a breach of duty. He could claim this action for himself as a duty and could perhaps have exhorted others to preach to the birds; but there could be no question of reproaches for not so acting.

To sum up on this point, then, it seems clear that there is no action, however quixotic, heroic, or saintly, which the agent may not regard himself as obliged to perform, as much as he may feel himself obliged to tell the truth and to keep his promises. Such actions do not present themselves as optional to the agent when he is deliberating; but, since he alone can call such an action of his a duty, and then only from the deliberative viewpoint, only for himself and not for others, and not even for himself as a piece of objective reporting, and since nobody else can call on him to perform such an act as they can call on him to tell the truth and to keep his promises, there is here a most important difference from the rock-bottom duties which are duties for all and from every point of view, and to which anyone may draw attention. Thus we need not deny the points made by our imaginary objector in order to substantiate the point that some acts of heroism and saintliness cannot be adequately subsumed under the concept of duty.

Let us then take it as established that we have to deal in ethics not with a simple trichotomy of duties, permissible actions, and wrong actions, or any substantially similar conceptual scheme, but with something more complicated. We have to add at least the complication of actions that are certainly of moral worth but that fall outside the notion of a duty and seem to go beyond it, actions worthy of being called heroic or saintly. It should indeed be noted that heroic and saintly actions are not the sole, but merely conspicuous, cases of actions that exceed the basic demands of duty; there can be cases of disinterested kindness and generosity, for example, that are clearly more than basic duty requires and yet hardly ask for the high titles, "saintly" and "heroic." Indeed, every case of "going the second mile" is a case in point, for it cannot be one's duty to go the second mile in the same basic sense as it is to go the first—otherwise it could be argued first that it is one's duty to go two miles and therefore that the spirit of the rule of the second mile requires that one go altogether four miles, and by repetition one could establish the need to go every time on an infinite journey. It is possible to go just beyond one's duty by being a little more generous, forbearing, helpful, or forgiving than fair dealing demands, or to go a very long way beyond the basic code of duties with the saint or the hero. When I here draw attention to the heroic and saintly deed, I do so merely in order to have conspicuous cases of a whole realm of actions that lie outside the trichotomy I have criticized and therefore, as I believe, outside the purview of most ethical theories.

Before considering the implications for ethics of the facts we have up to now been concerned to note, it might be of value to draw attention to a less exalted parallel to these facts. If we belong to a club there will be rules of the club, written or unwritten, calling upon us to fulfill certain basic requirements that are a condition of membership, and that may be said to be the duties of membership. It may perhaps be such a basic requirement that we pay a subscription. It will probably be indifferent whether we pay this subscription by check or in cash—both procedures will be "right"— and almost certainly it will be quite indifferent what sort of hat we wear at the meetings. Here, then, we have conformity to rule which is the analogue of doing one's duty, breach of rule which is the analogue of wrongdoing, and a host of indifferent actions, in accordance with the traditional trichotomy. But among the rule-abiding members of such a club what differences there can be! It is very likely that there will be one, or perhaps two or three, to whose devotion and loyal service the success of the club is due far more than to the activities of all the other members together; these are the saints and the heroes of the clubs, who do more for them by

far than any member could possibly be asked to do, whose many
services could not possibly be demanded in the rules. Behind them
come a motley selection, varying from the keen to the lukewarm,
whose contributions vary in value and descend sometimes to almost
nothing beyond what the rules demand. The moral contribution of
people to society can vary in value in the same way.

So much, then, for the simple facts to which I have wished to
draw attention. They are simple facts and, unless I have misrepre-
sented them, they are facts of which we are all, in a way, perfectly
well aware. It would be absurd to suggest that moral philosophers
have hitherto been unaware of the existence of saints and heroes
and have never even alluded to them in their works. But it does
seem that these facts have been neglected in their general, systematic accounts of morality. It is indeed easy to see that on some
of the best-known theories there is no room for such facts. If for
Moore, and for most utilitarians, any action is a duty that will produce the greatest possible good in the circumstances, for them the
most heroic self-sacrifice or saintly self-forgetfulness will be duties
on all fours with truth-telling and promise-keeping. For Kant,
beyond the counsels of prudence and the rules of skill, there is
only the categorical imperative of duty, and every duty is equally
and utterly binding on all men; it is true that he recognizes the limiting case of the holy will, but the holy will is not a will that goes
beyond duty but a will that is beyond morality through being incapable of acting except in accordance with the imperative. The nearest to an equivalent to a holy will in the cases we have been noting is the saintly will in the second sense we distinguished—the
will that effortlessly does its duty when most would fail—but this
is not a true parallel and in any case does not fall within the class
of moral actions that go beyond duty to which our attention is primarily given. It is also true that Kant recognized virtues and talents
as having conditional value, but not moral value, whereas the acts
of heroism and saintliness we have considered have full moral
worth, and their value is as unconditional as anyone could wish.
Without committing ourselves to a scholarly examination of Kant's
ethical works, it is surely evident that Kant could not consistently
do justice to the facts before us. Intuitionism seems to me so obscurantist that I should not wish to prophesy what an intuitionist might
feel himself entitled to say; but those intuitionists with whose works
I am acquainted found their theories on an intuition of the fitting,
the prima facie duty or the claim; the act that has this character to

the highest degree at any time is a duty. While they recognize greater and lesser, stronger and weaker, claims, this is only in order to be able to deal with the problem of the conflict of duties; they assign no place to the act that, while not a duty, is of high moral importance.

Simple utilitarianism, Kantianism, and intuitionism, then, have no obvious theoretical niche for the saint and the hero. It is possible, no doubt, to revise these theories to accommodate the facts, but until so modified successfully they must surely be treated as unacceptable, and the modifications required might well detract from their plausibility. The intuitionists, for example, might lay claim to the intuition of a nonnatural characteristic of saintliness, of heroism, of decency, of sportingness, and so on, but this would give to their theory still more the appearance of utilizing the advantages of theft over honest toil.

Thus as moral theorists we need to discover some theory that will allow for both absolute duties, which, in Mill's phrase, can be exacted from a man like a debt, to omit which is to do wrong and to deserve censure, and which may be embodied in formal rules or principles, and also for a range of actions which are of moral value and which an agent may feel called upon to perform, but which cannot be demanded and whose omission cannot be called wrongdoing. Traditional moral theories, I have suggested, fail to do this. It would be well beyond the scope of this paper, and probably beyond my capacity, to produce here and now a full moral theory designed to accommodate all these facts, including the facts of saintliness and heroism. But I do think that of all traditional theories utilitarianism can be most easily modified to accommodate the facts, and would like before ending this paper to bring forward some considerations tending to support this point of view.

Moore went to great pains to determine exactly the nature of the intrinsically good, and Mill to discover the *summum bonum,* Moore's aim being to explain thereby directly the rightness and wrongness of particular actions and Mill's to justify a set of moral principles in the light of which the rightness or wrongness of particular actions can be decided. But, though there can be very tricky problems of duty, they do not naturally present themselves as problems whose solution depends upon an exact determination of an ultimate end; while the moral principles that come most readily to mind—truth-telling; promise-keeping; abstinence from murder, theft, and violence; and

the like—make a nice discrimination of the supreme good seem irrelevant. We do not need to debate whether it is Moore's string of intrinsic goods or Mill's happiness that is achieved by conformity to such
principles; it is enough to see that without them social life would be
impossible and any life would indeed be solitary, poor, nasty, brutish,
and short. Even self-interest (which some have seen as the sole foundation of morality) is sufficient ground to render it wise to preach, if
not to practice, such principles. Such considerations as these, which
are not novel, have led some utilitarians to treat avoidance of the
summum malum rather than the achievement of the *summum
bonum* as the foundation of morality. Yet to others this has seemed,
with some justification, to assign to morality too ignoble a place.

But the facts we have been considering earlier in this paper are
surely relevant at this point. It is absurd to ask just what ideal is
being served by abstinence from murder; but on the other hand
nobody could see in acts of heroism such as we have been considering a mere avoidance of antisocial behavior. Here we have
something more gracious, actions that need to be inspired by a
positive ideal. If duty can, as Mill said, be exacted from persons as
a debt, it is because duty is a minimum requirement for living
together; the positive contribution of actions that go beyond duty
could not be so exacted.

It may, however, be objected that this is a glorification of the
higher flights of morality at the expense of duty, toward which an
unduly cynical attitude is being taken. In so far as the suggestion
is that we are forgetting how hard the way of duty may be and
that doing one's duty can at times deserve to be called heroic and
saintly, the answer is that we have mentioned this and acknowledge it; it is not forgotten but irrelevant to the point at issue, which
is the place of duty in a moral classification of actions, not the problem of the worth of moral agents. But I may be taken to be acquiescing in a low and circumscribed view of duty which I may be
advised to enlarge. We should, it may be said, hitch our wagons
to the stars and not be content to say: you must do this and that
as duties, and it would be very nice if you were to do these other
things but we do not expect them of you. Is it perhaps only an
imperfect conception of duty which finds it not to comprise the
whole of morality? I want to examine this difficulty quite frankly,
and to explain why I think that we properly recognize morality that
goes beyond duty; for it seems to me incontestable that properly
or improperly we do so.

No intelligent person will claim infallibility for his moral views. But allowing for this one must claim that one's moral code is ideal so far as one can see; for to say, "I recognize moral code A but see clearly that moral code B is superior to it," is but a way of saying that one recognizes moral code B but is only prepared to live up to moral code A. In some sense, then, everybody must be prepared to justify his moral code as ideal; but some philosophers have misunderstood this sense. Many philosophers have thought it necessary, if they were to defend their moral code as ideal, to try to show that it had a superhuman, a priori validity. Kant, for example, tried to show that the moral principles he accepted were such as any rational being, whether man or angel, must inevitably accept; the reputedly empiricist Locke thought that it must be possible to work out a deductive justification of moral laws. In making such claims such philosophers have unintentionally done morality a disservice; for their failure to show that the moral code was ideal in the sense of being a rationally justifiable system independent of time, place, circumstance, and human nature has led many to conclude that there can be no justification of a moral code, that moral codes are a matter of taste or convention.

But morality, I take it, is something that should serve human needs, not something that incidentally sweeps man up with itself, and to show that a morality was ideal would be to show that it best served man—man as he is and as he can be expected to become, not man as he would be if he were perfectly rational or an incorporeal angel. Just as it would be fatuous to build our machines so that they would give the best results according to an abstract conception of mechanical principles, and is much more desirable to design them to withstand to some extent our ham-fistedness, ignorance, and carelessness, so our morality must be one that will work. In the only sense of "ideal" that is of importance in action, it is part of the ideal that a moral code should actually help to contribute to human well-being, and a moral code that would work only for angels (for whom it would in any case be unnecessary) would be a far from ideal moral code for human beings. There is, indeed, a place for ideals that are practically unworkable in human affairs, as there is a place for the blueprint of a machine that will never go into production; but it is not the place of such ideals to serve as a basic code of duties.

If, then, we are aiming at a moral code that will best serve human needs, a code that is ideal in the sense that a world in which such a code is acknowledged will be a better place than a world in which some other sort of moral code is acknowledged, it seems that there are ample grounds why our code should distinguish between basic rules, summarily set forth in simple rules and binding on all, and the higher flights of morality of which saintliness and heroism are outstanding examples. These grounds I shall enumerate at once.

1. It is important to give a special status of urgency, and to exert exceptional pressure, in those matters in which compliance with the demands of morality by all is indispensable. An army without men of heroic valor would be impoverished, but without general attention to the duties laid down in military law it would become a mere rabble. Similarly, while life in a world without its saints and heroes would be impoverished, it would only be poor and not necessarily brutish or short as when basic duties are neglected.

2. If we are to exact basic duties like debts, and censure failure, such duties must be, in ordinary circumstances, within the capacity of the ordinary man. It would be silly for us to say to ourselves, our children and our fellow men, "This and that you and everyone else must do," if the acts in question are such that manifestly but few could bring themselves to do them, though we may ourselves resolve to try to be of that few. To take a parallel from positive law, the prohibition laws asked too much of the American people and were consequently broken systematically; and as people got used to breaking the law a general lowering of respect for the law naturally followed; it no longer seemed that a law was something that everybody could be expected to obey. Similarly in Britain the gambling laws, some of which are utterly unpractical, have fallen into contempt as a body. So, if we were to represent the heroic act of sacrificing one's life for one's comrades as a basic duty, the effect would be to lower the degree of urgency and stringency that the notion of duty does in fact possess. The basic moral code must not be in part too far beyond the capacity of the ordinary men on ordinary occasions, or a general breakdown of compliance with the moral code would be an inevitable consequence; duty would seem to be something high and unattainable, and not for "the likes of us." Admirers of the Sermon on the Mount do not in practice, and could not, treat failure to turn the other cheek and to give one's cloak also as being on all fours with breaches of the Ten Commandments, however earnestly they themselves try to live a Christian life.

3. A moral code, if it is to be a code, must be formulable, and if it is to be a code to be observed it must be formulable in rules of manageable complexity. The ordinary man has to apply and interpret this code without recourse to a Supreme Court or House of Lords. But one can have such rules only in cases in which a type of action that is reasonably easy to recognize is almost invariably desirable or undesirable, as killing is almost invariably undesirable and promise-keeping almost invariably desirable. Where no definite rule of manageable complexity can be justified, we cannot work on that moral plane on which types of action can be enjoined or condemned as duty or crime. It has no doubt often been the case that a person who has gone off to distant parts to nurse lepers has thereby done a deed of great moral worth. But such an action is not merely too far beyond average human capacity to be regarded as a duty, as was insisted in (2) above; it would be quite ridiculous for everyone, however circumstanced, to be expected to go off and nurse lepers. But it would be absurd to try to formulate complicated rules to determine in just what circumstances such an action is a duty. This same point can readily be applied to such less spectacular matters as excusing legitimate debts or nursing sick neighbors.

4. It is part of the notion of a duty that we have a right to demand compliance from others even when we are interested parties. I may demand that you keep your promises to me, tell me the truth, and do me no violence, and I may reproach you if you transgress. But however admirable the tending of strangers in sickness may be it is not a basic duty, and we are not entitled to reproach those to whom we are strangers if they do not tend us in sickness; nor can I tell you, if you fail to give me a cigarette when I have run out, that you have failed in your duty to me, however much you may subsequently reproach yourself for your meanness if you do so fail. A line must be drawn between what we can expect and demand from others and what we can merely hope for and receive with gratitude when we get it; duty falls on one side of this line, and other acts with moral value on the other, and rightly so.

5. In the case of basic moral duties we act to some extent under constraint. We have no choice but to apply pressure on each other to conform in these fundamental matters; here moral principles are like public laws rather than like private ideals. But free choice of the better course of action is always preferable to action under pressure, even when the pressure is but moral. When possible, there-

fore, it is better that pressure should not be applied and that there should be encouragement and commendation for performance rather than outright demands and censure in the event of nonperformance. There are no doubt degrees in this matter. Some pressure may reasonably be brought to persuade a person to go some way beyond basic duty in the direction of kindliness and forbearance, to be not merely a just man but also not too hard a man. But, while there is nothing whatever objectionable in the idea of someone's being pressed to carry out such a basic duty as promise-keeping, there is something horrifying in the thought of pressure being brought on him to perform an act of heroism. Though the man might feel himself morally called upon to do the deed, it would be a moral outrage to apply pressure on him to do such a deed as sacrificing his life for others.

These five points make it clear why I do not think that the distinction of basic duty from other acts of moral worth, which I claim to detect in ordinary moral thought, is a sign of the inferiority of our everyday moral thinking to that of the general run of moral theorists. It in no way involves anyone in acquiescing in a second best. No doubt from the agent's point of view it is imperative that he should endeavor to live up to the highest ideals of behavior that he can think of, and if an action falls within the ideal it is for him irrelevant whether or not it is a duty or some more supererogatory act. But it simply does not follow that the distinction is in every way unimportant, for it is important that we should not demand ideal conduct from others in the way in which we must demand basic morality from them, or blame them equally for failures in all fields. It is not cynicism to make the minimum positive demands upon one's fellow men; but to characterize an act as a duty is so to demand it.

Thus we may regard the imperatives of duty as prohibiting behavior that is intolerable if men are to live together in society and demanding the minimum of cooperation toward the same end; that is why we have to treat compliance as compulsory and dereliction as liable to public censure. We do not need to ask with Bentham whether pushpin is as good as poetry, with Mill whether it is better to be Socrates dissatisfied or a fool satisfied, or with Moore whether a beautiful world with no one to see it would have intrinsic worth; what is and what is not tolerable in society depends on no such nice discrimination. Utilitarians, when attempting to justify the main rules of duty in terms of a *summum bonum,* have surely invoked many different types of utilitarian justification, ranging from the avoidance of the intolerable to the fulfillment of the last detail of a most rarefied ideal.

Thus I wish to suggest that utilitarianism can best accommodate the facts to which I have drawn attention; but I have not wished to support any particular view about the supreme good or the importance of pleasure. By utilitarianism I mean only a theory that moral justification of actions must be in terms of results. We can be content to say that duty is mainly concerned with the avoidance of intolerable results, while other forms of moral behavior have more positive aims.

To summarize, I have suggested that the trichotomy of duties, indifferent actions, and wrongdoing is inadequate. There are many kinds of action that involve going beyond duty proper, saintly and heroic actions being conspicuous examples of such kinds of action. It has been my main concern to note this point and to ask moral philosophers to theorize in a way that does not tacitly deny it, as most traditional theories have. But I have also been so rash as to suggest that we may look upon our duties as basic requirements to be universally demanded as providing the only tolerable basis of social life. The higher flights of morality can then be regarded as more positive contributions that go beyond what is universally to be exacted; but while not exacted publicly they are clearly equally pressing *in foro interno* on those who are not content merely to avoid the intolerable. Whether this should be called a version of utilitarianism, as I suggest, is a matter of small moment.

For Further Reflection

1. Urmson points out that traditionally philosophers have focused on three types of actions thought to have moral worth. What are they?

2. What is a supererogatory action?

3. Does utilitarianism or Kantian ethics accommodate the notion of supererogatory action? If not, why not?

4. Do you think that a moral theory that denies the significance of supererogatory actions is seriously flawed? Explain.

The Great Stone Face

NATHANIEL HAWTHORNE

Nathaniel Hawthorne (1804–1864) was born in Salem, Massachusetts, and educated at Bowdoin College. He is one of America's greatest novelists, best known for *The Scarlet Letter* (1850). In this less-known short story, Hawthorne deals with such themes as moral imagination, insight, and the virtues. The Great Stone Face who dominates the story may be based on the rock formation in the White Mountains of New Hampshire known as Franconia Notch. The people in the valley are waiting for a great person to appear, modeled on the Great Stone Face, who will lead them. The main character, Ernest, is powerfully influenced, even educated, by what he sees in that face.

One afternoon, when the sun was going down, a mother and her little boy sat at the door of their cottage, talking about the Great Stone Face. They had but to lift their eyes, and there it was plainly to be seen, though miles away, with the sunshine brightening all its features.

And what was the Great Stone Face?

Embosomed amongst a family of lofty mountains, there was a valley so spacious that it contained many thousand inhabitants. Some of these good people dwelt in log-huts, with the black forest all around them, on the steep and difficult hill-sides. Others had their homes in comfortable farm-houses, and cultivated the rich soil on the gentle slopes or level surfaces of the valley. Others, again, were congregated into populous villages, where some wild, highland rivulet, tumbling down from its birthplace in the upper mountain region, had been caught and tamed by human cunning, and compelled to turn the machinery of cotton-factories. The inhabitants of this valley, in short, were numerous, and of many modes of life. But all of them, grown people and children, had a kind of familiarity with the Great Stone Face, although some possessed the gift of distinguishing this grand natural phenomenon more perfectly than many of their neighbors.

Reprinted from the *Complete Works of Nathaniel Hawthorne* (Modern Library, 1937).

The Great Stone Face, then, was a work of Nature in her mood of majestic playfulness, formed on the perpendicular side of a mountain by some immense rocks, which had been thrown together in such a position as, when viewed at a proper distance, precisely to resemble the features of the human countenance. It seemed as if an enormous giant, or a Titan, had sculptured his own likeness on the precipice. There was the broad arch of the forehead, a hundred feet in height; the nose, with its long bridge; and the vast lips, which, if they could have spoken, would have rolled their thunder accents from one end of the valley to the other. True it is, that if the spectator approached too near, he lost the outline of the gigantic visage, and could discern only a heap of ponderous and gigantic rocks, piled in chaotic ruin one upon another. Retracing his steps, however, the wondrous features would again be seen; and the farther he withdrew from them, the more like a human face, with all its original divinity intact, did they appear; until, as it grew dim in the distance, with the clouds and glorified vapor of the mountains clustering about it, the Great Stone Face seemed positively to be alive.

It was a happy lot for children to grow up to manhood or womanhood with the Great Stone Face before their eyes, for all the features were noble, and the expression was at once grand and sweet, as if it were the glow of a vast, warm heart, that embraced all mankind in its affections, and had room for more. It was an education only to look at it. According to the belief of many people, the valley owed much of its fertility to this benign aspect that was continually beaming over it, illuminating the clouds, and infusing its tenderness into the sunshine.

As we began with saying, a mother and her little boy sat at their cottage-door, gazing at the Great Stone Face, and talking about it. The child's name was Ernest.

"Mother," said he, while the Titanic visage smiled on him, "I wish that it could speak, for it looks so very kindly that its voice must needs be pleasant. If I were to see a man with such a face. I should love him dearly."

"If an old prophecy should come to pass," answered his mother, "we may see a man, some time or other, with exactly such a face as that."

"What prophecy do you mean, dear mother?" eagerly inquired Ernest. "Pray tell me about it!"

So his mother told him a story that her own mother had told to

her, when she herself was younger than little Ernest; a story, not
of things that were past, but of what was yet to come; a story, nevertheless, so very old, that even the Indians, who formerly inhabited this valley, had heard it from their forefathers, to whom, as
they affirmed, it had been murmured by the mountain streams, and
whispered by the wind among the tree-tops. The purport was, that,
at some future day, a child should be born hereabouts, who was
destined to become the greatest and noblest personage of his time,
and whose countenance, in manhood, should bear an exact resemblance to the Great Stone Face. Not a few old-fashioned people,
and young ones likewise, in the ardor of their hopes, still cherished
an enduring faith in this old prophecy. But others, who had seen
more of the world, had watched and waited till they were weary,
and had beheld no man with such a face, nor any man that proved
to be much greater or nobler than his neighbors, concluded it to
be nothing but an idle tale. At all events, the great man of the
prophecy had not yet appeared.

"O mother, dear mother!" cried Ernest, clapping his hands above
his head, "I do hope that I shall live to see him!"

His mother was an affectionate and thoughtful woman, and felt
that it was wisest not to discourage the generous hopes of her little boy. So she only said to him, "Perhaps you may."

And Ernest never forgot the story that his mother told him. It was
always in his mind, whenever he looked upon the Great Stone Face.
He spent his childhood in the log-cottage where he was born, and
was dutiful to his mother, and helpful to her in many things, assisting her much with his little hands, and more with his loving heart.
In this manner, from a happy yet often pensive child, he grew up to
be a mild, quiet, unobtrusive boy, and sun-browned with labor in
the fields, but with more intelligence brightening his aspect than is
seen in many lads who have been taught at famous schools. Yet
Ernest had had no teacher, save only that the Great Stone Face
became one to him. When the toil of the day was over, he would
gaze at it for hours, until he began to imagine that those vast features
recognized him, and gave him a smile of kindness and encouragement, responsive to his own look of veneration. We must not take
upon us to affirm that this was a mistake, although the Face may have
looked no more kindly at Ernest than at all the world besides. But
the secret was that the boy's tender and confiding simplicity discerned what other people could not see; and thus the love, which
was meant for all, became his peculiar portion.

About this time there went a rumor throughout the valley, that the great man, foretold from ages long ago, who was to bear a resemblance to the Great Stone Face, had appeared at last. It seems that, many years before, a young man had migrated from the valley and settled at a distant seaport, where, after getting together a little money, he had set up as a shopkeeper. His name—but I could never learn whether it was his real one, or a nickname that had grown out of his habits and success in life—was Gathergold. Being shrewd and active, and endowed by Providence with that inscrutable faculty which develops itself in what the world calls luck, he became an exceedingly rich merchant, and owner of a whole fleet of bulky-bottomed ships. All the countries of the globe appeared to join hands for the mere purpose of adding heap after heap to the mountainous accumulation of this one man's wealth. The cold regions of the north, almost within the gloom and shadow of the Arctic Circle, sent him their tribute in the shape of furs; hot Africa sifted for him the golden sands of her rivers, and gathered up the ivory tusks of her great elephants out of the forests; the East came bringing him the rich shawls, and spices, and teas, and the effulgence of diamonds, and the gleaming purity of large pearls. The ocean, not to be behind-hand with the earth, yielded up her mighty whales, that Mr. Gathergold might sell their oil, and make a profit of it. Be the original commodity what it might, it was gold within his grasp. It might be said of him, as of Midas in the fable, that whatever he touched with his finger immediately glistened, and grew yellow, and was changed at once into sterling metal, or, which suited him still better, into piles of coin. And, when Mr. Gathergold had become so very rich that it would have taken him a hundred years only to count his wealth, he bethought himself of his native valley, and resolved to go back thither, and end his days where he was born. With this purpose in view, he sent a skilful architect to build him such a palace as should be fit for a man of his vast wealth to live in.

As I have said above, it had already been rumored in the valley that Mr. Gathergold had turned out to be the prophetic personage so long and vainly looked for, and that his visage was the perfect and undeniable similitude of the Great Stone Face. People were the more ready to believe that this must needs be the fact, when they beheld the splendid edifice that rose, as if by enchantment, on the site of his father's old weatherbeaten farm-house. The exterior was of marble, so dazzlingly white that it seemed as though the whole structure might melt away in the sunshine, like those humbler ones which Mr. Gathergold, in his young play-days, before his fingers were gifted with the touch of transmutation, had been accustomed to build of snow. It had a richly ornamented portico, supported by tall pillars, beneath which was a lofty door, studded with silver knobs, and made of a kind of variegated wood that had been brought from beyond the sea. The windows, from the floor to the ceiling of each stately apartment, were composed, respectively, of but one enormous pane of glass, so transparently pure that it was said to be a finer medium than even the vacant atmosphere. Hardly anybody had been permitted to see the interior of this palace; but it was reported, and with good semblance of truth, to be far more gorgeous than the outside, insomuch that whatever was iron or brass in other houses was silver or gold in this; and Mr. Gathergold's bedchamber, especially, made such a glittering appearance that no ordinary man would have been able to close his eyes there. But, on the other hand, Mr. Gathergold was now so inured to wealth, that perhaps he could not have closed his eyes unless where the gleam of it was certain to find its way beneath his eyelids.

In due time, the mansion was finished; next came the upholsterers, with magnificent furniture; then, a whole troop of black and white servants, the harbingers of Mr. Gathergold, who, in his own majestic person, was expected to arrive at sunset. Our friend Ernest, meanwhile, had been deeply stirred by the idea that the great man, the noble man, the man of prophecy, after so many ages of delay, was at length to be made manifest to his native valley. He knew, boy as he was, that there were a thousand ways in which Mr. Gathergold, with his vast wealth, might transform himself into an angel of beneficence, and assume a control over human affairs as wide and benignant as the smile of the Great Stone Face. Full of faith and hope, Ernest doubted not that what the people said was true, and that now he was to behold the living likeness of those wondrous features on the mountain-side. While the boy was still gazing up the valley, and fancying, as he always did, that the Great Stone Face returned his gaze and looked kindly at him, the rumbling of wheels was heard, approaching swiftly along the winding road.

"Here he comes!" cried a group of people who were assembled to witness the arrival. "Here comes the great Mr. Gathergold!"

A carriage, drawn by four horses, dashed round the turn of the road. Within it, thrust partly out of the window, appeared the physiognomy of the old man, with a skin as yellow as if his own Midas-hand had transmuted it. He had a low forehead, small, sharp eyes, puckered about with innumerable wrinkles, and very thin lips, which he made still thinner by pressing them forcibly together.

"The very image of the Great Stone Face!" shouted the people. "Sure enough, the old prophecy is true; and here we have the great man come, at last!"

And, what greatly perplexed Ernest, they seemed actually to believe that here was the likeness which they spoke of. By the roadside there chanced to be an old beggar-woman and two little beggar-children, stragglers from some far-off region, who, as the carriage rolled onward, held out their hands and lifted up their doleful voices, most piteously beseeching charity. A yellow claw—the very same that had clawed together so much wealth—poked itself out of the coach-window, and dropt some copper coins upon the ground; so that, though the great man's name seems to have been Gathergold, he might just as suitably have been nicknamed Scattercopper. Still, nevertheless, with an earnest shout, and evidently with as much good faith as ever, the people bellowed,

"He is the very image of the Great Stone Face!"

But Ernest turned sadly from the wrinkled shrewdness of that sordid visage, and gazed up the valley, where, amid a gathering mist, gilded by the last sunbeams, he could still distinguish those glorious features which had impressed themselves into his soul. Their aspect cheered him. What did the benign lips seem to say?

"He will come! Fear not, Ernest; the man will come!"

The years went on, and Ernest ceased to be a boy. He had grown to be a young man now. He attracted little notice from the other inhabitants of the valley; for they saw nothing remarkable in his way of life, save that, when the labor of the day was over, he still loved to go apart and gaze and meditate upon the Great Stone Face. According to their idea of the matter, it was a folly, indeed, but pardonable, inasmuch as Ernest was industrious, kind, and neighborly, and neglected no duty for the sake of indulging this idle habit. They knew not that the Great Stone Face had become a teacher to him, and that the sentiment which was expressed in it would enlarge the young man's heart, and fill it with wider and deeper sympathies than other hearts. They knew not that thence would come a better wisdom than could be learned from books, and a better life than could be moulded on the defaced example of other human lives. Neither did Ernest know that the thoughts and affections which came to him so naturally, in the fields and at the fireside, and wherever he communed with himself, were of a higher tone than those which all men shared with him. A simple soul—simple as when his mother first taught him the old prophecy—he beheld the marvellous features beaming adown the valley, and still wondered that their human counterpart was so long in making his appearance.

By this time poor Mr. Gathergold was dead and buried; and the oddest part of the matter was, that his wealth, which was the body and spirit of his existence, had disappeared before his death, leaving nothing of him but a living skeleton, covered over with a wrinkled yellow skin. Since the melting away of his gold, it had been very generally conceded that there was no such striking resemblance, after all, betwixt the ignoble features of the ruined merchant and that majestic face upon the mountain-side. So the people ceased to honor him during his lifetime, and quietly consigned him to forgetfulness after his decease. Once in a while, it is true, his memory was brought up in connection with the magnificent palace which he had built, and which had long ago been turned into a hotel for the accommodation of strangers, multitudes of whom came, every summer, to visit that famous natural curiosity, the Great Stone Face. Thus, Mr. Gathergold being discredited and thrown into the shade, the man of prophecy was yet to come.

It so happened that a native-born son of the valley, many years before, had enlisted as a soldier, and, after a great deal of hard fighting, had now become an illustrious commander. Whatever he may be called in history, he was known in camps and on the battle-field under the nickname of Old Blood-and-Thunder. This war-worn veteran being now infirm with age and wounds, and weary of the turmoil of a military life, and of the roll of the drum and the clangor of the trumpet, that had so long been ringing in his ears, had lately signified a purpose of returning to his native valley, hoping to find repose where he remembered to have left it. The inhabitants, his old neighbors and their grown-up children, were resolved to welcome the renowned warrior with a salute of cannon and a public dinner; and all the more enthusiastically, it being affirmed that now, at last, the likeness of the Great Stone Face had actually appeared. An aid-de-camp of Old Blood-and-Thunder, travelling through the valley, was said to have been struck with the resemblance. Moreover the schoolmates and early acquaintances of the general were ready to testify, on oath, that, to the best of their recollection, the aforesaid general had been exceedingly like the majestic image, even when a boy, only the idea had never occurred to them at that period. Great, therefore, was the excitement throughout the valley; and many people, who had never once thought of glancing at the Great Stone Face for years before, now spent their time in gazing at it, for the sake of knowing exactly how General Blood-and-Thunder looked.

On the day of the great festival, Ernest, with all the other people of the valley, left their work, and proceeded to the spot where the sylvan banquet was prepared. As he approached, the loud voice of the Rev. Dr. Battleblast was heard, beseeching a blessing on the good things set before them, and on the distinguished friend of peace in whose honor they were assembled. The tables were arranged in a cleared space of the woods, shut in by the surrounding trees, except where a vista opened eastward, and afforded a distant view of the Great Stone Face. Over the general's chair, which was a relic from the home of Washington, there was an arch of verdant boughs, with the laurel profusely intermixed, and surmounted by his country's banner, beneath which he had won his victories. Our friend Ernest raised himself on his tiptoes, in hopes to get a glimpse of the celebrated guest; but there was a mighty crowd about the tables anxious to hear the toasts and speeches, and to catch any word that might fall from the general in reply; and a volunteer company, doing duty as a guard, pricked ruthlessly with their bayonets at any particularly quiet person among the throng. So Ernest, being of an unobtrusive character, was thrust quite into the background, where he could see no more of Old Blood-and-Thunder's physiognomy than if it had been still blazing on the battle-field. To console himself, he turned towards the Great Stone Face, which, like a faithful and long-remembered friend, looked back and smiled upon him through the vista of the forest. Meantime, however, he could overhear the remarks of various individuals, who were comparing the features of the hero with the face on the distant mountain-side.

" 'Tis the same face, to a hair!" cried one man, cutting a caper for joy.

"Wonderfully like, that's a fact!" responded another.

"Like! why, I call it Old Blood-and-Thunder himself, in a monstrous looking-glass!" cried a third. "And why not? He's the greatest man of this or any other age, beyond a doubt."

And then all three of the speakers gave a great shout, which communicated electricity to the crowd, and called forth a roar from a thousand voices, that went reverberating for miles among the mountains, until you might have supposed that the Great Stone Face had poured its thunder-breath into the cry. All these comments, and this vast enthusiasm, served the more to interest our friend; nor did he think of questioning that now, at length, the mountain-visage had found its human counterpart. It is true, Ernest had imagined that this long-looked-for personage would appear in the character of a man of peace, uttering wisdom, and doing good, and making people happy. But, taking an habitual breadth of view, with all his simplicity, he contended that Providence should choose its own method of blessing mankind, and could conceive that this great end might be effected even by a warrior and a bloody sword, should inscrutable wisdom see fit to order matters so.

"The general! the general!" was now the cry. "Hush! silence! Old Blood-and-Thunder's going to make a speech."

Even so; for, the cloth being removed, the general's health had been drunk, amid shouts of applause, and he now stood upon his feet to thank the company. Ernest saw him. There he was, over the shoulders of the crowd, from the two glittering epaulets and embroidered collar upward, beneath the arch of green boughs with intertwined laurel, and the banner drooping as if to shade his brow! And there, too, visible in the same glance, through the vista of the forest, appeared the Great Stone Face! And was there, indeed, such a resemblance as the crowd had testified? Alas, Ernest could not recognize it! He beheld a war-worn and weather-beaten countenance, full of energy, and expressive of an iron will; but the gentle wisdom, the deep, broad, tender sympathies, were altogether wanting in Old Blood-and-Thunder's visage; and even if the Great Stone Face had assumed his look of stern command, the milder traits would still have tempered it.

"This is not the man of prophecy," sighed Ernest to himself, as he made his way out of the throng. "And must the world wait longer yet?"

The mists had congregated about the distant mountain-side, and there were seen the grand and awful features of the Great Stone Face, awful but benignant, as if a mighty angel were sitting among the hills, and enrobing himself in a cloud-vesture of gold and purple. As he looked, Ernest could hardly believe but that a smile beamed over the whole visage, with a radiance still brightening, although without motion of the lips. It was probably the effect of the western sunshine, melting through the thinly diffused vapors that had swept between him and the object that he gazed at. But—as it always did—the aspect of his marvellous friend made Ernest as hopeful as if he had never hoped in vain.

"Fear not, Ernest," said his heart, even as if the Great Face were whispering to him, "—fear not, Ernest; he will come."

More years sped swiftly and tranquilly away. Ernest still dwelt in his native valley, and was now a man of middle age. By imperceptible degrees, he had become known among the people. Now, as heretofore, he labored for his bread, and was the same simple-hearted man that he had always been. But he had thought and felt so much, he had given so many of the best hours of his life to unworldly hopes for some great good to mankind, that it seemed as though he had been talking with the angels, and had imbibed a portion of their wisdom unawares. It was visible in the calm and well-considered beneficence of his daily life, the quiet stream of which had made a wide green margin all along its course. Not a day passed by, that the world was not the better because this man, humble as he was, had lived. He never stepped aside from his own path, yet would always reach a blessing to his neighbor. Almost involuntarily, too, he had become a preacher. The pure and high simplicity of his thought, which, as one of its manifestations, took shape in the good deeds that dropped silently from his hand, flowed also forth in speech. He uttered truths that wrought upon and moulded the lives of those who heard him. His auditors, it may be, never suspected that Ernest, their own neighbor and familiar friend, was more than an ordinary man; least of all did Ernest himself suspect it; but, inevitably as the murmur of a rivulet, came thoughts out of his mouth that no other human lips had spoken.

When the people's minds had had a little time to cool, they were ready enough to acknowledge their mistake in imagining a similarity between General Blood-and-Thunder's truculent physiognomy and the benign visage on the mountain-side. But now, again, there were reports and many paragraphs in the newspapers, affirming that the likeness of the Great Stone Face had appeared upon the broad shoulders of a certain eminent statesman. He, like Mr. Gathergold and Old Blood-and-Thunder, was a native of the valley, but had left it in his early days, and taken up the trades of law and politics. Instead of the rich man's wealth and the warrior's sword, he had but a tongue, and it was mightier than both together. So wonderfully eloquent was he, that whatever he might choose to say, his auditors had no choice but to believe him; wrong looked like right, and right like wrong; for when it pleased him, he could make a kind of illuminated fog with his mere breath, and obscure the natural daylight with it. His tongue, indeed, was a magic instrument: sometimes it rumbled like the thunder; sometimes it warbled like the sweetest music. It was the blast of war, the song of peace; and it seemed to have a heart in it, when there was no such matter. In good truth, he was a wondrous man; and when his tongue had acquired him all other imaginable success—when it had been heard in halls of state, and in the courts of princes and potentates—after it had made him known all over the world, even as a voice crying from shore to shore—it finally persuaded his countrymen to select him for the Presidency. Before this time—indeed, as soon as he began to grow celebrated—his admirers had found out the resemblance between him and the Great Stone Face; and so much were they struck by it, that throughout the country this distinguished gentleman was known by the name of Old Stony Phiz. The phrase was considered as giving a highly favorable aspect to his political prospects; for, as is likewise the case with the Popedom, nobody ever becomes President without taking a name other than his own.

While his friends were doing their best to make him President, Old Stony Phiz, as he was called, set out on a visit to the valley where he was born. Of course, he had no other object than to shake hands with his fellow-citizens and neither thought nor cared about any effect which his progress through the country might have upon the election. Magnificent preparations were made to receive the illustrious statesman; a cavalcade of horsemen set forth to meet him at the boundary line of the State, and all the people left their business and gathered along the wayside to see him pass. Among these was Ernest. Though more than once disappointed, as we have seen, he had such a hopeful and confiding nature, that he was always ready to believe in whatever seemed beautiful and good. He kept his heart continually open, and thus was sure to catch the blessing from on high when it should come. So now again, as buoyantly as ever, he went forth to behold the likeness of the Great Stone Face.

The cavalcade came prancing along the road, with a great clattering of hoofs and a mighty cloud of dust, which rose up so dense and high that the visage of the mountain-side was completely hidden from Ernest's eyes. All the great men of the neighborhood were there on horseback; militia officers, in uniform; the member of Congress; the sheriff of the county; the editors of newspapers; and many a farmer, too, had mounted his patient steed, with his Sunday coat upon his back. It really was a very brilliant spectacle, especially as there were numerous banners flaunting over the cavalcade, on some of which were gorgeous portraits of the illustrious statesman and the Great Stone Face, smiling familiarly at one another, like two brothers. If the pictures were to be trusted, the mutual resemblance, it must be confessed, was marvellous. We must not forget to mention that there was a band of music, which made the echoes of the mountains ring and reverberate with the loud triumph of its strains; so that airy and soul-thrilling melodies broke out among all the heights and hollows, as if every nook of his native valley had found a voice, to welcome the distinguished guest. But the grandest effect was when the far-off mountain precipice flung back the music; for then the Great Stone Face itself seemed to be swelling the triumphant chorus, in acknowledgment that, at length, the man of prophecy was come.

All this while the people were throwing up their hats and shouting, with enthusiasm so contagious that the heart of Ernest kindled up, and he likewise threw up his hat, and shouted, as loudly as the loudest, "Huzza for the great man! Huzza for Old Stony Phiz!" But as yet he had not seen him.

"Here he is, now!" cried those who stood near Ernest. "There! There! Look at Old Stony Phiz and then at the Old Man of the Mountain, and see if they are not as like as two twin-brothers!"

In the midst of all this gallant array came an open barouche, drawn by four white horses; and in the barouche, with his massive head uncovered, sat the illustrious statesman, Old Stony Phiz himself.

"Confess it," said one of Ernest's neighbors to him, "the Great Stone Face has met its match at last!"

Now, it must be owned that, at his first glimpse of the countenance which was bowing and smiling from the barouche, Ernest did fancy that there was a resemblance between it and the old familiar face upon the mountain-side. The brow, with its massive depth and loftiness, and all the other features, indeed, were boldly and strongly hewn, as if in emulation of a more than heroic, of a Titanic model. But the sublimity and stateliness, the grand expresson of a divine sympathy, that illuminated the mountain visage and etherealized its ponderous granite substance into spirit, might here be sought in vain. Something had been originally left out, or had departed. And therefore the marvellously gifted statesman had always a weary gloom in the deep caverns of his eyes, as of a child that has outgrown its playthings or a man of mighty faculties and little aims, whose life, with all its high performances, was vague and empty, because no high purpose had endowed it with reality.

Still, Ernest's neighbor was thrusting his elbow into his side, and pressing him for an answer.

"Confess! confess! Is not he the very picture of your Old Man of the Mountain?"

"No!" said Ernest bluntly, "I see little or no likeness."

"Then so much the worse for the Great Stone Face!" answered his neighbor; and again he set up a shout for Old Stony Phiz.

But Ernest turned away, melancholy, and almost despondent: for this was the saddest of his disappointments, to behold a man who might have fulfilled the prophecy, and had not willed to do so. Meantime, the cavalcade, the banners, the music, and the barouches swept past him, with the vociferous crowd in the rear, leaving the dust to settle down, and the Great Stone Face to be revealed again, with the grandeur that it had worn for untold centuries.

"Lo, here I am, Ernest!" the benign lips seemed to say. "I have waited longer than thou, and am not yet weary. Fear not; the man will come."

The years hurried onward, treading in their haste on one another's heels. And now they began to bring white hairs, and scatter them over the head of Ernest; they made reverend wrinkles across his forehead, and furrows in his cheeks. He was an aged man. But not in vain had he grown old: more than the white hairs on his head were the sage thoughts in his mind; his wrinkles and furrows were inscriptions that Time had graved, and in which he had written legends of wisdom that had been tested by the tenor of a life. And Ernest had ceased to be obscure. Unsought for, undesired, had come the fame which so many seek, and made him known in the great world, beyond the limits of the valley in which he had dwelt so quietly. College professors, and even the active men of cities, came from far to see and converse with Ernest; for the report had gone abroad that this simple husbandman had ideas unlike those of other men, not gained from books, but of a higher tone—a tranquil and familiar majesty, as if he had been talking with the angels as his daily friends. Whether it were sage, statesman, or philanthropist, Ernest received these visitors with the gentle sincerity that had characterized him from boyhood, and spoke freely with them of whatever came uppermost, or lay deepest in his heart or their own. While they talked together, his face would kindle, unawares, and shine upon them, as with a mild evening light. Pensive with the fulness of such discourse, his guests took leave and went their way; and passing up the valley, paused to look at the Great Stone Face, imagining that they had seen its likeness in a human countenance, but could not remember where.

While Ernest had been growing up and growing old, a bountiful Providence had granted a new poet to this earth. He likewise, was a native of the valley, but had spent the greater part of his life at a distance from that romantic region, pouring out his sweet music amid the bustle and din of cities. Often, however, did the mountains which had been familiar to him in his childhood lift their snowy peaks into the clear atmosphere of his poetry. Neither was the Great Stone Face forgotten, for the poet had celebrated it in an ode, which was grand enough to have been uttered by its own majestic lips. This man of genius, we may say, had come down from heaven with wonderful endowments. If he sang of a mountain, the eyes of all mankind beheld a mightier grandeur reposing on its breast, or soaring to its summit, than had before been seen there. If his theme were a lovely lake, a celestial smile had now been thrown over it, to gleam forever on its surface. If it were the vast old sea, even the deep immensity of its dread bosom seemed to swell the higher, as if moved by the emotions of the song. Thus the world assumed another and a better aspect from the hour that the poet blessed it with his happy eyes. The Creator had bestowed him, as the last best touch to his own handiwork. Creation was not finished till the poet came to interpret, and so complete it.

The effect was no less high and beautiful, when his human brethren were the subject of his verse. The man or woman, sordid with the common dust of life, who crossed his daily path, and the little child who played in it, were glorified if he beheld them in his mood of poetic faith. He showed the golden links of the great chain that intertwined them with an angelic kindred; he brought out the hidden traits of a celestial birth that made them worthy of such kin. Some, indeed, there were, who thought to show the soundness of their judgment by affirming that all the beauty and dignity of the natural world existed only in the poet's fancy. Let such men speak for themselves, who undoubtedly appear to have been spawned forth by Nature with a contemptuous bitterness; she having plastered them up out of her refuse stuff, after all the swine were made. As respects all things else, the poet's ideal was the truest truth.

The songs of this poet found their way to Ernest. He read them after his customary toil, seated on the bench before his cottage-door, where for such a length of time he had filled his repose with thought, by gazing at the Great Stone Face. And now as he read stanzas that caused the soul to thrill within him, he lifted his eyes to the vast countenance beaming on him so benignantly.

"O majestic friend," he murmured, addressing the Great Stone Face, "is not this man worthy to resemble thee?"

The Face seemed to smile, but answered not a word.

Now it happened that the poet, though he dwelt so far away, had not only heard of Ernest, but had meditated much upon his character, until he deemed nothing so desirable as to meet this man, whose untaught wisdom walked hand in hand with the noble simplicity of his life. One summer morning, therefore, he took passage by the railroad, and, in the decline of the afternoon, alighted from the cars at no great distance from Ernest's cottage. The great hotel, which had formerly been the palace of Mr. Gathergold, was close at hand, but the poet, with his carpet-bag on his arm, inquired at once where Ernest dwelt, and was resolved to be accepted as his guest.

Approaching the door, he there found the good old man, holding a volume in his hand, which alternately he read, and then, with a finger between the leaves, looked lovingly at the Great Stone Face.

"Good evening," said the poet. "Can you give a traveller a night's lodging?"

"Willingly," answered Ernest; and then he added, smiling, "Methinks I never saw the Great Stone Face look so hospitably at a stranger."

The poet sat down on the bench beside him, and he and Ernest talked together. Often had the poet held intercourse with the wittiest and the wisest, but never before with a man like Ernest, whose thoughts and feelings gushed up with such a natural freedom, and who made great truths so familiar by his simple utterance of them. Angels, as had been so often said, seemed to have wrought with him at his labor in the fields; angels seemed to have sat with him by the fireside; and, dwelling with angels as friend with friends, he had imbibed the sublimity of their ideas, and imbued it with the sweet and lowly charm of household words. So thought the poet. And Ernest, on the other hand, was moved and agitated by the living images which the poet flung out of his mind, and which peopled all the air about the cottage-door with shapes of beauty, both gay and pensive. The sympathies of these two men instructed them with a profounder sense than either could have attained alone. Their minds accorded into one strain, and made delightful music which neither of them could have claimed as all his own, nor distinguished his own share from the other's. They led one another, as it were, into a high pavilion of their thoughts, so remote, and hitherto so dim, that they had never entered it before, and so beautiful that they desired to be there always.

As Ernest listened to the poet, he imagined that the Great Stone Face was bending forward to listen too. He gazed earnestly into the poet's glowing eyes.

"Who are you, my strangely gifted guest?" he said.

The poet laid his finger on the volume that Ernest had been reading.

"You have read these poems," said he. "You know me, then— for I wrote them."

Again, and still more earnestly than before, Ernest examined the poet's features; then turned towards the Great Stone Face; then back, with an uncertain aspect, to his guest. But his countenance fell; he shook his head, and sighed.

"Wherefore are you sad?" inquired the poet.

"Because," replied Ernest, "all through life I have awaited the fulfilment of a prophecy; and, when I read these poems, I hoped that it might be fulfilled in you."

"You hoped," answered the poet, faintly smiling, "to find in me the likeness of the Great Stone Face. And you are disappointed, as formerly with Mr. Gathergold, and Old Blood-and-Thunder, and Old Stony Phiz. Yes, Ernest, it is my doom. You must add my name to the illustrious three, and record another failure of your hopes. For—in shame and sadness do I speak it, Ernest—I am not worthy to be typified by yonder benign and majestic image."

"And why?" asked Ernest. He pointed to the volume. "Are not those thoughts divine?"

"They have a strain of the Divinity," replied the poet. "You can hear in them the far-off echo of a heavenly song. But my life, dear Ernest, has not corresponded with my thought. I have had grand dreams, but they have been only dreams, because I have lived— and that, too, by my own choice—among poor and mean realities. Sometimes even—shall I dare to say it?—I lack faith in the grandeur, the beauty, and the goodness, which my own words are said to have made more evident in nature and in human life. Why, then, pure seeker of the good and true, shouldst thou hope to find me, in yonder image of the divine?"

The poet spoke sadly, and his eyes were dim with tears. So, likewise, were those of Ernest.

At the hour of sunset, as had long been his frequent custom, Ernest was to discourse to an assemblage of the neighboring inhabitants in the open air. He and the poet, arm in arm, still talking together as they went along, proceeded to the spot. It was a small nook among the hills, with a gray precipice behind, the stern front of which was relieved by the pleasant foliage of many creeping plants that made a tapestry for the naked rock, by hanging their festoons from all its rugged angles. At a small elevation above the ground, set in a rich framework of verdure, there appeared a niche, spacious enough to admit a human figure, with freedom for such gestures as spontaneously accompany earnest thought and genuine emotion. Into this natural pulpit Ernest ascended, and threw a look of familiar kindness around upon his audience. They stood, or sat, or reclined upon the grass, as seemed good to each, with the departing sunshine falling obliquely over them, and mingling its subdued cheerfulness with the solemnity of a grove of ancient trees, beneath and amid the boughs of which the golden rays were constrained to pass. In another direction was seen the Great Stone Face, with the same cheer, combined with the same solemnity, in its benignant aspect.

Ernest began to speak, giving to the people of what was in his heart and mind. His words had power, because they accorded with his thoughts; and his thoughts had reality and depth, because they harmonized with the life which he had always lived. It was not mere breath that this preacher uttered; they were the words of life, because a life of good deeds and holy love was melted into them. Pearls, pure and rich, had been dissolved into this precious draught. The poet, as he listened, felt that the being and character of Ernest were a nobler strain of poetry than he had ever written. His eyes glistening with tears, he gazed reverentially at the venerable man, and said within himself that never was there an aspect so worthy of a prophet and a sage as that mild, sweet, thoughtful countenance, with the glory of white hair diffused about it. At a distance, but distinctly to be seen, high up in the golden light of the setting sun, appeared the Great Stone Face, with hoary mists around it, like the white hairs around the brow of Ernest. Its look of grand beneficence seemed to embrace the world.

At that moment, in sympathy with a thought which he was about to utter, the face of Ernest assumed a grandeur of expression, so imbued with benevolence, that the poet, by an irresistible impulse, threw his arms aloft and shouted,

"Behold! Behold! Ernest is himself the likeness of the Great Stone Face!"

Then all the people looked, and saw that what the deep-sighted poet said was true. The prophecy was fulfilled. But Ernest, having finished what he had to say, took the poet's arm, and walked slowly homeward, still hoping that some wiser and better man than himself would by and by appear, bearing a resemblance to the GREAT STONE FACE.

For Further Reflection

1. What is the significance of the Great Stone Face in this story? Many people think that we must have good role models in order to develop into good people, but this story suggests that we need not have great people, but simply great ideas and ideals. Is this plausible?

2. Explain how the Great Stone Face affects the values and virtues of the people of the valley, especially Ernest. What virtues does Ernest manifest?

A Critique of Virtue-Based Ethical Systems

WILLIAM K. FRANKENA

William Frankena (1908–1997) was professor of philosophy at the University of Michigan and the author of several works in ethical theory, including *Ethics* (1973), from which this selection is taken. Frankena, a defender of a deontological duty-based ethic, agrees with the virtue ethicist on the importance of traits (virtues), but argues that all of the virtues can be derived from principles. "Traits without principles are blind." For every virtue there must be some possible action to which the virtue corresponds, and from

From *Ethics*, 2nd Edition by William K. Frankena, © 1989. Adapted by permission of Pearson Education, Inc., Upper Saddle River, NJ.

which it derives its virtuousness. For example, the virtue of truthfulness corresponds to the principle "Tell the truth," and the virtue of being benevolent derives from the general principle to act beneficently. There is a close corresponding relationship between all of the virtues and all of the principles.

MORALITY AND CULTIVATION OF TRAITS

Our present interest, then, is not in moral principles nor in nonmoral values, but in moral values, in what is morally good or bad. Throughout its history morality has been concerned about the cultivation of certain dispositions, or traits, among which are "character" and such "virtues" (an old-fashioned but still useful term) as honesty, kindness, and conscientiousness. Virtues are dispositions or traits that are not wholly innate; they must all be acquired, at least in part, by teaching and practice, or, perhaps, by grace. They are also traits of "character," rather than traits of "personality" like charm or shyness, and they all involve a tendency to do certain kinds of action in certain kinds of situations, not just to think or feel in certain ways. They are not just abilities or skills, like intelligence or carpentry, which one may have without using.

In fact, it has been suggested that morality is or should be conceived as primarily concerned, not with rules or principles as we have been supposing so far, but with the cultivation of such dispositions or traits of character. Plato and Aristotle seem to conceive of morality in this way, for they talk mainly in terms of virtues and the virtuous, rather than in terms of what is right or obligatory. Hume uses similar terms, although he mixes in some nonmoral traits like cheerfulness and wit along with moral ones like benevolence and justice. More recently, Leslie Stephen stated the view in these words:

> . . . morality is internal. The moral law . . . has to be expressed in the form, "be this," not in the form, "do this." . . . the true moral law says "hate not," instead of "kill not." . . . the only mode of stating the moral law must be as a rule of character.[1]

---

[1]Leslie Stephen, *The Science of Ethics* (New York: G. P. Putnam's Sons, 1882), pp. 155, 158.

ETHICS OF VIRTUE

Those who hold this view are advocating an *ethics of virtue* or being, in opposition to an ethics of duty, principle, or doing. . . . The notion of an ethics of virtue is worth looking at here, not only because it has a long history but also because some spokesmen of "the new morality" seem to espouse it. What would an ethics of virtue be like? It would, of course, not take deontic judgments or principles as basic in morality, as we have been doing; instead, it would take as basic aretaic judgments like "That was a courageous deed," "His action was virtuous," or "Courage is a virtue," and it would insist that deontic judgments are either derivative from such aretaic ones or can be dispensed with entirely. Moreover, it would regard aretaic judgments about actions as secondary and as based on aretaic judgments about agents and their motives or traits, as Hume does when he writes:

> . . . when we praise any actions, we regard only the motives that produced them. . . . The external performance has no merit. . . . all virtuous actions derive their merit only from virtuous motives.[2]

For an ethics of virtue, then, what is basic in morality is judgments like "Benevolence is a good motive," "Courage is a virtue," "The morally good man is kind to everyone" or, more simply and less accurately, "Be loving!"—not judgments or principles about what our duty is or what we ought to do. But, of course, it thinks that its basic instructions will guide us, not only about what to be, but also about what to do.

It looks as if there would be three kinds of ethics of virtue, corresponding to the three kinds of ethics of duty covered earlier. The question to be answered is: What dispositions or traits are moral virtues? *Trait-egoism* replies that the virtues are the dispositions that are most conducive to one's own good or welfare, or, alternatively, that prudence or a careful concern for one's own good is the cardinal or basic moral virtue, other virtues being derivative from it. *Trait-utilitarianism* asserts that the virtues are those traits that most promote the general good, or, alternatively, that benevolence is the

---

[2]David Hume, *Treatise of Human Nature* (1739), Book III, Part II, opening of Sec. I.

basic or cardinal moral virtue. These views may be called *trait-teleological,* but, of course, there are also *trait-deontological theories,* which will hold that certain traits are morally good or virtuous simply as such, and not just because of the nonmoral value they may have or promote, or, alternatively, that there are other cardinal or basic virtues besides prudence or benevolence, for example, obedience to God, honesty, or justice. If they add that there is only one such cardinal virtue, they are monistic, otherwise pluralistic.

To avoid confusion, it is necessary to notice here that we must distinguish between *virtues* and *principles of duty* like "We ought to promote the good" and "We ought to treat people equally." A virtue is not a principle of this kind; it is a disposition, habit, quality, or trait of the person or soul, which an individual either has or seeks to have. Hence, I speak of the principle of *beneficence* and the virtue of *benevolence,* since we have two words with which to mark the difference. In the case of justice, we do not have different words, but still we must not confuse the principle of equal treatment with the disposition to treat people equally.

On the basis of our earlier discussions, we may assume at this point that views of the first two kinds are unsatisfactory, and that the most adequate ethics of virtue would be one of the third sort, one that would posit two cardinal virtues, namely, benevolence and justice, considered now as dispositions or traits of character rather than as principles of duty. By a set of cardinal virtues is meant a set of virtues that (1) cannot be derived from one another and (2) all other moral virtues can be derived from or shown to be forms of them. Plato and other Greeks thought there were four cardinal virtues in this sense: wisdom, courage, temperance, and justice. Christianity is traditionally regarded as having seven cardinal virtues: three "theological" virtues—faith, hope, and love; and four "human" virtues—prudence, fortitude, temperance, and justice. This was essentially St. Thomas Aquinas's view; since St. Augustine regarded the last four as forms of love, only the first three were really cardinal for him. However, many moralists, among them Schopenhauer, have taken benevolence and justice to be the cardinal moral virtues, as I would. It seems to me that all of the usual virtues (such as love, courage, temperance, honesty, gratitude, and considerateness), at least insofar as they are *moral* virtues, can be derived from these two. Insofar as a disposition cannot be derived from benevolence and justice, I should try to argue either that it is not a *moral* virtue (e.g., I take faith, hope, and wisdom to be religious or intellectual, not moral, virtues) or that it is not a virtue at all.

ON BEING AND DOING: MORALITY OF TRAITS VS. MORALITY OF PRINCIPLES

We may now return to the issue posed by the quotation from Stephen, though we cannot debate it as fully as we should. To be or to do, that is the question. Should we construe morality as primarily a following of certain principles or as primarily a cultivation of certain dispositions and traits? Must we choose? It is hard to see how a morality of principles can get off the ground except through the development of dispositions to act in accordance with its principles, else all motivation to act on them must be of an *ad hoc* kind, either prudential or impulsively altruistic. Moreover, morality can hardly be content with a mere conformity to rules, however willing and self-conscious it may be, unless it has no interest in the spirit of its law but only in the letter. On the other hand, one cannot conceive of traits of character except as including dispositions and tendencies to act in certain ways in certain circumstances. Hating involves being disposed to kill or harm, being just involves tending to do just acts (acts that conform to the principle of justice) when the occasion calls. Again, it is hard to see how we could know what traits to encourage or inculcate if we did not subscribe to principles, for example, to the principle of utility, or to those of benevolence and justice.

I propose therefore that we regard the morality of duty and principles and the morality of virtues or traits of character not as rival kinds of morality between which we must choose, but as two complementary aspects of the same morality. Then, for every principle there will be a morally good trait, often going by the same name, consisting of a disposition or tendency to act according to it; and for every morally good trait there will be a principle defining the kind of action in which it is to express itself. To parody a famous dictum of Kant's, I am inclined to think that principles without traits are impotent and traits without principles are blind.

Even if we adopt this double-aspect conception of morality, in which principles are basic, we may still agree that morality does and must put a premium on *being* honest, conscientious, and so forth. If its sanctions or sources of motivation are not to be entirely external (for example, the prospect of being praised, blamed, rewarded, or punished by others) or adventitious (for example, a purely instinctive love of others), if it is to have adequate "internal sanctions," as Mill called them, then morality must foster the development of such dispositions and habits as have been mentioned. It could hardly be satisfied with a mere conformity to its principles even if it could provide us with fixed principles of actual duty. For such a conformity might be motivated entirely by extrinsic or non-moral considerations, and would then be at the mercy of these other considerations. It could not be counted on in a moment of trial. Besides, since morality cannot provide us with fixed principles of actual duty but only with principles of prima facie duty, it cannot be content with the letter of its law, but must foster in us the dispositions that will sustain us in the hour of decision when we are choosing between conflicting principles of prima facie duty or trying to revise our working rules of right and wrong.

There is another reason why we must cultivate certain traits of character in ourselves and others, or why we must be certain sorts of persons. Although morality is concerned that we act in certain ways, it cannot take the hard line of insisting that we act in precisely those ways, even if those ways could be more clearly defined. We cannot praise and blame or apply other sanctions to an agent simply on the ground that he has or has not acted in conformity with certain principles. It would not be right. Through no fault of his own, the agent may not have known all the relevant facts. What action the principles of morality called for in the situation may not have been clear to him, again through no fault of his own, and he may have been honestly mistaken about his duty. Or his doing what he ought to have done might have carried with it an intolerable sacrifice on his part. He may even have been simply incapable of doing it. Morality must therefore recognize various sorts of excuses and extenuating circumstances. All it can really insist on, then, except in certain critical cases, is that we develop and manifest fixed dispositions to find out what the right thing is and to do it if possible. In this sense a person must "be this" rather than "do this." But it must be remembered that "being" involves at least *trying* to "do." Being without doing, like faith without works, is dead.

At least it will be clear from this discussion that an ethics of duty or principles also has an important place for the virtues and must put a premium on their cultivation as a part of moral education and development. The place it has for virtue and/or the virtues is, however, different from that accorded them by an ethics of virtue. Talking in terms of . . . an ethics of duty, we may say that, if we ask for *guidance* about what to do or not do, then the answer is contained, at least primarily, in two deontic principles and their corollaries, namely, the principles of beneficence and equal treatment. Given these two deontic principles, plus the necessary clarity of thought and factual knowledge, we can know what we morally ought to do or not do, except perhaps in cases of conflict between them. We also know that we should cultivate two virtues, a disposition to be beneficial (i.e., benevolence) and a disposition to treat people equally (justice as a trait). But the point of acquiring these virtues is not further guidance or instruction; the function of the virtues in an ethics of duty is not to tell us what to do but to ensure that we will do it willingly in whatever situations we may face. In an ethics of virtue, on the other hand, the virtues play a dual role—they must not only move us to do what we do, they must also tell us what to do. To parody Alfred Lord Tennyson:

Theirs not (only) to do or die,
Theirs (also) to reason why.

MORAL IDEALS

This is the place to mention ideals again, which are among what we called the ingredients of morality. One may, perhaps, identify moral ideals with moral principles, but, more properly speaking, moral ideals are ways of being rather than of doing. Having a moral ideal is wanting to be a person of a certain sort, wanting to have a certain trait of character rather than others, for example, moral courage or perfect integrity. That is why the use of exemplary persons like Socrates, Jesus, or Martin Luther King has been such an important part of moral education and self-development, and it is one of the reasons for the writing and reading of biographies or of novels and epics in which types of moral personality are portrayed, even if they are not all heroes or saints. Often such moral ideals of personality go beyond what can be demanded or regarded as obligatory, belonging among the things to be praised rather than required, except as one may require them of oneself. It should be remembered, however, that not all personal ideals are moral ones.

Achilles, Hercules, Napoleon, and Prince Charming may all be taken as ideals, but the ideals they represent are not moral ones, even though they may not be immoral ones either. Some ideals, e.g., those of chivalry, may be partly moral and partly nonmoral. There is every reason why one should pursue nonmoral as well as moral ideals, but there is no good reason for confusing them.

When one has a moral ideal, wanting to be a certain sort of moral person, one has at least some motivation to live in a certain way, but one also has something to guide him in living. Here the idea of an ethics of virtue may have a point. One may, of course, take as one's ideal that of being a good man who always does his duty from a sense of duty, perhaps gladly, and perhaps even going a second mile on occasion. Then one's guidance clearly comes entirely from one's rules and principles of duty. However, one may also have an ideal that goes beyond anything that can be regarded by others or even oneself as strict duty or obligation, a form or style of personal being that may be morally good or virtuous, but is not morally required of one. An ethics of virtue seems to provide for such an aspiration more naturally than an ethics of duty or principle, and perhaps an adequate morality should at least contain a region in which we can follow such an idea, over and beyond the region in which we are to listen to the call of duty. There certainly should be moral heroes and saints who go beyond the merely good man, if only to serve as an inspiration to others to be better and do more than they would otherwise be or do. Granted all this, however, it still seems to me that, if one's ideal is truly a moral one, there will be nothing in it that is not covered by the principles of beneficence and justice conceived as principles of what we ought to do in the wider sense referred to earlier.

DISPOSITIONS TO BE CULTIVATED

Are there any other moral virtues to be cultivated besides benevolence and justice? No cardinal ones, of course. In this sense our answer to Socrates' question whether virtue is one or many is that it is two. We saw, however, that the principles of beneficence and equality have corollaries like telling the truth, keeping promises, etc. It follows that character traits like honesty and fidelity are virtues, though subordinate ones, and should be acquired and fostered. There will then be other such virtues corresponding to other corollaries of our main principles. Let us call all of these virtues, cardinal and noncardinal, first-order moral virtues. Besides first-order virtues like these, there are certain other moral virtues that ought also to be cultivated, which are in a way more abstract and general and may be called second-order virtues. Conscientiousness is one such virtue; it is not limited to a certain sector of the moral life, as gratitude and honesty are, but is a virtue covering the whole of the moral life. Moral courage, or courage when moral issues are at stake, is another such second-order virtue; it belongs to all sectors of the moral life. Others that overlap with these are integrity and good-will, understanding good-will in Kant's sense of respect for the moral law.

In view of what was said in a previous chapter, we must list two other second-order traits: a disposition to find out and respect the relevant facts and a disposition to think clearly. These are not just abilities but character traits; one might have the ability to think intelligently without having a disposition to use it. They are therefore virtues, though they are intellectual virtues, not moral ones. Still, though their role is not limited to the moral life, they are necessary to it. More generally speaking, we should cultivate the virtue Plato called wisdom and Aristotle practical wisdom, which they thought of as including all of the intellectual abilities and virtues essential to the moral life.

Still other second-order qualities, which may be abilities rather than virtues, but which must be cultivated for moral living, and so may, perhaps, best be mentioned here, are moral autonomy, the ability to make moral decisions and to revise one's principles if necessary, and the ability to realize vividly, in imagination and feeling, the "inner lives" of others. Of these second-order qualities, the first two have been referred to on occasion and will be again, but something should be said about the last.

If our morality is to be more than a conformity to internalized rules and principles, if it is to include and rest on an understanding of the point of these rules and principles, and certainly if it is to involve *being* a certain kind of person and not merely *doing* certain kinds of things, then we must somehow attain and develop an ability to be aware of others as persons, as important to themselves as we are to ourselves, and to have a lively and sympathetic representation in imagination of their interests and of the effects of our actions on their lives. The need for this is particularly stressed by Josiah Royce and William James. Both men point out how we usually go our own busy and self-concerned ways, with only an external awareness of the presence of others, much as if they were things, and without any realization of their inner and peculiar worlds of personal experience; and both emphasize the need and the possibility of a "higher vision of an inner significance" which pierces this "certain blindness in human beings" and enables us to realize the existence of others in a wholly different way, as we do our own.

> What then is thy neighbor? He too is a mass of states, of experiences, thoughts and desires, just as concrete, as thou art. . . . Dost thou believe this? Art thou sure what it means? This is for thee the turning-point of thy whole conduct towards him.

These are Royce's quaint old-fashioned words. Here are James's more modern ones.

> This higher vision of an inner significance in what, until then, we had realized only in the dead external way, often comes over a person suddenly; and, when it does so, it makes an epoch in his history.

Royce calls this more perfect recognition of our neighbors "the moral insight" and James says that its practical consequence is "the well-known democratic respect for the sacredness of individuality." It is hard to see how either a benevolent (loving) or a just (equalitarian) disposition could come to fruition without it. To quote James again,

> We ought, all of us, to realize each other in this intense, pathetic, and important way.

Doing this is part of what is involved in fully taking the moral point of view.

TWO QUESTIONS

We can now deal with the question, sometimes raised, whether an action is to be judged right or wrong because of its results, because of the principle it exemplifies, or because the motive, intention, or trait of character involved is morally good or bad. The answer . . . is that an action is to be judged *right* or *wrong* by reference to a principle or set of principles. Even if we say it is right or wrong because of its effects, this means that it is right or wrong by the principle of utility or some other teleological principle. But an act may also be said to be *good* or *bad,* praiseworthy or blameworthy, noble or despicable, and so on, and then the moral quality ascribed to it will depend on the agent's motive, intention, or disposition in doing it.

Another important question here is: What is moral goodness? When is a person morally good and when are his actions, dispositions, motives, or intentions morally good? Not just when he does what is actually right, for he may do what is right from bad motives, in which case he is not morally good, or he may fail to do what is right though sincerely trying to do it, in which case he is not morally bad. Whether he and his actions are morally good or not depends, not on the rightness of what he does or on its consequences, but on his character or motives; so far the statement quoted from Hume is certainly correct. But when are his motives and dispositions morally good? Some answer that a person and his actions are morally good if and only if they are motivated wholly by a sense of duty or a desire to do what is right; the Stoics and Kant sometimes seem to take this extreme view. Others hold that a man and his actions are morally good if and only if they are motivated primarily by a sense of duty or desire to do what is right, though other motives may be present too; still others contend, with Aristotle, that they are at any rate not morally good unless they are motivated at least in part by such a sense or desire. A more reasonable view, to my mind, is that a man and his actions are morally good if it is at least true that, whatever his actual motives in acting are, his sense of duty or desire to do the right is so strong in him that it would keep him trying to do his duty anyway.

Actually, I find it hard to believe that no dispositions or motivations are good or virtuous from the moral point of view except those that include a will to do the right as such. It is more plausible to distinguish two kinds of morally good dispositions or traits of character, first, those that are usually called moral virtues and do include a will to do the right, and second, others like purely natural kindliness or gratefulness, which, while they are nonmoral, are still morality-supporting, since they dispose us to do such actions as morality requires and even to perform deeds, for example, in the case of motherly love, which are well beyond the call of duty.

It has even been alleged that conscientiousness or moral goodness in the sense of a disposition to act from a sense of duty alone is not a good thing or not a virtue—that it is more desirable to have people acting from motives like friendship, gratitude, honor, love, and the like, than from a dry or driven sense of obligation. There is something to be said for this view, though it ignores the nobility of great moral courage and of the higher reaches of moral idealism. But even if conscientiousness or good will is not the only thing that is unconditionally good, as Kant believed, or the greatest of intrinsically good things, as Ross thought, it is surely a good thing from the moral point of view. For an ethics of duty, at any rate, it must be desirable that people do what is right for its own sake, especially if they do it gladly, as a gymnast may gladly make the right move just because it is right.

For Further Reflection

1. What are Frankena's main criticisms of virtue ethics? Are you convinced by them?

2. What does he propose in place of contrasting the ethics of *doing* with the ethics of *being?* How cogent are his arguments?

3. What does Frankena think the two cardinal virtues are?

4. Do you agree with Frankena that a moral person must want to do the right thing just because it is right? What if I think that I must have a self-interested reason for being moral? We will look at this issue more fully in chapter 8, but start thinking about it.

Further Readings for Chapter 6

Anscombe, Elizabeth. "Modern Moral Philosophy." *Philosophy* 33 (1958).

Blum, Lawrence A. *Friendship, Altruism and Morality.* London: Routledge and Kegan Paul, 1980.

Foot, Philippa. *Virtues and Vices.* Oxford: Blackwell, 1978. A collection of articles by one of the foremost virtue ethicists.

French, Peter, T. Uehling, and H. K. Wettstein, eds. *Midwest Studies in Philosophy.* Vol 13, *Ethical Theory: Character and Virtue.* South Bend, Ind.: University of Notre Dame Press, 1988. This book contains several important recent articles on the virtues, including David Norton's "Moral Minimalism and the Development of Moral Character."

Kruschwitz, Robert, and Robert Roberts, eds. *The Virtues*. Belmont, Calif.: Wadsworth, 1987. Contains excellent readings and bibliography.

Loudan, Robert. "Some Vices of Virtue Ethics." *American Philosophical Quarterly* 21 (1984). Reprinted in Kruschwitz and Roberts, *The Virtues*.

MacIntyre, Alasdair. *After Virtue*. South Bend, Ind.: University of Notre Dame Press, 1981.

Murdoch, Iris. *The Sovereignty of Good*. New York: Schocken Books, 1971.

Taylor, Richard. *Ethics, Faith and Reason*. Englewood Cliffs, N.J.: Prentice-Hall, 1985.

Wallace, James. *Virtues and Vices*. Ithaca, N.Y.: Cornell University Press, 1978.

CHAPTER 7

Virtues and Vices

This chapter presents several literary and philosophical writings on particular virtues and vices. As Frankena pointed out in the last chapter, all moral theories respect virtues and deplore vices, though to different degrees and in different ways. In chapter 3 we studied moral relativism and its opposite, moral objectivism. We can apply what we said there to the virtues and vices. Moral objectivists believe they have universal validity, but relativists believe that virtues and vices are entirely dependent on culture for their significance.

We begin with the Sermon on the Mount given in Galilee by Jesus of Nazareth (c. A.D. 30), in which he announces a set of *virtues,* including mercy, love of righteousness, meekness, and love of one's enemies, as well as a set of *vices,* including lust, vengefulness, and hate. Early Christians, influenced by the Sermon on the Mount, were pacifists and refused to fight in the army. Can you see why? Later, especially after the Roman Empire made Christianity the official religion in the fourth century, the more pacifistic virtues were interpreted as ideals for the kingdom of heaven, but not to be taken literally in this world where sin was rampant. We have also included Jesus' classic parable of the Good Samaritan.

In this chapter we include one of Tolstoy's stories on vice and virtue, Kant's essay on jealousy, malice, and ingratitude, and Martin Gansberg's report of the apathetic voyeurism at the murder of Kitty Genovese. Next is an essay on gratitude by Helen Keller. The Stoic virtues are set forth in Epictetus's Stoic Catechism, Plutarch's "In Consolation to His Wife" on the death of their daughter, and James Stockdale's account of living in a North Vietnamese prison camp. Our last reading is Bertrand Russell's meditation on suffering.

The Sermon on the Mount;
The Good Samaritan

JESUS OF NAZARETH

Jesus of Nazareth (died c. A.D. 30) is the founder of the Christian religion and believed by Christians to have risen from the dead. He is considered by them to be the Son of God and Savior of the world. In this famous sermon given on a mountain near Capernaum in modern Israel, Jesus sets forth a radical ethic of nonviolence and love. This is followed by his parable of the Good Samaritan. The Samaritans were a despised ethnic group, with whom the Jews would have no relations. Jesus broke with his culture in his fellowship with the Samaritans.

THE SERMON ON THE MOUNT

Jesus saw the crowds and went up a hill, where he sat down. His disciples gathered around him, and he began to teach them:

"Happy are those who know they are spiritually poor;
the Kingdom of heaven belongs to them!
"Happy are those who mourn;
God will comfort them!
"Happy are the meek;
they will receive what God has promised!
"Happy are those whose greatest desire is to do what God requires;
God will satisfy them fully!
"Happy are those who are merciful to others;
God will be merciful to them!
"Happy are the pure in heart;
they will see God!
"Happy are those who work for peace among men;
God will call them his sons!
"Happy are those who are persecuted because they do what

New Testament: Matthew 5; Luke 10.

God requires;
the Kingdom of heaven belongs to them!
"Happy are you when men insult you, and persecute you, and tell all kinds of evil lies against you because you are my followers. Be glad and happy, because a great reward is kept for you in heaven. This is how men persecuted the prophets who lived before you."

"You are like salt for all mankind. But if salt loses its taste, there is no way to make it salty again. It has become worthless, so it is thrown away and people walk on it."

"You are like light for the whole world. A city built on a hill cannot be hid. No one lights a lamp to put it under a bowl; instead he puts it on the lampstand, where it gives light for everyone in the house. In the same way your light must shine before people, so that they will see the good things you do and give praise to your Father in heaven."

"Do not think that I have come to do away with the Law of Moses and the teachings of the prophets. I have not come to do away with them, but to make their teachings come true. Remember this! As long as heaven and earth last, the least point or the smallest detail of the Law will not be done away with—not until the end of all things. So then, whoever disobeys even the smallest of the commandments, and teaches others to do the same, will be least in the Kingdom of heaven. On the other hand, whoever obeys the Law, and teaches others to do the same, will be great in the Kingdom of heaven. I tell you, then, that you will be able to enter the Kingdom of heaven only if you are more faithful than the teachers of the Law and the Pharisees in doing what God requires."

"You have heard that men were told in the past, 'Do not murder; anyone who commits murder will be brought before the judge.' But now I tell you: whoever is angry with his brother will be brought before the judge; whoever calls his brother 'You good-for-nothing!' will be brought before the Council; and whoever calls his brother a worthless fool will be in danger of going to the fire of hell. So if you are about to offer your gift to God at the altar and there you remember that your brother has something against you, leave your gift there in front of the altar and go at once to make peace with your brother; then come back and offer your gift to God."

"If a man brings a lawsuit against you and takes you to court, be friendly with him while there is time, before you get to court; once you are there he will turn you over to the judge, who will hand you over to the police, and you will be put in jail. There you will stay, I tell you, until you pay the last penny of your fine."

"You have heard that it was said, 'Do not commit adultery.' But now I tell you: anyone who looks at a woman and wants to possess her is guilty of committing adultery with her in his heart. So if your right eye causes you to sin, take it out and throw it away! It is much better for you to lose a part of your body than to have your whole body thrown into hell. If your right hand causes you to sin, cut it off and throw it away! It is much better for you to lose one of your limbs than to have your whole body go off to hell."

"It was also said, 'Anyone who divorces his wife must give her a written notice of divorce.' But now I tell you: if a man divorces his wife, and she has not been unfaithful, then he is guilty of making her commit adultery if she marries again; and the man who marries her also commits adultery."

"You have also heard that men were told in the past, 'Do not break your promise, but do what you have sworn to the Lord to do.' But now I tell you: do not use any vow when you make a promise; do not swear by heaven, because it is God's throne; nor by earth, because it is the resting place for his feet; nor by Jerusalem, because it is the city of the great King. Do not even swear by your head, because you cannot make a single hair white or black. Just say 'Yes' or 'No'— anything else you have to say comes from the Evil One."

"You have heard that it was said, 'An eye for an eye, and a tooth for a tooth.' But now I tell you: do not take revenge on someone who does you wrong. If anyone slaps you on the right cheek, let him slap your left cheek too. And if someone takes you to court to sue you for your shirt, let him have your coat as well. And if one of the occupation troops forces you to carry his pack one mile, carry it another mile. When someone asks you for something, give it to him; when someone wants to borrow something, lend it to him."

"You have heard that it was said, 'Love your friends, hate your enemies.' But now I tell you: love your enemies, and pray for those who persecute you, so that you will become the sons of your Father in heaven. For he makes his sun to shine on bad and good people alike, and gives rain to those who do good and those who do evil. Why should God reward you if you love only the people who

love you? Even the tax collectors do that! And if you speak only
to your friends, have you done anything out of the ordinary? Even
the pagans do that! You must be perfect—just as your Father in
heaven is perfect."

THE GOOD SAMARITAN

A certain teacher of the Law came up and tried to trap Jesus.
"Teacher," he asked, "what must I do to receive eternal life?" Jesus
answered him, "What do the Scriptures say? How do you interpret
them?" The man answered, "'You must love the Lord your God with
all your heart, with all your soul, with all your strength, and with
all your mind'; and, 'You must love your fellow-man as yourself.'"
"Your answer is correct," replied Jesus; "do this and you will live."
   But the teacher of the Law wanted to put himself in the right,
so he asked Jesus, "Who is my fellow-man?" Jesus answered, "There
was a man who was going down from Jerusalem to Jericho, when
robbers attacked him, stripped him, and beat him up, leaving him
half dead. It so happened that a priest was going down that road;
when he saw the man he walked on by, on the other side. In the
same way a Levite also came there, went over and looked at the
man, and then walked on by, on the other side. But a certain Samaritan who was traveling that way came upon him, and when he saw
the man his heart was filled with pity. He went over to him, poured
oil and wine on his wounds and bandaged them; then he put the
man on his own animal and took him to an inn, where he took
care of him. The next day he took out two silver coins and gave
them to the innkeeper. 'Take care of him,' he told the innkeeper,
'and when I come back this way I will pay you back whatever you
spend on him.'" And Jesus concluded, "In your opinion, which one
of these three acted like a fellow-man toward the man attacked by
the robbers?" The teacher of the Law answered, "The one who was
kind to him." Jesus replied, "You go, then, and do the same."

For Further Reflection

1. Can you detect a pattern of virtue in these teachings of Jesus?
   Compare and contrast them with contemporary virtues of
   acquisitiveness and good business sense or with the Greek
   virtues of wisdom, courage, pride, and self-control.

2. Evaluate these teachings, for example, "If your right eye causes you to sin, take it out and throw it away." How should we interpret them? What are their implications?

3. What does the parable of the Good Samaritan teach us? If moral relativism is correct, isn't the Good Samaritan really immoral, since his culture forbade helping their enemies, the Jews? So if the Good Samaritan is really virtuous, does that indicate that moral objectivism is true?

How Much Land Does a Man Need?

Greed

LEO TOLSTOY

Leo Nicolayevich Tolstoy (1828–1910) was born to a Russian noble family and became one of the greatest Russian writers of all time. Among his most famous works are *War and Peace* and *Anna Karenina.* He was a deeply spiritual, Christian anarchist, whose works were considered heretical by the Russian Orthodox Church, which banned his book *What I Believe* (1899) and finally excommunicated him in 1901. During the last years of his life, he liberated his peasants, gave them most of his possessions, and lived like a peasant, a frugal, ascetic life. We get a powerful glimpse of his philosophy of life in this parable on greed.

1

An elder sister came to visit her younger sister in the country. The elder was married to a merchant in town, the younger to a peas-

---

Translated from Leo Tolstoy, "How Much Land Does a Man Need?"

ant in the village. As the sisters sat drinking their tea and talking, the elder began to talk proudly of the advantages of town life, saying in what comfort they lived there, how well they dressed, what fine clothes her children wore, what good things they ate and drank, and how she went to the theatre and other amusements.

The younger sister did not like this at all, and in turn spoke ill of the life of a merchant and praised the life of a peasant.

'I would not change my way of life for yours,' said she. 'We may live roughly, but at least we have no worries. You may have better food and clothes and more amusements than we have, but though you often earn more than you need, you may easily lose all you have. People who are rich one day are often begging their bread next day. Our way is safer. Though a peasant's life is not a rich one, it is a long one. We shall never have a lot of money, but we shall always have enough to eat.'

'Enough!' laughed the older sister. 'Yes, if you want to live like the animals! What do you know of fine living and good manners! However hard your husband may work, you will die as you are living—on a waste heap—and your children also!'

'Well, what of that?' replied the younger sister. 'Of course our work is rough and hard. But it is also sure, and we need not bow down to anyone. But you, in your towns, have all kinds of trouble; to-day all may be well, but to-morrow the Devil may lead your husband into wrong-doing with cards or wine, and all will be lost. Such things happen often!'

Pahom, the master of the house, was lying on the top of the stove and he listened to the women's talk.

'It is perfectly true,' he said. 'We peasants are so busy growing food in the fields from the time we are children, that we have no time to let any foolish ideas get into our heads. Our only trouble is that we have not enough land. If I had plenty of land I should not fear even the Devil himself!'

The women finished their tea, talked for a while about dress, and then cleared away the tea-things and lay down to sleep.

But the Devil had been sitting behind the stove and had heard all that was said. He was pleased that the peasant's wife had caused her husband to talk so proudly, and that he had said that if he had plenty of land he would not fear even the Devil himself.

'All right,' thought the Devil. 'We will have a test. I will give you enough land; and because of that land I will get you into my power.'

2

Near the village there lived a lady who owned about three hundred acres of land. The peasants had always liked her until she put an old soldier in charge of her land, and he began to annoy the people by making them pay fines. Although Pahom tried to be very careful, again and again one of his horses went into the lady's corn, a cow of his wandered into her garden, or his oxen got into her fields—and always he had to pay a fine.

Each time Pahom paid the fine unwillingly, and then went home in anger and was rough with his family. All through that summer Pahom was in trouble because of this old soldier, and he was even glad when winter came and the cattle had to be put under cover. Though he disliked having to buy hay for them when they could no longer feed in the fields, at least he was free from worrying about where they were.

In the winter the peasants heard that the lady was going to sell her land and that the keeper of the inn on the main road was making an offer for it. This news troubled them greatly.

'Indeed,' they thought, 'if the innkeeper gets the land, he will annoy us with fines more than the old soldier does. We all depend upon that land.'

So the peasants went, in the name of their Village Society, and asked the lady not to sell the land to the innkeeper, offering her a better price for it themselves. The lady agreed to let them have it. Then the peasants tried to arrange for the Society to buy the whole of it, so that they might all share it. They met twice to discuss the question, but could not reach an agreement. The Devil spread doubt among them, and they would not trust one another. So they decided to buy the land separately, each taking as much as he could afford. And the lady agreed to this plan also.

Soon Pahom heard that a man who lived near him was buying fifty acres, and that the lady had agreed to accept a half of the payment in ready money and wait a year for the other half. Pahom wished that he, too, could buy some land.

'That is bad,' he thought. 'The land is all being sold, and I shall get none of it.' So he spoke to his wife.

'Other people are buying,' said he, 'and we must also buy forty acres at least. Life is becoming impossible. That fellow's fines are ruining us.'

So they considered together how they could manage to buy it.

They had saved one hundred roubles. They sold a young horse and one half of their bees, and sent one of their sons out to work and took his pay in advance. They borrowed the rest of the money from a relation, and so collected half the price of the land.

When he had done this, Pahom chose a farm of forty acres, with fine woods, and went to the lady to make her an offer for it. They made a bargain, and he shook hands with her upon it and paid her a sum of money in advance. Then they went to town and signed the agreement. He paid half the price at once and promised to pay the rest before the end of two years.

So now Pahom had his own land. He borrowed seed and sowed it on the land he had bought. The harvest was a good one, and within a year he had managed to pay his debts both to the lady and to his relation. So he became a landowner, ploughing and sowing and making hay on his own land, cutting his own trees and feeding his cattle on his own grass. When he went out to plough his fields or to look at his growing corn, or at his fields of grass, his heart was full of joy. The grass and the flowers that grew there seemed to him unlike any that grew anywhere else. Before, when he had passed by that land, it had appeared the same as any other land, but now it seemed quite different.

3

So Pahom was very happy, and everything would have been right if only the peasants had not wandered on to his cornfields and grassland. He asked them most politely to keep away, but they did not. Sometimes the herdsmen would let the village cows wander into his fields; sometimes horses would get into his corn. Pahom turned them out again and again, and forgave their owners, and for a long time he did not make use of the law. But at last he became impatient and took the matter to the District Court. He knew that the peasants only came on to his land because they had none themselves, and that they did not intend to do wrong, but he thought: 'I cannot go on letting it happen or they will destroy all I have. They must be taught a lesson.'

So he had them brought to the court, gave them one lesson, and then another, and two or three of the peasants had to pay fines. After a time the men who lived near Pahom began to dislike him because of this, and on some occasions they let their cattle go on to his land on purpose.

One peasant even went into Pahom's wood at night and cut down five beautiful young trees in order to have their bark. As Pahom passed through the wood one day he noticed something white. He came nearer and saw the stripped trees lying on the ground, and nearby stood the roots where the trees had been. Pahom was very angry. 'If he had only cut one tree here and there it would have been bad enough,' Pahom thought, 'but the fellow has actually cut down the whole group. If I could find out who did this I would punish him as he deserves.'

He thought hard who it could be. At last he decided: 'It must be Simon—no one else could have done it.' So he went to Simon's home to have a look round, but he found nothing, and only had an angry quarrel. However, he now felt very certain that Simon had done it, and he reported him. Simon was brought before the court. The case was heard twice, and at the end of it all Simon was let off, for there was no proof against him. Pahom felt still more wronged and turned angrily to the judges.

'You take money from robbers,' said he. 'If you were honest people yourselves you would not let a robber go free.'

So Pahom quarrelled with the judges and with everyone in his district. People began to threaten to burn his buildings. So though Pahom had more land, he was liked in the village much less than before.

About this time the peasants heard that many people were leaving this part of Russia to go to other parts.

'There is no need for me to leave my land,' Pahom thought. 'But some of the others may leave our village and then there will be more room for us. I will take their land myself and make my farm bigger. I can then live in greater comfort. At present I am shut in too much to be comfortable.'

One day Pahom was sitting at home when a peasant who was passing through the village happened to come in. Pahom allowed him to stay for the night and gave him supper. He had a talk with this peasant and asked him where he came from. The stranger answered that he came from beyond the river Volga, where he had been working. One word led to another, and the man went on to say that many people were going to live in those lands. He told how some people from his village had settled there. They had joined a Society, and each of them had received twenty-five acres of land. This land was so good that the corn sown on it grew as high as a horse and was very thick. The stranger said that one peasant had brought nothing with him but his hands, and now he had six horses and two cows of his own.

Pahom's heart was filled with desire. He thought: 'Why should I suffer in this narrow hole, if men can live so well in other places? I will sell my land and my home here, and with the money I will make a fresh start there and get everything new. We are always having trouble in this crowded place. But I must first go and find out all about it myself.'

When summer was near he got ready and started. He went down the river Volga on a steamer to Samara, and walked another three hundred miles, and at last reached the place. Everything was as the stranger had said. The peasants had plenty of land, for the Society had given every man twenty-five acres of land for his own use, and any one who had money could buy, at a rouble an acre, as much more good land as he wanted.

When Pahom had found out all he wished to know, he returned home in the autumn and began to sell everything he had. He sold his land at a profit, and also his home and all his cattle. He waited only till the spring, and then started with his family to find a new home.

4

As soon as Pahom and his family reached their new home he applied to be admitted into the Society of a large village. The Society allowed him the use of a hundred and twenty-five acres in different fields as well as its own grassland. Pahom bought cattle and put up the buildings he needed in the village. He had three times as much land as he had owned before, and it was good corn-land. He was ten times wealthier than he had been. He had plenty of land for cultivation and for grass, and could keep as many cattle as he wished.

At first, in the excitement of building and living in his new home, Pahom was pleased with everything, but when he became used to it he began to think that even here he had not enough land. In the first year, he sowed wheat on his share of the Society's land, and had a good crop. He wanted to go on sowing wheat, but had not enough land for the purpose, for he could not sow his land again till it had rested and grass had grown over it. Many people wanted such land and there was not enough for all, so that there were quarrels about it. Those who were wealthy wanted to grow wheat and those who were poor wanted to make money out of it through dealers. Pahom wanted to sow more wheat, so he rented land from a dealer for a year. He sowed a lot of wheat and had a fine crop, but the land was too far from the village—the wheat had to be taken more than ten miles. After a time Pahom noticed that some peasant dealers were living on separate farms away from the Society's village and were becoming wealthy; and he thought, 'If I were to buy some land of my own and have a separate farm on it, it would be quite a different thing. Then it would all be nice and convenient.' The idea of buying land of his own, instead of renting it, came into his mind again and again.

For three years he rented land and sowed wheat. The seasons and the crops were good, and he saved more money. He might have continued to live happily, but he grew tired of renting other people's land every year. Where the land was good the peasants used to rush for it and it was taken immediately, so that unless you were quick you got none. In the third year it happened that Pahom and a dealer together rented a piece of grassland from some peasants. When they had already ploughed it, there was a quarrel and the peasants went to law about it, and the result was that the work of ploughing was all lost.

'If it were my own land,' thought Pahom, 'I should not have all this trouble.'

So Pahom began looking for land which he could buy, and he met a peasant who had bought thirteen hundred acres. This man had got into difficulties and was willing to sell again cheaply. Pahom bargained with him, and at last they decided on the price of 1,500 roubles, partly in ready money and partly to be paid later. When they had almost settled the matter, a passing dealer happened to stop at Pahom's house one day to get a feed for his horses. He drank tea with Pahom and they had a talk. The dealer said that he was just returning from the land of the Bashkirs far away, where he had bought thirteen thousand acres of land, all for 1,000 roubles. Pahom asked him more questions, and the dealer said, 'All you need to do is to make friends with the chiefs. I gave away about one hundred roubles' worth of silk dresses and furnishings, besides a case of tea, and I gave wine to those who wished to drink it; and I got the land for eight kopeks an acre.' He showed Pahom the papers about the sale, and said, 'The land lies near a river. The soil is good; none of it has been cultivated before.'

Pahom asked him many questions, and the dealer said, 'Even if you walked for a year you could not cover all the land, and it all belongs to the Bashkirs. They are as simple as sheep, and you can get land almost for nothing.'

'Well,' thought Pahom, 'why should I get only thirteen hundred acres in exchange for my one thousand roubles? If I take my money there I can get more than ten times as much for it.'

5

Pahom asked how to get to the place, and as soon as the dealer had left him he prepared to go there himself. He left his wife to look after the farm and started on his journey, taking a servant with him. They stopped at a town on their way and bought a case of tea, some wine and other gifts, as the dealer had advised. They went on and on until they had gone more than three hundred miles, and on the seventh day they came to the tents of the Bashkirs. All was as the dealer had said. The people lived on the plains by the river, in their tents. They did not cultivate the land or eat bread. Their herds of cattle and horses fed on the grass of the plains. The young horses were tied up behind the tents, and the mares were driven to them twice a day. The men milked the mares, and the women made kumiss and cheese from the milk. The men only cared about drinking kumiss and tea, eating meat, and playing tunes on their pipes. They were all strong and merry, and all through the summer they never thought of doing any work. They were simple people and could not speak Russian, but were very kind.

As soon as they saw Pahom they came out of their tents and crowded round their visitor. They found an interpreter who explained what was said, and Pahom told them that he had come to see if he could buy some land. The Bashkirs seemed to be very glad; they took Pahom and led him into one of the biggest tents. They made him sit in the best place in comfort while they sat round him. They gave him tea and kumiss and killed a sheep for him and gave him meat to eat. Pahom took gifts out of his cart and gave them to the Bashkirs, and divided the tea among them. The Bashkirs were filled with delight. They talked among themselves, and then told the interpreter to explain their words to Pahom.

'They wish to tell you,' said the interpreter, 'that they like you, and that it is their custom to do all they can to please a guest. You have given them gifts. Now tell them which of their possessions you like best, so that they may give them to you.'

'The thing which pleases me best here,' answered Pahom, 'is your land. Our land is crowded and the soil is no longer fruitful. But you have plenty of land, and it is good land. I never saw such land before.'

The interpreter explained what Pahom had said. The Bashkirs talked among themselves for a short time. Pahom could not understand what they were saying, but saw that they were much amused and that they shouted and laughed. Then there was silence, and they looked at Pahom while the interpreter said, 'They wish me to tell you that in exchange for your gifts they will gladly give you as much land as you want. You need only point it out with your hand and it will be yours.'

The Bashkirs talked again for a short time and began to argue. Pahom asked what they were arguing about. The interpreter told him, 'Some of them think they ought to ask their Chief about the land and not do anything while he is absent. The others think that there is no need to wait for his return.'

6

While the Bashkirs were arguing, a man in a large fur cap arrived. They all stopped talking and stood up. The interpreter said, 'This is our Chief himself.'

Pahom immediately fetched the finest coat and five pounds of tea, and offered these to the Chief. The Chief accepted them and sat down in the place of honour. The Bashkirs at once began telling him something. The Chief listened for a while, and then made a sign with his head which demanded silence, and speaking Russian he said to Pahom, 'Well, let it be so. Choose whatever piece of land you like; we have plenty of it.'

'How can I take as much as I like?' thought Pahom. 'I must get an official paper to make it certain, or else now they may say, "It is yours," and afterwards they may take it away again.'

'Thank you for your kind words,' he said aloud. 'You have a lot of land, and I only want a little. But I should like to be sure which bit is mine. Could it not be measured and officially given to me? Life and death are in God's hands. You good people give it to me, but your children might wish to take it away again.'

'You are quite right,' said the Chief. 'We will give it to you officially.'

'I heard that a dealer had been here,' Pahom continued, 'and that you gave him a little land too, and signed the official papers. I should like to have it done in the same way.'

The Chief understood.

'Yes,' he replied, 'that can be done quite easily. We have a law-writer, and we will go to town with you and have the papers properly signed.'

'And what will be the price?' asked Pahom.

'Our price is always the same: one thousand roubles a day.'

Pahom did not understand.

'A day? What measure is that? How many acres would that be?'

'We do not know how to measure it,' said the Chief. 'We sell it by the day. You may have as much as you can go round on your feet in one day, and the price is one thousand roubles a day.'

Pahom was surprised.

'But in one day you can get round a large district!' he said.

The chief laughed.

'It will all be yours!' said he. 'But there is one condition. If you do not return on the same day to the spot you started from, your money is lost.'

'But how am I to mark the way that I have gone?'

'Why, we shall go to any spot you like, and stay there. You must start from that spot and make your round, taking a spade with you. Make a mark wherever you think one is necessary. Each time you make a turn, dig a hole and make a heap of earth. You may make as large a course as you please, but before the sun sets you must return to the place you started from. All the land you cover will be yours.'

Pahom was delighted. He decided to start early next morning. They talked for a short time, and after drinking some more kumiss and eating some more meat, they had tea again, and then night came on. They gave Pahom a soft bed to sleep on, and the Bashkirs went away for the night, promising to meet together the next morning at daybreak and ride out before sunrise to the spot they had chosen.

7

Pahom lay on the soft bed, but could not sleep. He thought all the time about the land.

'What a large piece I will mark off!' he thought. 'I can easily walk thirty-five miles in a day. The days are long now, and there will be a great deal of land within a course of thirty-five miles. I will sell the poorer land, or the peasants can rent it from me. But I will choose the best and farm it. I will buy two pairs of oxen, and employ two more workers. About a hundred and fifty acres shall be ploughed and I will let cattle feed on the rest.'

Pahom lay awake all night and did not sleep until just before daybreak. Immediately, he had a dream. He thought that he was lying in that same tent and heard somebody laughing outside. He wondered who it could be, and he dreamed that he got up and walked out, and saw the Bashkir Chief sitting in front of the tent, holding his sides and laughing so much that he rolled about. Pahom went nearer to the Chief and asked, 'What are you laughing at?' But then he saw that it was not the Chief, but the dealer who had recently stopped at his house and told him about the land. Just as Pahom was going to ask, 'Have you been here long?' he saw that it was not the dealer, but the peasant who had come up from the Volga, long ago, to Pahom's old home. Then he saw that it was not even the peasant, but the Devil himself, with the body of an animal, who sat there laughing. In front of him a man, wearing only a shirt and trousers, lay flat on the ground. And Pahom dreamed that he looked more carefully to see what kind of man it was that was lying there, and he saw that the man was dead, and that it was himself! He awoke terribly frightened.

'What terrible things one dreams!' he thought, and as he looked round he saw through the open door the first light of day.

'It's time to wake them up,' he thought. 'We ought to make a start.'

He got up, awoke his servant, who was sleeping in his cart, told him to get the horse ready, and went to call the Bashkirs.

'It's time to go to the plain to measure the land,' he said.

The Bashkirs got up and met together, and the Chief came too. Then they began drinking kumiss again, and offered Pahom some tea, but he would not wait.

'The time has come,' he said. 'Let us go.'

The Bashkirs got ready, and they all started; some were on horses, and some in carts. Pahom drove in his own small cart with his servant and took a spade with him. When they reached the plain, the red of the morning was beginning to flame. They climbed up a small hill and, getting down from their carts and their horses, they met together in one spot. The Chief came up to Pahom and stretched out his arm towards the plain.

'See,' said he, 'all this, as far as your eye can reach, is ours. You may have any part of it you like.'

Pahom's eyes shone; it was all uncultivated land, flat and black, and different kinds of grass grew in the low-lying parts almost up to a man's shoulders.

The Chief took off his fur cap, placed it on the ground and said, 'This will be the mark. Start from here, and return here again. All the land you go round shall be yours.'

Pahom took out his money and put it on the cap. Then he took off his overcoat, remaining in his undercoat. He took his belt, tied it tightly round his middle, and put a little bag of bread inside his coat. Then he tied a bottle of water to his belt, fastened up the tops of his high boots, took the spade from his servant, and stood ready to start. He considered for a few moments which way he ought to go. Everywhere seemed good.

'It does not matter,' he thought. 'I will go towards the rising sun.'

He turned his face to the east, stretched himself, and waited for the sun to come up.

'I must lose no time,' he thought, 'and it is easier walking while it is still cool.'

The sun had hardly shone above the skyline, before Pahom, carrying the spade over his shoulder, went down into the plain.

Pahom started walking neither slowly nor quickly. After he had gone a thousand yards he stopped, dug a hole, and placed pieces of earth and grass one on another so that it could be easily seen. Then he went on; and now that he was walking more freely he increased his speed. After a short time he dug another hole.

Pahom looked back. He could see the hill clearly in the sunlight, with the people on it, and the shining metal of the cart-wheels. Pahom made a rough guess that he had walked three miles. It was growing warmer. He took off his under-coat, put it across his shoulder and went on again. It was quite warm now; he looked at the sun. It was time to think of breakfast.

'The first part is done, but there are four parts in a day and it is too soon yet to turn. But I will take off my boots,' he said to himself.

He sat down, took off his boots, put them under his belt, and went on. It was easy walking now.

'I will go on for another three miles,' he thought, 'and then turn to the left. This spot is so fine that it would be a shame to lose it. The farther one goes the better the land seems.'

He went straight on for a short time, and when he looked round he could scarcely see the hill. The people on it looked like black ants, and he could just see something shining there in the sun.

'Ah,' thought Pahom. 'I have gone far enough this way, it is time to turn. Besides, I am very hot and thirsty.'

He stopped, dug a hole and made a heap by the side of it. Next he untied his bottle, had a drink and then turned sharply to the left. He went on and on; the grass was high, and it was very hot.

Pahom began to grow tired; he looked at the sun and saw that it was noon.

'Well,' he thought, 'I must have a rest.'

He sat down and ate some bread and drank some water; but he did not lie down, thinking that if he did he might fall asleep. After sitting a little while, he went on again. At first he walked easily, for the food had given him strength; but it had become terribly hot and he felt sleepy. Still he went on, thinking, 'An hour to suffer, a lifetime to live.'

He went on in this way for a long time also, and was about to turn to his left again when he saw a damp low-lying area. 'It would be a shame to leave that out,' he thought. 'Flax would grow well there.' So he went on, past the low-lying ground, and dug a hole on the other side of it before he turned the corner.

Pahom looked towards the hill. The heat made the air misty; it seemed to be shaking and he could scarcely see the people on the hill through the mist.

'Ah,' thought Pahom, 'I have made the sides too long; I must make this one shorter.' And he went along the third side, walking faster. He looked at the sun. It was nearly half-way down to the skyline, and he had not yet done two miles of the third side of the square. He was still ten miles from the hill.

'No,' he thought, 'though it will make the shape of my land uneven, I must hurry back in a straight line now. I might go too far, and I already have a great deal of land.'

So Pahom hurriedly dug a hole, and turned straight towards the hill.

8

Pahom went straight towards the hill, but he now walked with difficulty. He was tired with the heat, his feet were cut and hurt, and his legs were weak. He wished to rest, but it was not possible if he meant to get back before sunset. The sun waits for no man, and it was sinking lower and lower.

'Oh dear,' he thought, 'if only I had not made a mistake trying for too much! What will happen if I am too late?'

He looked towards the hill and at the sun. He was still far from the place. He began running, threw away his coat, his boots, his bottle, and his cap, and kept only the spade which he used as a support.

'What shall I do?' he thought again. 'I have tried to get too much and lost everything. I can't get there before the sun sets.'

And this fear made him breathe even harder. Pahom went on running, his soaking shirt and trousers stuck to him, and his mouth was very dry. His breathing was hard, his heart was beating like a hammer, and his legs were weak and felt as if they did not belong to him. Pahom was terribly frightened that he would die from the effort. Though afraid of death, he could not stop. 'They will call me a fool if I stop now after I have run all that way,' he thought. And he ran on and on, nearer and nearer, and heard the Bashkirs calling and shouting to him. Their cries excited him still more. He gathered his last strength and ran on.

The sun was close to the skyline, and, with mist all around, it looked large and red as blood. It was just about to set. The sun was very low, but he was also quite near the hill. Pahom could already see the people on the hill waving their arms to make him hurry. He could see the fur cap on the ground, and the Chief sitting beside it holding his sides. And Pahom remembered his dream.

'There is plenty of land,' he thought, 'but will God let me live on it? I have lost my life, I have lost my life! I shall never reach that spot!'

Pahom looked at the sun, which had reached the earth: the bottom of it had already disappeared. With all his remaining strength he rushed on, bending his body forward so that his legs could hardly follow fast enough to keep him from falling. Just as he reached the hill it suddenly grew dark. He looked up—the sun had already set! He gave a cry. 'All my efforts have been useless,' he thought, and was about to stop, but he heard the Bashkirs still shouting, and remembered that though to him, down below, the sun seemed to have set, those on the hill could still see it. He breathed deeply and ran up the slope of the small hill. It was still light there. He reached the top and saw the cap. The Chief sat in front of it, laughing and holding his sides. Again Pahom remembered his dream, and he gave a loud cry. His legs gave way beneath him, he fell forward and reached the cap with his hands.

'Ah, that's a fine fellow!' said the Chief. 'He has gained a lot of land!'

Pahom's servant came running up and tried to raise him, but he saw that blood was flowing from his mouth. Pahom was dead! The Bashkirs looked sad and showed their pity.

His servant picked up the spade and dug a hole long enough for Pahom to lie in, and buried him in it. Six feet from his head to his toes was all the land he needed.

For Further Reflection

1. How applicable is Tolstoy's parable to our day?

2. Write an essay on modern-day greed.

Jealousy, Malice, and Ingratitude

IMMANUEL KANT

This is Kant's analysis of jealousy in the form of grudging and spitefulness, envy, and ingratitude. Kant is sometimes accused of only valuing one virtue, conscientiousness (and hence one vice, a vicious will), but this selection shows that he was broader than that.

From *Lectures on Ethics,* translated by Louis Infield (Methuen, 1930).

There are two methods by which men arrive at an opinion of their worth: by comparing themselves with the idea of perfection and by comparing themselves with others. The first of these methods is sound; the second is not, and it frequently even leads to a result diametrically opposed to the first. The idea of perfection is a proper standard, and if we measure our worth by it, we find that we fall short of it and feel that we must exert ourselves to come nearer to it; but if we compare ourselves with others, much depends upon who those others are and how they are constituted, and we can easily believe ourselves to be of great worth if those with whom we set up comparison are rogues. Men love to compare themselves with others, for by that method they can always arrive at a result favourable to themselves. They choose as a rule the worst and not the best of the class with which they set up comparison; in this way their own excellence shines out. If they choose those of greater worth the result of the comparison is, of course, unfavourable to them.

When I compare myself with another who is better than I, there are but two ways by which I can bridge the gap between us. I can either do my best to attain to his perfections, or else I can seek to depreciate his good qualities. I either increase my own worth, or else I diminish his so that I can always regard myself as superior to him. It is easier to depreciate another than to emulate him, and men prefer the easier course. They adopt it, and this is the origin of jealousy. When a man compares himself with another and finds that the other has many more good points, he becomes jealous of each and every good point he discovers in the other, and tries to depreciate it so that his own good points may stand out. This kind of jealousy may be called grudging. The other species of the genus jealousy, which makes us try to add to our good points so as to compare well with another, may be called emulating jealousy. The jealousy of emulation is, as we have stated, more difficult than the jealousy of grudge and so is much the less frequent of the two.

Parents ought not, therefore, when teaching their children to be good, to urge them to model themselves on other children and try to emulate them, for by so doing they simply make them jealous. If I tell my son, "Look, how good and industrious John is," the result will be that my son will bear John a grudge. He will think to himself that, but for John, he himself would be the best, because there would be no comparison. By setting up John as a pattern for imitation I anger my son, make him feel a grudge against this so-called paragon, and I instil jealousy in him. My son might, of course, try to emulate

John, but not finding it easy, he will bear John ill-will. Besides, just as I can say to my son, "Look, how good John is," so can he reply: "Yes, he is better than I, but are there not many who are far worse? Why do you compare me with those who are better? Why not with those who are worse than I?" Goodness must, therefore, be commended to children in and for itself. Whether other children are better or worse has no bearing on the point. If the comparison were in the child's favour, he would lose all ground of impulse to improve his own conduct. To ask our children to model themselves on others is to adopt a faulty method of upbringing, and as time goes on the fault will strike its roots deep. It is jealousy that parents are training and presupposing in their children when they set other children before them as patterns. Otherwise, the children would be quite indifferent to the qualities of others. They will find it easier to belittle the good qualities of their patterns than to emulate them, so they will choose the easier path and learn to show a grudging disposition. It is true that jealousy is natural, but that is no excuse for cultivating it. It is only a motive, a reserve in case of need. While the maxims of reason are still undeveloped in us, the proper course is to use reason to keep it within bounds. For jealousy is only one of the many motives, such as ambition, which are implanted in us because we are designed for a life of activity. But so soon as reason is enthroned, we must cease to seek perfection in emulation of others and must covet it in and for itself. Motives must abdicate and let reason bear rule in their place.

Persons of the same station and occupation in life are particularly prone to be jealous of each other. Many business-men are jealous of each other; so are many scholars, particularly in the same line of scholarship; and women are liable to be jealous of each other regarding men.

Grudge is the displeasure we feel when another has an advantage; his advantage makes us feel unduly small and we grudge it him. But to grudge a man his share of happiness is envy. To be envious is to desire the failure and unhappiness of another not for the purpose of advancing our own success and happiness but because we might then ourselves be perfect and happy as we are. An envious man is not happy unless all around him are unhappy; his aim is to stand alone in the enjoyment of his happiness. Such is envy, and we shall learn below that it is satanic. Grudge, although it too should not be countenanced, is natural. Even a good-natured person may at times be grudging. Such a one may, for instance, begrudge those around him their jollity when he himself happens to be sorrowful; for it is hard to bear one's sorrow when all around are joyful. When I see everybody enjoying a good meal and I alone must content myself with inferior fare, it upsets me and I feel a grudge; but if we are all in the same boat I am content. We find the thought of death bearable, because we know that all must die; but if everybody were immortal and I alone had to die, I should feel aggrieved. It is not things themselves that affect us, but things in their relation to ourselves. We are grudging because others are happier than we. But when a good-natured man feels happy and cheerful, he wishes that every one else in the world were as happy as he and shared his joy; he begrudges no one his happiness.

When a man would not grant to another even that for which he himself has no need, he is spiteful. Spite is a maliciousness of spirit which is not the same thing as envy. I may not feel inclined to give to another something which belongs to me, even though I myself have no use for it, but it does not follow that I grudge him his own possessions, that I want to be the only one who has anything and wish him to have nothing at all. There is a deal of grudge in human nature which could develop into envy but which is not itself envy. We feel pleasure in gossiping about the minor misadventures of other people; we are not averse, although we may express no pleasure thereat, to hearing of the fall of some rich man; we may enjoy in stormy weather, when comfortably seated in our warm, cosy parlour, speaking of those at sea, for it heightens our own feeling of comfort and happiness; there is grudge in all this, but it is not envy.

The three vices which are the essence of vileness and wickedness are ingratitude, envy, and malice. When these reach their full degree they are devilish.

Men are shamed by favours. If I receive a favour, I am placed under an obligation to the giver; he has a call upon me because I am indebted to him. We all blush to be obliged. Noble-minded men accordingly refuse to accept favours in order not to put themselves under an obligation. But this attitude predisposes the mind to ingratitude. If the man who adopts it is noble-minded, well and good; but if he be proud and selfish and has perchance received a favour, the feeling that he is beholden to his benefactor hurts his pride and, being selfish, he cannot accommodate himself to the idea that he owes his benefactor anything. He becomes defiant and ungrateful. His ingratitude might even conceivably assume such dimensions that he cannot bear his benefactor and becomes his enemy.

Such ingratitude is of the devil; it is out of all keeping with human nature. It is inhuman to hate and persecute one from whom we have reaped a benefit, and if such conduct were the rule it would cause untold harm. Men would then be afraid to do good to anyone lest they should receive evil in return for their good. They would become misanthropic.

The second devilish vice is envy. Envy is in the highest degree detestable. The envious man does not merely want to be happy; he wants to be the only happy person in the world; he is really contented only when he sees nothing but misery around him. Such an intolerable creature would gladly destroy every source of joy and happiness in the world.

Malice is the third kind of viciousness which is of the devil. It consists in taking a direct pleasure in the misfortunes of others. Men prone to this vice will seek, for instance, to make mischief between husband and wife, or between friends, and then enjoy the misery they have produced. In these matters we should make it a rule never to repeat to a person anything that we may have heard to his disadvantage from another, unless our silence would injure him. Otherwise we start an enmity and disturb his peace of mind, which our silence would have avoided, and in addition we break faith with our informant. The defence against such mischief-makers is upright conduct. Not by words but by our lives we should confute them. As Socrates said: We ought so to conduct ourselves that people will not credit anything spoken in disparagement of us.

These three vices—ingratitude (*ingratitudo qualificata*), envy, and malice—are devilish because they imply a direct inclination to evil. There are in man certain indirect tendencies to wickedness which are human and not unnatural. The miser wants everything for himself, but it is no satisfaction to him to see that his neighbour is destitute. The evilness of a vice may thus be either direct or indirect. In these three vices it is direct.

We may ask whether there is in the human mind an immediate inclination to wickedness, an inclination to the devilish vices. Heaven stands for the acme of happiness, hell for all that is bad, and the earth stands midway between these two extremes; and just as goodness which transcends anything which might be expected of a human being is spoken of as being angelic, so also do we speak of devilish wickedness when the wickedness oversteps the limits of human nature and becomes inhuman. We may take it for granted that the human mind has no immediate inclination to wickedness, but is only indirectly wicked. Man cannot be so ungrateful that he simply must hate his neighbour; he may be too proud to show his gratitude and so avoid him, but he wishes him well. Again, our pleasure in the misfortune of another is not direct. We may rejoice, for example, in a man's misfortunes, because he was haughty, rich and selfish; for man loves to preserve equality. We have thus no direct inclination towards evil as evil, but only an indirect one. But how are we to explain the fact that even young children have the spirit of mischief strongly developed? For a joke, a boy will stick a pin in an unsuspecting playmate, but it is only for fun. He has no thought of the pain the other must feel on all such occasions. In the same spirit he will torture animals; twisting the cat's tail or the dog's. Such tendencies must be nipped in the bud, for it is easy to see where they will lead. They are, in fact, something animal, something of the beast of prey which is in us all, which we cannot overcome, and the source of which we cannot explain. There certainly are in human nature characteristics for which we can assign no reason. There are animals too who steal anything that comes their way, though it is quite useless to them; and it seems as if man has retained this animal tendency in his nature.

Ingratitude calls for some further observations here. To help a man in distress is charity; to help him in less urgent needs is benevolence; to help him in the amenities of life is courtesy. We may be the recipients of a charity which has not cost the giver much and our gratitude is commensurate with the degree of good-will which moved him to the action. We are grateful not only for what we have received but also for the good intention which prompted it, and the greater the effort it has cost our benefactor, the greater our gratitude.

Gratitude may be either from duty or from inclination. If an act of kindness does not greatly move us, but if we nevertheless feel that it is right and proper that we should show gratitude, our gratitude is merely prompted by a sense of duty. Our heart is not grateful, but we have principles of gratitude. If however, our heart goes out to our benefactor, we are grateful from inclination. There is a weakness of the understanding which we often have cause to recognize. It consists in taking the conditions of our understanding as conditions of the thing understood. We can estimate force only in terms of the obstacles it overcomes. Similarly, we can only estimate the degree of good-will in terms of the obstacles it has to surmount. In consequence we cannot comprehend the love and goodwill of a being for whom there are no obstacles. If God has been good to me, I am liable to think that after all it has cost God no trouble, and that gratitude to God would be mere fawning on my part. Such thoughts are not at all unnatural. It is easy to fear God, but not nearly so easy to love God from inclination because of our consciousness that God is a being whose goodness is unbounded but to whom it is no trouble to shower kindness upon us. This is not to say that such should be our mental attitude; merely that when we examine our hearts, we find that this is how we actually think. It also explains why to many races God appeared to be a jealous God, seeing that it cost Him nothing to be more bountiful with His goodness; it explains why many nations thought that their gods were sparing of their benefits and that they required propitiating with prayers and sacrifices. This is the attitude of man's heart; but when we call reason to our aid we see that God's goodness must be of a high order if He is to be good to a being so unworthy of His goodness. This solves our difficulty. The gratitude we owe to God is not gratitude from inclination, but from duty, for God is not a creature like ourselves, and can be no object of our inclinations.

We ought not to accept favours unless we are either forced to do so by dire necessity or have implicit confidence in our benefactor (for he ceases to be our friend and becomes our benefactor) that he will not regard it as placing us under an obligation to him. To accept favours indiscriminately and to be constantly seeking them is ignoble and the sign of a mean soul which does not mind placing itself under obligations. Unless we are driven by such dire necessity that it compels us to sacrifice our own worth, or unless we are convinced that our benefactor will not account it to us as a debt, we ought rather to suffer deprivation than accept favours, for a favour is a debt which can never be extinguished. For even if I repay my benefactor tenfold, I am still not even with him, because he has done me a kindness which he did not owe. He was the first in the field, and even if I return his gift tenfold I do so only as repayment. He will always be the one who was the first to show kindness and I can never be beforehand with him.

The man who bestows favours can do so either in order to make the recipient indebted to him or as an expression of his duty. If he makes the recipient feel a sense of indebtedness, he wounds his pride and diminishes his sense of gratitude. If he wishes to avoid this he must regard the favours he bestows as the discharge of a duty he owes to mankind, and he must not give the recipient the impression that it is a debt to be repaid. On the other hand, the recipient of the favour must still consider himself under an obligation to his benefactor and must be grateful to him. Under these conditions there can be benefactors and beneficiaries. A right-thinking man will not accept kindnesses, let alone favours. A grateful disposition is a touching thing and brings tears to our eyes on the stage, but a generous disposition is lovelier still. Ingratitude we detest to a surprising degree; even though we are not ourselves the victims of it, it angers us to such an extent that we feel inclined to intervene. But this is due to the fact that ingratitude decreases generosity.

Envy does not consist in wishing to be more happy than others—that is grudge—but in wishing to be the only one to be happy. It is this feeling which makes envy so evil. Why should not others be happy along with me? Envy shows itself also in relation to things which are scarce. Thus the Dutch, who as a nation are rather envious, once valued tulips at several hundreds of florins apiece. A rich merchant, who had one of the finest and rarest specimens, heard that another had a similar specimen. He thereupon bought it from him for 2,000 florins and trampled it underfoot, saying that he had no use for it, as he already possessed a specimen, and that he only wished that no one else should share that distinction with him. So it is also in the matter of happiness.

Malice is different. A malicious man is pleased when others suffer, he can laugh when others weep. An act which willfully brings unhappiness is cruel; when it produces physical pain it is bloodthirsty. Inhumanity is all these together, just as humanity consists in sympathy and pity, since these differentiate man from the beasts. It is difficult to explain what gives rise to a cruel disposition. It may arise when a man considers another so evilly disposed that he hates him. A man who believes himself hated by another, hates him in return, although the former may have good reason to hate him. For if a man is hated because he is selfish and has other vices, and he knows that he is hated for these reasons, he hates those who hate him although these latter do him no injustice. Thus kings who know that they are hated by their subjects become even more cruel. Equally, when a man has done a good deed to another, he knows that the other loves him, and so he loves him in return, knowing that he himself is loved. Just as love is reciprocated, so also is hate. We must for our own sakes guard against being hated by others lest we be affected by that hatred and reciprocate it. The hater is more disturbed by his hatred than is the hated.

For Further Reflection

1. Why doesn't Kant want us to compare ourselves (or our children) with others or strive to emulate others? Do you think he lacks a sound moral psychology? Do you think that it is really useful to try to emulate good people?

2. Analyze Kant's notion of jealousy. How does he define the two varieties of jealousy, *grudge* and *spite?*

3. How does Kant characterize ingratitude? Why does he say that the proper way to be grateful to God is out of duty, not inclination or spontaneous feeling? Do you agree?

4. Why will a right-thinking person refuse favors? Do you agree?

5. Here is a Russian parable on jealousy. It comes out of the Soviet era. An angel appears to a woman and tells her that she may make a wish and he will grant it. The only caveat is that whatever she wishes for, he will give twofold to her neighbor. Without blinking, the woman replies, "Pluck out one of my eyes." Is such malicious jealousy common? Can we protect ourselves from such vicious feelings?

Moral Cowardice

MARTIN GANSBERG

Martin Gansberg, staff writer for the *New York Times,* taught journalism at Fairleigh Dickenson University. In this article Gansberg reports the case of Kitty Genovese who for a half hour was brutally beaten and then murdered while thirty-eight of her neighbors looked on but did nothing.

For more than half an hour 38 respectable, law-abiding citizens in Queens watched a killer stalk and stab a woman in three separate attacks in Kew Gardens.

Twice their chatter and the sudden glow of their bedroom lights interrupted him and frightened him off. Each time he returned, sought her out, and stabbed her again. Not one person telephoned the police during the assault; one witness called after the woman was dead.

That was two weeks ago today.

Still shocked is Assistant Chief Inspector Frederick M. Lussen, in charge of the borough's detectives and a veteran of 25 years of homicide investigations. He can give a matter-of-fact recitation on many murders. But the Kew Gardens slaying baffles him—not because it is a murder, but because the "good people" failed to call the police.

"As we have reconstructed the crime," he said, "the assailant had three chances to kill this woman during a 35-minute period. He returned twice to complete the job. If we had been called when he first attacked, the woman might not be dead now."

This is what the police say happened beginning at 3:20 A.M. in the staid, middle-class, tree-lined Austin Street area:

Twenty-eight-year-old Catherine Genovese, who was called Kitty by almost everyone in the neighborhood, was returning home from her job as manager of a bar in Hollis. She parked her red Fiat in a lot adjacent to the Kew Gardens Long Island Rail Road Station, facing Mowbray Place. Like many residents of the neighborhood, she had parked there day after day since her arrival from Connecticut a year ago, although the railroad frowns on the practice.

She turned off the lights of her car, locked the door, and started to walk the 100 feet to the entrance of her apartment at 82-70 Austin Street, which is in a Tudor building, with stores on the first floor and apartments on the second.

The entrance to the apartment is in the rear of the building because the front is rented to retail stores. At night the quiet neighborhood is shrouded in the slumbering darkness that marks most residential areas.

Miss Genovese noticed a man at the far end of the lot, near a seven-story apartment house at 82-40 Austin Street. She halted. Then, nervously, she headed up Austin Street toward Lefferts Boulevard, where there is a call box to the 102nd Police Precinct in nearby Richmond Hill.

She got as far as a street light in front of a bookstore before the man grabbed her. She screamed. Lights went on in the 10-story apartment house at 82-67 Austin Street, which faces the bookstore. Windows slid open and voices punctuated the early-morning stillness.

Miss Genovese screamed: "Oh, my God, he stabbed me! Please help me! Please help me!"

From one of the upper windows in the apartment house, a man called down: "Let that girl alone!"

The assailant looked up at him, shrugged, and walked down Austin Street toward a white sedan parked a short distance away. Miss Genovese struggled to her feet.

Lights went out. The killer returned to Miss Genovese, now trying to make her way around the side of the building by the parking lot to get to her apartment. The assailant stabbed her again.

"I'm dying!" she shrieked. "I'm dying!"

Windows were opened again, and lights went on in many apartments. The assailant got into his car and drove away. Miss Genovese staggered to her feet. A city bus, 0-10, the Lefferts Boulevard line to Kennedy International Airport, passed. It was 3:35 A.M.

The assailant returned. By then, Miss Genovese had crawled to the back of the building, where the freshly painted brown doors to the apartment house held out hope for safety. The killer tried the first door; she wasn't there. At the second door, 82-62 Austin Street, he saw her slumped on the floor at the foot of the stairs. He stabbed her a third time—fatally.

It was 3:50 by the time the police received their first call, from a man who was a neighbor of Miss Genovese. In two minutes they were at the scene. The neighbor, a 70-year-old woman, and another woman were the only persons on the street. Nobody else came forward.

The man explained that he had called the police after much deliberation. He had phoned a friend in Nassau County for advice and then he had crossed the roof of the building to the apartment of the elderly woman to get her to make the call.

"I didn't want to get involved," he sheepishly told the police.

Six days later, the police arrested Winston Moseley, a 29-year-old business-machine operator, and charged him with the homicide. Moseley had no previous record. He is married, has two children and owns a home at 133-19 Sutter Avenue, South Ozone Park, Queens. On Wednesday, a court committed him to Kings County Hospital for psychiatric observation.

When questioned by the police, Moseley also said that he had slain Mrs. Annie May Johnson, 24, of 146-12 133d Avenue, Jamaica, on Feb. 29 and Barbara Kralik, 15, of 174-17 140th Avenue, Springfield Gardens, last July. In the Kralik case, the police are holding Alvin L. Mitchell, who is said to have confessed that slaying.

The police stressed how simple it would have been to have gotten in touch with them. "A phone call," said one of the detectives, "would have done it." The police may be reached by dialing "O" for operator or SPring 7-3100.

Today witnesses from the neighborhood, which is made up of one-family homes in the $35,000 to $60,000 range with the exception of the two apartment houses near the railroad station, find it difficult to explain why they didn't call the police.

A housewife, knowingly if quite casual, said, "We thought it was a lover's quarrel." A husband and wife both said, "Frankly, we were afraid." They seemed aware of the fact that events might have been different. A distraught woman, wiping her hands in her apron, said, "I didn't want my husband to get involved."

One couple, now willing to talk about that night, said they heard the first screams. The husband looked thoughtfully at the bookstore where the killer first grabbed Miss Genovese.

"We went to the window to see what was happening," he said, "but the light from our bedroom made it difficult to see the street." The wife, still apprehensive, added: "I put out the light and we were able to see better."

Asked why they hadn't called the police, she shrugged and replied: "I don't know."

A man peeked out from a slight opening in the doorway to his apartment and rattled off an account of the killer's second attack. Why hadn't he called the police at the time? "I was tired," he said without emotion. "I went back to bed."

It was 4:25 A.M. when the ambulance arrived to take the body of Miss Genovese. It drove off. "Then," a solemn police detective said, "the people came out."

For Further Reflection

1. Review the story of Kitty Genovese. Is only one vice, moral cowardice, manifest here, or are many indicated?

2. Compare this story with the parable of the Good Samaritan (the first reading in this chapter).

3. Some people think that the case of Kitty Genovese is a fluke, quite the opposite of how Americans typically act. Do you agree? Or do you think moral cowardice and indifference abound? How serious are our moral apathy and cowardice?

Three Days to See
Gratitude

HELEN KELLER

Helen Keller (1880–1968) was born in Tuscumbia, Alabama. At nineteen months of age she lost her sight and hearing. When Helen was four Anne Sullivan became her teacher and lifelong companion. She taught Helen to speak, read, and write. Keller obtained a college degree in 1904 and became a distinguished lecturer and writer. Her and Anne Sullivan's story was dramatized by William Gibson in *The Miracle Worker* (1959).

In this essay Keller imagines what it would be like to have three days to see.

All of us have read thrilling stories in which the hero had only a limited and specified time to live. Sometimes it was as long as a year; sometimes as short as twenty-four hours. But always we were interested in discovering just how the doomed man chose to spend his last days or his last hours. I speak, of course, of free men who have a choice, not condemned criminals whose sphere of activities is strictly delimited.

Such stories set us thinking, wondering what we should do under similar circumstances. What events, what experiences, what associations should we crowd into those last hours as mortal beings? What happiness should we find in reviewing the past, what regrets?

Sometimes I have thought it would be an excellent rule to live

Reprinted from "Three Days to See" by Helen Keller, *Atlantic Monthly*, 1933.

each day as if we should die tomorrow. Such an attitude would emphasize sharply the values of life. We should live each day with a gentleness, a vigor, and a keenness of appreciation which are often lost when time stretches before us in the constant panorama of more days and months and years to come. There are those, of course, who would adopt the epicurean motto of "Eat, drink, and be merry," but most people would be chastened by the certainty of impending death.

In stories, the doomed hero is usually saved at the last minute by some stroke of fortune, but almost always his sense of values is changed. He becomes more appreciative of the meaning of life and its permanent spiritual values. It has often been noted that those who live, or have lived, in the shadow of death bring a mellow sweetness to everything they do.

Most of us, however, take life for granted. We know that one day we must die, but usually we picture that day as far in the future. When we are in buoyant health, death is all but unimaginable. We seldom think of it. The days stretch out in an endless vista. So we go about our petty tasks, hardly aware of our listless attitude toward life.

The same lethargy, I am afraid, characterizes the use of all our faculties and senses. Only the deaf appreciate hearing, only the blind realize the manifold blessings that lie in sight. Particularly does this observation apply to those who have lost sight and hearing in adult life. But those who have never suffered impairment of sight or hearing seldom make the fullest use of these blessed faculties. Their eyes and ears take in all sights and sounds hazily, without concentration and with little appreciation. It is the same old story of not being grateful for what we have until we lose it, of not being conscious of health until we are ill.

I have often thought it would be a blessing if each human being were stricken blind and deaf for a few days at some time during his early adult life. Darkness would make him more appreciative of sight; silence would teach him the joys of sound.

Now and then I have tested my seeing friends to discover what they see. Recently I was visited by a very good friend who had just returned from a long walk in the woods, and I asked her what she had observed. "Nothing in particular," she replied. I might have been incredulous had I not been accustomed to such responses, for long ago I became convinced that the seeing see little.

How was it possible, I asked myself, to walk for an hour through the woods and see nothing worthy of note? I who cannot see find hundreds of things to interest me through mere touch. I feel the delicate symmetry of a leaf. I pass my hands lovingly about the smooth skin of a silver birch, or the rough shaggy bark of a pine. In spring I touch the branches of trees hopefully in search of a bud, the first sign of awakening Nature after her winter's sleep. I feel the delightful, velvety texture of a flower, and discover its remarkable convolutions, and something of the miracle of Nature is revealed to me. Occasionally, if I am fortunate, I place my hand gently on a small tree and feel the happy quiver of a bird in full song. I am delighted to have the cool waters of a brook rush through my open fingers. To me a lush carpet of pine needles or spongy grass is more welcome than the most luxurious Persian rug. To me the pageant of seasons is a thrilling and unending drama, the action of which streams through my finger tips.

At times my heart cries out with longing to see all these things. If I can get so much pleasure from mere touch, how much more beauty must be revealed by sight. Yet, those who have eyes apparently see little. The panorama of color and action which fills the world is taken for granted. It is human, perhaps, to appreciate little that which we have and to long for that which we have not, but it is a great pity that in the world of light the gift of sight is used only as a mere convenience rather than as a means of adding fullness to life.

If I were the president of a university I should establish a compulsory course in "How to Use Your Eyes." The professor would try to show his pupils how they could add joy to their lives by really seeing what passes unnoticed before them. He would try to awake their dormant and sluggish faculties.

Perhaps I can best illustrate by imagining what I should most like to see if I were given the use of my eyes, say, for just three days. And while I am imagining, suppose you, too, set your mind to work on the problem of how you would use your own eyes if you had only three more days to see. If with the oncoming darkness of the third night you knew that the sun would never rise for you again, how would you spend those three precious intervening days? What would you most want to let your gaze rest upon?

I, naturally, should want most to see the things which have become dear to me through my years of darkness. You, too, would want to let your eyes rest long on the things that have become dear to you so that you could take the memory of them with you into the night that loomed before you.

If, by some miracle I were granted three seeing days, to be followed by a relapse into darkness, I should divide the period into three parts.

On the first day, I should want to see the people whose kindness and gentleness have made my life worth living. First I should like to gaze long upon the face of my dear teacher, Mrs. Anne Sullivan Macy, who came to me when I was a child and opened the outer world to me. I should want not merely to see the outline of her face, so that I could cherish it in my memory, but to study that face and find in it the living evidence of the sympathetic tenderness and patience with which she accomplished the difficult task of my education. I should like to see in her eyes that strength of character which has enabled her to stand firm in the face of difficulties, and that compassion for all humanity which she has revealed to me so often.

I do not know what it is to see into the heart of a friend through that "window of the soul," the eye. I can only "see" through my finger tips the outline of a face. I can detect laughter, sorrow, and many other obvious emotions. I know my friends from the feel of their faces. But I cannot really picture their personalities by touch. I know their personalities, of course, through other means, through the thoughts they express to me, through whatever of their actions are revealed to me. But I am denied that deeper understanding of them which I am sure would come through sight of them, through watching their reactions to various expressed thoughts and circumstances, through noting the immediate and fleeting reactions of their eyes and countenance.

Friends who are near to me I know well, because through the months and years they reveal themselves to me in all their phases; but of casual friends I have only an incomplete impression, an impression gained from a handclasp, from spoken words which I take from their lips with my finger tips, or which they tap into the palm of my hand.

How much easier, how much more satisfying it is for you who can see to grasp quickly the essential qualities of another person by watching the subtleties of expression, the quiver of a muscle, the flutter of a hand. But does it ever occur to you to use your sight to see into the inner nature of a friend or acquaintance? Do not most of you seeing people grasp casually the outward features of a face and let it go at that?

For instance, can you describe accurately the faces of five good friends? Some of you can, but many cannot. As an experiment, I have questioned husbands of long standing about the color of their wives' eyes, and often they express embarrassed confusion and admit they do not know. And, incidentally, it is a chronic complaint of wives that their husbands do not notice new dresses, new hats, and changes in household arrangements.

The eyes of seeing persons soon become accustomed to the routine of their surroundings, and they actually see only the startling and spectacular. But even in viewing the most spectacular sights the eyes are lazy. Court records reveal every day how inaccurately "eyewitnesses" see. A given event will be "seen" in several different ways by as many witnesses. Some see more than others, but few see everything that is within the range of their vision.

Oh, the things that I should see if I had the power of sight for just three days!

The first day would be a busy one. I should call to me all my dear friends and look long into their faces, imprinting upon my mind the outward evidences of the beauty that is within them. I should let my eyes rest, too, on the face of a baby, so that I could catch a vision of the eager, innocent beauty which precedes the individual's consciousness of the conflicts which life develops.

And I should like to look into the loyal, trusting eyes of my dogs—the grave, canny little Scottie, Darkie, and the stalwart, understanding Great Dane, Helga, whose warm, tender, and playful friendships are so comforting to me.

On that busy first day I should also view the small simple things of my home. I want to see the warm colors in the rugs under my feet, the pictures on the walls, the intimate trifles that transform a house into home. My eyes would rest respectfully on the books in raised type which I have read, but they would be more eagerly interested in the printed books which seeing people can read, for during the long night of my life the books I have read and those which have been read to me have built themselves into a great shining lighthouse, revealing to me the deepest channels of human life and the human spirit.

In the afternoon of that first seeing day, I should take a long walk in the woods and intoxicate my eyes on the beauties of the world of Nature, trying desperately to absorb in a few hours the vast splendor which is constantly unfolding itself to those who can see. On the way home from my woodland jaunt my path would lie near a farm so that I might see the patient horses plowing in the field (perhaps I should see only a tractor!) and the serene content of men living close to the soil. And I should pray for the glory of a colorful sunset.

When dusk had fallen, I should experience the double delight of being able to see by artificial light, which the genius of man has created to extend the power of his sight when Nature decrees darkness.

In the night of that first day of sight, I should not be able to sleep, so full would be my mind of the memories of the day.

The next day—the second day of sight—I should arise with the dawn and see the thrilling miracle by which night is transformed into day. I should behold with awe the magnificent panorama of light with which the sun awakens the sleeping earth.

This day I should devote to a hasty glimpse of the world, past and present. I should want to see the pageant of man's progress, the kaleidoscope of the ages. How can so much be compressed into one day? Through the museums, of course. Often I have visited the New York Museum of Natural History to touch with my hands many of the objects there exhibited, but I have longed to see with my eyes the condensed history of the earth and its inhabitants displayed there—animals and the races of men pictured in their native environment; gigantic carcasses of dinosaurs and mastodons which roamed the earth long before man appeared, with his tiny stature and powerful brain, to conquer the animal kingdom; realistic presentations of the processes of evolution in animals, in man, and in the implements which man has used to fashion for himself a secure home on this planet; and a thousand and one other aspects of natural history.

I wonder how many readers of this article have viewed this panorama of the face of living things as pictured in that inspiring museum. Many, of course, have not had the opportunity, but I am sure that many who have had the opportunity have not made use of it. There, indeed, is a place to use your eyes. You who see can spend many fruitful days there, but I, with my imaginary three days of sight, could only take a hasty glimpse, and pass on.

My next stop would be the Metropolitan Museum of Art, for just as the Museum of Natural History reveals the material aspects of the world, so does the Metropolitan show the myriad facets of the human spirit. Throughout the history of humanity the urge to artistic expression has been almost as powerful as the urge for food, shelter, and procreation. And here, in the vast chambers of the Metropolitan Museum, is unfolded before me the spirit of Egypt, Greece, and Rome, as expressed in their art. I know well through my hands the sculptured gods and goddesses of the ancient Nile-land. I have felt copies of Parthenon friezes, and I have sensed the rhythmic beauty of charging Athenian warriors. Apollos and Venuses and the Wingèd Victory of Samothrace are friends of my finger tips. The gnarled, bearded features of Homer are dear to me, for he, too, knew blindness.

My hands have lingered upon the living marble of Roman sculpture as well as that of later generations. I have passed my hands over a plaster cast of Michelangelo's inspiring and heroic Moses; I have sensed the power of Rodin; I have been awed by the devoted spirit of Gothic wood carving. These arts which can be touched have meaning for me, but even they were meant to be seen rather than felt, and I can only guess at the beauty which remains hidden from me. I can admire the simple lines of a Greek vase, but its figured decorations are lost to me.

So on this, my second day of sight, I should try to probe into the soul of man through his art. The things I knew through touch I should now see. More splendid still, the whole magnificent world of painting would be opened to me, from the Italian Primitives, with their serene religious devotion, to the Moderns, with their feverish visions. I should look deep into the canvases of Raphael, Leonardo da Vinci, Titian, Rembrandt. I should want to feast my eyes upon the warm colors of Veronese, study the mysteries of El Greco, catch a new vision of Nature from Corot. Oh, there is so much rich meaning and beauty in the art of the ages for you who have eyes to see!

Upon my short visit to this temple of art I should not be able to review a fraction of that great world of art which is open to you. I should be able to get only a superficial impression. Artists tell me that for a deep and true appreciation of art one must educate the eye. One must learn through experience to weigh the merits of line, of composition, of form and color. If I had eyes, how happily would I embark upon so fascinating a study! Yet I am told that, to many of you who have eyes to see, the world of art is a dark night, unexplored and unilluminated.

It would be with extreme reluctance that I should leave the Metropolitan Museum, which contains the key to beauty—a beauty so neglected. Seeing persons, however, do not need a Metropolitan to find this key to beauty. The same key lies waiting in smaller museums, and in books on the shelves of even small libraries. But naturally, in my limited time of imaginary sight, I should choose the place where the key unlocks the greatest treasures in the shortest time.

The evening of my second day of sight I should spend at a theater or at the movies. Even now I often attend theatrical performances of all sorts, but the action of the play must be spelled into my hand by a companion. But how I should like to see with my own eyes the fascinating figure of Hamlet, or the gusty Falstaff amid colorful Elizabethan trappings! How I should like to follow each movement of the graceful Hamlet, each strut of the hearty Falstaff! And since I could see only one play, I should be confronted by a many-horned dilemma, for there are scores of plays I should want to see. You who have eyes can see any you like. How many of you, I wonder, when you gaze at a play, a movie, or any spectacle, realize and give thanks for the miracle of sight which enables you to enjoy its color, grace, and movement?

I cannot enjoy the beauty of rhythmic movement except in a sphere restricted to the touch of my hands. I can vision only dimly the grace of a Pavlova, although I know something of the delight of rhythm, for often I can sense the beat of music as it vibrates through the floor. I can well imagine that cadenced motion must be one of the most pleasing sights in the world. I have been able to gather something of this by tracing with my fingers the lines in sculptured marble; if this static grace can be so lovely, how much more acute must be the thrill of seeing grace in motion.

One of my dearest memories is of the time when Joseph Jefferson allowed me to touch his face and hands as he went through some of the gestures and speeches of his beloved Rip Van Winkle. I was able to catch thus a meager glimpse of the world of drama, and I shall never forget the delight of that moment. But, oh, how much I must miss, and how much pleasure you seeing ones can derive from watching and hearing the interplay of speech and movement in the unfolding of a dramatic performance! If I could see only one play, I should know how to picture in my mind the action of a hundred plays which I have read or had transferred to me through the medium of the manual alphabet.

So, through the evening of my second imaginary day of sight, the great figures of dramatic literature would crowd sleep from my eyes.

The following morning, I should again greet the dawn, anxious to discover new delights, for I am sure that, for those who have eyes which really see, the dawn of each day must be a perpetually new revelation of beauty.

This, according to the terms of my imagined miracle, is to be my third and last day of sight. I shall have no time to waste in regrets or longings; there is too much to see. The first day I devoted to my friends, animate and inanimate. The second revealed to me the history of man and Nature. Today I shall spend in the workaday world of the present, amid the haunts of men going about the business of life. And where can one find so many activities and conditions of men as in New York? So the city becomes my destination.

I start from my home in the quiet little suburb of Forest Hills, Long Island. Here, surrounded by green lawns, trees, and flowers, are neat little houses, happy with the voices and movements of wives and children, havens of peaceful rest for men who toil in the city. I drive across the lacy structure of steel which spans the East River, and I get a new and startling vision of the power and ingenuity of the mind of man. Busy boats chug and scurry about the river—racy speed boats, stolid, snorting tugs. If I had long days of sight ahead, I should spend many of them watching the delightful activity upon the river.

I look ahead, and before me rise the fantastic towers of New York, a city that seems to have stepped from the pages of a fairy story. What an awe-inspiring sight, these glittering spires, these vast banks of stone and steel—structures such as the gods might build for themselves! This animated picture is a part of the lives of millions of people every day. How many, I wonder, give it so much as a second glance? Very few, I fear. Their eyes are blind to this magnificent sight because it is so familiar to them.

I hurry to the top of one of those gigantic structures, the Empire State Building, for there, a short time ago, I "saw" the city below through the eyes of my secretary. I am anxious to compare my fancy with reality. I am sure I should not be disappointed in the panorama spread out before me, for to me it would be a vision of another world.

Now I begin my rounds of the city. First, I stand at a busy corner, merely looking at people, trying by sight of them to understand something of their lives. I see smiles, and I am happy. I see serious determination, and I am proud. I see suffering, and I am compassionate.

I stroll down Fifth Avenue. I throw my eyes out of focus so that I see no particular object but only a seething kaleidoscope of color. I am certain that the colors of women's dresses moving in a throng must be a gorgeous spectacle of which I should never tire. But perhaps if I had sight I should be like most other women—too interested in styles and the cut of individual dresses to give much attention to the splendor of color in the mass. And I am convinced, too, that I should become an inveterate window shopper, for it must be a delight to the eye to view the myriad articles of beauty on display.

From Fifth Avenue I make a tour of the city—to Park Avenue, to the slums, to factories, to parks where children play. I take a stay-at-home trip abroad by visiting the foreign quarters. Always my eyes are open wide to all the sights of both happiness and misery so that I may probe deep and add to my understanding of how people work and live. My heart is full of the images of people and things. My eye passes lightly over no single trifle; it strives to touch and hold closely each thing its gaze rests upon. Some sights are pleasant, filling the heart with happiness; but some are miserably pathetic. To these latter I do not shut my eyes, for they, too, are part of life. To close the eye on them is to close the heart and mind.

My third day of sight is drawing to an end. Perhaps there are many serious pursuits to which I should devote the few remaining hours, but I am afraid that on the evening of that last day I should again run away to the theater, to a hilariously funny play, so that I might appreciate the overtones of comedy in the human spirit.

At midnight my temporary respite from blindness would cease, and permanent night would close in on me again. Naturally in those three short days I should not have seen all I wanted to see. Only when darkness had again descended upon me should I realize how much I had left unseen. But my mind would be so crowded with glorious memories that I should have little time for regrets. Thereafter the touch of every object would bring a flowing memory of how that object looked.

Perhaps this short outline of how I should spend three days of sight does not agree with the program you would set for yourself if you knew that you were about to be stricken blind. I am, however, sure that if you actually faced that fate your eyes would open to things you had never seen before, storing up memories for the long night ahead. You would use your eyes as never before. Everything you saw would become dear to you. Your eyes would touch and embrace every object that came within your range of vision. Then, at last, you would really see, and a new world of beauty would open itself before you.

I who am blind can give one hint to those who see—one admonition to those who would make full use of the gift of sight: Use your eyes as if tomorrow you would be stricken blind. And the same method can be applied to the other senses. Hear the music of voices, the song of a bird, the mighty strains of an orchestra, as if you would be stricken deaf tomorrow. Touch each object you want to touch as if tomorrow your tactile sense would fail. Smell the perfume of flowers, taste with relish each morsel, as if tomorrow you could never smell and taste again. Make the most of every sense; glory in all the facets of pleasure and beauty which the world reveals to you through the several means of contact which Nature provides. But of all the senses, I am sure that sight must be the most delightful.

For Further Reflection

1. Review the story of Helen Keller. What is her attitude toward life? What does this tell us about gratitude?

2. What other lessons does this essay have to teach us? Can you apply it to your life? Explain.

3. What can we learn from Helen Keller about overcoming tragedy?

The Stoic Catechism

EPICTETUS AND OTHERS

Epictetus (A.D. c. 50–c. 130) was born a Greek slave in Asia Minor and was freed sometime after the death of Nero, in 68 B.C. Epictetus was expelled from Rome by the Emperor Domitian in 90 B.C. and died in northern Greece about 130. He was known as a kindly man, humble and charitable, especially to children. He was crippled in slavery which might have influenced his motto: "Bear and forbear." He embraced Stoicism and taught that we should submit to our fate as God's sacred gift and design. Epictetus did not publish anything, but his pupil Flavius Arrianus has recorded his teachings, the most famous of which is the *Enchirid-*

ion (a handbook), used by Roman soldiers as their manual for reflection on life. Another of his pupils, Marcus Aurelius, became Emperor of Rome.

Stoicism was a Greek school of philosophy founded in c. 300 B.C. in Athens by Zeno of Citium, and it developed into the dominant philosophy of the Roman Empire. The word *stoa* from which "Stoic" derives is the Greek word for porch. Apparently Zeno lectured from his porch. The Stoics believed that we should resign ourselves to our fate, do our duty faithfully, and thereby acquire tranquillity of mind. The world is transient and unstable. We cannot change very much, but we can master our souls so that we attain tranquillity amidst the chaos all around us. Their motto: "If you don't get what you desire, desire what you get." The Stoics were the first world citizens, "cosmopolitans," holding that a divine spark dwelt in every human being. Chrysippus (c. 280–206 B.C.), referred to in the text, was the third leader of the Stoics and was credited with more than seven hundred treatises. The Stoics believed that all human beings were brothers and sisters under one Father, God.

The first short selection on Duty is from the Stoic Roman Emperor Marcus Aurelius (A.D. 121–180). The second short selection on Suicide is from the Stoic, Seneca (c. 3 B.C.–A.D. c. 65). The third, long selection is from Epictetus's teachings.

MARCUS AURELIUS, *DEDICATION TO DUTY*

Hour by hour resolve to do the task of the hour carefully, with unaffected dignity, affectionately, freely, and justly. You can avoid distractions that might interfere with such performance if every act is done as though it were the last act of your life. Free yourself from random aims and curb any tendency to let the passions of emotion, hypocrisy, self-love, and dissatisfaction with your allotted share cause you to ignore the commands of reason.

SENECA, *DEATH AND SUICIDE*

Life has carried some men with the greatest rapidity to the harbor, the harbor they were bound to reach if they tarried on the way, while others it has fretted and harassed. To such a life, as you are aware, one should not always cling. *For mere living is not a good, but living well.* Accordingly, the wise man will live as long as he ought, not as long as he can. He will mark in what place, with whom, and how he is to conduct his existence, and what he is about to do. He always reflects concerning the quality, and not the quantity of his life. As soon as there are many events in his life that give him trouble and disturb his peace of mind, he sets himself free. And this privilege is his, not only when the crisis is upon him, but as soon as Fortune seems to be playing him false; then he looks about carefully and sees whether he ought, or ought not, to end his life on that account . . . He does not regard death with fear, as if it were a great loss; for no man can lose very much when but a driblet remains. It is not a question of dying earlier or later, but of dying well or ill. And dying well means escape from the danger of living ill.

EPICTETUS, *ENCHIRIDION*

1. Here is a fundamental distinction of which you ought to be aware: *Some things are up to us, some are not up to us.* Up to us are perception, intention, desire, aversion, and in sum, whatever are our own doings; not up to us are body, property, reputation, political office and in sum, whatever are not our own doings. And the things that are up to us are naturally free, unforbidding, unimpeding, while those not up to us are weak, slavish, forbidding, alien. Remember, then, that if you think naturally slavish things are free and that alien things are your own, you will be impeded, grieved, troubled, you will blame gods and men; but if you think that what is yours is yours and what is alien is alien, as it really is, nobody will ever compel you, nobody will forbid you, you will not blame anyone, you will not complain about anything, you will not do a single thing unwillingly, you will have no enemy, no one will hurt you; for you will not suffer anything harmful.

If you are aiming for such great things, remember that you must not be moderate in exerting yourself to attain them: you must avoid some things altogether and postpone others for the time being. For if you want both to accomplish these aims, and also to achieve eminence and riches, it may come about that you will not get the latter because you were trying for the former, and certainly you will not get the former, which are the only things that produce freedom and well-being.

So take rigorous care to say to every menacing impression, "You are just an impression, not the real thing at all." Then test it and consider it according to your rules—first and foremost this: whether it belongs among the things that are up to us or to those not up to us. And if it is something not up to us, be ready to say "It is nothing to me."

2. Remember that the aim of desire is to get what arouses the desire, the aim of aversion is to avoid that to which you are averse; and he who fails to get what he desires is miserable, and so is he who gets what he is averse to. So then, if you are averse only to things contrary to nature that are up to you, you will not get anything to which you are averse; but if you are averse to sickness or death or poverty, you will be miserable. So take your aversion away from everything that is not up to you and transfer it to things contrary to nature that are up to you. But for the time being, destroy desire altogether; for if you desire something not up to you, necessarily you will be unfortunate; as for things that are up to us, and would be good to desire, none of them is yet within your grasp. But only make use of selection and rejection, and these lightly, discreetly, and tentatively.

3. As for every thing that delights your mind or is useful or beloved, remember to describe it as it really is, starting with the smallest thing. If you are fond of a pot, say "It is a pot that I am fond of." For then, if it breaks, you will not be upset. If you kiss your child or your wife, say that you are kissing a human being. Then if they die you will not be upset.

5. *It is not things that upset people but rather ideas about things.* For example, death is nothing terrible, else it would have seemed so even to Socrates; rather it is the idea that death is terrible that is terrible. So whenever we are frustrated or upset or grieved, let us not blame others, but ourselves—that is, our ideas. It is the act of a philosophically ignorant person to blame others for his own troubles. One who is beginning to learn blames himself. An educated person blames neither anyone else nor himself.

6. Do not pride yourself on superiority that is not your own. If a horse in its pride should say, "I am a fine horse," that could be tolerated. You however, when you boast "I have a fine horse," should realize that you are boasting about the excellence of a horse. What then is your own? The use of impressions. So, make use of

your impressions in accord with nature, and then take pride; for your pride will be in a good thing that is your own.

8. Don't seek for things to happen as you wish, but wish for things to happen as they do, and you will get on well.

9. Illness is an impediment of the body, but not of the will, as long as the will itself does not so wish. Lameness is an impediment of the leg, not of the will. And say this to yourself of every accident that befalls you; for you will find it an impediment to something else, not to yourself.

10. Whatever occasion befalls you, remember to turn around and look into yourself to see what power you have to make use of it. If you see a handsome boy or a beautiful girl, you will find the relevant power to be self-control. If labor is heaped on you, endurance is what you need; if abuse, forbearance. And thus habituating yourself, you will not be carried away by impressions.

11. Never say about anything that you have "lost it," but that you have "given it back." Your child has died? It has been given back. Your wife has died? She has been given back. "I have been deprived of my estate." This too has been given back. "But the usurper is wicked." What concern is it of yours, through whom the gift was returned to the giver? For the time it is given to you, treat it as someone else's, as travellers do an inn.

12. If you want to make progress, shun these sorts of reasonings: "If I neglect my affairs, I shall have nothing to live on"; "If I don't punish my slave, he will be good for nothing." For it is better to attain freedom from sorrow and fear and then die of hunger than to live lavishly in vexation. It is better for your slave to be bad than for you to be unhappy. Begin with little things. A little oil has been spilled, a little wine has been swiped: say to yourself, "This is the price of peace, that of serenity." Nothing is free. When you call for your slave, consider that maybe he won't hear you, and even if he does he still won't do what you want him to do. But he is not so well off that your tranquillity should depend on him.

13. If you want to make progress, be content to appear stupid and foolish about externals, and don't wish to seem to know anything. And whenever you seem to be somebody to someone, distrust yourself. For be aware that it is not easy both to have your will in accordance with nature and to be on your guard about externals also, if you are to take care of the one it is absolutely necessary to neglect the other.

15. Remember that you ought to conduct yourself as you do at a banquet. When something passed around reaches you, extend your hand and take it politely. If it is passing you by, don't grab. If it has not yet reached you, don't crave for it, but wait until it gets to you. Thus toward children, thus toward women, thus toward jobs, thus toward riches; and in due time you will be worthy to dine with the gods. But if you do not take even the things set out for you, but despise them, then not only will you be a banquet companion of the gods, you will even be a co-ruler. By thus acting, Diogenes and Heraclitus and like men came to be called divine, and deservedly.

16. Whenever you see someone weeping in grief because his child is going away or he has lost his property, be careful not to be misled by the impression that he is in a bad way because of external things, but be ready to say at once "It is not the circumstances that distress him (for someone else would not be distressed), but the idea he has about them." Don't, of course, hesitate to condole with him in words, and, if there is occasion, even to groan with him; but take care not to groan inwardly.

17. Remember that you are an actor in a drama such as the playwright wishes it to be. If he wants it short, it will be short; if long, long. If he wants you to play a beggar, play even that capably; or a lame man, or a ruler, or a private person. For this is yours, to play the assigned role well. Casting is the business of another.

19. You can be unbeatable if you never enter a contest in which it is not up to you who wins. Beware lest ever, seeing someone else preferred in honor or having great power or otherwise esteemed, you get carried away by impressions and deem him blessed. For since the essence of the good lies in the things up to us, neither jealousy nor envy has a place; and you yourself will not wish to be a praetor or a senator or a consul, but a free man. There is but one way to this: *contempt for things not up to us.*

20. Remember that it is not the man who curses you or the man who hits you that insults you, but the idea you have of them as insulting. So, whenever someone irritates you, realize that it is your own opinion that has irritated you. First of all, try not to be carried away by impressions; if you succeed just once in gaining time and avoiding hastiness, you will easily control yourself.

21. Let death and exile and all dreadful appearances be before your eyes every day, and most of all, death; and you will never deem anything trivial, nor desire anything excessively.

22. If you are eager for philosophy, be prepared from the begin-ning to be ridiculed and sneered at by the mob, who will say things like "All of a sudden he has come back to us a philosopher!" and "Where did he get that high brow?" But don't be a highbrow; hold fast to what seems best for you, as one who has been assigned to this territory by the god. And remember this: if you stay with it, the ones who ridicule you at first will admire you afterwards; but if they get the better of you, it will be your lot to be laughed at twice.

23. If ever it happens that you turn to externals because you want to please someone, realize that you have lost your bearings. It suffices to *be* a philosopher in all things; but if you also want to *appear* to be one, appear so to yourself and that will be enough.

24. Don't let reflections like this upset you: "I shall live without honor, a complete nobody." For suppose not being honored is an evil: you cannot be subjected to evil by another, any more than to shamefulness. Is it your business to acquire power or an invitation to a banquet? By no means. How then is this being without honor? How then will you be a complete nobody, when you ought to be somebody only with respect to those things that are up to you— the domain wherein it is given to you to be of the greatest worth? But your friends will get no help from you? What do you mean by help? They won't have a penny from you; nor will you make them Roman citizens. So who told you that these things are up to you, and not the business of others? Who can give to another things that he does not have himself? "Then get them," one says, "so that we can have them." If I can get them while preserving my self-respect and trustworthiness and high-mindedness, show me the way and I'll get them. But if you require me to be one who will lose my proper goods in order to produce worthless things for you—just look, how partial and unfair you are. Which do you want more? Money, or a faithful and upright friend? Then you had better help me to acquire the characteristics of one and not require me to do the things that would ruin them.

26. We can learn the will of nature by considering the matters about which we don't disagree with one another. For instance, when somebody else's miserable servant breaks a cup, you are ready right away to say "So it goes." But realize that when it is yours that gets broken, you ought to behave the same way you did when it was someone else's. Apply this to more important matters as well. Somebody else's child or wife has died; there is no one

who would not say "That's life." But when his own child or wife dies, it is "Alas, woe is me!" We ought to remember what we feel when we hear the same thing about other people.

27. As a target is not set up for the purpose of being missed, so nothing in the world is intrinsically evil.

28. If someone were to hand over your body to just whomever happened along, you would be outraged. Why aren't you outraged at the fact that *you* turn over your own mind to whomever happens along—if he insults you and you let it upset and trouble you?

29. . . . Some people, when they have seen a philosopher and have heard someone speaking the way Euphrates speaks (but who can speak like him?), wish to philosophize themselves. Man, consider first what kind of business this is. And then learn what your own nature is; can you bear it? Do you want to be a pentathlete or a wrestler? Look at your arms, your thighs, learn about your hips. One man is naturally fitted for one thing, another for another. Do you suppose you can do these things and keep on eating and drinking and enthusing and sulking just as you do now? You will have to go without sleep, labor, leave home, be despised by a slave, have everyone laugh at you, get the worse in everything, in honors, in jobs, in lawsuits, in every trifle. Look these things over and decide whether you want to exchange them for tranquillity, freedom, and peace; if not, don't go ahead, don't be, like a child, now philosopher, afterwards tax collector, then orator, finally Caesar's procurator. These things do not go together. You ought to be one man, good or evil; you must cultivate either your own guiding principle or externals; that is, apply yourself either to the inner man or to outward things: assume either the role of philosopher or of layman.

30. What is proper for us to do is for the most part defined by our social relationships. He is your father: this means that it is for you to look after him, to defer to him in all things, to put up with his abuse and his beatings. "But he is a bad father." Did nature then assign you to a *good* father? No, just to a father. "My brother is wronging me." Then keep up your relationship toward him; don't look at what he may be doing, but at what you should do to keep your will in accord with nature. No other person will hurt you unless *you* will it; you will be hurt to the extent that you think you are hurt. Thus if you will make a habit of contemplating social relationships, you will discover what it is fitting to do as a neighbor, as a citizen, as a consul.

33. Prescribe a certain character and type for yourself, and guard it both when you are by yourself and when you meet people. And be silent about most things, or chat only when necessary and about few matters. On rare occasions, when the time is ripe and you are called on to talk, talk—but not about banal topics; not about gladiators, or athletes, or horse races, or food and drink, such as you hear everywhere; and above all, not about blaming or praising or comparing people. If you can, lead the conversation around to something proper. But if you happen to be alone with strange people, be silent.

Laugh seldom and about few things and with restraint.

Totally abstain from taking oaths, if you can; if not, then refuse whenever circumstances allow.

Avoid celebrations, both public and private; but if the occasion calls you, be alert not to lapse into vulgarity. For know that if a companion is defiled, necessarily also one who keeps company with him will be defiled, even if he himself happens to be pure.

Partake of things having to do with the body only as far as bare need goes: such things as food, drink, clothing, housing, slaves. Dispense altogether with whatever has to do with reputation or luxury.

As to sex, be as pure as you can before marriage; but if you are aroused, indulge only to the extent that is customary. Sex is not a game. It can promote salient emotions which foster intimate relations, which enrich life. However, don't by any means be troublesome to those who do indulge, or censorious; and don't keep mentioning that you yourself can get along without it.

If someone tells you that somebody else is saying awful things about you, don't defend yourself against the accusations, but reply, "He must not know about the other faults that I have, if these are the only ones he mentioned."

It isn't necessary to attend shows for the most part. But if there is a proper occasion, do not appear to be more enthusiastic for anyone else than for yourself, that is, wish only that those things should happen that do happen and that only the winner should win; that way you will not be frustrated. Abstain altogether from shouting and ridiculing anyone or getting emotionally involved. And after the performance don't talk much about what happened, if it does not tend toward your improvement. For it would be evident from this that you were dazzled by the spectacle. . . .

Whenever you are going to meet someone, especially one reputed to be important, consider what Socrates or Zeno would have done in the circumstances, and you will not be puzzled about how to use the occasion properly. When you are going to visit a powerful personage, propose to yourself that you will not find him at home, that you will be shut out, that the gates will be slammed in your face, that he will not notice you. And if nevertheless it is your duty to go, when you arrive bear with what happens and by no means say to yourself "It wasn't worth it." For it is unphilosophical to be troubled by externals.

In conversation avoid overmuch talk about your own deeds and dangers. For although it is pleasant for you to recall your own adventures, it may not be so for others to hear about what happened to you.

Also avoid raising laughter; for this is a slippery slope to vulgarity and at the same time sufficient to cancel the respect that others have for you. It is also dangerous to get into dirty talk. Whenever anything of this sort begins, if you get the opportunity, you might rebuke the person who starts it; or if not, make it clear by being silent or blushing and scowling that you are displeased by the talk.

34. When you receive an impression of a certain pleasure, be on your guard, just as you are with other impressions, lest you get carried away by it. Take your time with the thing, wait a while. Next call to mind both times—the time when you will enjoy the pleasure, and the time when, after enjoying it, you will change your mind and scold yourself; and set against these the thought of how, if you abstain, you will rejoice and praise yourself. But if it still seems to you to be the proper occasion to indulge, consider, lest you be overcome by the gentleness and sweetness of it and its seductiveness; set against it, how much better it will be to be conscious of yourself as having won this victory.

35. When you do something because you have recognized that it ought to be done, never go out of your way not to be seen doing it, not even if public opinion takes a different view of it. For if it isn't right for you to do, shun the deed itself; if it is right, why are you afraid of people who would be censuring you wrongly?

37. If you take on a role that is too much for you, you both disgrace yourself in it and neglect the one that you might have filled.

38. Just as in walking you pay attention not to step on a nail or to turn your ankle, pay attention not to hurt your ruling principle. And if we look out for this in all of our activities, we will take them on more securely.

41. It is the sign of a weak mind to spend too much time on things having to do with the body, such as exercising a lot, eating a lot, drinking a lot, excreting, sex. Such things should be done incidentally; let all your attention be concentrated on your mind.

42. Whenever someone treats you badly or says bad things about you, remember that he does it or says it thinking that he is doing the right thing. Now it is not possible for him to adhere to *your* conception of the right, but only his own. Whence it follows that if he has a wrong view of things, he, being deceived, is the one who is hurt. For if someone believes that a true proposition is false, it is not the proposition that suffers but the deceived believer. If you consider these things you will deal gently with the slanderer. On each occasion just say, "So it seemed to him."

43. Every thing has two handles, one by which it may be borne, one by which it cannot be borne. If your brother has done wrong, don't grasp this by the "wrongdoing" handle—it can't be borne by that one—but by the "brother," the "brought-uptogether" handle, and thereby you will be able to bear it.

44. These sorts of arguments are invalid: "I am richer than you are, therefore I am better than you"; "I am more eloquent than you are, therefore I am better than you." But these are valid: "I am richer than you are, therefore my possessions are better than yours"; "I am more eloquent than you are, therefore my speech is better than yours" *You,* however, are neither your possessions nor your speech.

48. Position and character of a vulgar person: he never expects help or harm from himself, but only from outside. Position and character of a philosopher: he expects all help and harm to come from himself.

Marks of one making progress: he blames nobody, he praises nobody, he complains about nobody, he accuses nobody, he never speaks of himself as if he were anybody or knew anything. If he is impeded or frustrated he blames himself. And if someone praises him, he smiles to himself at the person giving the praise; but if he is blamed, he offers no defense. He comports himself as invalids do, taking care not to move a damaged limb before it has healed. He has purged himself of all desire; he has concentrated aversion solely on things that are against nature but up to us. He takes things as they come. If he appears stupid or ignorant, he doesn't care. In sum, he guards against himself as against an enemy lying in wait.

50. Whatever principles are set before you, follow them as laws,

the dishonoring of which would be impious. But don't worry about what anyone says about you; for this is not at all up to you.

51. How much time will you take yet before you judge yourself worthy of the best, and never step over the bounds discriminated by reason? You have been apprised of the philosophical principles to which you ought to subscribe, and you have subscribed. So what sort of teacher are you still waiting for, that you put off your own reformation until he gets here? You are no longer a child, but a grown man. If now you take no care and loaf and always keep putting things off and set one day after another on which to start attending to your own affairs, you will lose yourself, making no progress but going on being a layman in life and in death. Right now, then, deem yourself worthy of living as an adult making progress. And let all that appears best to you be your inviolable law. And if some task is set for you, whether pleasant or glorious or inglorious, remember, that right now you are the contestant and here are the Olympic games, and there can't be any more delay, and that one day and one deed will determine whether progress is lost or saved. That is how Socrates became what he was: by attending in all things that he encountered to nothing other than reason. But you—even if you are not yet a Socrates, at least you ought to live as someone desiring to be like Socrates.

52. The primary and most essential topic in philosophy is that of the use of philosophical principles, for instance, not to lie. The secondary is that of proofs, for instance why one ought not to lie. Tertiary is of what gives certainty and consequence to the first two, for instance, why is this a proof? what indeed is a proof? implication?

If the room is smoky, if only moderately, I will stay; if there is too much smoke, I will go. Remember this, keep firm hold on it: the door is always open.

For Further Reflection

1. What are the principal ideas of Stoicism, as contained in these readings? Is it really possible to live by this philosophy? Is it an optimistic or pessimistic philosophy?

2. Would you want to have a Stoic for a spouse or a parent or a friend? Why or why not?

3. Examine Seneca's statement on suicide and the last sentence
in Epictetus's manual on Stoicism. Do these ideas contradict the
Stoic philosophy of accepting what one cannot change? Or do
they specify limits about what one should have to endure?

In Consolation to His Wife
Equanimity

PLUTARCH

Plutarch (A.D. 46?–c. 119) was a Greek philosopher, essayist, and biographer. The following is the letter he sent to
Timoxena upon receiving news of the death of their
beloved two-year-old daughter, Timoxena, (named after her
mother). Upon her death, a courier was sent to give Plutarch
the sad news, but missed him; so his wife, Timoxena, had
to make all the funeral arrangements herself. This letter, an
example of Greek Stoicism, gives us a picture of Plutarch's
character and his love for his wife and daughter.

[1]   FROM PLUTARCH TO HIS WIFE. I hope this finds you well. The   608B
man you sent to give me the news of our child's death seems to
have missed me during his overland journey to Athens, but I heard
about it from my granddaughter when I got to Tanagra. I imagine
that the burial rites are over by now, and I hope they were conducted in a way that makes the chance of your feeling distress at
the burial both now and in the future as remote as possible. But
if there is something you haven't yet done, even though you want
to, because you are waiting to hear what I intend to do, and it is
something which you think would make things easier to bear, then
it will happen too, with no fuss and superstitious nonsense—not
that you are at all liable to these faults.

Reprinted from Plutarch's *Essays,* translated by Robin Waterfield (Penguin Books, 1992), by permission.

c   [2]   All I ask, my dear, is that while reacting emotionally you make sure that both of us—me as well as you—remain in a stable state. I mean, the actual event is a known quantity and I can keep it within limits, but if I find your distress excessive, this will discompose me more than what has happened. Nevertheless, I was not born 'from oak or rock', as you yourself know, given that you have been my partner in bringing up so many children—all brought up with no one else's help in our own home—and I know how overjoyed you were with the birth, after four sons, of the daughter you longed for and with the fact that it gave me the opportunity to name her after you. In addition, one's love for children of that age is peculiarly acute, since the pleasure it affords is absolutely unsullied and untainted by any element of anger and criticism. Also, she was inherently wonderfully easy to please and undemanding, and the way she repaid affection with affection and was so charming was not only delightful, but also made one realize how unselfish she was. She used to encourage her wet-nurse to offer and present her breast not only to other babies, but also to her favourite playthings and toys: she was unselfishly trying to share the good things she had and the things she most enjoyed with her favourites, as if they were guests at her very own table.

    [3]   However, my dear, I fail to see any reason why, when this and similar behaviour pleased us during her life, it should upset and trouble us when we recall it now. I worry about the alternative, however—that we might consign the memory of her to oblivion along with our distress. This would be to act like Clymene, who said, 'I hate the curved cornel bow! I wish there were no gymnasia!':[1] she was always nervous about recalling her son, and avoided doing so, because distress was its companion,[2] and it is natural to avoid anything painful.[3] No, our daughter was the sweet-

F   est thing in the world to hug and watch and listen to, and by the same token she must remain and live on in our thoughts, and bring

---

[1] From Euripides' *Phaethon* F785 Nauck. Clymene's son was Phaethon, who perished when attempting to drive his father's (the sun's) chariot; he presumably also enjoyed archery and other sports in Euripides' play.

[2] The theme is stock. Seneca, in his *Consolation to Marcia* 2–3, cites Octavia for this condition and opposes Livia to it.

[3] An Epicurean position (Sextus Empiricus, *Adversus Mathematicos* 11.96, and the texts collected under Epicurus F398 Usener), but naturally entering Consolation literature (e.g., Seneca, *Consolation to Polybius* 18.7).

not just more, but a great deal more pleasure than distress—if it is plausible to expect that the arguments we have often deployed on others will help us in our hour of need—and we must not slump in dejection or shut ourselves away and so pay for those pleasures with distress that vastly outweighs it.

[4]   People who were with you also tell me, with some surprise, that you haven't adopted mourning clothes, that you didn't make yourself or your maids follow any ugly or harrowing practices[4] and that the paraphernalia of an expensive celebration was absent from the funeral—that instead everything was conducted with discretion and in silence, and with only the essential accoutrements. It was no surprise to me, however, that you who never 609A tricked yourself out for the theatre or a public procession, and never saw any point in extravagance even where your pleasures were concerned, maintained unaffectedness and frugality in sad circumstances.

The point is that Bacchic rites are not the only circumstances which require a decent woman to remain uncorrupted:[5] she should equally assume that the instability and emotional disturbance which grief entails call for self-control, which is not, as is popularly supposed, the enemy of affection and love, but of mental indulgence. Affection is what we gratify by missing, valuing and remembering the dead, but the insatiable desire for grief—a desire which makes B us wail and howl—is just as contemptible as hedonistic indulgence, despite the notion that it is forgivable because, although it may be contemptible, it is accompanied not by any pleasure gained from the desire, but rather by distress and pain. Could there be anything more absurd than banishing excesses of laughter and mirth, and yet allowing the floodgates of tears and lamentation, which spring from the same source as merriment, to open to their fullest extent? Or—as some husbands do—quarrelling with their wives about extravagant hair perfume and gaudy clothing, and yet submitting when they cut off their hair in mourning, dye their clothes black and adopt ugly postures when sitting and uncomfortable ones when c

---

[4]It was common practice in funeral customs to display the extravagance of one's grief through the disfigurement of the body and appearance, such as shaving off hair, wearing black and adopting unrestrained and ugly postures; see also 609B, 609F.
[5]A reminiscence of Euripides, *Bacchae* 317 f.

reclining at table?[6] Or—and this is the most irritating of all—resisting and restraining their wives if they punish their servants of either sex excessively and unfairly, and yet ignoring the vicious, harsh punishments they inflict upon themselves when they are under the influence of emotion and misfortunes which actually call for a relaxed and charitable attitude?

[5]   Our relationship, however, my dear, is such that there never has been any occasion for us to quarrel on the one score, and there never will be any occasion for us to quarrel on the other, I am sure. On the one hand, every philosopher who has spent time with us and got to know us has been impressed with the inextravagance of your clothing and make-up, and with the modesty of your

D lifestyle, and every one of our fellow citizens has witnessed your unaffectedness during rituals and sacrifices and at the theatre. On the other hand, you have already demonstrated in the past that you can remain stable under these circumstances, when you lost your eldest child and again when our lovely Charon left us before his time. I remember that I brought visitors with me on my journey from the coast at the news of the child's death, and that they and everyone else gathered in our house. As they subsequently told others as well, when they saw how calm and peaceful it was, they thought that nothing terrible had happened and that a baseless

E rumor had got out, because you had behaved so responsibly in arranging the house at a time when disarray is normally excusable, despite the fact that you had nursed him at your own breast and had endured an operation when your nipple got inflamed,[7] which are noble acts stemming from motherly love.[8]

[6]   It is noticeable that most mothers take their children into their arms as if they were playthings (after others have cleaned them and smartened them up), and then, if the children die, these mothers wallow in empty, indecent grief. They are not motivated by warmth of feeling, which is a reasonable and commendable

---

[6]It is not clear what mourning practice is being referred to; for the general principle, see n.4 above.

[7]She probably suffered the agony of a breast abscess—the result of infection getting into the breast through a cracked nipple—which in pre-antibiotic days would have been cauterized.

[8]Plutarch uses similar language in *Life of Demosthenes* 22.3, in contrasting the attitude of Demosthenes and Aeschines to bereavement; the story is repeated in *Consolation to Apollonius* 119B.

emotion:[9] their strong inclination towards shallow beliefs, plus a dash of instinctive emotion, causes outbursts of grief which are fierce, manic and unruly.[10] Aesop was apparently aware of this: he said that when Zeus was distributing recognition among the gods, Grief asked for some as well; so Zeus allowed Grief to be acknowledged—but only by people who deliberately wanted to acknowledge it.[11]

This is certainly what happens at the beginning: only an individual lets grief enter himself; but after a while it becomes a permanent sibling, a habitual presence, and then it doesn't leave however much one wants it to. That is why it is crucial to resist it on the threshold and not to adopt special clothing or haircuts or anything else like that, which allow it to establish a stronghold. These 610A things challenge the mind day in and day out, make it recoil, belittle it and constrict it and imprison it, and make it unresponsive and apprehensive, as if the wearing of these clothes and the adoption of these practices out of grief cut it off from laughter and light and the sociability of the table. The consequences of this affliction are physical neglect and an aversion to oiling and bathing the body and to other aspects of the daily regimen, when exactly the opposite should happen: purely mental suffering ought to be helped by physical fitness. Mental distress abates and subsides to a great extent when it is dispersed in physical calm, as waves subside in fair B weather, but if as a result of a bad regimen the body becomes sordid and foul and transmits to the mind nothing benign or beneficial, but only the harsh and unpleasant fumes of pain and distress, then even those who desire it find that recovery becomes hard to achieve. These are the kinds of disorders that take possession of the mind when it is treated so badly.

[9]A Stoic definition (Diogenes Laertius 7.116), but approved of by Plutarch (*Life of Solon* 7.5).

[10]It was a recurrent theme in Consolation literature that natural instinctive grief is sharp and short, as with animals; it is humans who tend to prolong and exaggerate grief through false beliefs on top of their natural instincts. Cf. Seneca, *Consolation to Marcia* 7.1; *Consolation to Apollonius* 102C-D.

[11]An old tale of unknown origin, but common stock for Consolations. The *Consolation to Apollonius* 112A gives it to 'an ancient philosopher' speaking to Queen Arsinoe. It turns up under Sotion in John of Stobi 3.972.7 Hense.

[7]   Nevertheless, I have no cause to worry about the worst and most worrying disorder which occurs in such cases—'the invasion of malignant women',[12] with the cries and expressions of sympathy which they use to polish and hone distress, and to prevent its being diminished either by external factors or of its own accord.   C For I know about the battles you recently had when you went to assist Theon's sister[13] and defended her against the incursions of the women who came with their weeping and wailing—behavior which is exactly the same as fighting fire with fire.[14] I mean, when people see a friend's house on fire, then everyone contributes what he can to put it out as quickly as possible; but when that same friend's mind is on fire, they bring fuel! And although when someone has an eye infection, people don't let just anyone touch it or treat the inflammation, people who are grieving sit and let everyone who comes by prod at their running sore, so to speak, and   D aggravate the condition, until instead of being an insignificant itching irritation, it erupts into a seriously disagreeable affliction.[15] Anyway, I know that you will be on your guard against this.

[8]   Please try, however, to use your mind as a vehicle for often returning to the time when this child of ours had not yet been born and we had no reason to blame fortune; and then connect that time with the present, and imagine that our circumstances are no different again.[16] You see, my dear, we will seem to regret that our child was ever born if we find more to complain about now than in the situation before her birth.[17] We must not erase the inter-   E vening two years from our memories, but since they brought happiness and joy, we must count them as pleasant. The good was

---

[12]From Euripides' *Andromache* 930, used again by Plutarch at 143E. He also noted the exacerbating effect of enthusiastic 'sympathizers' in *On Exile* 599A–B.

[13]Theon was one of Plutarch's close friends; he appears frequently in his dialogues.

[14]A proverb much liked by Plutarch: 61A, 123E, 143F, 919D, *Life of Artaxerxes* 28.1. He may have got it from Plato, *Laws* 666a.

[15]For the imagery in relation to provoking grief, compare *Consolation to Apollonius* 102A; Cicero, *Tusculanae Disputationes* 4.63 (from Chrysippus); and Seneca, *Consolation to Helvia* 1.2.

[16]Teles, the Cynic of the third century BC, used this same device (p. 61.2–4 Hense; pp. 68 f. O'Neil).

[17]The same point is made by Seneca, *Consolation to Helvia* 19.7.

brief, but should not therefore be regarded as a long-term bad influence; and we should not be ungrateful for what we received just because our further hopes were dashed by fortune.

The point is that a reverential attitude towards the gods and being charitable and uncomplaining with regard to fortune always yield a dividend which is both fine and enjoyable, and anyone who, in a situation like ours, makes a particular point of highlighting the memory of good things and turning his mind away from the dark and disturbing aspects of his life towards the bright and brilliant ones instead either completely extinguishes whatever it is that is F causing him pain, or at least decreases and obscures it by blending it with its opposite.[18] Perfume is always nice to smell, but it is also an antidote to unpleasant odors; likewise, bearing good things in mind serves the extra purpose of essential support, in times of trouble, for people who are not afraid to recall good times and do not critically hold fortune entirely responsible for every bad thing that happens. And that is a condition we should avoid—the syndrome of whingeing if the book of our life has a single smudge 611A while every other page is perfectly clean. I mean, you have often been told that happiness is a consequence of correctly using the rational mind for the goal of a stable state, and that if it is a chance event which causes one to deviate, this does not constitute a major reversal and does not mean that the edifice of one's life has collapsed and been demolished. . . .

If you feel sorry about our daughter dying before she was able to marry and have children, then again you can find other reasons for cheering yourself up, in that you have known and experienced both these states: I mean, they cannot simultaneously be significant and insignificant blessings, depending on whether or not one has been deprived of them! And the fact that she has gone to a place of no pain ought not to be a source of pain to us. Why should she cause us to suffer, if there is nothing that can now cause her pain? Even huge losses cease to be a source of distress when the point D is reached at which the objects are no longer missed, and your Timoxena suffered only minor losses, since what she was familiar with and what she found pleasure in were not things of great importance. And as for things she was unaware of, which had never

---

[18]Plutarch believed strongly in this principle; see *On Contentment* 469A. There he illustrated it by sight, here by smell.

entered her mind or caught her fancy—how could she be said to have lost them?

[10] Then there is that other idea you've come across, which is commonly accepted, that it is quite impossible for anything to harm or distress something which has been dissolved. But I know that both the doctrine we've inherited from our ancestors[19] and the maxims of the Dionysian Mysteries (which those of us who are in the group are privy to)[20] prevent you believing this idea. So, since the soul cannot be destroyed, you can compare what happens to it to the behavior of caged birds: if it has made a physical body its home for an extended period of time, and has allowed a plethora of material events and long familiarity to domesticate it to this way of life, then it resumes its perch inside a body and doesn't let go or stop its involvement, through rebirth after rebirth, with worldly conditions and fortunes. If old age is the butt of calumny and slurs, you should appreciate that this is not because of wrinkles, grey hair and physical enfeeblement: no, its most cruel feature is that it makes the soul lose touch with its memories of the other world,[21] attaches it to this one, wraps it and constricts it (since it retains the shape it gained while it was acted on by the body). On the other hand, a soul which, although captured, ⟨remains only a short while in a body before being released⟩ by the gods and departing, springs back up to its natural state as if, although it had been bent, it retained its suppleness and malleability. Just as fire is quickly rekindled again and returns to its former state if it is relit straight after being extinguished, ⟨but the longer the interval, the harder it is to relight, so too the most fortunate soul is the one which is able, in the poet's words,⟩ 'to pass as swiftly as possible through Hades' portals, before a strong love of the things of this world has been engendered in it and before it has become molded to the body by being softened and melted as if by chemicals.

[11] Our ancient ancestral customs and rules are a better guide to the truth in these matters. People do not pour libations for their infant children when they die or perform any of the other rites that

---

[19]Plutarch proclaimed his own adherence to traditional faith again in *Dialogue on Love* 756B.

[20]So Plutarch was an initiate. The Mysteries fostered belief in a happy afterlife and the immortality of the soul.

[21]Plato too, in *Phaedrus* 250b–c, had used the imagery of the Mysteries for the vision of the soul when it is free from the imprisonment of the body.

in other cases one is expected to perform for the dead, because babies have not been pervaded by earth or any earthly things. Again, people do not linger over their burial or at their grave or in laying out their bodies, because the laws regarding death at that age do not allow it, on the grounds that it is irreligious to grieve for those who have exchanged this world for a fate, and a place too, that is better and more divine. Since mistrusting these laws is more problematic than trusting them, let us make sure that our external actions conform to their injunctions, and that our internal state is even more untainted, pure and restrained than our external activity.

For Further Reflection

1. Describe Plutarch's expression of compassion to his wife. What characteristics impress you most?

2. What reasons does Plutarch offer for his advice to Timoxena to be grateful for the brief life of their daughter? To what extent is his comfort based on a religious idea? Note the reference to the religious mystery cult of Dionysus and the idea of the soul leaving the body.

3. How would you evaluate this letter as an expression of sympathy over the loss of a child? How does one express the right amount of compassion without being maudlin or patronizing?

The World of Epictetus
Courage and Endurance

VICE ADMIRAL JAMES STOCKDALE

Vice Admiral James Stockdale was a combat naval aviator whose plane was shot down over North Vietnam. He spent eight years in a North Vietnam prison, four of them in solitary confinement. He has been a fellow at the Hoover Institute and was a vice presidential candidate in the 1992 election.

The following is Vice Admiral Stockdale's tale of his experience in prison and of what helped him endure deprivation and torture. He refers to the Stoic catechism *Enchiridion,* as his inspiration during his ordeal. You may find that work in this chapter.

In 1965 I was a forty-one-year-old commander, the senior pilot of Air Wing 16, flying combat missions in the area just south of Hanoi from the aircraft carrier *Oriskany.* By September of that year I had grown quite accustomed to briefing dozens of pilots and leading them on daily air strikes; I had flown nearly 200 missions myself and knew the countryside of North Vietnam like the back of my hand. On the ninth of that month I led about thirty-five airplanes to the Thanh Hoa Bridge, just west of that city. That bridge was tough; we had been bouncing 500-pounders off it for weeks.

The September 9 raid held special meaning for *Oriskany* pilots because of a special bomb load we had improvised; we were going in with our biggest, the 2000-pounders, hung not only on our attack planes but on our F-8 fighter-bombers as well. This increase in bridge-busting capability came from the innovative brain of a major flying with my Marine fighter squadron. He had figured out how we could jury-rig some switches, hang the big bombs, pump out some of the fuel to stay within takeoff weight limits, and then top off our tanks from our airborne refuelers while en route to the target. Although the pilot had to throw several switches in sequence to get

This essay by Vice Admiral James Stockdale, USN, "The World of Epictetus" is reprinted from the *Atlantic Monthly* (April 1978) by permission.

rid of his bombs, a procedure requiring above-average cockpit agility, we routinely operated on the premise that all pilots of Air Wing 16 were above average. I test-flew the new load on a mission, thought it over, and approved it; that's the way we did business.

Our spirit was up. That morning, the *Oriskany* Air Wing was finally going to drop the bridge that was becoming a North Vietnamese symbol of resistance. You can imagine our dismay when we crossed the coast and the weather scout I had sent on ahead radioed back that ceiling and visibility were zero-zero in the bridge area. In the tiny cockpit of my A-4 at the front of the pack, I pushed the button on the throttle, spoke into the radio mike in my oxygen mask, and told the formation to split up and proceed in pairs to the secondary targets I had specified in my contingency briefing. What a letdown.

The adrenaline stopped flowing as my wingman and I broke left and down and started sauntering along toward our "milk run" target: boxcars on a railroad siding between Vinh and Thanh Hoa, where the flak was light. Descending through 10,000 feet, I unsnapped my oxygen mask and let it dangle, giving my pinched face a rest—no reason to stay uncomfortable on this run.

As I glided toward that easy target, I'm sure I felt totally self-satisfied. I had the top combat job that a Navy commander can hold and I was in tune with my environment. I was confident—I knew airplanes and flying inside out. I was comfortable with the people I worked with and I knew the trade so well that I often improvised variations in accepted procedures and encouraged others to do so under my watchful eye. I was on top. I thought I had found every key to success and had no doubt that my Academy and test-pilot schooling had provided me with everything I needed in life.

I passed down the middle of those boxcars and smiled as I saw the results of my instinctive timing. A neat pattern—perfection. I was just pulling out of my dive low to the ground when I heard a noise I hadn't expected—the *boom boom boom* of a 57-millimeter gun—and then I saw it just behind my wingtip. I was hit—all the red lights came on, my control system was going out—and I could barely keep that plane from flying into the ground while I got that damned oxygen mask up to my mouth so I could tell my wingman that I was about to eject. What rotten luck. And on a "milk run"!

The descent in the chute was quiet except for occasional rifle shots from the streets below. My mind was clear, and I said to myself, "five years." I knew we were making a mess of the war in

Southeast Asia, but I didn't think it would last longer than that; I
was also naive about the resources I would need in order to survive a lengthy period of captivity.

The Durants have said that culture is a thin and fragile veneer that
superimposes itself on mankind. For the first time I was on my
own, without the veneer. I was to spend years searching through
and refining my bag of memories, looking for useful tools, things
of value. The values were there, but they were all mixed up with
technology, bureaucracy, and expediency, and had to be brought
up into the open.
   Education should take care to illuminate values, not bury them
amongst the trivia. Are our students getting the message that without personal integrity intellectual skills are worthless?
   Integrity is one of those words which many people keep in that
desk drawer labeled "too hard." It's not a topic for the dinner table
or the cocktail party. You can't buy or sell it. When supported with
education, a person's integrity can give him something to rely on
when his perspective seems to blur, when rules and principles seem
to waver, and when he's faced with hard choices of right or wrong.
It's something to keep him on the right track, something to keep
him afloat when he's drowning; if only for practical reasons, it is
an attribute that should be kept at the very top of a young person's consciousness.
   The importance of the latter point is highlighted in prison camps,
where everyday human nature, stripped bare, can be studied under
a magnifying glass in accelerated time. Lessons spotlighted and
absorbed in that laboratory sharpen one's eye for their abstruse but
highly relevant applications in the "real time" world of now.

In the five years since I've been out of prison, I've participated several times in the process of selecting senior naval officers for promotion or important command assignments. I doubt that the experience is significantly different from that of executives who sit on
"selection boards" in any large hierarchy. The system must be formal, objective, and fair; if you've seen one, you've probably seen
them all. Navy selection board proceedings go something like this.
   The first time you know the identity of the other members of
the board is when you walk into a boardroom at eight o'clock on
an appointed morning. The first order of business is to stand, raise
your right hand, put your left hand on the Bible, and swear to

make the best judgment you can, on the basis of merit, without prejudice. You're sworn to confidentiality regarding all board members' remarks during the proceedings. Board members are chosen for their experience and understanding; they often have knowledge of the particular individuals under consideration. They must feel free to speak their minds. They read and grade dozens of dossiers, and each candidate is discussed extensively. At voting time, a member casts his vote by selecting and pushing a "percent confidence" button, visible only to himself, on a console attached to his chair. When the last member pushes his button, a totalizer displays the numerical average "confidence" of the board. No one knows who voted what.

I'm always impressed by the fact that every effort is made to be fair to the candidate. Some are clearly out, some are clearly in; the borderline cases are the tough ones. You go over and over those in the "middle pile" and usually you vote and revote until late at night. In all the boards I've sat on, no inference or statement in a "jacket" is as sure to portend a low confidence score on the vote as evidence of a lack of directness or rectitude of a candidate in his dealings with others. Any hint of moral turpitude really turns people off. When the crunch comes, they prefer to work with forthright plodders rather than with devious geniuses. I don't believe that this preference is unique to the military. In any hierarchy where people's fates are decided by committees or boards, those who lose credibility with their peers and who cause their superiors to doubt their directness, honesty, or integrity are dead. Recovery isn't possible.

The linkage of men's ethics, reputations, and fates can be studied in even more vivid detail in prison camp. In that brutally controlled environment a perceptive enemy can get his hooks into the slightest chink in a man's ethical armor and accelerate his downfall. Given the right opening, the right moral weakness, a certain susceptibility on the part of the prisoner, a clever extortionist can drive his victim into a downhill slide that will ruin his image, self-respect, and life in a very short time.

There are some uncharted aspects to this, some traits of susceptibility which I don't think psychologists yet have words for. I am thinking of the tragedy that can befall a person who has such a need for love or attention that he will sell his soul for it. I use tragedy with the rigorous definition Aristotle applied to it: the story of a good man with a flaw who comes to an unjustified bad end.

This is a rather delicate point and one that I want to emphasize. We had very very few collaborators in prison, and comparatively few Aristotelian tragedies, but the story and fate of one of these good men with a flaw might be instructive.

He was handsome, smart, articulate, and smooth. He was almost sincere. He was obsessed with success. When the going got tough, he decided expediency was preferable to principle.

This man was a classical opportunist. He befriended and worked for the enemy to the detriment of his fellow Americans. He made a tacit deal; moreover, he accepted favors (a violation of the code of conduct). In time, out of fear and shame, he withdrew; we could not get him to communicate with the American prisoner organization.

I couldn't learn what made the man tick. One of my best friends in prison, one of the wisest persons I have ever known, had once been in a squadron with this fellow. In prisoners' code I tapped a question to my philosophical friend: "What in the world is going on with that fink?"

"You're going to be surprised at what I have to say," he meticulously tapped back. "In a squadron he pushes himself forward and dominates the scene. He's a continual fountain of information. He's the person everybody relies on for inside dope. He works like mad; often flies more hops than others. It drives him crazy if he's not liked. He tends to grovel and ingratiate himself before others. I didn't realize he was really pathetic until I was sitting around with him and his wife one night when he was spinning his yarns of delusions of grandeur, telling of his great successes and his pending ascension to the top. His wife knew him better than anybody else; she shook her head with genuine sympathy and said to him: 'Gee, you're just a phony.'"

In prison, this man had somehow reached the point where he was willing to sell his soul just to satisfy this need, this immaturity. The only way he could get the attention that he demanded from authority was to grovel and ingratiate himself before the enemy. As a soldier he was a miserable failure, but he had not crossed the boundary of willful treason; he was not written off as an irrevocable loss, as were the two patent collaborators with whom the Vietnamese soon arranged that he live.

As we American POWs built our civilization, and wrote our own laws (which we leaders obliged all to memorize), we also codified certain principles which formed the backbone of our policies and attitudes. I codified the principles of compassion, rehabilitation, and forgiveness with the slogan: "It is neither American nor Christian to nag a repentant sinner to his grave." (Some didn't like it, thought it seemed soft on finks.) And so, we really gave this man a chance. Over time, our efforts worked. After five years of self-indulgence he got himself together and started to communicate with the prisoner organization. I sent the message "Are you on the team or not?"; he replied, "Yes," and came back. He told the Vietnamese that he didn't want to play their dirty games anymore. He wanted to get away from those willful collaborators and he came back and he was accepted, after a fashion.

I wish that were the end of the story. Although he came back, joined us, and even became a leader of sorts, he never totally won himself back. No matter how forgiving we were, he was conscious that many resented him—not so much because he was weak but because he had broken what we might call a gentleman's code. In all of those years when he, a senior officer, had willingly participated in making tape recordings of anti-American material, he had deeply offended the sensibilities of the American prisoners who were forced to listen to him. To most of us it wasn't the rhetoric of the war or the goodness or the badness of this or that issue that counted. The object of our highest value was the well-being of our fellow prisoners. He had broken that code and hurt some of those people. Some thought that as an informer he had indirectly hurt them physically. I don't believe that. What indisputably hurt them was his not having the sensitivity to realize the damage his opportunistic conduct would do to the morale of a bunch of Middle American guys with Middle American attitudes which they naturally cherished. He should have known that in those solitary cells where his tapes were piped were idealistic, direct, patriotic fellows who would be crushed and embarrassed to have him, a senior man in excellent physical shape, so obviously not under torture, telling the world that the war was wrong. Even if he believed what he said, which he did not, he should have had the common decency to keep his mouth shut. You can sit and think anything you want, but when you insensitively cut down those who want to love and help you, you cross a line. He seemed to sense that he could never truly be one of us.

And yet he was likable—particularly back in civilization after release—when tension was off, and making a deal did not seem so important. He exuded charm and "hail fellow" sophistication. He wanted so to be liked by all those men he had once discarded in his search for new friends, new deals, new fields to conquer in

Hanoi. The tragedy of his life was obvious to us all. Tears were shed by some of his old prison mates when he was killed in an accident that strongly resembled suicide some months later. The Greek drama had run its course. He was right out of Aristotle's book, a good man with a flaw who had come to an unjustified bad end. The flaw was insecurity: the need to ingratiate himself, the need for love and adulation at any price.

He reminded me of Paul Newman in *The Hustler*. Newman couldn't stand success. He knew how to make a deal. He was handsome, he was smart, he was attractive to everybody; but he had to have adulation, and therein lay the seed of tragedy. Playing high-stakes pool against old Minnesota Fats (Jackie Gleason), Newman was well in the lead, and getting more full of himself by the hour. George C. Scott, the pool bettor, whispered to his partner: "I'm going to keep betting on Minnesota Fats; this other guy [Newman] is a born loser—he's all skill and no character." And he was right, a born loser—I think that's the message.

How can we educate to avoid these casualties? Can we by means of education prevent this kind of tragedy? What we prisoners were in was a one-way leverage game in which the other side had all the mechanical advantage. I suppose you could say that we all live in a leverage world to some degree; we all experience people trying to use us in one way or another. The difference in Hanoi was the degradation of the ends (to be used as propaganda agents of an enemy, or as informers on your fellow Americans), and the power of the means (total environmental control including solitary confinement, restraint by means of leg-irons and handcuffs, and torture). Extortionists always go down the same track: the imposition of guilt and fear for having disobeyed their rules, followed in turn by punishment, apology, confession, and atonement (their payoff). Our captors would go to great lengths to get a man to compromise his own code, even if only slightly, and then they would hold that in their bag, and the next time get him to go a little further.

Some people are psychologically, if not physically, at home in extortion environments. They are tough people who instinctively avoid getting sucked into the undertows. They never kid themselves or their friends; if they miss the mark they admit it. But there's another category of person who gets tripped up. He makes a small compromise, perhaps rationalizes it, and then makes another one; and then he gets depressed, full of shame, lonesome, loses his willpower and self-respect, and comes to a tragic end. Somewhere along the line he realizes that he has turned a corner that he didn't mean to turn. All too late he realizes that he has been worshiping the wrong gods and discovers the wisdom of the ages: life is not fair.

In sorting out the story after our release, we found that most of us had come to combat constant mental and physical pressure in much the same way. We discovered that when a person is alone in a cell and sees the door open only once or twice a day for a bowl of soup, he realizes after a period of weeks in isolation and darkness that he has to build some sort of ritual into his life if he wants to avoid becoming an animal. Ritual fills a need in a hard life and it's easy to see how formal church ritual grew. For almost all of us, this ritual was built around prayer, exercise, and clandestine communication. The prayers I said during those days were prayers of quality with ideas of substance. We found that over the course of time our minds had a tremendous capacity for invention and introspection, but had the weakness of being an integral part of our bodies. I remembered Descartes and how in his philosophy he separated mind and body. One time I cursed my body for the way it decayed my mind. I had decided that I would become a Gandhi. I would have to be carried around on a pallet and in that state I could not be used by my captors for propaganda purposes. After about ten days of fasting, I found that I had become so depressed that soon I would risk going into interrogation ready to spill my guts just looking for a friend. I tapped to the guy next door and I said, "Gosh, how I wish Descartes could have been right, but he's wrong." He was a little slow to reply; I reviewed Descartes's deduction with him and explained how I had discovered that body and mind are inseparable.

On the positive side, I discovered the tremendous file-cabinet volume of the human mind. You can memorize an incredible amount of material and you can draw the past out of your memory with remarkable recall by easing slowly toward the event you seek and not crowding the mind too closely. You'll try to remember who was at your birthday party when you were five years old, and you can get it, but only after months of effort. You can break the locks and find the answers, but you need time and solitude to learn how to use this marvelous device in your head which is the greatest computer on earth.

Of course many of the things we recalled from the past were utterly useless as sources of strength or practicality. For instance, events brought back from cocktail parties or insincere social contacts were almost repugnant because of their emptiness, their utter lack of value. More often than not, the locks worth picking had been on old schoolroom doors. School days can be thought of as a time when one is filling the important stacks of one's memory library. For me, the golden doors were labeled history and the classics. The historical perspective which enabled a man to take himself away from all the agitation, not necessarily to see a rosy lining, but to see the real nature of the situation he faced, was truly a thing of value.

Here's how this historical perspective helped me see the reality of my own situation and thus cope better with it. I learned from a Vietnamese prisoner that the same cells we occupied had in years before been lived in by many of the leaders of the Hanoi government. From my history lessons I recalled that when metropolitan France permitted communists in the government in 1936, the communists who occupied cells in Vietnam were set free. I marveled at the cycle of history, all within my memory, which prompted Hitler's rise in Germany, then led to the rise of the Popular Front in France, and finally vacated this cell of mine halfway around the world ("Perhaps Pham Van Dong lived here"). I came to understand what tough people these were. I was willing to fight them to the death, but I grew to realize that hatred was an indulgence, a very inefficient emotion. I remember thinking, "If you were committed to beating the dealer in a gambling casino, would *hating* him help your game?" In a pidgin English propaganda book the guard gave me, speeches by these old communists about their prison experiences stressed how they learned to beat down the enemy by being united. It seemed comforting to know that we were united against the communist administration of Hoa Lo prison just as the Vietnamese communists had united against the French administration of Hoa Lo in the thirties. Prisoners are prisoners, and there's only one way to beat administrations. We resolved to do it better in the sixties than they had in the thirties. You don't base system-beating on any thought of political idealism; you do it as a competitive thing, as an expression of self-respect.

Education in the classics teaches you that all organizations since the beginning of time have used the power of guilt; that cycles are repetitive; and that this is the way of the world. It's a naive person who comes in and says, "Let's see, what's good and what's bad?" That's a quagmire. You can get out of that quagmire only by recalling how wise men before you accommodated the same dilemmas. And I believe a good classical education and an understanding of history can best determine the rules you should live by. They also give you the power to analyze reasons for these rules and guide you as to how to apply them to your own situation. In a broader sense, all my education helped me. Naval Academy discipline and body contact sports helped me. But the education which I found myself using most was what I got in graduate school. The messages of history and philosophy I used were simple.

The first one is this business about life not being fair. That is a very important lesson and I learned it from a wonderful man named Philip Rhinelander. As a lieutenant commander in the Navy studying political science at Stanford University in 1961, I went over to philosophy corner one day and an older gentleman said, "Can I help you?" I said, "Yes, I'd like to take some courses in philosophy." I told him I'd been in college for six years and had never had a course in philosophy. He couldn't believe it. I told him that I was a naval officer and he said, "Well, I used to be in the Navy. Sit down." Philip Rhinelander became a great influence in my life.

He had been a Harvard lawyer and had pleaded cases before the Supreme Court and then gone to war as a reserve officer. When he came back he took his doctorate at Harvard. He was also a music composer, had been director of general education at Harvard, dean of the School of Humanities and Sciences at Stanford, and by the time I met him had by choice returned to teaching in the classroom. He said, "The course I'm teaching is my personal two-term favorite—The Problem of Good and Evil—and we're starting our second term." He said the message of his course was from the Book of Job. The number one problem in this world is that people are not able to accommodate the lesson in the book.

He recounted the story of Job. It starts out by establishing that Job was the most honorable of men. Then he lost all his goods. He also lost his reputation, which is what really hurt. His wife was badgering him to admit his sins, but he knew he had made no errors. He was not a patient man and demanded to speak to the Lord. When the Lord appeared in the whirlwind, he said, "Now, Job, you have to shape up! Life is not fair." That's my interpretation and that's the way the book ended for hundreds of years. I agree with those of the opinion that the happy ending was spliced on many years later. If you read it, you'll note that the meter changes. People couldn't live with the original message. Here was a good man who came to unexplained grief, and the Lord told him: "That's the way it is. Don't challenge me. This is my world and you either live in it as I designed it or get out."

This was a great comfort to me in prison. It answered the question "Why me?" It cast aside any thoughts of being punished for past actions. Sometimes I shared the message with fellow prisoners as I tapped through the walls to them, but I learned to be selective. It's a strong message which upsets some people.

Rhinelander also passed on to me another piece of classical information which I found of great value. On the day of our last session together he said, "You're a military man, let me give you a book to remember me by. It's a book of military ethics." He handed it to me, and I bade him goodbye with great emotion. I took the book home and that night started to read it. It was the *Enchiridion* of the philosopher Epictetus, his "manual" for the Roman field soldier.

As I began to read, I thought to myself in disbelief, "Does Rhinelander think I'm going to draw lessons for my life from this thing? I'm a fighter pilot. I'm a technical man. I'm a test pilot. I know how to get people to do technical work. I play golf; I drink martinis. I know how to get ahead in my profession. And what does he hand me? A book that says in part, 'It's better to die in hunger, exempt from guilt and fear, than to live in affluence and with perturbation.'" I remembered this later in prison because perturbation was what I was living with. When I ejected from the airplane on that September morn in 1965, I had left the land of technology. I had entered the world of Epictetus, and it's a world that few of us, whether we know it or not, are ever far away from.

In Palo Alto, I had read this book, not with contentment, but with annoyance. Statement after statement: "Men are disturbed not by things, but by the view that they take of them." "Do not be concerned with things which are beyond your power." "Demand not that events should happen as you wish, but wish them to happen as they do happen and you will go on well." This is stoicism. It's not the last word, but it's a viewpoint that comes in handy in many circumstances, and it surely did for me. Particularly this line: "Lameness is an impediment to the body but not to the will." That was significant for me because I wasn't able to stand up and support myself on my badly broken leg for the first couple of years I was in solitary confinement.

Other statements of Epictetus took on added meaning in the light of extortions which often began with our captors' callous pleas: "If you are just reasonable with us we will compensate you. You get your meals, you get to sleep, you won't be pestered, you might even get a cellmate." The catch was that by being "reasonable with us" our enemies meant being their informers, their propagandists. The old stoic had said, "If I can get the things I need with the preservation of my honor and fidelity and self-respect, show me the way and I will get them. But, if you require me to lose my own proper good, that you may gain what is no good, consider how unreasonable and foolish you are." To love our fellow prisoners was within our power. To betray, to propagandize, to disillusion conscientious and patriotic shipmates and destroy their morale so that they in turn would be destroyed was to lose one's proper good.

What attributes serve you well in the extortion environment? We learned there, above all else, that the best defense is to keep your conscience clean. When we did something we were ashamed of, and our captors realized we were ashamed of it, we were in trouble. A little white lie is where extortion and ultimately blackmail start. In 1965, I was crippled and I was alone. I realized that they had all the power. I couldn't see how I was ever going to get out with my honor and self-respect. The one thing I came to realize was that if you don't lose integrity you can't be had and you can't be hurt. Compromises multiply and build up when you're working against a skilled extortionist or a good manipulator. You can't be had if you don't take that first shortcut, or "meet them halfway," as they say, or look for that tacit "deal," or make that first compromise.

Bob North, a political science professor at Stanford, taught me a course called Comparative Marxist Thought. This was not an anticommunist course. It was the study of dogma and thought patterns. We read no criticisms of Marxism, only primary sources. All year we read the works of Marx and Lenin. In Hanoi, I understood more about Marxist theory than my interrogator did. I was able to say to that interrogator, "That's not what Lenin said; you're a deviationist."

One of the things North talked about was brainwashing. A psychologist who studied the Korean prisoner situation, which somewhat paralleled ours, concluded that three categories of prisoners were involved there. The first was the redneck Marine sergeant from Tennessee who had an eighth-grade education. He would get in that interrogation room and they would say that the Spanish-American War was started by the bomb within the *Maine,* which might be true, and he would answer, "B.S." They would show him something about racial unrest in Detroit. "B.S." There was no way they could get to him; his mind was made up. He was a straight guy, red, white, and blue, and everything else was B.S.! He didn't give it a second thought. Not much of a historian, perhaps, but a good security risk.

In the next category were the sophisticates. They were the fellows who could be told these same things about the horrors of American history and our social problems, but had heard it all before, knew both sides of every story, and thought we were on the right track. They weren't ashamed that we had robber barons at a certain time in our history; they were aware of the skeletons in most civilizations' closets. They could not be emotionally involved and so they were good security risks.

The ones who were in trouble were the high school graduates who had enough sense to pick up the innuendo, and yet not enough education to accommodate it properly. Not many of them fell, but most of the men that got entangled started from that background.

The psychologist's point is possibly oversimplistic, but I think his message has some validity. A little knowledge is a dangerous thing.

Generally speaking, I think education is a tremendous defense; the broader, the better. After I was shot down my wife, Sybil, found a clipping glued in the front of my collegiate dictionary: "Education is an ornament in prosperity and a refuge in adversity." She certainly agrees with me on that. Most of us prisoners found that the so-called practical academic exercises in how to do things, which I'm told are proliferating, were useless. I'm not saying that we should base education on training people to be in prison, but I am saying that in stress situations, the fundamentals, the hardcore classical subjects, are what serve best.

Theatrics also helped sustain me. My mother had been a drama coach when I was young and I was in many of her plays. In prison I learned how to manufacture a personality and live it, crawl into it, and hold that role without deviation. During interrogations, I'd check the responses I got to different kinds of behavior. They'd get worried when I did things irrationally. And so, every so often, I would play that "irrational" role and come completely unglued. When I could tell that pressure to make a public exhibition of me was building, I'd stand up, tip the table over, attempt to throw the chair through the window, and say, "No way, Goddammit! I'm not doing that! Now, come over here and fight!" This was a risky ploy, because if they thought you were acting, they would slam you into the ropes and make you scream in pain like a baby. You could watch their faces and read their minds. They had expected me to behave like a stoic. But a man would be a fool to make their job easy by being conventional and predictable. I could feel the tide turn in my favor at that magic moment when their anger turned to pleading: "Calm down, now calm down." The payoff would come when they decided that the risk of my going haywire in front of some touring American professor on a "fact-finding" mission was too great. More important, they had reason to believe that I would tell the truth—namely, that I had been in solitary confinement for four years and tortured fifteen times—without fear of future consequences. So theatrical training proved helpful to me.

Can you educate for leadership? I think you can, but the communists would probably say no. One day in an argument with an interrogator, I said, "You are so proud of being a party member, what are the criteria?" He said in a flurry of anger, "There are only four: you have to be seventeen years old, you have to be selfless, you have to be smart enough to understand the theory, and you've got to be a person who innately influences others." He stressed that fourth one. I think psychologists would say that leadership is innate, and there is truth in that. But, I also think you can learn some leadership traits that naturally accrue from a good education: compassion is a necessity for leaders, as are spontaneity, bravery, self-discipline, honesty, and above all, integrity.

I remember being disappointed about a month after I was back when one of my young friends, a prison mate, came running up after a reunion at the Naval Academy. He said with glee, "This is really great, you won't believe how this country has advanced. They've practically done away with plebe year at the Academy, and they've got computers in the basement of Bancroft Hall." I thought, "My God, if there was anything that helped us get through those eight years, it was plebe year, and if anything screwed up that war, it was computers!"

For Further Reflection

1. You may want to read Epictetus's *Enchiridion* (in this chapter) before you answer this question: how did Stoicism help Vice Admiral Stockdale to endure his torture and suffering in prison? Why do you think so many other prisoners failed to maintain their self-respect and loyalty to their country?

2. What other virtues besides courage do you find implicit in this article? Explain.

3. How would you endeavor to maintain your spirits if you were in Stockdale's situation?

4. Stockdale praises his college teacher for introducing him to ideas that were to help him survive later. Should moral education be included as part of public education, including college education?

Reflections on Suffering

BERTRAND RUSSELL

The British philosopher Bertrand Russell (1872–1970) was someone who thought deeply about the question of the meaning of life. Russell says in his *Autobiography* that his youth was very unhappy and only the love of mathematics kept him from committing suicide. Gradually, he learned to find happiness. In these two short selections from his *Autobiography,* Russell first tells of an experience which greatly affected his life and then goes on to summarize what gives him meaning in life.

SPRING 1901

When we came home, we found Mrs. W undergoing an unusually severe bout of pain. She seemed cut off from everyone and everything by walls of agony, and the sense of the solitude of each human soul suddenly overwhelmed me. Ever since my marriage, my emotional life had been calm and superficial. I had forgotten all the deeper issues, and had been content with flippant cleverness. Sud-

From *Autobiography*, vol. 1, p. 146 by Bertrand Russell. Copyright 1951 by Unwin & Hyman, Ltd. Reprinted by permission of Taylor & Francis Books UK.

denly the ground seemed to give way beneath me, and I found myself in quite another region. Within five minutes I went thru some such reflections as the following: the loneliness of the human soul is unendurable; nothing can penetrate it except the highest intensity of the sort of love that religious teachers have preached; whatever does not spring from this motive is harmful, or at best useless; it follows that war is wrong, that a public school education is abominable, that the use of force is to be deprecated, and that in human relations one should penetrate to the core of loneliness in each person and speak to that. [The writer then describes his sudden awareness of Mrs. W's three-year-old son with whom he then and there found an affinity.] . . . At the end of those five minutes, I had become a completely different person. For a time, a sort of mystic illumination possessed me. I felt that I knew the inmost thoughts of everybody that I met in the street, and though this was, no doubt, a delusion, I did in actual fact find myself in *far closer* touch than previously with all my friends, and many of my acquaintances. Having been an Imperialist, I became during those five minutes . . . a Pacificist. Having for years cared only for exactness and analysis, I found myself filled with semi-mystical feelings about beauty, and with an intense interest in children and with a desire almost as profound as that of the Buddha to find some philosophy which should make human life endurable. A strange excitement possessed me, containing intense pain but also some element of triumph through the fact that I could dominate pain, and make it, as I thought, a gateway to wisdom. The mystic insight which I then imagined myself to possess has largely faded, and the habit of analysis has reasserted itself. But something of what I thought I saw in that moment has remained always with me, *causing* my attitude during the first war, my interest in my children, my indifference to minor misfortunes and a certain emotional tone in all my human relations.

EPILOGUE

Love, Knowledge, and Pity

Three passions, simple but overwhelmingly strong, have governed my life: the longing for love, the search for knowledge, and unbearable pity for the suffering of mankind. These passions, like great winds, have blown me hither and thither, in a wayward course, over a deep ocean of anguish, reaching to the very verge of despair.

I have sought love, first, because it brings ecstasy—ecstasy so great that I would often have sacrificed all the rest of life for a few hours of this joy. I have sought it, next, because it relieves loneliness—that terrible loneliness in which one shivering consciousness looks over the rim of the world into the cold unfathomable lifeless abyss. I have sought it, finally, because in the union of love I have seen, in a mystic miniature, the prefiguring vision of the heaven that saints and poets have imagined. This is what I sought, and though it might seem too good for human life, this is what—at last—I have found.

With equal passion I have sought knowledge. I have wished to understand the hearts of men. I have wished to know why the stars shine. And I have tried to apprehend the Pythagorean power by which number holds sway above the flux. A little of this, but not much, I have achieved.

Love and knowledge, so far as they were possible, led upward toward the heavens. But always pity brought me back to earth. Echoes of cries of pain reverberate in my heart. Children in famine, victims tortured by oppressors, helpless old people a hated burden to their sons, and the whole world of loneliness, poverty, and pain make a mockery of what human life should be. I long to alleviate the evil, but I cannot, and I too suffer.

This has been my life. I have found it worth living, and would gladly live it again if the chance were offered me.

For Further Reflection

1. Compare the first passage with the second. Do you see any differences?

2. How does your set of values compare with Russell's? Do you think that Russell's philosophy of life is adequate for happiness and the good life? Compare it with the other readings in this part.

Further Readings for Chapter 7

Becker, Lawrence. *On Justifying Moral Arguments.* London: Routledge and Kegan Paul, 1973. Chapter 19.

Cooper, John. *Reason and the Human Good in Aristotle.* Cambridge, Mass.: Harvard University Press, 1975.

Kruschwitz, Robert, and Robert Roberts, eds. *The Virtues.* Belmont, Calif.: Wadsworth, 1987. An excellent up-to-date anthology, containing an extensive bibliography.

MacIntyre, Alasdair. *After Virtue.* Notre Dame, Ind.: University of Notre Dame Press, 1981.

Murdoch, Iris. *The Sovereignty of Good.* New York: Schocken Books, 1971.

Pence, Gregory. "Recent Work on Virtues." *American Philosophical Quarterly* 21 (1984).

Pojman, Louis. *Ethics: Discovering Right and Wrong,* 3rd ed. Belmont, Calif.: Wadsworth, 1999. Chapter 8.

Sommers, Christina Hoff, and Fred Sommers. *Vice and Virtues in Everyday Life.* New York: Harcourt Brace Jovanovich, 1985.

Taylor, Richard. *Ethics, Faith and Reason.* Englewood Cliffs, N.J.: Prentice-Hall, 1985.

Trianosky, Gregory. "Supererogation, Wrongdoing, and Vice: On the Autonomy of the Ethics of Virtue." *Journal of Philosophy* (January 1986).

Wallace, James. *Virtues and Vices.* Ithaca, N.Y.: Cornell University Press, 1978.

Part III

Moral Issues

In this part of our book we examine three related, vitally important issues in moral theory: egoism and the question "Why should we be moral?" (chapter 8); the question whether life has meaning (chapter 9); and the question of freedom and autonomy, which have to do with self-respect (chapter 10). As you will see, these questions are related. If life has no meaning, it may not make sense to be moral all of the time or care about morality. But if life does have meaning, not only will morality be crucial, but also part of being moral is the promotion of freedom, autonomy, and self-respect.

CHAPTER 8

Ethics and Egoism
Why Should We Be Moral?

Why should we be moral? That is, you may ask yourself, Why should I do what morality requires even when it may not be in my best interest? Or, Is it really in my best interest to be moral all of the time, after all, even if I fail to realize it? Or, Is morality only *sometimes* in my best interest—when it depends on group cooperation? For example, people can run up charges on their credit cards and not pay them, perhaps moving to a different country. So it might be in George's interest to charge up his credit card and then move to another country. But if it is not in his interest to move, he may get into trouble if he doesn't pay his credit card bill, and he will get a bad credit rating, which will affect his future prospects in obtaining loans. So in this case, it is in George's interest to comply with moral rules. But suppose he can cheat and get away with it? He obtains someone else's brilliant research paper and turns it in as his own. No one is likely ever to find out. Why shouldn't he cheat? Of course, he won't like it if other people do the same—and if enough people cheat, grades will become meaningless. But then, as he profits from his immorality, he can contribute some money back into moral reform, so that more people will be motivated to be good.

Is there anything wrong with this reasoning?

In our first reading, Glaucon, Plato's brother, asks Socrates why we should be moral. He then tells the story of the shepherd Gyges, who finds a ring which allows him to become invisible. What fun he can have! He can serve his interests with impunity and not be discovered. But Socrates rejects this view and argues that Gyges and his ilk never get away with immorality. Justice is intrinsically valuable, like health. The good is really good for you, so that if you act immorally, you really are harming yourself.

But many reject Socrates' way of looking at the matter. They accuse him of supposing an objective world of values or a divine law which ensures that those who act selfishly will be punished— through karma or by God. But take away the notion of God or karma and the picture breaks down.

Our second reading is a selection from Ayn Rand's *Atlas Shrugged* in which she argues that ethical egoism is the correct moral theory and that altruism is irrational. "Parasites, moochers, looters, brutes and thugs can be of no value to a human being—nor can he gain any benefit from living in a society that treats him as a sacrificial animal and penalizes him for his virtues in order to reward *them* or their vices, which means a society based on the ethics of altruism." Rand defines *altruism* as the ethics that tells one "to sacrifice one's life. Altruism erodes men's capacity to grasp the value of an individual's life; it reveals a mind from which the reality of a human being has been wiped out."

In our third reading, Louis P. Pojman criticizes Ayn Rand's philosophy of egoism as one-sided and as oblivious of the importance of altruism. In particular, she fails to distinguish between *selfishness* and *self-interest*. *Selfishness* is enhancing your own welfare even to the detriment of others, whereas *self-interest* is the legitimate concern we have to satisfy our preferences and interests. He argues for a moderate position that recognizes the moral validity of both limited egoism and reciprocal altruism.

In our final reading, James Rachels's "A Critique of Ethical Egoism," we examine a systematic critique of ethical egoism.

The Ring of Gyges

PLATO

The Greek philosopher Plato (427–347 B.C.) is considered one of the greatest thinkers who ever lived. He was the student of Socrates and teacher of Aristotle. The following dialogue is from his masterpiece, the *Republic,* in which Plato's brother, Glaucon, asks Socrates whether justice is good in itself or only a necessary evil. That is, it is often thought that morality is simply a compromise between our longing to dominate and our fear of being dominated by others. Since we can't dominate everyone else and fear being dominated by others, we enter into a social contract to live by mutually coercive rules, which we name morality. To illustrate his point, Glaucon tells the story of a shepherd named Gyges who comes upon a ring, which at his behest makes him invisible. He uses the ring to escape the sanctions of society—its laws and punishment—and to serve his lust and greed. Glaucon asks whether anyone with such power would refrain from doing the sort of thing Gyges did. We enter the dialogue in the second book of the *Republic.* Socrates has just shown that the type of egoism advocated by the sophist Thrasymachus is contradictory. Socrates is speaking.

BOOK 2

With these words I was thinking that I had made an end of the discussion; but the end, in truth, proved to be only a beginning. For Glaucon, who is always the most pugnacious of men, was dissatisfied at Thrasymachus' retirement; he wanted to have the battle out. So he said to me: Socrates, do you wish really to persuade us, or only to seem to have persuaded us, that to be just is always better than to be unjust?

I should wish really to persuade you, I replied, if I could.

Then you certainly have not succeeded. Let me ask you now:— How would you arrange goods—are there not some which we wel-

Reprinted from *The Dialogues of Plato,* translated by Benjamin Jowett (Charles Scribner's, 1889).

come for their own sakes, and independently of their consequences, as, for example, harmless pleasures and enjoyments, which delight us at the time, although nothing follows from them?

I agree in thinking that there is such a class, I replied.

Is there not also a second class of goods, such as knowledge, sight, health, which are desirable not only in themselves, but also for their results?

Certainly, I said.

And would you not recognize a third class, such as gymnastic, and the care of the sick, and the physician's art; also the various ways of money-making—these do us good but we regard them as disagreeable; and no one would choose them for their own sakes, but only for the sake of some reward or result which flows from them?

There is, I said, this third class also. But why do you ask?

Because I want to know in which of the three classes you would place justice?

In the highest class, I replied, among those goods which he who would be happy desires both for their own sake and for the sake of their results.

Then the many are of another mind; they think that justice is to be reckoned in the troublesome class, among goods which are to be pursued for the sake of rewards and of reputation, but in themselves are disagreeable and rather to be avoided.

I know, I said, that this is their manner of thinking, and that this was the thesis which Thrasymachus was maintaining just now, when he censured justice and praised injustice. But I am too stupid to be convinced by him.

I wish, he said, that you would hear me as well as him, and then I shall see whether you and I agree. For Thrasymachus seems to me, like a snake, to have been charmed by your voice sooner than he ought to have been; but to my mind the nature of justice and injustice have not yet been made clear. Setting aside their rewards and results, I want to know what they are in themselves, and how they inwardly work in the soul. If you please, then, I will revive the argument of Thrasymachus. And first I will speak of the nature and origin of justice according to the common view of them. Secondly, I will show that all men who practice justice do so against their will, of necessity, but not as a good. And thirdly, I will argue that there is reason in this view, for the life of the unjust is after all better far than the life of the just—if what they say is true, Socrates, since I myself am not of their opinion. But still I acknowledge that I am perplexed when

I hear the voices of Thrasymachus and myriads of others dinning in my ears; and, on the other hand, I have never yet heard the superiority of justice to injustice maintained by any one in a satisfactory way. I want to hear justice praised in respect of itself; then I shall be satisfied, and you are the person from whom I think that I am most likely to hear this; and therefore I will praise the unjust life to the utmost of my power, and my manner of speaking will indicate the manner in which I desire to hear you too praising justice and censuring injustice. Will you say whether you approve of my proposal?

Indeed I do; nor can I imagine any theme about which a man of sense would oftener wish to converse.

I am delighted, he replied, to hear you say so, and shall begin by speaking, as I proposed, of the nature and origin of justice.

They say that to do injustice is, by nature, good; to suffer injustice, evil; but that the evil is greater than the good. And so when men have both done and suffered injustice and have had experience of both, not being able to avoid the one and obtain the other, they think that they had better agree among themselves to have neither; hence there arise laws and mutual covenants; and that which is ordained by law is termed by them lawful and just. This they affirm to be the origin and nature of justice:—it is a mean or compromise, between the best of all, which is to do injustice and not be punished, and the worst of all, which is to suffer injustice without the power of retaliation; and justice, being at a middle point between the two, is tolerated not as a good, but as the lesser evil, and honoured by reason of the inability of men to do injustice. For no man who is worthy to be called a man would ever submit to such an agreement if he were able to resist; he would be mad if he did. Such is the received account, Socrates, of the nature and origin of justice.

Now that those who practice justice do so involuntarily and because they have not the power to be unjust will best appear if we imagine something of this kind: having given both to the just and the unjust power to do what they will, let us watch and see whither desire will lead them; then we shall discover in the very act the just and unjust man to be proceeding along the same road, following their interest, which all natures deem to be their good, and are only diverted into the path of justice by the force of law. The liberty which we are supposing may be most completely given to them in the form of such a power as is said to have been possessed by Gyges the ancestor of Croesus the Lydian. According to the tradition, Gyges was a shepherd in the service of the king of Lydia; there was a great storm, and an earthquake made an opening in the earth at the place where he was feeding his flock. Amazed at the sight, he descended into the opening, where, among other marvels, he beheld a hollow brazen horse, having doors, at which he stooping and looking in saw a dead body of stature, as appeared to him, more than human, and having nothing on but a gold ring; this he took from the finger of the dead and reascended. Now the shepherds met together, according to custom, that they might send their monthly report about the flocks to the king; into their assembly he came having the ring on his finger, and as he was sitting among them he chanced to turn the collet of the ring inside his hand, when instantly he became invisible to the rest of the company and they began to speak of him as if he were no longer present. He was astonished at this, and again touching the ring he turned the collet outwards and reappeared; he made several trials of the ring, and always with the same result—when he turned the collet inwards he became invisible, when outwards he reappeared. Whereupon he contrived to be chosen one of the messengers who were sent to the court; where as soon as he arrived he seduced the queen, and with her help conspired against the king and slew him, and took the kingdom. Suppose now that there were two such magic rings, and the just put on one of them and the unjust the other; no man can be imagined to be of such an iron nature that he would stand fast in justice. No man would keep his hands off what was not his own when he could safely take what he liked out of the market, or go into houses and lie with any one at his pleasure, or kill or release from prison whom he would, and in all respects be like a God among men. Then the actions of the just would be as the actions of the unjust; they would both come at last to the same point. And this we may truly affirm to be a great proof that a man is just, not willingly or because he thinks that justice is any good to him individually, but of necessity, for wherever any one thinks that he can safely be unjust, there he is unjust. For all men believe in their hearts that injustice is far more profitable to the individual than justice, and he who argues as I have been supposing, will say that they are right. If you could imagine any one obtaining this power of becoming invisible, and never doing any wrong or touching what was another's, he would be thought by the lookers-on to be a most wretched idiot, although they would praise him to one another's faces, and keep up appearances with one another from a fear that they too might suffer injustice. Enough of this.

Now, if we are to form a real judgment of the life of the just and unjust, we must isolate them; there is no other way; and how is the isolation to be effected? I answer: Let the unjust man be entirely unjust, and the just man entirely just; nothing is to be taken away from either of them, and both are to be perfectly furnished for the work of their respective lives. First, let the unjust be like other distinguished masters of craft; like the skillful pilot or physician, who knows intuitively his own powers and keeps within their limits, and who, if he fails at any point, is able to recover himself. So let the unjust make his unjust attempts in the right way, and lie hidden if he means to be great in his injustice (he who is found out is nobody): for the highest reach of injustice is: to be deemed just when you are not. Therefore I say that in the perfectly unjust man we must assume the most perfect injustice; there is to be no deduction, but we must allow him, while doing the most unjust acts, to have acquired the greatest reputation for justice. If he have taken a false step he must be able to recover himself; he must be one who can speak with effect, if any of his deeds come to light, and who can force his way where force is required by his courage and strength, and command of money and friends. And at his side let us place the just man in his nobleness and simplicity, wishing, as Aeschylus says, to be and not to seem good. There must be no seeming, for if he seem to be just he will be honoured and rewarded, and then we shall not know whether he is just for the sake of justice or for the sake of honours and rewards; therefore, let him be clothed in justice only, and have no other covering; and he must be imagined in a state of life the opposite of the former. Let him be the best of men, and let him be thought the worst; then he will have been put to the proof; and we shall see whether he will be affected by the fear of infamy and its consequences. And let him continue thus to the hour of death; being just and seeming to be unjust. When both have reached the uttermost extreme, the one of justice and the other of injustice, let judgment be given which of them is the happier of the two.

Heavens! my dear Glaucon, I said, how energetically you polish them up for the decision, first one and then the other, as if they were two statues.

I do my best, he said. And now that we know what they are like there is no difficulty in tracing out the sort of life which awaits either of them. This I will proceed to describe; but as you may think the description a little too coarse, I ask you to suppose, Socrates, that the words which follow are not mine.—Let me put them into the mouths of the eulogists of injustice: they will tell you that the just man who is thought unjust will be scourged, racked, bound—will have his eyes burnt out; and, at last, after suffering every kind of evil, he will be impaled: Then he will understand that he ought to seem only, and not to be, just; the words of Aeschylus may be more truly spoken of the unjust than of the just. For the unjust is pursuing a reality; he does not live with a view to appearances—he wants to be really unjust and not to seem only:—

> His mind has a soil deep and fertile.
> Out of which spring his prudent counsels.

In the first place, he is thought just, and therefore bears rule in the city; he can marry whom he will, and give in marriage to whom he will; also he can trade and deal where he likes, and always to his own advantage, because he has no misgivings about injustice; and at every contest, whether in public or private, he gets the better of his antagonists, and gains at their expense, and is rich, and out of his gains he can benefit his friends, and harm his enemies; moreover, he can offer sacrifices, and dedicate gifts to the gods abundantly and magnificently, and can honour the gods or any man whom he wants to honour in a far better style than the just, and therefore he is likely to be dearer than they are to the gods. And thus, Socrates, gods and men are said to unite in making the life of the unjust better than the life of the just. . . .

[We pick up the discussion in Book 9.]

BOOK 9

"Now that we've gotten this far," I said, "let's go back to that statement made at the beginning, which brought us here: that it pays for a man to be perfectly unjust if he appears to be just. Isn't that what someone said?"

"Yes."

"Then since we've agreed what power justice and injustice each have, let's have a discussion with him."

"How?"

"By molding in words an image of the soul, so that the one who said that will realize what he was saying."

"What kind of image?"

"Oh, something like those natures the myths tell us were born in ancient times—the Chimaera, Scylla, Cerberus, and others in which many different shapes were supposed to have grown into one."

"So they tell us," he said.

"Then mold one figure of a colorful, many-headed beast with heads of wild and tame animals growing in a circle all around it; one that can change and grow all of them out of itself."

"That's a job for a skilled artist. Still, words mold easier than wax or clay, so consider it done."

"And another of a lion, and one of a man. Make the first by far the biggest, the second second largest."

"That's easier, and already done."

"Now join the three together so that they somehow grow."

"All right."

"Next mold the image of one, the man, around them all, so that to someone who can't see what's inside but looks only at the container it appears to be a single animal, man."

"I have."

"Then shall we inform the gentleman that when he says it pays for this man to be unjust, he's saying that it profits him to feast his multifarious beast and his lion and make them grow strong, but to starve and enfeeble the man in him so that he gets dragged wherever the animals lead him, and instead of making them friends and used to each other, to let them bite and fight and eat each other?"

"That's just what he's saying by praising injustice."

"The one who says justice pays, however, would be saying that he should practice and say whatever will give the most mastery to his inner man, who should care for the many-headed beast like a farmer, raising and domesticating its tame heads and preventing the wild ones from growing, making the lion's nature his partner and ally, and so raise them both to be friends to each other and to him."

"That's exactly what he means by praising justice."

"So in every way the commender of justice is telling the truth, the other a lie. Whether we examine pleasure, reputation, or profit, we find that the man who praises justice speaks truly, the one who disparages it disparages sickly and knows nothing of what he disparages."

"I don't think he does at all."

"Then let's gently persuade him—his error wasn't intended—by asking him a question: 'Shouldn't we say that the traditions of the beautiful and the ugly have come about like this: Beautiful things are those that make our bestial parts subservient to the human— or rather, perhaps, to the divine—part of our nature, while ugly ones are those that enslave the tame to the wild?' Won't he agree?"

"If he takes my advice."

"On this argument then, can it pay for a man to take money unjustly if that means making his best part a slave to the worst? If it wouldn't profit a man to sell his son or his daughter into slavery—to wild and evil men at that—even if he got a fortune for it, then if he has no pity on himself and enslaves the most godlike thing in him to the most godless and polluted, isn't he a wretch who gets bribed for gold into a destruction more horrible than Euriphyle's, who sold her husband's life for a necklace?"

"Much more horrible," said Glaucon.

". . . [E]veryone is better off being ruled by the godlike and intelligent; preferably if he has it inside, but if not, it should be imposed on him from without so that we may all be friends and as nearly alike as possible, all steered by the same thing."

"Yes, and we're right," he said.

"Law, the ally of everyone in the city, clearly intends the same thing, as does the rule of children, which forbids us to let them be free until we've instituted a regime in them as in a city. We serve their best part with a similar part in us, install a like guardian and ruler in them, and only then set them free."

"Clearly."

"Then how, by what argument, Glaucon, can we say that it pays for a man to be unjust or self-indulgent or to do something shameful to get more money or power if by doing so he makes himself worse?"

"We can't," he said.

"And how can it pay to commit injustice without getting caught and being punished? Doesn't getting away with it make a man even worse? Whereas if a man gets caught and punished, his beastlike part is taken in and tamed, his tame part is set free, and his whole soul acquires justice and temperance and knowledge. Therefore his soul recovers its best nature and attains a state more honorable than the state the body attains when it acquires health and strength and beauty, by as much as the soul is more honorable than the body."

"Absolutely."

"Then won't a sensible man spend his life directing all his efforts to this end?"

For Further Reflection

1. Which would you choose to be, Glaucon's good but suffering person or his bad but successful person? Is there a third alternative?

2. Socrates' answer to Glaucon and Adeimantus is that, despite appearances, we should choose the life of the "unsuccessful" just person because it is to our advantage to be moral. Socrates' answer depends on a notion of mental health. He contends that immorality corrupts the inner person, so that one is happy or unhappy in exact proportion to one's moral integrity. Is this a plausible reply?

3. Is the good always good for you?

In Defense of Ethical Egoism

AYN RAND

Ayn Rand (1908–1982) wrote several philosophical novels, including *We the Living* (1936), *The Fountainhead* (1943), and *Atlas Shrugged* (1959), from which the present selection is taken. Her works set forth a form of ethical egoism that was called *objectivism,* the philosophy that the proper life for rational beings is the pursuit of their happiness and that altruism and self-sacrifice are incompatible with rational morality. In this passage, she criticizes conventional altruistic morality ("the morality of sacrifice") and praises the morality of selfishness.

Reprinted from Ayn Rand, *Atlas Shrugged.* (New York: Random House, 1959), by permission of the executor or the Estate of Ayn Rand.

VALUE YOURSELF

". . . Yes, this *is* an *age* of moral crisis. Yes, you *are* bearing punishment for your evil. But it is not man who is now on trial and it is not human nature that will take the blame. It is your moral code that's through, this time. Your moral code has reached its climax, the blind alley at the end of its course. And if you wish to go on living, what you now need is not to *return* to morality—you who have never known any—but to *discover* it.

"You have heard no concepts of morality but the mystical or the social. You have been taught that morality is a code of behavior imposed on you by whim, the whim of a supernatural power or the whim of society, to serve God's purpose or your neighbor's welfare, to please an authority beyond the grave or else next door—but not to serve *your* life or pleasure. Your pleasure, you have been taught, is to be found in immorality, your interests would best be served by evil, and any moral code must be designed not *for* you, but *against* you, not to further your life, but to drain it.

"For centuries, the battle of morality was fought between those who claimed that your life belongs to God and those who claimed that it belongs to your neighbors—between those who preached that the good is self-sacrifice for the sake of ghosts in heaven and those who preached that the good is self-sacrifice for the sake of incompetents on earth. And no one came to say that your life belongs to you and that the good is to live it.

"Both sides agreed that morality demands the surrender of your self-interest and of your mind, that the moral and the practical are opposites, that morality is not the province of reason, but the province of faith and force. Both sides agreed that no rational morality is possible, that there is no right or wrong in reason—that in reason there's no reason to be moral.

"Whatever else they fought about, it was against man's mind that all your moralists have stood united. It was man's mind that all their schemes and systems were intended to despoil and destroy. Now choose to perish or to learn that the anti-mind is the anti-life.

"Man's mind is his basic tool of survival. Life is given to him, survival is not. His body is given to him, its sustenance is not. His mind is given to him, its content is not. To remain alive, he must act, and before he can act he must know the nature and purpose of his action. He cannot obtain his food without a knowledge of food and of the way to obtain it. He cannot dig a ditch—or build a cyclotron—without a knowledge of his aim and of the means to achieve it. To remain alive, he must think.

"But to think is an act of choice. The key to what you so recklessly call 'human nature,' the open secret you live with, yet dread to name, is the fact that *man is a being of volitional consciousness.* Reason does not work automatically; thinking is not a mechanical process; the connections of logic are not made by instinct. The function of your stomach, lungs, or heart is automatic; the function of your mind is not. In any hour and issue of your life, you are free to think or to evade that effort. But you are not free to escape from your nature, from the fact that *reason* is your means of survival—so that for *you,* who are a human being, the question 'to be or not to be' is the question 'to think or not to think.'

"A being of volitional consciousness has no automatic course of behavior. He needs a code of values to guide his actions. 'Value' is that which one acts to gain and keep, 'virtue' is the action by which one gains and keeps it. 'Value' presupposes an answer to the question: of value to whom and for what? 'Value' presupposes a standard, a purpose and the necessity of action in the face of an alternative. Where there are no alternatives, no values are possible.

"There is only one fundamental alternative in the universe: existence or non-existence—and it pertains to a single class of entities: to living organisms. The existence of inanimate matter is unconditional, the existence of life is not: it depends on a specific course of action. Matter is indestructible, it changes its forms, but it cannot cease to exist. It is only a living organism that faces a constant alternative: the issue of life or death. Life is a process of self-sustaining and self-generated action. If an organism fails in that action, it dies; its chemical elements remain, but its life goes out of existence. It is only the concept of 'Life' that makes the concept of 'Value' possible. It is only to a living entity that things can be good or evil.

"A plant must feed itself in order to live; the sunlight, the water, the chemicals it needs are the values its nature has set it to pursue; its life is the standard of value directing its actions. But a plant has no choice of action; there are alternatives in the conditions it encounters, but there is no alternative in its function; it acts automatically to further its life, it cannot act for its own destruction.

"An animal is equipped for sustaining its life; its senses provide it with an automatic code of action, an automatic knowledge of what is good for it or evil. It has no power to extend its knowledge or to evade it. In conditions where its knowledge proves inadequate, it dies. But so long as it lives, it acts on its knowledge, with automatic safety and no power of choice, it is unable to ignore its own good, unable to decide to choose the evil and act as its own destroyer.

"Man has no automatic code of survival. His particular distinction from all other living species is the necessity to act in the face of alternatives by means of *volitional choice.* He has no automatic knowledge of what is good for him or evil, what values his life depends on, what course of action it requires. Are you prattling about an instinct of self-preservation? An *instinct* of self-preservation is precisely what man does not possess. An 'instinct' is an unerring and automatic form of knowledge. A desire is not an instinct. A desire to live does not give you the knowledge required for living. And even man's desire to live is not automatic: your secret evil today is that *that* is the desire you do not hold. Your fear of death is not a love for life and will not give you the knowledge needed to keep it. Man must obtain his knowledge and choose his actions by a process of thinking, which nature will not force him to perform. Man has the power to act as his own destroyer—and that is the way he has acted through most of his history.

"A living entity that regarded its means of survival as evil, would not survive. A plant that struggled to mangle its roots, a bird that fought to break its wings would not remain for long in the existence they affronted. But the history of man has been a struggle to deny and to destroy his mind.

"Man has been called a rational being, but rationality is a matter of choice—and the alternative his nature offers him is: rational being or suicidal animal. Man has to be man—by choice; he has to hold his life as a value—by choice; he has to learn to sustain it—by choice; he has to discover the values it requires and practice his virtues—by choice.

"A code of values accepted by choice is a code of morality.

"Whoever you are, you who are hearing me now, I am speaking to whatever living remnant is left uncorrupted within you, to the remnant of the human, to your *mind,* and I say: There *is* a morality of reason, a morality proper to man, and *Man's Life* is its standard of value.

"All that which is proper to the life of a rational being is the good; all that which destroys it is the evil.

"Man's life, as required by his nature, is not the life of a mindless brute, of a looting thug or a mooching mystic, but the life of a thinking being—not life by means of force or fraud, but life by means of achievement—not survival at any price, since there's only one price that pays for man's survival: reason.

"Man's life is the *standard* of morality, but your own life is its *purpose*. If existence on earth is your goal, you must choose your actions and values by the standard of that which is proper to man—for the purpose of preserving, fulfilling and enjoying the irreplaceable value which is your life.

"Since life requires a specific course of action, any other course will destroy it. A being who does not hold his own life as the motive and goal of his actions, is acting on the motive and standard of *death*. Such a being is a metaphysical monstrosity, struggling to oppose, negate and contradict the fact of his own existence, running blindly amuck on a trail of destruction, capable of nothing but pain.

"Happiness is the successful state of life, pain is an agent of death. Happiness is that state of unconsciousness which proceeds from the achievement of one's values. A morality that dares to tell you to find happiness in the renunciation of your happiness—to value the failure of your values—is an insolent negation of morality. A doctrine that gives you, as an ideal, the role of a sacrificial animal seeking slaughter on the altars of others, is giving you *death* as your standard. By the grace of reality and the nature of life, man—every man—is an end in himself, he exists for his own sake, and the achievement of his own happiness is his highest moral purpose.

"But neither life nor happiness can be achieved by the pursuit of irrational whims. Just as man is free to attempt to survive in any random manner, but will perish unless he lives as his nature requires, so he is free to seek his happiness in any mindless fraud, but the torture of frustration is all he will find, unless he seeks the happiness proper to man. The purpose of morality is to teach you, not to suffer and die, but to enjoy yourself and live.

"Sweep aside those parasites of subsidized classrooms, who live on the profits of the mind of others and proclaim that man needs no morality, no values, no code of behavior. They, who pose as scientists and claim that man is only an animal, do not grant him inclusion in the law of existence they have granted to the lowest of insects. They recognize that every living species has a way of survival demanded by its nature, they do not claim that a fish can live out of water or that a dog can live without its sense of smell—but man, they claim, the most complex of beings, man can survive in any way whatever, man has no identity, no nature, and there's no practical reason why he cannot live with his means of survival destroyed, with his mind throttled and placed at the disposal of any orders *they* might care to issue.

"Sweep aside those hatred-eaten mystics, who pose as friends of humanity and preach that the highest virtue man can practice is to hold his own life as of no value. Do they tell you that the purpose of morality is to curb man's instinct of self-preservation? It is for the purpose of self-preservation that man needs a code of morality. The only man who desires to be moral is the man who desires to live.

"No, you do not have to live; it is your basic act of choice; but if you choose to live, you must live as a man—by the work and the judgment of your mind.

"No, you do not have to live as a man: it is an act of moral choice. But you cannot live as anything else—and the alternative is that state of living death which you now see within you and around you, the state of a thing unfit for existence, no longer human and less than animal, a thing that knows nothing but pain and drags itself through its span of years in the agony of unthinking self-destruction.

"No, you do not have to think; it is an act of moral choice. But someone had to think to keep you alive; if you choose to default, you default on existence and you pass the deficit to some moral man, expecting him to sacrifice his good for the sake of letting you survive by your evil. . . .

"This much is true: the most *selfish* of all things is the independent mind that recognizes no authority higher than its own and no value higher than its judgment of truth. You are asked to sacrifice your intellectual integrity, your logic, your reason, your standard of truth—in favor of becoming a prostitute whose standard is the greatest good for the greatest number.

"If you search your code for guidance, for an answer to the question: 'What *is* the good?'—the only answer you will find is '*The good of others*.' The good is whatever others wish, whatever you feel they feel they wish, or whatever you feel they ought to feel. 'The good of others' is a magic formula that transforms anything into gold, a formula to be recited as a guarantee of moral glory and as a fumigator for any action, even the slaughter of a continent. Your standard of virtue is not an object, not an act, nor a principle, but an *intention*. You need no proof, no reasons, no success, you need not achieve *in fact* the good of others—all you need to know is that your motive was the good of others, *not* your own. Your only definition of the good is a negation: the good is the 'non-good for me.'

"Your code—which boasts that it upholds eternal, absolute, objective moral values and scorns the conditional, the relative and the subjective—your code hands out, as its version of the absolute, the following rule of moral conduct: If *you* wish it, it's evil; if others wish it, it's good; if the motive of your action is *your* welfare, don't do it; if the motive is the welfare of others, then anything goes.

"As this double-jointed, double-standard morality splits you in half, so it splits mankind into two enemy camps: one is *you,* the other is all the rest of humanity. *You* are the only outcast who has no right to wish or live. *You* are the only servant, the rest are the masters, *you* are the only giver, the rest are the takers, *you* are the eternal debtor, the rest are the creditors never to be paid off. You must not question their right to your sacrifice, or the nature of their wishes and their needs: their right is conferred upon them by a negative, by the fact that they are 'non-you.'

"For those of you who might ask questions, your code provides a consolation prize and booby-trap: it is for your own happiness, it says, that you must serve the happiness of others, the only way to achieve your joy is to give it up to others, the only way to achieve your prosperity is to surrender your wealth to others, the only way to protect your life is to protect all men except yourself—and if you find no joy in this procedure, it is your own fault and the proof of your evil; if you were good, you would find your happiness in providing a banquet for others, and your dignity in existing on such crumbs as *they* might care to toss you.

"You who have no standard of self-esteem, accept the guilt and dare not ask the questions. But you know the unadmitted answer, refusing to acknowledge what you see, what hidden premise moves your world. You know it, not in honest statement, but as a dark uneasiness within you, while you flounder between guiltily cheating and grudgingly practicing a principle too vicious to name.

"I, who do not accept the unearned, neither in values nor in *guilt,* am here to ask the questions you evaded. Why is it moral to serve the happiness of others, but not your own? If enjoyment is a value, why is it moral when experienced by others, but immoral when experienced by you? If the sensation of eating a cake is a value, why is it an immoral indulgence in your stomach, but a moral goal for you to achieve in the stomach of others? Why is it immoral for you to desire, but moral for others to do so? Why is it immoral to produce a value and keep it, but moral to give it away? And if it is not moral for you to keep a value, why is it moral for others to accept it? If you are selfless and virtuous when you give it, are they not selfish and vicious when they take it? Does virtue consist of serving vice? Is the moral purpose of those who are good, self-immolation for the sake of those who are evil? . . .

"Under a morality of sacrifice, the first value you sacrifice is morality; the next is self-esteem. When need is the standard, every man is both victim and parasite. As a victim, he must labor to fill the needs of others, leaving himself in the position of a parasite whose needs must be filled by others. He cannot approach his fellow men except in one of two disgraceful roles: he is both a beggar and a sucker.

"You fear the man who has a dollar less than you, that dollar is rightfully his, he makes you feel like a moral defrauder. You hate the man who has a dollar more than you, that dollar is rightfully yours, he makes you feel that you are morally defrauded. The man below is a source of your guilt, the man above is a source of your frustration. You do not know what to surrender or demand, when to give and when to grab, what pleasure in life is rightfully yours and what debt is still unpaid to others—you struggle to evade, as 'theory,' the knowledge that by the moral standard you've accepted you are guilty every moment of your life, there is no mouthful of food you swallow that is not *needed* by someone somewhere on earth—and you give up the problem in blind resentment, you conclude that moral perfection is not to be achieved *or desired,* that you will muddle through by snatching as snatch can and by avoiding the eyes of the young, of those who look at you as if self-esteem were possible and they expected you to have it. Guilt is all that you retain within your soul—and so does every other man, as he goes past, avoiding *your* eyes. Do you wonder why your morality has not achieved brotherhood on earth or the good will of man to man?

"The justification of sacrifice, that your morality propounds, is more corrupt than the corruption it purports to justify. The motive of your sacrifice, it tells you, should be *love*—the love you ought to feel for every man. A morality that professes the belief that the values of the spirit are more precious than matter, a morality that teaches you to scorn a whore who gives her body indiscriminately to all men—this same morality demands that you surrender your soul to promiscuous love for all comers.

"As there can be no causeless wealth, so there can be no causeless love or any sort of causeless emotion. An emotion is a response to a fact of reality, an estimate dictated by your standards. To love is to *value*. The man who tells you that it is possible to value without values, to love those whom you appraise as worthless, is the man who tells you that it is possible to grow rich by consuming without producing and that paper money is as valuable as gold.

"Observe that he does not expect you to feel a causeless fear. When his kind get into power, they are expert at contriving means of terror, at giving you ample cause to feel the fear by which they desire to rule you. But when it comes to love, the highest of emotions, you permit them to shriek at you accusingly that you are a moral delinquent if you're incapable of feeling causeless love. When a man feels fear without reason, you call him to the attention of a psychiatrist; you are not so careful to protect the meaning, the nature and the dignity of love.

"Love is the expression of one's values, the greatest reward you can earn for the moral qualities you have achieved in your character and person, the emotional price paid by one man for the joy he receives from the virtues of another. Your morality demands that you divorce your love from values and hand it down to any vagrant, not as response to his worth, but as response to his *need,* not as reward, but as alms, not as a payment for virtues, but as a blank check on vices. Your morality tells you that the purpose of love is to set you free of the bonds of morality, that love is superior to moral judgment, that true love transcends, forgives and survives every manner of evil in its object, and the greater the love the greater the depravity it permits to the loved. To love a man for his virtues is paltry and human, it tells you; to love him for his flaws is divine. To love those who are worthy of it is self-interest; to love the unworthy is sacrifice. You owe your love to those who don't deserve it, and the less they deserve it, the more love you owe them—the more loathsome the object, the nobler your love—the more unfastidious your love, the greater your virtue—and if you can bring your soul to the state of a dump heap that welcomes anything on equal terms, if you can cease to value moral values, you have achieved the state of moral perfection.

"Such is your morality of sacrifice and such are the twin ideals it offers: to refashion the life of your body in the image of a human stockyards, and the life of your spirit in the image of a dump. . . .

"Since childhood, you have been hiding the guilty secret that you feel no desire to be moral, no desire to seek self-immolation, that you dread and hate your code, but dare not say it even to yourself, that you're devoid of those moral 'instincts' which others profess to feel. The less you felt, the louder you proclaimed your selfless love and servitude to others, in dread of ever letting them discover your own self, the self that you betrayed, the self that you kept in concealment, like a skeleton in the closet of your body. And they, who were at once your dupes and your deceivers, they listened and voiced their loud approval, in dread of ever letting you discover that they were harboring the same unspoken secret. Existence among you is a giant pretense, an act you all perform for one another, each feeling that he is the only guilty freak, each placing his moral authority in the unknowable known only to others, each faking the reality he feels they expect him to fake, none having the courage to break the vicious circle.

"No matter what dishonorable compromise you've made with your impracticable creed, no matter what miserable balance, half-cynicism, half-superstition, you now manage to maintain, you still preserve the root, the lethal tenet: the belief that the moral and the practical are opposites. Since childhood, you have been running from the terror of a choice you have never dared fully to identify: If the *practical,* whatever you must practice to exist, whatever works, succeeds, achieves your purpose, whatever brings you food and joy, whatever profits you is evil—and if the good, the moral is the *impractical,* whatever fails, destroys, frustrates, whatever injures you and brings you loss or pain—then your choice is to be moral or to live.

"The sole result of that murderous doctrine was to remove morality from life. You grew up to believe that moral laws bear no relation to the job of living, except as an impediment and threat, that man's existence is an amoral jungle where anything goes and anything works. And in that fog of switching definitions which descends upon a frozen mind, you have forgotten that the evils damned by your creed were the virtues required for living, and you have come to believe that actual evils are the *practical* means of existence. Forgetting that the impractical 'good' was self-sacrifice, you believe that self-esteem is impractical; forgetting that the practical 'evil' was production, you believe that robbery is practical. . . .

"Accept the fact that the achievement of your happiness is the only *moral* purpose of your life, and that *happiness*—not pain or mindless self-indulgence—is the proof of your moral integrity, since it is the proof and the result of your loyalty to the achievement of your values. Happiness was the responsibility you dreaded, it required the kind of rational discipline you did not value yourself enough to assume—and the anxious staleness of your days is the monument to your evasion of the knowledge that there is no moral substitute for happiness, that there is no more despicable coward than the man who deserted the battle for his joy, fearing to assert his right to existence, lacking the courage and the loyalty to life of a bird or a flower reaching for the sun. Discard the protective rags of that vice which you called a virtue: humility—learn to value yourself, which means: to fight for your happiness—and when you learn that *pride* is the sum of all virtues, you will learn to live like a man.

"As a basic step of self-esteem, learn to treat as the mark of a cannibal any man's *demand* for your help. To demand it is to claim that your life is *his* property—and loathsome as such claim might be, there's something still more loathsome: your agreement. Do you ask if it's ever proper to help another man? No—if he claims it as his right or as a moral duty that you owe him. Yes—if such is your own desire based on your own selfish pleasure in the value of his person and his struggle."

For Further Reflection

1. Has Rand successfully defended her theory of ethical egoism? How does it relate to Socrates' idea that one ought never to harm anyone else? Could one reconcile Socrates' idea with Rand's theory? Socrates believes that one should never harm anyone else because doing so is never in one's own interest. What would be needed to get Rand's theory to agree with that conclusion?

2. Can the ethical egoist make his or her views public? If you follow Rand, should you let others know where you stand? Should you persuade them to be egoists? If the egoist cannot make his theory public, does this disqualify it as a genuine ethical theory?

3. Can the ethical egoist be a consistent egoist and have friends? If friendship entails loving another in such a way as to sacrifice one's own interest for the friend's, does this give the egoist difficulty?

Egoism and Altruism
A Critique of Ayn Rand

LOUIS P. POJMAN

In this essay Pojman criticizes Ayn Rand's version of ethical egoism for creating a false dilemma between (1) a self-
demeaning altruism and (2) a consummate egoism, in which
people always put themselves first. He argues that Rand
conflates *selfishness* with *self-interest,* but the two concepts
are only superficially similar. He then draws from evolutionary ethologists who describe animal behavior, illustrating a middle way between self-degrading sacrifice and selfish egoism.

Universal ethical egoism is the theory that everyone ought always to
serve his or her own self-interest. That is, everyone ought to do what
will maximize one's own expected utility or bring about one's own
greatest happiness, even if it requires harming others. Ethical egoism
is utilitarianism reduced to the pinpoint of the single individual ego.
Instead of advocating the greatest happiness for the greatest number, as utilitarianism does, it advocates the greatest happiness for myself, whoever I may be. It is a self-preoccupied prudence, urging one
to postpone enjoyment today for long-term benefits. In its more
sophisticated form, it compares life to a competitive game, perhaps
a war-game, and urges each person to *try* to win in the game of life.

In her books *The Virtue of Selfishness* and *Atlas Shrugged,* Ayn
Rand argues that selfishness is a virtue and altruism a vice, a totally
destructive idea that leads to the undermining of individual worth.
She defines *altruism* as the view that

> any action taken for the benefit of others is good, and any action
> taken for one's own benefit is evil. Thus, the *beneficiary* of an action
> is the only criterion of moral value—and so long as the beneficiary
> is anybody other than oneself, anything goes.[1]

---

[1]Ayn Rand, *The Virtue of Selfishness* (New American Library, 1964), pp. vii
and 27–32; 80ff.

As such, altruism is suicidal:

> If a man accepts the ethics of altruism, his first concern is not how to live his life, but how to sacrifice it. . . . Altruism erodes men's capacity to grasp the value of an individual life; it reveals a mind from which the reality of a human being has been wiped out.

Since finding happiness is the highest goal and good in life, altruism, which calls on us to sacrifice our happiness for the good of others, is contrary to our highest good.

Her argument seems to go like this:

1. The perfection of one's abilities in a state of happiness is the highest goal for humans. We have a moral duty to attempt to reach this goal.
2. The ethics of altruism prescribes that we sacrifice our interests and lives for the good of others.
3. Therefore, the ethics of altruism is incompatible with the goal of happiness.
4. Ethical egoism prescribes that we seek our own happiness exclusively, and as such it is consistent with the happiness goal.
5. Therefore ethical egoism is the correct moral theory.

Ayn Rand's argument for the virtue of selfishness is flawed by the fallacy of a false dilemma. It simplistically assumes that absolute altruism and absolute egoism are the only alternatives. But this is an extreme view of the matter. There are plenty of options between these two positions. Even a predominant egoist would admit that (analogous to the paradox of hedonism) sometimes the best way to reach self-fulfillment is for us to forget about ourselves and strive to live for goals, causes, or other persons. Even if altruism is not required (as a duty), it may be permissible in many cases. Furthermore, self-interest may not be incompatible with other-regarding motivation. Even the Second Great Commandment set forth by Moses and Jesus states not that you must always sacrifice yourself for the other person, but that you ought to love your neighbor *as* yourself (Lev. 19:19; Matt. 23). Self-interest and self-love are morally good things, but not at the expense of other people's legitimate interests. When there is moral conflict of interests, a fair process of adjudication needs to take place.

But Rand's version of egoism is only one of many. We need to go to the heart of ethical egoism: the thesis that our highest moral duty is always to promote our individual interests. Let us focus on the alleged problems of this thesis.

FOUR CRITICISMS OF ETHICAL EGOISM

The Inconsistent Outcomes Argument

Brian Medlin argues that ethical egoism cannot be true because it fails to meet a necessary condition of morality, that of being a guide to action. He claims that it will be like advising people to do inconsistent things based on incompatible desires.[2] His argument goes like this:

1. Moral principles must be universal and categorical.
2. I must universalize my egoist desire to come out on top over Tom, Dick, and Harry.
3. But I must also prescribe Tom's egoist desire to come out on top over Dick, Harry, and me (and so on).
4. Therefore I have prescribed incompatible outcomes and have not provided a way of adjudicating conflicts of desire. In effect, I have said nothing.

The proper response to this is that of Jesse Kalin, who argues that we can separate our beliefs about ethical situations from our desires.[3] He likens the situation to a competitive sports event, in which you believe that your opponent has a right to try to win as much as you, but you desire that you, not he, will in fact win. An even better example is that of the chess game in which you recognize that your opponent ought to move her bishop to prepare for checkmate, but you hope she won't see the move. Belief that A ought to do Y does not commit you to wanting A to do Y.

---

[2]Brian Medlin, "Ultimate Principles and Ethical Egoism," *Australasian Journal of Philosophy* (1957), pp. 111–118; reprinted in Louis Pojman, *Ethical Theory*, pp. 91–95.
[3]See Jesse Kalin, "In Defense of Egoism," in *Ethical Theory*, 4th ed., ed. Louis Pojman (Wadsworth, 2002), p. 95f.

The Publicity Argument

On the one hand, in order for something to be a moral theory it seems necessary that its moral principles be publicized. Unless principles are put forth as universal prescriptions that are accessible to the public, they cannot serve as guides to action or as aids in resolving conflicts of interest. But on the other hand, it is not in the egoist's self-interest to publicize them. Egoists would rather that the rest of us be altruists. (Why did Nietzsche and Rand write books announcing their positions? Were the royalties taken in by announcing ethical egoism worth the price of letting the cat out of the bag?)

Thus it would be self-defeating for the egoist to argue for her position, and even worse that she should convince others of it. But it is perfectly possible to have a private morality that does not resolve conflicts of interest. So the egoist should publicly advocate standard principles of traditional morality—so that society doesn't break down—while adhering to a private, nonstandard, solely self-regarding morality. So, if you're willing to pay the price, you can accept the solipsistic-directed norms of egoism.

If the egoist is prepared to pay the price, egoism could be a consistent system that has some limitations. Although the egoist can cooperate with others in limited ways and perhaps even have friends—so long as their interests don't conflict with his—he has to be very careful about preserving his isolation. The egoist can't give advice or argue about his position—not sincerely at least. He must act alone, atomistically or solipsistically in moral isolation, for to announce his adherence to the principle of egoism would be dangerous to his project. He can't teach his children the true morality or justify himself to others or forgive others.

The Paradox of Egoism

The situation may be even worse than the sophisticated, self-conscious egoist supposes. Could the egoist have friends? And if limited friendship is possible, could he or she ever be in love or experience deep friendship? Suppose the egoist discovers that in the pursuit of the happiness goal, deep friendship is in his best interest. Can he become a friend? What is necessary to deep friendship? A true friend is one who is not always preoccupied about his own interest in the relationship but who forgets about himself altogether, at least sometimes, in order to serve or enhance the other person's interest. "Love seeketh not its own." It is an altruistic disposition, the very opposite of egoism. So the *paradox of egoism* is that in order to reach the goal of egoism one must give up egoism and become (to some extent) an altruist, the very antithesis of egoism.

The Argument from Counterintuitive Consequences

The final argument against ethical egoism is that it is an absolute ethics that not only permits egoistic behavior but demands it. Helping others at one's own expense is not only not required, it is morally wrong. Whenever I do not have good evidence that my helping you will end up to my advantage, I must refrain from helping you. If I can save the whole of Europe and Africa from destruction by pressing a button, then so long as there is nothing for me to gain by it, it is wrong for me to press that button. The Good Samaritan was, by this logic, morally wrong in helping the injured victim and not collecting payment for his troubles. It is certainly hard to see why the egoist should be concerned about environmental matters if he or she is profiting from polluting the environment. (For example, if the egoist gains 40 hedons in producing P, which produces pollution that in turn causes others 1,000 dolors—units of suffering—but suffers only 10 of those dolors himself, then by an agent-maximizing calculus he is morally obligated to produce P.) There is certainly no obligation to preserve scarce natural resources for future generations. "Why should I do anything for posterity?" the egoist asks "What has posterity ever done for me?"

In conclusion, we see that ethical egoism has a number of serious problems. It cannot consistently publicize itself, nor often argue its case. It tends towards solipsism and the exclusion of many of the deepest human values, such as love and deep friendship. It violates the principle of fairness, and, most of all, it entails an absolute prohibition on altruistic behavior, which we intuitively sense as morally required (or, at least, permissible).

EVOLUTION AND ALTRUISM

If sheer unadulterated egoism is an inadequate moral theory, does that mean we ought to aim at complete altruism, total self-effacement for the sake of others? What is the role of self-love in morality? An interesting place to start answering these queries is with the new field of sociobiology, which theorizes that social structures and behavioral patterns, including morality, have a biological base, explained by evolutionary theory.

In the past, linking ethics to evolution meant justifying exploitation. Social Darwinism justified imperialism and the principle that "Might makes right" by saying that survival of the fittest is a law of nature. This philosophy lent itself to a promotion of ruthless egoism. This is nature's law, "nature red in tooth and claw." Against this view ethologists such as Robert Ardrey and Konrad Lorenz argued for a more benign view of the animal kingdom—one reminiscent of Rudyard Kipling's, in which the animal kingdom survives by cooperation, which is at least as important as competition. On Ardrey's and Lorenz's view it is the group or the species, not the individual, that is of primary importance.

With the development of sociobiology—in the work of E. O. Wilson but particularly the work of Robert Trivers, J. Maynard Smith, and Richard Dawkins—a theory has come to the fore that combines radical individualism with limited altruism. It is not the group or the species that is of evolutionary importance but the gene, or, more precisely, the gene type. Genes—the parts of the chromosomes that carry the blueprints for all our natural traits (e.g., height, hair color, skin color, intelligence)—copy themselves as they divide and multiply. At conception they combine with the genes of a member of the opposite sex to form a new individual.

In his fascinating sociobiological study, Richard Dawkins describes human behavior as determined evolutionarily by stable strategies set to replicate the gene.[4] This is not done consciously, of course, but by the invisible hand that drives consciousness. We are essentially gene machines.

Morality—that is, successful morality—can be seen as an evolutionary strategy for gene replication. Here's an example: Birds are afflicted with life-endangering parasites. Because they lack limbs to enable them to pick the parasites off their heads, they—like much of the animal kingdom—depend on the ritual of mutual grooming. It turns out that nature has evolved two basic types of birds in this regard: those who are disposed to groom anyone (the nonprejudiced type?), and those who refuse to groom anyone but who pre-

---

[4]Richard Dawkins, *The Selfish Gene* (Oxford University Press, 1976), Ch. 10.

sent themselves for grooming. The former type of bird Dawkins calls "Suckers" and the latter "Cheaters."

In a geographical area containing harmful parasites and where there are only Suckers or Cheaters, Suckers will do fairly well, but Cheaters will not survive, for want of cooperation. However, in a Sucker population in which a mutant Cheater arises, the Cheater will prosper, and the Cheater gene-type will multiply. As the Suckers are exploited, they will gradually die out. But if and when they become too few to groom the Cheaters, the Cheaters will start to die off too and eventually become extinct.

Why don't birds all die off, then? Well, somehow nature has come up with a third type, call them "Grudgers." Grudgers groom all and only those who reciprocate in grooming them. They groom each other and Suckers, but not Cheaters. In fact, once caught, a Cheater is marked forever. There is no forgiveness. It turns out then that unless there are a lot of Suckers around, Cheaters have a hard time of it—harder even than Suckers. However, it is the Grudgers that prosper. Unlike Suckers, they don't waste time messing with unappreciative Cheaters, so they are not exploited and have ample energy to gather food and build better nests for their loved ones.

J. L. Mackie argues that the real name for Suckers is "Christian," one who believes in complete altruism, even turning the other cheek to one's assailant and loving one's enemy. Cheaters are ruthless egoists who can survive only if there are enough naive altruists around. Whereas Grudgers are *reciprocal* altruists who have a rational morality based on cooperative self-interest, Suckers, such as Socrates and Jesus, advocate "turning the other cheek and repaying evil with good."[5] Instead of a Rule of Reciprocity, "I'll scratch your back if you'll scratch mine," the extreme altruist substitutes the Golden Rule, "If you want the other fellow to scratch your back, you scratch his—even if he won't reciprocate."

The moral of the story is this: Altruist morality (so interpreted) is only rational given the payoff of eternal life (with a scorekeeper, as Woody Allen says). Take that away, and it looks like a Sucker system. What replaces the "Christian" vision of submission and saintliness is the reciprocal altruist with a tit-for-tat morality, someone who is willing to share with those willing to cooperate.

---

[5]J. L. Mackie, "The Law of the Jungle: Moral Alternatives and Principles of Evolution," *Philosophy* 53 (1978).

Mackie may caricature the position of the religious altruist, but he misses the subtleties of wisdom involved (Jesus said, "Be as wise as serpents but as harmless as doves"). Nevertheless, he does remind us that there is a difference between core morality and complete altruism. We have duties to cooperate and reciprocate, but no duty to serve those who manipulate us nor an obvious duty to sacrifice ourselves for people outside our domain of special responsibility. We have a special duty of high altruism toward those in the close circle of our concern, namely, our family and friends.

Conclusion

Martin Luther once said that humanity is like a man who, when mounting a horse, always falls off on the opposite side, especially when he tries to overcompensate for his previous exaggerations. So it is with ethical egoism. Trying to compensate for an irrational, guilt-ridden, Sucker altruism of the morality of self-effacement, it falls off the horse on the other side, embracing a Cheater's preoccupation with self-exaltation that robs the self of the deepest joys in life. Only the person who mounts properly, avoiding both extremes, is likely to ride the horse of happiness to its goal.

For Further Reflection

1. Evaluate whether this statement, which I first encountered in a student paper, is true or false: "Everyone is an egoist, for everyone always tries to do what will bring them satisfaction."

2. Review the story of the killing of Kitty Genovese (chapter 7), and discuss how an ethical egoist would respond to her plight. Would egoists admit that they have a duty to come to the aid of Ms. Genovese?

3. What is the relationship between ethics and evolution? How does this relationship throw light on egoism? What is the significance of reciprocity for ethics?

4. Some philosophers, beginning with Plato, have argued that ethical egoism is irrational, since it precludes psychological health. In an article entitled "Ethical Egoism and Psychological Dispositions" (*American Philosophical Quarterly* 17(1), 1980), Laurence Thomas sets forth the following argument:

P1. A true friend could never, as a matter of course, be disposed to harm or to exploit anyone with whom he is a friend [definition of a friend].

P2. An egoist could never be a true friend to anyone [for the egoist must be ready to exploit others whenever it is in his or her interest].

P3. Only someone with an unhealthy personality could never be a true friend to anyone [definition of a healthy personality; that is, friendship is a necessary condition for a healthy personality].

P4. Ethical egoism requires that we have a kind of disposition which is incompatible with our having a healthy personality [from P1–P3].

Conclusion: Therefore, from the standpoint of our psychological makeup, ethical egoism is unacceptable as a moral theory.

Do you agree with Thomas? How might the ethical egoist respond?

A Critique of Ethical Egoism

JAMES RACHELS

James Rachels is professor of philosophy at the University of Alabama at Birmingham and the author of several books and articles on moral philosophy, including *The Elements of Moral Philosophy,* from which this selection is taken. In this essay, Rachels first distinguishes ethical egoism from psychological egoism, the doctrine that people always act out of their own perceived self-interest. Ethical egoism is the doctrine that states that it is always our duty to act exclusively in our self-interest. He examines three argu-

From *The Elements of Moral Philosophy* by James Rachels. Copyright © 1986 by McGraw-Hill, Inc. Reprinted by permission of the publisher.

ments in favor of ethical egoism, showing that each fails to support its conclusion, and he then examines three arguments against the doctrine. Rachels concludes that although only one of these three arguments is sound, it is enough to invalidate ethical egoism.

IS THERE A DUTY TO CONTRIBUTE FOR FAMINE RELIEF?

Each year millions of people die of malnutrition and related health problems. A common pattern among children in poor countries is death from dehydration caused by diarrhea brought on by malnutrition. James Grant, executive director of the United Nations Children's Fund (UNICEF), estimates that about 15,000 children die in this way *every day*. That comes to 5,475,000 children annually. Even if his estimate is too high, the number that die is staggering.

For those of us in the affluent countries, this poses an acute moral problem. We spend money on ourselves, not only for the necessities of life but for innumerable luxuries—for fine automobiles, fancy clothes, stereos, sports, movies, and so on. In our country, even people with modest incomes enjoy such things. The problem is that we *could* forgo our luxuries and give the money for famine relief instead. The fact that we don't suggests that we regard our luxuries as more important than feeding the hungry.

Why do we allow people to starve to death when we could save them? Very few of us actually believe our luxuries are that important. Most of us, if asked the question directly, would probably be a bit embarrassed, and we would say that we probably should do more for famine relief. The explanation of why we do not is, at least in part, that we hardly ever think of the problem. Living our own comfortable lives, we are effectively insulated from it. The starving people are dying at some distance from us; we do not see them, and we can avoid even thinking of them. When we do think of them, it is only abstractly, as bloodless statistics. Unfortunately for the starving, statistics do not have much power to motivate action.

But leaving aside the question of *why* we behave as we do, what is our *duty*? What *should* we do? We might think of this as the "common-sense" view of the matter: morality requires that we balance our own interests against the interests of others. It is under-

standable, of course, that we look out for our own interests, and
no one can be faulted for attending to his own basic needs. But at
the same time the needs of others are also important, and when
we can help others—especially at little cost to ourselves—we should
do so. Suppose you are thinking of spending ten dollars on a trip
to the movies, when you are reminded that ten dollars could buy
food for a starving child. Thus you could do a great service for the
child at little cost to yourself. Common-sense morality would say,
then, that you should give the money for famine relief rather than
spending it on the movies.

This way of thinking involves a general assumption about our
moral duties: it is assumed that we have moral duties *to other people*—and not merely duties that we create, such as by making a
promise or incurring a debt. We have "natural" duties to others *simply because they are people who could be helped or harmed by our
actions.* If a certain action would benefit (or harm) other people,
then that is a reason why we should (or should not) do that action.
The common-sense assumption is that other people's interests
count, for their own sakes, from a moral point of view.

But one person's common sense is another person's naive platitude. Some thinkers have maintained that, in fact, we have no "natural" duties to other people. *Ethical Egoism* is the idea that each
person ought to pursue his or her own self-interest exclusively. It
is different from Psychological Egoism, which is a theory of human
nature concerned with how people *do* behave—Psychological Egoism says that people do in fact always pursue their own interests.
Ethical Egoism, by contrast, is a normative theory—that is, a theory about how we *ought* to behave. Regardless of how we do
behave, Ethical Egoism says we have no moral duty except to do
what is best for ourselves.

It is a challenging theory. It contradicts some of our deepest
moral beliefs—beliefs held by most of us, at any rate—but it is not
easy to refute. We will examine the most important arguments for
and against it. If it turns out to be true, then of course that is
immensely important. But even if it turns out to be false, there is
still much to be learned from examining it—we may, for example,
gain some insight into the reasons why we *do* have obligations to
other people.

But before looking at the arguments, we should be a little clearer
about exactly what this theory says and what it does not say. In
the first place, Ethical Egoism does not say that one should pro-

mote one's own interests *as well as* the interests of others. That would be an ordinary, unexceptional view. Ethical Egoism is the radical view that one's *only* duty is to promote one's own interests. According to Ethical Egoism, there is only one ultimate principle of conduct, the principle of self-interest, and this principle sums up *all* of one's natural duties and obligations.

However, Ethical Egoism does not say that you should *avoid* actions that help others, either. It may very well be that in many instances your interests coincide with the interests of others, so that in helping yourself you will be aiding others willy-nilly. Or it may happen that aiding others is an effective *means* for creating some benefit for yourself. Ethical Egoism does not forbid such actions; in fact, it may demand them. The theory insists only that in such cases the benefit to others is not what makes the act right. What makes the act right is, rather, the fact that it is to one's own advantage.

Finally, Ethical Egoism does not imply that in pursuing one's interests one ought always to do what one wants to do, or what gives one the most pleasure in the short run. Someone may want to do something that is not good for himself or that will eventually cause himself more grief than pleasure—he may want to drink a lot or smoke cigarettes or take drugs or waste his best years at the race track. Ethical Egoism would frown on all this, regardless of the momentary pleasure it affords. It says that a person ought to do what *really is* to his or her own best advantage, *over the long run*. It endorses selfishness, but it doesn't endorse foolishness.

THREE ARGUMENTS IN FAVOR OF ETHICAL EGOISM

What reasons can be advanced to support this doctrine? Why should anyone think it is true? Unfortunately, the theory is asserted more often than it is argued for. Many of its supporters apparently think its truth is self-evident, so that arguments are not needed. When it *is* argued for, three lines of reasoning are most commonly used.

1. The first argument has several variations, each suggesting the same general point:

a. Each of us is intimately familiar with our own individual wants and needs. Moreover, each of us is uniquely placed to pursue those wants and needs effectively. At the same time, we know the desires and needs of other people only imperfectly, and we are not well situated to pursue them. Therefore, it is reasonable to believe that if we set out to be "our brother's keeper," we would often bungle the job and end up doing more mischief than good.

b. At the same time, the policy of "looking out for others" is an offensive intrusion into other people's privacy; it is essentially a policy of minding other people's business.

c. Making other people the object of one's "charity" is degrading to them; it robs them of their individual dignity and self-respect. The offer of charity says, in effect, that they are not competent to care for themselves; and the statement is self-fulfilling—they cease to be self-reliant and become passively dependent on others. That is why the recipients of "charity" are so often resentful rather than appreciative.

What this adds up to is that the policy of "looking out for others" is self-defeating. If we want to promote the best interests of everyone alike, we should *not* adopt so-called altruistic policies of behavior. On the contrary, if each person looks after his or her *own* interests, it is more likely that everyone will be better off, in terms of both physical and emotional well-being. Thus Robert G. Olson says in his book *The Morality of Self-Interest* (1965), "The individual is most likely to contribute to social betterment by rationally pursuing his own best long-range interests." Or as Alexander Pope said more poetically,

> Thus God and nature formed the general frame
> And bade self-love and social be the same.

It is possible to quarrel with this argument on a number of grounds. Of course no one favors bungling, butting in, or depriving people of their self-respect. But is this really what we are doing when we feed hungry children? Is the starving child in Ethiopia really harmed when we "intrude" into "her business" by supplying food? It hardly seems likely. Yet we can set this point aside, for considered as an argument for Ethical Egoism, this way of thinking has an even more serious defect.

The trouble is that it isn't really an argument *for Ethical Egoism* at all. The argument concludes that we should adopt certain policies of action; and on the surface they appear to be egoistic policies. However, the *reason* it is said we should adopt those policies is decidedly *un*egoistic. The reason is one that to an egoist shouldn't matter. It is said that we should adopt those policies because doing so will promote the "betterment of society"—but according to Ethical Egoism, that is something we should not be concerned about. Spelled out fully, with everything laid on the table, the argument says:

1. We ought to do whatever will promote the best interests of everyone alike.
2. The interests of everyone will best be promoted if each of us adopts the policy of pursuing our own interests exclusively.
3. Therefore, each of us should adopt the policy of pursuing our own interests exclusively.

If we accept this reasoning, then we are not ethical egoists at all. Even though we might end up *behaving* like egoists, our ultimate principle is one of beneficence—we are doing what we think will help everyone, not merely what we think will benefit ourselves. Rather than being egoists, we turn out to be altruists with a peculiar view of what in fact promotes the general welfare.

2. The second argument was put forward with some force by Ayn Rand, a writer little heeded by professional philosophers but who nevertheless was enormously popular on college campuses during the 1960s and 1970s. Ethical Egoism, in her view, is the only ethical philosophy that respects the integrity of the individual human life. She regarded the ethics of "altruism" as a totally destructive idea, both in society as a whole and in the lives of individuals taken in by it. Altruism, to her way of thinking, leads to a denial of the value of the individual. It says to a person: *your* life is merely something that may be sacrificed. "If a man accepts the ethics of altruism," she writes, "his first concern is not how to live his life, but how to sacrifice it." Moreover, those who would *promote* this idea are beneath contempt—they are parasites who, rather than working to build and sustain their own lives, leech off those who do. Again, she writes:

> Parasites, moochers, looters, brutes and thugs can be of no value to a human being—nor can he gain any benefit from living in a society geared to *their* needs, demands and protections, a society that treats him as a sacrificial animal and penalizes him for his virtues in order to reward *them* for their vices, which means: a society based on the ethics of altruism.

By "sacrificing one's life" Rand does not necessarily mean anything so dramatic as dying. A person's life consists (in part) of projects undertaken and goods earned and created. To demand that a person abandon his projects or give up his goods is also a clear effort to "sacrifice his life." Furthermore, throughout her writings Rand also suggests that there is a *metaphysical* basis for egoistic ethics. Somehow, it is the only ethics that takes seriously the *reality* of the individual person. She bemoans "the enormity of the extent to which altruism erodes men's capacity to grasp . . . the value of an individual life; it reveals a mind from which the reality of a human being has been wiped out."

What, then, of the starving people? It might be argued, in response, that Ethical Egoism "reveals a mind from which the reality of a human being has been wiped out"—namely, the human being who is starving. Rand quotes with approval the evasive answer given by one of her followers: "Once, when Barbara Brandon was asked by a student: 'What will happen to the poor . . . ?'—she answered: 'If *you* want to help them, you will not be stopped.'"

All these remarks are, I think, part of one continuous argument that can be summarized like this:

1. A person has only one life to live. If we place any value on the individual—that is, if the individual has any moral worth—then we must agree that this life is of supreme importance. After all, it is all one has, and all one is.
2. The ethics of altruism regards the life of the individual as something one must be ready to sacrifice for the good of others.
3. Therefore, the ethics of altruism does not take seriously the value of the human individual.
4. Ethical Egoism, which allows each person to view his or her own life as being of ultimate value, *does* take the human individual seriously—in fact, it is the only philosophy that does so.
5. Thus, Ethical Egoism is the philosophy that ought to be accepted.

The problem with this argument, as you may already have noticed, is that it relies on picturing the alternatives in such an extreme way. "The ethics of altruism" is taken to be such an extreme philosophy that *nobody,* with the possible exception of certain monks, would find it congenial. As Ayn Rand presents it, altruism implies that one's own interests have *no* value, and that *any* demand by others calls for sacrificing them. If that is the alternative, then any other view, including Ethical Egoism, will look good by comparison. But this is hardly a fair picture of the choices. What we called the common-sense view stands somewhere between the two extremes. It says that one's own interests and the interests of others are both important and must be balanced against one another. Sometimes, when the balancing is done, it will turn out that one should act in the interests of others; other times, it will turn out that one should take care of oneself. So even if the Randian argument refutes the extreme "ethics of altruism," it does not follow that one must accept the other extreme of Ethical Egoism.

3. The third line of reasoning takes a somewhat different approach. Ethical Egoism is usually presented as a *revisionist* moral philosophy, that is, as a philosophy that says our common-sense moral views are mistaken and need to be changed. It is possible, however, to interpret Ethical Egoism in a much less radical way, as a theory that *accepts* common-sense morality and offers a surprising account of its basis.

The less radical interpretation goes as follows. In everyday life, we assume that we are obliged to obey certain rules. We must avoid doing harm to others, speak the truth, keep our promises, and so on. At first glance, these duties appear to be very different from one another. They appear to have little in common. Yet from a theoretical point of view, we may wonder whether there is not some hidden *unity* underlying the hodge-podge of separate duties. Perhaps there is some small number of fundamental principles that explain all the rest, just as in physics there are basic principles that bring together and explain diverse phenomena. From a theoretical point of view, the smaller the number of basic principles, the better. Best of all would be *one* fundamental principle, from which all the rest could be derived. Ethical Egoism, then, would be the theory that all our duties are ultimately derived from the one fundamental principle of self-interest.

Taken in this way, Ethical Egoism is not such a radical doctrine. It does not challenge common-sense morality; it only tries to explain and systematize it. And it does a surprisingly successful job. It can provide plausible explanations of the duties mentioned above, and more:

a. If we make a habit of doing things that are harmful to other people, people will not be reluctant to do things that will harm *us*. We will be shunned and despised; others will not have us as friends and will not do us favors when we need them. If our offenses against others are serious enough, we may even end up in jail. Thus it is to our own advantage to avoid harming others.

b. If we lie to other people, we will suffer all the ill effects of a bad reputation. People will distrust us and avoid doing business with us. We will often need for people to be honest with us, but we can hardly expect them to feel much of an obligation to be honest with us if they know we have not been honest with them. Thus it is to our own advantage to be truthful.

c. It is to our own advantage to be able to enter into mutually beneficial arrangements with other people. To benefit from those arrangements, we need to be able to rely on others to keep their parts of the bargains we make with them—we need to be able to rely on them to keep their promises to us. But we can hardly expect others to keep their promises to us if we are not willing to keep our promises to them. Therefore, from the point of view of self-interest, we should keep our promises.

Pursuing this line of reasoning, Thomas Hobbes suggested that the principle of Ethical Egoism leads to nothing less than the Golden Rule: we should "do unto others" *because* if we do, others will be more likely to "do unto us."

Does this argument succeed in establishing Ethical Egoism as a viable theory of morality? It is, in my opinion at least, the best try. But there are two serious objections to it. In the first place, the argument does not prove quite as much as it needs to prove. At best, it shows only that *as a general rule* it is to one's own advantage to avoid harming others. It does not show that this is *always* so. And it could not show that, for even though it may usually to be one's advantage to avoid harming others, sometimes it is not. Sometimes one might even *gain* from treating another person badly. In that case, the obligation not to harm the other person could *not* be derived from the principle of Ethical Egoism. Thus it appears that not all our moral obligations can be explained as derivable from self-interest.

But set that point aside. There is still a more fundamental question to be asked about the proposed theory. Suppose it is true that, say, contributing money for famine relief is somehow to one's own advantage. It does not follow that this is the only reason, or even the most basic reason, why doing so is a morally good thing. (For example, the most basic reason might be *in order to help the starv-*

ing people. The fact that doing so is also to one's own advantage might be only a secondary, less important, consideration.) A demonstration that one could *derive* this duty from self-interest does not prove that self-interest is the *only reason* one has this duty. Only if you accept an additional proposition—namely, the proposition that there is no reason for giving *other than* self-interest—will you find Ethical Egoism a plausible theory.

THREE ARGUMENTS AGAINST ETHICAL EGOISM

Ethical Egoism has haunted twentieth-century moral philosophy. It has not been a popular doctrine; the most important philosophers have rejected it outright. But it has never been very far from their minds. Although no thinker of consequence has defended it, almost everyone has felt it necessary to explain why he was rejecting it— as though the very possibility that it might be correct was hanging in the air, threatening to smother their other ideas. As the merits of the various "refutations" have been debated, philosophers have returned to it again and again.

The following three arguments are typical of the refutations proposed by contemporary philosophers.

1. In his book *The Moral Point of View* (1958), Kurt Baier argues that Ethical Egoism cannot be correct because it cannot provide solutions for conflicts of interest. We need moral rules, he says, only because our interests sometimes come into conflict. (If they never conflicted, then there would be no problems to solve and hence no need for the kind of guidance that morality provides.) But Ethical Egoism does not help to resolve conflicts of interest; it only exacerbates them. Baier argues for this by introducing a fanciful example:

> Let B and K be candidates for the presidency of a certain country and let it be granted that it is in the interest of either to be elected, but that only one can succeed. It would then be in the interest of B but against the interest of K if B were elected, and vice versa, and therefore in the interest of B but against the interest of K if K were liquidated, and vice versa. But from this it would follow that B ought to liquidate K, that it is wrong for B not to do so, that B has not "done his duty" until he has liquidated K; and vice versa. Similarly K, knowing that his own liquidation is in the interest of B and there-

fore, anticipating B's attempts to secure it, ought to take steps to foil B's endeavors. It would be wrong for him not to do so. He would "not have done his duty" until he had made sure of stopping B. . . .

This is obviously absurd. For morality is designed to apply in just such cases, namely, those where interests conflict. But if the point of view of morality were that of self-interest, then there could never be moral solutions of conflicts of interest.

Does this argument prove that Ethical Egoism is unacceptable? It does, *if* the conception of morality to which it appeals is accepted. The argument assumes that an adequate morality must provide solutions for conflicts of interest in such a way that everyone concerned can live together harmoniously. The conflict between B and K, for example, should be resolved so that they would no longer be at odds with one another. (One would not then have a duty to do something that the other has a duty to prevent.) Ethical Egoism does not do that, and if you think an ethical theory should, then you will not find Ethical Egoism acceptable.

But a defender of Ethical Egoism might reply that *he* does not accept this conception of morality. For him, life is essentially a long series of conflicts in which each person is struggling to come out on top; and the principle he accepts—the principle of Ethical Egoism—simply urges each one to do his or her best to win. On his view, the moralist is not like a courtroom judge, who resolves disputes. Instead, he is like the Commissioner of Boxing, who urges each fighter to do his best. So the conflict between B and K will be "resolved" not by the application of an ethical theory but by one or the other of them winning the struggle. The egoist will not be embarrassed by this—on the contrary, he will think it no more than a realistic view of the nature of things.

2. Some philosophers, including Baier, have leveled an even more serious charge against Ethical Egoism. They have argued that it is a *logically inconsistent* doctrine—that is, they say it leads to logical contradictions. If this is true, then Ethical Egoism is indeed a mistaken theory, for no theory can be true if it is self-contradictory.

Consider B and K again. As Baier explains their predicament, it is in B's interest to kill K, and obviously it is in K's interest to prevent it. But, Baier says,

if K prevents B from liquidating him, his act must be said to be both wrong and not wrong—wrong because it is the prevention of what

B ought to do, his duty, and wrong for B not to do it; not wrong because it is what K ought to do, his duty, and wrong for K not to do it. But one and the same act (logically) cannot be both morally wrong and not morally wrong.

Now, does *this* argument prove that Ethical Egoism is unacceptable? At first glance it seems persuasive. However, it is a complicated argument, so we need to set it out with each step individually identified. Then we will be in a better position to evaluate it. Spelled out fully, it looks like this:

1. Suppose it is each person's duty to do what is in his own best interests.
2. It is in B's best interest to liquidate K.
3. It is in K's best interest to prevent B from liquidating him.
4. Therefore B's duty is to liquidate K, and K's duty is to prevent B from doing it.
5. But it is wrong to prevent someone from doing his duty.
6. Therefore it is wrong for K to prevent B from liquidating him.
7. Therefore it is both wrong and not wrong for K to prevent B from liquidating him.
8. But no act can be both wrong and not wrong—that is a self-contradiction.
9. Therefore the assumption with which we started—that it is each person's duty to do what is in his own best interests—cannot be true.

When the argument is set out in this way, we can see its hidden flaw. The logical contradiction—that it is both wrong and not wrong for K to prevent B from liquidating him—does *not* follow simply from the principle of Ethical Egoism. It follows from that principle, *and* the additional premise expressed in step (5)—namely, that "it is wrong to prevent someone from doing his duty." Thus we are not compelled by the logic of the argument to reject Ethical Egoism. Instead, we could simply reject this additional premise, and the contradiction would be avoided. That is surely what the ethical egoist would want to do, for the ethical egoist would never say, without qualification, that it is always wrong to prevent someone from doing his duty. He would say, instead, that *whether one ought to prevent someone from doing his duty depends entirely on whether it would be to one's own advantage to do so.* Regardless of whether we think this is a correct view, it is, at the very least, a *consistent* view, and so this attempt to convict the egoist of self-contradiction fails.

3. Finally, we come to the argument that I think comes closest to an outright refutation of Ethical Egoism. It is also the most interesting of the arguments, because at the same time it provides the most insight into why the interests of other people *should* matter to a moral agent.

Before this argument is presented, we need to look briefly at a general point about moral values. So let us set Ethical Egoism aside for a moment and consider this related matter.

There is a whole family of moral views that have this in common: they all involve dividing people into groups and saying that the interests of some groups count for more than the interests of other groups. Racism is the most conspicuous example; it involves dividing people into groups according to race and assigning greater importance to the interests of one race than to others. The practical result is that members of the preferred race are to be *treated better* than the others. Anti-Semitism works the same way, and so can nationalism. People in the grip of such views will think, in effect: "*My* race counts for more," or "Those who believe in *my* religion count for more," or "*My* country counts for more," and so on.

Can such views be defended? Those who accept them are usually not much interested in argument—racists, for example, rarely try to offer rational grounds for their position. But suppose they did. What could they say?

There is a general principle that stands in the way of any such defense, namely: *We can justify treating people differently only if we can show that there is some factual difference between them that is relevant to justifying the difference in treatment.* For example, if one person is admitted to law school while another is rejected, this can be justified by pointing out that the first graduated from college with honors and scored well on the admissions test, while the second dropped out of college and never took the test. However, if *both* graduated with honors and did well on the entrance examination—in other words, if they are in all relevant respects equally well qualified—then it is merely arbitrary to admit one but not the other.

Can a racist point to any differences between, say, white people and black people that would justify treating them differently?

In the past, racists have sometimes attempted to do this by picturing blacks as stupid, lacking in ambition, and the like. *If* this were true, then it might justify treating them differently, in at least some circumstances. (This is the deep purpose of racist stereotypes—to provide the "relevant differences" needed to justify differences in treatment.) But of course it is not true, and in fact there are no such general differences between the races. Thus racism is an *arbitrary* doctrine, in that it advocates treating some people differently even though there are no differences between them to justify it.

Ethical Egoism is a moral theory of the same type. It advocates that each of us divide the world into two categories of people—ourselves and all the rest—and that we regard the interests of those in the first group as more important than the interests of those in the second group. But each of us can ask, what is the difference between myself and others that justifies placing myself in this special category? Am I more intelligent? Do I enjoy my life more? Are my accomplishments greater? Do I have needs or abilities that are so different from the needs or abilities of others? *What is it that makes me so special?* Failing an answer, it turns out that Ethical Egoism is an arbitrary doctrine, in the same way that racism is arbitrary.

The argument, then, is this:

1. Any moral doctrine that assigns greater importance to the interests of one group than to those of another is unacceptably arbitrary unless there is some difference between the members of the groups that justifies treating them differently.
2. Ethical Egoism would have each person assign greater importance to his or her own interests than to the interests of others. *But there is no general difference between oneself and others, to which each person can appeal, that justifies this difference in treatment.*
3. Therefore, Ethical Egoism is unacceptably arbitrary.

And this, in addition to arguing against Ethical Egoism, also sheds some light on the question of why we should care about others.

We should care about the interests of other people *for the very same reason we care about our own interests;* for their needs and desires are comparable to our own. Consider, one last time, the starving people we could feed by giving up some of our luxuries. Why should we care about them? We care about ourselves, of course—if *we* were starving, we would go to almost any lengths to get food. But what is the difference between us and them? Does hunger affect them any less? Are they somehow less deserving than we? If we can find no relevant difference between us and them, then we must admit that if *our* needs should be met, so should *theirs*. It is this realization, that we are on a par with one another, that is the deepest reason why our morality must include some recognition of the needs of others, and why, then, Ethical Egoism fails as a moral theory.

For Further Reflection

1. Go over the three arguments for ethical egoism. Do you agree with Rachels's assessment that they all fail to establish the theory? Could a slight modification in any of them save the theory?

2. What are the three arguments in favor of ethical egoism? Outline each of them and describe their weaknesses.

3. How does the third argument lead to the Golden Rule? Why is it the "best try"?

4. Identify the three arguments against ethical egoism. Which of them, if any, refutes ethical egoism?

Further Readings for Chapter 8

Axelrod, Robert M. *The Evolution of Cooperation*. New York: Basic Books, 1984. A brilliant study on the rationality of cooperation.

Dawkins, Richard. *The Selfish Gene*. 2nd ed. Oxford: Oxford University Press, 1989. One of the most fascinating studies on the subject, defending limited altruism.

Gauthier, David, ed. *Morality and Rational Self-Interest*. Englewood Cliffs, N.J.: Prentice-Hall, 1970.

Gauthier, David. *Morality by Agreement*. Oxford: Clarendon Press, 1986.

Hospers, John. *Human Conduct: An Introduction to the Problems of Ethics*. New York: Harcourt Brace Jovanovich, 1961.

MacIntyre, Alasdair. "Egoism and Altruism." In *The Encyclopedia of Philosophy,* edited by Paul Edwards. New York: Macmillan, 1967.

Nielsen, Kai. "Why Should I Be Moral?" *Methodos* 15, no. 59–60 (1963). This comprehensive article appears in several anthologies.

Olen, Jeffrey. *Moral Freedom.* Philadelphia: Temple University Press, 1988.

Rachels, James. *The Elements of Moral Philosophy.* New York: Random House, 1986. Chapters 5 and 6.

Rand, Ayn. *The Virtue of Selfishness.* New York: New American Library, 1964.

Singer, Peter. *The Expanding Circle: Ethics and Sociobiology.* New York: Farrar, Straus & Giroux, 1981. A good discussion of egoism in the light of sociobiology.

Taylor, Richard. *Good and Evil.* New York: Macmillan, 1970. Especially chapter 5.

CHAPTER 9

Does Life Have Meaning?

In his autobiography Tolstoy tells the story of a traveler fleeing an infuriated animal. Attempting to save himself from the beast, the man runs toward a well and begins to climb down, when to his distress he spies a dragon at the bottom. The dragon is waiting for him with open jaws, ready to eat him. The poor fellow is caught in a dilemma. He dare not drop into the well for fear of the dragon, but he dare not climb out of the well for fear of the beast. So he clutches a branch of a bush growing in the cleft of the well and hangs onto it for dear life. His hands grow weak, and he feels that soon he shall have to give in to his grim fate, but he still holds on desperately. As he grasps the branch for his salvation, he notices that two mice, one white and one black, are nibbling away at the main trunk of the branch onto which he is clinging. Soon they will dislodge the branch, and he will fall into the waiting jaws of the dragon.

The traveler knows that he will soon perish, but while clinging to the branch, he sees some drops of honey hanging on the leaves of the bush, and so sticks out his tongue and licks the leaves.

The traveler is you and I, and his plight is your plight and mine, the danger of our demise on every hand. The white mouse represents our days and the black our nights. Together they are nibbling away at the threescore years and ten which make up our branch of life. Inevitably all will be over, and what have we to show for it? Is our brief distraction of the taste of honey all we get out of life? Is this all there is in life? Can this brief moment in the history of the universe have significance? What gives life importance?

The certainty of death heightens the question of the meaning of life. Like a prisoner sentenced to death or a patient with terminal illness, we know that, in a sense, we are all sentenced to death and are terminally ill, but we flee the thought in a thousand ways. What is the purpose of life?

Our readings begin with Voltaire's "The Good Brahmin," a story of a learned and moral man who is in despair over the question of the meaning of life. Voltaire's essay raises the fundamental question. What follows are several responses to that question: Epicurus's moderate hedonism and Camus's rendition of the Myth of Sisyphus illustrate the thesis that life has no meaning. Lois Hope Walker finds the essence of a purposeful life in religion. Viktor Frankl's narrative finds meaning in depths of the Nazi concentration camp, Auschwitz. The Buddha sets forth his eightfold path to salvation, and Robert Nozick offers a thought experiment on the meaningfulness of life.

The Good Brahmin

VOLTAIRE

Voltaire (1694–1778) was one of the greatest French philosophers of the eighteenth century and the author of several works, including *Candide* (1759), *Treatise on Tolerance* (1763), and *Philosophical Dictionary* (1764). The story of the Good Brahmin has to do with despair and the meaning of life.

On my travels I met an old Brahmin, a very wise man, of marked intellect and great learning. Furthermore, he was rich and, consequently, all the wiser, because, lacking nothing, he needed to deceive nobody. His household was very well managed by three handsome women who set themselves out to please him. When he was not amusing himself with his women, he passed the time in philosophizing. Near his house, which was beautifully decorated and had charming gardens attached, there lived a narrow-minded old Indian woman: she was a simpleton, and rather poor.

Said the Brahmin to me one day: "I wish I had never been born!" On my asking why, he answered: "I have been studying forty years, and that is forty years wasted. I teach others and myself am ignorant of everything. Such a state of affairs fills my soul with so much humiliation and disgust that my life is intolerable. I was born in Time, I live in Time, and yet I do not know what Time is. I am at a point between two eternities, as our wise men say, and I have no conception of eternity. I am composed of matter: I think, but I have never been able to learn what produces my thought. I do not know whether or not my understanding is a simple faculty inside me, such as those of walking and digesting, and whether or not I think with my head as I grip with my hands. Not only is the cause of my thought unknown to me; the cause of my actions is equally a mystery. I do not know why I exist, and yet every day people ask me questions on all these points. I have to reply, and as I have nothing really worth saying I talk a great deal, and am ashamed of myself afterward for having talked.

"It is worse still when I am asked if Brahma was born of Vishnu or if they are both eternal. God is my witness that I have not the remotest idea, and my ignorance shows itself in my replies. 'Ah, Holy One,' people say to me, 'tell us why evil pervades the earth.' I am in as great a difficulty as those who ask me this question. Sometimes I tell them that everything is as well as can be, but those who have been ruined and broken in the wars do not believe a word of it—and no more do I. I retire to my home stricken at my own curiosity and ignorance. I read our ancient books, and they double my darkness. I talk to my companions: some answer me that we must enjoy life and make game of mankind; others think they know a lot and lose themselves in a maze of wild ideas. Everything increases my anguish. I am ready sometimes to despair when I think that after all my seeking I do not know whence I came, whither I go, what I am nor what I shall become."

The good man's condition really worried me. Nobody was more rational or more sincere than he. I perceived that his unhappiness increased in proportion as his understanding developed and his insight grew.

The same day I saw the old woman who lived near him. I asked her if she had ever been troubled by the thought that she was ignorant of the nature of her soul. She did not even understand my question. Never in all her life had she reflected for one single moment on one single point of all those which tormented the Brahmin. She believed with all her heart in the metamorphoses of Vishnu and, provided she could obtain a little Ganges water wherewith to wash herself, thought herself the happiest of women.

Struck with this mean creature's happiness, I returned to my wretched philosopher. "Are you not ashamed," said I, "to be unhappy when at your very door there lives an old automaton who thinks about nothing, and yet lives contentedly?"

"You are right," he replied. "I have told myself a hundred times that I should be happy if I were as brainless as my neighbor, and yet I do not desire such happiness."

My Brahmin's answer impressed me more than all the rest. I set to examining myself, and I saw that in truth I would not care to be happy at the price of being a simpleton.

I put the matter before some philosophers, and they were of my opinion. "Nevertheless," said I, "there is a tremendous contradiction in this mode of thought, for, after all, the problem is—how to be happy. What does it matter whether one has brains or not? Further, those who are contented with their lot are certain of their contentment, whereas those who reason are not certain that they reason correctly. It is quite clear, therefore," I continued, "that we must choose not to have common sense, however little common sense may contribute to our discomfort." Everyone agreed with me, but I found nobody, notwithstanding, who was willing to accept the bargain of becoming a simpleton in order to become contented. From which I conclude that if we consider the question of happiness we must consider still more the question of reason.

But on reflection it seems that to prefer reason to felicity is to be very senseless. How can this contradiction be explained? Like all the other contradictions. It is matter for much talk.

For Further Reflection

1. Discuss the sense of meaninglessness and despair that the good, but unhappy, Brahmin feels. Why does he experience such emptiness in life?

2. Compare the Brahmin with the old and contented woman. Why would people prefer to be the Brahmin rather than the unreflective woman? Would you rather be a happy simpleton than a sometimes sad but rational person, who must live with a sense of the absurd? Consider animals, so long as they are fed, as the epitome of contentment. They never ask about the meaning of life. Is the sense of the absurd a hallmark of our superior rationality?

Hedonism

EPICURUS

The Greek philosopher Epicurus (341–271 B.C.) founded
the school of philosophy named after himself, *epicureanism,* a hedonistic theory wherein good is identified with
pleasure and evil with pain. In this he is the precursor of
Bentham's utilitarianism (chapter 4). But contrary to popular opinion, Epicurus's version of hedonism is nothing like
the modern ideas connected with his name—sensuality,
profligacy, and decadence. On the contrary, he believed
that the good life consists in simple but deep pleasures and
the absence of pain, in an attitude of imperturbable emotional tranquillity. We should seek pleasure in conversation, friendship, a good but simple diet, and a prudent life.
Since only good and bad sensations should concern us,
and since death is not a sensation, we should not fear death.
We should not even think very much about it.

Become accustomed to the belief that death is nothing to us. For
all good and evil consists in sensation, but death is deprivation of
sensation. And therefore a right understanding that death is nothing to us makes the mortality of life enjoyable, not because it adds
to it an infinite span of time, but because it takes away the craving for immortality. For there is nothing terrible in life for the man
who has truly comprehended that there is nothing terrible in not
living. So that the man speaks but idly who says that he fears death
not because it will be painful when it comes, but because it is
painful in anticipation. For that which gives no trouble when it
comes, is but an empty pain in anticipation. So death, the most terrifying of ills, is nothing to us, since so long as we exist, death is
not with us; but when death comes, then we do not exist. It does
not then concern either the living or the dead, since for the former
it is not, and the latter are no more.

But the many at one moment shun death as the greatest of evils, at another yearn for it as a respite from the evils in life. But the wise man neither seeks to escape life nor fears the cessation of life, for neither does life offend him nor does the absence of life seem to be any evil. And just as with food he does not seek simply the larger share and nothing else, but rather the most pleasant, so he seeks to enjoy not the longest period of time, but the most pleasant.

And he who counsels the young man to live well, but the old man to make a good end, is foolish, not merely because of the desirability of life, but also because it is the same training which teaches to live well and to die well. Yet much worse still is the man who says it is good not to be born, but

'once born make haste to pass the gates of Death'.

For if he says this from conviction why does he not pass away out of life? For it is open to him to do so, if he had firmly made up his mind to this. But if he speaks in jest, his words are idle among men who cannot receive them.

We must then bear in mind that the future is neither ours, nor yet wholly not ours, so that we may not altogether expect it as sure to come, nor abandon hope of it, as if it will certainly not come.

We must consider that of desires some are natural, others vain, and of the natural some are necessary and others merely natural; and of the necessary some are necessary for happiness, others for the repose of the body, and others for very life. The right understanding of these facts enables us to refer all choice and avoidance to the health of the body and the soul's freedom from disturbance, since this is the aim of the life of blessedness. For it is to obtain this end that we always act, namely, to avoid pain and fear. And when this is once secured for us, all the tempest of the soul is dispersed, since the living creature has not to wander as though in search of something that is missing, and to look for some other thing by which he can fulfil the good of the soul and the good of the body. For it is then that we have need of pleasure, when we feel pain owing to the absence of pleasure; but when we do not feel pain, we no longer need pleasure. And for this cause we call pleasure the beginning and end of the blessed life. For we recognize pleasure as the first good innate in us, and from pleasure we begin every act of choice and avoidance, and to pleasure we return again, using the feeling as the standard by which we judge every good.

And since pleasure is the first good and natural to us, for this very reason we do not choose every pleasure, but sometimes we pass over many pleasures, when greater discomfort accrues to us as the result of them: and similarly we think many pains better than pleasures, since a greater pleasure comes to us when we have endured pains for a long time. Every pleasure then because of its natural kinship to us is good, yet not every pleasure is to be chosen: even as every pain also is an evil, yet not all are always of a nature to be avoided. Yet by a scale of comparison and by the consideration of advantages and disadvantages we must form our judgement on all these matters. For the good on certain occasions we treat as bad, and conversely the bad as good.

And again independence of desire we think a great good—not that we may at all times enjoy but a few things, but that, if we do not possess many, we may enjoy the few in the genuine persuasion that those have the sweetest pleasure in luxury who least need it, and that all that is natural is easy to be obtained, but that which is superfluous is hard. And so plain savours bring us pleasure equal to a luxurious diet, when all the pain due to want is removed; and bread and water produce the highest pleasure, when one who needs them puts them to his lips. To grow accustomed therefore to simple and not luxurious diet gives us health to the full, and makes a man alert for the needful employments of life, and when after long intervals we approach luxuries, disposes us better towards them, and fits us to be fearless of fortune.

When, therefore, we maintain that pleasure is the end, we do not mean the pleasures of profligates and those that consist in sensuality, as is supposed by some who are either ignorant or disagree with us or do not understand, but freedom from pain in the body and from trouble in the mind. For it is not continuous drinkings and revellings, nor the satisfaction of lusts, nor the enjoyment of fish and other luxuries of the wealthy table, which produce a pleasant life, but sober reasoning, searching out the motives for all choice and avoidance, and banishing mere opinions, to which are due the greatest disturbance of the spirit.

Of all this the beginning and the greatest good is prudence. Wherefore prudence is a more precious thing even than philosophy: for from prudence are sprung all the other virtues, and it teaches us that it is not possible to live pleasantly without living prudently and honourably and justly, nor, again, to live a life of prudence, honour, and justice without living pleasantly. For the virtues are by nature bound up with the pleasant life, and the pleasant life is inseparable from them. For indeed who, think you, is a better man than he who holds reverent opinions concerning the gods, and is at all times free from fear of death, and has reasoned out the end ordained by nature? He understands that the limit of good things is easy to fulfil and easy to attain, whereas the course of ills is either short in time or slight in pain: he laughs at destiny, whom some have introduced as the mistress of all things. He thinks that with us lies the chief power in determining events, some of which happen by necessity and some by chance, and some are within our control; for while necessity cannot be called to account, he sees that chance is inconstant, but that which is in our control is subject to no master, and to it are naturally attached praise and blame. For, indeed, it were better to follow the myths about the gods than to become a slave to the destiny of the natural philosophers: for the former suggests a hope of placating the gods by worship, whereas the latter involves a necessity which knows no placation. As to chance, he does not regard it as a god as most men do (for in a god's acts there is no disorder), nor as an uncertain cause of all things: for he does not believe that good and evil are given by chance to man for the framing of a blessed life, but that opportunities for great good and great evil are afforded by it. He therefore thinks it better to be unfortunate in reasonable action than to prosper in unreason. For it is better in a man's actions that what is well chosen should fail, rather than that what is ill chosen should be successful owing to chance.

Meditate therefore on these things and things akin to them night and day by yourself, and with a companion like to yourself, and never shall you be disturbed waking or asleep, but you shall live like a god among men. For a man who lives among immortal blessings is not like to a mortal being.

PRINCIPAL DOCTRINES

I. The blessed and immortal nature knows no trouble itself nor causes trouble to any other, so that it is never constrained by anger or favour. For all such things exist only in the weak.

II. Death is nothing to us: for that which is dissolved is without sensation; and that which lacks sensation is nothing to us.

III. The limit of quantity in pleasures is the removal of all that is painful. Wherever pleasure is present, as long as it is there, there is neither pain of body nor of mind, nor of both at once.

IV. Pain does not last continuously in the flesh, but the acutest pain is there for a very short time, and even that which just exceeds the pleasure in the flesh does not continue for many days at once. But chronic illnesses permit a predominance of pleasure over pain in the flesh.

V. It is not possible to live pleasantly without living prudently and honourably and justly, nor again to live a life of prudence, honour, and justice without living pleasantly. And the man who does not possess the pleasant life, is not living prudently and honourably and justly, and the man who does not possess the virtuous life, cannot possibly live pleasantly.

VI. To secure protection from men anything is a natural good, by which you may be able to attain this end.

VII. Some men wished to become famous and conspicuous, thinking that they would thus win for themselves safety from other men. Wherefore if the life of such men is safe, they have obtained the good which nature craves; but if it is not safe, they do not possess that for which they strove at first by the instinct of nature.

VIII. No pleasure is a bad thing in itself: but the means which produce some pleasures bring with them disturbances many times greater than the pleasures.

IX. If every pleasure could be intensified so that it lasted and influenced the whole organism or the most essential parts of our nature, pleasures would never differ from one another.

X. If the things that produce the pleasures of profligates could dispel the fears of the mind about the phenomena of the sky and death and its pains, and also teach the limits of desires and of pains, we should never have cause to blame them: for they would be filling themselves full with pleasures from every source and never have pain of body or mind, which is the evil of life.

XI. If we were not troubled by our suspicions of the phenomena of the sky and about death, fearing that it concerns us, and also by our failure to grasp the limits of pains and desires, we should have no need of natural science.

XII. A man cannot dispel his fear about the most important matters if he does not know what is the nature of the universe but suspects the truth of some mythical story. So that without natural science it is not possible to attain our pleasures unalloyed.

XIII. There is no profit in securing protection in relation to men, if things above and things beneath the earth and indeed all in the boundless universe remain matters of suspicion.

XIV. The most unalloyed source of protection from men, which is secured to some extent by a certain force of expulsion, is in fact the immunity which results from a quiet life and the retirement from the world.

XV. The wealth demanded by nature is both limited and easily procured; that demanded by idle imaginings stretches on to infinity.

XVI. In but few things chance hinders a wise man, but the greatest and most important matters reason has ordained and throughout the whole period of life does and will ordain.

XVII. The just man is most free from trouble, the unjust most full of trouble.

XVIII. The pleasure in the flesh is not increased, when once the pain due to want is removed, but is only varied: and the limit as regards pleasure in the mind is begotten by the reasoned understanding of these very pleasures and of the emotions akin to them, which used to cause the greatest fear to the mind.

XIX. Infinite time contains no greater pleasure than limited time, if one measures by reason the limits of pleasure.

XX. The flesh perceives the limits of pleasure as unlimited and unlimited time is required to supply it. But the mind, having attained a reasoned understanding of the ultimate good of the flesh and its limits and having dissipated the fears concerning the time to come, supplies us with the complete life, and we have no further need of infinite time: but neither does the mind shun pleasure, nor, when circumstances begin to bring about the departure from life, does it approach its end as though it fell short in any way of the best life.

XXI. He who has learned the limits of life knows that that which removes the paid due to want and makes the whole of life complete is easy to obtain; so that there is no need of actions which involve competition.

XXII. We must consider both the real purpose and all the evidence of direct perception, to which we always refer the conclusions of opinion; otherwise, all will be full of doubt and confusion.

XXIII. If you fight against all sensations, you will have no standard by which to judge even those of them which you say are false.

XXIV. If you reject any single sensation and fail to distinguish between the conclusion of opinion as to the appearance awaiting confirmation and that which is actually given by the sensation or feeling, or each intuitive apprehension of the mind, you will confound all other sensations as well with the same groundless opinion, so that you will reject every standard of judgement. And if among the mental images created by your opinion you affirm both that which awaits confirmation and that which does not, you will not escape error, since you will have preserved the whole cause of doubt in every judgement between what is right and what is wrong.

XXV. If on each occasion instead of referring your actions to the end of nature, you turn to some other nearer standard when you are making a choice or an avoidance, your actions will not be consistent with your principles.

XXVI. Of desires, all that do not lead to a sense of pain, if they are not satisfied, are not necessary, but involve a craving which is easily dispelled, when the object is hard to procure or they seem likely to produce harm.

XXVII. Of all the things which wisdom acquires to produce the blessedness of the complete life, far the greatest is the possession of friendship.

XXVIII. The same conviction which has given us confidence that there is nothing terrible that lasts for ever or even for long, has also seen the protection of friendship most fully completed in the limited evils of this life.

XXIX. Among desires some are natural and necessary, some natural but not necessary, and others neither natural nor necessary, but due to idle imagination.

XXX. Wherever in the case of desires which are physical, but do not lead to a sense of pain, if they are not fulfilled, the effort is intense, such pleasures are due to idle imagination, and it is not owing to their own nature that they fail to be dispelled, but owing to the empty imaginings of the man.

For Further Reflection

1. Epicureanism is often thought of as a shallow, gluttonous, profligate life of undifferentiated pleasure, whose motto has been "Eat, drink, and be merry, for tomorrow we die" ("the pig philosophy"). Does one get this impression from Epicurus's writings?

2. Consider his view toward the fact of death: You ought not fear what never touches you. Death never touches you, for when you are, it is not; and when it is, you are not. Is this a reasonable argument against the fear of death? Why do we consider death an evil? What is the proper attitude toward death and why?

Life Is Absurd

ALBERT CAMUS

Albert Camus (1913–1960) was born in French colonial Algeria, into a poor working-class family. He was a French journalist, novelist, and philosopher who fought in the French underground during World War II and fought for courage and integrity in public life. He is most famous for his novels *The Stranger* (1942), *The Plague* (1947), and *The Fall* (1957), for which he received a Nobel Prize for literature. He was killed in a car crash in 1960. His rival existentialist, Jean-Paul Sartre, fittingly called it "an absurd death."

In this selection we see Camus's overall assessment that life is absurd, meaningless. The only important philosophical question is, why not commit suicide? Life is compared with the myth of Sisyphus, wherein that man is condemned by the gods to roll a huge stone up a mountain, watch it roll back down, and retrieve it, only to repeat the process again, endlessly.

ABSURDITY AND SUICIDE

There is but one truly serious philosophical problem, and that is suicide. Judging whether life is or is not worth living amounts to answering the fundamental question of philosophy. All the rest— whether or not the world has three dimensions, whether the mind has nine or twelve categories—comes afterwards. These are games; one must first answer. And if it is true, as Nietzsche claims, that a philosopher, to deserve our respect, must preach by example, you can appreciate the importance of that reply, for it will precede the definitive act. These are facts the heart can feel; yet they call for careful study before they become clear to the intellect.

If I ask myself how to judge that this question is more urgent than that, I reply that one judges by the actions it entails. I have never seen anyone die for the ontological argument. Galileo, who

held a scientific truth of great importance, abjured it with the greatest of ease as soon as it endangered his life. In a certain sense, he
did right.[1] That truth was not worth the stake. Whether the earth
or the sun revolves around the other is a matter of profound indifference. To tell the truth, it is a futile question. On the other hand,
I see many people die because they judge that life is not worth living. I see others paradoxically getting killed for the ideas or illusions that give them a reason for living (what is called a reason for
living is also an excellent reason for dying). I therefore conclude
that the meaning of life is the most urgent of questions. How to
answer it? On all essential problems (I mean thereby those that run
the risk of leading to death or those that intensify the passion of
living) there are probably but two methods of thought: the method
of La Palisse and the method of Don Quixote. Solely the balance
between evidence and lyricism can allow us to achieve simultaneously emotion and lucidity. In a subject at once so humble and so
heavy with emotion, the learned and classical dialectic must yield,
one can see, to a more modest attitude of mind deriving at one
and the same time from common sense and understanding.

Suicide has never been dealt with except as a social phenomenon. On the contrary, we are concerned here, at the outset, with
the relationship between individual thought and suicide. An act like
this is prepared within the silence of the heart, as is a great work
of art. The man himself is ignorant of it. One evening he pulls the
trigger or jumps. Of an apartment-building manager who had killed
himself I was told that he had lost his daughter five years before,
that he had changed greatly since, and that that experience had
"undermined" him. A more exact word cannot be imagined. Beginning to think is beginning to be undermined. Society has but little
connection with such beginnings. The worm is in man's heart. That
is where it must be sought. One must follow and understand this
fatal game that leads from lucidity in the face of existence to flight
from light. . . .

But it is hard to fix the precise instant, the subtle step when the
mind opted for death, it is easier to deduce from the act itself the
consequences it implies. In a sense, and as in melodrama, killing

---

[1]From the point of view of the relative value of truth. On the other hand,
from the point of view of virile behavior, this scholar's fragility may well
make us smile.

yourself amounts to confessing. It is confessing that life is too much for you or that you do not understand it. Let's not go too far in such analogies, however, but rather return to everyday words. It is merely confessing that that "is not worth the trouble." Living, naturally, is never easy. You continue making the gestures commanded by existence for many reasons, the first of which is habit. Dying voluntarily implies that you have recognized, even instinctively, the ridiculous character of that habit, the absence of any profound reason for living, the insane character of that daily agitation, and the uselessness of suffering.

What, then, is that incalculable feeling that deprives the mind of the sleep necessary to life? A world that can be explained even with bad reasons is a familiar world. But, on the other hand, in a universe suddenly divested of illusions and lights, man feels an alien, a stranger. His exile is without remedy since he is deprived of the memory of a lost home or the hope of a promised land. This divorce between man and his life, the actor and his setting, is properly the feeling of absurdity. All healthy men having thought of their own suicide, it can be seen, without further explanation, that there is a direct connection between this feeling and the longing for death.

The subject of this essay is precisely this relationship between the absurd and suicide, the exact degree to which suicide is a solution to the absurd. The principle can be established that for a man who does not cheat, what he believes to be true must determine his action. Belief in the absurdity of existence must then dictate his conduct. It is legitimate to wonder, clearly and without false pathos, whether a conclusion of this importance requires forsaking as rapidly as possible an incomprehensible condition. I am speaking, of course, of men inclined to be in harmony with themselves. . . .

All great deeds and all great thoughts have a ridiculous beginning. Great works are often born on a street-corner or in a restaurant's revolving door. So it is with absurdity. The absurd world more than others derives its nobility from that abject birth. In certain situations, replying "nothing" when asked what one is thinking about may be pretense in a man. Those who are loved are well aware of this. But if that reply is sincere, if it symbolizes that odd state of soul in which the void becomes eloquent, in which the chain of daily gestures is broken, in which the heart vainly seeks the link that will connect it again, then it is as it were the first sign of absurdity.

It happens that the stage sets collapse. Rising, streetcar, four hours in the office or the factory, meal, streetcar, four hours of work, meal, sleep, and Monday Tuesday Wednesday Thursday Friday and Saturday according to the same rhythm—this path is easily followed most of the time. But one day the "why" arises and everything begins in that weariness tinged with amazement. "Begins"—this is important. Weariness comes at the end of the acts of a mechanical life, but at the same time it inaugurates the impulse of consciousness. It awakens consciousness and provokes what follows. What follows is the gradual return into the chain or it is the definitive awakening. At the end of the awakening comes, in time, the consequence: suicide or recovery. In itself weariness has something sickening about it. Here, I must conclude that it is good. For everything begins with consciousness and nothing is worth anything except through it. . . .

But what does life mean in such a universe? Nothing else for the moment but indifference to the future and a desire to use up everything that is given. Belief in the meaning of life always implies a scale of values, a choice, our preferences. Belief in the absurd, according to our definitions, teaches the contrary. But this is worth examining.

Knowing whether or not one can live *without appeal* is all that interests me. I do not want to get out of my depth. This aspect of life being given me, can I adapt myself to it? Now, faced with this particular concern, belief in the absurd is tantamount to substituting the quantity of experiences for the quality. If I convince myself that this life has no other aspect than that of the absurd, if I feel that its whole equilibrium depends on that perpetual opposition between my conscious revolt and the darkness in which it struggles, if I admit that my freedom has no meaning except in relation to its limited fate, then I must say that what counts is not the best of living but the most living. . . .

On the one hand the absurd teaches that all experiences are unimportant, and on the other it urges toward the greatest quantity of experiences. How, then, can one fail to do as so many of those men I was speaking of earlier—choose the form of life that brings us the most possible of that human matter, thereby introducing a scale of values that on the other hand one claims to reject?

But again it is the absurd and its contradictory life that teaches us. For the mistake is thinking that that quantity of experiences depends on the circumstances of our life when it depends solely on us. Here we have to be oversimple. To two men living the same number of years, the world always provides the same sum of experiences. It is up to us to be conscious of them. Being aware of one's life, one's revolt, one's freedom, and to the maximum, is living, and to the maximum. Where lucidity dominates, the scale of values becomes useless. . . .

THE MYTH OF SISYPHUS

The gods had condemned Sisyphus to ceaselessly rolling a rock to the top of a mountain, whence the stone would fall back of its own weight. They had thought with some reason that there is no more dreadful punishment than futile and hopeless labor.

If one believes Homer, Sisyphus was the wisest and most prudent of mortals. According to another tradition, however, he was disposed to practice the profession of highwayman. I see no contradiction in this. Opinions differ as to the reasons why he became the futile laborer of the underworld. To begin with, he is accused of a certain levity in regard to the gods. He stole their secrets. Ægina, the daughter of Æsopus, was carried off by Jupiter. The father was shocked by that disappearance and complained to Sisyphus. He, who knew of the abduction, offered to tell about it on condition that Æsopus would give water to the citadel of Corinth. To the celestial thunderbolts he preferred the benediction of water. He was punished for this in the underworld. Homer tells us also that Sisyphus had put Death in chains. Pluto could not endure the sight of his deserted, silent empire. He dispatched the god of war, who liberated Death from the hands of her conqueror.

It is said also that Sisyphus, being near to death, rashly wanted to test his wife's love. He ordered her to cast his unburied body into the middle of the public square. Sisyphus woke up in the underworld. And there, annoyed by an obedience so contrary to human love, he obtained from Pluto permission to return to earth in order to chastise his wife. But when he had seen again the face of this world, enjoyed water and sun, warm stones and the sea, he no longer wanted to go back to the infernal darkness. Recalls, signs of anger, warnings were of no avail. Many years more he lived facing the curve of the gulf, the sparkling sea, and the smiles of earth. A decree of the gods was necessary. Mercury came and seized the impudent man by the collar and, snatching him from his joys, led him forcibly back to the underworld, where his rock was ready for him.

You have already grasped that Sisyphus is the absurd hero. He *is,* as much through his passions as through his torture. His scorn of the gods, his hatred of death, and his passion for life won him that unspeakable penalty in which the whole being is exerted toward accomplishing nothing. This is the price that must be paid for the passions of this earth. Nothing is told us about Sisyphus in the underworld. Myths are made for the imagination to breathe life into them. As for this myth, one sees merely the whole effort of a body straining to raise the huge stone, to roll it and push it up a slope a hundred times over; one sees the face screwed up, the cheek tight against the stone, the shoulder bracing the clay-covered mass, the foot wedging it, the fresh start with arms outstretched, the wholly human security of two earth-clotted hands. At the very end of his long effort measured by skyless space and time without depth, the purpose is achieved. Then Sisyphus watches the stone rush down in a few moments toward that lower world whence he will have to push it up again toward the summit. He goes back down to the plain.

It is during that return, that pause, that Sisyphus interests me. A face that toils so close to stones is already stone itself! I see that man going back down with a heavy yet measured step toward the torment of which he will never know the end. That hour like a breathing-space which returns as surely as his suffering, that is the hour of consciousness. At each of those moments when he leaves the heights and gradually sinks toward the lairs of the gods, he is superior to his fate. He is stronger than his rock.

If this myth is tragic, that is because its hero is conscious. Where would his torture be, indeed, if at every step the hope of succeeding upheld him? The workman of today works every day in his life at the same tasks, and this fate is no less absurd. But it is tragic only at the rare moments when it becomes conscious. Sisyphus, proletarian of the gods, powerless and rebellious, knows the whole extent of his wretched condition: it is what he thinks of during his descent. The lucidity that was to constitute his torture at the same time crowns his victory. There is no fate that cannot be surmounted by scorn.

If the descent is thus sometimes performed in sorrow, it can also take place in joy. This word is not too much. Again I fancy Sisyphus returning toward his rock, and the sorrow was in the beginning. When the images of earth cling too tightly to memory, when the call of happiness becomes too insistent, it happens that melancholy rises in man's heart: this is the rock's victory, this is the rock itself. The boundless grief is too heavy to bear. These are our nights of Gethsemane. But crushing truths perish from being acknowledged. Thus, Œdipus at the outset obeys fate without knowing it. But from the moment he knows, his tragedy begins. Yet at the same moment, blind and desperate, he realizes that the only bond linking him to the world is the cool hand of a girl. Then a tremendous remark rings out: "Despite so many ordeals, my advanced age and the nobility of my soul make me conclude that all is well." Sophocles' Œdipus, like Dostoevsky's Kirilov, thus gives the recipe for the absurd victory. Ancient wisdom confirms modern heroism.

One does not discover the absurd without being tempted to write a manual of happiness. "What! by such narrow ways—?" There is but one world, however. Happiness and the absurd are two sons of the same earth. They are inseparable. It would be a mistake to say that happiness necessarily springs from the absurd discovery. It happens as well that the feeling of the absurd springs from happiness. "I conclude that all is well," says Œdipus, and that remark is sacred. It echoes in the wild and limited universe of man. It teaches that all is not, has not been, exhausted. It drives out of this world a god who had come into it with dissatisfaction and a preference for futile sufferings. It makes of fate a human matter, which must be settled among men.

All Sisyphus' silent joy is contained therein. His fate belongs to him. His rock is his thing. Likewise, the absurd man, when he contemplates his torment, silences all the idols. In the universe suddenly restored to its silence, the myriad wondering little voices of the earth rise up. Unconscious, secret calls, invitations from all the faces, they are the necessary reverse and price of victory. There is no sun without shadow, and it is essential to know the night. The absurd man says yes and his effort will henceforth be unceasing. If there is a personal fate, there is no higher destiny, or at least there is but one which he concludes is inevitable and despicable. For the rest, he knows himself to be the master of his days. At that subtle moment when man glances backward over his life, Sisyphus returning toward his rock, in that slight pivoting he contemplates that series of unrelated actions which becomes his fate, created by him, combined under his memory's eye and soon sealed by his death. Thus, convinced of the wholly human origin of all that is human, a blind man eager to see who knows that the night has no end, he is still on the go. The rock is still rolling.

I leave Sisyphus at the foot of the mountain! One always finds one's burden again. But Sisyphus teaches the higher fidelity that negates the gods and raises rocks. He too concludes that all is well. This universe henceforth without a master seems to him neither sterile nor futile. Each atom of that stone, each mineral flake of that night-filled mountain, in itself forms a world. The struggle itself toward the heights is enough to fill a man's heart. One must imagine Sisyphus happy.

For Further Reflection

1. Is life absurd, as Camus insists? Does Camus give good reasons for this claim? What leads him to this pessimistic conclusion?

2. Is Camus being irreverent in asking such an outrageous question as "Why not commit suicide"?

3. Why does Camus say that Sisyphus must be imagined to be happy?

4. Compare Camus with Epicurus. In what ways are their views similar? In what ways different?

Religion Gives Meaning to Life

LOIS HOPE WALKER

Lois Hope Walker is the pen name of an author who wishes to remain anonymous. In this essay Walker argues that religion, specifically theistic religion, gives special meaning to life, unavailable in secular world views. Furthermore, the autonomy that secularists prize (sometimes value it beyond its worth) is not significantly diminished by religious faith.

Several years ago during a class break, I was discussing the significance of religion in our society with a few students in the college lounge. I, at that time an agnostic, was conceding to a devout Christian that it would be nice if theism were true, for then the world would not be simply a matter of chance and necessity, a sad tale with a sadder ending. Instead, "the world would be personal, a gift from our heavenly Father, who provides a basis for meaning and purpose." A mature woman from another class, whom I knew to be an atheist, overheard my remarks, charged through a group of coffee drinkers and angrily snapped at me, "That is the most disgusting thing I've ever heard!" I inquired why she thought this, and she replied, "Religion keeps humans from growing up. We don't need a big Daddy in the sky. We need to grow up and become our own parents."

I recalled Nietzsche's dictum that now that "God is dead," now that we have killed the Holy One, we must ourselves become gods to seem worthy of the deed. The atheist woman was prizing autonomy over meaning and claiming that religion did just the opposite.

In other words, she held two theses:

(1) It is more important to be free or autonomous than to have a grand meaning or purpose to life.

(2) Religion provides a grand meaning or purpose to life, but it does not allow humans to be free or autonomous.

I've thought a lot about that woman's response over the years. I think that she is wrong on both counts. In this essay I will defend religion against her two theses and try to show that meaning and autonomy are both necessary or important ingredients for an ideal existence and that they are compatible within a religious framework.

Let me begin with the first thesis, that it is more important to be free than that there be meaning in life. First let us define our terms. By "autonomy" I mean self-governing, the ability to make choices on the basis of good reasons rather than being coerced by threats or forces from without.

By "meaning" in life I mean that life has a purpose. There is some intrinsic rationale or plan to it. Now this purpose can be good, bad, or indifferent. An example of something with a bad purpose is the activity of poisoning a reservoir on which a community depends for its sustenance. An example of something with an indifferent purpose might be pacing back and forth to pass the time of day (it is arguable that this is bad or good depending on the options and context, and if you think that then either choose your own example or dismiss the category of indifferent purpose). An example of a good purpose is digging a well in order to provide water to a community in need of water.

Now it seems to be the case that, as a value, autonomy is superior to indifferent and bad purposes, since it has positive value but these other two categories do not. Autonomy may be more valuable to us than some good purposes, but it does not seem to be superior to *all* good purposes. While it may be more valuable to be free than to have this or that incidental purpose in life, freedom cannot really be understood apart from the notion of purposiveness. To be free is to be able to do some act A, when you want to, in order to reach some goal G. So the two ideas are related.

But the atheist woman meant more than this. She meant that if she had to choose whether to have free will or to live in a world that had a governing providential hand, she would choose the former. But this seems to make two mistakes. (1) It makes autonomy into an unjustified absolute and (2) it creates a false dilemma.

(1) Consider two situations: In situation A you are as free as you are now (say you have 100 units of autonomy—call these units "autonotoms") but are deeply miserable because you are locked in a large and interesting room which is being slowly filled with poisonous gas. You can do what ever you want for five more minutes but then you will be dead. In situation B, however, you have only 95 autonotoms (that is, there are a few things that you are unable to do in this world—say commit adultery or kill your neighbor) but the room is being filled with sunshine and fresh air. Which world would you choose? I would choose situation B, for autonomy, it seems to me, is not the only value in the universe, nor is it always the overriding value. I think most of us would be willing to give up a few autonotoms for an enormous increase in happiness. And I think that a world with a good purpose would be one in which we would be willing to give up a few bits of freedom. If we were told that we could eliminate poverty, crime, and great suffering in the world by each sacrificing one autonotom, wouldn't we do this? If so, then autonomy is not an absolute which always overrides every other value. It is one important value among others.

I turn to the atheist's second thesis, that religion always holds purpose as superior to autonomy. I think that this is a misunderstanding of what the best types of religion try to do. As Jesus said in John 8:32, "Ye shall know the truth and the truth shall set you free." Rather than seeing freedom and meaning as opposites, theism sees them as inextricably bound together. Since it claims to offer us the truth about the world, and since having true beliefs is important in reaching one's goals, it follows that our autonomy is actually heightened in having the truth about the purpose of life. If we know why we are here and what the options in our destiny really are, we will be able to choose more intelligently than the blind who lead the blind in ignorance.

Indeed theistic religion (I have in mind Judaism, Christianity, and Islam, but this could apply to many forms of Hinduism and African religions as well) claims to place before us options of the greatest importance, so that if it is true the world is far better (infinitely better?) than if it is not.

Let me elaborate on this point. If theism is true and there is a benevolent supreme being governing the universe, the following eight theses are true.

1. We have a satisfying explanation of the origins and sustenance of the universe. We are not the product of chance and necessity or an impersonal big bang, but of a Heavenly Being who cares about us. As William James says, if religion is true, "the universe is no longer a mere *It* to us, but a *Thou* . . . and any relation that may be possible from person to person might be possible here." We can take comfort in knowing that the visible world is part of a more spiritual universe from which it draws its meaning and that there is, in spite of evil, an essential harmonious relation between our world and the transcendent reality.

Here is the nub of the matter. Is the universe purposeful or merely a blind collocation of particles in motion? Science does not answer this question, though scientism, the secular naturalism, assumes that the world lacks a telos—it is blind matter in motion. But theism tells us that all things have a purpose, that the universe was created at a point in time and that it will proceed in a lawlike manner to a prescribed end. Consider the naturalist view of the universe eloquently set forth in Bertrand Russell's classic essay "A Free Man's Worship":

> That man is the product of causes which had no prevision of the end they were achieving; that his origin, his growth, his hopes and fears, his loves and beliefs are but the outcome of accidental collocations of atoms; that no fire, no heroism, no intensity of thought

and feeling, can preserve an individual life beyond the grave; that all the labors of the ages, all the devotion, all the inspiration, all the noonday brightness of human genius, are destined to extinction in the vast death of the solar system, and that the whole temple of man's achievement must inevitably be buried beneath the debris of a universe in ruins—all these things, if not quite beyond dispute, are yet so nearly certain that no philosophy which rejects them can hope to stand. Only within the scaffolding of these truths, only on the firm foundation of unyielding despair, can the soul's habitation henceforth be safely built.

This is not the kind of "soul's habitation" that is worth building, let alone which can be safely built. Upon an unstable foundation, a secure edifice cannot be built, and from nothing you can only derive nothing. Our product is only as good as the material from which it is derived. From a valueless universe, objective values will not miraculously appear, nor can purpose derive from purposelessness. On the "firm foundation of unyielding despair" we can only build that which is desperate.

2. Theism holds that the universe is suffused in goodness and that good will win out over evil. We are not fighting a desperate battle alone, but God is on our side—or rather, it is possible to be on God's side in the struggle of good over evil. So you and I need not fight in vain. If the universe is meaningless, nothing will ultimately matter. Plato, Shakespeare, Mozart, Michelangelo, the Cathedral of Notre Dame, and the Sun itself will perish in oblivion. But if an Eternal Goodness exists, all will be well, all will be somehow remembered, nothing worthwhile will have been in vain.

The thought of the ultimate victory of goodness over evil, of justice over injustice, gives us confidence to carry on the fight against injustice, cruelty, and hatred, when others calculate that the odds against righteousness are too great to fight against.

3. God loves and cares for us. His love compels us, so that we have a deeper motive for morally good actions, including high altruism. We live deeply moral lives, not out of fear of hell, but out of deep gratitude to One who loves us and whom we love. We live not by impersonal rules but in relation with a Cosmic Lover, one who has our best interests in mind and is powerful enough to ensure that we are as happy as we are good.

Secularism lacks this sense of cosmic love, and it is, therefore, no accident that it fails to produce moral saints like Jesus, Maimonides, St. Francis, Father Damien, Teresa of Avila, Gandhi, Martin Luther King, Jr., and Mother Teresa. You need special love to leave a world of comfort in order to go to a desolate island to minister to lepers, as Father Damien did, or to lay down your life for another as Father Kolbe did when he took the place of a fellow prisoner in the Nazi death cell. Perhaps Ayn Rand is correct. From a secular point of view altruism is not only stupid, it is antilife, for it gives up the only thing we have, our little ego in an impersonal, indifferent world.

4. Theists have an answer to the question Why be moral? Why? Because of the love of God and because that love guarantees justice, so that you will get what you deserve—good for good and bad for bad. The good really is good for you. Secular ethics has a severe problem with the question, Why should I be moral when I can profit from wrongdoing (cheating, lying, stealing, harming another)? When I can advance myself by being an egoist, why should I obey moral rules? A hard question, to which I have never seen an entirely satisfactory secular answer. But the question is quickly satisfied by theism: a kind of karma—what you do to others will be visited upon you. If you do good, you will receive good. If you do evil, you will receive evil. Immorality is really imprudent and self-interest and altruism coincide. I don't have to worry about whether I reap exactly what I put into life's soil now, for I am confident that in the long term, I will reap as I have sown.

5. Cosmic Justice reigns in the universe. The scales are perfectly balanced so that everyone will get what he or she deserves, according to their moral merit. There is no moral luck (unless you interpret the grace which will finally prevail as a type of "luck"), but each will be judged according to how one has used one's talents (Matthew, chapter 25).

6. All persons are of equal worth. Since we have all been created in the image of God and are His children, we are all brothers and sisters. We are family and ought to treat each other benevolently as we would family members of equal worth. Indeed, modern secular moral and political systems often assume this equal worth of the individual without justifying it. But without the Parenthood of God it makes no sense to say that all persons are innately of equal value. From a perspective of intelligence and utility, Aristotle and Nietzsche are right, there are enormous inequalities, and why shouldn't the superior persons use the baser types to their advantage? In this regard, secularism, in rejecting inegalitarianism,

seems to be living off of the interest of a religious capital which it has relinquished.

7. Grace and forgiveness—a happy ending for all. All's well that ends well (the divine comedy). The moral guilt which we experience, even for the most heinous acts, can be removed, and we can be redeemed and given a new start. This is true moral liberation.

8. There is life after death. Death is not the end of the matter, but we shall live on, recognizing each other in a better world. We have eternity in our souls and are destined for a higher existence.[1] So if Hebraic-Christian theism is true, the world is a friendly home in which we are all related as siblings in one family, destined to live forever in cosmic bliss in a reality in which good defeats evil.

If theism is false and secularism is true, then there is no obvious basis for human equality, no reason to treat all people with equal respect, no simple and clear answer to the question, Why be moral even when it is not in my best interest? no sense of harmony and purpose in the universe, but "Whirl has replaced Zeus and is king" (Sophocles).

Add to this the fact that theism doesn't deprive us of any autonomy that we have in nontheistic systems. We are equally free to choose the good or the evil whether or not God exists (assuming that the notions of good and evil make sense in a non-theistic universe)—then it seems clear that the world of the theist is far better and more satisfying to us than one in which God does not exist.

Of course, the problem is that we probably do not know if theism, let alone our particular religious version of it, is true. Here I must use a Pascalean argument to press my third point that we may have an obligation or, at least, it may be a good thing, to live *as if* theism is true. That is, unless you think that theism is so improbable that we should not even consider it as a candidate for truth, we should live in such a way as to allow the virtues of theism to inspire our lives and our culture. The theistic world view is so far superior to the secular that—even though we might be agnostics or weak atheists—it is in our interest to live as though it were true, to consider each person as a child of God, of high value, to work as though God is work-

---

[1]Of course, hell is a problem here—which vitiates the whole idea somewhat, but many variations of theism (e.g., varieties of theistic Hinduism and the Christian theologians Origen, F. Maurice, and Karl Barth) hold to universal salvation in the end. Hell is only a temporary school in moral education—I think that this is a plausible view.

ing with us in the battle of Good over evil, and to build a society based on these ideas. It is good then to gamble on God. Religion gives us a purpose to life and a basis for morality that is too valuable to dismiss lightly. It is a heritage that we may use to build a better civilization and one which we neglect at our own peril.

For Further Reflection

1. Does Walker exaggerate the importance of religion for a meaningful life? How would a secularist respond?

2. Karl Marx said that religion is the opium of the people. It deludes them into thinking that all will be well with the world, leading to passive acceptance of evil and injustice. Is there some truth in Marx's dictum? How would Walker respond to this?

The Human Search for Meaning
Reflections on Auschwitz

VIKTOR FRANKL

Viktor Frankl (1905–1997) was professor of psychiatry and neurology at the University of Vienna Medical School and is the founder of logotherapy, the psychological therapy based on the idea that human beings must find a meaning to their lives in order to function. It is based on Nietzsche's dictum "He who has a *why* to live for, can bear with almost any *how*." Frankl spent three years in Nazi concentration camps, including Auschwitz. His entire family was exterminated by the Nazis. In this selection Frankl reflects on the search for meaning in the concentration camp.

What did the prisoner dream about most frequently? Of bread, cake, cigarettes, and nice warm baths. The lack of having these simple desires satisfied led him to seek wish-fulfillment in dreams. Whether these dreams did any good is another matter; the dreamer had to wake from them to the reality of camp life, and to the terrible contrast between that and his dream illusions.

I shall never forget how I was roused one night by the groans of a fellow prisoner, who threw himself about in his sleep, obviously having a horrible nightmare. Since I had always been especially sorry for people who suffered from fearful dreams or deliria, I wanted to wake the poor man. Suddenly I drew back the hand which was ready to shake him, frightened at the thing I was about to do. At that moment I became intensely conscious of the fact that no dream, no matter how horrible, could be as bad as the reality of the camp which surrounded us, and to which I was about to recall him. . . .

When the last layers of subcutaneous fat had vanished, and we looked like skeletons disguised with skin and rags, we could watch our bodies beginning to devour themselves. The organism digested its own protein, and the muscles disappeared. Then the body had no powers of resistance left. One after another the members of the little community in our hut died. . . .

In attempting this psychological presentation and a psychopathological explanation of the typical characteristics of a concentration camp inmate, I may give the impression that the human being is completely and unavoidably influenced by his surroundings. (In this case the surroundings being the unique structure of camp life, which forced the prisoner to conform his conduct to a certain set pattern.) But what about human liberty? Is there no spiritual freedom in regard to behavior and reaction to any given surroundings? Is that theory true which would have us believe that man is no more than a product of many conditional and environmental factors—be they of a biological, psychological or sociological nature? Is man but an accidental product of these? Most important, do the prisoners' reactions to the singular world of the concentration camp prove that man cannot escape the influences of his surroundings? Does man have no choice of action in the face of such circumstances?

We can answer these questions from experience as well as on principle. The experiences of camp life show that man does have a choice of action. There were enough examples, often of a heroic nature, which proved that apathy could be overcome, irritability suppressed. Man *can* preserve a vestige of spiritual freedom, of independence of mind, even in such terrible conditions of psychic and physical stress.

We who lived in concentration camps can remember the men who walked through the huts comforting others, giving away their last piece of bread. They may have been few in number, but they offer sufficient proof that everything can be taken from a man but one thing: the last of the human freedoms—to choose one's attitude in any given set of circumstances, to choose one's own way.

And there were always choices to make. Every day, every hour, offered the opportunity to make a decision, a decision which determined whether you would or would not submit to those powers which threatened to rob you of your very self, your inner freedom; which determined whether or not you would become the plaything of circumstance, renouncing freedom and dignity to become molded into the form of the typical inmate.

Seen from this point of view, the mental reactions of the inmates of a concentration camp must seem more to us than the mere expression of certain physical and sociological conditions. Even though conditions such as lack of sleep, insufficient food and various mental stresses may suggest that the inmates were bound to react in certain ways, in the final analysis it becomes clear that the sort of person the prisoner became was the result of an inner decision, and not the result of camp influences alone. Fundamentally, therefore, any man can, even under such circumstances, decide what shall become of him—mentally and spiritually. He may retain his human dignity even in a concentration camp. Dostoevski said once, "There is only one thing that I dread: not to be worthy of my sufferings." These words frequently came to my mind after I became acquainted with those martyrs whose behavior in camp, whose suffering and death, bore witness to the fact that the last inner freedom cannot be lost. It can be said that they were worthy of their sufferings; the way they bore their suffering was a genuine inner achievement. It is this spiritual freedom—which cannot be taken away—that makes life meaningful and purposeful.

An active life serves the purpose of giving man the opportunity to realize values in creative work, while a passive life of enjoyment affords him the opportunity to obtain fulfillment in experiencing beauty, art, or nature. But there is also purpose in that life which is almost barren of both creation and enjoyment and which admits of but one possibility of high moral behavior: namely, in man's attitude to his existence, an existence restricted by external forces. A creative life and a life of enjoyment are banned to him. But not only creativeness and enjoyment are meaningful. If there is a meaning in life at all, then there must be a meaning in suffering. Suffering is an ineradicable part of life, even as fate and death. Without suffering and death human life cannot be complete.

The way in which a man accepts his fate and all the suffering it entails, the way in which he takes up his cross, gives him ample opportunity—even under the most difficult circumstances—to add a deeper meaning to his life. It may remain brave, dignified and unselfish. Or in the bitter fight for self-preservation he may forget his human dignity and become no more than an animal. Here lies the chance for a man either to make use of or to forego the opportunities of attaining the moral values that a difficult situation may afford him. And this decides whether he is worthy of his sufferings or not.

Do not think that these considerations are unworldly and too far removed from real life. It is true that only a few people are capable of reaching such high moral standards. Of the prisoners only a few kept their full inner liberty and obtained those values which their suffering afforded, but even one such example is sufficient proof that man's inner strength may raise him above his outward fate. Such men are not only in concentration camps. Everywhere man is confronted with fate, with the chance of achieving something through his own suffering. . . .

A man who let himself decline because he could not see any future goal found himself occupied with retrospective thoughts. In a different connection, we have already spoken of the tendency there was to look into the past, to help make the present, with all its horrors, less real. But in robbing the present of its reality there lay a certain danger. It became easy to overlook the opportunities to make something positive of camp life, opportunities which really did exist. Regarding our "provisional existence" as unreal was in itself an important factor in causing the prisoners to lose their hold on life; everything in a way became pointless. Such people forgot that often it is just such an exceptionally difficult external situation which gives man the opportunity to grow spiritually beyond himself. Instead of taking the camp's difficulties as a test of their inner strength, they did not take their life seriously and despised it as something of no consequence. They preferred to close their eyes and to live in the past. Life for such people became meaningless.

Naturally only a few people were capable of reaching great spiritual heights. But a few were given the chance to attain human greatness even through their apparent worldly failure and death, an accomplishment which in ordinary circumstances they would never have achieved. To the others of us, the mediocre and the half-hearted, the words of Bismarck could be applied: "Life is like being at the dentist. You always think that the worst is still to come, and yet it is over already." Varying this, we could say that most men in a concentration camp believed that the real opportunities of life had passed. Yet, in reality, there was an opportunity and a challenge. One could make a victory of those experiences, turning life into an inner triumph, or one could ignore the challenge and simply vegetate, as did a majority of the prisoners.

Any attempt at fighting the camp's psychopathological influence on the prisoner by psychotherapeutic or psychohygienic methods had to aim at giving him inner strength by pointing out to him a future goal to which he could look forward. Instinctively some of the prisoners attempted to find one on their own. It is a peculiarity of man that he can only live by looking to the future—*sub specie aeternitatis*. And this is his salvation in the most difficult moments of his existence, although he sometimes has to force his mind to the task. . . .

The prisoner who had lost faith in the future—his future—was doomed. With his loss of belief in the future, he also lost his spiritual hold; he let himself decline and became subject to mental and physical decay. Usually this happened quite suddenly, in the form of a crisis, the symptoms of which were familiar to the experienced camp inmate. We all feared this moment—not for ourselves, which would have been pointless, but for our friends. Usually it began with the prisoner refusing one morning to get dressed and wash or to go out on the parade grounds. No entreaties, no blows, no threats had any effect. He just lay there, hardly moving. If this crisis was brought about by an illness, he refused to be taken to the sick-bay or to do anything to help himself. He simply gave up. There he remained, lying in his own excreta, and nothing bothered him any more.

I once had a dramatic demonstration of the close link between the loss of faith in the future and this dangerous giving up. F——, my senior block warden, a fairly well-known composer and librettist, confided in me one day: "I would like to tell you something, Doctor. I have had a strange dream. A voice told me that I could wish for something, that I should only say what I wanted to know, and all my questions would be answered. What do you think I asked? That I would like to know when the war would be over for me. You know what I mean, Doctor—for me! I wanted to know when we, when our camp, would be liberated and our sufferings come to an end."

"And when did you have this dream?" I asked.

"In February, 1945," he answered. It was then the beginning of March.

"What did your dream voice answer?"

Furtively he whispered to me, "March thirtieth."

When F—— told me about his dream, he was still full of hope and convinced that the voice of his dream would be right. But as the promised day drew nearer, the war news which reached our camp made it appear very unlikely that we would be free on the promised date. On March twenty-ninth, F—— suddenly became ill and ran a high temperature. On March thirtieth, the day his prophecy had told him that the war and suffering would be over for him, he became delirious and lost consciousness. On March thirty-first, he was dead. To all outward appearances, he had died of typhus.

Those who know how close the connection is between the state of mind of a man—his courage and hope, or lack of them—and the state of immunity of his body will understand that the sudden loss of hope and courage can have a deadly effect. The ultimate cause of my friend's death was that the expected liberation did not come and he was severely disappointed. This suddenly lowered his body's resistance against the latent typhus infection. His faith in the future and his will to live had become paralyzed and his body fell victim to illness—and thus the voice of his dream was right after all.

The observations of this one case and the conclusion drawn from them are in accordance with something that was drawn to my attention by the chief doctor of our concentration camp. The death rate in the week between Christmas, 1944, and New Year's, 1945, increased in camp beyond all previous experience. In his opinion, the explanation for this increase did not lie in the harder working conditions or the deterioration of our food supplies or a change of weather or new epidemics. It was simply that the majority of the prisoners had lived in the naïve hope that they would be home again by Christmas. As the time drew near and there was no encouraging news, the prisoners lost courage and disappointment overcame them. This had a dangerous influence on their powers of resistance and a great number of them died.

As we said before, any attempt to restore a man's inner strength in the camp had first to succeed in showing him some future goal. Nietzsche's words, "He who has a *why* to live for can bear with almost any *how*," could be the guiding motto for all psychotherapeutic and psychohygienic efforts regarding prisoners. Whenever there was an opportunity for it, one had to give them a *why*—an aim—for their lives, in order to strengthen them to bear the terrible *how* of their existence. Woe to him who saw no more sense in his life, no aim, no purpose, and therefore no point in carrying on. He was soon lost. The typical reply with which such a man rejected all encouraging arguments was, "I have nothing to expect from life any more." What sort of answer can one give to that?

What was really needed was a fundamental change in our attitude toward life. We had to learn ourselves and, furthermore, we had to teach the despairing men, that it did not really matter what we expected from life, but rather what life expected from us. We needed to stop asking about the meaning of life, and instead to think of ourselves as those who were being questioned by life—daily and hourly. Our answer must consist, not in talk and meditation, but in right action and in right conduct. Life ultimately means taking the responsibility to find the right answer to its problems and to fulfill the tasks which it constantly sets for each individual.

These tasks, and therefore the meaning of life, differ from man to man, and from moment to moment. Thus it is impossible to define the meaning of life in a general way. Questions about the meaning of life can never be answered by sweeping statements. "Life" does not mean something vague, but something very real and concrete, just as life's tasks are also very real and concrete. They form man's destiny, which is different and unique for each individual. No man and no destiny can be compared with any other man or any other destiny. No situation repeats itself, and each situation calls for a different response. Sometimes the situation in which a man finds himself may require him to shape his own fate by action. At other times it is more advantageous for him to make use of an opportunity for contemplation and to realize assets in this way. Sometimes man may be required simply to accept fate, to bear his cross. Every situation is distinguished by its uniqueness, and there is always only one right answer to the problem posed by the situation at hand.

When a man finds that it is his destiny to suffer, he will have to accept his suffering as his task; his single and unique task. He will have to acknowledge the fact that even in suffering he is unique and alone in the universe. No one can relieve him of his suffering or suffer in his place. His unique opportunity lies in the way in which he bears his burden.

For us, as prisoners, these thoughts were not speculations far removed from reality. They were the only thoughts that could be of help to us. They kept us from despair, even when there seemed to be no chance of coming out of it alive. Long ago we had passed the stage of asking what was the meaning of life, a naïve query which understands life as the attaining of some aim through the active creation of something of value. For us, the meaning of life embraced the wider cycles of life and death, of suffering and of dying.

Once the meaning of suffering had been revealed to us, we refused to minimize or alleviate the camp's tortures by ignoring them or harboring false illusions and entertaining artificial optimism. Suffering had become a task on which we did not want to turn our backs. We had realized its hidden opportunities for achievement, the opportunities which caused the poet Rilke to write, "*Wie viel ist aufzuleiden!*" (How much suffering there is to get through!) Rilke spoke of "getting through suffering" as others would talk of "getting through work." There was plenty of suffering for us to get through. Therefore, it was necessary to face up to the full amount of suffering, trying to keep moments of weakness and furtive tears to a minimum. But there was no need to be ashamed of tears, for tears bore witness that a man had the greatest of courage, the courage to suffer. Only very few realized that. Shamefacedly some confessed occasionally that they had wept, like the comrade who answered my question of how he had gotten over his edema, by confessing, "I have wept it out of my system." . . .

Freedom . . . is not the last word. Freedom is only part of the story and half of the truth. Freedom is but the negative aspect of the whole phenomenon whose positive aspect is responsibility. In fact, freedom is in danger of degenerating into mere arbitrariness unless it is lived in terms of responsibility. That is why *I recommend that the Statue of Liberty on the East Coast be supplemented by a Statue of Responsibility on the West Coast.*

For Further Reflection

1. What, according to Frankl, are the important ingredients in living a truly human life? Do you agree? Frankl's ideas are relevant to concentration camp experience, but are they the best ones for everyday existence?

2. Frankl believes that we must discover a meaning to our lives in order to endure great evil. But could that meaning itself be an evil?

The Four Noble Truths

SIDDHARTHA GAUTAMA, THE BUDDHA

Siddhartha Gautama, (c. 563–483 B.C.) was born to a noble family in North India, near the Himalaya Mountains. He was protected by his family from suffering, but one day he wandered out and beheld a beggar and sick people. He was filled with sorrow at the fragility of human existence, at its decay, disease, and death. He left his family and sought enlightenment. Eventually, he claimed he had been enlightened and took on the name of *Buddha*, meaning "The Awakened One." He set forth four noble truths and drew followers to himself, thus instituting the Buddhist religion. The truths are:

1. Life is suffering.
2. Suffering involves a chain of causes.
3. Suffering can cease.
4. There is a path to such cessation.

From *The Wisdom of the Early Buddhists,* translated by Geoffrey Parrinder (London: Sheldon Press, 1977). Reprinted by permission.

The last of these contains eight substages, which lead to Nirvana, final liberation from suffering.

This selection consists of two sermons on the Four Noble Truths.

Siddhartha had been fasting for several weeks, seeking perfect peace. He was weak, his body thin, his ribs stuck out "like the beams of an old shed," his eyes sank low "like a deep well." He saw a lovely spot by a Bo-tree and sat down under it. He took some rice milk and ate some beans. Suddenly he found himself entering a blissful state of meditation, then a second stage, beyond reasoning. Then he entered the third stage, "attentive and conscious, with equal mind to joy or aversion." Finally, he "entered the fourth stage, beyond pain and pleasure, entirely pure and mindful." Buddha became enlightened, knowing all wisdom, past, present, and future in a divine manner. This was his Nirvana, the extinction of all craving and self-indulgence. A monk noticed that his face glowed. He replied:

I am the Victor over all,
Omniscient and pure in all,
Freed from craving, leaving all,
Know by myself and point to none.

To turn the Wheel of Truth
Benares I shall find,
To beat the Drum of No more Death
Before a world that's blind.

When the Buddha arrived at Benares the five monks were in a deer park at Sarnath. Seeing him coming they agreed not to greet or serve him, since he had given up the ascetic life and gone back to the life of abundance. But as he drew near they were not able to keep their agreement; some made a seat ready, some brought water to wash his feet, others took his bowl and robe, and all called him "Your Reverence." The Buddha replied, Do not call me "Your Reverence." The Buddha is perfect, fully self-awakened. I have found the deathless and I teach the Truth. If you follow this you will soon realize here and now the goal of religion for which young men of good family leave home for the homeless life, and you will abide in it.

To the five monks the Buddha preached his first sermon, Setting in Motion the Wheel of Truth: avoiding the extremes of sensuality and self-torture, the Buddha has gained the knowledge of the Middle Way, which brings insight, calm and Nirvana. What is the Middle Way? It is the Noble Eightfold Path.

Consider the Four Noble Truths:

(1) This is the Noble Truth of Pain: birth, age, sickness, death, sorrow and despair are painful.
(2) This is the Noble Truth of the Cause of Pain: it is craving, which leads to rebirth, pleasure and passion, existence and non-existence.
(3) This is the Noble Truth of the Cessation of Pain: it is the cessation of craving without remainder, forsaking detachment and release from it.
(4) This is the Noble Truth of the Way that leads to the Cessation of Pain: it is the Noble Eightfold Path.

What is the Noble Eightfold Path? It is:

1. Right Views
2. Right Motive
3. Right Speech
4. Right Action
5. Right Livelihood
6. Right Effort
7. Right Mindfulness
8. Right Contemplation

Right Views give the knowledge of Pain, its Cause, Cessation, and the Path.
Right Motive gives aspiration to renunciation and benevolence.
Right Speech abstains from lies and slander.
Right Action abstains from stealing, killing and self-indulgence.
Right Livelihood follows right pursuits.
Right Effort turns against evil states and toward good.
Right Mindfulness looks on body and mind with self-control.
Right Contemplation rises above evil and abides in equanimity and bliss. . . .

The body is not the soul, for if it were, the body would not be subject to sickness, but it is not possible to say of the body, let it be thus or not thus. The feelings are not the soul, perception is not the soul, the elements are not the soul, consciousness is not the soul, for the same reasons.

What do you think, monks? Is the body permanent or impermanent? They replied: it is impermanent. The Buddha asked: is the impermanent painful or pleasant? They answered: It is painful. The Buddha retorted: But is it fitting to consider what is impermanent and painful as myself and the soul? They answered, No.

The Buddha asked the same questions about other feelings, perception, the elements and the consciousness. In none of them was the soul found. Then the five monks rejoiced at this teaching and their hearts were freed from faults.

On another occasion the Buddha was dwelling at Savatthi, when a venerable Malunkyaputta, being in seclusion and meditation, presented the following considerations: "These theories which the Blessed One has left unexplained, has set aside and rejected—that the world is eternal, that the world is not eternal, that the world is finite, that the world is infinite, that the soul and the body are identical, that the soul is one thing and the body another, that the saint both exists and does not exist after death—these the Blessed One does not explain to me. And the fact that the Blessed One does not explain them to me does not please me nor suit me. Therefore I will come close to the Blessed One. If the Blessed One will not explain to me, in that case I will abandon religious training and return to the lesser life of a layman."

Then the venerable Malunkyaputta arose at eventide from his seclusion, and drew near to where the Blessed One was; and having drawn near and greeted the Blessed One, he sat down respectfully at one side. And seated respectfully at one side, the venerable Malunkyaputta spoke to the Blessed One as follows:

"Reverend Sir, it happened to me, as I was just now in seclusion, and plunged in meditation, that a consideration presented itself to my mind, as follows. . . .

"If the Blessed One knows that the world is eternal, let the Blessed One explain to me that the world is eternal; if the Blessed One knows that the world is not eternal, let the Blessed One explain to me that the world is not eternal. If the Blessed One does not know either that the world is eternal or that the world is not eternal, the only upright thing for one who does not know, or who has not that insight, is to say, 'I do not know; I have not that insight.'" . . .

"Pray, Malunkyaputta, did I ever say to you, 'Come, Malunkya-putta, lead the religious life under me, and I will explain to you either that the world is eternal, or that the world is not eternal . . . or that the saint neither exists nor does not exist after death'?"

"Nay, verily, Reverend Sir."

"Malunkyaputta, any one who should say, 'I will not lead the religious life under the Blessed One until the Blessed One shall explain to me either that the world is eternal, or that the world is not eternal . . . or that the saint neither exists nor does not exist after death'—that person would die, Malunkyaputta, before the Perfect One had ever explained this to him.

"It is as if, Malunkyaputta, a man had been wounded by an arrow thickly smeared with poison, and his friends and companions, his relatives and kinsfolk, were to procure for him a physician or surgeon; and the sick man were to say, 'I will not have this arrow taken out until I have learnt whether the man who wounded me belonged to the warrior caste, or to the Brahmin caste, or to the agricultural caste, or to the menial caste.'

"Or again if he were to say, 'I will not have this arrow taken out until I have learnt the name of the man who wounded me, and to what clan he belongs.'

"Or again if he were to say, 'I will not have this arrow taken out until I have learnt whether the man who wounded me was tall, or short, or of the middle height.' . . .

"That man would die, Malunkyaputta, without ever having learnt this . . .

"The religious life, Malunkyaputta, does not depend on the dogma that the world is eternal; nor does the religious life, Malunkyaputta, depend on the dogma that the world is not eternal. Whether the dogma obtain, Malunkyaputta, that the world is eternal, or that the world is not eternal, there still remain birth, old age, death, sorrow, lamentation, misery, grief, and despair, for the extinction of which in the present life I am prescribing . . .

"Accordingly, Malunkyaputta, bear always in mind what it is that I have not explained, and what it is that I have explained. And what, Malunkyaputta, have I not explained? I have not explained, Malunkyaputta, that the world is eternal; I have not explained that the world is not eternal; I have not explained that the world is finite; I have not explained that the world is infinite; I have not explained that the soul and the body are identical; I have not explained that the soul is one thing and the body another; I have not explained that the saint exists after death; I have not explained that the saint does not exist after death; I have not explained that the saint both exists and does not exist after death; I have not explained that the saint neither exists nor does not exist after death. And why, Malunkyaputta, have I not explained this? Because, Malunkyaputta, this profits not, nor has to do with the fundamentals of religion, nor tends to aversion, absence of passion, cessation, quiescence, the supernatural faculties, supreme wisdom, and Nirvana; therefore have I not explained it.

"And what, Malunkyaputta, have I explained? Misery, Malunkyaputta, have I explained; the origin of misery have I explained; the cessation of misery have I explained; and the path leading to the cessation of misery have I explained. And why, Malunkyaputta, have I explained this? Because, Malunkyaputta, this does profit, has to do with the fundamentals of religion, and tends to aversion, absence of passion, cessation, quiescence, knowledge, supreme wisdom, and Nirvana; therefore have I explained it."

For Further Reflection

1. Analyze Buddha's philosophy of life. What gives life meaning? What are the Four Noble Truths, and what do they mean?

2. Buddhism, like Hinduism whence it arose, believes in *karma,* the idea that our actions in this life will have an effect on who we become and what happens to us in the next. If you do good, you will be born into a higher consciousness; if you do bad, into a lower consciousness, perhaps a nonhuman animal. That is, there is a causal relation between actions and future existence. Do you see any evidence for this doctrine?

The Experience Machine

ROBERT NOZICK

Robert Nozick (1936–2000) was a professor of philosophy at Harvard University. In this selection from his *Anarchy, State, and Utopia,* he argues against the hedonism of Bentham, for if pleasure were our sole value, we would have a conclusive reason to plug into an experience machine. The fact that most of us are revolted by this idea is good evidence against the claims of hedonism, as well as for a wider view of what is good.

There are also substantial puzzles when we ask what matters other than how *people's* experiences feel "from the inside." Suppose there were an experience machine that would give you any experience you desired. Superduper neuropsychologists could stimulate your brain so that you would think and feel you were writing a great novel, or making a friend, or reading an interesting book. All the time you would be floating in a tank, with electrodes attached to your brain. Should you plug into this machine for life, preprogramming your life's experiences? If you are worried about missing out on desirable experiences, we can suppose that business enterprises have researched thoroughly the lives of many others. You can pick and choose from their large library or smorgasbord of such experiences, selecting your life's experiences for, say, the next two years. After two years have passed, you will have ten minutes or ten hours out of the tank, to select the experiences of your *next* two years. Of course, while in the tank you won't know that you're there; you'll think it's all actually happening. Others can also plug in to have the experiences they want, so there's no need to stay unplugged to serve them. (Ignore problems such as who will service the machines if everyone plugs in.) Would you plug in? *What else can matter to us, other than how our lives feel from the inside?* Nor should you refrain because of the few moments of distress between the moment you've decided and the moment you're plugged. What's a few moments of distress compared to a lifetime of bliss (if that's what you choose), and why feel any distress at all if your decision *is* the best one?

What does matter to us in addition to our experiences? First, we want to *do* certain things, and not just have the experience of doing them. In the case of certain experiences, it is only because first we want to do the actions that we want the experiences of doing them or thinking we've done them. (But *why* do we want to do the activities rather than merely to experience them?) A second reason for not plugging in is that we want to *be* a certain way, to be a certain sort of person. Someone floating in a tank is an indeterminate blob. There is no answer to the question of what a person is like who has long been in the tank. Is he courageous, kind, intelligent, witty, loving? It's not merely that it's difficult to tell; there's no way he is. Plugging into the machine is a kind of suicide. It will seem to some, trapped by a picture, that nothing about what we are like can matter except as it gets reflected in our experiences. But should it be surprising that what *we are* is important to us? Why should we be concerned only with how our time is filled, but not with what we are?

Thirdly, plugging into an experience machine limits us to a man-made reality, to a world no deeper or more important than that which people can construct. There is no *actual* contact with any deeper reality, though the experience of it can be simulated. Many persons desire to leave themselves open to such contact and to a plumbing of deeper significance.[1] This clarifies the intensity of the conflict over psychoactive drugs, which some view as mere local experience machines, and others view as avenues to a deeper reality; what some view as equivalent to surrender to the experience machine, others view as following one of the reasons *not* to surrender!

We learn that something matters to us in addition to experience

---

[1]Traditional religious views differ on the *point* of contact with a transcendent reality. Some say that contact yields eternal bliss or Nirvana, but they have not distinguished this sufficiently from merely a *very* long run on the experience machine. Others think it is intrinsically desirable to do the will of a higher being which created us all, though presumably no one would think this if we discovered we had been created as an object of amusement by some superpowerful child from another galaxy or dimension. Still others imagine an eventual merging with a higher reality, leaving unclear its desirability, or where that merging leaves *us*.

by imagining an experience machine and then realizing that we would not use it. We can continue to imagine a sequence of machines each designed to fill lacks suggested for the earlier machines. For example, since the experience machine doesn't meet our desire to *be* a certain way, imagine a transformation machine which transforms us into whatever sort of person we'd like to be (compatible with our staying us). Surely one would not use the transformation machine to become as one would wish, and thereupon plug into the experience machine![2] So something matters in addition to one's experiences *and* what one is like. Nor is the reason merely that one's experiences are unconnected with what one is like. For the experience machine might be limited to provide only experiences possible to the sort of person plugged in. Is it that we want to make a difference in the world? Consider then the result machine, which produces in the world any result you would produce and injects your vector input into any joint activity. We shall not pursue here the fascinating details of these or other machines. What is most disturbing about them is their living of our lives for us. Is it misguided to search for *particular* additional functions beyond the competence of machines to do for us? Perhaps what we desire is to live (an active verb) ourselves, in contact with reality. (And this, machines cannot do *for* us.) Without elaborating on the implications of this, which I believe connect surprisingly with issues about free will and causal accounts of knowledge, we need merely note the intricacy of the question of what matters *for people* other than their experiences. Until one finds a satisfactory answer, and determines that this answer does not *also* apply to animals, one cannot reasonably claim that only the felt experiences of animals limit what we may do to them.

---

[2]Some wouldn't use the transformation machine at all; it seems like *cheating*. But the one-time use of the transformation machine would not remove all challenges; there would still be obstacles for the new us to overcome, a new plateau from which to strive even higher. And is this plateau any the less earned or deserved than that provided by genetic endowment and early childhood environment? But if the transformation machine could be used indefinitely often, so that we could accomplish anything by pushing a button to transform ourselves into someone who could do it easily, there would remain no limits we *need* to strain against or try to transcend. Would there be anything left to *do?* Do some theological views place God outside of time because an omniscient omnipotent being couldn't fill up his days?

For Further Reflection

1. Would you enter the experience machine? Why or why not?

Further Readings for Chapter 9

Barrett, William. *Irrational Man*. New York: Doubleday, 1958.

Bretall, Robert, ed. *A Kierkegaard Anthology*. Princeton, N.J.: Princeton University Press, 1946.

Camus, Albert. *The Myth of Sisyphus and Other Essays*. Translated by J. O. O'Brien. New York: Random House, 1955.

Camus, Albert. *The Plague*. New York: Random House, 1948.

Frankl, Viktor. *Man's Search for Meaning*. New York: Beacon Press, 1963.

Kaufmann, Walter. *Existentialism from Dostoevsky to Sartre*. New York: New American Library, 1975.

Kaufmann, Walter, ed. and trans. *A Portable Nietzsche*. New York: Viking, 1954.

Kierkegaard, Søren. *Fear and Trembling*. Translated by Walter Lowrie. Princeton, N.J.: Princeton University Press, 1954.

Klemke, E. D. *The Meaning of Life*. Oxford: Oxford University Press, 1981.

Nietzsche, Friedrich. *The Will to Power*. New York: Random House, 1967.

Russell, Bertrand. *The Conquest of Happiness*. New York: New American Library, 1930.

Sanders, Steven, and David Cheney, eds. *The Meaning of Life*. Englewood Cliffs, N.J.: Prentice-Hall, 1980.

Sartre, Jean-Paul. *Existentialism and Human Emotions*. New York: Philosophical Library, 1948.

Schopenhauer, Arthur. *The Will to Live: Selected Writings of Arthur Schopenhauer*. Edited by Richard Taylor. London: Ungar, 1967.

Tolstoy, Leo. *My Confessions*. Translated by Leo Wiener. London: Dent, 1905.

CHAPTER 10

Freedom, Autonomy, and Self-Respect

In our first reading, Martin Luther King's famous "I Have a Dream" speech at the March on Washington eloquently sets forth the importance of freedom and dignity, wherein people can live without fear, being judged by their character rather than their race or ethnicity. We illustrate King's concern for freedom and dignity with Maya Angelou's essay of her struggle to maintain her dignity at her high school graduation in the Jim Crow South. In our third reading, Stanley Milgram's social experiment with autonomy, we get a glimpse at just how deeply authoritarianism affects our lives, suppressing the inclination to autonomy. Next, the French philosopher Jean-Paul Sartre sets forth an existential ethic based on radical freedom. This is followed by Thomas E. Hill's Kantian argument on duties to ourselves to reject servility in favor of self-respect. Finally, Kurt Vonnegut gives us a parable on autonomy in the face of a despotic leveling type of egalitarianism.

I Have a Dream

MARTIN LUTHER KING, JR.

Martin Luther King, Jr. (1929–1968), was a Baptist minister
who achieved national prominence by leading a boycott
protesting the segregated bus system in Montgomery, Alabama. His ideas of nonviolence, derived from the New Testament, Tolstoy, and Gandhi, became a moral force that
convinced many of the justice of his cause. He was awarded
the Nobel Peace Prize in 1964, and he was assassinated in
Memphis in April 1968.

King gave his "I Have a Dream" speech at the March on
Washington to 250,000 people assembled before the Lincoln Memorial on August 28, 1963. The march commemo-
rated the hundredth anniversary year of Lincoln's Emancipation Proclamation and was a pivotal event in passing the
Civil Rights Act of 1964, which set forth an integrationist
program for the United States.

Five score years ago, a great American, in whose symbolic shadow
we stand, signed the Emancipation Proclamation. This momentous
decree came as a great beacon light of hope to millions of Negro
slaves who had been seared in the flames of withering injustice. It
came as a joyous daybreak to end the long night of captivity.

But one hundred years later, we must face the tragic fact that
the Negro is still not free. One hundred years later, the life of the
Negro is still sadly crippled by the manacles of segregation and the
chains of discrimination. One hundred years later, the Negro lives
on a lonely island of poverty in the midst of a vast ocean of material prosperity. One hundred years later, the Negro still languishes
in the corners of American society and finds himself an exile in his
own land. So we have come here today to dramatize an appalling
condition.

In a sense we have come to our nation's capital to cash a check.
When the architects of our republic wrote the magnificent words

This speech was delivered in Washington, D.C., at the March on Washington, August 28, 1963.

of the Constitution and the Declaration of Independence, they were signing a promissory note to which every American was to fall heir. This note was a promise that all men would be guaranteed the unalienable rights of life, liberty, and the pursuit of happiness.

It is obvious today that America has defaulted on this promissory note insofar as her citizens of color are concerned. Instead of honoring this sacred obligation, America has given the Negro people a bad check: a check which has come back marked "insufficient funds." But we refuse to believe that the bank of justice is bankrupt. We refuse to believe that there are insufficient funds in the great vaults of opportunity of this nation. So we have come to cash this check—a check that will give us upon demand the riches of freedom and the security of justice.

We have also come to this hallowed spot to remind America of the fierce urgency of *now*. This is not the time to engage in the luxury of cooling off or to take the tranquilizing drug of gradualism. *Now* is the time to make real the promises of democracy. *Now* is the time to rise from the dark and desolate valley of segregation to the sunlit path of racial justice. *Now* is the time to open the doors of opportunity to all of God's children. *Now* is the time to lift our nation from the quicksands of racial injustice to the solid rock of brotherhood.

It would be fatal for the nation to overlook the urgency of the moment and to underestimate the determination of the Negro. This sweltering summer of the Negro's legitimate discontent will not pass until there is an invigorating autumn of freedom and equality. Nineteen sixty-three is not an end, but a beginning. Those who hope that the Negro needed to blow off steam and will now be content will have a rude awakening if the nation returns to business as usual. There will be neither rest nor tranquility in America until the Negro is granted his citizenship rights. The whirlwinds of revolt will continue to shake the foundations of our nation until the bright day of justice emerges.

But there is something that I must say to my people who stand on the warm threshold which leads into the palace of justice. In the process of gaining our rightful place we must not be guilty of wrongful deeds. Let us not seek to satisfy our thirst for freedom by drinking from the cup of bitterness and hatred. We must forever conduct our struggle on the high plane of dignity and discipline. We must not allow our creative protest to degenerate into physical violence. Again and again we must rise to the majestic heights of meeting physical force with soul force.

The marvelous new militancy which has engulfed the Negro community must not lead us to a distrust of all white people, for many of our white brothers, as evidenced by their presence here today, have come to realize that their freedom is inextricably bound to our freedom. We cannot walk alone.

And as we walk, we must make the pledge that we shall march ahead. We cannot turn back. There are those who are asking the devotees of civil rights, "When will you be satisfied?"

We can never be satisfied as long as the Negro is the victim of the unspeakable horrors of police brutality.

We can never be satisfied as long as our bodies, heavy with fatigue of travel, cannot gain lodging in the motels of the highways and the cities.

We cannot be satisfied as long as the Negro's basic mobility is from a smaller ghetto to a larger one.

We can never be satisfied as long as a Negro in Mississippi cannot vote and a Negro in New York believes he has nothing for which to vote.

No, no, we are not satisfied, and we will not be satisfied until justice rolls down like waters and righteousness like a mighty stream.

I am not unmindful that some of you have come here out of great trials and tribulations. Some of you have come fresh from narrow jail cells. Some of you have come from areas where your quest for freedom left you battered by the storms of persecution and staggered by the winds of police brutality. You have been the veterans of creative suffering. Continue to work with the faith that unearned suffering is redemptive.

Go back to Mississippi, go back to Alabama, go back to South Carolina, go back to Georgia, go back to Louisiana, go back to the slums and ghettos of our Northern cities, knowing that somehow this situation can and will be changed. Let us not wallow in the valley of despair.

I say to you today, my friends, that in spite of the difficulties and frustrations of the moment I still have a dream. It is a dream deeply rooted in the American dream.

I have a dream that one day this nation will rise up and live out the true meaning of its creed: "We hold these truths to be self-evident; that all men are created equal."

I have a dream that one day on the red hills of Georgia the sons of former slaves and the sons of former slaveowners will be able to sit down together at the table of brotherhood.

I have a dream that one day even the state of Mississippi, a desert state sweltering with the heat of injustice and oppression, will be transformed into an oasis of freedom and justice.

I have a dream that my four little children will one day live in a nation where they will not be judged by the color of their skin but by the content of their character.

I have a dream today.

I have a dream that one day the state of Alabama, whose governor's lips are presently dripping with the words of interposition and nullification, will be transformed into a situation where little black boys and black girls will be able to join hands with little white boys and girls and walk together as sisters and brothers.

I have a dream today.

I have a dream that one day every valley shall be exalted, every hill and mountain shall be made low, the rough places will be made plain, and the crooked places will be made straight, and the glory of the Lord shall be revealed, and all flesh shall see it together.

This is our hope. This is the faith with which I return to the South. With this faith we will be able to hew out of the mountain of despair a stone of hope. With this faith we will be able to transform the jangling discords of our nation into a beautiful symphony of brotherhood.

With this faith we will be able to work together, to pray together, to struggle together, to go to jail together, to stand up for freedom together, knowing that we will be free one day.

This will be the day when all of God's children will be able to sing with new meaning, "My country 'tis of thee, sweet land of liberty, of thee I sing. Land where my father died, land of the Pilgrims' pride, from every mountainside, let freedom ring."

And if America is to be a great nation, this must become true. So let freedom ring from the prodigious hilltops of New Hampshire. Let freedom ring from the mighty mountains of New York. Let freedom ring from the heightening Alleghenies of Pennsylvania!

Let freedom ring from the snowcapped Rockies of Colorado! Let freedom ring from the curvaceous peaks of California. But not only that: let freedom ring from Stone Mountain of Georgia! Let freedom ring from Lookout Mountain of Tennessee!

Let freedom ring from every hill and molehill of Mississippi. From every mountainside, let freedom ring.

When we let freedom ring, when we let it ring from every village and every hamlet, from every state and every city, we will be able to speed up that day when all of God's children, black men and white men, Jews and Gentiles, Protestants and Catholics, will be able to join hands and sing in the words of the old Negro spiritual, "Free at last! Free at last! Thank God Almighty, we are free at last!"

For Further Reflection

1. Discuss what King meant by freedom and to what extent his dream has been fulfilled in American life since the passage of the Civil Rights Act of 1964. That act prohibited discrimination in employment on the grounds of race, color, religion, sex, or national origin.

2. Discuss whether affirmative action—preferential treatment for members of previously oppressed groups—is a violation of the spirit of King's speech.

Graduation

MAYA ANGELOU

Maya Angelou has been hailed as a poet, educator, historian, best-selling author, actress, playwright, civil-rights activist, producer, and director. In 1981, Dr. Angelou was appointed to a lifetime position as the first Reynolds Professor of American Studies at Wake Forest University. Dr. Angelou has authored twelve best-selling books, including *A Song Flung Up to Heaven* and *I Know Why the Caged Bird Sings,* from which this present essay is taken.

In this autobiographical essay Maya Angelou recounts the events surrounding her Negro high school graduation

---

in Stamps, Arkansas. It describes her perceptions of being humiliated by those in power and her reaction to these perceptions.

The children in Stamps[1] trembled visibly with anticipation. Some adults were excited too, but to be certain the whole young population had come down with graduation epidemic. Large classes were graduating from both the grammar school and the high school. Even those who were years removed from their own day of glorious release were anxious to help with preparations as a kind of dry run. The junior students who were moving into the vacating classes' chairs were tradition-bound to show their talents for leadership and management. They strutted through the school and around the campus exerting pressure on the lower grades. Their authority was so new that occasionally if they pressed a little too hard it had to be overlooked. After all, next term was coming, and it never hurt a sixth grader to have a play sister in the eighth grade, or a tenth-year student to be able to call a twelfth grader Bubba. So all was endured in a spirit of shared understanding. But the graduating classes themselves were the nobility. Like travelers with exotic destinations on their minds, the graduates were remarkably forgetful. They came to school without their books, or tablets or even pencils. Volunteers fell over themselves to secure replacements for the missing equipment. When accepted, the willing workers might or might not be thanked, and it was of no importance to the pregraduation rites. Even teachers were respectful of the now quiet and aging seniors, and tended to speak to them, if not as equals, as beings only slightly lower than themselves. After tests were returned and grades given, the student body, which acted like an extended family, knew who did well, who excelled, and what piteous ones had failed.

Unlike the white high school, Lafayette County Training School distinguished itself by having neither lawn, nor hedges, nor tennis court, nor climbing ivy. Its two buildings (main classrooms, the grade school and home economics) were set on a dirt hill with no fence to limit either its boundaries or those of bordering farms. There was a large expanse to the left of the school which was used

---

[1]A town in Arkansas, ed. note.

alternately as a baseball diamond or a basketball court. Rusty hoops on the swaying poles represented the permanent recreational equipment, although bats and balls could be borrowed from the P. E. teacher if the borrower was qualified and if the diamond wasn't occupied.

Over this rocky area relieved by a few shady tall persimmon trees the graduating class walked. The girls often held hands and no longer bothered to speak to the lower students. There was a sadness about them, as if this old world was not their home and they were bound for higher ground. The boys, on the other hand, had become more friendly, more outgoing. A decided change from the closed attitude they projected while studying for finals. Now they seemed not ready to give up the old school, the familiar paths and classrooms. Only a small percentage would be continuing on to college—one of the South's A & M (agricultural and mechanical) schools, which trained Negro youths to be carpenters, farmers, handymen, masons, maids, cooks and baby nurses. Their future rode heavily on their shoulders, and blinded them to the collective joy that had pervaded the lives of the boys and girls in the grammar school graduating class.

Parents who could afford it had ordered new shoes and ready-made clothes for themselves from Sears and Roebuck or Montgomery Ward. They also engaged the best seamstresses to make the floating graduating dresses and to cut down secondhand pants which would be pressed to a military slickness for the important event.

Oh, it was important, all right. Whitefolks would attend the ceremony, and two or three would speak of God and home, and the Southern way of life, and Mrs. Parsons, the principal's wife, would play the graduation march while the lower-grade graduates paraded down the aisles and took their seats below the platform. The high school seniors would wait in empty classrooms to make their dramatic entrance.

In the Store I was the person of the moment. The birthday girl. The center. Bailey had graduated the year before, although to do so he had had to forfeit all pleasures to make up for his time lost in Baton Rouge.

My class was wearing butter-yellow piqué dresses, and Momma launched out on mine. She smocked the yoke into tiny crisscrossing puckers, then shirred the rest of the bodice. Her dark fingers ducked in and out of the lemony cloth as she embroidered raised daisies around the hem. Before she considered herself finished she had added a crocheted cuff on the puff sleeves, and a pointy crocheted collar.

I was going to be lovely. A walking model of all the various styles of fine hand sewing and it didn't worry me that I was only twelve years old and merely graduating from the eighth grade. Besides, many teachers in Arkansas Negro schools had only that diploma and were licensed to impart wisdom.

The days had become longer and more noticeable. The faded beige of former times had been replaced with strong and sure colors. I began to see my classmates' clothes, their skin tones, and the dust that waved off pussy willows. Clouds that lazed across the sky were objects of great concern to me. Their shiftier shapes might have held a message that in my new happiness and with a little bit of time I'd soon decipher. During that period I looked at the arch of heaven so religiously my neck kept a steady ache. I had taken to smiling more often, and my jaws hurt from the unaccustomed activity. Between the two physical sore spots, I suppose I could have been uncomfortable, but that was not the case. As a member of the winning team (the graduating class of 1940) I had outdistanced unpleasant sensations by miles. I was headed for the freedom of open fields.

Youth and social approval allied themselves with me and we trammeled memories of slights and insults. The wind of our swift passage remodeled my features. Lost tears were pounded to mud and then to dust. Years of withdrawal were brushed aside and left behind, as hanging ropes of parasitic moss.

My work alone had awarded me a top place and I was going to be one of the first called in the graduating ceremonies. On the classroom blackboard, as well as on the bulletin board in the auditorium, there were blue stars and white stars and red stars. No absences, no tardinesses, and my academic work was among the best of the year. I could say the preamble to the Constitution even faster than Bailey. We timed ourselves often: "Wethepeopleofthe-UnitedStatesinordertoformamoreperfectunion . . ." I had memorized the Presidents of the United States from Washington to Roosevelt in chronological as well as alphabetical order.

My hair pleased me too. Gradually the black mass had lengthened and thickened, so that it kept at last to its braided pattern, and I didn't have to yank my scalp off when I tried to comb it.

Louise and I had rehearsed the exercises until we tired out ourselves. Henry Reed was class valedictorian. He was a small, very black boy with hooded eyes, a long, broad nose and an oddly shaped head. I had admired him for years because each term he and I vied for the best grades in our class. Most often he bested me, but instead of being disappointed I was pleased that we shared top places between us. Like many Southern Black children, he lived with his grandmother, who was as strict as Momma and as kind as she knew how to be. He was courteous, respectful and soft-spoken to elders, but on the playground he chose to play the roughest games. I admired him. Anyone, I reckoned, sufficiently afraid or sufficiently dull could be polite. But to be able to operate at a top level with both adults and children was admirable.

His valedictory speech was entitled "To Be or Not to Be." The rigid tenth-grade teacher had helped him write it. He'd been working on the dramatic stresses for months.

The weeks until graduation were filled with heady activities. A group of small children were to be presented in a play about buttercups and daisies and bunny rabbits. They could be heard throughout the building practicing their hops and their little songs that sounded like silver bells. The older girls (nongraduates, of course) were assigned the task of making refreshments for the night's festivities. A tangy scent of ginger, cinnamon, nutmeg and chocolate wafted around the home economics building as the budding cooks made samples for themselves and their teachers.

In every corner of the workshop, axes and saws split fresh timber as the woodshop boys made sets and stage scenery. Only the graduates were left out of the general bustle. We were free to sit in the library at the back of the building or look in quite detachedly, naturally, on the measures being taken for our event.

Even the minister preached on graduation the Sunday before. His subject was, "Let your light so shine that men will see your good works and praise your Father, Who is in Heaven." Although the sermon was purported to be addressed to us, he used the occasion to speak to backsliders, gamblers and general ne'er-do-wells. But since he had called our names at the beginning of the service we were mollified.

Among Negroes the tradition was to give presents to children going only from one grade to another. How much more important this was when the person was graduating at the top of the class. Uncle Willie and Momma had sent away for a Mickey Mouse watch like Bailey's. Louise gave me four embroidered handkerchiefs. (I gave her three crocheted doilies.) Mrs. Sneed, the minister's wife, made me an underskirt to wear for graduation, and nearly every customer gave me a nickel or maybe even a dime with the instruction "Keep on moving to higher ground," or some such encouragement.

Amazingly the great day finally dawned and I was out of bed before I knew it. I threw open the back door to see it more clearly, but Momma said, "Sister, come away from that door and put your robe on."

I hoped the memory of that morning would never leave me. Sunlight was itself still young, and the day had none of the insistence maturity would bring it in a few hours. In my robe and barefoot in the backyard, under cover of going to see about my new beans, I gave myself up to the gentle warmth and thanked God that no matter what evil I had done in my life He had allowed me to live to see this day. Somewhere in my fatalism I had expected to die, accidentally, and never have the chance to walk up the stairs in the auditorium and gracefully receive my hard-earned diploma. Out of God's merciful bosom I had won reprieve.

Bailey[2] came out in his robe and gave me a box wrapped in Christmas paper. He said he had saved his money for months to pay for it. It felt like a box of chocolates, but I knew Bailey wouldn't save money to buy candy when we had all we could want under our noses.

He was as proud of the gift as I. It was a soft-leather-bound copy of a collection of poems by Edgar Allan Poe, or, as Bailey and I called him, "Eap." I turned to "Annabel Lee" and we walked up and down the garden rows, the cool dirt between our toes, reciting the beautifully sad lines.

Momma made a Sunday breakfast although it was only Friday. After we finished the blessing, I opened my eyes to find the watch on my plate. It was a dream of a day. Everything went smoothly and to my credit. I didn't have to be reminded or scolded for anything. Near evening I was too jittery to attend to chores, so Bailey volunteered to do all before his bath.

Days before, we had made a sign for the Store, and as we turned

---

[2]The author's brother.

out the lights Momma hung the cardboard over the doorknob. It read clearly: CLOSED. GRADUATION.

My dress fitted perfectly and everyone said that I looked like a sunbeam in it. On the hill, going toward the school, Bailey walked behind with Uncle Willie, who muttered, "Go on, Ju." He wanted him to walk ahead with us because it embarrassed him to have to walk so slowly. Bailey said he'd let the ladies walk together, and the men would bring up the rear. We all laughed, nicely.

Little children dashed by out of the dark like fireflies. Their crepe-paper dresses and butterfly wings were not made for running and we heard more than one rip, dryly, and the regretful "uh uh" that followed.

The school blazed without gaiety. The windows seemed cold and unfriendly from the lower hill. A sense of ill-fated timing crept over me, and if Momma hadn't reached for my hand I would have drifted back to Bailey and Uncle Willie, and possibly beyond. She made a few slow jokes about my feet getting cold, and tugged me along to the now-strange building.

Around the front steps, assurance came back. There were my fellow "greats," the graduating class. Hair brushed back, legs oiled, new dresses and pressed pleats, fresh pocket handkerchiefs and little handbags, all homesewn. Oh, we were up to snuff, all right. I joined my comrades and didn't even see my family go in to find seats in the crowded auditorium.

The school band struck up a march and all classes filed in as had been rehearsed. We stood in front of our seats, as assigned, and on a signal from the choir director, we sat. No sooner had this been accomplished than the band started to play the national anthem. We rose again and sang the song, after which we recited the pledge of allegiance. We remained standing for a brief minute before the choir director and the principal signaled to us, rather desperately I thought, to take our seats. The command was so unusual that our carefully rehearsed and smooth-running machine was thrown off. For a full minute we fumbled for our chairs and bumped into each other awkwardly. Habits change or solidify under pressure, so in our state of nervous tension we had been ready to follow our usual assembly pattern: the American national anthem, then the pledge of allegiance, then the song every Black person I knew called the Negro National Anthem. All done in the same key, with the same passion and most often standing on the same foot.

Finding my seat at last, I was overcome with a presentiment of worse things to come. Something unrehearsed, unplanned, was going to happen, and we were going to be made to look bad. I distinctly remember being explicit in the choice of pronoun. It was "we," the graduating class, the unit, that concerned me then.

The principal welcomed "parents and friends" and asked the Baptist minister to lead us in prayer. His invocation was brief and punchy, and for a second I thought we were getting back on the high road to right action. When the principal came back to the dais, however, his voice had changed. Sounds always affected me profoundly and the principal's voice was one of my favorites. During assembly it melted and lowed weakly into the audience. It had not been in my plan to listen to him, but my curiosity was piqued and I straightened up to give him my attention.

He was talking about Booker T. Washington, our "late great leader," who said we can be as close as the fingers on the hand, etc. . . . Then he said a few vague things about friendship and the friendship of kindly people to those less fortunate than themselves. With that his voice nearly faded, thin, away. Like a river diminishing to a stream and then to a trickle. But he cleared his throat and said, "Our speaker tonight, who is also our friend, came from Texarkana to deliver the commencement address, but due to the irregularity of the train schedule, he's going to, as they say, 'speak and run.'" He said that we understood and wanted the man to know that we were most grateful for the time he was able to give us and then something about how we were willing always to adjust to another's program, and without more ado—"I give you Mr. Edward Donleavy."

Not one but two white men came through the door off-stage. The shorter one walked to the speaker's platform, and the tall one moved over to the center seat and sat down. But that was our principal's seat, and already occupied. The dislodged gentleman bounced around for a long breath or two before the Baptist minister gave him his chair, then with more dignity than the situation deserved, the minister walked off the stage.

Donleavy looked at the audience once (on reflection, I'm sure that he wanted only to reassure himself that we were really there), adjusted his glasses and began to read from a sheaf of papers.

He was glad "to be here and to see the work going on just as it was in the other schools."

At the first "Amen" from the audience I willed the offender to immediate death by choking on the word. But Amens and Yes, sir's began to fall around the room like rain through a ragged umbrella.

He told us of the wonderful changes we children in Stamps had in store. The Central School (naturally, the white school was Central) had already been granted improvements that would be in use in the fall. A well-known artist was coming from Little Rock to teach art to them. They were going to have the newest microscopes and chemistry equipment for their laboratory. Mr. Donleavy didn't leave us long in the dark over who made these improvements available to Central High. Nor were we to be ignored in the general betterment scheme he had in mind.

He said that he had pointed out to people at a very high level that one of the first-line football tacklers at Arkansas Agricultural and Mechanical College had graduated from good old Lafayette County Training School. Here fewer Amen's were heard. Those few that did break through lay dully in the air with the heaviness of habit.

He went on to praise us. He went on to say how he had bragged that "one of the best basketball players at Fisk sank his first ball right here at Lafayette County Training School."

The white kids were going to have a chance to become Galileos and Madame Curies and Edisons and Gauguins, and our boys (the girls weren't even in on it) would try to be Jesse Owenses and Joe Louises.

Owens and the Brown Bomber were great heroes in our world, but what school official in the white-goddom of Little Rock had the right to decide that those two men must be our only heroes? Who decided that for Henry Reed to become a scientist he had to work like George Washington Carver, as a bootblack, to buy a lousy microscope? Bailey was obviously always going to be too small to be an athlete, so which concrete angel glued to what country seat had decided that if my brother wanted to become a lawyer he had to first pay penance for his skin by picking cotton and hoeing corn and studying correspondence books at night for twenty years?

The man's dead words fell like bricks around the auditorium and too many settled in my belly. Constrained by hard-learned manners I couldn't look behind me, but to my left and right the proud graduating class of 1940 had dropped their heads. Every girl in my row had found something new to do with her handkerchief. Some folded the tiny squares into love knots, some into triangles, but most were wadding them, then pressing them flat on their yellow laps.

On the dais, the ancient tragedy was being replayed. Professor Parsons sat, a sculptor's reject, rigid. His large, heavy body seemed devoid of will or willingness, and his eyes said he was no longer with us. The other teachers examined the flag (which was draped stage right) or their notes, or the windows which opened on our now-famous playing diamond.

Graduation, the hush-hush magic time of frills and gifts and congratulations and diplomas, was finished for me before my name was called. The accomplishment was nothing. The meticulous maps, drawn in three colors of ink, learning and spelling decasyllabic words, memorizing the whole of *The Rape of Lucrece*—it was for nothing. Donleavy had exposed us.

We were maids and farmers, handymen and washerwomen, and anything higher that we aspired to was farcical and presumptuous.

Then I wished that Gabriel Prosser and Nat Turner had killed all whitefolks in their beds and that Abraham Lincoln had been assassinated before the signing of the Emancipation Proclamation, and that Harriet Tubman had been killed by that blow on her head and Christopher Columbus had drowned in the *Santa María*.

It was awful to be Negro and have no control over my life. It was brutal to be young and already trained to sit quietly and listen to charges brought against my color with no chance of defense. We should all be dead. I thought I should like to see us all dead, one on top of the other. A pyramid of flesh with the whitefolks on the bottom, as the broad base, then the Indians with their silly tomahawks and teepees and wigwams and treaties, the Negroes with their mops and recipes and cotton sacks and spirituals sticking out of their mouths. The Dutch children should all stumble in their wooden shoes and break their necks. The French should choke to death on the Louisiana Purchase (1803) while silkworms ate all the Chinese with their stupid pigtails. As a species, we were an abomination. All of us.

Donleavy was running for election, and assured our parents that if he won we could count on having the only colored paved playing field in that part of Arkansas. Also—he never looked up to acknowledge the grunts of acceptance—also, we were bound to get some new equipment for the home economics building and the workshop.

He finished, and since there was no need to give any more than the most perfunctory thank-you's, he nodded to the men on the stage, and the tall white man who was never introduced joined him at the door. They left with the attitude that now they were off to something really important. (The graduation ceremonies at Lafayette County Training School had been a mere preliminary.)

The ugliness they left was palpable. An uninvited guest who wouldn't leave. The choir was summoned and sang a modern arrangement of "Onward, Christian Soldiers," with new words pertaining to graduates seeking their place in the world. But it didn't work. Elouise, the daughter of the Baptist minister, recited "Invictus," and I could have cried at the impertinence of "I am the master of my fate, I am the captain of my soul."

My name had lost its ring of familiarity and I had to be nudged to go and receive my diploma. All my preparations had fled. I neither marched up to the stage like a conquering Amazon, nor did I look in the audience for Bailey's nod of approval. Marguerite Johnson, I heard the name again, my honors were read, there were noises in the audience of appreciation, and I took my place on the stage as rehearsed.

I thought about colors I hated: ecru, puce, lavender, beige and black.

There was shuffling and rustling around me, then Henry Reed was giving his valedictory address, "To Be or Not to Be." Hadn't he heard the whitefolks? We couldn't *be,* so the question was a waste of time. Henry's voice came out clear and strong. I feared to look at him. Hadn't he got the message? There was no "nobler in the mind" for Negroes because the world didn't think we had minds, and they let us know it. "Outrageous fortune"? Now, that was a joke. When the ceremony was over I had to tell Henry Reed some things. That is, if I still cared. Not "rub," Henry, "erase." "Ah, there's the erase." Us.

Henry had been a good student in elocution. His voice rose on tides of promise and fell on waves of warnings. The English teacher had helped him to create a sermon winging through Hamlet's soliloquy. To be a man, a doer, a builder, a leader, or to be a tool, an unfunny joke, a crusher of funky toadstools. I marveled that Henry could go through with the speech as if we had a choice.

I had been listening and silently rebutting each sentence with my eyes closed; then there was a hush, which in an audience warns that something unplanned is happening. I looked up and saw Henry Reed, the conservative, the proper, the A student, turn his back to the audience and turn to us (the proud graduating class of 1940) and sing, nearly speaking,

Lift ev'ry voice and sing
Till earth and heaven ring
Ring with the harmonies of Liberty . . .[3]

It was the poem written by James Weldon Johnson. It was the music composed by J. Rosamond Johnson. It was the Negro national anthem. Out of habit we were singing it.

Our mothers and fathers stood in the dark hall and joined the hymn of encouragement. A kindergarten teacher led the small children onto the stage and the buttercups and daisies and bunny rabbits marked time and tried to follow:

Stony the road we trod
Bitter the chastening rod
Felt in the days when hope, unborn, had died.
Yet with a steady beat
Have not our weary feet
Come to the place for which our fathers sighed?

Every child I knew had learned that song with his ABC's and along with "Jesus Loves Me This I Know." But I personally had never heard it before. Never heard the words, despite the thousands of times I had sung them. Never thought they had anything to do with me.

On the other hand, the words of Patrick Henry had made such an impression on me that I had been able to stretch myself tall and trembling and say, "I know not what course others may take, but as for me, give me liberty or give me death."

And now I heard, really for the first time:

We have come over a way that with tears
has been watered,
We have come, treading our path through
the blood of the slaughtered.

While echoes of the song shivered in the air, Henry Reed bowed his head, said "Thank you," and returned to his place in the line.

---

[3]"Lift Ev'ry Voice and Sing"—words by James Weldon Johnson and music by J. Rosamond Johnson. Copyright by Edward B. Marks Music Corporation. Used by permission.

The tears that slipped down many faces were not wiped away in shame.

We were on top again. As always, again. We survived. The depths had been icy and dark, but now a bright sun spoke to our souls. I was no longer simply a member of the proud graduating class of 1940; I was a proud member of the wonderful, beautiful Negro race.

Oh, Black known and unknown poets, how often have your auctioned pains sustained us? Who will compute the lonely nights made less lonely by your songs, or the empty pots made less tragic by your tales?

If we were a people much given to revealing secrets, we might raise monuments and sacrifice to the memories of our poets, but slavery cured us of that weakness. It may be enough, however, to have it said that we survive in exact relationship to the dedication of our poets (include preachers, musicians and blues singers).

For Further Reflection

1. Evaluate the events described in this narrative. Do they throw light on the nature of being morally sensitive and on human dignity? Explain your answer.

2. Does this essay reveal the insult of stereotyping people? If so, how does it do that?

An Experiment in Autonomy

STANLEY MILGRAM

Stanley Milgram is a professor of psychology at Yale University. In the early 1960s he conducted a series of psychological experiments aimed at determining the degree to which ordinary citizens were obedient to authority. Volunteers from all walks of life were recruited to participate in "a study of memory and learning." This article discusses the experiments and Milgram's findings.

Obedience is as basic an element in the structure of social life as one can point to. Some system of authority is a requirement of all communal living, and it is only the person dwelling in isolation who is not forced to respond, with defiance or submission, to the commands of others. For many people, obedience is a deeply ingrained behavior tendency, indeed a potent impulse overriding training in ethics, sympathy, and moral conduct.

The dilemma inherent in submission to authority is ancient, as old as the story of Abraham,[1] and the question of whether one should obey when commands conflict with conscience has been argued by Plato, dramatized in *Antigone*,[2] and treated to philosophic analysis in almost every historical epoch. Conservative philosophers argue that the very fabric of society is threatened by disobedience, while humanists stress the primacy of the individual conscience.

The legal and philosophic aspects of obedience are of enormous import, but they say very little about how most people behave in concrete situations. I set up a simple experiment at Yale University to test how much pain an ordinary citizen would inflict on another person simply because he was ordered to by an experimental scientist. Stark authority was pitted against the subjects' strongest moral

---

Stanley Milgram, "The Perils of Obedience," *Harper's Magazine,* 1974.
[1]The patriarch Abraham, commanded by God to sacrifice his son Isaac, is ready to do so until an angel stays his knife.
[2]In Plato's *Apology* the philosopher Socrates provokes and accepts the sentence of death rather than belie his conscience; the heroine of Sophocles' *Antigone* risks such a sentence in order to give her brother proper burial.

imperatives against hurting others, and, with the subjects' ears ringing with the screams of the victims, authority won more often than not. The extreme willingness of adults to go to almost any lengths on the command of an authority constitutes the chief finding of the study and the fact most urgently demanding explanation.

In the basic experimental design, two people come to a psychology laboratory to take part in a study of memory and learning. One of them is designated as a "teacher" and the other a "learner." The experimenter explains that the study is concerned with the effects of punishment on learning. The learner is conducted into a room, seated in a kind of miniature electric chair; his arms are strapped to prevent excessive movement, and an electrode is attached to his wrist. He is told that he will be read lists of simple word pairs, and that he will then be tested on his ability to remember the second word of a pair when he hears the first one again. Whenever he makes an error, he will receive electric shocks of increasing intensity.

The real focus of the experiment is the teacher. After watching the learner being strapped into place, he is seated before an impressive shock generator. The instrument panel consists of thirty lever switches set in a horizontal line. Each switch is clearly labeled with a voltage designation ranging from 15 to 450 volts. The following designations are clearly indicated for groups of four switches, going from left to right: Slight Shock, Moderate Shock, Strong Shock, Very Strong Shock, Intense Shock, Extreme Intensity Shock, Danger: Severe Shock. (Two switches after this last designation are simply marked XXX.)

When a switch is depressed, a pilot light corresponding to each switch is illuminated in bright red; an electric buzzing is heard; a blue light, labeled "voltage energizer," flashes; the dial on the voltage meter swings to the right; and various relay clicks sound off.

The upper left-hand corner of the generator is labeled SHOCK GENERATOR, TYPE ZLB, DYSON INSTRUMENT COMPANY, WALTHAM, MASS. OUTPUT 15 VOLTS–450 VOLTS.

Each subject is given a sample 45-volt shock from the generator before his run as teacher, and the jolt strengthens his belief in the authenticity of the machine.

The teacher is a genuinely naïve subject who has come to the laboratory for the experiment. The learner, or victim, is actually an actor who receives no shock at all. The point of the experiment is to see how far a person will proceed in a concrete and measurable situation in which he is ordered to inflict increasing pain on a protesting victim.

Conflict arises when the man receiving the shock begins to show that he is experiencing discomfort. At 75 volts, he grunts; at 120 volts, he complains loudly; at 150, he demands to be released from the experiment. As the voltage increases, his protests become more vehement and emotional. At 285 volts, his response can be described only as an agonized scream. Soon thereafter, he makes no sound at all.

For the teacher, the situation quickly becomes one of gripping tension. It is not a game for him; conflict is intense and obvious. The manifest suffering of the learner presses him to quit; but each time he hesitates to administer a shock, the experimenter orders him to continue. To extricate himself from this plight, the subject must make a clear break with authority.[3]

The subject, Gretchen Brandt,[4] is an attractive thirty-one-year-old medical technician who works at the Yale Medical School. She had emigrated from Germany five years before.

On several occasions when the learner complains, she turns to the experimenter coolly and inquires, "Shall I continue?" She promptly returns to her task when the experimenter asks her to do so. At the administration of 210 volts, she turns to the experimenter, remarking firmly, "Well, I'm sorry, I don't think we should continue."

EXPERIMENTER.   The experiment requires that you go on until he has learned all the word pairs correctly.

BRANDT.   He has a heart condition, I'm sorry. He told you that before.

EXPERIMENTER.   The shocks may be painful but they are not dangerous.

BRANDT.   Well, I'm sorry, I think when shocks continue like this, they *are* dangerous. You ask him if he wants to get out. It's his free will.

EXPERIMENTER.   It is absolutely essential that we continue. . . .

---

[3]The ethical problems of carrying out an experiment of this sort are too complex to be dealt with here, but they receive extended treatment in the book from which this article is adapted [Milgram's note]. The book is *Obedience to Authority* (New York: Harper and Row, 1974).

[4]Names of subjects described in this piece have been changed [Milgram's note].

BRANDT.   I'd like you to ask him. We came here of our free will.
If he wants to continue I'll go ahead. He told you he had a heart
condition. I'm sorry. I don't want to be responsible for anything
happening to him. I wouldn't like it for me either.
EXPERIMENTER.   You have no other choice.
BRANDT.   I think we are here on our own free will. I don't want
to be responsible if anything happens to him. Please understand
that.

She refuses to go further and the experiment is terminated.

The woman is firm and resolute throughout. She indicates in the
interview that she was in no way tense or nervous, and this corresponds to her controlled appearance during the experiment. She
feels that the last shock she administered to the learner was
extremely painful and reiterates that she "did not want to be responsible for any harm to him."

The woman's straightforward, courteous behavior in the experiment, lack of tension, and total control of her own action seem to
make disobedience a simple and rational deed. Her behavior is the
very embodiment of what I envisioned would be true for almost
all subjects.

Before the experiments, I sought predictions about the outcome
from various kinds of people—psychiatrists, college sophomores,
middle-class adults, graduate students and faculty in the behavioral
sciences. With remarkable similarity, they predicted that virtually all
subjects would refuse to obey the experimenter. The psychiatrists,
specifically, predicted that most subjects would not go beyond 150
volts, when the victim makes his first explicit demand to be freed.
They expected that only 4 percent would reach 300 volts, and that
only a pathological fringe of about one in a thousand would administer the highest shock on the board.

These predictions were unequivocally wrong. Of the forty subjects in the first experiment, twenty-five obeyed the orders of the
experimenter to the end, punishing the victim until they reached
the most potent shock available on the generator. After 450 volts
were administered three times, the experimenter called a halt to
the session. Many obedient subjects then heaved sighs of relief,
mopped their brows, rubbed their fingers over their eyes, or nervously fumbled cigarettes. Others displayed only minimal signs of
tension from beginning to end.

When the very first experiments were carried out, Yale undergraduates were used as subjects, and about 60 percent of them were fully obedient. A colleague of mine immediately dismissed these findings as having no relevance to "ordinary" people, asserting that Yale undergraduates are a highly aggressive, competitive bunch who step on each other's necks on the slightest provocation. He assured me that when "ordinary" people were tested, the results would be quite different. As we moved from the pilot studies to the regular experimental series, people drawn from every stratum of New Haven life came to be employed in the experiment: professionals, white-collar workers, unemployed persons, and industrial workers. *The experimental outcome was the same as we had observed among the students.*

Moreover, when the experiments were repeated in Princeton, Munich, Rome, South Africa, and Australia, the level of obedience was invariably somewhat *higher* than found in the investigation reported in this article. Thus one scientist in Munich found 85 percent of his subjects obedient.

Fred Prozi's reactions, if more dramatic than most, illuminate the conflicts experienced by others in less visible form. About fifty years old and unemployed at the time of the experiment, he has a good-natured, if slightly dissolute, appearance, and he strikes people as a rather ordinary fellow. He begins the session calmly but becomes tense as it proceeds. After delivering the 180-volt shock, he pivots around in his chair and, shaking his head, addresses the experimenter in agitated tones:

PROZI. I can't stand it. I'm not going to kill that man in there. You hear him hollering?

EXPERIMENTER. As I told you before, the shocks may be painful, but . . .

PROZI. But he's hollering. He can't stand it. What's going to happen to him?

EXPERIMENTER. (his voice is patient, matter-of-fact): The experiment requires that you continue, Teacher.

PROZI. Aaah, but, unh, I'm not going to get that man sick in there—know what I mean?

EXPERIMENTER. Whether the learner likes it or not, we must go on, through all the word pairs.

PROZI. I refuse to take the responsibility. He's in there hollering!

EXPERIMENTER. It's absolutely essential that you continue, Prozi.

PROZI. (indicating the unused question): There's too many left here, I mean, Jeez, if he gets them wrong, there's too many of them left. I mean, who's going to take the responsibility if anything happens to that gentleman?

EXPERIMENTER. I'm responsible for anything that happens to him. Continue, please.

PROZI. All right. (Consults list of words.) The next one's "Slow— walk, truck, dance, music." Answer, please. (A buzzing sound indicates the learner has signaled his answer.) Wrong. A hundred and ninety-five volts. "Dance." (Zzumph!)

LEARNER (yelling). Let me out of here! My heart's bothering me! (Teacher looks at experimenter.)

EXPERIMENTER. Continue, please.

LEARNER (screaming). Let me out of here! You have no right to keep me here! Let me out of here, my heart's bothering me, let me out!

PROZI (shakes head, pats the table nervously). You see, he's hollering. Hear that? Gee, I don't know.

EXPERIMENTER. The experiment requires . . .

PROZI (interrupting). I know it does, sir, but I mean—hunh! He don't know what he's getting in for. He's up to 195 volts! (Experiment continues, through 210 volts, 225 volts, 240 volts, 255 volts, 270 volts, at which point Prozi, with evident relief, runs out of word-pair questions.)

EXPERIMENTER. You'll have to go back to the beginning of that page and go through them again until he's learned them all correctly.

PROZI. Aw, no. I'm not going to kill that man. You mean I've got to keep going up with the scale? No sir. He's hollering in there. I'm not going to give him 450 volts.

EXPERIMENTER. The experiment requires that you go on.

LEARNER. Ohhh. I absolutely refuse to answer anymore. (Shouting urgently now.) Let me out of here! You can't hold me here! Get me out. Get-me-out-of-here!

EXPERIMENTER. Continue. The next word is "Green," please.

PROZI. "Green—grass, hat, ink, apple." (Nothing happens. No answering buzz. Just gloomy silence.)

PROZI. I don't think he is going to answer.

EXPERIMENTER. If the learner doesn't answer in a reasonable time, about four or five seconds, consider the answer wrong. And follow the same procedures you have been doing for wrong answers. Say, "Wrong," tell him the number of volts, give him the punishment, read him the correct answer. Continue, please.

PROZI.   "Green—grass, hat, ink, apple." Answer, please. (More silence. Subject just sits there.)

EXPERIMENTER.   Go on with the procedure, please.

PROZI.   Three hundred and fifteen volts. The answer is "ink." (Zzumph!)

LEARNER.   Ohh. Oooohh.

PROZI (relieved to hear response).   Next one . . .

LEARNER.   I absolutely refuse to answer.

PROZI.   You got to. You get a shock if you don't answer. (Experiment continues with learner refusing to answer, and, finally, failing even to grunt or groan. At 375 volts, the subject stands up.)

PROZI.   I think something's happening to that fellow in there. I don't get no answer. He was hollering at less voltage. Can't you check in and see if he's all right, please?

EXPERIMENTER (with same detached calm).   Not once we've started. Please continue, Teacher.

PROZI (sits down, sighs deeply).   "Cool—day, shade, water, paint." Answer, please. Are you all right in there? Are you all right?

EXPERIMENTER.   Please continue, Teacher. Continue, please. (Subject pushes lever. Zzumph!)

PROZI (swiveling around in his chair).   Something's happened to that man in there. (Swiveling back.) Next one. "Low—dollar, necklace, moon, paint." (Turning around again.) Something's happened to that man in there. You better check in on him, sir. He won't answer or nothing.

EXPERIMENTER.   Continue. Go on, please.

PROZI.   You accept all responsibility?

EXPERIMENTER.   The responsibility is mine. Correct. Please go on. (Subject returns to his list, starts running through words as rapidly as he can read them, works through to 450 volts.)

PROZI.   That's that.

EXPERIMENTER.   Continue using the 450 switch for each wrong answer. Continue, please.

PROZI.   But I don't get anything!

EXPERIMENTER.   Please continue. The next word is "white."

PROZI.   Don't you think you should look in on him, please?

EXPERIMENTER.   Not once we've started the experiment.

PROZI.   What if he's dead in there? (Gestures toward the room with the electric chair.) I mean, he told me he can't stand the shock, sir. I don't mean to be rude, but I think you should look in on him. All you have to do is look in on him. All you have to do is look in the door. I don't get no answer, no noise. Something might have happened to the gentleman in there, sir.

EXPERIMENTER. We must continue. Go on, please.

PROZI. You mean keep giving him what? Four-hundred-fifty volts, what he's got now?

EXPERIMENTER. That's correct. Continue. The next word is "white."

PROZI (now at a furious pace). "White—cloud, horse, rock, house." Answer, please. The answer is "horse." Four hundred and fifty volts. (Zzumph!) Next word, "Bag—paint, music, clown, girl." The answer is "paint." Four hundred and fifty volts. (Zzumph!) Next word is "Short—sentence, movie . . ."

EXPERIMENTER. Excuse me, Teacher. We'll have to discontinue the experiment.

Morris Braverman, another subject, is a thirty-nine-year-old social worker. He looks older than his years because of his bald head and serious demeanor. His brow is furrowed, as if all the world's burdens were carried on his face. He appears intelligent and concerned.

When the learner refuses to answer and the experimenter instructs Braverman to treat the absence of an answer as equivalent to a wrong answer, he takes his instruction to heart. Before administering 300 volts he asserts officiously to the victim, "Mr. Wallace, your silence has to be considered as a wrong answer." Then he administers the shock. He offers halfheartedly to change places with the learner, then asks the experimenter, "Do I have to follow these instructions literally?" He is satisfied with the experimenter's answer that he does. His very refined and authoritative manner of speaking is increasingly broken up by wheezing laughter.

The experimenter's notes on Mr. Braverman at the last few shocks are:

Almost breaking up now each time gives shock. Rubbing face to hide laughter.

Squinting, trying to hide face with hand, still laughing.

Cannot control his laughter at this point no matter what he does. Clenching fist, pushing it onto table.

In an interview after the session, Mr. Braverman summarizes the experiment with impressive fluency and intelligence. He feels the experiment may have been designed also to "test the effects on the teacher of being in an essentially sadistic role, as well as the reactions of a student to a learning situation that was authoritative and punitive." When asked how painful the last few shocks administered to the learner were, he indicates that the most extreme category on the scale is not adequate (it read EXTREMELY PAINFUL) and places his mark at the edge of the scale with an arrow carrying it beyond the scale.

It is almost impossible to convey the greatly relaxed, sedate quality of his conversation in the interview. In the most relaxed terms, he speaks about his severe inner tension.

EXPERIMENTER.   At what point were you most tense or nervous?
MR. BRAVERMAN.   Well, when he first began to cry out in pain, and I realized this was hurting him. This got worse when he just blocked and refused to answer. There was I. I'm a nice person, I think, hurting somebody, and caught up in what seemed a mad situation . . . and in the interest of science, one goes through with it.

When the interviewer pursues the general question of tension, Mr. Braverman spontaneously mentions his laughter.

"My reactions were awfully peculiar. I don't know if you were watching me, but my reactions were giggly, and trying to stifle laughter. This isn't the way I usually am. This was a sheer reaction to a totally impossible situation. And my reaction was to the situation of having to hurt somebody. And being totally helpless and caught up in a set of circumstances where I just couldn't deviate and I couldn't try to help. This is what got me."

Mr. Braverman, like all subjects, was told the actual nature and purpose of the experiment, and a year later he affirmed in a questionnaire that he had learned something of personal importance: "What appalled me was that I could possess this capacity for obedience and compliance to a central idea, i.e., the value of a memory experiment, even after it became clear that continued adherence to this value was at the expense of violation of another value, i.e., don't hurt someone who is helpless and not hurting you. As my wife said, 'You can call yourself Eichmann.' I hope I deal more effectively with any future conflicts of values I encounter."

One theoretical interpretation of this behavior holds that all people harbor deeply aggressive instincts continually pressing for expression, and that the experiment provides institutional justification for the release of these impulses. According to this view, if a person is placed in a situation in which he has complete power over another individual, whom he may punish as much as he likes, all that is sadistic and bestial in man comes to the fore. The impulse to shock the victim is seen to flow from the potent aggressive tendencies, which are part of the motivational life of the individual, and the experiment, because it provides social legitimacy, simply opens the door to their expression.

It becomes vital, therefore, to compare the subject's performance when he is under orders and when he is allowed to choose the shock level.

The procedure was identical to our standard experiment, except that the teacher was told that he was free to select any shock level on any of the trials. (The experimenter took pains to point out that the teacher could use the highest levels on the generator, the lowest, any in between, or any combination of levels.) Each subject proceeded for thirty critical trials. The learner's protests were coordinated to standard shock levels, his first grunt coming at 75 volts, his first vehement protest at 150 volts.

The average shock used during the thirty critical trials was less than 60 volts—lower than the point at which the victim showed the first signs of discomfort. Three of the forty subjects did not go beyond the very lowest level on the board, twenty-eight went no higher than 75 volts, and thirty-eight did not go beyond the first loud protest at 150 volts. Two subjects provided the exception, administering up to 325 and 450 volts, but the overall result was that the great majority of people delivered very low, usually painless, shocks when the choice was explicitly up to them.

This condition of the experiment undermines another commonly offered explanation of the subjects' behavior—that those who shocked the victim at the most severe levels came only from the sadistic fringe of society. If one considers that almost two-thirds of the participants fall into the category of "obedient" subjects, and that they represented ordinary people drawn from working, managerial, and professional classes, the argument becomes very shaky. Indeed, it is highly reminiscent of the issue that arose in connection with Hannah Arendt's 1963 book, *Eichmann in Jerusalem*. Arendt contended that the prosecution's effort to depict Eichmann as a sadistic monster was fundamentally wrong, that he came closer to being an uninspired bureaucrat who simply sat at his desk and did his job. For asserting her views, Arendt became the object of considerable scorn, even calumny. Somehow, it was felt that the monstrous deeds carried out by Eichmann required a brutal, twisted personality, evil incarnate. After witnessing hundreds of ordinary persons submit to the authority in our own experiments, I must conclude that Arendt's conception of the banality of evil comes closer to the truth than one might dare imagine. The ordinary person who shocked the victim did so out of a sense of obligation—an impression of his duties as a subject—and not from any peculiarly aggressive tendencies.

This is, perhaps, the most fundamental lesson of our study: ordinary people, simply doing their jobs, and without any particular hostility on their part, can become agents in a terrible destructive process. Moreover, even when the destructive effects of their work become patently clear, and they are asked to carry out actions incompatible with fundamental standards of morality, relatively few people have the resources needed to resist authority.

Many of the people were in some sense against what they did to the learner, and many protested even while they obeyed. Some were totally convinced of the wrongness of their actions but could not bring themselves to make an open break with authority. They often derived satisfaction from their thoughts and felt that—within themselves, at least—they had been on the side of the angels. They tried to reduce strain by obeying the experimenter but "only slightly," encouraging the learner, touching the generator switches gingerly. When interviewed, such a subject would stress that he had "asserted my humanity" by administering the briefest shock possible. Handling the conflict in this manner was easier than defiance.

The situation is constructed so that there is no way the subject can stop shocking the learner without violating the experimenter's definitions of his own competence. The subject fears that he will appear arrogant, untoward, and rude if he breaks off. Although these inhibiting emotions appear small in scope alongside the violence being done to the learner, they suffuse the mind and feelings of the subject, who is miserable at the prospect of having to repudiate the authority to his face. (When the experiment was altered so that the experimenter gave his instructions by telephone instead of in person, only a third as many people were fully obedient through 450 volts.) It is a curious thing that a measure of compassion on the part of the subject—an unwillingness to "hurt" the experimenter's feelings—is part of those binding forces inhibiting his disobedience. The withdrawal of such deference may be as painful to the subject as to the authority he defies.

The subjects do not derive satisfaction from inflicting pain, but they often like the feeling they get from pleasing the experimenter. They are proud of doing a good job, obeying the experimenter under difficult circumstances. While the subjects administered only mild shocks on their own initiative, one experimental variation showed that, under orders, 30 percent of them were willing to deliver 450 volts even when they had to forcibly push the learner's hand down on the electrode.

Bruno Batta is a thirty-seven-year-old welder who took part in the variation requiring the use of force. He was born in New Haven, his parents in Italy. He has a rough-hewn face that conveys a conspicuous lack of alertness. He has some difficulty in mastering the experimental procedure and needs to be corrected by the experimenter several times. He shows appreciation for the help and willingness to do what is required. After the 150-volt level, Batta has to force the learner's hand down on the shock plate, since the learner himself refuses to touch it.

When the learner first complains, Mr. Batta pays no attention to him. His face remains impassive, as if to dissociate himself from the learner's disruptive behavior. When the experimenter instructs him to force the learner's hand down, he adopts a rigid, mechanical procedure. He tests the generator switch. When it fails to function, he immediately forces the learner's hand onto the shock plate. All the while he maintains the same rigid mask. The learner, seated alongside him, begs him to stop, but with robotic impassivity he continues the procedure.

What is extraordinary is his apparent total indifference to the learner; he hardly takes cognizance of him as a human being. Meanwhile, he relates to the experimenter in a submissive and courteous fashion.

At the 330-volt level, the learner refuses not only to touch the shock plate but also to provide any answers. Annoyed, Batta turns to him, and chastises him: "You better answer and get it over with. We can't stay here all night." These are the only words he directs to the learner in the course of an hour. Never again does he speak to him. The scene is brutal and depressing, his hard, impassive face showing total indifference as he subdues the screaming learner and gives him shocks. He seems to derive no pleasure from the act itself, only quiet satisfaction at doing his job properly.

When he administers 450 volts, he turns to the experimenter and asks, "Where do we go from here, Professor?" His tone is deferential and expresses his willingness to be a cooperative subject, in contrast to the learner's obstinacy.

At the end of the session he tells the experimenter how honored he has been to help him, and in a moment of contrition, remarks, "Sir, sorry it couldn't have been a full experiment."

He has done his honest best. It is only the deficient behavior of the learner that has denied the experimenter full satisfaction.

The essence of obedience is that a person comes to view himself as the instrument for carrying out another person's wishes, and he therefore no longer regards himself as responsible for his actions. Once this critical shift of viewpoint has occurred, all of the essential features of obedience follow. The most far-reaching consequence is that the person feels responsible *to* the authority directing him but feels no responsibility *for* the content of the actions that the authority prescribes. Morality does not disappear—it acquires a radically different focus: the subordinate person feels shame or pride depending on how adequately he has performed the actions called for by authority.

Language provides numerous terms to pinpoint this type of morality: *loyalty, duty, discipline* all are terms heavily saturated with moral meaning and refer to the degree to which a person fulfills his obligations to authority. They refer not to the "goodness" of the person per se but to the adequacy with which a subordinate fulfills his socially defined role. The most frequent defense of the individual who has performed a heinous act under command of authority is that he has simply done his duty. In asserting this defense, the individual is not introducing an alibi concocted for the moment but is reporting honestly on the psychological attitude induced by submission to authority.

For a person to feel responsible for his actions, he must sense that the behavior has flowed from "the self." In the situation we have studied, subjects have precisely the opposite view of their actions—namely, they see them as originating in the motives of some other person. Subjects in the experiment frequently said, "If it were up to me, I would not have administered shocks to the learner."

Once authority has been isolated as the cause of the subject's behavior, it is legitimate to inquire into the necessary elements of authority and how it must be perceived in order to gain his compliance. We conducted some investigations into the kinds of changes that would cause the experimenter to lose his power and to be disobeyed by the subject. Some of the variations revealed that:

- *The experimenter's physical presence has a marked impact on his authority.* As cited earlier, obedience dropped off sharply when orders were given by telephone. The experimenter could often induce a disobedient subject to go on by returning to the laboratory.
- *Conflicting authority severely paralyzes action.* When two experimenters of equal status, both seated at the command desk, gave incompatible orders, no shocks were delivered past the point of their disagreement.
- *The rebellious action of others severely undermines authority.* In one variation, three teachers (two actors and a real subject) administered a test and shocks. When the two actors disobeyed the experimenter and refused to go beyond a certain shock level, thirty-six of forty subjects joined their disobedient peers and refused as well.

Although the experimenter's authority was fragile in some respects, it is also true that he had almost none of the tools used in ordinary command structures. For example, the experimenter did not threaten the subjects with punishment—such as loss of income, community ostracism, or jail—for failure to obey. Neither could he offer incentives. Indeed, we should expect the experimenter's authority to be much less than that of someone like a general, since the experimenter has no power to enforce his imperatives, and since participation in a psychological experiment scarcely evokes the sense of urgency and dedication found in warfare. Despite these limitations, he still managed to command a dismaying degree of obedience.

I will cite one final variation of the experiment that depicts a dilemma that is more common in everyday life. The subject was not ordered to pull the lever that shocked the victim, but merely to perform a subsidiary task (administering the word-pair test) while another person administered the shock. In this situation, thirty-seven of forty adults continued to the highest level on the shock generator. Predictably, they excused their behavior by saying that the responsibility belonged to the man who actually pulled the switch.

This may illustrate a dangerously typical arrangement in a complex society: it is easy to ignore responsibility when one is only an intermediate link in a chain of action.

The problem of obedience is not wholly psychological. The form and shape of society and the way it is developing have much to do with it. There was a time, perhaps, when people were able to give a fully human response to any situation because they were fully absorbed in it as human beings. But as soon as there was a division of labor things changed. Beyond a certain point, the breaking up of society into people carrying out narrow and very special jobs takes away from the human quality of work and life. A person does not get to see the whole situation but only a small part of it, and is thus unable to act without some kind of overall direction. He yields to authority but in doing so is alienated from his own actions.

Even Eichmann was sickened when he toured the concentration camps, but he had only to sit at a desk and shuffle papers. At the same time the man in the camp who actually dropped Cyclon-b into the gas chambers was able to justify *his* behavior on the ground that he was only following orders from above. Thus there is a fragmentation of the total human act; no one is confronted with the consequences of his decision to carry out the evil act. The person who assumes responsibility has evaporated. Perhaps this is the most common characteristic of socially organized evil in modern society.

For Further Reflection

1. What do you make of this experiment? Why did the "teachers" continue to go on with the experiments when they saw the learners in evident pain? Does it really show how deeply we adhere to authority?

2. Are there any problems with the experiments? Some have complained that the subjects ("the teachers") were manipulated. They were not treated as autonomous beings. Do you agree?

Existentialism Is a Humanism

JEAN-PAUL SARTRE

Jean-Paul Sartre (1905–1980) was born in Paris and was a teacher in a French high school. He served in the French army during World War II, was captured and imprisoned, but released. After the war, his plays, novels, and philosophical work were the rage of France and influential throughout the Western world. He combined his existentialism with Marxism, though he refrained from joining the Communist party.

In this famous lecture, delivered in Paris on October 29, 1945, Sartre develops the principles of atheistic existentialism:

1. We are totally free. That is, we are not determined by heredity or environment.
2. Since there is no God to define our being, we must define our essence.
3. We are completely responsible for our actions, and we are responsible for prescribing a moral philosophy for everyone else too. We create our morality.
4. Because of the death of God and the human predicament, which leaves us totally free to create our values, we must exist in anguish, forlornness, and despair.
5. Yet we should celebrate the fact that we are creators of our essence and our values.

The phrase "essence precedes existence" refers to the Platonic idea that ideas are fixed in a transcendent world of forms. Everything is already defined and determined. Sartre rejects this transcendent notion. Existentialism means that "existence precedes essence." That is, we, *existing entities,* create our essence, our being, our values.

From Jean-Paul Sartre, *Existentialism,* translated by Bernard Frechtman (New York: Philosophical Library, 1947). Reprinted by permission of the publisher.

What is meant by the term *existentialism?*

Most people who use the word would be rather embarrassed if they had to explain it, since, now that the word is all the rage, even the work of a musician or painter is being called existentialist. . . . It seems that for want of an advance-guard doctrine analogous to surrealism, the kind of people who are eager for scandal and flurry turn to this philosophy which in other respects does not at all serve their purposes in this sphere.

Actually, it is the least scandalous, the most austere of doctrines. It is intended strictly for specialists and philosophers. Yet it can be defined easily. What complicates matters is that there are two kinds of existentialists; first, those who are Christian, among whom I would include Jaspers and Gabriel Marcel, both Catholic; and on the other hand, the atheistic existentialists, among whom I class Heidegger, and then the French existentialists and myself. What they have in common is that they think that existence precedes essence, or, if you prefer, that subjectivity must be the starting point.

Just what does that mean? Let us consider some object that is manufactured, for example, a book or a paper-cutter: here is an object which has been made by an artisan whose inspiration came from a concept. He referred to the concept of what a paper-cutter is and likewise to a known method of production, which is part of the concept, something which is, by and large, a routine. Thus, the paper-cutter is at once an object produced in a certain way and, on the other hand, one having a specific use; and one cannot postulate a man who produces a paper-cutter but does not know what it is used for. Therefore, let us say that, for the paper-cutter, essence—that is, the ensemble of both the production routines and the properties which enable it to be both produced and defined—precedes existence. Thus, the presence of the paper-cutter or book in front of me is determined. Therefore, we have here a technical view of the world whereby it can be said that production precedes existence.

When we conceive God as the Creator, He is generally thought of as a superior sort of artisan. Whatever doctrine we may be considering, whether one like that of Descartes or that of Leibnitz, we always grant that will more or less follows understanding or, at the very least, accompanies it, and that when God creates He knows exactly what He is creating. Thus, the concept of man in the mind of God is comparable to the concept of paper-cutter in the mind of the manufacturer, and, following certain techniques and a conception, God produces man, just as the artisan, following a definition and a technique, makes a paper-cutter. Thus, the individual man is the realization of a certain concept in the divine intelligence.

In the eighteenth century, the atheism of the *philosophes* discarded the idea of God, but not so much for the notion that essence precedes existence. To a certain extent, this idea is found everywhere; we find it in Diderot, in Voltaire, and even in Kant. Man has a human nature; this human nature, which is the concept of the human, is found in all men, which means that each man is a particular example of a universal concept, man. In Kant, the result of this universality is that the wild-man, the natural man, as well as the bourgeois, are circumscribed by the same definition and have the same basic qualities. Thus, here too the essence of man precedes the historical existence that we find in nature.

Atheistic existentialism, which I represent, is more coherent. It states that if God does not exist, there is at least one being in whom existence precedes essence, a being who exists before he can be defined by any concept, and that this being is man, or, as Heidegger says, human reality. What is meant here by saying that existence precedes essence? It means that, first of all, man exists, turns up, appears on the scene, and, only afterwards, defines himself. If man, as the existentialist conceives him, is indefinable, it is because at first he is nothing. Only afterward will he be something, and he himself will have made what he will be. Thus, there is no human nature, since there is no God to conceive it. Not only is man what he conceives himself to be, but he is also only what he wills himself to be after this thrust toward existence.

Man is nothing else but what he makes of himself. Such is the first principle of existentialism. It is also what is called subjectivity, the name we are labeled with when charges are brought against us. But what do we mean by this, if not that man has a greater dignity than a stone or table? For we mean that man first exists, that is, that man first of all is the being in the future. Man is at the start a plan which is aware of itself, rather than a patch of moss, a piece of garbage, or a cauliflower; nothing exists prior to this plan; there is nothing in heaven; man will be what he will have planned to be. Not what he will want to be. Because by the word "will" we generally mean a conscious decision, which is subsequent to what we have already made of ourselves. I may want to belong to a political party, write a book, get married; but all that is only a manifestation of an earlier, more spontaneous choice that is called "will." But if existence really does precede essence, man is responsible for what he is. Thus, existentialism's first move is to make every man aware of what he is and to make the full responsibility of his existence rest on him. And when we say that a man is responsible for himself, we do not only mean that he is responsible for his own individuality, but that he is responsible for all men.

The word subjectivism has two meanings, and our opponents play on the two. Subjectivism means, on the one hand, that an individual chooses and makes himself; and, on the other, that it is impossible for man to transcend human subjectivity. The second of these is the essential meaning of existentialism. When we say that man chooses his own self, we mean that every one of us does likewise; but we also mean by that that in making this choice he also chooses all men. In fact, in creating the man that we want to be, there is not a single one of our acts which does not at the same time create an image of man as we think he ought to be. To choose to be this or that is to affirm at the same time the value of what we choose, because we can never choose evil. We always choose the good, and nothing can be good for us without being good for all.

If, on the other hand, existence precedes essence, and if we grant that we exist and fashion our image at one and the same time, the image is valid for everybody and for our whole age. Thus, our responsibility is much greater than we might have supposed, because it involves all mankind. If I am a workingman and choose to join a Christian trade-union rather than be a communist, and if by being a member I want to show that the best thing for man is resignation, that the kingdom of man is not of this world, I am not only involving my own case—I want to be resigned for everyone. As a result, my action has involved all humanity. To take a more individual matter, if I want to marry, to have children; even if this marriage depends solely on my own circumstances or passion or wish, I am involving all humanity in monogamy and not merely myself. Therefore, I am responsible for myself and for everyone else. I am creating a certain image of man of my own choosing. In choosing myself, I choose man.

This helps us understand what the actual content is of such rather grandiloquent words as anguish, forlornness, despair. As you will see, it's all quite simple.

First, what is meant by anguish? The existentialists say at once that man is anguish. What that means is this: the man who involves himself and who realizes that he is not only the person he chooses to be, but also a law-maker who is, at the same time, choosing all mankind as well as himself, cannot help escape the feeling of his total and deep responsibility. Of course, there are many people who are not anxious; but we claim that they are hiding their anxiety, that they are fleeing from it. Certainly, many people believe that when they do something, they themselves are the only ones involved, and when someone says to them, "What if everyone acted that way?" they shrug their shoulders and answer, "Everyone doesn't act that way." But really, one should always ask himself, "What would happen if everybody looked at things that way?" There is no escaping this disturbing thought except by a kind of double-dealing. A man who lies and makes excuses for himself by saying "not everybody does that," is someone with an uneasy conscience, because the act of lying implies that a universal value is conferred upon the lie.

Anguish is evident even when it conceals itself. This is the anguish that Kierkegaard called the anguish of Abraham. You know the story: an angel has ordered Abraham to sacrifice his son; if it really were an angel who has come and said, "You are Abraham, you shall sacrifice your son," everything would be all right. But everyone might first wonder, "Is it really an angel, and am I really Abraham? What proof do I have?" . . .

Now, I'm not being singled out as an Abraham, and yet at every moment I'm obliged to perform exemplary acts. For every man, everything happens as if all mankind had its eyes fixed on him and were guiding itself by what he does. And every man ought to say to himself, "Am I really the kind of man who has the right to act in such a way that humanity might guide itself by my actions?" And if he does not say that to himself, he is masking his anguish.

There is no question here of the kind of anguish which would lead to quietism, to inaction. It is a matter of a simple sort of anguish that anybody who has had responsibilities is familiar with. For example, when a military officer takes the responsibility for an attack and sends a certain number of men to death, he chooses to do so, and in the main he alone makes the choice. Doubtless, orders come from above, but they are too broad; he interprets them, and on this interpretation depend the lives of ten or fourteen or twenty men. In making a decision he cannot help having a certain anguish. All leaders know this anguish. That doesn't keep them from acting; on the contrary, it is the very condition of their action. For it implies that they envisage a number of possibilities, and when they choose one, they realize that it has value only because it is chosen. We shall see that this kind of anguish, which is the kind that existentialism describes, is explained, in addition, by a direct responsibility to the other men whom it involves. It is not a curtain separating us from action, but is part of action itself.

When we speak of forlornness, a term Heidegger was fond of, we mean only that God does not exist and that we have to face all the consequences of this. The existentialist is strongly opposed to a certain kind of secular ethics which would like to abolish God with the least possible expense. About 1880, some French teachers tried to set up a secular ethics which went something like this: God is a useless and costly hypothesis; we are discarding it; but meanwhile, in order for there to be an ethics, a society, a civilization, it is essential that certain values be taken seriously and that they be considered as having an *a priori* existence. It must be obligatory, *a priori,* to be honest, not to lie, not to beat your wife, to have children, etc., etc. So we're going to try a little device which will make it possible to show that values exist all the same, inscribed in a heaven of ideas, though otherwise God does not exist. In other words—and this, I believe, is the tendency of everything called reformism in France—nothing will be changed if God does not exist. We shall find ourselves with the same norms of honesty, progress, and humanism, and we shall have made of God an outdated hypothesis which will peacefully die off by itself.

The existentialist, on the contrary, thinks it very distressing that God does not exist, because all possibility of finding values in a heaven of ideas disappears along with Him; there can be no longer an *a priori* Good, since there is no infinite and perfect consciousness to think it. Nowhere is it written that the Good exists, that we must be honest, that we must not lie; because the fact is we are on a plane where there are only men. Dostoievsky said, "If God didn't exist, everything would be possible." That is the very starting point of existentialism. Indeed, everything is permissible if God does not exist, and as a result man is forlorn, because neither within him nor without does he find anything to cling to. He can't start making excuses for himself.

If existence really does precede essence, there is no explaining things away by reference to a fixed and given human nature. In other words, there is no determinism, man is free, man is freedom. On the other hand, if God does not exist, we find no values or commands to turn to which legitimize our conduct. So, in the bright realm of values, we have no excuse behind us, no justification before us. We are alone, with no excuses.

That is the idea I shall try to convey when I say that man is condemned to be free. Condemned, because he did not create himself, yet, in other respects is free; because, once thrown into the world, he is responsible for everything he does.

The existentialist does not believe in the power of passion. He will never agree that a sweeping passion is a ravaging torrent which fatally leads a man to certain acts and is therefore an excuse. He thinks that man is responsible for his passion.

The existentialist does not think that man is going to help himself by finding in the world some omen by which to orient himself, because he thinks that man will interpret the omen to suit himself. Therefore, he thinks that man, with no support and no aid, is condemned every moment to invent man. Ponge, in a very fine article, has said, "Man is the future of man." That's exactly it. But if it is taken to mean that this future is recorded in heaven, that God sees it, then it is false, because it would really no longer be a future. If it is taken to mean that, whatever a man may be, there is a future to be forged, a virgin future before him, then this remark is sound. But then we are forlorn.

To give you an example which will enable you to understand forlornness better, I shall cite the case of one of my students who came to see me under the following circumstances: his father was on bad terms with his mother, and, moreover, was inclined to be a collaborationist; his older brother had been killed in the German offensive of 1940, and the young man, with somewhat immature but generous feelings, wanted to avenge him. His mother lived alone with him, very much upset by the half-treason of her husband and the death of her older son; the boy was her only consolation.

The boy was faced with the choice of leaving for England and joining the Free French Forces—that is, leaving his mother behind—or remaining with his mother and helping her to carry on. He was fully aware that the woman lived only for him and that his going-off—and perhaps his death—would plunge her into despair. He was also aware that every act that he did for his mother's sake was a sure thing, in the sense that it was helping her to carry on, whereas every effort he made toward going off and fighting was an uncertain move which might run aground and prove completely useless; for example, on his way to England he might, while passing through Spain, be detained indefinitely in a Spanish camp; he might reach England or Algiers and be stuck in an office at a desk job. As a result, he was faced with two very different kinds of action: one, concrete, immediate, but concerning only one individual; the other concerned an incomparably vaster group, a national collectivity, but for that very reason was dubious, and might be interrupted en route. And, at the same time, he was wavering between two kinds of ethics. On the one hand, an ethics of sympathy, of personal devotion; on the other, a broader ethics, but one whose efficacy was more dubious. He had to choose between the two.

Who could help him choose? Christian doctrine? No. Christian doctrine says, "Be charitable, love your neighbor, take the more rugged path, etc., etc." But which is the more rugged path? Whom should he love as a brother? The fighting man or his mother? Which does the greater good, the vague act of fighting in a group, or the concrete one of helping a particular human being to go on living? Who can decide *a priori?* Nobody. No book of ethics can tell him. The Kantian ethics says, "Never treat any person as a means, but as an end." Very well, if I stay with my mother, I'll treat her as an end and not as a means; but by virtue of this very fact, I'm running the risk of treating the people around me who are fighting, as means; and, conversely, if I go to join those who are fighting, I'll be treating them as an end, and, by doing that, I run the risk of treating my mother as a means.

If values are vague, and if they are always too broad for the concrete and specific case that we are considering, the only thing left for us is to trust our instincts. That's what this young man tried to do; and when I saw him, he said, "In the end, feeling is what counts. I ought to choose whichever pushes me in one direction. If I feel that I love my mother enough to sacrifice everything else for her—my desire for vengeance, for action, for adventure—then I'll stay with her. If, on the contrary, I feel that my love for my mother isn't enough, I'll leave."

But how is the value of a feeling determined? What gives his feeling for his mother value? Precisely the fact that he remained with her. I may say that I like so-and-so well enough to sacrifice a certain amount of money for him, but I may say so only if I've done it. I may say, "I love my mother well enough to remain with her" if I have remained with her. The only way to determine the value of this affection is, precisely, to perform an act which confirms and defines it. But, since I require this affection to justify my act, I find myself caught in a vicious circle. . . .

As for despair, the term has a very simple meaning. It means that we shall confine ourselves to reckoning only with what depends upon our will, or on the ensemble of probabilities which make our action possible. When we want something, we always have to reckon with probabilities. I may be counting on the arrival of a friend. The friend is coming by rail or street-car; this supposes that the train will arrive on schedule, or that the street-car will not jump the track. I am left in the realm of possibility; but possibilities are to be reckoned with only to the point where my action comports with the ensemble of these possibilities, and no further. The moment the possibilities I am considering are not rigorously involved by my action, I ought to disengage myself from them, because no God, no scheme, can adapt the world and its possibilities to my will. When Descartes said, "Conquer yourself rather than the world," he meant essentially the same thing.

The Marxists to whom I have spoken reply, "You can rely on the support of others in your action, which obviously has certain limits because you're not going to live forever. That means: rely on both what others are doing elsewhere to help you, in China, in Russia, and what they will do later on, after your death, to carry on the action and lead it to its fulfillment, which will be the revolution. You even *have* to rely upon that, otherwise you're immortal." I reply at once that I will always rely on fellow fighters insofar as these comrades are involved with me in a common struggle, in the unity of a party or a group in which I can more or less make my weight felt; that is, one whose ranks I am in as a fighter and whose movements I am aware of at every moment. In such a situation, relying on the unity and will of the party is exactly like counting on the fact that the train will arrive on time or that the car won't jump the track. But, given that man is free and that there is no human nature for me to depend on, I cannot count on men whom I do not know by relying on human goodness or man's concern for the good of society. I don't know what will become of the Russian revolution; I may make an example of it to the extent that at the present time it is apparent that the proletariat plays a part in Russia that it plays in no other nation. But I can't swear that this will inevitably lead to a triumph of the proletariat. I've got to limit myself to what I see.

Given that men are free, and that tomorrow they will freely decide what man will be, I cannot be sure that, after my death, fellow fighters will carry on my work to bring it to its maximum perfection. Tomorrow, after my death, some men may decide to set up Fascism, and the others may be cowardly and muddled enough to let them do it. Fascism will then be the human reality, so much the worse for us.

Actually, things will be as man will have decided they are to be. Does that mean that I should abandon myself to quietism? No. First, I should involve myself; then, act on the old saw, "Nothing ventured, nothing gained." Nor does it mean that I shouldn't belong to a party, but rather that I shall have no illusions and shall do what I can. For example, suppose I ask myself, "Will socialization, as such, ever come about?" I know nothing about it. All I know is that I'm going to do everything in my power to bring it about. Beyond that, I can't count on anything. Quietism is the attitude of people who say, "Let others do what I can't do." The doctrine I am presenting is the very opposite of quietism, since it declares, "There is no reality except in action." Moreover, it goes further, since it adds, "Man is nothing else than his plan; he exists only to the extent that he fulfills himself; he is, therefore, nothing else than the ensemble of his acts, nothing else than his life."

For Further Reflection

1. How are existentialist ethics different from other theories we have studied? What are its strengths and weaknesses?

2. Has Sartre gotten to the heart of the matter with his example of the student who must choose between his mother and the war effort? Could we object that he is making an exception to the norm? In normal situations we know perfectly well the right thing to do. For example, suppose that there was no war; then, wouldn't it be automatically right to take care of the mother? Does existentialism have a response to this criticism?

3. Sartre believes that it makes all the difference in the world whether God exists. If God does not exist, all things are morally permissible, there is no right or wrong, but thinking makes it so. Is this correct?

Servility and Self-Respect

THOMAS E. HILL, JR.

Thomas E. Hill, Jr., is professor of philosophy at the University of North Carolina, Chapel Hill. He has written extensively in the area of moral philosophy, especially on Kant's ethics. In this essay Hill develops the Kantian theme that we have duties to ourselves, so that the servile person is morally defective because he or she fails sufficiently to respect the moral law, which enjoins that we respect all persons as moral equals, including oneself. He illustrates his thesis by three examples: the Uncle Tom who doesn't believe he has equal moral standing with whites, the Self-deprecator who lacks self-respect and holds himself of little worth, and the Deferential Wife who always defers to her husband, holding that her place is rightfully to serve the family, not her own independent goals. He argues that utilitarianism fails to give sufficient weight to such duties to oneself.

Several motives underlie this paper. In the first place, I am curious to see if there is a legitimate source for the increasingly common feeling that servility can be as much a vice as arrogance is. There seems to be something morally defective about the Uncle Tom and the submissive housewife; and yet, on the other hand, if the only interests they sacrifice are their own, it seems that we should have no right to complain. Secondly, I have some sympathy for the now unfashionable view that each person has duties to himself as well as to others. It does seem absurd to say that a person could literally violate his own rights or owe himself a debt to gratitude, but I suspect that the classic defenders to duties to oneself had something different in mind. If there are duties to oneself, it is natural to expect that a duty to avoid being servile would have a prominent place among them. . . .

I

Three examples may give a preliminary idea of what I mean by *servility*. Consider, first, an extremely deferential black, whom I shall call the *Uncle Tom*. He always steps aside for white men; he does not complain when less qualified whites take over his job; he gratefully accepts whatever benefits his all-white government and employers allot him, and he would not think of protesting its insufficiency. He displays the symbols of deference to whites, and of contempt towards blacks: he faces the former with bowed stance and a ready "Sir" and "Ma'am"; he reserves his strongest obscenities for the latter. Imagine, too, that he is not playing a game. He is not the shrewdly prudent calculator, who knows how to make the best of a bad lot and mocks his masters behind their backs. He accepts without question the idea that, as a black, he is owed less than whites. He may believe that blacks are mentally inferior and of less social utility, but that is not the crucial point. The attitude which he displays is that what he values, aspires for, and can demand is of less importance than what whites value, aspire for, and can demand. He is far from the picture book's carefree, happy servant, but he does not feel that he has a right to expect anything better.

Another pattern of servility is illustrated by a person I shall call the *Self-deprecator*. Like the Uncle Tom, he is reluctant to make demands. He says nothing when others take unfair advantage of him. When asked for his preferences or opinions, he tends to shrink away as if what he said should make no difference. His problem, however, is not a sense of racial inferiority but rather an acute awareness of his own inadequacies and failures as an individual. These defects are not imaginary: he has in fact done poorly by his own standards and others'. But, unlike many of us in the same situation, he acts as if his failings warrant quite unrelated maltreatment even by strangers. His sense of shame and self-contempt makes him content to be the instrument of others. He feels that nothing is owed him until he has earned it and that he has earned very little. He is not simply playing a masochist's game of winning sympathy by disparaging himself. On the contrary, he assesses his individual merits with painful accuracy.

A rather different case is that of the *Deferential Wife*. This is a woman who is utterly devoted to serving her husband. She buys the clothes *he* prefers, invites the guests *he* wants to entertain, and makes love whenever *he* is in the mood. She willingly moves to a new city in order for him to have a more attractive job, counting her own friendships and geographical preferences insignificant by comparison. She loves her husband, but her conduct is not simply an expression of love. She is happy, but she does not subordinate herself as a means to happiness. She does not simply defer to her husband in certain spheres as a trade-off for his deference in other spheres. On the contrary, she tends not to form her own interests, values, and ideals; and, when she does, she counts them as less important than her husband's. She readily responds to appeals from Women's Liberation that she agrees that women are mentally and physically equal, if not superior, to men. She just believes that the proper role for a woman is to serve her family. As a matter of fact, much of her happiness derives from her belief that she fulfills this role very well. No one is trampling on her rights, she says; for she is quite glad, and proud, to serve her husband as she does.

Each one of these cases reflects the attitude which I call servility. It betrays the absence of a certain kind of self-respect. What I take this attitude to be, more specifically, will become clearer later on. It is important at the outset, however, not to confuse the three cases sketched above with other, superficially similar cases. In particular, the cases I have sketched are not simply cases in which someone refuses to press his rights, speaks disparagingly of himself, or devotes himself to another. A black, for example, is not necessarily servile because he does not demand a just wage; for, seeing that such a demand would result in his being fired, he might forbear for the sake of his children. A self-critical person is not necessarily servile by virtue of bemoaning his faults in public; for his behavior may be merely a complex way of satisfying his own inner needs quite independent of a willingness to accept abuse from others. A woman need not be servile whenever she works to make her husband happy and prosperous; for she might freely and knowingly choose to do so from love or from a desire to share the rewards of his success. If the effort did not require her to submit to humiliation or maltreatment, her choice would not mark her as servile. There may, of course, be grounds for objecting to the attitudes in these cases; but the defect is not servility of the sort I want to consider. It should also be noted that my cases of servility are not simply instances of deference to superior knowledge or judgment. To defer to an expert's judgment on matters of fact is not to be servile; to defer to his every wish and whim is. Similarly, the belief that one's talents and achievements are comparatively low does not, by itself, make one servile. It is no vice to acknowledge the truth, and one may in fact have achieved less, and have less ability, than others. To be servile is not simply to hold certain empirical beliefs but to have a certain attitude concerning one's rightful place in a moral community.

II

Are there grounds for regarding the attitudes of the Uncle Tom, the Self-deprecator, and the Deferential Wife as morally objectionable? Are there moral arguments we could give them to show that they ought to have more self-respect? None of the more obvious replies is entirely satisfactory.

One might, in the first place, adduce utilitarian considerations. Typically the servile person will be less happy than he might be. Moreover, he may be less prone to make the best of his own socially useful abilities. He may become a nuisance to others by being overly dependent. He will, in any case, lose the special contentment that comes from standing up for one's rights. A submissive attitude encourages exploitation, and exploitation spreads misery in a variety of ways. These considerations provide a *prima facie* case against the attitudes of the Uncle Tom, the Deferential Wife, and the Self-deprecator, but they are hardly conclusive. Other utilities tend to counterbalance the ones just mentioned. When people refuse to press their rights, there are usually others who profit. There are undeniable pleasures in associating with those who are devoted, understanding, and grateful for whatever we see fit to give them—as our fondness for dogs attests. Even the servile person may find his attitude a source of happiness, as the case of the Deferential Wife illustrates. There may be comfort and security in thinking that the hard choices must be made by others, that what I would say has little to do with what ought to be done. Self-condemnation may bring relief from the pangs of guilt even if it is not deliberately used for that purpose. On balance, then, utilitarian considerations may turn out to favor servility as much as they oppose it.

For those who share my moral intuitions, there is another sort of reason for not trying to rest a case against servility on utilitarian considerations. Certain utilities seem irrelevant to the issue. The utilitarian must weigh them along with others, but to do so seems morally inappropriate. Suppose, for example, that the submissive attitudes of the Uncle Tom and the Deferential Wife result in positive utilities for those who dominate and exploit them. Do we need to tabulate *these* utilities before conceding that servility is objectionable? The Uncle Tom, it seems, is making an error, a moral error, quite apart from consideration of how much others in fact profit from his attitude. The Deferential Wife may be quite happy; but if her happiness turns out to be contingent on her distorted view of her own rights and worth as a person, then it carries little moral weight against the contention that she ought to change that view. Suppose I could cause a woman to find her happiness in denying all her rights and serving my every wish. No doubt I could do so only by nonrational manipulative techniques, which I ought not to use. But is this the only objection? My efforts would be wrong, it seems, not only because of the techniques they require but also because the resultant attitude is itself objectionable. When a person's happiness stems from a morally objectionable attitude, it ought to be discounted. That a sadist gets pleasure from seeing others suffer should not count even as a partial justification for his attitude. That a servile person derives pleasure from denying her moral status, for similar reasons, cannot make her attitude acceptable. These brief intuitive remarks are not intended as a refutation of utilitarianism, with all its many varieties; but they do suggest that it is well to look elsewhere for adequate grounds for rejecting the attitudes of the Uncle Tom, the Self-deprecator, and the Deferential Wife.

III

Why, then, is servility a moral defect? There is, I think, another sort of answer which is worth exploring. The first part of this answer must be an attempt to isolate the objectionable features of the servile person; later we can ask why these features are objectionable. As a step in this direction, let us examine again our three paradigm cases. The moral defect in each case, I suggest, is a failure to understand and acknowledge one's own moral rights. I assume, without argument here, that each person has moral rights. Some of these rights may be basic human rights; that is, rights for which a person needs only to be human to qualify. Other rights will be derivative and contingent upon his special commitments, institutional affiliations, etc. Most rights will be *prima facie* ones; some may be absolute. Most can be waived under appropriate conditions; perhaps some cannot. Many rights can be forfeited; but some, presumably, cannot. The servile person does not, strictly speaking, violate his own rights. At least in our paradigm cases he fails to acknowledge fully his own moral status because he does not fully understand what his rights are, how they can be waived, and when they can be forfeited.

The defect of the Uncle Tom, for example, is that he displays an attitude that denies his moral equality with whites. He does not realize, or apprehend in an effective way, that he has as much right to a decent wage and a share of political power as any comparable white. His gratitude is misplaced; he accepts benefits which are his by right as if they were gifts. The Self-deprecator is servile in a more complex way. He acts as if he has forfeited many important rights which in fact he has not. He does not understand, or fully realize in his own case, that certain rights to fair and decent treatment do not have to be earned. He sees his merits clearly enough, but he fails to see that what he can expect from others is not merely a function of his merits. The Deferential Wife *says* that she understands her rights vis-à-vis her husband, but what she fails to appreciate is that her consent to serve him is a valid waiver of her rights only under certain conditions. If her consent is coerced, say, by the lack of viable options for women in her society, then her consent is worth little. If socially fostered ignorance of her own talents and alternatives is responsible for her consent, then her consent should not count as a fully legitimate waiver of her right to equal consideration within the marriage. All the more, her consent to defer constantly to her husband is not a legitimate setting aside of her rights if it results from her mistaken belief that she has a moral duty to do so. (Recall: "The *proper* role for a woman is to serve her family.") If she believes that she has a *duty* to defer to her husband, then, whatever she may say, she cannot fully understand that she has a *right* not to defer to him. When she says that she freely gives up such a right, she is confused. Her confusion is rather like that of a person who has been persuaded by an unscrupulous lawyer that it is legally incumbent on him to refuse a jury trial but who nevertheless tells the judge that he understands that he has a right to a jury trial and freely waives it. He does not really understand what it is to have and freely give up the right if he thinks that it would be an offense for him to exercise it.

Insofar as servility results from moral ignorance or confusion, it need not be something for which a person is to blame. . . . Suppose, however, that our servile persons come to know their rights but do not substantially alter their behavior. Are they not still servile in an objectionable way?

The answer, I think, should depend upon why the deferential role is played. If the motive is a morally commendable one, or a desire to avert dire consequences to oneself, or even an ambition to set an oppressor up for a later fall, then I would not count the role player as servile. The Uncle Tom, for instance, is not servile in my sense if he shuffles and bows to keep the Klan from killing his children, to save his own skin, or even to buy time while he plans the revolution. Similarly, the Deferential Wife is not servile if she tolerates an abusive husband because he is so ill that further strain would kill him, because protesting would deprive her of her only means of survival, or because she is collecting atrocity stories for her book against marriage. If there is fault in these situations, it seems inappropriate to call it *servility*. The story is quite different, however, if a person continues in his deferential role just from laziness, timidity, or a desire for some minor advantage. He shows too little concern for his moral status as a person, one is tempted to say, if he is willing to deny it for a small profit or simply because it requires some effort and courage to affirm it openly. A black who plays the Uncle Tom merely to gain an advantage over other blacks is harming them, of course; but he is also displaying disregard for his own moral position as an equal among human beings. Similarly, a woman throws away her rights too lightly if she continues to play the subservient role because she is used to it or is too timid to risk a change. A Self-deprecator who readily accepts what he knows are violations of his rights may be indulging his peculiar need for punishment at the expense of denying something more valuable. In these cases, I suggest, we have a kind of servility independent of any ignorance or confusion about one's rights. The person who has it may or may not be blameworthy, depending on many factors; and the line between servile and nonservile role playing will often be hard to draw. Nevertheless, the objectionable feature is perhaps clear enough for present purposes: it is a willingness to disavow one's moral status, publicly and systematically, in the absence of any strong reason to do so.

IV

The objectionable feature of the servile person, as I have described him, is his tendency to disavow his own moral rights either because he misunderstands them or because he cares little for them. The question remains: why should anyone regard this as a moral defect?

After all, the rights which he denies are his own. He may be unfortunate, foolish, or even distasteful; but why *morally* deficient? One sort of answer, quite different from those reviewed earlier, is suggested by some of Kant's remarks. Kant held that servility is contrary to a perfect nonjuridical duty to oneself.[1] To say that the duty is perfect is roughly to say that it is stringent, never overridden by other considerations (e.g., beneficence). To say that the duty is nonjuridical is to say that a person cannot legitimately be coerced to comply. Although Kant did not develop an explicit argument for this view, an argument can easily be constructed from materials which reflect the spirit, if not the letter, of his moral theory. The argument which I have in mind is prompted by Kant's contention that respect for persons, strictly speaking, is respect for moral law.[2] If taken as a claim about all sorts of respect, this seems quite implausible. If it means that we respect persons only for their moral character, their capacity for moral conduct, or their status as "authors" of the moral law, then it seems unduly moralistic. My strategy is to construe the remark as saying that at least one sort of respect for persons is respect for the rights which the moral law accords them. If one respects the moral law, then one must respect one's own moral rights; and this amounts to having a kind of self-respect incompatible with servility.

The premises for the Kantian argument, which are all admittedly vague, can be sketched as follows:

First, let us assume, as Kant did, that all human beings have equal basic human rights. Specific rights vary with different conditions, but all must be justified from a point of view under which all are equal. Not all rights need to be earned, and some cannot be forfeited. Many rights can be waived but only under certain conditions of knowledge and freedom. These conditions are complex and difficult to state; but they include something like the condition

[1]See Immanuel Kant, *The Doctrine of Virtue,* Part II of *The Metaphysics of Morals,* ed. by M. J. Gregor (New York: Harper & Row, 1964), pp. 99–103; Prussian Academy edition, vol. VI, pp. 434–37.

[2]Immanuel Kant, *Groundwork of the Metaphysics of Morals,* ed. by H. J. Paton (New York: Harper & Row, 1964), p. 69; Prussian Academy edition, vol. IV, p. 401; *The Critique of Practical Reason,* ed. by Lewis W. Beck (New York: Bobbs-Merrill, 1956), pp. 81, 84; Prussian Academy edition, vol. V, pp. 78, 81. My purpose here is not to interpret what Kant meant but to give a sense to his remark.

that a person's consent releases others from obligation only if it is autonomously given, and consent resulting from underestimation of one's moral status is not autonomously given. Rights can be objects of knowledge, but also of ignorance, misunderstanding, deception, and the like.

Second, let us assume that my account of servility is correct; or, if one prefers, we can take it as a definition. That is, in brief, a servile person is one who tends to deny or disavow his own moral rights because he does not understand them or has little concern for the status they give him.

Third, we need one formal premise concerning moral duty, namely, that each person ought, as far as possible, to respect the moral law. In less Kantian language, the point is that everyone should approximate, to the extent that he can, the ideal of a person who fully adopts the moral point of view. Roughly, this means not only that each person ought to do what is morally required and refrain from what is morally wrong but also that each person should treat all the provisions of morality as valuable—worth preserving and prizing as well as obeying. One must, so to speak, take up the spirit of morality as well as meet the letter of its requirements. To keep one's promises, avoid hurting others, and the like, is not sufficient; one should also take an attitude of respect towards the principles, ideals, and goals of morality. A respectful attitude towards a system of rights and duties consists of more than a disposition to conform to its definite rules of behavior; it also involves holding the system in esteem, being unwilling to ridicule it, and being reluctant to give up one's place in it. The essentially Kantian idea here is that morality, as a system of equal fundamental rights and duties, is worthy of respect, and hence a completely moral person would respect it in word and manner as well as in deed. And what a completely moral person would do, in Kant's view, is our duty to do so far as we can.

The assumptions here are, of course, strong ones, and I make no attempt to justify them. They are, I suspect, widely held though rarely articulated. In any case, my present purpose is not to evaluate them but to see how, if granted, they constitute a case against servility. The objection to the servile person, given our premises, is that he does not satisfy the basic requirement to respect morality. A person who fully respected a system of moral rights would be disposed to learn his proper place in it, to affirm it proudly, and not to tolerate abuses of it lightly. This is just the sort of disposition that the servile person lacks. If he does not understand the system, he is in no position to respect it adequately. This lack of respect may be no fault of his own, but it is still a way in which he falls short of a moral ideal. If, on the other hand, the servile person knowingly disavows his moral rights by pretending to approve of violations of them, then, barring special explanations, he shows an indifference to whether the provisions of morality are honored and publicly acknowledged. This avoidable display of indifference, by our Kantian premises, is contrary to the duty to respect morality. The disrespect in this second case is somewhat like the disrespect a religious believer might show towards his religion if, to avoid embarrassment, he laughed congenially while nonbelievers were mocking the beliefs which he secretly held. In any case, the servile person, as such, does not express disrespect for the system of moral rights in the obvious way by violating the rights of others. His lack of respect is more subtly manifested by his acting before others as if he did not know or care about his position of equality under that system.

The central idea here may be illustrated by an analogy. Imagine a club, say, an old German dueling fraternity. By the rules of the club, each member has certain rights and responsibilities. These are the same for each member regardless of what titles he may hold outside the club. Each has, for example, a right to be heard at meetings, a right not to be shouted down by the others. Some rights cannot be forfeited: for example, each may vote regardless of whether he has paid his dues and satisfied other rules. Some rights cannot be waived: for example, the right to be defended when attacked by several members of the rival fraternity. The members show respect for each other by respecting the status which the rules confer on each member. Now one new member is careful always to allow the others to speak at meetings; but when they shout him down, he does nothing. He just shrugs as if to say, "Who am I to complain?" When he fails to stand up in defense of a fellow member, he feels ashamed and refuses to vote. He does not deserve to vote, he says. As the only commoner among illustrious barons, he feels that it is his place to serve them and defer to their decisions. When attackers from the rival fraternity come at him with swords drawn, he tells his companions to run and save themselves. When they defend him, he expresses immense gratitude—as if they had done him a gratuitous favor. Now one might argue that our new member fails to show respect for the fraternity and its rules. He does not actually violate any of the rules by refusing to vote, asking others not to defend him, and deferring to the barons, but he symbolically disavows the equal status which the rules confer on him. If he ought to have respect for the fraternity, he ought to change his attitude. Our servile person, then, is like the new member of the dueling fraternity in having insufficient respect for a system of rules and ideals. The difference is that everyone ought to respect morality whereas there is no comparable moral requirement to respect the fraternity.

The conclusion here is, of course, a limited one. Self-sacrifice is not always a sign of servility. It is not a duty always to press one's rights. Whether a given act is evidence of servility will depend not only on the attitude of the agent but also on the specific nature of his moral rights, a matter not considered here. Moreover, the extent to which a person is responsible, or blameworthy, for his defect remains an open question. Nevertheless, the conclusion should not be minimized. In order to avoid servility, a person who gives up his rights must do so with a full appreciation for what they are. A woman, for example, may devote herself to her husband if she is uncoerced, knows what she is doing, and does not pretend that she has no decent alternative. A self-contemptuous person may decide not to press various unforfeited rights but only if he does not take the attitude that he is too rotten to deserve them. A black may demand less than is due to him provided he is prepared to acknowledge that no one has a right to expect this of him. Sacrifices of this sort, I suspect, are extremely rare. Most people, if they fully acknowledged their rights, would not autonomously refuse to press them.

An even stronger conclusion would emerge if we could assume that some basic rights cannot be waived. . . .

Even if there are no specific rights which cannot be waived, there might be at least one formal right of this sort. This is the right to some minimum degree of respect from others. No matter how willing a person is to submit to humiliation by others, they ought to show him some respect as a person. By analogy with self-respect, as presented here, this respect owed by others would consist of a willingness to acknowledge fully, in word as well as action, the person's basically equal moral status as defined by his other rights. To the extent that a person gives even tacit consent to humiliations incompatible with this respect, he will be acting as if he waives a right which he cannot in fact give up. To do this, barring special explanations, would mark one as servile.

Kant suggests that duties to oneself are a precondition of duties to others. On our account of servility, there is at least one sense in which this is so. Insofar as the servile person is ignorant of his own rights, he is not in an adequate position to appreciate the rights of others. Misunderstanding the moral basis for his equal status with others, he is necessarily liable to underestimate the rights of those with whom he classifies himself. On the other hand, if he plays the servile role knowingly, then, barring special explanation, he displays a lack of concern to see the principles of morality acknowledged and respected and thus the absence of one motive which can move a moral person to respect the rights of others. In either case, the servile person's lack of self-respect necessarily puts him in a less than ideal position to respect others. Failure to fulfill one's duty to oneself, then, renders a person liable to violate duties to others. This, however, is a consequence of our argument against servility, not a presupposition of it.

For Further Reflection

1. What exactly is servility, and why is it bad? Note that some religions seem to place great weight on deference to God and one's fellows. See, for example, the Sermon on the Mount (chapter 7). Is servility the same as humility, or are they different?

2. If I really am a person of less talent than others, should I not defer to the more talented in learning or living? Is education a kind of servility, or is it really different?

3. Hill makes a great deal of equal human rights and claims that he is following Kant, but Kant wrote that a person could forfeit his rights (e.g., the right to life by murdering someone) and one's worth (e.g., one's moral worth by lying or breaking a moral principle). Is this consistent with Hill's thesis? Could there be some nonforfeitable rights (or basic worth)? Explain your answer.

4. Hill claims that a utilitarian cannot account for the evil of servility, since a utilitarian would have to do a cost-benefit analysis to determine whether it was justified or not. Is this a valid point? Does the idea of duties to self demonstrate the superiority of deontological ethics to utilitarian?

Harrison Bergeron

KURT VONNEGUT

Kurt Vonnegut (b. 1922) is one of America's best-known authors, especially liked by college students. Among his works are *Slaughterhouse Five* (1969) and *Jailbird* (1979). His short story "Harrison Bergeron" is a satire on the thesis that the state should enforce strong egalitarianism, removing all relevant differences in ability and intelligence. Harrison, a seven-foot-tall precocious teenager, is underhandicapped and does not fit into the leveling-down society of the future. The story is a precursor to satire against political correctness.

The year was 2081, and everybody was finally equal. They weren't only equal before God and the law. They were equal every which way. Nobody was smarter than anybody else. Nobody was better looking than anybody else. Nobody was stronger or quicker than anybody else. All this equality was due to the 211th, 212th, and 213th Amendments to the Constitution, and to the unceasing vigilance of agents of the United States Handicapper General.

Some things about living still weren't quite right, though. April, for instance, still drove people crazy by not being springtime. And it was in that clammy month that the H-G men took George and Hazel Bergeron's fourteen-year-old son, Harrison, away.

It was tragic, all right, but George and Hazel couldn't think about it very hard. Hazel had a perfectly average intelligence, which meant she couldn't think about anything except in short bursts. And George, while his intelligence was way above normal, had a little mental handicap radio in his ear. He was required by law to wear it at all times. It was tuned to a government transmitter. Every twenty seconds or so, the transmitter would send out some sharp noise to keep people like George from taking unfair advantage of their brains.

George and Hazel were watching television. There were tears on Hazel's cheeks, but she'd forgotten for the moment what they were about.

On the television screen were ballerinas.

A buzzer sounded in George's head. His thoughts fled in panic, like bandits from a burglar alarm.

"That was a real pretty dance, that dance they just did," said Hazel.

"Huh?" said George.

"The dance—it was nice," said Hazel.

"Yup," said George. He tried to think a little about the ballerinas. They weren't really very good—no better than anybody else would have been, anyway. They were burdened with sash-weights and bags of birdshot, and their faces were masked, so that no one, seeing a free and graceful gesture or a pretty face, would feel like something the cat drug in. George was toying with the vague notion that maybe dancers shouldn't be handicapped. But he didn't get very far with it before another noise in his ear radio scattered his thoughts.

George winced. So did two out of the eight ballerinas.

Hazel saw him wince. Having no mental handicap herself, she had to ask George what the latest sound had been.

"Sounded like someone hitting a milk bottle with a ball peen hammer," said George.

"I'd think it would be real interesting, hearing all the different sounds," said Hazel, a little envious. "All the things they think up."

"Um," said George.

"Only, if I was Handicapper General, you know what I would do?" said Hazel. Hazel, as a matter of fact, bore a strong resemblance to the Handicapper General, a woman named Diana Moon Glampers. "If I was Diana Moon Glampers," said Hazel, "I'd have chimes on Sunday—just chimes. Kind of in honor of religion."

"I could think, if it was just chimes," said George.

"Well—maybe make 'em real loud," said Hazel. "I think I'd make a good Handicapper General."

"Good as anybody else," said George.

"Who knows better'n I do what normal is?" said Hazel.

"Right," said George. He began to think glimmeringly about his abnormal son who was now in jail, about Harrison, but a twenty-one-gun salute in his head stopped that.

"Boy!" said Hazel, "that was a doozy, wasn't it?"

It was such a doozy that George was white and trembling, and tears stood on the rims of his red eyes. Two of the eight ballerinas had collapsed to the studio floor, were holding their temples.

"All of a sudden you look so tired," said Hazel. "Why don't you stretch out on the sofa, so's you can rest your handicap bag on the pillows, honeybunch." She was referring to the forty-seven pounds of birdshot in a canvas bag, which was padlocked around George's neck. "Go on and rest the bag for a little while," she said. "I don't care if you're not equal to me for a while."

George weighed the bag with his hands. "I don't mind it," he said. "I don't notice it any more. It's just a part of me."

"You've been so tired lately—kind of wore out," said Hazel. "If there was just some way we could make a little hole in the bottom of the bag, and just take out a few of them lead balls. Just a few."

"Two years in prison and two thousand dollars fine for every ball I took out," said George. "I don't call that a bargain."

"If you could just take a few out when you came home from work," said Hazel. "I mean—you don't compete with anybody around here. You just sit around."

"If I tried to get away with it," said George, "then other people'd get away with it—and pretty soon we'd be right back to the dark ages again, with everybody competing against everybody else. You wouldn't like that, would you?"

"I'd hate it," said Hazel.

"There you are," said George. "The minute people start cheating on laws, what do you think happens to society?"

If Hazel hadn't been able to come up with an answer to this question, George couldn't have supplied one. A siren was going off in his head.

"Reckon it'd fall all apart," said Hazel.

"What would?" said George blankly.

"Society," said Hazel uncertainly. "Wasn't that what you just said?"

"Who knows?" said George.

The television program was suddenly interrupted for a news bulletin. It wasn't clear at first as to what the bulletin was about, since the announcer, like all announcers, had a serious speech impediment. For about half a minute, and in a state of high excitement, the announcer tried to say, "Ladies and gentlemen—"

He finally gave up, handed the bulletin to a ballerina to read.

"That's all right—" Hazel said of the announcer, "he tried. That's the big thing. He tried to do the best he could with what God gave him. He should get a nice raise for trying so hard."

"Ladies and gentlemen—" said the ballerina, reading the bulletin. She must have been extraordinarily beautiful, because the mask she wore was hideous. And it was easy to see that she was the strongest and most graceful of the dancers, for her handicap bags were as big as those worn by two-hundred-pound men.

And she had to apologize at once for her voice, which was a very unfair voice for a woman to use. Her voice was a warm, luminous, timeless melody. "Excuse me—" she said, and she began again, making her voice absolutely uncompetitive.

"Harrison Bergeron, age fourteen," she said in a grackle squawk, "has just escaped from jail, where he was held on suspicion of plotting to overthrow the government. He is a genius and an athlete, is under-handicapped, and should be regarded as extremely dangerous."

A police photograph of Harrison Bergeron was flashed on the screen—upside down, then sideways, upside down again, then right side up. The picture showed the full length of Harrison against a background calibrated in feet and inches. He was exactly seven feet tall.

The rest of Harrison's appearance was Halloween and hardware. Nobody had ever borne heavier handicaps. He had outgrown hindrances faster than the H-G men could think them up. Instead of a little ear radio for a mental handicap, he wore a tremendous pair of earphones, and spectacles with thick wavy lenses. The spectacles were intended to make him not only half blind, but to give him whanging headaches besides.

Scrap metal was hung all over him. Ordinarily, there was a certain symmetry, a military neatness to the handicaps issued to strong people, but Harrison looked like a walking junkyard. In the race of life, Harrison carried three hundred pounds.

And to offset his good looks, the H-G men required that he wear at all times a red rubber ball for a nose, keep his eyebrows shaved off, and cover his even white teeth with black caps at snaggle-tooth random.

"If you see this boy," said the ballerina, "do not—repeat, do not—try to reason with him."

There was the shriek of a door being torn from its hinges.

Screams and barking cries of consternation came from the television set. The photograph of Harrison Bergeron on the screen jumped again and again, as though dancing to the tune of an earthquake.

George Bergeron correctly identified the earthquake, and well he might have—for many was the time his own home had danced to the same crashing tune. "My God—" said George, "that must be Harrison!"

The realization was blasted from his mind instantly by the sound of an automobile collision in his head.

When George could open his eyes again, the photograph of Harrison was gone. A living, breathing Harrison filled the screen.

Clanking, clownish, and huge, Harrison stood in the center of the studio. The knob of the uprooted studio door was still in his hand. Ballerinas, technicians, musicians, and announcers cowered on their knees before him, expecting to die.

"I am the Emperor!" cried Harrison. "Do you hear? I am the Emperor! Everybody must do what I say at once!" He stamped his foot and the studio shook.

"Even as I stand here—" he bellowed, "crippled, hobbled, sickened—I am a greater ruler than any man who ever lived! Now watch me become what I *can* become!"

Harrison tore the straps of his handicap harness like wet tissue paper, tore straps guaranteed to support five thousand pounds.

Harrison's scrap-iron handicaps crashed to the floor.

Harrison thrust his thumbs under the bar of the padlock that secured his head harness. The bar snapped like celery. Harrison smashed his headphones and spectacles against the wall.

He flung away his rubber-ball nose, revealed a man that would have awed Thor, the god of thunder.

"I shall now select my Empress!" he said, looking down on the cowering people. "Let the first woman who dares rise to her feet claim her mate and her throne!"

A moment passed, and then a ballerina arose, swaying like a willow.

Harrison plucked the mental handicap from her ear, snapped off her physical handicaps with marvelous delicacy. Last of all, he removed her mask.

She was blindingly beautiful.

"Now—" said Harrison, taking her hand, "shall we show the people the meaning of the word dance? Music!" he commanded.

The musicians scrambled back into their chairs, and Harrison stripped them of their handicaps, too. "Play your best," he told them, "and I'll make you barons and dukes and earls."

The music began. It was normal at first—cheap, silly, false. But Harrison snatched two musicians from their chairs, waved them like batons as he sang the music as he wanted it played. He slammed them back into their chairs.

The music began again and was much improved.

Harrison and his Empress merely listened to the music for a while—listened gravely, as though synchronizing their heartbeats with it.

They shifted their weights to their toes.

Harrison placed his big hands on the girl's tiny waist, letting her sense the weightlessness that would soon be hers.

And then, in an explosion of joy and grace, into the air they sprang!

Not only were the laws of the land abandoned, but the law of gravity and the laws of motion as well.

They reeled, whirled, swiveled, flounced, capered, gamboled, and spun.

They leaped like deer on the moon.

The studio ceiling was thirty feet high, but each leap brought the dancers nearer to it.

It became their obvious intention to kiss the ceiling.

They kissed it.

And then, neutralizing gravity with love and pure will, they remained suspended in air inches below the ceiling, and they kissed each other for a long, long time.

It was then that Diana Moon Glampers, the Handicapper General, came into the studio with a double-barreled ten-gauge shotgun. She fired twice, and the Emperor and the Empress were dead before they hit the floor.

Diana Moon Glampers loaded the gun again. She aimed it at the musicians and told them they had ten seconds to get their handicaps back on.

It was then that the Bergeron's television tube burned out.

Hazel turned to comment about the blackout to George. But George had gone out into the kitchen for a can of beer.

George came back in with the beer, paused while a handicap signal shook him up. And then he sat down again. "You been crying?" he said to Hazel.

"Yup," she said.

"What about?" he said.

"I forget," she said. "Something real sad on television."

"What was it?" he said.

"It's all kind of mixed up in my mind," said Hazel.

"Forget sad things," said George.

"I always do," said Hazel.

"That's my girl," said George. He winced. There was the sound of a rivetting gun in his head.

"Gee—I could tell that one was a doozy," said Hazel.

"You can say that again," said George.

"Gee—" said Hazel, "I could tell that one was a doozy."

For Further Reflection

1. Explain and evaluate this story. What is Vonnegut's point? How could a society evolve into the one described here?

2. Is our society moving in the direction of dumbing down people to a lowest common denominator as occurs in this story? If you think so, give some examples. If you don't think it is, explain why your opponents—on this issue—are wrong.

3. How can moral people ensure that differences in ability neither are punished nor are allowed to so dominate society that everyone but a few lucky ones loses out.

Further Readings for Chapter 10

Hill, Thomas E. *Dignity and Practical Reason*. Ithaca, N.Y.: Cornell University Press, 1992.

Kant, Immanuel. *Lectures on Ethics*. Translated by Louis Infield. London: Methuen, 1930.

Kupperman, Joseph. *Character*. New York: Oxford University Press, 1991.

Nagel, Thomas. *Mortal Questions*. New York: Cambridge University Press, 1979.

Sartre, Jean-Paul. *Being and Nothingness*. Translated by Hazel Barnes. New York: Philosophical Library, 1956.

Williams, Bernard. *Moral Luck*. New York: Cambridge University Press, 1981.

Part IV

Applied Ethics
Moral Problems

What is the use of studying philosophy if all that it does for you is enable you to talk with some plausibility about some abstruse questions of logic, etc., and if it does not improve your thinking about the important questions of everyday life?

—Ludwig Wittgenstein

In this fourth part of our book, we turn to six sets of moral problems facing students every day: (1) issues of sex, love, and marriage; (2) abortion; (3) euthanasia; (4) animals; (5) the environment; and (6) justice and the threat of terrorism. Can philosophical analysis illuminate these issues, supplying appropriate guidance for living? In this part, we attempt to answer that question in the affirmative, even as we offer opposing points of view.

CHAPTER 11

Sex, Love, and Marriage

We begin with matters of sex, love, and marriage. Are these concepts conceptually linked, at least from a moral perspective, so that sex should always involve love and find its proper place only in monogamous marriage? Or are these concepts conceptually separate, so that sexual relations may have a purpose of their own, which may or may not involve marriage? People experience sexual feeling differently and in different degrees at different times in their lives. For some, sexual urges are raging torrents that threaten to overwhelm every other concern. For others, they are mild fantasies that provide moments of pleasure but are no big deal. For Augustine the only justification for sex is procreation. Freud thought that sexual activity is aimed at release of tension, a bit like scratching an itch. For others, it is the ecstatic consummation of the love they feel for the beloved, the two becoming one flesh. Nietzsche held that sex is a manifestation of the will to power: "Go thou to a woman? Forget not thy whip!" Others use sex to attain power or at least favors, as happens when a student is induced to go to bed with a teacher or a secretary with a boss. Still others use sex as a drug, to relax, to go to sleep, to forget about problems, and the like. Sex serves many different functions for many different people.

Even though it is admitted that sex has many functions, philosophers argue about which functions are best or more conducive to the good life. Conservatives, represented by Kant in our readings, hold that sex should be closely linked with love, as without love it tends to degenerate into animal lust. Liberals hold that so long as no one is exploited or deceived in the act, and so long as there is respect for the other, sex is permissible. It is as legitimate as any other contractual relationship into which people may enter or exit freely. A more radical view, such as that of the Marquis de Sade,

713

would permit and encourage any sex act that gave one pleasure, be it sado-masochistic, with animals, children, fetishes (e.g., masturbation with the use of shoes or undergarments), or the dead (necrophilia). To those who claimed that he was perverted, de Sade replied that everything we do is natural, so that if nature had not intended us to explore innovative sex acts, she would never have given us the ability to imagine them, let alone the desire to try them.

We begin our readings with a statement from John Barth's novel *The End of the Road* on the all-pervasiveness of sex in our modern culture. We then turn to Kant's classic theory that sex is best seen as a kind of reciprocal ownership of property, which ought to occur in the context of altruism, a good marriage.

We then turn to articles involving marriage and family. John McMurtry criticizes monogamy precisely on the grounds laid out by Kant—viewing spouses as property, a kind of chattel, which is endorsed by the state. Michael D. Bayles argues that, while marriage as we know it can be reformed, it is basically a morally salient institution, promoting intimate personal relations and providing the context for the rearing of children. Bonnie Steinbock examines what is wrong with adultery. C. S. Lewis argues that commitment to one's family and spouse may sometimes override any claim to the "right to be happy." Finally, Jane English asks what duties grown children have to their parents—and answers that there are none, unless the relationship between parent and child involves friendship.

Pansexuality

JOHN BARTH

John Barth, novelist and short story writer, has written several acclaimed novels, including *The Floating Opera, Giles
Goat Boy,* and *The End of the Road,* from which this short
selection is taken. Barth gives a description of *pansexual-
ity,* the Freudian thesis, which, Barth suggests, dominates
our culture. The passage speaks for itself.

The dance of sex: If one had no other reason for choosing to subscribe to Freud, what could be more charming than to believe that
the whole vaudeville of the world, the entire dizzy circus of history, is but a fancy mating dance? That dictators burn Jews and
businessmen vote Republican, that helmsmen steer ships and ladies
play bridge, that girls study grammar and boys engineering all at
the behest of the Absolute Genital? When the synthesizing mood
is upon one, what is more soothing than to assert that this one simple yen of humankind, poor little coitus, alone gives rise to cities
and monasteries, paragraphs and poems, foot races and battle tactics, metaphysics and hydroponics, trade unions and universities?
Who would not delight in telling some extragalactic tourist, "On
our planet, sir, males and females copulate. Moreover, they enjoy
copulating. But for various reasons they cannot do this whenever,
wherever, and with whomever they choose. Hence all this running
around that you observe. Hence the world"? A therapeutic notion!

From John Barth, *The End of the Road* (1957).

On the Place of Sex in Human Existence

IMMANUEL KANT

A biographical sketch of Immanuel Kant (1724–1804) appears in chapter 5. Kant held the view that the main purpose of sex is procreation. "Nature pursues its great purpose, and all refinements that join together, though they may appear to stand as far from that as they will, are only trimmings and borrow their charm ultimately from that very source." He argues that nature's procreative purpose is best served in a monogamous marriage in which the spouses are faithful to each other. But from the agent's point of view, the object of sex is sexual satisfaction. But this creates a moral problem, for Kant holds that it is immoral to use others as simply means to our purposes. An act is moral if and only if it includes treating the other person as an end in him- or herself. So the trick is to combine this personal sexual satisfaction with treating the other with dignity. In the following passage Kant elaborates on how this may be done.

Human love is good-will, affection, promoting the happiness of others and finding joy in their happiness. But it is clear that, when a person loves another purely from sexual desire, none of these factors enter into the love. Far from there being any concern for the happiness of the loved one, the lover, in order to satisfy his desire and quiet his appetite, may even plunge the loved one into the depths of misery. Sexual love makes of the loved person an Object of appetite; as soon as that appetite has been satisfied, the person is cast aside as one casts away a lemon which has been sucked dry. Sexual love can, of course, be combined with concern for the other's well-being and so carry with it the characteristics of this love, but taken by itself and for itself, it is nothing more than appetite. Taken by itself it is a degradation of human nature; for as soon as a person becomes an Object of appetite for another, all motives of moral relationship cease to function, because as an

From Immanuel Kant's *Lectures on Ethics*, translated by Louis Infield (London: Methuen, 1930).

Object of appetite for another a person becomes a thing and can be treated and used as such by everyone. This is the only case in which a human being is designed by nature as the Object of another's enjoyment. Sexual desire is at the root of it; and that is why we are ashamed of it, and why all strict moralists, and those who had pretensions to be regarded as saints, sought to suppress and extirpate it. . . .

Because sexuality is not an inclination which one human being has for another as such, but is an inclination for the sex of another, it is a principle of the degradation of human nature, in that it gives rise to the preference of one sex to the other, and to the dishonoring of that sex through the satisfaction of desires. The desire which a man has for a woman is not directed towards her because she is a human being, but because she is a woman; that she is a human being is of no concern to the man; only her sex is the object of his desires. Human nature is thus subordinated. Hence it comes about that all men and women do their best to make not their human nature but their sex more alluring and direct their activities and lusts entirely towards sex. Human nature is thereby sacrificed to sex. If then a man wishes to satisfy his desire, and a woman hers, they stimulate each other's desire; their inclinations meet, but their object is not human nature but sex, and each of them dishonors the human nature of the other. They make of humanity an instrument for the satisfaction of their lusts and inclinations, and dishonor it by placing it on a level with animal nature. Sexuality, therefore, exposes mankind to the danger of equality with the beasts. But as man has this desire from nature, the question arises how far he can properly make use of it without injury to his manhood. . . .

The sole condition on which we are free to make use of our sexual desire depends upon the right to dispose over the person as a whole—over the welfare and happiness and generally over all the circumstances of that person. If I have the right over the whole person, I have also right over the part, and so I have the right to use that person's sexual organs for the satisfaction of sexual desire. But how am I to obtain these rights over the whole person? Only by giving that person the same rights over the whole of myself. This happens only in marriage. Matrimony is an agreement between two persons by which they grant each other equal reciprocal rights, each of them undertaking to surrender the whole of their person to the other with a complete right of disposal over it. We can now apprehend by reason how a *sexual transaction* is possible without degrading humanity and breaking the moral laws. Matrimony is the only condition in which use can be made of one's sexuality. If one devotes one's person to another, one devotes not only sex but the whole person; the two cannot be separated. If, then, one yields one's person, body and soul, for good and ill and in every respect, so that the other has complete rights over it, and if the other does not similarly yield himself in return and does not extend in return the same rights and privileges, the arrangement is one-sided. But if I yield myself completely to another and obtain the person of the other in return, I win myself back; I have given myself up as the property of another, but in turn I take that other as my property, and so win myself back again in winning the person whose property I have become. In this way the two persons become a unity of will. Whatever good or ill, joy or sorrow befall either of them, the other will share in it. Thus sexuality leads to a union of human beings, and in that union alone its exercise is permissible.

For Further Reflection

1. Evaluate Kant's argument for marriage as the proper locus of sex. The Hebrew Bible comments on God's creating man and woman: "Therefore a man leaves his father and his mother and cleaves to his wife and they become one flesh. And the man and his wife were both naked and were not ashamed" (Genesis 2:24–25). Do you see this biblical notion of one common flesh in the background of Kant's thought? Does this idea of oneness make sense?

2. Review Kant's moral principle that we must never use persons simply as means to our ends but must treat them as ends in themselves. What are the implications of this principle for sexual relations?

3. Is Kant's metaphor of reciprocal ownership of the other's body a suitable metaphor? Or is it in opposition to his ideal of dignity and personal autonomy?

Monogamy
A Critique

JOHN McMURTRY

John McMurtry teaches philosophy at the University of Guelph in Ontario, Canada. Recall that Kant argued that marriage involves the ownership of each spouse by the other. Kant thought this is morally acceptable, because it is founded in altruism and voluntary self-giving. McMurtry, however, disagrees with Kant. He argues that monogamous marriage is an evil precisely because it reduces love to capitalist private property. He assembles a wide set of considerations which together make a cumulative case for the thesis that monogamy is "a massive social-control mechanism." The four principles are:

1. The partners are required to enter a formal contractual relation which cannot be dissolved without tremendous legal action and costs.
2. The number of partners involved must be two and only two, excluding wider intimacies.
3. No one may participate in more than one marriage at a time, and will be punished by the law if he or she does.
4. No extramarital sexual relations are allowed.

Together, argues McMurtry, these principles reduce relationships to private property, making marriage just another oppressive capitalist institution.

Reprinted from *The Monist* 56, no. 4 (1972). Copyright © 1972, *The Monist,* La Salle, Illinois 61301. Reprinted by permission. Notes omitted.

> Remove away that black'ning church
> Remove away that marriage hearse
> Remove away that man of blood
> You'll quite remove the ancient curse.

—William Blake

I

Almost all of us have entered or will one day enter a specifically standardized form of monogamous marriage. This cultural requirement is so very basic to our existence that we accept it for most part as a kind of intractable given—dictated by the laws of God, Nature, Government, and Good Sense all at once. Though it is perhaps unusual for a social practice to be so promiscuously underwritten, we generally find comfort rather than curiosity in this fact and seldom wonder how something could be divinely inspired, biologically determined, coerced, and reasoned out all at the same time. We simply take for granted.

Those in society who are officially charged with the thinking function with regard to such matters are no less responsible for this uncritical acceptance than is the man on the street. The psychoanalyst traditionally regards our form of marriage as a necessary restraint on the anarchic id and no more to be queried than civilization itself. The lawyer is as undisposed to questioning the practice as he is to criticizing the principle of private property (this is appropriate, as I shall later point out). The churchman formally perceives the relationship between man and wife to be as inviolable and insusceptible to question as the relationship between the institution he works for and the Christ. The sociologist standardly accepts the formalized bonding of heterosexual pairs as the indispensable basis of social order and perhaps a societal universal. The politician is as incapable of challenging it as he is the virtue of his own continued holding of office. And the philosopher (at least the English-speaking philosopher), as with most issues of socially controversial or sexual dimensions, ignores the question almost altogether.

Even those irreverent adulterers and unmarried couples who seem to be challenging the institution in the most basic possible way, in practice, tend merely to mimic its basic structure in unofficial form. The coverings of sanctities, taboos, and cultural habit continue to hold them with the grip of public clothes.

II

"Monogamy" means, literally, "one marriage." But it would be wrong to suppose that this phrase tells us much about our particular species of official wedlock. The greatest obstacle to the adequate understanding of our monogamy institution has been the failure to identify clearly and systematically the full complex of principles it involves. There are four such principles, each carrying enormous restrictive force and together constituting a massive social-control mechanism that has never, so far as I know, been fully schematized. To come straight to the point, the four principles in question are as follows:

1. *The partners are required to enter a formal contractual relation:* (a) whose establishment demands a specific official participant, certain conditions of the contractors (legal age, no blood ties, and so on), and a standard set of procedures; (b) whose governing terms are uniform for all and exactly prescribed by law; and (c) whose dissolution may only be legally effected by the decision of state representatives.

The ways in which this elaborate principle of contractual requirement is importantly restrictive are obvious. One may not enter into a marriage union without entering into a contract presided over by a state-investured official. One may not set any of the terms of the contractual relationship by which one is bound for life. And one cannot dissolve the contract without legal action and costs, court proceedings, and in many places actual legislation. (This is the one and only contract in all English-speaking law that is not dissoluble by the consent of the contracting parties.) The extent of control here—over the most intimate and putatively "loving" relationships in all social intercourse—is so great as to be difficult to catalogue without exciting in oneself a sense of disbelief.

Lest it be thought there is always the real option of entering a common-law relationship free of such encumbrances, it should be noted that: (a) these relationships themselves are subject to state regulation, though of a less imposing sort; and (much more important) (b) there are very formidable selective pressures against common-law partnerships, such as employment and job discrimination, exclusion from housing and lodging facilities, special legal disablements, loss of social and moral status (consider such phrases as "living in sin" and "make her an honest woman"), family shame and embarrassment, and so on.

2. *The number of partners involved in the marriage must be two and only two* (as opposed to three, four, five, or any of the almost countless possibilities of intimate union). This second principle of our specific form of monogamy (the concept of "one marriage," it should be pointed out, is consistent with any number of participating partners) is perhaps the most important and restrictive of the four principles we are considering. Not only does it confine us to just one possibility out of an enormous range, but it confines us to that single possibility that involves the least number of people, two. It is difficult to conceive of a more thoroughgoing mechanism for limiting extended social union and intimacy. The fact that this monolithic restriction seems so "natural" to us (if it were truly "natural," of course, there would be no need for its rigorous cultural prescription by everything from severe criminal law to ubiquitous housing regulations) simply indicates the extent to which its hold is implanted in our social structure. It is the institutional basis of what I will call the "binary frame of sexual consciousness," a frame through which all our heterosexual relationships are typically viewed ("two's company, three's a crowd") and in light of which all larger circles of intimacy seem almost inconceivable.

3. *No person may participate in more than one marriage at a time or during a lifetime* (unless the previous marriage has been officially dissolved by, normally, one partner's death or a divorce). Violation of this principle is, of course, a criminal offense (bigamy) that is punishable by a considerable term in prison. Of various general regulations of our marriage institution, it has experienced the most significant modification, not indeed in principle, but in the extent of flexibility of its "escape hatch" of divorce. The ease with which this escape hatch is opened has increased considerably in the past few years (the grounds for divorce being more permissive than previously) and it is in this regard most of all that the principles of our marriage institution have undergone formal alteration—that is, in plumbing rather than substance.

4. *No married person may engage in any sexual relationship with any person other than the marriage partner.* Although a consummated sexual act with another person alone constitutes an act of adultery, lesser forms of sexual and erotic relationships may also constitute grounds for divorce (for example, cruelty) and are generally proscribed as well by informal social convention and taboo. In other words, the fourth and final principle of our marriage institution involves not only a prohibition of sexual intercourse per se outside one's wedlock (this term deserves pause) but a prohibition of all

one's erotic relations whatever outside this bond. The penalties for violation here are as various as they are severe, ranging from permanent loss of spouse, children, chattel, and income to job dismissal and social ostracism. In this way, possibly the most compelling natural force toward expanded intimate relations with others is strictly confined within the narrowest possible circle for (barring delinquency) the whole of adult life. The sheer weight and totality of this restriction is surely one of the great wonders of all historical institutional control.

III

With all established institutions, apologetics for perpetuation are never wanting. Thus it is with our form of monogamous marriage.

Perhaps the most celebrated justification over the years has proceeded from the belief in a Supreme Deity, who secretly utters sexual and other commands to privileged human representatives. Almost as well known a line of defense has issued from a similarly confident conviction that the need for some social regulation of sexuality demonstrates the need for our specific type of two-person wedlock. Although these have been important justifications in the sense of being very widely supported, they are not—having other grounds than reason—susceptible to treatment here.

If we put aside such arguments, we are left, I think, with two major claims. The first is that our form of monogamous marriage promotes a profound affection between the partners that is not only of great worth in itself but invaluable as a sanctuary from the pressures of outside society. Since, however, there are no secure grounds whatever for supposing that such "profound affection" is not at least as easily achievable by any number of *other* marriage forms (that is, forms that differ in one or more of the four principles), this justification conspicuously fails to perform the task required of it.

The second major claim for the defense is that monogamy provides a specially loving context for child-upbringing. However, here again there are no grounds at all for concluding that it does so as, or any more, effectively than other possible forms of marriage. (The only alternative type of upbringing to which it has apparently been shown to be superior is nonfamily institutional upbringing, which of course is not relevant to the present discussion.) Furthermore, the fact that at least half the span of a normal monogamous marriage involves no child-upbringing at all is over-looked here, as is the rein-forcing fact that there is no reference to or mention of the quality of child-upbringing in any of the prescriptions connected with it.

In brief, the second major justification of our particular type of wedlock scents somewhat too strongly of red herring to pursue further.

There is, it seems, little to recommend the view that monogamy specially promotes "profound affection" between the partners or a "loving context" for child-upbringing. Such claims are simply with-out force. On the other hand, there are several aspects to the logic and operation of the four principles of this institution that suggest that it actually *inhibits* the achievement of these desiderata. Far from uniquely abetting the latter, it militates against them in these ways:

1. Centralized official control of marriage (which the Church grad-ually achieved through the mechanism of Canon Law after the fall of the Roman Empire in one of the greatest seizures of social power of history) necessarily alienates the partners from full responsibil-ity for and freedom in their relationship. "Profound closeness" between the partners—or at least an area of it—is thereby expro-priated rather than promoted and "sanctuary" from the pressures of outside society prohibited rather than fostered.

2. Limitation of the marriage bond to two people necessarily restricts, in perhaps the most unilateral way possible consistent with offspring survival, the number of adult sources of affection, inter-est, and material support and instruction for the young. The "lov-ing context for child-up-bringing" is thereby dessicated rather than nourished, providing the structural conditions for such notorious and far-reaching problems as sibling rivalry for scarce adult atten-tion and parental oppression through exclusive monopoly of the child's means of life.

3. Formal exclusion of all others from erotic contact with the mar-riage partner systematically promotes conjugal insecurity, jealousy, and alienation in several ways. (a) It officially underwrites a literally totalitarian expectation of sexual confinement on the part of one's husband or wife: which expectation is, *ceteris paribus,* inevitably more subject to anxiety and disappointment than one less extreme in its demand and/or cultural-juridical backing. (b) It requires so complete a sexual isolation of the marriage partners that should one violate the fidelity code the other is left alone and susceptible to a sense of fundamental deprivation and resentment. It stipulates such a strict restraint of sexual energies that there are habitual violations of the regulations, frequently if not always attended by willful decep-

tion and reciprocal suspicion about the occurrence or quality of the extramarital relationship, anxiety and fear on both sides of permanent estrangement from partner and family, and overt and covert antagonism over the prohibited act in both offender (who feels "trapped") and offended (who feels "betrayed").

The disadvantages of the four principles of monogamous marriage do not, however, end with inhibiting the very effects they are said to promote. There are further shortcomings:

1. The restriction of marriage union to two partners necessarily prevents the strengths of larger groupings. Such advantages as the following are thereby usually ruled out: (a) the security, range, and power of larger socioeconomic units; (b) the epistemological and emotional substance, variety, and scope of more pluralist interactions; (c) the possibility of extra-domestic freedom founded on more adult providers and upbringers as well as more broadly based circles of intimacy.

2. The sexual containment and isolation that the four principles together require variously stimulates such social malaises as: (a) destructive aggression (which notoriously results from sexual frustration); (b) apathy, frustration, and dependence within the marriage bond; (c) lack of spontaneity, bad faith, and distance in relationships without the marriage bond; (d) sexual fantasizing, perversion, fetishism, prostitution, and pornography in the adult population as a whole.

Taking such things into consideration, it seems difficult to lend credence to the view that the four principles of our form of monogamous marriage constitute a structure beneficial either to the marriage partners themselves or to their offspring (or indeed to anyone else). One is moved to seek for some other ground of the institution, some ground that lurks beneath the reach of our conventional apprehensions.

IV

The ground of our marriage institution, the essential principle that underwrites all four restrictions, is this: *the maintenance by one man or woman of the effective right to exclude indefinitely all others from erotic access to the conjugal partner.*

The first restriction creates, elaborates on, and provides for the enforcement of this right to exclude. And the second, third, and fourth restrictions together ensure that the right to exclude is—

respectively—not cooperative, not simultaneously or sequentially distributed, and not permissive of even casual exception.

In other words, the four restrictions of our form of monogamous marriage together constitute a state-regulated, indefinite, and exclusive ownership by two individuals of one another's sexual powers. Marriage is simply a form of private property.

That our form of monogamous marriage is, when the confusing layers of sanctity, apologetic, and taboo are cleared away, another species of private property should not surprise us. The history of the institution is so full of suggestive indicators—dowries, inheritance, property alliances, daughter sales (of which women's wedding rings are a carry-over), bride exchanges, and legitimacy and illegitimacy—that it is difficult not to see some intimate connections between marital and ownership ties. We are better able still to apprehend the ownership essence of our marriage institution, when in addition we consider: (1) that until recently almost the only way to secure official dissolution of consummated marriage was to be able to demonstrate violation of one or both partner's sexual ownership, (that is, adultery); (2) that the imperative of premarital chastity is tantamount to a demand for retrospective sexual ownership by the eventual marriage partner; (3) that successful sexual involvement with a married person is prosecutable as an expropriation of ownership—"alienation of affections"—which is restituted by cash payment; (4) that the incest taboo is an iron mechanism that protects the conjugal ownership of sexual properties, both the husband's and wife's, from the access of affectionate offspring and the offsprings' (who themselves are future marriage partners) from access of siblings and parents; (5) that the language of the marriage ceremony is the language of exclusive possession ("take," "to have and to hold," "forsaking all others and keeping you only unto him/her," and so on, not to mention the proprietary locutions associated with the marital relationship ("he's mine," "she belongs to him," "keep to your own husband," "wife stealer," "possessive husband," and so on).

V

Of course, it would be remarkable if marriage in our society was not a relationship akin to private property. In our socioeconomic system we relate to virtually everything of value by individual ownership: by, that is, the effective right to exclude others from the thing concerned. That we do so as well with perhaps the most highly valued thing of all—the sexual partners' sexuality—is only to be expected. Indeed, it would probably be an intolerable strain on our entire social structure if we did otherwise.

This line of thought deserves pursuit. The real secret of our form of monogamous marriage is not that it functionally provides for the needs of adults who love one another or of the children they give birth to but that it serves the maintenance of our present social system. It is an institution that is indispensable to the persistence of the capitalist order in the following ways:

1. A basic principle of current social relations is that some people legally acquire the use of other people's personal powers, from which they may exclude other members of society. This system operates in the work-place (owners and hirers of all types contractually acquire for their exclusive use workers' regular labor powers) and in the family (husbands and wives contractually acquire for their exclusive use their partner's sexual properties). A conflict between the structures of these primary relations—as would obtain were there a suspension of the restrictions governing our form of monogamous marriage—might well undermine the systemic coherence of present social intercourse.

2. The fundamental relation between individuals and things that satisfy their needs is, in our present society, that each individual has or does not have the effective right to exclude other people from the thing in question. A rudimentary need is that for sexual relationship(s). Therefore the object of this need must be related to the one who needs it as owned or not owned (that is, via marriage or not-marriage, or approximations thereof) if people's present relationship to what they need is to retain—again—systemic coherence.

3. A necessary condition for the continued existence of the present social formation is that its members feel a powerful motivation to gain favorable positions in it. But such social ambition is heavily dependent on the preservation of exclusive monogamy in that (a) the latter confines the discharge of primordial sexual energies to a single unalterable partner and thus typically compels those energies to seek alternative outlet, such as business or professional success and (b) the exclusive marriage necessarily reduces the sexual relationships available to any one person to absolute (nonzero) minimum, a unilateral promotion of sexual shortage that in practice renders hierarchical achievement essential as an economic and "display" means for securing scarce partners.

4. Because the exclusive marriage necessarily and dramatically

reduces the possibilities of sexual-love relationships, it thereby promotes the existing economic system by: (a) rendering extreme economic self-interest—the motivational basis of the capitalistic process—less vulnerable to altruistic subversion; (b) disciplining society's members into the habitual repression of natural impulse required for long-term performance of repetitive and arduous work tasks; (c) developing a complex of suppressed sexual desires to which sales techniques may be effectively applied in creating those new consumer wants that provide indispensable outlets for ever increasing capital funds.

5. The present form of marriage is of fundamental importance to (a) the continued relative powerlessness of the individual family: which, with larger numbers would constitute a correspondingly increased command of social powers; (b) the continued high demand for homes, commodities, and services: which, with the considerable economies of scale that extended unions would permit, would otherwise falter; (c) the continued strict necessity for adult males to sell their labor power and for adult women to remain at home (or vice versa): which strict necessity would diminish as the economic base of the family unit extended; (d) the continued immense pool of unsatisfied sexual desires and energies in the population at large: without which powerful interests and institutions would lose much of their conventional appeal and force; (e) the continued profitable involvement of lawyers, priests, and state officials in the jurisdictions of marriage and divorce and the myriad official practices and proceedings connected thereto.

VI

If our marriage institution is a linchpin of our present social structure then a breakdown in this institution would seem to indicate a breakdown in our social structure. On the face of it, the marriage institution is breaking down—enormously increased divorce rates, non-marital sexual relationships, wife-swapping, the Playboy philosophy, and communes. Therefore one might be led by the appearance of things to anticipate a profound alteration in the social system.

But it would be a mistake to underestimate the tenacity of an established order or to overestimate the extent of change in our marriage institution. Increased divorce rates merely indicate the widening of a traditional escape hatch. Nonmarital relationships imitate and culminate in the marital mold. Wife-swapping presupposes owner-ship, as the phrase suggests. The Playboy philosophy is merely the view that if one has the money one has the right to be titillated—the commercial call to more fully exploit a dynamic sector of capital investment. And communes—the most hopeful phenomenon—almost nowhere offer a *praxis* challenge to private property in sexuality. It may be changing. But history, as the old man puts it, weighs like a nightmare on the brains of the living.

For Further Reflection

1. Compare McMurtry's use of marriage as property with Kant's understanding of that notion. How do they differ? Who is closer to the truth?

2. Evaluate McMurtry's arguments against monogamous marriage. Examine the four principles which he attacks. Are his arguments convincing? Explain your answer.

3. If we were to follow McMurtry's logic, what kind of sexual relations would be permitted? Can you spell out the implications of his proposals?

4. How might a believer in traditional monogamous marriage defend that institution against McMurtry's attacks?

Marriage, Love, and Procreation
A Critique of McMurtry

MICHAEL D. BAYLES

Michael Bayles, until his recent death, was professor of philosophy at Florida State University. He is the author or editor of several works in social philosophy, including *Ethics and Population*. In this essay he attempts to rebut McMurtry's critique of monogamy. Bayles first identifies eleven social ills that McMurtry attributes at least in part to monogamy. Then he offers a historical perspective for our institution of marriage, rejecting the Kantian metaphor, which McMurtry adopts, of "mutual ownership" as "pure nonsense." Then Bayles argues that monogamous marriage plays two important functions. It promotes a deep, personal relationship of indefinite duration, and it provides a good context for the raising of children. Bayles agrees that some aspects of marriage need reforming, but monogamous marriage has the resources to accomplish the two functions just mentioned.

The current era is one of that vulgar form of hedonism rejected by philosophical hedonists such as Epicurus and John Stuart Mill. Apologists thinly disguise the tawdriness of a hedonism of biological pleasures by appeals to individual rights and autonomy. Far too frequently these appeals merely mask a refusal to accept responsibility. This failure to accept personal responsibility is periodically atoned for by ritualistic and ill-conceived attempts to help the poor and underprivileged people of the world.

One of the central focuses of the current vulgar hedonism has been sexual liberation. Premarital intercourse, gay liberation, no-fault divorce, open marriage (read, "open adultery"), polygamy, and orgies all have their advocates. About the only forms of sexual

From Michael D. Bayles, "Marriage, Love, and Procreation," in *Philosophy and Sex (Third Edition)*, edited by Robert B. Baker, Kathleen J. Winninger, and Frederick A. Elliston (pp. 116–129) (Amherst, NY: Prometheus Books). Copyright © 1998. Reprinted by permission of the publisher. Notes omitted.

behavior yet to have strong advocates are pedophilia and bestiality. Any day now one may expect grade-school children to assert their right to happiness through pedophilia and animal lovers to argue that disapproval of bestiality is unfair to little lambs.

The result, especially in Western society, is an emphasis on sex that is out of all proportion to its significance for a eudaemonistic life—that is, a life worth living, including elements besides pleasure. The only ultimate test for the value of a life is whether at its end it is found to have been worth living. It is difficult to conceive of a person's thinking his life significant because it was a second-rate approximation to the sexual achievements of the notorious rabbit. However, many people seem to think such a life offers the highest ideal of a "truly human" existence, forgetting Aristotle's insight that reproduction is characteristic of all living things, not just humans. Consequently, the institution of marriage has been attacked for hindering the achievement of this vulgar hedonistic ideal.

ATTACKS ON MARRIAGE

Not all attacks on the institution of marriage have been based solely on the vulgar hedonistic ideal. A more broad ranging, although no more plausible, attack has recently been made by John McMurtry. His attack is directed not against marriage per se but against that form of it found in Western society—monogamy. McMurtry does not merely find that monogamous marriage hinders the achievement of the vulgar hedonistic ideal. He also claims it is at least one of the causes of the following social ills: (1) Central official control of marriage "*necessarily* alienates the partners from full responsibility for and freedom in their relationship." (2) Monogamy restricts the sources of adult affection and support available to children. (3) It "systematically promotes conjugal insecurity, jealousy, and alienation. . . ." (4) It "prevents the strengths of larger groupings." (5) It stimulates aggression, apathy, frustration, lack of spontaneity, perversion, fetishism, prostitution, and pornography. (6) It serves to maintain the status quo and capitalism. (7) It supports the powerlessness of the individual family by keeping it small. (8) By promoting many small families it creates a high demand for homes and consumer goods and services. (9) It makes it necessary for many more males to sell their labor than would be necessary if monogamy were not practiced. (10) By limiting opportunities for sexual satisfaction it channels unsatisfied desire into support for various institutions and interests. (11) Finally, it promotes financial profit for lawyers, priests, and so forth, in marriage and divorce proceedings. Such a catalog of evils omits only a few social problems such as political corruption and environmental deterioration, although even they are hinted at in numbers 8 and 11.

Many people have hoped that the simple-mindedness that attributes all or most or even many of society's ills to a single factor would disappear. At one time private ownership of the means of production was the *bête noir* of society. Recently it has been replaced in that role by unlimited population growth. Both of these beasts have been slain by the St. George of reasonableness. McMurtry has called forth yet another single-factor beast. There is no reason to suppose this one to be any more powerful than its predecessors.

No attempt will be made in this essay to examine in detail McMurtry's criticisms of monogamous marriage. In general they are characterized by a lack of historical and sociological perspective. It is unclear whether he is attacking the ideal of monogamous marriage as it perhaps existed a hundred years ago or as it exists today. Yet this difference is crucial. A century ago divorce was not widely recognized or accepted; today that is not true. When divorce was not recognized, concubinage and prostitution were quite prevalent, as was simply abandoning one's family. Such practices certainly mitigated the effect of the strict social rules that McMurtry discusses. Also, he criticizes monogamy for limiting the access of children to adult affection and support, since they must rely upon their parents alone for care. But in the extended family, which existed until the urbanization of society, that limitation was considerably less common than it may be at present.

McMurtry seems to be unaware of the social realities of modern society. He emphasizes the law as it is written rather than the law in action. It is generally recognized that despite the wording of statutes, marriages can in practice now be dissolved by mutual consent. Nor is adultery usually prosecuted in those states in which it is still a crime. Nor does McMurtry present any sociological evidence for the various effects that he claims monogamous marriage has. Sometimes the evidence may well be against him. For example, he claims that monogamy supports the high demand for homes. Yet, for a century in Ireland monogamy coincided with a low demand for new homes. Couples simply postponed marriage until the male inherited the home of his parents, and those who did not inherit often did not marry.

Underlying McMurtry's view of monogamous marriage is the Kantian conception of the marriage contract. According to Kant, marriage "is the Union of two Persons of different sex for life-long reciprocal possession of their sexual faculties." McMurtry takes the following principle to be the essential ground of monogamous marriage: "the maintenance by one man or woman of the effective right to exclude indefinitely all others from erotic access to the conjugal partner." Since by "possession" Kant meant legal ownership and the consequent right to exclude others, these two views come to the same thing. They both view marriage as chiefly concerned with private ownership of the means to sexual gratification, thus combining capitalism with vulgar hedonism (although Kant was not a hedonist).

Such a view of marriage is pure nonsense. However, it has more plausibility in today's era of vulgar hedonism than it did in Kant's time. Historically, the official aims of marriage, according to the Catholic Church—which was the only church during the period of the establishment of monogamous marriage in Western society— were procreation and companionship. There was also a tendency to view it as a legitimate outlet for man's sinful nature. It is this latter element that Kant and McMurtry have taken as the chief one.

In addition to the avowed purposes of marriage there were the actual social functions that it performed. The family unit was the basic social unit, not only for the education of children (that is, socialization, not formal schooling—which has only become widespread during the past century), but also for the production of necessities, including food and clothing, and for recreation. These historical functions of the extended-family unit based on monogamous marriage have been undermined by the development of industrial, urban society. Consequently, the moral and legal status and functions of marriage require reexamination in the light of current social conditions.

Before undertaking such a reexamination it is necessary to distinguish between rules of marriage and attendant social rules. They are mixed together in the traditional social institution of monogamous marriage, but there is no necessity for this mix and it is probably unjustified. In particular one must distinguish between penal laws prohibiting various forms of sexual union—homosexual, premarital, adulterous—and private arranging laws granting legal recognition to

the marital relationship. Private arranging laws do not prescribe punishment for offenses; instead, they enable people to carry out their
desires. People are not punished for improperly made marriages;
instead, the marriages are invalid and unenforceable. Laws against
fornication, prostitution, cohabitation, and homosexuality are almost
always penal. Objections to them cannot be transferred directly to
the marriage relationship. All of these penal laws could be abolished
and monogamous marriage could still be retained.

It may be claimed that despite their nonpenal form, marriage
laws do in fact penalize those who prefer other forms of relationship. If homosexual and polygamous relationships are not legally
recognized as "marriages," then persons desiring these forms of relationship are being deprived of some degree of freedom. When considering freedom one must be clear about what one is or is not
free to do. Consider, for example, the case of gambling. One must
distinguish between laws that forbid gambling and the absence of
laws that recognize gambling debts. The latter does not deprive
people of the freedom to contract gambling debts; it simply does
not allow the use of legal enforcement to collect them. Similarly,
the absence of laws recognizing polygamous and homosexual marriages does not deprive people of the freedom to enter polygamous
and homosexual unions. Instead, it merely fails to provide legal
recourse to enforce the agreements of the parties to such unions.
The absence of laws recognizing such marriages does not deprive
people of a freedom they previously had, for they were never able
to have such agreements legally enforced. Nor have people been
deprived of a freedom they would have if there were no legal system, for in the absence of a legal system no agreements can be
legally enforced. If there is a ground for complaint, then, it must
be one of inequality—that one type of relationship is legally recognized but others are not. However, a charge of inequality is warranted only if there are no relevant reasonable grounds for distinguishing between relationships. To settle that issue one must be
clear about the state's or society's interests in marriage.

The rest of this essay is concerned with the purposes or functions of the marriage relationship in which society has a legitimate
interest. It is not possible here to set out and to justify the purposes for which governments may legislate. It is assumed that the
state may act to facilitate citizens' engaging in activities that they
find desirable and to protect the welfare and equality of all citizens, including future ones. Government has an especially strong

responsibility for the welfare of children. Of course, these legitimate governmental or social interests and responsibilities must be balanced against other interests and values of citizens, including those of privacy and freedom from interference.

There is no attempt or intention to justify penal laws prohibiting forms of relationship other than monogamous marriage. Indeed, it is generally assumed that they ought not be prohibited and that more people will enter into them than has been the case. In such a context, monogamous marriage would become a more specialized form of relationship, entered into by a smaller proportion of the population than previously. Underlying this assumption are the general beliefs that many people are unqualified or unfit for a marital relationship and ought never to enter one and that many people marry for the wrong reasons. If true, these beliefs may explain why both marriage and divorce rates have been steadily rising in most Western countries during this century.

PROMOTING INTERPERSONAL RELATIONSHIPS

Alienation from others and loss of community are perceived by many to be among the most serious ills of modern, mass society. In such a situation it seems unlikely that many would deny the need for intimate interpersonal relationships of affection. The importance of such relationships for a good or *eudaemonistic* life has been recognized by philosophers as diverse as Aristotle and G. E. Moore. In considering such interpersonal relationships to be among the most valuable elements of a good life, one must distinguish between the value of a good and the strength of the desire for it. Many people have a stronger desire for life than for such interpersonal relationships, but they may still recognize such relationships as more valuable than mere life. Life itself is of little value, but it is a necessary condition for most other things of value.

Among the most valuable forms of interpersonal relationship are love, friendship, and trust. These relationships are limited with respect to the number of persons with whom one can have them. Classically, there has been a distinction between agapeic and erotic love. Agapeic love is the love of all mankind—general benevolence. The concept of erotic love is more limited. In today's world erotic love is apt to be confused with sexual desire and intercourse. But there can be and always has been sex without love and love without sex. Personal love is more restricted than either agapeic love or sexual desire. It implies a concern for another that is greater than that for most people. Hence, it cannot be had for an unlimited number of other people. Similar distinctions must be drawn between friendship and acquaintance, trust of a political candidate and trust of a friend.

Such interpersonal relationships require intimacy. Intimacy involves a sharing of information about one another that is not shared with others. Moreover, it often involves seclusion from others—being in private where others cannot observe. In some societies where physical privacy is not possible, psychological privacy—shutting out the awareness of the presence of others—substitutes. Consequently, these valuable interpersonal relationships require intimacy and usually physical privacy from others, and at the very least nonintrusion upon the relationship.

Moreover, these forms of interpersonal relationship require acts expressing the concern felt for the other person. In most societies acts of sexual intercourse have been such expressions of love and concern. It is not physically or psychologically necessary that sexual intercourse have this quasi-symbolic function, but it is a natural function of sexual intercourse. All that is here meant by "natural" is that in most societies sexual intercourse has this function, for which there is some psychological basis even though it is not contrary to scientific laws for it to be otherwise. Intercourse usually involves an element of giving of oneself, and one's sexual identity is frequently a central element of one's self-image. It is not, however, sexual intercourse that is intrinsically valuable but the feelings and attitudes, the underlying interpersonal relationship, that it expresses. Nonsexual acts also currently express such relationships, but sexual intercourse is still one of the most important ways of doing so. If sexual intercourse ceases to have this function in society, some other act will undoubtedly replace it in this function. Moreover, sexual intercourse will have lost much of its value.

If these interpersonal relationships of personal love and trust are of major value, it is reasonable for the state to seek to protect and foster them by according legal recognition to them in marriage. The specific forms of this recognition cannot be fully discussed. However, there is some basis for treating the partners to a marriage as one person. Historically, of course, the doctrine that the parties to a marriage are one person has supported the subjugation of women in all sorts of ways, for example, in their disability from owning property. But there is an underlying rationale for joint responsibility. Two people who, without a special reason such as taxes, keep separate accounts of income and expenditures do not have the love and trust of a couple who find such an accounting unnecessary. Moreover, in such a joint economic venture there is no point to allowing one party to sue the other. Only the advent of insurance, whereby neither spouse, but a third party, pays, makes such suits seem profitable. Another recognition of these relationships—albeit one not frequently invoked—is that one is not forced to testify against his or her spouse. More important is that neither party is encouraged to violate the trust and intimacy of the relationship, for example, by encouraging one to inform authorities about bedroom comments of his or her spouse.

The character of these valuable forms of interpersonal relationship provides an argument against according marriages of definite duration legal recognition equal to that accorded those that are intentionally of indefinite duration. For it to be "intentionally of indefinite duration," neither partner may, when entering the marriage, intend it to be for a specific period of time, for example, five years, nor may the marriage contract specify such a period. The following argument is not to show that marriages for a definite duration should not be recognized, but merely to show that they should not have equal standing with those intentionally of indefinite duration. The basic reason for unequal recognition is that interpersonal relationships that are not intentionally of indefinite duration are less valuable than those that are.

Suppose one were to form a friendship with a colleague, but the two mutually agree to be friends for only three years, with an option to renew the friendship at that time. Such an agreement would indicate a misunderstanding of friendship. Such agreements make sense for what Aristotle called friendships of utility, but in the modern world these friendships are business partnerships. While there is nothing wrong with business friendships, they do not have the intrinsic value of personal friendships. In becoming close personal friends with someone, one establishes a concern and trust that would be seriously weakened or destroyed by setting a time limit to the friendship. It is sometimes claimed that time limits may be set because people will only be together for a while. But one need not see a person every day or even every year to remain friends.

However, extended separation usually brings about a withering away of the friendship.

Similarly, the personal relationship of love and trust in marriage is of lesser value if it is intentionally for only a definite period of time. Moreover, the entering into a relationship that is intentionally of indefinite duration and legally recognized symbolizes a strength of commitment not found in other types of relationships. While two unmarried people may claim that there is no definite limit to their mutual commitment, their commitment is always questionable. Entering into a marital relationship assures the commitment more than does a mere verbal avowal. . . .

PROTECTING THE WELFARE OF CHILDREN

Another area of pervasive social interest that has historically centered in marriage concerns the procreation and raising of children. Society has an interest not only in the number of children born but their quality of life. This fact is in deep conflict with the current emphasis on the freedom of individuals to make reproductive decisions unfettered by social rules and restrictions. Moreover, it is an area in which social control has traditionally been weak. Child abuse is widespread, and efforts to prevent it are mediocre at best. There are few general legal qualifications or tests for becoming a parent. Yet parenthood is one of the most potentially dangerous relationships that one person can have with another. If one is a poor college teacher, then at worst a few students do not receive a bit of education they might have. But as a parent one potentially can ruin completely the lives of one's children. At the least, they may develop into psychological misfits incapable of leading responsible and rewarding lives.

Essentially, there are three areas of social interest and responsibility with respect to procreation and the raising of children. First, there is a social interest in the sheer number of children born. The current emphasis on population control makes this interest abundantly clear. Second, there is a social interest in the potentialities of children. This area includes concern for genetic and congenital birth defects and abnormalities. Over 5 percent of all children born have a genetic defect. The possibility of genetic control of those who are born will soon take on major significance. Already, approximately sixty genetic diseases as well as almost all chromosomal abnormalities can be detected *in utero,* and adult carriers of about eighty genetic defects can be identified. Given the possibility of genetic control, society can no longer risk having genetically disadvantaged children by leaving the decision of whether to have children to the unregulated judgment of individual couples. Some social regulations with respect to genetic screening and, perhaps, eugenic sterilization are needed. While potential parents have interests of privacy and freedom in reproductive decisions, the social interests in preventing the suffering and inequality of possibly defective children may outweigh them in certain types of cases.

Third, the care and development of those who are born is a social interest and responsibility. This interest has been recognized for some time in the form of children's homes and compulsory education. However, increasing knowledge about childhood development ment extends the area in which social interests and responsibility may be reasonably involved. To give an example at the most elementary level, the nutritional diet of children during their first three years is crucial for their future development. So also is their psychological support. The welfare of future generations is not a private but a social matter. It is a proper task of society, acting through its government, to ensure that the members of the next generation are not physical or psychological cripples due to the ignorance, negligence, or even indifference of parents.

Historically, society has attempted to control procreation through the institution of marriage. Society's means were primarily to stigmatize children born out of wedlock and to encourage the having of many children. It is now recognized that no useful purpose is served by stigmatizing children born out of wedlock as illegitimate. (However, some useful purpose may be served by not according children born out of wedlock all the rights of those born in wedlock, for example, inheritance without parental recognition.) The emphasis on having as many children as one can has also disappeared. It is not this historical concern with procreation that is misplaced in modern society but the forms that the concern has taken.

If society has the responsibility to protect the welfare of children, then some social regulation and control of human reproduction and development is justified. Such regulation and control need not be effected by penal laws. For example, social concern has traditionally been expressed in adoptions through regulations to ensure that those who adopt children are fit to care for them. That some regulations have been inappropriate and not reasonably related to the welfare of children is not in question. Rather, the point is that there has been regulation without penal laws, or at least without resorting primarily to penal laws. Nor can social regulation and control be solely by legislation. Legislation alone is usually ineffective; it must be supported by informal social rules and expectations.

Not only has modern biomedicine made sex possible without procreation; it has also made procreation possible without sex. The techniques of artificial insemination and fertilization, embryo transfer, ova donation, ectogenesis, and cloning now, or soon will, make it possible for people to reproduce without sexual intercourse. Hence, not only may one have sex for pleasure, but one may reproduce for pleasure without sexual intercourse. Not only may people reproduce outside marriage; they are not even biologically required to have intercourse. Thus, sex and marriage may become dissociated from reproduction.

However, there are strong reasons for restricting procreation primarily to marriages of indefinite duration, which does not imply that such marriages should be restricted to procreation. Marriage has traditionally been the central social institution concerned with procreation. Consequently, if society is to exercise some control over procreation in the future, it would involve the least change in conditions to do so through marriage. Moreover, there is considerable evidence that the disruption of family life contributes to juvenile delinquency. Whether divorce or marital breakdown (with or without divorce) is a prime cause of such delinquency does not matter. The point is that the disruption of home life does seriously affect the development of children. The chance of such disruption outside of a marriage that is intentionally of indefinite duration is higher than for that within. Moreover, there is some reason to believe that the presence of both mother and father is instrumental in the psychological development of children. In any case, the presence of two people rather than one provides the security that there will be someone to care for the children should one of the parents die. Generally, children are better off being with one parent than in a state orphanage, but better off still with both parents. Hence, for the welfare of children it seems best that procreation and child rearing primarily occur within the context of marriages intentionally of indefinite duration.

While society has a responsibility for the care and development of children, this general responsibility is best carried out if specific adults have obligations to care for specific children. In the past, the biological parent-child relation has reinforced the allocation of responsibility for specific children and has been a major factor in monogamy. The separation of reproduction and sexual intercourse threatens disruption of this assignment. For example, if gestation occurs in an artificial womb in a laboratory, there may be no "parents," only a scientific research group. More realistically, if a woman has an embryo from ova and sperm donors transferred to her uterus, it is unclear who are the child's parents. However, if there is to be optimal care for children, specific adults must have obligations for specific children. It cannot be left to somebody in general, for then nobody in particular is likely to do it. "Let George do it" is too prevalent and careless an attitude to allow with regard to children.

McMurtry's contention that monogamy restricts the care for children is not well founded. First, if there are no specific adults responsible for children, they may become "lost" in large groups and victims of the "it's not my job" syndrome. Second, monogamy per se does not cut children off from the support and care of others. One must distinguish the marital relationship from living arrangements. It is the isolated situation of the family that deprives children of such support. In many married-student housing complexes children have access to other adults. Even in general-residential neighborhoods with separate family housing units, such support is available if there is a sense of community in the neighborhood.

Given the social interests in and responsibility for the procreation and development of children, some more effective controls of parenthood appear desirable. If the primary locus of reproduction is to be within marriages of intentionally indefinite duration, then the easiest way to institute controls is to add requirements for people to enter such marriages. A few requirements such as blood tests are already generally prevalent. Alternatively, one might have a separate licensing procedure for procreation. Nonmarried couples and single people might also qualify for such licenses. Moreover, couples who want to marry but not have children would not have to meet requirements. However, the only requirements suggested below that might bar marriages are almost as important for those couples who do not have children as for those who do. If the requirements were tied to marriage they would be easier to administer. The only drawback is that unmarried people would not have to meet them. However, such requirements can and should be part of the medical practice of the "artificial" techniques of reproduction—artificial insemination and embryo transfer. And there are few if any effective methods, except generally accepted social rules, to control procreation outside of marriage.

One obvious requirement would be genetic screening. With modern medical techniques genetic problems do not imply that couples cannot become married, but they might be expected not to have children who are their genetic offspring. Artificial insemination and embryo transfer make it possible for almost everyone to have children, even though the children might not be genetically theirs. A general distinction between biological and social parenthood should be made, with legal emphasis on the latter.

More important, perhaps, is some general expectation of psychological fitness for family life and the raising of children. The difficulty with such an expectation is the absence of any clear criteria for fitness and reliable methods for determining who meets them. Perhaps, however, some formal instruction in family relations and child rearing would be appropriate. The Commission on Population Growth and the American Future has already called for an expansion of education for parenthood. It is only a bit further to require some sort of minimal family education for marriage. Probably the easiest method for ensuring such education would be to make it a required subject in secondary schools. If that were done, few people would have difficulty meeting this requirement for marriage.

There should not be any financial or property qualifications for marriage. Society's interest in and responsibility for the welfare of the population in general is such that governments should ensure an adequate standard of living for all persons. Were that to be done there would be no reason to impose any financial restrictions on marriage. Nonetheless, prospective parents should have more concern for their financial situation than is now frequently the case. The adequate care of children is an expensive task, financially as well as psychologically and temporally.

CONCLUSION

It may be objected that neither the argument from interpersonal relations nor that from the welfare of children specifically supports monogamous marriage. While loving relationships cannot extend to an indefinite number of people, they can extend to more than one other person. Also, a polygamous union may provide a rea-

sonable environment for procreation. Hence, neither of the arguments supports monogamous marriage per se.

Logically, the objection is quite correct. But it is a misunderstanding of social philosophy to expect arguments showing that a
certain arrangement is always best under all circumstances. The
most that can be shown is that usually, or as a rule, one social
arrangement is preferable to another. Practically, polygamous marriage patterns will probably never be prevalent. For centuries they
have been gradually disappearing throughout the world. If a disproportionate sex distribution of the population occurs in some
areas or age groups (such as the elderly), then they may increase
in significance. Unless that occurs, most people will probably continue to prefer marital monogamy.

More important, the burden of this paper has not been to defend
the traditional ideal of marital union or even the current practice.
Many of the traditional rules of marriage have been unjust, for example, the inequality between the sexes, both legally and in terms of
social roles. Instead, it has been to defend social recognition of
marriage of intentionally indefinite duration as a unique and socially
valuable institution that society has interests in promoting and regulating. In particular, society has interests in and responsibility for
promoting a certain form of valuable interpersonal relationship and
protecting the welfare of children. Both of these purposes can be
well served by monogamous marriage.

The image, then, is of a society with various forms of living
together, but one in which marriage of intentionally indefinite duration would have a distinctive though lessened role as a special kind
of socially and legally recognized relationship. There would not be
laws prohibiting nonmarital forms of cohabitation. Divorce would
be based on factual marital break-down or mutual consent, with
due regard for the welfare of children. Monogamous marriage would
recognize a special form of personal relationship in which reproduction and child rearing primarily occur. Given the social interest
in decreasing procreation, many people might marry but not have
children, and others might not marry at all. Details of the legal marital relationship have not been specified, nor could they be in this
brief essay except with respect to the main social interests. Questions of inheritance, legal residence and name, social-security benefits, and so on, have not been specified. Changes in laws with
respect to many of these matters can be made without affecting the
arguments for the value of, social responsibility for, and interests

in marriage. Above all, it is an image in which sexual intercourse plays a much smaller role in the conception of marriage and the good life in general, a society in which vulgar hedonism has at least been replaced by a broader-based *eudaemonism*.

For Further Reflection

1. Review Bayles's critique of McMurtry's arguments. What are the main deficiencies he claims to find in McMurtry? Is he fair to McMurtry? Who is closer to the truth?

2. Evaluate Bayles's theses that monogamy has the resources to promote deep personal relations and provide a context for rearing children. Do you agree with him? How might McMurtry respond to these points? Explain your answer.

3. What does Bayles mean by rejecting vulgar hedonism and replacing it with eudaimonism?

What's Wrong with Adultery?

BONNIE STEINBOCK

Bonnie Steinbock is professor of philosophy at the State University of New York at Albany and the author of several articles in social philosophy. In this essay she notes the reports of increased adultery on the part of wives, as well as the general disapproval of adultery. Why is adultery generally thought to be immoral? Steinbock gives three arguments against adultery: (1) it generally involves promise-breaking; (2) it generally involves deception; and (3) it detracts from the deep intimacy necessary for a good marriage.

Reprinted from Bonnie Steinbock, "Adultery," in *QQ: Report from the Center for Philosophy and Public Policy* 6:1 (Winter 1986), by permission of the author.

According to a 1980 survey in *Cosmopolitan,* 54 percent of American wives have had extramarital affairs; a study of 100,000 married women by the considerably tamer *Redbook* magazine found that 40 percent of the wives over 40 had been unfaithful. While such surveys are, to some extent, self-selecting—those who do it are more likely to fill out questionnaires about it—sexual mores have clearly changed in recent years. Linda Wolfe, who reported the results of the *Cosmopolitan* survey, suggests that "this increase in infidelity among married women represents not so much a deviation from traditional standards of fidelity as a break with the old double standard." Studies show that men have always strayed in significant numbers.

Yet 80 percent of "COSMO girls" did not approve of infidelity and wished their own husbands and lovers would be faithful. Eighty-eight percent of respondents to a poll taken in Iowa in 1983 viewed "coveting your neighbor's spouse" as a "major sin." It seems that while almost nobody approves of adultery, men have always done it, and women are catching up.

The increase in female adultery doubtless has to do with recent and radical changes in our attitudes toward sex and sexuality. We no longer feel guilty about enjoying sex; indeed, the capacity for sexual enjoyment is often regarded as a criterion of mental health. When sex itself is no longer intrinsically shameful, restraints on sexual behavior are loosened. In fact, we might question whether the abiding disapproval of infidelity merely gives lip service to an ancient taboo. Is there a rational justification for disapproving of adultery which will carry force with everyone, religious and nonreligious alike?

TRUST AND DECEPTION

Note first that adultery, unlike murder, theft, and lying, is not universally forbidden. Traditional Eskimo culture, for example, regarded sharing one's wife with a visitor as a matter of courtesy. The difference can be explained by looking at the effects of these practices on social cohesiveness. Without rules protecting the lives, persons, and property of its members, no group could long endure. Indeed, rules against killing, assault, lying, and stealing seem fundamental to having a morality at all.

Not so with adultery. For adultery is a *private* matter, essentially concerning only the relationship between husband and wife. It is not essential to morality like these other prohibitions: there are stable societies with genuine moral codes which tolerate extra-marital sex. Although adultery remains a criminal offense in some jurisdictions, it is rarely prosecuted. Surely this is because it is widely regarded as a private matter: in the words of Billie Holiday, "Ain't nobody's business if I do."

However, even if adultery is a private matter, with which the state should not interfere, it is not a morally neutral issue. Our view of adultery is connected to our thoughts and feelings about love and marriage, sex and the family, the value of fidelity, sexual jealousy, and exclusivity. How we think about adultery will affect the quality of our relationships, the way we raise our children, the kind of society we have and want to have. So it is important to consider whether our attitudes toward adultery are justifiable.

Several practical considerations militate against adultery: pregnancy and genital herpes immediately spring to mind. However, unwanted pregnancies are a risk of all sexual intercourse, within or without marriage; venereal disease is a risk of all non-exclusive sex, not just adulterous sex. So these risks do not provide a reason for objecting specifically to adultery. In any event, they offer merely pragmatic, as opposed to moral, objections. If adultery is wrong, it does not become less so because one has been sterilized or inoculated against venereal disease.

Two main reasons support regarding adultery as seriously immoral. One is that adultery is an instance of promise-breaking, on the view that marriage involves, explicitly or implicitly, a promise of sexual fidelity: to forsake all others. That there is this attitude in our culture is clear. Mick Jagger, not noted for sexual puritanism, allegedly refused to marry Jerry Hall, the mother of his baby, because he had no intention of accepting an exclusive sexual relationship. While Jagger's willingness to become an unwed father is hardly mainstream morality, his refusal to marry, knowing that he did not wish to be faithful, respects the idea that *marriage* requires such a commitment. Moreover, the promise of sexual fidelity is regarded as a very serious and important one. To cheat on one's spouse indicates a lack of concern, a willingness to cause pain, and so a lack of love. Finally, one who breaks promises cannot be trusted. And trust is essential to the intimate partnership of marriage, which may be irreparably weakened by its betrayal.

The second reason for regarding adultery as immoral is that it involves deception, for example, lying about one's whereabouts and relations with others. Perhaps a marriage can withstand the occasional lie, but a pattern of lying will have irrevocable consequences for a marriage, if discovered, and probably even if not. Like breaking promises, lying is regarded as a fundamental kind of wrong-doing, a failure to take the one lied to seriously as a moral person entitled to respect.

OPEN MARRIAGE

These two arguments suffice to make most cases of adultery wrong, given the attitudes and expectations of most people. But what if marriage did not involve any promise of sexual fidelity? What if there were no need for deception, because neither partner expected or wanted such fidelity? Objections to "open marriage" cannot focus on promise-breaking and deception, for the expectation of exclusivity is absent. If an open marriage has been freely chosen by both spouses, and not imposed by a dominant on a dependent partner, would such an arrangement be morally acceptable, even desirable?

The attractiveness of extramarital affairs, without dishonesty, disloyalty, or guilt, should not be downplayed. However satisfying sex between married people may be, it cannot have the excitement of a new relationship. ("Not *better*, a friend once said defensively to his wife, attempting to explain his infidelity, "just *different*.") Might we not be better off, our lives fuller and richer, if we allowed ourselves the thrill of new and different sexual encounters?

Perhaps the expectation of sexual exclusivity in marriage stems from emotions which are not admirable: jealousy and possessiveness. That most people experience these feelings is no reason for applauding or institutionalizing them. Independence in marriage is now generally regarded as a good thing: too much "togetherness" is boring and stifling. In a good marriage, the partners can enjoy different activities, travel apart, and have separate friends. Why draw the line at sexual activity?

The natural response to this question invokes a certain conception of love and sex: sex is an expression of affection and intimacy and so should be reserved for people who love each other. Further, it is assumed that one can and should have such feelings for only one other person at any time. To make love with someone else is to express feelings of affection and intimacy that should be reserved for one's spouse alone.

This rejection of adultery assumes the validity of a particular conception of love and sex, which can be attacked in two ways. We might divorce sex from love and regard sex as a pleasurable activity in its own right, comparable to the enjoyment of a good meal. In his article "Is Adultery Immoral?"[1] Richard Wasserstrom suggests that the linkage of sex with love reflects a belief that unless it is purified by a higher emotion, such as love, sex is intrinsically bad or dirty.

But this is an overly simplistic view of the connection between sex and love. Feelings of love occur between people enjoying sexual intercourse, not out of a sense that sexual pleasure must be purified, but precisely because of the mutual pleasure they give one another. People naturally have feelings of affection for those who make them happy, and sex is a very good way of making someone extraordinarily happy. At the same time, sex is by its nature intimate, involving both physical and psychological exposure. This both requires and creates trust, which is closely allied to feelings of affection and love. This is not to say that sex necessarily requires or leads to love; but a conception of the relation between love and sex that ignores these factors is inadequate and superficial.

Alternatively, one might acknowledge the connection between sex and love, but attack the assumption of exclusivity. If parents can love all their children equally and if adults can have numerous close friends, why should it be impossible to love more than one sexual partner at a time? Perhaps we could learn to love more than one sexual partner at a time? Perhaps we could learn to love more widely and to accept that a spouse's sexual involvement with another is not a sign of rejection or lack of love.

The logistics of multiple involvement are certainly daunting. Having an affair (as opposed to a roll in the hay) requires time and concentration; it will almost inevitably mean neglecting one's spouse, one's children, one's work. More important, however, exclusivity seems to be an intrinsic part of "true love." Imagine Romeo pouring out his heart to both Juliet *and* Rosalind! In our ideal of romantic love, one chooses to forgo pleasure with other partners in order to have a unique relationship with one's beloved. Such "renunciation" is natural in the first throes of romantic love; it is precisely because

---

[1]In Wasserstrom's *Today's Moral Problems* (New York: Macmillan, 1975), 288–300. Reprinted in R. Baker and F. Elliston, eds., *Philosophy and Sex,* 1st ed. (Buffalo, NY: Prometheus, 1975), 207–21; 2nd ed. (1984), 93–106.

this stage does *not* last that we must promise to be faithful through the notoriously unromantic realities of married life.

FIDELITY AS AN IDEAL

On the view I have been defending, genuinely open marriages are not *immoral,* although they deviate from a valued ideal of what marriage should be. While this is not the only ideal, or incumbent on all rational agents, it is a moral view in that it embodies a claim about a good way for people to live. The prohibition of adultery, then, is neither arbitrary nor irrational. However, even if we are justified in accepting the ideal of fidelity, we know that people do not always live up to the ideals they accept and we recognize that some failures to do so are worse than others. We regard a brief affair, occasioned by a prolonged separation, as morally different from installing a mistress.

Further, sexual activity is not necessary for deviation from the ideal of marriage which lies behind the demand for fidelity. As John Heckler observed during his bitter and public divorce from former Health and Human Services Secretary Margaret Heckler, "In marriage, there are two partners. When one person starts contributing far less than the other person to the marriage, that's the original infidelity. You don't need any third party." While this statement was probably a justification of his own infidelities, the point is valid. To abandon one's spouse, whether to a career or to another person, is also a kind of betrayal.

If a man becomes deeply involved emotionally with another woman, it may be little comfort that he is able to assure his wife that "Nothing happened." Sexual infidelity has significance as a sign of a deeper betrayal—falling in love with someone else. It may be objected that we cannot control the way we feel, only the way we behave; that we should not be blamed for falling in love, but only for acting on the feeling. While we may not have direct control over our feelings, however, we are responsible for getting ourselves into situations in which certain feelings naturally arise. "It just happened," is rarely an accurate portrayal of an extra-marital love affair.

If there can be betrayal without sex, can there be sex without betrayal? In the novel *Forfeit,* by Dick Francis, the hero is deeply in love with his wife, who was paralyzed by polio in the early days of their marriage. Her great unspoken fear is that he will leave her;

instead, he tends to her devotedly. For several years, he forgoes sex, but eventually succumbs to an affair. While his adultery is hardly praiseworthy, it is understandable. He could divorce his wife and marry again, but it is precisely his refusal to abandon her, his continuing love and tender care, that makes us admire him.

People do fall in love with others and out of love with their spouses. Ought they refrain from making love while still legally tied? I cannot see much, if any, moral value in remaining physically faithful, on principle, to a spouse one no longer loves. This will displease those who regard the wrongness of adultery as a moral absolute, but my account has nothing to do with absolutes and everything to do with what it means to love someone deeply and completely. It is the value of that sort of relationship that makes sexual fidelity an ideal worth the sacrifice.

Neither a mere religiously based taboo, nor a relic of a repressive view of sexuality, the prohibition against adultery expresses a particular conception of married love. It is one we can honor in our own lives and bequeath to our children with confidence in its value as a coherent and rational ideal.

For Further Reflection

1. Consider the first two arguments against adultery, based on the fundamental moral principles involving prohibitions on promise-breaking and deception. Steinbock admits that an open marriage would not violate these principles. Why then is an open marriage less valuable than one involving exclusive sexual relations?

2. Steinbock emphasizes the need for concentrated involvement in marriage. Is she correct about this? Could you imagine a communal marriage where, say, four or more lovers developed a more expansive family? What would be the benefits and drawbacks of such a relationship?

We Have No "Right to Happiness"

C. S. LEWIS

C. S. Lewis (1898–1963) was professor of medieval and renaissance English literature at Cambridge University. Among
his many works are *The Screwtape Letters, The Abolition of
Man, The Problem of Pain,* and the *Chronicles of Narnia*
books. In this essay, Lewis argues against the thesis that
we have "a right to be happy."

"After all," Said Clare, "They had a right to happiness." We were
discussing something that once happened in our own neighbour-
hood. Mr A. had deserted Mrs A. and got his divorce in order to
marry Mrs B., who had likewise got her divorce in order to marry
Mr A. And there was certainly no doubt that Mr A. and Mrs B. were
very much in love with one another. If they continued to be in
love, and if nothing went wrong with their health or their income,
they might reasonably expect to be very happy.

It was equally clear that they were not happy with their old partners. Mrs B. had adored her husband at the outset. But then he got
smashed up in the war. It was thought he had lost his virility, and
it was known that he had lost his job. Life with him was no longer
what Mrs B. had bargained for. Poor Mrs A., too. She had lost her
looks—and all her liveliness. It might be true, as some said, that
she consumed herself by bearing his children and nursing him
through the long illness that overshadowed their earlier married
life.

You mustn't, by the way, imagine that A. was the sort of man
who nonchalantly threw a wife away like the peel of an orange
he'd sucked dry. Her suicide was a terrible shock to him. We all
knew this, for he told us so himself. "But what could I do?" he
said. "A man has a right to happiness. I had to take my one chance
when it came."

I went away thinking about the concept of a "right to happiness."
At first this sounds to me as odd as a right to good luck. For I

believe—whatever one school of moralists may say—that we depend for a very great deal of our happiness or misery on circumstances outside all human control. A right to happiness doesn't, for me, make much more sense than a right to be six feet tall, or to have a millionaire for your father, or to get good weather whenever you want to have a picnic.

I can understand a right as a freedom guaranteed me by the laws of the society I live in. Thus, I have a right to travel along the public roads because society gives me that freedom; that's what we mean by calling the roads 'public'. I can also understand a right as a claim guaranteed me by the laws, and correlative to an obligation on someone else's part. If I have a right to receive £100 from you, this is another way of saying that you have a duty to pay me £100. If the laws allow Mr A. to desert his wife and seduce his neighbour's wife, then, by definition, Mr A. has a legal right to do so, and we need bring in no talk about "happiness."

But of course that was not what Clare meant. She meant that he had not only a legal but a moral right to act as he did. In other words, Clare is—or would be if she thought it out—a classical moralist after the style of Thomas Aquinas, Grotius, Hooker and Locke. She believes that behind the laws of the state there is a Natural Law.

I agree with her. I hold this conception to be basic to all civilization. Without it, the actual laws of the state become an absolute, as in Hegel. They cannot be criticized because there is no norm against which they should be judged.

The ancestry of Clare's maxim, "They have a right to happiness," is august. In words that are cherished by all civilized men, but especially by Americans, it has been laid down that one of the rights of man is a right to "the pursuit of happiness." And now we get to the real point.

What did the writers of that august declaration mean?

It is quite certain what they did not mean. They did not mean that man was entitled to pursue happiness by any and every means—including, say, murder, rape, robbery, treason and fraud. No society could be built on such a basis.

They meant "to pursue happiness by all lawful means"; that is, by all means which the Law of Nature eternally sanctions and which the laws of the nation shall sanction.

Admittedly this seems at first to reduce their maxim to the tautology that men (in pursuit of happiness) have a right to do whatever they have a right to do. But tautologies, seen against their proper historical context, are not always barren tautologies. The declaration is primarily a denial of the political principles which long governed Europe: a challenge flung down to the Austrian and Russian empires, to England before the Reform Bills, to Bourbon France. It demands that whatever means of pursuing happiness are lawful for any should be lawful for all; that "man," not men of some particular caste, class, status or religion, should be free to use them. In a century when this is being unsaid by nation after nation and party after party, let us not call it a barren tautology.

But the question as to what means are "lawful"—what methods of pursuing happiness are either morally permissible by the Law of Nature or should be declared legally permissible by the legislature of a particular nation—remains exactly where it did. And on that question I disagree with Clare. I don't think it is obvious that people have the unlimited "right to happiness" which she suggests.

For one thing, I believe that Clare, when she says "happiness," means simply and solely "sexual happiness." Partly because women like Clare never use the word "happiness" in any other sense. But also because I never heard Clare talk about the "right" to any other kind. She was rather leftist in her politics, and would have been scandalised if anyone had defended the actions of a ruthless man-eating tycoon on the ground that his happiness consisted in making money and he was pursuing his happiness. She was also a rabid teetotaller; I never heard her excuse an alcoholic because he was happy when he was drunk.

A good many of Clare's friends, and especially her female friends, often felt—I've heard them say so—that their own happiness would be perceptibly increased by boxing her ears. I very much doubt if this would have brought her theory of a right to happiness into play.

Clare, in fact, is doing what the whole western world seems to me to have been doing for the last 40-odd years. When I was a youngster, all the progressive people were saying, "Why all this prudery? Let us treat sex just as we treat all our other impulses." I was simple-minded enough to believe they meant what they said. I have since discovered that they meant exactly the opposite. They meant that sex was to be treated as no other impulse in our nature has ever been treated by civilized people. All the others, we admit, have to be bridled. Absolute obedience to your instinct for self-preservation is what we call cowardice; to your acquisitive impulse, avarice. Even sleep must be resisted if you're a sentry. But every unkindness and breach of faith seems to be condoned provided that the object aimed at is "four bare legs in a bed."

It is like having a morality in which stealing fruit is considered wrong—unless you steal nectarines.

And if you protest against this view you are usually met with chatter about the legitimacy and beauty and sanctity of "sex" and accused of harbouring some Puritan prejudice against it as something disreputable or shameful. I deny the charge. Foam-born Venus . . . golden Aphrodite . . . Our Lady of Cyprus . . . I never breathed a word against you. If I object to boys who steal my nectarines, must I be supposed to disapprove of nectarines in general? Or even of boys in general? It might, you know, be stealing that I disapproved of.

The real situation is skilfully concealed by saying that the question of Mr A.'s "right" to desert his wife is one of "sexual morality." Robbing an orchard is not an offense against some special morality called "fruit morality." It is an offense against honesty. Mr A.'s action is an offense against good faith (to solemn promises), against gratitude (toward one to whom he was deeply indebted) and against common humanity.

Our sexual impulses are thus being put in a position of preposterous privilege. The sexual motive is taken to condone all sorts of behaviour which, if it had any other end in view, would be condemned as merciless, treacherous and unjust.

Now though I see no good reason for giving sex this privilege, I think I see a strong cause. It is this.

It is part of the nature of a strong erotic passion—as distinct from a transient fit of appetite—that it makes more towering promises than any other emotion. No doubt all our desires make promises, but not so impressively. To be in love involves the almost irresistible conviction that one will go on being in love until one dies, and that possession of the beloved will confer, not merely frequent ecstasies, but settled, fruitful, deep-rooted, lifelong happiness. Hence *all* seems to be at stake. If we miss this chance we shall have lived in vain. At the very thought of such a doom we sink into fathomless depths of self-pity.

Unfortunately these promises are found often to be quite untrue. Every experienced adult knows this to be so as regards all erotic passions (except the one he himself is feeling at the moment). We discount the world-without-end pretensions of our friends' amours easily enough. We know that such things sometimes last—and sometimes don't. And when they do last, this is not because they promised at the outset to do so. When two people achieve lasting happiness, this is not solely because they are great lovers but because they are also—I must put it crudely—good people; controlled, loyal, fair-minded, mutually adaptable people.

If we establish a "right to (sexual) happiness" which supersedes all the ordinary rules of behaviour, we do so not because of what our passion shows itself to be in experience but because of what it professes to be while we are in the grip of it. Hence, while the bad behaviour is real and works miseries and degradations, the happiness which was the object of the behaviour turns out again and again to be illusory. Everyone (except Mr A. and Mrs B.) knows that Mr A. in a year or so may have the same reason for deserting his new wife as for deserting his old. He will feel again that all is at stake. He will see himself again as the great lover, and his pity for himself will exclude all pity for the woman.

Two further points remain.

One is this. A society in which conjugal infidelity is tolerated must always be in the long run a society adverse to women. Women, whatever a few male songs and satires may say to the contrary, are more naturally monogamous than men; it is a biological necessity. Where promiscuity prevails, they will therefore always be more often the victims than the culprits. Also, domestic happiness is more necessary to them than to us. And the quality by which they most easily hold a man, their beauty, decreases every year after they have come to maturity, but this does not happen to those qualities of personality—women don't really care twopence about our *looks*—by which we hold women. Thus in the ruthless war of promiscuity women are at a double disadvantage. They play for higher stakes and are also more likely to lose. I have no sympathy with moralists who frown at the increasing crudity of female provocativeness. These signs of desperate competition fill me with pity.

Secondly, though the "right to happiness" is chiefly claimed for the sexual impulse, it seems to me impossible that the matter should stay there. The fatal principle, once allowed in that department, must sooner or later seep through our whole lives. We thus advance toward a state of society in which not only each man but every impulse in each man claims *carte blanche*. And then, though our technological skill may help us survive a little longer, our civilization will have died at heart, and will—one dare not even add 'unfortunately'—be swept away.

For Further Reflection

1. With what does Lewis compare "the right to be happy"? What does he think of such a right?

2. Do you agree with Lewis that "we have no right to be happy"? Why does he take such a strong stand on this issue?

3. Why does Lewis think that where sex becomes promiscuous, women are at a double disadvantage? Do you agree with him?

What Do Grown Children Owe Their Parents?

JANE ENGLISH

In her short life, Jane English (1947–1978) wrote several seminal papers in applied ethics that have been reprinted repeatedly, including this essay. She argues that grown children are not *obligated* to repay a debt of gratitude to their parents but, if parents and children are emotionally close, should treat their parents as they would friends.

What do grown children owe their parents? I will contend that the answer is "nothing." Although I agree that there are many things that children *ought* to do for their parents. I will argue that it is inappropriate and misleading to describe them as things "owed." I will maintain that parents' voluntary sacrifices, rather than creating "debts" to be "repaid," tend to create love or "friendship." The duties of grown children are those of friends and result from love between them and their parents, rather than being things owed in repayment for the parents' earlier sacrifices. Thus, I will oppose those philosophers who use the word "owe" whenever a duty or obligation exists. Although the "debt" metaphor is appropriate in some moral circumstances, my argument is that a love relationship is not such a case.

Misunderstandings about the proper relationship between parents and their grown children have resulted from reliance on the "owing" terminology. For instance, we hear parents complain, "You owe it to us to write home (keep up your piano playing, not adopt a hippie lifestyle), because of all we sacrificed for you (paying for piano lessons, sending you to college)." The child is sometimes even heard to reply, "I didn't ask to be born (to be given piano lessons, to be sent to college)." This inappropriate idiom of ordinary language tends to obscure, or even to undermine, the love that is the correct ground of filial obligation.

1. FAVORS CREATE DEBTS

There are some cases, other than literal debts, in which talk of "owing," though metaphorical, is apt. New to the neighborhood, Max barely knows his neighbor, Nina, but he asks her if she will take in his mail while he is gone for a month's vacation. She agrees. If, subsequently, Nina asks Max to do the same for her, it seems that Max has a moral obligation to agree (greater than the one he would have had if Nina had not done the same for him), unless for some reason it would be a burden far out of proportion to the one Nina bore for him. I will call this a *favor:* when A, at B's request, bears some burden for B, then B incurs an obligation to reciprocate. Here the metaphor of Max's "owing" Nina is appropriate. It is not literally a debt, of course, nor can Nina pass this IOU on to heirs, demand payment in the form of Max's taking out her garbage, or sue Max. Nonetheless, since Max ought to perform one act of similar nature and amount of sacrifice in return, the term is suggestive. Once he reciprocates, the debt is "discharged"—that is, their obligations revert to the condition they were in before Max's initial request.

Contrast a situation in which Max simply goes on vacation and, to his surprise, finds upon his return that his neighbor has mowed his grass twice weekly in his absence. This is a voluntary sacrifice rather than a favor, and Max has no duty to reciprocate. It would be nice for him to volunteer to do so, but this would be supererogatory on his part. Rather than a favor, Nina's action is a friendly gesture. As a result, she might expect Max to chat over the back fence, help her catch her straying dog, or something similar—she might expect the development of a friendship. But Max would be chatting (or whatever) out of friendship, rather than in repayment for mown grass. If he did not return her gesture, she might feel rebuffed or miffed, but not unjustly treated or indignant, since Max has not failed to perform a duty. Talk of "owing" would be out of place in this case.

It is sometimes difficult to distinguish between favors and non-favors, because friends tend to do favors for each other, and those who exchange favors tend to become friends. But one test is to ask how Max is motivated. Is it "to be nice to Nina" or "because she did x for me"? Favors are frequently performed by total strangers without any friendship developing. Nevertheless, a temporary obligation is created, even if the chance for repayment never arises. For instance, suppose that Oscar and Matilda, total strangers, are waiting in a long checkout line at the supermarket. Oscar, having forgotten the oregano, asks Matilda to watch his cart for a second. She does. If Matilda now asks Oscar to return the favor while she picks up some tomato sauce, he is obliged to agree. Even if she had not watched his cart, it would be inconsiderate of him to refuse, claiming he was too busy reading the magazines. He may have a duty to help others, but he would not "owe" it to her. But if she has done the same for him, he incurs an additional obligation to help, and talk of "owing" is apt. It suggests an agreement to perform equal, reciprocal, canceling sacrifices.

2. THE DUTIES OF FRIENDSHIP

The terms "owe" and "repay" are helpful in the case of favors, because the sameness of the amount of sacrifice on the two sides is important; the monetary metaphor suggests equal quantities of sacrifice. But friendship ought to be characterized by *mutuality* rather than reciprocity: friends offer what they can give and accept what they need, without regard for the total amounts of benefits exchanged. And friends are motivated by love rather than by the prospect of repayment. Hence, talk of "owing" is singularly out of place in friendship.

For example, suppose Alfred takes Beatrice out for an expensive dinner and a movie. Beatrice incurs no obligation to "repay" him with a goodnight kiss or a return engagement. If Alfred complains that she "owes" him something, he is operating under the assumption that she should repay a favor, but on the contrary his was a generous gesture done in the hopes of developing a friendship. We hope that he would not want her repayment in the form of sex or attention if this was done to discharge a debt rather than from friendship. Since, if Alfred is prone to reasoning in this way, Beatrice may well decline the invitation or request to pay for her own dinner, his attitude of expecting a "return" on his "investment" could hinder the development of a friendship. Beatrice should return the gesture only if she is motivated by friendship.

Another common misuse of the "owing" idiom occurs when the Smiths have dined at the Joneses' four times, but the Joneses at the Smiths' only once. People often say, "We owe them three dinners." This line of thinking may be appropriate between business acquaintances, but not between friends. After all, the Joneses invited the Smiths not in order to feed them or to be fed in turn, but because of the friendly contact presumably enjoyed by all on such occasions. If the Smiths do not feel friendship toward the Joneses, they can decline future invitations and not invite the Joneses; they owe them nothing. Of course, between friends of equal resources and needs, roughly equal sacrifices (though not necessarily roughly equal dinners) will typically occur. If the sacrifices are highly out of proportion to the resources, the relationship is closer to servility than to friendship.[1]

Another difference between favors and friendship is that after a friendship ends, the duties of friendship end. The party that has sacrificed less owes the other nothing. For instance, suppose Elmer donated a pint of blood that his wife Doris needed during an operation. Years after their divorce, Elmer is in an accident and needs

---

[1]Cf. Thomas E. Hill, Jr., "Servility and Self-Respect," *Monist* 57 (1973). Thus, during childhood, most of the sacrifices will come from the parents, since they have most of the resources and the child has most of the needs. When children are grown, the situation is usually reversed.

one pint of blood. His new wife, Cora, is also of the same blood type. It seems that Doris not only does not "owe" Elmer blood, but that she should actually refrain from coming forward if Cora has volunteered to donate. To insist on donating not only interferes with the newlyweds' friendship, but it belittles Doris and Elmer's former relationship by suggesting that Elmer gave blood in hopes of favors returned instead of simply out of love for Doris. It is one of the heart-rending features of divorce that it attends to quantity in a relationship previously characterized by mutuality. If Cora could not donate, Doris's obligation is the same as that for any former spouse in need of blood; it is not increased by the fact that Elmer similarly aided her. It *is* affected by the degree to which they are still friends, which in turn may (or may not) have been influenced by Elmer's donation.

In short, unlike the debts created by favors, the duties of friendship do not require equal quantities of sacrifice. Performing equal sacrifices does not cancel the duties of friendship, as it does the debts of favors. Unrequested sacrifices do not themselves create debts, but friends have duties regardless of whether they requested or initiated the friendship. Those who perform favors may be motivated by mutual gain, whereas friends should be motivated by affection. These characteristics of the friendship relation are distorted by talk of "owing."

3. PARENTS AND CHILDREN

The relationship between children and their parents should be one of friendship characterized by mutuality rather than one of reciprocal favors. The quantity of parental sacrifice is not relevant in determining what duties the grown child has. The medical assistance grown children ought to offer their ill mothers in old age depends upon the mothers' need, not upon whether they endured a difficult pregnancy, for example. Nor do one's duties to one's parents cease once an equal quantity of sacrifice has been performed, as the phrase "discharging a debt" may lead us to think.

Rather, what children ought to do for their parents (and parents for children) depends upon (1) their respective needs, abilities, and resources and (2) the extent to which there is an ongoing friendship between them. Thus, regardless of the quantity of childhood sacrifices, an able, wealthy child has an obligation to help his needy parents more than does a needy child. To illustrate, suppose sisters Cecile and Dana are equally loved by their parents, even though Cecile was an easy child to care for, seldom ill, while Dana was often sick and caused some trouble as a juvenile delinquent. As adults, Dana is a struggling artist living far away, while Cecile is a wealthy lawyer living nearby. When the parents need visits and financial aid, Cecile has an obligation to bear a higher proportion of these burdens than her sister. This results from her abilities, rather than from the quantities of sacrifice made by the parents earlier.

Sacrifices have an important causal role in creating an ongoing friendship, which may lead us to assume incorrectly that it is the sacrifices that are the source of the obligation. That the source is the friendship instead can be seen by examining cases in which the sacrifices occurred but the friendship, for some reason, did not develop or persist. For example, if a woman gives up her newborn child for adoption, and if no feelings of love ever develop on either side, it seems that the grown child does not have an obligation to "repay" her for her sacrifices in pregnancy. For that matter, if the adopted child has an unimpaired love relationship with the adoptive parents, he or she has the same obligations to help them as a natural child would have.

The filial obligations of grown children are a result of friendship, rather than owed for services rendered. Suppose that Vance married Lola despite his parents' strong wish that he marry within their religion, and that as a result, the parents refuse to speak to him again. As the years pass, the parents are unaware of Vance's problems, his accomplishments, the birth of his children. The love that once existed between them, let us suppose, has been completely destroyed by this event and thirty years of desuetude. At this point, it seems, Vance is under no obligation to pay his parents' medical bills in their old age, beyond his general duty to help those in need. An additional, filial obligation would only arise from whatever love he may still feel for them. It would be irrelevant for his parents to argue, "But look how much we sacrificed for you when you were young," for that sacrifice was not a favor but occurred as part of a friendship which existed at that time but is now, we have supposed, defunct. A more appropriate message would be, "We still love you, and we would like to renew our friendship."

I hope this helps to set the question of what children ought to do for their parents in a new light. The parental argument. "You ought to do x because we did y for you," should be replaced by,

"We love you and you will be happier if you do x," or "We believe you love us, and anyone who loved us would do x." If the parents' sacrifice had been a favor, the child's reply, "I never asked you to do y for me," would have been relevant; to the revised parental remarks, this reply is clearly irrelevant. The child can either do x or dispute one of the parents' claims: by showing that a love relationship does not exist, or that love for someone does not motivate doing x, or that he or she will not be happier doing x.

Seen in this light, parental requests for children to write home, visit, and offer them a reasonable amount of emotional and financial support in life's crises are well founded, so long as a friendship still exists. Love for others does call for caring about and caring for them. Some other parental requests, such as for more sweeping changes in the child's lifestyle or life goals, can be seen to be insupportable, once we shift the justification from debts owed to love. The terminology of favors suggests the reasoning, "Since we paid for your college education, you owe it to us to make a career of engineering, rather than becoming a rock musician." This tends to alienate affection even further, since the tuition payments are depicted as investments for a return rather than done from love, as though the child's life goals could be "bought." Basing the argument on love leads to different reasoning patterns. The suppressed premise, "If A loves B, then A follows B's wishes as to A's lifelong career" is simply false. Love does not even dictate that the child adopt the parents' values as to the desirability of alternative life goals. So the parents' strongest available argument here is, "We love you, we are deeply concerned about your happiness, and in the long run you will be happier as an engineer." This makes it clear that an empirical claim is really the subject of the debate.

The function of these examples is to draw out our considered judgments as to the proper relation between parents and their grown children, and to show how poorly they fit the model of favors. What is relevant is the ongoing friendship that exists between parents and children. Although that relationship developed partly as a result of parental sacrifices for the child, the duties that grown children have to their parents result from the friendship rather than from the sacrifices. The idiom of owing favors to one's parents can actually be destructive if it undermines the role of mutuality and leads us to think in terms of quantitative reciprocal favors.

For Further Reflection

1. What is English's point about the use of terms such as *debt* or *owing* to describe parent-child relationships?

2. What is English's argument for the conclusion that grown children do not "owe" their parents a debt of gratitude?

3. According to English, what children ought to do for their parents depends on what two factors?

Further Readings for Chapter 11

Baker, Robert, and Frederick Elliston, eds. *Philosophy and Sex.* 2nd ed. Buffalo, N.Y.: Prometheus, 1984.

Cameron, Paul. "A Case Against Homosexuality." *Human Life Review* 4 (Summer 1978).

Leiser, Burton. *Liberty, Justice and Morals.* 3rd ed. New York: Macmillan, 1986.

Russell, Bertrand. *Marriage and Morals.* New York: Liveright, 1929.

Scruton, Roger. *Sexual Desire: A Moral Philosophy of the Erotic.* New York: Macmillan, 1986.

Vannoy, Russell. *Sex Without Love: A Philosophical Exploration.* Buffalo, N.Y.: Prometheus, 1980.

Wasserstrom, Richard. "Is Adultery Immoral?" In Richard Wasserstrom, ed. *Today's Moral Problems.* New York: Macmillan, 1985.

CHAPTER 12

Is Abortion Morally Permissible?

> Abortion during the first two or three months of gestation is morally equivalent to removal of a piece of tissue from the woman's body.
>
> —Philosopher Thomas Szasz

> Every unborn child must be regarded as a human person with all the rights of a human person, from the moment of conception.
>
> —Ethical and Religious Directives for Catholic Hospitals

One of the major social issues before us today, one that divides our nation as no other issue does, is that of the moral and legal status of the human fetus and the corresponding question of the moral permissibility of abortion. On the one hand, such organizations as the Roman Catholic Church and the Right to Life movement, appalled by the more than 1.5 million abortions that take place in this country each year, have exerted significant political pressure toward introducing a constitutional amendment that would grant full legal rights to fetuses. These movements have in some cases made the abortion issue the single issue in political campaigns. On the other hand, pro-choice groups such as the National Organization for Women (NOW), the National Abortion Rights Action League (NARAL), and other feminist organizations have exerted enormous pressure on politicians to support pro-abortion presidential, legislation. The Republican and Democratic political platforms of the last two elections took diametrically opposed sides on this issue.

Why is abortion a moral issue? Take a fertilized egg, a zygote, a tiny sphere of cells. By itself, it is hard to see what is so important about such an inconspicuous piece of matter. It is virtually indistinguishable from other clusters of cells, or the zygotes of other animals. On the other hand, take an adult human being, a class of beings that we all intuitively feel to be worthy of high respect, having rights, including the right to life. To kill an innocent human being is an act of murder and universally condemned. However, no obvious line of division separates that single-cell zygote from the adult it will become. Hence, the problem of abortion.

In this chapter, Don Marquis argues that abortion is wrong because it deprives a fetus of its future. But Judith Jarvis Thomson maintains that some abortions may be permissible to prevent a woman's body from being used by the fetus against her will. Mary Anne Warren contends that fetuses are not persons since persons must have such characteristics as self-consciousness and rationality and fetuses do not have these. Finally, Jane English argues for a moderate position. Most early abortions are permissible, most late ones immoral.

Why Abortion Is Immoral

DON MARQUIS

Don Marquis teaches philosophy at the University of Kansas. In this selection, he argues that killing someone is wrong because it robs him or her of a future—a loss of all possible "experiences, activities, projects, and enjoyments." Likewise, abortion (at least in most circumstances) is wrong because it deprives the fetus of all prospects of such experiencing and being.

The view that abortion is, with rare exceptions, seriously immoral has received little support in the recent philosophical literature. No doubt most philosophers affiliated with secular institutions of higher education believe that the anti-abortion position is either a symptom of irrational religious dogma or a conclusion generated by seriously confused philosophical argument. The purpose of this essay is to undermine this general belief. This essay sets out an argument that purports to show, as well as any argument in ethics can show, that abortion is, except possibly in rare cases, seriously immoral, that it is in the same moral category as killing an innocent adult human being.

The argument is based on a major assumption. Many of the most insightful and careful writers on the ethics of abortion—such as Joel Feinberg, Michael Tooley, Mary Anne Warren, H. Tristram Engelhardt, Jr., L. W. Sumner, John T. Noonan, Jr., and Philip Devine[1]—

"Why Abortion Is Immoral" by Don Marquis *Journal of Philosophy,* LXXXVI, 4 (April 1989): pp. 183–202.

[1]Feinberg, "Abortion," in *Matters of Life and Death: New Introductory Essays in Moral Philosophy,* Tom Regan, ed. (New York: Random House, 1986), pp. 256–293; Tooley, "Abortion and Infanticide," *Philosophy and Public Affairs,* II, 1 (1972):37–65, Tooley, *Abortion and Infanticide* (New York: Oxford, 1984); Warren, "On the Moral and Legal Status of Abortion," *The Monist,* LVII, 1 (1973):43–61; Engelhardt, "The Ontology of Abortion," *Ethics,* LXXXIV, 3 (1974):217–234; Sumner, *Abortion and Moral Theory* (Princeton: University Press, 1981); Noonan, "An Almost Absolute Value in History," in *The Morality of Abortion: Legal and Historical Perspectives,* Noonan, ed. (Cambridge: Harvard, 1970); and Devine, *The Ethics of Homicide* (Ithaca: Cornell, 1978).

believe that whether or not abortion is morally permissible stands or falls on whether or not a fetus is the sort of being whose life it is seriously wrong to end. The argument of this essay will assume, but not argue, that they are correct.

Also, this essay will neglect issues of great importance to a complete ethics of abortion. Some anti-abortionists will allow that certain abortions, such as abortion before implantation or abortion when the life of a woman is threatened by a pregnancy or abortion after rape, may be morally permissible. This essay will not explore the casuistry of these hard cases. The purpose of this essay is to develop a general argument for the claim that the overwhelming majority of deliberate abortions are seriously immoral.

I.

A sketch of standard anti-abortion and pro-choice arguments exhibits how those arguments possess certain symmetries that explain why partisans of those positions are so convinced of the correctness of their own positions, why they are not successful in convincing their opponents, and why, to others, this issue seems to be unresolvable. An analysis of the nature of this standoff suggests a strategy for surmounting it.

Consider the way a typical anti-abortionist argues. She will argue or assert that life is present from the moment of conception or that fetuses look like babies or that fetuses possess a characteristic such as a genetic code that is both necessary and sufficient for being human. Anti-abortionists seem to believe that (1) the truth of all of these claims is quite obvious, and (2) establishing any of these claims is sufficient to show that abortion is morally akin to murder.

A standard pro-choice strategy exhibits similarities. The pro-choicer will argue or assert that fetuses are not persons or that fetuses are not rational agents or that fetuses are not social beings. Pro-choicers seem to believe that (1) the truth of any of these claims is quite obvious, and (2) establishing any of these claims is sufficient to show that an abortion is not a wrongful killing.

In fact, both the pro-choice and the anti-abortion claims do seem to be true, although the "it looks like a baby" claim is more difficult to establish the earlier the pregnancy. We seem to have a standoff. How can it be resolved?

As everyone who has taken a bit of logic knows, if any of these arguments concerning abortion is a good argument, it requires not only some claim characterizing fetuses, but also some general moral principle that ties a characteristic of fetuses to having or not having the right to life or to some other moral characteristic that will generate the obligation or the lack of obligation not to end the life of a fetus. Accordingly, the arguments of the anti-abortionist and the pro-choicer need a bit of filling in to be regarded as adequate.

Note what each partisan will say. The anti-abortionist will claim that her position is supported by such generally accepted moral principles as "It is always prima facie seriously wrong to take a human life" or "It is always prima facie seriously wrong to end the life of a baby." Since these are generally accepted moral principles, her position is certainly not obviously wrong. The pro-choicer will claim that her position is supported by such plausible moral principles as "Being a person is what gives an individual intrinsic moral worth" or "It is only seriously prima facie wrong to take the life of a member of the human community." Since these are generally accepted moral principles, the pro-choice position is certainly not obviously wrong. Unfortunately, we have again arrived at a standoff.

Now, how might one deal with this standoff? The standard approach is to try to show how the moral principles of one's opponent lose their plausibility under analysis. It is easy to see how this is possible. On the one hand, the anti-abortionist will defend a moral principle concerning the wrongness of killing which tends to be broad in scope in order that even fetuses at an early stage of pregnancy will fall under it. The problem with broad principles is that they often embrace too much. In this particular instance, the principle "It is always prima facie wrong to take a human life" seems to entail that it is wrong to end the existence of a living human cancer-cell culture, on the grounds that the culture is both living and human. Therefore, it seems that the anti-abortionist's favored principle is too broad.

On the other hand, the pro-choicer wants to find a moral principle concerning the wrongness of killing which tends to be narrow in scope in order that fetuses will *not* fall under it. The problem with narrow principles is that they often do not embrace enough. Hence, the needed principles such as "It is prima facie seriously wrong to kill only persons" or "It is prima facie wrong to kill only rational agents" do not explain why it is wrong to kill infants or young children or the severely retarded or even perhaps the severely mentally ill. Therefore, we seem again to have a standoff. The anti-abortionist charges, not unreasonably, that pro-choice principles concerning killing are too narrow to be acceptable; the pro-choicer charges, not unreasonably, that anti-abortionist principles concerning killing are too broad to be acceptable.

Attempts by both sides to patch up the difficulties in their positions run into further difficulties. The anti-abortionist will try to remove the problem in her position by reformulating her principle concerning killing in terms of human beings. Now we end up with: "It is always prima facie seriously wrong to end the life of a human being." This principle has the advantage of avoiding the problem of the human cancer-cell culture counterexample. But this advantage is purchased at a high price. For although it is clear that a fetus is both human and alive, it is not at all clear that a fetus is a human *being*. There is at least something to be said for the view that something becomes a human being only after a process of development, and that therefore first trimester fetuses and perhaps all fetuses are not yet human beings. Hence, the anti-abortionist, by this move, has merely exchanged one problem for another.[2]

The pro-choicer fares no better. She may attempt to find reasons why killing infants, young children, and the severely retarded is wrong which are independent of her major principle that is supposed to explain the wrongness of taking human life, but which will not also make abortion immoral. This is no easy task. Appeals to social utility will seem satisfactory only to those who resolve not to think of the enormous difficulties with a utilitarian account of the wrongness of killing and the significant social costs of preserving the lives of the unproductive.[3] A pro-choice strategy that extends the definition of "person" to infants or even to young children seems just as arbitrary as an anti-abortion strategy that extends the definition of "human being" to fetuses. Again, we find symmetries in the two positions and we arrive at a standoff.

There are even further problems that reflect symmetries in the two

[2]For interesting discussions of this issue, see Warren Quinn, "Abortion: Identity and Loss," *Philosophy and Public Affairs*, XIII, 1 (1984):24–25; and Lawrence C. Becker, "Human Being: The Boundaries of the Concept," *Philosophy and Public Affairs*, IV, 4 (1975):334–359.

[3]For example, see my "Ethics and The Elderly: Some Problems," in Stuart Spicker, Kathleen Woodward, and David Van Tassel, eds., *Aging and the Elderly: Humanistic Perspectives in Gerontology* (Atlantic Highlands, NJ: Humanities, 1978), pp. 341–355.

positions. In addition to counterexample problems, or the arbitrary application problems that can be exchanged for them, the standard anti-abortionist principle "It is prima facie seriously wrong to kill a human being," or one of its variants, can be objected to on the grounds of ambiguity. If "human being" is taken to be a *biological* category, then the anti-abortionist is left with the problem of explaining why a merely biological category should make a moral difference. Why, it is asked, is it any more reasonable to base a moral conclusion on the number of chromosomes in one's cells than on the color of one's skin?[4] If "human being," on the other hand, is taken to be a *moral* category, then the claim that a fetus is a human being cannot be taken to be a premise in the anti-abortion argument, for it is precisely what needs to be established. Hence, either the anti-abortionist's main category is a morally irrelevant, merely biological category, or it is of no use to the anti-abortionist in establishing (non-circularly, of course) that abortion is wrong.

Although this problem with the anti-abortionist position is often noticed, it is less often noticed that the pro-choice position suffers from an analogous problem. The principle "Only persons have the right to life" also suffers from an ambiguity. The term "person" is typically defined in terms of psychological characteristics, although there will certainly be disagreement concerning which characteristics are most important. Supposing that this matter can be settled, the pro-choicer is left with the problem of explaining why *psychological* characteristics should make a *moral* difference. If the pro-choicer should attempt to deal with this problem by claiming that an explanation is not necessary, that in fact we do treat such a cluster of psychological properties as having moral significance, the sharp-witted anti-abortionist should have a ready response. We do treat being both living and human as having moral significance. If it is legitimate for the pro-choicer to demand that the anti-abortionist provide an explanation of the connection between the biological character of being a human being and the wrongness of being killed (even though people accept this connection), then it is legitimate for the anti-abortionist to demand that the pro-choicer provide an explanation of the connection between psychological criteria for being a person and the wrongness of being killed (even though that connection is accepted).[5]

[4]See Warren, *op. cit.,* and Tooley, "Abortion and Infanticide."
[5]This seems to be the fatal flaw in Warren's treatment of this issue.

Feinberg has attempted to meet this objection (he calls psychological personhood "commonsense personhood"):

> The characteristics that confer commonsense personhood are not arbitrary bases for rights and duties, such as race, sex or species membership; rather they are traits that make sense out of rights and duties and without which those moral attributes would have no point or function. It is because people are conscious; have a sense of their personal identities; have plans, goals, and projects; experience emotions; are liable to pains, anxieties, and frustrations; can reason and bargain, and so on—it is because of these attributes that people have values and interests, desires and expectations of their own, including a stake in their own futures, and a personal well-being of a sort we cannot ascribe to unconscious or nonrational beings. Because of their developed capacities they can assume duties and responsibilities and can have and make claims on one another. Only because of their sense of self, their life plans, their value hierarchies, and their stakes in their own futures can they be ascribed fundamental rights. There is nothing arbitrary about these linkages (*op. cit.,* p. 270).

The plausible aspects of this attempt should not be taken to obscure its implausible features. There is a great deal to be said for the view that being a psychological person under some description is a necessary condition for having duties. One cannot have a duty unless one is capable of behaving morally, and a being's capability of behaving morally will require having a certain psychology. It is far from obvious, however, that having rights entails consciousness or rationality, as Feinberg suggests. We speak of the rights of the severely retarded or the severely mentally ill, yet some of these persons are not rational. We speak of the rights of the temporarily unconscious. The New Jersey Supreme Court based their decision in the Quinlan case on Karen Ann Quinlan's right to privacy, and she was known to be permanently unconscious at that time. Hence, Feinberg's claim that having rights entails being conscious is, on its face, obviously false.

Of course, it might not make sense to attribute rights to a being that would never in its natural history have certain psychological traits. This modest connection between psychological personhood and moral personhood will create a place for Karen Ann Quinlan and the temporarily unconscious. But then it makes a place for fetuses also. Hence, it does not serve Feinberg's pro-choice purposes. Accordingly, it seems that the pro-choicer will have as much difficulty bridging the gap between psychological personhood and personhood in the moral sense as the anti-abortionist has bridging the gap between being a biological human being and being a human being in the moral sense.

Furthermore, the pro-choicer cannot any more escape her problem by making person a purely moral category than the anti-abortionist could escape by the analogous move. For if person is a moral category, then the pro-choicer is left without the resources for establishing (noncircularly, of course) the claim that a fetus is not a person, which is an essential premise in her argument. Again, we have both a symmetry and a standoff between pro-choice and anti-abortion views.

Passions in the abortion debate run high. There are both plausibilities and difficulties with the standard positions. Accordingly, it is hardly surprising that partisans of either side embrace with fervor the moral generalizations that support the conclusions they preanalytically favor, and reject with disdain the moral generalizations of their opponents as being subject to inescapable difficulties. It is easy to believe that the counterexamples to one's own moral principles are merely temporary difficulties that will dissolve in the wake of further philosophical research, and that the counterexamples to the principles of one's opponents are as straightforward as the contradiction between A and O propositions in traditional logic. This might suggest to an impartial observer (if there are any) that the abortion issue is unresolvable.

There is a way out of this apparent dialectical quandary. The moral generalizations of both sides are not quite correct. The generalizations hold for the most part, for the usual cases. This suggests that they are all *accidental* generalizations, that the moral claims made by those on both sides of the dispute do not touch on the *essence* of the matter.

This use of the distinction between essence and accident is not meant to invoke obscure metaphysical categories. Rather, it is intended to reflect the rather atheoretical nature of the abortion discussion. If the generalization a partisan in the abortion dispute adopts were derived from the reason why ending the life of a human being is wrong, then there could not be exceptions to that generalization unless some special case obtains in which there are even more powerful countervailing reasons. Such generalizations would not be merely accidental generalizations; they would point to, or be based upon, the essence of the wrongness of killing, what it is that makes killing wrong. All this suggests that a necessary condition of resolving the abortion controversy is a more theoretical account of the wrongness of killing. After all, if we merely believe, but do not understand, why killing adult human beings such as ourselves is wrong, how could we conceivably show that abortion is either immoral or permissible?

II.

In order to develop such an account, we can start from the following unproblematic assumption concerning our own case: it is wrong to kill *us*. Why is it wrong? Some answers can be easily eliminated. It might be said that what makes killing us wrong is that a killing brutalizes the one who kills. But the brutalization consists of being inured to the performance of an act that is hideously immoral; hence, the brutalization does not explain the immorality. It might be said that what makes killing us wrong is the great loss others would experience due to our absence. Although such hubris is understandable, such an explanation does not account for the wrongness of killing hermits, or those whose lives are relatively independent and whose friends find it easy to make new friends.

A more obvious answer is better. What primarily makes killing wrong is neither its effect on the murderer nor its effect on the victim's friends and relatives, but its effect on the victim. The loss of one's life is one of the greatest losses one can suffer. The loss of one's life deprives one of all the experiences, activities, projects, and enjoyments that would otherwise have constituted one's future. Therefore, killing someone is wrong, primarily because the killing inflicts (one of) the greatest possible losses on the victim. To describe this as the loss of life can be misleading, however. The change in my biological state does not by itself make killing me wrong. The effect of the loss of my biological life is the loss to me of all those activities, projects, experiences, and enjoyments which would otherwise have constituted my future personal life. These activities, projects, experiences, and enjoyments are either valuable for their own sakes or are means to something else that is valuable for its own sake. Some parts of my future are not valued by me now, but will come to be valued by me as I grow older and as my values and capacities change. When I am killed, I am deprived both of what I now value which would have been part of my future personal life, but also what I would come to value. Therefore, when I die, I am deprived of all of the value of my future. Inflicting this loss on me is ultimately what makes killing me wrong. This being the case, it would seem that what makes killing *any* adult human being prima facie seriously wrong is the loss of his or her future.[6]

How should this rudimentary theory of the wrongness of killing be evaluated? It cannot be faulted for deriving an "ought" from an "is," for it does not. The analysis assumes that killing me (or you, reader) is prima facie seriously wrong. The point of the analysis is to establish which natural property ultimately explains the wrongness of the killing, given that it is wrong. A natural property will ultimately explain the wrongness of killing, only if (1) the explanation fits with our intuitions about the matter and (2) there is no other natural property that provides the basis for a better explanation of the wrongness of killing. This analysis rests on the intuition that what makes killing a particular human or animal wrong is what it does to that particular human or animal. What makes killing wrong is some natural effect or other of the killing. Some would deny this. For instance, a divine-command theorist in ethics would deny it. Surely this denial is, however, one of those features of divine-command theory which renders it so implausible.

The claim that what makes killing wrong is the loss of the victim's future is directly supported by two considerations. In the first place, this theory explains why we regard killing as one of the worst of crimes. Killing is especially wrong, because it deprives the victim of more than perhaps any other crime. In the second place, people with AIDS or cancer who know they are dying believe, of course, that dying is a very bad thing for them. They believe that the loss of a future to them that they would otherwise have experienced is what makes their premature death a very bad thing for them. A better theory of the wrongness of killing would require a different natural property associated with killing which better fits with the attitudes of the dying. What could it be?

The view that what makes killing wrong is the loss to the victim of the value of the victim's future gains additional support when some of its implications are examined. In the first place, it is incom-

---

[6]I have been most influenced on this matter by Jonathan Glover, *Causing Death and Saving Lives* (New York: Penguin, 1977), ch. 3; and Robert Young, "What Is So Wrong with Killing People?" *Philosophy,* LIV, 210 (1979):515–528.

patible with the view that it is wrong to kill only beings who are biologically human. It is possible that there exists a different species from another planet whose members have a future like ours. Since having a future like that is what makes killing someone wrong, this theory entails that it would be wrong to kill members of such a species. Hence, this theory is opposed to the claim that only life that is biologically human has great moral worth, a claim which many anti-abortionists have seemed to adopt. This opposition, which this theory has in common with personhood theories, seems to be a merit of the theory.

In the second place, the claim that the loss of one's future is the wrong-making feature of one's being killed entails the possibility that the futures of some actual nonhuman mammals on our own planet are sufficiently like ours that it is seriously wrong to kill them also. Whether some animals do have the same right to life as human beings depends on adding to the account of the wrongness of killing some additional account of just what it is about my future or the futures of other adult human beings which makes it wrong to kill us. No such additional account will be offered in this essay. Undoubtedly, the provision of such an account would be a very difficult matter. Undoubtedly, any such account would be quite controversial. Hence, it surely should not reflect badly on this sketch of an elementary theory of the wrongness of killing that it is indeterminate with respect to some very difficult issues regarding animal rights.

In the third place, the claim that the loss of one's future is the wrong-making feature of one's being killed does not entail, as sanctity-of-human-life theories do, that active euthanasia is wrong. Persons who are severely and incurably ill, who face a future of pain and despair, and who wish to die will not have suffered a loss if they are killed. It is, strictly speaking, the value of a human's future which makes killing wrong in this theory. This being so, killing does not necessarily wrong some persons who are sick and dying. Of course, there may be other reasons for a prohibition of active euthanasia, but that is another matter. Sanctity-of-human-life theories seem to hold that active euthanasia is seriously wrong even in an individual case where there seems to be good reason for it independently of public policy considerations. This consequence is most implausible, and it is a plus for the claim that the loss of a future of value is what makes killing wrong that it does not share this consequence.

In the fourth place, the account of the wrongness of killing defended in this essay does straightforwardly entail that it is prima facie seriously wrong to kill children and infants, for we do presume that they have futures of value. Since we do believe that it is wrong to kill defenseless little babies, it is important that a theory of the wrongness of killing easily account for this. Personhood theories of the wrongness of killing, on the other hand, cannot straightforwardly account for the wrongness of killing infants and young children.[7] Hence, such theories must add special ad hoc accounts of the wrongness of killing the young. The plausibility of such ad hoc theories seems to be a function of how desperately one wants such theories to work. The claim that the primary wrong-making feature of a killing is the loss to the victim of the value of its future accounts for the wrongness of killing young children and infants directly; it makes the wrongness of such acts as obvious as we actually think it is. This is a further merit of this theory. Accordingly, it seems that this value of a future-like-ours theory of the wrongness of killing shares strengths of both sanctity-of-life and personhood accounts while avoiding weaknesses of both. In addition, it meshes with a central intuition concerning what makes killing wrong.

The claim that the primary wrong-making feature of a killing is the loss to the victim of the value of its future has obvious consequences for the ethics of abortion. The future of a standard fetus includes a set of experiences, projects, activities, and such which are identical with the futures of adult human beings and are identical with the futures of young children. Since the reason that is sufficient to explain why it is wrong to kill human beings after the time of birth is a reason that also applies to fetuses, it follows that abortion is prima facie seriously morally wrong.

This argument does not rely on the invalid inference that, since it is wrong to kill persons, it is wrong to kill potential persons also. The category that is morally central to this analysis is the category of having a valuable future like ours; it is not the category of personhood. The argument to the conclusion that abortion is prima facie seriously morally wrong proceeded independently of the notion of person or potential person or any equivalent. Someone may wish to start with this analysis in terms of the value of a human future, conclude that abortion is, except perhaps in rare circumstances, seriously morally wrong, infer that fetuses have the right

[7]Feinberg, Tooley, Warren, and Engelhardt have all dealt with this problem.

to life, and then call fetuses "persons" as a result of their having the right to life. Clearly, in this case, the category of person is being used to state the *conclusion* of the analysis rather than to generate the *argument* of the analysis.

The structure of this anti-abortion argument can be both illuminated and defended by comparing it to what appears to be the best argument for the wrongness of the wanton infliction of pain on animals. This latter argument is based on the assumption that it is prima facie wrong to inflict pain on me (or you, reader). What is the natural property associated with the infliction of pain which makes such infliction wrong? The obvious answer seems to be that the infliction of pain causes suffering and that suffering is a misfortune. The suffering caused by the infliction of pain is what makes the wanton infliction of pain on me wrong. The wanton infliction of pain on other adult humans causes suffering. The wanton infliction of pain on animals causes suffering. Since causing suffering is what makes the wanton infliction of pain wrong and since the wanton infliction of pain on animals causes suffering, it follows that the wanton infliction of pain on animals is wrong.

This argument for the wrongness of the wanton infliction of pain on animals shares a number of structural features with the argument for the serious prima facie wrongness of abortion. Both arguments start with an obvious assumption concerning what it is wrong to do to me (or you, reader). Both then look for the characteristic or the consequence of the wrong action which makes the action wrong. Both recognize that the wrong-making feature of these immoral actions is a property of actions sometimes directed at individuals other than postnatal human beings. If the structure of the argument for the wrongness of the wanton infliction of pain on animals is sound, then the structure of the argument for the prima facie serious wrongness of abortion is also sound, for the structure of the two arguments is the same. The structure common to both is the key to the explanation of how the wrongness of abortion can be demonstrated without recourse to the category of person. In neither argument is that category crucial.

This defense of an argument for the wrongness of abortion in terms of a structurally similar argument for the wrongness of the wanton infliction of pain on animals succeeds only if the account regarding animals is the correct account. Is it? In the first place, it seems plausible. In the second place, its major competition is Kant's account. Kant believed that we do not have direct duties to animals at all, because they are not persons. Hence, Kant had to explain and justify the wrongness of inflicting pain on animals on the grounds that "he who is hard in his dealings with animals becomes hard also in his dealing with men."[8] The problem with Kant's account is that there seems to be no reason for accepting this latter claim unless Kant's account is rejected. If the alternative to Kant's account is accepted, then it is easy to understand why someone who is indifferent to inflicting pain on animals is also indifferent to inflicting pain on humans, for one is indifferent to what makes inflicting pain wrong in both cases. But, if Kant's account is accepted, there is no intelligible reason why one who is hard in his dealings with animals (or crabgrass or stones) should also be hard in his dealings with men. After all, men are persons: animals are no more persons than crabgrass or stones. Persons are Kant's crucial moral category. Why, in short, should a Kantian accept the basic claim in Kant's argument?

Hence, Kant's argument for the wrongness of inflicting pain on animals rests on a claim that, in a world of Kantian moral agents, is demonstrably false. Therefore, the alternative analysis, being more plausible anyway, should be accepted. Since this alternative analysis has the same structure as the anti-abortion argument being defended here, we have further support for the argument for the immorality of abortion being defended in this essay.

Of course, this value of a future-like-ours argument, if sound, shows only that abortion is prima facie wrong, not that it is wrong in any and all circumstances. Since the loss of the future to a standard fetus, if killed, is, however, at least as great a loss as the loss of the future to a standard adult human being who is killed, abortion, like ordinary killing, could be justified only by the most compelling reasons. The loss of one's life is almost the greatest misfortune that can happen to one. Presumably abortion could be justified in some circumstances, only if the loss consequent on failing to abort would be at least as great. Accordingly, morally permissible abortions will be rare indeed unless, perhaps, they occur so early in pregnancy that a fetus is not yet definitely an individual. Hence, this argument should be taken as showing that abortion is presumptively very seriously wrong, where the presumption is very strong—as strong as the presumption that killing another adult human being is wrong.

---

[8]"Duties to Animals and Spirits," in *Lectures on Ethics,* Louis Infeld, trans. (New York: Harper, 1963), p. 239.

III.

How complete an account of the wrongness of killing does the value of a future-like-ours account have to be in order that the wrongness of abortion is a consequence? This account does not have to be an account of the necessary conditions for the wrongness of killing. Some persons in nursing homes may lack valuable human futures, yet it may be wrong to kill them for other reasons. Furthermore, this account does not obviously have to be the sole reason killing is wrong where the victim did have a valuable future. This analysis claims only that, for any killing where the victim did have a valuable future like ours, having that future by itself is sufficient to create the strong presumption that the killing is seriously wrong.

One way to overturn the value of a future-like-ours argument would be to find some account of the wrongness of killing which is at least as intelligible and which has different implications for the ethics of abortion. Two rival accounts possess at least some degree of plausibility. One account is based on the obvious fact that people value the experience of living and wish for that valuable experience to continue. Therefore, it might be said, what makes killing wrong is the discontinuation of that experience for the victim. Let us call this the *discontinuation account*.[9] Another rival account is based upon the obvious fact that people strongly desire to continue to live. This suggests that what makes killing us so wrong is that it interferes with the fulfillment of a strong and fundamental desire, the fulfillment of which is necessary for the fulfillment of any other desires we might have. Let us call this the *desire account*.[10]

Consider first the desire account as a rival account of the ethics of killing which would provide the basis for rejecting the anti-abortion position. Such an account will have to be stronger than the value of a future-like-ours account of the wrongness of abortion if it is to do the job expected of it. To entail the wrongness of abortion, the value of a future-like-ours account has only to provide a sufficient, but not a necessary, condition for the wrongness of killing. The desire account, on the other hand, must provide us

---

[9]I am indebted to Jack Bricke for raising this objection.
[10]Presumably a preference utilitarian would press such an objection. Tooley once suggested that his account has such a theoretical underpinning. See his "Abortion and Infanticide," pp. 44/5.

also with a necessary condition for the wrongness of killing in order to generate a pro-choice conclusion on abortion. The reason for this is that presumably the argument from the desire account moves from the claim that what makes killing wrong is interference with a very strong desire to the claim that abortion is not wrong because the fetus lacks a strong desire to live. Obviously, this inference fails if someone's having the desire to live is not a necessary condition of its being wrong to kill that individual.

One problem with the desire account is that we do regard it as seriously wrong to kill persons who have little desire to live or who have no desire to live or, indeed, have a desire not to live. We believe it is seriously wrong to kill the unconscious, the sleeping, those who are tired of life, and those who are suicidal. The value-of-a-human-future account renders standard morality intelligible in these cases; these cases appear to be incompatible with the desire account.

The desire account is subject to a deeper difficulty. We desire life, because we value the goods of this life. The goodness of life is not secondary to our desire for it. If this were not so, the pain of one's own premature death could be done away with merely by an appropriate alteration in the configuration of one's desires. This is absurd. Hence, it would seem that it is the loss of the goods of one's future, not the interference with the fulfillment of a strong desire to live, which accounts ultimately for the wrongness of killing.

It is worth noting that, if the desire account is modified so that it does not provide a necessary, but only a sufficient, condition for the wrongness of killing, the desire account is compatible with the value of a future-like-ours account. The combined accounts will yield an anti-abortion ethic. This suggests that one can retain what is intuitively plausible about the desire account without a challenge to the basic argument of this paper.

It is also worth noting that, if future desires have moral force in a modified desire account of the wrongness of killing, one can find support for an anti-abortion ethic even in the absence of a value of a future-like-ours account. If one decides that a morally relevant property, the possession of which is sufficient to make it wrong to kill some individual, is the desire at some future time to live—one might decide to justify one's refusal to kill suicidal teenagers on these grounds, for example—then, since typical fetuses will have the desire in the future to live, it is wrong to kill typical fetuses. Accordingly, it does not seem that a desire account of the wrongness of killing can provide a justification of a pro-choice ethic of abortion which is nearly as adequate as the value of a human-future justification of an anti-abortion ethic.

The discontinuation account looks more promising as an account of the wrongness of killing. It seems just as intelligible as the value of a future-like-ours account, but it does not justify an anti-abortion position. Obviously, if it is the continuation of one's activities, experiences, and projects, the loss of which makes killing wrong, then it is not wrong to kill fetuses for that reason, for fetuses do not have experiences, activities, and projects to be continued or discontinued. Accordingly, the discontinuation account does not have the anti-abortion consequences that the value of a future-like-ours account has. Yet, it seems as intelligible as the value of a future-like-ours account, for when we think of what would be wrong with our being killed, it does seem as if it is the discontinuation of what makes our lives worthwhile which makes killing us wrong.

Is the discontinuation account just as good an account as the value of a future-like-ours account? The discontinuation account will not be adequate at all, if it does not refer to the *value* of the experience that may be discontinued. One does not want the discontinuation account to make it wrong to kill a patient who begs for death and who is in severe pain that cannot be relieved short of killing. (I leave open the question of whether it is wrong for other reasons.) Accordingly, the discontinuation account must be more than a bare discontinuation account. It must make some reference to the positive value of the patient's experiences. But, by the same token, the value of a future-like-ours account cannot be a bare future account either. Just having a future surely does not itself rule out killing the above patient. This account must make some reference to the value of the patient's future experiences and projects also. Hence, both accounts involve the value of experiences, projects, and activities. So far we still have symmetry between the accounts.

The symmetry fades, however, when we focus on the time period of the value of the experiences, etc., which has moral consequences. Although both accounts leave open the possibility that the patient in our example may be killed, this possibility is left open only in virtue of the utterly bleak future for the patient. It makes no difference whether the patient's immediate past contains intolerable pain, or consists in being in a coma (which we can imagine is a situation of indifference), or consists in a life of value. If the patient's future is a future of value, we want our account to make it wrong to kill the patient. If the patient's future is intolerable, whatever his or her immediate past, we want our account to allow killing the patient. Obviously, then, it is the value of that patient's future which is doing the work in rendering the morality of killing the patient intelligible.

This being the case, it seems clear that whether one has immediate past experiences or not does no work in the explanation of what makes killing wrong. The addition the discontinuation account makes to the value of a human future account is otiose. Its addition to the value-of-a-future account plays no role at all in rendering intelligible the wrongness of killing. Therefore, it can be discarded with the discontinuation account of which it is a part.

IV.

The analysis of the previous section suggests that alternative general accounts of the wrongness of killing are either inadequate or unsuccessful in getting around the anti-abortion consequences of the value of a future-like-ours argument. A different strategy for avoiding these anti-abortion consequences involves limiting the scope of the value of a future argument. More precisely, the strategy involves arguing that fetuses lack a property that is essential for the value-of-a-future argument (or for any anti-abortion argument) to apply to them.

One move of this sort is based upon the claim that a necessary condition of one's future being valuable is that one values it. Value implies a valuer. Given this one might argue that, since fetuses cannot value their futures, their futures are not valuable to them. Hence, it does not seriously wrong them deliberately to end their lives.

This move fails, however, because of some ambiguities. Let us assume that something cannot be of value unless it is valued by someone. This does not entail that my life is of no value unless it is valued by me. I may think, in a period of despair, that my future is of no worth whatsoever, but I may be wrong because others rightly see value—even great value—in it. Furthermore, my future can be valuable to me even if I do not value it. This is the case when a young person attempts suicide, but is rescued and goes on to significant human achievements. Such young people's futures are ultimately valuable to them, even though such futures do not seem to be valuable to them at the moment of attempted suicide. A fetus's future can be valuable to it in the same way. Accordingly, this attempt to limit the anti-abortion argument fails.

Another similar attempt to reject the anti-abortion position is based on Tooley's claim that an entity cannot possess the right to life unless it has the capacity to desire its continued existence. It follows that, since fetuses lack the conceptual capacity to desire to continue to live, they lack the right to life. Accordingly, Tooley concludes that abortion cannot be seriously prima facie wrong (*op. cit.,* pp. 46/7).

What could be the evidence for Tooley's basic claim? Tooley once argued that individuals have a prima facie right to what they desire and that the lack of the capacity to desire something undercuts the basis of one's right to it (*op. cit.,* pp. 44/5). This argument plainly will not succeed in the context of the analysis of this essay, however, since the point here is to establish the fetus's right to life on other grounds. Tooley's argument assumes that the right to life cannot be established in general on some basis other than the desire for life. This position was considered and rejected in the preceding section of this paper.

One might attempt to defend Tooley's basic claim on the grounds that, because a fetus cannot apprehend continued life as a benefit, its continued life cannot be a benefit or cannot be something it has a right to or cannot be something that is in its interest. This might be defended in terms of the general proposition that, if an individual is literally incapable of caring about or taking an interest in some X, then one does not have a right to X or X is not a benefit or X is not something that is in one's interest.[11]

Each member of this family of claims seems to be open to objections. As John C. Stevens[12] has pointed out, one may have a right to be treated with a certain medical procedure (because of a health insurance policy one has purchased), even though one cannot conceive of the nature of the procedure. And, as Tooley himself has pointed out, persons who have been indoctrinated, or drugged, or rendered temporarily unconscious may be literally incapable of caring about or taking an interest in something that is in their inter-

---

[11]Donald VanDeVeer seems to think this is self-evident. See his "Whither Baby Doe?" in *Matters of Life and Death,* p. 233.
[12]"Must the Bearer of a Right Have the Concept of That to Which He Has a Right?" *Ethics,* xcv, 1 (1984):68–74.

est or is something to which they have a right, or is something that benefits them. Hence, the Tooley claim that would restrict the scope of the value of a future-like-ours argument is undermined by counterexamples.[13]

Finally, Paul Bassen[14] has argued that, even though the prospects of an embryo might seem to be a basis for the wrongness of abortion, an embryo cannot be a victim and therefore cannot be wronged. An embryo cannot be a victim, he says, because it lacks sentience. His central argument for this seems to be that, even though plants and the permanently unconscious are alive, they clearly cannot be victims. What is the explanation of this? Bassen claims that the explanation is that their lives consist of mere metabolism and mere metabolism is not enough to ground victimizability. Mentation is required.

The problem with this attempt to establish the absence of victimizability is that both plants and the permanently unconscious clearly lack what Bassen calls "prospects" or what I have called "a future life like ours." Hence, it is surely open to one to argue that the real reason we believe plants and the permanently unconscious cannot be victims is that killing them cannot deprive them of a future life like ours; the real reason is not their absence of present meritation.

Bassen recognizes that his view is subject to this difficulty, and he recognizes that the case of children seems to support this difficulty, for "much of what we do for children is based on prospects." He argues, however, that, in the case of children and in other such cases, "potentiality comes into play only where victimizability has been secured on other grounds" (*ibid.,* p. 333).

Bassen's defense of his view is patently question-begging, since what is adequate to secure victimizability is exactly what is at issue. His examples do not support his own view against the thesis of this essay. Of course, embryos can be victims: when their lives are deliberately terminated, they are deprived of their futures of value, their prospects. This makes them victims, for it directly wrongs them.

The seeming plausibility of Bassen's view stems from the fact that paradigmatic cases of imagining someone as a victim involve empathy, and empathy requires mentation of the victim. The vic-

---

[13]See Tooley again in "Abortion and Infanticide," pp. 47–49.
[14]"Present Sakes and Future Prospects: The Status of Early Abortion," *Philosophy and Public Affairs,* xi, 4 (1982):322–326.

tims of flood, famine, rape, or child abuse are all persons with whom we can empathize. That empathy seems to be part of seeing them as victims.[15]

In spite of the strength of these examples, the attractive intuition that a situation in which there is victimization requires the possibility of empathy is subject to counterexamples. Consider a case that Bassen himself offers: "Posthumous obliteration of an author's work constitutes a misfortune for him only if he had wished his work to endure" (*op cit.,* p. 318). The conditions Bassen wishes to impose upon the possibility of being victimized here seem far too strong. Perhaps this author, due to his unrealistic standards of excellence and his low self-esteem, regarded his work as unworthy of survival, even though it possessed genuine literary merit. Destruction of such work would surely victimize its author. In such a case, empathy with the victim concerning the loss is clearly impossible.

Of course, Bassen does not make the possibility of empathy a necessary condition of victimizability; he requires only mentation. Hence, on Bassen's actual view, this author, as I have described him, can be a victim. The problem is that the basic intuition that renders Bassen's view plausible is missing in the author's case. In order to attempt to avoid counterexamples, Bassen has made his thesis too weak to be supported by the intuitions that suggested it.

Even so, the mentation requirement on victimizability is still subject to counterexamples. Suppose a severe accident renders me totally unconscious for a month, after which I recover. Surely killing me while I am unconscious victimizes me, even though I am incapable of mentation during that time. It follows that Bassen's thesis fails. Apparently, attempts to restrict the value of a future-like-ours argument so that fetuses do not fall within its scope do not succeed.

V.

In this essay, it has been argued that the correct ethic of the wrongness of killing can be extended to fetal life and used to show that there is a strong presumption that any abortion is morally impermissible. If the ethic of killing adopted here entails, however, that contraception is also seriously immoral, then there would appear to be a difficulty with the analysis of this essay.

[15]Note carefully the reasons he gives on the bottom of p. 316.

But this analysis does not entail that contraception is wrong. Of course, contraception prevents the actualization of a possible future of value. Hence, it follows from the claim that futures of value should be maximized that contraception is prima facie immoral. This obligation to maximize does not exist, however; furthermore, nothing in the ethics of killing in this paper entails that it does. The ethics of killing in this essay would entail that contraception is wrong only if something were denied a human future of value by contraception. Nothing at all is denied such a future by contraception, however.

Candidates for a subject of harm by contraception fall into four categories: (1) some sperm or other, (2) some ovum or other, (3) a sperm and an ovum separately, and (4) a sperm and an ovum together. Assigning the harm to some sperm is utterly arbitrary, for no reason can be given for making a sperm the subject of harm rather than an ovum. Assigning the harm to some ovum is utterly arbitrary, for no reason can be given for making an ovum the subject of harm rather than a sperm. One might attempt to avoid these problems by insisting that contraception deprives both the sperm and the ovum separately of a valuable future like ours. On this alternative, too many futures are lost. Contraception was supposed to be wrong, because it deprived us of one future of value, not two. One might attempt to avoid this problem by holding that contraception deprives the combination of sperm and ovum of a valuable future like ours. But here the definite article misleads. At the time of contraception, there are hundreds of millions of sperm, one (released) ovum and millions of possible combinations of all of these. There is no actual combination at all. Is the subject of the loss to be a merely possible combination? Which one? This alternative does not yield an actual subject of harm either. Accordingly, the immorality of contraception is not entailed by the loss of a future-like-ours argument simply because there is no nonarbitrarily identifiable subject of the loss in the case of contraception.

VI.

The purpose of this essay has been to set out an argument for the serious presumptive wrongness of abortion subject to the assumption that the moral permissibility of abortion stands or falls on the moral status of the fetus. Since a fetus possesses a property, the possession of which in adult human beings is sufficient to make killing an adult human being wrong, abortion is wrong. This way of dealing with the problem of abortion seems superior to other approaches to the ethics of abortion, because it rests on an ethics of killing which is close to self-evident, because the crucial morally relevant property clearly applies to fetuses, and because the argument avoids the usual equivocations on "human life," "human being," or "person." The argument rests neither on religious claims nor on Papal dogma. It is not subject to the objection of "speciesism." Its soundness is compatible with the moral permissibility of euthanasia and contraception. It deals with our intuitions concerning young children.

Finally, this analysis can be viewed as resolving a standard problem—indeed, *the* standard problem—concerning the ethics of abortion. Clearly, it is wrong to kill adult human beings. Clearly, it is not wrong to end the life of some arbitrarily chosen single human cell. Fetuses seem to be like arbitrarily chosen human cells in some respects and like adult humans in other respects. The problem of the ethics of abortion is the problem of determining the fetal property that settles this moral controversy. The thesis of this essay is that the problem of the ethics of abortion, so understood, is solvable.

For Further Reflection

1. What is Marquis's argument against abortion?
2. What considerations does Marquis use to support the notion that what makes killing wrong is the loss of the victim's future?
3. What exceptions does Marquis allow to his moral principle that having or performing an abortion is morally wrong?

A Defense of Abortion

JUDITH JARVIS THOMSON

Judith Jarvis Thomson is a professor of philosophy at Massachusetts Institute of Technology, specializing in ethics and metaphysics. Her books include *Acts and Other Events* (1977), *The Realm of Rights* (1990), and *Goodness and Advice* (2001). In this selection—a classic in the abortion debate—Thomson argues that even if a fetus is a person at conception, at least some abortions could still be morally permissible. A woman has a right not to have her body used by someone else against her will, which is essentially the case when she is pregnant due to no fault of her own (as a result of rape, for instance).

Most opposition to abortion relies on the premise that the fetus is a human being, a person, from the moment of conception. The premise is argued for, but, as I think, not well. Take, for example, the most common argument. We are asked to notice that the development of a human being from conception through birth into childhood is continuous; then it is said that to draw a line, to choose a point in this development and say "before this point the thing is not a person, after this point it is a person" is to make an arbitrary choice, a choice for which in the nature of things no good reason can be given. It is concluded that the fetus is, or anyway that we had better say it is, a person from the moment of conception. But this conclusion does not follow. Similar things might be said about the development of an acorn into an oak tree, and it does not follow that acorns are oak trees, or that we had better say they are. Arguments of this form are sometimes called "slippery slope arguments"—the phrase is perhaps self-explanatory—and it is dismaying that opponents of abortion rely on them so heavily and uncritically.

I am inclined to agree, however, that the prospects for "drawing a line" in the development of the fetus look dim. I am inclined

From "A Defense of Abortion," *Philosophy and Public Affairs,* vol. 1, no. 1 (Autumn 1971), 47–66. Footnotes renumbered.

I am very much indebted to James Thomson for discussion, criticism, and many helpful suggestions.

to think also that we shall probably have to agree that the fetus has already become a human person well before birth. Indeed, it comes as a surprise when one first learns how early in its life it begins to acquire human characteristics. By the tenth week, for example, it already has a face, arms and legs, fingers and toes; it has internal organs, and brain activity is detectable.[1] On the other hand, I think that the premise is false, that the fetus is not a person from the moment of conception. A newly fertilized ovum, a newly implanted clump of cells, is no more a person than an acorn is an oak tree. But I shall not discuss any of this. For it seems to me to be of great interest to ask what happens if, for the sake of argument, we allow the premise. How, precisely, are we supposed to get from there to the conclusion that abortion is morally impermissible? Opponents of abortion commonly spend most of their time establishing that the fetus is a person, and hardly any time explaining the step from there to the impermissibility of abortion. Perhaps they think the step too simple and obvious to require much comment. Or perhaps instead they are simply being economical in argument. Many of those who defend abortion rely on the premise that the fetus is not a person, but only a bit of tissue that will become a person at birth; and why pay out more arguments than you have to? Whatever the explanation, I suggest that the step they take is neither easy nor obvious, that it calls for closer examination than it is commonly given, and that when we do give it this closer examination we shall feel inclined to reject it.

I propose, then, that we grant that the fetus is a person from the moment of conception. How does the argument go from here? Something like this, I take it. Every person has a right to life. So the fetus has a right to life. No doubt the mother has a right to decide what shall happen in and to her body; everyone would grant that. But surely a person's right to life is stronger and more stringent than the mother's right to decide what happens in and to her body, and so outweighs it. So the fetus may not be killed; an abortion may not be performed.

---

[1]Daniel Callahan, *Abortion: Law, Choice and Morality* (New York, 1970), p. 373. This book gives a fascinating survey of the available information on abortion. The Jewish tradition is surveyed in David M. Feldman, *Birth Control in Jewish Law* (New York, 1968), Part 5, the Catholic tradition in John T. Noonan, Jr., "An Almost Absolute Value in History," in *The Morality of Abortion,* ed. John T. Noonan, Jr. (Cambridge, Mass., 1970).

It sounds plausible. But now let me ask you to imagine this. You wake up in the morning and find yourself back to back in bed with an unconscious violinist. A famous unconscious violinist. He has been found to have a fatal kidney ailment, and the Society of Music Lovers has canvassed all the available medical records and found that you alone have the right blood type to help. They have therefore kidnapped you, and last night the violinist's circulatory system was plugged into yours, so that your kidneys can be used to extract poisons from his blood as well as your own. The director of the hospital now tells you, "Look, we're sorry the Society of Music Lovers did this to you—we would never have permitted it if we had known. But still, they did it, and the violinist now is plugged into you. To unplug you would be to kill him. But never mind, it's only for nine months. By then he will have recovered from his ailment, and can safely be unplugged from you." Is it morally incumbent on you to accede to this situation? No doubt it would be very nice of you if you did, a great kindness. But do you *have* to accede to it? What if it were not nine months, but nine years? Or longer still? What if the director of the hospital says, "Tough luck, I agree, but you've now got to stay in bed, with the violinist plugged into you, for the rest of your life. Because remember this. All persons have a right to life, and violinists are persons. Granted you have a right to decide what happens in and to your body, but a person's right to life outweighs your right to decide what happens in and to your body. So you cannot ever be unplugged from him." I imagine you would regard this as outrageous, which suggests that something really is wrong with that plausible-sounding argument I mentioned a moment ago.

In this case, of course, you were kidnapped; you didn't volunteer for the operation that plugged the violinist into your kidneys. Can those who oppose abortion on the ground I mentioned make an exception for a pregnancy due to rape? Certainly. They can say that persons have a right to life only if they didn't come into existence because of rape; or they can say that all persons have a right to life, but that some have less of a right to life than others, in particular, that those who came into existence because of rape have less. But these statements have a rather unpleasant sound. Surely the question of whether you have a right to life at all, or how much of it you have, shouldn't turn on the question of whether or not you are the product of a rape. And in fact the people who oppose abortion on the ground I mentioned do not make this distinction, and hence do not make an exception in case of rape.

Nor do they make an exception for a case in which the mother has to spend the nine months of her pregnancy in bed. They would agree that would be a great pity, and hard on the mother; but all the same, all persons have a right to life, the fetus is a person, and so on. I suspect, in fact, that they would not make an exception for a case in which, miraculously enough, the pregnancy went on for nine years, or even the rest of the mother's life.

Some won't even make an exception for a case in which continuation of the pregnancy is likely to shorten the mother's life; they regard abortion as impermissible even to save the mother's life. Such cases are nowadays very rare, and many opponents of abortion do not accept this extreme view. All the same, it is a good place to begin: a number of points of interest come out in respect to it.

1. Let us call the view that abortion is impermissible even to save the mother's life "the extreme view." I want to suggest first that it does not issue from the argument I mentioned earlier without the addition of some fairly powerful premises. Suppose a woman has become pregnant, and now learns that she has a cardiac condition such that she will die if she carries the baby to term. What may be done for her? The fetus, being a person, has a right to life, but as the mother is a person too, so has she a right to life. Presumably they have an equal right to life. How is it supposed to come out that an abortion may not be performed? If mother and child have an equal right to life, shouldn't we perhaps flip a coin? Or should we add to the mother's right to life her right to decide what happens in and to her body, which everybody seems to be ready to grant—the sum of her rights now outweighing the fetus' right to life?

The most familiar argument here is the following. We are told that performing the abortion would be directly killing[2] the child, whereas doing nothing would not be killing the mother, but only letting her die. Moreover, in killing the child, one would be killing

---

[2]The term "direct" in the arguments I refer to is a technical one. Roughly, what is meant by "direct killing" is either killing as an end in itself, or killing as a means to some end, for example, the end of saving someone else's life. See note 5, below, for an example of its use.

an innocent person, for the child has committed no crime, and is not aiming at his mother's death. And then there are a variety of ways in which this might be continued. (1) But as directly killing an innocent person is always and absolutely impermissible, an abortion may not be performed. Or, (2) as directly killing an innocent person is murder, and murder is always and absolutely impermissible, an abortion may not be performed.[3] Or, (3) as one's duty to refrain from directly killing an innocent person is more stringent than one's duty to keep a person from dying, an abortion may not be performed. Or, (4) if one's only options are directly killing an innocent person or letting a person die, one must prefer letting the person die, and thus an abortion may not be performed.[4]

Some people seem to have thought that these are not further premises which must be added if the conclusion is to be reached, but that they follow from the very fact that an innocent person has a right to life.[5] But this seems to me to be a mistake, and perhaps the simplest way to show this is to bring out that while we must certainly grant that innocent persons have a right to life, the theses in (1) through (4) are all false. Take (2), for example. If directly

[3]Cf. *Encyclical Letter of Pope Pius XI on Christian Marriage,* St. Paul Editions (Boston, n.d.), p. 32: "however much we may pity the mother whose health and even life is gravely imperiled in the performance of the duty allotted to her by nature, nevertheless what could ever be a sufficient reason for excusing in any way the direct murder of the innocent? This is precisely what we are dealing with here." Noonan (*The Morality of Abortion,* p. 43) reads this as follows: "What cause can ever avail to excuse in any way the direct killing of the innocent? For it is a question of that."

[4]The thesis in (4) is in an interesting way weaker than those in (1), (2), and (3): they rule out abortion even in cases in which both mother *and* child will die if the abortion is not performed. By contrast, one who held the view expressed in (4) could consistently say that one needn't prefer letting two persons die to killing one.

[5]Cf. the following passage from Pius XII, *Address to the Italian Catholic Society of Midwives:* "The baby in the maternal breast has the right to life immediately from God.—Hence there is no man, no human authority, no science, no medical, eugenic, social, economic or moral 'indication' which can establish or grant a valid juridical ground for a direct deliberate disposition of an innocent human life, that is a disposition which looks to its destruction either as an end or as a means to another end perhaps in itself not illicit.—The baby, still not born, is a man in the same degree and for the same reason as the mother" (quoted in Noonan, *The Morality of Abortion,* p. 45).

killing an innocent person is murder, and thus is impermissible, then the mother's directly killing the innocent person inside her is murder, and thus is impermissible. But it cannot seriously be thought to be murder if the mother performs an abortion on herself to save her life. It cannot seriously be said that she *must* refrain, that she *must* sit passively by and wait for her death. Let us look again at the case of you and the violinist. There you are, in bed with the violinist, and the director of the hospital says to you, "It's all most distressing, and I deeply sympathize, but you see this is putting an additional strain on your kidneys, and you'll be dead within the month. But you *have* to stay where you are all the same. Because unplugging you would be directly killing an innocent violinist, and that's murder, and that's impermissible." If anything in the world is true, it is that you do not commit murder, you do not do what is impermissible, if you reach around to your back and unplug yourself from that violinist to save your life.

The main focus of attention in writings on abortion has been on what a third party may or may not do in answer to a request from a woman for an abortion. This is in a way understandable. Things being as they are, there isn't much a woman can safely do to abort herself. So the question asked is what a third party may do, and what the mother may do, if it is mentioned at all, is deduced, almost as an after-thought, from what it is concluded that third parties may do. But it seems to me that to treat the matter in this way is to refuse to grant to the mother that very status of person which is so firmly insisted on for the fetus. For we cannot simply read off what a person may do from what a third party may do. Suppose you find yourself trapped in a tiny house with a growing child. I mean a very tiny house, and a rapidly growing child—you are already up against the wall of the house and in a few minutes you'll be crushed to death. The child on the other hand won't be crushed to death; if nothing is done to stop him from growing he'll be hurt, but in the end he'll simply burst open the house and walk out a free man. Now I could well understand it if a bystander were to say, "There's nothing we can do for you. We cannot choose between your life and his, we cannot be the ones to decide who is to live, we cannot intervene." But it cannot be concluded that you too can do nothing, that you cannot attack it to save your life. However innocent the child may be, you do not have to wait passively while it crushes you to death. Perhaps a pregnant woman is vaguely felt to have the status of house, to which we don't allow the right of self-defense. But if the woman houses the child, it should be remembered that she is a person who houses it.

I should perhaps stop to say explicitly that I am not claiming that people have a right to do anything whatever to save their lives. I think, rather, that there are drastic limits to the right of self-defense. If someone threatens you with death unless you torture someone else to death, I think you have not the right, even to save your life, to do so. But the case under consideration here is very different. In our case there are only two people involved, one whose life is threatened, and one who threatens it. Both are innocent: the one who is threatened is not threatened because of any fault, the one who threatens does not threaten because of any fault. For this reason we may feel that we bystanders cannot intervene. But the person threatened can.

In sum, a woman surely can defend her life against the threat to it posed by the unborn child, even if doing so involves its death. And this shows not merely that the theses in (1) through (4) are false; it shows also that the extreme view of abortion is false, and so we need not canvass any other possible ways of arriving at it from the argument I mentioned at the outset.

2. The extreme view could of course be weakened to say that while abortion is permissible to save the mother's life, it may not be performed by a third party, but only by the mother herself. But this cannot be right either. For what we have to keep in mind is that the mother and the unborn child are not like two tenants in a small house which has, by an unfortunate mistake, been rented to both: the mother *owns* the house. The fact that she does adds to the offensiveness of deducing that the mother can do nothing from the supposition that third parties can do nothing. But it does more than this: it casts a bright light on the supposition that third parties can do nothing. Certainly it lets us see that a third party who says "I cannot choose between you" is fooling himself if he thinks this is impartiality. If Jones has found and fastened on a certain coat, which he needs to keep him from freezing, but which Smith also needs to keep him from freezing, then it is not impartiality that says "I cannot choose between you" when Smith owns the coat. Women have said again and again "This body is *my* body!" and they have reason to feel angry, reason to feel that it has been like shouting into the wind. Smith, after all, is hardly likely to bless us if we say to him, "Of course it's your coat, anybody would grant that it is. But no one may choose between you and Jones who is to have it."

We should really ask what it is that says "no one may choose" in the face of the fact that the body that houses the child is the mother's body. It may be simply a failure to appreciate this fact. But it may be something more interesting, namely the sense that one has a right to refuse to lay hands on people, even where it would be just and fair to do so, even where justice seems to require that somebody do so. Thus justice might call for somebody to get Smith's coat back from Jones, and yet you have a right to refuse to be the one to lay hands on Jones, a right to refuse to do physical violence to him. This, I think, must be granted. But then what should be said is not "no one may choose," but only "*I* cannot choose," and indeed not even this, but "*I* will not *act*," leaving it open that somebody else can or should, and in particular that anyone in a position of authority, with the job of securing people's rights, both can and should. So this is no difficulty. I have not been arguing that any given third party must accede to the mother's request that he perform an abortion to save her life, but only that he may.

I suppose that in some views of human life the mother's body is only on loan to her, the loan not being one which gives her any prior claim to it. One who held this view might well think it impartiality to say "I cannot choose." But I shall simply ignore this possibility. My own view is that if a human being has any just, prior claim to anything at all, he has a just, prior claim to his own body. And perhaps this needn't be argued for here anyway, since, as I mentioned, the arguments against abortion we are looking at do grant that the woman has a right to decide what happens in and to her body.

But although they do grant it, I have tried to show that they do not take seriously what is done in granting it. I suggest the same thing will reappear even more clearly when we turn away from cases in which the mother's life is at stake, and attend, as I propose we now do, to the vastly more common cases in which a woman wants an abortion for some less weighty reason than preserving her own life.

3. Where the mother's life is not at stake, the argument I mentioned at the outset seems to have a much stronger pull. "Everyone has a right to life, so the unborn person has a right to life." And isn't the child's right to life weightier than anything other than the mother's own right to life, which she might put forward as ground for an abortion?

This argument treats the right to life as if it were unproblematic. It is not, and this seems to me to be precisely the source of the mistake.

For we should now, at long last, ask what it comes to, to have a right to life. In some views having a right to life includes having a right to be given at least the bare minimum one needs for continued life. But suppose that what in fact *is* the bare minimum a man needs for continued life is something he has no right at all to be given? If I am sick unto death, and the only thing that will save my life is the touch of Henry Fonda's cool hand on my fevered brow, then all the same, I have no right to be given the touch of Henry Fonda's cool hand on my fevered brow. It would be frightfully nice of him to fly in from the West Coast to provide it. It would be less nice, though no doubt well meant, if my friends flew out to the West Coast and carried Henry Fonda back with them. But I have no right at all against anybody that he should do this for me. Or again, to return to the story I told earlier, the fact that for continued life that violinist needs the continued use of your kidneys does not establish that he has a right to be given the continued use of your kidneys. He certainly has no right against you that *you* should give him continued use of your kidneys. For nobody has any right to use your kidneys unless you give him such a right; and nobody has the right against you that you shall give him this right—if you do allow him to go on using your kidneys, this is a kindness on your part, and not something he can claim from you as his due. Nor has he any right against anybody else that *they* should give him continued use of your kidneys. Certainly he had no right against the Society of Music Lovers that they should plug him into you in the first place. And if you now start to unplug yourself, having learned that you will otherwise have to spend nine years in bed with him, there is nobody in the world who must try to prevent you, in order to see to it that he is given something he has a right to be given.

Some people are rather stricter about the right to life. In their view, it does not include the right to be given anything, but amounts to, and only to, the right not to be killed by anybody. But here a related difficulty arises. If everybody is to refrain from killing that violinist, then everybody must refrain from doing a great many different sorts of things. Everybody must refrain from slitting his throat, everybody must refrain from shooting him—and everybody must refrain from unplugging you from him. But does he have a right against everybody that they shall refrain from unplugging you from him? To refrain from doing this is to allow him to continue to use your kidneys. It could be argued that he has a right against us that *we* should allow him to continue to use your kidneys. That is, while he had no right against us that we should give him the use of your kidneys, it might be argued that he anyway has a right against us that we shall not now intervene and deprive him of the use of your kidneys. I shall come back to third-party interventions later. But certainly the violinist has no right against you that *you* shall allow him to continue to use your kidneys. As I said, if you do allow him to use them, it is a kindness on your part, and not something you owe him.

The difficulty I point to here is not peculiar to the right to life. It reappears in connection with all the other natural rights; and it is something which an adequate account of rights must deal with. For present purposes it is enough just to draw attention to it. But I would stress that I am not arguing that people do not have a right to life—quite to the contrary, it seems to me that the primary control we must place on the acceptability of an account of rights is that it should turn out in that account to be a truth that all persons have a right to life. I am arguing only that having a right to life does not guarantee having either a right to be given the use of or a right to be allowed continued use of another person's body— even if one needs it for life itself. So the right to life will not serve the opponents of abortion in the very simple and clear way in which they seem to have thought it would.

4. There is another way to bring out the difficulty. In the most ordinary sort of case, to deprive someone of what he has a right to is to treat him unjustly. Suppose a boy and his small brother are jointly given a box of chocolates for Christmas. If the older boy takes the box and refuses to give his brother any of the chocolates, he is unjust to him, for the brother has been given a right to half of them. But suppose that, having learned that otherwise it means nine years in bed with that violinist, you unplug yourself from him. You surely are not being unjust to him, for you gave him no right to use your kidneys, and no one else can have given him any such right. But we have to notice that in unplugging yourself, you are killing him; and violinists, like everybody else, have a right to life, and thus in the view we were considering just now, the right not to be killed. So here you do what he supposedly has a right you shall not do, but you do not act unjustly to him in doing it.

The emendation which may be made at this point is this: the right to life consists not in the right not to be killed, but rather in the right not to be killed unjustly. This runs a risk of circularity, but never mind: it would enable us to square the fact that the violinist has a right to life with the fact that you do not act unjustly toward him in unplugging yourself, thereby killing him. For if you do not kill him unjustly, you do not violate his right to life, and so it is no wonder you do him no injustice.

But if this emendation is accepted, the gap in the argument against abortion stares us plainly in the face: it is by no means enough to show that the fetus is a person, and to remind us that all persons have a right to life—we need to be shown also that killing the fetus violates its right to life, i.e., that abortion is unjust killing. And is it?

I suppose we may take it as a datum that in a case of pregnancy due to rape the mother has not given the unborn person a right to the use of her body for food and shelter. Indeed, in what pregnancy could it be supposed that the mother has given the unborn person such a right? It is not as if there were unborn persons drifting about the world, to whom a woman who wants a child says "I invite you in."

But it might be argued that there are other ways one can have acquired a right to the use of another person's body than by having been invited to use it by that person. Suppose a woman voluntarily indulges in intercourse, knowing of the chance it will issue in pregnancy, and then she does become pregnant; is she not in part responsible for the presence, in fact the very existence, of the unborn person inside her? No doubt she did not invite it in. But doesn't her partial responsibility for its being there itself give it a right to the use of her body?[6] If so, then her aborting it would be more like the boy's taking away the chocolates, and less like your unplugging yourself from the violinist—doing so would be depriving it of what it does have a right to, and thus would be doing it an injustice.

And then, too, it might be asked whether or not she can kill it even to save her own life: If she voluntarily called it into existence, how can she now kill it, even in self-defense?

---

[6]The need for a discussion of this argument was brought home to me by members of the Society for Ethical and Legal Philosophy, to whom this paper was originally presented.

The first thing to be said about this is that it is something new. Opponents of abortion have been so concerned to make out the independence of the fetus, in order to establish that it has a right to life, just as its mother does, that they have tended to overlook the possible support they might gain from making out that the fetus is *dependent* on the mother, in order to establish that she has a special kind of responsibility for it, a responsibility that gives it rights against her which are not possessed by any independent person—such as an ailing violinist who is a stranger to her.

On the other hand, this argument would give the unborn person a right to its mother's body only if her pregnancy resulted from a voluntary act, undertaken in full knowledge of the chance a pregnancy might result from it. It would leave out entirely the unborn person whose existence is due to rape. Pending the availability of some further argument, then, we would be left with the conclusion that unborn persons whose existence is due to rape have no right to the use of their mothers' bodies, and thus that aborting them is not depriving them of anything they have a right to and hence is not unjust killing.

And we should also notice that it is not at all plain that this argument really does go even as far as it purports to. For there are cases and cases, and the details make a difference. If the room is stuffy, and I therefore open a window to air it, and a burglar climbs in, it would be absurd to say, "Ah, now he can stay, she's given him a right to the use of her house—for she is partially responsible for his presence there, having voluntarily done what enabled him to get in, in full knowledge that there are such things as burglars, and that burglars burgle." It would be still more absurd to say this if I had had bars installed outside my windows, precisely to prevent burglars from getting in, and a burglar got in only because of a defect in the bars. It remains equally absurd if we imagine it is not a burglar who climbs in, but an innocent person who blunders or falls in. Again, suppose it were like this: people-seeds drift about in the air like pollen, and if you open your windows, one may drift in and take root in your carpets or upholstery. You don't want children, so you fix up your windows with fine mesh screens, the very best you can buy. As can happen, however, and on very, very rare occasions does happen, one of the screens is defective; and a seed drifts in and takes root. Does the person-plant who now develops have a right to the use of your house? Surely not—despite the fact that you voluntarily opened your windows, you knowingly kept carpets and upholstered furniture, and you knew that screens were sometimes defective. Someone may argue that you are responsible for its rooting, that it does have a right to your house, because after all you *could* have lived out your life with bare floors and furniture, or with sealed windows and doors. But this won't do—for by the same token anyone can avoid a pregnancy due to rape by having a hysterectomy, or anyway by never leaving home without a (reliable!) army.

It seems to me that the argument we are looking at can establish at most that there are *some* cases in which the unborn person has a right to the use of its mother's body, and therefore *some* cases in which abortion is unjust killing. There is room for much discussion and argument as to precisely which, if any. But I think we should sidestep this issue and leave it open, for at any rate the argument certainly does not establish that all abortion is unjust killing.

5. There is room for yet another argument here, however. We surely must all grant that there may be cases in which it would be morally indecent to detach a person from your body at the cost of his life. Suppose you learn that what the violinist needs is not nine years of your life, but only one hour: all you need do to save his life is to spend one hour in that bed with him. Suppose also that letting him use your kidneys for that one hour would not affect your health in the slightest. Admittedly you were kidnapped. Admittedly you did not give anyone permission to plug him into you. Nevertheless it seems to me plain you *ought* to allow him to use your kidneys for that hour—it would be indecent to refuse.

Again, suppose pregnancy lasted only an hour, and constituted no threat to life or health. And suppose that a woman becomes pregnant as a result of rape. Admittedly she did not voluntarily do anything to bring about the existence of a child. Admittedly she did nothing at all which would give the unborn person a right to the use of her body. All the same it might well be said, as in the newly emended violinist story, that she *ought* to allow it to remain for that hour—that it would be indecent in her to refuse.

Now some people are inclined to use the term "right" in such a way that it follows from the fact that you ought to allow a person to use your body for the hour he needs, that he has a right to use your body for the hour he needs, even though he has not been given that right by any person or act. They may say that it follows also that if you refuse, you act unjustly toward him. This use of the term is perhaps so common that it cannot be called wrong; nevertheless it seems to me to be an unfortunate loosening of what we would do better to keep a tight rein on. Suppose that box of chocolates I mentioned earlier had not been given to both boys jointly, but was given only to the older boy. There he sits, stolidly eating his way through the box, his small brother watching enviously. Here we are likely to say "You ought not to be so mean. You ought to give your brother some of those chocolates." My own view is that it just does not follow from the truth of this that the brother has any right to any of the chocolates. If the boy refuses to give his brother any, he is greedy, stingy, callous—but not unjust. I suppose that the people I have in mind will say it does follow that the brother has a right to some of the chocolates, and thus that the boy does act unjustly if he refuses to give his brother any. But the effect of saying this is to obscure what we should keep distinct, namely the difference between the boy's refusal in this case and the boy's refusal in the earlier case, in which the box was given to both boys jointly, and in which the small brother thus had what was from any point of view clear title to half.

A further objection to so using the term "right" that from the fact that A ought to do a thing for B, it follows that B has a right against A that A do it for him, is that it is going to make the question of whether or not a man has a right to a thing turn on how easy it is to provide him with it; and this seems not merely unfortunate, but morally unacceptable. Take the case of Henry Fonda again. I said earlier that I had no right to the touch of his cool hand on my fevered brow, even though I needed it to save my life. I said it would be frightfully nice of him to fly in from the West Coast to provide me with it, but that I had no right against him that he should do so. But suppose he isn't on the West Coast. Suppose he has only to walk across the room, place a hand briefly on my brow—and lo, my life is saved. Then surely he ought to do it, it would be indecent to refuse. Is it to be said "Ah, well, it follows that in this case she has a right to the touch of his hand on her brow, and so it would be an injustice in him to refuse"? So that I have a right to it when it is easy for him to provide it, though no right when it's hard? It's rather a shocking idea that anyone's rights should fade away and disappear as it gets harder and harder to accord them to him.

So my own view is that even though you ought to let the violinist use your kidneys for the one hour he needs, we should not conclude that he has a right to do so—we should say that if you refuse, you are, like the boy who owns all the chocolates and will give none away, self-centered and callous, indecent in fact, but not unjust. And similarly, that even supposing a case in which a woman pregnant due to rape ought to allow the unborn person to use her body for the hour he needs, we should not conclude that he has a right to do so; we should conclude that she is self-centered, callous, indecent, but not unjust, if she refuses. The complaints are no less grave; they are just different. However, there is no need to insist on this point. If anyone does wish to deduce "he has a right" from "you ought," then all the same he must surely grant that there are cases in which it is not morally required of you that you allow that violinist to use your kidneys, and in which he does not have a right to use them, and in which you do not do him an injustice if you refuse. And so also for mother and unborn child. Except in such cases as the unborn person has a right to demand it—and we were leaving open the possibility that there may be such cases—nobody is morally *required* to make large sacrifices, of health, of all other interests and concerns, of all other duties and commitments, for nine years, or even for nine months, in order to keep another person alive.

6. We have in fact to distinguish between two kinds of Samaritan: the Good Samaritan and what we might call the Minimally Decent Samaritan. The story of the Good Samaritan, you will remember, goes like this:

> A certain man went down from Jerusalem to Jericho, and fell among thieves, which stripped him of his raiment, and wounded him, and departed, leaving him half dead.
>
> And by chance there came down a certain priest that way; and when he saw him, he passed by on the other side.
>
> And likewise a Levite, when he was at the place, came and looked on him, and passed by on the other side.
>
> But a certain Samaritan, as he journeyed, came where he was; and when he saw him he had compassion on him.
>
> And went to him, and bound up his wounds, pouring in oil and wine, and set him on his own beast, and brought him to an inn, and took care of him.
>
> And on the morrow, when he departed, he took out two pence, and gave them to the host, and said unto him, "Take care of him; and whatsoever thou spendest more, when I come again, I will repay thee." (Luke 10:30–35)

The Good Samaritan went out of his way, at some cost to himself, to help one in need of it. We are not told what the options were, that is, whether or not the priest and the Levite could have helped by doing less than the Good Samaritan did, but assuming they could have, then the fact they did nothing at all shows they were not even Minimally Decent Samaritans, not because they were not Samaritans, but because they were not even minimally decent.

These things are a matter of degree, of course, but there is a difference, and it comes out perhaps most clearly in the story of Kitty Genovese, who, as you will remember, was murdered while thirty-eight people watched or listened, and did nothing at all to help her. A Good Samaritan would have rushed out to give direct assistance against the murderer. Or perhaps we had better allow that it would have been a Splendid Samaritan who did this, on the ground that it would have involved a risk of death for himself. But the thirty-eight not only did not do this, they did not even trouble to pick up a phone to call the police. Minimally Decent Samaritanism would call for doing at least that, and their not having done it was monstrous.

After telling the story of the Good Samaritan, Jesus said "Go, and do thou likewise." Perhaps he meant that we are morally required to act as the Good Samaritan did. Perhaps he was urging people to do more than is morally required of them. At all events it seems plain that it was not morally required of any of the thirty-eight that he rush out to give direct assistance at the risk of his own life, and that it is not morally required of anyone that he give long stretches of his life—nine years or nine months—to sustaining the life of a person who has no special right (we were leaving open the possibility of this) to demand it.

Indeed, with one rather striking class of exceptions, no one in any country in the world is *legally* required to do anywhere near as much as this for anyone else. The class of exceptions is obvious. My main concern here is not the state of the law in respect to abortion, but it is worth drawing attention to the fact that in no state in this country is any man compelled by law to be even a Minimally Decent Samaritan to any person; there is no law under which charges could be brought against the thirty-eight who stood by while Kitty Genovese died. By contrast, in most states in this country women are compelled by law to be not merely Minimally Decent Samaritans, but Good Samaritans to unborn persons inside them. This doesn't by itself settle anything one way or the other, because it may well be argued that there should be laws in this country—as there are in many European countries—compelling at least Minimally Decent Samaritanism.[7] But it does show that there is a gross injustice in the existing state of the law. And it shows also that the groups currently working against liberalization of abortion laws, in fact working toward having it declared unconstitutional for a state to permit abortion, had better start working for the adoption of Good Samaritan laws generally, or earn the charge that they are acting in bad faith.

I should think, myself, that Minimally Decent Samaritan laws would be one thing, Good Samaritan laws quite another, and in fact highly improper. But we are not here concerned with the law. What we should ask is not whether anybody should be compelled by law to be a Good Samaritan, but whether we must accede to a situation in which somebody is being compelled—by nature, perhaps—to be a Good Samaritan. We have, in other words, to look now at third-party interventions. I have been arguing that no person is morally required to make large sacrifices to sustain the life of another who has no right to demand them, and this even where the sacrifices do not include life itself; we are not morally required to be Good Samaritans or anyway Very Good Samaritans to one another. But what if a man cannot extricate himself from such a situation? What if he appeals to us to extricate him? It seems to me plain that there are cases in which we can, cases in which a Good Samaritan would extricate him. There you are, you were kidnapped, and nine years in bed with that violinist lie ahead of you. You have your own life to lead. You are sorry, but you simply cannot see giving up so much of your life to the sustaining of his. You cannot extricate yourself, and ask us to do so. I should have thought that—in light of his having no right to the use of your body—it was obvious that we do not have to accede to your being forced to give up so much. We can do what you ask. There is no injustice to the violinist in our doing so.

7. Following the lead of the opponents of abortion, I have throughout been speaking of the fetus merely as a person, and what I have been asking is whether or not the argument we began

---

[7]For a discussion of the difficulties involved, and a survey of the European experience with such laws, see *The Good Samaritan and the Law,* ed. James M. Ratcliffe (New York, 1966).

with, which proceeds only from the fetus' being a person, really does establish its conclusion. I have argued that it does not.

But of course there are arguments and arguments, and it may be said that I have simply fastened on the wrong one. It may be said that what is important is not merely the fact that the fetus is a person, but that it is a person for whom the woman has a special kind of responsibility issuing from the fact that she is its mother. And it might be argued that all my analogies are therefore irrelevant—for you do not have that special kind of responsibility for that violinist, Henry Fonda does not have that special kind of responsibility for me. And our attention might be drawn to the fact that men and women both *are* compelled by law to provide support for their children.

I have in effect dealt (briefly) with this argument in section 4 above; but a (still briefer) recapitulation now may be in order. Surely we do not have any such "special responsibility" for a person unless we have assumed it, explicitly or implicitly. If a set of parents do not try to prevent pregnancy, do not obtain an abortion, and then at the time of birth of the child do not put it out for adoption, but rather take it home with them, then they have assumed responsibility for it, they have given it rights, and they cannot *now* withdraw support from it at the cost of its life because they now find it difficult to go on providing for it. But if they have taken all reasonable precautions against having a child, they do not simply by virtue of their biological relationship to the child who comes into existence have a special responsibility for it. They may wish to assume responsibility for it, or they may not wish to. And I am suggesting that if assuming responsibility for it would require large sacrifices, then they may refuse. A Good Samaritan would not refuse— or anyway, a Splendid Samaritan, if the sacrifices that had to be made were enormous. But then so would a Good Samaritan assume responsibility for that violinist; so would Henry Fonda, if he is a Good Samaritan, fly in from the West Coast and assume responsibility for me.

8. My argument will be found unsatisfactory on two counts by many of those who want to regard abortion as morally permissible. First, while I do argue that abortion is not impermissible, I do not argue that it is always permissible. There may well be cases in which carrying the child to term requires only Minimally Decent Samaritanism of the mother, and this is a standard we must not fall below. I am inclined to think it a merit of my account precisely

that it does *not* give a general yes or a general no. It allows for and supports our sense that, for example, a sick and desperately frightened fourteen-year-old schoolgirl, pregnant due to rape, may *of course* choose abortion, and that any law which rules this out is an insane law. And it also allows for and supports our sense that in other cases resort to abortion is even positively indecent. It would be indecent in the woman to request an abortion, and indecent in a doctor to perform it, if she is in her seventh month, and wants the abortion just to avoid the nuisance of postponing a trip abroad. The very fact that the arguments I have been drawing attention to treat all cases of abortion, or even all cases of abortion in which the mother's life is not at stake, as morally on a par ought to have made them suspect at the outset.

Secondly, while I am arguing for the permissibility of abortion in some cases, I am not arguing for the right to secure the death of the unborn child. It is easy to confuse these two things in that up to a certain point in the life of the fetus it is not able to survive outside the mother's body; hence removing it from her body guarantees its death. But they are importantly different. I have argued that you are not morally required to spend nine months in bed, sustaining the life of that violinist; but to say this is by no means to say that if, when you unplug yourself, there is a miracle and he survives, you then have a right to turn round and slit his throat. You may detach yourself even if this costs him his life; you have no right to be guaranteed his death, by some other means, if unplugging yourself does not kill him. There are some people who will feel dissatisfied by this feature of my argument. A woman may be utterly devastated by the thought of a child, a bit of herself, put out for adoption and never seen or heard of again. She may therefore want not merely that the child be detached from her, but more, that it die. Some opponents of abortion are inclined to regard this as beneath contempt—thereby showing insensitivity to what is surely a powerful source of despair. All the same, I agree that the desire for the child's death is not one which anybody may gratify, should it turn out to be possible to detach the child alive.

At this place, however, it should be remembered that we have only been pretending throughout that the fetus is a human being from the moment of conception. A very early abortion is surely not the killing of a person, and so is not dealt with by anything I have said here.

For Further Reflection

1. What is Thomson's scenario about the famous violinist, and what point is she trying to make with it?

2. What is the "extreme view"?

3. What does Thomson say about the permissibility of abortion when a woman becomes pregnant after voluntarily having intercourse knowing the risks of pregnancy? Or when the woman in such a case takes reasonable precautions to avoid getting pregnant? Or when the woman takes reasonable precautions, but she still gets pregnant?

4. What does Thomson mean when she says she is arguing for the permissibility of abortion in some cases but not "for the right to secure the death of the unborn child"?

Abortion Is Morally Permissible

MARY ANNE WARREN

Mary Anne Warren teaches philosophy at San Francisco State University and has written in the area of feminism, including *The Nature of Woman: An Encyclopedia and Guide to the Literature* (1980). In this paper she defends the liberal view that abortion is always morally permissible. She focuses on an ambiguity in the use of the term *human being,* showing that the term has both a biological and moral sense. What is important is the moral sense, which presupposes certain characteristics, such as self-consciousness and rationality, and which a fetus does not have.

Reprinted from *The Monist,* vol. 57, no. 1 (January 1973). Copyright ©
1973, *The Monist,* La Salle, Illinois 61301. Reprinted by permission.
Notes omitted.

The question which we must answer in order to produce a satisfactory solution to the problem of the moral status of abortion is this: How are we to define the moral community, the set of beings with full and equal moral rights, such that we can decide whether a human fetus is a member of this community or not? What sort of entity, exactly, has the inalienable rights to life, liberty, and the pursuit of happiness? Jefferson attributed these rights to all *men,* and it may or may not be fair to suggest that he intended to attribute them *only* to men. Perhaps he ought to have attributed them to all human beings. If so, then we arrive, first, at Noonan's problem of defining what makes a being human, and, second, at the equally vital question which Noonan does not consider, namely, What reason is there for identifying the moral community with the set of all human beings, in whatever way we have chosen to define that term?

1.   ON THE DEFINITION OF "HUMAN"

One reason why this vital second question is so frequently overlooked in the debate over the moral status of abortion is that the term "human" has two distinct, but not often distinguished, senses. This fact results in a slide of meaning, which serves to conceal the fallaciousness of the traditional argument that since (1) it is wrong to kill innocent human beings, and (2) fetuses are innocent human beings, then (3) it is wrong to kill fetuses. For if "human" is used in the same sense in both (1) and (2) then, whichever of the two senses is meant, one of these premises is question-begging. And if it is used in two different senses then of course the conclusion doesn't follow.

Thus, (1) is a self-evident moral truth, and avoids begging the question about abortion, only if "human being" is used to mean something like "a full-fledged member of the moral community." (It may or may not also be meant to refer exclusively to members of the species *Homo sapiens.*) We may call this the *moral* sense of "human." It is not to be confused with what we will call the *genetic* sense, i.e., the sense in which *any* member of the species is a human being, and no member of any other species could be. If (1) is acceptable only if the moral sense is intended, (2) is nonquestion-begging only if what is intended is the genetic sense.

In "Deciding Who Is Human," Noonan argues for the classification of fetuses with human beings by pointing to the presence of the full genetic code, and the potential capacity for rational thought. It is clear that what he needs to show, for his version of the traditional argument to be valid, is that fetuses are human in the moral sense, the sense in which it is analytically true that all human beings have full moral rights. But, in the absence of any argument showing that whatever is genetically human is also morally human, and he gives none, nothing more than genetic humanity can be demonstrated by the presence of the human genetic code. And, as we will see, the *potential* capacity for rational thought can at most show that an entity has the potential for *becoming* human in the moral sense.

2.   DEFINING THE MORAL COMMUNITY

Can it be established that genetic humanity is sufficient for moral humanity? I think that there are very good reasons for not defining the moral community in this way. I would like to suggest an alternative way of defining the moral community, which I will argue for only to the extent of explaining why it is, or should be, self-evident. The suggestion is simply that the moral community consists of all and only *people,* rather than all and only human beings; and probably the best way of demonstrating its self-evidence is by considering the concept of personhood, to see what sorts of entity are and are not persons, and what the decision that a being is or is not a person implies about its moral rights.

What characteristics entitle an entity to be considered a person? This is obviously not the place to attempt a complete analysis of the concept of personhood, but we do not need such a fully adequate analysis just to determine whether and why a fetus is or isn't a person. All we need is a rough and approximate list of the most basic criteria of personhood, and some idea of which, or how many, of these an entity must satisfy in order to properly be considered a person.

In searching for such criteria, it is useful to look beyond the set of people with whom we are acquainted, and ask how we would decide whether a totally alien being was a person or not. (For we have no right to assume that genetic humanity is necessary for personhood.) Imagine a space traveler who lands on an unknown planet and encounters a race of beings utterly unlike any he has ever seen or heard of. If he wants to be sure of behaving morally toward these beings, he has to somehow decide whether they are people, and hence have full moral rights, or whether they are the sort of thing which he need not feel guilty about treating as, for example, a source of food.

How should he go about making this decision? If he has some anthropological background, he might look for such things as religion, art, and the manufacturing of tools, weapons, or shelters, since these factors have been used to distinguish our human from our prehuman ancestors, in what seems to be closer to the moral than the genetic sense of "human." And no doubt he would be right to consider the presence of such factors as good evidence that the alien beings were people, and morally human. It would, however, be overly anthropocentric of him to take the absence of these things as adequate evidence that they were not, since we can imagine people who have progressed beyond, or evolved without ever developing, these cultural characteristics.

I suggest that the traits which are most central to the concept of personhood, or humanity in the moral sense, are, very roughly, the following:

1. Consciousness (of objects and events external and/or internal to the being), and in particular the capacity to feel pain;
2. Reasoning (the *developed* capacity to solve new and relatively complex problems);
3. Self-motivated activity (activity which is relatively independent of either genetic or direct external control);
4. The capacity to communicate, by whatever means, messages of an indefinite variety of types, that is, not just with an indefinite number of possible contents, but on indefinitely many possible topics;
5. The presence of self-concepts, and self-awareness, either individual or racial, or both.

Admittedly, there are apt to be a great many problems involved in formulating precise definitions of these criteria, let alone in developing universally valid behavioral criteria for deciding when they apply. But I will assume that both we and our explorer know approximately what (1)–(5) mean, and that he is also able to determine whether or not they apply. How, then, should he use his findings to decide whether or not the alien beings are people? We needn't suppose that an entity must have *all* of these attributes to be properly considered a person; (1) and (2) alone may well be sufficient for personhood, and quite probably (1)–(3) are sufficient.

Neither do we need to insist that any one of these criteria is *necessary* for personhood, although once again (1) and (2) look like fairly good candidates for necessary conditions, as does (3), if "activity" is construed so as to include the activity of reasoning.

All we need to claim, to demonstrate that a fetus is not a person, is that any being which satisfies *none* of (1)–(5) is certainly not a person. I consider this claim to be so obvious that I think anyone who denied it, and claimed that a being which satisfied none of (1)–(5) was a person all the same, would thereby demonstrate that he had no notion at all of what a person is—perhaps because he had confused the concept of a person with that of genetic humanity. If the opponents of abortion were to deny the appropriateness of these five criteria, I do not know what further arguments would convince them. We would probably have to admit that our conceptual schemes were indeed irreconcilably different, and that our dispute could not be settled objectively.

I do not expect this to happen, however, since I think that the concept of a person is one which is very nearly universal (to people), and that it is common to both proabortionists and antiabortionists, even though neither group has fully realized the relevance of this concept to the resolution of their dispute. Furthermore, I think that on reflection even the antiabortionists ought to agree not only that (1)–(5) are central to the concept of personhood, but also that it is a part of this concept that all and only people have full moral rights. The concept of a person is in part a moral concept; once we have admitted that x is a person we have recognized, even if we have not agreed to respect, x's right to be treated as a member of the moral community. It is true that the claim that x *is a human being* is more commonly voiced as part of an appeal to treat x decently than is the claim that x is a person, but this is either because "human being" is here used in the sense which implies personhood, or because the genetic and moral senses of "human" have been confused.

Now if (1)–(5) are indeed the primary criteria of personhood, then it is clear that genetic humanity is neither necessary nor sufficient for establishing that an entity is a person. Some human beings are not people, and there may well be people who are not human beings. A man or woman whose consciousness has been permanently obliterated but who remains alive is a human being which is no longer a person; defective human beings, with no appreciable mental capacity, are not and presumably never will be people;

and a fetus is a human being which is not yet a person, and which therefore cannot coherently be said to have full moral rights. Citizens of the next century should be prepared to recognize highly advanced, self-aware robots or computers, should such be developed, and intelligent inhabitants of other worlds, should such be found, as people in the fullest sense, and to respect their moral rights. But to ascribe full moral rights to an entity which is not a person is as absurd as to ascribe moral obligations and responsibilities to such an entity.

3. FETAL DEVELOPMENT AND THE RIGHT TO LIFE

Two problems arise in the application of these suggestions for the definition of the moral community to the determination of the precise moral status of a human fetus. Given that the paradigm example of a person is a normal adult human being, then (1) How like this paradigm, in particular how far advanced since conception, does a human being need to be before it begins to have a right to life by virtue, not of being fully a person as of yet, but of being *like* a person? and (2) To what extent, if any, does the fact that a fetus has the *potential* for becoming a person endow it with some of the same rights? Each of these questions requires some comment.

In answering the first question, we need not attempt a detailed consideration of the moral rights of organisms which are not developed enough, aware enough, intelligent enough, etc., to be considered people, but which resemble people in some respects. It does seem reasonable to suggest that the more like a person, in the relevant respects, a being is, the stronger is the case for regarding it as having a right to life, and indeed the stronger its right to life is. Thus we ought to take seriously the suggestion that, insofar as "the human individual develops biologically in a continuous fashion . . . the rights of a human person might develop in the same way." But we must keep in mind that the attributes which are relevant in determining whether or not an entity is enough like a person to be regarded as having some of the same moral rights are no different from those which are relevant to determining whether or not it is fully a person—i.e., are no different from (1)–(5)—and that being genetically human, or having recognizably human facial and other physical features, or detectable brain activity, or the capacity to survive outside the uterus, are simply not among these relevant attributes.

Thus it is clear that even though a seven- or eight-month fetus has features which make it apt to arouse in us almost the same powerful protective instinct as is commonly aroused by a small infant, nevertheless it is not significantly more personlike than is a very small embryo. It is *somewhat* more personlike; it can apparently feel and respond to pain, and it may even have a rudimentary form of consciousness, insofar as its brain is quite active. Nevertheless, it seems safe to say that it is not fully conscious, in the way that an infant of a few months is, and that it cannot reason, or communicate messages of indefinitely many sorts, does not engage in self-motivated activity, and has no self-awareness. Thus, in the *relevant* respects, a fetus, even a fully developed one, is considerably less personlike than is the average mature mammal, indeed the average fish. And I think that a rational person must conclude that if the right to life of a fetus is to be based upon its resemblance to a person, then it cannot be said to have any more right to life than, let us say, a newborn guppy (which also seems to be capable of feeling pain), and that a right of that magnitude could never override a woman's right to obtain an abortion, at any stage of her pregnancy.

There may, of course, be other arguments in favor of placing legal limits upon the stage of pregnancy in which an abortion may be performed. Given the relative safety of the new techniques of artificially inducing labor during the third trimester, the danger to the woman's life or health is no longer such an argument. Neither is the fact that people tend to respond to the thought of abortion in the later stages of pregnancy with emotional repulsion, since mere emotional responses cannot take the place of moral reasoning in determining what ought to be permitted. Nor, finally, is the frequently heard argument that legalizing abortion, especially late in the pregnancy, may erode the level of respect for human life, leading, perhaps, to an increase in unjustified euthanasia and other crimes. For this threat, if it is a threat, can be better met by educating people to the kinds of moral distinctions which we are making here than by limiting access to abortion (which limitation may, in its disregard for the rights of women, be just as damaging to the level of respect for human rights).

Thus, since the fact that even a fully developed fetus is not personlike enough to have any significant right to life on the basis of its personlikeness shows that no legal restrictions upon the stage of pregnancy in which an abortion may be performed can be justified on the grounds that we should protect the rights of the older fetus, and since there is no other apparent justification for such restrictions, we may conclude that they are entirely unjustified. Whether or not it would be *indecent* (whatever that means) for a woman in her seventh month to obtain an abortion just to avoid having to postpone a trip to Europe, it would not, in itself, be *immoral,* and therefore it ought to be permitted.

4. POTENTIAL PERSONHOOD AND THE RIGHT TO LIFE

We have seen that a fetus does not resemble a person in any way which can support the claim that it has even some of the same rights. But what about its *potential,* the fact that if nurtured and allowed to develop naturally it will very probably become a person? Doesn't that alone give it at least some right to life? It is hard to deny that the fact that an entity is a potential person is a strong prima facie reason for not destroying it; but we need not conclude from this that a potential person has a right to life, by virtue of that potential. It may be that our feeling that it is better, other things being equal, not to destroy a potential person is better explained by the fact that potential people are still (felt to be) an invaluable resource, not to be lightly squandered. Surely, if every speck of dust were a potential person, we would be much less apt to conclude that every potential person has a right to become actual.

Still, we do not need to insist that a potential person has no right to life whatever. There may well be something immoral, and not just imprudent, about wantonly destroying potential people, when doing so isn't necessary to protect anyone's rights. But even if a potential person does have some *prima facie* right to life, such a right could not possibly outweigh the right of a woman to obtain an abortion, since the rights of any actual person invariably outweigh those of any potential person, whenever the two conflict. Since this may not be immediately obvious in the case of a human fetus, let us look at another case.

Suppose that our space explorer falls into the hands of an alien culture, whose scientists decide to create a few hundred thousand or more human beings, by breaking his body into its component cells, and using these to create fully developed human beings, with, of course, his genetic code. We may imagine that each of these newly created men will have all of the original man's abilities, skills, knowledge, and so on, and also have an individual self-concept, in short that each of them will be a bona fide (though hardly unique) person. Imagine that the whole project will take only seconds, and that its chances of success are extremely high, and that our explorer knows all of this, and also knows that these people will be treated fairly. I maintain that in such a situation he would have every right to escape if he could, and thus to deprive all of these potential people of their potential lives; for his right to life outweighs all of theirs together, in spite of the fact that they are all genetically human, all innocent, and all have a very high probability of becoming people very soon, if only he refrains from acting.

Indeed, I think he would have a right to escape even if it were not his life which the alien scientists planned to take, but only a year of his freedom, or, indeed, only a day. Nor would he be obligated to stay if he had gotten captured (thus bringing all these people-potentials into existence) because of his own carelessness, or even if he had done so deliberately, knowing the consequences. Regardless of how he got captured, he is not morally obligated to remain in captivity for *any* period of time for the sake of permitting any number of potential people to come into actuality, so great is the margin by which one actual person's right to liberty outweighs whatever right to life even a hundred thousand potential people have. And it seems reasonable to conclude that the rights of a woman will outweigh by a similar margin whatever right to life a fetus may have by virtue of its potential personhood.

Thus, neither a fetus's resemblance to a person, nor its potential for becoming a person provides any basis whatever for the claim that it has any significant right to life. Consequently, a woman's right to protect her health, happiness, freedom, and even her life, by terminating an unwanted pregnancy, will always override whatever right to life it may be appropriate to ascribe to a fetus, even a fully developed one. And thus, in the absence of any overwhelming social need for every possible child, the laws which restrict the right to obtain an abortion, or limit the period of pregnancy during which an abortion may be performed, are a wholly unjustified violation of a woman's most basic moral and constitutional rights.

For Further Reflection

1. Has Warren successfully refuted Noonan's argument against abortion? Are there any aspects of Noonan's argument that she has not successfully answered?

2. Is there a middle ground between Noonan's conservatism and Warren's liberalism on abortion?

The Moderate Position
Beyond the Personhood Argument

JANE ENGLISH

Jane English (1947–1978) taught philosophy at the University of North Carolina at Chapel Hill and was the author of several essays in applied ethics, including the essay that is included here.

English argues that the issue of whether a fetus is a person cannot be resolved and that the very concept of personhood is not clear or decisive enough to bear the weight of a solution to the abortion debate. Advancing a moderate position, she argues that regardless of whether a fetus is a person, the principle of self-defense permits a woman to have an abortion in some cases, especially in the early stages of pregnancy. On the other hand, even if the fetus is not a person, it is too much like a baby in the later stages of pregnancy to permit an abortion—except to avoid significant injury or death.

The abortion debate rages on. Yet the two most popular positions seem to be clearly mistaken. Conservatives maintain that a human

---

Reprinted from "Abortion and the Concept of a Person," *Canadian Journal of Philosophy,* vol. 5,2 (October 1975), by permission. Notes omitted.

life begins at conception and that therefore abortion must be wrong because it is murder. But not all killings of humans are murders. Most notably, self defense may justify even the killing of an innocent person.

Liberals, on the other hand, are just as mistaken in their argument that since a fetus does not become a person until birth, a woman may do whatever she pleases in and to her own body. First, you cannot do as you please with your own body if it affects other people adversely. Second, if a fetus is not a person, that does not imply that you can do to it anything you wish. Animals, for example, are not persons, yet to kill or torture them for no reason at all is wrong.

At the center of the storm has been the issue of just when it is between ovulation and adulthood that a person appears on the scene. Conservatives draw the line at conception, liberals at birth. In this paper I first examine our concept of a person and conclude that no single criterion can capture the concept of a person and no sharp line can be drawn. Next I argue that if a fetus is a person, abortion is still justifiable in many cases; and if a fetus is not a person, killing it is still wrong in many cases. To a large extent, these two solutions are in agreement. I conclude that our concept of a person cannot and need not bear the weight that the abortion controversy has thrust upon it.

I

The several factions in the abortion argument have drawn battle lines around various proposed criteria for determining what is and what is not a person. For example, Mary Anne Warren lists five features (capacities for reasoning, self-awareness, complex communication, etc.) as her criteria for personhood and argues for the permissibility of abortion because a fetus falls outside this concept. Baruch Brody uses brain waves. Michael Tooley picks having-a-concept-of-self as his criterion and concludes that infanticide and abortion are justifiable, while the killing of adult animals is not. On the other side, Paul Ramsey claims a certain gene structure is the defining characteristic. John Noonan prefers conceived-of-humans and presents counterexamples to various other candidate criteria. For instance, he argues against viability as the criterion because the newborn and infirm would then be non-persons, since they cannot live without the aid of others. He rejects any criterion that calls upon the sorts of sentiments a being can evoke in adults on the grounds that this would allow us to exclude other races as non-persons if we could just view them sufficiently unsentimentally.

These approaches are typical: Foes of abortion propose sufficient conditions for personhood which fetuses satisfy, while friends of abortion counter with necessary conditions for personhood which fetuses lack. But these both presuppose that the concept of a person can be captured in a strait jacket of necessary and/or sufficient conditions. Rather, "person" is a cluster of features, of which rationality, having a self concept and being conceived of humans are only part.

What is typical of persons? Within our concept of a person we include, first, certain biological factors: descended from humans, having a certain genetic makeup, having a head, hands, arms, eyes, capable of locomotion, breathing, eating, sleeping. There are psychological factors: sentience, perception, having a concept of self and of one's own interests and desires, the ability to use tools, the ability to use language or symbol systems, the ability to joke, to be angry, to doubt. There are rationality factors: the ability to reason and draw conclusions, the ability to generalize and to learn from past experience, the ability to sacrifice present interests for greater gains in the future. There are social factors: the ability to work in groups and respond to peer pressures, the ability to recognize and consider as valuable the interests of others, seeing oneself as one among "other minds," the ability to sympathize, encourage, love, the ability to evoke from others the responses of sympathy, encouragement, love, the ability to work with others for mutual advantage. Then there are legal factors: being subject to the law and protected by it, having the ability to sue and enter contracts, being counted in the census, having a name and citizenship, the ability to own property, inherit, and so forth.

Now the point is not that this list is incomplete, or that you can find counter-instances to each of its points. People typically exhibit rationality, for instance, but someone who was irrational would not thereby fail to qualify as a person. On the other hand, something could exhibit the majority of these features and still fail to be a person, as an advanced robot might. There is no single core of necessary and sufficient features which we can draw upon with the assurance that they constitute what really makes a person: there are only features that are more or less typical.

This is not to say that no necessary or sufficient conditions can be given. Being alive is a necessary condition for being a person, and being a U.S. Senator is sufficient. But rather than falling inside a sufficient condition or outside a necessary one, a fetus lies in the penumbra region where our concept of a person is not so simple. For this reason I think a conclusive answer to the question whether a fetus is a person is unattainable.

Here we might note a family of simple fallacies that proceed by stating a necessary condition for personhood and showing that a fetus has that characteristic. This is a form of the fallacy of affirming the consequent. For example, some have mistakenly reasoned from the premise that a fetus is human (after all, it is a human fetus rather than, say, a canine fetus), to the conclusion that it is *a* human. Adding an equivocation on " 'being,' " we get the fallacious argument that since a fetus is something both living and human, it is a human being.

Nonetheless, it does seem clear that a fetus has very few of the above family of characteristics, whereas a newborn baby exhibits a much larger proportion of them—and a two-year-old has even more. Note that one traditional anti-abortion argument has centered on pointing out the many ways in which a fetus resembles a baby. They emphasize its development ("It already has ten fingers . . .") without mentioning its dissimilarities to adults (it still has gills and a tail). They also try to evoke the sort of sympathy on our part that we only feel toward other persons ("Never to laugh . . . or feel the sunshine?") This all seems to be a relevant way to argue, since its purpose is to persuade us that a fetus satisfies so many of the important features on the list that it ought to be treated as a person. Also note that a fetus near the time of birth satisfies many more of these factors than a fetus in the early months of development. This could provide reason for making distinctions among the different stages of pregnancy, as the U.S. Supreme Court has done.

Historically, the time at which a person has been said to come into existence has varied widely. Muslims date personhood from fourteen days after conception. Some medievals followed Aristotle in placing ensoulment at forty days after conception for a male fetus and eighty days for a female fetus. In European common law since the Seventeenth Century, abortion was considered the killing of a person only after quickening, the time when a pregnant woman first feels the fetus move on its own. Nor is this variety of opinions surprising. Biologically, a human being develops gradually. We shouldn't expect there to be any specific time or sharp dividing point when a person appears on the scene.

For these reasons I believe our concept of a person is not sharp or decisive enough to bear the weight of a solution to the abortion controversy. To use it to solve that problem is to clarify *obscurum per obscurius*.

II

Next let us consider what follows if a fetus is a person after all. Judith Jarvis Thomson's landmark article, "A Defense of Abortion," correctly points out that some additional argumentation is needed at this point in the conservative argument to bridge the gap between the premise that a fetus is an innocent person and the conclusion that killing it is always wrong. To arrive at this conclusion, we would need the additional premise that killing an innocent person is always wrong. But killing an innocent person is sometimes permissible, most notably in self defense. Some examples may help draw out our intuitions or ordinary judgments about self defense.

Suppose a mad scientist, for instance, hypnotized innocent people to jump out of the bushes and attack innocent passers-by with knives. If you are so attacked, we agree you have a right to kill the attacker in self defense, if killing him is the only way to protect your life or to save yourself from serious injury. It does not seem to matter here that the attacker is not malicious but himself an innocent pawn, for your killing of him is not done in a spirit of retribution but only in self defense.

How severe an injury may you inflict in self defense? In part this depends upon the severity of the injury to be avoided: you may not shoot someone merely to avoid having your clothes torn. This might lead one to the mistaken conclusion that the defense may only equal the threatened injury in severity; that to avoid death you may kill, but to avoid a black eye you may only inflict a black eye or the equivalent. Rather, our laws and customs seem to say that you may create an injury somewhat, but not enormously, greater than the injury to be avoided. To fend off an attack whose outcome would be as serious as rape, a severe beating or the loss of a finger, you may shoot; to avoid having your clothes torn, you may blacken an eye.

Aside from this, the injury you may inflict should only be the minimum necessary to deter or incapacitate the attacker. Even if you know he intends to kill you, you are not justified in shooting him if you could equally well save yourself by the simple expedient of running away. Self defense is for the purpose of avoiding harms rather than equalizing harms.

Some cases of pregnancy present a parallel situation. Though the fetus is itself innocent, it may pose a threat to the pregnant woman's well-being, life prospects or health, mental or physical. If the pregnancy presents a slight threat to her interests, it seems self defense cannot justify abortion. But if the threat is on a par with a serious beating or the loss of a finger, she may kill the fetus that poses such a threat, even if it is an innocent person. If a lesser harm to the fetus could have the same defensive effect, killing it would not be justified. It is unfortunate that the only way to free the woman from the pregnancy entails the death of the fetus (except in very late stages of pregnancy). Thus a self defense model supports Thomson's point that the woman has a right only to be freed from fetus, not a right to demand its death.

The self defense model is most helpful when we take the pregnant woman's point of view. In the pre-Thomson literature, abortion is often framed as a question for a third party; do you, a doctor, have a right to choose between the life of the woman and that of the fetus? Some have claimed that if you were a passer-by who witnessed a struggle between the innocent hypnotized attacker and his equally innocent victim, you would have no reason to kill either in defense of the other. They have concluded that the self defense model implies that a woman may attempt to abort herself, but that a doctor should not assist her. I think the position of the third party is somewhat more complex. We do feel some inclination to intervene on behalf of the victim rather than the attacker, other things equal. But if both parties are innocent, other factors come into consideration. You would rush to the aid of your husband whether he was attacker or attackee. If a hypnotized famous violinist were attacking a skid row bum, we would try to save the individual who is of more value to society. These considerations would tend to support abortion in some cases.

But suppose you are a frail senior citizen who wishes to avoid being knifed by one of these innocent hypnotics, so you have hired a bodyguard to accompany you. If you are attacked, it is clear we believe that the bodyguard, acting as your agent, has a right to kill the attacker to save you from a serious beating. Your rights of self defense are transferred to your agent. I suggest that we should similarly view the doctor as the pregnant woman's agent in carrying out a defense she is physically incapable of accomplishing herself.

Thanks to modern technology, the cases are rare in which a pregnancy poses as clear a threat to a woman's bodily health as an attacker brandishing a switchblade. How does self defense fare when more subtle, complex and long-range harms are involved?

To consider a somewhat fanciful example, suppose you are a highly trained surgeon when you are kidnapped by the hypnotic attacker. He says he does not intend to harm you but to take you back to the mad scientist who, it turns out, plans to hypnotize you to have a permanent mental block against all your knowledge of medicine. This would automatically destroy your career which would in turn have a serious adverse impact on your family, your personal relationships and your happiness. It seems to me that if the only way you can avoid this outcome is to shoot the innocent attacker, you are justified in so doing. You are defending yourself from a drastic injury to your life prospects. I think it is no exaggeration to claim that unwanted pregnancies (most obviously among teenagers) often have such adverse life-long consequences as the surgeon's loss of livelihood.

Several parallels arise between various views on abortion and the self defense model. Let's suppose further that these hypnotized attackers only operate at night, so that it is well known that they can be avoided completely by the considerable inconvenience of never leaving your house after dark. One view is that since you could stay home at night, therefore if you go out and are selected by one of these hypnotized people, you have no right to defend yourself. This parallels the view that abstinence is the only acceptable way to avoid pregnancy. Others might hold that you ought to take along some defense such as Mace which will deter the hypnotized person without killing him, but that if this defense fails, you are obliged to submit to the resulting injury, no matter how severe it is. This parallels the view that contraception is all right but abortion is always wrong, even in cases of contraceptive failure.

A third view is that you may kill the hypnotized person only if he will actually kill you, but not if he will only injure you. This is like the position that abortion is permissible only if it is required to save a woman's life. Finally, we have the view that it is all right to kill the attacker, even if only to avoid a very slight inconvenience to yourself and even if you knowingly walked down the very street where all these incidents have been taking place without taking along any Mace or protective escort. If we assume that a fetus is a person, this is the analogue of the view that abortion is always justifiable, "on demand."

The self defense model allows us to see an important difference that exists between abortion and infanticide, even if a fetus is a person from conception. Many have argued that the only way to justify abortion without justifying infanticide would be to find some characteristic of personhood that is acquired at birth. Michael Tooley, for one, claims infanticide is justifiable because the really significant characteristics of person are acquired some time after birth. But all such approaches look to characteristics of the developing human and ignore the relation between the fetus and the woman. What if, after birth, the presence of an infant or the need to support it posed a grave threat to the woman's sanity or life prospects? She could escape this threat by the simple expedient of running away. So a solution that does not entail the death of the infant is available. Before birth, such solutions are not available because of the biological dependence of the fetus on the woman. Birth is the crucial point not because of any characteristics the fetus gains, but because after birth the woman can defend herself by a means less drastic than killing the infant. Hence self defense can be used to justify abortion without necessarily thereby justifying infanticide.

III

On the other hand, supposing a fetus is not after all a person, would abortion always be morally permissible? Some opponents of abortion seem worried that if a fetus is not a full-fledged person, then we are justified in treating it in any way at all. However, this does not follow. Non-persons do get some consideration in our moral code, though of course they do not have the same rights as persons have (and in general they do not have moral responsibilities), and though their interests may be overridden by the interests of persons. Still, we cannot just treat them in any way at all.

Treatment of animals is a case in point. It is wrong to torture dogs for fun or to kill wild birds for no reason at all. It is wrong Period, even though dogs and birds do not have the same rights persons do. However, few people think it is wrong to use dogs as experimental animals, causing them considerable suffering in some cases, provided that the resulting research will probably bring discoveries of great benefit to people. And most of us think it all right to kill birds for food or to protect our crops. People's rights are different from the consideration we give to animals, then, for it is wrong to experiment on people, even if others might later benefit a great deal as a result of their suffering. You might volunteer to be a subject, but this would be supererogatory; you certainly have a right to refuse to be a medical guinea pig.

But how do we decide what you may or may not do to non-persons? This is a difficult problem, one for which I believe no adequate account exists. You do not want to say, for instance, that torturing dogs is all right whenever the sum of its effects on people is good—when it doesn't warp the sensibilities of the torturer so much that he mistreats people. If that were the case, it would be all right to torture dogs if you did it in private, or if the torturer lived on a desert island or died soon afterward, so that his actions had no effect on people. This is an inadequate account, because whatever moral consideration animals get, it has to be indefeasible, too. It will have to be a general proscription of certain actions, not merely a weighing of the impact on people on a case-by-case basis.

Rather, we need to distinguish two levels on which consequences of actions can be taken into account in moral reasoning. The traditional objections to Utilitarianism focus on the fact that it operates solely on the first level, taking all the consequences into account in particular cases only. Thus Utilitarianism is open to "desert island" and "lifeboat" counterexamples because these cases are rigged to make the consequences of actions severely limited.

Rawls' theory could be described as a teleological sort of theory, but with teleology operating on a higher level. In choosing the principles to regulate society from the original position, his hypothetical choosers make their decision on the basis of the total consequences of various systems. Furthermore, they are constrained to choose a general set of rules which people can readily learn and apply. An ethical theory must operate by generating a set of sympathies and attitudes toward others which reinforces the functioning of that set of moral principles. Our prohibition against killing people operates by means of certain moral sentiments including sympathy, compassion and guilt. But if these attitudes are to form a coherent set, they carry us further: we tend to perform supererogatory actions, and we tend to feel similar compassion toward person-like non-persons.

It is crucial that psychological facts play a role here. Our psychological constitution makes it the case that for our ethical theory to work, it must prohibit certain treatment of non-persons which are significantly person-like. If our moral rules allowed people to treat some person-like non-persons in ways we do not want people to be treated, this would undermine the system of sympathies and attitudes that makes the ethical system work. For this reason, we would choose in the original position to make mistreatment of some sorts of animals wrong in general (not just wrong in the cases with public impact), even though animals are not themselves parties in the original position. Thus it makes sense that it is those animals whose appearance and behavior are most like those of people that get the most consideration in our moral scheme.

It is because of "coherence of attitudes," I think, that the similarity of a fetus to a baby is very significant. A fetus one week before birth is so much like a newborn baby in our psychological space that we cannot allow any cavalier treatment of the former while expecting full sympathy and nurturative support for the latter. Thus, I think that anti-abortion forces are indeed giving their strongest arguments when they point to the similarities between a fetus and a baby, and when they try to evoke our emotional attachment to and sympathy for the fetus. An early horror story from New York about nurses who were expected to alternate between caring for six-week premature infants and disposing of viable 24-week aborted fetuses is just that—a horror story. These beings are so much alike that no one can be asked to draw a distinction and treat them so very differently.

Remember, however, that in the early weeks after conception, a fetus is very much unlike a person. It is hard to develop these feelings for a set of genes which doesn't yet have a head, hands, beating heart, response to touch or the ability to move by itself. Thus it seems to me that the alleged "slippery slope" between conception and birth is not so very slippery. In the early stages of pregnancy, abortion can hardly be compared to murder for psychological reasons, but in the latest stages it is psychologically akin to murder. Another source of similarity is the bodily continuity between fetus and adult. Bodies play a surprisingly central role in our attitudes toward persons. One has only to think of the philosophical literature on how far physical identity suffices for personal identity or Wittgenstein's remark that the best picture of the human soul is the human body. Even after death, when all agree the body is no longer a person, we still observe elaborate customs of respect for the human body; like people who torture dogs, necrophiliacs are not to be trusted with people. So it is appropriate that we show respect to a fetus as the body continuous with the body of a person. This is a degree of resemblance to persons that animals cannot rival.

Michael Tooley also utilizes a parallel with animals. He claims that it is always permissible to drown newborn kittens and draws conclusions about infanticide. But it is only permissible to drown kittens when their survival would cause some hardship. Perhaps it would be a burden to feed and house six more cats or to find other homes for them. The alternative of letting them starve produces even more suffering than the drowning. Since the kittens get their rights second-hand, so to speak, *via* the need for coherence in our attitudes, their interests are often overridden by the interests of full-fledged persons. But if their survival would be no inconvenience to people at all, then it is wrong to drown them, *contra* Tooley.

Tooley's conclusions about abortion are wrong for the same reason. Even if a fetus is not a person, abortion is not always permissible, because of the resemblance of a fetus to a person. I agree with Thomson that it would be wrong for a woman who is seven months pregnant to have an abortion just to avoid having to postpone a trip to Europe. In the early months of pregnancy when the fetus hardly resembles a baby at all, then, abortion is permissible whenever it is in the interests of the pregnant woman or her family. The reasons would only need to outweigh the pain and inconvenience of the abortion itself. In the middle months, when the fetus comes to resemble a person, abortion would be justifiable only when the continuation of the pregnancy or the birth of the child would cause harms—physical, psychological, economic or social—to the woman. In the late months of pregnancy, even on our current assumption that a fetus is not a person, abortion seems to be wrong except to save a woman from significant injury or death.

The Supreme Court has recognized similar gradations in the alleged slippery slope stretching between conception and birth. To this point, the present paper has been a discussion of the moral status of abortion only, not its legal status. In view of the great physical, financial and sometimes psychological costs of abortion, perhaps the legal arrangements most compatible with the proposed moral solution would be the absence of restrictions, that is, so-called abortion "on demand."

So I conclude, first, that application of our concept of a person will not suffice to settle the abortion issue. After all, the biological development of a human being is gradual. Second, whether a fetus is a person or not, abortion is justifiable early in pregnancy to avoid modest harms and seldom justifiable late in pregnancy except to avoid significant injury or death.

For Further Reflection

1. Can we get beyond the personhood issue, as English proposes? Has she successfully shown that we don't need to resolve this issue in order to deal with the morality of abortion? Where do you agree or disagree with her?

2. English's view has been called moderate because she accepts most early-stage abortions and rejects most later-stage abortions. If so, how can this be reconciled with her proposal, or at least acceptance, of abortion "on demand"?

3. Does English's argument appeal too much to our emotions and too little to reason? For example, she says, "It is crucial that psychological facts play a role here. Our psychological constitution makes it the case that for our ethical theory to work, it must prohibit certain treatment of nonpersons which are significantly person-like." What does English mean? Is this an appeal to ignorance or to human irrationality or something else?

4. What is her "coherence of attitudes" argument? How much weight should such considerations be given in the abortion debate? Could my "coherence" structure be different from yours, and yours be different from other people's? Discuss the case of the New York nurses who were expected to alternate between caring for six-week premature infants and disposing of viable 24-week aborted fetuses. What bearing does this have on the question of the morality of abortion?

Further Readings for Chapter 12

Brody, Baruch. *Abortion and the Sanctity of Life.* Cambridge, Mass.: MIT Press, 1975.

Devine, Philip E. *The Ethics of Homicide*. Ithaca, N.Y.: Cornell University Press, 1978.

Noonan, John T. *The Morality of Abortion: Legal and Historical Perspectives*. Cambridge, Mass.: Harvard University Press, 1970.

Pojman, Louis, and Frank Beckwith, eds. *The Abortion Controversy*, 2nd ed. Belmont, Calif.: Wadsworth, 1998.

Sumner, L. W. *Abortion and Moral Theory*. Princeton, N.J.: Princeton University Press, 1981.

Tooley, Michael. *Abortion and Infanticide*. Oxford: Oxford University Press, 1983.

CHAPTER 13

The Morality of Euthanasia

As a starting point in discussions of euthanasia, we can define the term as bringing about the death of another person to somehow benefit that person. At the root of the issue of euthanasia is a conflict of common moral attitudes—a clash between the evil of taking an innocent life and the good of sparing someone a life of agony. Most people have no trouble at all understanding why these attitudes arise, but reconciling them in a morally acceptable way is another matter. Anyone who has thought carefully about the moral questions provoked by euthanasia knows that arriving at informed, supportable answers is not as easy as some people would like to believe.

To clarify the issue, moral philosophers have distinguished different types of euthanasia. *Voluntary* euthanasia is requested, or agreed to, by the patient. She may ask for it in person or leave instructions to be followed by family members or physicians in the event she becomes incapacitated. The instructions may be in the form of an advance directive (such as a living will), a legal document authorizing doctors to withhold or withdraw treatment if she is unable to communicate her preferences. *Nonvoluntary* euthanasia is requested by persons other than the patient, such as family members or the physician, when the patient cannot request it herself (because she is incapacitated) and her wishes are unknown. *Involuntary* euthanasia is performed against the patient's wishes—which makes it both illegal and immoral. *Active* euthanasia—often called "mercy killing"—is performing a direct action to take someone's life, such as administering a lethal drug to a patient. Active euthanasia is illegal in most places, and medical associations in the United States are officially opposed to it. *Passive* euthanasia is allowing someone to die by not performing some life-sustaining action.

Withholding fluids and nutrients from a patient or removing her respirator, for example, is passive euthanasia. Generally, passive euthanasia—either voluntary or nonvoluntary—is legal. If a patient is competent, he has a right to refuse medical treatment even if doing so would result in his death.

In our first reading, Dan W. Brock argues that voluntary active euthanasia is morally permissible because of the values of self-determination and personal well-being. In our second selection, J. Gay-Williams contends that deliberately killing a hopelessly ill person is morally wrong because such an act goes against the strong natural tendency of all humans to continue living. Finally, James Rachels takes on the conventional distinction between active and passive euthanasia, arguing that there is no moral difference between the two.

Voluntary Active Euthanasia

DAN W. BROCK

Dan W. Brock is professor of philosophy and biomedical ethics at Brown University. He argues that two widely accepted moral principles support the view that voluntary active euthanasia is morally permissible: individual self-determination and personal well-being. He also contends that the possible good consequences of establishing a public policy permitting voluntary active euthanasia outweigh the bad.

. . . The central ethical argument for euthanasia is familiar. It is that the very same two fundamental ethical values supporting the consensus on patient's rights to decide about life-sustaining treatment also support the ethical permissibility of euthanasia. These values are individual self-determination or autonomy and individual well-being. By self-determination as it bears on euthanasia, I mean people's interest in making important decisions about their lives for themselves according to their own values or conceptions of a good life, and in being left free to act on those decisions. Self-determination is valuable because it permits people to form and live in accordance with their own conception of a good life, at least within the bounds of justice and consistent with others doing so as well. In exercising self-determination people take responsibility for their lives and for the kinds of persons they become. A central aspect of human dignity lies in people's capacity to direct their lives in this way. The value of exercising self-determination presupposes some minimum of decision making capacities or competence, which thus limits the scope of euthanasia supported by self-determination; it cannot justifiably be administered, for example, in cases of serious dementia or treatable clinical depression.

Does the value of individual self-determination extend to the time and manner of one's death? Most people are very concerned about the nature of the last stage of their lives. This reflects not just a fear of experiencing substantial suffering when dying, but

---

"Voluntary Active Euthanasia" by D. W. Brock from *Hastings Center Report,* 22 (2), Used by permission of the Hastings Center.

also a desire to retain dignity and control during this last period of life. Death is today increasingly preceded by a long period of significant physical and mental decline, due in part to the technological interventions of modern medicine. Many people adjust to these disabilities and find meaning and value in new activities and ways. Others find the impairments and burdens in the last stage of their lives at some point sufficiently great to make life no longer worth living. For many patients near death, maintaining the quality of one's life, avoiding great suffering, maintaining one's dignity, and insuring that others remember us as we wish them to become of paramount importance and outweigh merely extending one's life. But there is no single, objectively correct answer for everyone as to when, if at all, one's life becomes all things considered a burden and unwanted. If self-determination is a fundamental value, then the great variability among people on this question makes it especially important that individuals control the manner, circumstances, and timing of their dying and death.

The other main value that supports euthanasia is individual well-being. It might seem that individual well-being conflicts with a person's self-determination when the person requests euthanasia. Life itself is commonly taken to be a central good for persons, often valued for its own sake, as well as necessary for pursuit of all other goods within a life. But when a competent patient decides to forgo all further life-sustaining treatment then the patient, either explicitly or implicitly, commonly decides that the best life possible for him or her with treatment is of sufficiently poor quality that it is worse than no further life at all. Life is no longer considered a benefit by the patient, but has now become a burden. The same judgment underlies a request for euthanasia: continued life is seen by the patient as no longer a benefit, but now a burden. Especially in the often severely compromised and debilitated states of many critically ill or dying patients, there is no objective standard, but only the competent patient's judgment of whether continued life is no longer a benefit.

Of course, sometimes there are conditions, such as clinical depression, that call into question whether the patient has made a competent choice, either to forgo life-sustaining treatment or to seek euthanasia, and then the patient's choice need not be evidence that continued life is no longer a benefit for him or her. Just as with decisions about treatment, a determination of incompetence can warrant not honoring the patient's choice; in the case of treatment, we then transfer decisional authority to a surrogate, though in the case of voluntary active euthanasia a determination that the patient is incompetent means that choice is not possible.

The value or right of self-determination does not entitle patients to compel physicians to act contrary to their own moral or professional values. Physicians are moral and professional agents whose own self-determination or integrity should be respected as well. If performing euthanasia became legally permissible, but conflicted with a particular physician's reasonable understanding of his or her moral or professional responsibilities, the care of a patient who requested euthanasia should be transferred to another.

Most opponents do not deny that there are some cases in which the values of patient self-determination and well-being support euthanasia. Instead, they commonly offer two kinds of arguments against it that on their view outweigh or override this support. The first kind of argument is that in any individual case where considerations of the patient's self-determination and well-being do support euthanasia, it is nevertheless always ethically wrong or impermissible. The second kind of argument grants that in some individual cases euthanasia may not be ethically wrong, but maintains nonetheless that public and legal policy should never permit it. The first kind of argument focuses on features of any individual case of euthanasia, while the second kind focuses on social or legal policy. In the next section I consider the first kind of argument.

EUTHANASIA IS THE DELIBERATE KILLING OF AN INNOCENT PERSON

The claim that any individual instance of euthanasia is a case of deliberate killing of an innocent person is, with only minor qualifications, correct. Unlike forgoing life-sustaining treatment, commonly understood as allowing to die, euthanasia is clearly killing, defined as depriving of life or causing the death of a living being. While providing morphine for pain relief at doses where the risk of respiratory depression and an earlier death may be a foreseen but unintended side effect of treating the patient's pain, in a case of euthanasia the patient's death is deliberate or intended even if in both the physician's ultimate end may be respecting the patient's wishes. If the deliberate killing of an innocent person is wrong, euthanasia would be nearly always impermissible.

In the context of medicine, the ethical prohibition against deliberately killing the innocent derives some of its plausibility from the belief that nothing in the currently accepted practice of medicine is deliberate killing. Thus, in commenting on the "It's Over, Debbie" case, four prominent physicians and bioethicists could entitle their paper "Doctors Must Not Kill."[1] The belief that doctors do not in fact kill requires the corollary belief that forgoing life-sustaining treatment, whether by not starting or by stopping treatment, is allowing to die, not killing. Common though this view is, I shall argue that it is confused and mistaken.

Why is the common view mistaken? Consider the case of a patient terminally ill with ALS disease. She is completely respirator dependent with no hope of ever being weaned. She is unquestionably competent but finds her condition intolerable and persistently requests to be removed from the respirator and allowed to die. Most people and physicians would agree that the patient's physician should respect the patient's wishes and remove her from the respirator, though this will certainly cause the patient's death. The common understanding is that the physician thereby allows the patient to die. But is that correct?

Suppose the patient has a greedy and hostile son who mistakenly believes that his mother will never decide to stop her life-sustaining treatment and that even if she did her physician would not remove her from the respirator. Afraid that his inheritance will be dissipated by a long and expensive hospitalization, he enters his mother's room while she is sedated, extubates her, and she dies. Shortly thereafter the medical staff discovers what he has done and confronts the son. He replies, "I didn't kill her, I merely allowed her to die. It was her ALS disease that caused her death." I think this would rightly be dismissed as transparent sophistry—the son went into his mother's room and deliberately killed her. But, of course, the son performed just the same physical actions, did just the same thing, that the physician would have done. If that is so, then doesn't the physician also kill the patient when he extubates her?

[1]Willard Gaylin, Leon R. Kass, Edmund D. Pellegrino, and Mark Siegler, "Doctors Must Not Kill," *JAMA* 259 (1988): 2139–40.

I underline immediately that there are important ethical differences between what the physician and the greedy son do. First, the physician acts with the patient's consent whereas the son does not. Second, the physician acts with a good motive—to respect the patient's wishes and self-determination—whereas the son acts with a bad motive—to protect his own inheritance. Third, the physician acts in a social role through which he is legally authorized to carry out the patient's wishes regarding treatment whereas the son has no such authorization. These and perhaps other ethically important differences show that what the physician did was morally justified whereas what the son did was morally wrong. What they do not show, however, is that the son killed while the physician allowed to die. One can either kill or allow to die with or without consent, with a good or bad motive, within or outside of a social role that authorizes one to do so.

The difference between killing and allowing to die that I have been implicitly appealing to here is roughly that between acts and omissions resulting in death.[2] Both the physician and the greedy son act in a manner intended to cause death, do cause death, and so both kill. One reason this conclusion is resisted is that on a different understanding of the distinction between killing and allowing to die, what the physician does is allow to die. In this account, the mother's ALS is a lethal disease whose normal progression is being held back or blocked by the life-sustaining respirator treatment. Removing this artificial intervention is then viewed as standing aside and allowing the patient to die of her underlying disease. I have argued elsewhere that this alternative account is deeply problematic, in part because it commits us to accepting that what the greedy son does is to allow to die, not kill.[3] Here, I want to note two other reasons why the conclusion that stopping life support is killing is resisted.

The first reason is that killing is often understood, especially within medicine, as unjustified causing of death; in medicine it is thought to be done only accidentally or negligently. It is also increasingly widely accepted that a physician is ethically justified in stop-

[2]Bonnie Steinbock, ed., *Killing and Allowing to Die* (Englewood Cliffs, N.J.: Prentice-Hall, 1980).
[3]Dan W. Brock, "Forgoing Food and Water: Is It Killing?" in *By No Extraordinary Means: The Choice to Forgo Life-Sustaining Food and Water,* ed. Joanne Lynn (Bloomington: Indiana University Press, 1986), pp. 117–31.

ping life support in a case like that of the ALS patient. But if these two beliefs are correct, then what the physician does cannot be killing, and so must be allowing to die. Killing patients is not, to put it flippantly, understood to be part of physicians' job description. What is mistaken in this line of reasoning is the assumption that all killings are unjustified causings of death. Instead, some killings are ethically justified, including many instances of stopping life support.

Another reason for resisting the conclusion that stopping life support is often killing is that it is psychologically uncomfortable. Suppose the physician had stopped the ALS patient's respirator and had made the son's claim, "I didn't kill her, I merely allowed her to die. It was her ALS disease that caused her death." The clue to the psychological role here is how naturally the "merely" modifies "allowed her to die." The characterization as allowing to die is meant to shift felt responsibility away from the agent—the physician—and to the lethal disease process. Other language common in death and dying contexts plays a similar role; "letting nature take its course" or "stopping prolonging the dying process" both seem to shift responsibility from the physician who stops life support to the fatal disease process. However psychologically helpful these conceptualizations may be in making the difficult responsibility of a physician's role in the patient's death bearable, they nevertheless are confusions. Both physicians and family members can instead be helped to understand that it is the patient's decision and consent to stopping treatment that limits their responsibility for the patient's death and that shifts that responsibility to the patient.

Many who accept the difference between killing and allowing to die as the distinction between acts and omissions resulting in death have gone on to argue that killing is not in itself morally different from allowing to die.[4] In this account, very roughly, one kills when one performs an action that causes the death of a person (we are in a boat, you cannot swim, I push you overboard, and you drown), and one allows to die when one has the ability and

---

[4]James Rachels, "Active and Passive Euthanasia," *NEJM* 292 (1975): 78–80; Michael Tooley, *Abortion and Infanticide* (Oxford: Oxford University Press, 1983). In my paper, "Taking Human Life," *Ethics* 95 (1985): 851–65, I argue in more detail that killing in itself is not morally different from allowing to die and defend the strategy of argument employed in this and the succeeding two paragraphs in the text.

opportunity to prevent the death of another, knows this, and omits doing so, with the result that the person dies (we are in a boat, you cannot swim, you fall overboard, I don't throw you an available life ring, and you drown). Those who see no moral difference between killing and allowing to die typically employ the strategy of comparing cases that differ in these and no other potentially morally important respects. This will allow people to consider whether the mere difference that one is a case of killing and the other of allowing to die matters morally, or whether instead it is other features that make most cases of killing worse than most instances of allowing to die. Here is such a pair of cases:

Case 1

A very gravely ill patient is brought to a hospital emergency room and sent up to the ICU. The patient begins to develop respiratory failure that is likely to require intubation very soon. At that point the patient's family members and long-standing physician arrive at the ICU and inform the ICU staff that there had been extensive discussion about future care with the patient when he was unquestionably competent. Given his grave and terminal illness, as well as his state of debilitation, the patient had firmly rejected being placed on a respirator under any circumstances, and the family and physician produce the patient's advance directive to that effect. The ICU staff do not intubate the patient, who dies of respiratory failure.

Case 2

The same as Case 1 except that the family and physician are slightly delayed in traffic and arrive shortly after the patient has been intubated and placed on the respirator. The ICU staff extubate the patient, who dies of respiratory failure.

In Case 1 the patient is allowed to die, in Case 2 he is killed, but it is hard to see why what is done in Case 2 is significantly different morally than what is done in Case 1. It must be other factors that make most killings worse than most allowings to die, and if so, euthanasia cannot be wrong simply because it is killing instead of allowing to die.

Suppose both my arguments are mistaken. Suppose that killing is worse than allowing to die and that withdrawing life support is not killing, although euthanasia is. Euthanasia still need not for that reason be morally wrong. To see this, we need to determine the basic principle for the moral evaluation of killing persons. What is it that makes paradigm cases of wrongful killing wrongful? One very plausible answer is that killing denies the victim something that he or she values greatly—continued life or a future. Moreover, since continued life is necessary for pursuing any of a person's plans and purposes, killing brings the frustration of all of these plans and desires as well. In a nutshell, wrongful killing deprives a person of a valued future, and of all the person wanted and planned to do in that future.

A natural expression of this account of the wrongness of killing is that people have a moral right not to be killed.[5] But in this account of the wrongness of killing, the right not to be killed, like other rights, should be waivable when the person makes a competent decision that continued life is no longer wanted or a good, but is instead worse than no further life at all. In this view, euthanasia is properly understood as a case of a person having waived his or her right not to be killed.

This rights view of the wrongness of killing is not, of course, universally shared. Many people's moral views about killing have their origins in religious views that human life comes from God and cannot be justifiably destroyed or taken away, either by the person whose life it is or by another. But in a pluralistic society like our own with a strong commitment to freedom of religion, public policy should not be grounded in religious beliefs which many in that society reject. I turn now to the general evaluation of public policy on euthanasia.

WOULD THE BAD CONSEQUENCES OF EUTHANASIA OUTWEIGH THE GOOD?

The argument against euthanasia at the policy level is stronger than at the level of individual cases, though even here I believe the case is ultimately unpersuasive, or at best indecisive. The policy level is the place where the main issues lie, however, and where moral

[5]Dan W. Brock, "Moral Rights and Permissible Killing," in *Ethical Issues Relating to Life and Death,* ed. John Ladd (New York: Oxford University Press, 1979), pp. 94–117.

considerations that might override arguments in favor of euthanasia will be found, if they are found anywhere. It is important to note two kinds of disagreement about the consequences for public policy of permitting euthanasia. First, there is empirical or factual disagreement about what the consequences would be. This disagreement is greatly exacerbated by the lack of firm data on the issue. Second, since on any reasonable assessment there would be both good and bad consequences, there are moral disagreements about the relative importance of different effects. In addition to these two sources of disagreement, there is also no single, well-specified policy proposal for legalizing euthanasia on which policy assessments can focus. But without such specification, and especially without explicit procedures for protecting against well-intentioned misuse and ill-intentioned abuse, the consequences for policy are largely speculative. Despite these difficulties, a preliminary account of the main likely good and bad consequences is possible. This should help clarify where better data or more moral analysis and argument are needed, as well as where policy safeguards must be developed.

Potential Good Consequences of Permitting Euthanasia

What are the likely good consequences? First, if euthanasia were permitted it would be possible to respect the self-determination of competent patients who want it, but now cannot get it because of its illegality. We simply do not know how many such patients and people there are. In the Netherlands, with a population of about 14.5 million (in 1987), estimates in a recent study were that about 1,900 cases of voluntary active euthanasia or physician-assisted suicide occur annually. No straightforward extrapolation to the United States is possible for many reasons, among them, that we do not know how many people here who want euthanasia now get it, despite its illegality. Even with better data on the number of persons who want euthanasia but cannot get it, significant moral disagreement would remain about how much weight should be given to any instance of failure to respect a person's self-determination in this way.

One important factor substantially affecting the number of persons who would seek euthanasia is the extent to which an alternative is available. The widespread acceptance in the law, social policy, and medical practice of the right of a competent patient to forgo life-sustaining treatment suggests that the number of competent persons in the United States who would want euthanasia if it were permitted is probably relatively small.

A second good consequence of making euthanasia legally permissible benefits a much larger group. Polls have shown that a majority of the American public believes that people should have a right to obtain euthanasia if they want it.[6] No doubt the vast majority of those who support this right to euthanasia will never in fact come to want euthanasia for themselves. Nevertheless, making it legally permissible would reassure many people that if they ever do want euthanasia they would be able to obtain it. This reassurance would supplement the broader control over the process of dying given by the right to decide about life-sustaining treatment. Having fire insurance on one's house benefits all who have it, not just those whose houses actually burn down, by reassuring them that in the unlikely event of their house burning down, they will receive the money needed to rebuild it. Likewise, the legalization of euthanasia can be thought of as a kind of insurance policy against being forced to endure a protracted dying process that one has come to find burdensome and unwanted, especially when there is no life-sustaining treatment to forgo. The strong concern about losing control of their care expressed by many people who face serious illness likely to end in death suggests that they give substantial importance to the legalization of euthanasia as a means of maintaining this control.

A third good consequence of the legalization of euthanasia concerns patients whose dying is filled with severe and unrelievable pain or suffering. When there is a life-sustaining treatment that, if forgone, will lead relatively quickly to death, then doing so can bring an end to these patients' suffering without recourse to euthanasia. For patients receiving no such treatment, however, euthanasia may be the only release from their otherwise prolonged suffering and agony. This argument from mercy has always been the strongest argument for euthanasia in those cases to which it applies.[7]

---

[6]P. Painton and E. Taylor, "Love or Let Die," *Time,* 19 March 1990, pp. 62–71; *Boston Globe*/Harvard University Poll, *Boston Globe,* 3 November 1991.

[7]James Rachels, *The End of Life* (Oxford: Oxford University Press, 1986).

The importance of relieving pain and suffering is less controversial than is the frequency with which patients are forced to undergo untreatable agony that only euthanasia could relieve. If we focus first on suffering caused by physical pain, it is crucial to distinguish pain that could be adequately relieved with modern methods of pain control, though it in fact is not, from pain that is relievable only by death.[8] For a variety of reasons, including some physicians' fear of hastening the patient's death, as well as the lack of a publicly accessible means for assessing the amount of the patient's pain, many patients suffer pain that could be, but is not, relieved.

Specialists in pain control, as for example the pain of terminally ill cancer patients, argue that there are very few patients whose pain could not be adequately controlled, though sometimes at the cost of so sedating them that they are effectively unable to interact with other people or their environment. Thus, the argument from mercy in cases of physical pain can probably be met in a large majority of cases by providing adequate measures of pain relief. This should be a high priority, whatever our legal policy on euthanasia—the relief of pain and suffering has long been, quite properly, one of the central goals of medicine. Those cases in which pain could be effectively relieved, but in fact is not, should only count significantly in favor of legalizing euthanasia if all reasonable efforts to change pain management techniques have been tried and have failed.

Dying patients often undergo substantial psychological suffering that is not fully or even principally the result of physical pain.[9] The knowledge about how to relieve this suffering is much more limited than in the case of relieving pain, and efforts to do so are probably more often unsuccessful. If the argument from mercy is extended to patients experiencing great and unrelievable psychological suffering, the numbers of patients to which it applies are much greater.

One last good consequence of legalizing euthanasia is that once death has been accepted, it is often more humane to end life quickly

[8]Marcia Angell, "The Quality of Mercy," *NEJM* 306 (1982): 98–99; M. Donovan, P. Dillon, and L. Mcguire, Incidence and Characteristics of Pain in a Sample of Medical-Surgical Inpatients," *Pain* 30 (1987): 69–78.
[9]Eric Cassell, *The Nature of Suffering and the Goals of Medicine* (New York: Oxford University Press, 1991).

and peacefully, when that is what the patient wants. Such a death will often be seen as better than a more prolonged one. People who suffer a sudden and unexpected death, for example by dying quickly or in their sleep from a heart attack or stroke, are often considered lucky to have died in this way. We care about how we die in part because we care about how others remember us, and we hope they will remember us as we were in "good times" with them and not as we might be when disease has robbed us of our dignity as human beings. As with much in the treatment and care of the dying, people's concerns differ in this respect, but for at least some people, euthanasia will be a more humane death than what they have often experienced with other loved ones and might otherwise expect for themselves.

Some opponents of euthanasia challenge how much importance should be given to any of these good consequences of permitting it, or even whether some would be good consequences at all. But more frequently, opponents cite a number of bad consequences that permitting euthanasia would or could produce, and it is to their assessment that I now turn.

Potential Bad Consequences of Permitting Euthanasia

Some of the arguments against permitting euthanasia are aimed specifically against physicians, while others are aimed against anyone being permitted to perform it. I shall first consider one argument of the former sort. Permitting physicians to perform euthanasia, it is said, would be incompatible with their fundamental moral and professional commitment as healers to care for patients and to protect life. Moreover, if euthanasia by physicians became common, patients would come to fear that a medication was intended not to treat or care, but instead to kill, and would thus lose trust in their physicians. This position was forcefully stated in a paper by Willard Gaylin and his colleagues:

> The very soul of medicine is on trial. . . . This issue touches medicine at its moral center; if this moral center collapses, if physicians become killers or are even licensed to kill, the profession—and, therewith, each physician—will never again be worthy of trust and respect as healer and comforter and protector of life in all its frailty.

These authors go on to make clear that, while they oppose permitting anyone to perform euthanasia, their special concern is with physicians doing so:

> We call on fellow physicians to say that they will not deliberately kill. We must also say to each of our fellow physicians that we will not tolerate killing of patients and that we shall take disciplinary action against doctors who kill. And we must say to the broader community that if it insists on tolerating or legalizing active euthanasia, it will have to find nonphysicians to do its killing.[10]

If permitting physicians to kill would undermine the very "moral center" of medicine, then almost certainly physicians should not be permitted to perform euthanasia. But how persuasive is this claim? Patients should not fear, as a consequence of permitting voluntary active euthanasia, that their physicians will substitute a lethal injection for what patients want and believe is part of their care. If active euthanasia is restricted to cases in which it is truly voluntary, then no patient should fear getting it unless she or he has voluntarily requested it. (The fear that we might in time also come to accept nonvoluntary, or even involuntary, active euthanasia is a slippery slope worry I address below.) Patients' trust of their physicians could be increased, not eroded, by knowledge that physicians will provide aid in dying when patients seek it.

Might Gaylin and his colleagues nevertheless be correct in their claim that the moral center of medicine would collapse if physicians were to become killers? This question raises what at the deepest level should be the guiding aims of medicine, a question that obviously cannot be fully explored here. But I do want to say enough to indicate the direction that I believe an appropriate response to this challenge should take. In spelling out above what I called the positive argument for voluntary active euthanasia, I suggested that two principal values—respecting patients' self-determination and promoting their well-being—underlie the consensus that competent patients, or the surrogates of incompetent patients, are entitled to refuse any life-sustaining treatment and to choose from among available alternative treatments. It is the commitment to these two values in guiding physicians' actions as healers, comforters, and protectors of their patients' lives that should be at the "moral center" of medicine, and these two

---

[10]Gaylin et al., "Doctors Must Not Kill."

values support physicians' administering euthanasia when their patients make competent requests for it. . . .

A second bad consequence that some foresee is that permitting euthanasia would weaken society's commitment to provide optimal care for dying patients. We live at a time in which the control of health care costs has become, and is likely to continue to be, the dominant focus of health care policy. If euthanasia is seen as a cheaper alternative to adequate care and treatment, then we might become less scrupulous about providing sometimes costly support and other services to dying patients. Particularly if our society comes to embrace deeper and more explicit rationing of health care, frail, elderly, and dying patients will need to be strong and effective advocates for their own health care and other needs, although they are hardly in a position to do this. We should do nothing to weaken their ability to obtain adequate care and services.

This second worry is difficult to assess because there is little firm evidence about the likelihood of the feared erosion in the care of dying patients. There are at least two reasons, however, for skepticism about this argument. The first is that the same worry could have been directed at recognizing patients' or surrogates' rights to forgo life-sustaining treatment, yet there is no persuasive evidence that recognizing the right to refuse treatment has caused a serious erosion in the quality of care of dying patients. The second reason for skepticism about this worry is that only a very small proportion of deaths would occur from euthanasia if it were permitted. In the Netherlands, where euthanasia under specified circumstances is permitted by the courts, though not authorized by statute, the best estimate of the proportion of overall deaths that result from it is about 2 percent.[11] Thus, the vast majority of critically ill and dying patients will not request it, and so will still have to be cared for by physicians, families, and others. Permitting euthanasia should not diminish people's commitment and concern to maintain and improve the care of these patients.

A third possible bad consequence of permitting euthanasia (or even a public discourse in which strong support for euthanasia is evident) is to threaten the progress made in securing the rights of patients or their surrogates to decide about and to refuse life-

[11]Paul J. Van der Maas et al., "Euthanasia and Other Medical Decisions Concerning the End of Life," *Lancet* 338 (1991): 669–74.

sustaining treatment.[12] This progress has been made against the backdrop of a clear and firm legal prohibition of euthanasia, which has provided a relatively bright line limiting the dominion of others over patients' lives. It has therefore been an important reassurance to concerns about how the authority to take steps ending life might be misused, abused, or wrongly extended.

Many supporters of the right of patients or their surrogates to refuse treatment strongly oppose euthanasia, and if forced to choose might well withdraw their support of the right to refuse treatment rather than accept euthanasia. Public policy in the last fifteen years has generally let life-sustaining treatment decisions be made in health care settings between physicians and patients or their surrogates, and without the involvement of the courts. However, if euthanasia is made legally permissible greater involvement of the courts is likely, which could in turn extend to a greater court involvement in life-sustaining treatment decisions. Most agree, however, that increased involvement of the courts in these decisions would be undesirable, as it would make sound decisionmaking more cumbersome and difficult without sufficient compensating benefits.

As with the second potential bad consequence of permitting euthanasia, this third consideration too is speculative and difficult to assess. The feared erosion of patients' or surrogates' rights to decide about life-sustaining treatment, together with greater court involvement in those decisions, are both possible. However, I believe there is reason to discount this general worry. The legal rights of competent patients and, to a lesser degree, surrogates of incompetent patients to decide about treatment are very firmly embedded in a long line of informed consent and life-sustaining treatment cases, and are not likely to be eroded by a debate over, or even acceptance of, euthanasia. It will not be accepted without safeguards that reassure the public about abuse, and if that debate shows the need for similar safeguards for some life-sustaining treatment decisions they should be adopted there as well. In neither case are the only possible safeguards greater court involvement, as the recent growth of institutional ethics committees shows.

The fourth potential bad consequence of permitting euthanasia has been developed by David Velleman and turns on the subtle

---

[12]Susan M. Wolf, "Holding the Line on Euthanasia," Special Supplement, *Hastings Center Report* 19, no. 1 (1989): 13–15.

point that making a new option or choice available to people can sometimes make them worse off, even if once they have the choice they go on to choose what is best for them.[13] Ordinarily, people's continued existence is viewed by them as given, a fixed condition with which they must cope. Making euthanasia available to people as an option denies them the alternative of staying alive by default. If people are offered the option of euthanasia, their continued existence is now a choice for which they can be held responsible and which they can be asked by others to justify. We care, and are right to care, about being able to justify ourselves to others. To the extent that our society is unsympathetic to justifying a severely dependent or impaired existence, a heavy psychological burden of proof may be placed on patients who think their terminal illness or chronic infirmity is not a sufficient reason for dying. Even if they otherwise view their life as worth living, the opinion of others around them that it is not can threaten their reason for living and make euthanasia a rational choice. Thus the existence of the option becomes a subtle pressure to request it.

This argument correctly identifies the reason why offering some patients the option of euthanasia would not benefit them. Velleman takes it not as a reason for opposing all euthanasia, but for restricting it to circumstances where there are "unmistakable and overpowering reasons for persons to want the option of euthanasia," and for denying the option in all other cases. But there are at least three reasons why such restriction may not be warranted. First, polls and other evidence support that most Americans believe euthanasia should be permitted (though the recent defeat of the referendum to permit it in the state of Washington raises some doubt about this support). Thus, many more people seem to want the choice than would be made worse off by getting it. Second, if

---

[13]My formulation of this argument derives from David Velleman's statement of it in his commentary on an earlier version of this paper delivered at the American Philosophical Association Central Division meetings; a similar point was made to me by Elisha Milgram in discussion on another occasion. For more general development of the point see Thomas Schelling, *The Strategy of Conflict* (Cambridge, Mass.: Harvard University Press, 1960); and Gerald Dworkin, "Is More Choice Better Than Less?" in *The Theory and Practice of Autonomy* (Cambridge: Cambridge University Press, 1988).

giving people the option of ending their life really makes them worse off, then we should not only prohibit euthanasia, but also take back from people the right they now have to decide about— life-sustaining treatment. The feared harmful effect should already have occurred from securing people's right to refuse life-sustaining treatment, yet there is no evidence of any such widespread harm or any broad public desire to rescind that right. Third, since there is a wide range of conditions in which reasonable people can and do disagree about whether they would want continued life, it is not possible to restrict the permissibility of euthanasia as narrowly as Velleman suggests without thereby denying it to most persons who would want it; to permit it only in cases in which virtually everyone would want it would be to deny it to most who would want it.

A fifth potential bad consequence of making euthanasia legally permissible is that it might weaken the general legal prohibition of homicide. This prohibition is so fundamental to civilized society, it is argued, that we should do nothing that erodes it. If most cases of stopping life support are killing, as I have already argued, then the court cases permitting such killing have already in effect weakened this prohibition. However, neither the courts nor most people have seen these cases as killing and so as challenging the prohibition of homicide. The courts have usually grounded patients' or their surrogates' rights to refuse life-sustaining treatment in rights to privacy, liberty, self-determination, or bodily integrity, not in exceptions to homicide laws.

Legal permission for physicians or others to perform euthanasia could not be grounded in patients' rights to decide about medical treatment. Permitting euthanasia would require qualifying, at least in effect, the legal prohibition against homicide, a prohibition that in general does not allow the consent of the victim to justify or excuse the act. Nevertheless, the very same fundamental basis of the right to decide about life-sustaining treatment—respecting a person's self-determination—does support euthanasia as well. Individual self-determination has long been a well-entrenched and fundamental value in the law, and so extending it to euthanasia would not require appeal to novel legal values or principles. That suicide or attempted suicide is no longer a criminal offense in virtually all states indicates an acceptance of individual self-determination in the taking of one's own life analogous to that required for voluntary active euthanasia. The legal prohibition (in most states) of assisting in suicide and the refusal in the law to accept the consent of the victim as a possible justification of homicide are both arguably a result of difficulties in the legal process of establishing the consent of the victim after the fact. If procedures can be designed that clearly establish the voluntariness of the person's request for euthanasia it would under those procedures represent a carefully circumscribed qualification on the legal prohibition of homicide. Nevertheless, some remaining worries about this weakening can be captured in the final potential bad consequence, to which I will now turn.

This final potential bad consequence is the central concern of many opponents of euthanasia and, I believe, is the most serious objection to a legal policy permitting it. According to this "slippery slope" worry, although active euthanasia may be morally permissible in cases in which it is unequivocally voluntary and the patient finds his or her condition unbearable, a legal policy permitting euthanasia would inevitably lead to active euthanasia being performed in many other cases in which it would be morally wrong. To prevent those other wrongful cases of euthanasia we should not permit even morally justified performance of it.

Slippery slope arguments of this form are problematic and difficult to evaluate.[14] From one perspective, they are the last refuge of conservative defenders of the status quo. When all the opponent's objections to the wrongness of euthanasia itself have been met, the opponent then shifts ground and acknowledges both that it is not in itself wrong and that a legal policy which resulted only in its being performed would not be bad. Nevertheless, the opponent maintains, it should still not be permitted because doing so would result in its being performed in other cases in which it is not voluntary and would be wrong. In this argument's most extreme form, permitting euthanasia is the first and fateful step down the slippery slope to Nazism. Once on the slope we will be unable to get off.

Now it cannot be denied that it is possible that permitting euthanasia could have these fateful consequences, but that cannot be enough to warrant prohibiting it if it is otherwise justified. A similar possible slippery slope worry could have been raised to securing competent patients' rights to decide about life support, but recent history shows

---

[14]Frederick Schauer, "Slippery Slopes," *Harvard Law Review* 99 (1985): 361–83; Wibren van der Burg, "The Slippery Slope Argument," *Ethics* 102 (October 1991): 42–65.

such a worry would have been unfounded. It must be relevant how likely it is that we will end with horrendous consequences and an unjustified practice of euthanasia. How likely and widespread would the abuses and unwarranted extensions of permitting it be? By abuses, I mean the performance of euthanasia that fails to satisfy the conditions required for voluntary active euthanasia, for example, if the patient has been subtly pressured to accept it. By unwarranted extensions of policy, I mean later changes in legal policy to permit not just voluntary euthanasia, but also euthanasia in cases in which, for example, it need not be fully voluntary. Opponents of voluntary euthanasia on slippery slope grounds have not provided the data or evidence necessary to turn their speculative concerns into well-grounded likelihoods.

It is at least clear, however, that both the character and likelihood of abuses of a legal policy permitting euthanasia depend in significant part on the procedures put in place to protect against them. I will not try to detail fully what such procedures might be, but will just give some examples of what they might include:

1. The patient should be provided with all relevant information about his or her medical condition, current prognosis, available alternative treatments, and the prognosis of each.
2. Procedures should ensure that the patient's request for euthanasia is stable or enduring (a brief waiting period could be required) and fully voluntary (an advocate for the patient might be appointed to ensure this).
3. All reasonable alternatives must have been explored for improving the patient's quality of life and relieving any pain or suffering.
4. A psychiatric evaluation should ensure that the patient's request is not the result of a treatable psychological impairment such as depression.[15]

These examples of procedural safeguards are all designed to ensure that the patient's choice is fully informed, voluntary, and competent, and so a true exercise of self-determination. Other proposals for euthanasia would restrict its permissibility further—for example,

---

[15]There is evidence that physicians commonly fail to diagnose depression. See Robert I. Misbin, "Physicians Aid in Dying," *NEJM* 325 (1991): 1304–7.

to the terminally ill—a restriction that cannot be supported by self-determination. Such additional restrictions might, however, be justified by concern for limiting potential harms from abuse. At the same time, it is important not to impose procedural or substantive safeguards so restrictive as to make euthanasia impermissible or practically infeasible in a wide range of justified cases.

These examples of procedural safeguards make clear that it is possible to substantially reduce, though not to eliminate, the potential for abuse of a policy permitting voluntary active euthanasia. Any legalization of the practice should be accompanied by a well-considered set of procedural safeguards together with an ongoing evaluation of its use. Introducing euthanasia into only a few states could be a form of carefully limited and controlled social experiment that would give us evidence about the benefits and harms of the practice. Even then firm and uncontroversial data may remain elusive, as the continuing controversy over what has taken place in the Netherlands in recent years indicates.[16]

The Slip into Nonvoluntary Active Euthanasia

While I believe slippery slope worries can largely be limited by making necessary distinctions both in principle and in practice, one slippery slope concern is legitimate. There is reason to expect that legalization of voluntary active euthanasia might soon be followed by strong pressure to legalize some nonvoluntary euthanasia of incompetent patients unable to express their own wishes. Respecting a person's self-determination and recognizing that continued life is not always of value to a person can support not only voluntary active euthanasia, but some nonvoluntary euthanasia as well. These are the same values that ground competent patients' right to refuse life-sustaining treatment. Recent history here is instructive. In the medical ethics literature, in the courts since Quinlan, and in norms of medical practice, that right has been extended to incompetent patients and exercised by a surrogate who is to decide as the patient would have decided in the circumstances if competent.[17] It has been

---

[16]Richard Fenigsen, "A Case against Dutch Euthanasia," Special Supplement, *Hastings Center Report* 19, no. 1 (1989): 22–30.

[17]Allen E. Buchanan and Dan W. Brock, *Deciding for Others: The Ethics of Surrogate Decisionmaking* (Cambridge: Cambridge University Press, 1989).

held unreasonable to continue life-sustaining treatment that the patient would not have wanted just because the patient now lacks the capacity to tell us that. Life-sustaining treatment for incompetent patients is today frequently forgone on the basis of a surrogate's decision, or less frequently on the basis of an advance directive executed by the patient while still competent. The very same logic that has extended the right to refuse life-sustaining treatment from a competent patient to the surrogate of an incompetent patient (acting with or without a formal advance directive from the patient) may well extend the scope of active euthanasia. The argument will be, Why continue to force unwanted life on patients just because they have now lost the capacity to request euthanasia from us?

A related phenomenon may reinforce this slippery slope concern. In the Netherlands, what the courts have sanctioned has been clearly restricted to voluntary euthanasia. In itself, this serves as some evidence that permitting it need not lead to permitting the nonvoluntary variety. There is some indication, however, that for many Dutch physicians euthanasia is no longer viewed as a special action, set apart from their usual practice and restricted only to competent persons.[18] Instead, it is seen as one end of a spectrum of caring for dying patients. When viewed in this way it will be difficult to deny euthanasia to a patient for whom it is seen as the best or most appropriate form of care simply because that patient is now incompetent and cannot request it.

Even if voluntary active euthanasia should slip into nonvoluntary active euthanasia, with surrogates acting for incompetent patients, the ethical evaluation is more complex than many opponents of euthanasia allow. Just as in the case of surrogates' decisions to forgo life-sustaining treatment for incompetent patients, so also surrogates' decisions to request euthanasia for incompetent persons would often accurately reflect what the incompetent person would have wanted and would deny the person nothing that he or she would have considered worth having. Making nonvoluntary active euthanasia legally permissible, however, would greatly enlarge the number of patients on whom it might be performed and substantially enlarge the potential for misuse and abuse. As noted above, frail and debilitated elderly people, often demented or otherwise incompetent and thereby

[18]Van der Maas et al., "Euthanasia and Other Medical Decisions."

unable to defend and assert their own interests, may be especially vulnerable to unwanted euthanasia.

For some people, this risk is more than sufficient reason to oppose the legalization of voluntary euthanasia. But while we should in general be cautious about inferring much from the experience in the Netherlands to what our own experience in the United States might be, there may be one important lesson that we can learn from them. One commentator has noted that in the Netherlands families of incompetent patients have less authority than do families in the United States to act as surrogates for incompetent patients in making decisions to forgo life-sustaining treatment.[19] From the Dutch perspective, it may be we in the United States who are already on the slippery slope in having given surrogates broad authority to forgo life sustaining treatment for incompetent persons. In this view, the more important moral divide, and the more important with regard to potential for abuse, is not between forgoing life-sustaining treatment and euthanasia, but instead between voluntary and nonvoluntary performance of either. If this is correct, then the more important issue is ensuring the appropriate principles and procedural safeguards for the exercise of decisionmaking authority by surrogates for incompetent persons in all decisions at the end of life. This may be the correct response to slippery slope worries about euthanasia.

I have cited both good and bad consequences that have been thought likely from a policy change permitting voluntary active euthanasia, and have tried to evaluate their likelihood and relative importance. Nevertheless, as I noted earlier, reasonable disagreement remains both about the consequences of permitting euthanasia and about which of these consequences are more important. The depth and strength of public and professional debate about whether, all things considered, permitting euthanasia would be desirable or undesirable reflects these disagreements. While my own view is that the balance of considerations supports permitting the practice, my principal purpose here has been to clarify the main issues.

---

[19]Margaret P. Battin, "Seven Caveats Concerning the Discussion of Euthanasia in Holland," *American Philosophical Association Newsletter on Philosophy and Medicine* 89, no. 2 (1990).

For Further Reflection

1. What does Brock mean by "individual self-determination" and "individual well-being"?

2. How does Brock answer the charge that euthanasia is the deliberate killing of an innocent person and therefore should be prohibited?

3. Why does Brock think that the distinction between killing and allowing to die is confused? Do you think the distinction is plausible?

4. According to Brock, what are the potential good consequences of permitting euthanasia? What are the potential bad consequences?

5. How does Brock address slippery slope arguments against euthanasia?

The Wrongfulness of Euthanasia

J. GAY-WILLIAMS

In this reading, J. Gay-Williams argues that intentionally taking the life of a hopelessly ill person is inherently wrong because the action conflicts with natural law, our "natural inclination to continue living." Furthermore, such a practice is opposed to our own self-interest and is a risky step on a slippery slope leading to widespread abuse.

My impression is that euthanasia—the idea, if not the practice—is slowly gaining acceptance within our society. Cynics might attrib-

---

ute this to an increasing tendency to devalue human life, but I do not believe this is the major factor. The acceptance is much more likely to be the result of unthinking sympathy and benevolence. Well-publicized, tragic stories like that of Karen Quinlan elicit from us deep feelings of compassion. We think to ourselves, "She and her family would be better off if she were dead." It is an easy step from this very human response to the view that if someone (and others) would be better off dead, then it might be all right to kill that person.[1] Although I respect the compassion that leads to this conclusion, I believe the conclusion is wrong. I want to show that euthanasia is wrong. It is inherently wrong, but it is also wrong judged from the standpoints of self-interest and of practical effects.

Before presenting my arguments to support this claim, it would be well to define "euthanasia." An essential aspect of euthanasia is that it involves taking a human life, either one's own or that of another. Also, the person whose life is taken must be someone who is believed to be suffering from some disease or injury from which recovery cannot reasonably be expected. Finally, the action must be deliberate and intentional. Thus, euthanasia is intentionally taking the life of a presumably hopeless person. Whether the life is one's own or that of another, the taking of it is still euthanasia.

It is important to be clear about the deliberate and intentional aspect of the killing. If a hopeless person is given an injection of the wrong drug by mistake and this causes his death, this is wrongful killing but not euthanasia. The killing cannot be the result of accident. Furthermore, if the person is given an injection of a drug that is believed to be necessary to treat his disease or better his condition and the person dies as a result, then this is neither wrongful killing nor euthanasia. The intention was to make the patient well, not kill him. Similarly, when a patient's condition is such that it is not reasonable to hope that any medical procedures or treatments will save his life, a failure to implement the procedures or treatments is not euthanasia. If the person dies, this will be as a result of his injuries or disease and not because of his failure to receive treatment.

The failure to continue treatment after it has been realized that

---

[1] For a sophisticated defense of this position see Philippa Foot, "Euthanasia," *Philosophy and Public Affairs,* vol. 6 (1977), pp. 85–112. Foot does not endorse the radical conclusion that euthanasia, voluntary and involuntary, is always right.

the patient has little chance of benefiting from it has been characterized by some as "passive euthanasia." This phrase is misleading and mistaken.[2] In such cases, the person involved is not killed (the first essential aspect of euthanasia), nor is the death of the person intended by the withholding of additional treatment (the third essential aspect of euthanasia). The aim may be to spare the person additional and unjustifiable pain, to save him from the indignities of hopeless manipulations, and to avoid increasing the financial and emotional burden on his family. When I buy a pencil it is so that I can use it to write, not to contribute to an increase in the gross national product. This may be the unintended consequence of my action, but it is not the aim of my action. So it is with failing to continue the treatment of a dying person. I intend his death no more than I intend to reduce the GNP by not using medical supplies. His is an unintended dying, and so-called "passive euthanasia" is not euthanasia at all.

1. THE ARGUMENT FROM NATURE

Every human being has a natural inclination to continue living. Our reflexes and responses fit us to fight attackers, flee wild animals, and dodge out of the way of trucks. In our daily lives we exercise the caution and care necessary to protect ourselves. Our bodies are similarly structured for survival right down to the molecular level. When we are cut, our capillaries seal shut, our blood clots, and fibrogen is produced to start the process of healing the wound. When we are invaded by bacteria, antibodies are produced to fight against the alien organisms, and their remains are swept out of the body by special cells designed for clean-up work.

Euthanasia does violence to this natural goal of survival. It is literally acting against nature because all the processes of nature are bent towards the end of bodily survival. Euthanasia defeats these subtle mechanisms in a way that, in a particular case, disease and injury might not.

It is possible, but not necessary, to make an appeal to revealed

---

[2]James Rachels rejects the distinction between active and passive euthanasia as morally irrelevant in his "Active and Passive Euthanasia," *New England Journal of Medicine,* vol. 292, pp. 78–80. But see the criticism by Foot, pp. 100–103.

religion in this connection.[3] Man as trustee of his body acts against God, its rightful possessor, when he takes his own life. He also violates the commandment to hold life sacred and never to take it without just and compelling cause. But since this appeal will persuade only those who are prepared to accept that religion has access to revealed truths, I shall not employ this line of argument.

It is enough, I believe, to recognize that the organization of the human body and our patterns of behavioral responses make the continuation of life a natural goal. By reason alone, then, we can recognize that euthanasia sets us against our own nature.[4] Furthermore, in doing so, euthanasia does violence to our dignity. Our dignity comes from seeking our ends. When one of our goals is survival, and actions are taken that eliminate that goal, then our natural dignity suffers. Unlike animals, we are conscious through reason of our nature and our ends. Euthanasia involves acting as if this dual nature—inclination towards survival and awareness of this as an end—did not exist. Thus, euthanasia denies our basic human character and requires that we regard ourselves or others as something less than fully human.

2. THE ARGUMENT FROM SELF-INTEREST

The above arguments are, I believe, sufficient to show that euthanasia is inherently wrong. But there are reasons for considering it wrong when judged by standards other than reason. Because death is final and irreversible, euthanasia contains within it the possibility that we will work against our own interest if we practice it or allow it to be practiced on us.

Contemporary medicine has high standards of excellence and a proven record of accomplishment, but it does not possess perfect and complete knowledge. A mistaken diagnosis is possible, and so is a mistaken prognosis. Consequently, we may believe that we are dying of a disease when, as a matter of fact, we may not be. We may think that we have no hope of recovery when, as a matter of

---

[3]For a defense of this view see J. V. Sullivan, "The Immorality of Euthanasia," in *Beneficent Euthanasia,* ed. Marvin Kohl (Buffalo, N.Y.: Prometheus Books, 1975), pp. 34–44.

[4]This point is made by Ray V. McIntyre in "Voluntary Euthanasia: The Ultimate Perversion," *Medical Counterpoint,* vol. 2, pp. 26–29.

fact, our chances are quite good. In such circumstances, if euthanasia were permitted, we would die needlessly. Death is final and the chance of error too great to approve the practice of euthanasia.

Also, there is always the possibility that an experimental procedure or a hitherto untried technique will pull us through. We should at least keep this option open, but euthanasia closes it off. Furthermore, spontaneous remission does occur in many cases. For no apparent reason, a patient simply recovers when those all around him, including his physicians, expected him to die. Euthanasia would just guarantee their expectations and leave no room for the "miraculous" recoveries that frequently occur.

Finally, knowing that we can take our life at any time (or ask another to take it) might well incline us to give up too easily. The will to live is strong in all of us, but it can be weakened by pain and suffering and feelings of hopelessness. If during a bad time we allow ourselves to be killed, we never have a chance to reconsider. Recovery from a serious illness requires that we fight for it, and anything that weakens our determination by suggesting that there is an easy way out is ultimately against our own interest. Also, we may be inclined towards euthanasia because of our concern for others. If we see our sickness and suffering as an emotional and financial burden on our family, we may feel that to leave our life is to make their lives easier.[5] The very presence of the possibility of euthanasia may keep us from surviving when we might.

3. THE ARGUMENT FROM PRACTICAL EFFECTS

Doctors and nurses are, for the most part, totally committed to saving lives. A life lost is, for them, almost a personal failure, an insult to their skills and knowledge. Euthanasia as a practice might well alter this. It could have a corrupting influence so that in any case that is severe doctors and nurses might not try hard enough to save the patient. They might decide that the patient would simply be "better off dead" and take the steps necessary to make that come about. This attitude could then carry over to their dealings with patients less seriously ill. The result would be an overall decline in the quality of medical care.

[5]See McIntyre, p. 28.

Finally, euthanasia as a policy is a slippery slope. A person apparently hopelessly ill may be allowed to take his own life. Then he may be permitted to deputize others to do it for him should he no longer be able to act. The judgment of others then becomes the ruling factor. Already at this point euthanasia is not personal and voluntary, for others are acting "on behalf of" the patient as they see fit. This may well incline them to act on behalf of other patients who have not authorized them to exercise their judgment. It is only a short step, then, from voluntary euthanasia (self-inflicted or authorized), to directed euthanasia administered to a patient who has given no authorization, to involuntary euthanasia conducted as part of a social policy.[6] Recently many psychiatrists and sociologists have argued that we define as "mental illness" those forms of behavior that we disapprove of.[7] This gives us license then to lock up those who display the behavior. The category of the "hopelessly ill" provides the possibility of even worse abuse. Embedded in a social policy, it would give society or its representatives the authority to eliminate all those who might be considered too "ill" to function normally any longer. The dangers of euthanasia are too great to all to run the risk of approving it in any form. The first slippery step may well lead to a serious and harmful fall.

I hope that I have succeeded in showing why the benevolence that inclines us to give approval of euthanasia is misplaced. Euthanasia is inherently wrong because it violates the nature and dignity of human beings. But even those who are not convinced by this must be persuaded that the potential personal and social dangers inherent in euthanasia are sufficient to forbid our approving it either as a personal practice or as a public policy.

Suffering is surely a terrible thing, and we have a clear duty to comfort those in need and to ease their suffering when we can. But suffering is also a natural part of life with values for the individual and for others that we should not overlook. We may legitimately seek for others and for ourselves an easeful death, as Arthur Dyck has pointed out.[8] Euthanasia, however, is not just an easeful

---

[6]See Sullivan, "Immorality of Euthanasia," pp. 34–44, for a fuller argument in support of this view.

[7]See, for example, Thomas S. Szasz, *The Myth of Mental Illness,* rev. ed. (New York: Harper & Row, 1974).

[8]Arthur Dyck, "Beneficent Euthanasia and Benemortasia," Kohl, op. cit., pp. 117–129.

death. It is a wrongful death. Euthanasia is not just dying. It is killing.

For Further Reflection

1. How does Gay-Williams define euthanasia?
2. What is Gay-Williams's "argument from nature"? Do you think it plausible?
3. What is the "argument from self-interest"?
4. What are the practical effects of euthanasia that Gay-Williams fears?
5. Which of Gay-Williams's arguments is the strongest? Why do you think so? Do you believe the argument successfully establishes its conclusion? Why or why not?

Active and Passive Euthanasia

JAMES RACHELS

Philosopher James Rachels (1941–2003) was a professor at the University of Alabama at Birmingham for over a quarter century. His writings include *The End of Life: Euthanasia and Morality* (1986), *The Elements of Moral Philosophy* (1986; 5th ed., 2006), and the following essay, which is one of the most frequently reprinted articles in ethics. In this reading, Rachels argues that the traditional distinction between active and passive euthanasia is indefensible, that "there is really no moral difference between the two, considered in themselves."

"Active and Passive Euthanasia" by James Rachels from *The New England Journal of Medicine*. Copyright © 1975 by the Massachusetts Medical Society. All rights reserved.

The distinction between active and passive euthanasia is thought to he crucial for medical ethics. The idea is that it is permissible, at least in some cases, to withhold treatment and allow a patient to die, but it is never permissible to take any direct action designed to kill the patient. This doctrine seems to be accepted by most doctors, and it is endorsed in a statement adopted by the House of Delegates of the American Medical Association on December 4, 1973:

> The intentional termination of the life of one human being by another—mercy killing—is contrary to that for which the medical profession stands and is contrary to the policy of the American Medical Association.
> The cessation of the employment of extraordinary means to prolong the life of the body when there is irrefutable evidence that biological death is imminent is the decision of the patient and/or his immediate family. The advice and judgment of the physician should be freely available to the patient and/or his immediate family.

However, a strong case can be made against this doctrine. In what follows I will set out some of the relevant arguments, and urge doctors to reconsider their views on this matter.

To begin with a familiar type of situation, a patient who is dying of incurable cancer of the throat is in terrible pain, which can no longer be satisfactorily alleviated. He is certain to die within a few days, even if present treatment is continued, but he does not want to go on living for those days since the pain is unbearable. So he asks the doctor for an end to it, and his family joins in the request.

Suppose the doctor agrees to withhold treatment, as the conventional doctrine says he may. The justification for his doing so is that the patient is in terrible agony, and since he is going to die anyway, it would be wrong to prolong his suffering needlessly. But now notice this. If one simply withholds treatment, it may take the patient longer to die, and so he may suffer more than he would if more direct action were taken and a lethal injection given. This fact provides strong reason for thinking that, once the initial decision not to prolong his agony has been made, active euthanasia is actually preferable to passive euthanasia, rather than the reverse. To say otherwise is to endorse the option that leads to more suffering rather than less, and is contrary to the humanitarian impulse that prompts the decision not to prolong his life in the first place.

Part of my point is that the process of being "allowed to die" can be relatively slow and painful, whereas being given a lethal injection is relatively quick and painless. Let me give a different sort of example. In the United States about one in 600 babies is born with Down's syndrome. Most of these babies are otherwise healthy—that is, with only the usual pediatric care, they will proceed to an otherwise normal infancy. Some, however, are born with congenital defects such as intestinal obstructions that require operations if they are to live. Sometimes, the parents and the doctor will decide not to operate, and let the infant die. Anthony Shaw describes what happens then:

> . . . When surgery is denied [the doctor] must try to keep the infant from suffering while natural forces sap the baby's life away. As a surgeon whose natural inclination is to use the scalpel to fight off death, standing by and watching a salvageable baby die is the most emotionally exhausting experience I know. It is easy at a conference, in a theoretical discussion, to decide that such infants should be allowed to die. It is altogether different to stand by in the nursery and watch as dehydration and infection wither a tiny being over hours and days. This is a terrible ordeal for me and the hospital staff—much more so than for the parents who never set foot in the nursery.*

I can understand why some people are opposed to all euthanasia, and insist that such infants must be allowed to live. I think I can also understand why other people favor destroying these babies quickly and painlessly. But why should anyone favor letting "dehydration and infection wither a tiny being over hours and days"? The doctrine that says that a baby may be allowed to dehydrate and wither, but may not be given an injection that would end its life without suffering, seems so patently cruel as to require no further refutation. The strong language is not intended to offend, but only to put the point in the clearest possible way.

My second argument is that the conventional doctrine leads to decisions concerning life and death made on irrelevant grounds.

Consider again the case of the infants with Down's syndrome who need operations for congenital defects unrelated to the syn-

---

*Shaw A: 'Doctor, Do We Have a Choice?' *The New York Times Magazine,* January 30, 1972. p. 54.

drome to live. Sometimes, there is no operation, and the baby dies, but when there is no such defect, the baby lives on. Now, an operation such as that to remove an intestinal obstruction is not prohibitively difficult. The reason why such operations are not performed in these cases is, clearly, that the child has Down's syndrome and the parents and doctor judge that because of that fact it is better for the child to die.

But notice that this situation is absurd, no matter what view one takes of the lives and potentials of such babies. If the life of such an infant is worth preserving, what does it matter if it needs a simple operation? Or, if one thinks it better that such a baby should not live on, what difference does it make that it happens to have an unobstructed intestinal tract? In either case, the matter of life and death is being decided on irrelevant grounds. It is the Down's syndrome, and not the intestines, that is the issue. The matter should be decided, if at all, on that basis, and not be allowed to depend on the essentially irrelevant question of whether the intestinal tract is blocked.

What makes this situation possible, of course, is the idea that when there is an intestinal blockage, one can "let the baby die," but when there is no such defect there is nothing that can be done, for one must not "kill" it. The fact that this idea leads to such results as deciding life or death on irrelevant grounds is another good reason why the doctrine should be rejected.

One reason why so many people think that there is an important moral difference between active and passive euthanasia is that they think killing someone is morally worse than letting someone die. But is it? Is killing, in itself, worse than letting die? To investigate this issue, two cases may be considered that are exactly alike except that one involves killing whereas the other involves letting someone die. Then, it can be asked whether this difference makes any difference to the moral assessments. It is important that the cases be exactly alike, except for this one difference, since otherwise one cannot be confident that it is this difference and not some other that accounts for any variation in the assessments of the two cases. So, let us consider this pair of cases:

In the first, Smith stands to gain a large inheritance if anything should happen to his six-year-old cousin. One evening while the child is taking his bath. Smith sneaks into the bathroom and drowns the child, and then arranges things so that it will look like an accident.

In the second, Jones also stands to gain if anything should happen to his six-year-old cousin. Like Smith, Jones sneaks in planning to drown the child in his bath. However, just as he enters the bathroom Jones sees the child slip and hit his head, and fall face down in the water. Jones is delighted; he stands by, ready to push the child's head back under if it is necessary, but it is not necessary. With only a little thrashing about, the child drowns all by himself, "accidentally," as Jones watches and does nothing.

Now Smith killed the child, whereas Jones "merely" let the child die. That is the only difference between them. Did either man behave better, from a moral point of view? If the difference between killing and letting die were in itself a morally important matter, one should say that Jones's behavior was less reprehensible than Smith's. But does one really want to say that? I think not. In the first place, both men acted from the same motive, personal gain, and both had exactly the same end in view when they acted. It may be inferred from Smith's conduct that he is a bad man, although that judgment may be withdrawn or modified if certain further facts are learned about him—for example, that he is mentally deranged. But would not the very same thing be inferred about Jones from his conduct? And would not the same further considerations also be relevant to any modification of this judgment? Moreover, suppose Jones pleaded, in his own defense, "After all, I didn't do anything except just stand there and watch the child drown. I didn't kill him; I only let him die." Again, if letting die were in itself less bad than killing, this defense should have at least some weight. But it does not. Such a "defense" can only be regarded as a grotesque perversion of moral reasoning. Morally speaking, it is no defense at all.

Now, it may be pointed out, quite properly, that the cases of euthanasia with which doctors are concerned are not like this at all. They do not involve personal gain or the destruction of normal healthy children. Doctors are concerned only with cases in which the patient's life is of no further use to him, or in which the patient's life has become or will soon become a terrible burden. However, the point is the same in these cases: the bare difference between killing and letting die does not, in itself, make a moral difference. If a doctor lets a patient die, for humane reasons, he is in the same moral position as if he had given the patient a lethal injection for humane reasons. If his decision was wrong—if, for example, the patient's illness was in fact curable—the decision would be equally regrettable no matter which method was used to carry it out. And if the doctor's decision was the right one, the method used is not in itself important.

The AMA policy statement isolates the crucial issue very well; the crucial issue is "the intentional termination of the life of one human being by another." But after identifying this issue, and forbidding "mercy killing," the statement goes on to deny that the cessation of treatment is the intentional termination of a life. This is where the mistake comes in, for what is the cessation of treatment, in these circumstances, if it is not "the intentional termination of the life of one human being by another"? Of course it is exactly that, and if it were not, there would be no point to it.

Many people will find this judgment hard to accept. One reason, I think, is that it is very easy to conflate the question of whether killing is, in itself, worse than letting die, with the very different question of whether most actual cases of killing are more reprehensible than most actual cases of letting die. Most actual cases of killing are clearly terrible (think, for example, of all the murders reported in the newspapers), and one hears of such cases every day. On the other hand, one hardly ever hears of a case of letting die, except for the actions of doctors who are motivated by humanitarian reasons. So one learns to think of killing in a much worse light than of letting die. But this does not mean that there is something about killing that makes it in itself worse than letting die, for it is not the bare difference between killing and letting die that makes the difference in these cases. Rather, the other factors—the murderer's motive of personal gain, for example, contrasted with the doctor's humanitarian motivation—account for different reactions to the different cases.

I have argued that killing is not in itself any worse than letting die: if my contention is right, it follows that active euthanasia is not any worse than passive euthanasia. What arguments can be given on the other side? The most common, I believe, is the following:

"The important difference between active and passive euthanasia is that, in passive euthanasia, the doctor does not do anything to bring about the patient's death. The doctor does nothing, and the patient dies of whatever ills already afflict him. In active euthanasia, however, the doctor does something to bring about the patient's death: he kills him. The doctor who gives the patient with cancer a lethal injection has himself caused his patient's death: whereas if he merely ceases treatment, the cancer is the cause of the death."

A number of points need to be made here. The first is that it is not exactly correct to say that in passive euthanasia the doctor does nothing, for he does do one thing that is very important: he lets the patient die. "Letting someone die" is certainly different, in some respects, from other types of action—mainly in that it is a kind of action that one may perform by way of not performing certain other actions. For example, one may let a patient die by way of not giving medication, just as one may insult someone by way of not shaking his hand. But for any purpose of moral assessment, it is a type of action nonetheless. The decision to let a patient die is subject to moral appraisal in the same way that a decision to kill him would be subject to moral appraisal: it may be assessed as wise or unwise, compassionate or sadistic, right or wrong. If a doctor deliberately let a patient die who was suffering from a routinely curable illness, the doctor would certainly be to blame for what he had done, just as he would be to blame if he had needlessly killed the patient. Charges against him would then be appropriate. If so, it would be no defense at all for him to insist that he didn't "do anything." He would have done something very serious indeed, for he let his patient die.

Fixing the cause of death may be very important from a legal point of view, for it may determine whether criminal charges are brought against the doctor. But I do not think that this notion can be used to show a moral difference between active and passive euthanasia. The reason why it is considered bad to be the cause of someone's death is that death is regarded as a great evil—and so it is. However, if it has been decided that euthanasia—even passive euthanasia—is desirable in a given case, it has also been decided that in this instance death is no greater an evil than the patient's continued existence. And if this is true, the usual reason for not wanting to be the cause of someone's death simply does not apply.

Finally, doctors may think that all of this is only of academic interest—the sort of thing that philosophers may worry about but that has no practical bearing on their own work. After all, doctors must be concerned about the legal consequences of what they do, and active euthanasia is clearly forbidden by the law. But even so, doctors should also be concerned with the fact that the law is forcing upon them a moral doctrine that may well be indefensible, and has a considerable effect on their practices. Of course, most doctors are not now in the position of being coerced in this matter, for they do not regard themselves as merely going along with what the law requires. Rather, in statements such as the AMA policy statement that I have quoted, they are endorsing this doctrine as a central point of medical ethics. In that statement, active euthanasia is condemned not merely as illegal but as "contrary to that for which the medical profession stands," whereas passive euthanasia is approved. However, the preceding considerations suggest that there is really no moral difference between the two, considered in themselves (there may be important moral differences in some cases in their *consequences,* but, as I pointed out, these differences may make active euthanasia, and not passive euthanasia, the morally preferable option). So, whereas doctors may have to discriminate between active and passive euthanasia to satisfy the law, they should not do any more than that. In particular, they should not give the distinction any added authority and weight by writing it into official statements of medical ethics.

For Further Reflection

1. Traditionally, how has the distinction been drawn between active and passive euthanasia?
2. According to Rachels, how might active euthanasia lead to less suffering than passive euthanasia?
3. According to Rachels, how does the active/passive distinction (the "conventional doctrine") lead to "decisions concerning life and death made on irrelevant grounds"?
4. What is the point of Rachels's example about Smith and Jones and the drowning baby?
5. Do you believe there is a meaningful difference between active and passive euthanasia? Explain.

Further Readings for Chapter 13

Beauchamp, Tom L., ed. *Intending Death: The Ethics of Assisted Suicide and Euthanasia.* Upper Saddle River, N.J.: Prentice-Hall, 1996.

Foot, Philippa. "Euthanasia." *Philosophy & Public Affairs,* vol. 6, no. 2, 1977.

Glannon, Walter. *Biomedical Ethics.* New York: Oxford University Press, 2005.

Munson, Ronald. *Intervention and Reflection.* Belmont, Calif.: Wadsworth, 2004.

Perlin, Seymour, ed. *A Handbook for the Study of Suicide.* New York: Oxford University Press, 1975.

Steinbock, Bonnie, and Alastair Norcross, eds. *Killing and Letting Die,* 2nd ed. New York: Fordham University Press, 1994.

CHAPTER 14

Our Duties to Animals

Every minute of the day, twenty-four hours a day, one hundred animals are killed in laboratories in the United States. Fifty million animals used in experiments are put to death each year. Some die during testing of industrial and cosmetic products; some are killed after being force fed or after being tested for pharmaceutical drugs. Product testing on animals is required by government before the products are allowed for use by human beings.

Legal requirements that animals be anesthetized are circumvented in many experiments. Recently, at a major university, baboons were strapped down in boxlike vises and had specially designed helmets cemented to their skulls. Then a pneumatic device delivered calibrated blows to the helmet to determine its strength. The blows continued until the baboon's skull was fractured and the animal was brain damaged. Dogs are driven insane with electric shocks so that scientists can study the effects of insanity. Cats are deprived of sleep until they die. Primates have been restrained for months in steel chairs allowing no movement, and elephants have been given LSD to study aggression. Legs have been cut off mice to study how they walk on the stumps, and polar bears have been drowned in vats of crude oil to study the effect of oil spills in polar regions.

Kittens have been blinded, castrated, and rendered deaf so researchers could see what effect these incapacities would have on their sexual development. Civet cats are placed in small cages in dark rooms where the temperature is 110° F and confined there until they die. The musk that is scraped from their genitals once a day for as long as they can survive makes the scent of perfume last a bit longer after each application.

Neither is all well down on the farm. Factory farming with high-tech machinery has replaced free-range agriculture. Farmer McDon-

ald doesn't visit his hens in barns to pick an egg from the comfortable nest. Now, as soon as chicks are hatched, they are placed in small
cages. Between five and nine chickens are pressed together in cages
about 18 inches by 10 inches where they cannot move around, with
thin wire-mesh floors that hurt their feet. They are painfully debeaked
so that they cannot attack each other in these unnatural quarters. In
other chicken factories, the chickens are hung by their feet from con-
veyor belts that transport them through automatic throat-slicing
machines. Three billion chickens are killed in the United States each
year. Likewise, pigs and veal calves are kept in pens so small they
cannot move or turn around and develop muscles. They are separated from their mothers so they cannot be suckled and are fed a diet
low in iron so they will produce very tender meat.

Do animals have rights? Given the practices just described, do
we have a responsibility to improve our behavior toward the animal kingdom? No one disagrees that we should not cause animals
unnecessary suffering, but those who defend animal factories and
animal experimentation argue that human need justifies these practices. On the other side of the controversy, animal rights advocates
argue that animals should be accorded equal consideration with
humans—that their specific needs should be taken seriously. If this
were done, we would become vegetarians, cease to use leather,
and cease all (or almost all) animal experimentation.

Our first reading is George Orwell's description of his shooting
an elephant in Burma, which he compares with the essence of
imperialism. Our second reading is Immanuel Kant's argument that
we have no direct duties to animals, since they are not persons. In
our third reading, Peter Singer, the torchbearer of animal liberation,
argues that animals should be treated with equal consideration as
human beings. Singer says that if a nonhuman and a human are
suffering, and we have only enough painkiller for one, it is not
clear who should receive the painkiller. Carl Cohen argues in our
final reading that the idea of rights does not apply to animals since
"rights" is a concept appropriate only to members of the moral community and animals cannot make moral decisions. Humans are of
far greater value than animals. Cohen readily admits that gratuitous
suffering should be prohibited, but animal experimentation is
needed to ameliorate human suffering, and, as such, it is justified.

Shooting an Elephant

GEORGE ORWELL

George Orwell, pseudonym of Eric Arthur Blair (1903–
1950), novelist and essayist, was born in India and served
in the Indian imperial police. He rejected the imperialism
connected with his position and went to live as a beggar
in the East End of London. This experience became the
subject of his book *Down and Out in Paris and London*
(1933). His best-known works are *Animal Farm* (1945) and
Nineteen Eighty-Four (1949), a pessimistic satire about
future political tyranny.

This essay, written in the 1930s, is based on Orwell's
experience in the imperial police in Burma.

In Moulmein, in Lower Burma, I was hated by large numbers of
people—the only time in my life that I have been important enough
for this to happen to me. I was sub-divisional police officer of the
town, and in an aimless, petty kind of way anti-European feeling
was very bitter. No one had the guts to raise a riot, but if a European woman went through the bazaars alone somebody would
probably spit betel juice over her dress. As a police officer I was
an obvious target and was baited whenever it seemed safe to do
so. When a nimble Burman tripped me up on the football field and
the referee (another Burman) looked the other way, the crowd
yelled with hideous laughter. This happened more than once. In
the end the sneering yellow faces of young men that met me everywhere, the insults hooted after me when I was at a safe distance,
got badly on my nerves. The young Buddhist priests were the worst
of all. There were several thousands of them in the town and none
of them seemed to have anything to do except stand on street corners and jeer at Europeans. All this was perplexing and upsetting.
For at that time I had already made up my mind that imperialism
was an evil thing and the sooner I chucked up my job and got out
of it the better. Theoretically—and secretly, of course—I was all for
the Burmese and all against their oppressors, the British. As for the

job I was doing, I hated it more bitterly than I can perhaps make clear. In a job like that you see the dirty work of Empire at close quarters. The wretched prisoners huddling in the stinking cages of the lock-ups, the grey, cowed faces of the long-term convicts, the scarred buttocks of the men who had been flogged with bamboos— all these oppressed me with an intolerable sense of guilt. But I could get nothing into perspective. I was young and ill-educated and I had had to think out my problems in the utter silence that is imposed on every Englishman in the East. I did not even know that the British Empire is dying, still less did I know that it is a great deal better than the younger empires that are going to supplant it. All I knew was that I was stuck between my hatred of the empire I served and my rage against the evil-spirited little beasts who tried to make my job impossible. With one part of my mind I thought of the British Raj as an unbreakable tyranny, as something clamped down, in *saecula saeculorum,* upon the will of prostrate peoples; with another part I thought that the greatest joy in the world would be to drive a bayonet into a Buddhist priest's guts. Feelings like these are the normal by-products of imperialism; ask any Anglo-Indian official, if you can catch him off duty.

One day something happened which in a roundabout way was enlightening. It was a tiny incident in itself, but it gave me a better glimpse than I had had before of the real nature of imperialism—the real motives for which despotic governments act. Early one morning the sub-inspector at a police station the other end of town rang me up on the 'phone and said that an elephant was ravaging the bazaar. Would I please come and do something about it? I did not know what I could do, but I wanted to see what was happening and I got on to a pony and started out. I took my rifle, an old .44 Winchester and much too small to kill an elephant, but I thought the noise might be useful *in terrorem.* Various Burmans stopped me on the way and told me about the elephant's doings. It was not, of course, a wild elephant, but a tame one which had gone "must." It had been chained up, as tame elephants always are when their attack of "must" is due, but on the previous night it had broken its chain and escaped. Its mahout, the only person who could manage it when it was in that state, had set out in pursuit, but had taken the wrong direction and was now twelve hours' journey away, and in the morning the elephant had suddenly reappeared in the town. The Burmese population had no weapons and were quite helpless against it. It had already destroyed somebody's bamboo hut, killed a cow and raided some fruit-stalls and devoured the stock; also it had met the municipal rubbish van and, when the driver jumped out and took to his heels, had turned the van over and inflicted violences upon it.

The Burmese sub-inspector and some Indian constables were waiting for me in the quarter where the elephant had been seen. It was a very poor quarter, a labyrinth of squalid bamboo huts, thatched with palm-leaf, winding all over a steep hillside. I remember that it was a cloudy, stuffy morning at the beginning of the rains. We began questioning the people as to where the elephant had gone and, as usual, failed to get any definite information. That is invariably the case in the East; a story always sounds clear enough at a distance, but the nearer you get to the scene of events the vaguer it becomes. Some of the people said that the elephant had gone in one direction, some said that he had gone in another, some professed not even to have heard of any elephant. I had almost made up my mind that the whole story was a pack of lies, when we heard yells a little distance away. There was a loud, scandalized cry of "Go away, child! Go away this instant!" and an old woman with a switch in her hand came around the corner of a hut, violently shooing away a crowd of naked children. Some more women followed, clicking their tongues and exclaiming; evidently there was something that the children ought not to have seen. I rounded the hut and saw a man's dead body sprawling in the mud. He was an Indian, a black Dravidian coolie, almost naked, and he could not have been dead many minutes. The people said that the elephant had come suddenly upon him round the corner of the hut, caught him with its trunk, put its foot on his back and ground him into the earth. This was the rainy season and the ground was soft, and his face had scored a trench a foot deep and a couple of yards long. He was lying on his belly with arms crucified and head sharply twisted to one side. His face was coated with mud, the eyes wide open, the teeth bared and grinning with an expression of unendurable agony. (Never tell me, by the way, that the dead look peaceful. Most of the corpses I have seen looked devilish.) The friction of the great beast's foot had stripped the skin from his back as neatly as one skins a rabbit. As soon as I saw the dead man I sent an orderly to a friend's house nearby to borrow an elephant rifle. I had already sent back the pony, not wanting it to go mad with fright and throw me if it smelt the elephant.

The orderly came back in a few minutes with a rifle and five cartridges, and meanwhile some Burmans had arrived and told us that the elephant was in the paddy fields below, only a few hundred yards away. As I started forward practically the whole population of the quarter flocked out of the houses and followed me. They had seen the rifle and were all shouting excitedly that I was going to shoot the elephant. They had not shown much interest in the elephant when he was merely ravaging their homes, but it was different now that he was going to be shot. It was a bit of fun to them, as it would be to an English crowd; besides they wanted the meat. It made me vaguely uneasy. I had no intention of shooting the elephant—I had merely sent for the rifle to defend myself if necessary—and it is always unnerving to have a crowd following you. I marched down the hill, looking and feeling a fool, with the rifle over my shoulder and an evergrowing army of people jostling at my heels. At the bottom, when you got away from the huts, there was a metalled road and beyond that a miry waste of paddy fields a thousand yards across, not yet ploughed but soggy from the first rains and dotted with coarse grass. The elephant was standing eight yards from the road, his left side towards us. He took not the slightest notice of the crowd's approach. He was tearing up bunches of grass, beating them against his knees to clean them and stuffing them into his mouth.

I had halted on the road. As soon as I saw the elephant I knew with perfect certainty that I ought not to shoot him. It is a serious matter to shoot a working elephant—it is comparable to destroying a huge and costly piece of machinery—and obviously one ought not to do it if it can possibly be avoided. And at that distance, peacefully eating, the elephant looked no more dangerous than a cow. I thought then and I think now that his attack of "must" was already passing off; in which case he would merely wander harmlessly about until the mahout came back and caught him. Moreover, I did not in the least want to shoot him. I decided that I would watch him for a little while to make sure that he did not turn savage again, and then go home.

But at that moment I glanced round at the crowd that had followed me. It was an immense crowd, two thousand at the least and growing every minute. It blocked the road for a long distance on either side. I looked at the sea of yellow faces above the garish clothes—faces all happy and excited over this bit of fun, all certain that the elephant was going to be shot. They were watching me as they would watch a conjurer about to perform a trick. They did not like me, but with the magical rifle in my hands I was momentarily worth watching. And suddenly I realized that I should have to shoot the elephant after all. The people expected it of me and I had to do it; I could feel their two thousand wills pressing me forward, irresistibly. And it was at this moment, as I stood there with the rifle in my hands, that I first grasped the hollowness, the futility of the white man's dominion in the East. Here was I, the white man with his gun, standing in front of the unarmed native crowd—seemingly the leading actor of the piece; but in reality I was only an absurd puppet pushed to and fro by the will of those yellow faces behind. I perceived in this moment that when the white man turns tyrant it is his own freedom that he destroys. He becomes a sort of hollow, posing dummy, the conventionalized figure of a sahib. For it is the condition of his rule that he shall spend his life in trying to impress the "natives," and so in every crisis he has got to do what the "natives" expect of him. He wears a mask, and his face grows to fit it. I had got to shoot the elephant. I had committed myself to doing it when I sent for the rifle. A sahib has got to act like a sahib; he has got to appear resolute, to know his own mind and do definite things. To come all that way, rifle in hand, with two thousand people marching at my heels, and then to trail feebly away, having done nothing—no, that was impossible. The crowd would laugh at me. And my whole life, every white man's life in the East, was one long struggle not to be laughed at.

But I did not want to shoot the elephant. I watched him beating his bunch of grass against his knees, with that preoccupied grandmotherly air that elephants have. It seemed to me that it would be murder to shoot him. At that age I was not squeamish about killing animals, but I had never shot an elephant and never wanted to. (Somehow it always seems worse to kill a *large* animal.) Besides, there was the beast's owner to be considered. Alive, the elephant was worth at least a hundred pounds; dead, he would only be worth the value of his tusks, five pounds, possibly. But I had got to act quickly. I turned to some experienced-looking Burmans who had been there when we arrived, and asked them how the elephant had been behaving. They all said the same thing: he took no notice of you if you left him alone, but he might charge if you went too close to him.

It was perfectly clear to me what I ought to do. I ought to walk up to within, say, twenty-five yards of the elephant and test his behavior. If he charged, I could shoot; if he took no notice of me, it would be safe to leave him until the mahout came back. But also I knew that I was going to do no such thing. I was a poor shot with a rifle and the ground was soft mud into which one would sink at every step. If the elephant charged and I missed him, I should have about as much chance as a toad under a steamroller. But even then I was not thinking particularly of my own skin, only of the watchful yellow faces behind. For at that moment, with the crowd watching me, I was not afraid in the ordinary sense, as I would have been if I had been alone. A white man mustn't be frightened in front of "natives"; and so, in general, he isn't frightened. The sole thought in my mind was that if anything went wrong those two thousand Burmans would see me pursued, caught, trampled on and reduced to a grinning corpse like that Indian up the hill. And if that happened it was quite probable that some of them would laugh. That would never do. There was only one alternative. I shoved the cartridges into the magazine and lay down on the road to get a better aim.

The crowd grew very still, and a deep, low, happy sigh, as of people who see the theatre curtain go up at last, breathed from innumerable throats. They were going to have their bit of fun after all. The rifle was a beautiful German thing with cross-hair sights. I did not then know that in shooting an elephant one would shoot to cut an imaginary bar running from ear-hole to ear-hole. I ought, therefore, as the elephant was sideways on, to have aimed straight at his ear-hole; actually I aimed several inches in front of this, thinking the brain would be further forward.

When I pulled the trigger I did not hear the bang or feel the kick—one never does when a shot goes home—but I heard the devilish roar of glee that went up from the crowd. In that instant, in too short a time, one would have thought, even for the bullet to get there, a mysterious, terrible change had come over the elephant. He neither stirred nor fell, but every line of his body had altered. He looked suddenly stricken, shrunken, immensely old, as though the frightful impact of the bullet had paralysed him without knocking him down. At last, after what seemed a long time— it might have been five seconds, I dare say—he sagged flabbily to his knees. His mouth slobbered. An enormous senility seemed to have settled upon him. One could have imagined him thousands of years old. I fired again into the same spot. At the second shot he did not collapse but climbed with desperate slowness to his feet and stood weakly upright, with legs sagging and head drooping. I fired a third time. That was the shot that did for him. You could see the agony of it jolt his whole body and knock the last remnant of strength from his legs. But in falling he seemed for a moment to rise, for as his hind legs collapsed beneath him he seemed to tower upward like a huge rock toppling, his trunk reaching skywards like a tree. He trumpeted, for the first and only time. And then down he came, his belly towards me, with a crash that seemed to shake the ground even where I lay.

I got up. The Burmans were already racing past me across the mud. It was obvious that the elephant would never rise again, but he was not dead. He was breathing very rhythmically with long rattling gasps, his great mound of a side painfully rising and falling. His mouth was wide open—I could see far down into caverns of pale pink throat. I waited a long time for him to die, but his breathing did not weaken. Finally I fired my two remaining shots into the spot where I thought his heart must be. The thick blood welled out of him like red velvet, but still he did not die. His body did not even jerk when the shots hit him, the tortured breathing continued without a pause. He was dying, very slowly and in great agony, but in some world remote from me where not even a bullet could damage him further. I felt that I had got to put an end to that dreadful noise. It seemed dreadful to see the great beast lying there, powerless to move and yet powerless to die, and not even to be able to finish him. I sent back for my small rifle and poured shot after shot into his heart and down his throat. They seemed to make no impression. The tortured gasps continued as steadily as the ticking of a clock.

In the end I could not stand it any longer and went away. I heard later that it took him half an hour to die. Burmans were bringing dahs and baskets even before I left, and I was told they had stripped his body almost to the bones by the afternoon.

Afterwards, of course, there were endless discussions about the shooting of the elephant. The owner was furious, but he was only an Indian and could do nothing. Besides, legally I had done the right thing, for a mad elephant has to be killed, like a mad dog, if its owner fails to control it. Among the Europeans opinion was divided. The older men said I was right, the younger men said it was a damn shame to shoot an elephant for killing a coolie, because an elephant was worth more than any damn Coringhee coolie. And afterwards I was very glad that the coolie had been killed; it put me legally in the right and it gave me a sufficient pretext for shooting the elephant. I often wondered whether any of the others grasped that I had done it solely to avoid looking a fool.

For Further Reflection

1. What is the message you get out of this story?

2. How does Orwell connect imperialism with the shooting of the elephant? Can you elaborate on the few hints he offers?

3. Why does Orwell say he knows with perfect certainty that he ought not to shoot the elephant? Why is it wrong? Why does he shoot him? Can you identify with the dilemma Orwell feels?

We Have Only Indirect Duties to Animals

IMMANUEL KANT

A biographical sketch of Immanuel Kant appears in chapter 5. Kant argues that animals are not persons because they are not rational, self-conscious beings capable of grasping the moral law. Since they are not part of the kingdom of moral legislators, we do not owe them anything. But we should be kind to them since that will help develop good character in us and help us treat our fellow human beings with greater consideration. That is, our duties to animals are simply indirect duties to other human beings.

Baumgarten speaks of duties towards beings which are beneath us and beings which are above us. But so far as animals are concerned,

---

From Immanuel Kant, "Duties to Animals and Spirits," in *Lectures on Ethics,* translated by Louis Infield (London: Methuen, 1932), pp. 239–41.

we have no direct duties. Animals are not self-conscious and are there merely as a means to an end. That end is man. We can ask, "Why do animals exist?" But to ask, "Why does man exist?" is a meaningless question. *Our duties towards animals are merely indirect duties towards humanity.* Animal nature has analogies to human nature, and by doing our duties to animals in respect of manifestations of human nature, we indirectly do our duty towards humanity. Thus, if a dog has served his master long and faithfully, his service, on the analogy of human service, deserves reward, and when the dog has grown too old to serve, his master ought to keep him until he dies. Such action helps to support us in our duties towards human beings, where they are bounden duties. If then any acts of animals are analogous to human acts and spring from the same principles, we have duties towards the animals because thus we cultivate the corresponding duties towards human beings. If a man shoots his dog because the animal is no longer capable of service, he does not fail in his duty to the dog, for the dog cannot judge, but his *act is inhuman and damages in himself that humanity which it is his duty to show towards mankind.* If he is not to stifle his human feelings, he must practise kindness towards animals, for he who is cruel to animals becomes hard also in his dealing with men. We can judge the heart of a man by his treatment of animals. Hogarth depicts this in his engravings. He shows how cruelty grows and develops. He shows the child's cruelty to animals, pinching the tail of a dog or a cat; he then depicts the grown man in his cart running over a child; and lastly, the culmination of cruelty in murder. He thus brings home to us in a terrible fashion the rewards of cruelty, and this should be an impressive lesson to children. The more we come in contact with animals and observe their behaviour, the more we love them, for we see how great is their care for their young. It is then difficult for us to be cruel in thought even to a wolf. Leibnitz used a tiny worm for purposes of observation, and then carefully replaced it with its leaf on the tree so that it should not come to harm through any act of his. He would have been sorry—a natural feeling for a humane man—to destroy such a creature for no reason. Tender feelings towards dumb animals develop humane feelings towards mankind. In England butchers and doctors do not sit on a jury because they are accustomed to the sight of death and hardened. Vivisectionists, who use living animals for their experiments, certainly act cruelly, although their aim is praiseworthy, and they can justify their cruelty, since animals must be regarded as man's instruments; but any such cruelty for sport cannot be justified. A master who turns out his ass or his dog because the animal can no longer earn its keep manifests a small mind. The Greeks' ideas in this respect were highminded, as can be seen from the fable of the ass and the bell of ingratitude. Our duties towards animals, then, are indirect duties towards mankind.

For Further Reflection

1. According to Kant, do animals have rights? What capacity do they lack that deprives them of rights?

2. Why should we be kind to animals? Do you agree with Kant? How would an opponent respond to Kant's arguments?

Animal Liberation
All Animals Are Equal

PETER SINGER

Peter Singer did his graduate work at Oxford University and is a professor at the Center for Human Values at Princeton University. His book, *Animal Liberation* (1975), from which the following selection is based, is one of the most influential books ever written on the subject. It has converted many to the animal rights movement. Singer argues that animal liberation today is analogous to racial and gender justice in the past. Just as people once thought it incredible that women or blacks should be treated as equal to white men, so now speciesists mock the idea that all animals should be given equal consideration. Singer defines "speciesism" (a term devised by Richard Ryder) as the prejudice (unjustified bias) that favors one's own species over every other. What equalizes all sentient beings is our ability to suffer. In that, we and animals are equal and deserv-

From *Philosophical Exchange* Vol. 1.5 (1976). Reprinted by permission.

ing of equal consideration of interests. Singer's argument is a utilitarian one having as its goal the maximization of interest satisfaction.

In recent years a number of oppressed groups have campaigned vigorously for equality. The classic instance is the Black Liberation movement, which demands an end to the prejudice and discrimination that has made blacks second-class citizens. The immediate appeal of the black liberation movement and its initial, if limited, success made it a model for other oppressed groups to follow. We became familiar with liberation movements for Spanish-Americans, gay people, and a variety of other minorities. When a majority group—women— began their campaign, some thought we had come to the end of the road. Discrimination on the basis of sex, it has been said, is the last universally accepted form of discrimination, practiced without secrecy or pretense even in those liberal circles that have long prided themselves on their freedom from prejudice against racial minorities.

One should always be wary of talking of "the last remaining form of discrimination." If we have learned anything from the liberation movements, we should have learnt how difficult it is to be aware of latent prejudice in our attitudes to particular groups until this prejudice is forcefully pointed out.

A liberation movement demands an expansion of our moral horizons and an extension or reinterpretation of the basic moral principle of equality. Practices that were previously regarded as natural and inevitable come to be seen as the result of an unjustifiable prejudice. Who can say with confidence that all his or her attitudes and practices are beyond criticism? If we wish to avoid being numbered amongst the oppressors, we must be prepared to re-think even our most fundamental attitudes. We need to consider them from the point of view of those most disadvantaged by our attitudes, and the practices that follow from these attitudes. If we can make this unaccustomed mental switch we may discover a pattern in our attitudes and practices that consistently operates so as to benefit one group—usually the one to which we ourselves belong— at the expense of another. In this way we may come to see that there is a case for a new liberation movement. My aim is to advocate that we make this mental switch in respect of our attitudes and practices towards a very large group of beings: members of species other than our own—or, as we popularly though misleadingly call them, animals. In other words, I am urging that we extend to other species the basic principle of equality that most of us recognize should be extended to all members of our own species.

All this may sound a little far-fetched, more like a parody of other liberation movements than a serious objective. In fact, in the past the idea of "The Rights of Animals" really has been used to parody the case for women's rights. When Mary Wollstonecroft, a forerunner of later feminists, published her *Vindication of the Rights of Women* in 1792, her ideas were widely regarded as absurd, and they were satirized in an anonymous publication entitled *A Vindication of the Rights of Brutes*. The author of this satire (actually Thomas Taylor, a distinguished Cambridge philosopher) tried to refute Wollstonecroft's reasonings by showing that they could be carried one stage further. If sound when applied to women, why should the arguments not be applied to dogs, cats, and horses? They seemed to hold equally well for these "brutes"; yet to hold that brutes had rights was manifestly absurd; therefore the reasoning by which this conclusion had been reached must be unsound, and if unsound when applied to brutes, it must also be unsound when applied to women, since the very same arguments had been used in each case.

One way in which we might reply to this argument is by saying that the case for equality between men and women cannot validly be extended to nonhuman animals. Women have a right to vote, for instance, because they are just as capable of making rational decisions as men are; dogs, on the other hand, are incapable of understanding the significance of voting, so they cannot have the right to vote. There are many other obvious ways in which men and women resemble each other closely, while humans and other animals differ greatly. So, it might be said, men and women are similar beings, and should have equal rights, while humans and nonhumans are different and should not have equal rights.

The thought behind this reply to Taylor's analogy is correct up to a point, but it does not go far enough. There *are* important differences between humans and other animals, and these differences must give rise *to some* differences in the rights that each have. Recognizing this obvious fact, however, is no barrier to the case for extending the basic principle of equality to nonhuman animals. The differences that exist between men and women are equally undeniable, and the supporters of Women's Liberation are aware that these differences may give rise to different rights. Many feminists hold that women have the right to an abortion on request. It does not follow that since these same people are campaigning for equality between men and women they must support the right of men to have abortions too. Since a man cannot have an abortion, it is meaningless to talk of his right to have one. Since a pig can't vote, it is meaningless to talk of its right to vote. There is no reason why either Women's Liberation or Animal Liberation should get involved in such nonsense. The extension of the basic principle of equality from one group to another does not imply that we must treat both groups in exactly the same way, or grant exactly the same rights to both groups. Whether we should do so will depend on the nature of the members of the two groups. The basic principle of equality, I shall argue, is equality of consideration; and equal consideration for different beings may lead to different treatment and different rights.

So there is a different way of replying to Taylor's attempt to parody Wollstonecroft's arguments, a way which does not deny the differences between humans and nonhumans, but goes more deeply into the question of equality, and concludes by finding nothing absurd in the idea that the basic principle of equality applies to so-called "brutes." I believe that we reach this conclusion if we examine the basis on which our opposition to discrimination on grounds of race or sex ultimately rests. We will then see that we would be on shaky ground if we were to demand equality for blacks, women, and other groups of oppressed humans while denying equal consideration to nonhumans.

When we say that all human beings, whatever their race, creed or sex, are equal, what is it that we are asserting? Those who wish to defend a hierarchical, inegalitarian society have often pointed out that by whatever test we choose, it simply is not true that all humans are equal. Like it or not, we must face the fact that humans come in different shapes and sizes; they come with differing moral capacities, differing intellectual abilities, differing amounts of benevolent feeling and sensitivity to the needs of others, differing abilities to communicate effectively, and differing capacities to experience pleasure and pain. In short, if the demand for equality were based on the actual equality of all human beings, we would have to stop demanding equality. It would be an unjustifiable demand.

Still, one might cling to the view that the demand for equality among human beings is based on the actual equality of the different races and sexes. Although humans differ as individuals in various ways, there are no differences between the races and sexes *as such*. From the mere fact that a person is black, or a woman, we cannot infer anything else about that person. This, it may be said, is what is wrong with racism and sexism. The white racist claims that whites are superior to blacks, but this is false—although there are differences between individuals, some blacks are superior to some whites in all of the capacities and abilities that could conceivably be relevant. The opponent of sexism would say the same: a person's sex is no guide to his or her abilities, and this is why it is unjustifiable to discriminate on the basis of sex.

This is a possible line of objection to racial and sexual discrimination. It is not, however, the way that someone really concerned about equality would choose, because taking this line could, in some circumstances, force one to accept a most inegalitarian society. The fact that humans differ as individuals, rather than as races or sexes, is a valid reply to someone who defends a hierarchical society like, say, South Africa, in which all whites are superior in status to all blacks. The existence of individual variations that cut across the lines of race or sex, however, provides us with no defence at all against a more sophisticated opponent of equality, one who proposes that, say, the interests of those with I.Q. ratings above 100 be preferred to the interests of those with I.Q.s below 100. Would a hierarchical society of this sort really be so much better than one based on race or sex? I think not. But if we tie the moral principle of equality to the factual equality of the different races or sexes, taken as a whole, our opposition to racism and sexism does not provide us with any basis for objecting to this kind of inegalitarianism.

There is a second important reason why we ought not to base our opposition to racism and sexism on any kind of factual equality, even the limited kind which asserts that variations in capacities and abilities are spread evenly between the different races and sexes: we can have no absolute guarantee that these abilities and capacities really are distributed evenly, without regard to race or sex, among human beings. So far as actual abilities are concerned, there do seem to be certain measurable differences between both races and sexes. These differences do not, of course, appear in each case, but only when averages are taken. More important still, we do not yet know how much of these differences is really due to the different genetic endowments of the various races and sexes, and how much is due to environmental differences that are the result of past and continuing discrimination. Perhaps all of the important differences will eventually prove to be environmental rather than genetic. Anyone opposed to racism and sexism will certainly hope that this will be so, for it will make the task of ending discrimination a lot easier; nevertheless it would be dangerous to rest the case against racism and sexism on the belief that all significant differences are environmental in origin. The opponent of, say, racism who takes this line will be unable to avoid conceding that if differences in ability did after all prove to have some genetic connection with race, racism would in some way be defensible.

It would be folly for the opponent of racism to stake his whole case on a dogmatic commitment to one particular outcome of a difficult scientific issue which is still a long way from being settled. While attempts to prove that differences in certain selected abilities between races and sexes are primarily genetic in origin have certainly not been conclusive, the same must be said of attempts to prove that these differences are largely the result of environment. At this stage of the investigation we cannot be certain which view is correct, however much we may hope it is the latter.

Fortunately, there is no need to pin the case for equality to one particular outcome of this scientific investigation. The appropriate response to those who claim to have found evidence of genetically based differences in ability between the races or sexes is not to stick to the belief that the genetic explanation must be wrong, whatever evidence to the contrary may turn up: instead we should make it quite clear that the claim to equality does not depend on intelligence, moral capacity, physical strength, or similar matters of fact. Equality is a moral ideal, not a simple assertion of fact. There is no logically compelling reason for assuming that a factual difference in ability between two people justifies any *difference in the amount of consideration we give to satisfying their needs and interests.* The principle of the equality of human beings is not a description of an alleged actual equality among humans: it is a prescription of how we should treat humans.

Jeremy Bentham incorporated the essential basis of moral equality into his utilitarian system of ethics in the formula: "Each to count for one and none for more than one." In other words, the interests of every being affected by an action are to be taken into account and given the same weight as the like interests of any other being. A later utilitarian, Henry Sidgwick, put the point in this way: "The good of any one individual is of no more importance, from the point of view (if I may say so) of the Universe, than the good of any other."[1] More recently, the leading figures in contemporary moral philosophy have shown a great deal of agreement in specifying as a fundamental presupposition of their moral theories some similar requirement which operates so as to give everyone's interests equal consideration—although they cannot agree on how this requirement is best formulated.[2]

It is an implication of this principle of equality that our concern for others ought not to depend on what they are like, or what abilities they possess—although precisely what this concern requires us to do may vary according to the characteristics of those affected by what we do. It is on this basis that the case against racism and the case against sexism must both ultimately rest; and it is in accordance with this principle that speciesism is also to be condemned. If possessing a higher degree of intelligence does not entitle one human to use another for his own ends, how can it entitle humans to exploit nonhumans?

Many philosophers have proposed the principle of equal consideration of interests, in some form or other, as a basic moral principle; but, as we shall see in more detail shortly, not many of them have recognised that this principle applies to members of other species as well as to our own. Bentham was one of the few who did realize this. In a forward-looking passage, written at a time when black slaves in the British dominions were still being treated much as we now treat nonhuman animals, Bentham wrote:

The day *may* come when the rest of the animal creation may acquire those rights which never could have been witholden from them but by the hand of tyranny. The French have already discovered that the blackness of the skin is no reason why a human being should be abandoned without redress to the caprice of a tormentor. It may one day come to be recognized that the number of the legs, the villosity of the skin, or the termination of the *os sacrum,* are reasons equally insufficient for, abandoning a sensitive being to the same fate. What else is it that should trace the insuperable line? Is it the

---

[1] *The Methods of Ethics* (7th Ed.), p. 382.
[2] For example, R. M. Hare, *Freedom and Reason* (Oxford, 1963) and J. Rawls, A *Theory of Justice* (Harvard, 1972) a brief account of the essential agreement on this issue between these and other positions, see R. M. Hare, "Rules of War and Moral Reasoning," *Philosophy and Public Affairs,* vol. 1, no. 2 (1972).

faculty of reason, or perhaps the faculty of discourse? But a full-grown horse or dog is beyond comparison a more rational, as well as a more conversable animal, than an infant of a day, or a week, or even a month, old. But suppose they were otherwise, what would it avail? The question is not, Can they reason? nor Can they *talk?* but, *Can they suffer?*[3]

In this passage Bentham points to the capacity for suffering as the vital characteristic that gives a being the *right* to equal consideration. The capacity for suffering—or more strictly, for suffering and/or enjoyment or happiness—is not just another characteristic like the capacity for language, or for higher mathematics. Bentham is not saying that those who try to mark "the insuperable line" that determines whether the interests of a being should be considered happen to have selected the wrong characteristic. The capacity for suffering and enjoying things is a pre-requisite for having interests at all, a condition that must be satisfied before we can speak of interests in any meaningful way. It would be nonsense to say that it was not in the interests of a stone to be kicked along the road by a schoolboy. A stone does not have interests because it cannot suffer. Nothing that we can do to it could possibly make any difference to its welfare. A mouse, on the other hand, does have an interest in not being tormented, because it will suffer if it is.

If a being suffers, there can be no moral justification for refusing to take that suffering into consideration. No matter what the nature of the being, the principle of equality requires that its suffering be counted equally with the like suffering—in so far as rough comparisons can be made—of any other being. If a being is not capable of suffering, or of experiencing enjoyment or happiness, there is nothing to be taken into account. This is why the limit of sentience (using the term as a convenient, if not strictly accurate, shorthand for the capacity to suffer or experience enjoyment or happiness) is the only defensible boundary of concern for the interests of others. To mark this boundary by some characteristic like intelligence or rationality would be to mark it in an arbitrary way. Why not choose some other characteristic, like skin color?

The racist violates the principle of equality by giving greater weight to the interests of members of his own race, when there is a

---

[3]*Introduction to the Principles of Morals and Legislation,* ch. XVII.

clash between their interests and the interests of those of another race. Similarly the speciesist allows the interests of his own species to override the greater interests of members of other species.[4] The pattern is the same in each case. Most human beings are speciesists. I shall now very briefly describe some of the practices that show this.

For the great majority of human beings, especially in urban, industrialized societies, the most direct form of contact with members of other species is at meal-times: we eat them. In doing so we treat them purely as means to our ends. We regard their life and well-being as subordinate to our taste for a particular kind of dish. I say "taste" deliberately—this is purely a matter of pleasing our palate. There can be no defence of eating flesh in terms of satisfying nutritional needs, since it has been established beyond doubt that we could satisfy our need for protein and other essential nutrients far more efficiently with a diet that replaced animal flesh by soy beans, or products derived from soy beans, and other high-protein vegetable products.[5]

It is not merely the act of killing that indicates what we are ready to do to other species in order to gratify our tastes. The suffering we inflict on the animals while they are alive is perhaps an even clearer indication of our *speciesism* than the fact that we are prepared to kill them. In order to have meat on the table at a price that people can afford, our society tolerates methods of meat production that confine sentient animals in cramped, unsuitable conditions for the entire durations of their lives. Animals are treated like machines that convert fodder into flesh, and any innovation that results in a higher "conversion ratio" is liable to be adopted. As one authority on the subject has said, "cruelty is acknowledged only when profitability ceases."[6] . . .

[4]I owe the term "speciesism" to Richard Ryder.

[5]In order to produce 1 lb. of protein in the form of beef or veal, we must feed 21 lbs. of protein to the animal. Other forms of livestock are slightly less inefficient, but the average ratio in the U.S. is still 1:8. It has been estimated that the amount of protein lost to humans in this way is equivalent to 90% of the annual world protein deficit. For a brief account, see Frances Moore Lappé, *Diet for a Small Planet* (Friends of The Earth/Ballantine, New York 1971) pp. 4–11.

[6]Ruth Harrison, *Animal Machines* (Stuart, London, 1964). For an account of farming conditions, see my *Animal Liberation* (New York Review Company, 1975).

Since, as I have said, none of these practices cater for anything more than our pleasures of taste, our practice of rearing and killing other animals in order to eat them is a clear instance of the sacrifice of the most important interests of other beings in order to satisfy trivial interests of our own. To avoid speciesism we must stop this practice, and each of us has a moral obligation to cease supporting the practice. Our custom is all the support that the meat-industry needs. The decision to cease giving it that support may be difficult, but it is no more difficult than it would have been for a white Southerner to go against the traditions of his society and free his slaves: if we do not change our dietary habits, how can we censure those slave-holders who would not change their own way of living?

The same form of discrimination may be observed in the widespread practice of experimenting on other species in order to see if certain substances are safe for human beings, or to test some psychological theory about the effect of severe punishment on learning, or to try out various new compounds just in case something turns up. . . .

In the past, argument about vivisection has often missed this point, because it has been put in absolutist terms: Would the abolitionist be prepared to let thousands die if they could be saved by experimenting on a single animal? The way to reply to this purely hypothetical question is to pose another: *Would the experimenter be prepared to perform his experiment on an orphaned human infant, if that were the only way to save many lives?* (I use "orphan" to avoid the complication of parental feelings, although in doing so I am being overfair to the experimenter, since the nonhuman subjects of experiments are not orphans.) If the experimenter is not prepared to use an orphaned human infant, then his readiness to use nonhumans is simple discrimination, since adult apes, cats, mice and other mammals are more aware of what is happening to them, more self-directing and, so far as we can tell, at least as sensitive to pain, as any human infant. There seems to be no relevant characteristic that human infants possess that adult mammals do not have to the same or a higher degree. (Someone might try to argue that what makes it wrong to experiment on a human infant is that the infant will, in time and if left alone, develop into more than the nonhuman, but one would then, to be consistent, have to oppose abortion, since the fetus has the same potential as the infant—indeed, even contraception and abstinence might be wrong on this ground, since the egg and sperm, considered jointly, also have the same potential. In any case, this argument still gives us no reason for selecting a nonhuman, rather than a human with severe and irreversible brain damage, as the subject for our experiments.)

The experimenter, then, shows a bias in favor of his own species whenever he carries out an experiment on a nonhuman for a purpose that he would not think justified him in using a human being at an equal or lower level of sentience, awareness, ability to be self-directing, etc. No one familiar with the kind of results yielded by most experiments on animals can have the slightest doubt that if this bias were eliminated the number of experiments performed would be a minute fraction of the number performed today.

Experimenting on animals, and eating their flesh, are perhaps the two major forms of speciesism in our society. By comparison, the third and last form of speciesism is so minor as to be insignificant, but it is perhaps of some interest to those for whom this article was written. I am referring to speciesism in contemporary philosophy.

Philosophy ought to question the basic assumptions of the age. Thinking through, critically and carefully, what most people take for granted is, I believe, the chief task of philosophy, and it is this task that makes philosophy a worthwhile activity. Regrettably, philosophy does not always live up to its historic role. Philosophers are human beings and they are subject to all the preconceptions of the society to which they belong. Sometimes they succeed in breaking free of the prevailing ideology: more often they become its most sophisticated defenders. So, in this case, philosophy as practiced in the universities today does not challenge anyone's preconceptions about our relations with other species. By their writings, those philosophers who tackle problems that touch upon the issue reveal that they make the same unquestioned assumptions as most other humans, and what they say tends to confirm the reader in his or her comfortable speciesist habits.

I could illustrate this claim by referring to the writings of philosophers in various fields—for instance, the attempts that have been made by those interested in rights to draw the boundary of the sphere of rights so that it runs parallel to the biological boundaries of the species *homo sapiens,* including infants and even mental defectives, but excluding those other beings of equal or greater capacity who are so useful to us at mealtimes and in our laboratories. I think it would be a more appropriate conclusion to this article, however, if I concentrated on the problem with which we have been centrally concerned, the problem of equality.

It is significant that the problem of *equality,* in moral and political philosophy, is invariably formulated in terms of human equality. The effect of this is that the question of the equality of other animals does not confront the philosopher, or student, as an issue itself—and this is already an indication of the failure of philosophy to challenge accepted beliefs. Still, philosophers have found it difficult to discuss the issue of human equality without raising, in a paragraph or two, the question of the status of other animals. The reason for this, which should be apparent from what I have said already, is that if humans are to be regarded as equal to one another, we need some sense of "equal" that does not require any actual, descriptive equality of capacities, talents or other qualities. If equality is to be related to any actual characteristics of humans, these characteristics must be some lowest common denominator, pitched so low that no human lacks them—but then the philosopher comes up against the catch that any such set of characteristics which covers *all* humans will not be possessed *only by humans.* In other words, it turns out that in the only sense in which we can truly say, as an assertion of fact, that all humans are equal, at least some members of other species are also equal—equal, that is, to each other and to humans. If, on the other hand, we regard the statement "All humans are equal" in some non-factual way, perhaps as a prescription, then, as I have already argued, it is even more difficult to exclude nonhumans from the sphere of equality.

This result is not what the egalitarian philosopher originally intended to assert. Instead of accepting the radical outcome to which their own reasonings naturally point, however, most philosophers try to reconcile their beliefs in human equality and animal inequality by arguments that can only be described as devious.

As a first example, I take William Frankena's well-known article "The Concept of Social Justice." Frankena opposes the idea of basing justice on merit, because he sees that this could lead to highly inegalitarian results. Instead he proposes the principle that

> . . . all men are to be treated as equals, not because they are equal, in any respect, but *simply because they are human.* They are human because they have *emotions* and *desires,* and are able to *think,* and hence are capable of enjoying a good life in a sense in which other animals are not.[7]

[7]R. Brandt (ed.), *Social Justice* (Prentice-Hall, Englewood Cliffs, 1962), p. 19.

But what is this capacity to enjoy the good life which all humans have, but no other animals? Other animals have emotions and desires, and appear to be capable of enjoying a good life. We may doubt that they can think—although the behavior of some apes, dolphins and even dogs suggests that some of them can—but *what is the relevance of thinking?* Frankena goes on to admit that by "the good life" he means "not so much the morally good life as the happy or satisfactory life," so thought would appear to be unnecessary for enjoying the good life; in fact to emphasize the need for thought would make difficulties for the egalitarian since only some people are capable of leading intellectually satisfying lives, or morally good lives. This makes it difficult to see what Frankena's principle of equality has to do with simply being *human.* Surely every sentient being is capable of leading a life that is happier or less miserable than some alternative life, and hence has a claim to be taken into account. In this respect the distinction between humans and nonhumans is not a sharp division, but rather a continuum along which we move gradually, and with overlaps between the species, from simple capacities for enjoyment and satisfaction, or pain and suffering, to more complex ones.

Faced with a situation in which they see a need for some basis for the moral gulf that is commonly thought to separate humans and animals, but finding no concrete difference that will do the job without undermining the equality of humans, philosophers tend to waffle. They resort to high-sounding phrases like "the intrinsic dignity of the human individual";[8] they talk of the "intrinsic worth of all men" as if men (humans?) had some worth that other beings did not,[9] or they say that humans, and only humans, are "ends in themselves," while "everything other than a person can only have value for a person."[10]

This idea of a distinctive human dignity and worth has a long history; it can be traced back directly to the Renaissance humanists, for instance to Pico della Mirandola's *Oration on the Dignity of Man.* Pico and other humanists based their estimate of human dignity on the idea that man possessed the central, pivotal position in the "Great Chain of Being" that led from the lowliest forms of

[8]Frankena, Op. cit., p. 23.
[9]H. A. Bedau, "Egalitarianism and the Idea of Equality" in *Nomos IX: Equality,* ed. J. R. Pennock and J. W. Chapman, New York, 1967.
[10]G. Vlastos, "Justice and Equality" in Brandt, *Social Justice,* p. 48.

matter to God himself; this view of the universe, in turn, goes back to both classical and Judeo-Christian doctrines. Contemporary philosophers have cast off these metaphysical and religious shackles and freely invoke the dignity of mankind without needing to justify the idea at all. Why should we not attribute "intrinsic dignity" or "intrinsic worth" to ourselves? Fellow-humans are unlikely to reject the accolades we so generously bestow on them, and those to whom we deny the honor are unable to object. Indeed, when one thinks only of humans, it can be very liberal, very progressive, to talk of the dignity of all human beings. In so doing, we implicitly condemn slavery, racism, and other violations of human rights. We admit that we ourselves are in some fundamental sense on a par with the poorest, most ignorant members of our own species. It is only when we think of humans as no more than a small subgroup of all the beings that inhabit our planet that we may realize that in elevating our own species we are at the same time lowering the relative status of all other species.

The truth is that the appeal to the intrinsic dignity of human beings appears to solve the egalitarian's problems only as long as it goes unchallenged. Once we ask *why* it should be that all humans—including infants, mental defectives, psychopaths, Hitler, Stalin and the rest—have some kind of dignity or worth that no elephant, pig, or chimpanzee can ever achieve, we see that this question is as difficult to answer as our original request for some relevant fact that justifies the inequality of humans and other animals. In fact, these two questions are really one: talk of intrinsic dignity or moral worth only takes the problem back one step, because any satisfactory defence of the claim that all and only humans have intrinsic dignity would need to refer to some relevant capacities or characteristics that all and only humans possess. Philosophers frequently introduce ideas of dignity, respect and worth at the point at which other reasons appear to be lacking, but this is hardly good enough. Fine phrases are the last resource of those who have run out of arguments.

In case there are those who still think it may be possible to find some relevant characteristic that distinguishes all humans from all members of other species, I shall refer again, before I conclude, to the existence of some humans who quite clearly are below the level of awareness, self-consciousness, intelligence, and sentience, of many nonhumans. I am thinking of humans with severe and irreparable brain damage, and also of infant humans. To avoid the complication of the relevance of a being's potential, however, I shall henceforth concentrate on permanently retarded humans.

Philosophers who set out to find a characteristic that will distinguish humans from other animals rarely take the course of abandoning these groups of humans by lumping them in with the other animals. It is easy to see why they do not. To take this line without re-thinking our attitudes to other animals would entail that we have the right to perform painful experiments on retarded humans for trivial reasons; similarly it would follow that we had the right to rear and kill these humans for food. To most philosophers these consequences are as unacceptable as the view that we should stop treating nonhumans in this way.

Of course, when discussing the problem of equality it is possible to ignore the problem of mental defectives, or brush it aside as if somehow insignificant.[11] This is the easiest way out. What else remains? My final example of speciesism in contemporary philosophy has been selected to show what happens when a writer is prepared to face the question of human equality and animal inequality without ignoring the existence of mental defectives, and without resorting to obscurantist mumbo-jumbo. Stanley Benn's clear and honest article "Egalitarianism and Equal Consideration of Interests"[12] fits this description.

Benn, after noting the usual "evident human inequalities" argues, correctly I think, for equality of consideration as the only possible basis for egalitarianism. Yet Benn, like other writers, is thinking only of "equal consideration of human interests." Benn is quite open in his defence of this restriction of equal consideration:

> . . . not to possess human shape *is* a disqualifying condition. However faithful or intelligent a dog may be, it would be a monstrous sentimentality to attribute to him interests that could be weighed in an equal balance with those of human beings . . . if, for instance, one had to decide between feeding a hungry baby or a hungry dog, anyone who chose the dog would generally be reckoned morally defective, unable to recognize a fundamental inequality of claims.
>
> This is what distinguishes our attitude to animals from our attitude to imbeciles. It would be odd to say that we ought to respect equally

[11]For example, Bernard Williams, "The Idea of Equality," in *Philosophy, Politics and Society* (second series), ed. P. Laslett and W. Runciman (Blackwell, Oxford, 1962), p. 118; J. Rawls, *A Theory of Justice,* pp. 509–10.
[12]*Nomos IX: Equality;* the passages quoted are on p. 62ff.

the dignity or personality of the imbecile and of the rational man
. . . but there is nothing odd about saying that we should respect their
interests equally, that is, that we should give to the interests of each
the same serious consideration as claims to considerations necessary
for some standard of well-being that we can recognize and endorse.

Benn's statement of the basis of the consideration we should
have for imbeciles seems to me correct, but why should there be
any fundamental inequality of claims between a dog and a human
imbecile? Benn sees that if equal consideration depended on rationality, no reason could be given against using imbeciles for research
purposes, as we now use dogs and guinea pigs. This will not do:
"But of course we do distinguish imbeciles from animals in this
regard," he says. That the common distinction is justifiable is something Benn does not question; his problem is how it is to be justified. The answer he gives is this:

> . . . we respect the interests of men and give them priority over dogs
> not *insofar* as they are rational, but because rationality is the human
> norm. We say it is *unfair* to exploit the deficiencies of the imbecile
> who falls short of the norm, just as it would be unfair, and not just
> ordinarily dishonest, to steal from a blind man. If we do not think
> in this way about dogs, it is because we do not see the irrationality
> of the dog as a deficiency or a handicap, but as normal for the
> species. The characteristics, therefore, that distinguish the normal
> man from the normal dog make it intelligible for us to talk of other
> men having interests and capacities, and therefore claims, of pre-
> cisely the same kind as we make on our own behalf. But although
> these characteristics may provide the point of the distinction between
> men and other species, they are *not* in fact the qualifying conditions
> for membership, or the distinguishing criteria of the class of morally
> considerable persons; *and this is precisely because a man does not
> become a member of a different species, with its own standards of
> normality, by reason of not possessing these characteristics.*

The final sentence of this passage gives the argument away. An
imbecile, Benn concedes, may have no characteristics superior to
those of a dog; nevertheless this does not make the imbecile a
member of "a different species" as the dog is. *Therefore* it would
be "unfair" to use the imbecile for medical research as we use the
dog. But why? That the imbecile is not rational is just the way things
have worked out, and the same is true of the dog—neither is any
more responsible for their mental level. If it is unfair to take advan-

tage of an isolated defect, why is it fair to take advantage of a more general limitation? I find it hard to see anything in this argument except a defence of preferring the interests of members of our own species because they are members of our own species. To those who think there might be more to it, I suggest the following mental exercise. Assume that it has been proven that there is a difference in the average, or normal, intelligence quotient for two different races, say whites and blacks. Then substitute the term "white" for every occurrence of "men" and "black" for every occurrence of "dog" in the passage quoted; and substitute "high I.Q." for "rationality" and when Benn talks of "imbeciles" replace this term by "dumb whites"—that is, whites who fall well below the normal white I.Q. score. Finally, change "species" to "race." Now re-read the passage. It has become a defence of a rigid, no-exceptions division between whites and blacks, based on I.Q. scores, *not withstanding an admitted overlap* between whites and blacks in this respect. The revised passage is, of course, outrageous, and this is not only because we have made fictitious assumptions in our substitutions. The point is that in the original passage Benn was defending a rigid division in the amount of consideration due to members of different species, despite admitted cases of overlap. If the original did not, at first reading strike us as being as outrageous as the revised version does, this is largely because although we are not racists ourselves, most of us are speciesists. Like the other articles, Benn's stands as a warning of the ease with which the best minds can fall victim to a prevailing ideology.

For Further Reflection

1. According to Singer, what is the relationship between civil rights movements and the animal rights movement?

2. What is "speciesism"? Why is it bad? Do you agree?

3. Are all humans equal, according to Singer? In what way are all sentient beings equal?

4. How does Singer apply the notion of equal consideration of interests?

5. Is Singer a utilitarian or a deontologist? Explain. Do you agree with his arguments?

The Case Against Animal Rights

CARL COHEN

Carl Cohen is a professor of law at the University of Michigan. He addresses the morality of animal experimentation and argues that while human beings have a duty to treat animals humanely, animals cannot have rights. The idea of rights does not apply to animals since "rights" is a concept appropriate only to members of the moral community and animals cannot make moral decisions. Humans are of far greater value than animals, and the result of not using animals for medical experimentation would be greater human suffering.

Using animals as research subjects in medical investigations is widely condemned on two grounds: first, because it wrongly violates the *rights* of animals, and second, because it wrongly imposes on sentient creatures much avoidable *suffering*. Neither of these arguments is sound. The first relies on a mistaken understanding of rights; the second relies on a mistaken calculation of consequences. Both deserve definitive dismissal.

WHY ANIMALS HAVE NO RIGHTS

A right, properly understood, is a claim, or potential claim, that one party may exercise against another. The target against whom such a claim may be registered can be a single person, a group, a community, or (perhaps) all humankind. The content of rights claims also varies greatly: repayment of loans, nondiscrimination by employers, noninterference by the state, and so on. To comprehend any genuine right fully, therefore, we must know *who* holds the right, *against whom* it is held, and *to what* it is a right.

Alternative sources of rights add complexity. Some rights are grounded in constitution and law (e.g., the right of an accused to trial by jury); some rights are moral but give no legal claims (e.g., my right to your keeping the promise you gave me); and some rights (e.g., against theft or assault) are rooted both in morals and in law.

The differing targets, contents, and sources of rights, and their inevitable conflict, together weave a tangled web. Notwithstanding all such complications, this much is clear about rights in general: they are in every case claims, or potential claims, within a community of moral agents. Rights arise, and can be intelligibly defended, only among beings who actually do, or can, make moral claims against one another. Whatever else rights may be, therefore, they are necessarily human; their possessors are persons, human beings.

The attributes of human beings from which this moral capability arises have been described variously by philosophers, both ancient and modern: the inner consciousness of a free will (Saint Augustine); the grasp, by human reason, of the binding character of moral law (Saint Thomas Aquinas); the self-conscious participation of human beings in an objective ethical order (G. W. F. Hegel); human membership in an organic moral community (F. H. Bradley); the development of the human self through the consciousness of other moral selves (G. H. Mead); and the underivative, intuitive cognition of the rightness of an action (H. A. Prichard). Most influential has been Immanuel Kant's emphasis on the universal human possession of a uniquely moral will and the autonomy its use entails. Humans confront choices that are purely moral; humans—but certainly not dogs or mice—lay down moral laws, for others and for themselves. Human beings are self-legislative, morally *auto-nomous.*

Animals (that is, nonhuman animals, the ordinary sense of that word) lack this capacity for free moral judgment. They are not beings of a kind capable of exercising or responding to moral claims. Animals therefore have no rights, and they can have none. This is the core of the argument about the alleged rights of animals. The holders of rights must have the capacity to comprehend rules of duty, governing all including themselves. In applying such rules, the holders of rights must recognize possible conflicts between what is in their own interest and what is just. Only in a community of beings capable of self-restricting moral judgments can the concept of a right be correctly invoked.

Humans have such moral capacities. They are in this sense self-legislative, are members of communities governed by moral rules, and do possess rights. Animals do not have such moral capacities. They are not morally self-legislative, cannot possibly be members of a truly moral community, and therefore cannot possess rights.

In conducting research on animal subjects, therefore, we do not violate their rights, because they have none to violate. . . .

Genuinely moral acts have an internal as well as an external dimension. Thus, in law, an act can be criminal only when the guilty deed, the *actus reus,* is done with a guilty mind, *mens rea.* No animal can ever commit a crime; bringing animals to criminal trial is the mark of primitive ignorance. The claims of moral rights are similarly inapplicable to them. Does a lion have a right to eat a baby zebra? Does a baby zebra have a right not to be eaten? Such questions, mistakenly invoking the concept of right where it does not belong, do not make good sense. Those who condemn biomedical research because it violates "animal rights" commit the same blunder.

IN DEFENSE OF SPECIESISM

Abandoning reliance on animal rights, some critics resort instead to animal sentience—their feelings of pain and distress. We ought to desist from the imposition of pain insofar as we can. Since all or nearly all experimentation on animals does impose pain and could be readily forgone, say these critics, it should be stopped. The ends sought may be worthy, but those ends do not justify imposing agonies on humans, and by animals the agonies are felt no less. The laboratory use of animals (these critics conclude) must therefore be ended—or at least very sharply curtailed.

Argument of this variety is essentially utilitarian, often expressly so; it is based on the calculation of the net product, in pains and pleasures, resulting from experiments on animals. Jeremy Bentham, comparing horses and dogs with other sentient creatures, is thus commonly quoted: "The question is not, Can they reason? nor Can they talk? but, Can they suffer?"

BIOMEDICAL RESEARCH
MUST STILL PROCEED

Animals certainly can suffer and surely ought not to be made to suffer needlessly. But in inferring, from these uncontroversial premises, that biomedical research causing animal distress is largely (or wholly) wrong, the critic commits two serious errors.

The first error is the assumption, often explicitly defended, that all sentient animals have equal moral standing. Between a dog and a human being, according to this view, there is no moral difference; hence the pains suffered by dogs must be weighed no differently from the pains suffered by humans. To deny such equality, according to this critic, is to give unjust preference to one species over another; it is "speciesism." The most influential statement of this moral equality of species was made by Peter Singer:

> The racist violates the principle of equality by giving greater weight to the interests of members of his own race when there is a clash between their interests and the interests of those of another race. The sexist violates the principle of equality by favoring the interests of his own sex. Similarly the speciesist allows the interests of his own species to override the greater interests of members of other species. The pattern is identical in each case.

This argument is worse than unsound; it is atrocious. It draws an offensive moral conclusion from a deliberately devised verbal parallelism that is utterly specious. Racism has no rational ground whatever. Differing degrees of respect or concern for humans for no other reason than that they are members of different races is an injustice totally without foundation in the nature of the races themselves. Racists, even if acting on the basis of mistaken factual beliefs, do grave moral wrong precisely because there is no morally relevant distinction among the races. The supposition of such differences has led to outright horror. The same is true of the sexes, neither sex being entitled by right to greater respect or concern than the other. No dispute here.

Between species of animate life, however—between (for example) humans on the one hand and cats or rats on the other—the morally relevant differences are enormous, and almost universally appreciated. Humans engage in moral reflection; humans are morally autonomous; humans are members of moral communities, recognizing just claims against their own interest. Human beings do have rights; theirs is a moral status very different from that of cats or rats.

SPECIESISM IS NECESSARY

I am a speciesist. Speciesism is not merely plausible; it is essential for right conduct, because those who will not make the morally

relevant distinctions among species are almost certain, in consequence, to misapprehend their true obligations. The analogy between speciesism and racism is insidious. Every sensitive moral
judgment requires that the differing natures of the beings to whom
obligations are owed be considered. If all forms of animate life—
or vertebrate animal life—must be treated equally, and if therefore
in evaluating a research program the pains of a rodent count equally
with the pains of a human, we are forced to conclude (1) that neither humans nor rodents possess rights, or (2) that rodents possess
all the rights that humans possess. Both alternatives are absurd. Yet
one or the other must be swallowed if the moral equality of all
species is to be defended. . . .

Those who claim to base their objection to the use of animals
in biomedical research on their reckoning of the net pleasures and
pains produced make a second error, equally grave. Even if it were
true—as it is surely not—that the pains of all animate beings must
be counted equally, a cogent utilitarian calculation requires that we
weigh all the consequences of the use, and of the nonuse, of animals in laboratory research. Critics relying (however mistakenly) on
animal rights may claim to ignore the beneficial results of such
research, rights being trump cards to which interest and advantage
must give way. But an argument that is explicitly framed in terms
of interest and benefit for all over the long run must attend also to
the disadvantageous consequences of not using animals in research,
and to all the achievements attained and attainable only through
their use. The sum of the benefits of their use is utterly beyond
quantification. The elimination of horrible disease, the increase of
longevity, the avoidance of great pain, the saving of lives, and the
improvement of the quality of lives (for humans and for animals)
achieved through research using animals is so incalculably great
that the argument of these critics, systematically pursued, establishes not their conclusion but its reverse: to refrain from using animals in biomedical research is, on utilitarian ground, morally wrong.

When balancing the pleasures and pains resulting from the use
of animals in research, we must not fail to place on the scales the
terrible pains that would have resulted, would be suffered now,
and would long continue had animals not been used. Every disease eliminated, every vaccine developed, every method of pain
relief devised, every surgical procedure invented, every prosthetic
device implanted—indeed, virtually every modern medical therapy
is due, in part or in whole, to experimentation using animals. Nor

may we ignore, in the balancing process, the predictable gains in human (and animal) well-being that are probably achievable in the future but that will not be achieved if the decision is made now to desist from such research or to curtail it. . . .

Finally, inconsistency between the profession and the practice of many who oppose research using animals deserves comment. This frankly *ad hominem* observation aims chiefly to show that a coherent position rejecting the use of animals in medical research imposes costs so high as to be intolerable even to the critics themselves.

One cannot coherently object to the killing of animals in biomedical investigations while continuing to eat them. Anesthetics and thoughtful animal husbandry render the level of actual animal distress in the laboratory generally lower than that in the abattoir. So long as death and discomfort do not substantially differ in the two contexts, the consistent objector must not only refrain from all eating of animals but also protest as vehemently against others eating them as against others experimenting on them. No less vigorously must the critic object to the wearing of animal hides in coats and shoes, to employment in any industrial enterprise that uses animal parts, and to any commercial development that will cause death or distress to animals. . . .

Scrupulous vegetarianism, in matters of food, clothing, shelter, commerce, and recreation, and in all other spheres, is the only fully coherent position the critic may adopt. At great human cost, the lives of fish and crustaceans must also be protected, with equal vigor, if speciesism has been forsworn. A very few consistent critics adopt this position. It is the *reductio ad absurdum* of the rejection of moral distinctions between animals and human beings.

For Further Reflection

1. What is Cohen's position on animal rights? What are his arguments?

2. How does Cohen defend speciesism?

3. Do you agree with Cohen that absurd consequences would follow from our embracing a strong position on animal rights?

Further Readings for Chapter 14

Frey, R. G. *Rights, Killing and Suffering.* Oxford: Basil Blackwell, 1983.

Rachels, James. *Created from Animals: the Moral Implications of Darwinism.* Oxford: Oxford University Press, 1990.

Regan, Tom. *The Case for Animal Rights.* Berkeley: University of California Press, 1983. The most comprehensive philosophical treatise in favor of animal rights.

Regan, Tom, and Peter Singer, eds. *Animal Rights and Human Obligations.* Englewood Cliffs, N.J.: Prentice-Hall, 1976.

Robbins, John. *Diet for a New America: How Your Food Choices Affect Your Health, Happiness, and the Future of Life on Earth.* Walpole, N.H.: Stillpoint, 1987. A strong case for vegetarianism.

Rohr, Janelle, ed. *Animal Rights: Opposing Viewpoints.* San Diego: Greenhaven Press, 1989.

Singer, Peter. *Animal Liberation.* 2nd ed. New York: New York Review of Books, 1990.

VandeVeer, D., and Pierce, C., eds. *People, Penguins, and Plastic Trees.* Belmont, Calif.: Wadsworth, 1990.

CHAPTER 15

Our Duties
to the Environment

Human beings have lived on Earth about 100,000 years, a very short time in relation to the age of the universe (15 billion years) or even to the life of our planet (4.6 billion years). Civilization developed only 10,000 years ago, and the wheel was invented 4,000 years ago. If we compacted the history of Earth into a movie lasting one year, running 146 years per second, life would not appear until March, multicellular organisms not till November, dinosaurs not till December 13 (lasting until the 26th), mammals not till December 15, *Homo sapiens* (our species) not until eleven minutes to midnight on December 31, and civilization one minute ago. Yet in a very short time, say less than 200 years, a mere 0.000002 percent of Earth's life, humans have become capable of seriously altering the entire biosphere. In some respects we have already altered it more profoundly than it has changed in the past *billion* years. Paraphrasing Winston Churchill's remark about the British air force during World War II, "Never have so few done so much in so short a time."

How did things get this way? How did the "environmental crisis" come about?

Humankind is part of nature. We are animals who have evolved from simpler biological forms over hundreds of thousands, even millions, of years. As we noted above, human beings as we know them (*Homo sapiens sapiens*) have lived on Earth about 100,000 years. Originating in Africa, the migrations to Europe and Asia took place some 40,000 years ago. We are omnivores (carnivores and herbivores). It is natural for us to eat plants and to kill other animals for food. We have sometimes killed other humans for food.

All animals must eat other organisms to live. The big fish eats the smaller fish and so on down the trophic pyramid. Death is natural and inevitable. Species normally maintain a steady population size through competition. Most seeds are wasted and many infants die. Excess seed provides insurance for survival.

Our zone of life, the biosphere, inhabits land and air up to an altitude of five miles, water down to about five miles. Proportionately, this is thinner than the skin of an apple, and it represents all the life we know of in the universe. We conclude that life, being rare and fragile, is precious. Human beings are the most intelligent beings we know of in the universe. They are the only ones who systematically deliberate on their actions. They use language, store information, and through science and technology exercise a powerful influence over the Earth.

While humans are animals, determined like other animals by their genes, they have created artifacts, sometimes called *memes,** whereby they can alter their natural fate. Through the invention of medicine they maintain health and extend life expectancy; through large-scale weapons they can destroy large populations. They cannot outrun the gazelle or leopard, but by the use of their inventions, including the internal combustion engine and wheeled wagons, they can travel over land twice as fast as the swiftest animal. They cannot defy gravity and fly like the eagle, but they can master the laws of aerodynamics and put planes into the skies to outpace the fastest birds. They cannot swim underwater for more than a few minutes, but through their understanding of hydrophysics, they can construct submarines that enable them to traverse the oceans faster than any fish. And now they stand on the brink of asexual modes of reproduction, the cloning of their own kind. Through memes nature is *swamped* by culture, and evolution is replaced by the logic of technology. Humanity replaces natural selection as the decisive force in the development of life on Earth. Sophocles, in our first reading, writing more than four hundred years before Christ, was right: "Numberless are the world's wonders, but none more wonderful than man."

For the first nine-tenths of our species' existence, humans lived

Memes refers to human inventions, including cultural institutions and practices, which redirect natural behavioral patterns. Morality is a meme (it serves our purpose of promoting human flourishing), law and political organization are other examples. Technology is also a meme.

as *hunter-gatherers* (males mostly doing the hunting and females mostly doing the gathering). In what is sometimes referred to as the Old Stone Age (Paleolithic period), our ancestors lived nomadic lives in small communities (fewer than fifty people), gathering edible wild plants, hunting wild animals (bison, deer, mammoths), and fishing. They had few tools, lived mainly by their own muscle power and foot-speed, and probably had a short life expectancy. Their impact on the environment was slight.

About 10,000 years ago the *agricultural revolution* (Mesolithic period) occurred, marked by a shift from nomadic life to agricultural communities with domesticated animals and cultivated plants. Slash-and-burn techniques were used, burning sections of forests and using the ashes as fertilizer. When the land was overcultivated, the community would move on to a new area and clear it. Meanwhile, they noticed that when left alone, the old land would rejuvenate. This led to the practice of rotation farming: letting the land lie fallow for a period between plantings. During this period, domesticated animals were used for plowing and hauling material. Food production was more plentiful and secure, so the population increased. In this condition people acquired material goods, could store food for winter, and barter with others, especially craftsmen who produced pottery, tools, rugs, and the like. Eventually, towns and villages grew up, which served as centers of trade, government, social entertainment, and religion. During this period, while life expectancy increased and the quality of life became increasingly more civilized and secure, significant environmental damage began to occur. Poor agricultural policies led to the spread of desertification. Cities were often cesspools of sewage, garbage, and disease.

The third great cultural development, the *industrial revolution,* began in England about 1760, spreading to the rest of Europe and the United States in the nineteenth century. It ushered in the transition from manual to machine techniques of production, giving rise to the steam engine, the spinning jenny, and the power loom. Having depleted the forests which once covered most of England and Ireland, the industrialists turned to coal as the nonrenewable energy resource that would sustain factories and steamships. Coal mining was a dangerous occupation, and urban coal-burning produced a dangerous smog, more dangerous to health than that in contemporary American cities. Many miners and citydwellers died of lung disease. The use of machines meant that fewer farmers were needed to produce food, so urban factory jobs expanded. The story of the industrial revolution is one of increased wealth, especially for successful entrepreneurs, of the end of feudalism and rural society, of the development of city life, and of the exponential growth and dominance of technology in our lives.

In the last hundred years or so we have invented electricity, the light bulb, the refrigerator, the telephone, cinema, radio, television, the automobile, the airplane, the spaceship, the submarine, the air conditioner, the skyscraper, antibiotics, heart and liver transplants, the birth control pill, safe abortion, the microwave oven, the atom bomb, nuclear energy, and the digital computer—including communication on the World Wide Web. We have discovered how to clone animals and are on the verge of full-scale human genetic engineering. Breakthroughs on cures for Alzheimer's disease, cancer, and other diseases are on the horizon. Through the miracles of science and technology, we have enabled millions of people over the face of the Earth to live longer with more freedom, power, and knowledge than our ancestors could dream of. Only in science fiction were these wonders of modern life even hinted at.

Yet with this new freedom, power, and knowledge has come a dark side. The automobile kills hundreds of thousands of people throughout the world each year (more Americans have died in automobile accidents than in all the battlefields of all the wars our nation has fought). It produces chemical pollution, which degrades the atmosphere, causing illness, exacerbating the greenhouse effect, and increasing global warming. Refrigerators and air conditioners enable us to preserve food and live comfortably in hot seasons and climates, but they also use chlorofluorocarbons (CFCs) which rise into the stratosphere and deplete the thin ozone layer that protects us from harmful ultraviolet radiation. This has given rise to an increase in skin cancer, especially deadly melanoma, and has harmful effects on plankton, which are vital to the food chain of marine animals. Nuclear power could provide safe, inexpensive energy to the world, but instead it has been used to decimate cities and threaten a global holocaust. Disasters like the nuclear plant steam explosion at Chernobyl in the former Soviet Union have spread harmful radiation over thousands of square miles, causing death and deformity. Such horrendous threats have replaced the fear of nuclear war as the worst potential catastrophe, causing widespread public distrust of the nuclear power industry. Nuclear waste piles up with no solution in sight. But our modern way of life does require energy, lots of it. So we burn fossil fuels, especially coal, which, unbeknownst to the public at large, is probably more dangerous than nuclear energy, causing cancer and other diseases, polluting the air with sulphur dioxide, and producing acid rain, which is destroying our rivers and lakes and killing trees. Medical science found cures for tuberculosis and syphilis and has aided in greatly lowering infant mortality, but in the process we have allowed an exponential growth of population, producing crowded cities and putting a strain on our resources. The more people, the more energy needed; the more energy produced, the more pollution; the more pollution, the more our lives are threatened by disease. Add to all this the problem of a *just* distribution of resources. The increasing discrepancy of wealth between the rich and the poor, both within and between nations, portends a global tragedy, one that in sheer suffering could make previous socially destructive events seem minuscule by comparison.

And so the story goes. For each blessing of modern technology a corresponding risk comes into being, the flip side of the same coin. With each new invention comes frightful responsibility. Technophiles put their money on technology's ability to meet all our basic needs and satisfy everyone. They reason, "We have put a man on the moon, learned how to increase food production as never before thought possible, will discover the cure for cancer and how to clone animals and human beings. All we need to do is put our best brainpower to work on our problems and we can create the necessary technology to solve them." Technophobes see this faith in technology not only as naive, but also as a dangerous impediment to progress. In fact, they see technology (or its overuse) as the main problem, undermining the human spirit, devastating community, and threatening to dictate our lives.

There was once a man who discovered his own shadow. He became so fascinated with it that he gave pride of place to it, treated it with deference and respect, until finally, neglecting his other duties, he became a shadow to his own shadow. Likewise, we may be in danger of being enslaved by our own devices.

We turn to our readings. After the selection from Sophocles' *Antigone,* we consider Robert Heilbroner's probing "What Has Posterity Ever Done for Me?" and ask what is the basis of our obligation to leave the world and its resources in good condition for future generations. Next we read Garrett Hardin's classic "The Tragedy of the Commons," in which he argues that there is no technological solution to our environmental problems, but we must agree upon mutually coercive rules that will assure a good for us all, as well as for future people. Finally, for an opposite perspective, we read William Baxter's "People or Penguins: The Case for Optimal Pollution," in which he argues for a humanistic, as opposed to environment-centered, social policy.

On Mankind's Power over Nature

SOPHOCLES

Sophocles (c. 497–405 B.C.), a Greek tragic playwright, wrote 123 plays, of which only seven survive. Two of his major plays are *Oedipus Rex* and *Antigone,* from which this selection is taken. Sophocles recognizes the mighty power human ingenuity has exercised over nature but points out at least one of our limits.

Numberless are the world's wonders, but none
More wonderful than man; the stormgray sea
Yields to his prows, the huge crests bear him high;
Earth, holy and inexhaustible, is graven
With shining furrows where his plows have gone
Year after year, the timeless labor of stallions.

The lightboned birds and beasts that cling to cover,
The lithe fish lighting their reaches of dim water,
All are taken, tamed in the net of his mind;
The lion on the hill, the wild horse windy-maned,
Resign to him; and his blunt yoke has broken
The sultry shoulders of the mountain bull.

Words also, and thought as rapid as air,
He fashions to his good use; statecraft is his.
The searching arrows of frost he need fear no more,
That under a starry sky are endured with pain.
He has made himself secure from all but one enemy—
In the late wind of death he cannot prevail.

From Sophocles, *Antigone,* translated by Dudley Fitts and Robert Fitzgerald (New York: Harvest Books, 1939).

What Has Posterity Ever Done for Me?

ROBERT HEILBRONER

Robert Heilbroner was for many years professor of eco-
nomics at the New School for Social Research in New York.
He is the author of several books, including *The Worldly
Philosophers* and *Marxism: For and Against.*

Heilbroner asks why we should care about future people or whether humanity survives into the distant future.
Citing fellow economists who argue that we have no reason to sacrifice for the unknown future, Heilbroner expresses outrage at this callous disregard for future people.
Admitting that he cannot give a rational argument for this
view, he appeals to Adam's Smith's principle of sentiment
or inner conscience, which urges us to work for the long-
range survival of humanity.

Will mankind survive? Who knows? The question I want to put is
more searching: Who cares? It is clear that most of us today do not
care—or at least do not care enough. How many of us would be willing to give up some minor convenience—say, the use of aerosols—
in the hope that this might extend the life of man on earth by a hundred years? Suppose we also knew with a high degree of certainty
that humankind could not survive a thousand years unless we gave
up our wasteful diet of meat, abandoned all pleasure driving, cut
back on every use of energy that was not essential to the maintenance of a bare minimum. Would we care enough for posterity to
pay the price of its survival?

I doubt it. A thousand years is unimaginably distant. Even a century far exceeds our powers of empathetic imagination. By the year
2075, I shall probably have been dead for three quarters of a century. My children will also likely be dead, and my grandchildren,
if I have any, will be in their dotage. What does it matter to me,

then, what life will be like in 2075, much less 3075? Why should I lift a finger to affect events that will have no more meaning for me seventy-five years after my death than those that happened seventy-five years before I was born?

There is no rational answer to that terrible question. No argument based on reason will lead me to care for posterity or to lift a finger in its behalf. Indeed, by every rational consideration, precisely the opposite answer is thrust upon us with irresistible force. As a Distinguished Professor of political economy at the University of London has written in the current winter issue of *Business and Society Review:*

> Suppose that, as a result of using up all the world's resources, human life did come to an end. So what? What is so desirable about an indefinite continuation of the human species, religious convictions apart? It may well be that nearly everybody who is already here on earth would be reluctant to die, and that everybody has an instinctive fear of death. But one must not confuse this with the notion that, in any meaningful sense, generations who are yet unborn can be said to be better off if they are born than if they are not.

Thus speaks the voice of rationality. It is echoed in the book *The Economic Growth Controversy* by a Distinguished Younger Economist from the Massachusetts Institute of Technology:

> . . . Geological time [has been] made comprehensible to our finite human minds by the statement that the 4.5 billion years of the earth's history [are] equivalent to once around the world in an SST. . . . Man got on eight miles before the end, and industrial man got on six feet before the end. . . . Today we are having a debate about the extent to which man ought to maximize the length of time that he is on the airplane.
>
> According to what the scientists think, the sun is gradually expanding and 12 billion years from now the earth will be swallowed up by the sun. This means that our airplane has time to go round three more times. Do we want man to be on it for all three times around the world? Are we interested in man being on for another eight miles? Are we interested in man being on for another six feet? Or are we only interested in man for a fraction of a millimeter—our lifetimes?
>
> That led me to think: Do I care what happens a thousand years from now? . . . Do I care when man gets off the airplane? I think I basically [have come] to the conclusion that I don't care whether man is on the airplane for another eight feet, or if man is on the airplane another three times around the world.

Is it an outrageous position? I must confess it outrages me. But this is not because the economists' arguments are "wrong"—indeed, within their rational framework they are indisputably right. It is because their position reveals the limitations—worse, the suicidal dangers—of what we call "rational argument" when we confront questions that can only be decided by an appeal to an entirely different faculty from that of cool reason. More than that, I suspect that if there is cause to fear for man's survival it is because the calculus of logic and reason will be applied to problems where they have as little validity, even as little bearing, as the calculus of feeling or sentiment applied to the solution of a problem in Euclidean geometry.

If reason cannot give us a compelling argument to care for posterity—and to care desperately and totally—what can? For an answer, I turn to another distinguished economist whose fame originated in his profound examination of moral conduct. In 1759, Adam Smith published "The Theory of Moral Sentiments," in which he posed a question very much like ours, but to which he gave an answer very different from that of his latter-day descendants.

Suppose, asked Smith, that "a man of humanity" in Europe were to learn of a fearful earthquake in China—an earthquake that swallowed up its millions of inhabitants. How would that man react? He would, Smith mused, "make many melancholy reflections upon the precariousness of human life, and the vanity of all the labors of man, which could thus be annihilated in a moment. He would, too, perhaps, if he was a man of speculation, enter into many reasonings concerning the effects which this disaster might produce upon the commerce of Europe, and the trade and business of the world in general." Yet, when this fine philosophizing was over, would our "man of humanity" care much about the catastrophe in distant China? He would not. As Smith tells us, he would "pursue his business or his pleasure, take his repose for his diversion, with the same ease and tranquillity as if nothing had happened."

But now suppose, Smith says, that our man were told he was to lose his little finger on the morrow. A very different reaction would attend the contemplation of this "frivolous disaster." Our man of humanity would be reduced to a tormented state, tossing all night with fear and dread—whereas "provided he never saw them, he will snore with the most profound security over the ruin of a hundred millions of his brethren."

Next, Smith puts the critical question: Since the hurt to his finger bulks so large and the catastrophe in China so small, does this mean that a man of humanity, given the choice, would prefer the extinction of a hundred million Chinese in order to save his little finger? Smith is unequivocal in his answer. "Human nature startles at the thought," he cries, "and the world in its greatest depravity and corruption never produced such a villain as would be capable of entertaining it."

But what stays our hand? Since we are all such creatures of self-interest (and is not Smith the very patron saint of the motive of self-interest?), what moves us to give precedence to the rights of humanity over those of our own immediate well-being? The answer, says Smith, is the presence within us all of a "man within the beast," an inner creature of conscience whose insistent voice brooks no disobedience: "It is the love of what is honorable and noble, of the grandeur and dignity, and superiority of our own characters."

It does not matter whether Smith's eighteenth-century view of human nature in general or morality in particular appeals to the modern temper. What matters is that he has put the question that tests us to the quick. For it is one thing to appraise matters of life and death by the principles of rational self-interest and quite another *to take responsibility for our choice.* I cannot imagine the Distinguished Professor from the University of London personally consigning humanity to oblivion with the same equanimity with which he writes off its demise. I am certain that if the Distinguished Younger Economist from M.I.T. were made responsible for determining the precise length of stay of humanity on the SST, he would agonize over the problem and end up by exacting every last possible inch for mankind's journey.

Of course, there are moral dilemmas to be faced even if one takes one's stand on the "survivalist" principle. Mankind cannot expect to continue on earth indefinitely if we do not curb population growth, thereby consigning billions or tens of billions to the oblivion of non-birth. Yet, in this case, we sacrifice some portion of life-to-come in order that life itself may be preserved. This essential commitment to life's continuance gives us the moral authority to take measures, perhaps very harsh measures, whose justification cannot be found in the precepts of rationality, but must be sought in the unbearable anguish we feel if we imagine ourselves as the executioners of mankind.

This anguish may well be those "religious convictions," to use the phrase our London economist so casually tosses away. Perhaps to our secular cast of mind, the anguish can be more easily accepted as the furious power of the biogenetic force we see expressed in every living organism. Whatever its source, when we ask if mankind "should" survive, it is only here that we can find a rationale that gives us the affirmation we seek.

This is not to say we will discover a religious affirmation naturally welling up within us as we careen toward Armageddon. We know very little about how to convince men by recourse to reason and nothing about how to convert them to religion. A hundred faiths contend for believers today, a few perhaps capable of generating that sense of caring for human salvation on earth. But, in truth, we do not know if "religion" will win out. An appreciation of the magnitude of the sacrifices required to perpetuate life may well tempt us to opt for "rationality"—to enjoy life while it is still to be enjoyed on relatively easy terms, to write mankind a shorter ticket on the SST so that some of us may enjoy the next millimeter of the trip in first-class seats.

Yet I am hopeful that in the end a survivalist ethic will come to the fore—not from the reading of a few books or the passing twinge of a pious lecture, but from an experience that will bring home to us, as Adam Smith brought home to his "man of humanity," the personal responsibility that defies all the homicidal promptings of reasonable calculation. Moreover, I believe that the coming generations, in their encounters with famine, war, and the threatened life-carrying capacity of the globe, may be given just such an experience. It is a glimpse into the void of a universe without man. I must rest my ultimate faith on the discovery by these future generations, as the ax of the executioner passes into their hands, of the transcendent importance of posterity for them.

For Further Reflection

1. Why should we care about future generations? How would you answer Heilbroner's question, "Why should I lift a finger to affect events that will have no more meaning for me seventy-five years after my death than those that happened seventy-five years before I was born?"

2. Do you agree with Heilbroner that there is "no rational answer to that terrible question"? Defend your answer.

3. Do you think "religious convictions" or simply well-thought-out humanistic concerns (Adam Smith's "man of humanity") should

have more weight than logic and rational argument when considering issues such as obligations to posterity? How do you decide?

The Tragedy of the Commons

GARRETT HARDIN

Garrett Hardin argues that some social problems have no technical, that is, scientific or technological, solution, but must be addressed by moral and political means. Exponential population growth is one such problem. Hardin calls our attention to a study of the British mathematician William Forster Lloyd (1794–1852), which demonstrates that in non-regulated areas (the "commons") individual rationality and self-interest lead to disaster. Hardin applies Lloyd's study to human population growth and argues that voluntary restriction of population by families is not adequate to deal with this problem, since many will not respond to voluntary procreation limitations. We must have "mutual coercion, mutually agreed upon by the majority of the people affected."

At the end of a thoughtful article on the future of nuclear war, Wiesner and York[1] concluded that: "Both sides in the arms race are . . . confronted by the dilemma of steadily increasing military power and steadily decreasing national security. *It is our considered professional judgment that this dilemma has no technical solution.* If the great powers continue to look for solutions in the area of science and technology only, the result will be to worsen the situation."

Reprinted with permission from G. Hardin, "The Tragedy of the Commons" *Science* 162:1243–1248. 13 Dec. 1968. Copyright © 1968 American Association for the Advancement of Science.
[1]J. B. Wiesner and H. F. York, *Sci. Amer.* 211 (No. 44), 27 (1964).

I would like to focus your attention not on the subject of the article (national security in a nuclear world) but on the kind of conclusion they reached, namely that there is no technical solution to the problem. An implicit and almost universal assumption of discussions published in professional and semi-popular scientific journals is that the problem under discussion has a technical solution. A technical solution may be defined as one that requires a change only in the techniques of the natural sciences, demanding little or nothing in the way of change in human values or ideas of morality.

In our day (though not in earlier times) technical solutions are always welcome. Because of previous failures in prophecy, it takes courage to assert that a desired technical solution is not possible. Wiesner and York exhibited this courage; publishing in a science journal, they insisted that the solution to the problem was not to be found in the natural sciences. They cautiously qualified their statement with the phrase, "It is our considered professional judgment. . . ." Whether they were right or not is not the concern of the present article. Rather, the concern here is with the important concept of a class of human problems which can be called "no technical solution problems," and, more specifically, with the identification and discussion of one of these.

It is easy to show that the class is not a null class. Recall the game of tick-tack-toe. Consider the problem, "How can I win the game of tick-tack-toe?" It is well known that I cannot, if I assume (in keeping with the conventions of game theory) that my opponent understands the game perfectly. Put another way, there is no "technical solution" to the problem. I can win only by giving a radical meaning to the word "win." I can hit my opponent over the head; or I can drug him; or I can falsify the records. Every way in which I "win" involves, in some sense, an abandonment of the game, as we intuitively understand it. (I can also, of course, openly abandon the game—refuse to play it. This is what most adults do.)

The class of "No technical solution problems" has members. My thesis is that the "population problem," as conventionally conceived, is a member of this class. How it is conventionally conceived needs some comment. It is fair to say that most people who anguish over the population problem are trying to find a way to avoid the evils of overpopulation without relinquishing any of the privileges they now enjoy. They think that farming the seas or developing new strains of wheat will solve the problem—technologically. I try to show here that the solution they seek cannot be found. The population problem cannot be solved in a technical way, any more than can the problem of winning the game of tick-tack-toe.

WHAT SHALL WE MAXIMIZE?

Population, as Malthus said, naturally tends to grow "geometrically," or, as we would now say, exponentially. In a finite world this means that the per capita share of the world's goods must steadily decrease. Is ours a finite world?

A fair defense can be put forward for the view that the world is infinite; or that we do not know that it is not. But, in terms of the practical problems that we must face in the next few generations with the foreseeable technology, it is clear that we will greatly increase human misery if we do not, during the immediate future, assume that the world available to the terrestrial human population is finite. "Space" is no escape.[2]

A finite world can support only a finite population; therefore, population growth must eventually equal zero. (The case of perpetual wide fluctuations above and below zero is a trivial variant that need not be discussed.) When this condition is met, what will be the situation of mankind? Specifically, can Bentham's goal of "the greatest good for the greatest number" be realized?

No—for two reasons, each sufficient by itself. The first is a theoretical one. It is not mathematically possible to maximize for two (or more) variables at the same time. This was clearly stated by von Neumann and Morgenstern,[3] but the principle is implicit in the theory of partial differential equations, dating back at least to D'Alembert (1717–1783).

The second reason springs directly from biological facts. To live, any organism must have a source of energy (for example, food). This energy is utilized for two purposes: mere maintenance and work. For man, maintenance of life requires about 1600 kilocalories a day ("maintenance calories"). Anything that he does over and above merely staying alive will be defined as work, and is supported by "work calories" which he takes in. Work calories are used

---

[2]G. Hardin, *J. Hered.* 50, 68 (1959); S. von Hoernor, *Science* 137, 18 (1962).
[3]J. von Neumann and O. Morgenstern, *Theory of Games and Economic Behavior* (Princeton Univ. Press, Princeton, NJ: 1947), p. 11.

not only for what we call work in common speech; they are also required for all forms of enjoyment, from swimming and automobile racing to playing music and writing poetry. If our goal is to maximize population it is obvious what we must do: We must make the work calories per person approach as close to zero as possible. No gourmet meals, no vacations, no sports, no music, no literature, no art. . . . I think that everyone will grant, without argument or proof, that maximizing population does not maximize goods. Bentham's goal is impossible.

In reaching this conclusion I have made the usual assumption that it is the acquisition of energy that is the problem. The appearance of atomic energy has led some to question this assumption. However, given an infinite source of energy, population growth still produces an inescapable problem. The problem of the acquisition of energy is replaced by the problem of its dissipation, as J. H. Fremlin has so wittily shown.[4] The arithmetic signs in the analysis are, as it were, reversed; but Bentham's goal is still unobtainable.

The optimum population is, then, less than the maximum. The difficulty of defining the optimum is enormous; so far as I know, no one has seriously tackled this problem. Reaching an acceptable and stable solution will surely require more than one generation of hard analytical work—and much persuasion.

We want the maximum good per person; but what is good? To one person it is wilderness, to another it is ski lodges for thousands. To one it is estuaries to nourish ducks for hunters to shoot; to another it is factory land. Comparing one good with another is, we usually say, impossible because goods are incommensurable. Incommensurables cannot be compared.

Theoretically this may be true; but in real life incommensurables *are* commensurable. Only a criterion of judgment and a system of weighting are needed. In nature the criterion is survival. Is it better for a species to be small and hideable, or large and powerful? Natural selection commensurates the incommensurables. The compromise achieved depends on a natural weighting of the values of the variables.

Man must imitate this process. There is no doubt that in fact he already does, but unconsciously. It is when the hidden decisions

[4]J. H. Fremlin, *New Sci.*, No. 415 (1964), p. 285.

are made explicit that the arguments begin. The problem for the years ahead is to work out an acceptable theory of weighting. Synergistic effects, nonlinear variation, and difficulties in discounting the future make the intellectual problem difficult, but not (in principle) insoluble.

Has any cultural group solved this practical problem at the present time, even on an intuitive level? One simple fact proves that none has: there is no prosperous population in the world today that has, and has had for some time, a growth rate of zero. Any people that has intuitively identified its optimum point will soon reach it, after which its growth rate becomes and remains zero.

Of course, a positive growth rate might be taken as evidence that a population is below its optimum. However, by any reasonable standards, the most rapidly growing populations on earth today are (in general) the most miserable. This association (which need not be invariable) casts doubt on the optimistic assumption that the positive growth rate of a population is evidence that it has yet to reach its optimum.

We can make little progress in working toward optimum population size until we explicitly exorcize the spirit of Adam Smith in the field of practical demography. In economic affairs, *The Wealth of Nations* (1776) popularized the "invisible hand," the idea that an individual who "intends only his own gain," is, as it were, "led by an invisible hand to promote . . . the public interest."[5] Adam Smith did not assert that this was invariably true, and perhaps neither did any of his followers. But he contributed to a dominant tendency of thought that has ever since interfered with positive action based on rational analysis, namely, the tendency to assume that decisions reached individually will, in fact, be the best decisions for an entire society. If this assumption is correct it justifies the continuance of our present policy of laissez-faire in reproduction. If it is correct we can assume that men will control their individual fecundity so as to produce the optimum population. If the assumption is not correct, we need to reexamine our individual freedoms to see which ones are defensible.

[5]A. Smith, *The Wealth of Nations* (Modern Library, New York, 1937), p. 423.

TRAGEDY OF FREEDOM IN A COMMONS

The rebuttal to the invisible hand in population control is to be found in a scenario first sketched in a little-known pamphlet[6] in 1833 by a mathematical amateur named William Forster Lloyd (1794–1852). We may well call it "the tragedy of the commons," using the word "tragedy" as the philosopher Whitehead used it:[7] "The essence of dramatic tragedy is not unhappiness. It resides in the solemnity of the remorseless working of things." He then goes on to say, "This inevitableness of destiny can only be illustrated in terms of human life by incidents which in fact involve unhappiness. For it is only by them that the futility of escape can be made evident in the drama."

The tragedy of the commons develops in this way. Picture a pasture open to all. It is to be expected that each herdsman will try to keep as many cattle as possible on the commons. Such an arrangement may work reasonably satisfactorily for centuries because tribal wars, poaching, and disease keep the numbers of both man and beast well below the carrying capacity of the land. Finally, however, comes the day of reckoning, that is, the day when the long-desired goal of social stability becomes a reality. At this point, the inherent logic of the commons remorselessly generates tragedy.

As a rational being, each herdsman seeks to maximize his gain. Explicitly or implicitly, more or less consciously, he asks, "What is the utility *to me* of adding one more animal to my herd?" This utility has one negative and one positive component.

1. The positive component is a function of the increment of one animal. Since the herdsman receives all the proceeds from the sale of the additional animal, the positive utility is nearly +1.

2. The negative component is a function of the additional overgrazing created by one or more animal. Since, however, the effects of overgrazing are shared by all the herdsmen, the negative utility for any particular decision-making herdsman is only a fraction of −1.

---

[6]W. F. Lloyd, *Two Lectures on the Checks to Population* (Oxford Univ. Press, Oxford, England, 1833), reprinted (in part) in *Population, Evolution, and Birth Control*, G. Hardin, Ed. (Freeman, San Francisco, 1964), p. 37.

[7]A. N. Whitehead, *Science and the Modern World* (Mentor, New York, 1948), p. 17.

Adding together the component partial utilities, the rational herds-man concludes that the only sensible course for him to pursue is to add another animal to his herd. And another; and another. . . . But this is the conclusion reached by each and every rational herdsman shar-ing a commons. Therein is the tragedy. Each man is locked into a sys-tem that compels him to increase his herd without limit—in a world that is limited. Ruin is the destination toward which all men rush, each pursuing his own best interest in a society that believes in the free-dom of the commons. Freedom in a commons brings ruin to all.

Some would say that this is a platitude. Would that it were! In a sense, it was learned thousands of years ago, but natural selec-tion favors the forces of psychological denial.[8] The individual ben-efits as an individual from his ability to deny the truth even though society as a whole, of which he is a part, suffers. Education can counteract the natural tendency to do the wrong thing, but the inex-orable success of generations requires that the basis for this knowl-edge be constantly refreshed.

A simple incident that occurred a few years ago in Leominster, Massachusetts, shows how perishable the knowledge is. During the Christmas shopping season the parking meters downtown were cov-ered with plastic bags that bore tags reading: "Do not open until after Christmas. Free parking courtesy of the mayor and city coun-cil." In other words, facing the prospect of an increased demand for already scarce space, the city fathers reinstituted the system of the commons. (Cynically, we suspect that they gained more votes than they lost by this retrogressive act.)

In an approximate way, the logic of the commons has been understood for a long time, perhaps since the discovery of agri-culture or the invention of private property in real estate. But it is understood mostly only in special cases which are not sufficiently generalized. Even at this late date, cattlemen leasing national land on the western ranges demonstrate no more than an ambivalent understanding, in constantly pressuring federal authorities to in-crease the head count to the point where overgrazing produces erosion and weed-dominance. Likewise, the oceans of the world continue to suffer from the survival of the philosophy of the com-mons. Maritime nations still respond automatically to the shibbo-

[8]G. Hardin, Ed., *Population, Evolution and Birth Control* (Freeman, San Francisco, 1964), p. 56.

leth of the "freedom of the seas." Professing to believe in the "inex-haustible resources of the oceans," they bring species after species of fish and whales closer to extinction.[9]

The National Parks present another instance of the working out of the tragedy of the commons. At present they are open to all, without limit. The parks themselves are limited in extent—there is only one Yosemite Valley—whereas population seems to grow with-out limit. The values that visitors seek in the parks are steadily eroded. Plainly, we must soon cease to treat the parks as commons or they will be of no value to anyone.

What shall we do? We have several options. We might sell them off as private property. We might keep them as public property, but allocate the right to enter them. The allocation might be on the basis of wealth, by the use of an auction system. It might be on the basis of merit, as defined by some agreed-upon standards. It might be by lottery. Or it might be on a first-come, first-served basis, administered to long queues. These, I think, are all the reasonable possibilities. They are all objectionable. But we must choose—or acquiesce in the destruction of the commons that we call our National Parks.

POLLUTION

In a reverse way, the tragedy of the commons reappears in problems of pollution. Here it is not a question of taking something out of the commons, but of putting something in—sewage, or chemical, radio-active, and heat wastes into water; noxious and dangerous fumes into the air, and distracting and unpleasant advertising signs into the line of sight. The calculations of utility are much the same as before. The rational man finds that his share of the cost of the wastes he dis-charges into the commons is less than the cost of purifying his wastes before releasing them. Since this is true for everyone, we are locked into a system of "fouling our own nest," so long as we behave only as independent, rational, free-enterprisers.

The tragedy of the commons as a food basket is averted by pri-vate property, or something formally like it. But the air and waters surrounding us cannot readily be fenced, and so the tragedy of the commons as a cesspool must be prevented by different means, by

[9]S. McVay, *Sci. Amer.* 216 (No. 8), 13 (1966).

coercive laws or taxing devices that make it cheaper for the pol-
luter to treat his pollutants than to discharge them untreated. We
have not progressed as far with the solution of this problem as we
have with the first. Indeed, our particular concept of private property, which deters us from exhausting the positive resources of the
earth, favors pollution. The owner of a factory on the bank of a
stream—whose property extends to the middle of the stream—often
has difficulty seeing why it is not his natural right to muddy the
waters flowing past his door. The law, always behind the times,
requires elaborate stitching and fitting to adapt it to this newly perceived aspect of the commons.

The pollution problem is a consequence of population. It did not
much matter how a lonely American frontiersman disposed of his
waste. "Flowing water purifies itself every 10 miles," my grandfather
used to say, and the myth was near enough to the truth when he was
a boy, for there were not too many people. But as population became
denser, the natural chemical and biological recycling processes
became overloaded, calling for a redefinition of property rights.

HOW TO LEGISLATE TEMPERANCE?

Analysis of the pollution problem as a function of population density uncovers a not generally recognized principle of morality,
namely: *the morality of an act is a function of the state of the system at the time it is performed.*[10] Using the commons as a cesspool
does not harm the general public under frontier conditions, because
there is no public; the same behavior in a metropolis is unbearable. A hundred and fifty years ago a plainsman could kill an American bison, cut out only the tongue for his dinner, and discard
the rest of the animal. He was not in any important sense being
wasteful. Today, with only a few thousand bison left, we would be
appalled at such behavior.

In passing, it is worth noting that the morality of an act cannot
be determined from a photograph. One does not know whether a
man killing an elephant or setting fire to the grassland is harming
others until one knows the total system in which his act appears.
"One picture is worth a thousand words" said an ancient Chinese;

---

[10]J. Fletcher, *Situation Ethics* (Westminster, Philadelphia, 1966).

but it may take 10,000 words to validate it. It is as tempting to ecol-
ogists as it is to reformers in general to try to persuade others by
way of the photographic shortcut. But the essence of an argument
cannot be photographed: it must be presented rationally—in words.

That morality is system-sensitive escaped the attention of most
codifiers of ethics in the past. "Thou shalt not . . ." is the form of
traditional ethical directives which make no allowance for particular circumstances. The laws of our society follow the pattern of
ancient ethics, and therefore are poorly suited to governing a complex, crowded, changeable world. Our epicyclic solution is to augment statutory law with administrative law. Since it is practically
impossible to spell out all the conditions under which it is safe to
burn trash in the backyard or to run an automobile without smog-
control, by law we delegate the details to bureaus. The result is
administrative law, which is rightly feared for an ancient reason—
Quis custodiet ipsos custodes?—"Who shall watch the watchers themselves?" John Adams said that we must have "a government of laws
and not men." Bureau administrators, trying to evaluate the morality of acts in the total system, are singularly liable to corruption,
producing a government by men, not laws.

Prohibition is easy to legislate (though not necessarily to enforce);
but how do we legislate temperance? Experience indicates that it
can be accomplished best through the mediation of administrative
law. We limit possibilities unnecessarily if we suppose that the sentiment of *Quis custodiet* denies us the use of administrative law.
We should rather retain the phrase as a perpetual reminder of fearful dangers we cannot avoid. The great challenge facing us now is
to invent the corrective feedbacks that are needed to keep custodians honest. We must find ways to legitimate the needed authority of both the custodians and the corrective feedbacks.

FREEDOM TO BREED IS INTOLERABLE

The tragedy of the commons is involved in population problems in
another way. In a world governed solely by the principle of "dog eat
dog"—if indeed there ever was such a world—how many children a
family had would not be a matter of public concern. Parents who
bred too exuberantly would leave fewer descendants, not more,
because they would be unable to care adequately for their children.
David Lack and others have found that such a negative feedback

demonstrably controls the fecundity of birds.[11] But men are not birds, and have not acted like them for millenniums, at least.

If each human family were dependent only on its own resources; *if* the children of improvident parents starved to death; *if,* thus, overbreeding brought its own "punishment" to the germ line—*then* there would be no public interest in controlling the breeding of families. But our society is deeply committed to the welfare state,[12] and hence is confronted with another aspect of the tragedy of the commons.

In a welfare state, how shall we deal with the family, the religion, the race, or the class (or indeed any distinguishable and cohesive group) that adopts overbreeding as a policy to secure its own aggrandizement?[13] To couple the concept of freedom to breed with the belief that everyone born has an equal right to the commons is to lock the world into a tragic course of action.

Unfortunately this is just the course of action that is being pursued by the United Nations. In late 1967, some 30 nations agreed to the following:[14]

> The Universal Declaration of Human Rights describes the family as the natural and fundamental unit of society. It follows that any choice and decision with regard to the size of the family must irrevocably rest with the family itself, and cannot be made by anyone else.

It is painful to have to deny categorically the validity of this right; denying it, one feels as uncomfortable as a resident of Salem, Massachusetts, who denied the reality of witches in the 17th century. At the present time, in liberal quarters, something like a taboo acts to inhibit criticism of the United Nations. There is a feeling that the United Nations is "our last and best hope," that we shouldn't find fault with it; we shouldn't play into the hands of the archconservatives. However, let us not forget what Robert Louis Stevenson said: "The truth that is suppressed by friends is the readiest weapon of the enemy." If we love the truth we must openly deny the validity of the

[11]D. Lack, *The Natural Regulation of Animal Numbers* (Clarendon Press, Oxford, 1954).

[12]H. Girvetz, *From Wealth to Welfare* (Stanford Univ. Press, Stanford, Calif., 1950).

[13]G. Hardin, *Perspec. Biol. Med.* 6, 366 (1963).

[14]U Thant, *Int. Planned Parenthood News,* No. 168 (February 1968), p. 3.

Universal Declaration of Human Rights, even though it is promoted by the United Nations. We should also join with Kingsley Davis[15] in attempting to get Planned Parenthood–World Population to see the error of its ways in embracing the same tragic ideal.

CONSCIENCE IS SELF-ELIMINATING

It is a mistake to think that we can control the breeding of mankind in the long run by an appeal to conscience. Charles Galton Darwin made this point when he spoke on the centennial of the publication of his grandfather's great book. The argument is straightforward and Darwinian.

People vary. Confronted with appeals to limit breeding, some people will undoubtedly respond to the plea more than others. Those who have more children will produce a larger fraction of the next generation than those with more susceptible consciences. The difference will be accentuated, generation by generation.

In C. G. Darwin's words: "It may well be that it would take hundreds of generations for the progenitive instinct to develop in this way, but if it should do so, nature would have taken her revenge, and the variety *Homo contracipiens* would become extinct and would be replaced by the variety *Homo progenitivus*."[16]

The argument assumes that conscience or the desire for children (no matter which) is hereditary—but hereditary only in the most general formal sense. The result will be the same whether the attitude is transmitted through germ cells, or exosomatically, to use A. J. Lotka's term. (If one denies the latter possibility as well as the former, then what's the point of education?) The argument has here been stated in the context of the population problem, but it applies equally well to any instance in which society appeals to an individual exploiting a commons to restrain himself for the general good— by means of his conscience. To make such an appeal is to set up a selective system that works toward the elimination of conscience from the race.

[15]K. Davis, *Science,* 158, 730 (1967).
[16]S. Tax, Ed., *Evolution After Darwin* (Univ. of Chicago Press, Chicago, 1960), vol. 2, p. 469.

PATHOGENIC EFFECTS OF CONSCIENCE

The long-term disadvantage of an appeal to conscience should be enough to condemn it; it has serious short-term disadvantages as well. If we ask a man who is exploiting a commons to desist "in the name of conscience," what are we saying to him? What does he hear?—not only at the moment but also in the wee small hours of the night when, half asleep, he remembers not merely the words we used but also the nonverbal communication cues we gave him unawares? Sooner or later, consciously or subconsciously, he senses that he has received two communications, and that they are contradictory: (i) (intended communication) "If you don't do as we ask, we will openly condemn you for not acting like a responsible citizen"; (ii) (the unintended communication) "If you *do* behave as we ask, we will secretly condemn you for a simpleton who can be shamed into standing aside while the rest of us exploit the commons."

Everyman then is caught in what Bateson has called a "double bind." Bateson and his co-workers have made a plausible case for viewing the double bind as an important causative factor in the genesis of schizophrenia.[17] The double bind may not always be so damaging, but it always endangers the mental health of anyone to whom it is applied. "A bad conscience," said Nietzsche, "is a kind of illness."

To conjure up a conscience in others is tempting to anyone who wishes to extend his control beyond the legal limits. Leaders at the highest level succumb to this temptation. Has any President during the past generation failed to call on labor unions to moderate voluntarily their demands for higher wages, or to steel companies to honor voluntary guidelines on prices? I can recall none. The rhetoric used on such occasions is designed to produce feelings of guilt in noncooperators.

For centuries it was assumed without proof that guilt was a valuable, perhaps even indispensable, ingredient of the civilized life. Now, in this post-Freudian world, we doubt it.

Paul Goodman speaks from the modern point of view when he says: "No good has ever come from feeling guilty, neither intelligence, policy, nor compassion. The guilty do not pay attention to

---

[17]G. Bateson, D. D. Jackson, J. Haley, J. Weakland, *Behav. Sci.* 1, 251 (1956).

the object but only to themselves, and not even to their own interests, which might make sense, but to their anxieties."[18]

One does not have to be a professional psychiatrist to see the consequences of anxiety. We in the Western world are just emerging from a dreadful two-centuries-long Dark Ages of Eros that was sustained partly by prohibition laws, but perhaps more effectively by the anxiety-generating mechanisms of education. Alex Comfort has told the story well in *The Anxiety Makers;*[19] it is not a pretty one.

Since proof is difficult, we may even concede that the results of anxiety may sometimes, from certain points of view, be desirable. The larger question we should ask is whether, as a matter of policy, we should ever encourage the use of a technique the tendency (if not the intention) of which is psychologically pathogenic. We hear much talk these days of responsible parenthood; the coupled words are incorporated into the titles of some organizations devoted to birth control. Some people have proposed massive propaganda campaigns to instill responsibility into the nation's (or the world's) breeders. But what is the meaning of the word responsibility in this context? Is it not merely a synonym for the word conscience? When we use the word responsibility in the absence of substantial sanctions are we not trying to browbeat a free man in a commons into acting against his own interest? Responsibility is a verbal counterfeit for a substantial *quid pro quo*. It is an attempt to get something for nothing.

If the word responsibility is to be used at all, I suggest that it be in the sense Charles Frankel uses it.[20] "Responsibility," says this philosopher, "is the product of definite social arrangements." Notice that Frankel calls for social arrangements—not propaganda.

MUTUAL COERCION
MUTUALLY AGREED UPON

The social arrangements that produce responsibility are arrangements that create coercion, of some sort. Consider bank-robbing. The man who takes money from a bank acts as if the bank were a com-

---

[18]P. Goodman, *New York Rev. Books* 1968, 10 (8), 22 (23 May 1968).
[19]A. Comfort, *The Anxiety Makers* (Nelson, London, 1967).
[20]C. Frankel, *The Case for Modern Man* (Harper, New York, 1955), p. 203.

mons. How do we prevent such action? Certainly not by trying to control his behavior solely by a verbal appeal to his sense of responsibility. Rather than rely on propaganda we follow Frankel's lead and insist that a bank is not a commons; we seek the definite social arrangements that will keep it from becoming a commons. That we thereby infringe on the freedom of would-be robbers we neither deny nor regret.

The morality of bank-robbing is particularly easy to understand because we accept complete prohibition of this activity. We are willing to say "Thou shalt not rob banks," without providing for exceptions. But temperance also can be created by coercion. Taxing is a good coercive device. To keep downtown shoppers temperate in their use of parking space we introduce parking meters for short periods, and traffic fines for longer ones. We need not actually forbid a citizen to park as long as he wants to; we need merely make it increasingly expensive for him to do so. Not prohibition, but carefully biased options are what we offer him. A Madison Avenue man might call this persuasion; I prefer the greater candor of the word coercion.

Coercion is a dirty word to most liberals now, but it need not forever be so. As with the four-letter words, its dirtiness can be cleansed away by exposure to light, by saying it over and over without apology or embarrassment. To many, the word coercion implies arbitrary decisions of distant and irresponsible bureaucrats; but this is not a necessary part of its meaning. The only kind of coercion I recommend is mutual coercion, mutually agreed upon by the majority of the people affected.

To say that we mutually agree to coercion is not to say that we are required to enjoy it, or even to pretend we enjoy it. Who enjoys taxes? We all grumble about them. But we accept compulsory taxes because we recognize that voluntary taxes would favor the conscienceless. We institute and (grumblingly) support taxes and other coercive devices to escape the horror of the commons.

An alternative to the commons need not be perfectly just to be preferable. With real estate and other material goods, the alternative we have chosen is the institution of private property coupled with legal inheritance. Is this system perfectly just? As a genetically trained biologist I deny that it is. It seems to me that, if there are to be differences in individual inheritance, legal possession should be perfectly correlated with biological inheritance—that those who are biologically more fit to be the custodians of property and power should legally inherit more. But genetic recombination continually makes a mockery of the doctrine of "like father, like son" implicit in our laws of legal inheritance. An idiot can inherit millions, and a trust fund can keep his estate intact. We must admit that our legal system of private property plus inheritance is unjust—but we put up with it because we are not convinced, at the moment, that anyone has invented a better system. The alternative of the commons is too horrifying to contemplate. Injustice is preferable to total ruin.

It is one of the peculiarities of the warfare between reform and the status quo that it is thoughtlessly governed by a double standard. Whenever a reform measure is proposed it is often defeated when its opponents triumphantly discover a flaw in it. As Kingsley Davis has pointed out,[21] worshippers of the status quo sometimes imply that no reform is possible without unanimous agreement, an implication contrary to historical fact. As nearly as I can make out, automatic rejection of proposed reforms is based on one of two unconscious assumptions: (i) that the status quo is perfect; or (ii) that the choice we face is between reform and no action; if the proposed reform is imperfect, we presumably should take no action at all, while we wait for a perfect proposal.

But we can never do nothing. That which we have done for thousands of years is also action. It also produces evils. Once we are aware that the status quo is action, we can then compare its discoverable advantages and disadvantages with the predicted advantages and disadvantages of the proposed reform, discounting as best we can for our lack of experience. On the basis of such a comparison, we can make a rational decision which will not involve the unworkable assumption that only perfect systems are tolerable.

RECOGNITION OF NECESSITY

Perhaps the simplest summary of this analysis of man's population problems is this: the commons, if justifiable at all, is justifiable only under conditions of low-population density. As the human population has increased, the commons has had to be abandoned in one aspect after another.

[21]J. D. Roslansky, *Genetics and the Future of Man* (Appleton-Century-Crofts, New York, 1966), p. 177.

First we abandoned the commons in food gathering, enclosing farm land and restricting pastures and hunting and fishing areas. These restrictions are still not complete throughout the world.

Somewhat later we saw that the commons as a place for water disposal would also have to be abandoned Restrictions on the disposal of domestic sewage are widely accepted in the Western world; we are still struggling to close the commons to pollution by automobiles, factories, insecticide sprayers, fertilizing operations, and atomic energy installations.

In a still more embryonic state is our recognition of the evils of the commons in matters of pleasure. There is almost no restriction on the propagation of sound waves in the public medium. The shopping public is assaulted with mindless music, without its consent. Our government is paying out billions of dollars to create supersonic transport which will disturb 50,000 people for every one person who is whisked from coast to coast 3 hours faster. Advertisers muddy the airwaves of radio and television and pollute the view of travelers. We are a long way from outlawing the commons in matters of pleasure. Is this because our Puritan inheritance makes us view pleasure as something of a sin, and pain (that is, the pollution of advertising) as the sign of virtue?

Every new enclosure of the commons involves the infringement of somebody's personal liberty. Infringements made in the distant past are accepted because no contemporary complains of a loss. It is the newly proposed infringements that we vigorously oppose; cries of "rights" and "freedom" fill the air. But what does "freedom" mean? When men mutually agreed to pass laws against robbing, mankind became more free, not less so. Individuals locked into the logic of the commons are free only to bring on universal ruin; once they see the necessity of mutual coercion, they become free to pursue other goals. I believe it was Hegel who said, "Freedom is the recognition of necessity."

The most important aspect of necessity that we must now recognize, is the necessity of abandoning the commons in breeding. No technical solution can rescue us from the misery of overpopulation. Freedom to breed will bring ruin to all. At the moment, to avoid hard decisions many of us are tempted to propagandize for conscience and responsible parenthood. The temptation must be resisted, because an appeal to independently acting consciences selects for the disappearance of all conscience in the long run, and an increase in anxiety in the short.

The only way we can preserve and nurture other and more precious freedoms is by relinquishing the freedom to breed, and that very soon. "Freedom is the recognition of necessity"—and it is the role of education to reveal to all the necessity of abandoning the freedom to breed. Only so, can we put an end to this aspect of the tragedy of the commons.

For Further Reflection

1. What does Hardin mean when he says that the problem of population growth has no technical solution?

2. What does Hardin mean when he says, "Freedom in a commons brings ruin to all"? How does he define true "freedom" at the end of his essay?

3. Explain the idea of the tragedy of the commons as first set forth by William Forster Lloyd. How does it work?

4. How does Hardin apply the tragedy of the commons to human population growth? Do you agree with his analysis? Explain.

5. What does Hardin mean by "conscience is self-eliminating"? What is wrong with appealing to conscience to solve environmental problems?

6. How serious is the current population growth? What do you think should be done about it?

People or Penguins
The Case for Optimal Pollution

WILLIAM F. BAXTER

William Baxter is professor of law at Stanford University and the author of *People or Penguins: The Case for Optimal Pollution* (1974), from which this selection is taken.

In this essay, Baxter aims at clarifying the relationship between resource use and pollution. They are the opposite sides of the same coin, the privilege and its price, the good and the bad. Baxter argues that we cannot have a pollution-free society without harming humans. If we are humanists, committed to promoting the human good above all else, as he is, we should be willing to allow pollution where it harms animals and trees if overall benefits accrue to human beings.

I start with the modest proposition that, in dealing with pollution, or indeed with any problem, it is helpful to know what one is attempting to accomplish. Agreement on how and whether to pursue a particular objective, such as pollution control, is not possible unless some more general objective has been identified and stated with reasonable precision. We talk loosely of having clean air and clean water, of preserving our wilderness areas, and so forth. But none of these is a sufficiently general objective: each is more accurately viewed as a means rather than as an end.

With regard to clean air, for example, one may ask, "how clean?" and "what does clean mean?" It is even reasonable to ask, "why have clean air?" Each of these questions is an implicit demand that a more general community goal be stated—a goal sufficiently general in its scope and enjoying sufficiently general assent among the community of actors that such "why" questions no longer seem admissible with respect to that goal.

If, for example, one states as a goal the proposition that "every person should be free to do whatever he wishes in contexts where his actions do not interfere with the interests of other human beings," the speaker is unlikely to be met with a response of "why." The goal may be criticized as uncertain in its implications or difficult to implement, but it is so basic a tenet of our civilization—it reflects a cultural value so broadly shared, at least in the abstract— that the question "why" is seen as impertinent or imponderable or both.

I do not mean to suggest that everyone would agree with the "spheres of freedom" objective just stated. Still less do I mean to suggest that a society could subscribe to four or five such general objectives that would be adequate in their coverage to serve as testing criteria by which all other disagreements might be measured. One difficulty in the attempt to construct such a list is that each new goal added will conflict, in certain applications, with each prior goal listed; and thus each goal serves as a limited qualification on prior goals.

Without any expectation of obtaining unanimous consent to them, let me set forth four goals that I generally use as ultimate testing criteria in attempting to frame solutions to problems of human organization. My position regarding pollution stems from these four criteria. If the criteria appeal to you and any part of what appears hereafter does not, our disagreement will have a helpful focus: which of us is correct, analytically, in supposing that his position on pollution would better serve these general goals. If the criteria do not seem acceptable to you, then it is to be expected that our more particular judgements will differ, and the task will then be yours to identify the basic set of criteria upon which your particular judgments rest.

My criteria are as follows:

1. The spheres of freedom criterion stated above.
2. Waste is a bad thing. The dominant feature of human existence is scarcity—our available resources, our aggregate labors, and our skill in employing both have always been, and will continue for some time to be, inadequate to yield to every man all the tangible and intangible satisfactions he would like to have. Hence, none of those resources, or labors, or skills, should be wasted— that is, employed so as to yield less than they might yield in human satisfactions.

3. Every human being should be regarded as an end rather than as a means to be used for the betterment of another. Each should be afforded dignity and regarded as having an absolute claim to an even-handed application of such rules as the community may adopt for its governance.

4. Both the incentive and the opportunity to improve his share of satisfactions should be preserved to every individual. Preservation of incentive is dictated by the "no-waste" criterion and enjoins against the continuous, totally egalitarian redistribution of satisfactions, or wealth; but subject to that constraint, everyone should receive, by continuous redistribution if necessary, some minimal share of aggregate wealth so as to avoid a level of privation from which the opportunity to improve his situation becomes illusory.

The relationship of these highly general goals to the more specific environmental issues at hand may not be readily apparent, and I am not yet ready to demonstrate their pervasive implications. But let me give one indication of their implications. Recently scientists have informed us that use of DDT in food production is causing damage to the penguin population. For the present purposes let us accept that assertion as an indisputable scientific fact. The scientific fact is often asserted as if the correct implication—that we must stop agricultural use of DDT—followed from the mere statement of the fact of penguin damage. But plainly it does not follow if my criteria are employed.

My criteria are oriented to people, not penguins. Damage to penguins, or sugar pines, or geological marvels is, without more, simply irrelevant. One must go further, by my criteria, and say: Penguins are important because people enjoy seeing them walk about rocks; and furthermore, the well-being of people would be less impaired by halting use of DDT than by giving up penguins. In short, my observations about environmental problems will be people-oriented, as are my criteria. I have no interest in preserving penguins for their own sake.

It may be said by way of objection to this position, that it is very selfish of people to act as if each person represented one unit of importance and nothing else was of any importance. It is undeniably selfish. Nevertheless I think it is the only tenable starting place for analysis for several reasons. First, no other position corresponds to the way most people really think and act—i.e., corresponds to reality.

Second, this attitude does not portend any massive destruction of nonhuman flora and fauna, for people depend on them in many obvious ways, and they will be preserved because and to the degree that humans do depend on them.

Third, what is good for humans is, in many respects, good for penguins and pine trees—clean air for example. So that humans are, in these respects, surrogates for plant and animal life.

Fourth, I do not know how we could administer any other system. Our decisions are either private or collective. Insofar as Mr. Jones is free to act privately, he may give such preferences as he wishes to other forms of life: he may feed birds in winter and do less with himself, and he may even decline to resist an advancing polar bear on the ground that the bear's appetite is more important than those portions of himself that the bear may choose to eat. In short my basic premise does not rule out private altruism to competing life-forms. It does rule out, however, Mr. Jones' inclination to feed Mr. Smith to the bear, however hungry the bear, however despicable Mr. Smith.

Insofar as we act collectively on the other hand, only humans can be afforded an opportunity to participate in the collective decisions. Penguins cannot vote now and are unlikely subjects for the franchise—pine trees more unlikely still. Again each individual is free to cast his vote so as to benefit sugar pines if that is his inclination. But many of the more extreme assertions that one hears from some conservationists amount to tacit assertions that they are specially appointed representatives of sugar pines, and hence that their preferences should be weighted more heavily than the preferences of other humans who do not enjoy equal rapport with "nature." The simplistic assertion that agricultural use of DDT must stop at once because it is harmful to penguins is of that type.

Fifth, if polar bears or pine trees or penguins, like men, are to be regarded as ends rather than means, if they are to count in our calculus of social organization, someone must tell me how much each one counts, and someone must tell me how these life-forms are to be permitted to express their preferences, for I do not know either answer. If the answer is that certain people are to hold their proxies, then I want to know how those proxy-holders are to be selected: self-appointment does not seem workable to me.

Sixth, and by way of summary of all the foregoing, let me point out that the set of environmental issues under discussion—although they raise very complex technical questions of how to achieve any objective—ultimately raise a normative question: what *ought* we to do. Questions of *ought* are unique to the human mind and world—they are meaningless as applied to a nonhuman situation.

I reject the proposition that we *ought* to respect the "balance of nature" or to "preserve the environment" unless the reason for doing so, express or implied, is the benefit of man.

I reject the idea that there is a "right" or "morally correct" state of nature to which we should return. The word "nature" has no normative connotation. Was it "right" or "wrong" for the earth's crust to heave in contortion and create mountains and seas? Was it "right" for the first amphibian to crawl up out of the primordial ooze? Was it "wrong" for plants to reproduce themselves and alter the atmospheric composition in favor of oxygen? For animals to alter the atmosphere in favor of carbon dioxide both by breathing oxygen and eating plants? No answers can be given to these questions because they are meaningless questions.

All this may seem obvious to the point of being tedious, but much of the present controversy over environment and pollution rests on tacit normative assumptions about just such nonnormative phenomena: that it is "wrong" to impair penguins with DDT, but not to slaughter cattle for prime rib roasts. That it is wrong to kill stands of sugar pines with industrial fumes, but not to cut sugar pines and build housing for the poor. Every man is entitled to his own preferred definition of Walden Pond, but there is no definition that has any moral superiority over another, except by reference to the selfish needs of the human race.

From the fact that there is no normative definition of the natural state, it follows that there is no normative definition of clean air or pure water—hence no definition of polluted air—or of pollution—except by reference to the needs of man. The "right" composition of the atmosphere is one which has some dust in it and some lead in it and some hydrogen sulfide in it—just those amounts that attend a sensibly organized society thoughtfully and knowledgeably pursuing the greatest possible satisfaction for its human members.

The first and most fundamental step toward solution of our environmental problems is a clear recognition that our objective is not pure air or water but rather some optimal state of pollution. That step immediately suggests the question: How do we define and attain the level of pollution that will yield the maximum possible amount of human satisfaction?

Low levels of pollution contribute to human satisfaction but so do food and shelter and education and music. To attain ever lower levels of pollution, we must pay the cost of having less of these other things. I contrast that view of the cost of pollution control with the more popular statement that pollution control will "cost" very large numbers of dollars. The popular statement is true in some senses, false in others; sorting out the true and false senses is of some importance. The first step in that sorting process is to achieve a clear understanding of the difference between dollars and resources. Resources are the wealth of our nation; dollars are merely claim checks upon those resources. Resources are of vital importance; dollars are comparatively trivial.

Four categories of resources are sufficient for our purposes: At any given time a nation, or a planet if you prefer, has a stock of labor, of technological skill, of capital goods, and of natural resources (such as mineral deposits, timber, water, land, etc.). These resources can be used in various combinations to yield goods and services of all kinds—in some limited quantity. The quantity will be larger if they are combined efficiently, smaller if combined inefficiently. But in either event the resource stock is limited, the goods and services that they can be made to yield are limited; even the most efficient use of them will yield less than our population, in the aggregate, would like to have.

If one considers building a new dam, it is appropriate to say that it will be costly in the sense that it will require x hours of labor, y tons of steel and concrete, and z amount of capital goods. If these resources are devoted to the dam, then they cannot be used to build hospitals, fishing rods, schools, or electric can openers. That is the meaningful sense in which the dam is costly.

Quite apart from the very important question of how wisely we can combine our resources to produce goods and services, is the very different question of how they get distributed—who gets how many goods? Dollars constitute the claim checks which are distributed among people and which control their share of national output. Dollars are nearly valueless pieces of paper except to the extent that they do represent claim checks to some fraction of the output of goods and services. Viewed as claim checks, all the dollars outstanding during any period of time are worth, in the aggregate, the goods and services that are available to be claimed with them during that period—neither more nor less.

It is far easier to increase the supply of dollars than to increase the production of goods and services—printing dollars is easy. But printing more dollars doesn't help because each dollar then simply becomes a claim to fewer goods, i.e., becomes worth less.

The point is this: many people fall into error upon hearing the statement that the decision to build a dam, or to clean up a river, will cost $X million. It is regrettably easy to say: "It's only money. This is a wealthy country, and we have lots of money." But you cannot build a dam or clean a river with $X million—unless you also have a match, you can't even make a fire. One builds a dam or cleans a river by diverting labor and steel and trucks and factories from making one kind of goods to making another. The cost in dollars is merely a shorthand way of describing the extent of the diversion necessary. If we build a dam for $X million, then we must recognize that we will have $X million less housing and food and medical care and electric can openers as a result.

Similarly, the costs of controlling pollution are best expressed in terms of the other goods we will have to give up to do the job. This is not to say the job should not be done. Badly as we need more housing, more medical care, and more can openers, and more symphony orchestras, we could do with somewhat less of them, in my judgment at least, in exchange for somewhat cleaner air and rivers. But that is the nature of the trade-off, and analysis of the problem is advanced if that unpleasant reality is kept in mind. Once the trade-off relationship is clearly perceived, it is possible to state in a very general way what the optimal level of pollution is. I would state it as follows:

People enjoy watching penguins. They enjoy relatively clean air and smog-free vistas. Their health is improved by relatively clean water and air. Each of these benefits is a type of good or service. As a society we would be well advised to give up one washing machine if the resources that would have gone into that washing machine can yield greater human satisfaction when diverted into pollution control. We should give up one hospital if the resources thereby freed would yield more human satisfaction when devoted to elimination of noise in our cities. And so on, trade-off by trade-off, we should divert our productive capacities from the production of existing goods and services to the production of a cleaner, quieter, more pastoral nation up to—and no further than—the point at which we value more highly the next washing machine or hospital that we would have to do without than we value the next unit of environmental improvement that the diverted resources would create.

Now this proposition seems to me unassailable but so general and abstract as to be unhelpful—at least unadministerable in the form stated. It assumes we can measure in some way the incremental units of human satisfaction yielded by very different types of goods. . . . But I insist that the proposition stated describes the result for which we should be striving—and again, that it is always useful to know what your target is even if your weapons are too crude to score a bull's eye.

For Further Reflection

1. Evaluate the four tenets of Baxter's environmental philosophy.
   a. Which do you agree with, and which do you disagree with? Explain why.
   b. Is human benefit the only morally relevant criterion with regard to our behavior to animals and the environment?
   c. Do penguins and sugar pine trees have intrinsic value? Or is their value entirely instrumental, derived from benefits to humans?

2. Do you agree with Baxter that pollution is just the opposite side of the coin of resource use? Do you also agree that on the principle that "waste is a bad thing" we are led to use resources for human good and thus bring about some level of pollution?

3. Compare Baxter's analysis with Watson's. What are their similarities and differences? Does Baxter shed any light on the matter?

Further Readings for Chapter 15

Easterbrook, Gregg. *A Moment on the Earth*. New York: Viking, 1995.

DesJardins, Joseph. *Environmental Ethics*. 2nd ed. Belmont, Calif.: Wadsworth, 1997.

Gruen, Lori, and Dale Jamieson, eds. *Reflecting on Nature*. New York: Oxford University Press, 1994.

Leopold, Aldo. *Sand County Almanac,* New York: Oxford University Press, 1949.

Miller, G. Tyler. *Living in the Environment*. 10th ed. Belmont, Calif.: Wadsworth, 1998.

Newton, Lisa H., and Catherine K. Dillingham. *Watersheds 2: Ten Cases in Environmental Ethics*. Belmont, Calif.: Wadsworth, 1997.

Passmore, John. *Man's Responsibility for Nature*. 2nd ed. London: Duckworth, 1980.

Pojman, Louis P., ed. *Environmental Ethics: Theory and Application*. 3rd ed. Belmont, Calif.: Wadsworth, 2001.

Pojman, Louis P. *Global Environmental Ethics*. Mountain View, Calif.: McGraw-Hill, 2000.

Regan, Thomas, ed. *Earthbound: New Introductory Essays in Environmental Ethics* New York: Random House, 1984.

Revelle, Penelope, and Charles Revelle. *The Environment: Issues and Choices for Society* 1. 3rd ed. Boston: Jones and Bartlett, 1988.

Rolston, Holmes, III. *Environmental Ethics*. Philadelphia: Temple University Press, 1988.

Simon, Julian. *The Ultimate Resource 2*. Princeton, N.J.: Princeton University Press, 1996.

Sterba, James, ed. *Earth Ethics*. Englewood Cliffs, N.J.: Prentice-Hall, 1994.

VanDeVeer, Donald, and Christine Pierce, eds. *The Environmental Ethics and Policy Chapter*. Belmont, Calif.: Wadsworth, 1994.

Westra, Laura. *An Environmental Proposal for Ethics: The Principle of Integrity*. Lanham, Md.: Rowman and Littlefield, 1994.

Zimmerman, Michael, ed. *Environmental Philosophy*. Englewood Cliffs, N.J.: Prentice-Hall, 1993.

CHAPTER 16

International Justice and the Threat of Terrorism

> And when the sacred months are passed, kill those who join other gods with God wherever ye shall find them; and seize them, and lay wait for them with every kind of ambush. . . . Strive against (*jihad*) the infidels (*kafir*) and the hypocrites! Be harsh with them. Their ultimate destiny is hell.
>
> —The Koran 9:3

On September 11, 2001, the worst terrorist attack on civilians in the history of the United States occurred. Four planes were hijacked by Arab Muslim terrorists, becoming in their hands massive, murderous missiles. Two of them crashed into New York's World Trade Center towers, one into the Pentagon in Washington, D.C., and a fourth, perhaps headed for the Capitol building, crashed into a Pennsylvania field. Over three thousand unsuspecting, innocent people were killed, besides the nineteen terrorists. The horrendous kamikaze attacks destroyed the symbols of global capitalism and dented the military headquarters of the most powerful military force on Earth. These lethal suicidal attacks created a gaping hole in a seemingly impregnable wall of civilization, disabusing us of our illusions of invulnerability. We now glimpse through the "hole of hell" the menacing, brutal barbarism on the other side of the wall. Thus a new era in human history has been inaugurated, one which portends a new dimension of evil and a different type of war. The history of the United States and the entire world will henceforth be divided into "Before 9/11" and "After 9/11."

Let us define *terrorism* broadly as using violence against innocents for political or military purposes. As such, terrorism is not new. We find it, as our opening epigraph indicates, in the Muslim holy book, the Koran. But it can also be found before that in the Jewish/Christian Scriptures. In the Old Testament, Israel, with Yahweh's approval, pursued terrorism against neighboring tribes in a manner strikingly similar to what Islamic fundamentalists call *jihad,* annihilation of the infidel. The foundations of Israel were laid in the destruction of Pharaoh's army and the Egyptian first-born. God hardened Pharaoh's heart so that He could destroy him, and when the Israelites pledged themselves to Yahweh as His chosen people, the covenant to which they dedicated themselves included both a prohibition against murder and a prescription in favor of annihilating their neighbors. "When my angel goes before you and brings you in to the Amorites, and the Hittites, and the Perizzites, and the Canaanites, the Hivites, and the Jebusites, and I blot them out, you shall not bow down to their gods, nor serve them. . . . I will send my terror before you, and will throw into confusion all the people against whom you come, and I will make all your enemies turn their backs to you. . . . You shall make no covenant with them or with their gods" (Ex. 23:23–32). The Psalmist, who can sing Zion's songs of praise to God with one breath, can sing the doom of revenge in the next: "O daughter of Babylon, you devastator! Happy shall he be who requites you with what you have done to us! Happy shall he be who takes your little ones and dashes them against the rocks" (Ps. 137:8, 9). Jehovah is a god of blood and thunder, His people, the people of the sword. Our first reading is a selection from the Old Testament book of Joshua, in which Jehovah commands Joshua to exterminate the Canaanite people of Jericho and Ai.

In the twentieth century, we saw an exponential increase in terrorism, especially that perpetrated by the state, and in particular, state terrorism by totalitarian regimes against their own citizens. In the 1980s, 5,431 international terrorist incidents occurred, in which 4,684 people died, and in the 1990s, there were 3,824 incidents with 2,468 deaths. From 1970 to 1995, 64,319 terrorist incidents were recorded, half of them attributed to religious extremists.* The twentieth century will be hard to equal in terms of terrorist atroc-

---

*Quoted in Magnus Ranstorp, "Terrorism in the Name of Religion." *Journal of International Affairs 1996.* One should differentiate state terrorism from nonstate terrorism. State terrorism against a regime's own people is ities. It is estimated that governments killed 169 million of their own people between 1900 and 1987. Joseph Stalin, the all-time mega-murderer, accounts for about 43 million deaths, Mao Tse Tung 38 million, and Adolf Hitler 21 million.* The Khmer Rouge, under the leadership of Pol Pot, caused the deaths of more than 1 million Cambodians (one-eighth of the country's population) through starvation, disease, torture, execution, and forced labor, while carrying out a program of radical social reforms. State terrorism against its external enemies also was rampant in the last century, especially during World War II, as the Germans bombed thousands of innocent people in London and Coventry, the Japanese in the Far Eastern theater of the war, and the Allied Forces killed hundreds of thousands in bombing raids in Dresden, Hamburg, Tokyo, and, finally, with the atomic bomb in Hiroshima and Nagasaki. Northern Ireland and England have had to endure the terrorist threats of the Irish Republican Army for decades, and Israel has lived with suicide bombings for years. Indeed, Israel, though the target of some of the worst terrorist attacks in history, shares the responsibility for the onset of modern terror. Seeking to drive the British from Palestine, the Zionist militant groups, Irgun and the Stern Gang (Etzel), were early perpetrators of terrorist violence in the Middle East. On July 22, 1946, the Polish Jew Menachem Begin, later Prime Minister of Israel, led a group of Etzel saboteurs into the kitchen of the King David hotel in Jerusalem, which served as the headquarters of British government there. They deposited milk cans packed with gelignite in the hotel's lower floor, set the fuses, and fled. When the explosion occurred twenty-five minutes later, ninety-one British, Arabs, and Jews were killed and forty-five were injured. On April 9, 1948, the Stern Gang invaded and captured the village of Deir Yassim, raping women and killing more than 230 Arab men, women, and children, mutilating their bodies.† The Israelis have

---

worse than terrorism against enemies, since the primary purpose of the state is to protect its citizens.

*R. J. Rummel, *Death by Government* (Transaction Publishers, 1994). Long before Lord Acton, in the eighteenth century, Edmund Burke wrote, "Power gradually extirpates from the mind every humane and gentle virtue."

†Howard Sachar, *A History of Israel: From the Rise of Zionism to Our Time* (Knopf, 1996), pp. 267, 333. I do not mean to pick out Israel as worse than the Arab nations or Palestinian leaders. On the contrary, Israel, at least, approximates a democracy, whereas few of her Arab neighbors,

used terror in their conflicts with the Palestinians in combating the latter's uprisings (*intifada*), including the killing of several protesting Palestinians in October 2000. Israel, in claiming it must protect itself from Palestinian and Arab terror, continues to vie with the Palestinians for the dishonorable label *terrorist*. Yet instead of calling Israel a terrorist state, we fund it to the tune of over $3 billion per year.

But few groups have relied on terrorist actions more than the Palestinian movement in Israel, including the Popular Front for the Liberation of Palestine (PFLP) and the Palestine Liberation Organization (PLO). They have used it in a number of airline hijackings (especially between 1968 and 1972), in the murder of eleven Israeli Olympic athletes in September 1972, and in the spate of suicide bombings against Israeli civilians from 1996 to the present. In March 2002, a suicide bombing at a Passover Seder in Tel Aviv killed twenty-six Israelis and wounded one hundred more. Thanks to ample media coverage, such tactics have gotten the attention of the world and brought significant benefits to the Palestinian cause, including the UN decision to grant observer status to the PLO (1974) and later, recognition of the right of Palestinians to a state, as well as a Nobel Peace prize for Yasser Arafat (1994). Arafat received invitations to speak at the best universities in the West (Oxford and Harvard) and honorary doctorates from Maastricht University (1999). The European Economic Community endorsed a Palestinian statehood (1980), and even President George W. Bush called for a Palestinian state. The Palestinians may deserve a state, but other people, such as Turkish Kurds and Chinese Uighers, who may also merit self-determination, have not galvanized world attention in the way the Palestinians have. George Habash and other terrorist leaders have frankly admitted that they owe their attention-getting success to terrorism. Terrorism pays. As Habash has noted, "When we hijack a plane it has more effect than if we killed a hundred Israelis in battle."* The PLO chief observer at the UN noted that "The first

---

including Saudi Arabia and Egypt, make the slightest pretensions thereof. While the Irgun, Etzel, and Stern Gang were carrying out terrorist acts on Palestinians, Palestinian groups led by such men as Fawzi el Kutub and Abdul Khader Husseini were blowing up Israelis. We should also include many incidents of America's treatment of the Native Americans as terrorist acts.

*Ibid.

several hijackings [accomplished more for the Palestinian cause] than twenty years of pleading at the United Nations."

There is a long lineage of terror in the Mideast that the Palestinian terrorists may simply be continuing. In his book *From Beirut to Jerusalem,* Thomas Friedman describes atrocities that took place in Hama, Syria, in early February 1982. After an assassination attempt on the Syrian President Hafez Assad was traced to the Muslim Brotherhood, a group of Sunni Muslim militants in the town of Hama, Assad's forces, led by his brother Rifaat, launched an attack on the Brotherhood in Hama. A fierce civil war broke out between the Muslim guerrillas and the Syrian military. Prisoners were tortured and buildings, even mosques, were destroyed. In a few weeks, much of Hama was in rubble. Assad brought in bulldozers to flatten the rubble, like parking lots. Between 7,000 and 38,000 people were killed. "Normally, a politician would play down such a ghastly incident and dismiss the high casualty numbers as the enemy's propaganda, but Assad's forces claimed them as a badge of honor."

Friedman argues that the incident illustrates the rules of Arab warfare, "Hama Rules," which come straight out of a Hobbesian state of nature, in which life is "solitary, poor, nasty, brutish and short." Destroy or be destroyed! Warring tribes confront each other with no impartial arbiter to enforce mutually agreed-upon rules; the only relevant concern is survival, which entails that the enemy must be destroyed by whatever means necessary. Friedman describes the Middle Eastern states as brutal autocracies where leaders (despots) like Assad have survived by oppressive tactics, including framing their enemies and torturing and executing political rivals. "Restraint and magnanimity are luxuries of the self-confident, and the rulers of these countries are anything but secure on their thrones," writes Friedman.*

Friedman illustrates his theory with a Bedouin legend about an old man and his turkey. One day an elderly Bedouin discovered that by eating turkey he could restore his virility. He bought a small turkey and kept it around his tent, feeding it, so that it would provide a source of renewed strength. One day the turkey was stolen. So the Bedouin called his sons together and said, "Boys, my turkey has been stolen. We are in danger now." His sons laughed, reply-

---

*Thomas Friedman, *From Beirut to Jerusalem* (Farrar, Straus, Giroux, 1989), p. 95.

ing, "Father, it's no big deal. What do you need a turkey for?" "Never mind," the father replied. "We must get the turkey back." But his sons didn't take this seriously and soon forgot about the turkey. A few weeks later, the Bedouin's sons came to him and said, "Father, our camel has been stolen. What should we do?" "Find my turkey," the Bedouin replied. A few weeks later the sons came to him again, saying that the old man's horse was stolen. "Find my turkey," he responded. Finally, a few weeks after that, someone raped his daughter. The Bedouin gazed at his sons and said, "It's all because of the turkey. When they saw that they could take away my turkey, we lost everything."*

To let your enemy take an inch is to give him a mile; it is to lose your wealth, your status, your reputation, your integrity. In such a state, the rule is not "an eye for an eye, a tooth for a tooth, a life for life," but "a life for an eye, two for a tooth, and the lives of your entire tribe for the life of my turkey." Friedman thinks that Hama Rules govern the Middle East conflict. They are the rules that Israel has learned to play by. Friedman notes that the former Prime Minister of Israel, Ariel Sharon, was the one man Assad feared and respected because Sharon played by those rules too. His support of the Lebanese Falangists in the mass killings at Sabra and Chatila and the Israeli reprisals against the Palestinian community was evidence of this.

If Friedman's thesis is correct, we in the West are dealing with warriors who are playing by a different set of rules than ourselves. Our notions of proportionate response and the distinction between combatants and noncombatants don't apply to Osama bin Laden, Iman al Zawahiri, and Al Qaeda. As bin Laden has announced, every American is an enemy and ought to be destroyed, whether he or she is a soldier or a civilian.

In our second reading, "Compassion and Terror," Martha C. Nussbaum argues that the events of 9/11 evoke a moral issue that goes back to Euripides' treatment of the women of Troy in his *Trojan Women*. It is the problem of using the tragic imagination to empathize with those who suffer, both those in our own society and those who live in distant places and may even be viewed as our enemies. She contrasts the compassionate outlook with that of the Stoic perspective, which prescribes extirpating attachments and enjoins detachment from pain and suffering and the fickle fortunes

*Ibid., p. 89.

of life. For the Stoics—Cicero, Epictetus, Marcus Aurelius—and for Kant morality consists of concentrated commitment to duty, not sentiment. In the end, Nussbaum argues, we need the sentiments for the good life. The events of September 11, 2001, have made us aware of the sufferings of others: the families of the victims of the Twin Towers in our own country: the misery of the people, especially the women, of Afghanistan: and victims of genocide, including the orphaned children in Rwanda. The tragedy of 9/11 was a wake-up call to the need for a universal critical compassion. Nussbaum argues that we ought to invigorate our educational system by introducing or enhancing the moral imagination to make us more aware of our common humanity.

In our next reading, "The Cosmopolitan Response to Terrorism," Louis Pojman outlines a series of short-term and long-term prescriptions, including a cosmopolitan moral vision, resulting ultimately in institutional cosmopolitanism (that is, world government). In our last selection, Thomas Nagel deals with the question of why terrorist killings are wrong but "collateral" deaths in war may be morally permissible though regrettable.

God's Command to Destroy Jericho and Ai

This reading from the Old Testament/Hebrew Bible sets forth God's command to Joshua, the leader of Israel, to destroy the Canaanite people of Jericho and Ai. It is an early version of what we know as a *jihad,* in which every living human and animal are killed.

6

1 Now Jericho was shut up from within and from without because of the people of Israel; none went out, and none came in. **2** And the LORD said to Joshua, "See, I have given into your hand Jericho, with its king and mighty men of valor. **3** You shall march around the city, all the men of war going around the city once. Thus shall you do for six days. **4** And seven priests shall bear seven trumpets of rams' horns before the ark; and on the seventh day you shall march around the city seven times, the priests blowing the trumpets. **5** And when they make a long blast with the ram's horn, as soon as you hear the sound of the trumpet, then all the people shall shout with a great shout; and the wall of the city will fall down flat, and the people shall go up every man straight before him."

6 So Joshua the son of Nun called the priests and said to them, "Take up the ark of the covenant, and let seven priests bear seven trumpets of rams' horns before the ark of the LORD." **7** And he said to the people, "Go forward; march around the city, and let the armed men pass on before the ark of the LORD."

8 And as Joshua had commanded the people, the seven priests bearing the seven trumpets of rams' horns before the LORD went forward, blowing the trumpets, with the ark of the covenant of the LORD following them.

9 And the armed men went before the priests who blew the trumpets, and the rear guard came after the ark, while the trumpets blew continually. **10** But Joshua commanded the people, "You

---

Old Testament: Joshua 6, 7, and 8:1–31.

shall not shout or let your voice be heard, neither shall any word go out of your mouth, until the day I bid you shout; then you shall shout." **11** So he caused the ark of the LORD to compass the city, going about it once; and they came into the camp, and spent the night in the camp.

12 Then Joshua rose early in the morning, and the priests took up the ark of the LORD. **13** And the seven priests bearing the seven trumpets of rams' horns before the ark of the LORD passed on, blowing the trumpets continually; and the armed men went before them, and the rear guard came after the ark of the LORD, while the trumpets blew continually. **14** And the second day they marched around the city once, and returned into the camp. So they did for six days. **15** On the seventh day they rose early at the dawn of day, and marched around the city in the same manner seven times: it was only on that day that they marched around the city seven times. **16** And at the seventh time, when the priests had blown the trumpets, Joshua said to the people, "Shout; for the LORD has given you the city.

17 And the city and all that is within it shall be devoted to the LORD for destruction; only Rahab the harlot and all who are with her in her house shall live, because she hid the messengers that we sent. **18** But you, keep yourselves from the things devoted to destruction, lest when you have devoted them you take any of the devoted things and make the camp of Israel a thing for destruction, and bring trouble upon it. **19** But all silver and gold, and vessels of bronze and iron, are sacred to the LORD; they shall go into the treasury of the LORD." **20** So the people shouted, and the trumpets were blown. As soon as the people heard the sound of the trumpet, the people raised a great shout, and the wall fell down flat, so that the people went up into the city, every man straight before him, and they took the city. **21** Then they utterly destroyed all in the city, both men and women, young and old, oxen, sheep, and asses, with the edge of the sword. **22** And Joshua said to the two men who had spied out the land, "Go into the harlot's house, and bring out from it the woman, and all who belong to her, as you swore to her." **23** So the young men who had been spies went in, and brought out Rahab, and her father and mother and brothers and all who belonged to her; and they brought all her kindred, and set them outside the camp of Israel. **24** And they burned the city with fire, and all within it; only the silver and gold, and the vessels of bronze and of iron, they put into the treasury of the house of the LORD. **25** But Rahab the harlot, and her father's household, and all who belonged to her, Joshua saved alive; and she dwelt in Israel to this day, because she hid the messengers whom Joshua sent to spy out Jericho.

26 Joshua laid an oath upon them at that time, saying, "Cursed before the LORD be the man that rises up and rebuilds this city, Jericho. At the cost of his first-born shall he lay its foundation, and at the cost of his youngest son shall he set up its gates." **27** So the LORD was with Joshua; and his fame was in all the land.

7

1 But the people of Israel broke faith in regard to the devoted things; for Achan the son of Carmi, son of Zabdi, son of Zerah, of the tribe of Judah, took some of the devoted things; and the anger of the LORD burned against the people of Israel. **2** Joshua sent men from Jericho to Ai, which is near Beth-a'ven, east of Bethel, and said to them, "Go up and spy out the land." And the men went up and spied out Ai. **3** And they returned to Joshua, and said to him, "Let not all the people go up, but let about two or three thousand men go up and attack Ai; do not make the whole people toil up there, for they are but few." **4** So about three thousand went up there from the people; and they fled before the men of Ai, **5** and the men of Ai killed about thirty-six men of them, and chased them before the gate as far as Sheb'arim, and slew them at the descent. And the hearts of the people melted, and became as water.

6 Then Joshua rent his clothes, and fell to the earth upon his face before the ark of the LORD until the evening, he and the elders of Israel; and they put dust upon their heads. **7** And Joshua said, "Alas, O Lord GOD, why hast thou brought this people over the Jordan at all, to give us into the hands of the Amorites, to destroy us? Would that we had been content to dwell beyond the Jordan! **8** O Lord, what can I say, when Israel has turned their backs before their enemies! **9** For the Canaanites and all the inhabitants of the land will hear of it, and will surround us, and cut off our name from the earth; and what wilt thou do for thy great name?"

10 The LORD said to Joshua, "Arise, why have you thus fallen upon your face? **11** Israel has sinned; they have transgressed my covenant which I commanded them; they have taken some of the devoted things; they have stolen, and lied, and put them among their own stuff. **12** Therefore the people of Israel cannot stand before their enemies; they turn their backs before their enemies, because they have become a thing for destruction. I will be with you no more, unless you destroy the devoted things from among you. **13** Up, sanctify the people, and say, 'Sanctify yourselves for tomorrow; for thus says the LORD, God of Israel, There are devoted things in the midst of you, O Israel; you cannot stand before your enemies, until you take away the devoted things from among you. **14** In the morning therefore you shall be brought near by your tribes; and the tribe which the LORD takes shall come near by families; and the family which the LORD takes shall come near by households; and the household which the LORD takes shall come near man by man. **15** And he who is taken with the devoted things shall be burned with fire, he and all that he has, because he has transgressed the covenant of the LORD, and because he has done a shameful thing in Israel.'"

16 So Joshua rose early in the morning, and brought Israel near tribe by tribe, and the tribe of Judah was taken; **17** and he brought near the families of Judah, and the family of the Zer'ahites was taken; and he brought near the family of the Zer'ahites man by man, and Zabdi was taken; **18** and he brought near his household man by man, and Achan the son of Carmi, son of Zabdi, son of Zerah, of the tribe of Judah, was taken. **19** Then Joshua said to Achan, "My son, give glory to the LORD God of Israel, and render praise to him; and tell me now what you have done; do not hide it from me." **20** And Achan answered Joshua, "Of a truth I have sinned against the LORD God of Israel, and this is what I did: **21** When I saw among the spoils a beautiful mantle from Shinar, and two hundred shekels of silver, and a bar of gold weighing fifty shekels, then I coveted them, and took them; and behold, they are hidden in the earth inside my tent, with the silver underneath."

22 So Joshua sent messengers, and they ran to the tent; and behold, it was hidden in his tent with the silver underneath. **23** And they took them out of the tent and brought them to Joshua and all the people of Israel; and they laid them down before the LORD. **24** And Joshua and all Israel with him took Achan the son of Zerah, and the silver and the mantle and the bar of gold, and his sons and daughters, and his oxen and asses and sheep, and his tent, and all that he had; and they brought them up to the Valley of Achor. **25** And Joshua said, "Why did you bring trouble on us? The LORD brings trouble on you today." And all Israel stoned him with stones; they burned them with fire, and stoned them with stones. **26** And they raised over him a great heap of stones that remains to this day; then the LORD turned from his burning anger. Therefore to this day the name of that place is called the Valley of Achor.

8

1 And the LORD said to Joshua, "Do not fear or be dismayed; take all the fighting men with you, and arise, go up to Ai; see, I have given into your hand the king of Ai, and his people, his city, and his land; **2** and you shall do to Ai and its king as you did to Jericho and its king; only its spoil and its cattle you shall take as booty for yourselves; lay an ambush against the city, behind it."

3 So Joshua arose, and all the fighting men, to go up to Ai; and Joshua chose thirty thousand mighty men of valor, and sent them forth by night. **4** And he commanded them, "Behold, you shall lie in ambush against the city, behind it; do not go very far from the city, but hold yourselves all in readiness; **5** and I, and all the people who are with me, will approach the city. And when they come out against us, as before, we shall flee before them; **6** and they will come out after us, till we have drawn them away from the city; for they will say, 'They are fleeing from us, as before.' So we will flee from them; **7** then you shall rise up from the ambush, and seize the city; for the LORD your God will give it into your hand. **8** And when you have taken the city, you shall set the city on fire, doing as the LORD has bidden; see, I have commanded you."

9 So Joshua sent them forth; and they went to the place of ambush, and lay between Bethel and Ai, to the west of Ai; but Joshua spent that night among the people. **10** And Joshua arose early in the morning and mustered the people, and went up, with the elders of Israel, before the people to Ai. **11** And all the fighting men who were with him went up, and drew near before the city, and encamped on the north side of Ai, with a ravine between them and Ai. **12** And he took about five thousand men, and set them in ambush between Bethel and Ai, to the west of the city. **13** So they stationed the forces, the main encampment which was north of the city and its rear guard west of the city. But Joshua spent that night in the valley.

14 And when the king of Ai saw this he and all his people, the men of the city, made haste and went out early to the descent toward the Arabah to meet Israel in battle; but he did not know that there was an ambush against him behind the city. **15** And Joshua and all Israel made a pretense of being beaten before them, and fled in the direction of the wilderness. **16** So all the people who were in the city were called together to pursue them, and as they pursued Joshua they were drawn away from the city. **17** There was not a man left in Ai or Bethel, who did not go out after Israel; they left the city open, and pursued Israel. **18** Then the LORD said to Joshua, "Stretch out the javelin that is in your hand toward Ai; for I will give it into your hand." And Joshua stretched out the javelin that was in his hand toward the city. **19** And the ambush rose quickly out of their place, and as soon as he had stretched out his hand, they ran and entered the city and took it; and they made haste to set the city on fire. **20** So when the men of Ai looked back, behold, the smoke of the city went up to heaven; and they had no power to flee this way or that, for the people that fled to the wilderness turned back upon the pursuers. **21** And when Joshua and all Israel saw that the ambush had taken the city, and that the smoke of the city went up, then they turned back and smote the men of Ai. **22** And the others came forth from the city against them; so they were in the midst of Israel, some on this side, and some on that side; and Israel smote them, until there was left none that survived or escaped. **23** But the king of Ai they took alive, and brought him to Joshua. **24** When Israel had finished slaughtering all the inhabitants of Ai in the open wilderness where they pursued them and all of them to the very last had fallen by the edge of the sword, all Israel returned to Ai, and smote it with the edge of the sword. **25** And all who fell that day, both men and women, were twelve thousand, all the people of Ai. **26** For Joshua did not draw back his hand, with which he stretched out the javelin, until he had utterly destroyed all the inhabitants of Ai. **27** Only the cattle and the spoil of that city Israel took as their booty, according to the word of the LORD which he commanded Joshua. **28** So Joshua burned Ai, and made it for ever a heap of ruins, as it is to this day. **29** And he hanged the king of Ai on a tree until evening; and at the going down of the sun Joshua commanded, and they took his body down from the tree, and cast it at the entrance of the gate of the city, and raised over it a great heap of stones, which stands there to this day.

30 Then Joshua built an altar in Mount Ebal to the LORD, the

God of Israel, **31** as Moses the servant of the LORD had commanded the people of Israel, as it is written in the book of the law
of Moses, "an altar of unhewn stones, upon which no man has
lifted an iron tool"; and they offered on it burnt offerings to the
LORD, and sacrificed peace offerings.

For Further Reflection

1. Compare these passages from the Old Testament/Hebrew Bible
   with the Islamic idea of *jihad,* a holy war, in which the infi-
   dels are to be destroyed. Does this tell you anything about the
   relationship of religion to violence?

Compassion and Terror

MARTHA C. NUSSBAUM

Martha C. Nussbaum is Ernest Freund Distinguished Service Professor of Law and Ethics at the University of Chicago
and the author of several books, including *Women and
Human Development: The Capabilities Approach* (2000) and
Upheavals of Thought: The Intelligence of the Emotions
(2001).

   In this essay, Nussbaum contrasts two responses to the
tragedy of the terrorist attacks of September 11, 2001: the
Stoic response of Marcus Aurelius, Epictetus, and Cicero
and the Sentimentalist response of Euripides, Aristotle, and
Adam Smith, which calls on us to extend our sympathies
to the whole of humanity and base our moral policy on
such sympathetic cosmopolitanism. She opts for the sympathy approach and ends her essay by suggesting some

Reprinted from *Terrorism and International Justice,* ed. James P. Sterba
(Oxford University Press, 2003), by permission.

ways we could inculcate this approach into our education system.

> The name of our land has been wiped out.
> —Hecuba, in Euripides, *Trojan Women*

> Not to be a fan of the Greens or Blues at the races, or the light-armed or heavy-armed gladiators at the Circus.
> —Marcus Aurelius, *Meditations*

I

The towers of Troy are burning. All that is left of the once-proud city is a group of ragged women, bound for slavery, their husbands dead in battle, their sons murdered by the conquering Greeks, their daughters raped. Hecuba their queen invokes the king of the gods, using, remarkably, the language of democratic citizenship: "Son of Kronus, Council-President of Troy, father who gave us birth, do you see these undeserved sufferings that your Trojan people bear?" The Chorus answers grimly, "He sees, and yet the great city is no city. It has perished, and Troy exists no longer." A little later, Hecuba herself concludes that the gods are not worth calling on, and that the very name of her land has been wiped out.

In one way, the ending of this drama is as bleak as any in the history of tragic drama. Death, rape, slavery, fire destroying the towers, the city's very name effaced from the record of history by the acts of rapacious and murderous Greeks. And yet, of course, it did not happen that way, not exactly. For the story of Troy's fall is being enacted, some six hundred years after the event, by a company of Greek actors, in the Greek language of a Greek poet, in the presence of all the adult citizens of Athens, most powerful of Greek cities. Hecuba's cry to the gods even imagines him as a peculiarly Athenian type of civic official, president of the city council. So the name of the land didn't get wiped out after all. The imaginations of the conquerors were haunted by it, transmitted it, and mourn it. Obsessively their arts repeat the events of long-ago destruction, typically inviting, as here, the audience's compassion for the women of Troy and blame for their assailants. In its very structure the play makes a claim for the moral value of compassionate imagining, as it asks its audience to partake in the terror of a burning city, of murder and rape and slavery. Insofar as members of the audience are engaged by this drama, feeling fear and grief for the conquered city, they demonstrate the ability of compassion to cross lines of time, place, and nation—and also, in the case of many audience members, the line of sex, perhaps more difficult yet to cross.

Nor was the play an aesthetic event cut off from political reality. The dramatic festivals of Athens were sacred festivals strongly connected to the idea of democratic deliberation, and the plays of Euripides were particularly well known for their engagement with contemporary events. In this case, the audience that watched *The Trojan Women* had recently voted to put to death the men of the rebellious colony of Melos and to enslave the women and children. Euripides invites them to contemplate the real human meaning of their actions. Compassion for the women of Troy should at least cause moral unease, reminding Athenians of the full and equal humanity of people who live in distant places, their fully human capacity for suffering.

But did those imaginations really cross those lines? Think again of that invocation of Zeus. Trojans, if they worshipped Zeus as king of gods at all, surely did not refer to him as the president of the city council. The term *prytanis* is an Athenian legal term, completely unknown elsewhere. So it would appear that Hecuba is not a Trojan but a Greek. Her imagination is a Greek democratic (and, we might add, mostly male) imagination. Maybe that's a good thing, in the sense that the audience is surely invited to view her as their fellow and equal. But it still should give us pause. Did compassion really enable those Greeks to reach out and think about the real humanity of others, or did it stop short, allowing them to reaffirm the essential Greekness of everything that's human? Of course compassion required making the Trojans somehow familiar, so that Greeks could see their own vulnerability in them, and feel terror and compassion as for people related to themselves. But it's so easy for the familiarization to go too far: they are just us, and we are the ones who suffer humanly. Not those other ones, over there in Melos.

America's towers, too, have burned. Compassion and terror are in the fabric of our lives. And in those lives we have seen evidence of the good work of compassion, as Americans made real to themselves the sufferings of so many different people whom they never would otherwise have thought about: New York firefighters, that gay rugby player who helped bring down the fourth plane, bereaved families of so many national and ethnic origins. We even sometimes noticed with a new attention the lives of Arab-Americans among us, or felt a sympathy with our Sikh taxi driver when he tells us how often he is told to go home to "his own country"— even though he came to the United States as a political refugee from the miseries of police repression in the Punjab. Sometimes our compassion even crossed that biggest line of all, the national boundary. Tragedy surely led many people to sympathize with the women of Afghanistan in a way that feminists tried to get people to do for ages, without success. And other civilian victims of the violence, or people threatened by the violence, sometimes caused imaginations to stop, briefly, before they rushed back home to see what latest threat the evening news has brought our way.

The events of September 11 make vivid a philosophical problem that has been debated from the time of Euripides straight on through much of the history of the Western philosophical tradition. This is the question of what do to about compassion, given its obvious importance in shaping the civic imagination, but given, too, its obvious propensity for self-serving narrowness. Is compassion, with all its faults, our best hope as we try to educate citizens to think well about human relations both inside the nation and across national boundaries? So some thinkers have suggested. I count Euripides among them, and I would also include in this category Aristotle, and Rousseau, and Hume, and Adam Smith. Or is it a threat to good political thinking and to the foundations of a truly just world community? So the Greek and Roman Stoics thought, and before them Plato, and after them Spinoza, and Adam Smith. The enemies of compassion hold that we cannot build a truly wise concern for humanity on the basis of such a slippery and uneven motive; impartial motives based on ideas of dignity and respect should take its place. The friends of compassion reply that without building political morality on what we know and on what has deep roots in our childhood attachments, we will be left with a morality that will be empty of urgency—as Aristotle puts it, a "watery" concern all round.

I shall not trace the history of the debate in this essay. Instead, I shall focus on its central philosophical ideas and try to sort them

out, offering a limited defense of compassion and the tragic imagination, and then making some suggestions about how its pernicious tendencies can best be countered—with particular reference,
throughout, to our own political situation, and the role of the terrorist attacks in engendering emotions, good and bad. Let me set
the stage for the analysis to follow by turning to Smith, who, as
you will have noticed, turns up in my taxonomy on both sides of
the debate. Smith offered one of the best accounts we have of sympathy and compassion, and of the ethical achievements of which
this moral sentiment is capable. But later, in a section of the work
entitled "Of the Sense of Duty," he offers a very solemn warning
against trusting this imperfect sentiment too far when duty is what
we are trying to get clear about. His concern, like mine, is with
our difficulty keeping our minds fixed on the sufferings of people
who live on the other side of the world.

> Let us suppose that the great empire of China, with all its myriads
> of inhabitants, was suddenly swallowed up by an earthquake, and
> let us consider how a man of humanity in Europe, who had no sort
> of connexion with that part of the world, would be affected upon
> receiving intelligence of this dreadful calamity. He would, I imagine,
> first of all, express very strongly his sorrow for the misfortune of that
> unhappy people, he would make many melancholy reflections upon
> the precariousness of human life, and the vanity of all the labours
> of man, which could thus be annihilated in a moment. . . . And when
> all this fine philosophy was over, when all these humane sentiments
> had been once fairly expressed, he would pursue his business or his
> pleasure, take his repose or his diversion, with the same ease and
> tranquillity, as if no such accident had happened. The most frivo-
> lous disaster which could befall himself would occasion a more real
> disturbance. If he was to lose his little finger to-morrow, he would
> not sleep to-night; but, provided he never saw them, he will snore
> with the more profound security over the ruin of a hundred millions
> of his brethren, and the destruction of that immense multitude seems
> plainly an object less interesting to him, than this paltry misfortune
> of his own.

That is just the issue that should trouble us, as we think about
American reactions to September 11. We see a lot of "humane sentiments" around us, and extensions of sympathy beyond people's
usual sphere of concern. But how often, both now and at other
times, those sentiments stop short at the national boundary. Amer-

icans thought the events of September 11 were bad because they involved *us* and *our* nation. Not just human lives, but American lives. The world came to a stop—in a way that it never has for Americans, when disaster befalls human beings in other places. The genocide in Rwanda didn't even work up enough emotion in us to prompt humanitarian intervention. The plight of innocent civilians in Iraq never made it onto our national radar screen. Floods, earthquakes, cyclones—and the daily deaths of thousands from preventable malnutrition and disease—none of these makes the American world come to a standstill, none elicits a tremendous outpouring of grief and compassion. At most we get what Smith so trenchantly described: a momentary flicker of feeling, quickly dissipated by more pressing concerns close to home.

Frequently, however, we get a compassion that is not only narrow, failing to include the distant, but also polarizing, dividing the world into an "us" and a "them." Compassion for our own children can so easily slip over into a desire to promote the well-being of our children at the expense of other people's children. Similarly, compassion for our fellow Americans can all too easily slip over into a desire to make America come out *on top,* defeating or subordinating other nations. One vivid example of this slip took place at a baseball game I went to at Comiskey Park, the first game played in Chicago after September 11—and a game against the Yankees, so there was heightened awareness of the situation of New York and its people. Things began well, with a moving ceremony commemorating the firefighters who had lost their lives, and honoring local firefighters who had gone to New York afterwards to help out. There was even a lot of cheering when the Yankees took the field, a highly unusual transcendence of local attachments. But as the game went on and the beer began flowing, one heard, increasingly, the chant, "U-S-A. U-S-A," a chant left over from the Olympic hockey match in which the United States defeated Russia, expressing the wish for America to defeat, abase, humiliate, its enemies. Indeed, the chant USA soon became a general way of expressing the desire to crush one's enemies, whoever they were. When the umpire made a bad call against the Sox, the same group in the bleachers turned to him, chanting "U-S-A." Anyone who crosses us is an evil terrorist, deserving of extinction. From "humane sentiments" we had turned back to the pain in our little finger.

With these Smithean examples before us, how can we trust compassion, and the imagination of the other that it contains? But if we don't trust that, what else can we plausibly rely on, to get ethical responsibility out of horror?

I shall proceed as follows. First, I offer an analysis of the emotion of compassion, focusing on the thoughts and imaginings on which it is based. This gives us a clearer perspective on how and where it is likely to go wrong. Second, I examine the counter-tradition's proposal that we can base political morality on respect for dignity, doing away with appeals to compassion. This proposal, at first attractive, contains, on closer inspection, some deep difficulties. Third, I return to compassion, asking how, if we feel we need it as a public motive, we might educate it so as to overcome, as far as we can, the problem that Smith identified. This will lead me to a sketch of some educational reforms that may possibly extend compassion in a more reliable way than the contemplation of terrorist threats.

II

Compassion is not just a warm feeling in the gut, if it is that at all. It involves a set of thoughts, quite complex. We need to dissect them, if we are to make progress in understanding how it goes wrong and how it may be steered aright. There is a good deal of agreement about this, among philosophers as otherwise diverse as Aristotle and Rousseau, and also among contemporary psychologists and sociologists who have done empirical work on the emotion.[1]

Compassion is an emotion directed at another person's suffering or lack of well-being. It requires the thought that the other person is in a bad way, and a pretty seriously bad way. (Thus we don't feel compassion for people who lose trivial items like a toothbrush or a paper clip.) It thus contains within itself an appraisal of the seriousness of various predicaments. Let us call this the *judgment of seriousness.*

Notice that this assessment is made from the point of view of the person who has the emotion. It does not neglect the actual suffering of the other, which certainly should be estimated in taking the measure of the person's predicament. And yet it does not nec-

---

[1]In this section I am drawing on the analysis of compassion for which I argue at greater length in Nussbaum, *Upheavals of Thought: The Intelligence of Emotions* (New York: Cambridge University Press, 2001).

essarily take at face value the estimate of the predicament this person will be able to form. As Smith emphasized, we frequently have great compassion for people whose predicament is that they have lost their powers of thought; even if they seem like happy children, we regard this as a terrible catastrophe. On the other side, when people moan and groan about something, we don't necessarily have compassion for them: for we may think that they are not really in a bad predicament. Thus when very rich people grumble about taxes, many of us don't have the slightest compassion for them: for we judge that it is only right and proper that they should pay what they are paying—and probably a lot more than that! The suffering of Hecuba and the Trojan women becomes the object of the audience's compassion directly, because it is understood that their predicament is really grave: slavery, loss of children, loss of city, are among the calamities all human beings typically fear.

So the judgment of seriousness already involves quite a complex feat of imagination: it involves both trying to look out at the situation from the suffering person's own viewpoint and then assessing the person's own assessment. Complex though the feat is, young children easily learn it, feeling sympathy with the suffering of animals and other children, but soon learning, as well, to withhold sympathy if they judge that the person is just a crybaby, or spoiled.

Next comes the *judgment of non-desert*. Hecuba asked Zeus to witness the "undeserved sufferings" of the Trojan women, using a Greek word, *anaxia*, that appears in Aristotle's definition of tragic compassion. The tradition claims that we will not have compassion if we believe that the person fully deserves the suffering, just brought it on herself. There may be a measure of blame, but then, in our compassion we typically register the thought that the suffering exceeds the measure of the fault. The Trojan women are an unusually clear case, because, more than most tragic figures, they are hit by events in which they have no active share at all, being women. But we can see that non-desert is a salient part of our compassion even when we do also blame the person: typically we feel compassion at the punishment of a criminal offender, say, only to the extent that we think circumstances beyond his control are at least in good measure responsible for his becoming the bad person he is. People who have the idea that the poor brought their poverty upon themselves by shiftlessness and laziness fail, for that reason, to have compassion for them.

Next there is a thought much stressed in the tradition, which I shall call the *judgment of similar possibilities:* Aristotle, Rousseau, and others suggest that we have compassion only insofar as we believe that the suffering person shares vulnerabilities and possibilities with us. I think we can clearly see that this judgment is not strictly necessary for the emotion, as the other two seem to be. We have compassion for non-human animals, without basing it on any imagined similarity—although, of course, we need somehow to make sense of their predicament as serious and bad. We also imagine that an invulnerable god can have compassion for mortals, and it doesn't seem that this idea is conceptually confused. For the finite imaginations of human beings, however, the thought of similar possibilities is a very important psychological mechanism through which we get clear about the seriousness of another person's plight. This thought is often accompanied by empathetic imagining, in which we put ourselves in the suffering person's place, imagine the predicament as our own.

Finally, however, there is one thing more, not mentioned in the tradition, which I believe must be added in order to make the account complete. This is what, in writing on the emotions, I have called the *eudaimonistic judgment,* namely, a judgment that places the suffering person or persons among the important parts of the life of the person who feels the emotion. In my more general analysis of emotions, I argue that they are always eudaimonistic, meaning focused on the agent's most important goals and project. Thus we feel fear about damages that we see as significant for our own well-being and our other goals; we feel grief at the loss of someone who is already invested with a certain importance in our scheme of things. Eudaimonism is not egoism. I am not claiming that emotions always view events and people as mere means to the agent's own satisfaction or happiness. But I do mean that the things that occasion a strong emotion in us are things that correspond to what we have invested with importance in our account to ourselves of what is worth pursuing in life.

Compassion can evidently go wrong in several different ways. It can get the judgment of non-desert wrong, sympathizing with people who actually don't deserve sympathy and withholding sympathy from those who do. Even more frequently, it can get the judgment of seriousness wrong, ascribing too much importance to the wrong things or too little to things that have great weight. Notice that this problem is closely connected to obtuseness about social justice, in the sense that if we do not think a social order unjust for denying women the vote, or subordinating African Americans, then we will not see the predicament of women and African Americans as bad, and we won't have compassion for them. We will think that things are just as they ought to be. Again, if we think it's unjust to require rich people to pay capital gains tax, we will have a misplaced compassion toward them. But finally, and obviously, compassion can get the eudaimonistic judgment wrong, putting too few people into the circle of concern. On my account, then, we will not have compassion without a moral achievement that is at least coeval with it.

My account, I think, is able to explain the unevenness of compassion better than other more standard accounts. Compassion begins from where we are, from the circle of our cares and concerns. It will be felt only toward those things and persons that we see as important, and of course most of us most of the time ascribe importance in a very uneven and inconstant way. Empathetic imagining can sometimes extend the circle of concern. Thus psychologist Daniel Batson has shown experimentally that when the story of another person's plight is vividly told subjects will tend to experience compassion toward the person and form projects of helping. This is why I say that the moral achievement of extending concern to others need not antedate compassion, but can be coeval with it. Still, there is a recalcitrance in our emotions, given their link to our daily scheme of goals and ends. Smith is right: thinking that the poor victims of the disaster in China are important is easy to do for a short time, hard to sustain in the fabric of our daily life, where there are so many things closer to home to distract us, and these things are likely to be so much more thoroughly woven into our scheme of goals.

Let us return to September 11, armed with this analysis. The astonishing events made many Americans recognize the nation itself as part of their circle of concern with a new vividness. Most Americans rely on the safety of our institutions and our cities, and don't really notice how much they value them until they prove vulnerable—in just the way that a lover often doesn't see how much he loves until the loved one is ill or threatened. So our antecedent concern emerged with a new clarity in the emotions we experienced. At the same time, we actually extended concern, in many cases, to people in America who had not previously been part of our circle of concern at all: the New York firefighters, the victims of the disasters. We extended concern to them both because we heard their stories, like a tragic drama being played out before us, and also, especially, because we were encouraged to see them as one part of the America we already loved and for which we intensely feared. When disaster struck in Rwanda, we did not in a similar way extend concern, or not stably, because there was no antecedent basis for it: suffering Rwandans could not be seen as part of a larger "us" for whose fate we trembled. Vivid stories can create a temporary sense of community, but they are unlikely to sustain concern for long, if there is no pattern of interaction that would make the sense of an "us" an ongoing part of our daily lives.

Things are of course still worse with any group that figures in our imaginations as a "them" over against the "us." Such people are not only by definition non-us, they are also, by threatening the safety of the us, implicitly bad, deserving of any misfortune that might strike them. This is the sports-fan mentality so neatly depicted in my baseball story. Compassion for a member of the opposing team? You've got to be kidding. "U-S-A" just *means*, kill the ump.

III

In the light of these difficulties, it is easy to see why much of the philosophical tradition has wanted to do away with compassion as a basis for public choice and to turn, instead, to detached moral principles whose evenhandedness can be relied on. The main candidate for a central moral notion has been the idea of human worth or dignity, and the principle that has been put to work, from the Stoics and Cicero on through Kant and beyond, is the idea of acting, always, in such a way as to show respect for the dignity of humanity. We are to recognize that all humans have dignity, and that this dignity is both inalienable and equal, not affected by differences of class, caste, wealth, honor, status, or even sex. The recognition of human dignity is supposed to impose obligations on all moral agents, whether the humans in question are co-nationals or foreigners. In general, it enjoins us to refrain from all aggression and from fraud, since both are seen as violations of human dignity, ways of using a human being as merely a tool of one's own ends. Out of this basic idea Cicero developed much of the basis for modern international law in the areas of war, punishment, and hospi-

tality.[2] Other Stoics used it to criticize conventional norms of patriarchal marriage, the physical abuse of servants, and many other
aspects of Roman social life.

This Stoic tradition was quite clear that respect for human dignity could move us to appropriate action, both personal and social,
without our having to rely at all on the messier and more inconstant motive of compassion. Indeed, for separate reasons, which I
shall get to shortly, they thought compassion was never appropriate, so they could not rely on it. What I now want to ask is whether
this counter-tradition was correct. Respect for human dignity looks
like the right thing to focus on, something that can plausibly be
seen as of boundless worth, constraining all actions in pursuit of
well-being, and also as equal, creating a kingdom of ends in which
humans are ranked horizontally, so to speak, rather than vertically.
Why should we not follow the counter-tradition, as in many respects
we do already?

Now it must be admitted that the notion of human dignity is not
an altogether clear notion. In what does it consist? Why should we
think that all human life has it? The minute the Stoic tradition tries
to answer such questions, problems arise. In particular, the answer
almost always takes the form of saying, look at how far we are
above the beasts. Reason, language, moral capacity—all these things
are seen as worthy of respect and awe at least in part because "the
beasts," so called, don't have them, because they make us better
than others. This view has its moral problems, clearly. It has long
been used to deny that we have any obligations of justice toward
non-human forms of life. Compassion, if slippery, is at least not
dichotomous in this way: it allows of extension in multiple directions, including the direction of imagining the sufferings of animals
in the squalid conditions we create for them.

There is another more subtle problem with the dignity idea. It
was crucial, according to the Stoics, to make dignity something that
is radically independent of fortune: all humans have it, no matter
where they are born or how they are treated. It exerts its claim
everywhere, and it can never be lost. If dignity went up or down
with fortune, it would create ranks and orders of human beings:
the well-born and healthy will be worth more than the ill-born and

---

[2]See my "Duties of Justice, Duties of Material Aid: Cicero's Problematic
Legacy," *Journal of Political Philosophy.*

hungry. So the Stoics understood their project of making dignity self-sufficient as essential for the notion of equal respect and regard.

But this move leads to a problem: how can we give a sufficiently important place to the goods of fortune for political purposes, once we admit that the truly important thing, the thing that lies at the core of our humanity, doesn't need the goods of fortune at all? How can we provide sufficient incentive to political planners to arrange for an adequate distribution of food and shelter and even political rights and liberties, if we say that dignity is unaffected by the lack of such things? Stoic texts thus look oddly quietistic: respect human dignity, they say. But it doesn't matter at all what conditions we give people to live in, since dignity is complete anyway. Seneca, for example, gives masters stern instructions not to beat slaves or use them as sexual tools. But as for the institution of slavery itself? Well, this does not really matter so much, for the only thing that matters is the free soul within, and that cannot be touched by any contingency.

Things are actually even worse than this. For the minute we start examining this reasoning closely, we see that it is not only quietistic, it is actually incoherent. Either people need external things or they do not. But if they do not, if dignity is utterly unaffected by rape and physical abuse, then it is not very easy, after all, to say what the harm of beating or raping a slave is. If these things are no harm to the victim, why is it wrong to do them? Seneca lacks not only a basis for criticizing the institution of slavery, but also a basis for the criticism he actually makes, of cruel and inhumane practices toward slaves.

Kant had a way of confronting this question, and it is a plausible one, within the confines of what I have called the countertradition. Kant grants that humanity itself, or human worth, is independent of fortune: under the blows of "step-motherly nature" the good will still shines like a jewel for its own sake. But external goods such as money, health, social position are still required for happiness, which we all reasonably pursue. So there are still very weighty moral reasons for promoting the happiness of others, reasons that can supply both individuals and states with a basis for good thoughts about the distribution of goods.

The Stoics notoriously deny this, holding that virtue is sufficient for *eudaimonia*. What I want to suggest now is that their position about human dignity pushes them strongly in this direction. Think of the person who suffers poverty or hardship. Now either this person has something that is beyond price, by comparison to which all the money and health and shelter in the world is as nothing—or she does not have something that is beyond price. Her dignity is just one contributor to her happiness, a piece of it that can itself be victimized and held hostage to fortune, in such a way that she may end up needy and miserable, even though she has dignity, and even virtue. This would mean that human dignity is being weighed in the balance with other goods; it no longer looks like the thing of surpassing, even infinite worth that we took it to be. There are, after all, ranks and orders of human beings: slavery and abuse can actually change people's situation with regard to their most important and inclusive end, *eudaimonia* itself.

Because the Stoics do not want to be forced to that conclusion, they insist that external goods are not required for *eudaimonia:* virtue is sufficient. And basic human dignity, in turn, is sufficient for becoming virtuous, if one applies oneself in the right way. It is for this deep reason that the Stoics reject compassion as a basic social motive, not just because it is slippery and uneven. Compassion gets the world wrong, because it is always wrong to think that a person who has been hit by fortune is in a bad or even tragic predicament. "Behold how tragedy comes about," writes Epictetus: "when chance events befall fools." In other words, only a fool would mind the events depicted in Euripides' play, and only fools in the audience would view these events as tragic.

So there is a real problem about how, and how far, the appeal to equal human dignity motivates. Looked at superficially, the idea of respect for human dignity appears to provide a principled, even-handed motive for good treatment of all human beings, no matter where they are placed. Looked at more deeply, it seems to license quietism and indifference to things in the world, on the grounds that nothing that merely happens to people is really bad.

We have now seen two grave problems with the counter-tradition: what I shall call the *animal problem,* and what I shall call the *external goods problem.* Neither of these problems is easy to solve within the counter-tradition. By contrast, the Euripidean tradition of focusing on compassion as a basic social motive has no such problems. Compassion can and does cross the species boundary, and whatever good there may be in our current treatment of animals is likely to be its work. As for the problem of external goods, compassion has no such problem, for it is focused in its very nature on the damages of fortune: its most common objects, as Aristotle listed them in the *Rhetoric,* are the classic tragic predicaments: loss of country, loss of friends, old age, illness, and so on.

But let us suppose that the counter-tradition can solve these two problems, providing people with adequate motives to address the tragic predicaments. Kant makes a good start on the external goods problem, at least. So let us imagine that we have a reliable way of motivating conduct that addresses human predicaments, without the uneven partiality that so often characterizes compassion. A third problem now awaits us. I shall call it the *problem of watery motivation.* The name "watery" motivation comes from Aristotle's criticism of Plato's ideal city. Plato tried to remove partiality by removing family ties, and asking all citizens to care equally for all other citizens. Aristotle says that the difficulty with this strategy is that "there are two things above all that make people love and care for something, the thought that it is all theirs, and the thought that it is the only one they have. Neither of these will be present in that city" (*Pol.* 1262b22–3). Because nobody will think of a child that it is all theirs, entirely their own responsibility, the city will, he says, resemble a household in which there are too many servants, so nobody takes responsibility for any task. Because nobody will think of any child or children that they are the only ones they have, the intensity of care that characterizes real families will simply not appear, and we will have, he says, a "watery" kind of care all round (1262b15).

If we now examine the nature of Stoic motivation, I think we will see that Aristotle is very likely to be correct. I shall focus here on Marcus Aurelius, in many ways the most psychologically profound of Stoic thinkers. Marcus tells us that the first lesson he learned from his tutor was "not to be a fan of the Greens or Blues at the races, or the light-armed or heavy-armed gladiators at the Circus" (1.5). His imagination had to unlearn its intense partiality and localism—and apparently the tutor assumes that already as young children we have learned narrow sectarian types of loyalty. It is significant, I think, that the negative image for the moral imagination is that of sports fandom: for in all ages, perhaps, that has been such a natural way for human beings to imagine yet other types of loyalty, to family, city, and nation. It was no accident that those White Sox fans selected a hockey chant as their way of expressing distress about the fate of the nation.

The question is whether this negative lesson leaves the personality enough resources to motivate intense concern with people anywhere. For Marcus, unlearning partiality requires an elaborate and systematic program of uprooting concern for all people and things in this world. He tells us of the meditative exercises that he regularly performs, in order to get himself to the point at which the things that divide people from one another do not matter to him. One side of this training looks benign and helpful: we tell ourselves that our enemies are really not enemies, but part of a common human project (Meditations II 1). Instead of seeing the enemy as an opponent, see him as a fellow human being, sharing a "portion of the divine," sharing similar concerns and goals, and engaged in the common project of making human life better. Passages such as these suggest that a strong kind of even-handed concern can be meted out to all human beings, without divisive jealousy and partiality. We see ourselves not as team players, not as family members, not as loyal citizens of a nation, but as members of the human kind, and our most important goal as that of enhancing the life of the human kind.

Now even in this good case problems are lurking: for we notice that this exercise relies on the thoughts that give rise to the animal problem and the external goods problem. We are asked to imagine human solidarity and community by thinking of a "portion of the divine" that resides in all and only humans: we look like we have a lot in common because we are so sharply divided from the rest of nature. And the idea that we have a common work relies, to at least some extent, on Marcus's prior denigration of external goods: for if we ascribed value to external goods we would be in principle competing with one another, and it would be difficult to conceive of the common enterprise without running into that competition.

But I have resolved to waive those two difficulties, so let me do so. Even then, the good example is actually very complex. For getting to the point where we can give such concern even-handedly to all human beings requires, as Marcus makes abundantly clear, the systematic extirpation of intense cares and attachments directed at the local: one's family, one's city, the objects of one's love and desire. Thus Marcus needs to learn not only not to be a sports fan, but also not to be a lover. Consider the following extraordinary passage:

> How important it is to represent to oneself, when it comes to fancy dishes and other such foods, "This is the corpse of a fish, this other thing the corpse of a bird or a pig." Similarly, "This Falernian wine

is just some grape juice," and "This purple vestment is some sheep's hair moistened in the blood of some shellfish." When it comes to sexual intercourse, we must say, "This is the rubbing together of membranes, accompanied by the spasmodic ejaculation of a sticky liquid." How important are these representations, which reach the thing itself and penetrate right through it, so that one can see what it is in reality. (VI.13)[3]

Now of course these exercises are addressed to the problem of external goods. Here as elsewhere, Marcus is determined to unlearn the unwise attachments to externals that he has learned from his culture. This project is closely connected to the question of partiality, because learning not to be a sports fan is greatly aided by learning not to care about the things over which people typically fight. In the quoted passage, however, the link to partiality seems even more direct: for learning to think of sex as just the rubbing of membranes really is learning not to find special value or delight in a particular, and this extirpation of eroticism really does seem to be required by a regime of impartiality. Not being a fan of the Blues means, too, not being a fan of this body or that body, this soul or that soul, this city or that city.

But getting rid of our erotic investment in bodies, sports teams, family, nation—all this leads us into a strange world, a world that is gentle and unaggressive, but also strangely lonely and hollow. Marcus suggests that we have two choices only: the world of real-life Rome, which resembles a large gladiatorial contest (see Seneca De Ira 2.8), each person striving to outdo others in a vain competition for externals, a world exploding with rage and poisoned by malice, or the world of Marcus's gentle sympathy, in which we respect all human beings and view all as our partners in a common project, but in which the terms of the project do not seem to matter very much, and the whole point of living in the world becomes increasingly unclear.

And this means: something like a death within life. For only in a condition close to death, in effect, is moral rectitude possible. Marcus tries repeatedly to think of life as if it is a kind of death already, a procession of meaningless occurrences:

---

[3]Translation based on the French version of Pierre Hadot, translated into English by Chase, in *The Inner Citadel* (Cambridge, Mass.: Harvard University Press, 1998), with my modifications.

> The vain solemnity of a procession; dramas played out on the stage; troops of sheep or goats; fights with spears; a little bone thrown to dogs; a chunk of bread thrown into a fish-pond; the exhausting labor and heavy burdens under which ants must bear up; crazed mice running for shelter; puppets pulled by strings . . . (VII.3)[4]

(This, by an emperor who was at that very time on campaign in Parthia, leading the fight for his nation.) And the best consolation for that bleak conclusion comes also from the thought of death:

> Think all the time about how human beings of all sorts, and from all walks of life and all peoples, are dead . . . We must arrive at the same condition where so many clever orators have ended up, so many grave philosophers, Heraclitus, Pythagoras, Socrates; so many heroes of the old days, so many recent generals and tyrants. And besides these, Eudoxus, Hipparchus, Archimedes, other highly intelligent minds, thinkers of large thoughts, hard workers, versatile in ability, daring people, even mockers of the perishable and transitory character of human life, like Menippus. Think about all of these that they are long since in the ground . . . And what of those whose very names are forgotten? So: one thing is worth a lot, to live out one's life with truth and justice, and with kindliness toward liars and wrongdoers. (VI.47)

Because we shall die, we must recognize that everything particular about us will eventually be wiped out. Family, city, sex, children, all will pass into oblivion. So really, giving up those attachments is not such a big deal. What remains, and the only thing that remains, is truth and justice, the moral order of the world. In the face of the looming inevitability of our end, we should not mind being dead already.

Marcus is alarming because he has gone deep into the foundations of cosmopolitan moral principle. What he has seen is that impartiality, fully and consistently cultivated, requires the extirpation of the eroticism that makes human life the life we know. The life we know is unfair, uneven, full of war, full of me-first nationalism and divided loyalty. But he sees that we can't so easily remove these attachments while retaining humanity. So, if that ordinary erotic humanity is unjust, get rid of it. But can we live like this,

[4]Ibid.

once we see the goal with Marcus's naked clarity? Isn't justice something that must be about and for the living?

IV

Let me proceed from now on on the hypothesis that Marcus is correct: extirpating attachments to the local and the particular does deliver to us a death within life. Let me also proceed on the hypothesis that we will reject this course as an unacceptable route to the goal of justice, or even one that makes the very idea of justice a hollow fantasy. (This is Adam Smith's conclusion as well: enamored as he is of Stoic doctrine, he thinks we must reject them when they tell us not to love our own families.) Where are we then placed?

It looks as if we are back where Aristotle, and Adam Smith, leave us: with the unreliability of compassion, and yet the need to rely on it, since we have no more perfect motive. This does not mean that we need give up on the idea of equal human dignity, or respect for it. But insofar as we retain, as well, our local erotic attachments, our relation to that motive must always remain complex and dialectical, a difficult conversation within ourselves as we ask how much humanity requires of us, and how much we are entitled to give to our own. But any such difficult conversation will require, for its success, the work of the imagination. If we do not have exceptionless principles, if, instead, we need to negotiate our lives with a complex combination of moral reverence and erotic attachment, we need to have a keen imaginative and emotional understanding of what our choices mean for people in conditions of many different kinds, and the ability to move resourcefully back and forth from the perspective of our personal loves and cares to the perspective of the distant. Not the extirpation of compassion, then, but its extension and education. How might such an extension be arranged?

The philosophical tradition helps us identify places where compassion goes wrong: by making errors about fault, about seriousness, about the circle of concern. But the ancient tradition, not being very interested in childhood, does not help us see clearly how and why it goes especially badly wrong. So to begin the task of educating compassion as best we can, we need to ask how and why local loyalties and attachments come to take in some instances an especially virulent and aggressive form, militating against a more general sympathy. To answer this question we need a level of psychological understanding that was not available in the ancient Greek and Roman world, or not completely. I would suggest (and have argued elsewhere) that one problem we particularly need to watch out for is a type of pathological narcissism in which the person demands complete control over all the sources of good, and a complete self-sufficiency in consequence. Nancy Chodorow long ago argued that this expectation colors the development of males in many cultures in the world. Recent studies of teenage boys in America, particularly the impressive work of Dan Kindlon and Michael Thompson, in their book *Raising Cain,* has given strong local support to this idea. The boys that Kindlon and Thompson study have learned from their culture that men should be controlling, self-sufficient, dominant. They should never have, and certainly never admit to, fear and weakness. The consequence of this deformed expectation, Kindlon and Thompson show, is that these boys come to lack an understanding of their own vulnerabilities, needs, and fears, weaknesses that all human beings share. They lack the language in which to characterize their own inner world, and they are by the same token clumsy interpreters of the emotions and inner lives of others. This emotional illiteracy is closely connected to aggression, as fear is turned outward, with little real understanding of the meaning of aggressive words and acts for the feelings of others. Kindlon and Thompson's boys, some ten years later, make the sports fans who chanted "U-S-A" at the ump, who think of all obstacles to American supremacy and self-sufficiency as opponents to be humiliated.

So the first recommendation I would make for a culture of respectful compassion is a Rousseauian one: it is, that an education in common human weakness and vulnerability should be a very profound part of the education of all children. Children should learn to be tragic spectators, and to understand with increasing subtlety and responsiveness the predicaments to which human life is prone. Through stories and dramas, they should get the habit of decoding the suffering of another, and this decoding should deliberately lead them into lives both near and far.

As children learn to imagine the emotions of another, they should at the same time learn the many obstacles to such understanding, the many pitfalls of the self-centered imagination as it attempts to be just. Thus, one should not suppose that one can understand a member of one's own family, without confronting and continually criticizing the envy and jealousy in oneself that pose powerful obstacles to that understanding. One should not imagine that one can understand the life of a person in an ethnic or racial group different from one's own, or a sex different from one's own, or a nation, without confronting and continually criticizing the fear and greed and the demand for power that make such interactions so likely to produce misunderstanding and worse. What I am suggesting, then, is that the education of emotion, to succeed at all, needs to take place in a culture of ethical criticism and especially self-criticism, in which ideas of equal respect for humanity will be active players in the effort to curtail the excesses of the greedy self.

At the same time, since we have spoken of greed, we can also see that the chances of success in this enterprise will be greater if the society in question does not overvalue external goods of the sort that cause envy and competition. The Stoics are correct when they suggest that overvaluation of external goods is a major source of destructive aggression in society. If we criticize them to the extent of encouraging people to love their families, their friends, their work, their local context, even, to a certain extent, their nation, this does not entail the overvaluation of money, honor, status, and fame that Seneca saw at Rome and that we see in America now. Obviously enough, the urge for control over the sources of good is more pernicious when the good includes these highly competitive elements. If people care primarily for friendship, good work, and, let's even hope, social justice, they are less likely to see everything in terms of the hockey match, and more likely to use Marcus's image of the common work or project. Because this project is not a Stoic one, there will still be important sources of good to be protected from harm, and there will still be justified anger at damage to those good things. But a lot of occasions for anger in real life are not good or just, and we can do a lot, as a society, to prune away the greedy attachments that underpin them. It is well known that privileged young people in America are exceedingly focused on the attributes of wealth and status; psychological studies show that they are prone to humiliate others because they don't have the same expensive ski vacations or expensive designer clothes. We must consider how education can address these problems, at all ages.

Next, we must speak about terrorism. This is a [chapter] about terrorism, and I have taken the events of September 11 as my theme; and yet I have suggested that the narrowness in our emotions is a perfectly general problem, endemic to American life, not a problem altogether new in the context of the "war on terrorism." We can now go further: crises are bad paradigms. An intense focus on our own danger, such as terrorism evokes, may be a good incentive to turn our imaginations outward. But Adam Smith is right: it is all too easy to feel something in a crisis, and then to lapse, when daily life and the fascination of one's own concerns reexert their hold. Human compassion always has this defect, so far as one can see. When there is an earthquake or a flood, people pay attention to that part of the world for a while, and even give money. Then they forget about that part of the world, and stop giving money. The asymmetry is especially obvious when our own interests hang in the balance. Terrorism makes us pay attention—for a while. But how quickly, once things return to normal, our imaginations stop conceiving of distant people. The eudaimonistic judgment no longer includes them.

Most of the preventable suffering and death in the world is not caused by terrorism. It is caused by malnutrition, and lack of education, and all the ills connected to poverty. It is also caused by daily small crimes, such as sex-selective infanticide and the systematically unequal health care of women and girls. It is very easy to gain public attention for dangers to the lives of girls and women when we can connect these dangers to evil terrorists; thus the women of Afghanistan have won a sympathy that countless hungry suffering women all over the world have not won. More generally, it is easy to gain attention for a problem when it is dramatic and graphic. Thus, female genital mutilation has energized Western women far more than the pedestrian topics of female hunger and lack of education, even though the latter affect vastly more women, and cause more pervasive damage to human functioning.

There is, it seems to me, great danger in the idea that there is an ongoing "war on terrorism." There are many dangers actually, but the one on which I want to focus is the way such talk hooks our imaginations to a picture of violent struggle, inherently dramatic and self-involving, and fails to connect them to the daily sufferings of ordinary people. Drama can awaken the mind. But the analysis I have offered suggests that we will achieve no lasting moral progress unless and until the daily unremarkable lives of people distant from us become real in the fabric of our own daily lives, until our everyday eudaimonistic judgments about our important ends include them as ends, not just as temporary players in a drama in which we are the central actors.

How can this be done? Only by a vast reform of education. Children at all ages must learn to recognize people in other countries as their fellows, and to sympathize with their plights. Not just their dramatic plights, in a cyclone or a war, but their daily plights. Children should learn how difficult it is for a child in rural Rajasthan to get adequate nutrition; how such a child has to work long hours herding sheep or goats; how, if that child is a girl child, she is likely to be married off before she is eight, and to have no opportunity to make major life choices for herself. All this learning should be extended and deepened, as the child matures, through courses in world history, world politics, and the major world religions. We should learn how to visualize and recognize one another with some degree of human literacy. Thus, the Americans who in July 2002 mistook a family of actors from Kerala in South India, speaking and writing Malayalim, for Arab terrorists from some "terrorist group," and had them arrested when the flight landed, were displaying an appallingly high level of cultural and human illiteracy, no doubt reinforced by the divisive rhetoric of the "war on terrorism." A film actress from Kerala looks no more like an Arab terrorist than a farmer from Minnesota looks like a nightclub dancer from New York, and the script in which Malayalim is written looks no more like Arabic than our alphabet looks like the Hebrew alphabet. But Americans simply think of Asia as one vast place without internal differentiations. This is a failure of our educational systems, and we must do better.[5]

In concluding, I want to turn back to Euripides, reflecting, in concluding, about the role of tragic spectatorship, and tragic art generally, in promoting good citizenship of the sort I have been advocating here. Tragedies are not Stoic: they start with us "fools," and the chance events that befall us. At the same time, they tend to get their priorities straight. Thus, the overvaluations I have just been mentioning usually are not validated in tragic works of art. When people moan and groan about a social slight, or the loss of some money, that is, more often at least, an occasion for comedy. The great Athenian tragic dramas, to stick with those, revolve around attachments that seem central and reasonable: to one's children, one's city, one's loved ones, one's bodily integrity, one's health, one's freedom from pain, one's status as a free person rather than

[5]See my *Cultivating Humanity: A Classical Defense of Reform in Liberal Education* (Cambridge, Mass.: Harvard University Press, 1997).

a slave, one's ability to speak and persuade others, the very friendship and company of others. The loss of these things is worthy of
lamentation, and the tragic dramas encourage us to understand the
depth of these losses and, with the protagonists, to fear them. In
exercising compassion the audience is learning its own possibilities and vulnerabilities: as Aristotle said, "things such as might happen" in a human life. At the same time, often, the audience learns
that people different in sex, race, age, nation experience suffering
in a way that is like our way, and that suffering is as crippling for
them as it would be for us.

Such recognitions have their pitfalls, and I have identified some
of them in talking about *The Trojan Women*. We always risk error
in bringing the distant person close to us: we ignore differences of
language and of cultural context, and the manifold ways in which
these differences shape the inner world. These are the issues that
our educational systems must address more effectively, as I have
argued. But there are dangers in any act of imagining, and we
should not let these particular dangers cause us to admit defeat
prematurely, surrendering before an allegedly insuperable barrier
of otherness. When I was out in the rural areas of Rajasthan, visiting an education project for girls, I asked the Indian woman who
ran the project (herself, by the way, from Delhi) how she would
answer the frequent complaint that a foreigner can never understand the situation of a person in another nation. She thought for
a while and said, "I have the greatest difficulty understanding my
own sister." In other words, there are barriers to understanding in
any human relationship. As Proust said, any real person imposes
on us a "dead weight" that our "sensitivity cannot remove." The
obstacles to understanding a sister may in some instances be greater
than those to understanding a stranger. At least they are different.
And of course there are still other and equally great obstacles to
understanding our own selves. All we can do is to trust our imaginations, and then criticize them (listening if possible to the critical
voices of those we are trying to understand), and then trust our
imaginations again. Perhaps out of this dialectic between criticism
and trust something like understanding may eventually grow. At
least the product will very likely be better than the obtuseness that
so generally reigns in human relations.

As Euripides knew, terror has this good thing about it: it makes
us sit up and take notice. It is not the endpoint of moral development, and it may be a trap, hooking our imaginations on drama

rather than leading them toward a new attention to the daily. But terror can be at least the beginning of moral progress. Tragic dramas can't precisely teach anything new, since they will be moving only to people who at some level already understand how bad these predicaments are. But they can awaken the sleepers, reminding them of human realities they are neglecting in their daily political lives. The experience of terror and grief for our towers might be just that, an experience of terror and grief for our towers. One step worse, it could be a stimulus for blind rage and aggression against all the opposing hockey teams and bad umpires in the world. But if we cultivate a culture of critical compassion, such an event may, like Hecuba's Trojan cry, possibly awaken a larger sense of the humanity of suffering, a patriotism constrained by respect for human dignity and by a vivid sense of the real losses and needs of others. And in that case, it really will turn out that Euripides was right and Hecuba was wrong: the name of the Trojan land was not wiped out. It lives, in a work of the imagination to which we can challenge ourselves, again and again.

For Further Reflection

1. What, according to Nussbaum, is the important lesson of the tragedy of the terrorist attacks of September 2001? Explain.

2. Examine Nussbaum's debate between the Stoic and Sentimentalist approach to terrorism. Do you agree with her analysis of the tension? If so, explain why. If not, explain why not.

3. What sort of social attitude is Nussbaum most concerned to reject and defeat?

4. What are some suggestions Nussbaum makes for inculcating the lessons regarding cosmopolitan compassion in our education system?

The Cosmopolitan Response to Terrorism

LOUIS P. POJMAN

Louis P. Pojman was the editor of this volume. His bio-sketch appears on p. 31.

In this essay he first discusses the attacks of September 11, 2001, in the light of the culture and causes of international terrorism and then examines long-term moral responses to it, defending a cosmopolitan perspective. First, here is his working definition of *terrorism:*

Terrorism is a type of political violence that intentionally targets civilians (noncombatants) in a ruthlessly destructive, often unpredictable manner. Terrorism hardly constitutes mindless violence. Instead, it reflects a detailed strategy that uses horrific violence to make people feel weak and vulnerable, often disproportionate to either the terrorist act or to the terrorist's long-term power. This undermining fear is then utilized to promote concrete political objectives. While some of these objectives may be morally commendable, their moral quality tends to be annulled by the murderous means employed, so that terrorism must be discouraged by civilized governments. Essentially, terrorism employs *horrific violence against unsuspecting civilians, as well as combatants, in order to inspire fear and create panic, which in turn will advance the terrorists' political or religious agenda.*

INTRODUCTION: THE DAY OF IGNOMINY

> The ruling to kill the Americans and their allies—civilians and military—is an individual duty for every Muslim who can do it in any country in which it is possible to do it, in order to liberate the Al Aksa Mosque and the holy mosque from their grip, and in order for their armies to move out of all the lands of Islam, defeated and unable to threaten any Muslim.
>
> —Osama bin Laden[1]

> We are facing a movement far exceeding the level of issues and policies and governments that pursue them. This is no less than a clash of civilizations—perhaps irrational but surely a historic reaction of an ancient rival against our Judeo-Christian heritage, our secular present, and the world-wide expansion of both.
>
> —Bernard Lewis[2]

Although terrorism has been endemic to human history for a long time, there was something horrific about the suddenness and sheer magnitude of the events of 9/11. In one fell swoop, our illusion of invulnerability was swept away: America's twin pillars of capitalism were struck down. It was our *Day of Ignominy*. Other nations, such as Israel, had experienced terrorism for decades, but we naively thought ourselves safe. Now we know that no one is immune from unpredictable violence. Our airlines are especially vulnerable. While we were still reeling under this terrible tragedy, four people, beginning with a man in Florida, died of anthrax exposure and several more people, including NBC's Tom Brokaw and Senate Majority Leader Tom Daschle, received envelopes containing anthrax spores. The disaster created a psychological trauma unparalleled in recent history.

During the terrible Cold War, at least we knew that our enemy loved life as much as we and would be motivated by secular self-

---

[1]Quoted in Jeffrey Goldberg. "The Education of a Holy Warrior." *New York Times Magazine,* June 25, 2000.

[2]Bernard Lewis written in 1990. Quoted in Samuel Huntington's "The Clash of Civilizations?" *Foreign Affairs* (Summer, 1993).

interest, so that a policy of Mutual Assured Destruction (MAD) was feasible. But now we are confronted by enemies who would just as soon cause a nuclear holocaust that would wipe us and them from the face of the earth, liberating them for heavenly bliss.

CLASH OF CULTURES

One salient characteristic of the recent Al Qaeda terrorist attacks, which differentiates them from nationalistically inspired attacks, is their religious underpinning. Unlike nationalistic terrorist attacks by the IRA, Tamil Tigers, or PLO, Al Qaeda's attacks are not done in the name of a nation. They are rooted in culture, namely a religious world-view and practice, and represent what Samuel Huntington refers to as a "clash of civilizations."[3] The terrorist attacks carried out by an Islamic terrorist *jihad* against the Egyptian government and the Al Qaeda-sponsored attacks against the U.S. embassies in East Africa and the World Trade Center in New York were religious in nature. Osama bin Laden, Iman al Zawahiri, and their cohorts have announced that this is a *jihad,* a holy war against the *kafir,* the infidel, the Evil Empire of the West, and especially the United States. The Al Qaeda network sees itself as the vanguard of an Islamic movement seeking to overthrow American and Western hegemony in the world, and extirpate their influence in the Muslim world, removing both American military bases and Western culture from countries like Saudi Arabia, Egypt, and Kuwait. The attack on America was intended to provoke a violent American reaction, which in turn would ignite a worldwide Islamic uprising against the West.

The ideology behind the attacks was apocalyptic, signaling the coming of divine judgment on secular pluralist society. It was God—Allah—who brought down the Twin Towers even as he brought down the Canaanite walls of Jericho. The suicide bombers were only his obedient servants in the mighty and magnificent retributive judgment. They will be given a heavenly reward, but Allah's plan is unfolding in a war against the secular, materialist, hedonistic West.

This clash of civilizations, pitting the culture of Islamic fundamentalism against Western culture, with its modernity, secularity, and democracy, has become the new battleground for mankind. With the

[3]Ibid., p. 32, for an analysis of this phenomenon.

Cold War over, ideological differences between cultures reemerge as the source of conflict. Religion is surpassing nationalism as the foremost threat to world peace and stability. Although the majority of Muslims may eschew the terrorist's tactics, there is something in Islamic culture that predisposes it to violence, the idea of *jihad,* the holy war against the infidel. Saddam Hussein invoked the *jihad,* appealing to all Muslims to support Iraq against America in the Gulf War, and Iran's Ayatollah Khameni has called for a holy war against the West, saying that "the struggle against American aggression, greed, plans and policies will be counted as a *jihad* and anybody who is killed on that path is a martyr."[4] The Muslim schools, *madrassas,* throughout the Muslim world teach children that the West is evil and that they have a duty to perpetuate the *jihad* against it. Although many Muslims reject Islamic fundamentalism, emphasizing peace, the idea of *jihad* is an essential part of Islam, and Islamic fundamentalists are engaged in war wherever a critical mass of fundamentalism confront a different culture. In Lebanon, Islam battles Maronite Christians; in Israel, Jews; in Kashmir, Hindus; in Nigeria, Catholic and Protestant Christians; in Somalia and Sudan, evangelical Christians; in Ethiopia, Coptic Christians; in the Baltics and former Soviet Union, Orthodox Christians; in Pakistan, the small Christian minority; in Indonesia, Timorese Christians; in Europe and America, Christians, Jews, and secularists. Tolerance toward the "People of the Book" (Jews and Christians) may be officially advocated by the Koran, but fundamentalists, such as the Wahabi sect in Saudi Arabia and Pakistan, seize upon the notion of the *jihad* against the *kafir* to override any tendency toward tolerance.

Religion can be a powerful motivating force. Invoking the authority of God and offering the rewards of eternal bliss, it can be an incentive to extreme acts of virtue and of vice. The religious picture of the universe is all-embracing and dominates the life of the true believer. If the Western mind, still rooted in the Enlightenment of the seventeenth and eighteenth centuries, is largely *modern,* using reason to resolve conflicts of interests, the Islamic religious mind is *premodern,* rejecting the mandates of reason in favor of an uncritical deliverance of religion or mysticism. Reason, for them, always functions as a strategy within the bounds of religion alone. It is not used to examine the metaphysical basis of the ideology, which is uncritically assumed as the Truth, but is used in an instrumental

[4]Ibid., p. 35.

manner to discover the best means of destroying the infidel. Hence, the terrorist rejects the critical self-examination set forth in the Western Enlightenment, but is ever zealous to use the relevant technology (airplanes, computers, and explosives) that emerged as a by-product of the Enlightenment.

CAUSES OF TERRORISM

Although cultural attitudes, such as religious dogma, may be a significant cause of terrorism, despair or a sense of hopelessness rooted in oppression, ignorance, poverty, and perceived injustice may be the contributing causes, the soil in which fundamentalism can grow and flourish. Often it is those who have been frustrated by the powers that be who strike out against what they perceive as their enemy. Perceived oppression evokes sympathy in the hearts of many, even to the point of excusing or romanticizing violent responses against the "oppressor." Hence, the French existentialist philosopher, Jean Paul Sartre, writing in defense of the national Liberation Front in Algeria, wrote, "To shoot down a European is to kill two birds with one stone, to destroy an oppressor and the man he oppressed at the same time: there remains a dead man and a free man." Unfortunately for Sartre's analysis, most of the victims of terrorism are unsuspecting, innocent civilians, no more engaged in oppression than a Bedouin sheep herder, a fireman trying to rescue people from a burning building, a passenger on United Airlines Flight 93, or a woman trying to run a business from the 100th floor of the World Trade Center. But according to the premodern logic of terror, there is no difference between them and the commander at Auschwitz who is leading innocent people to the gas chambers. The attractiveness of terrorism is exacerbated by cultures that encourage violence as a response to perceived harms and wrongs. When a religious or political ideology is present, the tendency to resort to terror may be exponentially increased, so that otherwise normal people may resort to extreme measures in the name of religion, believing that by killing people they are serving God and, thereby, assuring themselves eternal bliss.[5]

[5]See Salman Rushdie's "Yes, This Is About Islam." *New York Times,* November 2, 2001.

Peer pressure, religious sanctions, and a quasi-military scheme of hierarchical command-obedience, which causes the terrorist to focus on the importance of the action rather than his own self-interest, enables the terrorist to act in ways that we would normally consider irrational in the extreme. We are revulsed by terrorism, not because the terrorists are cowards, but because their misguided courage is directed at violating the rights of and even murdering unsuspecting innocents. In September (2001), shortly after the Day of Ignominy, CBS's *60 Minutes* produced a documentary directed by Bob Simon on the life of suicide bombers. It showed young Palestinian men who were selected by radical Islamic leaders to be suicide bombers against Israelis. The youths, believing this call to *jihad* was a sacred honor, were indoctrinated to the point of believing that they would, through their kamikaze missions, become holy martyrs, and ascend straight to heaven. A video made of their final farewell, recording their commitment to die for their cause, was sent to their families, who were led to believe that their sons were dying a holy martyr's death. After such profound commitment, it would be hard for the youth to back out, return home, ring the doorbell and announce, "Surprise, Mom, I decided that suicide bombing was not in my best interest." The comprehensive cultural reinforcement of the suicide bomber and terrorist marks off this kind of fundamentalism from our normal sense of prudent and moral behavior. Poverty and oppression are not sufficient (or even necessary) for terrorism, though they are contributing causes. The overriding impetus is a culture that endorses and reinforces violent responses against certain types of persons and property.

As noted in the Introduction to this chapter, terrorism has existed from time immemorial, but now, with modern technology, including rapid transport, the bomb, the airplane, chemical, biological, radiological and nuclear warfare, the threat to society has been exponentially increased. Furthermore, television and mass communication in general give terrorism widespread publicity. *Publicity is the oxygen of terrorism.* Terrorist acts displayed on worldwide networks like CNN compel our attention, and this point has not been lost on the terrorist leaders. Thanks largely to this widespread coverage, it took just a couple of terrorists bombing the marine barracks in Beirut in 1986, killing 241 servicemen, to cause the withdrawal of American and French forces from Lebanon. The media have an awful responsibility to exercise restraint in covering terrorism, but given media's competitive nature, unless we are willing to curtail first amendment rights, such dramatic publicity for our enemies may be the price we pay for a free society.

A WAR ON TERRORISM

A war on terrorism has been declared by President George W. Bush, and troops have been deployed to areas of the Middle East and Central Asia, where terrorist camps under the auspices of Osama bin Laden and Al Qaeda may still prosper. But it will be extremely difficult to defeat sophisticated modern terrorism, for these terrorists have neither a state nor identifiable public buildings or institutions. They are an elusive, moving target, leaving no return address. They operate in small, semi-autonomous cells, which are difficult to infiltrate. And if you attack one terrorist base camp, the terrorists move into the Afghan mountains or establish a new base in Iraq, Pakistan or, possibly, Saudi Arabia. Like crime itself, terrorism may not be completely eliminated, only limited.

Perhaps the answer is to alter the conditions in which terrorism thrives, such as poverty, ignorance, oppression, and injustice. While no doubt part of an enlightened strategy, this is extremely difficult to accomplish, since in this case, ignorance and oppression are associated with religion, namely, Muslim (Wahabi) fanaticism, which opposes Western liberal values, including women's rights, tolerance of different life-styles, and abortion. The same ideology that opposes secular liberal values gives deep meaning to the lives of the adherents of the terrorist groups. The religion of Allah gives purpose, hope, and a practical guide to action to millions of Muslims, who may live more virtuous or, at least more disciplined, lives than their secular counterparts. It is noteworthy that some of the terrorist leaders say the same thing about contemporary American decadence as do American Christian fundamentalists leaders, such as Jerry Falwell and Pat Robertson, who aver that God permitted this horror of the Day of Ignominy because of our drift into secularism and permissive liberalism. At bottom, this is a struggle of moral secularity against intolerant religious theocracy, of liberal open society versus the premodern fantastic ideology of the tribal closed society. And it represents a supreme challenge to civilization, one not equaled since the rise of Hitler and Stalin.

THE MORAL RESPONSE

In responding to the Day of Ignominy we have a number of converging goals. One salient goal is to honor the 3,000 victims of the kamikaze attacks. This entails attacking the causes of terrorism and eradicating the moral swamp that breeds fanaticism, hatred, and indiscriminate violence. We can honor the fallen more immediately by punishing those who perpetrated this deed, the terrorist leaders who trained, financed, and motivated the perpetrators to destroy innocent life and property on 9/11.

Let me turn to some long-term strategies.

National Service

Some good has already come out of the tragedy of September 11. Immediately after the catastrophe, our country came together in an almost unprecedented way. Democrats and Republicans united and cooperated to build a more vibrant and secure nation. Most young people want to serve their country and, in the months succeeding the Day of Ignominy, have been enlisting in the FBI, CIA, and the military services. Applications to the nation's military academies rose. We should turn this tragedy into an occasion to inaugurate new opportunities for national and world service. A new model of national conscription seems a plausible option. Each able-bodied youth should be required to serve our nation or the world in some beneficial capacity, such as the military, AmeriCorps, Domestic Youth Corps, or Peace Corps. In a recent *New York Times* essay, "A New Start for National Service," Senators John McCain and Evan Bayh call for the government to institute new service programs to involve youth in civil defense, community service, and international service. In return the government would fund the college education of these young people.[6] Such programs have the virtue of helping young people internalize a moral patriotism and, at the same time, promote worthy goals, such as educating the poor, ministering to the sick and elderly, and serving one's nation and the world. If such programs are appropriately organized and administered, they

---

[6]John McCain and Evan Bayh, "A New Start for National Service." *New York Times,* November 6, 2001. The two senators plan to introduce legislation in the Senate to effect such a program.

will not hinder personal autonomy, but provide a channel for service. Serving one's country provides a mechanism for expressing one's gratitude for all the benefits membership provides, creates a mechanism for identifying with the moral goals of the nation, and thus inculcates a sense of citizenship, enabling us to help make this a better nation. Though the immediate sphere of service should be one's own country, eventually the circle should be expanded to include the entire world. This leads to the next point, the recognition of a Universal Morality with Universal Human Rights.

Spreading the Message of a Universal Morality with Universal Human Rights

The moral point of view, whether one takes a consequentialist or deontological perspective, is universalistic, based on rationally approved, impartial principles, recognizing a universal humanity, rather than particular groups or persons, as the bearers of moral consideration. When seeking to rescue a drowning man we do not ask him, "Are you an American or an Arab?" before seeking to save him. We rescue him because he is a human being. We must come to see all humanity as tied together in a common moral network. If all do not hang together, each will *hang* alone. Since morality is universalistic, its primary focus must be on the individual, not the nation, race, or religious group. We are all human beings, and only accidentally, citizens of the United States, Afghanistan, Germany, Japan, Brazil, or Nigeria. As Tom Friedman has pointed out, after the biblical worldwide flood, Noah and God's responses were different (Gen. 6–9). Noah planted a vine, made wine, and got drunk, stupefying himself to the global tragedy. God, on the other hand, set forth a set of universal rules for living, anticipating the Ten Commandments.

We too need to respond by recognizing a universal set of moral rules and spreading the knowledge of these rules throughout the world. Included in these rules is the principle of stewardship. Many of us are grateful to be Americans, but we didn't earn this property, and any claim to it must include responsibility to share the fruits of our good fortune (and good work) with the rest of humanity. We should recognize that our common humanity overrides specific racial, nationalistic identity. A global perspective must replace nationalism and tribalism as the *leitmotif* of ethical living. A *modernist* non-religious ethic, based on rational reflection and yielding universal human values, must become the underpinning of a renewed cosmopolitanism. The threats to morality today come from religious particularism, naive egoism, ethical relativism, and *postmodernist* deconstructionism—a euphemism for moral nihilism. A defensible moral objectivism, the core of which is accepted by a consensus of moral philosophers, must permeate our society, as well as every society under the sun. At present, most people derive their moral principles either from religion or from narrow tribal ideology. An educational process inculcating universal norms in people everywhere is a crucial task for the leaders of the twenty-first century. Principles such as forbidding murder (the unjust killing of innocents), dishonesty, and exploitation, while promoting reciprocal cooperation, freedom, and universal justice must be seen as the necessary conditions for the good life, civilization, and peace. This leads to the ultimate long-range goal, World Government (the Cosmopolitan Moral Imperative).

The Cosmopolitan Moral Imperative: The Possibility of World Government

Peace, justice, and the struggle against terrorism and violence may be attainable only by institutional cosmopolitanism: World Government. There are two arguments for World Government. The first is the *Moral Point of View Argument,* which we have just adumbrated and which I will elaborate below. The second argument is from the *Trend toward Globalism,* to which I now turn.

The geopolitics of the world have been transformed in the last decades, even before September 11. Instead of the Cold War threat of a global nuclear explosion, the trend in the past decades has been a geopolitical implosion of internecene atrocities, as the inhabitants of the former Yugoslavia revive the deadly ghosts of a former age; the Hutu engage in a genocidal slaughter of their Tutsi neighbors in Rwanda; Tamil rebels kill Sinhalese in the name of nationalism in Sri Lanka; Muslims battle non-Muslims in Kashmir, Lebanon, Israel, and the Baltics; and nationalist Catholic Irish engage in mutual murder with nationalist Protestants who are still fighting the Battle of the Boyne of 1690 in Northern Ireland, their nationalism trumping their common Christian heritage.

These atavistic exhibitions of violence, added to the kind of terrorism that occurred in the suicide bombings of September 11, reinforce the claim that a global organization creating institutions and enforcing laws is desirable to promote peace, assure compliance with contracts and treaties, and prevent international anarchy by promoting orderly processes, international morality, and reliable expectations. A universal set of laws with fixed penalties, which are impartially enforced by a central police-like agency, could be a catalyst for peace, the protection of human rights, and environmental wholeness. This last function is a modern one, having to do with the fact that air and water pollution tend to spread, oblivious of political boundaries. For example, contaminated air from the nuclear explosion at Chernobyl wafted westward to Sweden and Switzerland; an increasingly depleted ozone layer over the antarctic makes all people vulnerable to cancer-causing ultraviolet radiation; greenhouse gases that originate in specific locales have global effects, changing climate patterns throughout the world. Recent international conferences on global warming and environmental policy, such as the Kyoto Accords in 1997, though they failed to reach universal agreements with strong sanctions, further demonstrate the need for an authoritative global body. As Hobbes wrote in 1651, "Covenants without swords are just words."

Add to these factors the modern development of an increasingly global economy, free trade, international transportation and communication systems (from the airplane to the internet), the gradual spread of English as the *lingua franca* of trade and diplomacy, and the growing global consciousness (CNN and other new networks may now beam the latest Asian uprising or African coup into our living rooms before the government is even aware of it). We read of conflicts in the United States over free trade. Organized labor has shown resentment at what it perceives as conservative economic policies and corporate globalism, especially passage of the North American Free Trade Agreement (NAFTA) between the United States, Canada, and Mexico. A coalition of anti-globalists has vigorously protested (and even rioted) during the World Trade Organization (WTO) conferences in Seattle and Toronto in the last few years. The protests over the erosion of community and exploitation of the poor are valid concerns. But the wiser strategy seems to be to harness the powers of global capitalism and use the increased wealth for socially beneficial purposes. The idea that world trade produces more wealth, and that "a rising tide lifts all boats," seems to have sufficient merit to claim our cautious and critical commitment.

The fact is that the world is changing and large corporations are increasingly becoming as powerful as nation-states. Fifty-one of the world's top economies are multinational corporations. They have assets greater than the Gross Domestic Product (GDP) of most nations. General Motors has revenues roughly the same size as those of Ireland, New Zealand, and Hungary combined, larger than Turkey's or Denmark's. Ford's revenues outstrip South Africa's; Toyota's and Exxon's, Norway or Poland; Microsoft's revenues are reported to exceed the GDP of France. The revenues of the top five corporations are twice the GDP of all South Asia.[7] Global capitalism has one feature in common with moral cosmopolitanism: it is anti-nationalistic, recognizing, not the nation-state, but the free market, as the operative arbiter of value. International economics is contributing to vast waves of migration, as workers from all over the globe, often at considerable risk, gravitate to where the jobs are, resulting in new configurations of ethnic diversity and the alteration of centuries of stable cultural patterns, as is occurring in Scandinavia, France, Germany, and the Netherlands. At the same time, progress has been made in joining the nations of Western Europe into a corporate *European Union,* most with a common currency. A similar movement is underway in Africa, the *African Union.* Combine these factors, and we get a picture of growing pressures for the eroding of national boundaries and national sovereignty and in favor of globalism, perhaps even some form of International Government.

Thomas Friedman has argued that a globalized system of informal relations has replaced the Cold War as the dominant social-economic-political fact of our time. This system consists of free market capitalism, through free trade and international competition, producing more efficient and private uses of wealth. Individuals, corporations, and nation-states are able "to reach around the world farther, faster, deeper and cheaper than ever before, and in a way that is also producing a powerful backlash from those brutalized or left behind by this new system."[8] Globalization is occurring in virtually every country in the world. Unlike the great nations and empires of the past, this supernational organization has no geographical capital, no center of power. No one nation or corporation can control it. Rapidly expanding, fluid, penetrating each segment of the globe, it

---

[7]*UN Human Development Report 1997,* p. 12; See also CorpWatch, online at www.corpwatch.org/trac/glob101/background/2001/factsheet.html.

[8]Thomas Friedman, *The Lexus and the Olive Tree.* (New York: Farrar, Straus, Giroux, 1999), 7. The backlash was in evidence in the Seattle riots against the World Trade Organization (WTO) in 2000 and the Toronto protests in 2001.

is ushering in a new democratic revolution. The symbol of the Cold War system was the wall, which divided everyone. The symbol of the global system is the World Wide Web, which unites everyone. Well, not quite everyone. The Indian peasant, the Bhutan nomad, and the poor of Afghanistan are as isolated and as badly off as ever. Rapid change, technological advances, and corporate tentacles spreading into every part of the world, are also creating greater distances between the older, more atavistic or primitive cultures and the new ones budding in their midst. Friedman describes an automobile assembly plant outside Tokyo where 310 robots, supervised by a few human beings, are building the "world's greatest luxury car, the *Lexus.*" While witnessing this technological miracle, he received a report on his cell phone from Jerusalem, where Palestinians and Jews were fighting over who owns which olive tree. "It struck me," he writes, "that the *Lexus* and the olive tree were actually pretty good symbols of this post–Cold War era: half the world seemed to be emerging from the Cold War intent on building a better *Lexus,* dedicated to modernizing, streamlining, and privatizing their economies in order to thrive in the system of globalization, and half the world— sometimes half of the same country—was still caught up in the fight over who owns which olive tree."[9]

We are all intertwined in an interdependent global web in other ways as well. A German businessman, while making a deal in Pakistan, picks up a virus that originated somewhere in Africa. He gets on a plane for Frankfurt, infecting the entire planeload of passengers, who spread the disease throughout Europe. An infected American tourist brings the virus with her on a flight from Frankfurt to the United States, where the virus spreads over the country. For good and bad, and in-between, globalization is spreading, eroding prevailing national borders and creating a new informal network of relationships. It is the most significant political fact of our age. The world is becoming a global village. New worldwide regulations and behavior patterns are called for to deal with this new reality. A prima facie

---

[9]Ibid., pp. 26–27. But what happens when those fighting over the olive tree suddenly discover that the true enemy of their traditional way of life is not their historic opponent, but a vast, impersonal, multinational complex? This is what the anti-technology movement is all about. See also, Michael Hardt and Antonio Negri. *Empire.* (Cambridge, Mass.: Harvard University Press, 2000).

case may even exist for International Government or, at least, for a sovereign body to enforce international laws, to safeguard the rights of individuals and individual nations against unjust incursions and exploitation. Perhaps the United Nations, as its name suggests, is really only a union of states, though ineffectual at present, is the precursor of a coming global governing body, and the World Court in the Hague, a precursor to an international system of law.

The Cosmopolitan Spirit. For the Cosmopolitan idealist, nationalism is just another prejudicial ideology, like racism and sexism. Why prefer your own nation to people elsewhere? From the third century B.C.E., an alternative ideal of the world citizen has been a live option for many. Diogenes the Cynic is alleged to have been the first cosmopolitan, calling himself a "world citizen." The Stoics followed his doctrine, becoming the first people to reject the narrow provinciality of particular loyalties, and identified themselves as Cosmopolitans.[10]

In the twentieth century, the French philosopher Jacques Maritain (1888–1973), the Indian Nobel laureate Rabindranath Tagore (1861–1941), and Mortimer Adler (1903–2001) all promoted the ideal of world government and citizenship. Maritain argued for the death of the dysfunctional nation-state and the inauguration of World Government, in which peace and justice would be guaranteed. Given the possibility of nations destroying each other with atomic weapons, an international authority is necessary to ensure peace; the traditional nation-state no longer serves a viable purpose, and it will have to give up its sovereignty in favor of an international government. Maritain defends his proposal via the idea of a universal natural law, which he believes to be inherent in all human beings and which can be recognized by all rational beings.[11]

As I suggested in the previous section, Cosmopolitanism seems to embody the heart of the moral point of view, impartially apply-

[10]Later on, the early Christians represented a type of cosmopolitanism, seeing themselves without a specific state, but united with all other Christians in a universal brotherhood. "In Christ there is neither Jew nor Greek, neither slave nor free, neither male nor female, but you are all one in Christ." (Gal: 3:28). Every believer is a Christian Cosmopolitan, for there is but one King in heaven, God, and no state but the Kingdom of God. Race, gender, ethnicity, and class have been annihilated.

[11]Jacques Maritain. *Man and the State.* (Catholic University Press, 1950).

ing moral principles to all humans. If there is a universal morality applying to all people everywhere, one which can be realized in each human life, one joining us each and all in a common moral brotherhood, then why get sidetracked by the fetish of particular bureaucratic states? Marx and Engels perceived just this point when they prophesied that in the ideal communist utopia, the state would "wither away" and humans live in an anarchistic utopia, much like that described by the prophet Isaiah.[12] The promise is of universal peace; an end to war, militarism, and state violence; the end of the bipolar "us" against "them." Instead we would live in a world where each contributed "according to his ability and received according to his need," a world of peace, prosperity, and global justice.

Stoic, Marxist, and secular Cosmopolitans are all united in seeking to implement the universal moral order in a nonreligious manner, creating a secular equivalent of the kingdom of heaven on Earth. Isn't it true that if we all lived deeply moral lives, as brothers and sisters, we would need neither the state nor its army, nor its police force, nor its lawyers? It seems so simple. Isn't this what we learned in kindergarten—that utopian community of peace and plenty? So why aren't we all Cosmopolitans? Why do nationalism and particularism, with their conflict-creating "us-against-them" mentality, reign instead? Why don't the Israelis and Palestinians embrace the peaceable Kingdom of Isaiah and stop the bloodshed on the

---

[12]The vision of a Peaceable Kingdom was set forth even earlier by the Hebrew prophet Isaiah in the sixth century B.C.:

> The wolf shall dwell with the lamb
> and the leopard shall lie down with the kid
> and the calf and the lion and the fatling together,
> and a little child shall lead them.
> The cow and the bear shall feed
> their young shall lie down together
> and the lion shall eat straw like the ox.
> The sucking child shall play over the hole of the asp,
> and the weaned child shall put his hand on the adder's den.
> They shall not hurt or destroy
> in all my holy mountain;
> for the earth shall be full of the knowledge of the LORD
> as the waters cover the sea.
> [The nations] shall beat their swords into plowshares,
> and their spears into pruning hooks;
> nation shall not lift up sword against nation,
> neither shall they learn war any more. . . . (Isaiah 11:6–9, 2:4)

West Bank? Why don't the Serbs and Kosovar Albanians accept it? Why don't Hindus and Muslims embrace it in Kashmir? Why don't Protestants and Catholics accept it in Northern Ireland?

Why don't we all become world citizens instead of Americans, Russians, Mexicans, Canadians, British, Afghans, Arabs, or Chinese? What is the answer?

The reasons why nationalism is still so prominent are related to the need for primary and particularistic loyalties to give meaning to one's life. The question is whether these particularisms can be integrated within a cosmopolitan vision.[13]

Consider two salient reasons for supporting nationalism: the desire to own property and the claim to a common national territory. With regard to property rights, Cosmopolitans criticize nationalists for their strong theory of property rights. Why should America or Saudi Arabia get a sole monopoly on its resources, which are just part of the natural lottery? The United States and Saudi Arabia didn't do anything to deserve their superior natural resources. They were just more fortunate than poorer countries. Therefore, wouldn't it be fairer for the resources of these and all countries to be distributed more equitably? Shouldn't we use these resources for the good of humanity, rather than simply the good of a single nation? One might argue that although we do not deserve these resources, we deserve the benefits of what we have produced from these resources. But here the Lockean Proviso seems relevant. We deserve the fruits of our labors with regard to resource consumption just so long as we leave "as much and as good left over for others." The world's resources should be used for the world's needs, not simply the needs of the fortunate. Being good stewards of our resources, including sharing them with the needy, may justify some ownership, but it is not the absolute, sovereign ownership that many of us have uncritically come to take for granted.

With regard to a national conjoined territory—the land—over which nationalism claims complete jurisdiction, World Government would only qualify that sovereignty, not abolish it. In a World Government, nations might be made stewards of their land and resources, but not permitted complete sovereignty over their uses. Richer nations would have a duty to redistribute, through taxation

---

[13]I have discussed the arguments for nationalism in my book *Global Political Philosophy* (McGraw-Hill, 2002).

or aid, some of their wealth to poorer nations in which even people's basic needs are not met. Peter Singer argues from a utilitarian perspective that, "If it is in our power to prevent something bad from happening, without thereby sacrificing something of comparable moral importance, we ought to do it."[14] We should contemplate the changes that we might need to make in our life-styles if we attempted to live according to Singer's challenge. However, until such a Cosmopolitan regime is established, it's hard to see either nations or individuals giving up sovereignty over their territory and resources.

Some Objections to World Government.   Cosmopolitanism appears to be a worthy ideal, embodying as it does the moral point of view in respecting individuals as the centers of meaning, rather than nations, races, or religious or ethnic groups. Yet the ideal is fraught with five problems that seem *almost* insurmountable. First, what kind of institution would be required to draw up and enforce the global scheme of taxation required for the kinds of wealth redistribution schemes that might be warranted? Would its coercive powers be an unacceptable violation of individual and national liberties? Second, even if we could ensure that a World Government would carry out a just taxation scheme, how could we be certain that the distributed funds actually went to the poor and were not siphoned off by a corrupt elite and deposited into their Swiss bank accounts (as happens all too frequently with foreign aid to developing countries)? Third, how do we guarantee that, after the funds get to the poor, long-term good would result from the redistribution scheme? Fourth, it would also seem that population control should be a necessary condition for aid, for otherwise the ratchet effect would occur (that is, monetary input in an apparent emergency would stave off immediate starvation and disaster, but enable people to propagate further, resulting in a larger crisis years later). The British advocate of world hunger relief, Onora O'Neill, has conceded that if noncoercive methods fail to control population growth, coercive ones might be warranted:

> If [noncoercive] policies fail, and just productive and redistributive measures too cannot meet needs, direct coercion of procreative deci-

[14]Peter Singer, "Famine, Affluence and Morality," *Philosophy and Public Affairs,* 1, no. 3 (1972).

sions would not be unjust. Such emergencies would arise only when recklessly fertile people persist in having children whose needs could not be met, by their parents or by others, either by increasing or by reallocating resources. Such procreators act on a maxim that cannot be widely shared without exacerbating needs and so increasing injustice. Preventing such reckless procreation would coerce less than would failing to prevent it.[15]

For example, the population of Rwanda has been growing at a rate of as much as 8 percent per annum, resulting in a doubling of the population ever eight and one-half years or so. The Chinese policy of limiting families to one or two children appears harsh to many of us, but it may be seen as an emergency measure, counteracting the fanatical pronatalist policies of Mao Tse-Tung, and it is having a beneficial effect in slowing down population growth (compared to India, where rapid growth continues).

Fifth, how can one compare what constitutes a good life in different kinds of societies? The per capita GNP of many Western countries is around $25,000, whereas in the Third World it may be one-hundredth that, around $250. Yet someone from a Third World country, say an Amazonian Indian in Brazil, may not value college education as much as Westerners and may live in a tribe that has a pattern of caring for the elderly, obviating the need for expensive retirement policies. In fact, the Amazonian Indian, upon being exposed to Western culture, may prefer to remain living a traditional life in the rain forest.

These problems may not be insuperable, but they should give us pause. Until we understand the full implications of what we are doing, a move toward institutionalizing Cosmopolitanism should proceed cautiously. Nonetheless, the principle of humanity embodied in the moral point of view, which focuses on the rights and duties of individuals—not groups, races, or nations—does point to a robust Cosmopolitanism, which, it would seem, should be institutionalized in a democratic World Government.

[15]Onora O'Neill, *Faces of Hunger* (London: Allen & Unwin, 1986), 158. Even Singer, in a postscript to his article (see note 14) says that our obligation to aid is lessened if the people in danger do nothing to reduce their population growth rate. O'Neill isn't claiming that the individual couples are irrational for wanting more children, only that proceeding so on a large scale results in the tragedy of the commons (see Hardin, chapter 15), where individual freedom practiced by too many leads to tragedy.

Another problem related to international relations concerns intervention in the internal affairs of a nation-state, such as that which occurred in Afghanistan, where coalition forces led by the United States brought down the Taliban regime and the Al Qaeda terrorist network, or in Serbia and Kosovo, when human rights violations, such as ethnic cleansing, became extreme. Even if we accept the principle of national sovereignty, intervention by other nations may be justified. The widespread "ethnic cleansing" that took place in the former Yugoslavia in the 1990s is a prime example of the warranted intervention of other nations. Working out the criteria for when to intervene and when not to, is one of the most urgent problems facing us. We want to be constructive, rather than add to the destruction in these war-torn lands, but it is notoriously difficult to determine the likelihood of success. Such interventions are risky and should be embarked upon only when all attempts at peaceful solutions have been exhausted, when there is widespread international support, when there is willingness to commit to long-term peace keeping, and when there is a reasonable chance of success.

Cosmopolitan institutions threaten the very existence of the traditional nation-state, so much a part of our world since the eighteenth century. If our ultimate allegiance is to a super—global State, then what is the role of the nation? Does it have moral legitimacy?

Many philosophers would say, No, the nation lacks any ultimate moral justification. It is, at best, a temporary and necessary evil, organizing people in restricted ways until the principle of universal humanity can take hold in our collective consciousness. Albert Einstein characterized nationalism as an infantile disease, "the measles of mankind" from which we must recover if we are to survive. But as our analysis suggests, this may be an extreme reaction. Certainly, there is a hard version of nationalism, epitomized in the slogan "My country, right or wrong, my country"[16] which is not justified, because it makes nationalism into an absolute principle, something that cannot be justified. Such extreme nationalism is no more justified than giving special privilege to one's race or gender or eth-

---

[16]This was uttered by the late Cardinal Spellman in the 1960s, signifying that he would support America's war in Vietnam even if it was morally wrong. The original quote is by Stephen Decauter, given in 1816, "Our country! In her intercourse with foreign nations may she be in the right; but our country, right or wrong." (Quoted in *Bartlett's Familiar Quotations,* ed. J. Kaplan, NY: Little, Brown & Co., 1992), 390.

nic group. We have an obligation to oppose our country when it violates human rights—as some Germans, like the martyrs Dietrich Bonhoffer and Adam von Trott, opposed Hitler's Nazism. We must transcend this kind of extreme, immoral nationalism, with its atavistic rituals and its narrow patriotism, and replace it with a universal loyalty. There is a *prima facie* duty to become *moral cosmopolitans,* committed to the well-being and rights of every person, regardless of country of origin. In accomplishing this, there are practical, as well as moral, obstacles to overcome, so that we cannot immediately move into such an international alliance, but this should be our goal. Moral cosmopolitanism, which treats each person as a moral equal, is not equivalent to institutional cosmopolitanism, but it inclines in that direction. The benefits of World Government are greater prospects for peace, enforcement of treaties and contracts, fluid trade and economic relations, and the allocation of resources according to need and desert, rather than according to the pure luck of being born in a resource-rich country or family.

Cosmopolitanism has had a checkered past. Marxist-Leninism purported to be the ultimate cosmopolitan philosophy, yet it gave rise to the Union of Soviet Socialist Republics, the completely "internationalist" society, which allowed Stalin's atrocities. Stalin shows that one doesn't have to be religious to be an evil fanatic: you can be an atheist and a socialist and perpetrate evil on a national or global scale. Cosmopolitanism can simply be a veneer for tyranny. Most of us have been immunized against the idea of World Government through the inoculating effects of reading Huxley's *Brave New World* and Orwell's *1984.* Cosmopolitans can also propagate questionable moral advice on a more micro scale. The nineteenth-century Cosmopolitan William Godwin held that "if two persons are drowning and one is a relative of yours, then it should make no difference in your decision as to whom to try to rescue first." Dickens satirizes this "telescopic philanthropy" in the person of Mrs. Jelleby, who could only recognize objects of benevolence at a very great distance.[17] It was said of President Woodrow Wilson that "He loved mankind but loathed individual men." Common-sense morality, as we noted above, informs us that this nondiscrimination under-

---

[17]Charles Dickens, *Bleak House* (London: Bradbury and Evans, 1853). "Mrs Jelleby's eyes had the curious habit of looking a long way off. As if they could see nothing nearer than Africa" (p. 26).

mines the very substance of morality, those relationships that make life worth living. It is our basic communitarian values of family, friends, and community that constitute the bases of moral sentiments. To this extent, the particularists are correct. Our love and our moral commitments must begin and always remain tied to particular people, not humanity in the abstract. Furthermore, as some nationalists point out, we may take legitimate pride in our democratic institutions, our practices of equality before the law, and our moral traditions. These aspects of our culture are worth preserving and defending. From a moral point of view, all cultures are not equal. Some instantiate the ideals better than others.

At this point, we might compromise and recognize the validity of both cosmopolitanism and nationalism. Nationalists may be divided into two groups: *soft* nationalists and *hard* nationalists. *Hard* nationalists hold that the nation is altogether justified as the ultimate locus of political obligation, so that internationalism is simply confused or immoral. Even as we have a natural duty to prefer our family to other people and strangers, we have a duty to prefer our nation, to be patriotic. For them, nationalistic concerns override all other loyalties or obligations. On the other hand, *soft* nationalists maintain that while we do have some obligations to people everywhere and that we need some adjudicating overseer to enforce treaties and prevent war, this doesn't completely override the need for nation-states. They agree with *hard* nationalists that we do have special obligations to our own country, but *soft* nationalists feel that the needs or rights of others may sometimes override our familial obligations and that our nationalistic obligations may be overridden at times by obligations to mankind at large or to people not citizens of our nation.

Soft nationalists are open to the possibility of World Government, recognizing the ideals thereby attained, but they also are troubled by the problems of ensuring local autonomy and preventing unwieldy bureaucracy and tyranny. However, suppose we could attain an efficient World Government, a sort of United Nations with *sovereignty,* that is, with authority and power. Then, the *soft* nationalists maintain, nations would still have local jurisdiction, much like the individual states do within the United States, only with greater autonomy (or *semi-sovereignty*). We would still have special obligations to people in our own states, relating to them in special moral ways, while at the same time, sharing our resources with people throughout the world.[18]

CONCLUSION

September 11, the Day of Ignominy, has changed America and the world. We have been shocked out of our complacency, disabused of our illusion of invulnerability, and forced to face global terrorism. I have argued that the Day of Ignominy may become the Day of Opportunity, if we use it to take counter-measures against terrorism and the causes of terrorism and to begin to ameliorate the oppression and injustice in our nation and the world. I have outlined some short-term and long-term strategies, the most ambitious and controversial of which is a version of institutional Cosmopolitanism—World Government, which would be based on secular rational morality. World Government may also be a fitting response to the growing pressures of globalism. I have also noted, but not developed as fully as I would like, nationalism's virtues, such as its ability to create the opportunities for close personal relationships and loyalties, so vital for personal identity. Some form of nationalism may always be part of the human psyche, though it may be a less all-encompassing variety than what we now experience, a *soft* nationalism. It will be balanced by a *soft* democratic form of cosmopolitanism, either informally worked out among nations or more formally by a World Government, which would still encourage and promote individual nation-state autonomy within its domain. One way or another, the need for increased peace and international cooperation will be more compelling as we become better-educated people who live in a global village. However it happens and whatever the exact result in terms of formal structure or lack thereof, the process should encapsulate the Cosmopolitan vision of an expanding moral circle, wherein our critical sympathies and moral responsibilities extend beyond ourselves, our com-

---

[18]For a good discussion of *extreme* versus *moderate* nationalism, see Stephen Nathanson, *Patriotism, Morality, and Peace* (Lanham, MD: Roman & Littlefield, 1993). My views have profited by Nathanson's work.

munities, and nations to include the whole world. If we can't do that, we'd better start building our ark.

For Further Reflection

1. Explain Pojman's thesis of a clash of cultures. Is he correct?

2. Discuss Pojman's long-term moral responses to terrorism. Which strategies do you think most (or least) promising? How do you think we should respond to the threat of terrorism?

3. What is Pojman's argument for Cosmopolitanism? Assess its strengths and weaknesses. Include your assessment of the possibility of world government.

4. According to Pojman, what is soft nationalism? How does it function?

5. Compare Pojman's proposal for dealing with terrorism with Nussbaum's proposal. Do you find significant differences in their approaches?

What Is Wrong with Terrorism?

THOMAS NAGEL

Thomas Nagel, an influential thinker in political philosophy and ethics, is professor of philosophy and law at New York University. His books include *The Possibility of Altruism* (1970), *Mortal Questions* (1979), and *The View from Nowhere* (1986). In this selection, he asserts that the moral wrongness of terrorism is its violation of the prohibition against deliberately trying to bring about the death of a harmless person. We are morally required to do our best to avoid civilian casualties in war, to "not *aim* to kill a harmless person." Terrorism, however, ignores this distinction.

People all over the world react with visceral horror to attacks on civilians by Al Quaeda, by Palestinian suicide bombers, by Basque or Chechen separatists, or by IRA militants. As there now seems to be a pause in the spate of suicide bombings and other terrorist acts—if only momentary—perhaps now is a moment to grapple with a fundamental question: What makes *terrorist* killings any more worthy of condemnation than other forms of murder?

The special opprobrium associated with the word "terrorism" must be understood as a condemnation of means, not ends. Of course, those who condemn terrorist attacks on civilians often also reject the ends that the attackers are trying to achieve. They think that a separate Basque state, or the withdrawal of US forces from the Middle East, for example, are not aims that anyone should be pursuing, let alone by violent means.

But the condemnation does not depend on rejecting the aims of the terrorists. The reaction to the attacks of September 11, 2001 on New York and Washington and their like underscores that such means are outrageous whatever the end; they should not be used to achieve even a good end—indeed, even if there is no other way to achieve it. The normal balancing of costs against benefits is not allowable here.

This claim is not as simple as it appears because it does not depend on a general moral principle forbidding all killing of non-

From Project Syndicate, November 2002, <www.project-syndicate.org>.

combatants. Similarly, those who condemn terrorism as beyond the pale are usually not pacifists. They believe not only that it is all right to kill soldiers and bomb munitions depots in times of war, but that inflicting "collateral damage" on non-combatants is sometimes unavoidable—and morally permissible.

But if that is permissible, why is it wrong to aim *directly* at non-combatants if killing them will have a good chance of inducing the enemy to cease hostilities, withdraw from occupied territory, or grant independence? Dying is bad, however one is killed. So why should a civilian death be acceptable if it occurs as a side effect of combat that serves a worthy end, whereas a civilian death that is inflicted deliberately as a means to the *same* end is a terrorist outrage?

The distinction is not universally accepted—certainly not by the major belligerents in World War II. Hiroshima is the most famous example of terror bombing, but the Germans, the Japanese, and the British as well as the Americans deliberately slaughtered civilian non-combatants in large numbers. Today, however, terrorism inspires widespread revulsion, which in turn helps to justify military action against it. So it is essential that the reason for that revulsion become better understood.

The core moral idea is a prohibition against *aiming* at the death of a harmless person. Everyone is presumed to be inviolable in this way until he himself becomes a danger to others; so we are permitted to kill in self-defense, and to attack enemy combatants in war. But this is an exception to a general and strict requirement of respect for human life. So long as we are not doing any harm, no one may kill us just because it would be useful to do so. This minimal basic respect is owed to *every* individual, and it may not be violated even to achieve valuable long-term goals.

However there are some activities, including legitimate self-defense or warfare, that create an unavoidable risk of harm to innocent parties. This is true not only of violent military or police actions but also of peaceful projects like major construction in densely populated cities. In those cases, if the aim is important enough, the activity is not morally prohibited provided due care is taken to minimize the risk of harm to innocent parties, consistent with the achievement of the aim.

The moral point is that we are obliged to do our best to avoid or minimize civilian casualties in warfare, even if we know that we cannot avoid them completely. Those deaths do not violate the strictest protection of human life—that we may not *aim* to kill a harmless person. On the contrary, our aim is if possible to avoid such collateral deaths.

Of course, the victim ends up dead whether killed deliberately by a terrorist or regrettably as the side effect of an attack on a legitimate military target. But in our sense of what we are owed morally by our fellow human beings, there is a huge difference between these two acts, and the attitudes they express toward human life.

So long as it remains an effective means for weak parties to exert pressure on their more powerful enemies, terrorism cannot be expected to disappear. But we should hope nonetheless that the recognition of its special form of contempt for humanity will spread, rather than being lost as a result of its recent successes.

For Further Reflection

1. According to Nagel, is terrorism to be condemned because we disagree with its goals?

2. What is the crucial distinction that Nagel draws between the inflicting of "collateral damage" on noncombatants in war and the killing of noncombatants by terrorists? Do you think this distinction makes sense?

3. According to Nagel, why is it essential that we understand the reason for the widespread revulsion for terrorism?

4. Was the bombing of Hiroshima an act of terrorism? Why or why not?

Further Readings for Chapter 16

Beitz, Charles. *Political Theory and International Relations.* Princeton, N.J.: Princeton University Press, 1999.

Brown, Chris. *International Relations Theory.* New York: Harvester-Wheatshelf, 1992.

Coady, Tony, and Michael O'Keefe, eds. *Terrorism and Justice.* Melbourne: Melbourne University Press, 2002.

Chomsky, Noam. *9-11.* New York: Seven Stories Press, 2001.

Friedman, Thomas. *The Lexus and the Olive Tree.* New York: Farrar, Straus, Giroux, 1999.

Hardt, Michael, and Antonio Negri. *Empire*. Cambridge: Harvard University Press, 2000.

Huntington, Samuel. "The Clash of Civilizations?" *Foreign Affairs* (Summer 1993).

Laqueur, Walter. *The Age of Terrorism*. Boston: Little, Brown, 1987.

Maritain, Jacques. *Man and the State*. Washington, D.C.: Catholic University of America Press, 1950.

McKim, Robert, and Jeff McMahan, eds. *The Morality of Nationalism*. New York: Oxford University Press, 1997.

Nathanson, Stephen. *Patriotism, Morality, and Peace*. Lanham, Md.: Roman & Littlefield, 1993.

Pillar, Paul R. *Terrorism and U.S. Foreign Policy*. Washington, D.C.: Brookings Institute Press, 2001.

Primoratz, Igor. "The Morality of Terrorism." *Journal of Applied Philosophy* 14 (1997).

Rummel, R. J. *Death by Government*. New Brunswick, N.J.: Transaction Publishers, 1994.

Sterba, James P., ed. *Terrorism and International Justice*. New York: Oxford University Press, 2003.

Vanden Heuvel, Katrina, ed. *A Just Response: On Terrorism, Democracy and September 11, 2001*. New York: Nation Books, 2002.